Contemporary
Literary Criticism

Guide to Gale Literary Criticism Series

For criticism on	Consult these Gale series
Authors now living or who died after December 31, 1999	*CONTEMPORARY LITERARY CRITICISM (CLC)*
Authors who died between 1900 and 1999	*TWENTIETH-CENTURY LITERARY CRITICISM (TCLC)*
Authors who died between 1800 and 1899	*NINETEENTH-CENTURY LITERATURE CRITICISM (NCLC)*
Authors who died between 1400 and 1799	*LITERATURE CRITICISM FROM 1400 TO 1800 (LC)* *SHAKESPEAREAN CRITICISM (SC)*
Authors who died before 1400	*CLASSICAL AND MEDIEVAL LITERATURE CRITICISM (CMLC)*
Authors of books for children and young adults	*CHILDREN'S LITERATURE REVIEW (CLR)*
Dramatists	*DRAMA CRITICISM (DC)*
Poets	*POETRY CRITICISM (PC)*
Short story writers	*SHORT STORY CRITICISM (SSC)*
Black writers of the past two hundred years	*BLACK LITERATURE CRITICISM (BLC)* *BLACK LITERATURE CRITICISM SUPPLEMENT (BLCS)*
Hispanic writers of the late nineteenth and twentieth centuries	*HISPANIC LITERATURE CRITICISM (HLC)* *HISPANIC LITERATURE CRITICISM SUPPLEMENT (HLCS)*
Native North American writers and orators of the eighteenth, nineteenth, and twentieth centuries	*NATIVE NORTH AMERICAN LITERATURE (NNAL)*
Major authors from the Renaissance to the present	*WORLD LITERATURE CRITICISM, 1500 TO THE PRESENT (WLC)* *WORLD LITERATURE CRITICISM SUPPLEMENT (WLCS)*

ISSN 0091-3421

Volume 128

Contemporary
Literary Criticism

Criticism of the Works
of Today's Novelists, Poets, Playwrights,
Short Story Writers, Scriptwriters, and
Other Creative Writers

Jeffrey W. Hunter
EDITOR

Jenny Cromie
Justin Karr
ASSOCIATE EDITORS

Rebecca J. Blanchard
Vince Cousino
Linda Pavlovski
ASSISTANT EDITORS

GALE GROUP

Detroit
New York
San Francisco
London
Boston
Woodbridge, CT

STAFF

Janet Witalec, *Managing Editor, Literature Product*
Jeffrey W. Hunter, *Editor*
Mark W. Scott, *Publisher, Literature Product*

Jenny Cromie, Justin Karr, *Associate Editors*
Rebecca J. Blanchard, Vince Cousino, Linda Pavlovski, *Assistant Editors*
Patti A. Tippett, Timothy J. White, *Technical Training Specialists*
Kathleen Lopez Nolan, Lynn M. Spampinato, *Managing Editors*
Susan M. Trosky, *Content Director*

Maria L. Franklin, *Permissions Manager*
Sarah Tomasek, *Permissions Associate*

Victoria B. Cariappa, *Research Manager*
Tracie A. Richardson, *Project Coordinator*
Tamara C. Nott, *Research Associate*
Scott Floyd, Timothy Lehnerer, Ron Morelli, *Research Assistants*

Dorothy Maki, *Manufacturing Manager*
Stacy L. Melson, *Buyer*

Mary Beth Trimper, *Manager, Composition and Electronic Prepress*
Carolyn Fischer, *Composition Specialist*

Michael Logusz, *Graphic Artist*
Randy Bassett, *Image Database Supervisor*
Robert Duncan, Dan Newell, *Imaging Specialists*
Pamela A. Reed, *Imaging Coordinator*
Kelly A. Quin, *Image Editor*

Library of Congress Catalog Card Number 76-46132
ISBN 0-7876-3203-1
ISSN 0091-3421
Printed in the United States of America

10 9 8 7 6 5 4 3 2 1

Contents

Preface vii

Acknowledgments xi

Preface

Named "one of the twenty-five most distinguished reference titles published during the past twenty-five years" by *Reference Quarterly,* the *Contemporary Literary Criticism* (*CLC*) series provides readers with critical commentary and general information on more than 2,000 authors now living or who died after December 31, 1999. Volumes published from 1973 through 1999 include authors who died after December 31, 1959. Previous to the publication of the first volume of *CLC* in 1973, there was no ongoing digest monitoring scholarly and popular sources of critical opinion and explication of modern literature. *CLC,* therefore, has fulfilled an essential need, particularly since the complexity and variety of contemporary literature makes the function of criticism especially important to today's reader.

Scope of the Series

CLC provides significant passages from published criticism of works by creative writers. Since many of the authors covered in *CLC* inspire continual critical commentary, writers are often represented in more than one volume. There is, of course, no duplication of reprinted criticism.

Authors are selected for inclusion for a variety of reasons, among them the publication or dramatic production of a critically acclaimed new work, the reception of a major literary award, revival of interest in past writings, or the adaptation of a literary work to film or television.

Attention is also given to several other groups of writers—authors of considerable public interest—about whose work criticism is often difficult to locate. These include mystery and science fiction writers, literary and social critics, foreign authors, and authors who represent particular ethnic groups.

Each *CLC* volume contains individual essays and reviews taken from hundreds of book review periodicals, general magazines, scholarly journals, monographs, and books. Entries include critical evaluations spanning from the beginning of an author's career to the most current commentary. Interviews, feature articles, and other published writings that offer insight into the author's works are also presented. Students, teachers, librarians, and researchers will find that the general critical and biographical material in *CLC* provides them with vital information required to write a term paper, analyze a poem, or lead a book discussion group. In addition, complete biographical citations note the original source and all of the information necessary for a term paper footnote or bibliography.

Organization of the Book

A *CLC* entry consists of the following elements:

- The **Author Heading** cites the name under which the author most commonly wrote, followed by birth and death dates. Also located here are any name variations under which an author wrote, including transliterated forms for authors whose native languages use nonroman alphabets. If the author wrote consistently under a pseudonym, the pseudonym will be listed in the author heading and the author's actual name given in parentheses on the first line of the biographical and critical information. Uncertain birth or death dates are indicated by question marks. Single-work entries are preceded by a heading that consists of the most common form of the title in English translation (if applicable) and the original date of composition.

- A **Portrait of the Author** is included when available.

- The **Introduction** contains background information that introduces the reader to the author, work, or topic that is the subject of the entry.

- The list of **Principal Works** is ordered chronologically by date of first publication and lists the most important works by the author. The genre and publication date of each work is given. In the case of foreign authors whose works have been translated into English, the English-language version of the title follows in brackets. Unless otherwise indicated, dramas are dated by first performance, not first publication.

- Reprinted **Criticism** is arranged chronologically in each entry to provide a useful perspective on changes in critical evaluation over time. The critic's name and the date of composition or publication of the critical work are given at the beginning of each piece of criticism. Unsigned criticism is preceded by the title of the source in which it appeared. All titles by the author featured in the text are printed in boldface type. Footnotes are reprinted at the end of each essay or excerpt. In the case of excerpted criticism, only those footnotes that pertain to the excerpted texts are included.

- A complete **Bibliographical Citation** of the original essay or book precedes each piece of criticism.

- Critical essays are prefaced by brief **Annotations** explicating each piece.

- Whenever possible, a recent **Author Interview** accompanies each entry.

- An annotated bibliography of **Further Reading** appears at the end of each entry and suggests resources for additional study. In some cases, significant essays for which the editors could not obtain reprint rights are included here. Boxed material following the further reading list provides references to other biographical and critical sources on the author in series published by Gale.

Indexes

A **Cumulative Author Index** lists all of the authors that appear in a wide variety of reference sources published by the Gale Group, including *CLC*. A complete list of these sources is found facing the first page of the Author Index. The index also includes birth and death dates and cross references between pseudonyms and actual names.

A **Cumulative Nationality Index** lists all authors featured in *CLC* by nationality, followed by the number of the *CLC* volume in which their entry appears.

A **Cumulative Topic Index** lists the literary themes and topics treated in the series as well as in *Literature Criticism from 1400 to 1800, Nineteenth-Century Literature Criticism, Twentieth-Century Literary Criticism,* and the *Contemporary Literary Criticism* Yearbook, which was discontinued in 1998.

An alphabetical **Title Index** accompanies each volume of *CLC*. Listings of titles by authors covered in the given volume are followed by the author's name and the corresponding page numbers where the titles are discussed. English translations of foreign titles and variations of titles are cross-referenced to the title under which a work was originally published. Titles of novels, dramas, nonfiction books, and poetry, short story, or essay collections are printed in italics, while individual poems, short stories, and essays are printed in roman type within quotation marks.

In response to numerous suggestions from librarians, Gale also produces an annual paperbound edition of the *CLC* cumulative title index. This annual cumulation, which alphabetically lists all titles reviewed in the series, is available to all customers. Additional copies of this index are available upon request. Librarians and patrons will welcome this separate index; it saves shelf space, is easy to use, and is recyclable upon receipt of the next edition.

Citing *Contemporary Literary Criticism*

When writing papers, students who quote directly from any volume in the Literary Criticism Series may use the following general format to footnote reprinted criticism. The first example pertains to material drawn from periodicals, the second to material reprinted from books.

Alfred Cismaru, "Making the Best of It," *The New Republic* 207, no. 24 (December 7, 1992): 30, 32; excerpted and reprinted in *Contemporary Literary Criticism,* vol. 85, ed. Christopher Giroux (Detroit: The Gale Group, 1995), 73-4.

Yvor Winters, *The Post-Symbolist Methods* (Allen Swallow, 1967), 211-51; excerpted and reprinted in *Contemporary Literary Criticism,* vol. 85, ed. Christopher Giroux (Detroit: The Gale Group, 1995), 223-26.

Suggestions are Welcome

Readers who wish to suggest new features, topics, or authors to appear in future volumes, or who have other suggestions or comments are cordially invited to call, write, or fax the Managing Editor:

Managing Editor, Literary Criticism Series
The Gale Group
27500 Drake Road
Farmington Hills, MI 48331-3535
1-800-347-4253 (GALE)
Fax: 248-699-8054

Acknowledgments

The editors wish to thank the copyright holders of the excerpted criticism included in this volume and the permissions managers of many book and magazine publishing companies for assisting us in securing reproduction rights. We are also grateful to the staffs of the Detroit Public Library, the Library of Congress, the University of Detroit Mercy Library, Wayne State University Purdy/Kresge Library Complex, and the University of Michigan Libraries for making their resources available to us. Following is a list of the copyright holders who have granted us permission to reproduce material in this volume of *CLC*. Every effort has been made to trace copyright, but if omissions have been made, please let us know.

COPYRIGHTED EXCERPTS IN *CLC*, VOLUME 128, WERE REPRODUCED FROM THE FOLLOWING PERIODICALS:

America, October 23, 1993. © 1993. All rights reserved. Reproduced with permission of America Press, Inc.,106 West 56th Street, New York, NY 10019.—*The Black Scholar,* v. 16, November-December, 1985; March-April, 1986. Copyright 1985, 1986 by The Black Scholar. Both reproduced by permission.—*Book World—The Washington Post,* November 18, 1990 for "Born to be Wild" by Deborah Tannen/ August 8, 1993 for "Sacred and Profane" by Lisa Zeidner/ October 10, 1993, for "The Demon Seed" by Elizabeth Hand/ March 27, 1994 for "Yearning for a Home" by Constance Casey/ August 6, 1995 for "The Last of Lestat" by Kevin Allman/ November 6, 1998 for "The Night Has a Thousand Eyes," by E. F. Bleiler. © 1990, 1993, 1994, 1995, 1998 Washington Post Book World Service/Washington Post Writers Group. All reproduced by permission of the authors.—*Bucknell Review,* v. XV, 1967. Copyright © Bucknell Review 1967. Reproduced by permission of the publisher.—*Chicago Tribune Books,* July 5, 1989. © 1989 Tribune Media Services, Inc. All rights reserved. Reproduced by permission./ May 10, 1987 for "Piercy's Big War: 'Soldiers' is Not the 'Good' Fight Nostalgia Recalls" by Judith Wynn; April 17, 1994 for "Marge Piercy Tells a Cautionary Tale of Women on the Edge" by Judith Wynn. © 1987, 1994 Tribune Media Services, Inc. All rights reserved. Both reproduced by permission of the authors.—*The Christian Century,* February 15, 1995. Copyright 1995 Christian Century Foundation. Reproduced by permission from *The Christian Century.*—*Commentary,* v. 79, June, 1985 for "The Secret of Mary Gordon's Success" by Carol Iannone. Copyright © 1985 by the American Jewish Committee. All rights reserved. Reproduced by permission of the publisher and the author.— *Commonweal,* June 19, 1981; August 12, 1988; February 9, 1990; February 25, 1994; January 13, 1995; May 19, 1995; May 17, 1996; April 10, 1998. Copyright © 1981, 1988, 1990, 1994, 1995, 1996, 1998 Commonweal Publishing Co., Inc. All reproduced by permission of Commonweal Foundation.—*Contemporary Literature,* v. XXIV, Winter, 1983. © 1983 by the Board of Regents of the University of Wisconsin. Reproduced by permission of The University of Wisconsin Press.— *Contemporary Review,* v. 269, September, 1996. Reproduced by permission.—*Critique: Studies in Modern Fiction,* v. XXVII, Summer, 1986. Copyright © 1986 Helen Dwight Reid Educational Foundation. Reproduced with permission of the Helen Dwight Reid Educational Foundation, published by Heldref Publications, 119 18th Street, N. W., Washington, DC 20036-1802.—*Cross Currents,* v. XXXVII, Summer-Fall, 1987. Copyright 1987 by Cross Currents Inc. Reproduced by permission.—*The Dalhousie Review,* v. 72, Summer, 1992 for "In Iron John's Sloshy Swamp, There is a Bitterly Cold Undercurrent" by Anne Compton. Reproduced by permission of the publisher and the author.—*English Studies in Canada,* v. 22, December, 1996 for "Dieting and Damnation: Anne Rice's 'Interview with the Vampire'" by Sandra Tomc. © Association of Canadian University Teachers of English 1996. Reproduced by permission of the publisher and the author.— *English Studies,* Netherlands, v. 64, June, 1983. © 1983 by Swets & Zeitlinger B. V. Reproduced by permission.—*Essays in Literature,* v. 17, Spring, 1990. Copyright 1990 by Western Illinois University. Reproduced by permission.—*Extrapolation,* v. 37, Winter, 1996. Copyright © 1996 by The Kent State University Press. Reproduced by permission.—*The French Review,* v. 70, December, 1996. Copyright 1996 by the American Association of Teachers of French. Reproduced by permission.—*The Hudson Review,* v. XL, Summer, 1987. Copyright © 1987 by The Hudson Review, Inc. Reproduced by permission.—*Iowa Review,* v. 3, Summer, 1972 for "Robert Bly Alive in Darkness" by Anthony Libby. Copyright © 1972 by The University of Iowa. Reproduced by permission of the author.—*Komparatistische Hefte,* v. 8, 1983 for "Buchi Emecheta: The Shaping of a Self" by Chikwenye Okonjo Ogunyemi. Reproduced by permission of the author.—*Los Angeles Times,* December 29, 1985. Copyright, 1985, Los Angeles Times. Reproduced by permission.—*Los Angeles Times Book Review,* December 19, 1982; August 12, 1984; November 6, 1988; November 18, 1990; October 25, 1992; November 6, 1994. Copyright, 1982, 1984, 1988, 1990, 1992, 1994, Los Angeles Times. All reproduced by permission.— *The Massachusetts Review,* v. XVIII, Spring, 1977. © 1977. Reproduced from *The Massachusetts Review,* The Massachusetts Review, Inc. by permission.—*The Modern Language Review,* v. 89, January, 1994 for "Absurdist Estrangement and the Subversion of Narrativity in 'La Plage'" by Yoseph Milman. © Modern Humanities Association 1994. Reproduced by permission of the publisher.—*Mosaic,* v. 25, Summer, 1992. © *Mosaic* 1992. Acknowledgment of previous publication

Robert Bly
1926-

(Full name Robert Elwood Bly) American poet, critic, nonfiction writer, editor, and translator.

The following entry presents an overview of Bly's career through 1996. For further information on his life and works, see *CLC,* Volumes 1, 2, 5, 10, 15, and 38.

INTRODUCTION

A charismatic literary impresario, social critic, and spiritual father of the contemporary men's movement, Robert Bly is among the most prominent and influential American poets of the postwar generation. During the 1960s, he emerged as a leading proponent of "deep imagism," a school of poetry distinguished for its preoccupation with the surrealism, Jungian archetypes, and elemental description of the natural world and visionary emotional states. His first two collections of poetry, *Silence in the Snowy Fields* (1962) and *The Light Around the Body* (1967), an award-winning volume of antiwar poetry, established Bly as a major contemporary poet and passionate spokesperson for the healing powers of literature and myth. A popular guest on public television and at writing workshops, poetry readings, and men's gatherings, Bly is credited with rejuvenating public interest in poetry and the imaginative arts. His best-selling book about male initiation, *Iron John* (1990), catapulted him to the forefront of the men's movement and its attendant controversies. The prolific author of literary criticism, translations, and anthologies, Bly's best-selling dissertation on American culture, *The Sibling Society* (1996), also appealed to a broad mainstream audience.

BIOGRAPHICAL INFORMATION

Born Robert Elwood Bly in rural Madison, Minnesota, Bly was raised on a nearby farm operated by his father. After graduating from high school, he served in the United States Navy from 1944 to 1946. Discharged at the conclusion of the Second World War, he attended St. Olaf College in Minnesota for a year, then transferred to Harvard University, where he earned a bachelor's degree in English literature in 1950. While at Harvard, Bly served as editor of the *Harvard Advocate,* the campus literary magazine in which he published his first essays and poetry. Several of his classmates at Harvard, poets Donald Hall, John Ashbery, and Frank O'Hara, also went on to literary fame. After leaving Harvard, Bly lived and wrote in an isolated North Minnesota cabin before relocating to New York City, where he worked menial jobs while concentrating on

his writing and self-education in philosophy and foreign languages. He then pursued graduate studies at the University of Iowa, where he earned a master's degree in creative writing in 1956. Bly married writer Carol McLean in 1955. In 1956 he received a Fulbright grant to travel to Norway, his ancestral homeland, where he translated and studied Scandinavian poetry. Returning to the United States the next year, he settled on a Minnesota farm and founded *The Fifties,* a literary magazine devoted to translations of foreign works and poetry that rejected the formalism of T. S. Eliot and Allen Tate. The magazine was retitled *The Sixties* and *The Seventies*, in subsequent decades.

With the publication of his first volume of poetry, *Silence in the Snowy Fields*, Bly received growing critical recognition. In 1964 he was awarded an Amy Lowell fellowship and the first of two Guggenheim fellowships; he received a second Guggenheim in 1972. He also received a National Institute of Arts and Letters Award in 1965 and a Rockefeller Foundation Fellowship in 1967. His second volume of poetry, *The Light Around the Body*, won a National

Book Award in 1968. During the late 1960s, Bly became increasingly active in political and social causes. In 1966 he helped organize American Writers Against the Vietnam War, a protest group that conducted poetry "read-ins" on college campuses throughout the country. He was arrested during a 1967 rally at the Pentagon. While living in Minnesota, Bly maintained a steady output of poetry over the next two decades, including the volumes *Sleepers Joining Hands* (1973), *This Tree Will Be Here for a Thousand Years* (1979), *The Man in the Black Coat Turns* (1981), and *Loving a Woman in Two Worlds* (1987). He also published translations of the poetry that influenced his own work, notably that of Rainer Maria Rilke, Antonio Machado, Pablo Neruda, and the fifteenth-century Indian mystic Kabir. Bly divorced his first wife in 1979 and remarried Jungian analyst Ruth Counsell the next year. During the 1980s, Bly became interested in the psychological and spiritual rehabilitation of men, culminating in the 1990 publication of *Iron John,* its companion videotape *A Gathering of Men* (1990), and a PBS interview with Bill Moyers that established him as a leading figure of the men's movement.

MAJOR WORKS

Bly's "deep image" poetry is largely concerned with unconscious awareness, spiritual revelation, and solitary communion with the natural world. Reacting against the intellectualized academic verse of the 1950s, particularly the emphasis on technical virtuosity and artifice, Bly sought to infuse contemporary American poetry with emotionalism and spontaneity achieved through free association and nonrational subjectivity. His important early essays, "A Wrong Turning in American Poetry" and "Looking for Dragon Smoke," evince his strong opposition to the strictures of formalism and the devaluation of imagery which he attributed to the critical theories of T. S. Eliot. The "country poems" of Bly's first volume, *Silence in the Snowy Fields,* introduce the pastoral Midwest landscapes, surreal observations, and direct, personal idiom of his subsequent work. As does much of his writing, many of these poems feature a moment of awestruck clarity in which the speaker revels in private harmony with the world. One of his best-known poems from this volume, "Driving Toward the Lac Qui Parle River," relates the speaker's euphoric connectedness to the weathered Minnesota landscape while returning home at dusk. In another, "Poem in Three Parts," the speaker declares, "Oh, on an early morning I think I shall live forever! / I am wrapped in my joyful flesh."

The Light Around the Body, a much different collection, marks Bly's attempt to merge the personal and public in his art, resulting in a new didacticism that became a prominent feature of his work. In these overtly political poems, Bly adopts a polemical tone to condemn U.S. foreign policy and military involvement in Vietnam. Poems such as "Listening to President Kennedy Lie About the Cuban Invasion" and "Hatred of Men with Black Hair"

express Bly's psychic despair over betrayals of conscience associated with American imperialism and the degradation of war. His next major volume of poetry, *Sleepers Joining Hands,* also contains powerful references to the Vietnam War, notably in "The Teeth Mother Naked at Last," though returns to the more serene style of *Silence in the Snowy Fields.* Informed by his study of Jungian psychology, many of these poems express Bly's disdain for masculine elements of the subconscious associated with aggression, morality, and analytic reasoning. In "I Came Out of the Mother Naked," an essay from this volume, Bly extols the virtues of the Great Mother culture that preceded patriarchal ascendancy in the ancient world. With *This Tree Will Be Here For a Thousand Years* Bly returned to the bucolic settings and visionary transformations of *Silence in the Snowy Fields.* Focusing on the duality of consciousness, these poems embody Bly's effort to unite the inner and outer realms of experience, often resulting in a melancholy realization of emptiness and loss. In *The Man in the Black Coat Turns,* which includes several prose poems, Bly turned his attention to father-son relationships, the primal bonds of parentage, and male sorrow, reflecting a return to masculine awareness and Bly's need to reconcile with his own alcoholic father. *Loving a Woman in Two Worlds* explores themes of love, intimacy, and the possibility of cosmic union in human relationships. Typical of his poetry, the meditative imagery of stars, water, trees, farms, and wildlife suggests a profound, hidden knowledge in all things.

In *Iron John,* an interpretative study of a Brothers Grimm fairy tale of the same title, Bly presents his ideas about masculinity and the importance of folk tradition, mentoring, and ritual initiation for the healthy socialization of men. In the fable that frames Bly's commentary a young prince is abducted by a frightening "Wild Man" named Iron John and educated far from his parents in the mysterious depths of the forest, where he learns the virtues of self-discipline, fortitude, and courage. Drawing broadly upon insights from mythology, psychology, social science, and poetry, Bly contends that the modern "soft male" is afflicted with self-destructive grief, anger, and passivity stemming from a lack of guidance from older men and over-identification with feminine traits. Bly expands upon similar themes in *The Sibling Society,* a sociological treatise in which he links the decline of American culture, education, and civil discourse with a state of perpetual adolescence fostered by youth-oriented cultural values that encourage immediate gratification, self-centeredness, and disposable relationships. As Bly observes, adults are unwilling to accept their responsibilities as role models and leaders, and children, witnessing the inadequacies of their immature parents, do not aspire to become adults. As in *Iron John,* Bly stresses the significance of intergenerational mentoring and underscores his message with wide-ranging anecdotes from myth, folklore, and psychology.

CRITICAL RECEPTION

Bly is widely recognized as a gifted poet, provocative social commentator, and captivating public speaker whose advocacy of spiritual introspection and creativity is responsible for a resurgence of popular interest in contemporary poetry. He has been compared to Henry David Thoreau for his individualism and transcendental vision, to Ezra Pound for his broad literary influence, and to Joseph Campbell as a popularizer of world mythology. Though few dismiss Bly's considerable intelligence and remarkable ability to convey the excitement of poetic expression to a general audience, critical evaluation of his own poetry is mixed. While many praise the meditative simplicity, luminous imagery, and colloquial voice of Bly's verse, others find fault in his tendency toward sentimentality, banality, and empty exhortation. Most regard *Silence in the Snowy Fields* and *The Light Around the Body* as his most significant works, though he has also garnered critical approval for *The Man in the Black Coat Turns, Loving a Woman in Two Worlds,* and his *Selected Poems* (1986), which includes several new compositions and prefatory remarks. With the enormous success of *Iron John,* Bly won a mass readership and celebrity as a leading spokesperson of the men's movement in America. While reviewers appreciated Bly's perceptive analysis of sexual identity and the demoralization of men in post-industrial society, many objected to Bly's patriarchal assumptions about traditional sex roles, his deprecation of motherhood, and ambiguous promotion of "fierceness" among men, considered by some an implicit threat to feminism. Despite such controversy, Mihaly Csikszentmihalyi writes, "In terms of what it tries to accomplish, Mr. Bly's book is important and timely." Bly's subsequent nonfiction study, *The Sibling Society,* was similarly praised for its ambitious subject, though some reviewers noted flaws in its methodology and unsubstantiated claims. As Winifred Gallagher concludes, "In an age of experts and specialization, Bly's eclectic jeremiad, drawn from politics, folk tales, behavioral science, economics and mythology, is testament to the kind of everyman's literacy and love of learning he mourns."

PRINCIPAL WORKS

Twenty Poems of Georg Trakl [translator; with James Wright] (poetry) 1961

Silence in the Snowy Fields (poetry) 1962

Chrysanthemums (poetry) 1967

Hunger [by Knut Hamsun; translator] (novel) 1967

The Light Around the Body (poetry) 1967

Ducks (poetry) 1968

The Morning Glory: Another Thing That Will Never Be My Friend (poetry) 1969

The Fish in the Sea Is Not Thirsty: Versions of Kabir [translator] (poetry) 1971

Selected Poems of Pablo Neruda and César Vallejo [editor and translator] (poetry) 1971

The Teeth Mother Naked at Last (poetry) 1971

Christmas Eve Service at Midnight at St. Michael's (poetry) 1972

Water Under the Earth (poetry) 1972

The Dead Seal Near McClure's Beach (poetry) 1973

Jumping Out of Bed (poetry) 1973

Selected Poems of Federico Garcia Lorca and Juan Ramon Jimenez [translator] (poetry) 1973

Sleepers Joining Hands (poetry) 1973

Point Reyes Poems (poetry) 1974

Old Man Rubbing His Eyes (poetry) 1975

The Kabir Book: Forty-Four of the Ecstatic Poems of Kabir [translator] (poetry) 1977

The Loon (poetry) 1977

This Body Is Made of Camphor and Gopherwood (poetry) 1977

Twenty Poems of Rolf Jacobsen [translator] (poetry) 1977

I Never Wanted Fame [by Antonio Machado; translator] (poetry) 1979

This Tree Will Be Here for a Thousand Years (poetry) 1979

Visiting Emily Dickinson's Grave and Other Poems (poetry) 1979

Canciones [by Antonio Machado; translator] (poetry) 1980

News of the Universe: Poems of Twofold Consciousness [editor] (poetry) 1980

Finding an Old Ant Mansion (poetry) 1981

The Man in the Black Coat Turns (poetry) 1981

Night and Sleep [by Rumi; translator] (poetry) 1981

Selected Poems of Rainer Maria Rilke: Translation from the German and Commentary [editor and translator] (poetry) 1981

Four Ramages (poetry) 1983

Times Alone: Selected Poems of Antonio Machado [translator] (poetry) 1983

The Whole Moisty Night (poetry) 1983

Mirabai Versions (poetry) 1984

Out of the Rolling Ocean (poetry) 1984

In the Mouth of May (poetry) 1985

A Love of Minute Particulars (poetry) 1985

Selected Poems (poetry) 1986

Loving a Woman in Two Worlds (poetry) 1987

The Pillow and the Key: Commentary on the Fairy Tale Iron John (criticism) 1987

The Moon on a Fencepost (poetry) 1988

The Apple Found in the Plowing (poetry) 1989

American Poetry: Wilderness and Domesticity (criticism) 1990

Iron John: A Book about Men (nonfiction) 1990

Angels of Pompeii (poetry) 1991

The Rag and Bone Shop of the Heart: Poems for Men [editor] (poetry) 1992

What Have I Ever Lost by Dying?: Collected Prose Poems (poetry) 1992

Gratitude to Old Teachers (poetry) 1993

Meditations on the Insatiable Soul: Poems (poetry) 1994

The Soul Is Here for Its Own Joy [editor] (poetry) 1995

The Sibling Society (nonfiction) 1996

Lorca and Jimenez: Selected Poems [editor and translator] (poetry) 1997

Morning Poems (poetry) 1997

The Maiden King [with Marion Woodman] (nonfiction) 1998

CRITICISM

Anthony Libby (essay date Summer 1972)

SOURCE: "Robert Bly Alive in Darkness," in *Iowa Review,* Vol. 3, No. 3, Summer, 1972, pp. 78-91.

[*In the following essay, Libby examines irrational elements of mysticism and transcendence in Bly's poetry from* Silence in the Snowy Fields *and* The Light Around the Body. *According to Libby, "undeniably his strongest poetry evokes some sort of truth all the more forceful because it exists beneath or beyond any reasoned response."*]

Often self-consciously, poetry now reassumes its ancient forms. When at Antioch College in the autumn of 1970 Robert Bly began a reading with an American Indian peyote chant, he seemed merely to be accepting a hip convention almost expected by an audience accustomed to Ginsberg and Snyder. Bly chanted for the usual reason, "to lower the consciousness down, until it gets into the stomach and into the chest and farther on." But no such convention had existed in the early fifties, when Bly began to publish his intimations of physical transcendence, poetry of the mystical body, and the conventional mystical terms that have since become so easily available are still inadequate to describe what happens in his unique poetry. To use a characteristic phrase of Bly's, "something important is hidden in there that we don't understand."

Because of the elusively compelling force of its "deep images," Bly's poetry demands interpretation as much as it seems to resist it. When it does not consist of simple deliberately prosy statement, much of it seems obscure, distant, but at the same time it conveys a sense of meaning immediately perceived though seldom paraphrasable in any but its own terms. It is difficult to explain Bly's surrealist poetry, hard to say why some of his imagery moves us so basically and why some appears comparatively contrived, but undeniably his strongest poetry evokes some sort of truth all the more forceful because it exists beneath or beyond any reasoned response. However, what the stomach feels, the mind wants to know. Perhaps the best way to appreciate Bly's irrational evocations is to attempt to explain them logically. If this seems paradoxical, such paradoxes are implicit in the act of analyzing almost all poetry, not merely surrealist poetry, and in any case Bly himself provides ample precedent. Like many mystical poets he writes with large patterns in mind, and behind his explorations into darkness there stands not only a complex poetic theory but also a highly articulated scheme of the psychological development of civilization. This scheme, also like that of other mystical poets (Blake, for instance), is frequently based on logical antithesis suspended in paradox, and only through an understanding of paradoxes simple and profound can we come to terms with Bly's poetry.

He begins with the intention of creating a truly free associationalism, radically opposed to what he considers the calculated and artificially logical associationalism of Eliot and Pound. In an essay called **"Looking for Dragon Smoke"** he argues that the formalist obsessions of modern American poets (from Eliot to Charles Olson) have obscured the true psychic bases of poetry. "Our task is not to invent and encourage jargon about 'open form' and breath patterns, but to continue to open new corridors into the psyche by association." His associative and implicitly irrationalist poetry depends not on form but on imagery, primarily on the conception of the "subjective image" developed by Bly and such friends of his as William Duffy and James Wright. The successful subjective image (or "deep image") strikes us with the force of a newly discovered archetype, minor or major, coming from the depths of the poet's subjectivity with a paradoxically universal force, his private revelation made ours. In Bly's **"Depression,"** for instance, the poet describes his psychic state in images which despite their novelty seem more discovered than made.

> I dreamt that men came toward me, carrying thin wires;
> I felt the wires pass in, like fire; they were old Tibetans;
> Dressed in padded clothes, to keep out cold;
> Then three work gloves, lying fingers to fingers,
> In a circle, came toward me, and I awoke.

Like these, Bly's images are almost invariably marked by a surrealist concreteness; not only are psychological or spiritual states felt in material form, but all substances seem to seek greater density. In various poems in *Silence in Snowy Fields,* air frequently becomes water ("the quiet waters of the night"), darkness "drifts down like snow," snow becomes "jewels," moonlight becomes "The sound of the deaf hearing through the bones of their heads," etc. Even when this metaphorical transposition of substances could be interpreted as moving in the opposite direction, toward a reduction of density ("Waterfalls of stone deep in mountains, / Or a wing flying alone beneath the earth") still we feel a pervasive sense of heaviness, a downward drift.

This imagery suggests the constant preoccupation of *Silence*; the metaphorical flow into greater concreteness reflects the spiritual movement enacted or wished for in most of the poems, a sinking into things, into the earth, usually into darkness, finally into death. Often, as Richard Howard explains in *Alone with America,* spiritual immersion becomes a literal immersion in water. Howard's intelligent though rhetorically somewhat convoluted introduction to Bly centers on the "latent" waters of "that Minnesota mariner," which Howard connects with "the stream the Greeks called *Lethe.*" As Bly writes in **"Return to Solitude,"**

> We want to go back, to return to the sea,
> The sea of solitary corridors,
> And halls of wild nights,
> Explosions of grief,
> Diving into the sea of death,
> Like the stars of the wheeling Bear.

But though transcendent death by water suggests ancient mystic patterns, Bly's vision of the death which feeds life is neither exactly traditional nor really transcendental. Another main current of imagery in *Silence* suggests interpenetration of body and world. Animism ("The dawn stood there with a quiet gaze; / Our eyes met through the top leaves of the young ash") is complemented by a sort of bodily surrealism ("Inside me there is a confusion of swallows"). As the psyche is crowded with arcane corporeal images, so the body contains the objects of the world. In the past, for instance in Thoreau, such body-world parallelism and interpenetration has been used to suggest a higher spiritual reality which penetrates all physical being. More recently, in, say, the poetry of Sylvia Plath, the same pattern of imagery has grown into a vision of all physical substance as grotesquely alien to the perceiving consciousness, the body a dead husk imprisoning a sickened spirit, things endowed with terrifying life. While obviously closer to Thoreau, Bly is essentially similar to neither. His animism stems from a perception of vitality in things which connects with the vitality in the body, but which is neither separable from states of physical being nor basically alien to consciousness. Dying into the darkness at the heart of Bly's poetry is not a transcendence of the body but an immersion in the body in turn immersed in the corporeal flow of things. If this elusive immersion is achieved, the body in its fullness contains and is contained by "the inner world," which is this world, not illuminated but condensed to its deepest indivisible essence.

So behind the traditional mystical paradox—the praise of ordinarily negative states, grief and "the death we love," as avenues to holy joy—there exists in Bly the further paradox that spiritual union with the universe must be sought in physical terms. Perhaps for this reason trees play a constant symbolic role in *Silence*, reaching toward emptiness, but always rooted in the earth. In **"Poem in Three Parts"**:

> The strong leaves of the box-elder tree,
> Plunging in the wind, call us to disappear
> Into the wilds of the universe,
> Where we shall sit at the foot of a plant,
> And live forever, like the dust.

The dust, which appears frequently in Bly's poetry, suggests the most corporeal vision of union with the cosmos, a union spiritually more meaningful than the traditional theological dreams of death if only because of its physical inevitability. Bly compares the two visions in **"At the Funeral of Great-Aunt Mary."**

> The minister tells us that, being
> The sons and daughters of God,
> We rejoice at death, for we go
> To the mansions prepared
> From the foundations of the world.
> Impossible. No one believes it.
>
>   III
> Out on the bare, pioneer field,
> The frail body must wait till dusk

> To be lowered
> In the hot and sandy earth.

The sense of death as physical union with everything becomes a spiritual or moral force in life because it celebrates a loss of self into the other which is more absolute than the ego-loss presumably implied by the death of transcendence; the traditional mystic soul united with god as often seems swollen as lost in oneness. Also the sense of corporeal dissolution of self is, Bly suggests, always with us. Every sleep is a bodily premonition of death. Much of *Silence* concerns periods of transition between waking and sleep, between light and darkness. During such periods the deep image comes close to the surface because the mind sinks to the depths of the body, the body opens to the world.

> The day shall never end, we think:
> We have hair that seems born for the daylight;
> But, at last, the quiet waters of the night will rise,
> And our skin shall see far off, as it does under water.

Perhaps it no longer seems paradoxical that the state of "approaching sleep" is most fully described in **"Awakening."**

> We are approaching sleep: the chestnut blossoms in the mind
> Mingle with the thoughts of pain
>
> . . .
>
> Bodies give off darkness, and chrysanthemums
> Are dark, and horses, . . .
> As the great wheel turns around, grinding
> The living in water.
> . . . the living awakened at last like the dead.

In his second collection of poems, *The Light Around the Body,* Bly's paradoxes are deepened because much of his poetry spreads into another world. Like various other American mystics, most conspicuously Thoreau, Bly becomes interested in the politics of American imperialism, a subject at least superficially uncongenial to mysticism. All but one of the sections of *Light* begin with quotations from Jacob Boehme, the Protestant mystic who influenced the American transcendentalists (through Emerson, who knew him as "Behemen"). "For according to the outward man, we are in this world and according to the inward man, we are in the inward world . . . Since then we are generated out of both worlds, we speak in two languages, and we must be understood also by two languages." The poems of *Light* concern the conflict between the two worlds, in the poet, and in America. So inevitably these poems bring together the two languages of which Boehme speaks, doubling Bly's paradoxes, sometimes confusingly. *Light* still praises grief and maps the progress of the body toward that death which is fulfillment, but while *Silence* emphasized intimations of ultimate union *Light* focuses on obstacles to the good death, one of which is, paradoxically, another sort of death. **"Smothered by the World"** describes a purgatory between life and death.

> Once more the heavy body mourns!
> It howls outside the hedges of life,
> Pushed out of the enclosure.
> Now it must meet the death outside the death.
> Living outside the gate is one death,
> Cold faces gather along the wall,
> A bag of bones warms itself in a tree.

This death results from basic spiritual distortion in the world. Bly describes it in the same physical terms he used to connect the body and the world, but here the connection has become grotesque. Human consciousness inhabits objects only to suggest a general despair, as in **"Those Being Eaten by America."**

> The wild houses go on
> With long hair growing from between their toes
> The feet at night get up
> And run down the long white roads by themselves
>
> The dams reverse themselves and want to go stand
> alone in the desert

The sterile death that follows this despair is occasionally described in terms of whiteness, often snow, but even the darkness which in *Silence* was always the medium of visions has in *Light* changed, become corrupted. "There is another darkness," Bly writes in **"Listening to President Kennedy Lie about the Cuban Invasion."** "There is a bitter fatigue, adult and sad."

The other darkness, in poems like **"Hatred of Men with Black Hair,"** is described as inhabiting the same deep realms as the darkness of vision.

> The State Department floats in the heavy jellies near
> the bottom
> Like exhausted crustaceans, like squids who are
> confused,
> Sending out beams of black light to the open sea,

Both darknesses exist at the root of the mind, which is the source of politics as well as poetry. As the title of **"Hatred"** suggests, the destructive darkness results from a refusal to acknowledge that more primitive darkness which is the way to union. The American dream of self-proclaimed innocence, so shot through with unacknowledged blackness, leads to a death which cannot reinforce life, if only because it strikes so unnaturally. This vision is dramatized most fully in Bly's later poem **"The Teeth Mother Naked at Last,"** but it is suggested in **"At a March against the Vietnam War,"** which appears in *Light.* Bly says of "a boat / Covered with machine guns:"

> It is black,
> The hand reaches out
> And cannot touch it—
> It is that darkness among pine boughs
> That the Puritans brushed
> As they went out to kill turkeys
>
> At the edge of the jungle clearing
> It explodes
> On the ground

> We long to abase ourselves
>
> We have carried around this cup of darkness
> We have longed to pour it over our heads

Always, however individually, the poet reflects his time. Primarily *Silence* contains poetry written in the 1950s, a time of comparative political innocence (or naiveté) for American literature, when literary rebellion against America was usually considered a rather solitary and apolitical experience. *Silence* is a book of solitude, of Bly alone with the world; even its few love poems do not involve a recognizable other. *Light* is a book of the sixties, a predominantly political book, like many other books of poetry published since 1966 (the year Bly organized American Writers Against the Vietnam War). But while Bly's development must obviously be understood in terms of our recent history, he might probably have undergone similar changes in any historical context, for in *Light* he is only dramatizing a tension implicit in the paradoxes of *Silence.*

Traditionally, mysticism has existed in potential or actual conflict with more earthly approaches to morality; the conflict surfaces when the mystic theorizes about evil. Having accepted grief and the dissolution of his body as aspects of a vital flow into "the wilds of the universe," Bly must logically confront experiences of grief and death, perhaps unnecessary grief and premature death, much less palatable to those who suffer them. The mystic always returns to the world of men. The perception of dominant and perhaps inherent evil there can blunt his mystic acceptance, or it can become the basis for more strenuous efforts toward transcendence, a denial of the essential reality of certain aspects of the world in favor of higher realities. Allen Ginsberg, for instance, plays more or less seriously with the latter response when he chants, in "Wichita Vortex Sutra": "I here declare the end of the War / Ancient days' Illusion." But because Bly's mysticism remains untranscendental ("The two worlds are both in this world") neither traditional response is really possible. The social fact of pointless death forces a deeper examination of the idea of death as a spiritual good, but Bly is unwilling to deny either vision.

What he attempts to do instead, besides suggesting how the primitive sense of union has been lost, how death has been corrupted, is to create a vision of process toward a new world in which paradoxes resolve themselves. But the approach of this world is itself paradoxical, a terrible movement toward communal death which, like the individual death of *Silence,* is also the approach of birth. As the tension between inner and outer worlds grows more extreme Bly suggests that the center will not hold; however the approaching apocalypse is also described as evolution. The final section of *Light* is called **"A Body Not Yet Born."** Like the rest of the book it contains images of despairing death, as in **"Hurrying Away from the Earth."**

> Some men have pierced the chest with a long needle
> To stop the heart from beating any more;

. . .

The time for exhortation is past. I have heard
The iron chairs scraping in asylums,

. . .

Men cry when they hear stories of someone rising
from the dead.

If the dark night of the soul has become a universal darkness, it carries implications of universal illumination. In
"When the Dumb Speak," Bly describes

. . . a joyful night in which we lose
Everything, and drift
Like a radish
Rising and falling, and the ocean
At last throws us into the ocean

One ocean flows from the waters of inner experience
described throughout much of *Silence,* but the other
spreads through time as well as space. **"When the Dumb
Speak"** ends with "images" which evoke traditional
Christian visions of the world ending in apocalypse.

Images of the body shaken in the grave,
And the grave filled with seawater;
Fires in the sea

. . .

The house fallen,
The gold sticks broken,

But **"Evolution from the Fish,"** as its title indicates,
describes what is to come not as a Christian end but as an
evolutionary change which parallels earlier changes. Here
the loss of "everything," which is a loss of self, becomes a
participation in the physical development of life from the
beginning. "The grandson of fishes" is described

. . . moving toward his own life
Like fur, walking. And when the frost comes, he is
Fur, mammoth fur, growing longer

. . .

He moves toward the animal, the animal with furry
head!

As the poem moves into our time the furry-headed one
becomes specific, individual, "this long man with the
student girl," but in the end he is embarking on another
voyage, in darkness, through sleep.

Serpents rise from the ocean floor with spiral motions,
A man goes inside a jewel, and sleeps. Do
Not hold my hands down! Let me raise them!
A fire is passing up through the soles of my feet!

An earlier version of **"Evolution"** appeared in 1962 in a
brief anthology of poems by Bly, Duffy, and Wright, *The*

Lion's Tail and Eyes. Indicatively, it included one additional last line: "I am curving back into the mammoth
pool!" By omitting the backward curve Bly alters the final
direction of the poem from the past to the future; now the
subject is not repeating cycles of existence but a continuing upward spiral into new states of being.

Bly is at his most difficult, to follow and to accept, when
he begins to describe the particular nature of the apocalypse
to come, and the evolution it heralds. A premonitory poem
in *Light,* **"Romans Angry about the Inner World,"**
describes that world as "A jagged stone / Flying toward
them out of the darkness" and suggests the final articulation of Bly's evolutionary vision. In the poem "executives" watch Roman executioners torture "a woman /
Who has seen our mother / In the other world." Specifically the
lines refer to the mystical cult of Magna Mater, eventually
suppressed by the Romans. But the anachronistic presence
of the executives implies a comparison between imperial
Rome and neo-imperialist America, a comparison that
goes beyond ordinary politics. Later Bly will elaborate the
theory that the mother-goddesses smothered by one empire
are returning to haunt the psyche of the other. In his long
introduction to **"The Teeth Mother Naked at Last"** at
the Antioch reading, Bly explained a vision of mythic
development largely based on the psychological and
historical investigations of Jung's disciple Erich Neumann.
Originally, as Bly explains Neumann, the world's great
religions were based on worship of the female principle,
the Great Mother; the Romans and the Jews fought to
substitute male gods for the female goddesses, beginning
the long western tradition of primacy of the masculine
consciousness. Bly defines sexual consciousness in Jungian terms: masculine consciousness involves logic, ef-
ficiency, the advancement of material civilization, repression, and control of the natural world; and feminine
consciousness involves intuition, creativity, mystic acceptance of the world. Because only women are biologically creative, it is usually the man who feels the aesthetic
urge to create with materials outside his own body.
However he is truly inspired only if he makes "the great
turn" toward the mother, accepting the guidance of the
(always female) Muse, and exploring his own feminine
consciousness (Jung's anima). Now, though, not only artists but the whole culture is beginning, psychologically, to
turn to the Great Mother. "America looks down in the
psyche now," Bly said at Antioch, "and it sees the mothers
coming up." "That's what's been happening in America in
the last fifteen years, that the father consciousness civilization is dying and the mothers are returning."

As the mythic forms of the mothers suggest, this can be a
destructive as well as liberating process. Drawing on various mythologies for examples Bly describes the four great
mothers in opposed pairs, constructive and destructive: the
mother of fertility (Demeter) balanced by the mother of
destruction (Kali), the ecstatic mother (Artemis) balanced
by the stone mother (Medusa). In this relation to each
other they form a cross, or the four main compass points
of a circle, and the teeth mother hovers on the circumfer-

ence between death and stone mothers. To prove his theory, Bly cites widely various bits of evidence of the return of the different mothers. One manifestation of the destructive mothers in the aesthetic consciousness appears, for instance, in deKooning's paintings; Bly is perhaps thinking of works like "Woman I." In a very different sphere, Bly attributes the American violence of Vietnam, often directed against women and children, to our pathologically masculine soldier' fear of the female, of the mothers, whom they see only in the form of the death mother or the teeth mother. On the other side, Bly sees in hip and liberated life styles the influence of the ecstatic mother, though he explains that the search for the ecstatic mother can fail in a long fall toward the stone mother—the use of drugs, too, dramatizes this paradox, and Bly the comedian does not hesitate to play on the colloquial sense of "stoned."

To those moved by the visionary qualities of Bly's poetry, this theory may present serious problems. How much of it is really believable, how literally does Bly intend it, how necessary is it as a basis for his poetry? Indicatively, little of the theory actually appears in **"The Teeth Mother Naked at Last,"** though it provides a striking title. Bly's vision of the great evolutionary change is felt more convincingly in his poetry—explorations into "the inward world . . . thoughts we have not yet thought" which involve little detailed reference to the mothers—than in his spoken and very explicit explanations of what he thinks now. Bly the performer is enormously compelling, a constantly disarming mixture of vaudeville comedian and oracle, but in retrospect, beyond the range of his personal vibrations, his archetypal sociology does not fully convince. Perhaps in our time any extreme definition of the opposition between male and female consciousness must seem suspect. More important, though, is the tension between Bly's use of the old Jungian archetypes to describe our future, and the constant suggestions in his poetry that the present movement of human consciousness is something new, now hardly dreamed of. Somehow it seems inadequate to describe "the body not yet born" in terms of ancient myths, however they are blended or transmuted to define the world to come. Better to accept Bly's explanations as metaphor, his poems as reality.

For it is the sense of deeply perceived reality in the poetry that leads us in the first place to consider the prose articulation of the theory, and in fact Bly the poet, as he points out, was using the conflict between "masculine" and "feminine" as a metaphor long before he read Neumann and developed his theory. In *Light,* for instance, **"The Busy Man Speaks"** defines "the mother" in terms of "art," "sorrow," "the ocean"; and "the father" in terms of "The stones of cheerfulness, the steel of money." Still earlier, in *Silence,* women are often associated with liberating death, as in **"With Pale Women in Maryland"**: "Like those before, we move to the death we love / With pale women in Maryland."

To see Bly's poetry as dependent on anyone's theory, on Jung's, Neumann's, or even Bly's own, is not only to deny his belief in the irrational psychic sources of poetry but also to dilute the unique force of his poems. If we turn to Jung for explanations, we can say simply that the origin of Bly's deep images is the collective unconscious, that the conflict between the inner and outer worlds is a conflict between anima and persona, that Bly's water imagery is, given his concerns, predictable. Water, Jung says in "Archetypes of the Collective Unconscious," is "no figure of speech, but a living symbol of the dark psyche," the realm "where I experience the other in myself." Even Bly's paradoxical discovery of vitality in death can be explained in terms of Jung's contention, in "Psychological Aspects of the Mother Archetype," that "Nothing can exist without its opposite; the two were one in the beginning and will be one again in the end. Consciousness can only exist through continual recognition of the unconscious, just as everything that lives must pass through many deaths." But to interpret Bly basically in these terms is to oversimplify his paradoxes without really explaining them, as Jung's archetypes inevitably tend to reduce and oversimplify complex individual states of being. Descending into realms initially explored by Jung and later by Neumann, Bly goes beyond both. His greatest strength is his ability to discover in the darkness images that are not archetypal, at least not in the Jungian sense, because they are only beginning to loom into view.

But even if we remain unconvinced by the details of Bly's theory we cannot deny that it remains a fascinating metaphor for states as yet not analytically describable. More important, the mothers metaphor enables Bly to develop and enrich the paradoxes that float up from his inner darkness. He has constructed a vision of mystic evolution that not only refuses to deny but explains the moral dissolution that forms the primary vision of *Light.* The tension between the ecstatic mother and the stone mother provides a theoretical basis for Bly's double conception of darkness, the inspiring darkness of the inner world held in suspension with the terrifying blackness of the outer. **"The Teeth Mother Naked at Last,"** a map of the psychological politics behind an imperial war, is also a record of the collision between inner and outer worlds.

"Teeth Mother," though marked throughout by Bly's characteristic surrealist imagery, differs basically from his earlier poetry. So far it is his only really extensive poem, and its coherence is more theoretical than imagistic. Frequently its deep images give way to flat, almost prosy statement, often far less striking than the visions of *Light,* but in some ways more moving. Bly adopts different tactics in this poem partly because he is writing a sort of propaganda based on juxtaposition of certain facts, but also because it seems impossible, and probably not desirable, to assimilate the actuality of Vietnam into poetry as Bly has previously written it. The Vietnam poems in *Light* primarily concerned the reverberations of war; **"Teeth Mother"** is often a simple contemplation of unbearable facts. But it also implies an explanation.

> Helicopters flutter overhead. The death-
> bee is coming. Supersabres

like knots of neurotic energy sweep
around and return.
This is Hamilton's triumph.
This is the advantage of a centralized bank.

Destructive—"neurotic"—machines dominate the poem; despite his moral revulsion, Bly's ability to immerse himself in things enables him to evoke the alien world of machines and mechanical men as fully as he evokes the inner world. Vietnam represents the desperate end of the "masculine" rage for order, the force that created American prosperity but a force basically corrupted by its denial of the inner world. The warrior mentality, recreating itself in machines, opposes not only nature ("800 steel pellets fly through the vegetable walls") but the dark flow of its own humanity, its movement toward the death which completes life. The desire for death as fulfillment, corrupted, becomes a desire for death as grotesque destruction.

> The ministers lie, the professors lie, the television lies,
>   the priests lie . . .
> These lies mean that the country wants to die.
>
> . . .
>
> It is a desire to take death inside,
> to feel it burning inside, pushing out strong hairs,
> like a clothes brush in the intestines

In a series of awkward but often striking juxtapositions, Bly suggests that the American rejection of grief and darkness, made possible by wealth, creates the grief of Vietnam, It is:

> because we have so few tears falling on our own hands
> that the Supersabre turns and screams down toward
> the earth

In the face of this there appears no adequate response, no praise of the grief that follows the denial of grief, no mystical acceptance. Bly the political moralist presents, ironically undercut, the plea of the contemplative dreamer, who sees the corporeal flow of existence very much in terms that suggest *Silence.*

> Tell me about the particles of Babylonian thought that
>   still pass through the earthworm every day,
> Don't tell me about "the frightening laborers who do
>   not read books"

But the dehumanizing outer darkness prevails:

> if one of those children came near that we have set on
> fire,
> came toward you like a gray barn, walking,
> you would howl like a wind tunnel in a hurricane
> you would tear at your shirt with blue hands,

No response to this, and yet, paradoxically, Bly suggests a response, or at least a way of understanding it. The horribly catalogued violence against human and vegetable nature can be seen in a more distant sense as a natural aspect of the apocalyptic evolutionary change described in

more positive terms in the final pages of *Light.* One voice in **"Teeth Mother,"** looking for solace, suggests of the violence of "the Marine battalion," "This happens when the seasons change / this happens when the leaves begin to drop from the trees too early." Bly undercuts the suggestion of solace, but the comparison remains. Vietnam, in some sense the death of American dreams, is not an end but a transition, in which the teeth mother necessarily appears as an aspect of the ecstatic mother.

> Now the whole nation starts to whirl
>
> . . .
>
> pigs rush toward the cliff,
> the waters underneath part: in one ocean luminous
> globes
>   float up (in them hairy and ecstatic rock musi-
> cians)—
> in the other, the teeth mother, naked at last.

The balance, and the sense of cycles evolving, provide no cure to present agony. Bly knows it is the false transcendence of agony, with its attendant repression, which distorts human consciousness in the first place. But the vision of evolution enables Bly to sustain his paradoxical suspension of despair and mystic hope, his sense of death as life. Perhaps that paradox will always defy resolution, but in his latest poetry Bly continues to offer hope for evolution into a state of consciousness in which despair can be replaced by that grief which attends the natural movement of life, which is not inconsistent with joy. At the end of a recent poem read at Antioch, Bly suggests, through paradox now expressed with a clear simplicity, that the conflict between the father and the mother may be resolved by that consciousness now being born.

> More of the fathers are dying each day,
> It's time for the sons.
> Bits of darkness are gathering around the sons,
> The darkness appears as flakes of light.
>   . . . . .
>
> So Much Is Not Spoken
> Oh yes, I love you, book of my confessions,
> when the swallowed begins to rise from the earth
> again,
> and the deep hungers
> from the wells. So much is still inside me—like cows
> eating
> in a collapsed strawpile all winter to get out.
> Everything we need now is buried,
> it's far back into the mountain,
> it's under the water guarded by women.
>
> These lines themselves are sunk to the waist in the
> dusk under the odorous cedars,
> each rain will only drive them deeper,
> they will leave a faint glow in the dead leaves.
> You too are weeping in the low shade of the pine
> branches,
> you feel yourself about to be buried too,
> you are a ghost stag shaking his antlers in the herony
> light,

what is beneath us will be triumphant
in the cool air made fragrant by owlfeathers.

I am only half-risen.
I see how carefully I covered my tracks as I wrote,
how well I have brushed over the past with my tail.
I enter rooms full of photographs of the dead.
My hair stands up
as a badger crosses my path in the moonlight.

I see faces looking at me in the shallow waters
where I have thrown them down.
Mother and father pushed into the dark.
That shows how close I am to the dust that fills the
cracks on the ocean floor,
how much I love to fly in the rain,
how much I love to see the jellyfish pulsing at the
cold borders of the universe.

I have piled up people like dead flies between the
storm windows and the kitchen pane.
I stand at the edges of the light, howling to come in!
        So much is not spoken! And yet
all at once I follow the wind through open holes in
the blood . . .
So much ecstasy . . .
long evenings when the leopard leaps up to the stars,
and in an instant we understand all the rocks in the
world.

And I am there, prowling like a limp-footed bull
outside the circle of the fire,
praying, meditating,
full of energy, like a white horse, saddled, alone on
the unused fields.

A consciousness is hovering under the mind's feet,
climbing at times up on a shoelace!
It is a willow that knows of water under the earth.
I am a father who dips as he passes over underground
rivers,
who can feel his children through all distance and
time!

          ANOTHER POEM FOR WALLACE STEVENS
You are Isis, and I, a hen
picking among chaff,
move my thin head.
You flow, over rocks
and around reeds,
searching, as Isis
for her child, who will play
again by the sacks
of grain, shadowed in the shadowy barn.
We too, your readers, hollys of darkness,
mistletoes of winter, wait
for the Shining One, with whom
we will flee over the littered and wind blown roads.

               WATER RECONCILIATION
When your privacy is beginning over,
how beautiful the things that you did not notice!
A few sweetclover plants in the ditch
along the road to Bellingham,
culvert mouths in driveway approaches,
wooden corncribs, leaning,

what no one loves, no one rushes toward or shouts
about,
what lives like the new moon,
and the wind
blowing against the rumps of grazing cows.

Telephone wires stretched across water,
the drowning sailor standing at the foot of his mother's
bed,
grandfathers and grandsons sitting together.

                                                  Robert Bly

Lawrence Kramer (essay date Winter 1983)

SOURCE: "A Sensible Emptiness: Robert Bly and the
Poetics of Immanence," in *Contemporary Literature,* Vol.
XXIV, No. 4, Winter, 1983, pp. 449-62.

[*In the following essay, Kramer discusses the conventions
of Bly's "deep image" poetry and the presentation of immediate experience in* Silence in the Snowy Fields *and*
This Tree Will Be Here For a Thousand Years.]

The poetry of Robert Bly probably evokes the phrase "deep
image" for most readers. Deep images are supposed to tap
unconscious sources of energy, and the poetry that uses
them is thought to give only a sketchy account of the
phenomenal world. Everyday reality is only a surface; it
becomes significant insofar as it is disturbed by dark forces
that rise up from below. Bly has often endorsed this way
of looking at his work, in part perhaps because to do so
frees him from the burdens of a poetic tradition. The
context for his poetry is not a genre or a movement among
poetic generations; it is a primary truth, known to intuition
and expressible in myth. But Bly's poetry does not always
comply with the aesthetics of the deep image. There are
many lyrics that seem to celebrate pure immediacy for its
own sake:

It is the morning. The country has slept the whole
winter.
Window seats were covered with fur skins, the yard
was full
Of stiff dogs, and hands that clumsily held heavy
books.

Now we wake, and rise from bed, and eat breakfast!—
Shouts rise from the harbour of the blood,
Mists, and masts rising, the knock of wooden tackle
in the sunlight.

                                   (**"Waking from Sleep"**)

Lines like these have poetic affiliations that Bly's deep image poetry obscures and even denies. My aim in this essay
is to argue that Bly's successful poetry always depends on
a poetic rather than on an esoteric context, and that his
genuine achievement as a poet has little to do with deep
images.

Bly's poetic tradition is a specifically American one, and
he shares it with several other poets of his generation,

especially Gary Snyder and James Wright. What these poets have in common is a feeling for the numinous value of objects divorced from all transcendental glamor. Their values depend on simple, tangible, elemental things, confronted almost without thought. Unlike the thing-intoxicated early Williams, they are not indiscriminate in their appropriation of reality; they are closer to the spirit of Frost's "The fact is the sweetest dream that labor knows," and even closer to the definition of a poetics of immanence given by Walt Whitman:

> An American literat fills his own place . . .
> As he emits himself, facts are showered over with light,
> The day-light is lit with more volatile light—the deep between the setting and rising sun goes deeper many fold,
> Each precise object, condition, combination, process, exhibits a beauty.

> **("Waking from Sleep")**

The contemporary poem of immanence is written to be a fragment of a lost, privileged presence; it is not concerned with words but with things. Such a poem is meant to carry the facticity of things over into their representation by using a language in which the qualities of bodies—weight, position, texture, mass—is paramount. The logic of argument or narrative breaks down in favor of cinematic cuts from one item to another; Bly's poetry moves by groping forward metonymically:

> The storm is coming. The small farmhouse in Minnesota
> Is hardly strong enough for the storm.
> Darkness, darkness in grass, darkness in trees.
> Even the water in wells trembles.
> Bodies give off darkness, and chrysanthemums
> Are dark, and horses, who are bearing great loads of hay
> To the deep barns where the dark air is moving from corners.

> **("Awakening,")**

In lines like these, where the enveloping authority of a Whitmanian ego is lacking, value does not derive from a harmonization of subject and object but from the unspoken assimilation of both to a third, more primitive category. With the help of a rhetoric that shifts freely between personification and objectification, subjects are reduced and objects heightened so that both appear as prereflective fusions of consciousness and materiality—in other words, as bodies. Unrelated presences—horses, chrysanthemums, the corners of barns, the consciousness of the speaker—are drawn together as bodies in the medium of darkness, which is itself a kind of larger body here, diffused but tangible and animate. The traditional emphasis on "materials," as Whitman called them, is exaggerated to such a degree that physical proximity appears as a form of primary awareness or intentionality. Things fill space as materializations of perception: bodies "give off" darkness instead of being dark, and the trembling of water in wells

registers an anxious anticipation that belongs to no one in particular, yet belongs where it is. At the same time, subjectivity loses the indeterminate depth that it characteristically derives from subject-object opposition. Any sense of self is primarily physical; any sense of relationship is primarily spatial.

Bly's first book, *Silence in the Snowy Fields* (1962), is an important example of the poetics of immanence. Even before it was published, Donald Hall had celebrated its intimation of "a subjective life which is *general,* and which corresponds to an old objective life of shared experience and knowledge." Already in *Silence,* however, other strains were apparent in Bly's work, and over the years they have become dominant. Political outrage, fueled by the Vietnam war and expressed most stridently in *The Light Around the Body* (1967), led Bly to attempt a fusion of lyric with prophecy. The ambition to tap a collective unconscious impelled him to an archetypal, irrationalist style that many readers, myself included, find histrionic or merely pedantic—a doctrinaire surrealism or Jungian evangelism. But in 1979, Bly published a small book of striking austerity, *This Tree Will Be Here For A Thousand Years.* Collecting poems written since the publication of *Silence,* the new volume tries to recapture the heightened immediacy and "thingy spirit" of the first.

Tree, in fact, is Bly's explicit attempt to return to his origins, both personal and poetic. In his preface, he announces that the newly collected poems are not meant to form a sequel to *Silence* but to complete it; "the two books," he says, "make one book." And the new half of that book is openly nostalgic, crowded with images that mark moments of origin and departure: first snows, first frosts, first glimpses, first perceptions of physical or emotional distance. Bly's *Tree*-graft is arguably the best measure of his work to date. The double book not only puts his approach to a poetics of immanence into sharp focus, but also—perhaps unwillingly—admits some of the limitations that constrain him.

Tree/Silence will occupy most of my space here, but before turning to it I want to eliminate its competition. It is as important to reject Bly as a poet of deep images as it is to acknowledge him as a poet of bodies and spaces, so for a little while I will be polemical. Bly's style is motivated by a will to subtraction, an urge to simplify that far outdoes Thoreau's. Bly wants experience reduced to its essential elements; to be a poet of space one must clear out the clutter. Part of this simplification is a restriction of the topics of the poetry to three: landscape, history, and the archetypal unconscious. But only the first of these can really endure a minimalist treatment. Bly's landscapes are bucolic, but their numinous physicality gives them the innocence of the pastoral, and it is as a pastoral poet that he must stand or fall. (American poets of immanence prefer pastoral as a genre; William Stafford and Wendell Berry, as well as Wright and Snyder, come to mind.) Bly's sense of history as a purely destructive force, all war and economic exploitation, is itself a pastoral convention: the complaint of Tityrus under the tree, the deserted village smothered by "Trade's unfeeling train." But the convention is maintained with defiant sentimentality; it dismisses the complexity of social good and evil for a melodrama of victims and victimizers. When Bly turns to visions of "the murdered pine" laid low by "Arabic numerals . . . dressed as bankers and sportsmen" (**"The Current Administration"**), or proclaims that "There are lives the executives / Know nothing of, / A leaping of the body, / The body rolling—and I have felt it—(**"Romans Angry about the Inner World"**), history is reduced to a gush of antibourgeois rhetoric that confuses—sometimes willfully, as here—prophetic rage with self-congratulation.

With archetypes, something similar happens. Bly takes a pentecostal view of the unconscious; he receives the irrational uncritically as a form of revelation. His commentary on the subject tends to be more enchanted than informed:

> You know Freud considered in the first half of his life Eros energy to be the most powerful energy in the unconscious; we could also call that Demeter energy or Good Mother energy. Then, during the First World War, he saw Europe committing suicide, and it came to him that there is another balancing energy involved, which might be called the Death Wish, or the desire to die.

The poetry rarely falls down this badly, but its trouble with archetypes is similar. As a poet, Bly reduces his irrational imagery to the reflex level by refusing to take it seriously enough. His dreamlike passages and surrealist fantasies are typically ambivalent, a blend of terror and ecstasy, delusion and vision. But the poetry is not ambivalent *about* them. The potentially devastating otherness of the mind is broken down into bundles of merely formal attributes, almost ornaments, while Bly unreservedly endorses the "joyful night in which we lose / Everything" in a primal darkness (**"When the Dumb Speak"**). This is easiest to see in poems like **"The Busy Man Speaks,"** where the plenitude of archetype is denied to the tribe of the poet's villainous executives. The Busy Man gives himself away to the paternal Chase National Bank with its "landscape of zeros" and rejects the maternal spirit that encompasses both "the night full of crickets" and "the suffering of death," both "the mother of the open fields" and "the mother of Christ." The poem satirizes this choice stridently but fails to confront the terrible rigor of the alternative. It is merely glib to say "I shall give myself away" to fertility and mystery when they embrace the kind of pain, isolation, and passivity that the images of the poem ascribe to them. Even in less tendentious pieces, this failure to suffer what is celebrated undermines the impact of Bly's admittedly striking images:

> The blind horse among the cherry trees—
> And bones, sticking from cool earth.
> The heart leaps
> Almost up to the sky!

> **("Wanting to Experience All Things")**

The echo of Wordsworth here is a subtle act of self-aggrandizement: Bly's images celebrate the very collision of life and death, wholeness and maiming, that threatens to depress Wordsworth's leaping heart. Yet Bly's easy confidence in the therapeutic value of elementals seems facile when it is set against the bewildered stubbornness with which, say, the narrator of **"Resolution and Independence"** struggles through "the fear that kills; / And hope that is unwilling to be fed" just to achieve a workable defense mechanism.

That leaves the landscape, and particularly the landscape of Bly's native Minnesota. The rugged countryside, with its severe winters, seems to heighten the bodiliness of everyone and everything within its borders. Even at its hardest and sparest, it remains a *locus amoenus,* one that displaces the pastoral values of abundance and innocence from "the sweet especial rural scene" into a depth of appreciation for a scene that may be neither special nor sweet. Perceived with archaic, animistic simplicity, Minnesota is an austere Arcadia, a parcel of ground that appears sacred because everything inessential has been subtracted from it.

The decisive poem in this pattern of apotheosis is a famous one from *Silence,* **"Driving Toward the Lac Qui Parle River."** Here, the Minnesota countryside appears as both an animating presence and an animate one. It fills its place like a large projected body, a *corpus* rather than a *genius loci.* To enter this space is to participate in an ecstasy of locations that spreads from one site to another as if handed or breathed around:

> I am driving; it is dusk; Minnesota.
> The stubble field catches the last growth of sun.
> The soybeans are breathing on all sides.
> Old men are sitting before their houses on car seats
> In the small towns. I am happy,
> The moon rising above the turkey sheds.

> **("Wanting to Experience All Things")**

Though the time of the scene indicates transience, the spatial relations point to a permanence of presence. Each depleted object is balanced by a vital one: stubble by breathing soybeans, the old men by the young poet, the car seats by the moving car, the failing sun by the rising moon, the empty houses by the turkey sheds. The happiness of the poet does not come from any particular part of the landscape, nor from a subjective integration of the details into a whole. It is simply a fact of being there, not to be distinguished—as the loose syntax indicates—from the fact of the rising moon stationed above the turkey sheds.

"Driving" establishes the mode that the poems of *Tree* would like to recapture: an awed sense of connectedness, a feeling for a perfect but nonrational, inexplicable order in things, a language of pure description that never merely describes. Bly's aim in *Tree* is to find a severe simplicity by submitting attention to a drastic discipline. He looks into his privileged landscape to single out two or three objects, not necessarily related ones, which animate each other or their horizon merely by existing together. The objects all belong to the life of rural work and its seasonal imperatives; they are all somehow innocent; and they are all sanctified by their participation in the primary mystery of natural space: "Sometimes when you put your hand into a hollow tree / you touch the dark places between the stars" (**"Women We Never See Again"**).

The *Tree* poems, like those of *Silence,* vacillate between observation and a sort of descriptive rapture. Their strongest impulse is to leap abruptly from bare perception to mystical vision, usually by finding that the merely physical objects at hand have a creaturely dimension, or even a primitive intentionality:

> In small towns the houses are built right on the ground;
> The lamplight falls on all fours in the grass.
>
> **("Driving Toward the Lac Qui Parle River")**
>
> The day is awake. The bark calls to the rain still in the cloud.
> "Never forget the lonely taste of the white dew."
>
> **("July Morning")**

The release of vision is often triggered, as it is here, by proximity to the earth, particularly the grass, and by the passivity—tranquil, but always tinged with melancholy—that Bly associates with it. Often, too, the threshold of vision is an actual space where a line is drawn between light and darkness—the hollow of a tree, or a lake with reeds: "In the Ashby reeds it is already night, / though it is still day out on the lake" (**"Pulling a Rowboat Up Among Lake Reeds"**).

Bly's animism is a literal attempt to register what he calls "the consciousness *out there* among plants and animals." "I've come to believe," he writes, "that it is important for everyone that the second consciousness appear somehow in the poem, merged or not. It's time. The 'human' poem can become transparent or porous at the end, so that the city, or objects, or the countryside enters" (**"The Two Presences,"** Preface to *Tree*). The self-conscious innocence of these remarks makes them a little disingenuous; nothing is really at stake here but an overly naturalistic solution to the problem of subject-object relations that has confronted poetry in English since the Romantics. Nevertheless, Bly's impulse is distinctive. He does not want to empathize with objects, subtly mastering them in the process, nor does he want to internalize them. What he seeks instead is an impersonal poise, a detachment from both himself and the objects that will allow him to meet them as equals on—literally—the same ground. Unhappy with the mind's tendency to humanize external reality, he tries to limit his own subjectivity by naturalizing it. Unlike Charles Olson, who resists "the lyrical interference of the individual as ego" by programmatically treating persons as things, Bly treats all significant things as living bodies, dispersed locations of sentience.

In *Silence,* Bly's efforts to incorporate himself with otherness usually take the form of oblique, half-acknowledged personifications, like the image of light on all fours from **"Driving."** In **"Solitude Late at Night in the Woods,"** birch trees paradoxically take on sentience when the poet seems to deny it to them:

> The body is like a November birch facing the full moon
> And reaching into the cold heavens.
> In these trees there is no ambition, no sodden body, no leaves,
> Nothing but bare trunks climbing like cold fire!
>
> **("July Morning")**

At first, the metaphorical identification of the solitary body with a desolate single birch tree suggests that the body has become inanimate, that its subjectivity has frozen. But the rhetorical equation of the lack of ambition and sodden body in winter birches with their lack of leaves reverses the implication. Feelings, like leaves, belong to the trees inherently; the birches' lack of ambition and soddenness is not an absence of mind but a passionate concentration of purpose that the poet's body shares. When the poem speaks of "bare trunks climbing like cold fire," the image can refer equally well to the stark positioning of the winter trees or to the strained intensity of their "second consciousness." Likewise, the poet's body can accept identification with both the inner and the outer trees. Their situations, in every sense of the term, are parallel:

> I must return to the trapped fields,
> To the obedient earth.
> The trees shall be reaching all the winter.
>
> **("July Morning")**

The same personification appears in a more attenuated, more disguised form in another poem from *Silence,* **"Hunting Pheasants in a Cornfield":**

> What is so strange about a tree alone in an open field?
> It is a willow tree. I walk around and around it.
> The body is strangely torn, and cannot leave it.
> At last I sit down beneath it.
>
> **("July Morning")**

Here, the tree's subjective presence manifests itself in the inexplicable pull of fellowship between its body and a man's. The strangeness of the experience comes from the poet's participation in the tree's solitude, a feeling, not an inanimate fact, which he feels compelled to cure for both of them. The two "torn" bodies heal into one when the restlessly moving poet sits under the willow, thereby accepting both the tree's stillness and its domination, and taking up Bly's position of richest consciousness, near the earth. The poem underlines this union later on when it refers to "the chill skin of the branches" and declares that "The mind has shed leaves alone for years." With the closing image, the intimacy with the tree dissolves, but the poet recognizes that his identity is that of a body, not a subject:

I am happy in this ancient place,
A spot easily caught sight of above the corn,
If I were a young animal ready to turn home at dusk.

("July Morning")

Of course, only a subject can perform such an act of self-reflection, but the poem will acknowledge no paradox; it simply doesn't care.

When the poems in *Tree* "return" to the consciousness *out there* first found in *Silence,* they do it, stringently, without personification. Bly seems to have rejected the figure as too rhetorical, tainted by lyrical interference. No matter how subtilized, it always retains its link to the eighteenth-century pictorial ode, where abstractions are forced to "posture" and naturalness is covertly denied as a value. To realize the "second consciousness" in *Tree,* Bly depends primarily on a movement of language that effaces the presence of his voice, and thus his presence as a subject, as the texture of the poem modulates from sparseness to richness. In recent years, many American poets have tried to acknowledge the power of otherness by writing in a peculiarly "quiet" language, simplified in syntax, sparing of metaphor, and commemorative in intent. The style is one that minimizes the poet's action; the object, the other, borrows his language and seems to write *through* him. Many of the poems in *Tree* begin in this mode, often to the accompaniment of unemphatic first-person pronouns that both signal the poet's presence and dissolve it into a minimalized, anonymous articulation. Then, as the second consciousness takes hold, the "I" is wholly obscured and the eye takes over. The poet's presence merges into the landscape's, and the language, now writing for both the self and the other, shifts from description to figuration or from transparent to intricate syntax.

Elaborate though it is in the telling, this pattern gives the effect of a heightened simplicity, and it can be remarkably compressed:

How lightly the legs walk over the snow-whitened fields!
I wander far off, like a daddy-longlegs blown over the water.
All day I worked alone, hour after hour.
It is January, easy walking, the big snows still to come.

("After a Day of Work")

Each couplet of this poem encapsulates the basic rhythm of dissolving subjectivity. In the first, the poet wavers on the edge of self-estrangement, half-lost in the movement of "the legs"—legs almost no longer his. He recovers his selfhood only long enough to record how far he wanders off from it into the mood of the snow-whitened fields. The image of the daddy-longlegs both completes his effacement—together with his transformation into pure body, a pair of legs that move lightly—and expresses the feathery inwardness that belongs to the fields. The first line of the second couplet brings the poet back to himself, but only in the past tense, which robs his returning identity of any im-

mediacy it might have had. Finally, the closing line absorbs him back into January, the frail, impersonal condition of "easy walking" that has already shaped his consciousness all day.

Another poem, **"Nailing a Dock Together,"** spontaneously discards the satisfactions of selfhood with a gesture that is half generous and half nostalgic. The poet lets his awareness shift away from the pleasure he takes in working with boards—"How I love / putting my wet foot / on the boards I sawed myself!"—to the charismatic presence of a penned horse whose inner freedom works with boards in another way:

It is a horse whose neck human
beings have longed to touch for centuries.
He stands in a stable of invisible wood.

("After a Day of Work")

Once again, there is a movement from reflective awareness to simple sentience, from mind to body—here, to an image of ideal bodiliness. But the visionary leap in this case rebukes the poet as well as obscuring his presence as a subject. His dock is "a ladder stretching back to land," a literal attachment linking him to the earth. It enables him to approach the horse's consciousness, but it also humbles him: the horse does not need such external props. It dwells in a space of its own making more fully than the human body, beset by a longing that spans centuries, can ever do. The seductive neck is not only untouched, but untouchable.

The rigor of Bly's engagement with the second consciousness in *Tree* diffuses itself in the ascetic, quietly mournful tone of the book, and marks it off in yet another way from *Silence,* that origin it can never quite reach. Many of the earlier poems are founded on a sense of irrepressible joy that surges up in the community of feeling between the human and the natural. In a world subject to personification, the mere physical energy of the self can seem to reflect a universal exuberance. Dazzled by bodily existence, the poet can bask in an illusion of innocence and permanence that seems to be a transparent appreciation of reality:

Oh, on an early morning I think I shall live for ever!
I am wrapped in my joyful flesh,
As the grass is wrapped in its clouds of green.

("Poem in Three Parts")

Outside of elegy, the will to personify is more often than not a will to celebrate. With personification stripped away, the consciousness of objects appears in a new light, rooted in the pathos of change and the vulnerability of being still or set in place. Bly remarks in his preface that "the second consciousness has a melancholy tone, the tear inside the stone, what Lucretius calls 'the tears of things,' an energy circling downward, felt often in autumn, or moving slowly around apple trees or stars" (**"The Two Presences"**). The surprising substitution of Lucretius for Virgil makes its own kind of sense: the melancholy of Bly's poems reflects a sense of fatality in natural process, an ominous undertone of "night being ripped away from day." The poetry of *Tree* is constantly envisioning things at a vanishing point. In **"Late Moon,"** the farm of the poet's father appears half moonlit, half dark, in "the west that eats it away," while Bly himself, about to go in, fades into his own shadow as he sees it reaching for the latch. Many of the poems end in startled isolation as something disappears: a rabbit scooting under a granary joist, snow falling from a window, a column of smoke rising over a distant field. *Silence* is also marked at times by the tear within the stone, but the mark is often erased by poems that close with an image of fullness or continuation: people talking in a boat in **"Driving,"** or the moonlit road of **"After Working"**:

> We know the road; as the moonlight
> Lifts everything, so in a night like this
> The road goes on ahead, it is all clear.
>
> (**"Poem in Three Parts"**)

Tree is consistent in refusing to balance its tilt towards desolation. Most of the poems close in muted sadness, some in despair, none in a pleasure without a shadow. The book as a whole is carefully framed between a falling away and a falling inward. The first poem, **"October Frost,"** ends with ears "reaching far away east in the early darkness," half lost, half (literally) reoriented. The last poem, **"Out Picking Up Corn,"** lapses into disorientation with the image of a blanket of fog near a cliff—not a description, but a closing metaphor for the self in danger from its own sense of depth.

Bly responds to this entropic movement by setting a new value on the barrenness it leaves behind. Emptiness, or a few objects lodged in a too-open space, is simply the extreme to which a poetics of subtraction can go. Naturally, such a blankness suggests death. The few scattered objects left to be seen turn into memorials, cenotaphic images, of a lost plenitude: "Clods rose above the snow in the plowing west, / like mountain tops, or the chest of graves" (**"Roads"**). One poem, **"A Long Walk Before the Snows Began,"** so surrounds the poet with remnants and absences—"a few grains of white sleet on the leaves," the tracks of mice and a deer—that he is forced to respond by positing his own death, which appears as the gradual withdrawal of other presences from his body:

> I see my body lying stretched out.
> A woman whose face I cannot see stands near my body.
> A column of smoke rises from Vonderharr's field.
>
> (**"Poem in Three Parts"**)

Yet the emptiness can also appear as a rent in the phenomenal world, a site of sudden epiphany like the hollow in the tree that encloses the space between the stars. Bly's ambivalence is genuine on this point. A blank space can stand as a bleak authenticity, the meager reward for the poet's devotion to otherness, or it can give rise to a third consciousness, beyond and including both the self's and the other's, that consoles the bleakness from which it arises: "There are women we love whom we never see again. / They are chestnuts shining in the rain" (**"Women We Never See Again"**). Another poem, **"Driving My Parents Home at Christmas,"** grasps both facets of emptiness at once and incidentally measures the lostness of all origins. On the drive, over a treacherous road, the parents recollect their lives in tiny fragments—"hauling water . . . eating an orange"—but their old age gives this the air of recalling the dead ("their frailty hesitates on the edge of a mountainside"). Ironically, their safe return home is their entry into emptiness: "When they open the door of their house, they disappear." Yet the abyss of their disappearance turns abruptly into a house without walls, in which their presence is recaptured by a dialectical image: "They sit so close to each other . . . as if pressed together by the snow" (ellipsis Bly's). Here, love and mortality fuse in their antagonism, each both repealing and heightening the other.

Bly calls such sensible emptiness as this "a place to live," and the poem that offers the phrase, **"An Empty Place,"** is the key text in *Tree.* It starts with prose, praising empty places as "white and light-footed": "There is a joy in emptiness. One day I saw an empty corncob on the ground, so beautiful, and where each kernel had been, there was a place to live." The joy here is the sleight of mind that turns the fleeting of things into the freedom of light-footedness, transience in time into movement in space; the beauty is the trick of sight that turns vacancy into plenitude, one empty corncob into a landscape of places to live. The poem shifts to verse for a gloss on these sentences, covertly giving them a quasi-scriptural status as a text for explication. The poet's eyes again turn to the ground and find a scattering of debris there. Some of it he reanimates, using figuration to connect the broken to the whole; some of it he leaves as a sign that all breakage is irreparable:

> The eyes are drawn to the dusty ground in fall—
> small pieces of crushed oyster shell,
> like doors into the earth made of mother-of-pearl;
> slivers of glass,
> a white chicken's feather that still seems excited by the warm blood.
>
> (**"Poem in Three Parts"**)

As a last fragment, the poem brings back the corncob, expanding "room after room in its endless palace." Unfortunately, this leads to a weak ending, a wishful rather than integral identification of the corncob "palace" with Christ's house of many mansions. But the poem's scanty particulars retain the warmth and luminosity that Bly's ascetic attention has given them: minuscule body-fragments, but still warm.

"An Empty Place" is not the only poem in *Tree* marred by tendentiousness. A few others play tired archetypal tricks. Most of the book, though, carries the austere conviction of a backward look that forgives what it cannot recover, and it achieves a somber intensity not present in Bly's work since the darker poems of **Silence,** which it surpasses in harshness and resonance. Taken together, in their essential *dis*continuity, the two books represent Bly and the style of immanence at their strongest. The power of this poetry is limited, but real, even if its "cosmic" proportions are sometimes more fuzzy than suggestive. When Bly's lyrics are ascetic about the memory of immanence, when they are stringent about the placement of bodies on the margins of an emptiness, the emptiness becomes a persuasive sign for the original presences that it displaces. The nostalgia of the text for lost immediacies becomes seductive because the language of the text appears as the impression—a scratch, a scuff, a bruise—left behind by what is not there.

Holly Prado (review date 29 December 1985)

SOURCE: A review of *Loving a Woman in Two Worlds,* in *Los Angeles Times Book Review,* December 29, 1985, p. 11.

[*In the following review, Prado offers tempered assessment of* Loving a Woman in Two Worlds.]

Robert Bly's latest book of poems is being presented as a volume of love poetry. It is, and it isn't. The phrase ". . . in Two Worlds," which makes up half the title is a clue that Bly is not only speaking of human relationship but also of an enigmatic, inner realm.

Bly has a history of exploring the feminine that lives within—in men as well as in women. "The peony says that we have been given a gift, / and it is not the gift of this world. / Behind the leaves of the peony / there is a world still darker, that feeds many." The dark, nourishing world is the mystery that moves us—the knowledge that nature is alive. In these poems, Bly worships the mystery rather than trying, as many have, to destroy it by forcing it to make rational sense. He suggests that accepting the rhythms of nature amounts to accepting the secret rhythms of our own lives. The message-threads of meaning that run behind the poems, aren't blatantly stated but intuited: "A power neither of us knows has spoken to us."

There's human love here, too, a distinct "you" to whom Bly speaks. But is she really an outer woman? Is she Bly's interior feminine, perhaps? "The night is moist, and nourishing as your mind / that lets everything around you live. / I saw you carry the plants inside tonight / over the grass to save them from the cold." Taken literally, someone has brought plants into the house; taken figuratively, a caring figure protects and tends nature in a way that has ever-deepening spiritual resonances. With the abundance of flat, me-me-me poetry being written today, it's wonderful to read poems that shimmer on more than one level of possibility.

Because Bly has been practicing the art of poetry for many years, the poems in **Loving a Woman in Two Worlds** are distilled, offering an informed simplicity that can be mistaken for simple-mindedness unless the reader pays attention. Bly now seems to trust that a reader can attend fully to his special voice; therefore, one wants to listen closely, to lean toward the poet and be whispered to about mysteries. **"What We Provide"** is a four-line piece that a reader could hear, whispered, and then want to hear again and again. "Every breath taken in by the man / who loves, and the woman who loves, / goes to fill the water tank / where the spirit horses drink." What are those horses doing there? Whose water tank? This isn't poetry to be analyzed intellectually but to be mused on in the quiet of the reader's questioning mind until the images gather the occult clarity that's a product of Bly's long journey into the psyche and into poetry.

Occasionally, there's disappointment in the poems. Although Bly's instinct for the right form and language carries him well most of the time, there are a few short poems that do have an oversimplified tone: A quick list of objects or animals is supposed to provide sudden revelation, but sometimes a list is only a list; the poet's vision falters. He is also tempted by preciousness from time to time—oddly strained lines, such as, "I am faithful as the ant with his small waist," can mar the distillation that he's achieved in the whole of the book. Small objections, but one of the best spiritual poets we have should consider them. We don't expect perfection, only the uninterrupted enchantment that Bly is capable of sustaining, that he does give us, often, that we deeply need.

Joyce Peseroff (review date 25 May 1986)

SOURCE: "Minnesota Transcendentalist," in *New York Times Book Review,* May 25, 1986, p. 2.

[*In the following review, Peseroff offers positive evaluation of Bly's* Selected Poems.]

I first heard Robert Bly read his poems in the mid-1970s, sitting in the drab, fluorescent-lighted cafeteria of a community college. Most of his audience of students had been brought by their teachers, and stoically waited to have culture imposed upon them. Within the first 30 minutes of a two-hour reading Mr. Bly had every listener leaning forward, enthralled by his stage presence and props as well as by the tenderness of **"The Dead Seal,"** and by the terror of **"Counting Small-Boned Bodies,"** which he recited from under an enormous straw mask in a high-pitched, witchy voice. Poetry was no embroidery, it was the fiber of life; a hundred people walked away convinced.

Mr. Bly has never believed that poetry makes nothing happen. For almost 30 years he has been a busy and energetic advocate for certain spiritual, political and literary values; a publisher, translator and shaman. A man who praises privacy and solitude, he writes poems that rush toward and embrace the world, both the outer world, acutely observed in its glory and decay, and the inner world, to him the source of the soul's ecstasy and grief. Reconciling these two worlds has always been his mission as he writes poems meant, in words he quotes from the French prose poet Francis Ponge, to "nourish the spirit of man by giving him the cosmos to suckle." In *Selected Poems,* his new collection, he has shaped from both worlds his record of the body's journey and the soul's quest. This is not just an anthology of Mr. Bly's best work; its 11 new essays and its particular method of organization require a fresh look at the poet's achievement.

The book is arranged in nine sections, each introduced by a short essay. Two longer essays, **"Whitman's Line as a Public Form"** and **"The Prose Poem as an Evolving Form,"** conclude the book. Although he begins with early poems previously uncollected and ends with excerpts from his most recent volume, Mr. Bly avoids strict chronology. Rather, each section is designed to illustrate a step in the evolution of his poetics.

The third section, for example, includes poems from *Silence in the Snowy Fields* (1962), written in a rhapsodic mode, as well as others written in the same mode ("adapted from Waley's translations of Chinese poems, Frank O'Connor's translations of Celtic poems, and my own translations of Machado, but a certain gaiety carries them along. The line breaks usually come where the thought ends, and bring a moment of "silence") but published only 17 years later in *This Tree Will Be Here for a Thousand Years.* Part Five—prose poems from *The Morning Glory* (1975) and some from *The Man in the Black Coat Turns* (1981)—precedes (heavily revised) selections from *Sleepers Joining Hands* (1973) in Part Six. This arrangement allows the poet to contrast prose poems, like **"The Starfish"** and **"A Bouquet of Ten Roses,"** that "carry us to the new place on their minute detail, on what they give us to see," with those written "to turn away from seeing. . . . While I was still writing the *Morning Glory* poems, I felt a longing to compose a radical or root poem that would speak to what has its back turned to me."

> I sent my brother away.
> I saw him turn and leave. It was a schoolyard.
> I gave him to the dark people passing.
> He learned to sleep alone on the high buttes.
>
>   **("Poem in Three Parts")**

That is from a poem originally titled **"The Shadow Goes Away,"** the long poem in *Sleepers Joining Hands* that immediately follows the poet's 20-page essay. **"I Came Out of the Mother Naked."** I regret alterations here to this poem and to other long poems. Mr. Bly omits his homage to the Great Mother, preferring to shift emphasis from the female *anima* to male images "suggesting Joseph's betrayal of his brother."

The volume becomes a quest to find a voice to fit the poet and a prosody to fit the poem. After abandoning the iambic

"lute of three loudnesses" described in Part One ("I loved the music so much I could have written such lines for the rest of my life, but something in them didn't fit me") and, I surmise, Harvard University, the poet moved to New York. He sank, through solitude, "past . . . stones, past Eros, past family affections." From this period of estrangement came poems of both despair and healing that Mr. Bly would publish 14 years later in *The Light Around the Body.* It is only after this period that the poet, who had married and returned to his native Minnesota, composed the poems published in his first book. Sympathy between the soul and the countryside is the subject of *Silence in the Snowy Fields:*

> Oh, on an early morning I think I shall live forever!
> I am wrapped in my joyful flesh,
> As the grass is wrapped in its clouds of green.
>
>   **("Poem in Three Parts")**

I know of no contemporary poet, except perhaps Allen Ginsberg in his exuberant poems about sex, who is so unafraid to write about joy.

One of the pleasures of reading *Selected Poems* is to discover themes, language and imagery that will recur, transformed, throughout the poet's body of work like DNA passed from the acorn to the oak. The poems in Part One may not sound much like Robert Bly, but titles like **"Dawn in Threshing Time"** and *from* **Four Seasons in the American Woods"** indicate subjects the poet would write about again and again. **"Where We Must Look for Help"** presages the "deep image" poems of psychic connections, mythic comparisons and unexpected junctures:

> The dove returns; it found no resting place,
> It was in flight all night above the shaken seas
> Beneath ark eaves
> The dove shall magnify the tiger's bed.
>
>   **("Poem in Three Parts")**

More surprising is **"Schoolcraft's Diary Written on the Missouri: 1830,"** a three-page dramatic monologue poem including a good deal of narrative. The speaker observes the conflict between "busy whites" with "steel traps hanging, swung from saddle thongs" and the Sioux, "as still as Hudson's blankets winding them." He joins a party of men armed to confront a mysterious white apparition stalking the camp.

> So armed in case of Sioux, to our surprise
> We found a white and wounded Northern Bear
> Shot in that day about the snout and head.
>
>   **("Poem in Three Parts")**

As well as demonstrating the poet's early and abiding interest in American history, this long poem marks the beginning of his lifelong reliance on narrative.

Throughout his later work he would adapt narrative techniques to the lyric, just as he would appropriate the rhythms of sentences to replace a prosody based on counting syllables:

The boy gets out of high school and reads no more
books; the son stops calling home.
The mother puts down her rolling pin and makes no
more bread.
And the wife looks at her husband one night at a party
and loves him no more.

("Poem in Three Parts")

Powerful, succinct, poignant, such stories make up another
sort of history. The personal connects us to the world's
master plot. In fact, Mr. Bly has been able to write successful poems about public events because, for him, the
political is personal. His response to the Vietnam War was
rooted in grief, not grievance, and he never excluded
himself from the darker manifestations of our national
consciousness:

We have carried around this cup of darkness.
We hesitate to anoint ourselves.
Now we pour it over our heads.

("Poem in Three Parts")

But Mr. Bly is a public poet even in poems without overt
political content. Although in Part Four he introduces **"The
Teeth Mother Naked at Last"** with a description of the
long, cadenced line inspired by the Bible, Christopher
Smart, William Blake and Walt Whitman—a line "that
embodies power in a direct way . . . that throws or
catapults itself into the outer world"—even his most
intimate and meditative poems, with their frequent use of
the pronoun "we," are designed to instruct and exhort.
These poems function like stained-glass windows in a
cathedral; their images direct us to wisdom and salvation.
Mr. Bly's impulse to teach (some would say preach) unites
him to Emerson on his platform, Bronson Alcott in his
lyceum and Thoreau (whose nature writings Mr. Bly likens
to prose poems) awake in Concord jail. He is, in a sense,
the most recent in a line of great American transcendentalist writers.

Selected Poems begins with images of "this smoking body
plough[ing] toward death" and ends with a series of love
poems, including the sexy **"At the Time of Peony Blos-
soming"**:

When I come near the red peony flower
I tremble as water does near thunder,
as the well does when the plates of earth move,
or the tree when fifty birds leave at once.

("Poem in Three Parts")

It is a mellow ending to a good journey, one that is not
over yet.

Robert Richman (essay date December 1986)

SOURCE: "The Poetry of Robert Bly," in *New Criterion*,
Vol. 5, No. 4, December, 1986, pp. 37-46.

[*In the following essay, Richman provides an overview of
Bly's poetry, literary career, and critical reception.*]

With the publication this year of Robert Bly's **Selected
Poems**—a volume preceded by a number of books
celebrating this writer's work—the time has surely come
to take a closer critical look at one of the most "radical"
poetic careers of our time. Robert Bly himself has always
insisted that, of the many poetic movements spawned during the Sixties, none was more radical than his. To
establish the priority of his own literary outlook, Bly has
spent much time belittling that of his rivals in this period—
the confessional and New York School poets, on the one
hand, and, on the other, the formalist poets who survived
the Sixties. In Bly's view, "both cooked and raw poetry in
a certain sense in the United States is head poetry." To
deal with the objects of the external world, as both the
confessionals and the New York School poets do, is, in his
view, to be in thrall to the "logic" of that world. True free-
associational surrealism, which is what Bly has long
advocated for poetry, is achieved by turning inward, "into"
the body and away from the "head" and the world. It is
therefore hardly surprising that the only criterion of quality for this poetry of "weird" and "deep images" is said to
be its resistance to analysis. Bly's best poetry, according
to William Heyen in *Robert Bly: When Sleepers Awake*,
has always "defied serious inquiry and involved [that is,
complex] explication." "The prized conditions," according
to Donald Wesling, another admirer of his work, "are Not
Understanding and Not Saying."

A look at the recent publications devoted to Bly's writing
suggests, however, that far from defying serious inquiry
and explication, Bly's poetry is as full of explicable matter
as *The Waste Land*. And the question of form in Bly's
poetry has also been recently opened for review. Bly
himself has lately abandoned the harsh antiformal polemics that used to be his stock-in-trade. In the new *Selected
Poems* he has chosen to include a few previously unpublished poems from the late Forties and early Fifties written
in iambic pentameter. In addition, Bly's comments,
interspersed throughout the book, show the poet far more
willing to make concessions to the value of form in general
and to acknowledge its presence in poems we had been
previously asked to perceive very differently. This is not to
say Bly has abandoned every vestige of his radical outlook.
Indeed, one of the more amusing things about the *Selected
Poems*—as well as many of Bly's prose writings of the
Eighties—is the rhetorical hole he digs himself into by
trying to maintain his old radical principles while flaunting
an admiration for form: "It is not iambic," he says about
one group of poems in the *Selected Poems,* "but free verse
with distinct memories of form." For a writer whose
unequivocal rantings against form and meaning were long
a familiar feature of the literary scene—most of them on
the order of, "I refuse to say anything at all about prosody.
What an ugly word it is!" and "It's so horrible in high
school when they say, 'What's the interpretation of this
poem?'"—even this small shift in outlook acquires a
certain significance. Clearly a concerted effort is being

made by Bly and his many supporters to present a more tempered picture of his aesthetic position for posterity. But does this revisionist view of Bly's poetry really account for what he has written and what he has claimed for it?

Robert Bly was born sixty years ago in the rural farming community of Madison, Minnesota. He belongs to the impressive generation of American poets that emerged in the years immediately following the war. Bly's fellow students at Harvard—he was there from 1947 to 1950—included Richard Wilbur, Donald Hall, Adrienne Rich, Kenneth Koch, and John Ashbery. Like many of his classmates, Bly was under the sway of the formalist impulse then governing American poetry. According to the chronology in Howard Nelson's *Robert Bly: An Introduction to the Poetry,* Bly had "virtually memorized" Robert Lowell's *Lord Weary's Castle,* which had been published the year before Bly entered Harvard. But unlike most of his contemporaries, he chose to withhold from publication the book of formalist poems, entitled *The Lute of Three Loudnesses,* which he had assembled after graduation. The work from this book that is now included in the **Selected Poems** reveals an immature but by no means inconsiderable talent:

> Spring has come; I look up and see
> The agile companies of April sit
> As quaint and graceful as medieval guilds.
> Grouse feathers float away on the still lake.
> Summer and reeds; summer and partridge chicks.
> Then bees: eaters of honey till their death.
> The honey gatherers, coming and going, drive
> Their endless honey circles to the hive.
>
> The sedge root in the river lifts and frees,
> And blackbirds join in flocks, their duties through.
> And now the last autumnal freedom comes,
> And Zumbrota acorns drop, sun-pushed as plums,
> To half-wild hogs in Carolina trees,
> And disappointed bees, with half-gold feet,
> Sail home. For me this season is most sweet,
> And winter will be stamping of the feet.

(**"Poem in Three Parts"**)

Bly's dissatisfaction with the poems of *The Lute of Three Loudnesses*—"I heard a whisper of Milton," writes Bly in the **Selected Poems,** and "something in it didn't fit me"—led to a period of self-imposed isolation in New York City and Cambridge from 1951 to 1954. These years of reading and reflection have taken on a considerable importance in the Bly mythology, almost as important as the suppressed first book of poems. According to Bly and his commentators, this period was crucial in the transformation of the writer from a craftsman in rhyme and meter (what Bly would later call "antique work") to a surrealist free-verse poet. For this period of loneliness, as Bly describes it in the **Selected Poems,** "made clear to me [the] . . . interior starvation" which had given birth to the formal poetry Bly had been so unhappy with.

In 1954 Bly enrolled in the writing program at the University of Iowa, and the following year he married Carolyn McLean. In 1956, Bly travelled to Norway on a Fulbright grant to translate Norwegian poetry. Bly is of Norwegian descent but knew no Norwegian at the time. It was in the Oslo Public Library that he encountered the work of the South American poets Pablo Neruda and Cesar Vallejo, the Spanish poet Juan Jiménez, and the German poet Georg Trakl. Overwhelmed by what he perceived to be the imaginative freshness of the work of these "surrealist" poets—far more authentic, Bly believed, than the French surrealists—Bly promptly started a literary magazine when he returned to the United States. Its express purpose was to provide a forum for translations of the work of these writers. But *The Fifties,* as the magazine was called (it would eventually become *The Sixties, The Seventies,* and *The Eighties*), was also used as a vehicle for attacks on the poetry establishment. The editorial in the inaugural issue, published in 1958, read, in part: "The editors of this magazine think that most of the poetry published in America is too old-fashioned." Bly sent copies to all the contributors to *The New Poets of England and America,* the anthology of formalist poetry edited by Donald Hall, Robert Pack, and Louis Simpson which had appeared that same year. By the time the second installment of *The Fifties* appeared in 1959—featuring the first surrealist-inspired work of James Wright, a young poet who, like Bly, had abandoned the formalist path—Bly's commitment to his new aesthetic was solidly established.

In 1958 and 1959 Bly interrupted work on the surrealist "country poems" that would appear in his first published book, **Silence in the Snowy Fields** (1962), in order to finish a book of political poems. It was called *Poems for the Ascension of J. P. Morgan,* and failed to find a publisher. (A few of these poems would turn up in **Silence in the Snowy Fields** and **The Light Around the Body,** Bly's second published book, which appeared in 1967). Bly remained undeterred in his sense of poetic mission. American poetry was then going through a tremendous upheaval: Allen Ginsberg's *Howl* had appeared in 1956 and Robert Lowell's *Life Studies* in 1959—and Bly was anxious to be a part of the new movement. In 1961 he brought out **Twenty Poems of Georg Trakl,** translated by himself and James Wright. By this time Bly had forged more alliances with poets, among them Donald Hall and Louis Simpson, two of the editors of *The New Poetry of England and America* who were experiencing crises of confidence in their own formalist verse. Bly also met Galway Kinnell and David Ignatow around this time, two more poets sympathetic to his cause.

Silence in the Snowy Fields was the first major contribution to Bly's burgeoning surrealist movement. The first poem in the volume, entitled **"Three Kinds of Pleasures,"** provided the movement with a kind of brief poetic agenda:

I

> Sometimes, riding in a car, in Wisconsin
> Or Illinois, you notice those dark telephone poles
> One by one lift themselves out of the fence line
> And slowly leap on the gray sky—
> And past them the snowy fields.

II

The darkness drifts down like snow on the picked
cornfields
In Wisconsin, and on these black trees
Scattered, one by one,
Through the winter fields—
We see stiff weeds and brownish stubble,
And white snow left now only in the wheeltracks of
the combine.

III

It is a pleasure, also, to be driving
Toward Chicago, near dark,
And see the lights in the barns.
The bare trees more dignified than ever,
Like a fierce man on his deathbed,
And the ditches along the road half full of a private
snow.

("Poem in Three Parts")

Bly's pleasures are indeed threefold: the surreal, as
tentatively evidenced in the image of the leaping telephone
poles in the first stanza; the freedom to assert one's
emotional state rather than conjure it through an elaborate
network of poetic devices, as in "It is a pleasure, also, to
be driving . . ."; and the freedom to construct a poem out
of a series of plain, if finely drawn, random observations.
Most of the other poems in the book are made up of
sequences of description—also occasionally interspersed
with "surreal" images—that are far more random than this.
As Bly remarked, "when the poems of *Silence in the
Snowy Fields* came, I set them down with very little
rewriting, maybe one or two lines only . . . they arrived
as complete as they came." They were, he said on another
occasion, finished "in the thirty or forty seconds that it
took to write the poem." The final stanza of **"Driving
Toward the Lac Qui Parle River"** seems to confirm Bly's
remarks:

> Nearly to Milan, suddenly a small bridge,
> And water kneeling in the moonlight.
> In small towns the houses are built right on the
> ground;
> The lamplight falls on all fours on the grass.
> When I reach the river, the full moon covers it.
> A few people are talking, low, in a boat.

("Poem in Three Parts")

By attempting to "penetrate down into an evolutionary
part of the mind," as Bly felt Neruda, Trakl, and Vallejo
had done, the poet challenged the orthodoxies not only of
the formalist poetry of the late Forties and early Fifties but
of the modernist poets as well. In the poetry of Eliot, for
example, seemingly disparate images and allusions are
united by an underlying intellectual structure. Bly's bursts
of private subjectivity, on the other hand, seek to do
without such structural links. If the imagery happens to
cohere, as Bly insisted, the poem had to be disposed of.
According to the poet, the most "genuine line" in a poem
is the "weirdest line . . . the one that apparently doesn't
make any sense. . . ." "To Pound an image meant 'petals
on a wet, black bough,'" said Bly. "To us an image is
'death on the deep roads of the guitar.'"

Silence in the Snowy Fields also repudiated Eliot's notion
of the objective correlative. In Bly's view, the emotion
that the correlative objectifies is destroyed by the very
process of its objectification. Bly's "deep" poetic images,
emerging from "within," purportedly contained purer emotions whose psychic energy was still intact: "If I reached
my hands down, near the earth, / I could take handfuls of
darkness!" or "The sun lies happily on my knees." Bly's
other way of challenging the objective correlative (for
which he is perhaps more famous) is to make simple statements of his feelings. Two well-known examples of this in
Silence in the Snowy Fields are "I have awakened at Mis-
soula, Montana, utterly happy" (the last line of **"In a
Train"**) and "Oh, on an early morning I think I shall live
forever!" (the first line of **"Poem in Three Parts"**).

It is easy to understand why Bly's aesthetic—or anti-
aesthetic—became so popular in the Sixties and Seventies. It
found sympathetic readers among the growing number
of people who resented the complexity of modernist—and
postwar—poetry. Eliot made no bones about the fact that
the poet must be learned and his work difficult. It was
those who felt themselves to be disenfranchised from Eliot's exclusive club that Bly claimed as his own. Being a
poet could not be simpler, he told them, because each one
of us

> has our own psychic rhythms . . . Anybody at his peak
> moment, who wants to sit down and write a poem, can
> write it . . .

All one needed was a little "inner animal imagery," or,
failing that, the ability to state that one was happy, sad, or
indifferent in a given town at a given time of day. The
idea spread like wildfire.

It is not surprising that many perceived Bly's poetry to be
a long-awaited resurgence of Romanticism. But the
nineteenth-century English Romantic poets' suffusion of
their being into the external world is vastly different from
Bly's solipsistic engorging of the world. As Robert Langbaum points out in *The Poetry of Experience* (1957), the
Romantic poets did not so much seek to overwhelm the
world with their subjective being as confirm their inner
experiences in the crucible of the world. "There remains,"
Langbaum tells us, "the hardheaded critical awareness [on
the part of the poets] that the self is something other than
the object" of the poet's attention. The Romantics never
sought, as Langbaum says, "to put the head to sleep." Putting the head to sleep is a perfectly apt description of the
poetic program of Robert Bly.

Silence in the Snowy Fields was not entirely devoid of
poetic virtue, however. There is something to be said for
the freshness of Bly's language, and for the poet's attempt
to bring a wide-eyed wonder to the Minnesota countryside.
But the solipsism of this poetry—perfectly embodied in
Bly's barren, unpopulated landscapes—all but obscures
the musicality of the language.

As appealing as the solipsistic poetry of *Silence in the
Snowy Fields* was, it lacked the single element crucial in

the Sixties for a truly popular—and critical—success: politics. This element was firmly entrenched in Bly's next book, *The Light Around the Body,* which was published in 1967 and received the National Book Award for poetry in 1968. The conflation of surrealism and politics—a practice Bly also borrowed from his South American models—is evident in **"War and Silence"**—

> The bombers spread out, temperature steady.
> A Negro's ear sleeping in an automobile tire.
> Pieces of timber float by, saying nothing.
>
> * * *
>
> Bishops rush about crying, "There is no war,"
> And bombs fall,
> Leaving a dust on the beech trees.
>
> * * *
>
> One leg walks down the road and leaves
> The other behind; the eyes part
> And fly off in opposite directions.
>
> * * *
>
> Filaments of death grow out.
> The sheriff cuts off his black legs
> And nails them to a tree.
>
> **("Poem in Three Parts")**

—as well as in **"Driving Through Minnesota During the Hanoi Bombings"**:

> The sergeant said,
> "I felt sorry for him
> And blew his head off with a shotgun."
> These instants become crystals,
> Particles
> The grass cannot dissolve. Our own gaiety
> Will end up
> In Asia, and you will look down in your cup
> And see
> Black Starfighters.
> Our own cities were the ones we wanted to bomb!
>
> **("Poem in Three Parts")**

In **"The Teeth Mother Naked at Last"**—first published by City Lights Books in 1970 and included three years later in *Sleepers Joining Hands*—surrealistic imagery is for the most part disposed of. Replacing it is a sustained, hate-filled invective against everything in American life that Bly loathed:

> Helicopters flutter overhead. The death-
> bee is coming. Super Sabres
> like knots of neurotic energy sweep
> around and return.
> This is Hamilton's triumph.
> This is the triumph of a centralized bank.
>
> * * *
>
> The ministers lie, the professors lie, the television

reporters lie, the priests lie.
What are these lies? It means that the country wants to die.

> * * *
>
> This is what it's like for a rich country to make war.
> This is what it's like to bomb huts (afterwards described as "structures").
> This is what it's like to kill marginal farmers (afterwards described as "Communists").
>
> * * *
>
> It's because the average hospital bed now costs two hundred dollars a day
> that we bomb the hospitals in the north . . .
>
> **("Poem in Three Parts")**

Any poet not mentioning the war in 1970 ran the risk, of course, of being implicated in the "genocide." All the same, this appeared to be an egregious about-face for Bly. Unlike the confessional poets, for whom politics was a logical next step, Bly had presented himself as the poet of interior life. He had claimed, again and again, that society and culture threatened the purity of the poet's psychic rhythms. He had vociferously campaigned against what he called the "journalistic mind" in poetry, and had criticized poetry in which the words, as he said, had "their energy corrupted" by evil external forces. If *Silence in the Snowy Fields* demanded a poetry truly free of the rhetoric of the world, then *The Light Around the Body* seemed to be an outright betrayal of the earlier book. It was a book swamped by the rhetoric of the world.

Bly had an explanation, of course. The political poems of *The Light Around the Body,* he reasoned, were attempts to show "that the political poem comes out of the deepest privacy." "Neruda, Vallejo, Antonio Machado, Aleixandre, and Lorca," says Bly in the preface to the section of poems from *The Light Around the Body* in the *Selected Poems,* taught him that it was "just and natural to write of important national griefs in one's poetry as well as of private griefs." As long as these "national griefs" emerged from one's body, insisted Bly, they were not simply political rhetoric but the authentic subjective eruptions of a deeply grieved person. And who was to say whether these poems emerged from one's inner soul or were the product of the fallen world? Why, the poet himself? What we were offered was, in short, the same old solipsism. And as before, anyone who dared to question whether political imagery could be of the requisite psychic depth was automatically accused of using the superannuated critical tools of a dying culture. In the Sixties and Seventies, few wanted to be guilty of this crime.

Even if we take *The Light Around the Body* and **"Teeth Mother"** in their own terms—as attempts to expiate the alleged sins (greed, commercialism, aggression) of America—they still miss their target. Bly's high moral fervor is undone by some gross miscalculations. Most obvious of these is Bly's repeated stereotyping of people. "No one in business can be a Christian," says Bly in one poem. Accountants, executives, advertising men, and Indians are all similarly typecast (the last in a poem entitled **"Hatred of Men with Black Hair"**). This alarming attitude crops up in Bly's other works and statements from this time as well. In an interview from 1966 Bly declared that "the typical football player . . . mistreats women, because he has always mistreated the woman that is inside him." What this stereotyping now looks like is the inevitable point of view of someone who has dwelled too long in the unpopulated landscapes of his own subjectivity.

Bly's political poetry corresponded to some real-life activism during these years. In 1966 he organized the first anti-war poetry readings at Reed College and the University of Washington. The same year he co-founded American Writers Against the Vietnam War. In 1967 he took part in a Pentagon demonstration, and was arrested for blocking the entrance to an induction center. And in 1968, at the ceremony for the National Book Awards, Bly in his acceptance speech urged the young people in the audience to defy the draft. At the same ceremony he donated his award money to the "resistance." Ten years later Bly was still castigating his fellow poets—John Berryman was his bête noire—for "refusing to get up on one of those [anti-war] stages." Much of the other work Bly produced during the late Sixties and early Seventies—*Twenty Poems of Pablo Neruda* (1969), translated by Bly and Wright, *The Morning Glory* (1969), a chapbook of prose poems, *Twenty Poems of Tomas Tranströmer* (1970), and *Neruda and Vallejo: Selected Poems* (1971)—was obscured by the running political commentary. In 1971 Bly predicted "a very swift disintegration of all the structures of society" replaced by a world of isolated, self-sufficient communes. Clearly, Bly's primary interest was in taking his solipsism to the streets.

"The Teeth Mother Naked at Last" was the first poem written following Bly's intensive reading of Jung, which had begun in 1969. Jung's association of the unconscious with femininity and the conscious mind with masculinity struck a responsive chord in Bly, who promptly caricatured it in his writings. As Bly explains it in the essay **"I Came Out of the Mother Naked"** in *Sleepers Joining Hands* (1973), masculine awareness—which Bly identified with rules and morality—defeated the feminine consciousness— identified with nature, compassion, intuition, and poetry—in a struggle for control of the planet. *Sleepers Joining Hands* was an attempt, in Bly's words, to "right [the] spiritual balance" on earth. But for Bly righting the balance naturally meant giving the mother consciousness the upper hand. Bly condemns everything associated (in his own mind, anyway) with the masculine impulse, from literary criticism to the desire to "go out and conquer Africa," and is full of praise for everything associated with the feminine outlook. What Bly really liked about Jung's theories, or what he saw in them, anyway, was their simplicity. The world was neatly divided into two camps: the good and the bad. One is to be disposed of and one is to be saved. All special circumstances, contingencies, and complexities are conveniently ignored.

Of course, the masculine attribute most roundly condemned by Bly during his Jungian phase was poetic form. In an interview published in *Craft* magazine in 1972, Bly went to considerable lengths to indicate that his poetry is written without the assistance of what he refers to as "the stiff part of the mind." After the interviewer gets Bly to admit grudgingly that the poems of *The Light Around the Body* are composed in "high" or poetic language, the interviewer—clearly relishing the idea that he'll go on record as the only person ever to have forced Robert Bly to admit that his poetry is crafted—proudly declares: "That's a matter of craft." But Bly retorts: ". . . what guides this craft is an instinctive sense for when a sentence is alive and when it's not. . . . " When it comes to his "technique" or to what gives birth to a poem, Bly is even more evasive. He simply does not say anything.

Not surprisingly, Bly tried to revise literary history along these same anti-formal lines. All "great poems," he said, "like the *Odyssey,* take[s] [their] form . . . without mind intervention." Bly sought to revolutionize the art of translating poetry in a similar fashion. Knowing the language well wasn't the most important factor in translating poetry, Bly insisted, since "[w]hat you are essentially doing is slipping for a moment into the mood of the other poet . . . into an emotion which you may possibly have experienced at some time." In truth, Bly's ideas about translation merely allowed the translator, as James Dickey put it, to take "as many liberties as [he] wants to take with the original, it being understood that this enables [him] somehow to approach the 'spirit' of the poem [he] is translating." The emergence of public readings of poetry during this time was also given encouragement in Bly's ideas. When you read poetry, Bly explained, the mind intervenes. When you hear poetry, on the other hand, there is less chance of the mind analyzing the work and thereby suppressing a deep subjective interaction with the poem. Criticism of poetry also underwent a drastic change, thanks in part to Bly's theories. Fewer and fewer writers on poetry analyzed what they read. Instead poetry was admired for—to borrow a phrase of Howard Nelson's—its "flowing, rushing, knotting, whirling" energy. An entire way of writing about poetry was quickly becoming obsolete, and it was Bly who had played a major role in drafting the blueprint of its destruction.

Bly provided the generation of poets coming of age in the Seventies with plenty of examples of anti-poetic poetry to accompany his anti-critical rhetoric. The following excerpt, for example, from Bly's **"Six Winter Privacy Poems"**— which opens the book *Sleepers Joining Hands*— reminded budding poets how easy it was to stand by whatever banality they had first put down on paper:

> My shack has two rooms; I use one,
> The lamplight falls on my chair and table
> and I fly into one of my poems—
> I can't tell you where—
> as if I appeared where I am now,
> in a wet field, snow falling. . . .

                    * * *

There is solitude like black mud!
Sitting in this darkness singing,
I can't tell if this joy
is from the body, or the soul, or a third place!

("Poem in Three Parts")

Bly wasn't through yet. After all, he was still using the stanza and line—"antiquated" poetic units of measure. The prose poems of ***The Morning Glory*** (1975) and ***This Body Is Made of Camphor and Gopherwood*** (1977) sought, in Bly's words, to "calm the language down" even more, thereby making it a truer reflection of the timeless flow of the inner body. "[I]t was as if I had descended into my body at last," says Bly in the ***Selected Poems,*** "and that immersion is the subject of the poems. The joy [of the poetry] lies in its being unfocused":

The cucumbers are thirsty, their big leaves turn away from the wind. I water them after supper; the hose curled near the rhubarb. The wind sound blows through the head. . . . What is comforted words help, the sunken islands speak to us. . . .

Is this world animal or vegetable? Others love us, the cabbages love the earth, the earth is fond of the heavens—A new age comes close through the dark, threatens much, so much is passing away. . . .

Even some of the critics who had previously supported Bly rebelled against ***This Body Is Made of Camphor and Gopherwood.*** One of them, Philip Dacey in a piece entitled "This Book is Made of Turkey Soup and Star Music," cited by Nelson, wrote:

Although Bly, a classic literary demagogue, rails against artifice in poetry . . . many of the prose poems in this book are more artificial—pieces clearly contrived in a language one is not likely to hear outside the poem—than virtually any of, say, Frost's poems in blank verse. Frost and countless others achieve the natural or a semblance of it through the artificial; Bly wishes to bypass the latter and ends up smack in the middle of it.

Apparently Bly was sensitive to the charges. His next book, ***This Tree Will Be Here for a Thousand Years*** (1979)—a group of surrealist country poems much in the vein of those in ***Silence in the Snowy Fields***—was an obvious effort to conciliate the critics and readers who had grown impatient with his work. But these poems, written at intervals during the previous sixteen years, are more literary and less spontaneous than their predecessors. The book was promptly attacked by Eliot Weinberger—never a supporter of Bly's—who began his review, which appeared in *The Nation* on November 17, 1979, with the sentence, "Robert Bly is a windbag, a sentimentalist, a slob in the language."

Bly attempted to start off the decade of the Eighties on a new foot. ***The Man in the Black Coat Turns*** (1981) was heralded as the poet's long overdue reconciliation with the masculine consciousness, a "return to the father," as Bly put it. "To be able to respect your father is such a beauti-

ful thing!" Bly declared in an interview at the time. Although the surface details of the poems in this book seem to be vaguely "about" masculinity, little else has changed. Indeed, the same undiluted anti-rationalism and anti-formalism that governed the earlier poetry governs almost everything here. This is from **"What the Fox Agreed to Do":**

And the shells, the mollusc shells, grow large.
Smoke twists up through water,
the moon rockets up from the sea floor.

The fox agrees to leap into the ocean.
The human being feels a splash around him.
Hebrews straddle the slippery dolphins.

("Poem in Three Parts")

And this is from the prose poem entitled **"Eleven O'Clock at Night"** (none of these prose poems were included in the ***Selected Poems***):

I lie alone in my bed; cooking and stories are over at last, and some peace comes. And what did I do today? I wrote down some thoughts on sacrifice that other people had, but couldn't relate them to my own life. I brought my daughter to the bus—on the way to Minneapolis for a haircut—and I waited twenty minutes with her in the somnolent hotel lobby. I wanted the mail to bring some praise for my ego to eat, and was disappointed. I added up my bank balance, and found only $65, when I need over a thousand to pay the bills for this month alone. So this is how my life is passing before the grave?

The critics in Bly's thrall—there were still many of them—responded to this book, as they almost always had, by relinquishing their critical powers: "I risk, of course," said one, "by trying to be too rational (male-conscious), damaging [Bly's] subtle fabrics."

Howard Nelson, in his recent book on Bly, does not view the poetry in ***The Man in the Black Coat Turns*** as another episode of solipsistic surrealism. He finds it not only full of meaning—an attempt, in his words, to "recover the past"—but full of allusions to the New Testament as well. But then Nelson discovers allusions, "sexual metaphors," "symbols," and coherent imagery everywhere in the Bly *oeuvre.* "The consciousness in the ***Snowy Fields,***" Nelson avers, "is in fact quite complicated." Nelson's ability to misconstrue Bly's poetry—not to mention his ignoring the poet's numerous statements of intention—is remarkable. Bly's defiantly illogical imagery is said by Nelson to be a "smooth arc of association"—a phrase more easily applied to the poetry of the despised Eliot than to that of Bly. Astonishingly, Nelson asserts that Bly

prizes spontaneity but also believes in revision. For him, the free flow of the mind in and of itself is neither avant-garde nor necessarily very interesting.

This is not the blatant contradiction of Bly's aesthetic it appears to be, or so Nelson claims. For the "intelligence" Nelson finds running rampant in Bly's poetry is not the mind's intelligence, but the "body's wisdom," the consciousness of nature. "The rational intelligence," explains Nelson, "is not the only intelligence."

John Unterecker, who has contributed a foreword to Nelson's book, resorts to a similar strategy in his discussion of Bly's musical effects. Bly's "high" poetic language, Unterecker says, is "probably largely uncalculated," "perhaps casual in composition," "half-conscious," and written "without a great deal of premeditation." Yet a few sentences later Unterecker acknowledges that Bly "trusts to an ear that he's trained by careful listening. . . ." Now *trained* is very much the opposite of *casual, half-conscious* and *uncalculated.* But Unterecker, like Nelson, wishes to honor Bly's free-associational method while simultaneously claiming some quality of mind for the poetry. Clearly, it is no easy task.

In truth, though, Unterecker and Nelson are only responding to a tack recently taken by Bly himself. In a 1981 essay called **"Form that Is Neither In nor Out"**—which begins, "I have been thinking lately that we have not been very faithful servants of art"—Bly declares:

> . . . I have often thought of form as a prison . . . a kind of dungeon in which heart material gets imprisoned. Suppose I were wrong on that. If so, we need to find a way to speak of form so that its wild or intense quality becomes clear. The distinction between form as prison and form as wildness may correspond to a distinction between kinds of form, in particular, the mechanical and the organic. . . . I maintain then that the more form a poem has—I mean living form—the closer it comes to the wild animal.

This view is reiterated in an essay in the *Selected Poems* entitled **"The Prose Poem as an Evolving Form,"** in which Bly speaks of how "form in art relies on form in nature for its model." But whether it is Nelson's "organic" form, Unterecker's "half-conscious" form, or Bly's "wild" and "living" form, it all bespeaks a willed effort to conflate two irreconcilable attitudes toward poetry. For Bly and his critics, it is not enough for poetry to appeal to a primitive level of consciousness. It must be "composed" by that consciousness too.

Intelligence and form have been praised by Bly in other recent essays and interviews too. "All artists love art," he says in one, "but we miss sometimes in Whitman reminders of what a triumph the intensely worked poem can be." "Before solitude can give any nourishment to the poet, evidently a certain level of literary culture has to be reached." "Writing poetry means a lot of study." "Obsession with image can become a psychic habit as much as obsession with persona."

Robert Bly's recent change of heart is interesting as a part of the cultural history of our time—and anyway, he has every right to change his mind. But his well-publicized shift does nothing to rescue the poems, the majority of which suffer from the two worst poetic excesses of the Sixties: politics and solipsism. This is unfortunate, because Bly has displayed from the start an enormous gift for

language, and these excesses have worked against his strongest talent. To this reader, only a handful of the pastoral poems in *Silence in the Snowy Fields,* an equally small number of the "thought" poems from the early Eighties, and the previously suppressed formalist work of the late Forties do not betray this gift. Here is a section of another early poem—entitled **"Schoolcraft's Diary Written on The Missouri: 1830"**—which we are now seeing for the first time:

> Now night grows old above this riverboat.
> Before I end, I shall include account
> Of incident tonight that moved my wonder.
> At dusk we tied the ship to trees on shore;
> No mortal boat in these night shoals can live.
> At first I heard a cry: then shufflings, steps.
> The muffled sounds on deckoak overhead
> Drew me on deck. The air was chill, and there
> I sensed, because these senses here are sharp
> And must be, something living and unknown.

> ("Poem in Three Parts")

Far from being evidence of "interior starvation," as Bly claimed they were, these youthful lines hint at what Bly's poetic achievement might have been had he not chosen to abandon formalism for the gratifications of a half-baked surrealism. What we have instead is poetry disfigured by politics and the supposed pleasures he derives from being "wrapped in my joyful flesh."

Dana Gioia (essay date Summer 1987)

SOURCE: "The Successful Career of Robert Bly," in *Hudson Review,* Vol. XL, No. 2, Summer, 1987, pp. 207-23.

[*In the following essay, Gioia offers critical analysis of Bly's poetry and an overview of his literary career and critical reception. According to Gioia, "Bly insists on being judged as a major poet, but his verse cannot bear the weight of that demand."*]

Robert Bly is one of the most famous and influential poets now writing in America. The author, editor, and translator of over eighty books and pamphlets, Bly has been a constant and outspoken presence in American poetry for the last three decades. Now at sixty, he is one of the few contemporary poets who, like a rock star or sports celebrity, seems bigger than life. Indeed in parts of the academy Bly has already achieved canonic stature. His poetry has entered the curriculum and inspired a sizeable secondary literature of books, dissertations, and articles. He has demonstrated that it is still possible for a contemporary poet to become a public figure.

Bly's fame did not come by accident. He has not only poured immense energy into the solitary act of writing but also into developing his public personality as a writer. No contemporary poet (except Allen Ginsberg) has better understood the value of publicity or used it more aggressively to his own advantage. Bly realized early in his career how important it was for a poet to create an attractive public image independent of his work. There was little fame in the poetry world and many contenders. To become well-known one had to court a broader public— and not by poetry but personality. Bly knew that the mass media would always have room for a few poets, provided they were sufficiently colorful.

Bly created a series of timely public images, each suited to a particular decade. The sixties saw Bly as a fiery anti-war activist; the seventies as a mysterious shaman explaining the myths of contemporary culture; the eighties as a gentle spiritual counselor healing the psychic wounds of modern life. In the meantime, he gave more interviews than a Hollywood starlet, campaigned more miles than a presidential hopeful. He appeared on television, spoke on radio, made recordings, even engineered mass-market mailings to announce his books and seminars. Though he professes a preference for the contemplative life, Bly is not shy about sharing his talents. Traveling for months each year to give readings, performances, lectures, and workshops, he has probably reached a broader public than any American poet since Robert Frost.

Although Bly has achieved considerable literary fame, his position in contemporary letters remains curiously ambiguous. His importance to recent literary history seems incontestable, but his achievements as a poet are open to question. No comprehensive account of American poetry since 1950 can ignore Bly's manifold contributions as poet, translator, editor, critic, performer, and personality. One might even claim him as the most influential poet of the sixties and seventies. He helped introduce surrealism into American poetry, popularize Latin American verse, renew interest in literary translation, strengthen the identity of regional poetry from the Midwest, and lead the movement of political poetry during the Vietnam War. He also played a critical role in discrediting the American tradition of formal poetry, offering as an alternative his own vision of poems which would be, as Charles Molesworth has summarized, "more open in form, associative in structure, and ecstatic in intention."

This much Bly has certainly done. The debate begins when one stops chronicling and begins evaluating his achievements. Bly's advocates esteem him as a contemporary Ezra Pound, a multi-talented pioneer, who has used poetry, translation, and criticism innovatively to create an authentic and genuinely new style. His detractors see him as an industrious opportunist, a writer of immense but overwhelmingly pernicious influence and shallow achievement. Such controversy is not unexpected for so prolific and mercurial a writer. While criticism usually clarifies a writer's achievement, in Bly's case critics have been hard-pressed merely to keep up with his latest transformation. But now with the publication of his *Selected Poems* and the appearance of several critical books about his work, the time for an informed and frank appraisal has arrived.

Bly's work profits by being seen in the context of his life and background because he is one of the few twentieth-century American poets who has remained deeply rooted in his native landscape. Born in Madison, Minnesota in 1926, the poet grew up on a farm in the tightly knit, Norwegian/Lutheran society of the Great Plains. Although Bly left Minnesota to join the Navy in World War II and then spent more than a decade elsewhere, he returned to rural Minnesota in 1958 and has kept it as his base during his entire public literary life.

For all his later eccentricity, Bly began his literary career in the most conventional way for an ambitious young poet of his generation. In 1947 after a year at St. Olaf's, a stolid Lutheran college in Minnesota, Bly fled his native pastures for Harvard Yard. In those postwar years, Cambridge was the right place for an aspiring poet. John Ciardi and Archibald MacLeish were on the faculty. Richard Wilbur was a university fellow. Bly's fellow undergraduates included John Ashbery, Donald Hall, Kenneth Koch, Frank O'Hara, and L. E. Sissman, with Adrienne Rich at Radcliffe. Like everyone else literary, Bly competed for the staff of the *Harvard Advocate* and, as always, competition suited him. Eventually the *Advocate* not only made him a senior editor but also published his lively essays and awkward, metrical poems. In 1950 he left Harvard with a *magna cum laude* in English, and, not surprisingly, moved to New York City to write. This relocation proved unsuccessful, and he wrote very little. Several frustrating years later, Bly took the next conventional step and left for the University of Iowa to earn an M.A. in Creative Writing. His time at Iowa remains murky because he has maintained an uncharacteristic silence about this period, consistently skipping over it in his many autobiographical interviews and essays. Perhaps the most telling testimony of his years in the famed Writers' Workshop comes from his current advice to aspiring authors. When asked how to become a poet, Bly now replies that one should go off alone for two years and talk to no one. In 1956, however, having himself spent two years talking to his teachers and fellow graduate students, Bly left with his bride for Norway on a Fulbright. At the age of thirty, Bly seemed headed for a comfortable academic career.

Europe was the turning point in Bly's creative life. His subsidized scholarly project was to translate Norwegian poetry (although he knew no Norwegian at the time, Bly has never lacked self-confidence). Instead in Oslo he discovered modern European and Latin American poetry, especially the work of Georg Trakl and Pablo Neruda. Returning to the U.S. in 1958, he was filled with a religious mission to reform American poetry. His aim was to push aside the now decrepit "Puritan, American isolationist tradition" of Pound, Eliot, and Williams and replace it with a vital new international style. The old tradition, he claimed, strived for clarity and reason which created "a spare, bare poetry" with few images. The new movement would create *"poetry heavy with images from the unconscious"* (Bly's italics).

Bly saw himself at odds with the literary establishment— both in the academy and in New York—against which he waged a wily generational and geographical war. If rural Minnesota was remote from the center of American literary life, he would then bring it closer to the mainstream of world poetry. If he was a young man with no critical authority, he would discredit the older generation of literary arbiters. Not employed on any faculty, Bly could ignore the restraints of standard scholarly and critical writing and leap instead into polemic, satire, and speculation to accomplish his ends. He would overstep the narrow boundaries of academic departments and explore not only literatures in foreign languages but also ideas from sociology, psychology, and anthropology. He would fight on his own terms to transform the poetic standards of the coming decade.

To accomplish this transformation, Bly began what would become the most influential small poetry magazine of the next decade, *The Fifties* (later updated to *The Sixties* and briefly, before it expired, to *The Seventies*). Though it published the work of other writers, *The Fifties* was largely a one-man show with Bly supplying poems, translations, reviews, editorials, and fillers from cover to cover. For an average issue Bly wrote about two-thirds of the material, mostly under his own name but often under pseudonyms (including that of the arch-critic, Crunk). It was an exciting performance and one which quickly revealed Bly's strengths and weaknesses as a writer. His clarity of purpose gave vitality and directness to every page. His intellectual curiosity rejected the conventional limits for literary discourse set by the New Critics. He was not interested in careful, textual analysis but in ambitious cultural criticism. Bly responded to poetry with the whole of his intelligence, frequently making illuminating political, psychological, and sociological observations. One sensed a bold, original mind with a true talent for making unexpected associations. Bly also understood how a living literature needed innovation to avoid stagnation. In *The Fifties* he brought news to American poetry—news of foreign poets, critical alternatives, and revolutionary aesthetics.

The Fifties was an overtly didactic magazine, a paperbound church with Reverend Bly permanently at the pulpit. There might be a little poetic music to work up the crowd, but the sermon was the main attraction. There were souls to be saved. Bly's articles were not carefully crafted essays. Indeed the scholarship he proudly flaunts on all occasions often proves embarrassing under scrutiny, as when he analyzes Lucretius' image of "the tears of things" not realizing he is quoting one of Virgil's most famous phrases. The didactic impulse rarely leads to perfectionism, and too often the excitement of Bly's best prose often coincides with an enthusiastic hastiness.

Not only Bly's prose was spoiled by this didacticism. No where are its damaging effects more evident than in his copious translations. In *The Fifties* Bly translated the work of foreign writers, especially those involved in the surrealist and expressionist movements (which had not yet entered the mainstream of American literature) to illustrate how contemporary poems might be written. For all his

fascination with contemplative figures like Meister Eckhart, Bly has always chosen action and involvement. As a propagandist for a new poetics, he quickly discovered that translation was more important than his own poetry for demonstrating his theories in convincing, concrete terms. But as a translator, Bly reveals the aesthetic simplification inherent in his "deep image" school of poetry.

Bly's versions usually conveyed the surface sense and images of the original, but the careful shapes of sound which embody them and the nuances of meaning which enliven them were largely ignored. The main problem a translator of poetry faces is not in bringing across the surface sense. That task, at least in modern languages, is relatively easy. The difficulty comes in recreating the complex design of sound and connotation that charges the original with energy. Bly usually solved this problem by ignoring its existence. He merely provided prose translations, often curiously awkward ones, lineated as verse. His versions were usually good enough to make a particular critical point. Unfortunately they were rarely strong enough to bring the poetry itself across with the theory. In the pages of *The Fifties*, poetry truly became what got lost in translation.

Is this judgment an exaggeration? Here are the opening stanzas of two famous poems in the original French and German. (I offer two languages to increase the chances that the reader will be able to compare Bly's versions with the original text.) First the opening quatrain of Mallarmé's "Sonnet":

> *Sur les bois oubliés quand passe l'hiver sombre*
> *Tu te plains, ô captif solitaire du seuil,*
> *Que ce sépulcre à deux qui fera notre orgueil*
> *Hélas! du manque seul des lourds bouquets s'encombre* . . . .

> **("Poem in Three Parts")**

And now the beginning of Rilke's famous "Der Panther" describing a caged panther in the Jardin des Plantes in Paris:

> *Sien Blick ist vom Vorübergehn der Stäbe*
> *so müd geworden, dass er nichts mehr hält.*
> *Ihm ist, als ob es tausend Stäbe gäbe*
> *und hinter tausend Stäben keine Welt.*

> **("Poem in Three Parts")**

Here are Bly's versions. First the Mallarmé:

> While the dark winter is passing over the woods now forgotten
> Lonesome man imprisoned by the sill, you are complaining
> That the mausoleum for two which will be our pride
> Is unfortunately burdened down with the absence of masses of flowers . . .

> **("Poem in Three Parts")**

Now the Rilke:

From seeing and seeing the seeing has become so
exhausted
It no longer sees anything anymore.
The world is made of bars, a hundred thousand bars,
and behind the bars, nothing.

("Poem in Three Parts")

As an impromptu translation in a French II oral exam, the
Mallarmé might eke out a passing grade, but as poetry in
English it fails the most rudimentary test. Not only does it
not seem like the verse of an accomplished poet, it doesn't
even sound like the language of a native speaker. Nor does
the Rilke exhibit the virtues of a smooth literal translation.
It transforms the tight, musical German into loose, pretentious doggerel. In the first line, Bly gratuitously introduces
awkward, unidiomatic repetitions as equivalents to Rilke's
clean phrasing and substitutes a long limp line for the
original's appropriately controlled iambic pentameter.
("The Panther" is a poem about the repetition of confinement.) In the second line Bly indulges in more vague,
clumsy word play ("anything anymore") and meaning-
lessly varies the rhythm of the line from his opening, once
again betraying Rilke's tight stanza design for no apparent
benefit. In the third and fourth lines, Bly yet again shifts
the sense of rhythm and lineation with a jerky enjambment
falling in the middle of a phrase ("a hundred thousand /
bars") before tightening up his syntax suddenly.

If this language is indeed verse, it is verse of the most
amateurish variety. Not only are Rilke's subtle repetitions
vulgarized in Bly's heavy-handed language, but the intense
spiritual identification between the poet and the caged
animal is clumsily undercut in Bly's English. In the German Rilke carefully presents the panther as masculine. It
is "his glance" on the bars. The image of a thousand bars
occurs "to him." Of course this sexual identification comes
from the masculine gender of the German word for
"panther." But, like other great poets, Rilke uses the deep
structure of the language to heighten the meaning of his
images. Focusing such subtle connotations gives poetry its
intensity. Bly, who has repeatedly cited this particular
poem as a source for his theory of "twofold consciousness," misses this crucial nuance entirely. While understanding the central idea of the poem, Bly is strangely
deaf to the subtler side of its language, and he mechanically neuters this imprisoned masculine panther into an
"it," although English grammar can neatly duplicate German in this case, and common American speech uses
gender to personalize animals. What can one say about
translations so insensitive to both the sound and nuance of
the originals?

By propagating this minimal kind of translation Bly has
done immense damage to American poetry. Translating
quickly and superficially, he not only misrepresented the
work of many great poets, he also distorted some of the
basic standards of poetic excellence. His slapdash method
ignored both the obvious formal qualities of the originals
(like rhyme and meter) and, more crucially, those subtler
organizing principles such as diction, tone, rhythm, and

texture which frequently gave the poems their intensity.
Concentrating almost entirely on syntax and imagery, Bly
reduced the complex originals into abstract visual
blueprints. In his hands, dramatically different poets like
Lorca and Rilke, Montale and Machado, not only all
sounded alike, they all sounded like Robert Bly, and even
then not like Bly at his best. But as if that weren't bad
enough, Bly consistently held up these diminished versions as models of poetic excellence worthy of emulation.
In promoting his new poetics (based on his specially
chosen foreign models), he set standards so low that he
helped create a school of mediocrities largely ignorant of
the pre-modern poetry in English and familiar with foreign
poetry only through oversimplified translations.

Bly's weaknesses as a translator underscore his central
failings as a poet. He is simplistic, monotonous, insensitive to sound, enslaved by literary diction, and pompously
sentimental. Moreover these are not accidental faults. They
are the consequences of his poetic method and they are
exacerbated by his didactic impulse. Curiously Bly's prose
rarely exhibits these problems. Whatever its intellectual
failings, it is usually fresh, vigorous, and diverse. Much of
the poetry, however, suffers from being written according
to a method.

As *Selected Poems* makes clear, Bly's earliest work was
awful. A few lines written when the young Bly lived in
New York City will suffice to show his wisdom in waiting
till thirty-five to publish a book:

There is a joyful night in which we lose
Everything, and drift
Like a radish
Rising and falling, and the ocean
At last throws us into the ocean . . .

("Poem in Three Parts")

By the time his premier volume, *Silence in the Snowy
Fields,* appeared in 1962, Bly had developed a quiet,
personal style capable of creating fine short poems within
a limited range. The most noticeable qualities of this style
were simplicity, coolness, and compression. Even eighty
volumes later this strangely unified book remains the
central Bly collection, the one most often praised by critics and cherished by readers. Now in its thirteenth printing, it appears on many university course lists. Its contents
are frequently anthologized (not infrequently by Bly
himself), and in his *Selected Poems,* Bly preserves more
poems from it than any other collection. Here Bly created
a type of poem which would not only become his
trademark but also influence two generations of poets.
Here, too, one sees the beginning of the problems which
would weaken most of Bly's later work.

"Old Boards" from *Silence in the Snowy Fields* demonstrates the usual Bly manner:

I

I love to see boards lying on the ground in early
spring:

The ground beneath them is wet and muddy—
Perhaps covered with chicken tracks—
And they are dry and eternal.

II

This is the wood one sees on the decks of ocean ships,
Wood that carries us far from land,
With a dryness of something used for simple tasks,
Like a horse's tail.

III

This wood is like a man who has a simple life,
Living through the spring and winter on the ship of
his own desire.
He sits on dry wood surrounded by half-melted snow
As the rooster walks away springily over the dampened
hay.

("Poem in Three Parts")

"Old Boards" like all the "country poems" from *Silence in the Snowy Fields* is short and undeceptively simple. The rhythm is calm and deliberate. All of the lines are end-stopped with the line lengths matching the units of sense. The vocabulary is ordinary and traditional. One cannot find a single word or image which is distinctively modern. The diction is flat and old-fashioned or, to use Bly's more ambitious formulation, "dry and eternal." The tone, like the rhythm, never departs from a cheery peacefulness. Roman numerals have been placed between each stanza to slow the reader down and put each section in isolation. The first stanza presents an ordinary farm scene. Old boards have been laid over the muddy ground to make a walkway in spring. The second stanza equates this commonplace sight with something unexpected, the wood used to build the decks of ships which take men on voyages. The final stanza combines these notions to show how a farmer's seemingly ordinary life also encompasses a spiritual voyage. **"Old Boards"** is a simple, honest poem. While not particularly exciting or memorable, it has the modest virtues of brevity, directness, and precision.

The problem with Bly's work is that he has rewritten **"Old Boards"** several hundred times, usually less well. Not only is every poem in *Silence in the Snowy Fields* similar both technically and thematically, but so is most of Bly's subsequent verse. The style which this early book achieved through compression and discipline, quickly relaxed into an uninteresting set of mannerisms. Worse yet, as the style grew more slack, the intellectual demands Bly placed on it became more onerous. Bly's "country" style works best for simple, static scenes. It operates in isolated flashes that generate no complex narrative or intellectual energy. Despite their gestures of spiritual profundity, the poems operate too superficially to recreate any but the most elementary spiritual insights, and even these they usually assert rather than dramatize—and, as Bly develops, assert with increasing crudity. Bly's initial clarity and simplicity quickly became pious pretention like this section from **"Six Winter Privacy Poems,"** which opened *Sleepers Joining Hands* (1973):

There is a solitude like black mud!
Sitting in this darkness singing,

I can't tell if this joy
Is from the body, or the soul, or a third place!

("Poem in Three Parts")

This short poem deserves scrutiny because it is a microcosm of Bly's faults. It begins with the supposedly bold but ultimately corny "deep image" of solitude as "black mud." Anyone schooled in Bly's poetics will know that mud is a positive, profound symbol. It is earthy and elemental, especially when modified by black, the favorite "deep image" color after white. Although Bly's opening line is flat and abstract, he announces his metaphor in great excitement. (One can always tell when Bly is excited. He adds an exclamation point.) He then switches to an image which attests to his spiritual discipline. After all, how many of us desire spiritual growth strongly enough to spend time sitting alone singing in the dark? After one line of such grueling discipline, Bly is properly rewarded by a transfiguring joy which so confuses him that he is unable to determine whether it comes from his body, his soul or, in his inimitable phrase, "a third place" (second exclamation point). At this point the reader may want to go back to the beginning to see what he or she has missed. A second look will probably not help much. One may even begin to wonder what "black mud" is doing in the poem besides sitting around seeming profound. This indescribable quality is apparently what makes it a "deep image." Reaching the end a second time, the reader should simply appreciate the last line for what it is, a small masterpiece of bathos, a Hallmark Cards version of mysticism.

This poem also demonstrates the pompous sentimentality that pervades much of Bly's work. In poetry sentimentality represents the failure of language to carry the emotional weight an author intends. There is an excess of some lofty emotion which the reader understands but cannot participate in. Instead the reader remains outside the emotional action of the poem, a little embarrassed by it all, like a person sharing a train compartment with a couple whispering romantically in baby-talk.

This edifying sentimentality is one of the keys to Bly's popularity. Most people like sentimental art, as long as its emotions are stylish. The last century sentimentalized tender emotions like love and pity. This Old Sentimentality is now passé. The New Sentimentality prefers other ennobling qualities like alienation, loneliness, and especially sincerity. But traditional or contemporary, the sentimentalist always asks the reader to experience more emotion than the poem generates. Poets know that many readers will collaborate in the deception. A few bells will suffice to set off emotions readers want to experience anyway.

Reading Bly one continually comes across purple passages of the New Sentimentality like:

There is a restless gloom in my mind.
I walk grieving. The leaves are down.
I come at dusk
Where, sheltered by poplars, a low pond lies.
The sun abandons the sky, speaking through cold
leaves.

("Poem in Three Parts")

Is it possible for a stanza of poetry to be both unadorned and overwritten? Here every phrase contains at least one heavy-handed hint to the author's mood. (Excerpting these clues, one could easily compose a telegram version of the poem: "Restless gloom grieving down dusk low abandons cold.") But despite its crude overstatement, the language remains weirdly inert for a lyric poem. Characteristically Bly simply asserts his emotions. His utilitarian language does little to recreate them in the reader. Instead, in the manner of the New Sentimentality, he tries to bully the reader into an instant epiphany of alienation and self-pity.

If Bly writes this sentimentally about the weather, watch out when he talks about love, as in his recent volume, *Loving a Woman in Two Worlds* (1985). Here the Old and the New Sentimentality meet with truly gooey results. The gap between the intense emotions Bly intends and the tepid language he employs is broad enough for parody, but unfortunately, the poems are not intended to be funny. Sincerity alone cannot save a poem like **"Letter to Her"** which opens with this stanza:

> What I did I did.
> I knew that I loved you
> and told you that.
> Then I lied to you
> often so you would love me,
> hid the truth,
> shammed, lied.

("Poem in Three Parts")

Is Bly then only a sentimental poet with mystical pretentions? From much of his *Selected Poems* it would appear so, but then in the middle of all the early work one suddenly comes across sharp, startling poems like **"Counting the Small-Boned Bodies"**:

> Let's count the bodies over again.
>
> If we could only make the bodies smaller,
> the size of skulls,
> we could make a whole plain white with skulls in the moonlight
>
> If we could only make the bodies smaller,
> maybe we could fit
> a whole year's kill in front of us on a desk
>
> If we could only make the bodies smaller,
> we could fit
> a body into a finger ring, for a keepsake forever.

("Poem in Three Parts")

This remarkable short poem appeared in Bly's second full-length collection, *The Light Around the Body,* published in 1967 just as the movement against the Vietnam War hit full stride. This moment in American history became crucially important to Bly. His leadership in organizing poets to protest U.S. military involvement in Southeast Asia gave him national notoriety. His decision to write political poems incorporating the lessons he had learned from translating Neruda, Lorca, Vallejo, Trakl and others

produced his finest poems. And his cross-country trips to give readings against the Vietnam War created in him the hunger for celebrity and attention that characterized his later career. This historical episode was therefore doubly ironic for Bly. The political events, which cheapened the poetry of so many of his contemporaries, invigorated his work, while the occasion for his national fame eventually created the conditions for his literary decline. The politician produced a poet of rare quality just as the shaman degenerated into a showman.

One sees this transformation in the poems from *The Light Around the Body* and the pamphlet, *Teeth Mother Naked at Last* (1970). Several things happen there which rarely occur in his other work. First, the language breaks out of the monotonously literary diction of his "country" poems. Fresh, unexpected words and images appear. Second, the languid mood and syntax of the earlier poems acquire an urgency and excitement. Third, a powerful, illuminating anger disperses the fuzzy sentimentalism that weakens so much of his other work. Finally, Bly's view now broadens from his narrow private concerns to confront the rest of humanity. The poems no longer confine themselves to the easy juxtaposition of the poet alone with nature. They face the difficult world of human history. Bly seemed to be developing from the minor mode of his early work into a major new identity. In the process he wrote a few of the most stunning political poems in American literature—strange, frightening pieces like **"Romans Angry About the Inner World," "Johnson's Cabinet Watched by Ants,"** and especially **"Teeth Mother Naked at Last"** (which, like many of the *Selected Poems,* has now been significantly revised by the author). Here Bly truly created a new type of American poem driven by stunning images and startling associational connections for which nothing earlier in the national literature fully prepared one:

> Massive engines lift beautifully from the deck.
> Wings appear over the trees, wings with eight hundred rivets.
>
> Engines burning a thousand gallons of gasoline a minute sweep over the huts with dirt floors.
> Chickens feel the fear deep in the pits of their beaks.
> Buddha and Padma Sambhava.
>
> Meanwhile out on the China Sea
> immense gray bodies are floating,
> born in Roanoke,
> the ocean to both sides expanding, "buoyed on the dense marine."
>
> Helicopters flutter overhead. The death-
> bee is coming. Super Sabres
> like knots of neurotic energy sweep
> around and return.
> This is Hamilton's triumph.
> This is the triumph of a centralized bank.
> B-52s come from Guam. Teachers
> die in flames. The hopes of Tolstoy fall asleep in the ant heap.
> Do not ask for mercy.

("Poem in Three Parts")

Unfortunately, this exciting phase lasted only a few years. By the time **"Teeth Mother Naked at Last"** appeared in the volume, *Sleepers Joining Hands* (1973), Bly's political poetry had already dulled into a method as monotonous as his "country" poems. Bly's immense facility had again proven his undoing. The once frightening juxtaposition of myth and politics had become another easy routine. The new style and content were roughly similar to the best poems from *The Light Around the Body,* but the intensity and surprise had vanished. From now on Bly's writing becomes depressing to survey. When he risks large new themes as in the long poem, **"Sleepers Joining Hands,"** the work fails (as even he now senses, having broken this "too expansive and excitable" long poem into a number of shorter pieces in the *Selected Poems*). More often Bly remains content to revisit familiar themes with increasingly less compression and precision. A book like *This Tree Will Be Here For a Thousand Years* (1979) repeats self-consciously the mode of *Silence in the Snowy Fields.* Nor was this sentimental journey enough. As one of Bly's notes in *Selected Poems* makes clear, a third volume of "country poems" is on its way. This retrenchment would be less disappointing if Bly could still handle this mode as well as he did earlier in his career. Instead one sees a decline in quality as well as failure of real imaginative growth.

Bly's failure to build on the achievement of his best poems and his subsequent decline into self-parody makes *Selected Poems* a major disappointment. Whatever my reservations about Bly, I like the sensibility behind the work. I admire most of his basic values. I delight in his energy and irreverence. I want him to bring his poems to life—to dazzle, frighten and move me. Instead I read page after page of predictable, edifying poetic exercises. The experience would not be quite so bad if I did not hear the author so energetically applauding his own performances. Bly insists on being judged as a major poet, but his verse cannot bear the weight of that demand.

There is nothing subtle in Bly's bid for major stature. He has unabashedly organized his *Selected Poems* to demonstrate his own importance. He argues for this position overtly by chronicling each and every change in his poetry and equating them with growth. (One of the most interesting critical assumptions currently prevalent seems to be that the more a poet changes his work the more he grows in stature.) For Bly there is no subject so thoroughly engrossing as himself, and in recent years even his literary criticism, once so exciting and iconoclastic, has veered into pious autobiography. In *Selected Poems* this compulsion to annotate his own work proceeds unchecked by the Harper & Row editorial department. In only 204 pages of text the author has provided no fewer than 11 substantial prose commentaries. There is an introduction for each of the nine selections of the book plus two "afterthoughts" at the end, short essays which link the poet's technique with that of Smart, Blake, Whitman, Baudelaire, Ponge, and Jimenez. Of course, a *Selected Poems* should advertise a poet's achievement. Usually, however, a volume accomplishes this by presenting an author's best poems and letting the reader evaluate them. From the organization of this book, however, it would seem that Bly distrusts either his readers or his own work.

What use is poetry that cannot speak to its contemporary audience without the support of intermediary prose? Perhaps these insistent commentaries are only the miscalculations of an overly eager author. But in Bly's case even a sympathetic reader may begin to wonder about what is really going on. Reading the commentary in this volume is like watching a ball game from the stands while listening to someone describe it on the radio. The announcer, however, seems to be describing an altogether different game, one much more exciting than the humdrum contest down on the field. One should not be too surprised though. It is just that gift for self-marketing that has built Bly's successful career. Some readers enjoy the sales pitch enough to accept the poetry on faith. I advise a more critical reading of these *Selected Poems.* There are a few breathtaking moments here as well as many quiet revelations. If only one did not have to push through all the dullness and pretention to find them or shut out the author's eager guided tours along the way. Bly's best poems make this volume worth the effort, but, unfortunately, it is an effort.

Askold Melnyczuk (review date 1988)

SOURCE: "Robert Bly," in *Partisan Review,* Vol. LV, No. 1, 1988, pp. 167-71.

[In the following review, Melnyczuk offers analysis of Bly's poetry and artistic development in Selected Poems.*]*

My first thought on opening Robert Bly's *Selected Poems* was how much this volume could not contain. Like Ezra Pound half a century earlier, Bly has centered himself in poetry and proceeded to radiate his energies out to nearly all corners of the world of letters. He has been influential as an editor, translator, theorist, and publicist for his gifted contemporaries. Where Pound schooled us in Greek, Latin, and Chinese classics, Bly has tutored us in Spanish (Machado, Neruda, Vallejo), Swedish (Ekelof, Transtromer), Norwegian (Hamsun), German (Rilke, Trakl), and even Hindu (Kabir). His public persona has been that of a guru, a bard of the people's court, a hyper- vitaminized skald, a WASP shaman (some would insist on abbreviating that word), a kind of straight Allen Ginsberg. Bly also resembles Pound in his talent for vexing the soberer doctors of letters, who tend to tsk and hiss, *de haut en bas,* at the work of mere masters of spirit.

The *Selected,* like all Bly productions, is an idiosyncratic affair. It is divided into ten parts. Nine of these contain excerpts (often much revised) from both published and unpublished material. A final chapter, "Afterthoughts," offers two brief essays on prosody. Bly introduces the poetry sections with semi-autobiographical prefaces that are variously illuminating and irritating. He is capable of awesome banality: "All poems are journeys. They go from somewhere to somewhere else." His need to personalize the rhetoric of poetic convention produces some quaint locutions: he describes the "English melodic line" as "the lute of three loudnesses." But he also surfaces in these pages as a dues-paying guildsman tirelessly testing rhythm and pitch, carefully building the craft that will carry his voice. Like most of the poets born in the twenties, he began by writing in conventional meters. But "something in it did not fit" him; he continued to cast about until he discovered the loose and placid (though not flaccid) line that is his signature. The swivel and pivot of syllables and consonants in Bly's verse are quiet and regular as the plains and fields of his native Midwest.

Until recently, Bly's poetry has been Janus-faced, revealing alternately a public and a private aspect. Bly is aware of this dualism. He calls the work focusing on the inner life "poems of affinity," while those touching on social and political experience he labels "poems of judgment." In solitude, away from society, Bly suggests, we commune freely with nature and spirit and all that makes us feel large and whole. In community, however, we compromise and are compromised, we are driven by greed, motivated by fear, and live at the mercy of the *tamas gunas.* This book charts the poet's movement toward integrity and wholeness.

The earliest poems here reflect the poet's apprentice status. Tender sentiments are tritely expressed in a diction straightlaced with Wordsworthisms: "For me this season is most sweet," vows the young swain of autumn. The following line, however, redeems that confession by its engaging rhythm and evocative image: "And winter will be stamping of the feet." Had Bly developed along the lines he traced out for himself, he would have become a conventional taxidermist of nature: "The honey gatherers, coming and going, drive / Their endless circles to the hive." A notable exception is the longer **"Schoolcraft's Diary Written on the Missouri: 1830"** which, though a little fuzzy in details, convincingly fuses narrative, symbolism, and period diction to convey something of the awe and mystery that must have enveloped the forays of the American pioneers. Toward the poem's end, the speaker, having just seen a wounded white bear, declares: "I felt as I had once when through a door, / At ten or twelve, I'd seen my mother bathing." His memory of the accidental trespass of a human taboo illuminates the more public and deliberate violation of the American wilderness.

In later books Bly sought a language with which to limn the struggles of the inner man—or, rather, the interior city:

> Inside the veins there are navies setting forth,
> Tiny explosions at the water lines,
> And seagulls weaving in the wind of the salty blood.
>
> **"Waking from Sleep"**

The mood of the poems is generally ecstatic: "Oh, on an early morning I think I shall live forever." Bly's sense of the numinous probably owes something to his study of the Christian mystics Boehme and Eckhart, both of whom saw the divine as immanent rather than transcendent. Drawn mainly from *The Silence in the Snowy Fields,* and influenced by Waley's Chinese translations and his own versions of Machado, the best of these poems are lapidary and comprehensive:

> V. *Listening to Bach*
> Inside this music there is someone
> Who is not well described by the names
> Of Jesus, or Jehovah, or the Lord of Hosts!
>
> **"Six Winter Privacy Poems"**

The counterparts to these terse panegyrics are the public poems, many from the Vietnam era. To evoke the psychic dislocations of a nation divided, Bly deployed a brand of neosurrealism which came to be known as deep imagism. Simplifying grossly, the technique has the poet juxtapose radically disparate images aimed at detonating an emotional explosion in the reader. Here poems that fail lack inevitability. Their images seem arbitrary and cartoonish:

> Filaments of death grow out.
> The sheriff cuts off his black legs
> And nails them to a tree.
>
> **"War and Silence"**

But the blunt rhetorical strategies can also be unnervingly effective:

> Tonight they burn the rice supplies; tomorrow
> They lecture on Thoreau; tonight they move around
> the trees;
> Tonight they throw firebombs; tomorrow
> They read the Declaration of Independence; tomorrow
> they are in church.
>
> **"Johnson's Cabinet Watched by Ants"**

The war also inspired what may be Bly's finest single poem, **"The Teeth Mother Naked At Last."** Structurally reliant on Whitmanesque anaphora, the poem, part catalogue, part document, keens the loss of America's political innocence. A combination of *Mauberley,* a condensed *Cantos,* and *Howl,* it could be read as the bloody right parenthesis to "When Lilacs Last in the Dooryard Bloomed":

> I know that books are tired of us.
> I *know* they are chaining the Bible to chairs.
> Books don't want to remain in the same room with us
> anymore.
> New Testaments are escaping . . . dressed as women
> they slip out after dark.

Pasternak once remarked that a book is nothing more than a "cubic piece of burning, smoking conscience." The pyre Bly lit with his war poems continues to smoulder and disturb our night.

Bly's prose poems deserve an essay of their own. While his meditations on the prosody of prose are provocative, the things themselves embody and magnify some of the weaknesses of Bly's less successful verse. They can be obvious, *faux-naïf,* packed with posturings and banal observations. Memorable exceptions include **"The Hockey Poem"** with its Ovidian metamorphoses, and **"The Dead Seal"** which, as a meditation on death and physical decay, is every bit as good as Richard Eberhardt's much anthologized "The Groundhog."

A "selected poems" may become either a tombstone or a capstone to a career. In Bly's case, however, it appears to be a stepping stone. The poems included here from his last two books, ***The Man in the Black Coat Turns*** and ***Loving a Woman in Two Worlds*** are his finest yet. Previously Bly's community seemed comprised of trees, turtles, horses, and the poet's own soul. Now that humans have entered as subjects of the poems, the tensions between public and private, outward and inward, have diminished. Bly writes about trying to come to terms with his father and about learning his own limitations as a father and a lover:

> I know there is someone
> who tries to teach us.
> He has four ways
> to do that . . .
> . . . I usually ignore
> the earlier three,
> and learn by falling.

"Four Ways of Knowledge"

He speaks, with startling luminosity, about loving a woman simultaneously muse and mortal:

> And we did what we did, made love attentively, then
> dove into the river, and our bodies joined as calmly
> as the swimmer's shoulders glisten at dawn.

"The Good Silence"

And his meditations on the sources of our otherness are worth attending to:

> We are bees then; our honey is language.
> Now the honey lies stored in caves
> beneath us, and the sound of words
> carries what we do not.

"Words Rising"

The ebb and flow of the spirit now surges in every line. The separate profiles of Janus have merged and he looks out at us at last full face.

Deborah Tannen (review date 18 November 1990)

SOURCE: "Born to be Wild," in *Washington Post Book World,* November 18, 1990, pp. 1-2.

[*In the following review, Tannen offers a favorable evaluation of* Iron John.]

In addition to being one of our finest poets, Robert Bly has, over the last 10 years, inspired—through talks, workshops and tapes—a growing men's movement, conceived not to oppose the women's movement but to claim for men the strength and rejuvenation that he sees the women's movement giving women. *Iron John* is Bly's brilliantly eclectic written meditation on why men today are unhappy and how they can become happier. Iron John, in the Grimms' fairy tale, is a wild, hairy man living at the bottom of a pond deep in the forest. Since the story's gradual unfolding provides the book's suspense, I will not reveal it, but simply note that Bly sees Iron John as a metaphor for what men need.

Bly's premise is that the '60s and '70s created a "soft male" who is in touch with his feminine side, eschews violence and seeks harmony, is "a nice boy who pleases not only his mother but also the young woman he is living with"—and is full of grief. Suffering from passivity, na-iveté and numbness, what he needs to know is not only his feminine side (though it also is of value) but the "deep male" symbolized by Iron John. Making contact with (not becoming) the Wild Man entails forsaking parents for a male mentor. Though "a clean break from the mother is crucial," Bly refreshingly does not blame mothers when this break isn't made; he blames fathers, who abandon their sons, leaving a vacuum that mothers fill. He finds our society deficient in mythology and impoverished by the loss of ritual, especially initiation rituals by which older men take boys from the women and teach them how to be men.

The book is structured around Bly's colloquial rendering of the Iron John tale, told piece by piece, interspersed with commentary, snatches of tales from other traditions and mythologies, anthropological lore of non-literate cultures, Jungian insights and, most gloriously, poetry, much of it written or beautifully translated by Bly. The book is illuminated by the poet's image-rich vision and voice, generous in such wonderful phrasings as "old-man-minded farmer," "the Idaho of the mind" and "Men and women alike once called on men to pierce the dangerous places, carry handfuls of courage to the waterfalls, dust the tails of the wild boars."

The growth of the men's movement is testimony that Bly has struck a resonant chord: the need for ritual and for new stories and images to replace the ones that have worn out and let us down, the alienation of father and son in post-industrial society. He seeks to restore the terms "masculine" and "feminine" as legitimate, apolitical descriptions of the sexes as essentially different but not opposed. His observations about the differences between the sexes are true—and work both ways. Indeed, "how often every adult man has felt himself, when baffled by a woman's peculiar interpretation of his behavior—so different from his own—go into a sulk."

Though she may be more likely to talk than sulk, every adult woman, too, has been baffled by a man's peculiar interpretation of her behavior. Similarly, Bly correctly observes that mothers can distort their sons' views of their fathers: "Mothers can be right about the father's negative side, but the woman also can be judgmental about masculine traits that are merely different or unexpected," such as not talking about his feelings. This is important and also applies to fathers who give sons (and daughters) a view of their mothers as hysterical, manipulative, and illogical.

I am a bit nervous, not about Bly's own enlightened and enlightening vision, but about what might be made of it. He cautions that the Wild Man, who is fierce, should not be confused with the "savage man," who is aggressively destructive; yet the two are easily confused. Writer Trip Gabriel found that, during a men's retreat inspired (but not run) by Bly, the participants easily danced like savages but were at a loss when asked to dance like wild men. And I could imagine Bly cringing at a letter responding to Gabriel's article about the retreat in which a man claims to have displayed his Wild Man by fighting in gang brawls and beating on garbage cans during college keg parties.

A theme running through the book is that men must regain comfort with the sword, learn to fight, get in touch with their "inner warrior." Despite Bly's emphasis that the inner warrior is better expressed through ritual display, such as poetry, than by literal warfare, he uses much warlike imagery. For example, he says of the naive man, "If his wife or girlfriend, furious, shouts that he is 'chauvinist,' a 'sexist,' a 'man,' he doesn't fight back, but just takes it. He opens his shirt so that she can see more clearly where to put the lances. He ends with three or four javelins sticking out of his body, and blood running all over the floor." But then, my objection to such imagery serves to illustrate Bly's point about women's discomfort with male agonism—fighting or warlike behavior.

Bly overestimates the effect of the women's movement, of women's strength and self-assurance, of the change in men resulting from New Age thinking. It hardly seems that most men have rejected the sword, when child abuse, rape, wife-beating, street crime and war are increasingly evident. If, as Bly eloquently demonstrates, agonism is an inherent and essential part of male consciousness, he is also right that our hope lies in the rediscovery of ritual enactments to replace the literal enactments that have both our society and the future of the earth under siege. This rewarding book is an invaluable contribution to the gathering public conversation about what it means to be male—or female.

Mihaly Csikszentmihalyi (review date 9 December 1990)

SOURCE: "Bring on the Hairy Mentor," in *New York Times Book Review*, December 9, 1990, pp. 15-6.

[*In the following review, Csikszentmihalyi offers positive assessment of* Iron John, *though notes that "the overall style of the book is a bit disappointing."*]

It is refreshing these days to read a book that does not lay the blame for America's collective ills on social injustice, the savings and loan scandal, Iraq or the National Endowment for the Arts, but—get this—on defective mythology. The reason so many young people are ruined by drugs or senseless violence, according to Robert Bly (who is well known for his verse as well as for his recent forays into the reconstruction of the male psyche), is that to grow up as a wholesome adult one needs not only material comforts but the wise guidance of one's elders; and that is becoming increasingly scarce.

Anthropological literature is filled with accounts of how the Hopi Indians or the Arapesh of New Guinea nudge their youth into adulthood with the help of myths, symbols and initiation rituals. It is generally understood that such cultures would not endure unless elders spent a great deal of energy passing on their knowledge and values to the younger generation. But one could read a towering stack of enthnographies without encountering the suggestion that perhaps the same necessity holds also for us. Primitive people may need myths and rituals, because, well, they are primitive, aren't they? We, being rational, need none of that. Just give us the facts and the truth shall set us free.

It is with this dry Cartesian notion of human development that Mr. Bly takes issue. He starts with the assumption that boys don't become men or girls women by simply getting older and better informed. They also need a spiritual infusion from myths and mentors, in the form of a caring relationship that gradually discloses to the young what adulthood is all about. According to Mr. Bly, women in the last few decades have begun to rediscover what femininity means, while for men—separated from their fathers and from other male models—the concept of masculinity gets progressively blurred. To grow up healthy, young males need a positive ideal of manhood, and *Iron John* intends to provide it for them.

The model explored in this book is an archetypal character who recurs in myths and literature from the Gilgamesh to the brothers Grimm. Iron John is a hairy wild man who inhabits the forests and helps aimless young princes in their quest for fame and fortune. Mr. Bly's reading turns this Iron John into a perfect combination of untamed impulses and thoughtful self-discipline. This, and not the macho idols of the 1950s or the androgynous flower children of the 60s, should be our guiding ideal of mature masculinity. Although Iron John is an unregenerate male, man and woman can be whole only through each other. Mr. Bly does not believe that blurring the distinctions between the genders makes sense. As in biological development, integration requires prior differentiation; a fulfilling relationship requires a masculine man and a feminine woman.

It is possible that people who think of themselves as liberated will find Mr. Bly's theses somewhat reactionary. After all, why assume that the two genders need different myths, or that women can't initiate boys into manhood? Why not assume a generic human psyche, and unisex role models? To these questions Mr. Bly gives reasonably convincing answers. Four million years in which men and women prospered by maximizing complementary characteristics, eons that etched different patterns on the neural networks of the two genders, cannot—with all the good will in the world—be erased in a few decades. Nor can the subtle tendrils of culture, which entangle us in traditional gender roles, be cut without running the risk of bleeding the sap out of a growing man, or woman.

In terms of what it tries to accomplish, Mr. Bly's book is important and timely. We need powerful jogs such as this to help us remember that, moon shots and genetic engineering notwithstanding, we are still befuddled creatures needing all the help we can get from the distilled experience of the ancients of the tribe. It is easy to forget that culture gets transmitted from the psyche of one generation to the next, and that when the chain gets broken, savagery is likely to ensue. There is no question that Mr. Bly has focused on a real source of malaise. His prescriptions for a cure are more difficult to assess, partly because of his oracular prose, partly because the issues are too complex for a definitive judgment. Perhaps all one can do is repeat the Italian aphorism, *se non è vero, è ben trovato*, or, it need not be true as long as it is well said.

However, in this case it is not always well said. The overall style of the book is a bit disappointing. Donald Hall once commented, "Bly moves like a huge hummingbird from Jung flower to Zen Flower, from the Buddha to the Great Mother," and this *modus operandi* is very much in evidence in the present volume—except that the field of flowers has expanded to include a few up-to-date anthropologists, psychologists and the headlines of the daily papers. There is nothing inherently wrong with this approach, except that the shift in ontological and epistemological perspective implied when the author moves from legend to commentary to psychological interpretation to sociological aside disrupts the reader's involvement with the story. A well-written sociological treatise creates its own symbolic universe, just as a great novel or play does. But alternating genres is difficult, because the reader becomes aware of the artifice as one form passes into the other. The many voices of *Iron John* occasionally drown one another out, and none imposes itself with authority.

Mr. Bly, like other rehabilitators of ancient myths (such as Joseph Campbell, Robert Graves, Carlos Castaneda), tries to reflect the complexity of existence by making every symbol, image or event both good and bad, helpful and dangerous. Soon all the landscape is filled with ambivalent characters flashing red and green, stop and go, do this but watch out for the consequences. The great King is the ideal father not to be confused with the real father, and he is to be looked up to but escaped from, admired but abandoned, and so forth. This approach shows a sophisticated understanding of the dialectical nature of psychic reality, but it is also rather confusing. It suggests that a

young man better forget about growing up unless he has the sensitivity of a Jung, the brains of an Einstein and the determination of a General Patton, plus a good dose of luck. Yet one senses that the author holds a map that would insure a safe passage over the booby-trapped terrain, but he is coyly withholding it from the reader. The riotous ambivalence of the mythopoetic imagination makes one nostalgic for the simple-minded clarity of the scientific approach, in which different outcomes are explained in terms of general principles and necessary conditions.

It is easy to find fault with a book that tries to accomplish something as novel and difficult as this one does. *Iron John* is Mr. Bly's first full-length volume of prose, and one hopes that with successive excursions into the hermeneutics of myth he will develop a style that fits its subject. In the meantime there is much that is thought provoking in the present book, and whenever Mr. Bly shares with us his acerbic poet's vision, the provocation is very enjoyable.

Ted Solotaroff (essay date 9 September 1991)

SOURCE: "Captain Bly," in *Nation,* September 9, 1991, pp. 270-4.

[*In the following essay, Solotaroff provides an overview of Bly's literary career and intellectual development, and an analysis of* Iron John.]

Recently in these pages Gore Vidal remarked that instead of politics Americans have elections. One sees what he means, but it's not quite on the money, because elections matter mostly to the politicians, their PAC groups and their dwindling party loyalists. For the rest of America, elections are a peculiar form of TV entertainment in which the commercial has become the program. The affiliations and ideologies people care about are elsewhere, in what Theodore Roszak fifteen years ago termed "situational groups," the politics of the personal. "In less than a generation's time," he wrote, "every conceivable form of situational belonging has been brought out of the closet and has forced its grievances and its right to exist upon the public consciousness." He was writing about the mitosis of the counterculture, but his observation was no less prescient about its opposition—the pro-lifers, creationists, apocalyptics, neoconservatives, school vigilantes, et al. There are also the expressive therapeutic groups: The most influential ideology of change in America today is probably that of A. A., not only because it works so dramatically but because it provides a model of psychological and spiritual community, which is what the ethnic, racial, gender, sexual and other situational groups are partly about. The most interesting recent example is the men's movement, a complex phenomenon that appears to derive from A. A., feminism, New Age religion and therapy, environmentalism and the culture and charisma of Robert Bly.

That a poet is the spokesman of a broadly based movement as well as at the top of the charts has, of course, struck many readers but not, I imagine, many poets. They are used to Bly the group leader, publicist, ideologist, translator, mythologist, guru and scold, he having played these roles in the American poetry of the second half of the century, much as Ezra Pound did in that of the first half. Poets are also used to Bly the showman, his hit performance on Bill Moyers's program, which sent the men's movement into media orbit, having been preceded by hundreds of his sold-out poetry readings and seminar star turns.

Like most literary careers that last, Bly's has been formed from the ongoing play of oppositions, but his have been particularly intense: Lutheran and pagan, rural and international, reclusive and engaged, austere and grandiose. These contending traits and inclinations have generated Bly's high energy and also created a certain rhythm to his career that makes his present celebrity and function almost predictable. Also they are compacted into a strongly lived life that personalizes the mythopoetic structure and far-out counsel of *Iron John* and gives the book, for all of its discursiveness and highhandedness, an overall staying power and a kind of charmed ability to hit paydirt about every third page.

Iron John is less about male identity than it is about what Jungians, following John Keats, call "soul-making." Much of Bly's soul has been forged and refined by his relationship with the Wild Man, his favorite name for the tutelary figure in the fairy tale that he unpacks and unpacks, embroiders and embroiders to tell the reader how boys psychically become men and men remain psychically boys.

Bly grew up, as he says, a "Lutheran Boy-god" in Minnesota, being his mother's favorite, and in good Freudian fashion, drawing from that a heightened sense of entitlement as well as a tendency to see the world through her eyes and feel it with her heart, which means he didn't see or feel very much on his own. In Bly's terms his soul or psyche had a lot of conducting "copper" in it, which would come in handy as an editor, critic and translator, and not much of the "iron" of autonomy that he would later have to extract on his own from the mines of the archetypal warrior king in himself. In short, he grew up "soft," like the males of today to whom *Iron John* is mainly addressed. Bly's brother appears to have been his father's son, the one who took up the family occupation of farming, the hairy Esau to his tent-dwelling Jacob. His father was strong, kindly, intensely moral, and alcoholic, creating a particularly poignant remoteness that broods over *Iron John*, as it does in some of Bly's later poetry: "the man in the black coat" who appears only to turn away again and whose haunting absence, along with his mother's haunting presence, has created Bly's lifelong project and process of fathering one's soul, which is his particular contribution to the men's movement.

For the rest, Bly was a well-raised product of Madison, Minnesota, a small plains community with a Norwegian cultural accent. He was properly clean and godly, cheerful

and repressed, "asleep in the Law," as he puts it in his major autobiographical poem, **"Sleepers Joining Hands."** A Lutheran Boy-god who remains in this state is likely to become a minister, his grandiosity put into the service of interpreting doctrines and counseling the flock. Bly has, of course, taken the opposite road, "from the Law to the Legends," as he puts it in *Iron John,* but the deal he apparently made with his psyche is that the nascent preacher has gone with him and adapted to his various stages and purposes.

Bly doesn't talk about his Harvard experience in *Iron John*—he seldom has in a career otherwise rich in self-revelation—but it was a determinate stage in which this wounded Boy-god and naïve "ascender" was both endowed and banished, a literary version of the prince of his fairy tale. Here he is as an editor of the *Harvard Advocate,* reviewing a collection of British poetry edited by Kenneth Rexroth. One sentence tells the tale:

> Perhaps it is unfortunate that Rexroth should have been let loose on the Romantics; there is, I think, a difference between the desire to express personal emotion by increased direct reference to the world of nature, and the desire to overthrow all external discipline of morals of government.

This is, of course, the T. S. Eliot act that many young writers in the postwar era used to put themselves on the cutting edge of modernism. In Bly's case, it suggests that he was turning over in his sleep from the Lutheran law to the Anglican one. The literary air at the time was thick with conservative authority and decorum. It had an archbishop, Eliot; a set of bishops, the New Critics; a martyr, Pound; and lots of acolytes, who were becoming half paralyzed by the dogma that poetry was a hieratic vocation, that the imagination lived, worked and had its being within The Tradition. As Eliot had laid it down, it was mostly Dante and the metaphysical poets, the high Anglicans like himself. The dogma came equipped with Eliot's emphasis on the impersonal, objective image and with a set of literary heresies and fallacies that were meant to nip any revival of Romanticism in the bud.

To subscribe to this ethos typically led a young writer to graduate school or to the pits. Bly chose the latter, having become "overcommitted to what he was not," as Erik Erikson would say, and badly needing to find his way to his own "inner tradition." He ended up in New York, where he spent the next three years being mostly blocked, depressed and poor: the state of "ashes, descent, and grief" that forms a major early stage in his mythic prince's initiation. According to Bly, life reserves this "katabasis" particularly for the grandiose ascender, putting him in touch with the dark, wounded side he has tried to ignore and evade and ministering to the naïveté, passivity and numbness that comes with the apron strings of his entitlement. The road, in short, that leads "from the mother's house to the father's house."

The one poem that Bly published from this period, **"Where We Must Look for Help,"** is based on three types of birds that were sent forth from Noah's ark into the flooded world: the glamorous peaceful dove and the graceful swallows find no land, only the crow does:

> The crow, the crow, the spider-colored crow,
> The crow shall find new mud to walk upon.

("Poem in Three Parts")

As Bly was to tell Deborah Baker, who has written an excellent biographical essay about him, "It was the first time . . . I ran into the idea of the dark side of the personality being the fruitful one." After a year at the Iowa Writers' Workshop, Bly went to live on a farm his father had bought for him, and a year later, while visiting relatives in Norway, he discovered his new mud lying adjacent to his inner tradition.

In primitive societies, as Bly tells us in *Iron John,* the male initiation is viewed as a second birth, with the elders acting as a "male mother." Bly's were first Georg Trakl, a German, and Gunnar Ekelöf, a Swede. From them he began to grasp the subjective, intuitive, "wild" side of modernism as opposed to the objective, rationalist, "domesticated" one. In their work as in that of the French and Hispanic surrealists—Char, Michaux, Jiménez, Vallejo and Lorca, among others—Bly sensed the missing water, the unconscious, for lack of which he believed Anglo-American poetry was suffering vastation. Increasingly dry, ironical, exhausted, remote, it was itself The Wasteland, while the European poets were still fecund, passionate and present. Returning to the family farm, Bly started a magazine, *The Fifties,* to say so as aggressively as possible and to provide translations of the European and Latin American surrealists in three or four languages, as well as to give welcome to his contemporaries who showed signs of new life and put down those who were dead on their feet. Flying a woodcut of Woden as his logo, Bly almost single-handedly led the charge against the reign of the "Old Fathers" in the middle, joined by the New York School on his right and the West Coast Beats on his left. Neither wing was anywhere near as relentless, reductive and brutal as Bly. He was out to deauthorize as well as replace the Eliot-Pound-Tate tradition, stamping on it well into the next generation—Lowell, Berryman, Delmore Schwartz, Jarrell, Karl Shapiro, whomever. In *Iron John* he chides himself for contributing to the decline of "Zeus energy," attributing it to the demons in his father-wound: a false note from someone who has repeatedly insisted that literature advances by generational strife and deplored the absence of adversarial criticism among poets.

Be that as it may, in the late fifties Bly entered his warrior phase, developing the strategy and service to a cause that in *Iron John* distinguish the warrior from the soldier. Though his magazine was known mainly for its demolition jobs, it also blazed, paved and landscaped a new road. Bly wrote many essays that developed his concept of "leaping" and "wild poetry," both in concept and prosody. In **"Looking for Dragon Smoke,"** Bly hooked together a countertradition to the Christian-rational-industrial one that

provided a kind of culture of the Wild Man. It begins with *Gilgamesh,* in which the "psychic forces" of an early civilized society created the hairy, primitive Enkidu as the adversary and eventual companion of the golden Gilgamesh (the first harbinger of *Iron John*). After *Beowulf* (Bly's Nordic touchstone) the "dragon smoke" of inspired association with primal memories is not much in evidence until Blake arrives to give the lie to the Enlightenment, as do the associative freedom and "pagan and heretical elements" in his German contemporaries Novalis, Goethe and Hölderlin. With Freud and Jung the unconscious is back in business again, and the romantic/symbolist/surrealist wing of modernism provides Bly with a whole range of leaping, dragon smoke poets from Scandinavia south to Spain and across to Latin America to translate, publish and emulate.

Compared with Trakl's images ("On Golgotha God's eyes opened") or Lorca's ("Black horses and dark people are riding over the deep roads of the guitar"), Bly's own early leaps as a poet did not take him very far inward. About a horse wandering in the moonlight, he wrote: "I feel a joy, as if I had thought / Of a pirate ship ploughing through dark flowers." The poems of his first collection, *Silence in the Snowy Fields,* are noticeably restrained, wishing to be admired for the integrity of their mood, mostly a meditative one: a young pastoral poet getting his act together rather than appearing with snakes in his hair or as a messenger from the deeps.

Then, in the mid-sixties, Bly got caught up in the antiwar movement. He became a leading mobilizer of the literary community and provided one of the great moments in the theater of demonstrations when he gave his National Book Award check for his second collection, *The Light Around the Body,* to a draft resister while on the stage at Lincoln Center. Auden said of Yeats, "Mad Ireland hurt you into poetry"; the Vietnam War hurt Bly into writing the kind of poetry he had been calling for and that in places matched Neruda's in its creeping balefulness. Evoking the fallout of evil that has settled in Minnesota, he ends:

> Therefore we will have to
> Go far away
> To atone
> For the suffering of the stringy-chested
> And the short rice-fed ones, quivering
> In the helicopter like wild animals,
> Shot in the chest, taken back to be questioned.

("Poem in Three Parts")

In the course of writing these poems and of editing a collection of antiwar poetry, Bly developed his concept of the intuitive association to reconnect literature with politics, two realms that most criticism and most experience of their "bloody crossroads," in Lionel Trilling's phrase, counseled to keep apart. Bly's position was an early version of the statement, long before it became cant, that the personal was political. As he put it, "A modern man's spiritual life and his growth are increasingly sensitive to the tone and content of a regime." Since much of our foreign and domestic policy comes from more or less hidden impulses in the American psyche, and because that psyche is in the poet too, "the writing of political poetry is like the writing of personal poetry, a sudden drive by the poet inward."

Along with strengthening his own poetry, Bly's involvement turned him into a performer of it. His high-visibility poetry readings developed into a countercultural event, the Lutheran Boy-god and warrior now reappearing as the bard. I first caught his act in the early seventies, when he entered a symposium on literary editing dressed in a serape and tapping a Tibetan drum, as though he were a cross between Neruda and Chögyam Trungpa, the meditation guru Bly studied with. After his poetry reading, complete with primitive masks, the other Bly, the literary caretaker, appeared on the panel of editors—sharp, shrewd and no less dominating.

He supported himself by his public appearances; otherwise he remained on his farm, tending to his chores as an editor, publisher, critic and poet and using his solitude to nourish "the parts that grow when we are far from the centers of ambition." Through the writings of Jung, Joseph Campbell, James Hillman and other psychic/cultural explorers he developed his encyclopedic command of the great heuristic myths, legends and folklore that understand us, concentrating on those that involve the female side. He gave lectures on Freud and Jung, as well as on Grimms' Fairy Tales, in the church basement in Madison, his trial by fire in making the esoteric vivid and meaningful to the public. He turned from America's shadow to his own, producing eleven collections of poems, most of them inward, associative, naked—Bly fully joining the tradition he had been staking out. He put out only one issue of *The Seventies,* a noticeably temperate one. The warrior was giving way to the gardener and lover, two roles that Bly lived through and that noticeably "moistened" his poetry in the eighties. They also provided two more stages in the process of male initiation that he took into his work with the men's movement. So did certain personal experiences of shame, guilt and loss, along with the aging process through which the holds that a father and son put on each other can turn into a yearning embrace. So, too, did his awareness that the young men in the literary and New Age circles he visited and who visited him on his farm had been weakened by the feminism of the era, and that male consciousness was in short and despairing supply. It was time, as Bly would say, to do something for the hive again.

Iron John, then, grows not only out of Bly's experience during the past decade in the men's movement but out of the central meanings of his life. If he has bought into the confusion and anxiety of many younger men today, caught between the new sensitivity and the old machismo, he has done so with the capital he has earned from his own growth as a man, a poet, a thinker and a husbandman of the culture. The souled fierceness that he prescribes for staking out and protecting the borders of male identity has provided much of the motive energy for his career as a

literary radical. By the same token, his devotion to asserting and cultivating the primalness and primacy of the imagination in a highly domesticated and institutionalized literary culture has led him to view the condition of men in similar terms and to apply the learning he has acquired in the archeology and anthropology of the imagination to remedy it. This authority is finally what makes *Iron John* a serious, groundbreaking book.

The startling public appeal of Bly's therapeutic sermon is not hard to fathom. Based on Jungian psychology, it takes a much more positive measure of human potential for change than does the Freudian model, whose Great Father and Great Mother are pretty strictly one's own and give not much quarter to altering their influence: a foot of freedom here, a pound less grief there. Bly's pagan goodspell is that the gods are still around and within each of us, able to be mobilized or deactivated, as the case may be. Like Rilke's torso of Apollo, they search us out where it aches and command us to treat it and thereby change our lives.

Also, *Iron John* has a lot of specific insight and lore to teach men and employs a very effective method. It takes an old story and gives it a new spin, thereby enlisting the child in us who is still most open to learning and the adult who is keen to escape from his own banality. Along with combining therapy for men, or at the very least clarity, with a course in the world mythology and ethnography of male initiation, *Iron John* is also a spiritual poetry reading in which the words of Blake and Kabir, Rumi and Yeats and many others join Bly's own poems as a kind of accompaniment to the text.

The prominence of poetry in the men's movement is perhaps its most surprising feature; none of the other situational groups seem to be particularly disposed to it, and most poets would tend to agree with Auden that poetry "makes nothing happen." Perhaps it's only an aspect of Bly's influence, but I see it as part of the same reviving interest in the imagination signified by the increasing popularity of poetry readings.

Some people say that the men's movement will have to move into national politics, as the women's movement has done, if it is to survive its trendiness and become socially significant. I'm not so sure. As the bonanza of the Reagan era recedes and the midlife crisis of its favored generation draws on, there are a lot of men in America who have mainly their imaginations to fall back upon. As a social analysis of male distress, *Iron John* is pretty thin stuff; but that's not why it is being read. It's not the *Growing Up Absurd* of the nineties but rather a deeply based counsel of self-empowerment and change. Like the men's movement itself, it offers the sixties generation another crack at the imagination of alternatives they grew up on, right where they most inwardly live and hurt and quest. This is the imagination that they turned in to become Baby Boomers; if it can be let loose in America by this broad, influential and growing situational group, there's no telling what can happen.

Anne Compton (essay date Summer 1992)

SOURCE: "In Iron John's Sloshy Swamp, There Is a Bitterly Cold Undercurrent," in *Dalhousie Review,* Vol. 72, No. 2, Summer, 1992, pp. 273-82.

[*In the following essay, Compton objects to Bly's presentation of women and mothers in* Iron John. *Compton concludes,* "Iron John *is a reactionary book, and, I believe, a dangerous book."*]

The usual criticism of women these days focuses on their alleged inattention to their children's needs. A woman's pursuit of a career, so the argument runs, results in the breakdown of the family, an argument favored by right-wingers and the moral majority. But for those women who have successfully managed family and career, there is Robert Bly, American poet and winner, in 1968, of the National Book Award for Poetry, who will certainly dampen any sense of success. In *Iron John* Bly argues that for sons over twelve, or perhaps it is over two, or earlier—"One could say that the father now loses his son five minutes after birth"—the mother is bad news. "Mother love" cripples. Among other things, Bly worries about "certain kinds of intellectual conversations proceeding from her rationalist mind that the unconscious mother indulges in with her teenage son." He continues,

> We are aware of a disturbing rise in the number of sons who report sexual abuse by mothers, as well as by fathers, uncles, and older brothers; but the culture still does not take seriously the damage caused by psychic incest between mother and son. . . . Much sexual energy can be exchanged when the mother looks the son directly in the eyes and says, "Here is your new T-shirt, all washed."

This nonsense should not be taken seriously, except that so many do. *Iron John* is "a serious, groundbreaking book"; "a transforming book," offering "reassurance"; "Mr. Bly's book is important and timely." That so many applaud the book's advice without interrogating its context, makes *Iron John* a dangerous book. That, and other things.

Bly believes that "manhood doesn't happen by itself." "A boy becomes a man . . . only through the 'active intervention'" of an older man, a mentor who guides the boy into manhood. This advice is transfused through the Grimms' tale "Iron John," making the preachy palatable. Bly moves back and forth between tale and present-day circumstances—"men in crisis." Along the way, many other tales, poems, anecdotes, and statistics get told. "Iron John," an eight-staged story, recounts the Wild Man's leading the prince-turned-pauper into adulthood. The boy's father has caged the troublesome Wild Man, a swamp-dweller, responsible for the disappearance of some of the king's subjects. The boy, stealing the key from beneath his mother's pillow, frees the Wild Man and the adventures begin. These adventures, or stages in development, include: life with the Wild Man, the period of ashes and kitchen work, tending the garden, warriorhood, and a ritualized festival leading to marriage and kingship. Guided through-

out by Iron John, the boy takes on the energy and initiative of the Wild Man. The tale is entertaining; the advice is sound. Of course, boys need the company of male elders. How unfortunate, then (and how surprising), that one phrase in the tale—"'the key is under your mother's pillow'"—advances the anti-feminist tone of this work.

Even if it weren't offensive on that head, *Iron John* is unpleasant reading—boring and chaotic. Written in a style somewhere between a self-help manual and poetry, *Iron John* adopts a folksy tone: "Let's see what we've learned so far" kind of approach, as if it were a manual on fixing bathroom plumbing. Indeed, in one of the book's many metaphors, "children turn into copper wires." Sometimes these homely metaphors are affectedly coy:

> When the father-table, the groundwater, drops, so to speak, and there is too little father, instead of too much father, the sons find themselves in a new situation. What do they do: drill for new father water, ration the father water, hoard it, distill mother water into father water?

With all this plumbing, it is little wonder Iron John comes unstuck from his pond.

The book, however, lacks the clarity of a do-it-yourself repair guide. Bly introduces and repeats phrases that never get clarified as if repetition conferred authority. What anyway are "women's values," and how do you know when you have had too many of them? Distinctions are similarly asserted but never secured. There are times when "wild man" seems a good deal like "savage man," although Bly insists that they are different. Lacking rigorous distinctions, the book "swamps" us in the mythopoetic imagination so that, as Csikszentmihalyi says, "one [feels] nostalgic for the simple-minded clarity of the scientific approach. . . ." Bly could have made greater use of the "Logos-knife" that he himself recommends. Metaphor, myth, literature are all instrumental in this self-help manual, but when literature is an instrument serving thesis, as it is in this case, the effect is reductionist. Hamlet, we are told, is "stuck" on his mother (How about that criminal uncle for a mentor?), and Ophelia is reduced to an aspect of Hamlet: "We could say that some sentimental girl inside Hamlet, here called Ophelia, has gone mad at this clumsily performed move [to the father's world] and will 'die.'" Perhaps this bias—girls are merely aspects of boys—explains why girls do not need the careful mentoring that boys require: "A girl changes into woman on her own . . . ." Girls as well as boys need the father, and both children need the tutoring of the elders of both sexes, but as Jill Johnston points out, Bly's "only concern here [absentee fathers in relation to daughters] is the damaging effect of such deficits on 'the daughter's ability to participate . . . in later relationships with men.'"

Bly begins *Iron John* by outlining three historical stages—macho man, soft man, and wild man. Through the fairy tale "Iron John," Bly explores this third possibility—the wild man. Soft man is really quite unhappy; wild man must correct the soft man's problems. Responsibility for this softening rests with the feminists, who wanted sensitive men. This is a straw dog, straw bitch, I should say; what women actually wanted, and still want, is not men who easily weep, but fair men and just practices in gender relations.

Feminism, Bly argues, reconstituted the world, creating the new couple—softer men and harder women. The terms, of course, are phallic; women have appropriated phallic power, and power must be reclaimed. The new woman is described elsewhere in the book as "fierce" and as "warrior," and since fierce warrior is one of the forms, or stages, of the truly initiated man, it is not difficult to see that Bly's real worry is not "soft men" but "hard women." Bly sets out to remind us what men and women are supposed to be. He does this by staking out and fortifying the territory of the male identity. Men need to recover the twenty-thousand-year-old heritage of "'natural brutality.'" Natural is supposed to make the "brutal" all right, but as we all know, often what is passed off as "natural" is really a cultural construct. In the "natural," that is in the traditional order of things, men are hard and women are soft. To ensure male identity, boys must be kept safe from the contamination of mother love: "When women, even women with the best intentions, bring up a boy alone, he may in some way have no male face, or he may have no face at all." Readers who can get beyond the patronizing tone in this passage will appreciate Bly's lesson on how things "naturally" ought to be.

Essays on and reviews of *Iron John* have focussed, thus far, on the book's message for men; this is not surprising as it is sub-titled, "A Book About Men." Bly is seen as a "spokesman" for "the men's movement." *Iron John* is "an important text for anyone trying to make spiritual sense out of contemporary male development," but the book also has a good deal to say about women. The urgency in Bly's voice as he advises men on the need for the father, arises out of an equally urgent warning about the danger of the mother. It is time then to examine further Bly's view of women.

Bly contends that men have been enervated by the feminism of our era. Reading women's gains as men's damage, Bly renders recent cultural changes significant only to the extent that these affect men. The putative deleterious effects of feminism in recent decades—man's supposed softening—is equated with centuries of female powerlessness. "You think you have suffered, well look at what's happened to us," or as Neil Lyndon, British broadcaster and writer, puts it: "'Men are suffering from systematic disadvantages . . . [which] represent a body of grievous, institutionalised discrimination.'" In terms of sexual oppression, the twentieth century belongs to men. Bly writes:

> We know that nineteenth-century men characteristically failed to notice female suffering. *The Madwoman in the Attic,* by Sandra Gilbert and Susan Gubar, describes how strong that suffering was. In this century, men have added another inattention: they characteristically failed to notice their own suffering.

Bly's book is stirred by the emergence of the "strong" woman, the "fierce" woman, but Bly does not engage with this figure. Instead, he tackles the mother. Although Bly claims that it is not necessary to lay "a lot of blame on the mother," he does. *Iron John* is riddled with assumptions about maternal behavior, referring, for example, to "the possessiveness that mothers *typically* exercise on sons" [emphasis mine]. Boys need "more hardness than she could *naturally* give" [emphasis mine]. The mother's ascensionism imparts to the boy, Bly implies, a contempt for physical labor. D. H. Lawrence, learning too late an honor for his father and his father's work, is Bly's example here:

> The children of his [Lawrence's] generation deduced that their fathers had been doing something wrong all along, that men's physical work is wrong, and that those sensitive mothers who prefer white curtains and an elevated life are right and always have been.

"Women's values" are equated with "white curtains," with prettiness, and include a deprecation of physical work. In the household I live in, a mother taught sons to handle an axe, glaze a window, and dig a garden. Children, of course, must see work done, but work is not gendered. There is not man's work and woman's work. This notion that work and "values" are gendered widens the gender gap. Supposing a mother does "male work," should a boy avoid imitation because the work has been done by a woman, out of "women's values"? And if that were not confusing enough, there is, Bly tells us, "male initiation, female initiation, and human initiation." A life could be used up just getting through all that initiation.

If the work of women is a useless example for maturing boys, women's feelings, particularly the mother's feelings for the father, cripple masculinity: "when the son is introduced primarily by the mother to feeling, he will learn the female attitude toward masculinity and take a female view of his own father and of his own masculinity." In Bly's view of marriage, the mother cannot help but present a negative image of the father—marriage is imbricated with competition, with viciousness—so that the mother imposes on the son a "wounded image of his father." Throughout the work, Bly assumes there are sides in marriage—not a couple, and not a couple raising children—but sides, as in a debate, or a war. In the household I grew up in, my mother, the mother of five sons, passed on to her sons her feelings of respect, even veneration, for her husband, and he communicated the same about her. It is absurd to contend that mothers "naturally" undermine the image of the father, and it is equally absurd to deny a child exposure to the mother's feelings. Is he to be deprived knowledge of one half of the human race? But Bly imagines mothers so irresponsible as to impose their adult pain on their children: "When at five years old he sat at the kitchen table, his mother may have confided her suffering to him, and he felt flattered to be told of such things by a grown up. . . ." The mother who "confided her suffering" to her son is responsible for his becoming a "naive man," one who often lacks "'natural brutality.'"

Mother's work is a useless model to the male child; her feelings destroy his masculinity; her pain leads to his naïvete; and worse, her protection of him is numbing. The "Iron John" fable suggests, says Bly, "that a mother's protection, no matter how well intentioned, will not do as a substitute for the father's protection." Bad news that for all those single mothers trying to raise sons, but second best just won't do! Perhaps the numbness of mother and child has more to do with the fact that "[f]ifty-seven per cent of single-parent families headed by women live below the poverty line," a figure recorded in the 1992 report of the National Action Committee on the Status of Women.

In the "Iron John" tale, when the boy takes the key from under the mother's pillow, escaping her civilizing force, her possessiveness, the mentor, or male mother, enters the landscape, and in his presence, a "hint will come to us as to where our genius lies." Favorably reviewing Bly's book, John Bemrose says, "And with women taking on jobs that used to be held solely by males, it is no longer possible for a man to define his masculinity by occupations"; enter the "male mother," a new role for man, one which restores exclusivity.

In the company of Iron John, the prince, like any boy in the company of his mentor, learns about his genius (his gold finger); his acceptable instincts (his gold hair); and an intelligence in nature (his eyes reflected in the pond). When the boy leaves the forest and Iron John, he enters the "ashes" stage, the way down is the way out. The place of humiliation, of *katabasis*, for the prince is kitchen work (oddly enough, this is where women spend a good deal of their lives). To go through "ashes" is to give up the "safe life promised to the faithful mother's son." In initiation, the naïve boy, the comfort-loving boy dies. Unless the boy sheds the "earthly, conservative, possessive clinging part of the maternal feminine" and identifies with the king father, he will believe he is a defective male. In the "Iron John" fable, the kitchen boy has occasion to serve at the king's table, but making a mistake, he is fired, well, not actually fired, but relocated to the garden. All boys, Bly extrapolates, long to live with the king. To do so, they must honor the father's clear and helpful side, but this is difficult as "something in the culture wants us to be unfair to our father's masculine side . . . assume he is a monster, as some people say all men are." "Some people" have made fathers seem smaller, resulting in a world with "'too little father.'" Similarly, "[f]orces in contemporary society recently encouraged women to be warriors, while discouraging warrior hood in boys and men," and although these agents—"some people" and "forces"—remain vague and undefined, it is clear that woman's advance implies man's diminishment. As Jill Johnston points out, Bly's "program for men, as defined in *Iron John,* depends strictly on women playing their traditional roles at home." One wonders, then, if Bly doesn't actually mean to put the statement—"A man who cannot defend his own space [be a warrior], cannot defend women and children"—the other way around. Being a warrior depends on women staying in their "natural" place, in need of defence. Men aren't going to be able to play out the "Iron John" story unless women stay in place, at home. But why should we play out an ancient folk tale at all, and if this one, why not, let's say, "Bluebeard"? When my son, at three, was read the "Frog Prince" at nursery school, he tried to translate that story into action. If the princess, throwing the frog at the wall got a prince, he was sure that by throwing his cat at the wall, he would get something even better. Folk tales, fairy tales, are not the eight steps to deliverance, either from boredom or debilitation.

By the time a child in our culture is twelve, he "will be crippled by shame," his warrior weakened, stunted, or killed off. The mother's insistence on "improper intimacies," or the father's "improper belittling" causes shame, or "[t]o be without a supportive father" is "to be in shame." Mythologically, the boy's shame is a lamed horse; only the Wild Man can provide the magnificent mount which the boy needs for the battle; in our culture, only an older man, a mentor, can work to prevent further shaming. The boy, indeed the adult man, must raise a sword in battle to cut "his adult soul from his mother-bound soul." The warrior "can teach us how to hold boundaries" against too much merging, how to hold in oppositional tension the distinction between genders, and although Bly assures us that "living in the opposites does not mean identifying with one side and then belittling the other," a paragraph later, he says, "More and more women in recent decades have begun identifying with the female pole, and maintain that everything bad is male, and everything good is female," a fairly sweeping, condemnatory, and erroneous statement about his "opposite."

The encounter with the mentor, the awakening of the warrior within, enables the boy to replace his addiction to harmony and safety with a vigilant look-out for shamers. The mother is chief among shamers. One's personal mother is receptive or transparent to the great mother, who "doesn't want the boy to grow up," who wants to keep him "locked up." It is at this stage that Bly introduces the most offensive of ideas—"psychic incest between mother and son." "Psychic incest" occurs in intellectual conversations between mother and son, or as an earlier quotation illustrates, in the passing of a clean T-shirt. "Marian Woodman," Bly tells us, associates these dangerous intellectual conversations between mother and son with the "'false phallus.'" Is intellectual tutoring the prerogative of men? Who will accept, even for a moment, that bright women should silence their ideas, their learning, their language in the company of their sons?

That boys must have male mentors, that grown men must get in touch with the wild man within, is the tactic of regrouping. Using poetry, fairy tale, myth and personal story, General Bly attempts to rally the forces in a palisade which he believes to be besieged. Bly's *Iron John* is an insidious expression of the backlash because it pretends to approve women's gains in recent decades, but in fact, *Iron John* is oppositional and the opponent is woman, in particular, the mother. Using the fairy tale, Bly shows that woman is fine in her place, and her place comes at the end of the tale. She is the well-deserved reward—the king's daughter—at the end of the male quest: "Give me your daughter as my wife": *mine* and *yours,* and therefore owned. *Iron John* more than affirms the patriarchy; it shores it up. It sets up an exclusive, elitist world of boys and men, relegating women to the earliest stages of chil-drearing, and denominating them dangerous if they are participants in the later stages of a boy's development. As rewards, they are fine.

Bly devalues and contaminates "mother love," ignoring the fact that women learn to be mothers from their own mothers, a heritage equally as glorious, not to mention useful, as that passed from fathers to sons. Moreover, a mother's love is inclusive, not exclusive, and wide-ranging; it requires neither swamp nor desert for its expression; does not wait upon a developmental clock; is ignorant of stages; cherishes daughters as well as sons. In reading *Iron John* one cannot help but be struck by a similarity between Bly's mythic images ("Riding the Red, the White, and the Black Horses," for example) and those in Revela-tions. As I read this book, I remembered a particular im-age in Revelations: "And when the dragon saw that he was thrown down to the earth, he persecuted the woman who gave birth to the male child" (13: 13).

In making the case for the boy's deepening need for male elders, it was not necessary to deprecate mothers and tra-ditionalize women. *Iron John* is a reactionary book, and, I believe, a dangerous book. In insisting that a boy move from "the mother's house to the father's house," it proposes a diminished, an either/or, world.

Allen Hoey (review date Spring 1993)

SOURCE: A review of *American Poetry,* in *Southern Humanities Review,* Vol. XXVII, No. 2, Spring, 1993, pp. 189-92.

[*In the following review, Hoey offers evaluation of Bly's critical essays in* American Poetry.]

Perhaps no one has exerted greater single-handed influ-ence on the course of mainstream American poetry since the early sixties than Robert Bly. The rise of creative writ-ing programs coincided with Bly's energetic and broadcast polemicizing on behalf of a vision of a poetry revolution-ized, internationalized, and politicized. The simultaneous escalation of the war in Vietnam gave Bly even wider exposure and influence. His essays spoke to a generation impatient with the status quo, irritated at the slowness of change, and enraged at the obduracy of an obsolete establishment. How easy it was to spill politics into poetry;

the injustice of the war, of a national posture revealed in the Civil Rights movement, made Bly's message all the more urgent. And it didn't hurt that the ideas he advocated for poetry were easily applied in poetry workshops: focus on the image, on its psychological and political resonance, with little attention to the forms of verse, other than discarding the traditional (what worse condemnation?) trappings of rhyme and meter. Even the models he proposed were tailored to the political climate: Central Americans, Spanish surrealists, wild-eyed and free-spirited political activists or at least licensed outsiders.

Bly's essays are best read in light of this historic context. To this end, the essays bear the date of their initial publica-tion. The essays from the first of the book's three divi-sions, **"Looking for Dragon Smoke,"** represent his think-ing from the sixties through the early seventies, "sum[ming] up," as Bly writes, "the platform or viewpoint of my magazine, *The Fifties, The Sixties,* and *The Seven-ties.*" The second section consists of essays on twelve of Bly's contemporaries, culled from reviews and, in some instances, combining shorter reviews of a poet across a span of many years. Finally, **"Educating the Rider and the Horse"** concentrates on the evolving shape of American poetry over the past thirty or so years. Most interesting here are the essays, composed in the eighties, wherein Bly levels a critical eye at the workshop mentali-ty's effect on American poetry.

These essays show a concerned, synthetic imagination at work. References abound to politics (domestic, interna-tional, and historic), to psychology, and to a diverse group of writers. He has read widely, if selectively. Unfortunately, his scope of learning is not always matched by broadness of interpretation. In some instances this limitation seems to result from a too-narrow frame of reference, as when he translates the title of Baudelaire's "Correspondences" as "Intimate Associations," completely missing the title's al-lusion to the Medieval theory of correspondence. Or perhaps this alteration just stems from Bly's quirky tendency to overly Americanize his translations. In other cases, his failures seem to arise from a dedication to his program, his sense of what poetry has been and must be; true believers doctor the "truth," such as we can know it, in service to a higher vision. Bly's rendition of the main currents of American poetry too often suffers from being fed through his grinder. Writing of Pound, Bly avers that he "was not interested in the 'Voyage' or in the 'Holy Thing'. . . ." What, then, are we to make of "The Seafarer," of the voyage motif that runs through the early *Cantos,* and of Pound's concern with establishing an ideal city, a vision that includes what many readers have construed as the sacred?

Bly also tends to elevate what might be specific criticisms to the level of the general, and such pronouncements seem unapologetically ex cathedra. In his seminal 1963 essay, **"A Wrong Turning in American Poetry,"** while chiding his contemporaries and immediate predecessors for exclud-ing the unconscious from their poetry by concentrating on formal rather than imagistic aspects, he suggests that the work of finding rhymes is conducted by the conscious mind, by the will. While he may intend for this criticism to apply only to the particular poet under discussion, he implies that all poets rhyme consciously. That many of the poets Bly himself praises have worked—and worked extensively—in rhyme alone hints that his assertion fails when too broadly applied—or would if his translations of poets like Rainer Maria Rilke indicated that they used those outmoded devices. In fact, much of the strength of Bly's argument for what has come to be called the "deep-image" poem results from his comparing American poems he finds spiritually bankrupt to poems by European poets more in touch with the unconscious. How much does he beg the question by using his own translations of these poet' works to underscore his point? This essay in particular, with its valorization of the unconscious image and denigration of the conscious mind, its elevation of passion and untrammeled inspiration and dismissal of craft, has led to many of the excesses of what Bly's friend Donald Hall calls the "McPoem"—gratuitous use of image for its own sake and reliance on a facile and privatistic surrealism.

Although Bly never takes any credit for the promulgation of the "Workshop Esthetic" (as David Dooley calls it), his essays dating from the eighties, mostly included in the third section, are concerned with ways in which his own program took a wrong turn in its evolution. By the late seventies, Bly was castigating American poets for neglecting their responsibility to review poetry; what reviews appear, he complains, largely consist of uncritical praise, which he identifies as an outgrowth of the sixties "and its odd belief that criticism is an attempt to put down the young or minorities." To address this tendency, he suggests "that every person publishing poetry or fiction in this country take a vow to review two books every six months." In another essay, he clarifies a mistaken conception of the image, correcting the notion that to focus on image means forsaking the intellect: "A great image contains logic, that is, thinking." Most notably, two essays revise his ideas regarding form. Form now can be playful, can function to help mediate meaning in a poem, can itself even be "wild"—always here a term of praise. Form, he recognizes in **"Educating the Rider and the Horse,"** contains, certainly, but in giving shape it also imposes order, "something that chaos does not have." These musings bring him to "the threshold between domestic and wild form," a recognition that all forms of order cannot be discarded willy-nilly.

Bly's commentaries on his contemporaries provide an opportunity to see his critical program applied. He chooses primarily from the "mainstream" of post-World War II practitioners: James Wright, David Ignatow, Etheridge Knight, Denise Levertov, William S. Merwin, Thomas McGrath, Robert Lowell, Louis Simpson, James Dickey, Galway Kinnell, Donald Hall, and John Logan. Many of the pieces survey the whole of the poet's career; in the case of Wright and Kinnell, reviews written in the eighties

synthesize a view of what they have accomplished. More interestingly, essays on Ignatow, Simpson, and Dickey assemble reviews written as individual volumes appeared that span, in some cases, more than twenty years. The piece on Dickey combines a review of his first two books, in which Bly finds considerable imaginative power somewhat blunted by "a curious narcissism," with a scathing review of *Buckdancer's Choice,* a book whose content he finds morally repugnant. Bly quotes generously from Dickey's poems to argue that the speakers of such poems as "Firebombing" and "Slave Quarters" are not presented at a remove from the poet; Dickey was neither "outside of [n]or beside the poem. . . . On the contrary, the major characteristic of all these poems is their psychic blurriness." Yet "[r]eaders go on applying [New Critical ideas] anyway, in fear of the content they might have to face if they faced the poem as a human being." Borrowing a psychological term, Bly identifies this pervasive flaw as "inflation" and concludes that, although many American artists "collapse," "in Dickey's case the process seems accelerated, as in a nightmare, or a movie someone is running too fast."

These essays reveal Bly's mind at work—quirky, insightful, yet resistant to the "niceties" of prose style. He writes with little sense of transition, impatient to move to the next point, or too willing merely to repeat just to be sure the reader really, absolutely got it. Yet flawed as they are, taken together they represent the mind and manner of a writer who has had a profound impact on how poetry is written and read.

Robert Peters (essay date 1994)

SOURCE: "News From Robert Bly's Universe," in *Where the Bee Sucks: Workers, Drones and Queens of Contemporary American Poetry,* Asylum Arts, 1994, pp. 27-34.

[*In the following essay, Peters discusses Bly's artistic preoccupations and poetry in* The Man in the Black Coat Turns.]

Mountains, rivers, caves, and fields quicken us in solitude. We leap toward connections lost to our rational selves and defy logic. This, as Bly explains in *Leaping Poetry: An Idea with Poems and Translations* (1975), occurs when the newest of our three brains is activated. This, the Reptile Brain, acts coldly to preserve us against dangers real or imagined. The Mammal Brain, constituting the cortex, creates our institutions, affections, and sexual fervors. The third, and least-used brain, one lying as a one-eighth inch thick layer over the Mammal Brain, is the New Brain, the neo-cortex; this generates "wildness" and produces the "leaping poetry" written by Lorca, Rilke, Neruda, Takahashi, and Vallejo.

This activated New Brain evokes verbal miracles. "Watery syllables" well up from mythic depths, from the Dordogne caves and the aboriginal South Sea islands where men lived "under the cloak / of an animal's sniffing." Ancient angers explode. One of Bly's poems, **"Words Rising,"** echoes howls once declaimed by ancient priests in furs holding aloft luminous barley heads. They generate verbal wildness. We are "bees" with language for "honey." We express the inexpressive, the archetypal, what was residual long before the invention of the wheel. Both celebrant (priest) and sufferer (aborigine and political victim) dwell within our words:

> Wicker baskets and hanged men
> come to us as stanzas and vowels.
> We see a million hands with dusty
> palms turned up inside each verb,
> lifted. There are eternal vows
> held inside the word "Jericho"

("Poem in Three Parts")

As mystery, language reflects profound events unlimited by space. During meditation, cortextual cells generate dance and ecstasy.

I simplify, and urge readers to turn to Bly's provocative essays (in addition to **"Leaping Poetry"** see **"I Came Out of the Mother Naked"** in *Sleepers Joining Hands* (1973), and the prose sections of his Sierra Club anthology, *News of the Universe*). I wish here to employ his main distinctions as a way of perceiving his new poems. His verse techniques reflect his theories. No matter how good Bly was in the past—and he was good—this poetry is an impressive advance. *The Man in the Black Coat Turns* was one of the seminal works of the eighties.

Some readers complain that Bly's poems are almost completely devoid of living persons other than himself. Clear the stage is Bly's refrain. The creative occurs in a nurturing isolation. Forest, pasture, clearing, the isolated building, all suit him for meditation. His writing-shack is so private that even his wife doesn't know where it is, and he carries his own drinking water with him in jars. He recalls Thoreau with whom he has many similarities, and tangentially, Wordsworth. He would not hesitate to eat Thoreau's woodchuck raw if it would intensify his perceptions; and he would welcome the stark fear induced in Wordsworth by that shadow looming suddenly over the water at Mt. Skiddaw. "Urge and urge and urge," wrote Whitman: "Always the procreant urge of the world."

Bly is unlike other contemporary nature poets who seldom take themselves off very far from the boat landing or the fire tower. In him there's nothing genteel. His reclusiveness is itself a metaphor for toughness. He is no Sunday dabbler, taking nature trails through museum-forests which some placid ranger has marked for easy recognition. His secret places are invested with agents of psychic confrontation: mythic mothers and fathers bearing fangs; the male instincts to kill, waste, and subdue are omnipresent in our psyches, in conflict with our gentler, creative selves. Only in solitude is our mental subsoil activated, proving equal

to these conflicts, stilling the nagging, demanding Father who speaks for order, reason, and obedience. You can't build a birdhouse or haul much manure sitting on your haunches in a forest, or in the lotus position beside a stream.

To achieve quietude, Bly has explored various disciplines, including Tibetan ones. No matter the guides, he remains himself, quizzical, self-reliant, choosing from an eclectic feast only what will enhance his spirit. There is no wastage.

We observe Bly on his own mind-stage with minimal properties, peopled with a few souls acting out scenes as he invites them in. Like Whitman (about whom Bly has written a most valuable and perceptive essay, [in *Walt Whitman: The Measure of His Song,* ed. Jim Perlman, 1981] we "loaf" with him and share his urges and leapings, which drift to us like bird feathers, or leap with the brilliance of arcing trout, or does in meadows. Energy and largeness, two of Whitman's favorite concepts, for Bly induce ecstasy and insight. To adapt one of Mary Baker Eddy's images, Bly is utterly at ease in those natural vestibules where the material sense of things disappears.

Before scrutinizing Bly's new work, I should like to speculate briefly on Bly the Surrealist. Despite the fact that he sees his poems deriving from, or inspired by, poets he calls Surrealist—Rilke, Vallejo, Lorca, and Neruda, among others—I don't find the term useful when applied to him. Most obviously, Surrealism refers to that movement in the arts initiated by André Breton, c. 1924, attracting Aragon, Eluard, Desnos, Cocteau, Dali, and Tanguy, among other writers and artists. They sought juxtapositions of irrational images, often derived from easy associations. The result was an often trivial, zany melange produced by an imagery of pyrotechnics rather than one emergent from a substratum of psychic fears and joys, from dream and archetypal energies. Bly's surrealism is of these deeper perceptions. No Tinker Bell waves her wand over a gaggle of pastel oblivion ha-has. No snickering, skeleton-bone, Halloween belly-riffs here. Bly's images emerge from a neocortical loam, with an unpredictability and speed distressing to readers prizing the linear, the rational, the easily deciphered—readers with Mammal brains. Bly is a whirl of color in a field of cabbages.

"Visiting the Farallones" will clarify what I mean. Here Bly revisits concerns that have occupied his energies for years—the pollution of the environment and the insane destruction of natural life. While his fervor has not diminished, his approach has. He seems more content now to allow his rage a less programmatic, less didactic, breath. Imagery, rather than direct statements. He trusts his readers more.

Clubbing seals initiates the poem, followed by the decimation of whales and tortoises. The latter are crammed into shipholds. Often for Bly, the daily news triggers memories of past disasters. The plundering of the tortoises is a leap back to the nineteenth century (a.k.a. "The Age of Darwin") when sailing ships used tortoises for ballast and food. There are more connections, as Bly arraigns decadent human cultures. The Roman empire was the first universal culture to rot. The American frontier, symbolized by a wagon breaking to pieces on boulders, is gone, the landscape is now littered with beer cans and the air is befouled. "Darkness," Bly says, is reality—as is the feather he spies lying near him on snow, leading his gaze to the carcass of a half-eaten rooster. For most of us, a maimed bird is revolting, no matter how rich the thematic evocations. But if we are to be enlightened, Bly believes, we must scrutinize the gross and painful as well as the scenic and palatable. "Crumbling" is the word he employs to interweave these disparate materials. Animal species have crumbled, as have empires, and once vital frontiers.

Thus far, Bly has seen objects clearly. Now he turns to a fresh image, one not literally seen, contemporary, emblematic of all crumblings. In an old folks' home, life crumbles, wasted and brutalized. A sadistic society tucks these ancients out of sight, much as sailing ships stowed the turtles. There's a perversion/inversion here of a life principle. The death-mother works in loathsome ways her wonders to perform.

In **"Snowbanks North of the House,"** the mysterious man in black of the book's title starts up a hill, changes his mind, and returns to the bottom. Is he a minister? An undertaker? Is he Bly's father? Is he Death? What would he have found on the hill? Once more, Bly generates thematic leaps by an initial meditation on something concrete—here it's a great snowdrift stopped about six feet from a house, a phenomenon I witnessed often when I was a boy in northern Wisconsin. In meeting the house, vectored air currents kept the snow back. If the sweeps had piled themselves tight against the building, that building would be insulated and warm. This house, though, contains failed marriages and memories of children who don't write home. A son dies. The bereaved parents never speak to one another again. The church too fails, as the wine sours, and the minister "falls." These failures seem debris in some ocean of life, lifting and falling (failing) all night long. The saving image is the moon, as it proceeds through clouds and stars, achieving a splendid isolation, a symbol for the self apart, for a lone sufficiency bathed in moon-radiance.

Like the snow drifts, the man in the black coat, who eschews the hilltop, symbolizes the poet in isolation. He seems an "advocate of darkness" (see **"For My Son Noah, Ten Years Old"**), an associate of the Earth death-mother who appears to ease our way through life. He also suggests what Bly terms "the masculine soul" or "Father consciousness." In its "middle range," the masculine soul is "logic and fairness"; in its higher leapings it "hurries toward the spirit." Like the feminine consciousness, its counterpart and opposite, it is a "good," can't be eradicated and remains ever mysterious. It is a "veil," Bly says, drawn against the death so feared by men. The best we can hope

for, Bly writes, is to meld these two consciousnesses and experience what lies beyond the veil. Bly's best images possess a koan-like quality of unresolved suggestiveness—so also with the black-suited man. I shall return to him.

In another poem, "the walnut" of Bly's brain glows in solitude. Even when thus charged, his insights are not all they might be; he has mere intimations of the visionary, of deciphering the vast enigmas behind Shelley's veil. Even Albert Einstein reputedly utilized only a small part of his neocortex. By stimulating his third brain, Bly releases a genie who, alas, flies off to hover over some "car cemetery" and won't return to his bottle. We must accept the presence of such contradictions and our dimly realized visions. By accepting, we may be preparing for later insights of a hitherto unknown grandeur.

One of the best of Bly's efforts to reflect the glowings of that "walnut brain" appears in **"The Dried Sturgeon,"** a prose poem. Insight, ecstasy, growth, and death are the primary motifs. On an October walk along a riverbank, Bly finds a dried-out sturgeon which he examines. A "speckled nose-bone" leads back to an eye socket, behind which is a "dark hole" where soft gills once grew. This hole, a sort of cave, the poet enters to confront his female self. A hunchback appears and is made whole by the "sweet dark," a virgin with magical black stones in her cloak.

These seem elements in a fairy tale, evocative of the narrative inconsistencies children love. Our poet, himself flawed, enters his healing meditation via images of fish corpse, pine needle, sand, and hunchback. Underground, he thrills to the proximity of Death, a duende experience he prizes in other poets. As he returns to light, to Father consciousness symbolized by the sturgeon's scales which are "dry, swift, organized, tubular, straight and humorless as railway schedules, the big clamp of the boxcar, tapering into sleek womanly death," he is invigorated. In a sense, he closes up the rich female concavities of the "dark hole." Reason prevails, symbolized by the straight line, by schedules, by speed—antitheses for the female underworld. To this "womanly" region we shall return at our deaths, completing the circle that began on leaving the womb, on peregrinations to and through our father-selves.

Another striking presence of shadow/duende is in **"Mourning Pablo Neruda,"** written in brief lines reminiscent of the Chilean poet's own. Bly is driving to his shack. Beside him on the seat is a sweating jar of water. Glancing down, Bly observes that the jostling jar creates a wet shadow on the seat, a paradigm for Neruda's death, a shadowing itself of subtle, tragic effects. Bly drives through granite quarries, filled with blocks soon to be shaped into gravestones. A leap: our memories of the dead are watery traces within us, mere hints of the moisture still resident within granite. If we accept this diminution, we see that the dead have merely flowed "around us" to the Gulf Stream and out to the Eternal Sea.

Bly's techniques of moving from the concrete to the universal are well-realized in **"Finding an Old Ant Mansion,"** another prose poem. Asleep on a floor, he dreams that a rattlesnake is biting him. He rises, dresses, and goes to a pasture where he senses the ground beneath his shoes, their rubbery texture allowing feel in a way leather would not. He likes these "rolls and humps," and marvels that the earth "never lies flat." It must accommodate a varied debris both falling down upon it (trees) and emerging from its depths (stones). He passes through a strip of hardwoods to another pasture, and finds a chunk of wood on the ground, strangely etched into some sixteen layers by ants. He fetches the piece home and props it on his desk.

The cavities in the wood create doors into "cave-dark" places—Persephone redivivus. Leaps evoke memories: the shadows recall the "heavy brown of barn stalls" he knew as a boy, and other dark insights—a daughter understands her mother's silences. The ant artifact is a universe all its own, a paradigm for our psyches, so antlike and male, in their obsessions. We scurry to execute our father's hopes and wishes: "infant ants awaken to old father-worked halls, uncle-loved boards, walls that hold the sights of the pasture, the moos of confused cows . . . some motor cars from the road, held in the same wood, given shape by Osiris' love." According to designs taught us by our great benefactor and primal father image, himself son of Nut and Geb, the legendary Osiris, we shape our lives.

The ant-riddled wood suggests primeval forces (it recalls, perhaps, in its unchewed state, the erect father) and provides residences, "apartments," for spirits to inhabit. The ants, thus, have wrought "a place for our destiny" that sweep of time within which "we too labor, and no one sees our labor." Uncannily, and with a delicate compassion, Bly retrieves the specific from the universal, returning the motif to himself. He recalls his own father whose labors he has symbolically discovered in this chunk of wood. What follows? Who will discover Bly's labors when he dies? His wood will lie somewhere in a pasture "not yet found by a walker." This poem moves me: the gentle voice, so mature and exploring, is the exfoliation of a man large in both physique and spirit. Bly's leap into that image of our lives as wood pieces waiting for discovery resolves the poem profoundly in areas of the psyche hitherto untapped. To most observers, that ant-eaten, riddled hunk of dead fibers would deserve, if noticed at all, to be thrust aside by a boot.

Bly's gatherings of objects include many we normally feel squeamish about: a partially devoured bird, a dangling eyeball. A "sick" rose, as William Blake knew, is as conducive to insight as a healthy one. To see whole, Bly implies, we must encompass all of Experience we can, the positive and the negative, the creative and the destructive. In **"Kennedy's Inauguration,"** a Sister hands Bly the seed of a witch hazel tree, a globular fruit with hornlike projections. When it ripened, it discharged its seed in an explosive burst. The pod is as fertile, one feels, as Persephone's pomegranate. Now pinecone dry (an echo of the desiccated sturgeon), the pod is the size of a cow's eyeball. The seeing once possible there, like that in the eyeball, has "exploded out through the eye-holes," leaving behind a husk of spikes and dark vacancies resembling hen beaks "widening in fear."

Bly next reviews his day. He went on errands twice, both times avoiding the funeral parlor. He held three "distant" conversations (by phone?). The gift of the seed followed. Now, as he starts to meditate, the cow's eye reminds him of a Lorenzo shot by a cannonball that left his eye dangling from his face, a horror. Like the seedpod, history, exploding, is both germinative and sterile, humanizing and destructive. In this poem, though, it "seeds" the worst—mayhem and torture: a Papal candidate is murdered by an enemy. Belgian King Leopold's plantation overseer (ca. World War I) chops off the hands of an African youth and deposits them near his father. Fascists destroy contraceptive clinics and carry the women off to breeding brothels. Our drugged sex-mistress, Marilyn Monroe, lies dead on her bed. Young men are decimated in purposeless war, viz., the Vietnam conflict which Bly, as we know, protested vociferously and courageously. A Marine whose head and feet are shot off "cries" for a medic. John Kennedy, a vigorous, youthful man, stands in the cold, taking his oath of office. Nearby waits the old poet Robert Frost. Bly hopes that the inauguration will produce a new national destiny. Hindsight, of course, has it otherwise. The Reptile brain kills and wastes. A father ejects his seed from his loins, delaying his son's return to his primal mother. She, in imitation of Persephone, carries a round red fruit in her hand. Both figures draw us into magnetic fields; both must be departed from, abandoned, and returned to. The father, finally, may be the more difficult of the pair to please.

In **"The Prodigal Son,"** a son kneels on dried cobs in a swine pen and reflects on his hostile father. He hears the latter's death-fearing plea to the doctor: "Don't let me die!" and recalls a particularly venomous altercation. As he was dragging his father over the floor, the father saw a crack in the boards and shouted for him to stop: "I only dragged my father that far!" Brutal conflict seems the norm. As the son resists the father, he pursues his own maleness. His departure vexes not only the father but also the mother—both feel deserted by him (cf. the parents in **"Snowbanks North of the House"**). Before he can accept his father as an equal, the son must dance to his own music, honor his own dreams, and write poems.

In **"The Ship's Captain Looking Over the Rail,"** Bly observes that to tell a captain or a father that they are "good" is to say nothing; for these men conceal their true scars, limps, and blemishes from underlings—sailors and children. In **"Kneeling Down to Look Into a Culvert,"** the final poem in the book, Bly merges his own father and his sons. The culvert (as reason, rod, conduit) is a masculine image from which the female water is released into merry light. Bly imagines his children splashing in the brightness at the culvert's end, where they sense his presence, and where he performs a similar commemorative act for his own father.

"My Father's Wedding 1924" links Bly's father with that puzzling figure in the black coat. Once again a prosaic object, another chunk of wood, stripped of its bark, triggers leaps and recollections. What was Bly's father like, as a younger man? Was he a masked birdfather, Bhutanian, with giant teeth and a pig nose, dancing ritually on a bad leg? Was he really as assured as he seemed? No. He concealed a limp from his son. When he, Bly, fathered his own children, he saw that his father's limp reflected his craving to be loved. Showing affection has not been a desirable masculine trait. Like the log which once held bark, Bly's father kept people at a distance, even members of his family. He covered his vulnerabilities with a gnarled, rough exterior. At his wedding, his true bride was not the woman of flesh and blood beside him; rather, she stood invisible between him and his bride interposing herself as a kind of Fata Morgana. This strange ceremony was performed by a man in a black coat, a preacher who lifted his "book" and called "for order."

Who is the preacher? Possibly he serves as a father-spirit who marries us to our mythic mother, Death, as she waits in those shadowy concavities, death-spaces, burnished through eye sockets, wood, and culverts. The father in black appears when we wed ourselves to Death, which we do when we allow our emotions, our feminine selves, full play, thereby resolving our struggles with our father. Thus, partially fulfilled, we are able to proceed to our Mother (Death) with minimal fear. Male and female spirits balanced.

I don't pretend that my reading of the black figure as a kind of Robert Mitchum Bible-thumper who initiates our journey back to the womb is the only possible reading. The image remains complex. To read the figure merely as Death is facile. Finally, my efforts to sort meanings have made me aware of how male directed are my critical acts.

Walter Goodman (review date 19 June 1996)

SOURCE: "Fe, Fi, Fo, Whoa! The Inner Giant Has Taken Over," in *New York Times*, June 19, 1996, p. C15.

[*In the following review, Goodman offers tempered assessment of* The Sibling Society, *which he describes as "a mix of imagination, scholarship and remarkable silliness."*]

As you can discover in any chapter of Robert Bly's new jeremiad, he is outraged by a society in which children grow up without fathers and with rotten schools, their brains stupefied by television, their imaginations squelched by computers, their sensibilities coarsened by rock music and exploitative movies, their dreams corrupted by advertising. Instead of growing into maturity with the help of older mentors who can pass along the experience of generations, they remain in a state of perpetual adolescence: selfish, acquisitive, spiritually flattened, dangerous. *Welcome to The Sibling Society*.

The indictment, less original than the label, is a cousin to *Iron John,* Mr. Bly's best seller, which generated a sort of men's movement in America. Here again, he draws on myth, religion, fairy tales, poems and even science of sorts for evidence of the wisdom that he argues has been discarded by a society that disdains the past. To borrow his language, we now live laterally, keeping an envious eye on one another, rather than vertically, in the glow of wise authority.

The book begins with an elaborate exegesis of "Jack and the Beanstalk," especially the nature of the Giant whom Mr. Bly likens to the primitive human brain, to the *nafs,* which, he reports, is the ever-demanding soul of Muslim and Sufi tradition, and to the Freudian id, all of which keep human beings in perpetual battle to satisfy insatiable appetites. As for Jack, he "represents all men and women who live in a fatherless and, increasingly, motherless society."

Mr. Bly is an accomplished storyteller, and his affection for the tales of many peoples over many centuries can be catching. But when it comes to the contemporary condition, his propheteering arias seem as out of control as the nafs: "The teenagers in our inner cities are expressing the presence of the Giant, who is fundamentally opposed to life. He is the one who stabs people in the library and eats children." And beware: "We don't realize that when we put a computer or television in a child's own room, we are sending that child to be alone with the Giant."

Before you know it, Mr. Bly is attributing the growth of armed militias, unemployment and all manner of other ailments to siblingitis. For him, politics is psychology; he finds the roots of the North American Free Trade Agreement and the opposition to affirmative action in societal dysfunction.

Some of the presumable facts he losses in as evidence of the national disarray are risible. Lamenting the flat language bred by television, he writes: "A poll a few years ago revealed that the average American father talked to his child for about 10 minutes a day. We know by contrast that in certain parts of Russia, earlier in the century, the Russian father spent more like two hours engaging in such talk. Russians have a word for 'soul-talk,' and it wasn't unusual for a grandfather to say to a granddaughter, 'Let's go out by the tree and have some soul-talk.'"

And he combines a vacuum-cleaner approach to the world's problems with a salesman's bent for wildly disproportionate comparisons. After lumping together the slaughters in Bosnia, Rwanda, Somalia and Cambodia as expressions of siblingdom triumphant, he adds, "Our sibling society came into existence by different means, but there is a comparable elimination of elders, accompanied by increasing anger on the part of youth."

Toward the end of his new book, Mr. Bly complains that most reviewers, trapped in "the flat, literal or sociological mode in which there is only one world," treated ***Iron John*** in a simplistic way. But the notable thing about his first book of prose was its success. With help from a Bill Moyers interview on PBS, it stayed on the best-seller list of *The New York Times* for more than a year, several weeks as No. 1. It was like a second coming of Joseph Campbell. As for reviews, most of those I have read swallowed the whole thing.

Credit for that success must go largely to Mr. Bly's enthusiasm for myth, his talent as a storyteller and the fact that he was onto a serious subject, the pathology of sons without fathers. It also offered the novelty of a men's movement as a sort of counter to or sibling of the women's movement and the promise of self-improvement cultivated by public broadcasting.

The Sibling Society has some of the same appeals. It should also please liberals. Noting that "our first thoroughly sibling Congress" is not about to "defend children, nor wetlands, nor blacks, nor women, nor full-growth forests, nor the Alaska wilderness," he concludes, "Some sibling meanness has interrupted the understanding people had in the 1960s that we are all related." Was that really "the understanding" in the 1960s?

If I cannot rouse more enthusiasm for ***The Sibling Society,*** it may be because grandpa never took me out by the tree for some soul-talk. That is probably why I do not share the author's admiration for such hierarchical or God-directed communities as medieval monasteries, mistrust his treatment of history and find his rhapsodies to supposedly more spiritual cultures a touch smoky. ("Native Americans felt horror that white people would take peyote with no elders present, no one to clear the air or protect the souls from invasions by those spirits who do not wish us well.") And generally, the use of myth to make points in political argument strikes me as no favor either to myth or to politics.

The book ends with a charming telling of a great story from Sweden, the "Lind Wurm": When the queen is delivered of a tiny snake, as her first offspring, the midwife throws it out the window, with momentous consequences. Typically, Mr. Bly reduces a rich tale to fit his by now predictable litany: "Because of 'downsizing,' parental neglect and bad schools, almost every member of Generation X, or the Day-Care Generation, feels thrown out the window."

No, don't throw his book out the window. At least read the fairy tales. ***The Sibling Society*** is by turns engaging and exasperating, suggestive and tendentious, a mix of imagination, scholarship and remarkable silliness. Although he announces, in his take-no-prisoners way, "Television is the thalidomide of the 1990s," I wouldn't be surprised if Mr. Bly showed up on PBS again soon.

David Bromwich (review date 16-23 September 1996)

SOURCE: "The Young Republic," in *The New Republic,* September 16-23, 1996, pp. 31-4.

[*In the following review, Bromwich offers analysis of Bly's social concerns in* The Sibling Society.]

A child knows the world of the living. A grown-up knows something of those who are dead, and can think of those who are still to be born. So a society that has a past and looks to a future had better be a society with a fair ratio of grown-ups—a disheartening announcement in America today. Our passage from childhood has grown murky, and ten minutes with a TV or the Internet will show a country densely populated by childlike adults, people who would like to share everything and decide nothing.

To assist them and to increase their numbers, there has arisen a ghostly regime of mediators, prophets of arrested development who hold an undeclared interest in keeping the children just as they are. The entertainment-information complex has yielded symptoms hardly measurable in economic terms, and it is these that concern Robert Bly: above all, a loss of respect for the old, so that the very idea of elders has come to seem a quaintness. We are all one generation now, or getting close to it. Nobody knows how to stop the process, even though nobody much likes the generational tone: laid back, wised up, serviceable.

The Sibling Society is loosely written, in places hardly written at all, and if the author were capable of consecutive argument he would make a better show of it. Its texture is a Jung-and-Campbell soufflé of archetypes, its sole narrative device an ad hoc exegesis of fairy tales, from *Jack and the Beanstalk* to the story about the snake that ate its first twelve brides and was tamed by the thirteenth, a resourceful woman who strips off one of his skins for every wedding shirt she removes, scrubs him with lye and a wire brush and finds him changed to a man. Bly trots out the archetype-analysis side by side with his unorganized free reflections, and the only rule seems to be that anything may be said anywhere.

Yet Bly has lived in our society and watched it to some effect, and his title deserves to catch on. We lacked a name for what is happening when we are first-named by a sales clerk, a real-estate agent, an investment broker, or the doctor offering a gloomy prognosis, and for all its slackness of structure the book has a genuine firmness of purpose. We must work hard, it says, to restore the dignity of such lost categories as mentor, apprentice, leader and stranger—the last most of all, since it denotes the unfamiliar person to whom politeness, not intimacy, is owed.

Books of social criticism by Christopher Lasch, William Greider, Neil Postman and many others supply the background picture of American mores that Bly takes for granted, but his motive for writing seems to have come from a personal recognition:

> I was startled one day walking on Madison near Eighty-fifth Street, when I saw a poster that asked this question:
>
> *What is 24 stories tall, carries the most sophisticated armament on earth, and is run by a crew of 21 year olds?*

The answer was "an aircraft carrier," the poster being an advertisement for a program on the Discovery channel. The "most sophisticated armament on earth" means the ability to devastate entire countries—and this is to be run by a crew of twenty-one year olds? There is a lie involved, spoken to flatter young men and women: a lie that resides in the ambiguity of the word "run." The ad people want to have twenty-one year olds running the carrier; and the twenty-one year olds believe they can and should run it. We understand that they don't "run" a carrier, but why is this word made inexact? The confusion of who should run the carrier is a confusion deep in the sibling society. Freshman members of Congress believe they can and should run the government.

Advertising has become the universal solvent of education, and "those devoted to the bottom line," Bly suspects, "have effectively interposed themselves between the father and the family. Part of the effort has been to get at the children more easily. The more the parents' dignity and strength are damaged, the more open the children are to persuasion." Our long adolescence can now extend well into our 40s and 50s, and it routinely begins for children at the age of 9 or 10.

In every earlier generation, a rebellious child, turning against the rules of parents, could see beyond the hottest resentment a solid grown-up world whose behavior gave a reason for the opaqueness of the barrier. It was a different world: unattractive for the most part, but different. Bank clerks, teachers, ballplayers, shopkeepers, even journalists acted and looked like "men and women who knew how to have fun, but they had one foot in Necessity," as Bly reflects when comparing photographs of a baseball crowd in the '20s with the look of Americans on the streets of Europe today.

Square America, however, has died. We will never know who or what killed it, but one casualty was an ethic of reticence, the sense that a large part of life is not meant to be lived in reactions or even words. Reticence and decorum are close neighbors. When I was 7, the father of a friend, giving a lesson in manners, told me coolly to address him as "Mr." or "Sir" and never as just "you." It was an unpleasant moment and I thought him an unpleasant man, but the lesson was learned; and on the whole it probably gave childhood a freer feeling to have the assurance that grown-ups were different from one's friends.

A boy growing up today gets much more confusing signals. A lot of the authorities are trying to be cool, like him, and clever in a way not markedly different from his: they do not slow down and speak from a distance. Classwork in grade school has become largely an affair of peer education, the class divided into groups to "pool their resources," that is, to share their opinions and to dig up random facts before being called together to present an audiovisual product. Methods such as those of the Whittle corporation, whose Channel One broadcasts curricular films mixed in with commercials, were unthinkable a generation ago and would have been discountenanced. Our licensed amusers are preparing appetites to which the concept of the infomercial is in no way suspect.

It is perceptive of Bly to have noticed that this is a war of bad parents and nonparents against the right of children to grow up as thinking beings. He blames the academic left, among others, for lowering the tone of education, and calls its adepts "colonial administrators"—scions of a privileged class, who teach the undesirability of inheriting anything and so cheat their constituency of the powers of self-invention. This last point is not false, but it is not new and does not rise above the level of grousing annoyance. The word "deconstruction" appears in these pages as an approximate synonym for poison gas.

Bly's acquaintance with left-wing opinion lapsed after his service in the anti-war protests of the 1960s, and was only renewed with mutual shock at the scandalized reception of *Iron John,* his masculine self-help tract. Traces of the tribal-mythic homily of that book linger in this one: "We need to institute something like the Artemis bear-clan to protect young girls from the pressure of Junk culture or siblingism, and to institute as well rituals to honor their associations with the divine world." Not just the colonial administrators but also some of the natives may wonder what to make of that. But therapeutic proposals are a minor element in *The Sibling Society,* and it cannot be called anti-feminist since, according to Bly, every boy is in a worse fix than every girl from the moment "the nipple is inserted in his mouth; later he will have trouble with anything inserted." I cannot guess the meaning of such a passage. It seems put in to show new readers where the author was coming from, a matter of small interest compared to the things he is pointing to.

Bly writes mostly from the stance of a perplexed citizen, and once his leading observation has lodged itself in your mind, the evidence to confirm it is everywhere. Consider a symptom we never really bother to analyze—the enormous numbers of Americans who rage against taxes. The complaint is as old as the country, but the rage is not, and it ought to be unsettling. It is not that taxes are too high, or that people wish at least their property or their whiskey could be spared. Rather, it seems to many a transparent offense that there should be taxes at all.

Politicians, who cannot escape knowing better, only in rare instances have refrained from wheedling with this delusive style of resentment. They go along with the grievances because they want to be good siblings. In the years of the cold war, when money saved out of taxes might have helped to buy a bomb shelter and a shotgun to keep out the neighbors, nobody grudged the payments to support decently functioning police and fire departments, public schools and public parks. It would have been thought a low boast, the sign of a shady character, to be heard congratulating yourself about how cleverly you cheated the government. That kind of talk was for mob lawyers. Today the fact that a rule or a request or a protocol emanates from established authority is enough to warrant any brutality of abuse in the fight against it.

Violent resisters may be few, but they have many apologists. We make a poor show opposing the distrust by which citizens are recruited from believing that they have duties to society to believing that they have none. The prevalent view of authority in the middle classes is a generalized irony—a graceful attitude struck for its own sake—and one of the best speculative passages in Bly's book tells how this posture acquired its appeal:

> Parents of my generation taught our children the codes of responsibility, restraint, and renunciation, but also we taught them how to evade the codes. Stepping through the codes was a secret game among parents in the 1970s, a little payback for being a parent. That would be all right—at least humanly normal—if the code were strong. But widely varying codes from a dozen attractive cultures flood our receptors. If we want to evade a certain element in our code, the renunciation of selfishness or thievery, for example, we can always find another code—the codes by which the Hindu gods live, for example—in which the forbidden is allowed. Some of us spend our whole lives looking, success-fully, for holes in the codes. When our parents teach us how to do that at the dinner table, we find those les-sons very appealing. We could say that flatness lies in saying yes to everything.

And in saying no to nothing. For people in authority today, especially people in their 30s and 40s, have an extraordi-narily hard time saying no. They have a hard and endless time with cases that present a genuine test—turning down an honest plea or disappointing a party with a quasi-official entitlement for pleading. Negotiation postpones the final no and changes its meaning, and when the authorities do say it at last, they often show a visible reluctance with a bending of the head, knees or voice. The refusal is of the serial kind that lays the ground for a future request.

Freud thought that every group demands of its masters "strength, or even violence. It wants to be ruled and op-pressed and to fear its master." That was in a paternal society. Today the masters act in the self-fulfilling belief that the group wants to be their friend. Compare the Ste-ichen portrait of J. P. Morgan with the jacket photo on Bill Gates's corporate memoir: there a murderous father, perfect in his powers of repression; here a brother among brothers, superior only in his billions.

Our masters dominate now by the creation of spectacles, electronically proliferated. "Some sort of trance," writes Bly, "takes over if enough people are watching an event simultaneously," and the trance becomes harder to break when we have the mysterious knowledge that a given event is being watched by others just like ourselves. An elder in this setting is rather like a judge, and with none on the scene, the siblings are free to astonish each other. The judges in actual courtrooms today, if Lance Ito and Harold Baer are not anomalies, have a hard time carrying themselves like judges even in conditions of maximum exposure. Jurors in famous trials of the past two years have begun to share every detail of their deliberations: the task of private conscience seems a pointless renunciation, or an instruction they did not understand. Yet so fixed are American reflexes in these matters that opinion-makers can imagine the remedy lies in still more spectacle. It

would serve the cause of uniform justice, *The New York Times* lately suggested, to televise all criminal trials.

The want of humility in "our talking America," as Emer-son called it, has long been part of our eagerness for distinction. Citizens in a democracy are always looking for new grounds for approval. Practically, this means finding reasons connected with merit, or with social conformity, or both. No earlier observer could have guessed how sud-denly this would change to a quest for exemption from the social order—a contractual exclusion which itself becomes a source of distinction shared with others. Pausing to note the way impeccable political time-servers affect to speak from the margins, Bly brings together his cultural and educational themes in an aphorism: "If your arguments have been rejected by four or more institutions, they do not need any evidence at all to be accepted." I recently heard a high-school teacher attending a talk on Abraham Lincoln inform the speaker that Lincoln was a slave-owner. The truth was in some documents that had never been translated.

The Reagan years were a turning point. You will not find quite these words in *The Sibling Society,* but Bly says as much in other words, and his remarks on the subject are just wrong enough to be irritating. Reagan was "a poor father by all accounts," while leaving the impression of a good and fatherly person, but this need not be hypocrisy, nor does it follow that he was "utterly unable to stand for any important 'traditional' values." Stand for them is exactly what he did, as a mascot stands for a team. He felt the force of those values as a thing of the past, which gave a reflected glory to Americans in the present, and required in observance neither acts nor habits of self-sacrifice. "He managed to represent limitless acquisition, disguised as family," says Bly, but fondness for money was surely a recessive note in the Reagan personality, and that was part of his appeal. Familial piety was more important, and if he summoned only the echoes of paternal dignity, echoes can often succeed by their shallowness: the depth is supplied by our memory of the original.

Reagan's was a piety without a burden, a loyalty that floated free of specific duties, and we have only begun to see how much his illusions will cost. Yet Bly succumbs to an ordinary failure of observation when he says that this president showed an "envy of the rich." Reagan never conveyed a particle of that sentiment, being always utterly trustful of the rich and successful, an old man who shone with the confidence that "a boy like me," as he called himself at a late press conference, would have a house built for him and the future taken care of by the benevolent order that attends to such things. He conveyed gratitude extremely well—something that does not go with envy.

We could wish for a gratitude more discriminating of its patrons and less willing to bankrupt the future at their pleasure. That kind of moral and personal strength has few public exemplars today, and a more inquisitive mind than Bly's might ask why this is so. Gianni Vattimo in *The*

Transparent Society described philosophically many of the same phenomena as *The Sibling Society,* but he did his best to feel encouraged: the leveling of manners is democratic; the reluctance to blame or praise heroically, or to decide hard cases, may be a benign effect of tolerance; and with the dismantling of the Enlightenment ideas of reason, judgment and historical continuity citizens are arriving by default at the conclusion postmodern theory has reached by sophistication. The uneasy signs in our time of "disorientation" and "weak thinking"—words that Vattimo uses in a favorable sense—are therefore healthy and may foster less violence than their enlightened precursors. Once we have given up the idea of human nature, and realized that we are infinitely malleable, why not suppose our adjustment time will grow shorter and shorter?

A surprising number of intellectuals are comforted by some such view of contemporary life. Faith in progress was always strong in America, and it has never flourished more wildly than now, but progress for us means almost exclusively technological improvement: traveling faster, talking faster, making money faster. Capitalism lives on this faith as credulously as Marxism. If a piece of improvement can be executed all across the society, we ought to do it in a clean sweep, for the good that we lose is calculable, the good that we gain incalculable. But all the new tools a people master cannot assure their generous use. Technology travels a different road from political stability, moral well-being or aesthetic achievement, and it is for us to say whether a decent society is compatible with what the master siblings want to call progress. Anyway, the choice of manners is separate from the choice of materials. Bly's intuitions about the decomposition of authority may be confirmed or qualified by empirical observers, but in questions like this it is not only empirical answers that one wants. His call to "face the children," half formed as it is and half-unhinged, is also an earnest warning to count the casualties, the ones who will never grow up.

FURTHER READING

Criticism

Allen, Charlotte. "The Little Prince." *Commentary* 91, No. 5 (May 1991): 58-60.
    An unfavorable review of *Iron John.*

Beneke, Timothy. "Deep Masculinity as Social Control: Foucault, Bly, and Masculinity." In *The Politics of Manhood: Profeminist Men Respond to the Mythopoetic Men's Movement (And the Mythopoetic Leaders Answer),* edited by Michael S. Kimmel, pp. 151-63. Philadelphia: Temple University Press, 1995.
    Applies Michel Foucault's theories of knowledge, power, and authority to Bly's interpretation of masculinity in *Iron John.*

Bernard, April. "Sad, Sorry Critters." *New Republic* (7-14 September 1992): 43-5.
    A negative review of *The Rag and Bone Shop of the Heart.*

Chappell, Fred. "Sepia Photographs and Jazz Solos." *New York Times Book Review* (13 October 1985): 15.
    A review of *Loving a Woman in Two Worlds.*

Delville, Michel. "Deep Images and Things: The Prose Poems of Robert Bly." In *The American Prose Poem: Poetic Form and the Boundaries of Genre,* pp. 150-68. Gainesville, FL: University Press of Florida, 1998.
    Examines the major themes, artistic concerns, and significance of nature and inanimate objects in Bly's prose poems.

Doubiago, Sharon. "Enemy of the Mother: A Feminist Response to the Men's Movement." *Ms.* II, No. 5 (March-April 1992): 82, 84-5.
    Presents strong objection to Bly's interpretation of masculinity in *Iron John.*

"The Gifts of Growing Old: An Interview with Robert Bly." *Utne Reader* 75 (May-June 1996): 58-60.
    Bly discusses *The Sibling Society* and his views concerning art, myth, and parenthood in contemporary society.

Gutterman, David S. "A Woman for Every Wild Man: Robert Bly and His Reaffirmation of Masculinity." In *The Politics of Manhood: Profeminist Men Respond to the Mythopoetic Men's Movement (And the Mythopoetic Leaders Answer),* edited by Michael S. Kimmel, pp. 164-72. Philadelphia: Temple University Press, 1995.
    Examines Bly's interpretation of masculinity and heterosexual gender roles in *Iron John.*

Harris, Peter. "Separate Anthologies: Poems by Women, Poems for Men." *Virginia Quarterly Review* 70, No. 4 (Autumn 1994): 679-96.
    Offers evaluation of *The Rag and Bone Shop of the Heart.*

Johnston, Jill. "Why Iron John Is No Gift to Women." *New York Times Book Review* (23 February 1992): 1, 28-9, 31.
    Discusses Bly's attitudes toward male initiation and womanhood in *Iron John.*

Kakutani, Michiko. "Beyond Iron John? How About Iron Jane?" *New York Times* (27 August 1993): C1, C28.
    Discusses Bly's relationship to the men's movement and offers comparative analysis of *Iron John,* Marianne Williamson's *A Woman's Worth,* andClarissa Pinkola Estés's *Women Who Run with the Wolves.*

Kakutani, Michiko. "Man and Nature." *New York Times* (3 May 1986): C14.
    A review of *Selected Poems.*

Kooser, Ted. "Five Chapbooks Out of Many." *Georgia Review* XLVIII, No. 4 (Winter 1994): 812-21.

Provides a brief review of *Gratitude to Old Teachers*.

Kupers, Terry A. "Soft Males and Mama's Boys: A Critique of Bly." In *The Politics of Manhood: Profeminist Men Respond to the Mythopoetic Men's Movement (And the Mythopoetic Leaders Answer),* edited by Michael S. Kimmel, pp. 222-30. Philadelphia: Temple University Press, 1995.

Discusses positive and negative aspects of Bly's masculine ideal in *Iron John*. Though affirming Bly's call for forgiveness and sensitivity, Kupers objects to implicit sexism and homophobia in the book.

Lammon, Marty. "Something Hard to Get Rid Of: An Interview with Robert Bly." *Ploughshares* 8, No. 1 (1982): 11-23.

Bly discusses his poetry, his artistic concerns, and his relationship with poet Donald Hall.

Milne, Kristy. "Cubs in Charge." *New Statesman* (15 November 1996): 47-8.

A review of *The Sibling Society*.

Morrow, Lance. "The Child is Father of the Man." *Time* (19 August 1991): 53-4.

Provides an overview of Bly's life, career, and relationship to the men's movement.

Murry, Gordon. "Homophobia in Robert Bly's *Iron John*." In *The Politics of Manhood: Profeminist Men Respond to the Mythopoetic Men's Movement (And the Mythopoetic Leaders Answer),* edited by Michael S. Kimmel, pp. 207-12. Philadelphia: Temple University Press, 1995.

Discusses Bly's silence on the subject of male homosexuality in *Iron John* and among participants of the men's movement.

Perloff, Marjorie. "Soft Touch." *Parnassus* 10, No. 1 (Spring-Summer 1982): 209-30.

A review of *The Man in the Black Coat Turns*.

Savran, David. "The Sadomasochist in the Closet." In *Taking It Like a Man: White Masculinity, Masochism, and Contemporary American Culture,* pp. 161-210. Princeton: Princeton University Press, 1998.

Examines interpretations of masculinity presented in *Iron John* and Bly's relationship to the men's movement.

Schulman, Robert. "Boys Will Be Boys: Ode to the Old Days." *Wall Street Journal* (19 December 1990): A14.

A review of *Iron John*.

Shakarchi, Joseph. "An Interview with Robert Bly." *Massachusetts Review* XXIII, No. 2 (Summer 1982): 226-45.

Bly discusses his philosophical views, artistic influences, and interest in Eastern literature and spirituality.

Stitt, Peter. "Coherence Through Place in Contemporary Poetry." *Georgia Review* XL, No. 4 (Winter 1986): 1021-33.

A review of *Selected Poems*.

Warren, Catherine. "Myths Make the Man." *New Statesman & Society* (27 September 1991): 54.

A review of *Iron John*.

Additional coverage of Bly's life and career is contained in the following sources published by the Gale Group: *Contemporary Authors,* **Vols. 5-8R;** *Contemporary Authors New Revisions Series,* **Vols. 41, 73;** *Dictionary of Literary Biography,* **Vol. 5;** *DISCovering Authors Module: Poets;* **and** *Major 20th-Century Writers,* **Eds. 1, 2.**

Buchi Emecheta
1944-

(Full name Florence Onye Buchi Emecheta) Nigerian novelist, children's writer, screenplay writer, and autobiographer.

The following entry presents an overview of Emecheta's career through 1998. For further information on her life and works, see *CLC*, Volumes 14 and 48.

INTRODUCTION

Among the most important female authors to emerge from postcolonial Africa, Nigerian-born Buchi Emecheta is distinguished for her vivid descriptions of female subordination and conflicting cultural values in modern Africa. Her best-known novels, including *Second-Class Citizen* (1974), *The Bride Price* (1976), and *The Joys of Motherhood* (1979), expose the injustice of traditional, male-oriented African social customs that relegate women to a life of child-bearing, servitude, and victimization. Often regarded as a feminist writer, Emecheta illustrates the value of education and self-determination for aspiring young women who struggle against sexual discrimination, racism, and unhappy marital arrangements to achieve individuality and independence. While critical of patriarchal tribal culture, Emecheta's fiction evinces an abiding reverence for African heritage and folklore that reflects the divided loyalties of Africans torn between the competing claims of tradition and modernization. Noted for her realistic characters, conversational prose style, and sociological interest, Emecheta is highly regarded for introducing an authentic female perspective to contemporary African literature.

BIOGRAPHICAL INFORMATION

Born in Lagos, Nigeria, and raised in the nearby village of Ibuza, Emecheta received a traditional Ibo upbringing and early witnessed tensions between indigenous African culture and urban Western values. Orphaned as a young child and raised by extended family, she attributes her desire to write to the storytelling of her aunt, "Big Mother." Though schooling for girls was discouraged, Emecheta managed to receive an education at a missionary school, where she was taught English in addition to her several native languages. Bound by Ibo custom, she left school at age sixteen to marry a man to whom she had been engaged since she was eleven years old. Emecheta gave birth to their first child at age seventeen and by twenty-two was the mother of five. Shortly after her marriage she moved to London where her husband had already relocated to study.

While working odd jobs at the British Museum library and a youth center to support her family, Emecheta devoted herself to writing in her spare time. Despite efforts by her abusive husband to undermine her literary aspirations, Emecheta eventually published several of her diary entries in *New Statesman,* later becoming the material for her first book, *In the Ditch* (1972). Emecheta left her husband in 1966 and continued to work and write while raising her children and studying sociology at the University of London; she graduated with a bachelor's degree in 1972. While still in England she completed two additional books, *Second-Class Citizen* and *The Bride Price,* then moved to the United States where she supported herself as a social worker in Camden, New Jersey. Upon the publication of *The Slave Girl* (1977), a novel whose manuscript was once burned by her former husband, Emecheta received a Jock Campbell award from *New Statesman* and was selected as the Best Black British Writer in 1978. With the success of her 1979 novel *The Joys of Motherhood,* Emecheta was invited to work as a visiting professor at several American universities and as a research fellow at the University of Caliber in Nigeria before taking a permanent teaching position at the University of London in 1982. She also wrote several books for children and screenplays for British television. During the 1980s, Emecheta continued to establish her reputation with the novels *Double Yoke* (1982) and *The Rape of Shavi* (1983). She was named one of the Best British Young Writers in 1983. Her autobiography was published as *Head Above Water* (1984).

MAJOR WORKS

Emecheta's fiction focuses on the plight of African women who struggle against patriarchal family structures, unfair gender stereotypes, and contradictory social values in contemporary Africa. Her first two books, *In the Ditch* and *Second-Class Citizen,* are autobiographical accounts of her early life and marital difficulties as the fictionalized protagonist Adah. *In the Ditch* begins with Adah's separation from her husband and relates her demoralizing experiences while working, writing, and raising her five children on public assistance in a London tenement. Her economic privations are exacerbated by prejudice against her as an impoverished single mother and black African immigrant. *Second-Class Citizen* recounts Adah's childhood struggle to obtain an education in Nigeria, her emigration to England, and her determination to write despite the demands of motherhood and her tyrannical student husband who physically assaults her. Adah finally abandons her husband after he callously burns the completed manuscript of her first book, marking a defining moment in Adah's growing self-awareness and confidence. In *The Bride Price* Emecheta illustrates the injustice of male chauvinism and caste restrictions in her native country. Set in Lagos and Ibuza during the 1950s, the protagonist is Aku-nna, a young Nigerian girl whose father dies when she is thirteen, leaving her in the charge of her father's brother. Aku-nna manages to remain in school only because her uncle believes it will increase her bride price. However, she falls in love with her teacher, Chike, a descendant of slaves whose social status prohibits their involvement. Despite the protestations of her family and a potential suitor who kidnaps her, Aku-nna elopes with Chike and deprives her uncle of her dowry. In the end Aku-nna dies in childbirth, fulfilling the fateful superstition that a woman whose bride price is unpaid will not survive the birth of her first child.

The Slave Girl similarly depicts the limited opportunities and property status of women in Nigerian society. The female protagonist is Ojebeta, a young girl who is sold into domestic slavery by her brother after her parents die in an influenza epidemic. Stripped of her rights, Ojebeta is moved from her village to a busy town where she is converted to Christianity and taught to read and write. She is later married to a man who pays off her owner, drawing attention to the parallel institutions of slavery and marriage as Ojebeta is simply transferred from one master to another. *The Joys of Motherhood* describes the circum-scribed existence of protagonist Nnu Ego, a dutiful Nigerian wife and mother who suffers poverty and humiliation in a traditional polygamous marriage. Rejected by her first husband for failing to produce a child, Nnu Ego subsequently marries Naife, a cruel city man she finds unattractive but resigns herself to, and eventually bears several children. Exhausted by years of servitude and domestic conflict with her co-wife, Adaku, Nnu Ego finally returns to her village alone and unappreciated for her sacrifices, reflected in the novel's ironic title. A departure from the limited domestic settings of her previous books, *Destination Biafra* (1982) is a sweeping historical novel about civil unrest in Nigeria during the Biafran secession-ist movement of the late 1960s. The central figure is Debbie Ogedemgbe, daughter of a slain businessman who eschews passivity by joining the bloody struggle on the side of a united Nigeria. In *Double Yoke* Emecheta relates the disillusioning experiences of a female college student, Nko, whose personal relationships and educational goals are compromised by sexual politics on a Nigerian campus. Nko is scorned by her boyfriend for permitting premarital sex with him, then seduced by a manipulative professor with whom she becomes pregnant. The title refers to Nko's double bind as she realizes her equally degrading choice between prostitution as a traditional wife or as a liberated academic woman.

In *The Rape of Shavi* Emecheta presents an allegorical interpretation of European imperialism in Africa. The story relates the despoliation of the mythical Shavians, an idyl-lic tribe of African cattle farmers who are uncorrupted by contact with the West until a plane piloted by Englishmen crash lands among them. The white men abuse their trust, exploit their natural resources, and introduce guns and greed to their society, leaving the Shavians devastated by war, drought, and famine. Returning to the English setting of her first two books, *Gwendolyn* (1990) chronicles the difficult life of the title character, a young Jamaican im-migrant who endures rape, incest, and racism on the way to independence. Gwendolyn flees Jamaica, where she is molested by a family friend, to live with her parents in a poor London neighborhood. At age sixteen she becomes involved in an incestuous relationship with her father, bears his child, and, after her father's suicide, tentatively reconciles with her mother and boyfriend. *Kehinde* (1994) involves a middle-aged Nigerian woman who relinquishes a professional career in England to return to her native land with her husband. When Kehinde arrives in Nigeria after staying behind to sell their house, she discovers that her husband has taken a second wife, reducing her to insignificance despite her status as an educated woman and senior wife. Kehinde eventually leaves her polygamous marriage, returning to England where she gains new perspective on her life.

CRITICAL RECEPTION

Widely recognized as a leading female voice in contempo-rary African literature, Emecheta has attracted international attention for her compelling depiction of the female experience in African society and, in particular, her native Nigeria. Along with Bessie Head, Ama Ata Aidoo, and fellow Nigerian Flora Nwapa, Emecheta is credited with establishing an important female presence in the previously male-dominated literature of modern Africa. Commenting of Emecheta's contribution, Eustace Palmer writes, "Scarcely any other African novelist has succeeded in probing the female mind and displaying the female personality with such precision." Though often classified as a feminist writer, Emecheta differentiates her own Afrocentric perspective from that of her Western counterparts by describing herself as "an African feminist with a small f." Critics commend Emecheta's impressive narrative abilities, psychologically complex female protagonists, and powerful social critique of traditional African culture that, as reviewers note, is largely unencumbered by ideology or polemics. While *The Joys of Motherhood* is considered Emecheta's most accomplished work, she has won critical approval for *Second-Class Citizen, The Bride Price,* and *Double Yoke.* However, her attempts to depart from the highly personal subjects of these works in novels such as *Destination Biafra* and *The Rape of Shavi* have received mixed assessment. Some reviewers also find fault in uneven and occasionally repetitious elements of her fiction. Despite such criticisms, Emecheta is consistently praised for her engaging, compassionate rendering of African women, motherhood, and the impact of Westernization in postcolonial Nigeria.

PRINCIPAL WORKS

In the Ditch (novel) 1972

Second-Class Citizen (novel) 1974

The Bride Price (novel) 1976

The Slave Girl (novel) 1977

The Joys of Motherhood (novel) 1979

Titch the Cat (juvenilia) 1979

Nowhere to Play (juvenilia) 1980

The Wrestling Match (juvenilia) 1980

The Moonlight Bride (juvenilia) 1981

Destination Biafra (novel) 1982

Double Yoke (novel) 1982

Naira Power (juvenilia) 1982

Adah's Story [consists of *In the Ditch* and *Second-Class Citizen*] (novel) 1983

The Rape of Shavi (novel) 1983

Head Above Water (autobiography) 1984

Family Bargain (juvenilia) 1987

A Kind of Marriage (novel) 1987

Gwendolyn [published as *The Family* in the United States] (novel) 1990

Kehinde (novel) 1994

CRITICISM

Chikwenye Okonjo Ogunyemi (essay date 1983)

SOURCE: "Buchi Emecheta: The Shaping of a Self," in *Komparatistische Hefte,* Vol. 8, 1983, pp. 65-78.

[*In the following essay, Ogunyemi provides an overview of Emecheta's literary career and the major themes in her novels.*]

Easily the most poignant event in Nigeria's Buchi Emecheta's career as a novelist was her husband's crime in burning her first manuscript, a version of what, rewritten, would become *The Bride Price*. The manuscript had become an extension of Emecheta authenticating her unacknowledged and unacclaimed breadwinning role vis-à-vis her male dependents. The burning was therefore of great symbolic significance. It represented her husband's destroying what was left of their fragile marital relationship. It represented, in another sense, the immolating of Emecheta, the "second-class citizen," struggling to free herself from the bonds of her father, her brother, and, most especially, her husband. Her husband was intelligent enough to see the manuscript for what it really was: a violent threat to the *status quo* of his marriage. He acted accordingly to preserve what he thought was left of his manhood.

Undeterred by that incendiary act, or perhaps, incensed by it, Emecheta went on to write and has had published five important feminist novels. She is currently the most prolific and controversial of all black African female novelists. The novels are: *In the Ditch* (1972); *Second-Class Citizen* (1974); *The Bride Price* (1976); *The Slave Girl* (1977); and *The Joys of Motherhood* (1979). The first three novels I regard as apprentice pieces which prepared Emecheta for her fourth attempt whose promise has now been fulfilled in her much more mature novel, *The Joys of Motherhood*. As she moved from the autobiographical to a more fictive medium, she became more expansive. No longer are her talents restricted by the stifling egotism of the earlier novels. The subtle change is noticeable in the differing dedications to her works: the first novel is dedicated to her father; the second to her children; the third to her mother; the fourth to her friend and publisher, Margaret Busby; and the fifth to "all mothers." These dedications reveal an unconscious struggle involving a shift from the private, the personal, and the subjective to a feminist world that is quite public. Here, she attempts to reach out to a universal sisterhood where woman recognizes her peculiar predicament and yearns to become her sister's keeper. Outgrowing her father, she embraces her mother to emerge as a firebrand upholding the feminist faith.

Emecheta's shaping of herself took the form of an eighteen-year self-imposed exile in England that had the limiting effect of confining her to an outdated view of her country, Nigeria. It explains her inability to link the past meaningfully with the realities of present-day Nigeria. Indeed, the long exile has done her a greater harm. This manifests itself in her ambivalent attitude towards her material; her viewpoint shifts between shame and pride in her people, a feeling of inferiority interlaced with a need to be tough to gain approval of those who matter to her—her British audience. Her ambivalence reveals an English strain in her attitude towards life, a strain in constant conflict with her innate Africanness. Consequently the works tend to be pulled apart by the tensions of these opposing forces. Her circumstances have generated in her career an emotional and intellectual crisis which has in turn resulted in a crisis in the creative process. In *The Joys of Motherhood*, she resolves the impasse by seeming to come to terms with her Africanness.

In the Ditch and *Second-Class Citizen* are so slight and interconnected thematically and chronologically that they could have appeared as one novel. They function cathartically for Emecheta in expurgating the grossness of her childhood and marital life while fortifying her to endure the so-called joys of motherhood and creativity. She had to come to grips with her life before she could establish herself solidly in the imaginative world.

Adah, Emecheta's projection of herself in *Second-Class Citizen*, said she had a broad knowledge of black American writers, having come in contact with them through her job in different libraries. Her vast reading in black American literature has had its effect on *In the Ditch*, grounded as it is in the protest tradition of Richard Wright and his imitators. The opening skirmish with the rat and roaches are in the tradition of Wright's *Native Son*. But Emecheta's scene lacks the immediacy and the symbolic significance of Wright's account. Apparently the black rat, Adah, is surrounded by white rats waiting for the fairy godmother, the social worker who helps them to exist in the ditch and ultimately pulls them out of it. Emecheta's protest thus lacks the urgency and hopelessness of Wright's version of the black American situation since it excludes, to a large extent, the injustices associated with racism. Its feminist thrust is also weakened because, on the level of plot, it is the women's patience rather than their resistance to the authorities that is finally rewarded when they are rescued by the social workers.

The victim in this novel is woman. Her crime is that she is a woman and head of a single parent family. The victimizers (the authorities) are ready to listen (albeit reluctantly), a factor which unwittingly undercuts the necessity for Emecheta's elaborate protest. The weakness in the conception of the novel is further brought out by the character of Adah, who, in spite of her seeming unsureness, copes, supported by the very authorities Adah-Emecheta criticizes. The technical flaw in the book lies in Emecheta's preference for the historical perspective over the symbolic, which in a few concentrated scenes can underscore concisely yet pervasively and emotionally the quality of life in the ditch. We are made to see Pussy Mansions as an improvement on Adah's former abode, yet she still complains. She spreads herself thin and the reader soon becomes immune to her querulous tone.

In the Ditch concentrated on social problems as they affect the single woman with a family—problems of housing, child care, education, support, and male companionship. The work is tailored to suit feminist ideologies but its presentation of the heroine's dilemma is so wearyingly pedestrian as to reduce its cogency. Affected by vestiges of the oral tradition, misplaced in this milieu, the novel is an extended praise poem of Adah in her struggle to survive without a husband, tied down by five children, in a hostile environment. Adah is a heroine *par excellence*; she is remarkable for her strength of character in the black matriarchal tradition and the representativeness of her social predicament. Hence one would agree with Emecheta's publisher "that readers will expect to be told how Adah came to be in the predicament with which the story is concerned," which, we are promptly informed, "is to be the subject of another book."

Although the opening of Emecheta's first novel echoes the manner of *Native Son*, there is a strong African undercurrent in her sarcasm and humor. It is the ironic banter of the Igbo, west of the Niger, a verbal style that helps them endure pain and deprivation. The strain is obvious in this sentence: "One of the frightened cockroaches ran into Adah's hollow for maternal protection." This is protest literature with a humorous difference; Emecheta accepts herself. Unfortunately she fails to maintain the standard and the novel is mired in infelicities. Her inability to discriminate consistently between Adah and herself is apparent in the use of pronouns. A few examples will suffice to illustrate the point. "*She* did not feel like asking for grants just for the kids' Christmas presents. *I* want to give *my* children *my* own presents, what *I* actually work for . . . ideas came to *her* head" (emphasis supplied). The problem in delineating the inward flow of thought through the stream of consciousness technique remains unresolved until four novels later.

Another major problem with her preoccupation is that she protests on too many fronts: welfarism, racism, and sexism. She sacrifices character for her subject to such an extent that none of the characters besides Adah comes alive. Furthermore, her long sojourn in Britain has blurred her vision of Nigeria. She remarks for instance that during the Biafran War, "Most of them (Adah's people) had died from snake bites, running away to save their lives." Such gross misrepresentation of present-day Nigerian realities and her tendency towards exaggeration make her work inauthentic. Her bitter marital experience induces her to end the novel lamely with the white Whoopey impregnated by an African and with Adah empathizing by cursing "all African men for treating women the way they do." This sweeping statement reveals an attitude which intrudes again in another stereotype: "One of the boys (Adah's son) was shivering, his brown, bony naked body shaking as if doing an African sex dance." The tone of denigration is subdued in this first novel mainly because the other memorable characters are white. The conflict in the writer comes out into the open more explicitly in her next novel.

The second novel, *Second-Class Citizen*, is also feminist in ideology. It delineates the second-class citizenship of Adah in two senses: first as a black person in a predominantly white world, then as a woman in a male-controlled world. It has aroused some furor not for its radical stance for blackism and feminism but for its conservatism in projecting white paternalistic and/or stereotypical attitudes towards Africa. As one reviewer rightly complained, Emecheta dwells on those aspects of Nigerian life which "the average British would wish to hear about the African."

This tragic pass is apparent in the indiscriminate use of animal images which pervade the entire work and reveal her incredible and deep-seated alienation and contempt for the African. Unsurprisingly, Adah's husband, Francis, comes in for such debasement. On one occasion, he "reminded Adah of a snake spitting out venom. Francis had a small mouth, with tiny lips . . . so when he pouted those lips like that, he looked so unreal that he reminded the onlooker of other animals, not anything human." Later, Francis "was like an enraged bull," angered by Adah's refusing him sex, a typical Igbo female ploy. We can hardly miss the reference as she reaffirms his bestiality: "All that Francis needed to be taken for a gorilla was simply to bend his knees."

If her husband is an animal, she is (economically) the "goose that laid the golden eggs" and (sexually) the "wicked temptress luring her male to destruction." But she destroyed Francis with neither money nor seduction; rather, like a witch, by the magical power of the words which make up the novel, she devastated him. Her struggle is for emancipation from wifehood through motherhood to selfhood. For Adah sees the husband-wife relationship as destructive and corruptive, and the woman is victim. One of man's offensive weapons is the penis, used to break woman's individuality (frigidity to Francis), and needed to subjugate the woman through pregnancy and childbearing.

Emecheta therefore retaliates in typical western fashion with a Freudian weapon, the pen. In using her pen she declares her emancipation from her husband and Igbo patriarchal convention. The height of her newly acquired liberty is demonstrated in the boldness of her public narration of her private story. But like Okot p'Bitek's *Song of Lawino* in its defence of tradition, Adah's revolutionary statement of her case against tradition is so one-sided that we wish the "first-class citizen" could have been given the equal time that p'Bitek was compelled to provide with his *Song of Ocol*. If we were to imagine Emecheta stating her case before a group of Igbo elders (male and female), would they not have condemned her as much for the self-centered crudity of the telling as for the story itself?

Second-Class Citizen is a satire against Francis, who comes to represent the Igbo man or the African man; under criticism is man's vaunted role as breadwinner coupled with his exaggerated notions of manhood in which the woman is unjustifiably treated as a subordinate. As forceful as the attack might be from a feminist stance, the work nevertheless is both morally and aesthetically dissatisfying to a reader who comes from a culture where it is unethical to reveal the unpleasant details of a marital breakdown. The western Igbo avoid such impropriety by using the custom of "ikpo si ike," a procedure which allows a hostile spouse, privately, to bare the buttocks to the full view of the partner as a sign of divorce when a relationship has broken down irretrievably. Its finality saves the couple the enervating experience of a public proceeding. Emecheta, originally a western Igbo, was to use this neat means to effect a separation between Aku-nna's mother and her new husband in *The Bride Price*. Her treatment of the collapse of Adah's marriage in *Second-Class Citizen* is somewhat coarse when considered, as the novel must be, in an Igbo context. To an Igbo, Emecheta's acquired English sensibility is insensitive and distasteful.

From the foregoing, it is ironical that Adah was irritated by Francis' and Pa Noble's (the noble savage?) toadyish behavior towards white women. Of *Second-Class Citizen* we can ask Emecheta a modified version of what Adah in her anger asked Pa Noble: "Why did you not tell your white audience that your father had tails, Ma Emecheta . . . Why must you descend so low? Just to gain approval from these people?"

But then the novel is a *Bildungsroman* and Adah is confused at this point in the novel. She grows from ignorance to a slight awareness of her power, the extent of which she does not yet fully recognize. Her story itself is pathetic: the heroine develops a confused identity commencing from her arrival in London and culminating in the burning of her manuscript. The trauma speeds up her Anglicization and encourages her feminism to the detriment of her Africanness. Since Francis did not bargain for an English wife, he intentionally hurt her by insisting that they were not married, a statement of truth in conservative Igbo eyes, since the traditional bride price, symbol of female subjugation, was unpaid. As Francis performed his dastardly acts, Adah became the "monkey" poisoned by Francis and the "goat" lashed by him for not doing the impossible. In the image of the monkey is implied some mischief on Adah's part; her book is therefore a "monkey business," set out to destroy Francis while he in his turn makes her a scapegoat for his intellectual failure. In the final analysis, the weak Francis did have cause to fear the indefatigable Adah, whose resilience enabled her to reproduce a fresh version of her burnt manuscript from whose ashes emerged the dedicated feminist.

Having tackled her personal problems in two novels, Emecheta moves from the autobiographical to the more challenging fictive representation contained in her third work, *The Bride Price*. But the experiment in *The Bride Price* reveals a lack of expansive imagination; Aku-nna's story could have been hers; she duplicates thematic patterns, technique, and method of characterization already employed in the first two autobiographical novels.

The animal images which emerged in *In the Ditch* and *Second-Class Citizen* reach alarming proportions in *The*

Bride Price. Surprisingly, the heroine, Aku-nna, also comes in for this debasing treatment. At one point in the story all the noise Aku-nna could emit "was like that made by ageing frogs at the sides of marshy streams." The Yoruba traffic warden has "zebra-like tribal markings," while some Igbo men puff "thoughtfully on clay pipes like goats chewing grass." Igbo women are not left out; "the happy group were chattering like monkeys," while another female character is depicted "wagging her foot like a contented dog." These images are not carefully worked out to support, for example, a feminist stance. Rather, they betray Emecheta's half-conscious attitudes towards Africans, male and female. She unwittingly takes us back to the days of the anthropological researcher, stereotypically debating the nature of the African. Such writing has its consequences.

Besides this propensity for animal images, Emecheta employs other images that are equally reprehensible. The friends and relatives who mourn Aku-nna's father dance and "like mad Christians gone berserk would roll themselves into balls . . . working their bodies into lumpy or smooth shapes, like a huge dough being prepared for pastry." This level of writing speaks for itself.

The novel is further marred by the numerous explanations of customs, obviously meant for a foreign audience who would not notice such a flaw as narrating an essentially Igbo story using Yoruba proverbs. Such sweeping generalizations as "The bride usually won, and then the houseboy would go away in search of his own fortune somewhere else. It was always so, and it still is so among the Ibos in Lagos today. It is one of those unwritten norms which are here to stay" were, by the mid 70s, inapplicable with the advent of smuggling, military rule, civil war, and the beginning of free education in Nigeria. Other infelicities as "They (the male mourners) beat their chests to the rhythm of their agony, they hugged themselves this way and that like raging waves on a gloomy day, and on each face ran two rivers of tears which looked as though they would never dry" cannot bear close scrutiny. They are the signs of an unaccomplished writer. Her outsider's lack of empathetic interpretation shows that Emecheta partly absorbed her perspective not from James Baldwin, whom Adah confesses to have read, but from the Wright of Black Power. Like Wright, she writes about Africa with a western sensibility, so much so that her attack on the tradition of bride price with its feminist thrust becomes suspect; she is no longer "one of us."

Despite her style and anti-African images, in the denouement of *The Bride Price*, having prepared us in many ways, Emecheta attributes Aku-nna's death to the violation of tradition. Mutiso's observation about the dissident in the African novel is pertinent here. According to him, "The literature suggests that the modern African individualist is almost by definition a schizoid person. This word is not used lightly, but arises from the fact that whenever the individual has apparently shaken the operational aspects of the communal ethic, it nevertheless returns to haunt his

memory." Aku-nna's dissent haunts her in her last days. The link between *The Bride Price* and Ernest Hemingway's *A Farewell to Arms* is obvious in the scene where Chike puts a dried leaf on the path of a line of brown ants, disrupting them. The action is reminiscent of Henry's godlike role in his treatment of the ants on the burning log in *A Farewell to Arms*. The human being is equated to the ant; Chike informs Aku-nna that "each ant would be lost if it did not follow the footsteps of those in front, those who have gone on that very path before." Aku-nna's defiance of tradition brings about her end in a devastating way that cannot be compared to Adah's success. It is incongruous that the feminist Emecheta should permit such failure considering the fact that she (Emecheta) came out unscathed after her own deviation from the African norm.

We are further prepared for Aku-nna's death by the fact that the heroine, like the writer's mother to whom the novel is dedicated, is an "Ogbanje," destined to die and return time and again. This belief in reincarnation is however not in keeping with Emecheta's fundamental stance. What is more in tune with her Anglicized world view is the incorporation of Hemingway's use of the "biological trap." In Aku-nna's instance, the trap lies in her tender age, malnutrition, narrow hips, sickliness, and consequent weakness. That idyllic sojourn in Ughelli, with its reverberations of a "separate peace" and the sentimentality evoked by the lovesick couple, ends in the clinical, ascetic surrounding of a hospital bed, the would-be mother caught by the trap of nature as Catherine was in *A Farewell to Arms*.

Parallel to the development of the "biological trap" are others: the "psychological trap," the "superstition trap," and the "tradition trap." Emecheta overdoes it by making the odds against Aku-nna overwhelming. Thus Aku-nna's feminist revolt is foredoomed, battered as she is from several angles. If she represents woman-in-revolt with its tragic consequences, Ojebeta, the heroine in the fourth novel, *The Slave Girl*, represents contrastingly the tragic fate of woman acquiescent to the whims and caprices of society. Emecheta implies forebodingly that the woman is always a loser no matter what her attitude towards life is or the degree of her awareness of her socio-political predicament.

Perhaps it is a coincidence that the heroine of *The Slave Girl*, Alice Ogbanje Ojebeta, is named after Emecheta's mother, Alice Ogbanje Emecheta; or is Ojebeta's story a fictional version of Emecheta's mother's life? There are chronological and geographical parallels in both stories but it might be wise to leave that line of thought, interesting though it may be.

In *The Slave Girl*, set at the beginning of the twentieth century, Emecheta is a lot more inventive than before as she weaves a story based on the type of accounts that were rife among the western Igbo—stories of exile and return of members of the clan apparently sold into slavery. She has journeyed back in time. That journey motif is reflected in the name Ojebeta (literally did her journey start today?), a wry commentary on the frequency of the heroine's reincarnation. In the present phase of her existence, she is destined to continue moving back and forth from Ibuza to Onitsha back to Ibuza and off to Lagos. These incessant journeys remind us of the perilous one to Benin undertaken by her father on her behalf to ensure her survival. In her lifetime, Ojebeta journeys from one form of slavery into another as she plays in turns the role of daughter, sister, housemaid or rather pawn, niece, lover, wife and mother—roles which insistently subordinate her to men.

Besides the journey motif, there is implicit in Ojebeta's name, Alice, a connection with Alice in Wonderland. Ojebeta's life is romantic and her journey to Onitsha is fantastical particularly when we recall that her life there is far removed from the reality of her circumstances in Ibuza. Normalcy is restored when she wakes up, as it were, to the possibility of regaining her lost freedom and then returns from Onitsha to Ibuza.

As Ebeogu points out, Emecheta has destroyed the basis of the "propaganda" in this novel that protests against the exploitation of women in traditional society by depicting too many successful female characters such as Uteh, Umeadi, and most importantly, Ma Palagada. In contrast, only Ojebeta is made to represent the enslaved woman; because of the imbalance, Ojebeta's situation appears atypical, contrary to the author's intention. It seems therefore that it is not so much the society which has permitted many women to lead free, happy, productive lives that is to blame for Ojebeta's feminine predicament, but her orphanage, a stressful situation that could retard the progress of an average child in any culture. Ojebeta then emerges as an inadequate medium to convey Emecheta's feminist ideologies, while the more memorable figure of Ma Palagada, who dwarfs her husband and son, and even bequeaths them with a name, unwittingly serves as a forceful antithesis.

In spite of all these conceptual flaws, Emecheta examines the subject of woman's subjugation doggedly. There is new-found confidence in the work as she unifies Ojebeta's African heritage with her acquired Anglo-Christian ones, as signified in the names Ojebeta and Alice. Emecheta makes us believe that the innocent Ojebeta had been preserved not only by the love of her parents but by the talismanic bells and charms, symbols of that parental love. When Ojebeta abandons these ties with her ancestors and accepts a Christian God, life becomes more insecure for her, so that the promise that Ojebeta the child held is not fulfilled in the adult Alice. Her later difficulties can be attributed to her apostasy in the same way that her brother, Okolie, had had to suffer materially and spiritually for betraying the spirit of the ancestors by exchanging his sister for money. Before the end of the story, the reader gradually becomes aware of the fact that Ojebeta is Nigeria, "enslaved" by the British (represented by the bourgeoise Ma Palagada) through her betrayal by her own

people for mere bauble. Ojebeta's kith and kin, those to become the colonized, lacked the moral strength and the foresight to present a united front to fight the new, black elitist force which suicidally, would entrench British mores in the society. It must be noted that with reference to Ojebeta's traumatic experience, Okolie, her brother, is as much to blame as his elder brother who shirked the duties of the first son by abandoning his patrimony to settle in Lagos. Nigeria's fate, like Ojebeta's, has been determined on the one side by ignorant, disloyal people.

In this novel, Emecheta begins to get into the spirit of what it is to be an Igbo raconteur with her alienation against things African noticeably minimized. She has realized that a successful story-teller can criticize but cannot afford to be alienated from the people who provide the material for a work of art. Although Eze's voice might sound "like that of a hoarse frog," yet Ojebeta can stand "quaking like African water lilies on a windy day." In warming up to her subject, she becomes almost lyrical in parts. Eze's and Uteh's voices in argument "were like a rising song that started with a low tune and gained in volume till it was raised to the highest pitch." This is a more mature Emecheta. Although she has not completely relieved herself of the shackles of her English sensibility, she has come a long way in integrating her images and developing a more acceptable African world view.

Her improved skills are also obvious in the novel's strong ending. Images of death and corruption dominate *The Slave Girl* and so do those of avarice, selfishness, and dishonor; they represent the decadence of Nigerian society as encapsulated in Ojebeta's life. Emecheta manages to render these negative qualities from the viewpoint of an insider. In the end, she identifies the politico-cultural perspective of British infiltration into Nigeria with the Anglicization of Ojebeta and her illusory happiness at her lot in her husband's house. Considered in a political context, the tragic irony in the novel lies in Ojebeta's ignorance of the major event that will affect Nigeria— colonization—a large-scale slavery that will determine, socially, economically, and psychologically, the fate of every Nigerian, woman and man. The last paragraph of the novel is indicative of this new era: "So as Britain was emerging from war once more victorious, and claiming to have stopped the slavery which she had helped to spread in all her black colonies, Ojebeta, now a woman of thirty-five, was changing masters." Ojebeta was blind to her predicament just as Nigeria was in the dark as she drifted into colonialism. Nnu Ego, the heroine in Emecheta's latest feminist novel, finally sees the light which must precede a change.

With the publication of *The Joys of Motherhood*, Emecheta has come to her own. It is a much more substantial work than its predecessors. It covers the same grounds, thematically, but there is a marked technical development in the writing with its wry humor and underlying irony.

The psychological grounding of the novel is based on the story of a slave princess already narrated by the character,

Chiago, in *The Slave Girl*. The contrast between Chiago's narrative and its dramatization in *The Joys of Motherhood* shows the extent of Emecheta's growth as a writer. From mere reporting, she now conjures up her subject in vivid scenes as if she had learnt some lessons from Jane Austen. The stream of consciousness which she had hitherto handled awkwardly now finds occasional expression in the recording of the flow of thought in italics, in an almost Faulknerian fashion.

The first chapter is captivating; Emecheta excels herself in the tremendous sweep back in time to explain Nnu Ego's present psychological impasse. She treats in depth the role of one's *chi*, that is the guardian spirit, in the Igbo person's psychic disposition. In spite of the fact that she scoffs at the idea of a *dibia*'s omniscience, she manipulates the point of view so as to make us see and believe with Nnu Ego on the efficacy of the dibia's juju while we also understand and accept Oshia's disbelief in these local medicine men. Nnu Ego's difficult life stems from the unpleasant circumstances surrounding her half-brother's death blow on the slave princess destined to be her chi. Her inauspicious life becomes a case of a self-fulfilling prophecy as the drama unfolds.

The tempo of the first few chapters starts to flag with the sameness in Nnaife's many marriages, his fathering of children by Adaku, Adankwo, Okpo, and Nnu Ego, and Nnu Ego's numerous pregnancies. These are tales of woe that emphasize the hardships of unplanned families and subsistence living. The burden is the tragedy of woman.

Where then lie the "joys" of motherhood? In expressing the joys, Emecheta is at her best as a western Igbo story teller, for example in the irony implied in the title. Children give joy, we all agree. From that premise, she builds an elaborate story to demolish such nonsense, while at the same time pretending to uphold the age-long idea. She dramatizes the adage that "if you don't have children the longing for them will kill you, and if you do, the worrying over them will kill you." A mother of boys must be happy; the oldest mother in a polygynous household must be joyous. Such happiness should help woman bear the grind of poverty. But in the background is the motif of the loneliness of the prolific mother. Nnu Ego gradually realizes that motherhood has not brought fulfillment but enslavement to the children. Keenly aware of the "umbilical" ties with her father, husband, and sons; keenly aware of the hardship of numerous children; Nnu Ego ruminates: "God, when will you create a woman who will be fulfilled in herself, a full human being, not anybody's appendage?" Her tragedy, and, by extension woman's tragedy lies in our awareness of her wasted life.

Nnu Ego's epiphany emanates from her brief contact with the feminist character, her co-wife, Adaku. Nnu Ego, turning feminist herself, laments the female predicament in a monologue: "I am a prisoner of my own flesh and blood . . . But who made the law that we should not hope in our daughters? We women subscribe to that law more than

anyone. Until we change all this, it is still a man's world, which women will always help to build." These ideas push feminism to great heights though coming from Nnu Ego at that point in time they sound anachoristic and anachronistic. An Anglicized black female character like Adah would have been a more appropriate persona than Nnu Ego to voice such female discontent. What is more, several inconsistencies appear in Nnu Ego's character that demonstrate her inadequacy as a feminist. For example, in spite of her seeming revisionist stance, she is horrified at Adaku's bid for freedom from marital drudgery; she regards it as prostitution. Obviously she is an inheritor of traditional male brainwashing. Besides, her criterion as to who out of her children should be formally educated is based on sex rather than on ability, with preference given to the boys over the girls. She also insists on her daughters rather than her sons doing the household chores. Thus the two crucial sources for reeducating a people with a patriarchal heritage and changing the sexist *status quo*, namely, formal education and the division of labor in the home, remain unexplored by our "feminist" heroine. Emecheta heightens Nnu Ego's ambivalent attitude and so fails to let her grow into a radical, perhaps in a last-minute bid to retain verisimilitude rather than advance, through the heroine, the propagandist tenets which the reader had been made to expect.

Emecheta further confuses the reader about her own stance in her naming of some of the characters. The name Obiageli (she who has come to enjoy her father's and/or husband's wealth), given to one of the twins, seems to be a misnomer coming after Nnu Ego's epiphany since it underscores the stereotype of the parasitic nature of woman. On the other hand, Malachi (which should read Malechi—who knows what the morrow will bring?) generates some hope in its forward looking to a probable female emancipation. It is as if Emecheta herself is not sure of what she wants or is nostalgic about the past with its own order. Her ambivalence towards her subject had been apparent earlier in her portraits of strong women as minor characters in contrast to weak women as central characters (for example, the powerful Ma Palagada as opposed to the pawn Ojebeta in *The Slave Girl*). In *The Joys of Motherhood*, the economically independent Adaku and the emotionally strong Ona differ from Nnu Ego. Adaku, like Adah-Emecheta, easily rids herself of her husband in a bid for economic independence while still believing that men "do have their (sexual) uses." She prefers a man as a companion on a basis of equality rather than as husband and provider, a relationship which gives ground for female incapacitation, if the husband does provide; and for frustration, if he does not. One can only wish then that Emecheta had resolved her doubts during the creative process and made her central characters carry the weight of her feminist convictions.

Besides the diminution of obnoxious images in her writing, there is a further change in Emecheta. By using the pronoun "us" for the first time with herself included, she finally acknowledges her sense of belonging with Africa instead of emphasizing her spirit of dissociation. Her identity crisis seemingly over, the dynamic Emecheta might help to launch a feminist revolt having at last found her place in the Nigerian artistic world.

The organic unity of Emecheta's works lies in her treatment of themes, use of technique, and exploration of a particular sociological background. More often than not, she peoples her novels with impotent men. But within the narrow canvas she has chosen, she has been able to portray the development of both working-class and middle-class Ibuza women from the beginning of the twentieth century to the 1960s. She concentrates on what has been. Her western Igbo reader enjoys the unveiling of the past and feels at home with her irony, a carry-over from the western Igbo language. Her feminist disposition, more western than African, needs further grounding in the Nigerian indigenous cultural milieu to make the impact of her writing felt by those who can effect a change of heart and attitude (if the novels were overtly meant to bring that about)—that is, the African woman and the African man. For the functional purpose of change implicit in her novels, Africans, rather than the British, must serve as her primary audience; otherwise, Emecheta's stereotypic portraits of Africans can only provide light entertainment for the outsider. Fortunately, *The Joys of Motherhood* foreshadows what can legitimately be expected of a mature, Nigerian feminist literature.

Rolf Solberg (essay date June 1983)

SOURCE: "The Woman of Black Africa, Buchi Emecheta: The Woman's Voice in the New Nigerian Novel," in *English Studies*, Vol. 64, No. 3, June, 1983, pp. 247-62.

[*In the following essay, Solberg examines Emecheta's conflicted feminist perspective and the representation of African women and contemporary social themes in her fiction. According to Solberg, Emecheta's harsh criticism of male chauvinism is tempered by her respect for traditional African culture.*]

The changes that have taken place in sub-Saharan black Africa during the hundred odd years since the 'scramble for Africa' are probably more profound than one can readily comprehend when looking at things from Western Europe. Colonialism unsettled a number of well-balanced mechanisms in almost every sphere of the traditional society: ecologically, socially, politically, and not least concerning the roles of the sexes.

In most traditional African societies there was a fairly well-defined pattern of duties and responsibilities shared by males and females. By and large the male was the dominant partner, and most societies had a patrilineal kinship pattern. In some societies the woman had to show excessive deference to her husband. She had to address him as her master, was not allowed to eat at his table, and

had to kneel before him. She has often been referred to as a 'beast of burden'. On the other hand there were also matrilineal societies where women had considerable power and exercised political influence that women still lack in advanced western societies today. And even in tribes where male authority was largely unchallenged, such as the Ibo tribe of Eastern Nigeria, she often enjoyed a considerable amount of independence socially, and especially economically.

As modern industrialism developed in Africa, the ensuing urbanisation drove a wedge into the traditional sex-structure. The men often had to move to industrial centres for jobs, and this meant a redefinition of agricultural work duties. Large-scale farming projects had similar effects. Families had to live apart and marriage relations often became strained. The predominantly polygynous traditional marriage had as its main objective the preservation of the (male) kinship line, and was not based on 'romantic' love. With the extra load added on to the already heavy burden of the woman (with agricultural work, house-keeping and child-rearing) and with the lure of city life, more and more women began to migrate to the towns and cities. Polygyny has come to be questioned more and more strongly by such women, and the western type 'romantic' marriage is gaining support among western-oriented Africans; women are pressing for real equality in all walks of life: the axe lies at the root, it seems, of the old African extended family tradition.

Since Independence the changes in the social structures of the new African nations have been accelerated. A number of husbands have taken their families with them to the cities, and large numbers of unattached women have moved to the cities for education as well as for other city attractions (pleasure, less-demanding work, more personal independence). The professional debate among sociologists and anthropologists about the effects of the migration to the cities upon the women themselves does not as yet yield any clear picture of the situation, which one could hardly expect, as it is still a transitional period. What does seem to emerge from the debate, however, is a realization that the process is irreversible, and one that is bound to affect the situation of the women, and, indeed, almost every aspect of the African societies involved.

Male support for the feminist issue appears to be less than whole-hearted. Bearing in mind the reactions past and present of the western male on the question of equality, this is perhaps to be expected. In proceedings from conferences on Third World development the need to enlist the women's services in the modernization process is very heavily underlined, with reference being made to their important roles in traditional societies, especially as mothers and agricultural workers.

If one looks at feminist legislation all seems well. One would be hard put to name a new African nation where women are denied their civic rights—on the statute books. By and large they have full political rights, and on paper there is hardly any discrimination at all in the fields of education, industrial or professional life. However, except for odd examples like Guinea, where president Sécou Touré himself has worked actively to achieve full emancipation for his country's women, the picture is often very different when it comes down to practical politics. Politicians, who are mainly men, tend only to pay lip service to such legislation, and through manipulation effectively keep women out of important positions in politics and management. It would be wrong to jump from this fact to the conclusion that African women are downtrodden, placid beings unable to take a stand-up fight if necessary. African history shows several examples of the contrary. C. C. M. Mutiso makes the following comment:

> Probably no single charge about the nature of traditional African society has animated Africans more than the idea commonly held by most foreigners that the African woman is generally a pliable person.

And although African women need understanding and support in their fight for an equal share in the benefits as well as responsibilities of the modern world, they have little time for the attitudes of some of their feminist champions in the West. In reply to Germaine Greer a Nigerian journalist writes in a conference news sheet at the women's conference in Mexico City in 1975:

> It is presumptuous for anyone to presume that women of the Third World are unable to articulate their outrage at any issue that concerns them. As a member of the Third World, I repudiate that patronizing attitude and particularly the underlying intellectual imperialism. Women in the Third World do not need any more champions. We are bored and tired of any more Great White Hopes.

In other words one has to tread softly. One of the ways of correcting one's faulty image of the African woman would be through the reading of creative literature. But even there one is in danger of acquiring biased information, as Eleanor Wachtel points out in a paper entitled 'The Mother and the Whore: Image and Stereotype African Women'. Here she examines the image of the African woman as it appears through the work of a number of modern African writers. Most of these writers are men, and she concludes that the image is largely a stereotype generally distorted by males, some of whom appear downright mysogynist.

Obviously there are a number of distinguished exceptions to this. In writings by Chinua Achebe, Cyprian Ekwensi and Okot p'Bitek for example we find a very different picture. But what one should really look for is the African woman seen from the 'inside', in other words rendered by women. However, African women writers are few and far between. It is all the more exciting to come across Nigerian Buchi Emecheta, a writer with no less than five novels to her name, all published in the short span of seven years, from 1972 to 1979. The sixth is in the pipeline ready for publication. And what is more: they are all very readable books.

'Buchi Emecheta, 36, daughter of a railway worker, followed her husband from Nigeria to London in 1962 but was later separated from him and left with five children to bring up alone. She now earns her living by writing and lecturing . . . She also writes children's books'. This is part of the laconic introduction to the *Sunday Times Magazine* feature, 'A Life in the Day of Buchi Emecheta' of 23rd March 1980. Academically she got herself an education in Lagos as a librarian before taking a degree in sociology while on the dole in London. Her writer's career includes, apart from the novels and children's books, a couple of television plays and also some poetry. In this article we shall concentrate on Buchi Emecheta's novels. Her first four novels, in the reverse order of their publication, take us from her parent's and grandparents' Africa, from the Ibo territories of Eastern Nigeria and the city of Lagos, and through the post-war Lagos childhood of Adah, the protagonist of the two earliest novels.

The first two of them, ***In the Ditch*** (1972) and ***Second-Class Citizen*** (1975) are both strictly autobiographical. Through the account of Adah's struggle to get herself an education on equal terms with her brother we are introduced to the author's childhood, and when we read about Adah's early married life in Lagos and London in the early and mid-1960s, it is equally about Buchi Emecheta's personal struggle for plain survival for herself and her five small children in the London slum. Her plight, or Adah's, to keep within the framework of Buchi Emecheta's novels, is all the more onerous as she is fettered to a useless slob of a Nigerian student husband, whose ultimate act of disgrace is to 'kill her brain-child': he burns the manuscript of his wife's first novel, ***The Bride Price***. The novel was later rewritten and appeared in 1976 as Buchi Emecheta's third novel. The fourth is ***The Slave Girl*** (1977) and the fifth, ***The Joys of Motherhood***, was published in the summer of 1979.

The African novels, i.e. the last three, cover a period from about 1910 to roughly 1960. They are not in the same sense autobiographical as the London novels. But they all fan out from the central experience of the author's Lagos childhood, and she uses material from her own family. From this nucleus, described in the first two chapters of ***Second-Class Citizen***, and the opening of ***The Bride Price***, they take us into three different social and temporal environments. There is (i) the market town of Onitsha in ***The Slave Girl***, with the first real exposure of the protagonist Ogbanje Ojebeta Odi to the modern world (the 1930s) and the white man's values. (ii) In ***The Bride Price*** we meet Blackie, modelled on the same person as Ogbanje (probably the author's mother) but now as the mother of Aku-Nna, the main character of this novel. With her mother Blackie and her brother Nna-Nndo, Aku-Nna moves back to the family roots in the Ibo village of Ibuza after a period in Lagos where she and her brother have spent their early childhood years. She (as well as Adah) was born about the end of World War II, and Buchi Emecheta herself in 1944, so the identification seems fairly obvious. (iii) In her latest novel, ***The Joys of Motherhood***, we join the Ogbanje/Blackie generation again, but this time in the city environment of Lagos, exploring with Nnu

Ego the pangs of culture collision. Here we witness the struggle of the illiterate first generation town-dwellers to bring up the first generation of city-born Africans about the time of World War II.

In the following pages I want to examine, in broad outline, the image of the African woman as it appears in Buchi Emecheta's three African novels. The opening chapters of *Second-Class Citizen* called 'Childhood' and 'Escape into éliticism' form a kind of exposition of Buchi Emecheta's central themes as a writer. At the same time as they give us the necessary information to appreciate Adah's situation in London they also introduce the basic dichotomy between traditionalism and modernism in Africa, with the woman's position as the central theme, especially the idea of the woman as slave. Linked with the enslavement of women is the question of the impact on the woman's situation of the Christian religion as well as that of education.

That the issue is of paramount importance is suggested already on the very first page where we are buttonholed by the author:

> She [Adah] was not even quite sure that she was exactly eight, because, you see, she was a girl . . . since she was such a disappointment to her parents, to her immediate family, to her tribe, nobody thought of recording her birth.

This is the introduction of the protagonist, Adah, about the time when she decided she wanted an education:

> School—the Ibo never played with that! They were realizing fast that one's saviour from poverty and disease was education.

However, Adah is hardly typical of Ibo femalehood in the determined way in which she comes to grips with schooling and education. On her way to an educated life (although initially as a second-class citizen) in Britain, she flagrantly violates a number of Ibo traditions, and her motto is: 'Be as cunning as a snake but as harmless as a dove'.

She marries Francis without a bride-price being paid, and she goes to join her husband in Britain against the will of her father-in-law. On leaving for Britain she reflects, while thinking about her little brother who has come to wave her off:

> . . . he had accepted the fact that in Africa, and among the Ibos in particular, a girl was little more than a piece of property. Adah had been bought, though on credit [Francis being unable to pay her bride price], and she would never go back to being an Ofili [her patrilineal family name] any more. The tiny hands clutching her blouse were the hands of a big man in the making. Her duty was to them now. From now on her children came first.

The question begged by these thoughts is whether they express Adah's, and by implication Buchi Emecheta's own acceptance of the traditional pattern where the woman's primary duty is to raise a large family for her husband's

kinship line, accepting her own subordinate position, or if they mean a clean breach with tradition: her duties will now lie with the 'nuclear family'. The latter appears to be the more probable, especially in the light of her reflections when, according to Ibo tradition, her mother is taken over as a co-wife by her father's brother on the father's death:

> She hated Ma for marrying again, thinking it was a betrayal of Pa . . . She would never, never in her life get married to any man, rich or poor, to whom she would have to serve his food on bended knee: she would not consent to live with a husband whom she would have to treat as a master and refer to as 'Sir' even behind his back. She knew that all Ibo women did this, but she wasn't going to!

Adah's basic problem here is one that is obviously shared by the author, and one that is becoming increasingly urgent to the growing section of African women that are now flocking to the urban centres: should they accept the age-old polygamous family system, or should they opt for the monogamous nuclear family? We must look to the African novels for a discussion of this problem.

Having read the three first novels by Buchi Emecheta the reader will probably link the slave reference of *The Slave Girl* with the status of women in the traditional African society. That is a hotly disputed issue, not least because of its negative reflections on the African male. Buchi Emecheta, although she refuses, like Adah, to bend her knee to the obligations inherent in the traditional view of male/female roles, still appears to be drawn by the traditional values.

Turning back again, briefly, to the opening of *Second-Class Citizen*, we find a rather nostalgic description of the village women preparing for the homecoming of lawyer Nweze, the Ibuza 'been-to' who returns with his British education. The occasion is filled with expectations of future benefits to be showered on Ibuza through its illustrious son:

> It was a joy to hear and see these women, happy in their innocence . . . Their wants were easily met. Not like those of their children who later got caught up in the entangled web of industrialization . . .

We find the same apparent ambivalence in *The Bride Price* where 13-year-old Aku-Nna is on her way to her father's home town Ibuza:

> Nearly everyone in Ibuza was related. They all knew each other, the tales of one another's ancestors, their histories and heroic deeds. Nothing was hidden in Ibuza. It was the duty of every member of the town to find out and know his neighbour's business.
>
> For a while they all stood and chatted. The young men had that distinctive and good-humoured quality of ease which was the heritage of people who had long ago learned and absorbed the art of communal living . . .
>
> Her cousin did not know about stories in books, but she did know a great number of folk stories that were told by moonlight and handed down from generation to generation.

Comparing the people of Ibuza with the people of Lagos:

> There was something else different about the people
> here; they seemed more relaxed, more naturally beauti-
> ful than their relatives in Lagos. The women all had
> such long necks and carried their heads high, like
> ostriches, as if they had a special pride in themselves,
> and their gracefully thin legs lent their whole appear-
> ance extra height. It was only the old people who could
> be seen to stoop. Every other person moved with such
> bearing that gave them a natural, untutored elegance.

Already a couple of pages later follows a clear corrective
to this flattering presentation of the village people:

> The children stared in the direction their mother was
> pointing and saw about fifteen women trotting into the
> fast filling square that was to be the market place. They
> were carrying a heavy pile of damp cassava pulp . . .
> So heavy was it that the necks of the poor women car-
> riers (who were sweating profusely) . . . were com-
> pressed to half their normal sizes.

Aku-Nna's problem is not so much the question whether
the old Ibo way of life is good, bad or middling: it soon
becomes clear that the real problem of Aku-Nna and Buchi Emecheta's generation is the one mentioned above:
they are the children 'who got caught up in the entangled
web of industrialization'.

At the end of chapter 6 of *The Bride Price* the author
comments on the situation of Aku-Nna and her brother
Nna-Nndo after they have been transplanted into the
traditional society of Ibuza. They carry in their veins their
Lagos childhood, and on top of that a typical British education is inflicted on them even in the Ibuza primary school:

> Aku-Nna and Nna-Nndo soon grew accustomed to
> things at Ibuza, learning in school the European ways
> of living and coming home to be faced with the count-
> less and unchanging traditions of their own people. Yet
> they were like helpless fishes caught in a net; they
> could not as it were go back into the sea, for they were
> trapped fast, and yet they were still alive because the
> fisherman was busy debating within himself whether it
> was worth killing them to take home, seeing as they
> were such small fry.

The question of slave versus free-born gets a rather special
twist in this novel as Aku-Nna falls in love with her teacher
Chike, who comes from a slave family. Like other
categories of osus, outcasts, the descendants from slaves
tended to rise to important positions in public life more
frequently and quickly than the free-born during the
colonial administration. They stood to gain more through
the modern education introduced by the whites and through
untraditional careers than their high-born African brothers.

For the free-born to have normal everyday relations with
the descendants of slaves was quite usual and acceptable.
But when it came to vital matters like owning land, marriage, and religious offices, there was an unbridgeable gap
between the two groups in the traditional society.

When Chike and Aku-Nna elope, therefore, it is in open
defiance of Ibo marriage traditions and it is regarded as an
abomination. This is so even though Aku-Nna was
abducted in the first place by members of the family of
one of her suitors, whom she was determined she would
never accept as a husband. Chike rescues her from the
unwanted match after the two families involved have
agreed on bride price. The act of defiance is 'Tempting
Providence', as the last chapter of the novel is called.
Aku-Nna dies in child-birth in consequence:

> So it was that Chike and Aku-Nna substantiated the
> traditional superstition they had unknowingly set out to
> eradicate. Every girl born in Ibuza after Aku-Nna's
> death was told her story, to reinforce the old taboos of
> the land. If a girl wished to live long and see her
> children's children, she must accept the husband chosen
> for her by her people, and the bride price must be paid.
> If the bride price was not paid, she would never survive
> the birth of her first child. It was a psychological hold
> over every young girl that would continue to exist,
> even in the face of every modernization, until the
> present day. Why this is so is, as the saying goes,
> anybody's guess.

Aku-Nna's death is in several ways a contrast to
Okonkwo's in Achebe's novel *Things Fall Apart*. His
downfall is primarily a consequence of flaws in his own
nature—his inordinate pride and his fear of being thought
weak and effeminate. Aku-Nna is killed by forces entirely
outside her control, and not because of inherent moral
shortcomings. And whereas Okonkwo is the traditional
male hero who dies, in a sense, in defence of the old way
of life, Aku-Nna is a feeble woman defying tradition.

On the first reading of *The Bride Price* one feels less
prepared for the tragic outcome than one does for
Okonkwo's death in Achebe's novel, despite the anticipa-
tions accumulating especially in the last chapter of *The
Bride Price*. One explanation may be found in the
enigmatic final line of the novel, where the author comments on the psychological hold that the traditional taboos
have on the young girls: 'Why this is so is, as the saying
goes, anybody's guess'. She finds it difficult to put our
minds at ease, or she deliberately refuses to.

We have seen before that Emecheta expresses herself
ambiguously when it comes to the question of traditional
values. In *Second-Class Citizen* Adah gets away with her
'revolt' against tradition. But then she is a much more
robust character than Aku-Nna. And *her* marriage is based,
if not on family negotiations, then on cool reasoning. Aku-
Nna refuses to be a slave to tradition in her love life.
When her mother lets her know that Chike can be no match
for her she turns the whole matter over in her mind: 'Oh,
what kind of savage custom was it that could be so heartless and make so many people unhappy?' And she is
determined to kill herself rather than sleep with the young
man whose relatives have kidnapped her. But by obeying
her heart and choosing as her partner the slave Chike she
takes on more than she can cope with. She is ill equipped
to stand up to such strain, and like the fishes caught in the
net she is 'trapped fast' once Ibuza has made up its collective mind.

In a larger context one could see Aku-Nna's death as one
of redemption—redeeming the woman's lot. A key to such

a reading is the word *joy*, and before Aku-Nna's death Chike promises her that the baby girl shall be called Joy. Note also Chike's insistence that girls are 'love babies'.

Aku-Nna is herself unable to enjoy her love union, the modern marriage, beyond the brief spell of one pregnancy. But the fruit of her married bliss, Joy, points forward to the new order. The next generation may already be safely through the initial effects of the culture collision, which is in the final analysis what kills Aku-Nna.

The institution of marriage itself is given a much more thorough examination in *The Joys of Motherhood*. Marriage in the African tradition has as its first objective the continuation of the kinship line. In most traditional societies that means, as I have pointed out above, the patrilineal kin. With the high infant mortality as a natural background the institution of polygamous marriage was evolved, and with it came the extended-family system. Within the natural and social framework of black Africa the system appears to have functioned very well. In a collective society where even religion was family oriented (ancestor worship etc.) one can easily understand that the individual had also to be subordinated to the group when it came to the choice of partners in marriage. The 'romantic marriage' with its rather 'haphazard' matching of two individuals would not meet the needs of the traditional African agricultural society. Marriage was an agreement between families. Married 'love' the way one thinks of it in our culture was 'incidental', and certainly subordinated to the overriding goal of the continuation of the kinship line.

In *The Joys of Motherhood* the main character Nnu Ego is the daughter of Agbadi, the illustrious hunter and powerful chief, a man who had many wives and concubines. There was only one woman he loved the 'romantic' way, and that was the concubine Una, Nnu Ego's mother. Once again there is the motif of the love-child. Nnu Ego is the only issue of Agbadi and Una's love, and this time we are moved one generation back from Aku-Nna in *The Bride Price*. Nnu Ego is born into the Ibuza society and is in due course married to the farmer Amatokwu in the traditional way. The importance of children in marriage is stressed early on. As Nnu Ego remains childless after a couple of years Amatokwu divorces her:

> 'What do you want me to do?' Amatokwu asked, 'I am a busy man. I have no time to waste my precious seed on a woman who is infertile. I have to raise children for my line.'

After this her doting father Agbadi returns the bride price and decides that he

> would rather give his daughter to an old chief with a sense of the tried, traditional values than to some young man who only wanted her because of her family name.

He has promised her mother Una on her death-bed, though, 'to allow her a life of her own' and not to prevent her from being a full woman as *her* father did her. Despite the fact that she was in a sense the slave of two men,—her father and her lover, Una remained a proud and uncompromising woman. But that was probably because she fully accepted the conventions of her culture. She refused to marry her lover because she felt she owed it to her father to give him an heir, her own son, first, to continue *his* line. During Una's pregnancy with Nnu-Ego, Agbadi's senior wife, Agunwa, dies. As part of the traditional funeral rites a female slave is killed to go with her in the grave. As the slave woman is dying she cries out to Agbadi, who intervenes to lessen her pains,

> 'Thank you for your kindness Nwokotcha, the son of Agbadi. I shall come back to your household, but as a legitimate daughter. I shall come back.'

Nnu Ego, who was born shortly afterwards, was born with the slave woman's growth on her head, thus symbolically assuming the traditional woman's slave mark. After being rejected by Amatokwu as a barren woman, she is given away to the rather unattractive Nnaife who works as a house-boy for an English family in Lagos. With his she begins to have children. The first born, a 'clean-looking boy', suddenly dies. Then she gets another, accompanied by a strange dream. She picks up a baby boy left by a stream. Then she sees the slave woman, her CHI (personal god), who says to her: 'Yes, take the dirty, chubby babies. You can have as many of those as you want. Take them!' The rather indiscriminate reference by the slave woman to the 'dirty, chubby babies' could be significant in view of the further development. Nnu Ego has seven children who grow up, and three of them are boys. Due to that fact she is grateful to her lazy, floppy husband, while still dreaming at times of a

> . . . handsome young man, black and shiny of skin like carved ebony, tall, straight and graceful like the trunk of a palm tree, with no fat anywhere but strong bones set inside his perfect body.

Still, Nnaife has made her into a 'real woman': he has given her sons. Hence, what pleasure the illiterate Nnu Ego gets out of her first-generation city life she gets from her motherhood.

Through a repetitive style of writing the author brings out this merged motif of slaving motherhood against the almost opaque background of male infallibility. In the traditional society the blessing of children and especially sons, lay partly in the returns their parents could rightfully expect in old age. It functioned as the indigenous type of old age pension. In the late colonial era there was the extra inducement to educate one's sons, who would, like lawyer Nweze in *Second-Class Citizen*, make good in the world and return to take up lucrative posts in the administrative hierarchy, or in politics, and thus shed honour and riches on their parents and indeed on the entire village or clan, if all went as it should.

The sad irony of *The Joys of Motherhood* lies partly in the juxtaposition of the strong love story between the successful traditional chief and his proud mistress and the drab toil which the fruit of that relationship, Nnu Ego, is subjected to in order to bring up her large family of 'dirty, chubby babies', the off-shoots of slavery. And that story is unfolded against Nnu Ego's repeated self-deluding praises to the joys of motherhood.

One is again left mildly puzzled, as with the previous books, about the author's total attitude towards tradition/modernization. However, the criticism of male chauvinism is very clear, clearer than in the other novels:

> On her way back to their room, it occurred to Nnu Ego that she was a prisoner, imprisoned by her love for her children, imprisoned in her role as senior wife . . . It was not fair, she felt, the way men cleverly used a woman's sense of responsibility to actually enslave her.

Her co-wife Aduke remarks about Nnaife: '. . . But you can't deny that he is a selfish man.' 'All men are selfish. That's why they are men.'

It does not appear from this novel what kind of development the author envisages for the African woman. However, she drops a couple of significant hints. Before Nnaife is drafted and sent to Burmah to fight for the British in the Second World War he inherits Aduke from his elder brother who dies. (Later he takes a third wife in common marriage. His Christianity is only skin deep.) During his absence Aduke does well for herself as a petty trader, as Ibo women are famed to do, she abandons tradition and decides to go and live as an independent woman:

> 'My CHI be damned! I am going to be a prostitute. Damn my CHI!' she added again fiercely. . . . 'You mean you won't have to depend on men friends to do anything for you?' Nnu Ego asks. 'No', she replied. 'I want to be a dignified single woman. I shall work to educate my daughters, though I shall not be without male companionship.' She laughed again. 'They do have their uses.'

Nnu Ego, on the other hand, solidifies in her traditional role, but not without being aware, again as the Ibo are known to be, of the blessings of education:

> She and her husband were ill prepared for a life like this, where only the pen and not the mouth could really talk. Her children must learn.

She becomes painfully clear about her slavery towards the end of the novel, for all her acceptance of the traditional yoke. On having born her last girl twins she prays:

> 'God, when will you create a woman who will be fulfilled in herself, a full human being, not anybody's appendage?'

> 'When will I be free?' . . . 'Never, not even in death. I am a prisoner of my own flesh and blood . . . But who made the law that we should not hope in our daughters? We women subscribe to that law more than anyone. Until we change this, it is still a man's world, which women will always help to build.'

In other words she remains a slave all her life, in accordance with the curse of the slave woman of the opening pages. This comes out in a symbolic scene towards the end of the novel, where she has a miscarriage. She blames herself for the dead baby girl:

> Has she wanted the child to die—was that the interpretation of the slight relief she had experienced when she crawled to the dead child to check what sex it was? That it was a girl had lessened her sense of loss. Oh, God, she did not wish it . . . Please God, give her something to hold on to, some faith to assure her that she deliberately had not killed her own child in her heart. But the thought kept recurring, until she felt she was hearing it in the voice of her father: 'Nnu Ego, why did you not call for help when you were in labour? . . .'

This could be taken as an indictment against the male-oriented traditional society: this is what it can do to a mother's mind even.

Nnu Ego dies in middle age in her ancestral Ibuza, her mind having begun to wander. And she dies friendless. Her 'very clever children', and notably the two eldest sons, only remember her after she has died. While she was alive

> everybody referred to Nnu Ego, as she proudly carried back-breaking firewood up from the waterside, as the mother of very clever children.

The two sons who are studying in Canada and the U.S.A. forget even to write to their mother:

> And her reward? Did she not have the greatest funeral Ibuza had ever seen? It took Oshia three years to pay off the money he had borrowed to show the world what a good son he was.

One is again reminded of the slave-woman's reference to the 'dirty, chubby babies'. Also towards the end of *The Slave Girl* we find the slave-master motif related to the traditional marriage. Ogbanje has been released from her bondage on the death of the relative who brought her from Ogbanje's brother when she was a little girl. Now she is going to marry an Ibuza man, Jacob, who is, like herself, literate and a Christian:

> She had been a slave before against her wishes. If this time she was going to marry and belong to a man according to the custom of her people, she intended to do so with her eyes wide open . . . it would [be] better to be a slave to a master of her choice, than to one who didn't care or even know who you were.

This is when Christianity enters the picture. Opinions vary a lot when it comes to the general question of what blessings or curses the white man's religion has bestowed upon the African continent, and that is a problem beyond the scope of this article. However, the impact of Christianity on the African woman's lot is a question which Buchi Emecheta pronounces on fairly strongly:

> [Her family] wanted to know why it was essential for her to go to church and have those strange foreign words said over her, just because she was going to her husband's house . . . and the bride price had been paid.

What worried these people, and Ogbanje as well at the time, was what problems might arise later if the legally married wife did not produce children:

> Ogbanje did not know the answer to that one. (But years later Nigerian men solved the problem them-selves. A woman could be taken to church and a ring slipped on her finger as easily as a piece of string round a man's cattle to mark it out from another person's. But that did not mean that the man could have only her. What if he had enough money and could afford more wives, or if the first one married in church had no child? So men would simply take wives when they felt like it; while women, on the other hand, must have one husband, and only one.)

Love did not really enter into this relationship, no more than it did between Adah and Francis in *Second-Class Citizen*.

> There was certainly a kind of eternal bond between husband and wife, a bond produced by centuries of traditions, taboos, and, latterly, Christian dogma. Slave obey your master. Wife, honour your husband who is your father, your head, your heart, your soul . . .

And this is how Adah reflected on the impact of Christian-ity:

> Those god-forsaken missionaries! They had taught Adah all the niceties of life. They had taught her the Bible, where a woman was supposed to be ready to give in to the man at any time, and she was to be much more precious to a husband than rubies . . .

The Christian marriage in effect meant a double obligation to the African woman. So maybe the answer for the African woman is Aduke's: use men when you need them; otherwise do without them! That may be so. But it does not appear to be the author's position.

In the course of this article I have referred a couple of times to what I see in Buchi Emecheta as an ambivalent attitude towards traditionalism/modernisation. We find this expressed in her view of the man-woman relationship as well as reflections on the general development on the West African scene.

Her traditionalist leanings come out very clearly in the fol-lowing extract from the interview referred to above, where she comments on the ending of *The Bride Price*: '. . . you know towards the end of that book Aku Nna died because I felt that she went against her parents—you know that part of tradition . . .' And she talks about

> the traditional values [which] have been tried and ap-proved. There are certain parts of you that are so tied to them that if you don't adhere to traditions, you just die . . . What I am really saying is that what is good in the old values—let us keep it. I wish not to look down on everything we have as bad or backward just because it is not modern. And community life for example, I think we should keep that,—you know, just like that.

On the other hand there is—implicitly rather than explicitly—the criticism of the lingering effects of age-old institutions like slavery, and the drudgery of the village women's back-breaking toil, put in relief by, for example, one of Nnu Ego's rare glimpses of a better future for the African women:

> . . . I am beginning to think that there may be a future for educated women. I saw many young women teach-ing in schools. It would really be something for a woman to be able to earn some money monthly like a man.

It seems to me that Buchi Emecheta's dilemma is part and parcel of the Culture Conflict syndrome: her love and respect for the African heritage vying with the pains of having to define her attitudes towards the problems of the post-colonial reality. Some of the apparent paradox, of course, lies in the short lapse of time between the unified, old village tradition and the challenge posed by modern city life.

Returning again to the feminist issue, the author says of the tribal traditions '. . . some of them are still relevant—like a polygamous life. I think in village Africa you still need this tradition . . .'

Now this seems to throw a shadow of doubt on her feminist integrity—polygamy being considered a 'relevant' institution. (One should note, though, that the author is talking about 'village Africa', which is, after all, a far cry from modern or urban Africa.) She even disclaims the feminist label. Asked point blank whether she is a feminist she answered:

> Not in the western sense, no. Because I think our problem is beyond feminism. We still have the basic problems to solve. Now I think our men have an excuse to oppress us, because they are not free themselves, even in the so-called independent states. They cannot see that they are being used. So until they are free you can't really . . . claim to be a feminist.

And she adds for good measure: 'We need our men'.

The apparent dichotomy between tradition and 'development' or modernism, as we see it in the clash between Adah's revolt against polygamy in *Second-Class Citizen* and the mature author-cum-sociologist's comment just quoted, is one of the basic dynamisms of Buchi Emecheta's African novels up to *The Joys of Mother-hood*.

In my view this does not reduce the momentum of her feminist criticism. Her denunciation of the ill effects of the male dominance in the Ibo society is clear. In places her exposure of male chauvinism is scathing, although at times her veneration for the old way of life seems to take some of the sting out of her charges.

From the evidence we have in her published novels, and from the statements she made in the interview referred to, she still appears to be struggling to clarify her attitudes towards some of these fundamental problems. That may partly be the reason why she, and African women in general, are wary of accepting the ways suggested by western feminism. It is probably also true to say that at this stage Buchi Emecheta is an African writer first and a feminist second. Whether she chooses, or is able, to clarify her position in her future work remains to be seen, of course. We shall be looking for this in her next novel, due to appear shortly under the name of *Destination Biafra*. There she takes us into contemporary Africa. The scene is eastern Nigeria in the 1960s, and we are going to meet the educated young African woman.

What seems clear to me, though, is that the modern African woman of the future is not going to accept much longer a position ascribed to her by her male counterpart. The new African woman, whether she be conservative (in the best sense of the word) like Buchi Emecheta, or of a more radical brand, will probably wish to define the terms of her motherhood herself: the time of Achebe's Okonkwo and Emecheta's Agbadi is past.

Marilyn Richardson (essay date May 1985)

SOURCE: "A Daughter of Nigeria," in *Women's Review of Books*, Vol. II, No. 8, May, 1985, pp. 6-7.

[*In the following essay, Richardson offers an overview of Emecheta's literary career and fiction.*]

At a conference at the University of Ibadan in Nigeria, in 1982, I found myself seated on the dais in a large, windowless conference room. As I waited my turn to present my paper to a sizeable audience of academics, writers and students, the lights in the room flickered and went out. "Carry on," urged the chairman, addressing the panelist caught in mid-sentence. "You wrote the paper, surely you can tell us all what is in it." The only woman and the only black American up there, I cursed the Middle Passage; had I lost my birthright to the oral tradition? Clearly I was unprepared to sit in pitch darkness and recite a ten-page paper from memory. Whichever deity responded to my desperate importunings—and I called on a good cross-section, seated as I was in the heart of Yorubaland and a conscientious respecter of turf—I breathed a sigh of genuine gratitude when the lights came back on just before I was introduced. I whipped through my paper in record time, terrified of being plunged back into the abyss with the prospect of trying to enter into some trance-like state in order to retrieve, verbatim, the last of my footnotes.

It was, therefore, with the greatest sympathy and total willingness to suspend disbelief that I read Buchi Emecheta's account of student life in Nigeria in her 1982 novel, *Double Yoke*. Miss Bulewao, the new lecturer in Creative Writing, is in mid-harangue when, sure enough, the lights go out. As the lights flickered, the students "were well aware of what was coming, yet its suddenness was embarrassing to all. They felt embarrassed for Nigeria."

In Nigeria the electricity fails daily, the water comes and goes, and the telephones seldom work; all because of the pervasive and presumably ineradicable corruption and abuse of power at the heart of every government agency and public utility. They are as well at the thematic heart of this thoughtful and revealing novel.

Based on Emecheta's experiences as a faculty member in the Department of English and Literary Studies at the University of Calabar, *Double Yoke* is an exploration of the ways in which such corruption, taken for granted in public and business matters, corrodes the integrity of even the most intimate aspects of private life as well. In her understanding of the intersection of the public and the private in Nigerian life, Emecheta shows us the formidable adjustments facing young people, especially women, as they move from the traditions of village life to the independence of life in the university; from village social norms to the world of expediency and compromise beyond.

The many pressures encountered by young women of ability and ambition moving out of the traditional worlds and into careers and choices of their own are presented in excruciating detail in this novel of initiation. The student Nko understands that society will define her in one of two ways:

> She must either have her degree and be a bad, loose, feminist, shameless, career woman who would have to fight men all her life; or do without her degree, and be a good loving wife and Christian woman to [her fiancé] and meanwhile reduce herself and her family to beggars at [his] table.

And she herself must reconcile her own experience and background with her emerging identity as one professionally trained in the oppressor's methods. "How was she expected to study and be able to pass down to future generations the Nigerian culture which she would have to express in another language?" In a contemporary society where wealth, status and appearances are valued above individual rights and dignity, choices between old and new become life and death matters, for the body and the spirit.

While the title of the novel refers to the particular dilemmas h characters encounter, it could serve equally as a reference to the task the book itself performs. With this book, the two dominant, but up to this point quite distinct, elements of Emecheta's substantial literary output, converge. *Double Yoke* is the culmination of work begun in her earlier novels, *The Bride Price* (1976), *The Slave Girl* (1977) and *The Joys of Motherhood* (1979). While written out of chronological sequence, these novels together present a rich panorama of Nigerian life, rural and urban, before, during and after colonial domination. Above all they show us, as never before, Nigerian women's lives in their historical, social and personal complexity. Uniquely qualified by both her training and her experience to serve as a trustworthy guide, Emecheta is both a product and a chronicler of the worlds she describes.

Born in Lagos in 1944, she was married at seventeen and soon moved to London where her husband was a student.

They eventually separated and she stayed on to study for a degree in sociology and begin her career as a writer while supporting herself and five young children. Emecheta's earliest fiction, the frankly autobiographical *In the Ditch* (1972) and *Second-Class Citizen* (1974), recount her struggle to make it on her own.

Down but not out in London, Adah Obi, the heroine of both novels, has a job, is a part-time student, and nurtures a dream of becoming a successful writer. But she also has five children, all under the age of six, no husband, and black skin. Landlords will not rent to her, childcare is impossibly expensive, and her physically and psychologically abusive husband delights in withholding even the merest crumbs of child support. Adah soon finds herself caught in the quicksand of social service agencies whose assistance can be had only at the cost of abandoning all attempts at self-sufficiency. To receive even marginal public assistance, she must give up her job, move into garbage-strewn, rat-infested public housing, and struggle against the pull to resign herself to the inevitability of years of life on the dole.

Insider and outsider, client and social scientist simultaneously, Emecheta writes of being a black welfare mother. As she describes the pain, the camaraderie, and at times even the humor of life "in the ditch," she can nail the system's stupidities, blind spots, and cruelties as only a woman could who has not only studied that system, but, at risk of life and sanity, survived it. And in *Double Yoke* we see Adah triumphant, under another name perhaps, but a Nigerian novelist living in England who spends time as a visiting lecturer at a Nigerian university.

In her most recent book Emecheta takes a very different approach to the interaction of tradition and change in Nigerian society. *The Rape of Shavi* is an allegorical tale set in the isolated kingdom of Shavi, somewhere in present-day Africa. A land of gentle, creative and long-suffering people for whom "shame kills faster than disease." Shavi is ruled by good king Patayon and his council of elders. We learn something of the community's history, its economy and its dedication to pacifism. There is much to recommend the Shavis' communal moral code, although they are clearly heir to the profound sexism of much African tradition.

One day from out of the sky falls a flaming silver bird, bearing in its belly a group of pale, leprous-looking beings whose claim to membership in the human race is none too certain. The parable of the honest but naive tribal folk corrupted by contact with even well-meaning Europeans might with some imaginative reworking of predictable material sustain a short story. Paradoxically, it could as well lend itself to an elaborate and informative epic novel full of complex characters and motives. But Emecheta's version falls between two stools: its overlong recitation of the obvious, without benefit of intricacies of characterization or plot, succeeds only in indicting the potential for greed and arrogance in both worlds. The outsiders come,

they see, they corrupt, and in the end everyone left alive stands around scratching their heads and speculating on the real meaning of civilization.

While much that is wrong with *The Rape of Shavi* may be traced to the paucity of its conceptual framework, the novel has another shortcoming for which the book's editor or may be responsible. Throughout her work, Emecheta's narrative voice, while altered in ways appropriate to accommodate changes in time, place and circumstance, is distinctly and recognizably her own, grounded in oral tradition and enriched by a liberal dose of West African idiom and syntax. In what is presumably an attempt to preserve the purity of that voice, anachronisms, awkward usages, and just plain howlers have been allowed to stand, although they both detract from the credibility of the text and distract the reader unnecessarily. Maybe king Patayon sits on his palace "piazza"; maybe one village elder says to another, "the ball is in your court"; but would a daughter of the village really be taught to "keep her cool" under pressure?

Perhaps there are political reasons for the editorial laissez-faire in these numerous small matters and for the apparent absence of effort to thrash out and refine the basic assumptions and structures of the text. One wonders whether this African document was itself to be left "untouched" like some latter-day companion piece to the work of Emecheta's countryman Amos Tutuola.

The Rape of Shavi, while not a successful novel, is fundamentally a political statement, attuned to the bitter realities of drought, famine, conflicts between modern and traditional values, and above all the chaos that can ensue when a small nation reaches for unaccustomed power. In a 1982 novel, conceived and written on a boldly ambitious scale, Emecheta handles all of these matters much more deftly and convincingly.

Destination Biafra is an angry, bitter, impassioned novel of the civil war that engulfed Nigeria from 1967 until 1970. Here Emecheta rescues from oblivion the story of Ibuza, her family village and other places like it whose people endured almost unspeakable horror and suffering as pawns in an intricate and vicious political struggle.

The line of women in those novels set in previous generations, Ojebeta in *The Slave Girl*, Aku-nna in *The Bride Price*, and Nnu Ego in the ironically titled *Joys of Motherhood*, continues in the person of Debbie Ogedemgbe, "who is neither Ibo nor Yoruba nor Hausa, but simply a Nigerian." Emecheta's clear and distinctive voice serves her well as the insistent narrator of stories too painful to tell, too painful to leave untold. She dedicated the book to

> the memory of many relatives and friends who died in this war, especially my eight-year-old niece, Buchi Emecheta, who died of starvation, and her four-year-old sister Ndidi Emecheta who died two days afterwards of the same Biafran disease . . . also my aunt Ozili Emecheta and my maternal uncle Okile Okwuekwu,

both of whom died of snakebites as they ran into the bush the night the federal forces bombed their way into Ibuza.

I also dedicate **Destination Biafra** to the memory of those Ibuza women and children who were roasted alive in the bush at Nkoptu Ukpe.

This lengthy, graphic and precise roll-call of a dedication reflects a story which unfolds in eloquent and elegiac detail, capturing with reportorial immediacy the tragedy of Biafra in ways that are reduced to cold abstractions and metaphors in *The Rape of Shavi*. This is the story of a war in which little if any attempt was made to spare women and children; we hear their story from a woman who shares and identifies with their suffering. She identifies as well with the larger nation brought to the brink of self-immolation: "I am a woman and a woman of Africa. I am a daughter of Nigeria and if she is in shame, I shall stay and mourn with her in shame."

Buchi Emecheta is sometimes described as a protest writer, and indeed she does protest against the devaluing of women's humanity and potential wherever that occurs. She protests as well against European racism, and black as well as white hierarchies of caste and class. She protests against injustice as she locates, exposes and dissects in her writing the very roots of oppression. In her life and in her novels she struggles for change, but with the clear understanding that one can never really escape from the past, personal or historical. A woman who works at understanding her past, who moves with hope into the future, Emecheta takes her comment on the end of the Biafran war into a larger context: ". . . it is time to forgive, though only a fool will forget."

Jewelle Gomez (review date November-December 1985)

SOURCE: A review of *Double Yoke*, in *Black Scholar*, Vol. 16, No. 6, November-December, 1985, p. 51.

[*In the following review, Gomez offers a favorable assessment of* Double Yoke.]

Buchi Emecheta's new novel lays bare the schism between the limiting yet familiar comforts of traditional African roles, and the more expansive and sometimes dangerous choices offered by modern society. These forces buffet the lives of Ete Kamba and Nko, two young Nigerian university students who fall in love. Within the context of the most simple love story Emecheta opens up the complex world of tribal life and is able to make real both the values of ancient customs and the urgent need to revise them; to learn to take the best from both the old and the new.

But Emecheta is not a theoretician on polemicist. Her value is as a storyteller. Her characters are as rich as her thesis is compelling. Ete Kamba is full of boyish pride for his successful bid to win a scholarship and he is enthralled

with his first adult love, Nko, who has also gained admission to the school. Yet these triumphs precipitate confrontations for which neither is prepared. How can Ete Kamba, a traditional African man pledge marriage to a woman who gives herself to him without apology, who refuses the shame of lost virginity and who makes it clear that education is not merely a hobby for her? He is proud of Nko but cannot abide the shift in power her independent thinking implies.

Although Nko resists the more frivolous influences from the West like straightened hair and makeup, she is firm in her ambitions. The double standard threatens to strangle Nko's hopes for both a successful marriage and a good education. The mysterious waters of sexual politics are treacherous. When Ete Kamba spurns Nko and her university mentor conspires to seduce her, she must learn to accept the burden of her progressive vision and the fallibility of everyone, including Ete Kamba and herself.

The novel is both comic and tragic in its depiction of Nko's and Ete Kamba's youthful, emotional extravagances and the campus response to their transgressions. Here, as in Emecheta's other novels, she speaks with an undeniably Nigerian voice; makes clear the Nigerian woman's circumscribed position in society and her skillful adaptation to it.

Emecheta is able to depict the tribal and class structures which shape so much of African life: how the Hausa and the Ibo perceive of themselves in relationship to society; the rigid strata to which colonialist educational systems have given birth; and how the tenuous nature of economic security spawns both ambition and desperation in West African life.

Emecheta skillfully weaves the cloth of tribal tradition that has made survival possible in the face of colonialism but that has also bound women and men to pointlessly limited roles. Ete Kamba is too much 'man' to discuss his feelings of jealousy with Nko so instead berates her for not being the traditional virgin. By retreating he loses the opportunity to acknowledge his sincerity and receive insight or support from Nko who experiences some of the same conflicts. It is only when faced with the new woman lecturer that Ete Kamba must concede that he does not know everything. She too is an African woman but her accomplishments are known world wide. Her insistence that Ete Kamba confront the illogic of his choices, on paper, makes the independence Nko seeks less threatening.

A most appealing aspect of Emecheta's storytelling voice is her refusal to look scornfully upon these very real problems in modern African society. Each character represents not some polarized aspect of community prejudice, but an individual that the author knows and loves. It is Emecheta's crystal clear insight into the emotional underpinnings of cultural traditions and her abiding empathy for those caught in wrenching transitions that make *Double Yoke* an enduring love story.

Marie Linton Umeh (essay date 1986)

SOURCE: "Reintegration With the Lost Self: A Study of Buchi Emecheta's *Double Yoke*," in *Ngambika: Studies of Women in African Literature,* edited by Carole Boyce Davies and Anne Adams Graves, Africa World Press, 1986, pp. 173-80.

[*In the following essay, Umeh discusses Emecheta's social concerns and the presentation of female liberation and sex roles in* Double Yoke. *"Emecheta again campaigns against female subjugation and champions her case for female emancipation," writes Umeh.*]

Double Yoke is a love story told in the blues mode. The story laments a loss; yet it sings a love song. Its theme of the perilous journey of love, is a major preoccupation in author Buchi Emecheta's dramatic work. On an equally fundamental level, *Double Yoke* describes the tragic limitations of Nigerian women in pursuit of academic excellence and the anxiety of assimilation. Similar to her earlier novels, *Double Yoke* assesses the predicament of women in Africa. By describing the sexual and cultural politics in Nigerian society, Emecheta again campaigns against female subjugation and champions her case for female emancipation. Nko, the author's intellectually oriented heroine, provides some insight into the psyche of modern African women who are encumbered by traditional African misconceptions attached to the university-educated female.

Firstly, *Double Yoke* is a love story but with tragic implications. Buchi Emecheta is at her best in describing the anxiety lovers often experience because of mutual distrust at one time or another and the inability to reconcile their difficulties. According to the author, love, if betrayed, is directly responsible for the misery that afflicts the human soul. The tale of the terrifying journey of the possibilities and failures of love is then at the dramatic center of *Double Yoke*.

This theme of romantic conflict is not entirely new in African literature. The principle characters in Chinua Achebe's *No Longer At Ease*, Chukwuemeka Ike's *Toads For Supper*, Okot p'Bitek's *Song of Lawino*, and Flora Nwapa's *One Is Enough*, similarly narrate their personal traumas over lost loves. Diverging from her theme that Igbo women are enslaved to Igbo traditions which subjugate them to certain customs, Emecheta extends her metaphor by stating that Nigerian men are similarly enslaved. Ete Kamba, a central character in the story, is described as a traditional African man who is sorely disappointed when he falls in love with Nko, a modern African girl. Because Nko gives herself to Ete Kamba who has just gained admission into the university she is faced with untold hardships. Ete Kamba's love for Nko turns to distrust. He begins to question her virginity. This develops into a kind of neurosis, forcing him to lose sleep and cease concentration on his studies. He tells Nko, "You are not a virgin are you? Were you a virgin? There was not a drop of blood. You are a prostitute, a whore and you keep put-

ting on this air of innocence as if you were something else." Their problems are magnified when Ete Kamba consults a spiritual advisor, the Reverend Professor Ikot, who dissuades him from the love affair with ulterior motives:

> Nko is from my part. She is a true Efik from Duke Town, and women from our part have always brought great honour to their families. She will be in this university in a year or two. So what do you want a graduate wife for? Why don't you get a trained teacher or a nurse or something. Let us pray my boy, so that God will give you the wisdom to learn to sew your coat according to your measurement.

It is not long before Ikot succeeds in seducing and impregnating Nko. Ete Kamba, unnerved by Nko's air of independence and self-assertiveness, had set the stage for this fall. He therefore expresses his grief and the pain he feels about what has happened to him to Miss Bulewao, a character in the novel apparently speaking the mind of author Emecheta.

The significant tragic implication here is that Ete Kamba is not the modern African man. Despite his pursuit of western ideals, i.e., a university education and a university-educated wife, his reliance on traditional African mores stands out. His quest for a humble, chaste wife signifies one of Nigerian society's myopic perceptions of the making of the perfect African woman. Emecheta's dominant realization of women is that of a being limited by the dictates of men in a patriarchal society. Nko, with a feminist orientation, probes the root of things, questions where she is going and attempts to control her fate. Ete Kamba cannot cope with Nko's heightened sensibilities. He is unable to love and live with Nko on a plane of equality and mutual respect. Herein lies the tragedy. Although Ete Kamba wants a beautiful, educated and sophisticated wife to grace his home, his ideal seems to be the quiet, submissive, innocent female who looks after the children and the house, cooks, earns money and puts his interests before her own. For the African woman, the implications are more devastating. The African woman more so than the African man, is caught in a bind. In order to be liberated and fulfilled as a woman she must renounce her African identity because of the inherent sexism of many traditional African societies. Or, if she wishes to cherish and affirm her 'Africanness' she must renounce her claims to feminine independence and self-determination. Either way she stands to lose; either way she finds herself diminished, impoverished. It is Emecheta's growing awareness of the futility of attempting to resolve this dilemma that accounts for the growing bitterness that engulfs Nko. Emecheta, a sensitive artist and student of society, distinguishes between the idealization of womanhood and the realities of a woman's place in the African community. Ete Kamba's ambivalence towards Nko mirrors African society's unconscious hypocrisy towards women. It never occurs to Ete Kamba that it was Nko's innocence and purity of spirit that attracted her to him. It never occurs to him that he practically raped Nko the night she lost her virginity to him and that any resistance against his desperate advances would have been futile. He deflowers Nko, only to turn around and search for another virgin queen: someone he feels he can respect, someone his children can call mother. Ete Kamba's double standards are simply co-existent realities in his environment. The conflicting standards in Ete Kamba's perception of women is shared by his roommates. Their collective image of females is an idealized rather than a realistic portrait of the African woman's situation. The African man's perception of the educated African woman often ignores some of the realities of her sex.

Emecheta in another episode, illustrates how innocent young females are often turned into prostitutes at places one would least expect: academic institutions. When approached by the Reverend Professor Ikot, Nko retorts:

> Most girls here come to read for their degrees. If they become what you think, which is 'prostitutes Nigerian style', it is because people like you made them so. But with me sir, you are not going to be let off lightly. My reward is a good degree. I did not believe in bottom power until today sir.

One then asks, why does Nko submit to Reverend Ikot's advances? Why does she stray away from those goals she so clearly defined for herself? What is peculiar in all of Emecheta's novels up to the present time is a consistent female view that sometimes mars her art by its emphasis on the all-suffering, victimized female. However, author Emecheta generally attains a balance in that she looks at women not in the narrow advocacy of feminine rights but in a wider context of a concern for the female and by implication the species they represent. In describing some of the injustices that have been transcended, she captures the quintessential core of female discrimination in a male-dominated society as it has remained among the Nigerian ethnic groups and most other patriarchal social organizations. The answer also lies here. Nko is about to fully participate in Nigerian elitist society to a level much greater than most women. Perhaps the thought of this participation places too great a psychological strain on her. She lives with the fear of disappointing her parents and community by not succeeding in earning a good degree and helping her parents to train her younger sisters and brothers. She is obsessed with succeeding. It can also be said that she has internalized a narrow and limiting role pattern which casts her as a woman into subservient behaviour. Nko's inconsistent behaviour stems from her being brought up both formally and informally to believe that this is a man's world and that she is merely a woman, a second-class citizen. Feelings of anxiety about a degree, indoctrination into acceptable female roles and Ete Kamba's ambivalent and troubled feelings towards her, pressure Nko into surrendering herself to Reverend Professor Ikot. One needs courageous determination and encouragement to stir oneself out of being programmed into passivity and psychological servitude. A related problem is the questioning and disavowal of a woman's genuine, individual merit. It is almost a common assumption that a woman's merit resides in her sexuality. This of course is a

threat to the concept of female merit in institutions of higher learning. Thus Nko's reliance on stereotyped female wiles at this point is out of character. Additionally, it conflicts with Nko's inclination towards feminism, vividly portrayed in earlier parts of the novel in her struggles for equality and self-respect with Ete Kamba.

This idea which Emecheta explores introduces the elements of women's liberation and the correct role for women in Africa. The right path for them is not clear as Mrs. Nwaizu, a character in the novel, puts it: "We are still a long way from that yet. Here feminism means everything the society says is bad in women. Independence, outspokenness, immorality, all the ills you can think of. . . ." The feminine protest in this novel is not as subtle as in Flora Nwapa's *Idu* and *Efuru* or Efua Sutherland's *Edufa*. Nko vehemently protests against female victimization which brings her psychological strains. Similarly, university women today in Nigeria find themselves at the crossroads of losing their identity in male-female relationships (marriage) or attaining self realization by earning a degree thus forfeiting family life. In any event, in the novel the basic illustration is that Emecheta attacks certain masculine preserves such as having children out of wedlock and expectations of humility in women especially in the traditional sense. Miss Bulewao asks Ete Kamba, "Are you strong enough to be a modern African man? Nko is already a modern African lady, but you are still lagging . . . oh so far, far behind." Nko's characterization of a modern African lady though is not totally impressive. Moral laxity need not be equated with the New African woman. Ironically, Emecheta in her plot does not promote female liberation in Africa. Instead, she strengthens the belief of conservative Nigerians who fear that female education leads women to all sorts of corruption.

This leads us to another issue raised in *Double Yoke*, namely, the limitations of females in pursuit of self-realization in Nigerian society. This subjugation of women consistently emerges as one explores Nigerian society's history of raising women to perform the narrow, unidimensional, traditional role of wife/mother, while at the same time encouraging the male to expand and explore his capabilities to the fullest. Hence, society's division of sex roles limits woman's human capacity for the pursuit of self-realization thus destroying any attempt at fulfillment outside the family. In *Double Yoke* Emecheta unmasks areas of human experience so far subsumed under the myth of the decorous stable institution of marriage as witnessed in the social organization of Okonkwo's household in *Things Fall Apart* and Ezeulu's most equitable household in *Arrow of God*. Through Emecheta's characters we learn that this norm, prescribed by traditional African society is in fact abnormal. In *Double Yoke*, the female psyche emerges as an important quarry for concern. From multiple female voices such as Nko's, Mrs. Nwaizu's, Miss Bulewao, and Nko's roommates, emerge pertinent questions that put the nature of the female's well being at the heart of traditional African social organization.

Emecheta then surpasses Flora Nwapa, another Igbo writer, with her consistent unbiased exploration of the oppressed female psyche, although Flora Nwapa in *One Is Enough* is more decidedly feminist. Emecheta points out artistically, as have other feminist writers such as Simone de Beauvoir and Germaine Greer, that the very structure of patriarchal social organizations creates a suppressed individual by making an existential being an object for male subjectivity. Author Emecheta is not in a class of her own. She shows, like Kate Millet, that patriarchy is a power structured relationship that in most cases exploits women through a system of assigned and devalued roles. Through her characters she challenges some of the assumptions of traditional Igbo society which frustrate the gifted woman from the realization of herself as an entity. Through her heroine we realize with Catherine Mackinnon that gender is a learned quality not essentially a biological fact.

A sub-theme in *Double Yoke* is the exploration of the dilemma of men and women positioned between modernization and traditionalism in this instance on university campuses in Nigeria. Young adults become disoriented by conflicting standards of morality and the role of men and women in a changing society. Ete Kamba and Nko quarrel about whether or not the latter should attend the Reverend Elder Ikot's Revivalist meeting. They are trapped by conflicting standards in religious obligations and patriotism. Emecheta writes:

> How he [Ete Kamba] wished his girlfriend had been just a simple village girl to whom he could simply say, 'you must not go to the Revivalist meetings again, because I don't trust the head of the movement.' He could never say a thing like that to Nko. She would like to know all the reasons behind his orders.

At another time Ete Kamba demands Nko confess whether or not she is a virgin. He is trapped by conflicting standards in morality. What kind of woman makes the 'ideal wife'? One of his roommates rationalizes: 'Give me a fourteen-year-old village girl with uncomplicated background any time.'

Apart from Ete Kamba's inability to throw off the precepts of traditional African society which give certain prerogatives to men and deny them to women, author Emecheta points out that today's modern female is also torn between two worlds and unable to function properly in either. Nko is confused about the actual role the educated female should play in Nigerian society. The title of the book, *Double Yoke*, then is symbolic. According to the author, because educated Nigerian women are expected to play both the role of the submissive, gentle, docile female and the modern, sophisticated individual, there is confusion about which values to adopt: those of traditional African society or those of the west. Both African men and women are therefore in bondage. Living in two different cultures brings too much tension. Hence, they must live with a 'double yoke' for daring to walk where angels fear to tread.

There is satire too in *Double Yoke*. As well as the clash between the old and the new, there is a clash between the genuine and the false. In the character of Reverend Professor Ikot, pretentious and immoral university professors in Nigeria are attacked. Ikot, like the true trickster figure is shrewd, cunning and loquacious. Posing as a religious leader and educator, he dupes others but is rarely duped himself. His strong archetypal appeal, ability to outwit others and articulate his ideas enable him to exercise power and control over people. Even when caught in the act, he exploits the situation and emerges a winner. Note how he handles his confrontation with Ete Kamba in one of the most dramatic scenes in the book. Playing on the intelligence of his people, he fabricates a story knowing full well what the policemen want to hear. Emecheta, pointing to the exploitation of students on university campuses and the abuse of Christian teachings, protests against the corrupt, opportunistic nature of contemporary Nigerians. Rather than working towards the acquisition of souls or imparting knowledge to students, Ikot preoccupies himself with "getting a piece of the cake." Almost risking his chances of being the next Vice-Chancellor at Unical, he shamelessly destroys the lives of both Nko and Ete Kamba.

Finally, Ete Kamba exemplifies primacy of the group ethic over individual self-interests, which is so embedded in traditional African society, by sympathizing with Nko upon hearing of her father's death. Ete Kamba begins to realize that despite their inexperience they have to resolve their problems for no other reason than because they love each other. Ete Kamba and Nko choose to grow from their blunders and bear their double burden together. Ete Kamba's deep feeling of affection for Nko, despite a certain myopia which blinds him to manifest ambiguities within himself, helps him to understand that no one knows very much about the life of another. This ignorance becomes vivid, if you love another.

This ending is not altogether convincing even in these modern times. It then becomes obvious that author Emecheta is ascribing her personal modes of thought even though they may be way ahead of her audience. Most of us are still very conservative. In the fusing of the old and the new traditional African society's intolerance of one's right to choose one's destiny rather than consider the common good seems to be strengthened. In spite of this, *Double Yoke* is quite entertaining while it explores several political and social issues common in African literature. Emecheta's simplicity of style covers her exploration of these important issues in strikingly new and provocative twists.

Nancy Topping Bazin (essay date March-April 1986)

SOURCE: "Feminist Perspectives in African Fiction: Bessie Head and Buchi Emecheta," in *Black Scholar*, Vol. 17, No. 2, March-April, 1986, pp. 34-40.

[*In the following excerpt, Bazin provides an overview of feminist themes in the fiction of Emecheta and Bessie Head.*]

Bessie Head, born in 1937 in South Africa, has probably received more acclaim than any other black African woman novelist writing in English. Buchi Emecheta, born in 1944 in Nigeria, is rivaled only by Flora Nwapa, another Nigerian, for second place. Other black African women have published novels of distinction in either English or French. However, except for Lloyd W. Brown's *Women Writers in Black Africa* and a few articles, this growing body of literature has received a minimal amount of attention from critics. As Lloyd W. Brown has said, "Western male Africanists have contributed heavily to an old boy network of African studies in which the African woman simply does not exist as a serious or significant writer." The books and journals on African literature have accorded little or usually no space to women writers.

Leading African women writers' descriptions of the female experience are quite different from those that have emerged from works by most of their male colleagues. This is one reason that it is important to read their works, for many myths have circulated about black African women, even in feminist circles. One of the primary myths is that they have other priorities, such as economic development; therefore, sexual equality is not a topic they wish to discuss.

Tales of the wealthy market women in West Africa have led many to say that African women are already liberated. Cultural relativists also promote the myth that the African woman's situation is so different that one cannot and should not presume to judge what in it is unjust. Another myth erroneously attributes the African woman's problems only to colonialism and not at all to "indigenous mores." All of these myths are negated by the novels of the two leading African female novelists, Bessie Head and Buchi Emecheta. . . .

Their works reveal a great deal about the lives of African women and about the development of feminist perspectives. The first perspective evolves from personal experience. It requires personal growth on the part of the individual to extract herself from an oppressive environment. Personal growth leads into a second perspective that is social or communal. It demands an analysis of the causes of oppression within the social mores and the patriarchal power structure.

This perspective enables the woman to see that all women share problems such as "dependency, secondary existence, domestic labor, sexual exploitation, and the structuring of their role in procreation into a total definition of their existence." The third perspective allows women to see the similarities between the experience of women and that of other oppressed groups in all cultures, throughout history. In this framework, domination and oppression of all kinds are rejected. Finally, in the fourth perspective, problems of women are seen in a philosophical and moral dimension; principles of justice and equality become the basis for a new world view.

In the works of Buchi Emecheta, the feminist perspectives are primarily of the first two types— personal and social.

There are some insights into the third perspective where similarities are found between women's oppression and other forms of prejudice and exploitation. . . .

The chronological development of Emecheta's skill as a novelist suggests she is moving towards a vision that includes greater complexity and subtlety. Someday she may attain the philosophical or spiritual dimension present in the novels of Bessie Head.

This paper examines the novels of Bessie Head and Buchi Emecheta to determine what the nature of the black African women's experience is and how this experience can be analyzed in increasing depth and breadth by progressing through the four feminist perspectives—personal, social, multicultural, and spiritual/philosophical.

Both Buchi Emecheta and Bessie Head have recorded in their literary works the personal experiences that were the foundation of their feminist outlook. Buchi Emecheta clarified in an interview that the experiences of Adah in her second novel *Second-Class Citizen* were in fact, her own. Adah's parents were so bitterly disappointed when she was born, because her father "did not want a girl for his first child," that they did not even bother to record her birth.

Adah felt the pressures of son preference again when her daughter was born: "Everyone looked at her with an 'is that all?' look. . . . It was nine good months wasted. She paid for it though, by having [her son] Vicky soon afterwards." Emecheta's novels echo over and over again the difficulty she had in getting to stay in school as a child. Educating a girl who would just be turned over to her husband's family was viewed as a waste of scarce resources.

For example, in *Second-Class Citizen*, in order to get money for the "entrance examination fee," Adah had to pretend to lose the money she was given to buy meat. For "losing" it, she was beaten one hundred and three strokes. The beating made her happy because it enabled her to feel that she "had earned the two shillings." Ultimately, Adah was allowed to stay in school only because it would bring a bigger bride price for her.

Then, when Adah's father died, her "Ma was inherited by Pa's brother", as was the custom. In return for supporting her, the daughter, a relative would have her as a servant and eventuality receive her bride price. She finally married just to get away from home so she could have a place to study. The price Adah paid for this was a series of babies at an early age, and a husband who, after she followed him to London, exploited her ability to earn money by refusing to work at all to keep the family.

Yet he made the rules in the household that she was to obey, abused her physically, and refused to allow her to use any birth control. Adah's marriage, like Buchi Emecheta's, finally broke up because of her husband's reaction to her writing her first novel. Her husband refused to read it or to take her desire to write seriously, and he actually burned her completed manuscript. He insisted that "she would never be a writer because she was black and because she was a woman." In a September 1981 interview, Emecheta said people find it hard to believe that she has not exaggerated the truth in this autobiographical novel. The grimness of what is described does indeed make it painful to read. . . .

These personal experiences breed rebellious female protagonists in the fiction of both women. But the female protagonist's struggle often leads to a victory that is little more than just the courage to survive. This is so in Head's *A Question of Power* and in Emecheta's three novels *In the Ditch*, *Second-Class Citizen*, and *The Joys of Motherhood*. Sometimes the strong female protagonist ultimately succumbs to male power as in Head's *Maru* or in Emecheta's *The Slave Girl* or *The Bride Price*.

In the process of personal growth, the protagonists in the novels must acquire the feminist perspective that makes connections between a woman's personal experience and those shared by women as a group. This allows the protagonists to name the social and structural causes of their suffering. These causes are embedded in traditions often viewed as sacred or simply unchangeable. The protagonists in the novels of Head and Emecheta confront and only sometimes outwit the traditions that oppress them.

In the world described by Emecheta a girl may fear to announce her first menstrual period, because it means her parents will force her to marry. In this world, too, a woman is told that she is unclean when she is menstruating, thus restricting where she can go. She is likewise taught that an unpaid bride price will make her die in childbirth, or it will cause the marriage to fail or the children of that marriage to die. She also has to accept that when a father dies, the family ceases to exist.

In the novels of both Emecheta and Head a woman must accept the double standard of sexual freedom; it permits polygamy and infidelity for both Christian and non-Christian men but only monogamy for women. These books reveal the extent to which the African woman's oppression is engrained in the African mores.

FEMALE COMPLICITY

Both novelists demonstrate female complicity in their own victimization. Emecheta's *The Slave Girl* draws a parallel between Ojebeta's being bought as a wife and her having been bought as a slave years before. Indeed in her state of wifehood, she is worse off, but ironically she fails to see this. Even the rebellious women in these novels sometimes fail to recognize the extent to which they have been subjected to what Kate Millett calls "interior colonization."

Because of their patriarchal socialization, mostly by their own mothers, they too see life from a male perspective and often accept the value system and rules which follow from that. The novelists themselves demonstrate some blind spots that further illustrate that point. . . . Both Head and Emecheta frequently reveal through their fiction a longing for a strong, stable man who will save and protect them.

The best depiction of how the patriarchal system functions is in Emecheta's powerful novel The *The Joys of Motherhood*. Emecheta explores the evils not of motherhood but of what Adrienne Rich calls "the institution of motherhood"—that is, the way in which a woman's role as mother is used to render her an inferior, second-class citizen.

The Joys of Motherhood is about the life of Nnu Ego who marries but is sent home in disgrace because she fails to bear a child quickly enough. She then is sent to the city by her father to marry a man she has never seen. She is horrified when she meets this second husband because she finds him ugly, but she sees no alternative to staying with him. Poverty and repeated pregnancies wear her down; the pressure to bear male children forces her to bear child after child since the girls she has do not count.

She is particularly shamed when she bears female twins. The impact of son preference upon both mothers and daughters is clearly shown in this novel. The awareness of Emecheta's protagonist increases until she is able to make this statement:

> The men make it look as if we must aspire for children or die. That's why when I lost my first son I wanted to die, because I failed to live up to the standard expected of me by the males in my life, my father and my husband—and now I have to include my sons. But who made the law that we should not hope in our daughters? We women subscribe to that law more than anyone. Until we change all this, it is still a man's world, which women will always help to build.

The consequences of rapid urbanization, conflicts between old and new concepts of justice, and new educational opportunities abroad for African males are also revealed in the book. Despite rapid changes, however, the patriarchal attitudes prevail. As the aging mother Nnu Ego, impoverished and exhausted, returns to her village at the end of the book, with her two sons abroad and her husband in prison for attacking a potential son-in-law who was from the "wrong" tribe, she has to listen to a taxi driver complain: "'This life is very unfair to us men. We do all the work, you women take all the glory. You even live longer to reap the rewards. A son in America? You must be very rich, and I'm sure your husband is dead long ago.'" Like so many other women, Nnu Ego bears the burden of such attitudes silently.

> She did not think it worth her while to reply to this driver, who preferred to live in his world of dreams rather than face reality. What a shock he would have if she told him that her husband was in prison, or that the so-called son in America had never written to her directly, to say nothing of sending her money.

Only her daughters, not her sons, support her in her old age, so the primary reason for preferring sons that led her to bear so many children brought no benefit to her.

Despite her awakening, Nnu Ego gains status and decision-making power only after death when she is honored with a shrine for her fertility. The young women in her village pray to her spirit when they are unable to get pregnant or bear sons. But the spirit of Nnu Ego chooses not to grant the wishes of these women to bear many, especially male, children, for she has known personally the slave-like state created by this self-defeating practice.

The third feminist perspective draws parallels between the ego-mania that causes the domination of women and that inherent in Nazi anti-semitism, Ku Klux Klan behavior, Black Power fist raising in the United States, slavery within Africa, the treatment of the African male as Kaffir, and black Africans treatment of "Coloureds" and especially the Masarwa tribe (or Bushmen) in Botswana. . . .

Emecheta is aware of her dual burden of being black and female and how in England the African is made to suffer for both but one does not detect in her books the same desire to see domination and oppression more wholistically. Perhaps because she is younger and more instilled with middle-class values, she is not as far along on her journey from the personal on through the social and the multicultural to the spiritual/philosophical. Yet the sense of good and evil forces doing battle, intertwined within people and social conventions, does inform, to some extent, two of her more recent books *The Bride Price* (1976) and *The Slave Girl* (1977). . . .

Buchi Emecheta and Bessie Head speak for millions of black African women through their novels, for they describe what it is like to be female in patriarchal African cultures. Their feminist perspectives are solidly founded in their own personal lives. However, they grew to understand how son preference, bride price, polygamy, menstrual taboos, nine-month mourning periods for windows, male inheritance rights, wife beating, early marriages, early and unlimited pregnancies, arranged marriages, and male dominance in the home functioned to keep women powerless.

MAKING CONNECTIONS

Their analyses of the patriarchal system and attitudes led them to see connections among all forms of oppression. Buchi Emecheta saw parallels between sexual and racial discrimination and parallels between buying wives and buying slaves. . . .

Buchi Emecheta's novels remain more on the level of individual experience and social custom with less attention to spiritual questions and implications. Bessie Head explores good and evil within the soul and within society, and she emphasizes the philosophical framework that determines our social attitudes and behavior.

Bessie Head's is the larger vision and she perhaps the greater artist because she attempts more. However, Buchi Emecheta's later novels deal with serious themes within the controlled structure of tales someone might tell around a fire in an African village. These works not only have their aesthetic appeal but they are also rich in meaning. Emecheta is younger than Bessie Head and already her output is greater. Perhaps she is not as far along on her feminist journey from the personal to the philosophical, but she is certainly someone to watch. She is well on her way.

Buchi Emecheta (essay date 1988)

SOURCE: "Feminism with a Small 'f'!," in *Criticism and Ideology: Second African Writers' Conference,* edited by Kirsten Holst Petersen, Scandinavian Institute of African Studies, 1988, pp. 173-85.

[*In the following essay, Emecheta discusses her artistic concerns and feminist perspective. As Emecheta illustrates, African feminism differs significantly from Western feminism due to the distinct cultural values and sexual identity of African women.*]

I am just an ordinary writer, an ordinary writer who has to write, because if I didn't write I think I would have to be put in an asylum. Some people have to communicate, and I happen to be one of them. I have tried several times to take university appointments and work as a critic, but each time I have packed up and left without giving notice. I found that I could not bring myself to criticize other people's work. When my husband burned my first book, I said to him 'If you can burn my book, you can just as well burn my child, because my books are like my children, and I cannot criticize my children'. When I had my babies they were very, very ugly; they had big heads, like their father and their bodies looked like mine. But if anybody looked into the pram and said 'What an ugly baby', I would never talk to that person again. And I know that I am not the only writer who finds it hard to accept criticism. One critic asked me 'You have so much anger in you, how can you bear it?' 'Well', I said, 'I can't bear it, so I have to let it out on paper'. I started writing in 1972, and a few weeks ago I handed in my sixteenth novel. In order to make you understand how I work I will tell you about my background.

I was born in Lagos, Nigeria, and was raised partly there and partly in my village, Ibuza, and this explains my wish to tell stories when I was a child. My parents both came from Ibuza and moved to Lagos in search of work. As both of them were partly educated they embraced the C.M.S (Church Missionary Society) way of life. But being of the old Ibo kingdom they made sure that my brother and myself never lost sight of home, of life in Ibuza.

We worked at home during the rains, to help on the farm and to learn our ways. If I lived in Lagos I could start to have loose morals and speak Yoruba all the time. So my parents wanted me to learn the rigorous Ibo life. You can see that even in Nigeria we still discriminate against each other.

It was at home that I came across real story tellers. I had seen some Yoruba ones telling their stories and songs and beating their drums whilst we children followed them— Pied Piper like— from street to street. But the Ibo story teller was different. She was always one's mother. My Big Mother was my aunt. A child belonged to many mothers. Not just one's biological one. We would sit for hours at her feet mesmerized by her trance like voice. Through such stories she could tell the heroic deeds of her ancestors, all our mores and all our customs. She used to tell them in such a way, in such a sing-song way that until I was about fourteen I used to think that these women were inspired by some spirits. It was a result of those visits to Ibuza, coupled with the enjoyment and information those stories used to give us, that I determined when grew older that I was going to be a story teller, like my Big Mother.

I learned to my dismay at school in Lagos that if I wanted to tell stories to people from many places I would have to use a language that was not my first—neither was it my second, or third, but my fourth language. This made my stories lose a great deal of their colour, but I learned to get by. My English must have been very bad because when I first told my English teacher, who came from the Lake District, and who was crazy about Wordsworth that I was going to write like her favourite poet, she ordered me to go to the school chapel and pray for forgiveness, because she said: 'Pride goeth before a fall'. I did not go to the chapel to pray because even then I knew that God would have much more important things to do than to listen to my dreams. Dreams which for me, coming both from the exotic so-called Ibo bush culture and the historic Yoruba one, were not unattainable.

Some of these early missionaries did not really penetrate the African mind. That incident confirmed what I had always suspected as a child, that the art of communication, be it in pictures, in music, writing or in oral folklore is vital to the human.

I never learn from my experiences. My first attempt to write a book, called **The Bride Price** was resented by my husband. He too, like my English teacher, told me that 'Pride goeth before a fall'. I left him and I found myself at twenty-two, husbandless with five young children. I thought I would wait to be as old as Big Mother with a string of degrees before writing. But I had to earn my living and the only thing I could do was write. Whilst looking after my fast-growing family I decided to read for a degree that would help me master the English language and help me write about my society for the rest of the world. I chose sociology and continued writing. I had enough rejection slips to paper a room. But in 1972 the *New Statesman* started serializing my work and those recollections later appeared as my first book, **In the Ditch**.

I have been writing ever since, and I am now living entirely on my writing. Those babies of mine are now beginning to leave home. One of them has started to write as well, so perhaps writing runs in the family. I am not doing anything particularly clever. I am simply doing what my Big Mother was doing for free about thirty years ago. The only difference is that she told her stories in the moonlight, while I have to bang away at a typewriter I picked up from Woolworths in London. I am not good at reading, and sometimes when I write I can't even read my writing. Writing is a very lonely profession. One is there at one's desk, thinking of ideas and reasoning them out and putting them into works of fiction or stories, and if one is not careful, one will start living the life of the characters in the book. Conferences like this one save some of us from becoming strange.

Writers are often asked 'Who are you writing for?'. How am I supposed to know who is going to pick up my works from the library shelf? I wonder sometimes if people ask painters, when they are doing their paintings, who they are painting them for. The painter can control the picture while he is still painting it, but can we expect him to foretell who is going to love looking at it? A book is akin to a child on his mother's back. The mother knows she is carrying a baby on her back but the child can use its hands to lift anything that passes by, without the mother knowing. I find this question sometimes rather patronizing. In fact it is sometimes healthier not to think of one's readers at all. Writers are communicators. We chronicle everyday happenings, weave them into novels, poetry, documentary fiction, articles etc. The writer has the freedom to control, to imagine and to chronicle. I write for everybody.

The writer also has a crucial control over the subject s/he writes about. For myself, I don't deal with great ideological issues. I write about the little happenings of everyday life. Being a woman, and African born, I see things through an African woman's eyes. I chronicle the little happenings in the lives of the African women I know. I did not know that by doing so I was going to be called a feminist. But if I am now a feminist then I am an African feminist with a small f. In my books I write about families because I still believe in families. I write about women who try very hard to hold their family together until it becomes absolutely impossible. I have no sympathy for a woman who deserts her children, neither do I have sympathy for a woman who insists on staying in a marriage with a brute of a man, simply to be respectable. I want very much to further the education of women in Africa, because I know that education really helps the women. It helps them to read and it helps them to rear a generation. It is true that if one educates a woman, one educates a community, whereas if one educates a man, one educates a man. I do occasionally write about wars and the nuclear holocaust but again in such books I turn to write about the life and experiences of women living under such conditions.

Maybe all this makes me an ordinary writer. But that is what I want to be. An ordinary writer. I will read to you two pieces from my own observations. The style is simple but that is my way. I am a simple and unsophisticated person and cultural people really make me nervous. First I want to read a short piece about polygamy. People think that polygamy is oppression, and it is in certain cases. But I realize, now that I have visited Nigeria often, that some women now make polygamy work for them. What I am about to relate happened only a few weeks ago. I was in my bedroom in Ibuza listening to a conversation. It was cool and damp and I was debating whether to get up from my bed or not. I knew it was about six in the morning. I did not have to look at the clock. I just knew because I could hear the songs of the morning, children on their way to fetch water, a cock crowing here and there. Then the penetrating voice of Nwango, the senior wife of Obike came into my thoughts. 'Go away you stinking beast. Why will you not let me sleep? I have a full day ahead of me and you come harassing me so early in the morning. You are shameless. You don't even care that the children sleep next-door. You beast. Why don't you go to your new wife.' Now the man: 'All I have from you is your loud mouth. You are never around to cook for me, and when I come to your bed, you send me away. What did I pay the bride-price for?' The voice of Obike was slow and full of righteous anger. 'Go to your wife.' 'She is pregnant', said Obike. 'So what, get another woman. I need my energy for my farm and my trading, and today is the market-day', Nwango insisted. I was sorry to miss the end of the quarrel because my mother-in-law came in and told me not to mind them. 'They are always like that, these men. They are shameless. They think we women are here just to be their partners at night. He can marry another girl. But again which girl in her right senses will take him? He is too lazy to go regularly to his farm.' My mother-in-law should know. She had thirteen children. They lived in the capital, Lagos, and her husband did not have room to bring home another wife, so she had to do everything. If they had spent their life in the village it would have been different.

I know this is a situation which our Western sisters will find difficult to understand. Sex is important to us. But we do not make it the centre of our being, as women do here. In fact most of the Nigerian women who are promiscuous are so for economic reasons. The Yorubas have a saying that a woman must never allow a man to sleep with her if, at the end of the day she is going to be in debt. Few of our women go after sex *per se*. If they are with their husbands they feel they are giving something out of duty, love, or in order to have children. A young woman might dream of romantic love, but as soon as they start having children their loyalty is very much to them, and they will do everything in their power to make life easier for them. In the villages the woman will seek the company of her age-mates, her friends, and the women in the market, and for advice she goes either to her mother or to her mother-in-law. Another woman in the family will help share the housework, like Nwango cited earlier. The day her husband wanted her was an Eke day, a big market day. She had to be up early to be at the market. She had to contribute her twenty naira which is almost ten pounds, to the savings fund of the market women. That is the way we raise capital for our business without having to go to the bank, because most banks will not lend money to a woman. So she had

to contribute her twenty naira and later on in the evening, she had to put on her otuogu and she had to be at the Agbalani group, as they were going to dance at the second burial of the grandmother of one of their members. For that dance they had to tie the otuogu with the Akangwose style; all of which took them three years to save up for. They had to wear a navy-blue head-tie and carry a navy-blue Japanese fan and wear black flat shoes or slippers. None of these items was bought by their husbands. Nwango worked on her cassava farm four days of the week—we have a five-day week—and sold the garri made from the cassava on the fifth day, Eke market day. She gave twenty naira esusu of her profit to the collector who was one of the women in her group. It is from this esusu forced saving that she is sending her son to college, and she spends the rest exactly as she likes. At the funeral dance the group will give the bereaved lady a thousand naira (about five hundred pounds), from their fund to help out. And the dance will go on till very late. At about eight p.m. one will hear these women going home, singing their heads off. They drink anything from whisky, beer, gin, brandy, you name it, and no man dares tell them not to. Cooking for the husband, fiddle sticks! Get another woman to do it. Especially if the other woman is still a young seventeen- or eighteen-year old with her head full of romantic love. By the time she is twenty-five she will become wiser too. Nwango's husband is almost a stud. Not a nice word, but that is the way most village women feel.

Sex is part of life. It is not THE life. Listen to the Western feminists' claim about enjoying sex, they make me laugh. African feminism is free of the shackles of Western romantic illusions and tends to be much more pragmatic. We believe that we are here for many, many things, not just to cultivate ourselves, and make ourselves pretty for men. The beauty in sisterhood is when women reach the age of about forty. The women who cultivated sisters either through marriage or through the village age-group start reaping their reward. In England for example I belong to the war-babies. They call us 'the saltless babies'. That means we were born in Nigeria when they didn't have salt because of the war. So in our village we were called 'the Saltless Women'. There are about sixteen of my age-mates in London, and we have our own group here too. Last year a member of our group was in hospital and she said that other patients called her the Princess of Africa. On visiting days the nurses and doctors invariably shooed us away. She was there for three weeks, and the two days I went to visit her I had to wait over fifteen minutes before it came to my turn. I live in North London, a long way from her house, but those members who lived near her made sure she had visitors every night as well as her seven children. Her husband left her over three years ago to do some business in Nigeria, but we all know that he lives with another woman over there. Did our group member care? No. She is too busy to care. If he returns, good, if not, better still. She is training to be a hairdresser, now that all her children are at school. She is converting her large house into flats so that she and her older daughter can start a bed-and-breakfast business. And when she is ready she is going to come to our group and take an interest-free loan from our funds. If her husband had been around he would probably have been a help, just by being there, since he had no job anyway, but he could also be in the way of our member's self-realization. Looking after a man for sexual rewards does take a lot of time. I assure you.

In the West many women hurry to get married again after a divorce or a bereavement. Our women are slower. And many who have children don't even bother, because a new life opens for them. A new life among other women and friends. Women are very quarrelsome and jealous. We always make it up, especially after we have had a few brandies and consumed, I don't know how many chicken legs. This is because we realize that what we gain by forgiving one another is better than what we gain by being alone in order to avoid jealousy. In my book *Joys of Motherhood* I describe a family in which the women went on strike and refused to take the housekeeping money, because they knew that the husband was drinking the greater part of his income. I also describe a life of another woman who was so busy being a good mother and wife that she didn't cultivate her women friends. She died by the wayside, hungry and alone. In the same book I describe how jealous she was, when her husband brought home a new wife. Instead of going to sleep on the first night she stayed awake listening to the noise made by her husband and the new wife in love-making. She learned only a few days later that it would be better and to their mutual advantage, if she and the new wife became friends, rather than quarrel over their shared husband. They soon became so busy in their everyday life that sexuality was pushed into the background.

In many cases polygamy can be liberating to the woman, rather than inhibiting her, especially if she is educated. The husband has no reason for stopping her from attending international conferences like this one, from going back to University and updating her career or even getting another degree. Polygamy encourages her to value herself as a person and look outside her family for friends. It gives her freedom from having to worry about her husband most of the time and each time he comes to her, he has to be sure that he is in a good mood and that he is washed, and clean and ready for the wife, because the wife has now become so sophisticated herself that she has no time for a dirty, moody husband. And this in a strange way, makes them enjoy each other.

The small son of one of our group-members in London told his teacher that he had two Mummies. 'My Mummy number one is working. Mummy number two will come and collect me.' The teacher did not understand until she realized that his solicitor father had two wives, and the little child enjoys being loved and looked after by two women, his mother and the senior wife. What a good way to start one's life. In Ibuza it is the same. Once a woman starts making money she stops having children regularly.

This is because women who are lucky to find the work which they love and which they are good at derive the same kind of enjoyment from it as from sex. Many female writers, many English female writers I have spoken to claimed that they find their work, not only sexually satisfactory but sometimes masturbatory. I certainly find my work satisfying. Sex is part of our life—it shouldn't be THE life.

In this next section I will give you a quick overview of some issues concerning black women. In many parts of Africa only one's enemies will go out of their way to pray for a pregnant woman to have a girl-child. Most people want a man-child. The prayers will go: 'You will be safely delivered of a bouncing baby boy, a real man-child that we can and make jolly with whisky and beer.' The pregnant woman will not protest at this prayer because in her heart, she too would like to have a man-child, who will not be married away, but will stay in the family home and look after his mother when she becomes weak and old. In most African societies the birth of a son enhances a woman's authority in the family. Male children are very, very important. Yet, this girl-child that was not desired originally comes into her own at a very early age. From childhood she is conditioned into thinking that being the girl she must do all the housework, she must help her mother to cook, clean, fetch water and look after her younger brothers and sisters. If she moans or shows signs of not wanting to do any of this, she will be sharply reminded by her mother. 'But you are a girl! Going to be a woman.'

It is our work to bring the next generation into the world, nurture them until they are grown old enough to fly from the nest and then start their own life. It is hard. It could be boring and could sometimes in some places be a thankless job. But is it a mean job? I had my photograph taken once in my office where I do my writing. The photo-journalist was a staunch feminist, and she was so angry that my office was in my kitchen and a package of cereal was in the background. I was letting the woman's movement down by allowing such a photograph to be taken, she cried. But that was where I worked. Because it was warmer and more convenient for me to see my family while I put my typewriter to one side. I tried to tell her in vain that in my kitchen I felt I was doing more for the peace of the world than the nuclear scientist. In our kitchens we raise all Reagans, all Nkrumahs, all Jesuses. In our kitchens we cook for them, we send them away from home to be grown men and women, and in our kitchens they learn to love and to hate. What greater job is there? I asked. A mother with a family is an economist, a nurse, a painter, a diplomat and more. And we women do all that, and we form, we are told, over half of the world's population. And yet we are on the lowest rung. Men did not put us there, my sisters, I think sometimes we put ourselves there. How often do you hear colleagues say; 'Oh, I don't know anything I am only a housewife'?

There should be more choices for women, certainly women who wish to be like Geraldine Ferraro should be allowed to be so. We need more of her type, especially among the black women. We need more Golda Meirs, we need more Indira Gandhis, we even need more Margaret Thatchers. But those who wish to control and influence the future by giving birth and nurturing the young should not be looked down upon. It is not a degrading job. If I had my way, it would be the highest paid job in the world. We should train our people, both men and women to do housework. A few privileged African women are now breaking bonds. They live at home and work outside. Most of these women were lucky enough to come from families where the girls were allowed to go to school and to stay there long enough to acquire knowledge to equip them to live away from their families and to rub shoulders with men. Black women are succeeding in various fields along these lines.

This we must remember is not new to the black woman, because her kind has always worked. In the agrarian setting women do petty-trading. Usually, they have small children with them. They trade in anything from a few loaves of bread to a few packages of matches. The lucky ones have stalls or sheds. Others not so fortunate use the front of their house as their stall. Many Nigerian women live in the cities, collect their esusu profits and bank it when they think it is big enough. I have a great number of friends who have built up their families this way. This means that the others who were trained to do the lower-middle-class jobs of, for example, teaching have invariably given up their work in order to take up trading.

Being successful in whatever we undertake is not new to the women of Africa. The Aba riot is a case in point. This was a riot that spread from Owerri in Eastern Nigeria to Calabar among women who did not even speak the same language, and it included all the towns in the area to Onitsha by the river Niger and went further across the river to include women from the Asaba area. Although the white male chroniclers called it a riot, it was a real war. It was a marvel that women at that time were able to organize themselves; remember, there were no telephones, no letters, only bushtracks and dangerous rivers. The whole area was equivalent to the distance from London to Edinburgh. The actual war was organized with women from different groups wearing various headgears and all using their household utensils as weapons. The war, which took place in 1929 was in answer to British demands that women should pay taxes. The black women of that war were praised by all their menfolk. They received admiration not rebuke. And in desperation, the British administrators jailed all men whose wives took an active part in the war. They could not acknowledge that women, especially barbaric women, could organize themselves to achieve such a feat.

Working and achieving to great heights is nothing new to the woman of Africa, but there are still many obstacles in her way. Her family still prefers to educate the boy, while she stays at home to do the important jobs called 'women's duties'. And we accept the tag, knowing full well that the boy, however clever he is, would not be where he is today without the sacrifices made by his mother, his sweetheart, his wife or even his sister. The African woman has always been a woman who achieves. This does not necessarily mean that she becomes a successful international lawyer, a writer or a doctor, although African women in these professions are doing very well, and there are quite a few of us. But for the majority of women of Africa, real achievement—as I see it—is to make her immediate environment as happy as is possible under the circumstances, by tending the crops or giving comfort. But she still will have higher aspirations and achieve more when those cleverly structured artificial barriers are removed, when education is free and available to every child, male or female, when the male-dominated media does not give exposure to a black woman simply because she is a beautiful entertainer, thereby undermining our brain power, and when we ourselves have the confidence to value our contribution to the world. It is about time we start singing about our own heroic deeds.

Reginald McKnight (review date 29 April 1990)

SOURCE: "Lost in the Moder Kontry," in *New York Times Book Review*, April 29, 1990, p. 30.

[*In the following review, McKnight offers a favorable assessment of* The Family.]

"The writer with the tin ear," wrote John Gardener, in his book *On Becoming a Novelist*, who is good enough at other things, "may in the end write deeper, finer novels than the most eloquent verbal musicians." It was the writer's facility with those "other things"—the development of "character, action, setting" and ideas, which Gardner called "profluence"—that compelled the reader to turn the page.

There are, of course many novelists whose prose is both poetic and profluent: Margaret Atwood, Toni Morrison, Nathanael West. But some of the most highly regarded novelists (Balzac, Crane, Orwell), as Gardner suggested, are no poets at all.

Most readers, no doubt, would include the works of the Nigerian writer Buchi Emecheta in the latter category. The prose in her latest novel, The Family, like that of her earlier works (particularly *Double Yoke* and *The Slave Girl*) is generally vivid, plain and clear—the kind of prose that illuminates rather than buries the characters and settings it describes: "Winston was everything Gladys said he was, so why did she feel this eel of distrust coiled about [his] memory?" But there are times when the language is barely firm enough to carry images and ideas: "Gwendolen was not the cleverest of people. She could be slow, but she was not thick-skinned."

Nevertheless, occasional lapses such as this do not hinder our being moved and intrigued by the novel's principal character, Gwendolen Brillianton, a young girl from

Granville, Jamaica, whose mother and father leave her with her grandmother. Granny Naomi, to seek a better life for themselves in England, the "Moder Kontry." Very soon after their departure, a close family friend molests the 8-year-old Gwendolen. And because "she did not like Uncle Johnny troubling her at night, and she did not like to see Granny Naomi unhappy," Gwendolen flees to the home of her paternal grandmother, Elinor, who lives in Kingston. But before she is even fully reacquainted with her family in Kingston they rebuff her, intimating that because they are fair-skinned and Gwendolen dark, she does not belong. Thus far, less than one-tenth of the narrative has been traversed. Gwendolen will see and feel much, much more once her parents finally send for her.

In this rich, complex and fast-moving novel, one breathlessly follows Gwendolen from Granville to London in her search for love, family and a place "where she could be herself—happy, trusting Gwendolen again." And through this journey we see her suffer rape, incest, racism, teenage pregnancy and loneliness. She endures the indignities of illiteracy and remedial education, falls in love with a boy her mother describes as a "dirty white" and veers toward madness. We witness the social and economic dynamics that force both Gwendolen and her mother to "remain alive for others. . . . to look after members of their families, to boost the ego of the man in their lives, be the man a father, a husband, or even a son. And they were to nurture and act as agony aunts to their offspring. But to live for themselves was not to be."

In many ways Ms. Emecheta probably speaks from experience. Not only is she a novelist, a research fellow at the University of Calabar, Nigeria, and a member of Britain's Advisory Council to the Home Secretary on Race and Equality, but she is also a mother of five. She speaks from a vantage point that few of us know. Her London, for example, is a cold, gray, multicultural world, a world made up of Ibos, Anglos, Yorubas, Jamaicans—both fair and dark—Greeks, Indians, the educated, the undereducated, the dispossessed, the alienated. Ms. Emecheta's novel shows us—as do many other important works of African and African-American literature—that a large number of the problems that plague the African diaspora—rootlessness, "hue prejudice," self-hatred and perhaps even some of the sexual violence that nearly destroys Gwendolen— are the direct result of slavery and colonialism. But Buchi Emecheta is no ideologue; her characters do not utter or think words that would not come from them; they are not mere representatives of larger social movements but real, complex human beings, shaped by the vicissitudes of class, culture and sexual politics. She raise the right questions, but never harangues. She writes with subtlety, power and abundant compassion. The Family is a good book, and one not easily forgotten.

Adele S. Newson (review date Summer 1994)

SOURCE: A review of *Kehinde,* in *World Literature Today,* Vol. 68, No. 3, Summer, 1994, p. 867.

[*In the following review, Newson offers tempered praise for* Kehinde.]

Buchi Emecheta's latest novel, **Kehinde**, is a study of cultural traditions, adaptation, and transculturation, of how and when an adopted country becomes home. It is, in short, about choices of how to be in the world.

Kehinde Okolo is thirty-five years old, married with two children, and employed in a management position at Barclays Bank when the story opens. Her husband Albert is a forty-year-old shopkeeper who is intent on returning to Nigeria, where he hopes to be made a chief in his homeland. The couple have been living in England for some eighteen years and have managed to eke out a comfortable existence, but pressures from Albert's sisters in Nigeria and midlife pulls conspire to disrupt the current life of the couple.

Eventually the couple return to Nigeria. Albert and the two children precede Kehinde, who stays behind for more than a year in an effort to sell their house in London. When she arrives in Nigeria, she discovers that Albert has taken another wife, Rike, who has given birth to one child and is pregnant with a second. Although Kehinde is the senior wife who has lived abroad, she has little status or influence in her new life. In preparing for a journey to visit her children in boarding schools, Kehinde learns just how little status she has: "Kehinde made to sit in the front seat of the Jaguar, as she had done in London, daring Rike to challenge her right to sit next to Albert. Instead, Mama Kaduna's boisterous laughter halted her. . . . Kehinde squeezed into the back of the car with Rike, her baby and the maid." In addition to the humiliation of Albert's taking a second wife, Kehinde must defer to his sisters, who "take the place of honour" in his home.

Ultimately, Kehinde returns to England with a more informed perspective on the role of fond remembrances of home and on the reality of the choices in life open to African women at home and abroad. Along the way to self-awareness, she encounters many women, some of whom she judges, others of whom she cherishes, like her dead sister Taiwo, who is her twin. Significantly, Kehinde (the twin who follows behind) survives, although her mother and twin sister die. Kehinde's experiences in the womb can be read as the expression of sisterhood extending beyond familial ties.

> Together we fought against the skin that kept us captive. . . . We communicated with each other by touch and by sounds. Sounds which only we could understand. . . . Frustrated, we banged and shouted; and we kicked and cried in our limited space. Exhausted, I fell asleep. I felt even in sleep the cessation of the rhythmical movements I was accustomed to. I felt around me in the now warm thickening water for my sister, but she had become just a lump of lifeless flesh. I clung to her, because she had been the only living warmth that I knew. I called to her but there was no answer. I cried for her in my now lonely tomb. . . . As she dried, I had more space. I grew bigger. I survived. But I did

not eat my sister, as they said I did. There was only life enough for one of us.

In the acknowledgment Emecheta thanks her friends for the book's creation—with some she "spent hours debating about the so-called 'Black women's madness.'" By turns, the reader discovers that the black woman's madness arises from her acceptance of limited choices in life as to how she is to be in the world.

Kehinde's content is important as well as engaging. Its execution, however, is uneven. Emecheta is at her best when she testifies to female experience in Africa and abroad; she is most disappointing in managing the nuances of the larger narrative.

Mary E. Modupe Kolawole (essay date 1997)

SOURCE: "Metafiction, Autobiography, and Self-Inscription," in *Womanism and African Consciousness,* Africa World Press, 1997, pp. 167-79.

[*In the following excerpt, Kolawole discusses Emecheta's fictional use of autobiography in* Second-Class Citizen *to illustrate the reality of African women. "The intersection of personal problems, communal dilemmas, ethnicity, race, class, and gender problems," writes Kolawole, "is remarkably underscored in this novel."*]

SELF-INSCRIPTION AND THE INTERSECTION OF GENDER AND CULTURE

Metafiction has become popular with women writers because it highlights the struggles and the painful process of recreating oneself. The struggle to be a writer carries a special burden for the African woman who tries to negotiate a space in a hostile environment as she tries to tread on a male domain (modern literature has been a male domain for a long time). Nonetheless metafiction is a popular tool of women's self-expression. Gayle Greene explains this:

> It is a powerful tool of feminist critique, for, to draw attention to the structures of fiction is also to draw attention to the conventionality of the codes that govern human behaviour.

Metafiction as the device that draws attention to the process of fiction enables African writers to recreate the way certain values have been deployed to promote or delimit gender roles. Patricia Waugh observes that metafiction unveils "how the meanings and values of the world have been constructed and how, therefore, they can be challenged or changed." These writers are therefore not interested in Joycean self-effacement, nor are they keen on standing outside the work biting their fingernails. Disinterestedness is not a feature of the biographical works by these African writers.

Gendered literature is an aspect of the constant search for African aesthetics that fosters self-knowledge without indiscriminate separatism. To borrow Maya Angelou's words, "image-making is very important for every human being." It is even more so for African women writers who need to confront multiple levels of otherness . . . racial, cultural, regional, religious, third world, and post-colonial. Like other Black writers, to change her world is an imperative. Toni Morrison's view supports this:

> We are the subjects of our own narrative, witnesses to and participants in our own experience, and in no way coincidentally, in the experiences of those with whom we have come in contact. . . . And to read imaginative literature by and about us is to choose to examine centers of the self and to have the opportunity to compare these centers with the 'raceless' one with which we are all of us, most familiar.

The process of writing oneself is also the process of re-writing the collective self. So, the communal values that inform the unconscious also emerge in the literary production. This is true of the works of Buchi Emecheta. This writer, like Ama Ata Aidoo, has rejected the tag, 'feminist writer.' Yet, personal experience, which is at the center of her story, is a redemptive act. In Emecheta's novel *Second-Class Citizen*, dream and memory play important roles in the world of the heroines, both as vision and as hope. Emecheta's protagonist, Adah, is representative of the author's experience, personal and communal. Her birth at a time when a baby boy is expected is considered a personal, familial, and collective tragedy. It highlights the way traditional attitude entrenched into the society encourages gender differentiation.

> One clear demographic indicator of the relative value placed on males and females in a society is the extent to which parents show a marked preference for children of a particular sex.

This profound cultural world-view forms the foundation of the heroine's tragic life and experience:

> She was a girl who arrived when everyone was expecting and predicting a boy. So since she was such a disappointment to her parents, to her immediate family, to her tribe, nobody thought of recording her birth.

This story is one of the most profound depictions of gender bias in African societies in the fictional production of African women. Emecheta shows with a keen sense of familiarity how this often has a devastating effect in psychological and practical terms on the growing consciousness of young girls. Consequently, the heroine's life is predicated on this archetypal disadvantaged status cut out for women in the Igbo society that she grew up to know, a paradigm of the experience of girls in many other parts of Africa. Adah becomes disobedient, rebellious and despondent as the reality is presented to her, that although education is of a paramount importance among the Ibos, she is to be excluded from it because she happens to belong to the wrong gender: "School—the Ibos never played with that! They were realising that one's saviour from poverty and disease was education. Every Ibo family saw to it that their children attended school. Boys were usually given preference, though." This directly threatens Adah's dreams. She is presented as a determined ambitious girl whose consciousness is advanced for her age. One might even call her a genius, as we see later in the story. The family can not afford to send two children to school and their decision to send Boy to school as the wise solution to the problem elicits fundamental gender problems: "Even if she went to school, it was very doubtful whether it would be wise to let her stay long. A year or two would do, as long as she can write her name and count. Then she will learn to sew."

Adah refuses to be daunted and forces her agenda on the family blueprint by running off to school and forcing her parents to keep her there with the help of a neighbor who teaches in a nearby school, Mr. Cole. Adah's dream is aborted by her father's death, her mother's leviratic marriage to her late husband's brother, and the family's decision to send Adah to a maternal uncle to be the latter's servant. Subsequent decisions and the reasons motivating them are equally important in revealing the heroine's gender humiliation and degradation:

> It was decided that the money in the family, a hundred pounds or two, would be spent on Boy's education. So Boy was cut out for a bright future, with grammar school education and all that. Adah's schooling would have been stopped, but somebody pointed out that the longer she stayed in school, the bigger the dowry her future husband would pay for her. After all she was too young for marriage at the age of nine or so and moreover, the extra money she would fetch would tide Boy over.

Adah is allowed to stay in school for such an absurd reason but she takes advantage, excels, and forces her way into the secondary school, earning a full scholarship by her exceptional performance. The rest of Adah's story is a reiteration of a self-made woman struggling against ethnic, gender, and race bigotry. What is so spectacular about Adah's story is the close affinity between the heroine's experience and Emecheta's own background, life, and experience. In spite of some fictional devices that mediate the story initially, there is a keen resemblance to Emecheta's childhood in Lagos until her departure for England. Adah's unhappy marriage to Francis, his wickedness, indolence, as well as his callous treatment, sadistic brutalization, and abuse of his wife bear a closer link between the author's life and the protagonist's.

In the account of Adah's tortuous marital relationship, the veil of fiction is removed. Auteurist mediation becomes maximal and Emecheta's biography melts into Adah's story with an almost one-to-one correlation. Autobiography is often the most effective way of presenting the author's voice and many African women writers are not apologetic about this dispensation. It is a deliberate attempt to inscribe the writer's experience as a mode of collective writing or re-writing of African women's reality. One can clearly see Emecheta's story intruding on the fiction, and in this process she highlights issues of collective concern, as we see in the question of exploitative bride price. This is a recurrent theme in Igbo women's literature because, in reality, it is a major problem in this part of Nigeria. The attitude to women and child-bearing is also prominent. Being prolific in child-bearing is so highly valued that the woman can easily be reduced to this worth. Among the Ibos Emecheta observes that it is "the greatest asset a woman can have. A woman can be forgiven everything as long as she produced children."

The interference of relatives in the affairs of a family and the devastating effects on a young family occupies a central place in Emecheta's pre-occupations. In this we see Francis reduced to a puppet, "most of the decisions about their own lives had to be referred to Big Pa, Francis's father, then to his mother, then discussed among the brothers of the family, before Adah was referred to." Yet Adah is to finance such plans and when Francis is far apart from these family consultants, the Nigerian neighbors become his consultants and counsellors. In all these, personal experience is inseparable from larger problems confronting African women and in particular the peculiar problems of second-class citizens in Britain. The intersection of personal problems, communal dilemmas, ethnicity, race, class, and gender problems is remarkably underscored in this novel.

Second-Class Citizen as an autobiographical novel comes out most vividly as a metafiction and this unfolds the self-conscious self-inscription of Emecheta in an incontrovertible way. Any mask that the writer may have put on the real identity of Francis, the leech and indolent oppressive opportunist, is unveiled through metafiction. Adah becomes totally effaced and Buchi Emecheta comes out visibly and audibly in the last part of this novel. Emecheta's comment on the very process of fiction, the search for reviewers and the search for a publisher become overtly autobiographical. The turning point in Adah's ordeal is the possibility of working at home and writing the book, *The Bride Price*. The problems confronting Black women writers are unfolded here and Emecheta has reiterated these problems in interviews and in several of her writings. To Emecheta, like Adah, the most painful aspect is the rejection by her husband, who believes that a Black woman's dream of becoming a writer is a false dream. His narrow-minded and jaundiced vision is heightened by his reason for burning her manuscript: ". . . my family would never be happy if a wife of mine was permitted to write a book like that."

The details may vary but many African women writers have admitted facing similar obstacles and rejection by individuals or publishers. Adah's comments on the process of writing are profound; it is the first thing that brings a glimmer of hope and happiness into her bleak life:

> It was in that mood that she went . . . . and started to scribble down *The Bride Price*. The more she wrote, the more she knew she could write and the more she enjoyed writing. She was feeling this urge: *Write; go on and do it, you can write.* When she finished it and read it all through, she knew she had no message with a capital 'M' to tell the world. . . . The story was

over-romanticized. Adah had put everything lacking in her marriage into it.

To Emecheta and to several African women writers, writing as the brainchild of the author entails self-inscription as well as writing the collective identity for self-fulfillment. Memory and dream therefore play central roles in the process of fiction as recollection and as an idealization of the collective consciousness. *In the Ditch* takes off the story line from the end of *Second-Class Citizen* in a similar autobiographical and partly metafictional mode. Like Tsitsi Dangarembga's heroine, the sense of gender injustice motivates and validates the heroine's sense of inequality and gendered consciousness. One can therefore not separate Adah's primary experience from the collective consciousness. It is the second half of the novel that brings out more vividly a direct link between the fictional process and reality. Adah is unmistakably the auterist mouthpiece and a living proof of Emecheta's predicament and how she confronts the problem. The metafictional aspect reinforces Emecheta's real-life experience. Adah's attempt to write creative work is consistently thwarted by her irresponsible, indolent, and parasitic husband, Francis. The destruction of Adah's manuscript unveils reality and merges it with fiction. Her experience is a replica of the experience of Emecheta and many female writers. Some experience a psychological or sociological, even political opposition and/or censorship. Ama Ata Aidoo is an exile from her country, Ghana, like Micere Mugo. Nawal El Saadawi is a permanent political suspect in her own country too. They are victims of politics and exiles of conscience.

Emecheta is obviously speaking for several African women, and others like Ama Ata Aidoo have a similar song to sing. Aidoo confesses, "while all African writers have many constraints to deal with, African women writers have a double problem of being women and being African." The portrait of many of the fictional heroines is therefore a portrait of the artist as a woman of Africa trying to unload the double, often multiple yoke on her back. Through the artistic medium, she cries out for help. Like the average African woman whose dilemma she often fictionalizes, she is calling for help to balance her load, like her rural or traditional sister. Apart from domestic discouragement, Emecheta confesses the rejection of her manuscripts many times:

> . . . we marry very early in my own area, so by the time I was 22 I already had five children and the marriage had broken up [sic] . . . the only thing I could do was to write. After several years of failure and rejections my work was accepted for publication. . . .

Christine Loflin (essay date 1998)

SOURCE: "Mother Africa: African Women and the Land in West African Literature," in *African Horizons: The Landscapes of African Fiction*, Greenwood Press, 1998, pp. 35-54.

[*In the following excerpt, Loflin examines the significance of household environments and architecture in* The Joys of Motherhood *as indicative of tension between traditional Nigerian communal life and the social pressures of Western modernization.*]

AFRICAN WOMEN'S LITERATURE

African women writers are sensitive, perhaps to a fault, to the preexisting images of woman's space. Their preoccupation with motherhood and/or barrenness as the crucial element in women's lives, in novels such as *Efuru*, *The Joys of Motherhood*, *The Bride Price*, and *So Long A Letter* has led Obioma Nnaemeka to characterize these works as "motherhood literature." Elaine Savory Fido has identified the original "motherland" as the mother's body—that with which we identify, from which we learn to separate. The mother country is also the mother's cultural and national identity, which gives children their first social identity. Thus the mother is at the center of the motherland: "[she is] the one who is the starting point of all journeys and the point of reference for all destinations. . . . In a sense, we know that there is no homecoming unless mother is at the end of it." Fido uses this definition to explore the painful separations of Buchi Emecheta, Bessie Head, and Jean Rhys, not only from their mother countries, but from their mothers, and she sees this pattern replicated in their fiction: "Ona's death makes the condition of mother-loss the crucial factor in Nnu Ego's difficult life, and thus is Emecheta's own estrangement from her mother also re-enacted." Fido shows that women writers also may blur the distinctions between mother, The Mother and Mother Africa.

Within African women's literature, the equation of womanhood with motherhood is asserted, but it is also probed and questioned. African women writers explore the space of motherhood, sometimes exposing it as illusory (*The Joys of Motherhood*) or claiming it as a liberatory space for self-reflection and self-discovery (*So Long A Letter*). Ama Ata Aidoo's ambivalent attitude is typical: "Oh, being a mother! Traditionally, a woman is supposed to be nothing more valid than a mother. Sometimes one gets nervous of such total affirmation and total negation in relation to other roles that one has played. But I think that being a mother has been singularly enriching."

In every novel in this chapter, the central character is a woman who is or becomes a mother. African women's literature, by centering stories on the experience of motherhood, shapes the African landscape from a woman's perspective, moving outward from the family, with mothers and children at the core of the novel. African women writers, through their focus on womanhood and motherhood, are testing the boundaries and exploring the possibilities of that marginal "woman's space."

BUCHI EMECHETA

Buchi Emecheta was born near Lagos in 1944 and has been living in London since 1962. She has written ten novels, including the now-classic novel *The Joys of Motherhood* (1979). In *The Joys of Motherhood* Emecheta shows how the traditional background and experiences of a village woman, Nnu Ego, become dysfunctional in Lagos. Her attack on the "joys" of motherhood in Nigeria is a sophisticated analysis of the betrayal of women in colonial and postcolonial Africa.

Nnu Ego is brought to Lagos before World War II to marry Nnaife, a man she has never met. This is her second marriage. When she meets Nnaife, his potbelly, pale skin and demeaning job (washerman to a white family) are shocking to her. A friend of Nnu Ego's underscores the problem: "Men here are too busy being white men's servants to be men." Gender roles are dependent on appearance and status, as well as sex; without the appearance or the work of a typical male, Nnaife is seen as "a middle-aged woman." These remarks foreshadow Nnu Ego's own struggles to maintain her identity in the antagonistic urban space of Lagos.

At first, they live in one room in the "boys' quarters" belonging to Dr. and Mrs. Meers, Nnaife's employers. The name "boys' quarters" itself is a reminder that this is a space designed for the servants of Europeans, imagined, again, not to be men, but boys. Nnu Ego herself is not supposed to be present at all—these quarters were designed as if servants did not have families. To Nnu Ego, the place is initially disgusting: "This place, this square room painted completely white like a place of sacrifice." In this image, the squareness of the room and its whiteness identify it as a European-designed space, which, reinterpreted in Nnu Ego's aesthetic and architectural categories, is awkward, even ominous: "a place of sacrifice." The Meers' proximity to the boys' quarters controls certain aspects of Nnu Ego's behavior: she is not allowed to make noise, and her pregnancy has to be hidden from Mrs. Meers. When her baby son dies, even her grief has to be restrained. The arrangement of the Meers' compound, with the boys' quarters within the grounds but not actually part of the house, is a classic example of the architecture of colonialism. The architectural environment has political and social relations of power built into it.

Shaheen Haque has asserted in her discussion of British architects' plans for low-income housing in England that white male middle-class architects "create the physical environment in which we live and reinforce through their designs their problematic definitions of women, Black people and the working classes." Similarly, the Meers' compound suits their needs, but forces Nnu Ego to accept a foreign geometry and design for her home. Further, the design of the compound forces her to repress her feelings and make her behavior conform to the Meers' standards, not just in their presence, but even when she is alone within her apartment. The size, location and design of the boys' quarters reinforce the unequal relations of power between the white masters and the black servants.

Nnu Ego's pregnancy is supposed to reconcile her to her new situation; her husband says he has given her every-thing a woman wants. After the birth, Nnu Ego herself agrees to this, saying "He has made me into a real woman." Her motherhood is central to her sense of self, and makes her content with her husband Nnaife and their life in Lagos. Nnu Ego's baby son dies, however, when he is only four weeks old; Nnu Ego discovers his body lying on the floor mat in their apartment. The loss of her baby, the loss of motherhood, almost drives her insane. She flees through Lagos, gradually determining to drown herself by throwing herself off a bridge. These scenes, which open the novel, show Nnu Ego to be completely disassociated from her environment: "Nnu Ego backed out of the room, her eyes unfocused and glazed, looking into vacancy. Her feet were light and she walked as if in a daze, not conscious of using those feet. She collided with the door." Without her child, she feels no connection to her surroundings, and brushes past buildings and people without seeing them. Her grief is caused by the loss of her baby; Nnu Ego, who was barren in her first marriage, now feels that she will never have a child that lives, never be a mother.

Even in Lagos, the flight of a young woman so clearly in distress arouses people's concern: "She dodged the many who tried to help her." Emecheta shows that there is still a sense of community in Lagos' urban environment. On the bridge itself, a crowd grows as a man tries to prevent Nnu Ego from killing herself. Emecheta reveals both the crowd's idle curiosity and their underlying values:

> [The crowd] appreciated this free entertainment, though none of them wanted the woman to achieve her suicidal aim . . . a thing like that is not permitted in Nigeria; you are simply not allowed to commit suicide in peace, because everyone is responsible for the other person.

Here, Emecheta claims that there is a national ethic of behavior in Nigeria, a code that transcends ethnic and regional divisions. In Lagos, that code is present, but somewhat fragile; people are anxious to get to work, and can see Nnu Ego's behavior as entertainment, even as they try to stop her. Providentially, a friend of Nnaife's arrives and recognizes Nnu Ego, and he is able to convince her to return home. Only someone who knows her is able to dissuade her from suicide.

Nnu Ego gradually becomes accustomed to her new environment, and her one room apartment becomes a reflection of her state of mind. As she begins to accept Lagos standards of material wealth, she improves the room with her savings from petty trading: "They now had attractive mats on the floor, they had polished wooden chairs and new patterned curtains." When Nnu Ego is grieving for her son, Emecheta shows how Nnu Ego's friend Ato "reads" her home to discover the extent of her grief: "Nnu Ego led her into their room, which was unswept; the curtains had gone grey from lack of timely washing and the whole atmosphere was disorderly. Ato, knowing how clean and meticulous her friend normally was, tactfully said nothing."

Emecheta emphasizes the interrelationship between women and their immediate environment: their feelings, desires and creativity are written on the walls of the homes that they maintain. Traditionally, West African women decorate their own homes, painting the walls with designs and symbols that are drawn from their culture and are expressive of the individual woman's creativity. These designs continue to be produced today, examples of an African art form that is uniquely female: "Wall and body motifs . . . are a woman's response to the world around her and, above all, adorn her home, enhancing an otherwise cheerless landscape." Emecheta uses Ato's reading of Nnu Ego's room to show how Nnu Ego's creativity is limited to the choice of furnishings, and to the habit of cleanliness. She is unable, for example, to paint the outside walls of her home, or to add to them; living in the boys' quarters of the Meers' compound, she would not be allowed to express herself so publicly. Ato's readings of Nnu Ego's room are readings of the inadequate space alloted to African women in a Western-designed home.

Nnu Ego learns to adjust to Lagos; her husband gets a different job and they move into a new apartment with their growing family. Traditional practices clash with modern living when Nnaife's older brother dies and Nnaife inherits his four wives, one of whom comes to live in their one room apartment. The added burdens of the new wife, her daughter and the children she has by Nnaife ultimately cause a collapse of the family; so many people can't be fed on Nnaife's salary, or live under one roof. The urban compression of living space makes traditional polygamous relationships unbearable.

Ibuza, Nnu Ego's native village, is described in strong contrast to the impersonal, Westernized architecture and urban anonymity of Lagos. Here, where Nnu Ego was born, the organization of the compound reflects the social ordering within the family: her father's hut is in the middle of the courtyard, surrounded by the huts of his wives. In this world, Nnu Ego has an acknowledged and respected role. Emecheta, while acknowledging that motherhood is the central concern of women in Ibuza society, describes a society that can allow for exceptions. In Nnu Ego's first marriage, she fails to have a child and must return to her father's compound, yet the women there make her feel that she is a welcome member of their extended family. This is the environment in which Nnu Ego is most at ease: "Nnu Ego sat contentedly in front of the hut she had to herself, enjoying the cool of the evening." Here, the larger living spaces within the compound allow for less stressful relationships between family members, and the agricultural economy offers some security: "If it came to the worst, she could always plant her food at the back of her hut." Yet Nnu Ego finds only a temporary respite for herself in Ibuza. Having married Nnaife, whose work is in Lagos, she can only visit, not return to, her native village.

Nnu Ego's daily life is lived most intensely within the home. Lagos, for her, is made up of isolated locations: markets, bridges, and the places where she has lived. She has only a vague idea of the world outside of Lagos and Ibuza; she hears of the end of World War II "when people

began saying that the war was over, that the enemy, whoever he was, had killed himself." Nnu Ego's sketchy understanding of international events reflects her vision of the world, firmly centered on her family and her family's interests. The novel itself, however, is located within an international political and economic horizon: the Meers leave for England and Nnaife is sent off to Burma because of World War II; Nnu Ego's sons leave Nigeria for the United States and Canada in search of better economic opportunities. Lemuel Johnson's remark that "in *The Joys of Motherhood*, Emecheta is running Igbo culture through an enormously complex international geography" (personal communication) seems particularly apt. While Nnu Ego's perspective is limited, the reader can see that her family's history is caught in a web of international concerns.

Within *The Joys of Motherhood*, the significant boundaries are Ibuza, Lagos, and the international horizons of colonialism, World War II, and Western capitalism. National politics are conspicuously absent, in contrast to many African novels by men. Ibuza and Lagos, for example, are usually represented in opposition to each other, rather than as two aspects of a national Nigerian community. This may be the result of the circumstances of the creation of the text: although the novel is set in the time period around World War II, Emecheta wrote it after the Biafran war. The nascent Igbo nation-state was defeated, and forcibly reintegrated into Nigeria. Thus it is not surprising that *The Joys of Motherhood* does not have a strong national boundary. In addition, while the most significant contrast between Ibuza and Lagos is that between the traditional village and a Westernized city, there is also an ethnic difference. Lagos is primarily a Yoruba community, within which the Igbo immigrants are a small minority. Although Emecheta doesn't emphasize ethnic conflict in this novel, part of the characters' sense of isolation and alienation in Lagos comes from their position as part of a minority community.

Nnu Ego's life does have a larger, spiritual horizon, which is an integral part of her experience of the world. Nnu Ego's family believes that she inherited the malevolent spirit of a slave girl, murdered to serve her mistress (a member of Nnu Ego's family) in the afterlife. This spirit is blamed for Nnu Ego's initial inability to conceive a child, and figures in her dreams throughout her life, giving her babies but taunting her at the same time. Nnu Ego herself, after her death, is supplicated as a spirit by her grandchildren. Because she has had eight children, they believe she will help them conceive, yet she "refuses": "However many people appealed to her to make women fertile, she never did." This spiritual horizon expands the novel into the past and the future, and suggests that Nnu Ego, a tormented woman in human life, has freedom and power in the afterlife. The slave woman protests against her inhuman treatment; Nnu Ego protests the virtual enslavement of women in motherhood by refusing children to her descendants. Emecheta is very careful in her description of spiritual beliefs; her narrative neither asserts nor denies the validity of Nnu Ego's spiritual powers. The slave girl's spirit may be a real influence on Nnu Ego's life, or a dream figure, created by her family's mythology. Nnu Ego's "refusal" to help her grandchildren conceive may be simply the silence of the grave. Yet the image of the slave girl's spirit shows how Nnu Ego (and her family) sees her life interacting transgenerationally within the family, and the time span of the novel is extended beyond the limits of her own life.

In traditional Igbo societies, Nnu Ego's numerous children would have been her guarantee of an honorable and prosperous old age. Certainly, it would have been expected that her children would house and clothe her. Yet Nnu Ego is disappointed here as well, caught in the social upheaval created by Western colonization in Nigeria. Her two eldest male children, educated in British style schools, leave Nigeria for Canada and the United States. Their dislocation makes them unavailable to their mother, even if they had seen it as their duty to support her; Oshia, her eldest son, refuses his father's direct request for help with the family's expenses. Oshia has accepted Western ideas of individual ambition and self-sufficiency, and will not accept any responsibility for his extended family. Instead of being cared for by her children, Nnu Ego dies by the roadside: "She died quietly there, with no child to hold her hand and no friend to talk to her." Motherhood, which should have guaranteed and strengthened her connection to the land, has betrayed her; her death is the death of the homeless, the abandoned.

In the course of the novel, Emecheta provides a description of the disjunction between the urban, Westernized environment of colonial Lagos and Ibuza culture: the architecture of Lagos is itself hostile to the preservation of large, polygamous households. In this way, Emecheta emphasizes the interrelationship between society and landscape; the landscape of the village, the compound and the separate huts is created by and suited to a traditional life. Lagos, that amalgam of Western imitations, is hostile to it. The new urban landscape of Africa demands a new kind of society.

While Emecheta critiques contemporary attitudes towards women and the "double bind" of the collision of African and Western culture, she provides only a limited image of the African landscape. The contrast of the Westernized city and the traditional village is a commonplace in African literature, and reinforces the image of traditional societies as static havens from the modern world. Perhaps this is the result of Emecheta's own life history.

Emecheta did not grow up in a village. She describes herself as an observer of rural life: "I was intrigued by the whole way of life. For example, some women will sit for hours just peeling egusi (melon seed) or tying the edge of cloth." In *The Joys of Motherhood*, while Ibuza life is valued, there are few descriptions of what women's work entailed, other than the care of children; it may be that Emecheta did not feel she knew enough about other experiences in village life to describe them.

Before she became a writer, Emecheta left Nigeria for England, which has been her principal residence since that time (except for a stint at the University of Port Harcourt). In England, she has become critical of African English and African literature: "My vehicle is the English language and staying in this society, working in it, you master the nuances. Writing coming from Nigeria, from Africa (I know this because my son does the criticism) sounds quite stilted." She feels that women in Nigeria "are riddled with hypocrisy." For Emecheta, Nigeria has become a foreign country: "I find I don't fit in there anymore." In light of these feelings, it is easier to understand the sweeping criticism of Nigerian society in *The Joys of Motherhood*: no one in Ibuza or in Lagos is, finally, willing to support Nnu Ego. Her loneliness, and her death by the roadside, may be not only an appeal to Emecheta's audience to address the problems of African women, but also a figuration of the exile, alone in a strange land. The landscape of *The Joys of Motherhood* is a description written from a distance. It combines Emecheta's fond memories of village life with her reasons for leaving Nigeria; it is the landscape of memory and desire. Her most recent novels have focused on the experience of immigrants in Britain. The landscape of Africa, in Emecheta's life and works, has faded into the background.

FURTHER READING

Criticism

Andrade, Susan Z. "Rewriting History, Motherhood, and Rebellion: Naming an African Women's Literary Tradition." *Research in African Literature* 21, No. 1 (Spring 1990): 91-110.

> Addresses Western misrepresentations of African women's literary history and offers comparative analysis of Emecheta's *The Joys of Motherhood* and Flora Nwapa's *Efuru.*

Fido, Elaine Savory. "Mother/lands: Self and Separation in the Work of Buchi Emecheta, Bessie Head, and Jean Rhys." In *Motherlands: Black Women's Writing from Africa, the Caribbean, and South Asia,* edited by Susheila Nasta, pp. 330-49. New Brunswick: Rutgers University Press, 1992.

> Examines themes of alienation and dislocation in the autobiographic works of Emecheta, Bessie Head, and Jean Rhys, drawing attention to the significance of emigration and motherhood for each author.

Frank, Katherine. "*The Death of the Slave Girl*: African Womanhood in the Novels of Buchi Emecheta." *World Literature Written in English* 21 (1982): 476-97.

> Examines the changing social and political position of African women as reflected in Emecheta's novels *In*

the Ditch, Second Class Citizen, The Bride Price, The Slave Girl, and *The Joys of Motherhood.*

Gardner, Susan. "Culture Clashes." *Women's Review of Books* XII, No. 2 (November 1994): 22-3.

A review of Emecheta's *Kehinde* and Ama Ata Aidoo's *Changes: A Love Story.*

Newman, Judie. "'He Neo-Tarzan, She Jane?': Buchi Emecheta's *The Rape of Shavi.*" *College Literature* 22, No. 1 (February 1995): 161-70.

Examines Emecheta's presentation of sexual politics, Nigerian history, tensions between African tradition and Western modernity, and allusions to George Bernard Shaw in *The Rape of Shavi.*

Phillips, Maggi. "Engaging Dreams: Alternative Perspectives on Flora Nwapa, Buchi Emecheta, Ama Ata Aidoo, Bessie Head, and Tsitsi Dangarembga's Writing." *Research in African Literatures* 25, No. 4 (Winter 1994): 89-103.

A comparative study of dreams, spirituality, and communal identity in the works of Emecheta, Flora Nwapa, Ama Ata Aidoo, Bessie Head, and Tsitsi Dangarembga.

Umeh, Marie. "African Women in Transition in the Novels of Buchi Emecheta." *Présence Africaine* 116 (1980): 190-201.

Provides an overview of Emecheta's novels and her portrayal of female experience in African society.

Umeh, Marie. "*The Joys of Motherhood:* Myth or Reality?" *Colby Library Quarterly* XVIII, No. 1 (March 1982): 39-46.

Examines Emecheta's portrayal of African women and motherhood in *The Joys of Motherhood.*

Ward, Cynthia. "What They Told Buchi Emecheta: Oral Subjectivity and the Joys of 'Otherhood'." *PMLA: Publications of the Modern Language Association of America* 105, No. 1 (January 1990): 83-97.

Explores conflicting interpretations of authorial identity, Western notions of textual authority, and oral tradition in Emecheta's novels.

Mary Gordon
1949-

American novelist, short story writer, essayist, and memoirist.

The following entry presents an overview of Gordon's career. For further information on her life and works, see *CLC,* Volumes 13 and 22.

INTRODUCTION

Mary Gordon emerged as a highly respected contemporary novelist with the enormous critical and popular success of her debut novel, *Final Payments* (1978). Drawing heavily upon her own Catholic upbringing, Gordon examines the problematic and often contradictory claims of universal and particular love, Christian morality, domestic responsibility, sexual desire, and emotional fulfillment in the secular world. Distinguished for her well-crafted prose and engaging evocation of cloistered Catholic lives, Gordon focuses on the private struggles of modern women whose personal needs are sacrificed to the demands of selfless care-giving, marriage, motherhood, and religious conscience. While *Final Payments* and *The Company of Women* (1981) figure largely around Catholic themes, in subsequent novels such as *Men and Angels* (1985) and *Spending* (1998) Gordon expanded the settings and subjects of her novels to include female academics and artists who explore their conflicted feelings about romantic love and independence.

BIOGRAPHICAL INFORMATION

Born in Long Island, New York, Gordon was an only child raised in a devout Catholic home by her mother, a legal secretary of Irish and Italian descent, and her eccentric father, a Jewish convert to Catholicism and avowed anti-Semite who wrote speeches for Joseph McCarthy and published a string of unsuccessful right-wing Catholic magazines. Gordon shared a strong emotional bond with her doting father, who taught her Greek, French, and philosophy before suffering a fatal heart attack when she was seven. Gordon attended a Catholic parochial school and graduated from Mary Louis Academy, an all-girl Catholic high school. As a child she wrote poetry and considered a monastic life, though eventually rejected the Church as a teenager; Gordon still considers herself a Catholic despite objections to papal strictures against birth control, abortion, and the ordination of women.

In 1967 Gordon received a scholarship to attended Barnard College of Columbia University in New York. While at Barnard, Gordon studied writing with novelist Elizabeth Hardwick, an important early mentor who encouraged her to switch from poetry to prose. After graduating from Barnard in 1971, Gordon attended Syracuse University, where she earned a master's degree in writing in 1973 and started an unfinished doctoral dissertation on Virginia Woolf; Gordon counts Woolf, Jane Austen, Charlotte Brontë, and Ford Madox Ford among her most important literary influences. While at Syracuse, Gordon met her first husband, James Brain, an anthropologist. From 1974 to 1978 Gordon taught English at Dutchess Community College in Poughkeepsie, New York, where she began work on her first novel, *Final Payments,* which appeared in 1978. Gordon taught at Amherst College in 1979 and, during the same year, remarried to Arthur Cash, an English professor. During the 1980s, Gordon published several additional novels, *The Company of Women, Men and Angels,* and *The Other Side* (1989), and the short story collection *Temporary Shelter* (1987). She has taught English at Barnard College since 1988. Many of her critical essays and reviews are contained in *Good Boys and Dead Girls and Other Essays*

(1992). Gordon has since published novellas in *The Rest of Life* (1993), the memoir *The Shadow Man* (1996), and a fifth novel, *Spending*.

MAJOR WORKS

Final Payments introduces many of the recurring motifs and preoccupations in Gordon's fiction: the struggle to reconcile conflicting aspects of charitable and romantic love, emotional dependency, spiritual and family debts, and individual conscience and religious morality; rebellion against patriarchal authority; and the perverse allure of self-abnegation for the benefit of others, particularly among women. Set in working-class Queens, *Final Payments* is narrated by Isabel Moore, a thirty-year-old Irish Catholic woman who has devoted eleven years of her life to the constant care of her invalid father, a conservative Catholic and former professor of medieval literature; his debilitating paralysis stems from a stroke suffered after discovering Isabel in bed with one of his students. Upon her father's death—the novel opens at his funeral—Isabel is freed of her responsibilities and thrust into the world to establish an independent life. She finds an outlet for her long repressed sexual desire in two affairs—both with married men—which result in humiliation and self-loathing. To atone for her deep-seated guilt, Isabel resolves to care for her father's former housekeeper, Margaret Casey, an unlovable wretch whom she despises though views as a means to salvation. However, after enduring a period of penitent care-taking, Isabel abandons Margaret for a new life, leaving her a large sum of money from the sale of her father's home as a "final payment."

The Company of Women involves a group of five middle-aged, sexually dormant women who share a profound emotional attachment to Father Cyprian, a right-wing Catholic priest who has renounced his clerical order in protest of liberal church concessions. Much of the novel figures around Felicitas Taylor, the daughter of one of the widowed women, whom Cyprian cultivates as his spiritual disciple. Felicitas eventually rebels against Cyprian and enrolls at Columbia University, where she encounters the student radicalism of the late 1960s and enters into a manipulative sexual relationship with her professor, a self-styled revolutionary by whom she becomes pregnant. Returning to the unconditional love of the women and Cyprian, Felicitas and the others relocate to Cyprian's Upstate New York home, where Felicitas raises her daughter and resigns herself to a simple life of ordinary pleasures. *Men and Angels* focuses on Anne Foster, an art historian and working mother whose husband, a professor, is on sabbatical in France. Uncomfortable with her new independence, Anne hires Laura Post, an emotionally scarred religious zealot, to help care for her children while she works on a catalogue of artwork by Caroline Watson, an obscure early twentieth-century painter. Anne's research reveals that Watson was a callous mother who neglected her son, mirrored by Laura's own unhappy childhood and consequent insecurities. Laura's fanaticism, which ultimately leads her to suicide, wreaks havoc in the Foster home and threatens Anne's domestic security. Though Catholicism is absent from this novel, the themes of selfless love and renunciation come to the fore as Anne questions her inability to care for the unlovable Laura, as well as the responsibilities of motherhood and married life.

In *The Other Side* Gordon returned to the New York Irish Catholic milieu of her first novel. Set over a period of twenty-four hours, this generational saga revolves around the homecoming of Vincent MacNamara, an elderly man who returns to his Queens home and dying wife, Ellen, after several months in the hospital with a broken hip. Drawing upon the fragmentary, transcontinental experiences of a large cast of characters, Gordon reconstructs the complex web of infidelity, parental neglect, alcoholism, divorce, and sibling rivalry that has shaped the immigrant MacNamara family since the early years of the twentieth century. *Spending* features Monica Szabo, a witty, middle-aged artist, mother, and divorcee who enters into an ideal romantic arrangement with "B," a wealthy Wall Street trader and admiring collector of her paintings who offers unlimited emotional and financial support to facilitate her art. With "B" as her devoted lover, muse, and model, Monica produces "Spent Men," an acclaimed series of paintings that depicts Christ in a state of post-orgasmic exhaustion after his crucifixion. In addition to problems associated with her new celebrity, fortune, and controversial art, Monica reflects on the artistic process and the exigencies of modern life.

The Rest of Life contains three novellas, each of which features women who obsess over love, death, and isolation. The first, "Immaculate Man," involves a middle-aged female narrator who runs a shelter for battered women. She is entangled in an intense affair with Clement, an unchaste priest who she fears will leave her for a needier woman. In "Living at Home," the female narrator is a psychiatrist who works with autistic children. She lives in constant fear of losing her beloved third husband Lauro, an Italian photojournalist who frequently travels to dangerous foreign locales to cover war and revolution. The third novella, "The Rest of Life," involves Paolo, a septuagenarian who returns to her native Italy where, as a teenager, she failed to fulfill her half of a suicide pact with her boyfriend, Leo, and was ostracized by the community for his death. Though able to forgive herself and others, she laments her unrealized passion and Leo's untimely death.

Gordon's collection of short fiction, *Temporary Shelter,* contains twenty stories that previously appeared in publications such as *Granta, Antaeus, Redbook,* and *Mademoiselle.* As in her novels, these stories involve female protagonists—both young and adult—who relate the fragile security of loving relationships, particularly those between parents and children, spouses, and lovers. *Good Boys and Dead Girls* consists of book reviews, essays on literature and contemporary issues, and Gordon's personal reflections on diverse subjects such as abortion, Andy Warhol, the Gospel of Saint Mark, and writing. In *The Shadow*

Man Gordon retraces her effort to come to terms with the powerful memory of her long deceased father. Through painstaking research into the factual content of his biography, Gordon discovers that her father has lied about much; she learns, among other things, that his real name was Israel not David, he was born in Lithuania not Ohio, he never attend Harvard, or any college, as he claimed, and he edited a pornographic magazine during the 1920s. After scrutinizing his life and legacy, Gordon finally lays him to rest in a symbolic reburial that signifies closure.

CRITICAL RECEPTION

Gordon is highly regarded for her penetrating studies of self-denial, Catholic consciousness, and guilt-stricken women who are torn between external obligations and private desires. *Final Payments* was hailed as an impressive first novel and enthusiastically praised for its remarkable maturity, psychological depth, and unusual discussion of self-sacrifice and filial piety—concerns that seemed to run counter to the 1970s "me generation." As Pearl K. Bell notes, *Final Payments* "was acclaimed not only for the dazzling intensity of her prose, but for the indisputable authority of her portrayal of the Irish-Catholic working class in Queens." *The Company of Women,* which received mixed assessment, is considered by many an elaboration of the themes and personalities in *Final Payments.* Gordon garnered favorable reviews for *Men and Angels, The Other Side,* and the novellas of *The Rest of Life.* Along with *Final Payments, Men and Angels* and *The Other Side* are regarded as Gordon's most ambitious and accomplished works to date. Gordon is often compared to Victorian novelists Jane Austen and Charlotte Brontë, as well as Virginia Woolf for her subtle perception of female emotions, and to Flannery O'Connor for her interest in extreme religiosity. Best known as a novelist, Gordon has also received positive reviews for her short stories, essays, and memoir *The Shadow Man.* Though critics have cited flaws in Gordon's reliance on stereotyped characters, tenuous narrative structures, and faulty plots, she is consistently praised for her finely tuned prose, vivid descriptions, and keen insights regarding the complexities of reciprocal love.

PRINCIPAL WORKS

Final Payments (novel) 1978

The Company of Women (novel) 1981

Men and Angels (novel) 1985

Temporary Shelter (short stories) 1987

The Other Side (novel) 1989

Good Boys and Dead Girls and Other Essays (essays) 1992

The Rest of Life: Three Novellas (novellas) 1993

The Shadow Man (memoir) 1996

Spending (novel) 1998

CRITICISM

Ann Hulbert (review date 28 February 1981)

SOURCE: "Catholic Devotions," in *The New Republic,* February 28, 1981, pp. 33-4.

[*In the following review, Hulbert offers tempered evaluation of* The Company of Women.]

Like being singled out as a child to be the object of others' great love and hope, writing an acclaimed first novel can be a mixed blessing. Great expectations loom forever after. To judge from the importance of special daughters in Mary Gordon's fiction, she seems to have known the first fate, and has no doubt learned the second during the three years since her excellent first novel, *Final Payments,* was published. A second novel faces the challenge of showing new promise without betraying any of the old.

In *The Company of Women* Gordon pursues the theme she developed in *Final Payments:* a much-loved daughter's experience of the conflict between the anachronistic Catholic world she grows up in and the sexually liberated, politically radical America of the 1960s and 1970s she finds beyond it. Among the host of almost formulaic contemporary novels by women about women in search of love, *Final Payments* stood out for its depiction of working-class Catholic life, where a more demanding drama of giving and receiving love unfolded. Under the sway of the church, Gordon's women were ready to dedicate their lives to others—not to husbands or lovers, but to parents, children, one another, and priests. Now Gordon seems to be elaborating a formula of her own. Not only does she keep to her original theme, she also constructs a similar structure. Both Isabel Moore in *Final Payments* and Felicitas Maria Taylor in *The Company of Women* venture forth from their Catholic haven, no longer fortified by the faith but irrevocably influenced by Catholicism's unfashionable mores. They try out the ordinary world and are made unhappy in love. In trouble, they retreat to a new version of their former lives.

Where Gordon ventures beyond her own model is in narrative technique. In her first novel Gordon had Isabel tell her story in the first person, which she did with authority and wit. Gordon's prose was strikingly crafted, full of carefully chosen words, observations, and ironies, especially throughout the first part of Isabel's tale—the 11 years she spent nursing her fiercely orthodox father, just the two of them in their dark house in Queens, until he died when she was 30. In *The Company of Women* young Felicitas has six collaborators telling the first section of her story, which takes place in the summer of 1969: her mother, four of her mother's friends, and a priest, Father Cyprian, who is spiritual mentor to all of them and surrogate father to the child (whose real father is long dead). As an omniscient narrator this time, Gordon never stands far back. Instead she projects herself into each of her characters in turn, looking through their eyes, speaking in their voices.

Gordon's ambitious narrative effort, however, does not succeed in opening out onto a more crowded Catholic scene. Unhappily, Gordon's new company seems to be composed of characters lifted from the periphery of Isabel's world in *Final Payments* to stand on their own nearer the center of the new novel, which it soon becomes clear they're not substantial enough to do. Felicitas's mother, Charlotte, remarks on a penchant of Father Cyprian's, which Gordon unfortunately shares:

> Cyprian thought she was stupid. That was what he meant when he said, 'Charlotte is the salt of the earth.' He had to do that with people, have that one little sentence about everyone, as if he couldn't remember who was who without it. She was the salt of the earth and Elizabeth was one of God's doves and Clare had a mind like a man's and Mary Rose was a ray of sunlight and Muriel was an extraordinary soul.

Since these women, even stolid Charlotte, view themselves largely in Cyprian's terms, they tend to offer variations on his little epithets when Gordon gives them their chance to come forward. Not surprisingly, this makes for prose that is stylized and uneven, and characters who are closer to types than to fully imagined selves—and familiar types at that. Elizabeth and Clare are like maiden-aunt versions of, respectively, dreamy Eleanor and manly Liz, Isabel's best friends. Whining Muriel is a parody of Margaret in the earlier novel, who was a parody of the spinster with a martyr complex. Even Charlotte, whose personality is rounded out by the other characters' views of her, often lapses into caricatured saltiness when she speaks in her own voice, which Gordon loads with clichéd colloquialisms, "hells," and "goddamns." And Father Cyprian is cut from the same fierce, flawed, God-like cloth as Isabel's father; this adamant anti-sentimentalist who for years has been the anchor in the lives of these women is less compelling in the flesh than Mr. Moore was in Isabel's memory.

Only Felicitas, a younger and plainer version of Isabel, comes fully to life through others' doting visions of her and through her own voice, which inspires some of Gordon's best prose: "She believed she was worthy. Her soul she saw as glass filled with sky or water, as beautiful, as light, as silvery and important. That was her soul, light let through some transparent thing, cool light refreshed by water." This serious 14-year-old lives for the summers spent among the odd company in the New York countryside, for the trip to six p.m. mass in the red pickup alone with Father Cyprian, talking about the splendor of God, the illusory beauty of nature, the turpitude of mankind—though she would never dream of admitting this joy to the friends she has made back at school in Brooklyn.

But six years later at Columbia, at the height of student radicalism, a rebellious Felicitas is ready to ridicule those joys to win the approval of the liberated friends she is desperate to have. As in *Final Payments*, Gordon's ironic sense and psychological insight are thrown off their accurate course when she turns from the outdated virginal enclave to portray the secular world beyond it. Her version of the 1960s scene is a superficial caricature rather than a penetrating parody. Robert Cavendish, Felicitas's political science professor and seducer, is ludicrous from the moment he strides into class and starts pontificating about "St. Herbert" (Marcuse). Out of class he's even worse, as he generously donates his beautiful body to the cause of promoting "revolutionary consciousness" through sex—naturally without the "possessiveness trip." Robert's physique simply is not enough to explain why the once discriminating (often outright intolerant) Felicitas should fall for him and, with uncharacteristic piety, receive his attentions as "a blessing." Occasionally she has flashes of her old judgmental self and pierces the self-righteous vacuity of the Columbia crowd with jokes, which of course they never get. But mostly she suffers Robert's abuse, convinced she's happy and free for the first time. Only when she finds she's pregnant does she turn back to her Catholic company in misery and need.

They take her in and give her their unconditional love, which they also give her child, yet another in the line of special daughters "whose family life is peculiar." Gordon's feminine geneology is becoming all too familiar. But behind it lies a typology of love that gives Gordon's novels their uncommon clarity: the fierce love of God and the charity for all souls dictated by the Catholic faith; the selective but unswerving human love that flourishes in families, among friends (companies of women in Gordon's books); the sexual love between men and women. The fate of Gordon's heroines (unlike her other characters) is to know the competing claims of all three kinds of love and ultimately to choose the circumscribed love of a devoted enclave, which they took for granted when young and come to value, stoically rather than joyfully, in maturity. It is, as Felicitas says, an "isolated, difficult and formal" life, an anomaly in the "ordinary" world, where love is distributed differently. There, as Gordon showed in *Final Payments,* charity is left to government, which dispenses it "without the weights of love." And there, as she shows this time, sexual love is easy, indiscriminate. But that world knows little of the steadfast love among close souls. Despite the weaknesses of her second effort, Gordon clearly is an authority on such loyal companies.

Robert Towers (review date 19 March 1981)

SOURCE: "Reconciliations," in *New York Review of Books,* March 19, 1981, pp. 7-8.

[*In the following review, Towers offers tempered assessment of* The Company of Women, *which he describes as "a work at once excellent and flawed."*]

Since the rise and predominance of the art novel, the documentary aspect of fiction—regarded in the nineteenth century as a major strength of the genre—has figured little in critical discourse except among Marxists. Yet, stubbornly, the appeal of the documentary persists—and not only among unsophisticated readers. It is an impurity that cannot be strained out by the most finely textured filter of linguistically based criticism. Just as readers were once eager to be told *what it is like* to live in a coal mining town or to work in a grog shop in a Paris slum or to make one's way up as a businessman in Boston, so we still yearn for the revelation of modes of existence that are relatively unfamiliar, even when they involve large numbers of people living in our midst.

Too often, of course, the fiction that in these days gratifies that yearning has no literary pretensions whatsoever. What is it like to have grown up in an Irish-Catholic neighborhood in Queens, in a house that "had always been full of priests"? An exotic way of life? Hardly—except perhaps to the excessively secularized purveyors and consumers of "serious" literary culture. Yet I suspect that the careful, indeed loving, documentation of the mores of this world, arousing as it does the staring curiosity of the outsider and the pained or delighted recognition of the insider, had a good deal to do with the popular success of Mary Gordon's first novel, *Final Payments*.

Fortunately for her reputation, there was much more to the novel than that. Though imperfectly resolved, *Final Payments* is clearly the work of a gifted novelist, a writer whose stylistic attainments are on a level with her intelligence and insight. The story of the venturing into life of a "good Catholic girl" of thirty, who had devoted the previous eleven years to the unremitting care of her once formidable, then invalided, father, was in itself moving, and the moral perplexities she faced were handled with subtlety, humor, and compassion until the plot took a melodramatic turn that damaged the credibility of the last third of the book. Her new novel, *The Company of Women,* is likewise a fascinating document, likewise a work at once excellent and flawed. Though it is to some degree a reworking of the themes of the earlier novel, *The Company of Women* is, in its structure and scope, a very different sort of book.

The company referred to in the title consists of five middle-aged, sexually inactive Catholic women—two virgins, two widows, and the undivorced wife of a hopelessly insane man who had barely consummated his marriage before being institutionalized—permanently. Their status and occupations vary: the robust and wisecracking Charlotte works in an insurance office in Brooklyn: the delicate, impractical Elizabeth teaches school and reads Jane Austen; Clare, the only one with real money, manages a successful leather-goods business inherited from her father; Mary Rose, an usher in a Broadway movie house, maintains a friendly, platonic relationship with the theater's Jewish manager; and Muriel, embittered and envious, takes in typing and looks after her mother until the latter dies.

Somewhat reminiscent of the spinsterish Anglicans who populate the novels of Barbara Pym, these women are united not by temperament or background but by a common devotion to a spellbinding priest, Father Cyprian, who from 1932 to the Second World War conducted weekend retreats for working women. He has helped each one of the company in a time of crisis; he dominates them, exhorts them, feeds upon their love, and makes them (these "lame ducks no man wanted") feel, collectively, that they are "something." Ferociously right-wing, he detests the modern world and insists that there is no salvation outside the Church; scorning interfaith cooperation, "he would not let souls under his care risk eternal damnation to swim with Methodists, eat hot dogs with Baptists."

The offspring, so to speak, of the intense bonding between the women and Father Cyprian is Charlotte's daughter Felicitas, who is fourteen when we meet her in 1963. She is the pivotal figure of the novel. Left fatherless at the age of six months, Felicitas is the only child of the whole group, and as such she is the repository of the hopes and love of all the women except for Muriel, who like the bad fairy in "Sleeping Beauty," resents the fact that she was not invited to the child's baptism and begrudges the love that is showered upon her. For Father Cyprian, Felicitas is no less than the chosen one, the one who will embody, in her preferably celibate (though not cloistered) womanhood, all that is purest, hardest, and most brilliant in the austere faith that he cherishes.

When the novel opens, Father Cyprian, who has left his order (the Paracletists) in disgust over certain concessions to the slackness of the times, is a secular priest living in his hometown in upstate New York, where, with no church of his own, he sleeps in a furnished room and fills in for sick or vacationing priests. There the women visit him for three weeks every August, bringing along Felicitas; her adolescent feelings for the priest and for the faith are caught in a remarkable passage:

> There was no one she could tell about Father Cyprian. It would have been death for her to go a year without seeing him. But how could she say to her friends that the deepest pleasure of her life was riding to the six o'clock mass alone with Father Cyprian in the front of his red pickup? The light then made her see the world as fragile and beautiful. And there was the other light that came through the windows . . . the light she sat in, praying, with his back to her in his beautiful vestments—grass green for the feria, blue for feasts of Our Lady. She wanted always to be there kneeling, looking at his black shoes below the black cuffs of his trousers and the long white alb. They were serious and blessed and devotional. . . . Her soul she saw as glass filled with sky or water, as beautiful, as light, as silvery and as important. That was her soul, light let through some transparent thing, cool light refreshed by water. The side of God apart from punishment or care. The God that breathed, breathed over all. The thin, transparent God that barely left a shadow. She watched the feet of Father Cyprian as she opened her mouth. She prayed in her soul for light, a life of light, a life essential as those shoes, as serious.
>
> How could she tell all that to her friends, who were interested that year in TV doctors?

Father Cyprian's feelings for the girl are equally intense. When in the course of an accident (the priest's fault) Felicitas suffers a concussion, Father Cyprian lifts her from the truck, thinking, "If this child dies, then I will die." His love for her borders on the idolatrous. Yet he can be brutal with her, determined as he is to root out all that is sentimental, soft-headed, or "womanish" in her nature. I can think of few recent novels that begin so brilliantly, with such a plenitude of possibilities in their opening situations.

In Part II we move ahead to 1969-1970. The Second Vatican Council has taken place. Latin is no longer taught at St. Anne's College, to which Felicitas, who wants to major in classics, has won a scholarship; the little college's last professor of classics advises her to transfer to Columbia rather than Fordham. ("A Dominican, be preferred to see her educated by pagans rather than Jesuits.") By this time, Felicitas is in full rebellion against Father Cyprian and the sheltering company of women, whose lives she now perceives as bankrupt. In a furious argument with the priest over Vietnam, Felicitas maintains that Daniel Berrigan, whom Father Cyprian has denounced as a "snot-nosed limelighter," is "the only hero in the Church." Whereupon Father Cyprian stands up and bangs his fist on the table, "making the wine jump out of the glasses and spill like blood."

> He said, "How dare you speak to me like that?"
>
> Felicitas also stood up. It was a foolish move; she was half his size and he bulked above her.
>
> "I speak the truth," she said.
>
> "You have no humility," he shouted. "You have been corrupted by this proud and lying age."
>
> "I was not brought up to be humble. I was brought up to speak the truth."
>
> "You are a scandal to us all," he said.

That night he suffers a mild heart attack, the first of a series. Felicitas is sorry but unrepentant. She returns to New York, vowing to change her life.

What follows is nearly as disastrous for the novel as it is for Felicitas. At Columbia she falls slavishly in love with a handsome, posturing professor in his thirties, a self-proclaimed radical spokesman of the "Movement." A refugee from a life of privilege that included Exeter, Amherst, Harvard, and summers on the Vineyard, Robert Cavendish has left his wife and children and now shares a dingy apartment on Amsterdam Avenue with two emotionally disheveled women, one of whom has a child named Mao. Felicitas moves in—and submits to every indignity and outrage that the hip late Sixties could have invented for a nice Catholic girl.

The professor is given to remarks like the following:

> "I mean," he said, "I didn't know what women wanted because I was completely out of touch with the feminine side of myself. Now I wish I had been born a woman. A black woman. You know who I wish I had been born?"
>
> "Who?"

> "Billie Holiday. There was a woman who knew things."
>
> "I believe she was very unhappy," said Felicitas.
>
> "Of course, because she lived in this fucked-up culture. God, how I wish I'd been born Third World."

I will not elaborate on the details of Felicitas's degradation except to say that she ends up on the very brink of performing an act that, particularly in these times, would be considered the most horrendous sin an unmarried, pregnant Catholic girl might be tempted to commit. She pulls back—just in the nick—and the reader, Catholic or not, goes limp with relief.

The whole Columbia section rings false—not because the events described could not have happened, but because Mary Gordon abandons the delicacy of perception and the psychological subtlety that deepens the other sections and indulges in the sort of melodramatic excess that marred the last third of *Final Payments.* Robert Cavendish is a grossly drawn type, not a character at all; he seems to have been set up, like some mustache-twirling villain in an 1890s shocker, purely for the purpose of harrowing poor Felicitas and her admirers. And Felicitas herself is unaccountably deprived of the rather feisty intelligence that earlier characterized her.

Fortunately for the novel, an effective recovery is made in Part III, which is set in 1977. The company of women, now approaching old age, have reassembled in upstate New York, where Father Cyprian has built, on his family's old farm, a prisonlike house of cinder blocks, with a chapel in which he is able, with the bishop's permission, to perform the Latin mass in private. Their number is intact except for Mary Rose, who, freed at last by her insane husband's death, is able, in her sixties, to marry her Jewish boyfriend. She is greatly missed. Felicitas is there too, and with her is her child. The novel shifts from the third person to a series of first-person monologues in which the women and Father Cyprian sum up their attitudes toward their experience, individual and communal. These monologues are beautifully written and touching; they nearly all deal in one way or another with the theme of reconciliation: to old age, to the fallibilities of the flesh and spirit, to the humbling demands of ordinary human existence at odds with the exaltations of faith, and, in the case of Father Cyprian, to the failure, through spiritual pride, of his priestly mission and to the imminence of death.

The theme of reconciliation—of the need for charity toward oneself as well as toward others—is merely one of the many themes explored in *The Company of Women.* The role of women in relation to male authority and to the Church, the rhythms of submission and rebellion, the perception of human love as a form of entrapment, the conflicting needs for shelter and escape—such are some of the preoccupations of this most *thoughtful* of recent novels. This thematic abundance is more successfully realized in short episodes and ruminations than dramatized in the compelling sweep of a major action. Mary Gordon is a reflective, even meditative novelist, and the effective sustaining of a plot is not among her strengths, either here or in *Final Payments.* There were times when I felt that the themes had escaped the narrative frame designed to contain them and scattered in several directions at once.

The Company of Woman, with its extraordinary marshalling of forces in the opening section, promises more than it is ever able to deliver. Yet there is so much in this novel to admire and enjoy, to make the reading of it memorable. I will conclude with one striking example of Mary Gordon's artistry: her remarkable tact in handling the psychological alignments of the novel without so much as a Freudian nudge in the reader's ribs. She feels no compulsion to comment on or to underscore in any way what can be seen as Felicitas's quest for a father-surrogate or the veiled eroticism in the relationship between Father Cyprian and his flock. The veiling is thick indeed. Father Cyprian examines his spiritual state with great scrupulosity and precision and with never a consciously sexual thought; even his covert misogyny and his longing for an impassioned male friendship (such as he once enjoyed with Charlotte's long-dead husband) are given an entirely religious coloration. His tools are those of Catholic introspection, tools handed down from one priestly generation to the next. And not one of the older women voices the slightest concern or regret over the absence of sexual contact in their lives; better off without it, they would say. It is left for us to meditate, if we choose, upon the odd twists and turnings of sublimation.

Sally Fitzgerald (review date 19 June 1981)

SOURCE: "Harsh Love and Human Happiness," in *Commonweal,* June 19, 1981, pp. 375-7.

[*In the following review, Fitzgerald offers praise for* The Company of Women.]

St. Cyprian was a third-century bishop of Carthage, and an outspoken opponent of Pope Stephen's liberality toward lapsed members of the young church. He was martyred, and personally so revered that he was canonized, and his name has for centuries appeared among those of the early fathers in the Canon of the Mass. Some of his overly rigid views and writings were, however, rejected and officially Indexed as teaching error.

Whether or not by design, a modern Cyprian, who plays a central role in Mary Gordon's fine new book, is reminiscent of his ancient namesake. Father Cyprian—pure, elitist, tyrannical, but unquestionably dedicated to his priesthood—has seen his most cherished theological conceptions rejected, and priestly practices altered, by the postconciliar church. Unable to accept *aggiornamento,* he can neither live at peace with his Paracletist fellow-monks, nor effectively function as a secular priest, as he attempts to do after leaving his order. The only followers, or friends, left to him are his disprized "goose-girls," five working

women of disparate backgrounds, bound together by their devotion to him, and by the sustaining friendship that has grown up among at least four of their number. The only human being Cyprian can really love is the promising daughter of one of these women, the only child among them. Felicitas is well aware of the strangeness of her upbringing in this circle, of which she is the spoiled cynosure and greatest hope. As a young child, she fully returns Father Cyprian's love for her, even as she comes with time to realize what he will do to her life and mind if she does not escape his overweening presence.

Two of the women of the company are spinsters and two are widows. The fifth is manifestly a victim of Cyprian's purism and high-minded arrogation of authority to himself. Married briefly to a dangerous lunatic, Mary Rose is first saved from harm by Cyprian's practical action of leading her husband to Bellevue and doctors who adjudge him to be hopelessly insane. The priest then decides, however, quite on his own, that she is bound to this hapless marriage because her husband "wasn't insane when (she) married him." This without reference to expert medical opinion or higher canonical authority. So Mary Rose obediently spends the better part of her life alone and lonely, attended by the kindly old Jewish owner of the theater where she works, who patiently waits for her to be free so that they can marry.

The others, apart from impossible Muriel, whose only wish is to have Cyprian to herself to wait upon, are no less subservient to his thinking. Occasionally restive and resentful, they are nonetheless faithful to him as mentor and attentive to his personal needs. Neither he nor they seem to realize that he is as dependent upon them as they are upon him. Clare is a well-off career woman in New York, who has inherited from her father a high-fashion leather business which she conducts with taste and acumen. Cyprian's highest praise of her is that she "thinks like a man," and he is of course incapable of understanding that this implies an affront both to herself and her friends. "Womanish" is to him a pejorative term. Elizabeth is a gentle, fearful, but humorous schoolteacher, deserted by her husband after the death of their child. Bookish and bemused, she finds in Charlotte, the rough-tongued mother of Felicitas, a personality who calms her fears and provides the common sense, reciprocal humor, and reassuring warmth she needs to stay them. Charlotte, "whose real genius lay in never longing for what did not seem accessible," takes life as it comes, and deals with it effectively. Cyprian has offended her unforgivably (as, in one way or another, he has offended all these women) by the suggestion that he mourns the death of her husband far more than she. As she realizes, what he really mourns is her marriage to a friend of his, a former seminarian whom he has hoped to make his own disciple. Still, like the rest, she can not only forgive him, she would die for him.

"The salt of the earth," Cyprian calls her. She knows that this means he thinks she is stupid. "He had to do that with people, have that one little sentence about everyone, as if he couldn't remember who was who without it. She was the salt of the earth and Elizabeth was one of God's doves and Clare had a mind like a man's and Mary Rose was a ray of sunlight and Muriel was an extraordinary soul: Something in Cyprian made him do that, as if he had to pin people down so he wouldn't lose track of anybody.

In other words, Cyprian fits everyone into a flat and linear schema of his own. Felicitas matters much more to him than the others, but he sees her with an equally flattening eye: she is to embody the realization of all his hopes. Brilliant, studious, malleable, she is to be formed by himself into an infallible Héloïse, or a Catherine of Alexandria, Virgin, Doctor of the Church. He would make of her a denatured, desexed disciple, a mind perfected in his own image. But Felicitas, even at fourteen and still passionately devoted to him despite her growing rage, knows herself better, and his hopes scarcely resemble her own. She is able to appreciate and return the love her mother's other friends surround her with, but she knows that she can find no model for her own life in theirs. At nineteen, now fully defiant, she crashes through all plans to send her off to absorb further "Catholic" education and persuades her mother to let her go to Columbia University instead.

Here, by one of the awful accidents, or designs, of love, she encounters a very different sort of man, a fatally handsome, and fatuous, professor of modern political philosophy, Robert Cavendish. He has likewise been able to attract to himself a company of women, but far more slavish women, who live in the seraglio he has set up in the process of freeing them from the old—or any—order of existence. Pitiable, empty, without dignity or real hope of any kind, Iris and Sally live at armistice with each other, occupying his apartment with Sally's small son, Mao, whom the mother is careful to present as the product of a causal—free—encounter, lest she bore the professor with the knowledge of his parenthood. Conversation in this household is usually stoned, entirely predictable, and ineffably boring.

Father Cyprian has once terrified, and infuriated, the adolescent Felicitas, when she speaks of her pleasure in the beauty of the natural world, particularly in the fragrance of grasses, on a drive with him in the country one fine summer day. By way of punishment for this pantheistic failure of 'spirituality,' he stops with her at the run-down farm of an odious family he knows, where he introduces her violently to the smells which for him represent nature: handsful of cow dung, chicken dung, and pig dung, calling this last the most aromatic of all because, as he tells her, "pigs eat garbage, like the mind of modern man." Sickened and rebellious, Felicitas vows to herself never to forgive him, and it is a long time before she does. He has set her up for Robert's apparent health and beauty.

In this new establishment, 'nature' is exalted in theory, but in terms curiously similar to Cyprian's at the farm. Among her new friends, everything is either "good shit" or "bad shit," and "getting (one's) shit together" defines acceptable

thinking or performance. And again Felicitas has it thrust in her face *ad nauseam*. Transfixed by this unlikely academic, and with straightforward passion, Felicitas joins his absurd menage as a timid and unloved lover, taken more out of perversity than real attraction or interest on the philosopher's part. There she awaits his summons to bed as it pleases him, when her turn comes. The final indignity he imposes upon her is the suggestion that she further free herself and increase her experience by extending her favors to someone else, anyone else, say nondescript Richard, who lives downstairs with his three dogs, Ho, Che, and Jesus (which, of the nature-lovers, only Felicitas has the wit and will to feed properly and train). Less able to resist Professor Cavendish's guidance than Father Cyprian's, Felicitas obeys, only to find herself pregnant "by one of two men," as she must tell her mother and, eventually, the daughter who is born to her after she finds herself constitutionally unable to go through with an abortion. She is saved from utter despair by the simple, practical kindness of her mother and her mother's friends, including Cyprian, "people who had rigorously worked to banish instinct from their lives," but whose love for her, unjudgmental and resilient, makes it seem entirely natural to them to alter those lives in order to help her construct a new and sheltering one for herself and her child.

Even Cyprian rallies round with an offer to help build a simple house for them near the one he has built for himself on the site of his parents' old farm in upstate New York. Charlotte retires and moves there, too, and Elizabeth moves in to help. Clare pays for everything, cheerfully, and eventually begins the construction of her own house nearby. Poor paranoid Muriel, continuing to fume at the breach of her privilege of sole proximity to Father Cyprian, is no more able to love the child, Linda, than she has been able to love Felicitas or the others, but she does what she can, and she is not excluded.

Only Mary Rose leaves the company, to marry her faithful suitor, a week after she learns that her mad husband has finally died. But before she leaves she has "brought with her the one gift none of the other godmothers had brought to the christening," conventional responses. From Mary Rose and Joe, Felicitas gets the idea that the presence of a baby in the house is a simple pleasure, and for the first time she sees the child as weaker than herself, and as beautiful. Seven years later, Felicitas does not even remember when her life began to change—which is to say, return—and she is no longer desperate. She will marry the village hardware merchant, Leo. She will marry for shelter, she suspects, and to give Linda a father and "an ordinary life." She wants, too, to be more human, and to escape what she feels to be a growing cruelty of judgment in herself that she hopes will be assuaged by sexual love. She wants for her child a father who doesn't father her as if they were both bodiless, as Cyprian had fathered, driving her to extremes of revolt.

The novel, with the exception of the somehow contrived and unbelievable university scenes, is skillfully and richly narrated in its first two parts. The third part, however, is the finest of the book. It is composed of beautifully written and extremely moving meditations in the distinctive voices of each of these women, and of Father Cyprian, who must in effect now choose death or life, after a heart attack. From these we learn something of the composure each has reached as an unexpected outcome of the ordeal of Felicitas, and we learn that they are all, except hopeless Muriel, happier than they have ever been in their lives. As Charlotte reflects: "There they are, five old women waiting for an old man to die, living in the country with a young woman and a kid. When you put it that way, it sounds pretty goddamn flat. But you can always make your life sound wrong if you try to describe it in a hundred words or less."

Cyprian, reflecting on himself, and although aware that he, too, is happier than ever before, nevertheless suffers from a sense of failure on all scores, particularly in his priesthood. He is able to see the pride and fastidiousness that have moved him from the outset of his vocation, and to see what a trial he has been to his superiors and fellow-priests. Above all, he thinks about the aging women from whom he has received and accepted so much, even as he despised them all. He realizes how much he has needed them all, and how generously they have responded. He is able to decide that he will pray for the eventual ordination of women. His is a quantum leap in understanding, informed by a new awareness of the inestimable value and sweetness of human love. "I had to learn ordinary happiness," he thinks, "and from ordinary happiness the first real peace of my life, my life which I wanted full of splendor. I wanted to live in the unapproachable light, the light of the pure spirit. Now every morning is miraculous to me. I wake and see in the thin, early light the faces of my friends."

There seems less reason than before for him to fear, as he does, that he has betrayed his vocation in favor of the "terrible ringed accident of human love." Rather, he seems for the first time able to value what he has received, and to return it in kind, instead of forcing upon his friends that which in his vanity he supposed he could give them from his own borrowed splendor. Until he sees the *lumen lumens* he has always longed for, the "slant, imperfect sun" will suffice to reflect it. He is spared the knowledge of the damage he has done to Felicitas by his dualistic schooling. Nor is she aware of the change that has occurred in him. Ironically, now that he might correct and amplify his previous instruction, she can, or will, no longer talk to him about it. But Cyprian's "grand, impossible life," or the idea of it, she knows she will always need at the center of her own. He has made his most important point.

In this novel, Mary Gordon has undertaken something considerably more difficult than the subject of *Final Payments.* Uneven in execution it is nevertheless, I think, an even more impressive work, larger in scope, more deeply perceptive, richer in mystery, than the first book. A bravo performance. Encore, encore.

Michiko Kakutani (review date 20 March 1985)

SOURCE: "Books of the Times," in *The New York Times,* March 20, 1985, p. C21.

[*In the following review, Kakutani offers positive evaluation of* Men and Angels.]

For Mary Gordon's heroines, the choice between perfection of the life or of the work has always held center stage. Torn between the hope of "ordinary human happiness" and the pure, crystalline demands of an absolute vocation, between a need to fulfill personal imperatives and a need to submerge themselves in some kind of "clear, consuming work," they've frequently ended up in an emotional and spiritual limbo. Both Isabel in *Final Payments* and Felicitas in *The Company of Women* were raised on the romance of religion, on the idea of selfless devotion to a cause, and though both defected from the Church, they would later experience domestic life in the world of men and children as a come-down from the loftiness of their earlier ideals.

In *Men and Angels,* her fierce, shining new novel, Miss Gordon broadens her concept of vocation to include art, as well as religion—thereby moving beyond the insular, Catholic universe of her earlier fiction—and she also sets forth a new, more generous and humane vision of temporal life. Whereas Felicitas in *The Company of Women* bluntly refused the promises of romantic and sexual love ("it is for shelter that we marry and make love," she declared near the end of the book), Anne, the heroine of *Men and Angels,* embraces, however tentatively, the possibilities of "that other life, beautiful and heavy-scented as a dark fruit that grew up in shadow, the life of the family."

In doing so, Anne forgoes the consolations offered by the pristine, ordered realms of Art and Religion, and instead acknowledges all the messy entanglements and conditional values of humdrum daily life. Through painful experience, she comes to accept the fact that the heart cannot be moved at will, that it is subject to the vagaries of fate: and she realizes, too, that even the most potent love—between a parent and a child, between a man and a woman—is horribly limited. She can neither protect her children from the perils of everyday life—the hole in the icy pond, the slight suffered at school, the intractable fact of death—nor save them from unhappiness and misfortune.

When we first meet her, Anne has what seems to be a comfortable, comforting life, "ornamented with good fortune, like a spray of diamonds on the dark hair of a woman." At 38, she's happily married to Michael Foster, a handsome professor at Selby College; she has two wonderful kids, "Darling Peter, Darling Sarah," and a good job as an assistant director at the college art gallery. In addition, she's working on a monograph about an American Impressionist painter named Caroline Watson—the arc of whose life will come to counterpoint her own.

Writing in dense, lyrical prose that is as richly pictorial in its use of metaphor as Caroline's paintings, Miss Gordon conjures up Anne's world with extraordinary precision. Like Virginia Woolf, she has a gift for tracking the subtle ebb and flow of emotions, the insubstantial moon tide of feelings and moods; and she uses this gift to delineate Anne's inner life and to give the reader a sense of the social and moral rhythms at work in a small college town.

Anne worries, from time to time, that her life in Selby is too placid, that she has ignored her generation's feminist dictates by being mainly a wife and a mother, and her wish for change is soon fulfilled. When Michael is offered a fellowship abroad, she elects to stay behind with the children—in order to have time to complete her study of Caroline Watson. "She had done one courageous thing, had lived without him, had stayed at home to live a separate life while he went away," writes Miss Gordon. "Why had she imagined that nothing would be risked and nothing lost in the arrangement? It is what her generation always did, expected everything and was always shocked, like children, when something had to be given up."

Indeed Anne begins to see that all she had once taken for granted is subject to the terrifying flux of modern life. Caroline's story—she abandoned her 2-year-old son to pursue her career, traded a home and family for artistic achievement and a succession of hotel rooms—makes her wonder whether Art and Family are mutually exclusive notions. Her separation from Michael, coupled with the unexpected attraction she feels for another man, throws into question all her carefully packaged assumptions about marriage and fidelity. And the arrival of a pasty-faced au pair girl, named Laura, thoroughly disrupts the tranquility of her home.

There's something vaguely voyeuristic about Laura—she always seems to be eavesdropping, insinuating herself where she's not wanted. And thanks to Miss Gordon's use of shifting points of view, the reader also learns that she's a religious zealot, whose loneliness has twisted the teachings of the Bible into a strange, self-serving doctrine. Laura believes that she is one of God's chosen, that she's been sent to "save" Anne and her children by teaching them "that human love meant nothing," that "it was only the Love of God that could protect and lead and cover." In this sense, Laura seems like an extreme version of Father Cyprian in *The Company of Woman,* who preaches a doctrine of "hate the world and love God"—in her case, though, adherence to an absolute doctrine leads not to idealism but to simple madness.

One of the problems with Laura is that Miss Gordon uses her as a melodramatic device to keep the plot of *Men and Angels* ticking along—the reader can see the ending coming, a mile off—and to serve this end, she's frequently turned into a caricature of religious fanaticism. Readers may be distracted by other aspects of *Men and Angels* as well. Miss Gordon's insistence on giving a feminist reading to everything from sex appeal to artistic achievement (Nobody cares, complains one character, "if Monet was a bad father") becomes tiresome at times; and as in her previous books, her male characters remain mere shadows of her woman. These, however, are fairly minor quibbles with what is essentially a beautifully written and highly ambitious novel—a novel that marks a new turn in Miss Gordon's brilliant career.

Rosellen Brown (review date 29 April 1985)

SOURCE: "The Wages of Love," in *The New Republic,* April 29, 1985, pp. 34-6.

[*In the following review, Brown offers favorable assessment of* Men and Angels.]

In one of the Irish writer Mary Lavin's stories, a woman stands beside her dying husband's bed and hears bird-song for the first time in years, "so loud [had been] the noise of their love in her ears." This moment has always seemed the quintessential expression of the triumph and danger of a fulfilling love, conjugal or parental: even the healthiest of loves can be consuming, limiting, threatening to the world and to the self, which is implacably single. And yet—the question hangs beside its unambiguous but not uncomplicated answer—what is the self without profound engagement with others?

Mary Gordon's third novel, **Men and Angels,** is a fine amplification of Lavin's paradox. Gracefully written, with a sustained fierceness new to her work, it is complex in its vision of family and motherhood, and pained, finally, at the terms we must make, all of us (for if we are not all parents, we were all once children), with a universe that apportions love and its rewards unjustly.

Anne Foster, possessor of a Harvard Ph.D. in art history and of a household that contains her much loved husband, Michael, and a young son and daughter, is a woman haunted only by the fear that she has too much, has been too lucky, and therefore that she could at any moment lose it all. In this, her 38th year, she is at work with great absorption writing the catalog for an exhibition of the somewhat neglected paintings of an American woman, Caroline Watson, who went to Paris in the 1880s and had the misfortune "to be a merely first-rate painter in an age of geniuses."

Mary Gordon sends Anne's husband to France on an academic exchange, thus freeing her of the comfortable "noise" of her marriage to hear for the first time the birdcalls of many kinds of creatures. She concentrates on her work for its own sake, and so that "refreshed she could dive back down to the dense underworld, to her children." She is befriended by Jane, Caroline Watson's formidable daughter-in-law, who, together with Caroline, seems to have thrived on the inadequacy of Caroline's pathetic son, dead early of a lack of love and confidence. Suspecting her perfect husband of a dalliance in France, Anne falls in something like love with a young electrician whose wife's chronic illness makes him vulnerable. (To say this, incidentally, gives nothing away: Gordon, like Marge Piercy and others—perhaps we could go back to Jane Austen—has a formulaic weakness for certain male characters who, even in the face of momentary surliness or unseemly working-class occupations, are graced with aesthetically and morally impeccable habits, princes in disguise.)

The most decisive step Anne takes during this year of ostensible freedom is to reluctantly hire a young woman named Laura, because no mother can accomplish work that demands concentration without someone to help with her children. Unlovely and unloved, Laura arrives out of the limbo of utter homelessness, trusting in the Jesus who commanded that one leave one's parents, taking "neither gold nor silver . . . nor two tunics nor a staff," to serve, even to kill, for the Lord, to do anything necessary to advance righteousness in the world. She will, we know from the start, bring the whole house down, though not necessarily in the ways we (or Anne) might fear.

Men and Angels begins in Laura's consciousness, which is fixed, desperate, essentially mad. She has grown up the victim of one of many kinds of child abuse that fascinate Gordon—in this case, the monstrousness of a mother who does not love her and does not dissemble about it. The vengeful havoc Laura wreaks strips Anne and her children of the luck of their lifelong belovedness, of the carefully nurtured perfection of their life.

Men and Angels is lush with the details of family intimacy, unlike Gordon's first two novels. The life of Felicitas in *The Company of Women* was lived primarily among virgins and widows, under the beneficent reign of a priest who is impossible father and lover to them all. In *Final Payments* Isabel yields to the patriarchy of her bedridden father, his Irish-Catholic cronies, and their negligent contempt for women. *Men and Angels,* by contrast, portrays motherhood and wifehood relished in wonderfully seductive detail: "[The children] took turns measuring the cocoa, the sugar, the milk, the pinch of salt . . . There are my children, Anne said to herself, these are the ones I missed. She could smell their thin high sweat; they should have taken off their sweaters. But it was autumn and she understood their feelings: woolen clothes on such a day were a pleasure in themselves."

At the same time she recognizes the costs of such commitment: "Marriage muffled, it protected, it made it much more difficult to be generous because you were always kept back a little from the lives of others, and so from feeling their need," Anne reflects; and she finds that motherhood muffles further. "But now she was a woman with young children; she couldn't possibly do anything dangerous to them. The whole shape of her life must be constructed to make her children safe." Curious not merely about the work but about the life of Caroline Watson, Anne thinks "yet one wanted to know, when the women had accomplished something. Whom did they love in relation to their bodies? Whom were they connected to by blood? . . . But it wasn't the fact of connection that was interesting; it was how they got around it."

What binds all of Gordon's work together, whatever its differences, is her unique fascination with the idea of love and its derivatives, the lovable, the unlovable, the unloved, subcategories as ineluctable as election and damnation.

Most novelists, it goes without saying, entangle their characters in questions of love and the power it gives and withholds: its acquisition, its maintenance, its loss. But the capacity to love and be loved—abstract as a Platonic ideal, however graphic its realization as plot—is a fairly unique preoccupation these days. One thinks of Hawthorne's *Tales,* perhaps of the woman perfect but for the birthmark on her cheek; or the aftermath of such death-of-the-heart novels as Elizabeth Bowen's, or Antonia White's *Frost in May,* or Robb Forman Dew's recent *The Time of Her Life,* which makes the disillusion attendant on a child's loss of love a permanent incapacitating scar. But in those books events befall, they are not inevitable. People choose their fates; the end is not written in the beginning. I can't think of one of her contemporaries who shares quite the same psychological/aesthetic determinism as Mary Gordon, whose vision of a gated kingdom, of a fiery excluding sword raised against the charmless, seems to shimmer in her imagination constantly.

In Gordon's work, loving is not so much a process as it is a state, given like grace; a condition, like beauty, into which one is born. There is no appealing its presence or absence in one's life: it is absolute, untouchable even by the love of God, which "means nothing to a heart that is starved of human love." That is Mary Gordon's catch-22: for those who are most in need of its light, like flowers in a dark place, no love can penetrate or suffice. They are like instruments whose receptors are damaged, who give out a single mechanical cry of pain and need that, perversely, repels salvation.

In *The Company of Women,* Muriel, who has "a styptic heart," envies and resents Felicitas, the child of grace, even as she loves her. In *Final Payments,* Margaret, representing every ounce of salt and vinegar Gordon can conjure up, the life-denying constriction of nuns without bodies, fights for the soul of Isabel, who has just—barely—leaped free into the pleasures of the contemporary secular world. Finally, in *Men and Angels,* though the Catholic church is hardly mentioned (Laura represents her own distorted church, a religion of desperation and defensiveness), the agon is still familiar. Anne is elect, as are her children. Laura sues for her love and, losing, guarantees only one thing: that, having laid waste the kingdom of the graced by taking away the certainty of safety and sewing guilt and self-doubt, she will never be forgotten.

The girl's abjectness is echoed many times over. Caroline Watson, the painter whose letters Anne reads with fascination, is a terrible mother. She is given the single-mindedness of the artist too preoccupied to notice that her child is waiting patiently at the door while she works. (In fact it is worse: she hears him but does not respond.) Yet it appears to be her son's innate lack of appeal and force, not merely her need to get a day's work done, that keeps her from loving him. Cause and effect are a bit vague—undoubtedly both are true—yet Caroline at her death shoulders the blame for blighting him. And we are shown, conversely, how the (rather too simple) love of the electrician, Ed, saves his small son from the vagaries of a deranged mother's attentions.

On the way to the novel's conclusion, in which nothing is resolved except that there is no democracy of the affections, and that the emotionally hungry, whom we shall always have with us, will forever endanger the feasts of the fortunate, Gordon draws a hundred small moments beautifully. Anne, at 38, weeps because her parents no longer rush to succor her when she needs them. She buys tulip bulbs in too many colors because she "hadn't the courage for a unified field; she couldn't live with leaving so much out." Her six-year-old daughter is humiliated in a ballet performance, betrayed only by her youth and eagerness. Anne begins to comprehend the complexity of certain sexual charades, the "lively attentiveness that came only with sex" but might in fact mask other needs. The novel has its flaws—Laura frequently becomes as tedious in print as she is said to be in person, revealing herself to be the contrivance that holds together the skeleton of moral concerns beneath the book's more poignant flesh. The epilogue iterates too explicitly what we have seen, casting a skein of sentimentality over the rest that it doesn't deserve.

But **Men and Angels** is a beautifully written, passionate inquiry into many kinds of vulnerability and power, and an acknowledgment of the pain of trying to balance instinctual love with a more encompassing compassion. If compassion is inadequate, so be it, Mary Gordon says through Anne: "Perhaps she was an adult now . . . Children's terror, children's sorrow, was all based on disappointment; adults took their grief from certainty and loss." Such maturity becomes both character and author. This is Mary Gordon's finest book.

Carol Iannone (essay date June 1985)

SOURCE: "The Secret of Mary Gordon's Success," in *Commentary*, Vol. 79, No. 6, June, 1985, pp. 62-6.

[*In the following essay, Iannone discusses the interplay of religious and feminist themes in Gordon's fiction. "Miss Gordon's novels," concludes Iannone, "are at once the symptom and the artistic exemplification of the empty self-centeredness which happens to have become her subject."*]

Mary Gordon's first novel, **Final Payments** (1978), about the embattled coming of age of an Irish Catholic woman, was both a best-seller and the object of an astonishingly enthusiastic critical response, in which Miss Gordon was compared to Jane Austen and her novel was called a contemporary version of Joyce's *Portrait of the Artist*. Her second novel, **The Company of Women** (1981), also a best-seller, met with a slightly less rapturous but still highly respectful critical reception; Francine du Plessix Gray was typical in hailing Miss Gordon as her generation's "preeminent novelist of Roman Catholic mores and manners." After this novel Miss Gordon announced that she intended to expand her concerns, and indeed her third novel, **Men and Angels,** is ostensibly not about Catholicism. Except, of course, that it is; only the names have been changed to protect the guilty.

Mary Gordon's background has supplied her with some unique qualifications to write about present-day Catholicism. Her mother, whom she has described simply as "an Irish Catholic working-class girl," was the daughter of Irish and Italian immigrants. Her father, David, a Harvard-educated Jew, had belonged in the 20's to the colony of American expatriates in Paris, where he gradually grew disaffected with modern culture. His sympathy with what his daughter calls "the embarrassing side" in the Spanish Civil War led to his conversion to Catholicism, and a tendency to romanticize the Catholic working class led to his marrying Mary Gordon's mother. While his wife worked as a legal secretary, he made several attempts to found a right-wing Catholic periodical while staying at home to care for their only child (no doubt preparing the ground for Mary's later ardent feminism—she has remarked that for her, feminism comes nearest to Catholicism as an informing framework of values). He died when Mary was only seven, but had by then already begun to teach her Greek, philosophy, and French.

Perhaps partially because of the mixed colors of her personal history, Mary Gordon gradually came to resent her confinement in the Catholic "ghettoes" of Queens and Valley Stream, Long Island, where she attended parochial school through the 12th grade. A docile child—she wrote devout tracts entitled "What Is Prayer?"—she became a rebellious adolescent who once organized a bubble-gum-blowing demonstration to harass the "ignorant" nuns she had come to despise. Her bitter provincial exile ended with a scholarship to Barnard. There Miss Gordon began her advance beyond the pale into the mainstream of American life—which for her, it seems, is entirely, eternally, lyrically Protestant. (Her perception of the ethos formed by the two religions sometimes seems a caricature-in-reverse. For her, Catholics are morbid and intensely self-scrutinizing while Protestants are confident, masterful, disciplined, capable of "a deep unstated sympathy.") It being the turbulent '60s at Columbia, Miss Gordon found more effective ways to protest authority than by blowing bubble gum. She participated in student strikes and sit-ins, and thereby, presumably, gained the social consciousness that filters into some of her work as a liberating alternative to the burdensome demands of Catholic charity.

But Catholicism is not entirely a negative force for Miss Gordon. She has remarked on its profound idealism, and in her novels she depicts a species of Catholic manhood that is fiercely compelling. To her heroines, moreover, she accords a driving passion and qualities of clarity, insight, and penetration that at times can make the Protestants around them seem watery and complacent. Miss Gordon still calls herself a Catholic, or, as she puts it, "I have a real religious life in a framework which I think of as Catholic." But she doubts the Pope would be pleased with her: her views on birth control, abortion, and the ordination of women are unorthodox, and she has observed that "sexy people" leave the Church. On the other hand, her writing evinces a decided scorn for much of the updated Church of post-Vatican II and a certain nostalgia for the consuming seriousness of traditional Catholicism.

In some ways, Mary Gordon's own story, as well as the story she tells in her novels, is one of upward ethnic mobility. But it is a story with a twist: Catholicism, with its insistent ethic of self-renunciation, can make the achievement of worldly success seem not just difficult or forbidding, but positively evil. This tension between the mutually exclusive demands of the sacred and the profane gives Mary Gordon's writing its all-absorbing, almost obsessive intensity, and may well account for the excitement her work has provoked. In a generation of casually pervasive materialism, her protagonists' struggles to break free of the peremptory, otherworldly claims of the Church and to carve out a share of "ordinary human happiness" must seem both deliciously exotic and monumentally heroic. Without the defining element of religion, the resemblance of her novels to the genre known as "women's fiction" (in which omnicompetent heroines battle through impossible odds toward inevitable triumph) would no doubt have been more readily discerned.

This is not to suggest that Miss Gordon lacks technical skill; quite the contrary. She can be fabulously descriptive; her tightly packed sentences burst with metaphoric energy; her characters can be large, her situations affecting. Reviewers have praised her for all of this—and have as well cited her flaws, which include overwriting, a tendency to fall back on stereotypes, failure to sustain an overall narrative. But it is clear that they are ultimately impressed with something far greater than technical skill. With Miss Gordon's novels, it seems, they enter the presence of something almost, well, holy. A "painful, powerful transforming book, the monster we have all been waiting for," said the *Christian Science Monitor* of *Final Payments,* while the New York *Times* found *The Company of Women* to be a vision of "integrity," "chastity," "purity," ambition, and grandeur." Miss Gordon's concerns, asserted *Harper's,* are nothing less than "eschatological"; according to *Saturday Review,* she writes about "instinct and reason, submission and authority, the holiness of the flesh, and the awesome power of love to diminish, enrich, and immortalize." And when they are not agreeably dazzled in this manner, Mary Gordon's critics praise her for freeing us from "the false lessons of the past," for dethroning "the mythical nobility of suffering," and for exposing the charity that is really disguised masochism, the morality that is only a cover for hypocrisy.

This, then, with a few emendations and detours, and the determined imposition of feminist ideology, is the substance of the Gordon *oeuvre:* a muscular prohibitive orthodoxy crusades against a sunny mainline permissiveness, while the heroine, who embodies the best of both worlds, is torn between the righteousness of being Catholic and the freedom of being Protestant.

This struggle appears in Miss Gordon's first novel, *Final Payments,* in the form of a revisionist treatise on love and charity. Isabel Moore, Irish-Catholic born and bred, has made a sacrifice unusual for the self-seeking generation to which she belongs but (Miss Gordon implies) typical of the Catholic female with dreams of self-denial. When she was nineteen, her adored father, a widower, an ultra-conservative Catholic, and a professor of medieval literature at a small Catholic college in Queens, had discovered her in bed with his favorite student, and shortly thereafter suffered a stroke. Isabel has cared for him through eleven years of wretched invalidism, both hating and loving her self-imposed martyrdom. The novel opens at his funeral, when she realizes that she must "invent an existence for herself."

Once freed of her burden, Isabel eagerly plunges into the indulgences of the flesh. She sells her house and acquires an I.U.D., then takes on a new job, a new apartment (outside of Catholic Queens), and a couple of lovers (both married, one to a best friend); thirty years of Irish Catholic repression have obviously failed to dim her capacity for the sensual and the sexual. But Isabel soon finds living for the pleasures of this world more than she can bear. The repellent, self-pitying wife of one of her lovers humiliates her and triggers off a terrible episode of guilt and self-condemnation. Isabel determines to return to a life of self-sacrifice. With the willed perversity of the saints who drank the water in which they washed the lepers' feet, she undertakes the care of the aged and impoverished Margaret Casey, a onetime housekeeper for her father and herself.

Margaret is a selfish and sanctimonious woman whom Isabel has always despised but toward whom she still feels an intense obligation. She sets herself the task of learning to love this woman she hates in order to attain the pure, impersonal state of Christian charity. It is a mistake, concludes Isabel, to want to love uniquely and be loved uniquely; better to love "as God loved His creatures, impartially, impervious to their individual natures and thus incapable of being really hurt by them." But soon it becomes obvious to her that such forced sacrifice is itself illegitimate. At novel's end Isabel dispatches her debt to Margaret and resolves to seek a "reasonable life" of ordinary satisfactions.

Mary Gordon once expressed surprise that a novel of "sacrifice and old age" should have been so warmly received as was *Final Payments*—as if the esoteric ethic of self-renunciation were not this author's chief appeal. But "sacrifice and old age" are in any event only half the message of *Final Payments.* The other half is a treatise on how to overcome guilt, cut loose from life's losers, and buckle down to enjoying "the cares of this world" as soon as possible. Thus, much of the book is devoted to Miss Gordon's improvements on traditional morality. When Isabel commits adultery she suffers a sharp backlash of guilt, but the book reminds us that this "sin" breaks up a stagnant marriage and frees one of life's winners from one of its congenital losers. ("I was never any match for her, with all her deprivations," the defecting husband declares of his whining martyr of a wife.) In Isabel's job as a social worker (investigating home care for the aged), she comes across an old woman ready to commit suicide because of her need for particular love rather than the "generalized charity" she receives; Isabel does not hesitate to help her end her life, once again with the novel's quietly defiant endorsement.

It is here, in the dichotomy between the need for personal affection and the Catholic exhortation to universal love, that Miss Gordon repeatedly focuses her moral attention. But she has stacked the deck. Universal, unconditional love is for her largely the love of and for losers. People love God and seek to be loved in Him mostly because they are tired or defeated or because "their bodies . . . had not given them sufficient pleasure." These losers not only lack the courage to risk human love but never had much to recommend them to begin with—no beauty, grace, intelligence, humor, or sensuality, especially no sensuality. (Other models of loser-spirituality include Isabel's father, fanatical and often hateful, and Father Mulcahy, her pastor, loving and loyal but somewhat beside the point. The men of Isabel's choice love "conditionally.")

Personal human love is for the winners—for those with all the assets plus the guts to ask to be loved for themselves alone and "not for what we share with the rest of the human race." But once you admit your need for such love, you are vulnerable; "there was nothing worth living for once you lost it." Hence Isabel's sympathy for the old woman's desire to commit suicide. Life is "monstrous" in its "randomness" as to who gets the good stuff, and in its precariousness as to who gets to keep it, but there you have it; the winners accept the terms.

The problem is that Catholicism asks the contenders to care for the rejects. How to quiet this nagging demand with minimal energy and still stay on the fast track—that is the question that haunts Isabel, who recognizes, correctly, that the charity and sacrifice being demanded cannot be accomplished through a simple act of the will (she does not surmise that it can be achieved through grace). And so she rejects her parochial-school lessons—"Love is measured by sacrifice," and "Charity suffereth long and is kind"—in favor of something much simpler:

> Margaret's life would be more bearable if she did not have to worry about money. And I had money, money from the sale of the house. It occurred to me, simply, that I could give up my money; I did not have to give up my life.

By signing over her entire bank account to Margaret, making her "final payment," Isabel is freed from pointless self-

sacrifice and can begin her own life anew: "It was all the money I had in the world. But I was free of Margaret now, and I felt weightless. . . . There was nothing left between us. Margaret could not touch me now."

It seems awkward to have to remind such a self-reflective writer as Mary Gordon that in the very same chapter of I Corinthians from which she draws the title of her third book, *Men and Angels,* Paul gives a clear warning against precisely this kind of giving: "though I bestow all my goods to feed the poor . . . and have not charity, it profiteth me nothing." But Miss Gordon, who so arranges her moral landscape as to make *any* impulse toward transcendent love seem deluded, aims of course precisely to dismantle charity in its Christian sense. Indeed, even private philanthropy is not her idea of a model system for the necessary redistribution from winners to losers. Isabel's first lover, a pointedly crude, callous, and selfish man, nevertheless "really does a lot of good" in his position as overseer of county welfare programs: more good, it is implied, than can ever be done by trivial acts of self-sacrifice. "Governments gave money and did not ask for love. Money was beautiful . . . you could change lives without giving up your own life." Government is a "dealer in charity without the weights of love."

In her exposé of Christian charity, Mary Gordon thus inadvertently gives us a sudden compact insight into the much vaunted "compassion" of the Left. We may be seeing here just what is impelling so many Catholics to equate their religion with the welfare state: not so much compassion as guilt, and the desire to enjoy life's banquet disencumbered of Lazarus at the gate.

One reason *Final Payments* needs to be examined in detail is that it fixes the pattern of which Miss Gordon's later novels are progressive variants. *The Company of Women,* set partly in the pre-Vatican II period, draws the same sort of (loaded) dichotomy between universal and particular love. A group of unattached women, living separately, are linked by the guidance of a powerful conservative priest, Father Cyprian, who has in one way or another helped them, given meaning to their lives, and made them into "something." This little company places all its hopes for the future on a girl named Felicitas (after "the one virgin martyr whose name contained some hope for ordinary human happiness"), the daughter of one of their widowed members and the only child among them. But Felicitas gradually rejects the all-pervasive spirituality that Father Cyprian would impose upon her. She leaves her mother's Brooklyn apartment for Columbia University, briefly undertakes a radical style of life, gets herself pregnant, and returns to the group to have her baby. At this point the women build themselves houses near the now-retired Cyprian. Felicitas eventually agrees to marry (another man), and little by little begins "to have an ordinary life."

The novel makes conscious allusion to *Jane Eyre,* an allusion which Miss Gordon has underscored in interviews. Like Mr. Rochester, Cyprian must be symbolically castrated—Mary Gordon has warned us about her feminism—broken from his obsession with spirituality and made to accept his own need for human love. At the end of his life he is forced to admit that "the love of God, untouched by accident and preference and failure," still eludes him. As for the particular love of the women who surround him, this is the only real love he has felt—a fact he admits somewhat grudgingly: "They have dragged me down to the middling terrain of their conception of the world, half blood instinct, half the impulse of the womb." (Such ideas are among the elements that bring Miss Gordon closer to D. H. Lawrence than to the "female tradition" of Jane Austen and the Brontës she seems to believe she belongs to.) So much for putting your eggs in the basket of spirituality.

As for Felicitas, she continues the line, set by Isabel in *Final Payments,* of criticizing the ways of God to man: "I will not accept the blandishments of the religious life; I will not look to God for comfort, or for succor, or for sweetness. God will have to meet me on the high ground of reason, and there He's a poor contender." While the older women need a strict Catholicism to fill and order their otherwise diffuse and empty lives, Felicitas manages on what is revealed as a budding feminism. She turns away from sexual "liberation" when she sees how men exploit it for their own selfish pleasure. A graphic description of a mangled abortion, as well as a section telling how Felicitas at first hates her baby and learns to sympathize with abusive mothers, constitutes part of this novel's contribution to feminist suasion. (In *Final Payments* it was a defense of lesbianism and a glorification of female friendship; in *Men and Angels,* it is an object lesson in how to combine family and career.)

But the feminism in *The Company of Women* goes far beyond the promotion of various items on the liberationist agenda to become the new moral imperative. The doomed, savagely devout priest is obviously meant in a way to stand for the old Church itself, which pointedly needs to be cut loose from male spiritual chauvinism—"macho clericalism," as Miss Gordon has put it—humanized, feminized, and brought down to earth by (the company of) women. If it seems at first surprising that Miss Gordon is no supporter of the post-Vatican II changes in the Church, and indeed mocks many of their manifestations—priests in chinos, sappy new rites of penance, daisy-covered prayer cards, etc.—this is because her real hope for renewal derives from the mystical and salvific feminism evident in *The Company of Women.* It is the female principle that will save Catholicism from the death of orthodoxy—although how the replacement of one expansive orthodoxy by a second, much narrower one constitutes an improvement, she does not say.

At any rate, traditional Catholicism having been effectively consigned to the ash heap of history in *The Company of Women,* in her latest novel, *Men and Angels,* the ideal of an ascendant religious sensibility is no longer embodied in a compelling man like Cyprian, but in a quintessential

loser. Laura, a pathetic waif, bruisingly rejected by her family, seizes upon the idea of God's love to assuage the miserable loneliness of her existence. She becomes a mother's helper to Anne Foster, a Harvard Ph.D. in Art History and a winner who is not yet wholly secure about the fact. Anne has been happily making a home for her two children and her husband, a professor of French literature at a small northeastern college, when she is offered (at thirty-eight) a remarkable opportunity to prepare the catalogue for an exhibit of the works of Caroline Watson, an early 20th-century painter (a fictional composite of Cecilia Beaux, Mary Cassatt, and Suzanne Valadon), neglected in her own time but now being rediscovered thanks to the current interest in women. Taking the job requires that Anne stay home with her children while her husband goes off on a sabbatical to France.

Anne makes several attempts to be nice to Laura but really comes to despise her—for Laura, pathetic as she is, is also carefully presented as difficult and self-righteous. But Laura, falsely cheered by Anne's outward signs of affection, is so devastated when Anne fires her for negligence that she commits suicide by slitting her wrists in the family bathtub. Later Anne, learning of Laura's unhappy life, mourns her inability to have overcome her hatred of the girl and extend the love that might have saved her. But everyone assures her that such love is virtually impossible (they must have read Mary Gordon's previous novels); no matter how much she suffered, Laura was inherently unlovable.

Anne, like Isabel before her, finally accepts the "monstrous" precariousness of human life—illustrated in various ways throughout the novel—without the consolations of transcendent love. As Laura may or may not be winging her way to the God who let her down, Anne walks bravely away from the gravesite into the beatitude of husband, children, home, and career.

> She wept and wept. People were so weak, and life would raise its whip and bring it down again and again on the bare tender flesh of the most vulnerable. Love was what they needed, and most often it was not there. It was abundant, love, but it could not be called. It was won by chance; it was a monstrous game of luck.

Although Anne is presented as having no "religious life," her tendency to self-scrutiny, her insecurity about her place in the world of achievement, and her fear that she might someday be punished for the "great good fortune" life has handed her put her fairly in the line of Miss Gordon's Catholic heroines. In this novel the fanatical and antisensual religiosity has been filtered off into Laura, while the sunny Protestant version of "religious life" is represented by Jane, Caroline Watson's beloved daughter-in-law, a beautiful, intelligent, and proud old woman who lives comfortably by the "senses" rather than by "morals."

Actually, it turns out that Jane, in an access of guilt over the way she had treated her husband before his miserable, untimely death, had once sought and found forgiveness in

God. But her faith is of that highly qualified variety of which Miss Gordon approves: God's love (such as it is to begin with) will ever be "insufficient for the human heart," it "means nothing to the heart that is starved of human love." Thus the revisionist charity Miss Gordon advances as a gloss on the famous idealism from Paul that gives the book its title: "Though I speak with the tongues of men and angels, and have not charity, I am become as sounding brass, or a tinkling cymbal."

In her novels Mary Gordon goes over the same ground again and again—the precariousness and random unfairness of human existence, its value nonetheless, the right to enjoy it if one is a winner, the nagging problem of what to do with the losers. Miss Gordon's work in some ways resembles those books and articles on "having it all" that are written for women, with their advice on cramming in as much as possible, keeping track of one's needs, making sure they're satisfied, the whole informed by a lurking fear that nothing will really suffice.

Thus in the end the real question is not whether human love will serve in the absence of the divine, for Miss Gordon's books are not really about love at all; they are about the monumental self-centeredness released by the collapse of orthodoxy, the agitated emptiness that finds an expression in movements like feminism. It is a historical irony, no doubt inevitable, that this same agitation should be the presiding difficulty of the contemporary Church as well, with its restless movements and demands and its cries over the "monstrous" unfairness of being poor, of being female, of being deprived. Where there was once some ability to accept the simple grace of God's love even in the face of inequalities, and to work in one's own quiet way for His kingdom, now this entire dimension seems to have been lost, or perhaps destroyed. Yet it is hard to see how all the aimless revisionism, of the variety produced by the Church itself or proposed to it by the likes of Mary Gordon, is going to lead the way back to salvation. For Miss Gordon's novels are at once the symptom and the artistic exemplification of the empty self-centeredness which happens to have become her subject.

Sarah Gilead (essay date Summer 1986)

SOURCE: "Mary Gordon's *Final Payments* and the Nineteenth-Century English Novel," in *Critique: Studies in Modern Fiction,* Vol. XXVII, No. 4, Summer, 1986, pp. 213-27.

[*In the following essay, Gilead compares the theme and structure of* Final Payments *to the works of Victorian novelists such as Jane Austen, Charlotte Brontë, and George Eliot. According to Gilead, Gordon reinterprets the moral themes of canonical nineteenth-century women's fiction through the lens of contemporary feminism.*]

Mary Gordon's *Final Payments* may be read as a study of the problem of female identity in a culture characterized by changing, often conflicting moral ideals and behavioral directives. As such, *Final Payments* considers what the Victorians called "The Woman Question" and, appropriately, borrows or alludes to situations, characters, themes, and titles from nineteenth-century English novels dramatizing similar psycho-cultural crises. But iteration requires difference as well as similarity. Gordon's borrowings of and allusions to the conventions of a prior novelistic era do not reflect a lack of literary imagination, but imply the Bloomian notion that literary invention and authorial self-invention are generated by strong reading one's literary progenitors. Thus, in *Final Payments,* a parallel emerges between the plight of the heroine, adrift emotionally and socially after the death of her father, and the condition of the contemporary "belated" novelist in quest of authorly identity in the wake of the great traditions of the nineteenth century and modernist novels. Just as Isabel Moore owes "final payments" to her dead father and the traditional moral and behavioral codes he had instilled in her, Mary Gordon owes *Final Payments* to the "great tradition" of such novelists as Jane Austen, Charlotte Brontë, and George Eliot, a tradition she must both incorporate and modify.

Isabel Moore's first-person autobiographical narrative follows the traditional pattern of the Bildungsroman, in which the protagonist's moral education is dramatized through a series of crises and transformations best understood as rites of passage. Victor Turner's development of Van Gennep's concept of liminality illuminates the multiple significances of dramas of transformation, whether social or literary. Detached from social structure, the liminal passenger undergoes an ordeal in which her or his structural attributes are lost; then is "re-born" into social structure, newly inscribed within its values, meanings, and role functions. But during the liminal period, the individual is free of classificatory systems, is "betwixt and between the positions assigned and arrayed by law, custom, convention, and ceremonial." Though enacting a ritual process which will ultimately affirm law, custom, and convention, the passenger may, paradoxically, embody a critique of aspects of social structure. The numerous orphan-narratives of the nineteenth century novel are liminal in precisely this way. The orphan-protagonists of Dickens, Eliot, the Brontës and others are exiles or outsiders with respect to ordinary society, and as such dramatize a serious questioning of the mores, ideals, traditions, and power-structures of that society; but these orphan figures undergo transformations which are representative and symbolic of social and cultural change, and thus imply the possibility of reconciliation between the dissatisfied, disenfranchised, rebellious, or "lost" individual and a society whose injustices and constraints are revealed as ameliorating and thus tolerable: thus, the surprisingly conservative compromises that conclude originally critical novels like *Oliver Twist, Jane Eyre, Vanity Fair,* and *Middlemarch.*

Isabel Moore as fictional-autobiographical subject and narrator combines the character-attributes of the typical Victorian orphan-protagonist with those of the Austenian narrator. Isabel's narration reveals a self-critical, analytical, clear-thinking mind articulated in elegant, lucid prose. Descendant not only of the Austenian narrator but also of such Austenian heroines as Elizabeth Bennet, Emma Woodhouse, and Anne Elliot, Isabel's fine intelligence is particularly apt in perceiving the nuanced meanings of social behaviors, styles, clothing, body positions and movements, and facial expressions; and, what convention forbad Austen, in discussing with modern frankness the life of the body (there is delicious mockery both of contemporary interior decor and of Austen in Isabel's observation that her gynecologist's office "would have been a perfect setting for *Pride and Prejudice*"). As orphan, Isabel, like her Victorian predecessors, bears a more ambiguous relationship to her social environment and cultural heritage that does either the Austenian heroine or the modernist alienated anti-hero. Like Oliver Twist, David Copperfield, Jane Eyre, Becky Sharp, and other displaced persons in Victorian fiction, Isabel in her initial orphaned condition metaphorically expresses the inadequacy of the moral, social, and psychosexual givens of her traditional upbringing, of her father's and her community's narrow and unreflective conservatism. Yet, like her Victorian ancestors, the very modes in which she conceives and enacts her rejection of that conservatism are permeated by it, and necessitate not flight from but a series of painful confrontations with her past, confrontations which constitute the "final payments" she finds so difficult to make. Isabel's new life is based precisely on those principles and values her father and his world abhorred or misunderstood (social welfare, female independence, sexual liberty, self-actualization). But her newly won freedom leads to what Isabel cannot help but interpret as a reenactment of her sexual crime of eleven years ago, in guilty reaction against which she became her community's exemplar of its conservative religious and social ideals. In forging a new life, Isabel seems destined to reinscribe upon it the patterns of the old. Isabel, like many of the heroes and heroines of Dickens, Eliot, Thackeray and the Brontës, is a victim of the paradoxical mechanisms of guilt, by which intense desire for freedom and pleasure is bred in a life constrained by narrow ideology and limited social experience; but acting on that desire produces the self-punishing guilt which binds the actor even more tightly to the ideological and social constraints she had sought to overcome. The efforts to surmount value-conflicts only exacerbate them. New values, principles, and behaviors cannot simply replace the old; rather, a new formula must be found which can accommodate elements from both old and new. As discussed above, such formulae often underlie the ambiguous "compromise" endings of Victorian novels, and characterize the novels' particular mode of liminality.

Final Payments begins in the traditional fashion of the Victorian novel at a scene of orphaning (as do, for example, *Oliver Twist, David Copperfield, Great Expectations, Jane Eyre, Wuthering Heights*) in which the absence, death, or impotence of the father implies a whole range of social, cultural, and psychological problems, tentative solutions to which are enacted in the orphaned daughter's or son's liminal processes of mourning, wandering, ordeal, and transformation. Like the sons, the daughters are in quest of a stable social identity, tolerable gender self-concept, and source of moral authority, but are doubly dispossessed, by changing and unstable social structures and codes; and by the patriarchal nature of both traditional and modern culture. Like its Victorian predecessors, the beginning of *Final Payments* rehearses the heroine's generic, paradigmatic identity crisis whose deferred solutions form the ensuing narrative. For the first few paragraphs, all we know of the orphan-narrator is the fact of orphaning. The reader does not learn the narrator's gender, name, or age, as if the narrator is deprived even of the basic elements of identity-formation. The recounted inability to weep at the father's funeral suggests the broader inability to mourn for a lost or vitiated cultural heritage. Completed mourning both expresses guilt for abandoning or questioning that heritage and transforms that guilt into greater self-knowledge and into the creative energy needed, in turn, to transform the fragments and shards of cultural endowments into usable forms: Isabel Moore's "final payments" to her father's memory and to all that it represents will complete her mourning. Moore's Catholic heritage represents traditional norms and values in general (as Catholicism does occasionally in Victorian literature, for example in Browning's "Bishop Blougram's Apology," Thackeray's *Henry Esmond,* Charlotte Brontë's *Villette*); the priests who were her father's friends and co-religionists image the benevolent paternalism of most traditional cultures—benevolence which is protective and formative, and to which its inheritor is indebted for the very shape and solidity of the self (however illusory that solidity later proves to be). The traditional world of strong fathers represented at the priest-filled funeral of Isabel's father also recalls the passing of each individual's pre-Oedipal infancy, in which strong, idealized parents shelter and nurture the newly forming personality matrix. But the powerful claims of the past, whether cultural or personal, conflict with the need to adapt to change and to assert individuality.

Isabel as product of a "priest"-dominated community and family (her family for many years had consisted solely of her priest-like father and her father-devoted self) had lived out a modern version of the Victorian ideal of self-abnegating woman, who is indeed never "woman" alone but is always care-taking, felicity-making, comfort-bringing daughter, wife, mother, aunt; she is always primarily defined by her relationship to men. (As Mr. Wakem in *The Mill on the Floss* puts it, "We don't ask what a woman does, we ask whom she belongs to," Book 6, ch. 8.) For eleven years, until her father's death, Isabel had played the angel in the house, leading a celibate and monotonous life, nursing her sick, then dying, father and indulging herself in nothing but a sense of her own martyrdom. His death fails to free her. The "murderous importance" she still attaches to her father even after his death is murderous in several related senses, suggesting a kind of belated Oedipal guilt for her relief at his death and at her inability to weep for him; murderous too in that her fulfillment of the patriarchal ideal of angelic femininity has murdered eleven years of her life, and possibly more in the future; murderous perhaps in that she senses that to free herself from the intricate, strangling webs of the past, of its guilt and self-mistrust, of its half-acknowledged desires, rages, and fears, will require an act of violence, a radical repudiation or reinterpretation of the ideals, authority-structures, and self-images that had heretofore sustained her. She realizes, "I would have to invent an existence for myself"—such an act of self-generation indeed implying the annihilation of the "father" that had engendered and nurtured her past self.

Like many Victorian literary heroines, Isabel had succumbed to the addictive lures of self-sacrifice: "the day Dr. MacCauley told me about my father's stroke was of my whole life the day I felt most purely alive" because "certainty was mine; and purity; I was encased in meaning like crystals." But such achieved clarity of meaning also conceals acts of murder. Isabel's martyr's purity freezes nearly to death her ambition, egoism, rage, and sexuality, for all of which she is unable to find legitimate means of expression. Grasping at the opportunity for expiatory self-sacrifice, Isabel had sought in "visible martyrdom" to obliterate the humiliating memory of her father's having caught her, three weeks before his stroke, in bed with a man. Unlike such Victorian martyrs and near-martyrs as Dorothea Brooke, Jane Eyre, Amelia Sedley, and Lily Dale, Isabel with her Austenian analytical skill and post-Freudian conceptual framework is capable of sophisticated interpretations of her own motives. For example, she speculates on the possibility of having constructed, unconsciously, "the scene that would forbid me marriage during my father's lifetime, that would make impossible the one match he might have approved. . . . It is clear to me now that what I most feared was the possibility of my father's and my relationship becoming ordinary, or even assuming a texture that might seem comprehensible to an onlooker who had not known us all our lives." But Isabel's analytical superiority affords her no immediately discernible benefits; she seems as destined to "err," in the double sense of the word, as her nineteenth-century predecessors; better able than they to articulate the nature of her moral, emotional, and sexual problems, she is not better able to solve them.

The dispossessed orphans of nineteenth-century fiction find partial or provisional solutions to their individual problems of identity and to the larger cultural problems by revising the available models for selfhood, and thus both generating individuality and retaining links to the collective past. Similarly, both Mary Gordon as author and Isabel Moore as character/narrator revise their precursor texts in order to formulate their own. Isabel's most problematic relationships (those that reveal her insecurity and confusion) are with men; but in the histories of her relationships with women, Isabel quests for an adequate model of self; just as Gordon models her text on the texts of her literary predecessors, texts such as, in particular, *Jane Eyre* and *Pride and Prejudice.* For both author and character, revision and reinterpretation are strategies that prove creative, if problematic; for both Gordon and Moore, the sense of the past is a curious compound of intimacy, affection, and ironic resentment; the need to retain continuity with the past does not easily accord with the equally pressing need to avoid being crushed by the burden of the past. *Final Payments* is indeed, and in many important respects, modeled on prior nineteenth-century texts which it mentions by name; but it is far from being a simplistic or obvious revision of any one of them; the very fact that the text of *Final Payments* is imbued with aspects of not one but a number of prior texts suggests a complex intertextuality rather than straightforward influencing. Similarly, Isabel cannot simply model herself on a ready-made precursor—as for many nineteenth-century heroines, Isabel's orphanhood represents the absence of any fully adequate model of female selfhood, a lack which necessitates the heroine's ensuing narrative history as quest for such a model or for some personality structure otherwise sanctioned by either traditional or contemporary culture. The women of Isabel's past each represent a mode—at best, partially successful—of surviving in a patriarchal culture.

As in *Jane Eyre,* Isabel's self-narrated history traces her journeyings away from and toward the women who represent her own past as well as various options for the future. Margaret Casey, like Jane's Mrs. Reed, sometimes seems to be a kind of Oedipal mother who rivals, rejects, and breeds guilt in her daughter, and who has mysteriously and nightmarishly usurped the original good mother's place. At a broader level of symbolism, such meanly conventional-minded, ignorant, jealous "stepmothers" are dangerous doubles of their "daughters," threatening in that they represent a prevalent type of femalehood as ordained by a patriarchal society. As such, they embody a negative identity, subservient to strong, despotic males (Mrs. Reed is terrorized by the memory of her dead husband and slavishly devoted to her tyrannical son; Margaret Casey had been the secretly adoring housekeeper to Isabel's absolutist, "priestly" father). Both Mrs. Reed and Margaret Casey are hungry for power of their own; the only power they acquire is that which they exert over those females even weaker than themselves (the orphan child Jane; the guilt-ridden adult-orphan Isabel). Isabel, like Jane, is forced into a power-struggle with her unmaternal "mother," a struggle which she can win only at the cost of guilt. For Isabel, as for Jane and other Victorian heroines such as Maggie Tulliver, Dorothea Brooke, and Lucy Snowe, self-assertion, even when defensive, is for women always tainted with illegitimacy, and sooner or later generates its opposite, self-abnegation. Jane's childish rage at Mrs. Reed's coldness and cruelty toward her is an unconscious act of rebellion not only against what Mrs. Reed does but against what she represents: victim of a society which has consigned her to secondary roles, Mrs. Reed is also that society's enforcer. Margaret Casey is not only Mr. Moore's devoted housekeeper, she is the "creature" of the male-dominated culture he represents, a culture which defines female virtue in terms of domestic servitude but which simultaneously valorizes such "male" attributes as enterprise, ambition, individualism, self-aggrandizement, and achievement. Margaret bitterly resents and futilely attempts to quash Isabel's egotism, intellect, and independence; in turn, Isabel fears and loathes with a physical disgust Margaret's emotional, intellectual, sexual, and moral poverty.

As in countless Victorian novels, one's opposite, rival, or enemy is also one's double, a shadow or submerged self; or a criminal, libidinal, aggressive aspect of self. One recalls Orlick's symbolic relationship to Pip (*Great Expectations*), Uriah Heep's to David Copperfield, Hetty Sorrel's to Dinah Morris (*Adam Bede*), Madame Beck's to Lucy Snowe (*Villette*). Isabel recognizes in Margaret the negative image of herself, the image against which she has constituted herself ("I invented myself in her image, as her opposite"). But despite that insight, Margaret remains an embodiment of Isabel's deep-rooted emotional frailty, the guilt and self-contempt that is the obverse of her self-approbation, sexual vitality, and independence. Isabel can name Margaret as her haunting shadow-self, but cannot exorcise her: "She would come upon me, thinking she had surprised me, but she was not clever enough to be successfully furtive. . . . But she made me feel as if she had surprised me, as if she had found me with my hand somewhere shameful: in the cookie jar, in the money-box, in my own private parts." And Isabel is repeatedly threatened by Margaret as specter of her own possible future self. Isabel's father's legacy is double: like many women, Isabel has received conflicting cultural signals, having been inculcated with a strong sense of her individuality and a desire to achieve; but also with the paradigmatic Christian ethic of renunciation and self-sacrifice, always applied with special force to women. As different as Isabel is from Margaret, she is aware that her father's traditional world has the power virtually to eradicate the first set of personality components, to foster the second, and has the power to see her as merely another Margaret. Her family lawyer and her close friend Father Mulcahy can visualize no future for Isabel other than that of "paid companion," as one of the sisterhood of "good daughters who cared for their parents" and, if they were unable to play their ordained roles as daughter, wife, or mother, could be helped through the kindly offices of the Church to play surrogate daughter, wife, mother in some bereft family. Margaret had played, in Isabel's motherless family, a kind of debased governess. Like the many governesses in nineteenth-century English life and fiction, Margaret's role was anomalous, in the family yet not of it. Isabel, after her father's death, is faced with a similar anomalousness, and thinks of her situation in nineteenth-century terms: "If it were the nineteenth century, I'd have become a governess." Among her almost nonexistent professional qualifications is her capacity for devotion: "What a nineteenth century phrase, 'that young woman was devoted to her father.' In the nineteenth century, it would have had a resonance; now, devotion was something dogs had."

Isabel's final confrontation, discussed below, with her Margaret-double will be Isabel's most critical, liminal ordeal, but Margaret is not Isabel's only significant double. As for Jane Eyre, Isabel's relationships with women form a strangely assorted sisterhood symbolizing a complex self, at once fragmented, conflicted, and in process of change. Isabel is flanked by two girlhood friends, dramatically contrasted with each other, yet both representing Isabel's quest for continuity with the past. Liz and Eleanor, like many pairs of women in nineteenth-century literature, are dark versus light (like *Ivanhoe*'s Rebecca and Rowena, *The Woman in White*'s Marion and Laura, *The Mill on the Floss*'s Maggie and Lucy). Typically, the dark-haired woman is characterized by dangerous or excessive vitality, intelligence, passion, or ambition, whereas the light-haired woman tends to be passive, frail, conventional, and submissive. In *Jane Eyre,* salient aspects of such contrasting feminine types are present in two of Jane's associates, flanking her in allegorical fashion, Bertha Mason Rochester and Helen Burns. Jane's symbolic journeys leave a succession of houses of the past, with their binding structures of anticipation, routine, and memory; as Jane travels from Gateshead to Lowood to Thornfield to Marsh End to Ferndean, she confronts aspects of herself, each confrontation generating a transformative ordeal. At Lowood School, Jane admires, then emulates, then mourns the frail martyr Helen Burns, who represents in extreme form Jane's "Jane" self, guilt-prone, life-mistrusting, secretly resentful, and self-destructive. At Thornfield, Jane encounters Bertha, the dark-haired, corpulent, powerfully built madwoman in the attic and monstrous version of Jane's "Eyre" (eerie, airish) self. Isabel's Liz is dark haired, energetic, and passionate. She hammers a six-foot long post into the ground for the barn she is building to house her pregnant mare; she adores her female lover; she swims, rides, plays tennis, climbs mountains. Unlike Bertha, however, Liz is witty, tough, and precise. Despite her excessive vitality, she seems a kind of latter-day Elizabeth Bennet living in a parodied version of Pemberley. Liz "was capable of a fine malice; she had a cutting edge like a good French knife." Liz attributes to both herself and to Isabel "elegant perceptions like heroic couplets." However, Liz's version of Austenian "regulated hatred" is enriched by her awareness of her un-Austenian potentiality for rage and violence. In contrast, Eleanor is gentle, sexually fearful ("I feel much cleaner when I'm chaste"), and delicately blond ("she had the kind of face that would have driven a Victorian paterfamilias to strangled fantasies"). Liz feels contempt for Eleanor's fragility and passivity; Eleanor fears Liz's sharpness and sarcasm. But the tension between the two also represents Isabel's inner confusion and polarization. Indeed, the three names suggest this, the first syllable of "Isabel" repeated in the "iz" of Liz; the last syllable of "Isabel" repeated in the "el" of Eleanor.

Like Jane Eyre, Isabel's visits at the houses of her female doubles generate further symbolic journeys. Eleanor's apartment is tiny, tidy, and comfortable, an apt emblem for the reduced, almost miniaturized existence Eleanor has invented for herself perhaps as a kind of therapy for the emotional wounds sustained during her divorce, perhaps also as emblem of a defensively avoidant mode of coping with a brutal world. Eleanor, then, represents a passive-defensive model of personality which is a real potentiality within Isabel. Isabel is attracted to Eleanor and to the cosily domestic and male-free life Eleanor offers her [Eleanor: "I had worked out an elaborate fantasy that you'd get an apartment near here, and we'd meet for lunch, and go to concerts and take walks"]. But Isabel is also attracted to Liz and to Liz's house, the structure of self-meanings comprising passionate engagement with life, emotional risk-taking, and self-assertion. Isabel's stay at Eleanor's apartment is enjoyable but brief, and functions as a stepping-stone to the more significant visit with Liz, which leads to Isabel's new job and an apartment of her own: to a provisional, newly furbished set of social and private roles. Both Eleanor and Liz take Isabel shopping for new clothes, during which, naturally enough, Isabel faces her image in a mirror. As in similar "resartus" episodes in *Jane Eyre* (such as Jane's uneasy trying on of bridal garments), Isabel is also trying on new identities. Isabel experiences, alternately, dismay and pleasure as Eleanor helps her purchase new underwear, slacks, blouses; as Liz lends her an ill-fitting bikini, then takes her to town for a new swim-suit (Isabel's "accidental" forgetting to bring her old swimsuit recalls Jane Eyre's "accidental" loss, when she flees Rochester, of her bundle of relics from her not-yet-assimilated past).

Just as novelistic solutions borrowed from the conservative world of Jane Austen are attractive but inadequate (Liz half-jokingly offers Isabel the role of "aunt to the kids, a sister to me, a confidante to John. . . . Just like a Jane Austen novel"), so Isabel's bonds with women, necessary though they be, do not in themselves generate a complete self. Isabel needs to confront the male-dominated, larger-scaled public realm. Yet feminine bonding in *Final Payments* is not merely a regressive, deprived alternative to the social realities invented and legitimized by males; rather, such bonding is both a necessary prelude to surviving confrontation with patriarchal society and an equally necessary supplement to it. Both Liz and Eleanor—despite their intelligence, insight, and warmth—offer Isabel role-models which are only partially successful. Despite their differences in style and appearance, they reveal similar strategies for survival in a society which remains inimical to them and whose limitations they cannot fully overcome. Liz's lesbianism and Eleanor's celibacy imply rejection of conventional gender roles. Yet in other ways, their lives are based on acceptance of things as they are. Liz, despite her high-level energy, critical eye, and lucidity, leads a life which is only slightly less cloistered than Eleanor's. Liz and Eleanor remind the reader also of the provisional solutions to "The Woman Question" in the world of the Victorian novel, and remind us too of the tenuousness of these solutions. In this respect, Liz is a belated version of what might be termed the "domestic" solution; Eleanor, of the "independent spinster" solution. Liz's domesticity is like but even more unlike, say, Dorothea Brooke's marriage to the politically active Ladislaw (Liz's early respect

for her politician husband has become contempt and dislike). Eleanor's life recalls but also questions the value of the lives evolved by such spinster-survivors as Lucy Snowe, Nelly Dean, Madame Beck, and Lily Dale. Liz is trapped on her lovely country estate; her relationship with Erica appears doomed. Eleanor is trapped in her apartment. Thumbnail descriptions of their lives imply triviality and loneliness: Isabel observes, "Liz reads a lot of eighteenth-century history and she's building a barn." Eleanor responds, "And I take baths and read 'The New York Times.'" Thus, like Helen Burns and Bertha Mason Rochester respecting Jane Eyre, Liz and Eleanor function symbolically as threatening doubles as well as sisterly parallels to Isabel.

The description of Isabel's old house represents her past life as good daughter and her present lack of self-knowledge and self-respect: cluttered, dusty, uncared for, it had always measured her inadequacy in conventional feminine domesticity, but also her uniqueness as her father's spoiled, beloved, intellectual daughter—free of cares and skills ordinarily defined as feminine, but haunted by their lack. Isabel's remorse at her "own neglect of the house and its considerable spaces" ("I sat in the middle of the floor, weeping. I wept for my failure of love for the house that had kept me since childhood") mourns the irrevocability of the past and laments her present uncertainty. A paragraph beginning with her house becomes a paragraph about her person:

> I could have taken care of the house. I could have learned a language or knitting. I could have kept a journal or written a history. For all these years I was a servant to bodies, my father's body and my own, which had spread and softened from languor and neglect. I was always terribly tired.

Isabel's new job, fittingly, requires her to inspect private homes wherein aged individuals are cared for. Each inspection of these physical, emotional, and social structures in some way alters her own. Each visit re-enacts her own years of nursing her dying father, but now she plays the role of observer, a role which symbolizes her gradual adopting of new perspectives on her past. The penultimate house she visits, the Kiley's, most clearly signals her own disordered emotional and moral state. The house and its inmates are nightmarish versions both of Isabel's past life with her father and of her forthcoming sojourn with Margaret. The house features garbage on the lawn, a broken window, the pervasive smell of cat dung; Patricia Kiley, the caretaking daughter, is a twenty-eight-year-old version of what Isabel secretly fears she deserves to become (and will become at Margaret's house), a selfless woman. Patricia has no front teeth ("the mouth of an old woman"), dead eyes, pendulous breasts, a bad complexion. Her mother is "twisted excruciatingly" in a wheelchair, also has no teeth, and, like Isabel's father, her face sags on one side. Like Margaret, although literally, Mrs. Kiley's life is paralyzed and hopeless. The piles of magazines all over the house remind Isabel of her old house: "I understood how Patricia Kiley had let her life become like this. . . . I understood perfectly, because it was only luck that I had never looked like that girl, and that I read different magazines"—luck she seeks to eradicate by sacrificing herself for Margaret.

Patricia adumbrates Isabel's self-willed transformation into selflessness. As Margaret's care-taker, Isabel neglects herself, gets fat (her own breasts become pendulous), regresses to the simple orality of secret gluttony. But this flight from her married lover, Hugh Slade, and from the pain and guilt caused by their relationship, becomes, as does Jane's flight from Rochester, a liminal ordeal, a slow gathering of forces preparatory to a future transformation which will dramatize her growing maturity, courage, and independence. Jane's ordeal is precipitated by her encounter with the unlikely double, Bertha; Isabel's, by a very different though equally unlikely double, who like Jane's is also her lover's wife. Cynthia Slade, Isabel's rival, is nearly a point for point contrast, blond and stiff-haired, Protestant, middle-aged, and vulgar. Her crude denunciation of Isabel's affair with Hugh articulates Isabel's latent self-dislike, guilt, and the legacy of her father's values. In fact, Cynthia's presence is that of an accusatory ghost of the father, figuring forth the traditional moral authority embodied in the renunciatory doctrine of "thou shall not." Confronted by Cynthia, Isabel is literally paralyzed: "It did not occur to me that I could move in any way to avoid her; it did not seem possible that I could in any way prevent her reaching me, her doing whatever it was she wanted to do." As her father's daughter, Isabel thinks, "I could no more refuse my father than Mary could have refused the angel coming upon her, a finger of light." In contrast, "as Hugh's woman . . . I would have to calculate each new face I came upon: would it be open to me, or would it see me as the thief, to be cast out?" Although both alternatives depend on a relationship with a male, there is a significant difference between them, the difference between "daughter" and "woman," between the sanctuary of universal approbation earned by renunciation, and the uncertain life that questions accepted moral norms. As her father's nurse, Isabel "had bought sanctuary by giving up youth and freedom, sex and life"; the certain efficacy of past solutions to the problem of female identity is contrasted to "exposure" to future risk: "I saw myself as the public culprit, the woman carried naked through the town, head shaved, borne aloft in a parody of the procession in honor of the Virgin."

In accordance with the paradox of liminality, Isabel can strengthen her shaky belief in her own self-worth only by acting out, once more, the contrary role of self-abnegating "daughter." Isabel's description of her emotional situation appropriately draws upon the liminal imagery of darkness, falling, drowning, withdrawal, numbness, and death. Isabel retreats from life, risk, and choice and into the childish illusion of changeless selfhood: "I knew with my old childhood certainty that I would go on being like this. I was not going to change" (ironic, since she is undergoing critical experiences which will transform her not once but twice, first into Margaret-double and second into autonomous, adult woman).

Isabel's flight to Margaret's house brings about a revised version of Isabel's "good daughter" years of nursing her father. As then, Isabel shops and cooks for the aged and helpless parent (although Margaret is not an invalid, she is arthritic, impoverished, and alone). Unlike then, Isabel receives no recompense in the form of gratitude or love. Nursing the narrow-minded, censorious, embittered Margaret becomes for Isabel "a pure act, like the choice of a martyr's death which, we had been told in school, is the only inviolable guarantee of salvation." But this purity conceals Raskolnikovian murderousness. At the bus station on the way to Margaret, Isabel sees a hideous old woman reading, of all things, *Pride and Prejudice:* "The old woman caught my eye and laughed like an animal." Isabel's mental world is, at that moment, inconceivable in the terms of the Austenian fictional world. The incongruity between the illusory moral purity of her martyrdom and her actual anger and self-hatred is imaged in the incongruity of the repulsive Margaret-like woman's reading *Pride and Prejudice,* and in Isabel's violent fantasy: "I thought how easy it would be to kill a woman like that. You could lure her with coffee and doughnuts and then poison her or bash her skull in. To watch her die would be perfectly enjoyable."

Symbolically allying herself with the old, the dying, and the dead; Isabel simultaneously weds herself to the dead past and begins to kill it, to murder her old "angelic" self so that her new complex self may be born. She begins turning into Margaret: "In this light my face too was gray. It was the color of Margaret's face." She inhabits a world of death, of thick, exhausted, excessive sleep: "I slept too late every morning. And every morning I awoke as if there was a war outside, as if I had only to open my eyes to see the corpses and the shell-shocked wounded. . . . I feared a face outside the window, dead eyes looking in at me as I pulled out of sleep." "Dead eyes" recalls both Patricia Kiley, Isabel's proleptic alter ego, and Margaret, her current double. The shell-shocked wounded and the terrorizing voyeur mirror her own psyche, severely wounded by guilt and haunted by the unassimilated past. She cuts her hair, unconsciously fulfilling a ceremony in rite of passage, at once sacrificing her sexuality and vitality, and preparing for future growth. Her new but antiquated "bubble cut," combined with her thickening figure and dowdiness, make her a bloated parody of Margaret. Isabel re-creates herself in so repulsive an image that she is constrained to kill it, finally freeing herself from the hauntings of the past.

Isabel gains the courage to carry through that therapeutic killing only with the help of a secret literary sisterhood. Wishing to alleviate her boredom and at the same time please and educate Margaret, who likes reading cheap romances, Isabel reads aloud the great romance, *Jane Eyre.* At the fourth chapter, Margaret stops her: "All that stuff is old hat. . . . You can tell the person who wrote that was one of those unsatisfied women. Unfulfilled. I hate that kind of writing. It has no life to it." Enraged, Isabel throws the book on the floor (perhaps inspired by John Reed's throwing a book at Jane Eyre's head in the first chapter of

Jane Eyre): "Who are you to criticize Charlotte Brontë?" The realization that she cannot, after all, submerge her own identity comes about when she finds that she cannot submerge her powers of literary discrimination. She knows, even though she had tried to forget, that Charlotte Brontë is better than Regina Carey. Like the child Jane Eyre, Isabel tries to suppress her fury at the meanly domineering woman in whose house she is living as an alien; but just as Jane's anger helps to free her from the prison of Gateshead, so Isabel's helps free her from Margaret's house—that is, from the guilty self-abnegation and self-denial that currently "houses" her personality. But Isabel is not merely acting out a revised version of Jane's narrative. Like both Jane Eyre and Mary Gordon, she herself is able to revise the received texts of her culture. Unconsciously modeling herself on the fictional character created in the feminist countertradition, Isabel also, but consciously, models herself on her own revised interpretation of a biblical text. Thus, she integrates her two heritages, the feminist and the patriarchal, the unauthorized and the authorized. Father Mulcahy, the novel's gentlest representative of the latter tradition, suggests how that tradition may be revised without being violated. He views Isabel's self-sacrifice for Margaret as a sin against the fifth commandment: "thou shalt not kill," he points out, "means slow deaths, too." Soon after, Isabel interprets the biblical text, "the poor you have always with you" to mean that pleasure must be taken "because the accidents of death would deprive us soon enough. We must not deprive ourselves, our loved ones, of the luxury of our extravagant affections. We must not try to second-guess death by refusing to love the ones we loved in favor of the anonymous poor." On Good Friday, she interprets the death of Christ as symbolizing the inevitability of every death: "Christ had suffered in the body, and I too had a body. . . . Christ had been betrayed by His friends, but my friends had stood by me in a miracle of love when I had ceased to love them."

Liz and Eleanor overcome their mutual dislike in order to act together as midwives assisting at Isabel's rebirth (which takes place, appropriately, at pre-dawn); and Lavinia's job-offer awaits Isabel. A female community, loose, tentative, and unaware of itself as such is thus very faintly sketched. The early dawn when Isabel escapes from Margaret is "fragile" but also "exhilarating": "The three of us laughed. . . . And our laughter was solid. It stirred the air and hung above us like rings of bone that shivered in the cold, gradual morning." Isabel's reunion with Hugh appears imminent, but the final images of the book show Isabel's pleasure at the loyalty, understanding and sheer physical presence of the two women. Isabel's return to Hugh, like Jane's to Rochester, takes place in her own time and terms; but unlike Jane she will not be wholly defined by her relation to her lover. Equally significant are her friendships with women. Her "final payments" are, in one sense, the final exorcism of guilt vis-à-vis her own paternalistic morality; but are, in another sense, the novel's concluding, if understated, payment of praise to the sustaining power of female bonding.

Escaping from Margaret's house of death, Isabel effects a reconciliation, perhaps a fragile one, between contemporary liberal secularism and traditional Christian morality, just as Gordon effects a reinterpretation of the canonic nineteenth-century British novels by women, preserving elements of their structure and moral themes, but in an era of far greater self-consciousness in the questioning of patriarchal traditions. Isabel's problems in self-invention are paradigmatic for modern women in general and for women writers in particular. Like her Victorian forbears, Isabel is both beneficiary and victim of traditional religious, moral, and social directives and codes, and thus is faced with the imperative need to revise—neither mindlessly to accept nor mindlessly to abjure those directives and codes. Isabel's final act of interpretation frees her from the residual dead weight of the past because she has modified and internalized what for her are still usable aspects of that past. Similarly, Gordon fashions an authorly persona that is partly modeled on, yet not limited by, nineteenth-century literary traditions; that reinterprets, yet carries on and adds to, the feminist literary tradition, itself both canonical and unofficial, partly inscribed in the dominant "great tradition" in order to make itself heard within it, yet continually questioning its suppositions and principles.

Rachel Billington (review date 19 April 1987)

SOURCE: "Women at Bay," in *New York Times Book Review*, April 19, 1987, p. 8.

[*In the following review, Billington offers negative assessment of* Temporary Shelter.]

The keening of a frightened and suffering woman is never far from the surface of Mary Gordon's writing. These 20 stories—some long, others only a few pages, some about the Irish immigrant poor, others about the Long Island rich, some imbued with the spirit of the countryside, others set in cosmopolitan London or New York—all carry with them the same atmosphere of fatalistic depression, of lives lived with at best lack of hope and at worst something dangerously threatening.

This theme is most acutely expressed in the second story, just four pages long, called **"The Imagination of Disaster,"** which is written in a first person, present tense, stream of consciousness narrative. A housewife and mother going about her everyday tasks is obsessed by the dangers of the future. Faced by her daughter wanting help with modeling clay animals, she thinks with terror: "I cannot pervert her life so that she will be ready for the disaster. There is no readiness; there is no death in life."

The vulnerability that the Gordon woman feels about herself is increased and made obvious through her concern for her children. *Temporary Shelter,* the long title story, takes this process a stage further and makes the child's terrors central. It is one of several stories where the author speaks with a child's voice and deals with the loaded themes of class and religious differences. It is a more densely worked piece than **"The Neighborhood,"** where another small, unhappy child, also possessing a single unsatisfactory parent, searches for comfort. In **"The Neighborhood"** the child finds a moment of happiness with a warmhearted but sluttish Irish neighbor. In **"Temporary Shelter"** the child steps out bravely into the wide world. In neither case does the black curtain of gloom lift very far.

Adult gloom centers, hardly surprisingly, on the relationship between women and men. The divorced or otherwise single woman, usually with children she must cope with on her own, features in almost every story. **"The Other Woman"** is the simplest but most effective example. A happily married wife—a unique state in the book, expressed mainly through a comfortable physical relationship—discovers her husband weeping uncontrollably after reading a story about a husband who, out of love for his children, didn't leave his wife for his lover. It has reminded him of a similar sacrifice he made in the past. The happily married wife is horrified at his tragic tears, realizing he has never loved her so deeply. The moral comes out clearly: there is no security anywhere; only temporary shelter.

The alternative to the pain inherent in the male-female relationship is shown through one of the best stories, **"Out of the Fray."** Here a newly paired (though much-divorced) couple go to London, where they find a discarded wife. Apparently supremely self-sufficient, she is soon revealed to be emotionally crippled by the breakup of her marriage nearly 20 years ago. Moral: loneliness is as threatening as involvement. **"Out of the Fray"** is written in the personal, almost diarylike manner that seems to come most naturally to Ms. Gordon. It suits her aim for a high emotional content but tends to limit her to a one-tone voice.

Possibly she is aware of this problem, since one of the longest stories, **"Now I Am Married,"** is divided into a short prologue and five sections headed by the names of the women who speak. The narrator is a second wife visiting her husband's family in England. The other women talk to her. The technique does get around the problem to some extent, but it also appears as an admission of structural defeat.

Besides, here, as in the other stories, there is no real indication of an authorial point of view—a dangerous lack in stories aiming to be above glossy-magazine level. Perhaps this is another way of saying there is very little sense of morality, of choices made, for good or for ill, of guilt suffered rightly or wrongly, of the struggle to break the barriers of being merely human. Although Ms. Gordon's characters suffer, they do so in a numb and mindless kind of way. She is writing out of emotion, and it suffuses and blurs the writing.

"The Dancing Party" is the most stylishly written of the collection and comes nearest to breaking what seems to be the Gordon mold. The subject is the habitual one, and no less compelling for that, of the pairing or nonpairing of the sexes and is approached with the usual sense of foolish hopes sharpened by impending doom. However, the characters are dealt with separately, and their different thoughts and reactions during the course of the same event are cleverly counterpoised with each other. In one sense the story does Ms. Gordon a disservice because it points up the tendencies in the rest of her writing. Neither wit, irony, satire nor humor is on her agenda, all sacrificed, presumably on the altar of sensibility.

Ms. Gordon attempts to step beyond her limits with **"A Writing Lesson."** Sadly, the result is pretentiously obscure rather than thought-provoking: "If you are writing a fairy tale, you can begin by saying that they had built a house in the center of the woods. And they sat in the center of it, as if they were children, huddled, cringing against bears." Short stories are a testing ground for any novelist, particularly one whose talents lie rather in conveying the intimacies of a woman's mind than in any stylistic finesse. This sort of writing, in which Mary Gordon is most successful, is in danger of becoming indigestible in a collection of short fiction, needing the breadth of the novel form to give it background and air. Nevertheless, *Temporary Shelter* contains some stories that are touching, and some that are memorable.

Eleanor B. Wymward (essay date Summer-Fall 1987)

SOURCE: "Mary Gordon: Her Religious Sensibility," in *Cross Currents,* Vol. XXXVII, Nos. 2-3, Summer-Fall, 1987, pp. 147-58.

[*In the following essay, Wymward examines Gordon's religious concerns in her novels and short stories. According to Wymward, "Gordon's fiction is centered not on a narrowly sectarian creed or tradition, but on the essentials of Christian theology: sin, grace, incarnation, and redemption."*]

Mary Gordon's comments on the liaison between her religious beliefs and creativity have never equalled the boldness of Flannery O'Connor's revelation:

> I see from the standpoint of Christian orthodoxy. This means for me the meaning of life is centered on our Redemption by Christ and what I see in its relation to that. I don't think that this is a position that can be taken halfway or one that is particularly easy in these times to make transparent in fiction.

Nonetheless, Gordon willingly provides insight into the context of her religious values. To the question, "Are you still a believing Catholic?", Mary Gordon answered in a New York *Times* interview:

> I consider myself a Catholic. I have a real religious life in a framework which I think of as Catholic. But I don't think John Paul II would be pleased with it. . . . I think one of the things that helped me in life is Flan-

nery O'Connor's statement that you must remember that in this day and age one must suffer because of the church and not for the church.

In her first two novels, *Final Payments* (1978) and *The Company of Women* (1980), Gordon is distinctly Catholic, revealing an identifiable Catholic culture and theology. She laments the inability of the church to respond to a person's deepest spiritual needs, and satirizes priests who are unable to relate scripture to contemporary life. Consequently, Gordon's characters are left largely on their own to confront the terms of their personal salvation. Although the familiar Catholic landscape of *Final Payments* and *The Company of Women* is absent in *Men and Angels* (1985), Gordon's third novel, her theme regarding the neglect of the truth of scripture evolves with complexity and ambiguity. Ultimately, the characters in the three novels do find their center by confronting, through their own efforts, the mysteries of Christianity long obscured for them by rubrics and fossilized tradition. But in Gordon's first collection of short stories, *Temporary Shelter* (1987), formal religion is ostensibly absent, or, at best, useless when individuals are helpless. Gordon treats religion seriously and one feels her regret, though not necessarily her suffering, when it proves deficient. Her religious sense is basic to her vision of life.

Final Payments, Gordon's first novel, is the story of Isabel Moore, who has sacrificed eleven years of her young adulthood to care for her invalid father, a retired professor of medieval literature from St. Aloysius College. Fiercely conservative, he believed that the "refusal of anyone in the twentieth century to become part of the Catholic Church was not pitiable; it was malicious and willful." In the meantime, Isabel, without his knowledge, has for years substituted long walks for Sunday mass. During her father's funeral, the Moores' home is "full of priests," "faceless priests," Isabel later sees, who "blessed my father's coffin, who had sat at my table, who had never remembered my name." Gordon's priests live to be served, not to serve.

As a child, Isabel is her father's spiritual prodigy:

> My father had once looked at me and said, "I love you more than I love God. I love you more than God. I love you more than God loves you. . . . " I had studied [my catechism] with pure, delectable absorption. . . . That absorption gave me the right, at six, to turn to my father and say, "You mustn't say that. It's a sin." I had been right; it was wrong, what he had said, loving me more than God. I could not love with God's intensity. But I would choose His mode: the impartial, the invulnerable, removed from loss.

This confused concept of love and sacrifice haunts Isabel into adulthood, causing her to experience an intense emotional crisis. After her father's death, Isabel reenters life at age thirty to have some sexual encounters, but her breakdown occurs when she runs from a successful love relationship because of guilt. Always having felt responsible for her father's first stroke because he found her in bed with a young lover, Isabel identifies sexual pleasure

with extravagant selfishness. To atone for her sins, Isabel embraces her "father's equation, the Church's equation, between suffering and value" and moves from her apartment to care for the mean-spirited Margaret Casey, who had been the Moores' housekeeper for seventeen terrible years.

In an early review of *Final Payments,* Maureen Howard comments that "the reader will be tempted to hiss when Margaret comes on the scene, to cheer when Isabel, grown fat, idle and ugly, is saved by her own good sense." More than good sense, Isabel experiences a religious crisis that jolts her out of her confused notion of sainthood:

> I had wanted to give up all I loved so that I would never lose it. I had tried to kill all that had brought me pleasure so that I could not be susceptible. Why had I done it? For safety, certainly, for the priests, the faceless priests. . . . For them I would give up all I had most savored, those I had most treasured . . . so that those faceless priests could say, when they thought of me, "She is a saint."

Isabel is shocked back into life. She rescues herself in a moment where Gordon reveals the action of grace without sacrificing psychological credibility or dramatic technique. After a visit from Father Mulcahy, her father's lifetime friend, Isabel, enraged at Margaret's question—"What were you doing out there with him all that time?"—rightfully calls her a "wicked, wicked woman." When Margaret counters that she is simply a "poor woman," Isabel shouts, "'The poor you have always with you.'" Suddenly finding profound personal meaning in the gospel words she has blurted out, Isabel escapes from the ghosts of her past to pursue a new life in spiritual freedom. For the first time, Isabel understands:

> What Christ was saying, what he meant, was that the pleasure of that hair, that ointment, must be taken. . . . We must not deprive ourselves, our loved ones, of the luxury of extravagant affections. . . . And it came to me, fumbling in the hallway for the light, that I had been a thief. Like Judas, I had wanted to hide gold. . . . I knew now I must open the jar of ointment. I must open my life.

Isabel achieves this liberating insight from within herself, as she draws upon her deepest spiritual resources where the message of Jesus has taken root. The faceless priests who filled her father's home—metaphors for a church which never tries to reach her—routinely "argued about baptism of desire, knocking dishes of pickles onto the carpet in their ardor. They determined the precise nature of the Transubstantiation, fumbling for my name as I freshened their drinks." Their talk ignores the intrinsic connection between the life of Jesus and the individual person. Theirs is a church consistently quarreling with form, instead of renewing itself through spreading the hope of the incarnation. Preparing for the sacraments as a child, Isabel is concerned "for the perfection of the outward forms. Standing on line for Confession, for Communion, we were careful to keep our spines straight, to fold our hands so that they were Gothic steeples, not a mess of immigrant knuckles." Twenty-five years later, the priest who hears Isabel's confession after she moves in with Margaret Casey, also is obsessed with form:

> "Bless Me, Father, for I have sinned."
>
> I could see the priest's mouth tighten in exasperation.
>
> "Do you mind not interrupting me during the blessing?" he said.

His boredom is pierced only by Isabel's version of the Act of Contrition. "'Wait,' he interrupted. 'That's not it. You'll have to read it from the card in front of you.'"

Ironically, the Sacrament of Reconciliation offers little promise for Isabel's reconciling herself to living. Isabel is left on her own resources to hear the "good news" which frees her to pursue a new life. After her encounter with Margaret, she builds her strength further by reading the prayers of Holy Week while alone in her room. Refreshed by the Word, Isabel is, nonetheless, distanced from the Good Friday liturgy by having to kiss the giant crucifix: "That was vulgar. I regretted the priests doing that, wiping the feet of Christ with a tissue after the brush of every mouth. I wished they wouldn't do that; it made me wish I hadn't come today." For Gordon, the Vatican II church offers little promise of revitalization because it sentimentalizes the rich tradition which Isabel draws upon for her cure. Early in *Final Payments* when Father Mulcahy complains that he cannot adjust to the new church because it feels as if "someone's broken in [to] the house and stolen all the furniture," Isabel refrains from agreeing only because she does not want to "encourage his regret by making him appear to have allies in another generation." As her father's spiritual protégé, Isabel prides herself on her reconcilement of the secular and the sanctified, as well as her scorn for pietism and religiosity. She had always despised, for example, Margaret's perpetual novenas and devotions: "I used the missal my father had given me for confirmation. I, like him, followed the Latin of the Mass. . . . He wrote scornful letters to The Tablet about pastors who encouraged the faithful to say the Rosary during Mass." But the church of the sixties also neglects the cultivation of aesthetic and intellectual excellence, for St. Stanislaus', the scene of Isabel's confession, looks like a "firehouse, impromptu, unconsidered, American. . . . I imagined how my father would have stormed through this church."

If Gordon does not support changes in the post-Vatican II church, neither is she simply nostalgic for the rigor of traditional Catholicism. *The Company of Women,* her second novel, focuses on Father Cyprian Leonard, an ideological traditionalist, who isolates himself from his religious community to escape the corruption he perceives in the church of the sixties. Instead, Father Cyprian, formerly of the Paracletists, ministers to five single women, three of them widowed, who have remained excessively dependent upon him through various personal crises, since the days when "Father Cyp" conducted popular weekend retreats for working women. Cyprian's milieu is distinct from the world of traditional priest-heroes, for Gordon affirms the importance of women to his spiritual development. Because he has shared so deeply in the lives of the five women who have both comforted and disappointed him, the aging Cyprian gradually acknowledges the "enduring promise of plain human love [and] understand[s] the incarnation for, I believe, the first time: Christ took on flesh for love, because the flesh is lovable. . . ." Through the company of women, Cyprian celebrates the promise of the incarnation for himself.

To achieve this insight, Cyprian has had to struggle against his personal spiritual orientation which over a lifetime has caused him to substitute guilt for love, pursuing human perfection and scorning human frailty. Shaped by the same legacy Isabel Moore inherited from her medievalist father, Cyprian has yearned to live in "unapproachable light, the light of pure spirit," the impersonal state of Christian charity. But if life is going to have any truly human meaning for Gordon's characters, they must plunge into the ordinary and treasure the holiness of it. Gordon is therefore no iconoclast. She urges a necessary return to the essential Christian truth of incarnation, a mystery clouded by the guilt that accompanies, in the tradition of the church, a celebration of life. Convinced that the classical ideal of the priest requires detached human interactions, Cyprian suffers considerable conflict:

> I have had to be struck down by age and sickness to feel the great richness of the ardent, the extraordinary love I live among. . . . Now every morning is miraculous to me. I wake and see in the thin, early light the faces of my friends. But I fear that in loving as I do now I betray the priestly love I vowed to live by. There is no way in which my love can be objective or impersonal. . . . I am pulled down by irresistible gravity of affection and regard. These are the people I love: I choose to be with them above all others. These are the countenances that lift my heart.

Only at the end of his life does Cyprian learn to tolerate his own tender qualities, reconciling his deeply felt tension between the expression of personal and priestly love.

Cyprian renews his capacity for love and faith, especially through Felicitas, the daughter of Charlotte, the only one of the five women who is a mother as well as a widow. All of the women have focused their interests on Felicitas and have great expectations for her, but no more so than Cyprian. Even from her early childhood, Cyprian expects Felicitas to reach exceptional standards of intellectual prowess and spiritual development, just as Professor Moore does for his daughter. Indeed, Felicitas does not disappoint Cyprian, until she becomes a renegade from Catholic higher education. As a student at Columbia, she forsakes her classical studies, is the lover of a sadistic young professor and becomes pregnant. But after years of estrangement, Cyprian blesses Felicitas and grows in love for Linda, her daughter. Finally allowing Felicitas to stand for what she really is, a human being and not a god, Cyprian accepts her imperfection. To accept imperfection is to surrender to the mystery of the incarnation—that God Himself gave new meaning and value to life by living in the imperfect human condition.

Clearly, in his concluding monologue, Cyprian rediscovers the Word of scripture and seeks to participate in the creation of the world by assuming some responsibility for changing the situation of the modern church. Cyprian recognizes, for example, that the meaning of his own life is left finally "in the hands of God, in the hands of a girl," Felicitas' child, Linda. Because of this deep love for Felicitas, and then for her daughter, Cyprian comes into the presence of grace. Furthermore, interrupting Linda playing mass, Cyprian "was shocked, a girl child saying the sacred words of God." When challenged by Linda as to why she cannot be a priest, Cyprian thinks "of all the foolish, mediocre men who were permitted ordination because of the accident of sex. And I thought of this child, obviously superior to all others of her age in beauty, grace and wisdom. . . . And so each morning at my masses, I pray for the ordination of women."

Cyprian's prayers for the ordination of women might make it seem that Gordon has a hidden agenda in *The Company of Women.* Her panacea is not simply feminism, however. For example, when Felicitas "grew older, grew rebellious, [Cyprian] knew the bitterest of Jesus' sorrows: the agony within the Agony of Gethsemene, when Judas kissed and the three faithful slept." Using feminism, then, as her metaphor for change, Gordon asserts that the contemplation of Christian mystery allows the believer to see the world with new eyes. From this perspective, Gordon offers some hope for the future of the institutional church, not consigning traditional Catholicism to the "ash heap of history," as critic Carol Iannone has concluded. Gordon's quarrel is with a counterfeit church which stretches the dichotomy between the secular and sacred, thus becoming parochial, insular and anachronistic. Repressive policies and practices will change in the Church of Rome, Gordon implies, when the church returns to the gospels themselves as the source of Christian living and inspiration. The final wisdom of Cyprian, for example, is in his insight that belief in the incarnation requires his affirming and renewing the imperfect time in which he lives.

While Gordon's recognizably Catholic scene is not the context for *Men and Angels,* serious religious conflicts dominate the novel. The message of the title acquired from Paul—"Though I speak with the tongues of men and angels and have not charity, I am become as sounding brass, or a tinkling cymbal"—is left to an unlovable and fanatic evangelist, Laura Post. Nonetheless, Laura serves as a spiritual catalyst, shocking Anne Foster, the protagonist, to confront a dimension of reality she has previously either ignored or denied. In fact, Anne, who prizes herself as a rational woman responsible for her own acts, does not understand people who live a "religious life."

From the very first page of the novel, the dichotomy between Laura and Anne is established. Flying home from London after having been fired as a nanny for an American family, Laura is not frightened by having no job prospects, for, as she pores over her Bible, she is certain that the Lord will take care of her. A fellow passenger arranges for Laura to meet Anne, an art historian and an academic wife, who needs a mother's helper while her husband Michael is teaching for the year in France, and she stays at home to finish a monograph on Caroline Watson, a neglected American artist.

Obsessively religious, Laura is determined to save Anne, who is more and more repelled by Laura, but tries to compensate for her lack of personal warmth through gestures and gifts. In *Men and Angels,* Gordon's religious vision and fictional technique are strikingly close to Flannery O'Connor's. Less concerned with the eccentricities of the church which deter one from contemplating the ultimate Christian mysteries, Gordon uses the grotesque character to point out the need for salvation greater than ourselves. To this end, like Flannery O'Connor, she fears the false comforts of liberal compassion sponsored by respectable churches and a highly secularized urban society. Without implying any conscious emulation of O'Connor, one sees in *Men and Angels* proof of O'Connor's often quoted insight:

> Writers who see by the light of their Christian faith will have, in these times, the sharpest eye for the grotesque, for the perverse, and for the unacceptable. . . . Redemption is meaningless unless there is cause for it in the actual life we live, and for the past few centuries there has been operating in our culture the secular belief that there is no such cause.

> The novelist with Christian concerns will find in modern life distortions which are repugnant to him, and his problem will be to make these appear as distortions to an audience which is used to seeing them as natural, and he may well be forced to take even more violent means to get his vision across to this hostile audience. . . . To the hard of hearing you shout, and for the almost blind you draw large and startling figures.

No doubt Laura's religious commitment is compulsive, obsessive, even "mad." Anne finds Laura increasingly perverse and unacceptable. Through the dynamics of their interrelationship, Gordon gives credence to O'Connor's perception that if the "good person" is ever to confront the abrasive questions posed by Christian beliefs regarding faith in God, then he must be jolted violently. En route from London, before even meeting Anne, Laura ponders the words of Isaiah: "'Can a woman forget her suckling child, that she would have no compassion on the child of her womb? Even these may forget, yet I will not forget you.'" The mother/child relationships throughout the novel allow variations on this theme, but Anne's vision is expanded to include the deeper mystery of family and faith, the interconnection between good and evil. At Laura's funeral, Anne ruminates: "Had Caroline not lived, Laura would not be dead. . . . Each time now that she thought of her work on Caroline, she would have to wonder if Laura had been its sacrifice. Her death would touch even that. Had she not met me, she might not have died." This slow growth of Anne's awareness ends in a mild challenge to God as she listens to the words of the psalm:

> "I will lift mine eyes unto the hills, from whence cometh my help? My help cometh from the Lord, which made heaven and earth. . . ." It was so beautiful, and it was such a lie. . . . Yet she was glad the priest had read those words. Perhaps it was true for Laura now . . . or perhaps not. . . . She had never noticed it before, but the way the priest read it made it clear that the words were a question. From whence cometh my help?

At Laura's funeral, Anne experiences a religious crisis because she confronts the deepest and most conflicting elements of her life. The questions which Anne begins to ask, Gordon does not answer. But in the final paragraph of *Men and Angels,* Anne embraces the terrible terms of human experience:

> She could now say to her children—"This is life. What shall we make of it? For it is terrible, and shining, and our hearts are sore. Something dreadful had happened to us; more will happen; terrible, beautiful, there is no way of telling. And anything might lie and then recoil and strike, in silence, in the darkness."

Anne experiences authentic renewal, not wholesale conversion. She is not at peace, but she does make an act of faith, investing in the tremendous risk of love, as did Isabel and Cyprian.

Final Payments and *The Company of Women* offer strong critiques of the church, but both novels end significantly with liturgical rituals, a Good Friday service and Cyprian's private mass. However much the church fades into the background of *Men and Angels,* it is during Laura's funeral that Anne hears the compelling Old Testament words which move her to accept the mysterious reality of a divine force. Fact and mystery have a chance to be connected in the world of Mary Gordon when one truly hears and ponders Revelation. Gordon implies that any hope for the survival of the institutional Roman Church will be in its ability to make the word of God startlingly relevant to the realities of peoples' lives. Gordon's fiction is centered not on a narrowly sectarian creed or tradition, but on the essentials of Christian theology: sin, grace, incarnation and redemption.

But in *Temporary Shelter,* Gordon's collection of short stories, the word of God is neither preached nor heard. The characters in these nineteen stories are simply ordinary men, women and children who make up the world. Human as they are, their suffering is private and their victories are quiet indeed. At the core of Gordon's vision is the radical realism which marks *Men and Angels:* human beings are essentially alienated and alone, needing both hope and love to cope effectively with situations which are central to their individual existences. Characters who awaken to feelings of love and guilt through their suffering, finally assent to the mystery of being and see new meaning for themselves, gaining, in effect, temporary shelter. But

throughout the stories, religion is absent or useless when individuals are adrift, and, once again, one senses Gordon's disappointment.

The last short story in the collection, **"Mrs. Cassidy's Last Year,"** includes the celebration of two masses, one attended by Mr. Cassidy at his parish church, and the other a television mass watched and spat at by his senile wife at home. But different from Gordon's novels, the liturgies here bring no measure of peace to these disturbed characters.

Loyal to his vow never to institutionalize his wife, Mr. Cassidy suffers deeply from watching her humiliate herself and him with physical and verbal abuse. After days of enduring shame and curses, Mr. Cassidy kneels "before the altar of God" at Sunday mass and probes the guilt of his married life. Mr. Cassidy "knew he couldn't go to communion. He had sinned against charity. He had wanted his wife dead." He judges those who stay back from communion with him as being ersatz sinners because they have sinned "from the heat of their bodies . . . while he sat back from the coldness of his heart. . . . He had wished the one dead he had promised he would love forever." One does not expect much from Gordon's "boy-faced priest" who celebrates the mass, but the tone changes to describe his final gestures: "The boy priest blessed the congregation. Including Mr. Cassidy himself." Mr. Cassidy cannot accept himself, but God does, despite the priest who remains a distant figure.

After leaving mass, Mr. Cassidy spends a violent day at home while Mrs. Cassidy fights off his every attempt to care for her. She finally knocks him to the floor and wanders out onto the street as he writhes with a broken leg. Violence increases when Mr. Cassidy's only means of attracting attention to himself in order to save his wife from "wandering up and down the street in her nightgown," is to hurl figurines and crockery through the living room windows. "In the dark he lay and prayed that someone would come and get her. That was the only thing now to pray for; the one thing he had asked God to keep back." Even the most unswerving dedication to another human being, represented by Mr. Cassidy's commitment to his marriage vows, can provide only "temporary shelter" from the vicissitudes of Gordon's human condition.

"Mrs. Cassidy's Last Year" balances the first story, **"Temporary Shelter,"** where the main character, Joseph Kaszperkowski, a little boy who grows to adolescence, is actually victimized by two controlling adults. Determining his future are his bitter immigrant mother, Helen, and Dr. Meyers, a Jewish convert to Catholicism and a purveyor of pietistic liturgical art, for whom Helen keeps house and where she lives with her son. As a young child, Joseph liked to crawl "on Dr. Meyers' lean, dry lap, a lap of safety. Not like his mother's lap, which he had to share with her stomach." Joseph and Maria, Dr. Meyers' young daughter whose mother died soon after her birth, share every secret of childhood, especially magic moments in

Manhattan with Dr. Meyers at Rumpelmayers and St. Patrick's. Joseph's shelter with the Meyers is temporary, however, for as he grows older, he suspects Sister Berchmans, who hopes Maria will be a nun, of suggesting that he leave the Meyers' haven: "What did she see when she looked at him? And what had she told Dr. Meyers? Or did she never dare to speak to Dr. Meyers; had she spoken only in confession to Father Cunningham, who did the nun's bidding like a boy?"

Joseph's mother, seldom a source of solace for him, is never more cruel than when she remarks, "I guess you're okay to be her playmate, but God forbid anything else. And for a husband, let's face it, he's got something better in mind than some dumb Polack whose mother washed his shitty underwear for ten years straight."

Dr. Meyers chooses Sunday after mass at the end of a weekend retreat as the moment to tell Joseph of his decision to separate him from Maria by giving Helen a house of her own. Even while saying "thank you, sir," Joseph silently charges Meyers for being "guilty of the cruelty of sending me away. Of separating me from everything I love. Of sending me to live alone, in ugliness and hatred with the mother whom I cannot love." But Joseph quickly renews his dream of making Maria "want to marry him before they went to college," by seeing the advantages of accepting Meyers' offer to send him away for high school: "He would write to [Maria]. And his letters would make her think of him in the right way. Make her think of him so she would love him, want to live with him, the body life, and not the life that rose up past the body, not the life of Sister Berchmans and the white-faced nuns."

Gordon's ironic eye for the images, tone and atmosphere of the Catholic scene is sharp in **"Temporary Shelter."** Moreover, she draws from theology for her ultimate orientation. Characters in **"Temporary Shelter"** are identified by creed: Meyers, the Jew converted to Catholicism; Maria, the romantic Catholic, curious about Judaism; and Joseph, Catholic since birth. But Gordon does not create characters simply to fit a given solution; rather she presents them in very human situations which are open to theological interpretation. For example, when Maria and Joseph sneak into temple to observe a Yom Kippur service, Joseph feels at one with the liturgy:

> He rode the music, let it carry him. The sadness and the loneliness, the darkness and the hope. The winding music, thick and secret. Like the secrets of his heart. . . . The music that traveled to a God who listened, distant and invisible, and heard the sins of men and their atonement in darkness . . . but would give back to men the music they sent up, a thick braid of justice and kept promises and somber hope.

Joseph knows that the music which inspires him to embrace the world is different from the singing of the nuns that Maria loved, which made her want to "leave the body life . . . leave him and all their life together. The men singing in the temple did not want to rise up and leave. And that was why he liked them better. And why she did not."

This theme is familiar in Gordon's fiction. While her characters, like Maria, yearn to achieve absolute union with God, Gordon simultaneously recognizes that such an ideal can be achieved only by the individual's risking trust in human existence, thus denying faith in the mystery of the incarnation. Although the seventeen stories between **"Temporary Shelter"** and **"Mrs. Cassidy's Last Year"** may seem to make *Temporary Shelter* a book which has less religious concerns than the three novels, they reveal Gordon's versatility in probing the human condition. To achieve scope, she allows ordinary persons to confront the mysteries of their own separate lives. She insists upon the uniqueness of each human being, for the enigmas of existence always relate specifically to the individual character. The narrator in **"Billy,"** for example, expresses a perception that gives thematic unity to all of the stories. After Billy's death, the sympathetic narrator comments that Veronica, his mother, told "the truth to Billy, but too early, and too much. The world is cruel, she told him, it is frightening, and it will hurt you. She told him this with every caress, with every word of praise and spoon of medicine. And he believed her. Well, of course, he would. She was telling the truth; she was his mother." In each of the stories, characters experience the threat of evil, death and violence. Although life on Gordon's planet is to be embraced, it is lived, at best, in temporary shelters. The young, creative wife in **"The Imagination of Disaster,"** thinks:

> Perhaps I should kill us all now and save us from the degradation of disaster. Perhaps I should kill us while we are whole and dignified and full of our sane beauty. . . . We live with death, the stone in the belly, the terror on the road alone. People have lived with it always. But we live knowing not only that we will die, that we may suffer, but that all that we hold dear will finish; that there will be no more familiar. That the death we fear we cannot even imagine, it will not be the face of dream, or even nightmare. For we cannot dream the poisoned earth abashed, empty of all we know.

The goal of the artistic imagination, according to Gordon, is to realize with vivid truth all of the mysteries, paradoxes and ambiguities in the total life of the human situation. Thus when the priest in **"Mrs. Cassidy's Last Year"** blesses the congregation, Gordon accepts the premise that the world is a holy place. But faith, for Gordon, survives because it is Catholic and personal, not because of the efforts of the institutional church. Most of the characters in *Temporary Shelter* do not think in theological or religious terms, but throughout these stories one is aware of an unblinking eye revealing the mystery on which the scene is built, and a consistent voice saying that no alternative exists except to love. The young mother in **"Safe,"** filled with love for her husband and baby, has the chilling insight: "I could not live a moment without terror for myself. I know that I must live my life now knowing it is not my own. I can keep them from so little it must be the shape of my life to keep them at least from the danger I could bring them."

To end *Temporary Shelter,* Gordon adds a concluding essay, **"A Writing Lesson,"** where she proposes that fairy tales "have within them the content of all fiction. As an exercise, write the same story as a fairy tale, and then as the kind of fiction we are more used to. If you are writing a fairy tale, you can begin by saying that they had built a house in the center of the woods. And they sat in the center of it, as if they were children, huddled, cringing against bears." At the essay's close, Gordon offers further direction: "Once you have decided upon the path of your narrative and have understood its implications, go back to the beginning of the story. Describe the house."

While the essay will probably be valued in college writing classes for Gordon's comments on technique, her essential message is, "You must be sure that your values are clear to the reader." In other words, "Describe the house." For Gordon, the writer's responsibility is to her craft and to her readers. Gordon's house, then, is no temporary shelter, but one of faith. Faith informs Gordon's artistic vision in a way that Ralph Ellison describes well:

> St. Therese says, "I require of you only to *look*." Only to *look*. And this has traditionally been the genius of Incarnational faith when it has been in full possession of its sacramental vision—to empower men to face, without flinching, the arduous welter of nature and historical existence, since, frail though the flesh may be, it was proven by the Incarnation to be stout enough for the tabernacling of that than which nothing is more ultimate—namely, God Himself.

Gordon affirms the incarnate God of Christianity, but, as her canon develops, she loses confidence in the ability of the institutional church to make the message of the incarnation relevant to the problems of modern living. **"Temporary Shelter"** and **"Mrs. Cassidy's Last Year,"** stories strategically placed at the beginning and end of the collection, provide the context for this perspective. Each of the seventeen stories between them implies that individuals bring order and meaning to their lives by adopting ultimate values which will help them live with, and yet transcend, enduring problems. The milieu of the Irish Catholic home in **Final Payments** and the Catholic culture of **The Company of Women** provide a frame of reference for Gordon's religious perspective which frees her from contrivance. In **Men and Angels** and **Temporary Shelter,** she moves further away from a readily identifiable Catholic tradition, thus muting her theme of religious affirmation. Unless Gordon finds new vitality in the old liturgical rites and symbols, her fiction will become less recognizable as a celebration of the ultimate encounter between time and eternity. Her affirmation of the beauty, terror and mystery of existence will continue, but the feasts will be secular and the unseen world, perhaps, obscured.

Rosemary Booth (essay date 12 August 1988)

SOURCE: "A Concentration of Purpose: The Artistic Journey of Mary Gordon," in *Commonweal*, August 12, 1988, pp. 426-30.

[*In the following essay, Booth discusses Gordon's artistic development and the major themes in her novels. Accord-*ing to Booth, "The 'motion' in Mary Gordon's fiction, her novels in particular, has gone from a focus on defining a spiritually adult self, to defining a female self, to defining a parenting, creating self."]

> *"I guess as I began writing more and more and I began confronting in my writing a lot of the issues which really stemmed from my childhood, I began to see that I had a kind of religious hunger and that I had shaped many experiences in religious terms."*
>
> Mary Gordon in *Once A Catholic* by Peter Occhiogrosso

The poet Galway Kinnell has observed, "Everyone knows that human existence is incomplete. Among those who are especially troubled by this are those who turn to writing [which] is a way of trying to understand the incompleteness." Mary Gordon's work, more obviously than that of many writers, has evolved as a kind of investigation of this incompleteness. Her three novels—**Final Payments** (1978), **The Company of Women** (1980), **Men and Angels** (1985)—and book of short stories—**Temporary Shelter** (1986)—portray interior journeys of seeking. Religious issues have been the impetus for these travels, but not their end, for it is in the compelling nature of human affection and the artist's need to render it that the author finds resolution.

The "motion" in Mary Gordon's writings, her novels in particular, has gone from a focus on defining a spiritually adult self, to defining a female self, to defining a parenting, creating self. The process is an accretive one, like experience, so that the heroine of Gordon's latest novel, **Men and Angels,** is coping with a residue of issues faced by her predecessors in **Final Payments** and **The Company of Women.** By the same process, the author poses increasingly complex problems. **Men and Angels** thus involves an intricate calculus, one that will yield the answer to an old question: "What am I called to do?"—and its peculiarly twentieth-century corollary: "What are the balances to be struck?" If less satisfying as a novel than the earlier books, **Men and Angels** is also more ambitious in the scope of the questions it raises.

We see this development in the outpouring of themes that run like rivers through Gordon's novels and stories: the character of love; the sources of moral authority; the duty of parents; and the meaning (and demands) of sacrifice, intellectuality, passion or sensuality, loss, and creativity. The author launches these themes in terms of contrasts, contrasts between male and female, corporal and spiritual, Catholic and Protestant. Her characters often define themselves not by what they are, but by what they are not. Social class is less examined than alluded to, but is also a discernible motif.

The author's Roman Catholic background colors the terms of her arguments and accounts for the courts in which they are debated; that background also explains the seriousness and care with which her arguments are presented. Her heroines hone their own ethics—but in response to an accepted, orthodox mandate—to find a moral solution to their dilemmas. Their eventual understanding of charity, for example, may differ from the one they inherited (though the inheritance always affects how the subject is framed), but they cannot escape constructing a meaning that can be acted on in their own lives.

Mary Gordon says that she is interested in the novel "as a form of high gossip" and that "novels should be about people" (Diana Cooper-Clark, "An Interview with Mary Gordon," *Commonweal,* May 9, 1980). Her work, rooted in quotidian topics that carry great weight, from food to clothing, from phone calls to bus rides, reflects that bias. The stories abound in details supplied with the precision implied by a philosophical rootedness in the world and in things (e.g., a child in "Billy" is described as "'spoiled' . . . a terrible word, suggesting meat gone iridescent"), but nothing is at a trivial level. Although Mary Gordon's writing reflects her belief that the function of the novel is to give pleasure, perhaps the overriding note of the texts is her earnestness of purpose. In the short story, **"Now I Am Married,"** forty-year-old Gillian, a former schoolteacher, notes "Now I've gone back to writing. I don't know if I'm any good. I don't suppose it matters, really. It's a serious thing, and that's important." Over the decade of her writing, the questions which Gordon heroines confront have changed, but they all obey an urgent imperative to find satisfactory answers.

Mary Gordon's first novel, ***Final Payments,*** considers the overwhelming issue of establishing a self, distinct from one's parents, and, in particular, forming an independent moral conscience. The story follows thirty-year-old Isabel Moore in the months after her father's death, starting with his funeral. As in James Agee's *A Death in the Family,* all of the events are infused with the central fact of a father's dying. Unlike Agee's work, ***Final Payments*** is not elegiac in tone but forward-looking, a novel describing the aftermath of an event, not the prelude to it. Having been her father's sole caretaker for eleven years (and motherless since infancy), Isabel is suddenly free—compelled, really—to decide what she will do, where she will live, and, of crucial importance, who she will be.

Isabel searches desperately for an understanding of charity or love, of the way to relate to her fellow human beings, whom she must now engage. The fundamental choice she perceives (albeit an artificially stark one) is between the claims of the body and those of the spirit. Thus, she can indulge her nascent affections by lavishing them on those she genuinely loves, or she can follow what she recalls as the church's exhortation to a higher level of love through self-sacrifice. In the story, Isabel must choose between continuing an affair with Hugh, the (married) man she loves, and moving in with Margaret, who kept house for the family in the years following Mrs. Moore's death, until Isabel came of age and forced the housekeeper out. While the whole of Isabel's caring is for Hugh, she feels compelled—for a while, at any rate—to choose Margaret, to obey what she sees as the stronger moral imperative,

that of expiating her father's death by renouncing sensuality and joy in her own life.

Perhaps a novelist raised as a Protestant would have selected a different set of options from these. I think it's also likely that many Catholic novelists would pose the issues differently. After all, in choosing to stay with Margaret, Isabel would have been obeying the letter of the law but not its spirit, hardly a sanctified choice—but this reading gets too tangled. Ultimately, of course, the decision is understood as a broader one (Margaret can be offered a less drastic sacrifice), and this broadening forms the crux of Isabel's growth. Isabel considers the higher calling—to love others "as God loves His creatures, impartially, . . . without wanting anything in return"—and rejects it in favor of love realized "in the body." In doing so, she acknowledges her need to be loved for herself alone, in her own body, and in that way accepts herself as human. Isabel essentially refuses austere sanctity in favor of flawed life. This spiritual maturation allows her to cast off at once the moral authority of an anonymous church ("the faceless priests who blessed my father's coffin") and her guilt over her father's death ("my father had died, but I had not killed him"). In turn, she accepts the role of a person liable to experience pain and loss, because she is willing to risk loving someone whose love she also desires in return.

Final Payments illustrates Mary Gordon's skill at characterizing dilemmas by the use of contrast. In this case, the distinction between the repulsive Margaret and the emerging Isabel sharpens the choice to be made, for Margaret carries the multiple burdens of superstitious beliefs, frumpy appearance, obsolete taste, and a whining demeanor. The descriptions of her are some of the best in the book:

> You can imagine how unbearable the brown patches on her skin—they were not moles but large, irregular in shape, like the beginning of a cancer—were to a child, or even worse, to an adolescent. . . . All her clothes seemed damp, as if her body were giving off a tropical discharge. . . . Her feet were flat as a flash, except where the bunions developed like small crops of winter onions. The sound of her slopping around the house in her slippers is the sound of my nightmares. . . . How I hated her method of waking me. . . . It was Margaret, always, knocking on my door like some rodent trapped behind a wall.

In finally rejecting the old woman's claims, Isabel embraces instead a world of youth, passion, and culture. Although Margaret had nominally been the Moore family housekeeper, it is clear that she had also served psychologically as Isabel's mother, and it was only by rebelling against her mores, attitudes, and even appearance that Isabel could grow up. Unlike Joseph Moore, who had been a professor, Margaret is not an intellectual; her unforgivable sin in the young woman's eyes is to speak disparagingly of Jane Eyre. From the first chapter, Isabel affirms this dichotomy: "Margaret's unattractiveness and stupidity made the shape of my life possible. I always knew who I was; I was not Margaret."

Isabel's rejection of Margaret is complete, down to the last details (diet, haircut), and her consequent growth is into an acceptance of herself as a passionate, intellectual, and, in the end, loving individual. Yet, because Margaret is also impoverished and dull, Isabel is also renouncing any identification with the social class she represents. Like the slovenly Mrs. Delehanty (**"The Murderer Guest"**) or slatternly Mrs. Lynch (**"The Neighborhood"**), Margaret has a self so repulsive as to be grounds alone for rejection. At the same time, since her Catholicism is also of a lesser order (novenas and rosary beads rather than Latin missals and medieval paintings), refusing her is in effect a repudiation of a vulgar approach to religion.

If the heroine is *not* Margaret, who is she? Gender aside, she is clearly not identical with either of the two "fathers" in the story—the memory of Isabel's own father or the reality of his replacement, Father Mulcahy—who are intellectuals with passionate flaws. In fact, in shirking an alliance with Margaret, Isabel also discards the notions of the authoritarian spirituality she has imbibed from her father and the paternal priest.

The answer is more fully developed by Felicitas Taylor, the central character in **The Company of Women.** More rambling a story than **Final Payments,** this novel is also richer in its panoply of characters. The story takes place from 1963 through 1977. Its title invites two interpretations. In one sense, it means group, a reference to the band of five women who revolve like satellites (or disciples) around their energetic, dogmatic leader, Father Cyprian Leonard. One of the women has a daughter (but no husband, who died six months after the child was born), and it is the simultaneous development of this child from apprentice devotee to independent woman and of the priest from unassailable guru to admitted fellow traveler that forms the novel's plot. In a second sense, the title connotes companionship, an allusion to the mutual friendship which exists among the women. The two meanings converge in the corps itself, which is more than the sum of its members, who create, as the novel's epigraph suggests, a "common world between them."

In a 1981 interview, Mary Gordon described one of her themes in this novel as "the relationship between the male spiritual authority and the female" (Le Anne Schrieber, "A Talk with Mary Gordon," *New York Times Book Review,* February 15, 1981). On the one hand, there is Father Cyprian, the passionate absolutist, prescribing a view of the world; on the other, there are his middle-aged acolytes, forming among themselves a kind of composite woman. Like Mrs. Hastings in **"The Magician's Wife,"** the women absorb a feeling of privilege simply by association with the magicmaker.

Though none of the women themselves is remarkable, the collective weight of their personalities compels. Felicitas's attention: "When all of them came together, they were something." The women are not driven by an ideal, like Cyprian, but rather by their needs, which are ordinary.

Their habits vary, from a coarse earthiness, to a penchant for fine goods, to a love of literature, but the sights of all five are fixed on things of the world and they offer models of everyday nurturance. Felicitas is drawn to defining herself in relation to this corporate matriarchy as distinct from the priest, her relentless spiritual mentor, who, ignoring her sex, had singled the girl out to inherit his mantle.

The portraits of the women are wonderfully drawn, neither effusive nor restrained. In their complicated individuality they are sisters to the women in several of Mary Gordon's short stories, **"Now I Am Married," "Delia," "Agnes,"** or **"Eileen."** By contrast, Cyprian appears a creature of his tenets and philosophy, and his attraction comes from the authority of the dogma he preaches and its mesmerizing exhortations to heed a bygone tradition. The priest's words resemble those of the American followers of the conservative Archbishop Lefebvre, once described by Mary Gordon as opposing all the elements of modernism, from atheism and communism to liberalism, socialism, and democracy (**"More Catholic Than the Pope; Archbishop Lefebvre and a Romance of the One True Church,"** *Harper's,* July 1978).

Through her exposure to a decadent academic-hippie "group" that parodies the Cyprian discipleship, Felicitas grows skeptical of the priest's position and the women's role in perpetuating it. Subsequently, by deciding to bear the child she unwittingly conceives (and whose father is never known), Felicitas signals her decision to join the women, to accept her role as one of them. Ironically, it is by thwarting Cyprian's plans for her as a surrogate son—someone different from the women because intellectual, unsentimental, and independent—that Felicitas gains the moral authority she needs to confront the priest as an equal. She comes to recognize his limitations. "He had three ideas," she concludes, "the authority of the church, the corruption induced by original sin, and the wickedness of large-scale government. All the rest is instinct and effusion." This recognition in turn frees her to adopt Cyprian's intensity of conviction, his "compelling sense of the ideal" (*New York Times Book Review,* February 15, 1981), and adapt it for her own imaginative use.

It's hard not to compare Felicitas's perceptions about Cyprian with a feminist perspective on the Catholic church: Here is the elderly priest, whose word is taken without question by his pious handmaidens, dictating their very life choices, even as he derides their "Womanish" religion. The shakeup (such as it is) comes about almost by biological accident—Cyprian is confronted with the fact of Felicitas's pregnancy, and the recognition forces him to accept her femininity. Felicitas's child, who turns out to be a girl (Linda), ultimately augments the female ranks, and in the end Cyprian finds himself "surrounded by the muffling, consoling flesh of women . . . dragged . . . down to the middling terrain of their conception of the world, half blood instinct, half the impulse of the womb." Instead of adhering to his old ideal of "objective of impersonal" love, he will now be "pulled down by the irresistible gravity of affection and regard."

With Cyprian's capitulation comes a change in the women, too, who must face the end to one kind of ordering in their lives—that provided by a heretofore unassailable leader. They offer varying observations on this development, which can also be read as a spectrum of comments on changes in the church during the sixties and seventies. Felicitas's mother, the practical Charlotte, for example, is unfazed by what has happened, remarking. "You could look at us and say, There they are, five old women waiting for an old man to die . . . [but] we're a lot better off than a lot of people." Elizabeth, who spends her days reading poetry, sees the end (and Cyprian's eventual death) "in terms of the breakup of the neighborhood" and prays, "Let things stay as they are." Clare sees herself as the end of the line, the last of a dying race" and mourns the end of reverence for, "formal rules." While Cyprian feels defeated by the ascendancy of the female principle and its destruction of this moral ideal, the older women are nostalgic but more or less at peace over it. Felicitas admits to a defiant agnosticism but is philosophical, while her daughter, Linda, is jubilant at the new order. "I am running toward them. They are standing under the apple tree. My mother picks me up and holds me in her arms. My grandmother is laughing. My mother lifts me up into the leaves. We are not dying."

In *The Company of Women* Mary Gordon has developed a heroine who secures a female self by acknowledging the strengths and cadences of women and by accepting the fleshly, emotional side of human life. Just as Isabel needed to reject the role of martyr in order to take part in human events, so Felicitas had to refuse that of priest (the isolated, cerebral being) in order to embrace life as a woman. However, the new woman is not permitted one indulgence granted the old—that of dependence on a man. Instead, her maternity brings into relief her responsibility to protect others. "All the people I love are frailer than I," says Felicitas. "There is no person . . . for whom I do not have to watch out, who can take physical charge even for a little while. And if the physical charge is mine, the moral charge must be mine also."

Men and Angels again examines the theme of woman's spiritual role. Laura Post, a self-anointed prophet who preaches the perils of the flesh, is absorbed into the household of art historian Anne Foster, who hires her as a babysitter for her two children. Anne is enraptured with motherhood. The surface struggle is between Laura's and Anne's views of what matters in life: obedience to the spirit (articulated by Laura) or attention to the needs of the flesh (embodied in Anne's children and in her own sexual desires). But in fact a third viewpoint intrudes, that of the neglected, talented, early-twentieth-century painter, Caroline Watson. Anne is hired to write the catalogue notes for an exhibit of Caroline's work, and the duty to one's art or creative calling becomes one of the elements she must reconcile.

It is a particularly poignant issue for a woman, as Mary Gordon herself must realize, because of the conflicting demands posed by children and creative work, such as writing, "Caroline was a woman and had a child and had created art: because the three could be connected in some grammar, it was as though the pressure to do so were one of logic." Caroline had succeeded in creating great works of art, an achievement Anne admires. At the same time, she faults Caroline for neglecting her son, whom she more or less abandoned and who died young. The development that must occur in Anne, then, is to build a life that tends to multiple dimensions: the needs of her husband and children; the demands of her own body and soul; and the exigencies of her art, the work she is completing on Caroline Watson.

The needs of her husband and particularly her children seem primary. Anne enjoys a "primitive" exultation in her children's bodies, "flesh and flesh, bone, blood connection," and believes her primary charge is "to keep her children safe." In this outlook, she resembles other Gordon characters, such as the wife and mother in **"Safe,"** who says of her husband and baby, "It must be the shape of my life to keep them at least from the danger I could bring them." Yet after the violent upheaval of Laura's suicide, Anne recognizes that even if she expends all of her energies to protect her children, she will not succeed, for they will necessarily be exposed to events without her, some of them dangerous and all of them carrying risk. In her turn, although she is a mother, she takes part in activities that do not involve her children, realizing that a mother's love is "not all of life."

Another dimension that engages the author's imagination in *Men and Angels* is the purely spiritual, personified in the ill-fated Laura. The babysitter moves into the Foster household with the intention of teaching the family "that the flesh was nothing; a mother and her children, all that famous love, was nothing more than flesh to flesh, would drown them all, would keep them from the Spirit." As for marriage, "the idea of it disgusted her: choosing a partner for the urges of the flesh, in filth creating children to be hurt and caused to suffer." As the personification of a radical attitude—that the only reality worth pursuing is a spiritual one—Laura is understandable, but as a character she comes across as too thin and bloodless to compel attention. Because she commands so little sympathy, it is hard to feel the attraction of the spiritual perspective that she is intended to represent. Nevertheless, Laura's presence is ubiquitous (every other chapter of the twelve-chapter novel is told from her point of view) and we are forced to notice her, most graphically by her self-slaughter at the novel's conclusion.

Laura is like a young Margaret (of *Final Payments*), if Margaret were inclined to proselytize. Like Margaret, she lacks love but cannot even command pity, for she exerts no effort to make herself lovable. As a result, it is difficult to feel Anne's guilt and torment at not having loved Laura (or, by implication, having attended enough to her own spiritual needs), for even in life the babysitter seems ghost-like, an anemic imitation of a person. Anne's failure to love Laura, which precipitates the girl's suicide, is even less understandable as a failure of charity than Isabel's disdain of Margaret, for Laura is not only single-minded, but also mute and her hopes, verbalized silently, are seldom shared.

The most credible part of Anne's struggle is in the realm of her work, which she finds absorbing in a different way from her relationships with her family or Laura. Unlike the subjects of Anne's earlier research, Caroline Watson takes hold of the historian's feelings so that in writing about her Anne comes to see her task as that of "build-[ing] a house for the woman she loved." This realization moves catalogue-writing from the category of job to that of vocation, one in which Anne will try to discover the soul of her subject and thus enlighten herself. The product must not only be faithful to Keats's dicta—true and beautiful—but faithful to Anne's feelings, an expression of love. The process of writing promises at the same time to increase Anne's understanding of how to reconcile her own creative needs with her responsibilities to her husband and children. Some distance from them would be required, some cost in closeness. "The truth of the matter was that for a woman to have accomplished something, she had to get out of the way of her own body," Anne observes. "This was the trick people wanted to know about. Did she pull it off? . . . One wanted to believe that the price was not impossible, . . . that there were fathers, husbands, babies, beautifully flourishing beside the beautiful work. For there so rarely were."

In her essay, **"The Fate of Women of Genius"** (written as an introduction to a special edition of Virginia Woolf's *A Room of One's Own* and published in the *New York Times Book Review,* September 13, 1981), Mary Gordon wrote:

> Woolf's sense of the writer's vocation is religious in its intensity. The clarity of heart and spirit that she attributes to writers like Shakespeare and Jane Austen, who have expressed their genius "whole and entire," demands a radical lack of self and ego that might be required of a saint. Yet the writer cannot, for Woolf, work to be rid of the self.

The qualities that are called for in a writer, Gordon notes in the same essay, require an absence of personal grievance. She lists these qualities as "[s]erenity, selflessness, freedom from rage [words which] recall the mystics' counsels," but which in Virginia Woolf's case (and in Mary Gordon's) include an appreciation for the body and its pleasures. The artist—perhaps especially the woman artist—remains an outsider. She is like the narrator, Nora, in several of Mary Gordon's short stories, one of whose legs is shorter than the other and who feels herself odd and conspicuous as a result. Disclosure and consequent shame remain a constant possibility. However, in observing the damaged Agnes in a story of the same name, Nora realizes that, in spite of her handicap, "it might be possible to live a life of passion." What is called for in the artist (or writer) is not to remain aloof from passion, but to capture it in her art.

In the end, Anne recognizes too that her work will require a singularity of vision. She must achieve this, not by abdicating her role as wife and mother (nor by forswearing sensual pleasure) but by undertaking her writing task with a concentration of purpose. If Isabel Moore's fulfillment came through rejecting the role of victim, and Felicitas Taylor's in spurning that of priest, Anne Foster succeeds by accepting a calling akin to that of prophet, not in a religious sense (like Laura), but as someone proclaiming life, in its terrible as well as shining dimensions. She acknowledges in the end her resolve to begin, to:

> take her mind, sharpen it, make it single . . . [to] take the facts that she had learned, the words that there were for them. Join them together. . . . She would write . . . [h]ard words, formed words, white stones that she could hold and separate. And then, refreshed, she could dive back down to the dense underworld, to her children, and say, "This is life. What shall we make of it?"

From Isabel Moore to Felicitas Taylor and Anne Foster, the central figures in Mary Gordon's novels reflect a kind of early imprinting with the form and habit of asking religious questions, so that they can never quiet them later, but only dull their sound or attempt to ignore it. She presents people who have been permanently marked with a spiritual dimension. In the vividness of her characters and in the seriousness of their questionings, Mary Gordon has constructed an involving set of works, one that describes the intricacies of a moral life, in terms not exclusive to women but especially compelling for them. Finally, her books reflect Virginia Woolf's exhortation to the woman writer, "Above all, you must illumine your own soul."

John W. Mahon (essay date 1989)

SOURCE: "Mary Gordon: The Struggle with Love," in *American Women Writing Fiction: Memory, Identity, Family, Space,* edited by Mickey Pearlman, University Press of Kentucky, 1989, pp. 47-60.

[*In the following essay, Mahon examines the depiction of love, family, and personal attachments in Gordon's novels. "Gordon seeks in all her work," writes Mahon, "to explore how people love, or fail to love, each other in a world where belief in God is either a memory or an inconceivability."*]

Mary Gordon's third novel, *Men and Angels* (1985), introduces, for the first time in her fiction, a family in the ordinary sense of the word. Also for the first time, she eschews the Irish Catholic subculture that permeates her earlier novels, *Final Payments* (1978) and *The Company of Women* (1980). Despite this change in focus, Gordon seeks in all her work to explore how people love, or fail to love, each other in a world where belief in God is either a memory or an inconceivability. While the conventional family unit occupies the center of *Men and Angels,* Gordon's real concern extends beyond Anne and Michael Foster and their children to the wider human community outside their comfortable home.

In the first two novels, Gordon portrays communities where the traditional nuclear family plays little part. *Final Payments* opens on the day that Isabel's father is buried. Feeling responsible for her father's stroke eleven years before, she has devoted her life to nursing him. Ultimately, the novel is about coming to terms with death and accepting life with all its risks. It is only near the end that Isabel really mourns her father and begins to move beyond her guilt and self-hatred.

The narrative of *Final Payments* covers the several months following Joe Moore's death. Through flashback we learn that when Isabel is two her mother dies and her father hires the spinster Margaret Casey to keep house. Margaret, an odious, unlovable person, dislikes Isabel and schemes to marry Joe, but Isabel uses her influence on her doting father to secure Margaret's dismissal. For the next seventeen years, until Joe's death, Isabel's family consists of her father, her school friends Eleanor and Liz, and Father Mulcahy. She finds a home with these three at various times after her father's death, until she gets involved with the "saintly" Hugh Slade. Chastened by the violent reaction of Hugh's wife to this latest adultery, Isabel relinquishes self-indulgence in favor of masochistic denial; she moves in with the hideous Margaret Casey, who, as ever, makes Isabel's life an ordeal. In the end, Isabel makes a "final payment" to Margaret by writing a check for all the money her father left behind. She then escapes Margaret in the company of her friends Eleanor and Liz, determined to try again for happiness with Hugh.

In *The Company of Women,* Felicitas, named for the virgin martyr mentioned in the Canon of the Mass, loses her father when she is six months old. She grows up surrounded by widows and spinsters, all under the domination of the dictatorial Father Cyprian. The importance of community here is implicit both in the title—the working title for this second novel had been *Fields of Force*—and in the name of Felicitas, which appears in the Canon after these words: "We ask some share in the *fellowship* of your apostles and martyrs" (emphasis mine).

In Cyprian's look Felicitas reads the message: "You are the chosen one. Make straight the way of the Lord"; like Isabel she is Mary, not Martha, destined for contemplation and study rather than concern about practical problems (Luke 10:40). Trained in the doctrines and ritual of the Church, Felicitas as an adult will provide her elders with vicarious satisfaction as she defeats the dragons of the secular culture. But the precocious Felicitas chooses to rebel, converts to the counterculture of the late sixties, sleeps with Robert Cavendish and another member of his "turned-on" community, and gets pregnant. Deciding literally at the last minute against an abortion, she returns to her mother, who takes charge and moves them both upstate to live permanently near Cyprian. Eight years after Linda

is born, Felicitas elects to marry a local man who is simple but loving: "It is for shelter that we marry and make love."

In these first two novels, Gordon writes virtual allegories of the search for community and love after the collapse of old certainties. The dilemma is exemplified in the life of Cyprian Leonard, one of Gordon's most important "minor" characters. His baptismal name was Philip, but he took the name of the early Christian martyr Cyprian, Bishop of Carthage, when he entered the Paraclete Order. ("Paraclete," a title applied to the Holy Spirit, means "advocate," "intercessor.") Like Felicitas, Cyprian is invoked in the Canon of the Mass. He reacts to change in the Church by growing more conservative, until he feels unwelcome among the Paracletists and begins a long exile, moving from one diocese to another before settling permanently in his hometown on his parents' property. Thus, Philip Leonard rejects his nuclear family to embrace the community of Paracletists: feeling betrayed by change, Cyprian Leonard rejects the community, returns home, and develops his own community, the "company of women" with Felicitas as the promise of a new generation. His reaction to upheaval is rejection; he thus anticipates the rebellion of his protégé, Felicitas, against him.

The experience of Isabel Moore and Felicitas Taylor also mirror those of the Catholic community from which they spring and against which they rebel. Both women spend years in a cloistered existence, and their break with the "cloister" mirrors the experience of Catholicism, especially American Catholicism, following the Second Vatican Council—long years of life in a carefully guarded fortress vanish before the onrush of the secular world and all its blandishments. Both Isabel and Felicitas function on one level as types, confronted with fundamental changes and loss of personal faith, forced to abandon familiar patterns and live outside the Catholic ghetto.

Both women break free of their cloistered environment through sex, an obvious route for repressed Catholic girls of their generation. The strictness of the cloister accounts in part for the extremity of their breaks. Isabel visits a gynecologist to get "some kind of birth control" and chooses the IUD: "Never had I felt such pain, and there was an added sense of outrage in knowing that I had invited it." Desperate to leave the doctor's office, she makes light of the pain: "I tried to make myself look Protestant." After submitting in a moment of weakness to the odious John Ryan, husband of her friend Liz, she takes on the kindly Hugh Slade as a lover. Slade, every Catholic's idea of the solid WASP, talks of the "barbarous background" Isabel and her friends had; his unbelievably bland goodness is as grotesque as Ryan's chauvinism.

Felicitas rejects the control of the sternly conservative Cyprian only to fall into the lubricious arms of the odious Robert Cavendish, whose free-love harem is less attractive than the celibate community headed by Cyprian. Already under Cavendish's spell, Felicitas is unimpressed when her "aunt" Elizabeth tells her that Cyprian "loves you so much that he can hardly bear it." Felicitas responds that Cyprian "doesn't know anything about love." When Elizabeth observes that "None of us knows much," Felicitas thinks of Cavendish: "He knew about love." In fact, love in any meaningful sense is a dirty word to Cavendish, and Felicitas learns to appreciate, if grudgingly, the love and shelter offered by her extended family, the company of women.

Shelter is an important word in Gordon's work, sought by all of her characters with more or less success. (It is no accident that the title for her collection of short stories [1987] is *Temporary Shelter.*) In the first two novels, love and shelter must be searched for outside the traditional family setting. Both Isabel and Felicitas find themselves members of a family in the extended sense. Struck by Eleanor's jealousy of her friendship with Liz, Isabel realizes, "We are connected. . . . I am not entirely alone." Reflecting on the relationship among her friends, Felicitas's mother Charlotte realizes that "there was something between them, between all of them. They were connected to something, they stood for something. . . . When all of them came together, they were something." It is this "something" that Felicitas rejects, to seek security in the Cavendish ménage, "more like a family, and Felicitas needed a lot of support."

In *The Company of Women,* there is only one nuclear family, the one Cyprian leaves behind to enter the priesthood: "I would not be the son of my father, the brother of my brothers, bumbling and heavy and uncouth. I would be part of that glorious company, the line of the apostles. I would not be who I was." The few families in *Final Payments* lack love. Liz and John Ryan find marriage more of a convenience for raising two children than a meaningful relationship. Liz finds fulfillment in a lesbian liaison, while John regularly commits adultery. Cynthia Slade has tricked Hugh into marriage and now taunts him with his infidelities.

The real love in the novel is between Isabel and her friends. Liz loves Isabel enough to confront her on occasion with difficult questions: Why fall for John Ryan? Do you realize the complications involved in loving Hugh? When Isabel retreats into her masochistic shell, it is Liz who tells her to get out of bed and confront life. It should be noted that Hugh, also, tries to jolt Isabel out of her self-hatred. How, after all, can you love others if you do not love yourself? Ultimately pushing Isabel to the decision to leave Margaret Casey, Father Mulcahy offers her money to improve her appearance, reminding her of the commandment against self-destruction.

Isabel's work for the county involves visiting families who are paid by the government to provide shelter for old people. Shelter can be provided, but love is not so easy to come by. Visiting one women, Isabel wishes she could really help but thinks of St. Paul's statement in 1 Corinthians 13:4: "Charity suffereth long and is kind":

> That was it, unless you were willing to suffer in your kindness, you were nothing. Barbarous, Hugh would have said. He would have said that most people feel nothing, that you can be kind in simpler ways. But with me I carried the baggage of the idea. Love and charity. One was that feeling below the breast, and the other was doing something, anything, to take people's pain away. I remembered the lettering on a bulletin board at Anastasia Hall: LOVE IS MEASURED BY SACRIFICE. And I remembered thinking how wrong that was, because the minute I gave up something for someone I liked them less.
>
> "Ah," Sister Fidelis had said when I asked her, "you don't have to like someone to love them in God."
>
> But who wants to be loved in God? I had thought then, and still thought. We want to be loved for our singularity, not for what we share with the rest of the human race. We would rather be loved for the color of our hair or the shape of our ankle than because God loves us.

Isabel learns that some of the old people are happy while others are miserable. One old man gives her good advice about her relationship with Hugh and asks that, in return, she show him her breasts; she agrees. An old woman spends her days weeping and begs Isabel to recommend her transfer to a nursing home—there she can use the medication she has been saving to kill herself. She has, after all, nothing to live for, with both her son and husband dead: "What I want is to be with someone who wants me. Wants *me*. . . . Or else I want to die." Isabel agrees to recommend her transfer: "That was charity, then. You let someone die if they wanted to. . . . If that was what you wanted—someone to love you for yourself more than anyone else (What I wanted from Hugh)—there was nothing worth living for once you lost it."

In distinguishing between love and charity, Isabel blurs the seamless nature of love in the Christian understanding, which is that God has a deeply personal love for each human being. Christians believe in the uniqueness of the individual and hold the cognate belief that Jesus died not for the race but for each person. The obligation of the Christian is to love others as God has loved each of us. By this definition the real lovers in Gordon's work are the mothers, who would die for their children "without a thought" (*Men and Angels*); interestingly, Cyprian, not related to Felicitas by blood, feels the same way about her as Charlotte does and as Anne Foster feels about her children.

The "charity" that Isabel practices in exposing herself to the old man and helping the old woman commit suicide is a perversion of Christian love. Through the love of her son and her husband, the old woman *has* experienced the kind of deeply personal love God has for each individual, but she has failed to find in human love the promise of God's love that would keep her from despair and suicide. Instead of helping the old woman to recognize the richness of the love in her life and to confront the pain of loss, Isabel helps her to opt out and fears the same end for herself if she risks loving Hugh.

Isabel has only a dim sense of what she knows her father would call the "error" in this line of thought and action because, long before her father's death, she has lost her faith. Operating on the purely human level, she tries to give Hugh up and embrace life with Margaret: "If we can love the people we think are most unlovable, if we can get out of this ring of accident, of attraction, then it's pure act, love; then we mean something, we stand for something."

In fact, if she really loved Margaret, she would recognize her responsibility for Margaret's fate: Margaret reached out for human love with Isabel's father, but Isabel defeated the attempt. If she could love Margaret, Isabel would see her not as an ogre to be fobbed off with a check but as a person who has never been loved as Isabel herself feels people must be loved. If she really loved Margaret, who *has* hurt many people (including Father Mulcahy) and spread scandal, she would heed the advice of Jesus: "If thy brother shall trespass against thee, go and tell him his fault between thee and him alone: if he shall hear thee, thou hast gained thy brother" (Matt. 18:15). In short, if Isabel really loved Margaret, she would relate to her, and this she never does. Margaret Casey is an important "type" for Gordon, who will create a similar character in Laura Post in *Men and Angels.* Like Isabel, Anne Foster will encounter the unlovable; her actions will be somewhat different, but they too will be circumscribed by the limitations inherent in a response that cannot, or will not, transcend the human level.

Of course, Gordon's own experiences lie behind the struggle with love in all her work, behind the unconventional communities of the first two novels and behind the obsessive motherhood of the third. These experiences include her Catholic education in the fifties, when she would have learned by rote most of the Church's doctrines, as summarized in the Baltimore Catechism. My guess is that Mary Gordon, consciously or not, was profoundly influenced by the concept of the Mystical Body of Christ. In *The Company of Women,* Robert Cavendish praises Felicitas's abilities as a writer and declares: "'I think the three women in this room could be at the vanguard of the new movement. Felicitas the head, Sally the hands and Iris the heart.' The mystical body of Christ, Felicitas thought, but said nothing."

According to the Catechism, "the Catholic Church is called the Mystical Body of Christ because its members are united by supernatural bonds with one another and with Christ, their Head, thus resembling the members and head of the living human body." Since Catholics were also taught that every human being, either directly or by extension, belonged to the Church, the Mystical Body is, in fact, the human race with Christ as its head. The Church derives the notion of Mystical Body from Scripture: in John's gospel, Jesus says that "I am the vine, ye are the branches. He that abideth in me, and I in him, the same bringeth forth much fruit: for without me ye can do nothing" (15:5). Writing to the Ephesians, St. Paul says that the Father has made Jesus "head over all things to the church, which is his body" (1:22-3). In the chapter of I Corinthians that immediately precedes the famous disquisi-

tion on love that Gordon refers to in *Final Payments* and uses in the title *Men and Angels,* Paul writes most eloquently on this concept: "For as the body is one, and hath many members, and all the members of that one body being many, are one body: so also is Christ. For by one Spirit are we all baptized into one body. . . . And whether one member suffer, all the members suffer with it; or one member be honoured, all the members rejoice with it. Now ye are the body of Christ, and members in particular" (12:12-13; 26-27).

Every human being, then, is a member of the same family; blood ties matter far less than the unity all people share in Christ. The doctrine of the Mystical Body lies at the heart of Catholic belief; its concept of a community that makes no distinctions based on such human accidents as race or sex is an ideal the church has always sought to realize. Mary Gordon has said, "I guess what I see as valuable in the Church is a very high ethic of love which exists in the context of the whole of European civilization."

Schooled in this approach to life, Gordon explores the boundaries of love, hopelessly limited on the merely human level but transformed when viewed in relationship to the transcendent. Very revealing are her selections for a 1985 symposium on "The Good Books: Writer's Choices":

> Simone Weil, *Waiting for God,* George Herbert—a 17th-century poet—and the *Holy Sonnets* of John Donne. In Herbert, it is the perfection and the understatement of the language that allows for a simple encounter with the divine; the understatement allows for tremendous expansiveness. Simone Weil writes of a vision of God as love, and the relationship of the love of God to human life. It is rigorous, absolute, and passionate. In all three works, it is the link between spirituality and passion, as well as the absoluteness of vision. Much of my work deals with the limitation of human love; the vision of the absolute is the ideal that we as humans are striving against. If one talks about a spiritual quest, it is about this pursuit of absolute love.

Gordon's choice of preposition in the penultimate sentence says a great deal. "We . . . humans strive *against* [emphasis mine]," not *toward,* the vision of the absolute, the ideal explored by Weil, Herbert and Donne. So far, her fiction has avoided the "spiritual quest," which would make "absolute love" its goal, and has focused instead on "the limitation of human love."

Therefore, her protagonists fail to acknowledge the divine dimension in human love; like the narrator in Francis Thompson's "The Hound of Heaven," they flee from the demands of absolute love, which is God, and try desperately to find substitutes for transcendence. In the first two novels, Isabel and Felicitas reject the Church at least partly because they do not really understand the substance of Christianity that lies beneath the accidents of discipline and ritual. Isabel seeks in vain for shelter in sex or in masochism. Felicitas seeks in vain for shelter in sex or in motherhood.

In her review of *Men and Angels,* Margaret Drabble notes that "this is a deliberately domestic, at times claustrophobic novel," one, indeed, in which very little happens on the surface. The Fosters plan to spend a year in France, where Michael will teach while a French colleague replaces him at Selby College in Massachusetts. But Anne decides to stay in Selby with the two children because an old friend, the art dealer Ben Hardy, offers her an opportunity to write the catalogue for an exhibition of paintings by Caroline Watson, an American artist who died in 1938. "Her misfortune was to be a merely first-rate painter in an age of geniuses."

From the start, then, Gordon makes this "ordinary" family extraordinary by physically separating the parents; the Foster family is seriously weakened. Anne's decision to stay home precipitates the action, since she needs a live-in baby-sitter so that she can work. She reluctantly hires Laura Post, having conceived an instant dislike for this twenty-one-year-old who reads only the Bible. Laura is convinced that she is God's specially chosen creature (compare the status of Isabel and Felicitas!), destined to rescue Anne and her children from their pagan ways, their attachment to the flesh. Ultimately, she decides that she can rescue Anne only by taking her own life. Her suicide and its aftermath comprise the final movement of the novel.

In the earlier novels, the protagonist incorporates two extremes of behavior. Here, the extremes are split into two characters, who are meant to reflect one another; the masochist and the mother confront each other as distinct individuals. Early in the novel, Gordon goes to some trouble to suggest that Laura and Anne physically resemble each other. Thus, Anne has white skin and blue eyes, reddish hair, "a small bosom and no waist," and "comical size-eleven feet." Laura has "the light blue watery eyes of many redheads, which her thick glasses clouded and enlarged. There was something opulent about her skin: it was white, translucent." If Anne has big feet, Laura has "large, protruding ears." Later, Anne notes that Laura is wearing the same perfume and eye shadow Anne herself uses.

It would seem that no two people could be less alike than Laura and Anne, but this physical resemblance haunts the novel and forces the reader to consider that the all-too apparent obsessions of Laura are somehow related to the obsessive motherhood of Anne. Indeed, they share more than physical resemblance and makeup. With Michael they share the experience of mothers who failed them in one way or another. Lucy Foster, abandoned by her husband when Michael was four, could not handle domestic life: "Anne often wondered how Michael had physically survived his early childhood." By the age of eight, he did all the shopping, cooking, and cleaning. But he never had cause to doubt his mother's love for him, despite her neglect of the house. Anne's mother not only disliked home life and failed during the simplest domestic crises; she never cared for Anne as Anne's father does; the mother has always feared that Anne's success would overshadow her sister, who even in adulthood resents Anne. Both

Michael and Anne "had been, as children, mothers, both involved in the conspiracy at the center of the lives of children of deficient parents."

Anne's only real failure in life occurs in 1974, when she loses her job at Boston's Gardner Museum: "She had felt shame then, as she had never in her life felt it before. . . . She knew, for the first time then, that failure made you feel like a criminal." Unfortunately, Laura has never known success, and her lunacy derives directly from her brutal childhood. In *The Company of Women,* Felicitas recalls that, for some months, she was unable to treat Linda as her child: "I neglected Linda; I neglected her shamefully, but she is all right. I have read that a mother's rejection can cause autism and schizophrenia."

A mother at seventeen, Mrs. Post rejects Laura because Laura's birth represents the end of her freedom. (Interestingly, Anne and Mrs. Post are the same age: Anne could also have a twenty-one-year-old daughter; instead, her older child is only nine.) The damage is compounded by the passivity of Laura's father, who makes no effort to intervene when the mother mistreats Laura and favors their younger daughter. Mrs. Post withholds love from Laura and also destroys Laura's innocence, not only by tossing bloody menstrual napkins anywhere but by committing adultery in the middle of the afternoon.

The Spirit first comes to Laura after a particularly vicious attack by Mrs. Post; her mother's rejection causes her to "find the Lord." From the start Laura's "Christianity" scorns and fears human love; so badly hurt by her mother, she avoids risking love and thus cripples her Christianity. Rejecting the possibility of human love, Laura leaves home and takes up with a sect of religious fanatics whose leader insists that the Lord desires the joining of his body and Laura's "flesh to flesh." Later, she sleeps with Anne's philandering friend Adrian, whom earlier she had fantasized marrying, because she wants to keep him from Anne. "Laura did not understand marriage; the idea of it disgusted her: choosing a partner for the urges of the flesh, in filth creating children to be hurt and caused to suffer."

Laura abhors sex and fears human attachments. When she fantasizes about marrying Adrian in Anne's house and living with him nearby, she catches herself: "They would love her but she would not love back as much. Because she still would have the Spirit. They would have to stay but she might leave at any time because she knew that attachments meant nothing. . . . She would have to be careful. Careful that she did not start to need, careful to remember that it was all nothing." Ironically, Laura eventually dreams of a kind of celibate marriage with Anne; when Anne fires her for neglecting the children, she takes her life in order to win Anne's love, to win love that she has never known.

Presenting Laura with *Fear and Trembling* and *Waiting for God* as Christmas presents, Michael "tried to tell her about them. But she didn't care. Books would lead no one to the

Spirit. In the Scripture she found all she needed." Laura's tragedy is that she cannot find a human love to validate her love of God. She is completely isolated; she excommunicates herself from all human and religious community. Laura Post is the unloved child who never really understands the "whole point of the Gospels. She read them over and over, and she never got the point. . . . That she was greatly beloved." Unfortunately, "the love of God means nothing to a heart that is starved of human love." The deranged Laura kills herself to save Anne Foster; ironically, her suicide does have a lasting effect; it destroys forever Anne's illusion that she can shelter her children from life and its dangers simply by the force of her motherly will.

Desiring to save her children from life, Anne exposes them to it sooner than she ever was exposed herself—indeed, she doesn't learn how awful it can be until confronted by Laura's suicide. Isabel in *Final Payments* decides that life is "monstrous: what you had you were always in danger of losing. The greatest love meant only the greatest danger. That was life; life was monstrous." Anne recognizes this truth in the abstract, but it takes Laura to incarnate it for her, when she is thirty-eight years old. Gordon demonstrates Anne's obsessive love for her children in as much detail as she documents Laura's lunacy.

Anne's mother-love demonstrates the truth of a remark addressed to her at one point in the novel: "You're a great believer in the power of blood. A real primitive you are, aren't you?" Early in the story, Gordon writes: "No one would ever know the passion she felt for her children. It was savage, lively, volatile. It would smash, in one minute, the image people had of her of someone who lived life serenely, steering always the same sure, slow course. As it was, they would never know, she was rocked back and forth, she was lifted up and down by waves of passion: of fear, of longing, of delight."

At the crisis of the story, when Laura inadvertently allows the children to walk on an icy pond probably not firm enough to hold them, Anne brings the children to safety and then turns to Laura. "The desire to put her hands around Laura's throat, to take one of the large rocks on the shore and smash her skull, to break the ice and hold her head under the water till she felt her life give out was as strong as any passion Anne had ever known." The gravity of the situation justifies Anne's anger. But it is also clear that Anne lives far from the extended families of the earlier novels and is unfamiliar with the concept of the Mystical Body, with its promise that blood is not all-important, that there are relationships that transcend the physical.

Long before this crisis, Gordon makes clear that religious belief is foreign to the Fosters; Anne's mother admits that her daughters "were both brought up quite irreligiously. I went to convent school for twelve years and had all I could take. Perhaps that was rash." Consequently, "Anne

had never understood the religious life. She could be moved by it when it led to some large public generosity. . . . But there was another side to it she couldn't comprehend. People led religious lives in the way that people wrote poetry, heard music." As for the children, "Peter and Sarah hadn't been told anything about the devil."

Yet someone Anne greatly respects and admires, Caroline Watson's daughter-in-law Jane, has a religious life and articulates some of the most important insights in the novel. It is Jane who realizes that Laura missed the "whole point of the Gospels" and who identifies Anne as "a great believer in the power of blood." Out of a sense of guilt over the death of her husband, Stephen, Caroline's illegitimate son, Jane "turned to faith because it showed the possibility of forgiveness for the unforgivable."

Caroline's inability to love Stephen, her own flesh and blood, angers Anne, and Caroline's mistreatment of her son threatens Anne's ability to write about her objectively. "Whenever Anne thought of Caroline's treatment of Stephen she came upon a barrier between them that was as profound as one of language. . . . She couldn't imagine Peter or Sarah marrying anyone she would prefer to them, as Caroline had preferred Jane to Stephen." Stephen's death at the age of twenty-eight was the result.

When Michael returns from France for Christmas, the Fosters visit Jane Watson. Michael notes that she has many of Simone Weil's books. Ben comments:

> "Michael, be a dear boy and don't go on about Mademoiselle Weil. It's bound to make Jane and me come to blows. All that hatred of the flesh. . . ."
>
> "It was Simone Weil who brought me to a religious life. Well, she and George Herbert."
>
> "How so?" asked Michael.
>
> Anne was embarrassed. She thought that religious people shouldn't talk about such things in public. . . . But Michael, she knew, had no such qualms. To him a religious disposition was only one more example of odd human traits quite randomly bestowed, like buckteeth or perfect pitch. Anne felt it was something powerful and incomprehensible. It made people behave extraordinarily; it made them monsters of persecution, angels of self-sacrifice.

From her curious vantage point, Laura recognizes the emptiness of the lives around her. The reader is forced to wonder how long Anne and her family can survive in the culture of secular materialism that surrounds them. It is no accident, surely, that Laura's choice of suicide—slitting her wrists and bleeding to death in a bathtub that overflows down to the basement—destroys much of the fabric of the Foster home; possessions will not provide shelter, any more than mother-love can.

Laura's suicide is the desperate act of a deranged person. Yet it may force Anne to move beyond "blood" and mother-love to some concept of love that can embrace even the unlovable. Like Isabel with the old people in *Final Payments,* she practices "charity" on Laura, buying her beautiful clothing and fussing to celebrate her birthday. Unable to like Laura, Anne fails to love her, fails to provide her even a foster home. Loving Laura would mean taking some responsibility for her, providing her with real help, probably with psychiatric care.

Laura's death brings her the recognition she was denied in life: Anne could not love her, but she pledges to mourn for her. Weeping in Michael's arms, Anne reflects on the love that features so prominently in Gordon's work:

> People were so weak, and life would raise its whip and bring it down again and again on the bare tender flesh of the most vulnerable. Love was what they needed, and most often it was not there. It was abundant, love, but it could not be called. It was won by chance; it was a monstrous game of luck. Fate was too honorable a name for it. . . . [Laura] was starved, and she had died of it. And Anne let her husband's love feed her. Let the shade of its wing shelter her, cover her over. But no wing had ever covered Laura. The harsh light had exhausted her until she could only go mad. And then the whip had fallen. And Anne knew that she had helped the whip to descend.

In partially recognizing love's power, Anne may come to understand the love that transcends human love, that consoles even in cases like Laura's. At Laura's funeral service, for the first time in their lives, Peter and Sarah hear religious language as the priest recites several Psalms, including Psalm 121: "The Lord shall preserve thee from all evil: he shall preserve thy soul." The Fosters may come to recognize that familial love is not enough. But Gordon's focus, always, is on "the limitation of human love," and that limitation is nowhere more brilliantly presented than in *Men and Angels.*

Mary Gordon uses various strategies to explore how people live and relate to each other in the late twentieth century. In *Final Payments* and *The Company of Women,* she studies the Catholic subculture in disarray as certainties fade; shelter is offered by extended families, earthly echoes of the Mystical Body. But these families are flawed, even that of Father Cyprian, whose "company of women" is insular and isolated. There is no sense here of the universal community predicated by St. Paul or the Canon of the Mass. The third novel, *Men and Angels,* shifts the focus to an "average" American family. But the shelter offered here, in an a-religious environment, is so fragile that it cannot include the troubled Laura.

"Nobody wants to write about yuppies," Gordon herself has remarked. "It's much more interesting to write about a closed, slightly secret, marginal group." This preference explains the first two novels, some of the short stories, and the work in progress, a treatment of the Irish immigrant experience. Yet *Men and Angels* is her "yuppy novel." As such it dramatizes forcefully the dilemma of our culture, which has left God and Church behind but not yet found a satisfactory substitute—the best it can offer is a Foster family.

Madison Smartt Bell (review date 15 October 1989)

SOURCE: "Terrible, the Way It Was in Families," in *New York Times Book Review,* October 15, 1989, p. 9.

[*In the following review, Bell offers positive assessment of* The Other Side.]

Mary Gordon's earlier work has demonstrated her expertise in portraying the politics of family life, with its manifold misunderstandings and its complex struggles for power and love. In her fourth novel, she applies this ability to a much larger and more intricate situation than ever before, attempting to account for five generations of the MacNamara family within the space of 24 hours. On the day in question, the elderly Vincent MacNamara is expected to return from a sanitarium, where he has spent several months recuperating from a broken hip, to the house in Queens where his wife, Ellen, lies dying after a series of small strokes. Their children, grandchildren and great-grandchildren have gathered for his homecoming, thus supplying the book with some 20 major characters. It is a tribute to Ms. Gordon's artistry that she brings this dauntingly large cast so quickly and surely to life.

Her approach is to cut a cross section through the trunk of these interrelated lives to reveal how they appear at this particular moment to which their histories have brought them—and to expose the fibers that bind them together. Naturally, Vincent and Ellen, the heads of the house, are found at the center. "Terrible, the way it was in families," thinks Vincent. "He'd never understood it. Why they weren't what they were meant to be, what they could almost be so easily."

In the MacNamara family, love tends to skip generations. Ellen is uninterested in her daughters, Magdalene and Theresa, caring only for her son, John, who is killed in World War II. Afterward, she seizes his accidentally conceived son, Dan, away from his hapless mother and raises him as her own, while the remainder of her maternal affection goes to Magdalene's daughter, Cam, who has been effectively orphaned by her father's death and her mother's alcoholism. Ellen herself is the survivor of a wretched childhood in Ireland, which she served as the keeper of her insane mother, whom her father abandoned. Vincent's Irish family seems only a little kindlier, and he also arrives in America in flight. With vignettes of memory, the two reconstruct a classic immigrants' tale: lives as laborers, as union organizers, the ascent to the middle class.

The stories of all the MacNamara descendants are also given in marvelously economical capsules. Theresa's three children, John, Marilyn and Sheilah, are all in one way or another crippled by their mother's contempt, which seems to have been inspired by Ellen's indifference to her. That sort of repeating pattern in family history is itself a recurring feature of Ms. Gordon's work. Magdalene's daughter, Cam, and John's son, Dan, who were loved as children, break out of the pattern to some degree, but although they are successful in their partnership as divorce lawyers, they both lead ragged personal lives. Cam is stuck in the shell of a failed and childless marriage, and she cannot solve her perpetual quarrel with her mother, a drunken hypochondriac who hasn't left her room in years. The messily divorced Dan is tormented by guilt over what his departure has done to his own children. Both he and Cam find only limited comfort with their respective lovers, since both are still members of a Roman Catholic culture where adultery is regarded with great seriousness. "The stories told by the women in her family," Cam thinks, "were always in the service of this: this judgment, without whose proximity they could not, any of them, think of pleasure."

There's plot enough in **The Other Side** for several novels, but the main purpose of all the action is to illuminate individual character: what it is and how it comes to be. Ms. Gordon has set out to discover how each self is formed in relation to other selves, to learn to what extent identity is chosen and to what extent it is imposed. The agoraphobic Magdalene supplies a metaphor for this repeating uncertainty in the lives of all the characters: "She sees herself on the street. There is no self there, no shape, nothing to keep *her* from spilling over into air, into life, into anybody's life. Outside this room she can fly off, she will, there will be no more her, nothing will press down on her to create a shape."

As Magdalene is shaped by the walls of her room, so are the other characters by other people, by circumstantial relationships that mold for almost every one of them an identity that becomes hardened past any possibility of change. Of all the MacNamaras, only Vincent seems capable of imagining himself as something other than what he is; this capacity serves as a healing force in his marriage when he returns to Ireland to repair some of the damage done by Ellen's vengefully motivated departure many years earlier. But all the others (down to Dan's teenage daughters Darci and Staci) suffer that hardening of personality that may be an inheritance from Ellen, who is so powerfully intransigent as to break herself with her own strength. In her deathbed reverie, "she wants a stone now for a body, smooth, a weapon, closed. Now her body keeps nothing back." All the MacNamaras experience themselves as *formed,* inexorably: such is the tragedy of this family's life.

The spectacle of so many strong and good people so seriously failing one another and themselves would logically become, in a religious context, an image of the fallen world. Mary Gordon is consummately skilled at rendering nuances of religious devotion, which she has handled very differently in her very different books: **The Company of Women,** for example, treats religious mysticism respectfully and lovingly, while **Men and Angels** shows an extreme case of it as a psychopathological catastrophe. In this new novel, Catholicism appears more in its influence on ordinary life than in its mystery. The big religious questions are asked, but not dwelt upon. At one point, Vin-

cent tentatively characterizes God as "some person whom your tears will interest," then asks himself, "And have you made Him up?" The MacNamaras' predicament is presented existentially, and Deus (*ex machina* or otherwise) does not actually appear.

The Other Side is epic in scope but not in length, and in other hands it might have ended as a snarl of unfinished business. But Mary Gordon's painstakingly cultivated gift for zeroing in on the important emotions with unsentimental precision, and her talent for summing up character efficiently and accurately, make this the best of her several fine books. Although some threads of the plot go dangling, the strands turn out to matter much less than the web. Thus Vincent's questions of faith are answered, somewhat backhandedly, by Dan, who "realizes the nature of his faith. He believes in human frailty. He sees the wholeness of all life, the intricate connecting tissue. It is this, this terrible endeavor, this impossible endeavor. Simply to live a life."

"Each unhappy family," as Tolstoy put it, "is unhappy in its own way," and under the aspect of eternity the pursuit of happiness may be less important than the pursuer takes it to be. The idea that suffering is the catalyst that gives each soul its essential nature remains at least consistent with the Christian heritage of which Mary Gordon continues to partake. Like Tolstoy, she is a profoundly religious novelist who has obligated herself to understand the lives she invents in strictly human terms.

Pearl K. Bell (review date 18 December 1989)

SOURCE: "Last Exit to Queens," in *The New Republic,* December 18, 1989, pp. 39-41.

[*In the following essay, Bell offers an overview of Gordon's literary career and tempered evaluation of* The Other Side.]

Young writers do not as a rule take commanding possession of a literary world, religious or social, with a first novel. Their fictional property rights, so to speak, need to be confirmed in a continuing body of work. But when Mary Gordon published her first novel, **Final Payments,** at the age of 29, it was acclaimed not only for the dazzling intensity of her prose, but for the indisputable authority of her portrayal of the Irish-Catholic working class in Queens, that least urban and most provincial of the New York City boroughs. With that single novel she established her dominion as a writer in the time and the place she knew best.

There have been relatively few Catholic writers in the United States. The Protestant culture found its literary landscape in the small towns and rural regions of America, while Jewish writers in the last 40 years have dominated the urban scene. Most of the novelists born into Catholic families, like John O'Hara and F. Scott Fitzgerald, had no interest in writing about their religion. Except for J. F. Powers, who has portrayed the everyday life of parish priests in the Midwest with wry sympathy, no significant name comes to mind. (There are popular novelists like James Carroll and Andrew Greeley, but their work is entertainment, not art. Does anyone read James T. Farrell anymore?)

Nor are there many women who write as Catholics. In the South, Flannery O'Connor, a devout believer, envisioned the timeless mysteries of God and the Devil in grotesque and violent forms. But in Mary McCarthy's brittle novels about urban intellectuals, there's scarcely a hint of religion of any persuasion, and the very title of her autobiographical *Memories of a Catholic Girlhood* indicated that her ties to the Church were among the "childish things" she put away, not exactly in the spirit of St. Paul, when she grew up.

In her first two books, Gordon dealt with the conflicts that all young people experience in coming of age, though her particular terrain was Irish Catholic Queens. *Final Payments* and *The Company of Women* were abundantly rich in detail about Catholic ritual, custom, and belief, the kind of intimate knowledge only a cradle Catholic can possess. Yet each novel was a kind of bildungsroman. Each described a mettlesome young woman who slowly and painfully realizes that only by rejecting the repressive interdictions of the Church can she be free to enjoy "the rewards of a reasonable life."

In *Final Payments,* Isabel Moore has sacrificed a precious decade of youth to the care of an invalid father, a man whose faith is so unyielding and austere that he believes "the refusal of anyone in the 20th century to become part of the Catholic Church was not pitiable; it was malicious and willful." Even after she is released from filial bondage by her father's death, Isabel does not question her certainty that "what I came from was far more compelling than what I was." After a brief fling with a married man, she scuttles back to her cocoon of piety, and the specious purity of self-abnegation, to atone for her transgression. We are told that in time Isabel finds the courage to liberate herself, sexually and otherwise; but exactly how and why she managed this about-face remains unclear.

Of course such dramatically abrupt changes of heart and mind are a stock feature of coming-of-age novels, and Gordon did not resist their tidy appeal. What redeemed *Final Payments* from banality and predictability, however, was its descriptive eloquence and its metaphoric freshness. Though it seemed obvious that Gordon conceived her heroine's pursuit of "ordinary human happiness" in terms of worldly feminism, she emphatically declared in an interview that "I have a real religious life in a framework which I think of as Catholic."

Is it possible to be both a devout Catholic and a radical feminist? To someone who is neither it sounds, I confess, like an oxymoron. Feminists within the Church want to lift the ban on the ordination of women because they feel they deserve a share of hierarchical power. Yet their commitment to the Roman faith remains intact. They would not assent for a moment to the inimical judgment of divinity expressed by Felicitas, the young rebel in *The Company of Women,* who smugly announces at the end of the book that she has hardened her heart against God: "I will not accept the blandishments of the religious life; I will not look to God for comfort, or for succor, or for sweetness. God will have to meet me on the high ground of reason, and there he's a poor contender." How Flannery O'Connor would have shuddered at this self-righteous blasphemy.

There is ambivalence, there is confusion, at the heart of this second novel, and Gordon seemed unable, or unwilling, to deal with it. The conservative priest Father Cyprian has pinned his highest hopes on the child Felicitas. If she abides by his counsel, she will attain the spiritual purity that in his view is increasingly defiled in the modern world. But she cruelly rejects his dream, enrolls at Columbia rather than a Catholic college, has an affair with a dopey radical professor (heavy-handedly caricatured); becomes pregnant, and bears an illegitimate child. Cyprian is crushed by her rebellion. Still, even though Gordon obviously sees him as a representative of the old, intransigent, pre-Vatican II order of the Church, he is the most compelling and complex character in the novel. In the end, the anguished old priest has more profound moral weight, is more credibly human, than the arrogantly self-satisfied heroine.

Perhaps it was Gordon's inability to resolve the emotional tug-of-war between sanctity and emancipation that accounts for the absence of Catholicism from her third novel, *Men and Angels,* in which religion takes the menacing form of non-denominational lunacy. Anne Foster, a supposedly intelligent and sensitive woman, much given to tiresome rumination about the precariousness of human existence, has entrusted her children to a live-in baby sitter who's more than a little peculiar. We know it will all end horribly because Gordon spins out the demented girl's lurid fantasies about the Spirit of Vengeance and the Chosen of the Lord at tedious length, but exactly what this character is supposed to illustrate is hard to grasp.

If Gordon is trying to say that any form of religious fanaticism is a kind of madness, she doesn't convey this judgment persuasively. And if she means the novel to be a celebration of motherhood, Anne is too deplorably lacking in the common sense a mother must have to protect her children from danger. Gordon couldn't make up her mind, it seems, about any of the questions she raised in *Men and Angels,* and the result was a weak and muddled book lacking all conviction.

Gordon's new novel, *The Other Side* (as the Irish of Ireland called the beckoning land across the sea), is her most ambitious work so far, and it brings her back to where she started, to the Irish Catholics of Queens. Instead of a bravely independent young woman straining against the repressive leash of the Church, Gordon has expanded her sights to encompass five generations of a large family, each unhappy in its own fashion.

Shuttling restlessly between past and present, between the bogs of Ireland and the streets of New York, the story is framed by the events of one day in the summer of 1985, when the entire clan has gathered in Queens to await the homecoming of the patriarch, 88-year-old Vincent Mac-Namara. For months he has been recuperating in a nursing home from a broken hip. In the arresting episode that begins the family saga, we learn how he was injured: his 90-year-old wife, Ellen, battered by years of strokes, knocked him down in a sudden access of wild rage, and wandered out of the house in her nightgown. In the ensuing months she has become almost completely insensible, but she is fitfully tormented by memories of the past that whirl through her ruined head like the bits of colored glass in a kaleidoscope.

Indeed, anger has been Ellen's life-blood since childhood, the agitated sinews of her being, and even on her death-bed she can still cry out curses that terrify the family. In a bravura passage, Gordon summons up the soul of this difficult woman with majestic dread:

> Within the nearly visible skull, the brain, disintegrating fast, reaches back past houses, curtains, out to ships and over oceans, down to the sea's bottom, back, down, to the bog's soaked floor, to mud, then to the oozing beds of ancient ill will, prehistoric rage, vengeance, punishment in blood.

Neither time nor her husband's long-suffering devotion has pacified Ellen MacNamara, who has been raging against the ways of God and man through most of her 90 years. As a girl in Ireland she despised the priests, and hated her father for transforming her beautiful mother into a gibbering imbecile. Now, as the old woman tosses and raves in her bed, the bitter harvest of her unassuageable fury is reaped by her descendants. One daughter is a hard-hearted martinet armored in righteous Catholic piety, and the other has become a whining drunk wallowing in self-pity. Both of them blame everything that has gone wrong in their lives on the mother who could not love them.

Only two of the grandchildren, Camille and Dan, have known a gentler side of Ellen, and in the younger generation only they have felt an enduring affection for her. But it has not enabled them to straighten out their lives any more successfully than the others. Each of the grandchildren has been maimed in some way by thwarted hopes. They feel no pleasure in each other's company, and the air of the old house in Queens is soured by animosity and resentment.

We wait for the tension to break, for a storm to erupt. It does not happen. The novel's wavelike oscillation back and forth in time and space prevents the story from gathering the momentum it badly needs. The disjointed structure that Gordon has imposed on the MacNamara family saga, crosscutting nervously from one cousin's life story to another, makes it a considerable effort to keep the different characters firmly in mind.

It has been said that every modern American writer eventually tries a Hollywood novel and an immigrant novel. Not only Jewish writers, though they have perhaps been the most prolific, have been drawn to it time and again: the immigrant experience has been one of the great American subjects, indeed the unending American subject. Growing up in Nebraska, Willa Cather so fully absorbed the suffering and the triumphs of the Bohemian and Scandinavian pioneers flowing onto the prairie that she wrote some of her finest novels (*My Antonia, The Song of the Lark*) about those hardy European settlers, though she was not one of them.

As far as I know, the life of the immigrants from Ireland has been much less fully explored in American fiction, and it is this stream in the westward migration from Europe that has provided Gordon with the strongest sections of her new novel. She evokes with considerable power the harrowing life that Irish immigrants endured in New York before the First World War.

Just off the boat, not yet 20 years old, Vincent took the first job that came along, digging the I.R.T. subway tunnel in the bowels of the city. For the country boy from Cork, those were "terrible days at first, he couldn't get used to working underground. The heat, the stink. Exhaustion in the bones and worse; filth you could never get away from . . . the beast's work that required no mind: digging, nothing to understand." Ellen, just as young and green, thought herself lucky to find a job as maid to a woman she despised, then became a seamstress in a sweatshop, hunched over fancy gowns for endless hours, and sleeping in a dark basement room. We can begin to recognize the deep, gnarled roots of her irrepressible rage against fate.

Compared with the poverty and brutalizing labor that engulfed Ellen and Vincent at the start of their life in the new world, how petty and self-indulgent are the grievances and discontents of the younger generation. The pity of it is that Gordon hasn't done more with the immigrant past. Though the eldest MacNamaras are the most completely realized characters in the book, their early years in America are not rendered with the fullness and the depth they deserve. Gordon shifts away too abruptly from the past, which is the riveting heart of her story, to the present, which is far less interesting.

It may very well be that as a novelist Gordon has gone as far as she can with the Irish, and with the Catholic Church. Her feelings about Irishness and Ireland remain fixed in the tension between her two eldest protagonists: Ellen could feel only "anger at the Irish countryside, the harsh soil and the scrub growth, the gorse she hated," while Vincent never lost his loving memory of the rolling green land, his delight in "the tilled field . . . the elm or the potato, tender when in leaf." And, as we have seen, the

Catholic world of present-day Queens has become exhausted as well.

In Gordon's literary imagination, Catholicism has lost the vital urgency it had in her earlier work. For most of the present-day generations in *The Other Side,* the Church has no significance, not even as something they long to escape from. In the lives of the younger MacNamaras, as in the lives of the young in other ethnic worlds, the defining influence of religion and the European past has become meaningless, and they are of a piece with the rest of their age. Now that her world no longer holds together, where will this remarkable writer turn next?

John B. Breslin (review date 9 February 1990)

SOURCE: "The Blight in Their Baggage," in *Commonweal,* February 9, 1990, pp. 87-8.

[*In the following review, Breslin offers tempered evaluation of* The Other Side.]

Mary Gordon's latest novel is also her most ambitious both in length and, more importantly, in scope. That's the good news about the novel, and it is indeed good. The bad news is that the execution isn't quite as good as the idea.

The Other Side covers one day in the life of the Mc-Namara family, four generations of New York Irish-Americans who have most of the vices and some of the virtues of their kind. But that day extends backward over eight decades, and the novel's focus moves from the new world to the old and back.

In a Queens bedroom, the ninety-year-old matriarch, Ellen, lies angrily dying while a hundred miles east in a warmly lit nursing home her husband Vincent reluctantly waits to be brought back to her. In the meantime, their children, grandchildren, and great-grandchildren gather in Queens to await the reunion and live out the grudges, resentments, and affections that have grown up across the generations.

But the story of Ellen and Vincent has its roots in Ireland, the most obvious but not the only sense of the novel's evocative title. The dark strain in the McNamara family romance flows in an appropriately Freudian way from a sibling rivalry that sours Vincent's growing up and from a maternal breakdown that destroys Ellen's idyllic childhood and breeds an undying hatred of her ambitious father for abandoning his wife. The long passage of retrospect that limn their troubled departures from home reveal Gordon at her narrative and psychological best. I found that judgment confirmed when, at a reading I attended, she chose to read exclusively from these sections. Here's a sample taken from Ellen's memories of her father's infidelity:

"But it was her job to hate her father. To punish him for leaving them alone in the stone house with only two windows, for allowing Marin Monahan in the house that

had been once her mother's. To soil it with her filth. He'd made the mother darken, coarsen, till she looked out at the brown grasses from the moment of her awakening until dark, her only pleasure food, eaten fearfully, and greedily, like an animal. Her mother, once beautiful, now ruined, was her father's work."

And this from Vincent's recollection of his older brother's vicious killing of a pet lamb in a scene redolent of the Book of Genesis:

"While Vincent looked down at the animal's body, he knew everything. The first thing he took in with calm; it was simple: the animal was dead. The second made him frightened: he could see the remnants of life still within the animal. What happened had just happened. The third thing he knew made fear and anger grow inside his brain, like trees that grow from the same root beside each other, harmful and competitive, yet bound. His brother had done this to harm him. It was Vincent's throat, not the poor animal's, he would have liked to cut."

After such wounding, what healing? Surprisingly, for Ellen and Vincent, their marriage, tumultuous as its six decades prove to be, offers each the confidence and love they have lacked. Indeed, it is the only successful marriage in the whole novel. The blight they carried with them from the other side infects in one form or another all three of their children and most of the next two generations. It is not a happy family that gathers around Ellen to await Vincent's fulfillment of a vow she had extracted from him early in their marriage that he would never abandon her to an institution. Of all their descendants unto the third generation only Cam and Dan are presented as attractive individuals. Having alienated their daughters and lost their son in World War II, Ellen and Vincent attempt to recoup their losses through these two grandchildren whom they raise as their own. Cousins who become siblings, Cam and Dan inherit both Ellen's fierce determination to change the world and Vincent's calmer acceptance of life's anomalies. They also come to be partners in a local law firm specializing in divorce, a condition each knows intimately. Together they stand against their cousins and their aunts, intent on protecting Ellen and Vincent from their indifference and resentment.

What are we to make of this world of the McNamaras that Mary Gordon has created? Surely, it is an interesting one, especially in the persons of its matriarch and patriarch. The tangle of their love, as expressed in their own ruminations and in the deeply biased reflections of their progeny, confirms Tolstoy's observation about the uniqueness of unhappy families. When Vincent finally does return on the last page of the novel, he confirms what the story has already made abundantly clear:

"He walks through the living room, waving his hand at people, like a politician. He waves at his children, his grandchildren, his great-grandchildren. He has no time for them now.

"He is on his way to his wife."

In the end, Vincent and Ellen are alone together, more passionate and committed than any of their clan. All the rest, even Cam and Dan, fade into insignificance in the final ambiguous flaring of their lifelong love that closes the book:

"She hears his step in the room and opens up her eyes."

"He believes that she can see him, but he's not quite sure."

Vincent and Ellen dominate not only their family but Mary Gordon's novel as well, and both to questionable effect. Ellen's indifference toward her daughters is richly repaid by their hostility, just as her devotion to her son John is recompensed in the way of Irish fatalism with his death in battle. In setting out to do Tolstoy in Queens, Mary Gordon has taken as many risks as her heroine. If the list of family members and their interrelationships that prefaces the novel is a form of homage to her Russian models, it also should forewarn readers that exposition will be in short supply. The narrative shuttles from consciousness to consciousness with names being dropped in an entirely familial way, requiring many flips back to the list of dramatis personae. More seriously, the large cast dissipates both the narrative flow and the dramatic tension of the novel. Too many of the clan are more caricatures than characters, each with a special grudge or a special tic, like daughter Theresa's deadly combination of punishing remarks and charismatic prayers or grandson John's general ineffectualness. The protracted accounts of their unhappiness become tedious after a while, and the reader longs for the sharper passions of Ellen and Vincent which give the novel the genuine power it has.

In spite of these disappointments, I for one look forward eagerly (not anxiously) to Mary Gordon's next novel which I trust will be as daring in its way as *The Other Side.*

John M. Neary (essay date Spring 1990)

SOURCE: "Mary Gordon's *Final Payments:* A Romance of the One True Language," in *Essays in Literature,* Vol. 17, No. 1, Spring, 1990, pp. 94-110.

[*In the following essay, Neary examines the problem of linguistic authority, religious truth, and metaphysical uncertainty in* Final Payments. *According to Neary, Gordon reacts to "the loss of certainty" and its attendant disillusionment through humor and shifted focus on the aesthetic qualities of language.*]

"I was looking for miracle, mystery, and authority," Mary Gordon says in a 1978 issue of *Harper's,* consciously echoing Dostoevsky's Grand Inquisitor; "I was interested in style, in spirituality." Gordon is describing a visit to the Long Island headquarters of the Society of St. Pius X, a group of radically conservative followers of French Archbishop Marcel Lefebvre. But she could well be discussing the evolution of her first novel, *Final Payments:* this stylish, spiritual depiction of the American Catholic experience was published just a few months prior to the appearance of the *Harper's* article.

In the article, Gordon explains that the existence of the Lefebvrists represents for her the possible persistence of the Church of her childhood, a world of certainties—a world in which words and other signs represent, absolutely, the reality signified. And the fact that the society is located on Long Island just intensifies the nostalgia; Gordon feels on the verge of being swallowed up by the past:

> I grew up on Long Island among radically conservative Catholics, and there is a particular aptness for me in the coincidence of a movement that embodies what I have left and lost being placed in the physical world of my childhood.
>
> . . . My friends are worried. They kiss me on the forehead before I leave, as if they are afraid they will not see me again, as if they are seeing me off on a voyage of indeterminate length and destination in a vessel whose seaworthiness they seriously doubt.

That the society turns out to lack the miracle, mystery, and authority sought by Gordon may not be terribly surprising to readers of the article (we trust a smart contemporary novelist, a member of a breed who subsist on ambiguities and uncertainties, not to be entrapped by a band of absolutists). Gordon herself, however, after professing that she felt "relief" when she escaped from the society, says that "there is loss, as well, or more properly disappointment." And *Final Payments* is in fact about very similar loss and disappointment. The protagonist's central crisis is a realization that the human world and its symbols (particularly its linguistic ones) can no longer mediate an absolute, transcendent vision, a real presence of God, of parent, of ordered world.

But the vision presented in *Final Payments* is not tragic; this is a comic novel, filled with and even preoccupied with jokes and humor. The despair and loss experienced by the protagonist, Isabel Moore, is only half the story, just as Gordon's disappointment with the Lefebvrists is only half the story she has recorded of her adult relationship with the Church and with the idea of faith. Gordon tells the rest of the story in an article on her own devotion to the Virgin Mary published in a 1982 issue of *Commonweal.* This article is a corrective to the Lefebvre article; if the Lefebvrists merely reminded Gordon that the symbol-structure of her childhood Church had lost its ontological foundation for her, images of Mary suggest to Gordon that, even without metaphysical certainties, human symbols and words do have a tentative and at least hypothetical efficacy. A devotion to the Mother of God turns Gordon away from her yearning for a past, transcendent perfection—a perfection that seems predicated on a hatred of physicality—and toward an openness to the incarnate world of imperfect present and future contingency. And this is strikingly similar to the resolution achieved by Isabel in **Final Payments.**

The *Harper's* and the *Commonweal* articles, therefore, present in an expository form the problem and resolution that constitute the narrative movement of **Final Payments:** Isabel Moore nostalgically tries to regain her solid religious past, in which language transparently mediated divine reality, but the faith she finally achieves is founded on a new use of language—not fiercely literal but metaphorical, imaginative, lightly comic. So before examining Isabel's transformation of the grammar of her youth, it would be well to look at Gordon's articulation of these issues in the magazine articles.

The complete title of Mary Gordon's article on Archbishop Lefebvre contains the words, "a *Romance* of the One True Church" (my italics). And there is much about the idea of a lingering remnant of the pre-Vatican II Church that sparks in Gordon a girlish sense of romantic dreaminess:

> . . . *l'incident Lefebvre* engages my imagination. It inspires in me an embarrassing richness of nostalgic fantasy: sung Gregorian Masses, priests in gold, the silence of Benediction, my own sense of sanctity as an eight-year-old carrying a lily among a hundred other eight-year-olds on Holy Thursday.

At the most personal level, therefore, the existence of Lefebvre's radically conservative movement suggests to this woman who grew up in a now-changed Church the possible persistence of childhood innocence. Her ideas about Lefebvre's societies are all lovely and exciting, like a fairy tale. And the Archbishop himself, in Gordon's imagination, is decked out in dashing fairy-tale splendor; he is an elegant old French gentleman, a monarchist, a man who would surely not have been at home among those original, seedy Apostles, but who would have been "a smash with one of the Medici popes" in a world of "chateaux silver, ancient and perfect servants, a chapel near the tennis courts."

But for all the fancifulness, the rigor about what Lefebvre represents to Mary Gordon indicates a classical precision beneath Gordon's romanticism: "I was interested . . . in a movement that combined the classical ideal of the Gregorian mass with the romantic image of the foreign life." This paradoxically romantic classicism is founded on Gordon's desire for linguistic exactness, a desire to possess and utilize a body of language that has a solid base—that does not, in the Derridean sense, "defer" meaning, but that presents it purely and immediately.

In the very first paragraph of the Lefebvre article, Gordon describes her childhood Church as

> that repository of language never to be used again, words white-flat and crafted: "monstrance," "chasuble"; words shaped to fit into each other like spoons, words that overlap and do not overlap, words that mark a way of life that has a word for every mode, a category for each situation: "gifts of the Holy Ghost," "corporal works of mercy," "capital sins," "cardinal virtues."

There is a grandeur about the words that Gordon chooses to remember (surely, like most young Catholics, she linked the word "monstrance" with "monstrous"), but it is an absolutely clear grandeur. These are words that have no ambiguity; they describe definite objects that exist in one definite place, the Church. Even such seemingly huge categories as the "gifts of the Holy Ghost" and the "corporal works of mercy" have been precisely spelled out and delimited by the Baltimore Catechism: there are seven (that lucky number) of each, no more and no less.

And Gordon's description of Lefebvre, not surprisingly, focuses on his rhetoric, his grand and solid use of words:

> His rhetoric is desperate, and it has the excitement of desperation. It has the excitement, too, of an archaism revivified: it is the language of conflict, but a conflict that seems ancient, and consequently grand. . . . "You cannot marry truth and error," he said in a sermon delivered in Lille in 1976, "because that is like adultery, and the child will be a bastard—a bastard rite for mass, bastard sacraments, and bastard priests."
>
> Bastard. *Bâtard.* How exciting, from the mouth of an archbishop. The world is serious; the truth is obvious; the lines are clear.

Gordon is excited by the solidity the word "bastard" takes on in Lefebvre's mouth. It is not just a tag, a combination of sounds that has been arbitrarily granted meaning. It has substance, essence.

This is Gordon's notion of the language of pre-Vatican II Catholicism, which Lefebvre's societies are desperately attempting to keep alive in a hostile modern world. It is a language-system that leaves no gaps; it makes signified objects and concepts perfectly present, just as God is said to be simply and unambiguously present in the Eucharist. In her nostalgia for this lost linguistic perfection—best preserved, of course, in Latin, a language that has not been knocked around the common workaday world for several centuries—Gordon is exemplifying what Derrida calls "an ethic of nostalgia for origins, an ethic of archaic and natural innocence, of purity of presence and self-presence in speech."

Gordon does not find this "purity"; her romanticism is punctured. After beginning her article with a fanciful lyricism, Gordon ends up presenting a coolly ironic portrait of an actual Lefebvrist priest whom she interviewed. And although his notions of theology and sexuality are surprisingly enlightened, the priest is as repellently intolerant as the Grand Inquisitor himself; he thinks, for example, that the medieval way of dealing with Protestants was "perfectly acceptable": "They were more or less removed from the scene . . . [b]y being executed." Gordon's most deflatingly satirical touch, though, is a comically understated criticism not of the priest's cruelty but of his taste:

> He tells me they [the society] bought out the company that made St. Joseph Missals. I had one: I remember the glossy photographs beside appropriate feast days, the work of an artist who probably spent his secular life drawing for Ivory Snow. Before I know what I am

saying I exclaim, "But St. Joseph Missals were the tackiest of any of them." "Tacky?" he says, looking puzzled. I am again disappointed; I cannot take seriously the spiritual life of anyone for whom "the tacky" is not a lively concept.

This article is primarily a record of disillusionment. But it does reveal two important characteristics of Gordon's eventual strategy for dealing with the loss of certainty: beauty and humor. Though words and symbols no longer possess an absolute metaphysical base, Gordon finds that they can still be used with aesthetic care and tastefulness. (Indeed, the fact that the Society of St. Pius X displays not the elegance of the Middle Ages but the tackiness of the 1950s is one of her most severe disappointments.) And humor, people's ability to share a joke, gives language and erotic energy, a power to connect: comedy effects at least a hypothetical and analogous approach to the now-vanished presence. The Lefebvrist priest may be tasteless and bigoted, but Gordon maintains her own humanity and good spirits by writing about him gracefully and comically.

In her *Commonweal* article on the Virgin Mary, Gordon more explicitly sets forth her faith in the values of humor and of beauty, especially of *physical* beauty. The article begins, in fact, with a Catholic-school joke about the ridiculous lengths the Church used to go to in order to suppress bodily beauty:

> Queens in the nineteen sixties had almost as many Catholic high schools as bakeries. Towards the spring of the year, the approach of Senior Prom meant big business for local merchants. There was one store—which girls in my school were urged to patronize—that had a special section devoted to what were called "Mary-like gowns." The Mary-like gown was an invention of nuns and a coalition of sodalists, and its intent, I think, was to make prom dresses as much like habits as possible. We used to go and try the dresses on for a laugh. They were unbelievably ugly. The yardage of material could have dressed even an Irish family for a year.

This is a joke with deep significance, a joke that casts a shadow even on the grandest ages of that linguistically perfect Church. If the tackiness of the 1950s and the relativism of the 1960s had never occurred, Gordon might still have had serious problems with the Church: its focus on spiritual essences (attractive though that focus seems to Gordon in the Lefebvre article) has historically resulted in a denigration of the physical world. Particularly unsettling to Gordon is the fact that women have come under special attack: the desire of "nuns and a coalition of sodalists" to cloak girls' bodies under yards of ugly material is only a ludicrous modern version of the Church's long-time hatred of women and of all physical bodies.

The first section of this article, in fact, is not an attack on the styleless contemporary Church at all; this time it is the most revered thinkers of the Catholic tradition, the "Fathers of the Church," that Gordon criticizes. Their thinking, she maintains, was "poisoned by misogyny, and a hatred of the body, particularly female sexuality." She proceeds to quote hate-filled statements from Tertullian, Augustine, and Jerome, among others, pronouncements that must have seemed to them as serious, obvious, and clear as Archbishop Lefebvre's use of the word "bastard"; this time, however, Gordon is not charmed or excited. She ends her attack by quoting a statement made by St. John Chrysostom, a man whose nickname ("Chrysostom" means "golden-tongued") marks him as one of the supreme guardians of that ontologically solid linguistic system. Here is how Chrysostom describes female nature:

> The whole of her bodily beauty is nothing less than phlegm, blood, bile, rheum, and the fluid of digested food. . . . If you consider what is stored up behind those lovely eyes, the angle of the nose, the mouth and cheeks you will agree that the well-proportioned body is merely a whitened sepulcher.

The great tradition of the Church may have possessed a sublime and stylish vision of transcendent perfection, but it was not very good on the subjects of physicality and of women. Her realization about the position of women throughout history (and Gordon opines that Christianity has treated women a little better, at least, than many other groups) frees Gordon from what she calls "historical romanticism," in which she had indulged in the Lefebvre piece. Though the precision and the seeming solidity of the early Church remain enticing, the fact that she has a body—along with the fact that she is a woman—releases Gordon from her nostalgia for the past and pushes her in a new direction. And it is the image of Mary, the Mother of God, that forms the metaphorical bridge for Gordon, allowing her to take the best of the past Church (its spirituality, its clarity, and its aesthetic style) and project it into a limited, contingent world. One must, Gordon says, "sift through the nonsense and hostility that has characterized thought and writing about Mary, to find some images, shards, and fragments, glittering in the rubble." As Gordon shows us these images, shards, and fragments, a coherent portrait of Mary begins to emerge, colored by a mixture of earthiness and aestheticism.

Gordon sees Mary's purity, her virginity, as indicating not a distaste for the temporal—and physical—human world, but rather an openness to it, expressed by the very curves and rhythms of her body: "I think of the curve of the body of a thirteenth century statue of the young Mother with her child. At ease in its own nature, swinging almost with the rhythms of maternal love, ready for life; radically open to experience, to love." Mary's innocence, Gordon continues, is "an innocence that is rooted in the love of the physical world." Even as the Queen of Heaven, Mary is not divorced from the temporal world, lost in some infinitely transcendent perfection; she is "enthroned, not above her children, but in the midst of them."

It is important to note that Gordon achieves this vision of Mary not by ignoring the Church's traditional symbol-system, but rather by entering that system carefully and selectively. She draws her striking, and rather erotic, image of Mary's rhythmically curved figure from a thirteenth-century statue of the Madonna, and in other sections of the essay she meditates on some of the Church's other great artworks: Annunciations by Leonardo and by Fra Angelica, a Winchester Cathedral sculpture, Pergolesi's *Stabat Mater,* Bellini's Pieta.

So even though the system of precise and definite symbols represented by Gordon's childhood Church has lost its vitality (being maintained, now, by a small band of Long Islanders who have no concept of "the tacky"), Gordon still finds value in clarity and precision—but these have become for her ethical and aesthetic rather than metaphysical qualities:

> I think, finally, it is through poetry, through painting, sculpture, music, through those human works that are magnificently innocent of the terrible strain of sexual hatred by virtue of the labor, craft, and genius of their great creators, that one finds the surest way back to the Mother of God.

Gordon's aesthetic basis for judging human sign-making no longer permits her to assert that words and images perfectly mediate a transcendent realm. Her own words about Mary cannot be final, a closed system like that presented by the Baltimore Catechism; they can only record a series of relations rooted within the contingent, temporal world:

> I offer here, no system, but a set of meditations. I offer no final words, since, for a woman to come to terms with this woman who endures beloved despite a history of hatred, she must move lightly and discard freely. . . . She must put out for those around her scattered treasure, isolates without a pattern whose accumulated meaning comes from the relations of proximity.

This is a highly qualified statement about our ability to know. Its relativism sounds very nearly postmodernist; Gordon seems to imply that one cannot write about things, but only about differences—gaps—between things. Nonetheless, Gordon's field of interest is clearly substantive rather than negative. Though she is unable to speak definitively, to mediate absolute presence, she can still meditate at least hypothetically on a woman who is no less than the mother of God.

So the Lefebvre and the Mary articles together reveal Gordon's replacement of a metaphysically solid, perfectly defined system of words and other signs with a fragile, temporally limited, "scattered treasure"—which is nonetheless clear, beautiful, and often funny (one of Gordon's favorite statues of the young Mary has the girl looking amused; "Her mouth, a thin identured curve, turns up with pleasure"). That previous perfect union with the ground of being has been exchange for a sort of aesthetic eroticism, a beautiful and humorous expression of radical openness to the world. And this movement from metaphysics to aesthetics, which Gordon describes in these articles, is much like the narrative movement of *Final Payments,* the story of a young woman who loses her religious certainty and then, after a period of despair, gains a real—though tentative and uncertain—religious and human faith.

The first chapter of *Final Payments* ends with Isabel Moore, the protagonist and narrator, thinking to herself, "This is no longer my father's house." The novel has opened with the funeral of Joseph Moore, Isabel's radically conservative Catholic father, whom Isabel—alone, without a single day's respite—has nursed for the past eleven years. And as if this were not enough to have made him the most significant figure in Isabel's life, Joseph Moore has been no ordinary father: with his fierce Catholic absolutism he has reigned over Isabel with the power of an autocratic medieval pope, banishing her only boyfriend and expecting her complete submission, body and soul, to his needs and dogmas. From the novel's first pages, Isabel vividly conveys the way Joseph Moore has, for her, been not just a father but an image of the Father, both dreadful and loving. Wilfrid Sheed claims, in fact, that despite his physical absence (like God's), Joseph Moore hovers over the novel as its most impressive and even attractive character:

> . . . astonishingly he emerges as the most impressive and attractive character in the book—especially astonishing since he is never on stage but has to dominate from the clouds, and from memory. Gordon has conveyed his mere emanations, his perfectionism, his intelligence, his sheer size of spirit so well that the reader too half-sees that after him the outside world would seem trashy and pointless. The religious vocation has been made incarnate.

So when Isabel says that the house is no longer her father's, she is not simply recording the fact that Joseph Moore has died and that the building in which she grew up, with all its books and knickknacks and furnishings, no longer belongs to him. Rather, the statement "This is no longer my father's house," with its unmistakably Biblical sound (it is as if the Holy of Holies had lost its holiness), points toward the novel's large philosophical and religious themes. Isabel has to live in a world in which "the Father" is no longer immediately present; the death of a parent has effected an absolutely metaphysical rupture in Isabel's life.

Derrida has described the "rupture" that effected the "destruction of the history of metaphysics," the advent of postmodernism:

> The event I called a rupture . . . presumably would have come about when the structurality of structure had begun to be thought. . . . Henceforth, it was necessary to begin thinking that there was no center, that the center could not be thought of in the form of a present-being, that the center had no natural site, that it was not a fixed locus but a function, a sort of nonlocus in which an infinite number of sign-substitutions came into play. This was the moment when language invaded the universal problematic, the moment when, in the absence of a center or origin, everything became discourse.

Isabel, with her nearly obsessive concern about centers ("center" is one of her favorite words), connects herself with these Derridean issues. Her father's bed, she tells us early in the novel, occupied the exact center of his bedroom; without that center, she feels painfully abandoned: "I thought of my father and his sureness, his body in the bed at the center of the room, and I wanted to cry out, 'I am terribly alone.'" Later she indicates that the loss of her father, her center, has even resulted in a loss of a permanent and unshifting self: "I was not [any longer] the person who lived with my father's body in the center of my life, in my father's house, with his bed at the center of it." Her unswervingly Catholic father was Isabel's "fixed locus," her guarantee that particular words and things had ontological substance and significance, that they could not be replaced by Derrida's "infinite number of sign-substitutions." We will see that Isabel's ultimate resolution of this problem of uncenteredness, like Gordon's in the Mary article, is a movement toward a tentative ethicality and faith rather than toward Derrida's "Nietzschean *affirmation . . .* of a world of signs without fault, without truth, and without origin"; although it addresses postmodernist issues, this is certainly not a deconstructive text in the manner of John Barth or Thomas Pynchon. Nonetheless, Isabel's problem—the loss of father, of center—looks distinctly like a "destruction of the history of metaphysics." So before leaping to Isabel's (and Gordon's) special resolution to the problem, we must look more closely at the problem itself and precisely identify the way in which Isabel has lost a "center." We should first examine, therefore, the character of Joseph Moore.

Joseph Moore, as Isabel describes him, takes on an exotic romanticism similar to that of Gordon's Archbishop Lefebvre. Like Lefebvre, Moore was a grand, and fiercely intolerant, aristocrat ("In history, his sympathies were with the Royalists in the French Revolution, the South in the Civil War, the Russian czar, the Spanish Fascists") whose mind had "the endurance of a great Renaissance sculpture." He was the "neighborhood intellectual," a professor of medieval literature at a small Catholic college on Long Island; even his McCarthyism and racism, therefore, were subordinate to a devotion to Old-World, aesthetic ideals. It is as if, like Wordsworth's quintessentially romantic Child, Joseph Moore trailed "clouds of glory":

> They should have had for his funeral a Mass of the Angels, by which children are buried in the Church. His mind had the brutality of a child's or an angel's: the finger of the angel points in the direction of hell, sure of the justice of the destination of the soul he transports.

Obviously, in spite of the references to angels and children and to medieval aestheticism, Moore—again, like Lefebvre—stood for a classical rigor rather than a romantic, lyrical softness; "softmindedness" was something he had no tolerance for. His childlikeness was brutal.

But he was most brutally childlike in his faith, which was absolute and unequivocal:

> For my father, the refusal of anyone in the twentieth century to become part of the Catholic Church was not pitiable; it was malicious and willful. Culpable ignorance, he called it. He loved the sense of his own orthodoxy, of holding out for the purest and the finest

and the most refined sense of truth against the slick hucksters who promised happiness on earth and the supremacy of human reason.

Predictably, Moore was not terribly interested in the frills of Catholicism—the rosary beads, the plastic Marys, the novena books held together with rubber bands. The tough core of the Church for him was the Mass, in Latin, with the responses recited by the congregation:

> He wrote scornful letters to *The Tablet* about pastors who encouraged the faithful to say the Rosary during Mass. The Mass, he said, was the Single Most Important Act in History. The Consecration, the Transubstantiation, was the central drama of Salvation.

Gordon's use of capital letters at this point is telling. These words, describing the events through which the Church mediates God's "real presence," have a powerful ontological weight for believing Catholics. According to orthodox Catholic theology, the recitation of five Latin words—"*Hoc est enim corpus meum*"—transforms the substance (the essential thingness) of bread and wine into the substance of the body and blood of Christ. It is hard to imagine language ever having a more substantive power to signify. And this, for Isabel, is the key to what her father and the Church of her childhood represent. When Isabel, after her father's death, expresses to her friend Liz a fear that her father was absurd, full of "sound and fury, signifying nothing," Liz's answer sums up Joseph Moore: "Oh no. Jesus Christ, he signified. He signified all over the place."

Isabel's eleven-year devotion to her disabled father has allowed her to live in this absolutely certain world in which words and symbols mediate a transcendent presence. She has given up her independence, her adulthood, her sexuality, but the spiritual returns have been enormous:

> Does it suggest both the monstrosity and the confusion of the issue if I say that the day Dr. MacCauley told me about my father's stroke was of my whole life the day I felt most purely alive? Certainty was mine, and purity; I was encased in meaning like crystal.

She calls the event a "monstrosity"—a weighty word (remember "monstrance"). It has offered her certainty and purity; it has encased her in meaning, "like crystal." Meaning—significance—has not been a fragile and arbitrary thing; it has possessed a diamond-hard solidity.

But it is a thing of the past. As the novel begins, Joseph Moore is being buried. The world of bodily contingency has fractured Isabel's crystalline certainty, has deprived her of her father's presence. Her first feeling after the funeral, when she finds herself alone in the house which is no longer her father's, is that the universe has opened up, that its center has lost its substantiality and become "airy":
. . . "life was space, the borders seemed so far away from the vast airy center that there was no help and I remembered my childhood dream of falling out of bed, through the floor, and simply falling." The physical world, which her father had always disdained, now seems to her the

only thing that is real. And its reality is merely the reality of change, of instability, of decay. This discovery horrifies her; when she sees broccoli "liquefying" in her refrigerator, she wants to "run away and set a match to the whole house."

Isabel does not set fire to the house, but what she does seems almost as bad to her father's staunchly conservative friends. She sells the house and moves upstate to Ringkill to direct a social-welfare project. (In this novel about substantial centers around which perfect circles—or rings—can spin, Isabel's move to a place called "Ringkill" has particular significance.) Almost immediately she has an affair with her friend's husband, the glamorous but oafishly insensitive politician John Ryan—it would be hard to imagine a man more different from her father. And she falls in love with another married man, Hugh Slade, a rational humanist who coolly describes her Catholic upbringing as "barbarous." And although Isabel maintains her sense of humor and her extraordinary care about clarity and precision, she is slowly and inexorably made aware that her life has no center, that her certainty has crumbled. Having once been enveloped by her father's faith that the world is a sort of Dantesque *commedia* with a metaphysical and everlasting significance, that human beings clearly and certainly were created to know, love, and serve God in this life and to share in God's happiness for all eternity, she must now confront the possibility that everything, including herself, is a signifier lacking a signified: "What," she wonders, "if you represented nothing but were only yourself?" If people and things represent "nothing" beyond themselves, then it seems to Isabel that there can be no larger order beneath the chaotic surface of everyday life; randomness is all.

As a social worker Isabel becomes even more aware of the randomness of human life; "there was no way," she asserts, "of predicting what would make people happy, no way of controlling it." In her own personal life, too, she is becoming dependent for happiness on Hugh Slade, a man who is not tied to her by blood or religion, but who in fact is tied to other people by marital and familial obligations. She is desperately troubled by the realization that she has become a slave to contingency, that her love for a particular person—a person who may die or leave her— throws her into a world in which everything is as unstable as the broccoli that liquefied in her refrigerator. When she is confronted by Hugh Slade's wife, who shrewdly argues that Isabel will have to give up Hugh to prove she is "a good person," she cracks; she makes a final, frantic attempt to reconstitute the world of absolute certainty by replacing love with "charity," by devoting herself not to people whom she cares about particularly and emotionally, but to someone whom she does not even like. She decides to move in with Margaret Casey.

Isabel was taught in school that love and charity—*eros* and *agape*—are very different things. And at that time she distinctly preferred *eros*:

> Love and charity. One was that feeling below the breast, and the other was doing something, anything, to take

people's pain away. I remembered the lettering on a bulletin board at Anastasia Hall: LOVE IS MEA- SURED BY SACRIFICE. And I remembered thinking how wrong that was, because the minute I gave up something for someone I liked them less.

> "Ah," Sister Fidelis had said when I asked her, "you don't have to like someone to love them in God."

> But who wants to be loved in God? . . . We want to be loved for our singularity, not for what we share with the rest of the human race. We would rather be loved for the color of our hair or the shape of our ankle than because God loves us.

Now, however, Isabel feels that she was caught in a terrible error. To prefer love—based on accidental singularities (hair color, ankle shape, feelings shared memories, jokes)—is to throw oneself into the randomness of the physical world, a world that can never have the sureness of Isabel's father and his solid pre-Vatican II Catholic religious system. Charity, according to Isabel and Sister Fidelis, cuts through the surface of accidents, making immediately present the metaphysical idea that all human beings possess an immortal soul designed in God's image. This notion of charity, in fact, is analogous to the dogma of Transubstantiation, which states that the accidents of the Eucharist (the physical appearances of bread and wine) are unimportant, that after the words of consecration are spoken, only the substance (Christ's body and blood) matters. So Isabel's decision to live a life of charity reflects an attempt to return to dogmatic Catholicism, with an absolute symbol-system that purports to mediate pure presence— purports to "mean," to "stand for." "If we can love the people we think are most unlovable," she says, "if we can get out of this ring of accident, of attraction, then it's a pure act, love; then we mean something, we stand for something."

Within this "ring of accident," Margaret Casey is, for Isabel, as unlovable as a person could be. The housekeeper who once wanted to marry Joseph Moore, Margaret is the one human being whom Isabel has always unequivocally loathed; the mere sound of her "slopping around the house in her slippers," Isabel says, "is the sound of my nightmares." Taking care of Margaret, therefore, seems to Isabel to be the purest of pure acts, an act that is utterly unconnected with the world of human particularity. Isabel will continue to feel disgust for this woman, and she surely will not be thanked; Margaret, incapable of gratitude, behaves as if Isabel's presence were in fact an imposition on her. But this now seems to Isabel much the better. Individual feelings, cravings for thanks, all partake of the random, accidental world; Isabel wants to experience perfect Catholic charity, unblemished by worldly *eros*:

> There would be no more talk or thought of love that could be gained or lost by accidents, by jokes or the angle of a shoulder. I would love Margaret now as God loved His creatures: impartially, impervious to their individual natures and thus incapable of being really hurt by them.

Faced with the reality of a world in which the certain meanings of her childhood have fled, in which things represent no larger reality but are only themselves, Isabel has built a fortress against things and their randomness. Using appropriately Catholic language, she calls it a "sanctuary." She has returned, she thinks, to her father's house.

But it is a house without a foundation, a sanctuary without God. Joseph Moore was able genuinely to represent for Isabel the certainty of the Catholic symbol-system; even after the grown-up Isabel began to lose her faith in the Church itself, her father continued to exist as a center, a "real presence." This new attempt to attain certainty, however, consists of forms without substance, of Catholic behavior without Catholic conviction. Isabel starts again to employ the language of the Church, but she no longer believes that it has meaning. She begins to pray the rosary with Margaret, suffering like a martyr ("The bones in my knees began to grow into the floor like roots; my back was stiff and painful with kneeling"), but the formerly efficacious words are now void of significance:

> . . . I could no longer imagine a face who would be interested in me above all others, who cared for the nature and the quality of my prayer. I said these prayers because it pleased Margaret. But they brought me no comfort; there was no face, wise, amused, and dangerously open, listening to the words I sent out like cigar-shaped missiles to the neutral, heated air.

The language of traditional Catholicism is supposed to mediate God's presence. But like Mary Gordon visiting the Lefebvrists, Isabel has returned to her Catholic past and found only an absence.

Furthermore, Isabel's new experience of charitable martyrdom lacks the crisp rigor which her charity possessed when she nursed her father; in that earlier time, she felt her "visible martyrdom" as "sheer relief: a grapefruit ice that cleanses the palate between courses of a heavy meal." But everything with Margaret seems hot and cloying rather than cool and invigorating. Isabel this time does not cleanse her palate; instead she grows fat eating sickeningly sweet foods that make her palate "heavy and dull." The purity of her love for her father encased Isabel, as we saw, "in meaning like crystal." Now, however, she sees herself "cased in the pink, sweating flesh of a pig; I could imagine my eyes grown small and light like a pig's. I wanted to sleep."

By charitably adopting Margaret, Isabel was trying to recapture the one true Language, the perfect sign-system in which words and symbols provide a perfectly crystallized meaning. But something has gone wrong. With Margaret, in fact, words—not just prayers and religious language, but all words—simply cease to matter, to be different from one another. Margaret's statements to Isabel are deadeningly trite ("Good afternoon. Get your beauty sleep?"). And even Isabel's rigorous need to differentiate between good literature and bad is quenched: when Margaret prefers tacky grocery-store romances, by authors like "Regina Carey," to *Jane Eyre,* Isabel represses her disgust. "It was caring about things so strongly," she says,

"whether Charlotte Brontë was better than Regina Carey, that had caused my trouble."

Isabel is overlooking the fact that a careful use of language, the sort of thing that distinguishes a Charlotte Brontë from a Regina Carey, was highly valued by the very sources of her present notion of charity: her father and the Catholic Church. Isabel has said that her father, unlike Margaret, "loved books, and jokes, and arguments, . . . loved my stories about impossible places when really I had just gone to the grocer's." And the Church's "white-flat and crafted" words ("monstrance," "chasuble," "gifts of the Holy Ghost," "cardinal virtues"), memorialized by Gordon in the Lefebvre article, are founded on the belief that distinctions can be made, that one thing is not another.

So Isabel's "charitable" flight to Margaret is not a return to past certainty at all; it is a lapse into a despairing state in which all words and things—whether certain or hypothetical—have been dissolved. It no longer makes any difference to Isabel what she says, what she does, what she looks like. Her body becomes heavier and heavier, and she is dragged by Margaret to a beauty salon where she receives a hideously archaic haircut (a "bubble cut"), yet her only response is, "What did it matter?"

But the novel ends optimistically. After her experiment with perfect charity toward Margaret has driven her to a nervous breakdown, Isabel returns to a tentative health. And her resolution of her problem is founded not on an acceptance of the Derridean *mise en abyme* but on a new understanding of the Catholic symbol-system itself; Isabel appropriates a sort of humorous, erotic Catholic aestheticism, similar to that articulated by her creator in the article on the Virgin Mary. Mary Gordon, as we saw, was able to reestablish a personal veneration for Mary, assembled from images and fragments gleaned from a largely misogynous storehouse. Gordon offered, in her article, "no system, but a set of meditations"—meditations filled with an earthy aestheticism and enlivened with humor. Likewise Isabel discovers that Catholic images and words, though for her no longer absolute, can have a hypothetical and perhaps metaphorical efficacy: the Greek root of the word "metaphor" (*metapherein*) means "to carry over," and Catholic images, words, and stories serve Isabel as a bridge between a classically rigorous system in which words *mean* and a decentered, fleshly world in which words and objects have no stable significance or substance. This bridge allows Isabel to carry over her care for clarity and beauty into the physical, temporal world.

And the bridge's keystone is the crucial Christian notion of the Incarnation. The final chapter of the novel presents a series of epiphanies; events occurring during Holy Week—a time when the Church celebrates the belief that Christ had a body, which died and rose—awaken in Isabel a realization of the value and beauty of the bodily world, and of words that talk about it carefully, elegantly, and humorously.

Holy Week begins with a visit from Father Mulcahy, the kindly old priest who has always loved Isabel. He is not a "perfect" Catholic like Joseph Moore (he is an alcoholic), and he is not capable of listening to the "absolute truth" (he has refused to hear Isabel's confession, afraid to learn about her recent un-Catholic activities). But he is a man with whom Isabel can laugh, sing, be human:

> His fine, cared-for fingers played chords. He began singing in his high, boy's voice, "I'll Take You Home Again, Kathleen."
>
> I joined in. I could sing the harmony; I had sung it with my father. And I had sung it with Hugh. I could never tell Father Mulcahy the truth about Hugh. But that was all right. I could not tell the truth, but we could sing at the piano.

The world of particular affections, of *eros,* is for Isabel given some symbolic—though not absolute—significance and value by virtue of the fact that a priest cares about the sensuous harmony of music. And the world of sexual pleasure is ritualistically joined with that of absolute religious rigor: Isabel has sung this harmony with both Hugh Slade and her father.

Father Mulcahy, furthermore, tells Isabel that even the Bible, the Word of God, can be interpreted as being concerned not just with transcendent substance (that absolute, suprapersonal perfection which Isabel has tried to make present for herself through her martyred practice of "charity") but with temporal, physical accidents (those things that are components of *eros*). The priest tells her to watch her weight, to take care of her body:

> "Thou shalt not kill? What does that have to do with it?"
>
> "It means slow deaths, too," he said.

Isabel's most striking Holy Week epiphany is about to be inspired by other words from the Bible—but these words will have an evocative, personal, associative significance for Isabel rather than an absolutely substantive meaning. When Margaret, after Father Mulcahy leaves, begins to behave particularly obnoxiously, whining that she is "a poor woman," Isabel explodes. Her feelings for this woman, which she has been repressing, come pouring out. And her emotions of anger and loathing borrow their particular form from a statement originally made by Jesus himself: " 'The poor you have always with you,' I shouted, slamming the kitchen door."

In the same epiphanic moment, Isabel discovers not only these words themselves, but the *meaning* of the words. And she discovers, in a broader way, that words carry their meanings not simply and unequivocally (the way, for example, policemen carry guns), but gently, contextually—within narratives, chains of shifting relations. Isabel's strikingly insightful, though also strikingly personal, interpretation of Jesus's cryptic words is based on her seeing the words relationally, both in relation to the other characters within a Biblical story (Martha and Mary, Judas) and in relation to her own current, particular situation. Her insight, therefore, should be looked at in its full context, so I must quote at length:

> It is one of the marvels of a Catholic education that the impulse of a few words can bring whole narratives to light with an immediacy and a clarity that are utterly absorbing. "The poor you have always with you." I knew where Christ had said that: at the house of Martha and Mary. Mary had opened a jar of ointment over Christ's feet. Spikenard, I remembered. And she wiped his feet with her hair. Judas had rebuked her; he had said that the ointment ought to be sold for the poor. But, St. John had noted, Judas had said that only because he kept the purse and was a thief. And Christ had said to Judas, Mary at his feet, her hair spread around him, "The poor you have always with you: but me you have not always."
>
> And until that moment, climbing the dark stairs in a rage to my ugly room, it was a passage I had not understood. It seemed to justify to me the excesses of centuries of fat, tyrannical bankers. But now I understood. What Christ was saying, what he meant, was that the pleasures of that hair, that ointment, must be taken. Because the accidents of death would deprive us soon enough. We must not deprive ourselves, our loved ones, of the luxury of our extravagant affections. . . .
>
> I knew now I must open the jar of ointment. I must open my life. I knew now that I must leave.

Religious language has regained a significance for Isabel, but it is a contextual, personal significance, involved with the changing world of human accident.

By the time Good Friday arrives, Isabel is ready to attend a service that will have meaning for her. But it will not be the sort of meaning that was mediated by the one true Language of her childhood Church, which purported to make present a transcendent substance or center, a permanent truth that is divorced from the human condition. The words and symbols of the Church now act as more limited—but also more rich and evocative—signifiers, simultaneously general and personal, tinged with tragedy and humanity:

> The church was dark with the number of the congregation. And the statues, covered in their purple cloth, stole what light there would have been available. . . . I thought of Christ, of the death of Christ. We were here to acknowledge the presence of death among us. We were here to acknowledge our own inevitable deaths.
>
> My father was dead; there was the pain. I had loved him, but my love had not been able to help him. . . . I would die; everyone in this church would die. Everyone I knew and loved would die. . . .
>
> That was what we were kneeling to acknowledge, all of us, on this dark afternoon. We were here to say that we knew about death, we knew about loss, that it would not surprise us. But of course it would surprise us; it had surprised even Christ in the garden.

A priest begins the service, reading "in the voice of God": "My people, what have I done to you? Or in what have I offended you, answer Me?" Isabel's reaction to the words of the service reflects a new compromise between the unquestioning dogmatism of her father and her own recent despairing attitude about the value of language. The issue of absolute truth or falsity no longer seems so pressing to her; the words of this service have an efficacy that is immanent and communal rather than transcendent:

. . . I had wanted to hear those words spoken, the harsh Old Testament words and then the words of John. I wanted to hear the story said aloud, and I wanted to hear about His rest in the dark tomb. I wanted to hear it in the presence of my kind.

For there was death; you had to know that, and betrayal, and the negligence of friends at crucial moments, and their sleep. I wanted that acknowledged in the presence of my kind also.

This realization of the certainty of death, of the ineluctable power of the world of decaying flesh, instills in Isabel a paradoxical appreciation of the value of bodies; if the death of bodies is important, even to God, then bodies themselves—"accidental" though they may be—are important:

I walked home with Margaret, feeling my body moving on its clever legs. Christ had suffered in the body, and I too had a body. I knew it false but capable of astonishing pleasures.

So the novel ends not with the nostalgic disappointment articulated by Gordon in the Lefebvre article, but rather with the sort of tentatively faithful meditativeness represented by Gordon's article on the Virgin Mary. When we demand that words refer to an absolute truth, the novel seems to say, they inevitably disappoint; language works, but even when it is used with aesthetic elegance and precise care it is capable only of expressing relative truths, of telling stories. At their best, though, these stories have an erotic energy, an ability to connect people (it is important to Isabel that she hear the Biblical words "in the presence of [her] kind"), by bringing the hearers more deeply and compassionately into the painful world of human accident.

Or by making them laugh. Although Isabel's story is painful, *Final Payments,* as I said earlier, is a comic novel. As Wilfrid Sheed has noted, the conditions Gordon has set for herself in this novel are "that the story must be sad, the telling funny."

Sheed, however, claims that the sadness is primary, and that the comedy is sardonic and wry—"the best way to talk about" the fact that God "has died in this century." But although he has appreciated Gordon's humor, Sheed has failed to note that this humor gives the novel a generous, affirmative tone. Gordon's comedy is about faith rather than despair; for Gordon, I think, one of the best proofs that words can signify, can go beyond mere self-referentiality, is that they unite people through laughter.

Indeed, after the long and moving church-service sequence, Gordon concludes *Final Payments* with a scene in which her characters' friendships are revivified by a joke. Isabel, in the final page of the novel, is escaping from Margaret; her long-time friends Eleanor and Liz have come to drive her away. It is the first time they have seen how she has allowed her physical appearance to deteriorate:

Liz looked at me, her eyes flicking up and down in quick judgment. "Who did your hair? Annette Funicello?"

This joke seems as filled with "miracle, mystery, and authority" as any Good Friday service; it is not about the death of God at all:

The three of us laughed. It was a miracle to me, the solidity of that joke. Even the cutting edge of it was a miracle. And our laughter was solid. It stirred the air and hung above us like rings of bone that shivered in the cold, gradual morning.

The death of her father had ruptured for Isabel the world's ontological solidity, effecting a Derridean "destruction of the history of metaphysics"; it had decentered the ring of her life, sending her to "Ringkill." And now a mere joke has created a new solidity, stirring the air like new rings— and these are as sturdy as bone. Language may no longer have the "white-flat and crafted," categorical certainty of pre-Vatican II Catholicism, but it still performs miracles.

The novel, in fact, implicitly affirms the value of language even in its gloomiest sequences: there are few novelistic characters for whom exactness of word choice and attention to the sheer beauty of language are more important than they are for Isabel Moore. Throughout the book, Isabel has used words like "clarity," "purity," "certainty," and especially "center" with such frequency and care that they begin to seem as solid as the word "bastard" sounded in Archbishop Lefebvre's mouth. Although it is her lover Hugh Slade who, according to Isabel, is able to take words like "devoted" and "duty" and "polish them like stones," it is really Isabel herself who is the novel's primary word-polisher. It is through her aesthetic, erotic, humorous care with language that a bridge has been created between the beautiful but rigid (and lost) world of Joseph Moore and the world of temporal humanity: "That, at least, I owed to my father—making the effort to find the proper words for things."

The absolute ontological foundations of words have for Isabel become relativized; language has become for her a collection of metaphors (a "scattered treasure," as Gordon calls it in the Mary article) rather than a closed system mediating "real presence." But Isabel shows that language nonetheless can effect at least partial and hypothetical communication between people—and maybe even between human beings and God—if the words are polished like stones, if they tell stories, and if they are employed with humor.

And by presenting Isabel's ultimate faith that human beings in the modern world can still articulate a religious vision if they employ a narrative rather than a doctrinal discourse, *Final Payments* seems to be making a larger statement about the efficacy of storytelling for pursuing religious questions; this is a religious novel about the religious value of novels. Gordon demonstrates here that narrative can consider religious issues imaginatively, metaphorically, even playfully, without freezing them into dogma. This means that, for Gordon, religious truths cannot be stated definitively; there is no One True (and Literal) Language. But there are plenty of metaphors to weave, tales to spin, jokes to tell. The last words of *Final Payments* are, appropriately, "There was a great deal I wanted to say."

Wendy Martin (review date 28 April 1991)

SOURCE: "Passions and Provocations," in *New York Times Book Review,* April 28, 1991, p. 9.

[*In the following review, Martin offers favorable assessment of* Good Boys and Dead Girls.]

Novelists who write essays on politics, education, religion, art and literature participate in a venerable tradition. In the 19th century, George Eliot, William Thackeray, Nathaniel Hawthorne, Henry James, Mark Twain and others demonstrated their prowess as critics; in the 20th, Virginia Woolf, Mary McCarthy, John Updike, Joyce Carol Oates, V. S. Naipaul, Salman Rushdie, Margaret Drabble and Margaret Atwood, among others, have also made it clear that creative and critical skills can enrich each other.

With the publication of *Good Boys and Dead Girls: And Other Essays,* Mary Gordon shows us once again that there need not be a schism between the esthetic and the analytical. The author of four novels (*Final Payments, The Company of Women, Men and Angels, The Other Side*) and a collection of short stories (*Temporary Shelter*), Ms. Gordon is at her best in these essays, as well as in her fiction, when writing about the impact of Irish Catholicism on art and life. No longer conventionally religious herself, Ms. Gordon admires those writers who take a moral position: she praises Edna O'Brien's "pervasive ironic morality," Flannery O'Connor's "conscious" Catholicism and Mary McCarthy's willingness to draw a "firm line."

In contrast to her fierce appreciation of the life-affirming work of the painters Georgia O'Keeffe, Mary Cassat and Berthe Morisot, Ms. Gordon is outraged by Andy Warhol, whom she decries as nihilistic as well as untalented. Convinced that Warhol lived in a moral vacuum, Ms. Gordon is depressed by his love of mass culture and the popular image. While Ms. Gordon's high-church assessment of Warhol's work is questionable in the larger context of art history, her passionate response is provocative and bracing.

Although Ms. Gordon sometimes takes the high ground in these wide-ranging essays (many of which originally appeared in such publications as *The Atlantic, Antaeus* and *The New York Times Book Review*), she often tempers her judgments with humor as she offers acerbic reflections on the complexities of abortion, marriage, pregnancy and motherhood, family politics and class consciousness. Describing the range of responses to abortion, she writes: "After having an abortion, some women get dressed and go to Burger King and some want to die." Similarly, her observations about her own religious childhood are funny yet poignant. She recalls putting thorns in her shoes "for

penance," pleading with the owner of the local gas station to take "the nude calendar off his wall," begging the proprietor of a candy store to remove the sex magazines from his shelves. Her pious efforts failed: the thorns were so painful she sacrificed beatitude for comfort; the gas station owner exiled her from the premises; the candy store proprietor stopped giving [her] free egg creams."

Ms. Gordon marvels at the difference between her own upbringing and that of her children. For her, the Devil "was real. And he was feared." Nevertheless, she tells her own young daughter that the Devil is "like the banshee or the Loch Ness monster." Noting the leap from the sacred to the secular in one generation, Ms. Gordon explores the contrast between believing in "seven capital sins, three theological virtues and four moral ones, seven sacraments, seven gifts of the Holy Ghost" and in appreciating the esthetic form of the Mass and the literary power of liturgical language.

The first two sections of Ms. Gordon's book contain essays on literature and contemporary issues, but the third, "Parts of a Journal," is more free in form. Here Ms. Gordon moves deftly, for example, from reflections on the female reproductive cycle to her interpretation of the Gospel of St. Mark, thereby creating her own hermeneutics. Reviewing her experience of pregnancy and motherhood, which she sees as inversely related to artistic accomplishment, she frets about the impact on her moral life of having children, describing "the membrane that my obsession with them creates between me and the outside world." Yet Ms. Gordon does not hesitate to assert the sensory, even sensuous, pleasures of mothering: "A film of moisture covers my flesh and my son's. Both of us drift in and out of sleep. . . . I am ancient, repetitive. In a life devoted to originality, I adore the animal's predictability."

Only the title essay, which is one of the few of these 28 pieces that have not been published previously, is disappointing. Arguing that American fiction and culture are too often based on the masculine "search for the unfettered self," Ms. Gordon bemoans the association of "females with stasis and death; males with movement and life." This bifurcation of active and passive spheres has been explored in greater literary complexity by feminist scholars in the past two decades. In addition, it lacks historical depth: what Ms. Gordon attributes to the American masculine imperative to escape "bruising authority" is in fact rooted in the more complex heritage of antinomianism—the conviction that subjective experience is as important as religious doctrine—that was the basis of the trial of Anne Hutchinson, the 17th-century Puritan who was tried as a heretic for holding Bible study sessions in her kitchen. Had Ms. Gordon more clearly understood the origins of the American insistence on autonomous selfhood and subjectivity (the "escape from fate," as she phrases it), she would no doubt have seen its relevance to her own development as a novelist and critic.

Despite this lapse, Ms. Gordon's book is both rewarding and challenging, for it chronicles a mind shaped and informed by religious experience, but not constrained by theological dogma. Through these essays, the reader understands that, like the work of the writers and painters she most admires, Mary Gordon's own writing is buttressed by a powerful moral vision.

Alison Lurie (review date 8 August 1993)

SOURCE: "Love Has Its Consequences," in *New York Times Book Review,* August 8, 1993, pp. 1, 25.

[*In the following review, Lurie offers praise for* The Rest of Life.]

We read fiction, in part, to widen our social circle: to make new friends effortlessly, receive their confidences and enter their worlds. Mary Gordon's remarkable new book, *The Rest of Life,* fulfills this purpose wonderfully. Her heroines are all wholly alive and complex contemporary women, and they conceal nothing from us, not even their most intimate secrets.

Though they are full of dramatic incident, the three novellas that make up *The Rest of Life* do not have plots in the traditional sense. Instead, Ms. Gordon works like a sculptor who shapes and reshapes a figure by pressing bits of clay onto a wire armature. We learn about her characters as we would a new friend: first we hear the basic facts, then gradually more and more is revealed, not necessarily in chronological order

The nameless narrator of the first and perhaps most striking story, *Immaculate Man,* runs a shelter for battered women and is having a passionate affair with a Roman Catholic priest, an affair that she describes in vivid sensual and emotional detail. She is middle-aged, plain and outspoken, willing to question everything, even her own identity: "How do any of us recognize ourselves? By being around familiar objects, by performing actions that have some similarity to the actions of the past. I think that's all."

Clement, the priest she loves, appears to her as beautiful, strong and perfect. When they meet he is a 43-year-old virgin who has never been close to another woman, and he declares that he will always love her, but she does not feel secure: "I'm a woman, how can I talk about possessing a man's body. How can you possess what you can't enter? What you don't invade, penetrate."

She is consumed with the fear that Clement will leave her for someone who is not only younger and prettier but who needs him even more than she does—most likely one of the injured women in her shelter. She holds the belief, more common 150 years ago than it is today, that the weaker and more helpless a woman is, the more attractive she is to men: "I feel quite angry at some of the women I'm supposed to help. . . . I feel they've gotten away with something. Or is it that I feel they've taken something

from me? The honored female place. The true, ancient name of woman? That in their supine posture, they arouse in men . . . the instinct to reach down and lift them up."

If she loses Clement, she believes, her whole identity will change, she will become one of those women who will not "ever again be prized," whose body "is of no concern to anyone except yourself. You worry that one day you might get sick, that you'll become a nuisance or a burden. But that's all. You know that's all your body will be to anybody else: a nuisance or a burden. No one will look at you again attentively or lovingly."

The heroine of *Living at Home,* Ms. Gordon's second novella, is also nameless; but initially she seems far more in control of her life. She is attractive, articulate, well educated and successful. As the psychiatrist in charge of a clinic for autistic children, she is famous for her understanding of her young patients, who are hauntingly described: "Aloneness is what life is about for them. . . . They create edifices or machines to separate themselves from the world. One child would speak only inside a construction of cardboard, wires, tins. . . . They can't predict, so they are safe only in sameness. They are so far from an experience of time that only space and its emptiness remains."

Yet she too is emotionally dependent on a man: an Italian journalist named Lauro who covers wars and revolutions for a London newspaper. She too is obsessed with losing her lover, in this case not to another woman but to illness or accidental death. When Lauro is about to have a tooth pulled she does not sleep the previous night, and blames herself for thinking that if he died in the dentist's chair she would not commit suicide.

She is also acutely jealous. She resents the fact that Lauro's visits cheer her invalid mother: "I wanted to take him away from her. I wanted to bring him home to the place where we live, where she doesn't live. . . . I was afraid she'd drain the life out of him. And I needed his life."

These fears and jealousies seem to be related to her view of women as naturally alone and lost, like the autistic children. "I've often imagined myself homeless," she says. "All women do, or many. They see themselves wandering, holding everything they own in a bag, sleeping against the warm sides of buildings in the freezing night." Essentially, this strong and gifted woman can help only those she sees as weaker than she. Infinitely patient and kind at work, she is impatient and unkind to Lauro when he's ill.

Paola, the heroine of Ms. Gordon's third novella, *The Rest of Life,* is also someone whose existence centers on—and indeed has been ruined by—men. As a girl in Italy in the 1920s, she is taught to devalue herself, to conceal her knowledge and defer to male opinions. At the age of 15 she is persuaded to enter into a suicide pact by her first lover, a brilliant and disturbed 16-year-old boy called Leo; but at the last minute she refuses to die with him. When this becomes known she is disgraced; Leo's family calls her a whore and a murderer, and her beloved father sends her to America and never sees her again. Though Paola marries and has children, she passes the next 63 years in a state of emotional numbness. Only when she returns to Turin at the age of 78 is Paola able to forgive others and herself. But even then her deepest sympathy is for men who, like Leo, have died young.

Women today are said to have "come a long way." Yet the heroines of the three novellas that compose *The Rest of Life* don't seem to have heard the news. Though they all have children they care for and full-time careers—perhaps typically, in what are called the "helping professions"—each of these women is focused on some man with whom she is involved in an obsessive, unequal sexual relationship.

What are we to make of this? Considering Mary Gordon's intelligence and her great gifts as a writer, I think we must read this book not as a post-feminist assertion of our essential emotional weakness but as a cautionary tale: a skilled and complex portrait of three strong, interesting and admirable women who have been deeply damaged by their dependence on men.

Lisa Zeidner (review date 8 August 1993)

SOURCE: "Sacred and Profane," in *Washington Post Book World,* August 8, 1993, p. 5.

[*In the following review, Zeidner offers positive assessment of* The Rest of Life.]

Since her first novel, the bestseller *Final Payments,* Mary Gordon's fiction has explored the tug-of-war between duty and desire. Her heroines are often good Catholic girls who sacrifice so much of their own happiness that their very identities become threatened. Gordon's mission is to shake up their complacency—to save them from cloistered virtue.

Her seventh book, *The Rest of Life,* comprises of three gentle, quiet novellas about Gordon's own brand of unassuming heroine. Two of these women are middle-aged, the third elderly, all at times in their lives when you'd expect them to have settled into cozy bargains with God. But they're still being tested, still having to struggle with the same old thorny issues: sex and death. As the pun in the title indicates, the rest of life isn't all that restful.

The 48-year-old narrator of *Immaculate Man,* a divorced mother who works in a shelter for battered women, was "brought up to be well-behaved. Brought up to practice all the minor virtues: thrift, honesty, politeness, temperance. All forms of moderation. Above all not to make a fuss." So she's surprised to find herself embroiled in a love affair with Clement, a 45-year-old priest. Only Father Boniface, the homosexual priest who encouraged Clement to join the church and fought for years against his own sexual

impulses towards his young charge, appreciates the depth and complexity of the narrator's hunger for her lover. The narrator's biggest fear is that Clement will leave her, that like Boniface she will have to confront death alone.

The narrator of *Living at Home* also fears death—her husband's. Lauro is a photo-journalist who travels gleefully to revolutions in remote countries. He's the narrator's third husband; she sets out to explain "why, although I'm far from irresponsible, I've left so many men, and why with Lauro I have been so happy."

Like *Immaculate Man, Living at Home* is a graceful meditation on the pains and pleasures of middle age. The narrator, a psychiatrist, works with autistic children; Gordon deftly uses autism as a metaphor for all of our isolation and detachment. "I've always felt," the narrator says, "that we all live so much of our lives as if we were in a sealed jar, the lid tight, looking out. Things tap on the outside—branches, fingers—but not hard enough. If they tapped too hard, there would be breakage and that mustn't be."

The 78-year-old widow in *The Rest of Life,* the last novella, hides as tightly wrapped in her sorrow as those autistic children. Sixty-three years ago, she fled Turin in shame when she failed to keep her part in a suicide pact with her young lover and was held responsible for his death. She endured a loveless marriage, raising her children numbly. Now she travels back to Italy for the first time since her banishment, accompanied by her grown son and his girlfriend, and is forced to question the very nature of the way she has "lived, day by day, watching, waiting, she has never known for what."

Only the title novella offers a plot, a set of events promising resolution. All of the tales are related in the present tense; pointedly, Gordon enters and exits in the middle of these lives, eschewing inflated climaxes and presenting instead a restrained contemplation about the fragility of daily happiness.

As a writer committed to Catholic themes, Gordon is unusual in that her characters search so hard for happiness—and often find it. Most Catholic novelists would agree with the Misfit in Flannery O'Connor's story "A Good Man is Hard to Find" that there's "no real pleasure in life." In some sense, the grimmer Catholic view of this world makes for a better story: It's bloodier and more dramatic. The ordinary people who populate Andre Dubus's fiction confront many of the same theological issues found here, but because they're often less sweet from the onset—they sin harder and more often—their stories have a more satisfying shape.

Unlike the novel, however, the novella form wears the lack of drama well. Gordon's prose isn't showy, but it's rich in image and connection. She excels in describing emotions in concrete physical terms—rooms, houses, landscapes, countries. Except for an occasional glut of rhetorical questions ("What does that mean, that she is living and he is not? What is the difference between life and death?"), *The Rest of Life* allow us to sink into the characters' thoughts as if sitting in a trellised garden in late afternoon, with nothing to do but enjoy the crisp solitude.

John B. Breslin (review date 25 February 1994)

SOURCE: "Between a Romp and Redemption," in *Commonweal,* February 25, 1994, pp. 24-5.

[*In the following review, Breslin offers positive assessment of* The Rest of Life.]

Three stories; three women; four men (one a father) to whom the women are bound by ties of obsession and memory; several children to whom the women are devoted, all but one boys, none fathered by their lovers. Such is the cast of characters in these novellas, Mary Gordon's first fiction since the generational saga of *The Other Side,* but what really matters here are the voices, in turn confessional, suspicious, celebratory, always questioning but finally, in the concluding story, grateful.

The first two stories, *Immaculate Man* and *Living at Home,* echo one another most closely. Both are first-person narratives by women in their forties who have been married and divorced, have achieved professional independence (significantly, as a social worker with battered women and a psychiatrist for autistic children), and have fallen in love, respectively, with a priest and a foreign journalist, men temperamentally unsuited to settling down, or, some might claim, to growing up. What links these two nameless women is their physical attachment to their lovers, their fear of displacement by abandonment or death. Each story ends with the words, "I don't know"; and what they don't know is how they'll live without their men, so binding has the covenant of the flesh become. And yet their voices rarely sound a self-pitying note; indeed, they often reveal a sharp-eyed realism. Father Clement's late sexual awakening restores the narrator's regard for her body, but it becomes wearying in its very devotion: "Sometimes," she reflects, "I want a romp: athletic, careless, and desanctified." The journalist's mortal fear of even the simplest medical procedure mocks his itch to be in the thick of violent revolutions.

At other times, however, the clarity gives way to the moral obtuseness of the age and the peculiar blindness of any *égoisme à deux:* despite her concern for autistic children, the second narrator has no serious qualms about having an abortion and confines her outrage to the journalist's insensitivity in planning a trip at the time of the procedure.

The perils—and delights—of romantic love experienced in middle age bind these couples together in a way that family or religious community failed to do. What Mary Gordon has so evocatively caught in her narrators' voices is

how precious and precarious such late-blooming pleasures can be, like the pleasures of the stories themselves with their shifting promises of meaning.

In the third and most moving of the novellas, *The Rest of Life,* the focus shifts to youth and old age, but of the same woman. It is a long and long-resisted exercise of memory by a seventy-eight-year-old grandmother returning to Turin from America six decades after she was sent away in disgrace by her adored father; at fifteen she had fallen in love with a Byronesque youth a year older who subsequently committed suicide in a pact she failed to honor. Guilt, shame, loss shadow her subsequent life as nurse, wife, and mother, for no attachment, even that to her youngest and best loved son, can make up for her infatuation with the teen-aged romantic or her despair at the eclipse of her father's devotion.

Memory for her means something quite different from nostalgia; not the peaceful stream to be navigated at will but "the cataract, the overwhelming flood" she has kept dammed up. Even the city of her childhood becomes a menace when she tries to lead her son and his fiancée on a walking tour. Relieved at first because she finds no incriminating names in the phone book and no buildings remaining that might silently accuse her of youthful crimes, she becomes lost in streets she cannot remember, surrounded by buildings and wires that cast surreal shadows and remind her of Turin's reputation for black magic and hidden malice. Memory's power to shape and distort the present becomes palpable, but not inescapable.

For memory can also be cathartic, as she discovers when she decides to retrace alone the final journey with Leo to the medieval tower of their broken pact. She finds it half-demolished, marked off with a warning sign: *Pericoloso,* a place for uncomplicated young boys, so unlike Leo, to play their games. What she discovers and reclaims is her will to live, that deep desire for a shared happiness that led her to offer her life to Leo but stopped her from taking it. What she leaves behind is her guilt, her bitterness at life's unfairness. Coming back to Turin, to her son and his African fiancée, she discovers, like Gabriel Conroy at the end of Joyce's short masterpiece, that the dead absolve more than they blame the living: "the dead, being one and many, knew there was nothing to forgive." And so the story that began in dread ends in gratitude, transmuting memory into a hymn of celebration for "all that has gone before us, everything, all things, the living and the dead. . . . *Si, grazie.*"

A rather different ending from the agnosticism of the heart that concludes the first two stories. Is it an epistemological advance or simply an idiosyncrasy of old age? Perhaps the lyricism of that ending, with all its echoes of "The Dead" ("A boy like you died here. It might have been because of me."), makes most sense as a testament of independence. For the achievement of this reluctant pilgrim has been to become her own woman, freed in memory now from lover and father as she had already been freed by widowhood from a husband she respected but could never love. It is a freedom her sister narrators might well envy but would likely want to postpone.

John Leonard (review date 6 May 1996)

SOURCE: "She Lost Her Father," in *The Nation,* May 6, 1996, pp. 24-6, 28.

[*In the following review, Leonard offers favorable evaluation of* The Shadow Man.]

"I love you more than God," David Gordon told his daughter, Mary, before dying of a heart attack when she was 7. His only child, than whom there's no brainier writer or reader, no more resourceful archeologist of hidden meanings, has worried this bone, like a hound of heaven, ever since: "I didn't know, and still don't, if he meant he loved me more than he loved God or more than God loved me. It almost doesn't matter. It was a serious thing to say and it scared me."

It also sounds like a curse. No one, not even a parent, should have such power over our imagining of ourselves. Nor ought any child need to love him back so much, at whatever cost. But David taught Mary to read when she was 3; to memorize the Latin Mass when she was 5; to dwell in libraries and ideas. "He ripped a picture of Beethoven out of the encyclopedia and hung it near my toy box." The only other picture allowed in the house was a print of Holbein's *Thomas More;* no landscapes, no still lifes, certainly not any modern art, which he considered "dangerous, and ugly, too." Not even any television. Instead, the Easter show at Radio City, where the Rockettes dressed up as angels and nuns. And *Six O'Clock Saints,* where Mary learned the story of Saint Nicholas, who reassembled little boys who had been dismembered and pickled. And in a magazine her father edited, *The Children's Hour,* tales of the super-dutiful daughters of Prospero, Rip Van Winkle and the Chinese mandarin Kuan-Yo.

In Lafcadio Hearn's "The Soul of the Bell," Kuan-Yo, an adviser to the emperor, supervises the construction of the world's most perfect bell. But the heated metals of gold, silver and brass won't blend, and the bell can't be cast. To save his life, Kuan-Yo consults the usual wise old man on the usual mountain, who explains that only the body of the usual spotless virgin can cause the metals to blend. Naturally, Kuan-Yo has just such a daughter, who promptly flings herself into the vat, crying "For thy sake, O father." Presto: ding-dong. "The perfect life," says a sarcastic Mary, "the perfect death, the graceful fall into the boiling metal. . . . Endlessly entombed, endlessly beloved, endlessly revered, the body turns to music, the perfection of the bell's tone repeats itself in the receptive and ecstatic air." And yet, not believing a word of Hearn, what she does in this aurora of a memoir is turn herself into a bell.

"Ecclesiastical language is full of names for vessels," she tells us: "chalice, ciborium, monstrance, pyx; there must be containers to enclose, keep safe, keep intact, keep protected from the world's contamination the sacred matter." The world contaminated her only father. Too late to protect him, Mary's bell will ring his vespers.

Because the David Gordon who wrote poems to his daughter—from whom she learned "the sovereignty of the mind and the imagination," after whom she named her son—was also the David Gordon who, in the twenties, edited a semi-porn girlie magazine called *Hot Dog;* and, in the late thirties and early forties, wrote anti-Semitic articles for *Catholic International* and the Jesuit weekly *America;* and, in the early fifties, wrote speeches for Joe McCarthy. Even his biography of the poet Paul Claudel, written a decade after the terrible news of the death camps, was actually a diatribe against André Gide, Modernism and "the infection of the Jews": "The Jew Proust. The Jew Bergson. The Jew Masoch . . ." More remarkably, David Gordon had himself been born a Jew, only converting to Roman Catholicism in 1937, just in time to side with Franco in the Spanish Civil War and to complain in *America* about the international brigades of "Jewish soldiers" gone to Spain "to help murder nuns in Lincoln's name."

So he died on her, this changeling, and his secrets with him: "I am in the dark room, waiting to be allowed to see him, to wave to him. I have always been. I have always been waiting. I have always known that if they let me see him, he will never die. I know what the sight of me means to him. Everything." And what the death of him meant to her was a fall into her mother's Irish-Sicilian world of grudge and grievance; of polio, alcoholism and Alzheimer's; of *My Little Margie* on Friday night television and something more mysterious on the bedroom wall: "a picture made of slats. You turned your head one way: it was the Scourging at the Pillar. Another turn of the head produced Jesus Crowned with Thorns. If you looked absolutely straight ahead, you saw the Agony in the Garden"—the world, in other words, of Mary Gordon's novels, of *Final Payments, The Company of Women, Men and Angels* and *The Other Side.*

Though she wouldn't discover *Hot Dog,* pressed between pages of the *Catholic Encyclopedia,* until she was 12, which bared breasts, provocative bums and Little Girtie Ginger sex jokes she flushed immediately down a toilet, it was not as if half-orphaned Mary, afraid of mayonnaise and gristle, hadn't known she was partly Jewish. Her father told her his ancestors had been wealthy and cultivated French Jews; that his grandfather had been a rabbi; that his father owned a saloon. (He also told her, or so she thinks she remembers, that he was an only child; that he had gone to Harvard with Walter Lippmann, seen Oxford's dreamy spires in the era of *Brideshead Revisited,* consorted in Left Bank cafes with poets like Claudel and been blacklisted by the Anti-Defamation League of B'nai B'rith, which was why he couldn't hold a job driving a taxi or tending a bar.) In his absence, moreover, her mother's family had always been there to remind her, whenever she was reading, dreaming or otherwise difficult: "That's the *Jew* in you."

The Jew in her? "For most of my life, I felt I had no right to claim Jewishness for myself because I hadn't suffered for it. . . . No one needed me to be a Jew. But what did *I* need?" A father, of course, who must have abandoned her because she hadn't been alert enough to love him more: "maybe he was not really dead but was missing or banished, a political exile, and I, by the right word or signal, would be able to recall him." A *writing* father, from whom she inherited, like a recessive gene, a predisposition to semicolons and parallelisms, argumentative paragraphs that end in punchy accusations and "some dream of purity, or style. Some way of naming and distinguishing. Some taste for exclusion and embellishment. And a desire for a point of silence, emptiness, and rest." A *film noir* father who "lived as a man drowning," with his missing teeth, torn trousers, broken shoes: "The figure behind every story. The stranger on the road. The double, feared and prized, approaching from the distance." Had he lived, this Shadow Man would have seen to it that his daughter went to college in Quebec, or Belgium, or Ireland, certainly not to godless Barnard, where she became the leftist-feminist and trained investigator who pursues him through these pages: the scholar, historian, literary critic, private eye and Magic Realist who looks for him in library catalogues, census reports, deed bins, immigration archives and other "caves of memory" in New York, New Haven, Providence and Cleveland, in photo albums, microfiche plates and dossiers marked "Loss," "Fascism" and "Kafka." The child Mary feared bicycles and seesaws and merry-go-rounds. The adult, a hedgehog and a fox, will go anywhere by any means to track her father down: "It's a less hopeless prospect for me to imagine that I can find him than to imagine that he can find me. I am, after all, the one who lost him. 'She lost her father,' I've often heard people say. 'She lost her father when she was very young.'"

Bad enough that David "did other things in his life than love me." It turns out he also lied a lot: "Facts nose their way into what I thought was the past like a dog sticking his nose under a lady's skirts. How I resent the insidious, relentless, somehow filthy nudging of these facts." He had been born not in Lorain, Ohio, but in Vilna, Lithuania. His first name had been Israel, not David; his first language Yiddish, not English. Nor was he an only child; sisters stashed in nursing homes and mental hospitals, relatives of whom she had no inkling, possessed snap-shots of little Mary, lovingly inscribed. Rather than owning a saloon, his father had worked in a dry-goods store. Instead of going to Harvard with Walter Lippmann, David was a railroad clerk. Far from rolling Oxford lawns with Evelyn Waugh, or Left Banking with right-wingers, he never graduated from high school, never applied for a passport. He'd even been previously married, to a flapper, and a stepfather to *her* son. Mary being Mary, she is more jealous of Yiddish than she is of any stepson. Yiddish was an elsewhere her

father could go to, leaving her behind without her even knowing it, as if "the legitimate daughter" were "too good" ever to meet "the love child"—this Other's discourse of shtetl and Ellis Island, of goose grease and cabbage leaves and steerage, of Chagall's dancing cows and dark men in fur hats "praying to a God who has no son or mother."

And so an angry daughter in mourning, the cracked bell, must imagine her father's passage from turn-of-the-century Midwest outcast ("the tumult, the vilification and self-hatred, the immigrant's terror, the weak son's dread, the Eastern Jew's American abashment") to the dandy, the autodidact and the convert who tried to pass by reading Matthew Arnold and Walter Pater, by dropping names like Ovid and Dante, by pretending his "natural habitations" were the open spaces of Rome, the dappled woods of the Middle Ages, the majestic palaces of the Renaissance, hoping in the cramped rooms above the store "one day to awake without reproach." Like a porcupine bristling with empathetic intelligence, every needle an optic nerve, Mary sees him flee his past into her future. She'll dream him up all over again, in an ecstatic trance, by meditation and incantation on such objects as his pink shirt, black comb, silver ring and a prayerbook with a lamb's paw; on such fragmentary texts as Father Coughlin and Father Feeney; on her "police artist" sketch of the face of his "stalker," with H. L. Mencken's mouth, Ezra Pound's hair, Henry Roth's eyes and Bernard Berenson's skull. Because we know and she knows that the shadow will always follow and fall on the fugitive, this luminous exertion breaks the heart:

> My father walks out of the meadow to the marble building. He is light with feverish joy but his forehead is cool. Words jump and dance but remain separate, do not swarm. Assisi. Provence. Languedoc. Toscana. Chartres. Words rise up, white and shining, images of iridescent ease, words that do not accuse but absorb accusation. No need to fear, no need to cringe or wait for the reproach. In the white silence rimmed with green or gold, the dream of Europe, swallowing loathsomeness and hatred, insult, terror, dread.

> Until it starts again. The buzz and hiss. The torment. "Everything you do is wrong."

This shadow fell as well on her, during *The Children's Hour* in the fifties, while her father was writing speeches for Joe McCarthy and loving Mary more than God. The political pathologizes the personal:

> I hear as if in a dream or through thick fog . . . the news of the execution of the Rosenbergs. Mrs. Rosenberg in her boxy coat, her hat, her pocketbook, like anybody's mother. I am told she, too, is trying to kill me. She is a mother, but the deaths of children mean nothing to her. Even the death of her own children would mean nothing to her. She is a Communist. This is what Joe McCarthy and Roy Cohn are protecting me from. But every time I see electric wires, a chain-link fence with barbed wire on top, or an electric power plant, sometimes even a water tower, anything sending something from one part of the official world into our private lives, I am afraid for Mrs. Rosenberg. For the electricity in her body. To save *me*? You don't need to do that to her, I want to tell everybody. It is impossible

that people like me will be saved. We will eventually be found out, and we know very well that you will be the ones to do it. We don't know what we've done, but you know. Then we will join Mrs. Rosenberg. Then our bodies will be shot through with electricity. We will be shocked. (I have felt it when I touched the plug of the electric toaster.) We will be shocked to death.

We are reminded of other memoirs, variously apposite. Some Sartre, surely, for the precocious Baby Writer: a bratty Jean-Paul inventing in *Words* a childhood self appropriate to his speed-freak metaphysics, in the absence of his dead father, gleefully certain he's free of superego. Some *Speak, Memory* Nabokov, for sheer lyrical anti-Freudian stubbornness: who claimed, as a child in prelapsarian Russia, to have seen through the dining-room window his father levitate, a glorious midair sprawl in a wind-rippled white summer suit against the cobalt-blue noon sky, hoisted by happy peasants, prefiguring the vaulted ceiling, wax tapers, swimming lights, funeral lilies and open coffin. Maybe even Philip Roth, about whom Gordon has written so brilliantly, who came to understand *Patrimony* during his custodianship of his dying father: a shaving mug handed down by generations of Jewish immigrants; the excrement Philip had to clean up, as once he'd been cleaned up after as a baby; their mutual obsession with memory, never forgetting *anything*; a distinctive voice: "He taught me the vernacular. He *was* the vernacular, unpoetic and expressive and point-blank, with all the vernacular's glaring limitations and all its durable force."

Or, for a female point of view on excess, secrecy and dysfunction: Germaine Greer, who tells us in *Daddy, We Hardly Knew You* that her father Reg had lied his whole life to his wife and children about almost everything, from his ersatz South African origins to his phony war as a cipher clerk at an underground decoding machine in Malta, meaning there had been no excuse at all for his daughter's growing up in Melbourne in a house without music, books, flowers, cheese or love. To which, add Carolyn See, who speaks in *Dreaming* of a grandfather dying drunk in a snowdrift, a grandmother blowing her head off with a shotgun, a father who churns out hard-core porn under a life-sized snap of a naked Marilyn Monroe and a mother playing tag at night inside a high-voltage power station with a pint of vodka in her Bible; of knowing that it's Thanksgiving because Uncle Bob sets himself on fire, and that it's Easter because you're in Las Vegas, where the Risen Christ is a topless dancer on a skating rink, performing "Spice on Ice."

But Gordon is sui generis, and so is her book: wounding, refulgent and redemptive. "The detective in love with her client," she warns, "usually ends up murdering or murdered." Besides, "We want the log of a voyage with a happy ending. The story we don't want to hear is the story of disintegration, diminishment, humiliation, loss. This is the America that we cannot imagine." Nevertheless: "There is some residue. . . . You didn't get it from your accusers; it was neither pitiable nor the stuff of shame. Perhaps it was the voice of God. The God of singleness and silence."

The font of pure, accepting love." Insisting: "His name is not David, or Israel. It is My Father." Finally: "This man owes me his life, and he will live forever."

In the last astonishing pages of *The Shadow Man,* having exhumed her father, she reburies him, in an elsewhere of her own choosing, in a ceremony of her own devising, in a coffin strewn with the severed heads of roses. Her friends think she is crazy. Well, so was Joan of Arc. And Simone Weil. And Antigone. And Hildegard von Bingen, the twelfth-century "Sybil of the Rhine," who wrote poems, plays, histories and sacred songs, and refused to yield to local authorities the body of a radical buried in her convent graveyard.

Maybe she just loved him more than God.

Sara Maitland (review date 17 May 1996)

SOURCE: "Final Payment," in *Commonweal,* May 17, 1996, pp. 17-8.

[*In the following review, Maitland offers negative assessment of* The Shadow Man.]

Mary Gordon has a well established record as a novelist deeply shaped by, although rather at odds with, her Roman Catholicism. I admire her work, and particularly *Final Payments.* So I came to this autobiographical memoir with some enthusiasm, though also with some doubts, as I have difficulties with books in the confessional genre by novelists. However, even uneasy amalgams can be interesting, and I was interested.

I was also feeling indirectly involved. Gordon writes of the death of her father when she was seven as the most important event of her life. My brother died last year leaving two small children, the older of whom is just seven. My family has talked a great deal about how one supports the children in preserving useful memories of their father, so I was open to a deeper understanding of loss and the way death complicates memory, knowledge, anger, and love.

I have spelled my position out in more detail than I might normally do, because I want to be fair to Gordon, but I have to say that *The Shadow Man* is quite simply a bad book. Nearly forty years after he died Gordon set out "in search" of her lost father, and the book is a record of the search. It ends up being more about Gordon's sensitivities than a biography of another person, but she was laboring under a particular difficulty—everything that she found out is pretty nasty. Her father was a liar (in large and small), a pornographer, a Jewish anti-Semite, a crypto-Nazi, and a grossly irresponsible husband.

It must be hard to discover all that about one's beloved father; and it was made more difficult still for Gordon because at the same time she was turning her attention to the task, her mother was collapsing into Alzheimer's disease, unable to offer more domestic balancing memories to her daughter. But "hard" is not, from the reader's point of view, enough of an excuse. I hope that were I to start out on such a project and found what Gordon found, I would sensibly abandon it, or fictionalize it, or not publish it. Instead the whole thing seems to have rotted Gordon's writerly intelligence (which she certainly has). The book is not simply ill-conceived, it is badly structured, sloppily written, and deplorably self-indulgent.

The best example of these qualities is the bizarre stylistic flourishes that adorn the book: I cannot find a single page which is not littered with preposterous rhetorical questions. Here is Gordon on the subject of her father's false teeth:

> But were the teeth his? Yes, of course, since he had bought them. Did he pay for them, or did my mother, or some anonymous benefactor with a taste for Orthodox Catholicism, literature with a fascist bite? But the teeth weren't his in that they didn't emanate from his body. They weren't flesh of his flesh as I was. So it is possible to say that I was his daughter but they were not his teeth. Then whose teeth were they?

This self-dramatizing quality might be justified in relation to her memories, but it continues into the period of her "search," all of which is unfortunately written in the present tense—giving a gushing flow, but undercutting any self-critical possibility.

> But I went to a place where I was not the only one [the public archives office] . . . who are all these people and how could I be one of them? What are they looking for? What is the evidence they need? Are they trying to find lost kin. . . . Or maybe someone with money, the money that can change their lives?

At the root of the book's failure is the fact that I simply cannot believe in the seven-year-old self whom Gordon remembers and describes—a seven-year-old whose beloved father has just died and who lies in bed and thinks

> I had to allow for the possibility that I might be only an idea—but in the mind of whom? Or what? Not God certainly. I knew it wasn't God; at that moment God was only one more instance of failed language.

(I don't think so. And this from the creator of the young girl in *The Company of Women*—we know Gordon knows better.)

Because she does not give us a credible child it is increasingly hard to believe in the sincerity, or even emotional capability, of the grown woman who is now the narrator. This is a double shame because it also undermines the potentially most interesting part of the book, when she turns her attention from this maudlin drivel to an exploration of her mother, her mother's retreat into amnesia, and the struggle Gordon therefore has in establishing the possibility of exhuming her father and reburying him. It has become, regrettably, almost impossible to believe anything she says.

The difficulty is enhanced, I would have to add, by some most peculiar lapses of taste: name-dropping the fact that Toni Morrison recommended the hotel in which Gordon stayed in Lorain, or telling us that she gave her children *French* bread with their omelet the day of her father's re-burial.

I think I feel a sincere pity for Gordon wrestling with what is obviously a devastating experience, but I feel as sorry for the reader having to read it in this form. At one point she exclaims

> Am I one of those modern people who don't know the difference between the public and the private? One of those people on "Oprah" or "Geraldo," one of those transsexual doctors or dominatrix twins who can't wait to tell their tales? Am I squandering my legacy by putting it out in the open, on the trail, where it can be consumed like Hansel and Gretel's crumbs, by pass-ersby?

The answer is "Yes you are."

William H. Pritchard (review date 26 May 1996)

SOURCE: "The Cave of Memory," in *New York Times Book Review,* May 26, 1996, p. 5.

[*In the following review, Pritchard offers tempered evaluation of* The Shadow Man.]

Mary Gordon's first novel, ***Final Payments,*** begins with a funeral, that of the heroine's father, whom she has cared for through 11 years and a series of strokes. The daughter's subsequent rediscovery of life. which this first-person narrative engagingly traces, concludes with a sentence predictive of Ms. Gordon's subsequent career as a writer: "There was a great deal I wanted to say."

Now, after three further novels, a collection of stories, three novellas and a book of essays, she has written a passionate and extravagant account of coming to terms with her own father, David Gordon, who died of a heart attack when she was 7 years old. Who and what David Gordon really was is the object of his daughter's search. She begins that search knowing or believing she knows, that he was a Jew whose earlier life involved a Midwestern boyhood, years at Harvard and in France, a certain amount of journalistic and literary production, a conversion to Roman Catholicism and marriage to her mother (herself a Catholic). But the "cave of memory" Ms. Gordon is about to enter turns out to be as she apply puts it, "a tourist trap."

For the "facts" about David Gordon are, to say the least, misleading. In the course of her investigations—which consist in part of reading her father's works in libraries, checking his family's birth records, traveling to Lorain, Ohio, and engaging in countless conversations with those who may or may not have known him or known about him—she finds that her father was in fact born in Vilna, Lithuania, that his first name was Israel, that he was not an only child, that there was no Harvard and no Paris in his "undergraduate years" (he worked for the B & O railroad), that he edited a mildly pornographic "humor" magazine in the 1920's, that after his conversion he became stridently anti-Semitic and right-wing, admiring radio's Father Coughlin and Cambridge's Father Feeney, that he was married once before, back in Ohio.

In the book's preface, referring to her love for this "passionate man" who once assured her that he loved her more than God, Ms. Gordon admits that "my desire not to move from that place led to a kind of memorializing that amounted to entombment." So the book is, figuratively and literally, about the disinterring of the father, and it concludes with his reburial in a different cemetery from the one where he had reposed with his Catholic in-laws.

It's nothing less than a matter of life and death, for the stakes are mortal ones. As suggested by her witty and serious play on the themes of entombment and memorializing, Ms. Gordon's success as a writer depends on how vividly and convincingly she can bring the dead to life. She uses the word "quest" to describe her attempts to get back in memory to the place she and her father once shared. That place turns out to be elusive, indeed delusive, but "quest" accurately describes her experience as both daughter and writer. As in fairy tales and ritual magic, there are obstacles to be surmounted, reverses to be endured. The right questions must be asked, the right (or the least wrong) moves made in order for the dead "shadow man" to yield up his lineaments, thereby removing a weight from the shoulders of his living daughter.

Ms. Gordon's narrative seeks to avoid the banalities of repetitive insistence by exploiting the lively paradoxes and incongruities of her situation. If the cliché has it that the living woman seeks to find the lost father, then the notion of losing must be examined. "I am my father's daughter. I am reading what he wrote as his daughter, desperate not to lose him because of the words he sent out to strangers, to the world. But how can I fail to lose him, reading what he wrote?"

At particular issue here are sentences the father published in the early 1940's about Jews, and looking at pages of his contributions to a journal called Catholic International she finds that "what he wrote, what I have made myself read, what I have waited so long to read properly, has taken away what I used to have, my joy in being with my father, with the man who took me to the city, who bought me books, wrote me poems." Such are the ambiguous gifts of trying to bring the father into full consciousness by somehow explaining him: "I know it's blasphemy to invent an inner life for a father, whose inner life literally produced you." Indeed, her identity as writer is in question since, she says, she is a writer because her father was one: "I write the way I do because of the way he wrote."

The narrative is strongest and liveliest when the daughter is able to see herself in incongruous relation to institutions and objects that are not, as she is, obsessed with a single passion. Some of the best pages of *The Shadow Man* are about books, about the libraries where Ms. Gordon looks up her father's writings. In Columbia's Butler Library, "temple to high Protestantism," where she has been coming for 27 years, she locates him in the Readers' Guide to Periodical Literature and finds an essay on an English poet by this "Ohio Jew" later turned Catholic. At Brown University's Hay Library, "a small Federal-style mansion with portraits of founders on the wall," she finds it absurd to be asking for the archives on Hot Dog, a magazine in which her father, under the name Jack Dinnsmore, wrote things like "Are Chorus Girls on the Square?" In Lorain, Ohio, her father's hometown after he came to America at the age of 6, she arrives in an ice storm and instead of concentrating on David Gordon's early education finds herself worrying about the fine leather coat she's brought along, exactly the wrong thing to wear in such weather. Meanwhile, her hotel caters to her uneasy heart only by serving "heart easy" pasta, a food slightly less than spiritually fulfilling.

But sometimes the atmosphere feels less enlivening than oppressively up close and personal. Ms. Gordon keeps raising the ante in this game for mortal stakes, and in what seems to me the least successful chapter ("Seeing Past the Evidence") she goes about placing her father in a police lineup with herself as "police artist," putting together his face from bits of Bernard Berenson, H. L. Mencken, Ezra Pound and Henry Roth. She tries, but fails, to "become" her father by impersonating him, telling him stories. "I cannot bear to be my father," she concludes, and she worries about her own balance. "Can I keep my own brain, sound and white, not seething, not fevered?"

Maybe. But her sentences do something like seethe and are, if not fevered, to my taste rather overheated. About her attempt to provide a "face" for her father she writes: "It must be a face without features. A face of light and air. A flame. Perhaps it is the face of music. Of beauty beyond the search for beauty. A face both human and inhuman. A face of love beyond the end of love." The sentence fragments—a general feature of the book's writing—are supposed to create an atmosphere of anguished sincerity. But eventually this reader's sympathies were with the father who, as she imagines him writing in torment, asks, "Why are you doing this to me?"

The book's final pages, in which Ms Gordon succeeds in having her father exhumed and reburied, are informed by a Shakespearean vision of herself as "the lunatic, the lover, and the poet," and she declares, proudly, that no obstacle will stop her. Nor does one. Her friends think she's "crazy" but loyally gather round; her mother, disposed originally to look on the project as a "wacky" idea, finally says "I'm so proud of you. My one and only." In the book's last paragraph, the heroine realizes "that I'm not sad at all. That I'm very happy." It is all a bit like Jane Eyre: the first person "I" endures and overcomes all obstacles as the world comes round to meet its demands.

In her preface, "To the Reader," Ms. Gordon's claim about her father is that "having lost him, once, twice, I will have him forever. He is always with me, always mine." By the end of *The Shadow Man,* that reader has seen the thing come to pass and must testify, if with some mixed feelings, to the dominance of such absolute literary power.

Christopher Lehmann-Haupt (review date 5 March 1998)

SOURCE: "A Male Muse Lacking Only a Name," in *The New York Times,* March 5, 1998, p. E12.

[*In the following review, Lehmann-Haupt offers unfavorable assessment of* Spending.]

"Where are the male Muses?" asks Monica Szabo at the end of the slide show of her paintings that begins Mary Gordon's new novel, *Spending: A Utopian Divertimento.*

"Right here," answers the man in the audience whom Monica chooses to call simply B in her account of the unusual love affair they are about to begin.

B is a feminist's fantasy come to life. A highly successful trader of commodities futures, he has bought four of Monica's paintings and fallen in love with her from afar. He believes her to be "a very, very good painter" who one day "might be great" if only she had the advantages of the great male artists of history.

"What do you think you need that would give you the optimum conditions for work?" he asks her.

"Space and time," she answers.

So they undertake the experiment that B proposes: that he become her patron and muse in every possible sense of those words.

In her earlier novels, *Final Payments, The Company of Women, Men and Angels* and *The Other Side,* Ms. Gordon was preoccupied with self-sacrifice. Now in the character of Monica Szabo, she has created a woman who not only wants it all back but also thinks it her due because she is an artist and a superior being.

Of course, Monica has certain qualms about her arrangement with B. As the egalitarian-minded daughter of working-class parents (her father was a baker), she insists she is uncomfortable with money and privilege. Worse, since she and B have immediately become lovers, for her to take money from him puts her in the position of a prostitute, or a "sex worker," as one of her twin daughters prefers to call it. And since B is sleeping with her anyway, shouldn't he also pose for her, as the lovers of the great male artists always did?

Yet thanks to a remarkable capacity for self-forgiveness, she manages to overcome these difficulties. Despite her supposed discomfort with luxury, she seems to know all about the best stores, restaurants, hotels and great cities in Europe. The pattern of her protests suggests that once she has aired her objections to accepting B's sexual attentions and money, she is free to do so to her heart's content. "I think the most important thing to say about why I did everything I did was that I always felt he liked me a great deal," she explains somewhat lamely.

As for his posing for her: "Can I think about it?" he asks.

"Yes, but not too long," she responds, only half teasing. "And you really need to bear in mind that you have a responsibility to do it. It's part of your bargain, remember. Think of all those women taking off their clothes for all those men. Think of all you have to make up for."

"The way you put it is so subtle, so full of possibility. I suppose I have no choice."

Despite Monica's excesses as a character, her story does draw the reader in after a hundred pages or so. Looking at B's sleeping, naked form, she conceives a series of paintings based on her perception that the deposed Christs of Renaissance art are not dead but postorgasmic. The resulting show wins her sales, fame, controversy and a second patron, who offers her still greater wealth and inspires her to further invention.

At the novel's high point, Monica goes on the "Charlie Rose Show" and defends her "Spent Men" series against a Roman Catholic critic who considers them blasphemous. "All I'm saying is that, as an artist, the way I look at what's before my eyes is partly determined by what other artists have seen before me," she declares. "I don't understand why that's a mockery."

But Monica wears on you after a while. Her assumptions of superiority and moral rationalizations become insufferable. Her concluding comparison of herself to a conquering emperor sounds megalomaniac, and the context in which she does this, namely during her preparations for a climactic celebratory party, recalls the far better written novel by Virginia Woolf, "Mrs. Dalloway." As for the sex she has with B: there is so much of it that you begin to feel exhausted on behalf of the characters. This may be the first novel I've ever read where you skim the sex scenes to find the talky parts.

Finally, you have to ask, is what happens to Monica all that it would take to produce the great painter she clearly thinks she has become, or would several generations of a restructured society be required to fulfill the conditions she implies are needed to create great female artists? Whatever the answer, the connection between her experience and her sudden flowering is hard to see. Given her self-assertiveness, she seems just as likely to have discovered herself without the attentions of B.

As for what her self-assertiveness does to the novel, one can't help noting her comments on a Vermeer show she visits at the National Gallery of Art in Washington. (Despite her egalitarian belief that everyone should have equal access to Vermeer, she painfully accepts an invitation to see the exhibit before what she refers to as "the ordinary viewers" arrive.)

At the show, she is inspired by what she sees not because she wants to "paint like Vermeer in the technical sense." She continues: "What I wanted was more an example of something I would have to call moral; that sense of his getting out of the way of his own vision, of not coming between the spectator and what the spectator wanted to see, the graciousness of a withdrawal so complete that there was space between the viewer and the image that made room for the whole world. I was thinking about how to bring silence into my paintings."

Because of Monica's almost bullying presence in her story, there is no space for the spectator to see what really is happening. There is no silence for the reader to hear. Which is probably just as well, because without Monica's self-inflation, *Spending* might easily collapse into nothing.

Hilary Mantel (review date 8 March 1998)

SOURCE: "For Art's Sake," in *New York Times Book Review,* March 8, 1998, p. 5.

[*In the following review, Mantel offers tempered assessment of* Spending.]

Sex, art, money: that's what it's all about. So we learn in the neatly chiseled opening sentences of Mary Gordon's new novel. Add in death and we would have a ferocious quaternity to frame the action. But in Monica Szabo's world, death is the gracious suspension of breath that she finds in the works of the great masters of religious art. It is a death that is curiously lifelike, but she does not notice this until one or two life crises have come and gone.

Monica is a painter: middle-aged, well preserved, amicably divorced. She has twin children, age 20, both of them bright and capable girls, and she has a small but growing reputation. She is ambitious. No post-modern jokiness will do for her. She believes in her work, and she is scrupulous in placing a divide between herself and those with a thinner talent. They are not artists; let them keep galleries. The notion of the "Sunday painter" makes her squirm.

Day to day, Monica's need is for space and time. She has struggled hard to find "someplace to live that didn't look like Lee Harvey Oswald was brought up there." Teaching eats into her working week, her New York studio is poorly lighted, her summer rental in Provincetown is cramped. What sort of a painter would she be if these irritations were removed? Along comes a man, like a genie out of a bottle, and offers to let her find out.

B, as she calls him, is unattached, sexually dynamic. He would like to be an artist, but isn't, and so he offers to be her muse. Unlike the traditional female muse, he is very rich. He is a futures trader. Monica doesn't know what this is and remains incurious until the late stages of the book ("He might have been an alchemist or a blacksmith for all the understanding I had of what he did"). On the night of their first meeting, she and B begin a passionate affair. He offers her enough money to quit teaching, to travel, to rent a new studio. Caviar and silk camisoles shall be hers, and first-class flights to Italy, and nights and mornings of orgasmic bliss.

Misgivings set in. Is she a whore? Call yourself a sex worker, suggests the less sympathetic of her daughters. Money is something Monica hates to deal with, even the thought of it makes her queasy. She has always put her work first. What is the relationship between desire and inspiration? Which impulse will win—early morning sex or the need to be out of bed and in the studio when the light is at its best?

The reader's misgivings are perhaps more profound that Monica's. If you are a painter, a writer or a musician, it may be that your struggle with daily life lends an importance and dignity to your work that it would lack if the struggle suddenly ended. When the external challenges are removed, you have to confront the inner ones. Is your work important? Perhaps only the effort to do it makes it seem so. What happens when the artist gets "the clean slate," "the clear field"? The leisure to examine one's talent might result in the alarming conclusion that it is not so great after all. These difficulties are suggested, but Monica is not paralyzed by them. Instead, a major project overtakes her, the project that will be the making of her.

In "Sexual Personae," Camille Paglia argues that Michelangelo's "Dying Slave" looks not so much moribund as post-orgasmic. It is, she says, a "pagan crucifixion." Monica takes a further step, focusing on the figure of Christ deposed, Christ in that difficult interval between cross and burial. She studies the paintings of the great artists and notices the coy crossed ankles, the voluptuous gleam of light on ribs elegantly speared. She discerns an exhaustion that does not correspond to death so much as to post-coital languor. (If she had half an eye, she would ask herself whether it is in Pietà figures that Christ is most sexualized; but this would not fit the plot.) Monica begins a series of paintings called "Spent Men," which will reinterpret masterpieces of Renaissance art. She decides to use her lover as a life model for the exhausted God.

For this piece of daring—personal and artistic—she is rewarded with a sell-out show. Gordon is articulate about Monica's passion for "painting vision," about her efforts to find a place to stand and look at a tradition that is European and male. Monica succeeds in finding an idiom where her work will "include the relation of the past—art and faith—to the present," incorporating "the working female artist" who is "touched by the past but not shaped by it entirely. A light, indelible impression. Not a crushing hoof."

And Gordon herself, in writing distinguished by its freshness and grace, demonstrates a devoted attention to the visual. "All I could think about," Monica confesses at one point, "was green skies, skies with small, dingy, disengaged smoky clouds in them, like smudges underneath an eyelid. Mascara the morning after."

The difficulty comes when Monica loses the thread of her argument with herself. She has already noted that painting Christ is not like, for instance, painting Achilles. Her Roman Catholic girlhood tells her that its resonances are different. Why, then, is she surprised when her show is picketed by a Catholic pressure group? The reader is not.

Indeed, the book seems to lose its ambition to surprise. Conflicts—internal and external—arise only to be waited away. The threat from the Catholic protesters simply dissolves, and though Monica has to go on talk shows and otherwise debase herself, her reputation is only enhanced. B loses his money, but gets some more, and it doesn't matter anyway because by then Monica is rich in her own right and has decided she likes him and will help him out.

Monica's spiky personality entertains the reader, and Gordon uncovers in her layers and layers of ambivalence. But Monica's guilts as woman, as mother, are the routine ones, and don't go deep. Gordon's snappy wit keeps the reader interested ("Try and Relax is a three-word oxymoron"), yet the book is slowed to a crawl by its heroine's need for introspection. After the one-third mark, we should know Monica for ourselves, but every shift in her psyche is monitored, made explicit. The reader is given little credit for having paid attention.

Mary Gordon is an honest and perceptive writer. She shows these virtues in her dealings with the reader, but then she turns them into vices. She seems unwilling to take a short route to any conclusion that involves human beings and the way they behave. This endows her narrative with calmness, realism and grace. It takes away, though, the conflict and drive that should power it.

Monica feels bad, then good, then bad again. The cycle will stop just when the author chooses. We are being manipulated, after all. There are times, early in the story, when Monica is refreshingly unlikable, and Gordon is good at describing how the self-abnegating nature of creative art can look to family and lovers like plain old selfishness. But she admires her heroine too much.

Despite the variety of prettily written sex scenes, the novel's end is an anti-climax. It is as if, for example, in a Faustian pact story, the devil took the bond sealed in blood and lost it through a hole in his pocket. There is no interest, and ultimately no life, in a narrator who—as artist, feminist, lover—is born to win. Gordon has subtitled her book "A Utopian Divertimento." The point is taken; this is not real life, this is not how real life proceeds, this is a fairy tale. But we end with lip-smacking naturalism over pubic hair and pasta. An early indication of irony does not protect the novel from its final coziness.

Robert H. Bell (review date 10 April 1998)

SOURCE: "All Expenses Paid," in *Commonweal,* April 10, 1998, pp. 28-9.

[*In the following review, Bell offers positive evaluation of* Spending.]

Mary Gordon's new novel is immensely engaging fun, a delightful romp by an author distinguished for narratives of rigorous self-denial, harrowing disillusionment, and painful self-discovery. If anyone deserves a holiday from conscience and an interlude with the pleasure principle, it's the writer of ***Final Payments, The Company of Women,*** and the recent memoir, ***The Shadow Man.*** As its subtitle suggests, ***Spending*** locates us in the land of make-believe, what if, and once-upon-a-time.

Gordon's premise is delicious: what if a fifty-year-old painter, divorced mother of twin girls, were offered patronage, and much more, all her heart desires, by a wealthy, sexy, adoring benefactor? Thus "B" presents himself, irresistibly, to the dedicated, talented Monica Szabo, our narrator and heroine. Monica knows very clearly what she wants and rather less clearly what she is, an incurable narcissist. Floating into intimacy with B, she thinks, "You can't possibly lose. He's watching you and you're watching yourself. And you know there's nothing you can do that he won't like. Your body weighs nothing. It would be quite easy to fly up, and float away. He would watch you, flying up, floating away, not at all surprised because the whole time he'd thought you were miraculous." ***Spending*** is "The Unbelievable Lightness of Being."

Gordon magically releases Monica from the restrictions of reality and cleverly reverses conventional patterns. Instead of being the objectified object of the male gaze, Monica stars in her own show. She is the maker, he is the model. What she creates is, like Monica herself, outrageous and irresistible, a series of postcoital variations on classic versions of Christ's passion (her theory being that the Christs of the old masters represented *le petit mort*). Hence the title of her series, "Spent Men," and the punning title of Gordon's novel.

B views Monica as miraculous. "I think you're a very, very good painter. I think one day you might be great." "When you were younger did you think you looked like Hedy Lamarr?" When she momentarily worries that she could afford to lose ten pounds, doting B responds, "My God, you don't know much, for all you think you know. Don't you know the incredible power of what you've got there? Of the appeal of that endless responsiveness, and all its variety?" Even his gesture, "you don't know much," yields to a paean of praise. To hear such stuff is a major motive to fall in love.

But B, love-struck, blind to cellulite and sag, not to mention his beloved's vanity and egocentricity, isn't the only character who feels Monica's "incredible power" and "appeal." A former student presents Monica with a bouquet. Her sister Helena says to B, "We have something else in common. We both think my sister's a great painter." Viewing Monica's new series, "Spent Men," Monica's agent exclaims, "It's the most exciting work I've seen in a long time. I knew the idea was great but the execution is a triumph." Monica has an insatiable need for praise, an urgent, incessant throb. She's got it half-right when she comments, "Maybe I have trouble accepting praise because my hunger for it is so boundless." She's closer to the artist's dirty little secret when she admits what she'd *really* like to hear: "Every other living painter's work is shit. Yours, only yours, is gold."

I found Monica a fully realized, compelling, intriguing figure. She describes the process of painting and works of art with vivid, passionate fervor. She's very nearly as persuasive depicting really good sex as she is describing Vermeer. And she is persistently smart and funny: "Nothing marks the death of desire like the moment when you find yourself thinking that the ex-wife had a point." Another of Monica's endearing qualities is a tenderness for humankind, including males.

A vibrant novel, *Spending* has limited ambitions and effects, and it eventually runs out of steam. Monica's benefactor B is insubstantial and flagrantly fantastic: a rock of support, a geyser of praise, a faithful, worshipful lover, amusing but never threatening, a Wall Street futures trader who wittily quotes T. S. Eliot, and who is ready, willing, and able to drop everything and serve Monica's purposes. Financing her project and modeling her subjects, he is her sugar daddy, spending lover, and savior. When his herniated disk requires Monica's ministration and some erotic accommodation, B is only temporarily grumpy and the problem just disappears. If only! So full of loving-kindness and devoted patience is B that he is an apt model of Christ.

Monica seems too abundantly endowed, the recipient of excessive authorial affection and regard, or perhaps an idealized, privileged surrogate for the author. (She's a wonderful synthesis of Lily Briscoe and Mrs. Ramsay in Woolf's *To the Lighthouse*). Monica is not only romantically and artistically enabled but blissfully freed from the exigencies of reality. Swimming naked, Monica thinks, "Movement is utterly easy; you're working against nothing, what you're in wants you to move in it, with it, it offers no resistance, only help." Encountering no resistance enables floating and fantasy but limits fiction and life. Without more intractability—vulnerabilities, inconsistency, orneriness—there's inadequate conflict between what Yeats terms "the perfection of the life or of the work." *Spending* romanticizes artistic experience without studying the costs of artistic commitment. Monica's adventures are amusing and entertaining but not richly dramatic. Still, if you're looking for an artful indulgence of appetite, and a joyous spring fling, *Spending* is your ticket. Soon, I predict, to be a major motion picture.

E. M. Broner (review date July 1998)

SOURCE: "Pigment of the Imagination," in *The Women's Review of Books,* Vol. XV, Nos. 10-11, July, 1998, pp. 25-6.

[*In the following review, Broner offers favorable assessment of* Spending.]

Mary Gordon has always taken on strong enemies: the church, memory, family. She is not averse to taking on the big bad boys either. Reviewing Norman Mailer's *The Gospel According to the Son* last year in *The Nation,* she wondered how he "could have the audacity to do something there was no need to do . . . that no one particularly wanted, that he knew nothing about and that he wasn't well suited for." Knocking out that kind of pugilistic male is no sweat for her.

She has created exactly the opposite in this book: a male supportive of the woman hero's work. *Spending* is a fairy tale with a Prince Charming (referred to as B, only named after he's earned it). Cinderella is Monica Szabo, smart-mouthed, a gifted artist and independent woman with too little time, too many jobs and inadequate studio space. Later there will be a fairy godmother who will save both prince and princess.

The title is clearly about money and sex, both to the point of exhaustion and total consumption. *The American Heritage* Dictionary defines spend as "To pass (time) . . . To throw away, waste, squander, to pay out or expend money," and *spent* as "consumed; used up; expended." But Gordon is too sophisticated and knowledgeable to confine herself to definition. Monica insists on defining herself, all the time, to everyone, herself, her twin daughters and her "Muse," the patron. (To him: "I didn't have to tell him that at my age I'd had rather a lot of sex. . . . [S]ometimes I wanted work more than love.")

Monica throws out a challenge at a show of her work: Where oh where is the male muse? There have always been female muses, servicing their lovers with sex and food, used as objects, as models. We have trained our daughters to be muses but not our sons. Suddenly a man—handsome and wealthy, it goes without saying—raises his hand. He will be the Muse. It will solve everything.

But from then on the conflicts are between independence and accepting a patron, between counting one's time as one's own to make art and repaying the Muse by making time for love. The demands Monica makes of B enlarge. Soon she finds she needs him not only as patron and lover but as model.

Watching B spent, after sex, Monica reflects:

> [H]e was sitting like Jesus in Carpaccio's *Meditation on Christ's Passion.* That relaxed weight, the heaviness. The loss of regard. The position of the limbs, the hands and feet. . . . The face unexpressive. . . .

I began thinking about other dead Christs, Pontormo's, Mantegna's. . . . And suddenly, I had an idea. Suppose all those dead Christs weren't dead, just postorgasmic?

That is the beginning of her series of paintings, *Spent Men, After the Masters.* The idea is playful and outrageous: what can possibly happen next, the reader wonders? Because it's a fairy tale, of course the paintings are completed, the show is sold out, there are great reviews in the *New York Times* and Monica discomfits her opponent from the Catholic Defense League, both invited for a public sparring on the *Charlie Rose Show.*

Every scene is visual. Monica describes one of her works: there is a

kind of spacy gray green. And a shadow of a table. In the foreground, a man wearing only his underwear, a very beautiful pair of green and white striped silk boxer shorts. I had a wonderful time doing those shorts, the pearliness of the white, absorbing that dim light, and the green stripes, the green of an Anjou pear, but waxier. . . .

Only subtly do we learn that the model has an erection, "a lot of brush work, a swelling and then just the tenderest hint of pink."

There is steamy and satisfying sex—on everything and everywhere: on beds, airplanes, movie theatres, on the Upper West Side, in a cottage on Cape Cod, in hotels in Washington, Milan and Rome. But in each place, there is also the satisfaction of looking for a long time at art— Vermeer in Washington at the National Gallery, or the Christs at the Metropolitan Museum of Art and in various museums in Italy where Monica's lover takes her for inspiration.

Everywhere the writer "paints" still lifes:

He laid the table on the deck with the yellow pottery. The table was cast-iron and glass, the chairs cast-iron. . . . He brought in royal blue place mats and napkins. The silver was Vienna Secessionist, I thought. There was coffee in a white pot, and a platter with slices of honeydew, cantaloupe and Persian melon arranged alternately.

One does not know which to enjoy more, the sexuality or the sensuality. Even the weather thrills:

It was 7:00, the twentieth of August. Two weeks before there wouldn't have been even a suggestion of dusk, but now there was and with it the slight anxiety of coming nightfall, or the end of one more precious summer day. The grass was damp and the air had a peppery smell.

Or the rare accuracy in the physicality of making of art:

My body felt used, worn out, fatigued, dirty, and yet overwrought. . . .

After working like that, I feel I have filth all over my hands, and at the same time I'm incandescent.

Monica is self-made, self-willed; she has always been responsible, moderate in her choices and independent. But now she changes from thrifty to spendthrift, gleefully going on spending sprees. In Milan she is offered clothing which "no living woman could possibly wear":

Shoes made of glass and metal, skirts of feathers, jackets of acid green or kumquat leather. But then we saw the pearl gray camisole that turned us both on. He bought it for me; we didn't look at what it cost. He bought a belt. I bought a scarf, the color of blue hydrangeas.

They spend and spend, and suddenly there's no more. The Muse is not amused. And is doubly deprived of his power. What can possibly happen next? Only a reversal of fortune, a role change, will do.

Despite the fun, *Spending* is not a summer beach book— though it would certainly be a turn-on to read while being oiled on a beach towel. But it's too smart. (Monica says of B's ex-wife, "If Brillo could talk, this is what it would sound like.") And it's too wise. Gordon can't help dishing out the metaphysics:

I've often thought that the problem of foolishness is more metaphysically vexing than the problem of evil. Evil is a hard dark point, or a hypnotizing vortex; it's humbling; you can learn something from it, if it doesn't destroy you. . . . But foolishness is an unworthy adversary; it just smothers you in its wet thickness.

Most of all, what carries this work above fantasy— "utopian," as Gordon calls it, or "an entertainment," as Mary Cantwell described it in *Vogue,* or even something megalomaniacal and Napoleonic, as the crusty, cranky critic said in the daily *New York Times*—is the truth of work, the knowledge of art. That's what keeps Gordon's mouthy, funny, prickly Monica always on earth.

FURTHER READING

Criticism

Akins, Ellen. "Worlds of Possibility." *Los Angeles Times Book Review* (29 August 1993): 2, 9.
   A positive review of *The Rest of Life.*

Becker, Alida. "The Arts of Love." *Washington Post Book World* (31 March 1985): 6.
   A positive review of *Men and Angels.*

Cooper-Clark, Diana. "An Interview with Mary Gordon." *Commonweal* (9 May 1980): 270-3.
   Gordon discusses her literary influences, religious views, and the critical reception of *Final Payments.*

Earnshaw, Doris. Review of *Good Boys and Dead Girls and Other Essays,* by Mary Gordon. *World Literature Today* 66, No. 2 (Spring 1992): 349-50.

A positive review of *Good Boys and Dead Girls*.

Eder, Richard. "Harp Harpy and Her Brood." *Los Angeles Times Book Review* (22 October 1989): 3, 12.
A tempered review of *The Other Side*.

Eder, Richard. Review of *Men and Angels*, by Mary Gordon. *Los Angeles Times Book Review* (14 April 1985): 3, 7.
An unfavorable review of *Men and Angels*.

Flanagan, Mary. "Threnody for Marriage." *New Statesman and Society* (2 February 1990): 34.
A positive review of *The Other Side*.

Gray, Paul. "Daughters." *Time* (20 April 1987): 74.
A favorable review of *Temporary Shelter*.

Gray, Paul. "Meditations on Motherhood." *Time* (1 April 1985): 77.
An unfavorable review of *Men and Angels*.

Hughes, Kathryn. "Great Divides." *New Statesman & Society* (28 January 1994): 38-9.
A favorable review of *The Rest of Life*.

Kakutani, Michiko. "After Faith and Family, Stories of Sexual Love." *The New York Times* (3 August 1993): C17.
A favorable review of *The Rest of Life*.

Kakutani, Michiko. "How Could He Have Been Her Wonderful Father?" *The New York Times* (3 May 1996): C29.
A positive review of *The Shadow Man*.

Kakutani, Michiko. "Past Traced to the Present in a Family's Intricate Story." *The New York Times* (10 October 1989): C21.
A positive review of *The Other Side*.

Kaye-Kantrowitz, Melanie. "In the New New World." *The Women's Review of Books* VII, No. 7 (April 1990): 7-9.
A positive review of *The Other Side*.

Knapp, Mona. Review of *The Rest of Life*, by Mary Gordon. *World Literature Today* 69, No. 1 (Winter 1995): 139.

A positive review of *The Rest of Life*.

Lehmann-Haupt, Christopher. "Books of the Times." *The New York Times* (9 April 1987): C25.
A positive review of *Temporary Shelter*.

Leonard, John. Review of *The Other Side*, by Mary Gordon. *The Nation* (27 November 1989): 653, 655.
A favorable review of *The Other Side*.

Milton, Edith. "Essayists of the Eighties." *The Women's Review of Books* VIII, Nos. 10-11 (July 1991): 20-1.
A positive review of *Good Boys and Dead Girls*.

O'Rourke, William. "A Father Father Figure." *The Nation* (28 February 1981): 245-6.
A negative review of *The Company of Women*.

Phillips, Robert. "A Language for Compassion." *Commonweal* (17 May 1985): 308-9.
A positive review of *Men and Angels*.

Reed, Kit. "The Devlins and Their Discontents." *Washington Post Book World* (8 October 1989): 4.
A tempered review of *The Other Side*.

Ruta, Suzanne. "Feet of Clay." *The Women's Review of Books* XIII, Nos. 10-11 (July 1996): 26-7.
A review of *The Shadow Man*.

See, Carolyn. Review of *Temporary Shelter*, by Mary Gordon. *Los Angeles Times Book Review* (12 July 1987): 10.
A positive review of *Temporary Shelter*.

Sheppard, R. Z. "A Prodigal Daughter Returns." *Time* (16 February 1981): 79.
A positive review of *The Company of Women*.

Skow, John. "Dad Revisited." *Time* (27 May 1996): 82-3.
A tempered review of *The Shadow Man*.

Weeks, Brigitte. "Group Portrait with Felicitas." *Washington Post Book World* (22 February 1981): 3.
A positive review of *The Company of Women*.

Additional coverage of Gordon's life and career is contained in the following sources published by the Gale Group: *Contemporary Authors*, **Vol. 102;** *Contemporary Authors New Revision Series*, **Vol. 44;** *Dictionary of Literary Biography*, **Vol. 6;** *Dictionary of Literary Biography Yearbook*, **Vol. 81; and** *Major 20th-Century Writers*.

Pope John Paul II
1920-

(Karol Wojtyla; also wrote under pseudonym Andrzej Jawien) Polish theologian, nonfiction writer, essayist, dramatist, critic, and poet.

The following entry presents an overview of Pope John Paul II's literary career through 1998.

INTRODUCTION

The first non-Italian pope in 455 years and the first Slavic pope ever, Pope John Paul II is internationally renowned as a devoted missionary for peace and the dynamic spiritual and moral leader of nearly one billion Roman Catholics worldwide. Ordained as pontiff in 1978, the former Cardinal Karol Wojtyla of Krakow—also a poet, playwright, and professor—is regarded as a formidable intellectual and radical conservative whose religious perspective is equally informed by Thomism and twentieth-century philosophy, particularly Marxism, existentialism, and phenomenology. A firm proponent of traditional theological strictures against sex out of wedlock, contraception, abortion, homosexuality, and the ordination of women, he has elicited much controversy for his uncompromising stand against the secularization of the church and strong criticism of moral degradation under both communist and capitalist economic systems. As "the strong conscience of the whole Christian world" and "the greatest of our modern popes," according to the Reverend Billy Graham, John Paul has attracted millions of Catholic and non-Catholic admirers through his warm personal style, his devotion to the cause of social justice and human dignity, and dedication to direct ministration before mass congregations around the world.

BIOGRAPHICAL INFORMATION

Born Karol Wojtyla in Wadowice, Poland, John Paul was the younger of two sons raised by devout Catholic parents. His mother, of Lithuanian descent, died when John Paul was nine and his father, a retired army officer, died in 1941. As a child John Paul excelled at school and athletics, developing lifelong passions for skiing, hiking, and canoeing. In 1938 he began studies in literature and philosophy at Jagiellonian University in Krakow, where he wrote poetry and participated in semiprofessional theater productions as an actor and playwright. During the Nazi occupation of Poland, John Paul worked as a laborer in a quarry and at a chemical factory while continuing his artistic activities. He wrote his first (now lost) play, *David,*

in 1939 and two others, *Job* and *Jeremiah,* in 1940. He cofounded the underground Rhapsodic Theater, or "theater of the word," with Mieczyslaw Kotlarczyk and appeared in more than twenty productions during the Second World War. In 1942 John Paul began clandestine studies for the priesthood at a seminary in Krakow. Following his ordination in 1944, he earned a doctorate in theology from Jagiellonian University in 1948 and continued postgraduate study under conservative French theologian Reginald Garrigou-Lagrange at the Pontifical Angelicum University in Rome; he completed a thesis on St. John of the Cross in 1950 and a habilitation thesis on the philosophy of Max Scheler in 1957.

John Paul worked as a university chaplain and professor of moral philosophy at Catholic University in Lublin, Poland, until his appointment as auxiliary bishop of Krakow in 1958. He was elevated to vicar capitular of the archdiocese of Krakow in 1962, archbishop of Krakow in 1964, and bestowed cardinalship by Pope Paul VI in 1967. During the 1960s and 1970s, John Paul participated in the

Second Vatican Council and rose to prominence at international bishops synods. He also published several plays, including *Sklep Jubüerski* (1960; *The Jeweler's Shop*), and the noted ethical and theological works *Milose i odpowiedzialnosc* (1960; *Love and Responsibility*), *Osoba i czyn* (1969; *The Acting Person*), and *Znaki sprzecznosci* (1976; *Sign of Contradiction*). John Paul served continuously as archbishop of Krakow until his appointment as Supreme Pontiff of the Roman Catholic Church on October 16, 1978. He succeeded Pope Paul VI and Pope John Paul I, both of whom died only months apart in 1978, to become the 264th pope in Church history and, at age fifty-eight, the youngest of the twentieth century. In 1979 he initiated the first of numerous international pilgrimages with a trip to Latin America. In 1981 John Paul survived a near fatal assassination attempt in St. Peter's Square at the Vatican. During the 1980s, he was an important catalyst in the democratic reforms that swept Eastern Europe, particularly the Solidarity movement in his native Poland, and met with numerous world leaders and heads of states. Despite weakened physical health since the early 1990s—it is widely reported that he suffers from Parkinson's disease—John Paul maintains a rigorous travel itinerary and remains an active proponent of world peace. His fluency in multiple languages, including Italian, English, German, French, and Spanish, in addition to Latin and his native tongue, has enabled him to speak directly to a large international audience.

MAJOR WORKS

John Paul wrote six plays between 1939 and 1964, five of which are contained in *The Collected Plays and Writings on Theater* (1987), along with several essays on drama. His early dramatic works, *Job* and *Jeremiah,* are written in verse and draw upon biblical themes to portray the suffering and martyrdom of the Polish nation during the Second World War; the first is modeled on Greek tragedy, the second on Symbolist theater. *Our God's Brother,* written during the late 1940s, centers upon the life of Adam Chmielowski (1845-1916), a Polish artist, political dissident, and advocate for the homeless known as Brother Albert whom he greatly admired. Characteristic of John Paul's "inner theater," this work exhibits a minimum of external dramatic action, focusing instead on the protagonist's spiritual conflicts and philosophical concerns in nonlinear progression. His last two dramas, *The Jeweler's Shop* and *The Radiation of Fatherhood* (1964), are comprised of long, interrelated monologues and meditations that resemble mystery plays in their archetypal themes and characterizations. *The Jeweler's Shop,* published under the pseudonym Andrzej Jawien, focuses on the separate relationships of three couples and their struggles with love, alienation, and parenthood.

Easter Vigil and Other Poems (1979) and *Collected Poems* (1982) contain English translations of his poetry, much of which was published in Catholic periodicals under the Jawien pseudonym. John Paul's overarching ethical,

philosophical, and religious principles are put forth in *The Acting Person,* a culmination of a decade's research and reflection in which he synthesizes elements of Thomism, existentialism, and phenomenology into a complex foundation for moral action. While defending the free will of the individual and maintaining that human experience is essentially understood in terms of action, he rails against Cartesian subjectivism and dismisses the existentialist notion that action itself defines the person. Drawing upon Aristotelian metaphysics, John Paul attempts to establish objective principles of right and wrong action by which the individual acts autonomously to qualitatively improve or degrade his or her life. According to John Paul, the highest order of self-determination and personal fulfillment is achieved through integration with others and participatory activity toward the common good. *Sign of Contradiction* consists of discourses presented to Pope Paul VI and the Roman Curia during a 1976 Lenten retreat. Drawing upon a wide array of scriptural, literary, and philosophical sources, including the early church fathers, St. Augustine, Shakespeare, Martin Heidegger, and Albert Camus, John Paul condemns totalitarianism, Western consumerism, and Third World poverty as primary sources of human suffering in the contemporary world. He also asserts that Jesus did not intend for his disciples to engage in overt political action, reflecting his disavowal of the Liberation Theology movement of Latin America. John Paul presents his views on love, marriage, and sexuality in *Love and Responsibility,* which derives from his university lectures, and *Fruitful and Responsible Love* (1979), based on an address delivered at a Milan conference on birth control in 1978. While extolling the sanctity of conjugal love in each, he condemns contraception, premarital and extramarital sex, and divorce. In *Love and Responsibility* he underscores the importance of transcendent love as a prerequisite for physical communion and warns against the exploitative objectification of one's partner for the sake of carnal gratification. Pleasure and procreation may coexist, he contends, but only among married partners who share a profound loving connection that supercedes the sex act itself.

In addition to his numerous addresses and apostolic letters, John Paul's major theological pronouncements are contained in his papal encyclicals. His first, *Redemptor Hominis* (1979; *The Redeemer of Man*), introduces John Paul's characteristic personal tone and international concern for the collective well-being and salvation of humanity, particularly the poor and disenfranchised in communist, capitalist, and Third World countries. In subsequent encyclicals he addressed spiritual aspects of labor (*Laborem Exercens,* 1981; *On Human Work*), the prohibition against the ordination of women as priests (*Mulieris Dignitatem,* 1988; *The Dignity and Vocation of Women*), the vying ambitions of Marxism and capitalism (*Sollicitudo Rei Socialis,* 1988; *The Social Concern of the Church*), the need for social justice in free market economies (*Centesimus Annus,* 1991; *On the Hundredth Anniversary*), the reunification of the Christian church (*Ut Unum Sint,* 1995; *That All May Be One*), and reaffirmed

Catholic moral tradition against relativism and revisionists (*Veritatis Splendor,* 1994; *The Splendor of Truth*). John Paul also offers insight into his religious and historical perspective in *"Be Not Afraid!"* (1984), an interview with French journalist André Frossard, and the international bestseller *Crossing the Threshold of Hope* (1994), which consists of John Paul's responses to questions on personal, theological, and metaphysical topics posed by Italian journalist Vittorio Messori.

CRITICAL RECEPTION

John Paul is admired throughout the world for his universal message of hope and numerous diplomatic peace missions. His literary experiments, moral philosophy, and papal writings have earned him recognition as a profound thinker who is equally at home with the modern philosophy and social theories of Scheler, Camus, John-Paul Sartre, and Paul Ricoeur as with the Bible and medieval theology. Though the revered figurehead of the Roman Catholic church, he has generated considerable controversy among both clergy and laity due to his unwavering opposition to abortion, birth control, artificial fertilization, homosexuality, and the ordination of women. His progressive detractors within the church, particularly in Holland and the United States, view his stand on these issues as archaic, sexist, and unnecessarily exclusionary. However, both supporters and critics alike praise his exceptional moral courage and integrity, for which he was honored as *Time* magazine's "Man of the Year" in 1994. As many critics note, John Paul's experiences under Nazi and communist regimes forged his abiding personal stake in the defense of political freedom and human rights. Commenting on John Paul's "prophetic humanism," Avery Dulles writes in *America,* "He is conscious of speaking to a world that is in the throes of crisis—a crisis of dehumanization. Like most prophets, he senses that he is faced with enormous opposition and that his is perhaps a lonely voice. He is not afraid to confront others in his struggle to salvage human dignity." John Paul has also won respect for his impressive erudition and intellectual rigor. Noting the sophistication of his commentary in *Crossing the Threshold of Hope,* a book ostensibly intended for a mass audience, Peter Steinfels writes in *Commonweal,* "it is justifiably satisfying that the current successor of Peter takes it for granted that serious questions demand not just piety and good will but also knowledge and intellectual effort."

PRINCIPAL WORKS

David (drama) 1939

Job (drama) 1940

Jeremiah (drama) 1940

Quaestio de fide apud s. Joannem a Cruce [as Karol Wojtyla; *Faith According to St. John of the Cross*] (doctoral thesis) 1950

Ocena mozliwoœci zbudowania etyki chrzeœcijañskiej przy zakozeniach systemu Maksa Schelera [as Karol Wojtyla; *An Evaluation of the Possibility of Constructing Christian Ethics on the Assumptions of Max Scheler's Philosophical System*] (doctoral thesis) 1957

Milose i odpowiedzialnosc: Studium etyczne [as Karol Wojtyla; *Love and Responsibility*] (philosophy) 1960

Sklep Jubüerski [as Andrzej Jawien; *The Jeweler's Shop*] (drama) 1960

Osoba i czyn [as Karol Wojtyla; *The Acting Person*] (philosophy) 1969

Znaki sprzecznosci [as Karol Wojtyla; *Sign of Contradiction*] (philosophy) 1976

Fruitful and Responsible Love (addresses) 1979

Easter Vigil and Other Poems [as Karol Wojtyla] (poetry) 1979

Redemptor Hominis [*The Redeemer of Man*] (encyclical) 1979

Dives in Misericordia [*On the Mercy of God*] (encyclical) 1980

Laborem Exercens [*On Human Work*] (encyclical) 1981

Collected Poems [as Karol Wojtyla] (poetry) 1982

"Be Not Afraid!": André Frossard in Conversation with Pope John Paul II (interview) 1984

Prayers and Devotions from Pope John Paul II: Selected Passages from His Writings and Speeches Arranged for Every Day of the Year (prayers) 1984

Slavorum Apostoli (encyclical) 1985

Dominum et Vivificantem (encyclical) 1986

The Collected Plays and Writings on Theater [as Karol Wojtyla] (drama and essays) 1987

Redemptoris Mater [*Mother of the Redeemer*] (encyclical) 1987

Sollicitudo Rei Socialis [*The Social Concern of the Church*] (encyclical) 1988

Mulieris Dignitatem [*The Dignity and Vocation of Women*] (encyclical) 1988

Centesimus Annus [*On the Hundredth Anniversary*] (encyclical) 1991

Crossing the Threshold of Hope (interview) 1994

Veritatis Splendor [*The Splendor of Truth*] (encyclical) 1994

Evangelium Vitae [*The Gospel of Life*] (encyclical) 1995

Ut Unum Sint [*That All May Be One*] (encyclical) 1995

Fides et ratio [*Faith and Reason*] (encyclical) 1998

CRITICISM

J. M. Cameron (review date 3 May 1979)

SOURCE: "Where the New Pope Stands," in *New York Review of Books,* May 3, 1979, pp. 14-20.

[*In the following review, Cameron examines John Paul's leadership, social vision, and thought in* Sign of Contradiction.]

Interest in the Papacy has increased since the short pontificate of John XXIII. The good nature and charm of John were irresistible. As a personality Paul VI was less expansive; the task of presiding over the consequences of the second Vatican Council was something he did with great ability, but he found it tormenting, and this was evident in the tone of his later speeches, plaintive, passionate, mournful. John Paul I was an instant success: it seemed as though Don Camillo had become Pope (just as John XXIII, in his humanity and holiness, seemed to have come out of the pages of *I Promessi Sposi*); but we had scarcely begun to enjoy his gentle belletrist approach to spiritual problems when death took him. (*Illustrissimi*, with its letters to Dickens, Scott, Saint Bernard, Goldoni, Figaro, Luke the Evangelist, and others, has a distinctively nineteenth-century charm).

Now, with John Paul II, we are presented with one who is altogether formidable: younger than his fifty-eight years, strong in body and mind, familiar with the political world of Eastern Europe, intensely masculine, a man of humble background and a former manual worker, well-educated, much better acquainted with modern philosophical thought than his immediate predecessors, a respectable poet, a weighty contributor to the Vatican II debates. The most immediately striking thing about him is that he is a Pole, a former archbishop of Krakow.

The Poles are a singular people in the contemporary world. Their national consciousness and their consciousness as Catholics are hard to prize apart. This is a fact so influential that the communist government finds itself, perhaps a little to its own surprise, giving the Church an amount of recognition without parallel in Eastern Europe or anywhere else under communist rule. Cardinal Wojtyla's own vivid feeling as a Pole—what it would scarcely be too strong to call his romanticism—overflowed into his first sermon as Pope, when, at the end, he turned to those who had come from Krakow to the Mass of his inauguration.

> What shall I say to you who come from my Krakow, from the see of St. Stanislaus of whom I was the unworthy successor for fourteen years . . .? Everything that I could say would fade into insignificance compared with what my heart feels at this moment. . . . I ask you: be with me at Jasna Gora and everywhere. Do not cease to be with the Pope who today prays with the words of the poet: "Mother of God, you who defend bright Czestochowa and shine at Ostrabrama." . . .

Sign of Contradiction appeared first in Italian in 1977. It is a set of discourses given during a retreat held for the Pope (Paul VI) and some of his collaborators. As Cardinal Wyszynski noted in his foreword to the Italian edition, it is free from professional jargon. The standpoint is solidly traditional, the way of handling problems fresh and direct. The range of reference is what distinguishes it from other works of this genre. As well as the references one would expect to Scripture, Augustine, Thomas, there are many references to the early Fathers. Irenaeus is clearly a favorite: his "The glory of God is man alive" is one of the

sayings to which he returns often. Of modern theologians the one he seems to find most sympathetic is Henri de Lubac, the leading figure among the Jesuits of the Lyon school; it is ironical that this group of men had a rough time under Pius XII. Then, there are references to Shakespeare and Goethe, to Feuerbach and to Rahner, Heidegger, Camus, Kolakowski, Ricoeur, and other contemporary thinkers. He has read much, and widely, and profited from his reading.

The following points in *Sign of Contradiction* seem of interest, as indicating John Paul II's style of thought.

He doesn't think that to be poor or to be oppressed by a dictatorship is the worst thing that can happen to a man. It is worse still to be "caught in the toils of consumerism and a prey to the hunger for status symbols that divides both the world and the hearts of men." He is anxious to avoid any kind of clericalism (this also came out in his Mexican speeches). In social and political matters the leading role should in principle be that of the laity. He seems to stress, as the great human evils of our time, first, totalitarianism, "the age of the concentration camp and the oven," then, the confusions and frustrations of men living in opulence in the liberal societies, lastly, the conditions of life in the Third World. Finally, there is an analysis of the policies of nominally Christian societies.

> The great poverty of many peoples, first and foremost the poverty of the peoples of the Third World, hunger, economic exploitation, colonialism—which is not confined to the Third World—all this is a form of opposition to Christ on the part of the powerful, irrespective of political regimes and cultural traditions. This form of contradiction of Christ often goes hand-in-hand with a partial acceptance of religion, of Christianity and the Church, an acceptance of Christ as an element present in culture, morality and even education.

The man who has no illusions about the nature of the people's democracies has no illusions about Western Europe and North America.

Judgments on the Pope and his policy must necessarily be tentative and provisional. His striking personality, as it moves the masses on the television screen, in the images of the press, in St. Peter's Square or in Mexico, is something that hasn't been seen, in such an office, for a very long time. The image—the figure in a Mexican hat carrying a small child, the pastor who breaks the protocol of centuries to bless the marriage of the daughter of a Roman garbage collector, the Pope who says "I," not "We," all the time and eschews the bland, obfuscating rhetoric of the curial speechwriters—is not so much a creation of the media as a gift to them. It is certainly not fabricated by Vatican image-makers, who, as working journalists will testify, have no skill in public relations and almost always make a botch of important occasions. No doubt some of the force of Wojtyla's effect springs from his being the first non-Italian Pope for so long and from his being, as it were, a veteran of famous wars in Eastern Europe. The expectations are so great that some are certain to be disappointed from time to time and in connection with this issue or that.

The visit to the conference of Latin American bishops at Puebla, in Mexico, was the first major test of his sagacity. What he had to say baffled much of the press and no final verdicts have as yet come in. The early reporting seemed intent upon deciding whether or not the Pope was "for" or "against" Liberation Theology. It wasn't made clear what this theology might be or if indeed there is a single school to which the label rightly belongs. It was generally known that under many of the military regimes in Latin America the Church had become a major factor in opposing the repressive policies of these regimes, a refuge for those hunted by the secret police, a defender of the collective enterprises of peasants, a protector of the rights of the native Indians. And it was also known that a considerable number of priests and religious, and even an occasional bishop, had been arrested, imprisoned, roughed up, tortured, killed by the police of the military dictators. It was also known that Latin American Catholics, especially the bishops, were divided about the wisdom of the policies that had led to such confrontations between the Church and the military rulers.

What isn't known and what even close students of the region are not agreed upon is how the socio-political situation of the Latin American countries is to be analyzed and what the remedy for the social and economic evils may be. There is a large amount of what looks like paranoia. External forces are sometimes blamed almost exclusively for the horrors, though of course the actual interventions of the CIA and of Castro are indisputable. Middle-class groups, where they exist in strength (notably in Chile), seem to lack basic skills in sustaining parliamentary regimes, and, terrified of "communism," place their liberties in the hands of soldiers and policemen. In some areas industrial and large-scale agricultural development is advancing at a great rate—Brazil is the obvious example—with all the suffering and social dislocation and inequality such development brings with it. The most evident sign of the dislocation caused by these changes and of the ineptitude of existing social elites is the growth, around all the great cities, of shanty towns, *bidonvilles,* with populations drawn from a countryside that has been neglected or given over to large scale farming.

The Puebla conference came ten years after the Medellin conference of the Latin American bishops. The Medellin conference, the conclusions of which were approved by Paul VI, though not by some of his Vatican advisers, has been described as "a decisive milestone in contemporary theology, inasmuch as it situated the full and integral liberation of mankind squarely at the center of Christian reflection and practice, not only in Latin America but in much of the rest of the world." From Medellin came the confrontation of the Church with the regimes, deep changes in the structure of religious communities, a variety of impressive personalities who seemed to incarnate the plight of Latin America (Dom Helder Camara is the best known in North America and Europe), and a great many new theological tendencies all brought under the umbrella-term Liberation Theology.

Nothing could have saved Puebla from being anticlimactic after Medellin; progress was disappointing and patchy, bishops were still divided, there was a savage backlash from sections of the Catholic bourgeoisie who patronize terrorist movements dedicated to the rescue of property, family, country. Some liberation themes seemed to have run into the sand; and as so often in the contemporary climate of thought, the discovery that the overcoming of great evils is a slow process provoked rage in some. John Paul II's decision to go to Puebla didn't save the conference from all its difficulties, but it gave it the world's attention.

The Pope's speech to the Puebla conference is a complex but not an evasive statement. It has to be taken as a whole, but to stress the following points will, I hope, reflect without too much distortion the emphases of the speech. Against the type of liberation theology that tries to bring Catholicism close to Marxism, treating the moment of revolution as a surrogate for the day of judgment, he urges that the "idea of Christ as a political figure, a revolutionary, as the subversive man from Nazareth" has no connection with the Church's tradition and goes against the evidence of the New Testament. At the center of preaching is the truth that (he argues) is peculiar to Christianity:

> The truth that we owe to man is . . . a truth about man. As witnesses of Jesus Christ we are heralds, spokesmen and servants of this truth. We cannot reduce it to the principles of a system of philosophy or to pure political activity. We cannot forget it or betray it.

(One remembers his moving Christmas Day sermon in which he invited us to attend, in the darkness of the first Christmas night, to "the wailing of the child," as to the cry of suffering humanity taken into the mystery of God's love; and one recalls his picking out of Irenaeus's aphorism. "The glory of God is man alive.")

He has, at the same time, a strong statement against the violation of human rights under all regimes. He links—doesn't divide—evangelization and social advancement and reaffirms what was said at Medellin about this. He argues that the Church has no business linking her mission to "ideological systems," and should "stay free with regard to the competing systems, in order to opt only for man."

> Whatever the miseries or sufferings that afflict man, it is not through violence, the interplay of power and political systems, but through the truth concerning man that he journeys towards a better future.

He attacks the "mechanisms that . . . produce on the international level rich people ever more rich at the expense of poor people ever more poor"; and argues that no theoretical device for changing this situation is likely to be effective unless there is a passion for justice.

Finally, we sense in John Paul II, here as in other of his speeches and writings, a strong feeling against clericalism in any form—it seems he sees an incipient clericalism in some radical trends among the clergy. Priests are not as such political leaders, nor are they servants of the state. "It is necessary to avoid supplanting the laity. . . . Is it not the laity who are called, by reason of their vocation in the Church, to make their contribution in the political and economic dimensions, and to be effectively present in the safeguarding and advancement of human rights?" Here the Pope is surely endorsing the policy of forming basic lay communities able to function largely without clerical leadership and concerning themselves with giving actual help to the poor and raising questions of social justice. Such communities have flourished in Brazil and it is perhaps not an accident that some of the most resourceful bishops (notably Cardinal Lortscheider) come from that country.

There was one startling omission from the Puebla speech, and from the other speeches in Mexico. Nothing was said about the many Christians who have suffered in the prisons and torture chambers of Latin America, and have died in defense of human rights and their Christian faith. To compare perhaps, small things with great, though here comparisons are hateful, this is like talking about Hitler's Germany or Stalin's Russia without referring to the martyrs of the death camps. One can only conclude that in this matter the Pope was badly advised.

The temper of the Pope's mind and his intellectual and social concerns are amplified in his first encyclical, *Redemptor Hominis*. The style is personal and direct: "I" is generally employed; good will toward the non-Christian religions and toward unbelievers is strongly marked; and there are many pungent statements. For example, after remarking that the pattern of world development represents a "gigantic development of the parable in the Bible of the rich banqueter and the poor man Lazarus," he adds:

> by submitting man to tensions created by himself, dilapidating at an accelerated pace material and energy resources, and compromising the geophysical environment, [men] unceasingly make the areas of misery spread, accompanied by anguish, frustration and bitterness. We have before us here a great drama that can leave nobody indifferent. . . . The drama is made still worse by the presence close at hand of the privileged social classes and of the rich countries, which accumulate goods to an excessive degree and the misuse of whose riches very often becomes the cause of various ills.

The central concerns of John Paul II are far from those of "progressive" Catholicism in North America and in such European countries as Holland. These groups are concerned to transform Catholic tradition in such matters as sexual morality, to change the role of women in the Church, to temper or abandon what they take to be the unseemly claims of Catholicism to any kind of exclusive connection with the truths of faith, and to move the ethos of Christianity away from what is harsh, exacting, and ascetical (what Hume called "the monkish virtues") to an ethos of self-fulfillment and self-realization. Hebblethwaite notes that a professor of theology at Boston College took the view (before the conclave that elected John Paul I) that a Pope

who emphasized continuity with the pontificate of Paul VI would "only intensify the frustration of both left and right alike."

There is in effect already a right-wing schism, or rather several schisms, with Archbishop Lefebvre's group the best known internationally. The same possibilities exist on the (ecclesiastical) left, though one suspects the left will cling as long as possible to the main body of the Church; they have, after all, captured many positions of strength, in the Catholic press and in publishing, in the religious orders, and in Catholic universities and colleges. In any case, the "left" covers very diverse groups of people, some of whom will rally to a strong and credible ecclesiastical leadership, even if it is conservative by their standards. Others would be happier, perhaps, in the now very relaxed atmosphere of mainstream Anglicanism or of other liberal Protestant groups. But these are the problems of middle-class Catholics in the rich societies and are not, could not be, serious problems for the man from Krakow. "The glory of God is man alive": I suspect that for John Paul II man is man as we encounter him in the sobriety and realism of the Biblical tradition and in the classic tradition of the Gentile epic and drama. "The abdication of belief / Makes the behavior small," wrote Emily Dickinson.

Karol Wojtyla, like the passionate Pole he is, sees man as large, heroic, with great pains and great joys. Some sense of the vastness of man's inner kingdom may pass from the Pope to many Catholics now dispirited by the times. The older among them were dispirited by Pius XII's great refusal when confronted with the Antichrist of National Socialism; John XXIII raised their spirits; John Paul II has the natural endowments and the intellectual formation to cheer and enliven them. May he prove to all men, believers and unbelievers, a point of light in the darkness of a naughty world.

Raymond A. Schroth (review date 24 June 1979)

SOURCE: "The Vicars of Christ on Earth," in *New York Times Book Review*, June 24, 1979, pp. 11, 44-5.

[*In the following review, Schroth discusses John Paul's theological views in* Fruitful and Responsible Love *and* Sign of Contradiction.]

It is almost a plunge into nostalgia now, only nine months after the events themselves, to relive the three months of the three Popes; when the television camera peered benevolently down like the eye of God on the wooden box holding the discolored corpse of the sad, sensitive, loving but not well-loved Giovanni Montini; when Dan Rather struggled to pronounce Castel Gandolfo and announced that the funeral mass was coming to an end though it had barely begun; when all those never-before and never-since-heard-of papal "candidates" popped full-color onto the covers of Newsweek and Time; and when the Roman

Catholic Church—briefly and imperfectly embodied in the 111 mostly elderly Cardinal electors of the Conclaves—paused, examined itself and picked two comparative strangers to be Vicars of Christ and, for many outside the church as well, moral leaders of the world.

It was the news story of the year, perhaps of the decade, one the news media were poorly prepared to cover because few journalists know theology or church history and because, in the standard man-bites-dog sense, religion is only occasionally "news." Then, when a right-to-lifer firebombs an abortion clinic, an anti-arms race priest digs a grave on the White House lawn, a bishop marries or a Pope dies, reporters must scurry around in search of a clerical spokesman (most of them are bland and noncommittal) to explain what is going on. Moreover, a certain kind of clerical mind prefers secrecy, knows little about journalism and is, at best, amused by what journalists call the public's "right-to-know." Thus, a papal election is to the religious journalist what a big fire is to a cub reporter—the challenge of his career, the chance, as I. F. Stone says, to have a "helluva good time," if he doesn't "forget it's really burning." . . .

The election of Karol Wojtyla to the papacy, said a commentator in The New Statesman last fall, had been expected in certain European intellectual circles for some time—an observation that may tell us something about the isolation of some intellectual circles from the general religious press now digging through his published philosophical and spiritual works for clues to the future of his church. Those who still see *Humanae Vitae* as a shadow threatening the future credibility of the papacy can take little comfort from *Fruitful and Responsible Love.* It consists of an address Cardinal Wojtyla gave to the June 1978 Milan International Congress on the birth-control encyclical sponsored by the International Center for the Study of Family Life, supplemented by a series of mostly fawning comments from authorities on the family. He emphasizes the importance of mutual love, the necessary connection between conjugal love and its fulfillment in parenthood, and the parents' responsibility to determine their family size with a free and upright conscience. But he jumps to the conclusion that "they will not have recourse to contraception, which is essentially opposed to love and parenthood," without explaining why, for couples who already have children, every conjugal act need necessarily be open to conception. Indeed, his personalist framework and emphasis on love is the argument many Catholics have used to practice contraception with a clear conscience.

Much of what John Paul II has said in his address to the Latin American bishops at Puebla, Mexico, and in his first, highly personal encyclical, *Redemptor Hominis,* he had already said to Paul VI and the Roman Curia in a Lenten retreat he preached to them in 1976. As Mr. Hebblethwaite remarks, "he became known to the Curia and the Curia liked what it saw." These spiritual exercises have now been published as *Sign of Contradiction.*

One of the paradoxes of John Paul II may well be that, as much as Catholic progressive intellectuals tend to appreciate a versatile and highly intelligent scholar-pope, they may have in Wojtyla a man almost too intelligent, a man—unlike John XXIII, who captivated the world by his openness and almost careless boldness—whose learning and convictions in a few crucial areas are so deep that he will find it hard to be educated by broader experience and what Father Greeley calls "the enormous leap from Cracow to Rome." "Karol Wojtyla," says Father Greeley, "is going to have to draw back from the attitudes, opinions, and perspectives of a lifetime to be fully effective in his new job."

Sign of Contradiction reveals a mind filled with the Scriptures and the Church Fathers, yet unfamiliar or uncomfortable with recent scriptural scholarship; at home with Thomistic philosophy, yet always reinterpreting it in existentialist or phenomenologist terms; absolutely convinced that the false gods of "progress"—consumerism, the hunger for status symbols, technology—diminish man's dignity and his freedom to love. John Paul II warns us that Jesus never intended his opposition to secular and religious authorities to have political implications, but he sees in Jesus carrying his cross the Jewish prisoners in Nazi extermination camps forced to bear quarry stones on their backs and workers ground down by their machines.

Whatever he may be, the new Pope seems a man thoroughly at home with himself. In the long run it will not matter much whether we have a pope who skis, jogs, canoes, sings, strums a guitar, writes poems and plays, tosses babies in the air, or even one who smiles. What matters is how well be reads the various spirits of his own time and can tell which movements enrich and complement Christian humanism and which the church must contradict. "It is the task of the church," he says, "to fight on the side of man, often against men themselves. Christ fought like that, and be goes on fighting through the ages in men's hearts and in the human conscience." With Karol Wojtyla's leadership, it will be a fight to see.

Andrzej Poltawski (review date 4 April 1980)

SOURCE: "Objectifying the Subjective," in *Times Literary Supplement,* April 4, 1980, p. 397.

[In the following review, Poltawski examines John Paul's moral and philosophical perspective in The Acting Person.*]*

This is the present Pope, Karol Wojtyla's, main philosophical work, in which he tries to give an outline of his philosophical anthropology. The point of departure is man as he is given to himself in and through his actions.

The author's position may be described as phenomenological realism. But this is not the realism criticized by Heidegger for introducing ready-made external things into the sense-bestowing human subjectivity; nor does it embrace the tendency of the traditional, cosmological approach to regard man as a thing among other things in the universe. If Wojtyla accepts the traditional Aristotelian metaphysics in its general outline, he at the same time shows its inadequacy when applied to human subjectivity. What the traditional approach could not give was precisely a direct access to subjectivity. It is not, therefore, the external point of view which he takes from tradition, but the vision of man as a dynamic unity. Being an organic unity acting in the world, man is in a sense objective in all his aspects. Nevertheless, according to Wojtyla, it is only the category of lived experience that makes possible the objectivation of human subjectivity and a genuine foundation of philosophical anthropology and ethics.

Consequently, we should not be deceived by the occurrence of traditional metaphysical terms (eg, *suppositum*) in the context of Wojtyla's considerations; they serve only as a general delimitation of the place where the genuine phenomenological work has to begin—the work which, in fact, gives those terms a new meaning. The starting point of the investigation is thus exactly opposite to that which is usual in school discussions, where ready-made categories are simply taken for granted. Moreover, Wojtyla's acceptance of the realistic attitude is motivated by his own analyses, in which he shows that originally and fundamentally man experiences himself as acting, and that it is only this experience which can give an adequate understanding of man.

Thus, the famous disagreement between Locke and Hume concerning the existence of "a clear and distinct idea of active power, as we have from reflexion on the operations of our mind", decided by modern sensualism and transcendentalism against Locke, seems, on a more thorough examination, to be judged in his favour; but it is precisely the activity of the integral man, not that of his mind, which is here being shown as given. In this perspective, human subjectivity, one of the main concerns of contemporary thought, appears not only as bestowing sense on things, but in the first place as the subject of actions and processes that take place in man; and cognizing also is a real action or process.

Human consciousness, "mirroring" ourselves and the world in which we live and thus revealing to us, one might say, the scene on which we act, has another function also of subjectivation: it makes our image of the world, as well as our actions, *our own*. But consciousness itself does not give us the power invoked by Locke; its mirroring of the world is, on the contrary, a consequence of real acts of cognition. It is the whole man alone who acts and cognizes and who can develop and perfect himself (or deteriorate) on the strength of his action.

Conceived in this way, Wojtyla's philosophical anthropology opens the way to an objective treatment of moral values. The characteristics of right and wrong, applying in the first place to free human actions, qualify secondarily the acting person, who is made better or worse by his ac-

tions. In fact, Wojtyla wrote this book in order to understand better the foundation of ethics, which is his main concern in philosophy.

The original and rich analyses of experience, the gist of which I have tried to convey, constitute Part 1 of the work. The main problems treated are: the relation of consciousness to efficacy (ie, our experience of "being the agent" of our actions) and the distinction between two modes of human activity—the mode of something merely happening in us and, on the other hand, that of genuine free, responsible action. (It is interesting to note that these analyses, in their main features, if not in their vocabulary and point of departure, are parallel to the ideas expressed by the French psychiatrist Henri Ey in his book *La conscience*.) It is shown that efficacy demands a particular transcendence of the person towards his action, and Part 2 is devoted to an analysis of this transcendence; while steering his actions, man at the same time shapes himself and, if his actions are right, fulfils himself. This needs—and brings—integration, and Part 3 describes this integration on its two levels, of the living body and the psyche. But the fulfilment of man seems, on examination, to be possible only if he cooperates, of his own accord, with other people and makes, so to speak, a gift of himself to others. This attitude, called by Wojtyla "participation", consists in a conscious acceptance of the common good and a striving to realize it. Part 4 of the book gives a sketch of this dimension of human existence (which is more fully developed in other works by Wojtyla).

If one wants really to understand what appears to some people as a surprising combination of conservatism and novelty in the teaching of Pope John Paul II, it is not enough to look at it from a pragmatical, sociological, political or other external point of view, or even from a purely theological one; we should also take into account Karol Wojtyla's perfectionist philosophy of man—a philosophy which, although in harmony with its theological prolongation, has an independent foundation and is deeply rooted in the problematics of our time.

The actual shape of the present English text needs some explanation. Translated by Andrzej Potocki from the second Polish corrected and enlarged edition and yet published), it was edited by A. T. Tymienieeka, who made many changes and rewrote some parts of the translation. The examination of these changes had only partly been made by the author before October 1978; it was subsequently passed by him to a committee of three people. However, the book was published before the results of this examination, as well as a great part of the translator's stylistic corrections, could reach the editor. And, while some sentences of the translation have been improved in the published version, some parts of the original have, unfortunately, been obscured and distorted. The editor often paraphrases the original loosely, occasionally introducing terms alien to the author's own vocabulary, like "constituting the object" and "noematic autopresentation" or "ideas". Moreover, the Latin term *suppositum*, which plays an important role in the original text, is rendered by a dozen or so different, sometimes very complicated phrases.

Boleslaw Taborski (essay date 1981)

SOURCE: "The 'Inner Theatre' of Karol Wojtyla," in *Polish Perspectives,* Vol. XXIV, No. 2, 1981, pp. 64-70.

[*In the following essay, Taborski discusses the style and major themes of John Paul's dramatic works.*]

The plays of Karol Wojtyla constitute an unusual, and even in certain respects, unique phenomenon. The reasons for it are certainly far more complex than the fact that this particular playwright became Pope. It would be best (though, perhaps, not now possible), if one could forget about the election to the highest office in the Church of the author of those plays. The fact that these plays have only now been revealed to the world at large is understandable, considering that the author never bothered to have them published or performed. But the plays would sooner or later be noticed and discovered on their own merit. It could happen however, rather later than sooner. These plays are somewhat removed from our habits and theatrical tastes, maybe also from our everyday interests. They are difficult and complex, unconventional and . . . experimental. In the days when theatre is open to all superficial sensations, experiences and excesses, they reach deep into man's psyche and their action often develops within the mind. To achieve this the author uses interesting formal means, even though form is not his main concern. In the natural course of things, it is possible that we were not yet ready to receive these works. Maybe this was to be left to future generations, just as we discovered Witkacy, or Przybyszewska. However, due to the great events connected with the person of the author, our acquaintance with these plays has been speeded up, as it were. It is *we* who are discovering them and, I hope, will accept them.

Karol Wojtyla's dramatic works are closely connected with his poetry. His poetry consists as a rule of long poems, subdivided into a number of parts, often structured like drama, containing monologues, or even dialogue, not unlike plays in their intensity.

His dramatic works, on the other hand, have a poetic character, in varying degree and expressed in different ways. They show also a strong affinity with Romantic and Neoromantic drama and the Polish literary tradition. There is nothing strange in this, considering the author's background of studies and reading, as well as theatre activity in his school and student days. This is equally true not only of the first three plays, related to one another by their biblical subjects and poetic style, which he wrote in the first year of the war, but also of the later plays. These were written after a ten-year gap. Karol Wojtyla realized

in them what I would call his 'Inner Theatre', modelled to a certain extent on Mieczyslaw Kotlarczyk's Rhapsodic Theatre, whose member he was during its wartime underground phase, and of which he remained a friend and follower to the end. Being a thinker and a poet, Karol Wojtyla felt the need to express himself also in drama, and he did this with amazing consistency.

His early plays were a result of intensive reading of the Old Testament in the first year of World War II. Wojtyla remained at that time in close contact with the great Polish actor and director, Juliusz Osterwa, for whom he made a new translation of Sophocles's *Oedipus.* At the end of December 1939, the nineteen-year-old Karol informed Kotlarczyk that he had written 'a drama, or more precisely, a dramatic poem', entitled *David* The text of that drama has not yet been found, but we know that it was written in prose, and in blank and rhymed verse. Just before Easter 1940, Karol informed his friend that he had written 'a new drama, Greek in form, Christian in spirit, eternal in its essence . . . a drama about suffering', entitled *Job.* Written entirely in verse, partly rhymed, partly blank, this earliest preserved literary text by Wojtyla (if we except a few cycles of early poems) is astonishingly mature in its structure and contents. The young author recreated the biblical story in an unpretentious and concise manner and endowed the title hero with great force of dramatic expression.

If, however, the figure of Job, as a prefiguration of Christ and martyred Fatherland imposed itself easily on Polish mentality—there were other plays written by Polish writers on the same subject during the war, such as *Sprawiedliwy (The Just Man)* by Jerzy Zawieyski—Wojtyla's next play expressed his thoughts on the reasons for Poland's downfall two centuries earlier. It was also an experiment in dramatic structure. In the summer of 1940, Karol, who had just turned twenty, wrote—as he himself confessed, 'in a flash'—his next biblical play, *Jeremiah.* In spite of the title, the main action is set in the 17th century, and its protagonist is the visionary Jesuit priest, Piotr Skarga, who in his sermons repeatedly warned the Polish nobles that unless they mended their ways, Poland would fall. It is in his visions that the story of the prophet Jeremiah's argument with the elders of Israel is shown. The young playwright develops the analogy between the Biblical story and the fate of Poland as a stylistic *tour-de-force.* He uses different kinds of blank and rhymed verse, varies the length of the line, the number of accents and syllables, uses also prose and—for the first time—extensive stage directions (something that is to become an important element in his later plays), suggesting some scenes as tableaux. Statues of angels come to life on the altar, a chorus of monks changes into elders of Israel, etc. It is a more complex work than *Job,* ending with an image characteristic of its author's theatrical imagination: 'Father Skarga takes up the Hetman's final utterance and throws it into the empty church, that is to say—into the filled auditorium'. A typical idea for a work dominated not so much by action as by spatially composed images. Within these images the characters express—in a poetic, though still somewhat flowery language—their inner experiences and visions. Such a structure is already a clear forecast of the author's later plays.

The period of nearly ten years since the writing of *Jeremiah* to the completion of his next play was of crucial importance in the life of Karol Wojtyla. During that time he worked as a labourer in a quarry, engaged in his most important theatre activity in the wartime underground Rhapsodic Theatre, carried on his clandestine studies first in philology than at the theological seminary, culminating in his ordination as priest, studies abroad and his first posting as an auxiliary priest in the village of Niegowiæ. It is significant that in spite of the radical turn his life took in another direction, his interest in the theatre did not wane and that towards the end of that period he returned to playwriting, making use of his many experiences and subordinating them to his main vocation. This does not mean that his work became 'devotional' in character. In his poetry and drama, Karol Wojtyla remained an artist, though he managed to use his talent to express things he considered close and important.

The person of Adam Chmielowski—Brother Albert—had fascinated him for some time. There is some evidence that while a student at the Angelicum in Rome immediately after the war, he recited for an international audience of students and professors fragments of a play about Brother Albert, not his own as yet, perhaps, but an earlier work by Nunsch. On the other hand, it could have been an early draft of his own work. The fact is that *Our God's Brother* exists in two versions. It is possible that the second draft resulted from his play not having been accepted by the *Znak* monthly, but he could have worked on it independently. I think that the final version emerged while the 29-year-old Father Wojtyla lived in Niegowiæ in 1949. He stayed there only a short time, but managed to establish a parish theatre and direct Zofia Kossak's *Spodziewany Goœæ* (*The Expected Guest*). In that play he performed the title role—of the guest, who turned out to be a beggar, who turned out to be Christ. Echoes of this found their way into Wojtyla's play where Adam sees Christ in the homeless beggar.

The fascination with Brother Albert could, to a certain extent, have a personal significance for Wojtyla. An artist who gave up art and artistic life in order to devote his life to God and work for the poor was certainly someone very close to Karol Wojtyla who, in a way, took a similar decision. But though there are similarities, it would not be proper to see autobiographical elements in his play about Brother Albert. But it was not the author's aim to write a biographical play either. Although its characters are authentic, the external events have been condensed, transposed in time, and many have been left out (Adam's youth, his novitiate with the Jesuits, nervous breakdown and cure, almost all the details regarding his activity). It is even difficult to pinpoint in time the action of Acts I and II. It is after 1884, when Adam has finally settled in Cra-

cow, and his decision to give up art and devote his life to the poor has matured in his mind. But at that time some of the characters in the play were not in fact alive: Maks (Gierymski—died 1874) and Lucjan (Siemieñski—died 1877), while Helena Modrzejewska emigrated to America in 1876 and returned to Cracow only as a guest, which is not at all clear in the play. Perhaps the action of Act III is most clearly defined in time, as it takes place in the last days of Brother Albert's life, ie. 1916. But even there the revolution, or disturbances, which break out at the close of the play, are a transposition of either earlier events (which did not take place mainly in Cracow) or later ones.

Such compression, selection and transposition in time has its origin in the fact that the author was not concerned with sketching out an external biography but—as he himself defined it in the introduction—with 'an attempt to penetrate the man', reaching 'to the sources of his humanity'. The author realized that as this 'is bound to a certain extent to steer clear of historical details it will leave something to be desired'. Fortunately for us, he did not give up his 'reaching', but followed his artistic instinct and the overall aims he set himself. Thanks to that, we have been spared a historical-biographical bore of a play, of which there have been plenty in the post-war period, and instead we have received an insight into the inner history of an unusual man, as Adam Chmielowski was; the history of his spiritual struggles and his progress to sanctity.

Those struggles are revealed on several levels. Adam's main problem of 'overcoming the artist in himself', of sacrificing art for the sake of life for the poor, is understandable and clear. It might seem surprising, though, that the problem of revolution has been extensively treated and assumes almost equal importance. It appears in Act I, in Adam's conversation with the Stranger, almost dominates the second half of Act II and finds its culmination at the close of the play. There is nothing strange in this. In the mind of an author so sensitive to these problems (as was later to be proved by his pronouncements in Mexico or Brazil), Adam *had* to tackle the question of social injustice and look for the means to abolish it, even to the extent of radical revolutionary solutions. It does not really matter whether the disturbances really erupted just before Brother Albert's death, and whether the character of the Stranger was really modelled on an authentic revolutionary. The problem lies *within Adam,* and the 'dialogue with revolution' is carried on in his mind. These struggles, too, go on till the end and lead to a significant conclusion: that there is no contradiction between great just anger 'which lasts' and the choice of a 'greater freedom' by Brother Albert. It is a positive synthesis at the end of the struggles within the hero of this drama and a still valid message *for us.*

Such an 'inner' approach to his hero by the author has in its turn important consequences for the style of the work. Not only has flat realism been rejected, but also the linear construction of the average play. For the first time the author introduces here the relativity of time, which makes it possible for characters and events from the past and the future to appear on stage in the present. (This relative use of time will become an almost basic principle of his later plays.)

The solution of this problem of performance lies in the mystery theatre. Mysteries have no limitations imposed by narrowly conceived realism. They take place within the limits of the Christian cosmos, as well as within the human soul; in the past as well as in the future, focussed into one point of stage present. From the vantage point of Providence human life is seen as a totality, not as a moment in time. And such a perspective in spite of remnants of other models and traditions, exists already in *Our God's Brother,* as a clear beginning of a new phase of Karol Wojtyla's 'Inner Theatre'.

In 1960, the Catholic monthly *Znak* published, under his literary pseudonym Andrzej Jawieñ, Bishop Wojtyla's drama *Sklep Jubiierski* (*The Jeweller's Shop*). Four years later Archbishop Wojtyla wrote a drama entitled *Promieniowanie Ojcostwa* (*The Radiation of Fatherhood*), not published till 1980.

The first work was described by its author as 'a meditation on the sacrament of matrimony, passing on occasion into a drama'; the second is now openly called 'a mystery'. In both these works, modelled on the style of the Rhapsodic Theatre, all semblance of realism and linear development of action have been abandoned. All external theatre effects have been toned down, but human problems have been shown in an even greater close-up: the problems of loneliness, fatherhood (motherhood), childhood in *The Radiation of Fatherhood.* Both works are constructed on the principle of inter-related monologues, spoken in long lines of blank verse; there is also prose. In the first work a chorus appears a couple of times, there are excerpts from letters; in the second, even some dialogue and visual mime scenes suggested by the stage directions. External action diminishes, giving way to the journey to the interior of the human soul.

The Radiation of Fatherhood is fully expressive of inner theatre. No external and 'material' factors detract from the expression of the essentials. But it would be wrong to assume that these are not plays at all, but superficially dramatized treatises. This author writes treatises too, and would write a treatise in this instance if this were his intention. The last two works are not in the nature of abstract dissertations, but reveal a moving drama of human existence and the human soul. If the characters in *The Radiation of Fatherhood* have something of symbols or archetypes about them, the drama abounds also in lyricism and in dramatic statements on the basic problems faced by man. *The Jeweller's Shop,* on the other hand, is a moving story about three couples and three aspects of love: one love that has survived death; another which withered; and, yet another which is born in young lovers. The subject is treated with insight, warmth, understanding

and delicacy. It is a highly imaginative work, which has proved itself, particularly in many radio productions.

It is remarkable to what extent the dramas of Karol Wojtyla, written over the period of a quarter century (1939-1964), for all their stylistic differences, are monolithic as far as their moral meaning and themes are concerned. They are consistent in what I would call their inner form. They appeal to the highest values in our culture, and also at a time when the word is totally degraded and devalued, they aim at its revaluation. Last but not least, they develop with amazing consistency a modern mystery theatre of the highest order. Even though the author of these works did not aim at theatre, they are a proposition which theatre ought seriously to consider. Karol Wojtyla has on a number of occasions stated that theatre has given him a great deal. But he too has certainly much to give to theatre, if only the latter will accept this gift.

I think that theatre has rightly made a start with *Our God's Brother,* a work none too easy, but, perhaps, closest to our theatre sensibilities. This significant link in his development as playwright is a discovery that widens our perception of drama. It increases also our knowledge of Brother Albert, still too little known. For that matter, many a problem raised in this work will sound topical and fresh, as if it were written for us today. And this, after all, is the test of good playwriting.

POSTSCRIPT

The above essay was written originally in connection with the first production of one of Karol Wojtyla's plays, *Our God's Brother*, at the Juliusz Slowacki Theatre in Cracow in December 1980 / directed by Krystyna Skuszanka/. In 1997 the Polish film director Krzysztof Zanussi made a movie based on my translation of the play, with Scott Wilson in the title role. It is also worth noting that in 1989 Pope John Paul II declared Brother Albert a saint / surely a unique event in the entire history of theatre in that the author canonized the protagonist of his own play/. I wish to add that although I expanded my thoughts on Karol Wojtyla's plays, notably in the introductions to his *Collected Plays and Writings on Theater*, published in my translations by University of California Press in 1987, my views have not substantially altered from those expressed in this essay.

                                                            B. Taborski

Kenneth Briggs (review date 9 September 1981)

SOURCE: "Rejoinder to the Sexual Revolution," in *New York Times Book Review,* September 20, 1981, p. 13.

[*In the following review, Briggs discusses John Paul's views on love and sexuality as delineated in* Love and Responsibility.]

Pope John Paul II has often spoken about sex and marriage during his nearly three-year reign. The impression left by these utterances, portraying the Pontiff as simply a pillar of traditional Catholic moral theology, does an injustice to the wider scope of his thinking. When he makes public statements, the well-developed conceptual underpinnings for his views unfortunately get left behind.

Moreover, the Pope is often a better teacher than disciplinarian, as this book, a revised version of a series of lectures on sexuality and love he gave over 20 years ago to Polish university students, aptly illustrates. A respected philosopher, he is at ease at the head of the class, carefully and rigorously building his case, projecting a positive stance against his intellectual opponents, such as Freud, who are often cited in support of a more sexually permissive standard. In no other book does he emerge more clearly as a thinker of independent bent, grounded in both an ethic that places the individual above rules and in a system of ideas that can affirm the church's doctrine with integrity.

When John Paul II made the comment at a Vatican audience that a man who lusts after his wife commits a sin, ridicule and scorn gushed forth from a variety of "liberated" critics. The essential idea behind his somewhat archaic wording was that exploitation in any form is wrong, a concept that presumably anyone could gladly endorse. He deserves a hearing, although the same difficulty that the Pope has had in translating complex concepts into the language of public pronouncements sometimes obscures his book's sensitive, though toughminded arguments.

The theme that runs through *Love and Responsibility* is that although sexuality is God-given, it may be degrading unless it is transcended by love. The Pope suggests that there are many aspects to love between two people, including physical attraction, emotional attachment, tenderness and comradeship, but that sensuality is dominant unless these are integrated by a love for the "truth of the person." People must learn that they are masters of their own sexuality, not slaves to instinct; unless they enhance love by ethical truth it lapses into "subjectivism," an unreliable guide.

Though human love, in the Pope's view, cannot be reduced simply to any of its psychological or physical components, all the elements play a constructive role. Sexual pleasure, apart from procreation (which John Paul II, like his predecessors, sees as the supreme purpose of sexuality), can be good and necessary for married couples; the body serves more than only a utilitarian goal. He asserts that "there exists a difference between carnal love and 'love of the body'—for the body as a component of the person may also be an object of love and not merely of concupiscence." He further cautions against seeing "pleasure itself as evil—pleasure in itself is a specific good," though he warns of the "moral evil involved in fixing the will on pleasure alone."

On the subject of love, the Pope's romanticism often soars above the colder dictates of logic. At other points, his logic founders on the need to reinforce doctrine, and he can come across as a stern naysayer who trades only in prohibitions. As would be expected, he solidly supports Roman Catholic teachings against premarital sex, extramarital sex, artificial birth control and divorce. But his personalistic philosophy appears to put him in tension with at least the last two stands. He holds out an ideal of a totally self-giving, committed marriage that benefits from sex without being dependent upon it for a marriage's survival. He talks constantly and sensitively about the need to value the dignity of the other person. He sets forth, sometimes with poetic flourish, a picture of marital perfection that may seem far beyond the capabilities of most people.

In many respects, Pope John Paul II has written a courageous apologetic. Aware that some might question the conclusions of a celibate male, he goes ahead with aplomb and authority; he shies from nothing, but avoids arrogance. He ponders a range of issues, from the Old Testament's accounts of polygamy (the effect, he says, was to degrade women), to the need for men to better serve the sexual needs of their wives, to the case for chastity. *Love and Responsibility* is a high-minded rejoinder to the sexual revolution, pervaded by an implicit commandment: "Thou shalt not use another for thine own sake."

Jaroslav Pelikan (review date 22 April 1984)

SOURCE: "Conversations With the Pope," in *New York Times Book Review,* April 22, 1984, p. 12.

[*In the following review, Pelikan discusses John Paul's theological views in* "Be Not Afraid!"]

When the Pope speaks ex cathedra (literally, from the throne)—"that is, in carrying out his office as the pastor and teacher of all Christians," as the First Vatican Council explained this phrase in 1870—he is believed to be preserved from any error in matters of faith and morals. But whatever someone's personal or theological views about this ex cathedra infallibility may be, it is in many ways more interesting and certainly more unusual when a pope elects to speak in public *extra cathedram,* that is, in a personal capacity.

That is what the current Pontiff has done in *"Be Not Afraid!,"* a book whose title comes from the words with which Karol Cardinal Wojtyla greeted the people of Rome after his election to the throne of Saint Peter in 1978. The book came out of a series of taped conversations with the French journalist André Frossard, an adult convert to the Roman Catholic faith. The conversations consisted of Mr. Frossard's questions and the Pope's answers. But as a skilled veteran of many kinds of interrogation from many quarters, Pope John Paul II managed to turn the questions in the direction of answers he wanted to give. As Mr. Frossard says, "the Pope is not averse to walking round a question before stepping into it."

Mr. Frossard's questions ranged from the conventional and catechetical—"Should infants be baptized?"—through the more controversial—"Can one deduce a political policy from the Gospel?"—to the plaintive—"Has [the world] got one last chance of escaping the logic of death in which it is gradually being enmeshed?" The Pope's answers also covered a wide territory, from a totally official recitation of the decrees of the Second Vatican Council of 1962-65 through an altogether personal comment on celibacy—"In this domain I have received more graces than battles to fight"—to observations on literature and philosophy—he likes to read Czeslaw Milosz and Rainer Maria Rilke and not only St. Thomas Aquinas but the phenomenologist Max Scheler.

No one will be surprised to find the Bishop of Rome declaring his allegiance to the continuity of the church, not merely the continuity of its institutions, moral teachings and theological doctrines but especially the continuity of its life of prayer and devotion. As the first Slavic pope, he is particularly devoted to Saints Cyril and Methodius, the ninth-century "apostles to the Slavs" whom he has designated as joint patron saints of Europe together with St. Benedict, the father of Western monasticism. As the first Polish Pope, moreover, he has found ever greater depths in that nation's dedication to the Virgin Mary, whose depiction in the icon of Our Lady of Czestochowa, the Black Madonna, hangs over the altar of his private chapel in the Vatican. "Our inner relation to the Mother of God derives from our connection with the mystery of Christ," he told Mr. Frossard, and added, "The more my inner life has been centered on the mystery of the Redemption, the more surrender to Mary . . . has seemed to me to be the best means of participating fruitfully and effectively in this reality." Carrying out a moral implication of this reality—he sees the entire human race as a family whose mother is the Virgin Mary—he called his would-be assassin, Mehmed All Agca, "brother." Mr. Frossard writes, "All round, I should have preferred this brother to find another means of entering the family." But his fraternal embrace of his attacker was also part of the Pope's continuing emphasis on the imperatives of the Gospel.

But this Pope, like any true conservative, is open to change. Believing as he does in those things that cannot be changed, he is able to be flexible about everything else; he is acutely aware not only of continuity in the church but also of the need for and inevitability of change. "We must," he says, "constantly seek a form of faith adapted to a world that is being continually renewed" and not seek to live in a "pre-Copernican" or "pre-Einsteinian" or "even pre-Kantian world." Despite his admiration for St. Thomas Aquinas, his own exposure to non-Thomist ways of thinking has helped him take time and history far more seriously, than some Thomists have; he sees that "man is a being involved in history," and thus he recognizes that "the Church writes her truth on the curving, muddled lines of history," a truth that is immutable in its divine origins but is obviously mutable in its human expressions.

The human and historical relativity of the absolute truth implies that the church's position on various practical issues must repeatedly be reformulated in light of the continuing progress of insight and understanding in scholarship and science. The Pope notes that the church's consideration of "usury and interest in connection with the development of the economic sciences" has been changing since the Middle Ages. And he suggests its position must change today as it formulates a view of "responsible paternity [parenthood] in connection with the development of the bio-physiological sciences." It is not clear what that somewhat cryptic comment may imply for a greater scientific (and theological) refinement in the interpretation of parenthood and sexuality than has been evident in the encyclicals of some of his predecessors in this century.

On the entire problem of unity with other believers, the Pope has concluded that historical honesty compels us to recognize the presence in ourselves and others of "a mentality marked by centuries of divisions and separations," but honesty also requires us to acknowledge that "what unites us is stronger than what divides us." To put it mildly, that is a recognition and acknowledgment that could not always be heard in the declaration of popes in their response to the Protestant Reformation during the 16th century, when it was still possible to do something about it.

Interspersed among these many examples of the Pope's wisdom are occasional—too rare, for my taste—flashes of his well-known wit. One object of the wit is Mr. Frossard himself, whom the Pope "accused . . . several times of presenting him in too favorable a light, of making him 'the hero of a romance.'" Elsewhere the Pope put question marks into the margin of the manuscript and charged Mr. Frossard with being too much of a "papalist," more of a papalist, presumably, than the Pope himself. Even a sympathetic reader will sometimes find Mr. Frossard's breathless attitude a bit excessive. The Pope's friendship may well be, as he declares, his most precious possession, and he may find "his presence at the head of the Church" the only remaining basis for any optimism about the world, but it is in keeping neither with the official spirit of Vatican II nor with the personal style of John Paul II for an interviewer to engage in the kind of Byzantine fawning that occasionally peeks through the pages of *"Be Not Afraid!"*

Yet even Mr. Frossard's deference cannot detract from the intellectual force, personal dynamism and spiritual authenticity that characterize the Pope when he converses *extra cathedram* as least as much as when he speaks *ex cathedra*.

Stanislaw Baranczak (review date 14 December 1987)

SOURCE: "Praying and Playing," in *The New Republic*, December 14, 1987, pp. 47-8.

[In the following review, Baranczak examines the style, central themes, and philosophical underpinnings of John Paul's plays.]

Two of the world's most powerful men were once actors. But only one of them was also smart enough to write his own lines. The appearance in English of *The Collected Plays and Writings on Theater* reminds us that before he became John Paul II, Karol Wojtyla's extraecclesiastic pastimes included not only philosophy, poetry, acting, skiing, and hiking, but also playwriting. To paraphrase Stalin, how many diversions does the pope have?

To be exact, Wojtyla stopped writing plays years before he moved to Rome. Between 1940 and 1964 he wrote six plays altogether, of which five have survived. Of these, three were written after he had become a priest. Only one, *The Jeweler's Shop,* was published (under a pseudonym) before his election to the papacy. Naturally all five were eagerly unearthed by the Polish Catholic publishing house Znak in the wake of the rejoicing in 1978, and were included in a volume of Wojtyla's collected poems and plays published in 1980. The poems have been available in English translation for several years; the present edition collects the plays and six brief essays on theater, all translated, annotated, and introduced with extreme care by John Paul's appointed English translator, the London-based poet and critic Boleslaw Taborski.

Though Wojtyla was virtually unknown as a playwright before 1980, dramaturgy was for him a more essential expression than poetry. As an eight-year-old he was involved with an amateur theater in his hometown of Wadowice; as a teenager he acted in some ten plays staged by his high school theater. After moving to Krakow and entering the university in 1938 (he majored in Polish literature), Wojtyla continued to perform with a semiprofessional theater group.

The outbreak of the war did not dissuade him from his literary and theatrical pursuits, even though the Nazi occupation forced Polish cultural activity underground. Working by day in a quarry and in a chemical factory, by night Wojtyla continued to study at the university, now clandestine, and to write poetry. In December 1939 he wrote his first play (eventually lost), *David;* in 1940 *Job* and *Jeremiah* followed. In these first years of the occupation he was also involved with an underground group of young actors, who staged plays in private apartments. These efforts were institutionalized, though still covert, after August 1941, when Wojtyla and his older friend Mieczyslaw Kotlarczyk founded the Rhapsodic Theater in Krakow.

The Rhapsodic Theater was not just another clandestine form of keeping Polish culture alive. It was an artistic experiment aimed at creating a special "theater of the word," in which scarcity of visual theatrical effect (a natural scarcity, under the circumstances) was part of a deliberate aesthetic. The performances were based on recitation rather than acting, and the repertory consisted of poems rather than plays. As Kotlarczyk put it, it was an attempt "to revolutionize theater through the *word.*"

Wojtyla took part in all 22 wartime performances of the Rhapsodic Theater. After 1946, when he was ordained a priest, his ties with the Theater became looser, of course, but they were never completely severed. On the contrary, he supported and defended the Theater throughout its postwar existence, which was particularly difficult during the years of Stalinism, until its final closure by the Gomulka regime in 1967.

The idea of a "rhapsodic theater," or "theater of the word," clearly informs Wojtyla's three later plays, *Our God's Brother* (1945-50), *The Jeweler's Shop* (1960), and *Radiation of Fatherhood* (1964). Compared with these works, his beginnings as a dramatist seem decidedly conventional. *Job* and *Jeremiah,* both written when he was 20, expose the workings of the young author's mind and show his familiarity with the Bible, and with the Polish Romantic and Neo-Romantic traditions, but they are not artistic feats in themselves. *Job* reflects on the problems of evil, suffering, and punishment, viewing Job's fate as a prefiguration of Christ's passion, and of mankind's martyrdom during the Second Word War. *Jeremiah* fuses biblical allusion with a segment of Poland's turbulent history in the early 17th century, thus creating a messianic vision of the nation's downfall and resurrection. *Job* is structured like a Greek tragedy, while *Jeremiah* is closer to Symbolist theater.

It is in their style, however, that both these plays are most marked by the future pope's attachment to a particular tradition, the choice of which was not exactly, well, infallible. Both plays, especially in the original, appear heavily influenced by the worst of the work of Stanislaw Wyspianski, the greatest Polish Symbolist playwright, namely his artificially elevated and pseudo-archaic language. These stylistic qualities are greatly toned down in Taborski's sensitive translation, but stiltedness remains. *Job* and *Jeremiah* were written by a 20-year-old sophomore, and in the Polish edition of Wojtyla's work both plays were listed as juvenilia.

The reader who opens this book in order to see the future pope's mind at work might well begin by reading Wojtyla's next play, *Our God's Brother.* As Taborski notes in his introduction, this play is unique if only because it doesn't happen very often that a playwright has the chance to beatify his play's protagonist. Wojtyla's lifelong fascination with the figure of the legendary Brother Albert (Adam Chmielowski, 1845-1916), a painter and political insurrectionist, protector of the homeless and founder of the order of Albertines, resulted first in his writing a play about him. More than 30 years later, his hero was finally beatified by the Church, and it was John Paul II who announced the event to one million people who came to hear him in Krakow during his second papal visit to Poland.

Our God's Brother opens the main chapter in Wojtyla's dramaturgy; it breaks with the conventions of Symbolist theater and offers a more innovative approach. The principles of "theater of the word" are already put into effect. The dramatic action and the stage movement are reduced to a minimum; the characters serve mainly as exponents of different ethical attitudes, presented in extensive philosophical exchanges. At the same time it is an example of what Kotlarczyk and Wojtyla called "inner theater." As an attempt to "penetrate the man" rather than simply to illustrate the course of his life, the action takes place in the inner space of the protagonist's mind. The dramatic scenes (if that is what they are) occur as if they belonged to external reality, but in fact they are reminiscences played out on the stage of the hero's thoughts.

Wojtyla made a further step in this direction in his two plays written in the early 1960s, *The Jeweler's Shop* and *Radiation of Fatherhood.* These two plays mark a decisive shift toward the mystery play. Their protagonists are modern Everymen of both sexes, who meditate on the problem of their entanglement in the web of relationships with God and other humans, and ponder the fundamental mysteries of love, marriage, and parenthood. This is indeed a theater of the word, or an even more ascetic theater of ideas, one that tries to prove, as Wojtyla put it in one of his essays on theater, that "not only events but also problems are dramatic."

Thus it is mainly the problem that "acts" here, while the actor serves mainly to "carry the problem." The dramatic action is minimized even more than before; each play is actually composed of long monologues, which, though interrelated by their content, are monologues nonetheless. Taborski notes properly that these are not monologues of the Harold Pinter variety, where the isolation of utterances serves to stress the characters' inability to communicate. Rather, these are monologues merely because meditation can be done only in solitude. On another plane, though, these separate meditations form a universal dialogue that permeates the human and divine world, "a conversation of prayers," as Dylan Thomas put it.

From a purely literary standpoint, Wojtyla's plays may provoke different reactions. Certainly not everybody needs this much seriousness and solemnity in art. But they should be required reading, along with his poems and philosophical writings, for anyone who wishes to understand the man, certainly for anybody who wishes to pass judgment on him. I don't mean that the plays clarify John Paul's specific ideas. (Although they do that too: *Our God's Brother,* for instance, contains a revealing discussion, of the problem of social injustice and revolution, which corresponds intriguingly with the pope's pronouncements in Latin America 30-odd years later.) I mean that they illuminate the character of this pope—particularly his open-mindedness, so seldom comprehended by those who are unwilling to see behind the rigid facade of the institution he represents.

Open-minded? The pope? I won't be surprised if I hear a roar of protest. The recent papal visit to this country, and

its largely moronic coverage by the media, left behind two images of John Paul: a Great Communicator and a great guy, or a reactionary bogeyman who denies the benefits of progress to women and gays. Between the lawn sprinkler in the shape of the pope marketed by some fast-thinking entrepreneur (Let Us Spray, it was called) and the practice target of the left there is really not much difference: both are made of plastic.

Behind those flat images an infinitely more complex personality waits to be discovered. What we usually see is John Paul the former actor. We should also see John Paul the former playwright—someone for whom theater means not so much showmanship as dialogue. The mind of a man for whom the theater has been a primary means of expression can hardly be dogmatic. Even when he has shifted from plays to encyclicals, his outlook is still imbued with his recognition of the world's dramatic plurality. The playwright's natural element, after all, is dialogue, the confusion and conversation of our prayers.

Richard Viladesau (essay date March 1992)

SOURCE: "Could Jesus Have Ordained Women? Reflections on *Mulieris Dignitatem,*" in *Thought,* Vol. 67, No. 264, March, 1992, pp. 5-20.

[*In the following essay, Viladesau examines John Paul's historical and anthropological arguments against the ordination of women as delineated in* Mulieris Dignitatem. *According to Viladesau,* Mulieris Dignitatem, *"suffers from weaknesses of questionable theological presumptions and faulty logic."*]

A priest of my acquaintance tells a story of his visit to the home of parishioners in rural Ireland. During the conversation the man of the house broached the subject of women in the church and asked why they could not be ordained. The priest reached into the depths of his theology and replied, "We can't ordain them, Pat, because the Lord Jesus didn't." At this point a strident female voice replied from the kitchen: "Sure, he *would* have if they hadn't killed the poor man so young!"

The issue of ordination of women remains significant in the church, despite or even because of reiterated rejections of its possibility by Rome. It raises not only the theological, exegetical, and historical questions implied by the woman in the anecdote—must the traditional prohibition of women's ordination in some way be linked to Jesus, and if so, on what basis?—but also philosophical and anthropological issues that go beyond the strictly theological realm and engage the interest and the competence of other thinkers.

Perhaps the most comprehensive official statement of the argument against ordination of women is found in the apostolic letter *Mulieris Dignitatem* of Pope John Paul II. This issue is not the principal focus of the document; it occupies a relatively minor place, and it would be a grave mistake to allow a concentration on this issue to overshadow the contribution the Pope's meditation makes to the cause of women in the church and in society. It is indeed a theologically ground-breaking statement on the dignity and complete equality of women, based on a reading of scriptural tradition in light of a philosophy of personalism. In this regard it has a significance beyond "women's" issues that bears on our vision of the human person.

Precisely because it is placed in such a positive context, however, the Pope's reasoning concerning the ordination of only males clarifies the principle he is defending and the theological method that underlies it. Pope John Paul makes abundantly clear that women are equal to men and share equally in the common baptismal priesthood of the faithful. Their exclusion from ministerial orders, therefore, is seen as based not on any intrinsic inferiority of women, but on the explicit will of Christ, which includes a differentiation of sexual roles in the economy of salvation. The essence of the argument is brief enough to be quoted at length.

> Against the broad background of the "great mystery" expressed in the spousal relationship between Christ and the church, it is possible to understand adequately the calling of the "Twelve." In calling only men as his apostles, Christ acted in a completely free and sovereign manner. In doing so, he exercised the same freedom with which, in all his behavior, he emphasized the dignity and the vocation of women without conforming to the prevailing customs and to the traditions sanctioned by the legislation of the time. Consequently, the assumption that he called men to be apostles in order to conform with the widespread mentality of his times does not at all correspond to Christ's way of acting. "Teacher, we know that you are true, and teach the way of God truthfully, and care for no man; for you do not regard the position of men" (Matt. 22.16). These words fully characterize Jesus of Nazareth's behavior. Here one also finds an explanation for the calling of the "Twelve." They are with Christ at the Last Supper. They alone receive the sacramental charge, "Do this in remembrance of me" (Luke 22.19; 1 Cor. 11.24), which is joined to the institution of the eucharist. . . .
>
> Since Christ in instituting the eucharist linked it in such an explicit way to the priestly service of the apostles, it is legitimate to conclude that he thereby wished to express the relationship between man and woman, between what is "feminine" and what is "masculine." It is a relationship willed by God both in the mystery of creation and in the mystery of redemption. It is the eucharist above all that expresses the redemptive act of Christ, the bridegroom, toward the church, the bride. This is clear and unambiguous when the sacramental ministry of the eucharist, in which the priest acts *in persona Christi,* is performed by a man.

The argument presented here has two dimensions, which may be characterized as "historical" and "anthropological." The historical argument is that the designation of males alone for ordained ministry was an explicit choice of Jesus. Jesus was free from the sexual role-conditioning of his time; thus he *could* have ordained women had he so wished; that he did not is proof of his positive will to

exclude women from such office. However, the Pope does not see Jesus's choice as arbitrary, but as one that reveals something intrinsic about the theological meaning of being male and female, in the orders of creation and of grace. The Pope's "anthropological" argument thus posits a sense in which Jesus *could not* have ordained women: he could not have willed to do so, not because of any limitation or conditioning of his freedom, but precisely because he was conscious of and wished to reveal an intrinsic unsuitability of women for this role.

In the following sections I shall examine each of these arguments in detail, attending to the issues they raise for theologians and others. I shall attempt to show that the historical argument, as presented in *Mulieris Dignitatem,* suffers from weaknesses of questionable theological presuppositions and faulty logic. The document's anthropological argument, I shall suggest, is more fundamental and more powerful, being based on the claim of an intrinsic analogy between masculinity and God's relationship to the world as revealed in Christ and represented in ministry. Yet this argument, as stated in the Pope's document and in the theology of Hans Urs von Balthasar, poses a dilemma: for I shall attempt to show that it can only be logically compelling insofar as it implicitly claims an exclusivity for the male analogy of God, and that this in turn implies a general superiority of males over women—positions that the Pope himself explicitly rejects. If this is so, then the force of this argument for exclusively male ministry is undermined. Finally, I shall suggest that a consideration of the theological problem of the ordination of women on either historical or anthropological grounds necessitates the posing of questions that are not addressed by *Mulieris Dignitatem.*

THE HISTORICAL ARGUMENT

The historical/Christological argument, as Pope John Paul notes, essentially repeats the reasoning of the 1977 declaration *"Inter Insigniores"* of the Sacred Congregation for the Doctrine of the Faith. The main points of the argument can be summarized in the following propositions that are either explicitly stated or presupposed:

1. Jesus transcended the mentality of his times with regard to the treatment of women.

2. Jesus chose only men to form the group of the Twelve.

3. The exclusion of women from this group was purposeful and expressed Jesus's sovereign freedom.

4. This choice of males only was not an accommodation to the mentality of the times.

5. The Twelve alone received the "sacramental charge" to celebrate the eucharist.

6. The Twelve were thus explicitly constituted as priests by Jesus.

7. By choosing only the male Twelve for this priestly and apostolic service, Jesus intended to reveal a truth about permanent male and female roles.

8. The priesthood of the church is the continuation of the priestly function of the Twelve.

9. Therefore only men may be admitted to this ministry, in accord with the explicit intention of Jesus.

This argument is clearly Christological, in that it is centered on the explicit will and actions of Jesus. It seems also to hold together only on the basis of a Christology in which Jesus completely transcends normal human limitations, in which he has a full and supra-human knowledge and is aware of all issues and is completely "free and sovereign" in his actions, and in which he foresees, explicitly wills, and concretely establishes the structures of the future church.

However, this Christological picture and the reasoning it supports appear at odds with much contemporary Christian theology on historical and logical grounds. First, the foundation of a number of these historical/Christological assertions seems open to question. In some instances they go beyond the scriptural and historical evidence; in others they apply anachronistic concepts to the data. Second, even if the assertions are accepted as true, the conclusions do not appear logically warranted by the premises.

The first contention, that Jesus's treatment of women "constitutes an 'innovation' with respect to the prevailing custom at that time," is clearly supported by a number of instances reported in the gospels, cited both here and in "*Inter Insigniores*" (John 4.27; Matt. 9.20ff.; Luke 7.37; John 8.11; Mark 10.2-11; Matt. 19.3-9), even if we must be cautious about attributing detailed historical accuracy to texts that clearly bear the stamp of the evangelists' theological purposes and contexts. Nevertheless, as "*Inter Insigniores*" admits, these texts give only isolated instances, and cannot be said clearly to demonstrate the contention. Taken together, they provide a kind of "convergence" that allows us to conclude that Jesus's attitude toward women was both liberated and liberating as compared with that of his contemporaries.

It would not be logically warranted, however, to generalize from this that Jesus must have been *totally* free of *all* societally conditioned attitudes regarding women, so that his every action regarding the female sex bespeaks a perfect freedom from the customs and ideas of his times. This position cannot be validly induced from the limited instances given in the New Testament, and drawing such a universal conclusion from such particular evidence could be warranted only on grounds of an *a priori* conviction that Jesus *must have* had a perfect attitude. This in turn seems grounded in the Christological position that holds Jesus's human mind to have possessed a superhuman and a historical mode of knowing that excluded all ignorance, limitation, and conditioning, at least in matters pertaining

to salvation. This seems part of the Christological presupposition of the Pope's meditation: "'the mysteries of the kingdom' were known to him in every detail. He also 'knew what was in man' [John 2.25], in his inmost being, in his 'heart.' He was a witness of God's eternal plan for the human being. . . . He was also perfectly aware of the consequences of sin . . . .'"

It is beyond the scope of this essay to enter into the classical theological problem of the consciousness of Christ, and in particular of the interaction between his fully human mind and the divine intellect. It must suffice to note that, in contrast to what is apparently implied in the Pope's statements, most contemporary theologians and scripture scholars hold that the human mind of Jesus was truly historically conditioned. That is, even though Jesus's humanity was inspired and transformed by his unity with God, the transcendent experience of that mystery ("hypostatic union") always necessarily expressed itself in a mind that remained truly human and therefore necessarily expressed even its deepest intuitions in time-conditioned language and categories. This does not mean, of course, that Jesus was simply subservient to the received categories of his time and place. Even ordinary intelligent people can expand and reformulate their ways of thinking and have new insights that go beyond their social conditioning; *a fortiori* it is clear that Jesus was constantly breaking through the thought and behavior patterns of his day in the light of his inner experience of God and God's Kingdom. But such breakthroughs would of their nature be concrete and progressive, not total or systematic; they would still be subject to the intrinsic limitations of even the best available mode of expression, and would necessarily occur within a linguistic and social context that could not be *completely* transcended.

Furthermore, there would always necessarily remain areas that were unknown because unexperienced: aspects of experience not yet integrated into a new vision, ideas taken for granted as part of the historical setting, and the normal possibility of mistaken memory or understanding. Thus, as Raymond Brown shows in his *Jesus God and Man,* despite the gospels' emphasis on his "superhuman" knowledge, certain passages nevertheless portray Jesus as sharing normal human ignorance about concrete matters and as both able and needing to learn in the normal human way (Mark 5.30-33; Luke 2.46, 52); he is credited with mistaken citations of scripture (Mark 2.26; Matt. 23.35); he takes for granted certain mistaken ideas of his times, like the Davidic authorship of the Psalms (Mark 12.36) and the historicity of the Book of Jonah (Matt. 12.39-41); he interprets the scriptures in the common rabbinic way, in violation of the sense of the texts (John 10.33-36; Mark 12.36); in many areas he apparently accepts without criticism the mythological world view of his times, with its demonology, its material conception of the afterlife, and its apocalyptic expectations (Mark 9.17-18; Matt. 12.43-45; Mark 9.43ff.; Matt. 9.48; Mark 13.24-25; Mark 13.7-8).

However, it remains true that Jesus appears to have made extraordinary breakthroughs on crucial religious issues, even if modern scholarship on the Judaism of Jesus's times forces us to be more cautious about attributing absolute novelty to all his teachings. Some of these breakthroughs regarded attitudes toward the Law, toward non-Jews, and toward women. Nevertheless, Jesus did not institute a program of complete liberation from observance of the Law, or of mission to the gentiles; these had to await the coming of the Spirit after his death and resurrection. His revolutionary attitudes were combined during his life with a certain acceptance of many prevailing attitudes of his context. In a Christology that acknowledges the true humanity of Jesus as one who was "like us in all things but sin," this fact need not be explained away as a conscious and purposeful accommodation to others' mentality; it is to be expected that Jesus's own mentality would in many ways remain within the conceptual and moral framework of his times, even while he transcended it both in its essential dynamism and in particular dramatic instances that came within the purview of his mission. There would be many things, however, that did not arise as issues for Jesus, and on which he would presumably accept the prevailing customs and understandings.

The assertion of "*Inter Insigniores*" and **Mulieris Digni-tatem** that Jesus's choice of males alone as members of "the Twelve" implies a deliberate and purposeful *exclusion* of women reveals a Christological perspective in which such normal conditionings and limitations of Jesus's mind and actions do not enter into consideration. Indeed, both documents seem to presume that the only possible alternative to a purposeful exclusion of women on Jesus's part would be an equally purposeful and knowing *concession* to the mentality of his times. They seem to assume, furthermore, that the latter represents the position of those who think that Jesus's action in this regard need not be normative today. Thus both documents take pains to refute the argument that Jesus avoided choosing women for the Twelve as an opportune concession to the customs of the day or "following the accepted mentality of his times," but neither seems to envisage the possibility that this mentality might have been shared or at least never completely critically examined by Jesus himself, or even that other accidental or time-conditioned factors might have been operative in Jesus's concrete choice.

Similar Christological presumptions seem to underlie other critical assertions in the Pope's argument. It appears taken for granted that Jesus explicitly foresaw and instituted the actual priestly ministry of the church by conferring it on the Twelve apostles alone at the Last Supper. However, although the essentially historical account of Jesus's command to commemorate him certainly implies a community gathered in his name and memory (and this in turn implies some kind of ministry), few scholars today would attribute to the historical Jesus an explicit foreknowledge and intention of the church in its concrete later institutions. Indeed, Jesus (like the earliest Christians) appears to have expected an imminent arrival of the eschatological Kingdom of God, whose coming his own death would somehow bring about; it is difficult to reconcile this with a clear vision of a permanent institutional church.

Furthermore, our limited information about the earliest church does not support the presumption that only the Twelve or those appointed by them presided at the Eucharist. As Raymond Brown writes, "there is simply no compelling evidence for the classic thesis that the members of the Twelve always presided when they were present, and that there was a chain of ordination passing the power of presiding at the Eucharist from the Twelve to missionary apostles to presbyter-bishops." It seems more likely that the very diverse early Christian communities took Jesus's charge to "do this" as addressed to the church in general, which the Twelve represent (an idea echoed in the present third Eucharistic prayer, in which we speak of Jesus commanding us to celebrate these mysteries), and that these communities designated ministers in different ways, according to their diverse structures. There is, Brown notes, at least some evidence that others than apostles and presbyters may at times have presided. Moreover, Brown shows convincingly that the episcopacy and priesthood of the church as they actually developed do not totally coincide with the notion or functions of the "apostles"; nor can an historical continuity of "ordination" from the latter be demonstrated.

Acceptance of such scholarship does not, of course, deny the emergence of the priesthood as the work of the Spirit in a church implicitly willed by Christ and in continuity with his mission, but it does seriously challenge the Christological foundation of the Pope's argument as summarized above, and in particular his conclusion that the norms for the present institution of the priesthood can be traced directly to an intent of Jesus to define masculine and feminine roles.

In summation, the Pope's historical-Christological argument against the ordination of women in **Mulieris Dignitatem** appears based on a "classicist" Christology that overlooks the findings of modern biblical scholarship and the theology that flows from them.

Even if one were to accept the Pope's Christological presuppositions, however, there is another difficulty with his argumentation, on the basis of logic. Another anecdote will perhaps serve to make the problem clear. In an episode of the British comedy series "Bless Me, Father," set in a Catholic parish in the 1950s, a woman taking convert instructions asks a young curate why women cannot be ordained. His reply indicates that the priesthood derives from the Twelve apostles, and that Jesus chose that all his apostles should be men. The prospective convert thinks for a moment, and then says: "But all of the apostles were also Jewish. Are *you* Jewish, Father?"

We might clarify the logical issue further by expanding the analogy that the anecdote suggests and by accepting the presuppositions of the Pope's argument. Jesus was clearly beyond the mentality of his times in dealing with gentiles. He broke customs and traditions sanctioned by his religious background. Hence, in calling only Jews to be apostles he could not have been simply conforming to the mentality of his society, but must have been acting in a completely sovereign and free manner. Since in instituting the Eucharist Christ linked it to the priestly service of the Twelve, it is legitimate to conclude that he wished to express thereby the permanent relationship between gentile and Jew in the church's ministry. Therefore only Jewish Christians may be admitted to the priesthood.

The fallacy in this argument is immediately apparent. Although it is true that all Jesus's disciples were Jews, it does not follow that he called them simply *because* they were Jews, or that this is a permanent and essential condition for priesthood (even if one accepts a derivation of priesthood from the Twelve); there were other factors overlooked in the argument. Does not the same reasoning apply to the sex of the apostles? Even if one holds that Jesus completely transcended all historical conditioning, we cannot read his mind to know what was "intended" by his actions. How can we know that male sex was an intrinsic and not an accidental factor in Jesus's *de facto* choice?

With this question we come to the second, anthropological element in the Pope's Christological meditation; for he argues that there is in fact something intrinsic about the difference between the sexes that is operative in and shown by Jesus's choice of male apostles.

The Anthropological Argument

In Pope John Paul's mind, Christ's choice of only males for the ministry of the Twelve was not an arbitrary act of will, but reveals a basic anthropological principle inherent in the nature of humanity from the creation, as well as a basic Christological principle inherent in the economy of salvation. This point is of great significance, for it means that this element is in principle separable from the historical arguments discussed above. Although the Pope sees his anthropological position as connected with Jesus's historical attitude, its validity does not depend on the presumed *de facto* connection, but can be asserted on the basis of independent theological reasoning.

This anthropological-Christological element is where Pope John Paul most significantly expands the treatment of "*Inter Insigniores*". The latter had enunciated the basic principle that the celebrant of the Eucharist must be male in order to provide a more adequate "natural" image of Christ, for whom he acts ("*in persona Christi*") in relation to the church. The document however had not clearly answered the objection referred to above: why is sharing Jesus's sex crucial to representing him, rather than sharing his Jewish race (or for that matter any of a number of other features of his historical person: color, physiognomy, culture, psychology)?

Pope John Paul implicitly replies to this difficulty by placing the entire question of priestly ministry within the wider context of a "spousal" theology based on the analogy of bridegroom and bride enunciated in the Letter to the Ephesians (5.25-32). This idea is already present in "*Inter Insigniores*," but Pope John Paul enlarges it and makes it central to his exposition. (It is to be noted that the treatment of "The Eucharist," where the ordination of women is dealt with in *Mulieris Dignitatem,* is a subdivision of the major section entitled "The Church—The Bride of Christ.") The male sex of the representative of Christ is significant because Christ's relation to the church is precisely that of bridegroom to bride, and this symbol, echoing the images of spousal love in the prophets, is in turn founded on the relationship of male to female established by God in creation. It is this that appears to lie behind the assertion that in establishing a male priesthood Jesus "wished to express the relationship between man and woman, between what is 'feminine' and what is 'masculine,' . . . a relationship willed by God both in the mystery of creation and in the mystery of redemption."

Not surprisingly, John Paul's treatment of this topic contains a number of striking similarities to the writings on the subject by the Pope's favorite theologian, Hans Urs von Balthasar, who was elevated to the cardinalate shortly before his death. Specifically, we can find in *Mulieris Dignitatem* echoes of von Balthasar's Marian and "spousal" theology of the church, as well as his exegesis of Ephesians 5.21-33, a text that plays a major part in the Pope's considerations. Since the Pope actually quotes from von Balthasar's essay on the ordination of women ("Frauenpriestertum?"), these similarities are clearly not fortuitous. But there are also aspects of *Mulieris Dignitatem* that seem to take it beyond von Balthasar's thought. A brief reference to this aspect of von Balthasar's theology can therefore perhaps help to illuminate both the background of Pope John Paul's views and their originality.

Von Balthasar is strongly committed to the idea of difference and complementarity between the sexes, and believes that the modern feminist movement is mistaken in trying to overcome such differences. The forgetfulness of the femininity of women is for him one of the defects of an era characterized by technology and positivism; the Catholic church because of its structure is a countervailing force to this failing of our age, and is perhaps the last bulwark in humanity of a true appreciation of the differences between the sexes. The female is related to values of being and meaning rather than those of accomplishment; woman's essential role is to provide reserves of safety and home for the ever-wandering and task-orienting male.

The genetic sexual differences between male and female are for von Balthasar the basis of a natural theological symbolism necessarily reflected in the different roles of males and females in the church. In the sexual act, von Balthasar says, the man is the initiator and leader, and the woman, even though not passive, is truly receptive ("Ein Wort"). Analogously, the entire creation is female (radically receptive) to God, who, as the Origin and

Source, is the male principle. This fundamental relationship is reflected and repeated in the relationship of Christ as the male principle to the church as his bride. Precisely as male, Christ represents the Origin, the Father, and the church is the woman made fruitful by him. In his meditation "The Conquest of the Bride," von Balthasar portrays Christ speaking these words: "Being God, I am the Source and am before every being, and for this reason the man is the glory of God and the source of the woman, and God-become-human is the man, while the Church is a woman, since the woman is the glory of the man." For this reason woman has the easier task, for "woman is being-created as such with regard to God and being-church with regard to Christ. She has nothing to represent which she is not herself, while the male must represent the Origin of all life, which he can never be."

Von Balthasar sees the primary model for the church as bride in Mary, whose "yes" to God is the paradigm of receptive readiness. In the perspective of the fundamental Marian nature of the church, the equality of women is not something that needs to be painfully striven for, since it is already present. This does not mean identity of roles, however. Mary is Queen of Apostles, but does not have apostolic office; she has something different and better. Likewise, women in general have a more fundamental role in the church than that of holding priestly office. Woman in fact incorporates the essence of the church, so that every member of the church, even priests, must assume a female/receptive attitude with regard to the Lord of the church. On the other hand, by their office the members of the male hierarchy are representatives of the bridegroom Christ within this encompassing femininity of the church. Because it is the bridegroom who is represented in the male role of leadership, and especially in the Eucharist, in which Christ continually "begets" the church, the office of the Twelve and their successors is essentially and not accidentally masculine, although exercised within the wider context of the essentially feminine and Marian church. Thus a woman who sought this office would be seeking a specifically masculine role, and in doing so would be forgetting the essential primacy of the feminine aspect of the church over the masculine.

Whether or not von Balthasar's theology is a specific source of Pope John Paul's Christology and anthropology, it clearly manifests parallel ideas and concerns and represents a powerful statement of the argument that an exclusively male priesthood is based not on an arbitrary command but on an intrinsic connection between Christ's masculinity and his salvific function. The "separate but equal" roles of men and women in the church, on this thesis, are based on two diverse ways of being human, each of which reflects in a distinct way the relationship of humanity to God.

Can one then argue, as von Balthasar and Pope John Paul do, from the idea of God or Christ as "bridegroom" of the church to the necessity of a male clergy to "represent" him? There seem to be major difficulties with this reasoning. First, the notion of "representation" needs close examination and clarification. In exactly what sense does a priest in fact "represent" God or Christ, and precisely *as* "bridegroom"? Is this a necessary and adequate way of describing the function of the Eucharistic celebrant, for example? Furthermore, even granting a clear meaning to the idea of "representation," could not the reasoning in fact be reversed: the priest "represents" the church and acts "*in persona ecclesiae*"; the church is female, and the bride of Christ; therefore, the priest ought to be female?

At the root of this difficulty is the fact that the argument attempts to draw specific conclusions from a *metaphor.* As Sallie McFague has shown, metaphors and models are crucial to theological thought, but by their very nature they demand plurality: there must be a number of complementary metaphors in order to express the richness and complexity of the relationships between God and God's creatures. When any single metaphor becomes so dominant as to be exclusive, or is implicitly thought to encompass every aspect of the human-divine relationship, then one ends by absolutizing certain aspects of that relationship, while losing others. In that case the transcendence of God is compromised by anthropomorphism, and the created term of the analogy is idolized. It is for this reason that Catholic theology rightfully insists on the negative moment in every analogy: God is like *x,* but is always more profoundly *un*like *x,* and possesses the qualities in question in an eminent and unimaginable way. It is also for this reason that no single analogy can ever suffice.

In the case at hand, it is clear that the metaphor of God (or Christ) as bridegroom, world (or church) as bride, is a legitimate one, and leads to fruitful reflection on the nature of creation and salvation. Can it be claimed, however, that *every* aspect of these realities is determined by a metaphor in which God is male with respect to a female world, or in which Christ is the spousal "other" to the female church? If so (as seems implied by certain of von Balthasar's statements), then this amounts to a claim for universal male superiority, no matter what protestations to the contrary may be made; for if God is *in every respect* more like a man than like a woman, then it follows that the male sex is more like God, more in God's image. If, on the other hand, one does not claim absoluteness for this metaphor, then other analogies are possible, and the question of *which* aspects of our humanity and of our relation to God are represented by each metaphor remains open. (If, for example, one admits that God is to be represented as "active" with regard to a "receptive" creation, then it may be allowed to follow that God is more like the male than the female *in the act of procreation.* But is this sexual act to be taken as the sole determinant of what is "intrinsically" masculine and feminine? If one takes the act of *bearing* a child as the metaphor, then God is more like the actively giving mother than like the receptive child or the helpless father. In this instance, the female principle is active, not receptive: the mother not only gives physical existence, but shares her very life, nourishes, houses, and finally brings forth her child, while the father awaits pas-sively. Could the metaphor of God's motherhood then apply to ministry? It is interesting that it was extensively so used in the Middle Ages.)

In *Mulieris Dignitatem* Pope John Paul II clearly avoids absolutizing the metaphors of God as male (Father or bridegroom) by adverting to the phenomenon of anthropomorphism and insisting on the negative moment in every analogy. Moreover, he explicitly refers to the possibility of female metaphors for God, in particular God as Mother. For the Pope, then, there is nothing intrinsically and exclusively masculine about the relationship of God to creation. In this John Paul goes beyond the texts cited above from von Balthasar. In doing so, however, he also weakens the theological case for the exclusivity of the bridegroom-bride metaphor with regard to Christ and the church; for this metaphor can no longer be regarded as grounded in a more basic analogy according to which humanity is *always* to be thought of as "female" with regard to God's (male) activity.

In fact, of course, there are other and more central metaphors for the relationship of Christ to the church that do not imply sexual differentiation: for example, the image of the church as the body or members of Christ, or the image of Christ as our "brother." As noted above, there are even instances in medieval spiritual writers (including such not inconsiderable figures as Anselm of Canterbury and Bernard of Clairvaux) of a female image being applied to Christ: like God in the Old Testament, Christ is portrayed as Mother in giving birth to the church and nurturing it; and, significantly, this function is attributed also to those with office in the church, particularly abbots.

As was observed above, the signal innovation of *Mulieris Dignitatem* over "*Inter Insigniores*" with regard to exclusion of women from ordination is the placing of the question within the framework of the "spousal" theology of the bridegroom; this ostensibly answers the question why the maleness of Jesus, rather than other accidental aspects of his historical person, is crucial to "representing" him to the community. But once it is admitted in principle that the spousal analogy is simply a metaphor, and not the only possible one, the rationale loses its force, and the question recurs: why should *this* metaphor, in which there is a sexual element, be determinative for office in the church?

The whole context of *Mulieris Dignitatem* seems to suggest that the centrality of this metaphor in the case of priesthood is based on a *prior* conviction concerning "natural" sexual role divisions, based on God's disposition of humanity in creation. This would return us to von Balthasar's assertion that church office is intrinsically masculine; but not simply on the basis of "representing" the male Christ, or because *every* activity of God with regard to the world is analogously "masculine," and must be so represented, but on the ground that *some* activities of the church on God's behalf—those specifically connected with sacramental leadership and order—*de facto* involve primarily masculine traits. Is there any anthropological basis for such an assertion?

It seems undeniable, in the light of contemporary studies, that there are significant genetically imprinted physical and psychological differences between men and women, and that some kinds of role differentiation stem from these. The *degree* of sexual divergence and the actual parameters of the sexual division of life and labor, however, seem to derive from cultural factors, and are to a large measure within the control of human decision. "Male" and "female" roles and characteristics are therefore not absolutely universal and static realities, but have a certain latitude of definition, even though grounded on a basic biological framework. Several questions then arise.

If there are roles at least indirectly sexually determined by innate genetic dispositions or tendencies, is the Christian sacramental priesthood among them, or is its association with the male sex determined purely by cultural and historical circumstances? Does the ordained ministry, in its essence, call for specifically masculine traits or simply for human traits? Are there aspects of such ministry that could call for specifically female traits? Has the ministerial priesthood been too narrowly realized because of its restriction to males? Until recently, none of the great world religions has admitted women to the clerical state. Is this because of something intrinsically masculine about the office, or because of the historical association of the so-called "higher" religions with Indo-European patriarchal societies worshipping a Father-god?

Positions of official leadership and power in the church and in society have historically been held by men, albeit with some notable exceptions in the secular world. Is there something intrinsically masculine about socio-political power? If so, should this be the model for office in the church, in which service and not lordship is supposed to be the norm for those who lead? Are the kinds of leadership and power exercised by men essentially or only accidentally unfeminine? Are they the only possible kinds? Women perform ministries in the church, and have a long history of leadership in certain aspects of Christian life (one may think of the orders of religious women in missionary and teaching roles, for example). How are these related to what is sacramentalized in ordination?

These and similar considerations seem to need examination if one is to attempt to examine the question of ordination of women on anthropological grounds.

CONCLUSION

I have examined only the two arguments against ordination of women that seem central to Pope John Paul II's thought. The historical-Christological argument seems not only to presuppose, but to depend on, certain positions that are (at least) questionable in light of contemporary scriptural and historical studies and of an adequate theological valuation of the true humanity of Jesus. Although some may deny the primacy of the historico-critical method in evaluating church doctrines and practices, such a method is certainly relevant to evaluation of an argument that purports to be based precisely on history. The anthropological-Christological argument as presented by von Balthasar and resumed by the Pope, starting from the "spousal" character of God's relationship to the world and Christ's relationship to the church, as well as the "Marian"-receptive character of the latter, seems based on the absolutizing of a particular metaphor. This appears inconsistent with the views on equality presented in earlier sections of the document, unless it can be grounded in another kind of anthropological argument, related to the Pope's analysis of a sexual differentiation willed by God from the creation. Such an argument, which goes beyond the scope of **Mulieris Dignitatem,** might attempt to draw support from the data of genetic and socio-biological studies. However, even if such support were found, this approach would still raise a number of questions about the very nature of ordained ministry that would have to be answered before any conclusions could be drawn on its basis. It is at least problematic that ordained ministry should *a priori* be restricted to aspects of service associated with "male" characteristics.

Of course, a critique of arguments for exclusively male ministry does not in itself constitute a positive argument in favor of the ordination of women. Moreover, it has been the purpose of this analysis to confine itself only to Christological/anthropological reflections raised by **Mulieris Dignitatem.** As was noted above, the case against ordination of women is not the central concern of this document; it is not to be expected, therefore, that every aspect of the question should be considered there. Aside from Christological and anthropological considerations there is also, for example, the important question of the church's long and constant historical tradition. This tradition might be argued by some to be normative, even if it is based on historically conditioned decisions that might *per se* have been determined otherwise. Such arguments, and the question of the criteria on which they might be judged, raise important methodological and ecclesiological (and hence also ecumenical) issues which go beyond the scope of present considerations. It is my hope, however, that these limited reflections may serve to advance the discussion by clarifying some critical issues, pointing out the more fundamental methodological problems which lie behind the explicit points at issue, and inviting further exchange of ideas in these areas.

Avery Dulles (essay date 23 October 1993)

SOURCE: "The Prophetic Humanism of John Paul II," in *America,* October 23, 1993, pp. 6-11.

[*In the following essay, Dulles examines John Paul's humanist view of individual conscience, communalism, political participation, and transcendent order. According to Dulles, "John Paul II evidently sees himself and the church as divinely commissioned to be the advocates of authentic humanity."*]

For some time I have been asking myself whether there is a single rubric under which it might be possible to summarize the message of the present pontificate. I have thought about the Pope's concern for the inner unity of the Catholic Church, the new evangelization, the dialogue between faith and culture, and reconstruction of the economic order. All these themes are clearly important to John Paul II, but no one of them permeates his teaching as a whole. In seeking a more comprehensive theme, I have hit upon the idea of prophetic humanism.

In the case of this Pope, as in the case of any other, it is difficult to ascertain which of his statements are actually composed by himself and which are simply accepted by him after having been drafted by others. I have no inside information to help me in tiffs discernment. My method will be to rely principally on books and articles that he published under the name of Karol Wojtyla before he became Pope, and then inspect documents from his papacy that closely resemble these in style and in substance. Several of his encyclicals are so personal in tone that it seems safe to attribute them to himself, even though he presumably had assistants in the final process of editing. Most of his major documents are amply furnished with footnotes that he would scarcely have had time to compose.

1. The Concept of Prophetic Humanism

The concept of prophetic humanism requires some explanation. Any humanism must be a system of thought centered on the human person. The Pope himself generally uses the term "man," which, at least in Latin, has no reference to gender. In quoting or paraphrasing his statements I shall sometimes use the English word "man" to mean an individual member of the human race. Near-synonyms such as "person" are not always satisfactory, given the Pope's understanding of personalization.

Humanism, moreover, implies a high esteem for the human as having intrinsic value. As we shall see, the defense of the dignity of the human person and the promotion of human rights stand at the very center of the Pope's program.

This program may be called prophetic for several reasons. A prophet is someone who speaks out of a strong conviction and with a sense of vocation. John Paul II evidently sees himself and the church as divinely commissioned to be advocates of authentic humanity. The prophet speaks with a certain sense of urgency. Karol Wojtyla, even when he writes as a philosopher, is never the detached academic. He is conscious of speaking to a world that is in the throes of a crisis—a crisis of dehumanization. Like most prophets, he senses that he is faced with enormous opposition and that his is perhaps a lonely voice. He is not afraid to confront others in his struggle to salvage human dignity.

Yet the Pope is no pessimist. He is convinced that in the face of human needs God has provided an answer in

Christ, who came that we might have life to the full. He sees the Gospel as a message of hope, love and truth, not for Christians or Catholics alone, but for every human being. The church, he believes, has an essential contribution to make to the task of making the world more human. He repeatedly quotes from Vatican II the statement that the church is called to be a sign and safeguard of the transcendence of the human person ("Pastoral Constitution on the Church in the Modern World," No. 76).

The central and unifying task of the church, for John Paul II, is to rediscover and promote the inviolable dignity of every human person. "Man," as he puts it in his first encyclical, is the way of the church—"man in the full truth of his existence, of his personal being and also of his community and social being" (*Redemptor Hominis* [1979], No. 14). The church's mission must therefore be carried out with a view to humanity, and for that very reason with a view to God. Following Christ, who is both God and man, the church must link anthropocentrism and theocentrism in a deep and organic way (*Dives in Misericordia* [1980], No. 1).

2. Human Dignity

The first point is to consider the Pope's understanding of what it means to be human. Especially in his major philosophical work, *The Acting Person* (1969, revised 1977, English version 1979), he develops an original anthropology that owes something to classical Thomism and something to modern personalist phenomenology, especially as represented by Max Scheler (1874-1928). He is also conscious of points of contact with the philosophy of action of Maurice Blondel (d. 1949). In place of the Cartesian cogito ("I think"), which begins with the thinking subject, John Paul prefers to begin with action. "I act, therefore I am," might fairly characterize his starting point. Through action, he maintains, one can come to know the real character of the human being as a free, creative, responsible subject. By my free actions, he asserts, I make myself what I am.

Although John Paul's focus is initially on man as subject, his analysis brings out the necessary role of the object. As free and intelligent beings we are called to make decisions, and for these decisions to be meaningful they must conform to the truth. The root of human dignity consists in the capacity to transcend mere self-interest and embrace what is objectively true and good. One element in this objective order is the existence of other human beings with the same essential dignity as my own. With an explicit reference to Kant, Wojtyla declares that human beings must always be treated as ends, never as mere means. He frequently quotes from Vatican II the statement that, alone among all creatures on earth, man exists for his own sake.

For Wojtyla the ethical dimension is determinative for the value of all human action. When I act according to truth, I fulfill the deepest dynamism of my being and become good. When I do not act according to the truth, I do not fulfill myself and I become bad. In his philosophical works Wojtyla does not explain very clearly how a person intuits the truth. As George Hunston Williams remarks, he "fails to provide the reader with what the conditions are for coming to the truth" (*The Mind of John Paul II,* 1981). Williams hints that the operative ethics behind Wojtyla's proposal come from Christian revelation and Catholic tradition, and I suspect he is correct.

Speaking prophetically, the Pope formulates his doctrine of freedom in opposition to a merely negative concept, according to which freedom would consist in not being coerced or not being obligated by law. Already at Vatican II Bishop Wojtyla had pleaded successfully for amendments to the "Declaration on Religious Freedom" to specify that freedom is not a mere entitlement to do whatever one pleases. During his first visit as Pope to the United States in 1979, he warned that the concept of freedom should not be used as a pretext for moral anarchy, as though it could justify conduct that violates the moral order. Freedom, he insisted, is not an end in itself. It is a capacity to fulfill one's deepest aspirations by choosing the true and the good. In this connection the Pope likes to quote the saying of Jesus, "The truth shall make you free" (Jn. 8:32). When freedom is rightly understood, moral norms do not appear as a limitation. Truth is the guide to meaningful action, action in accordance with conscience.

We can, of course, disobey the voice of conscience and act against the truth as we perceive it. Violations of conscience do not bring about self-fulfillment; they result in anti-values and frustration. The very ability to commit sin testifies in favor of the dignity of the person. Because we have the capacity freely to embrace the good, we also have the power to reject it. "To erase the notion of sin," says the Pope, "would be to impoverish man in a fundamental part of his experience of his humanity" (*'Be Not Afraid!': André Frossard in Conversation with Pope John Paul II,* 1984). The loss of the sense of sin, which seems to be an affliction of our time, is evidence of the failure to see man as a responsible moral subject oriented toward truth and goodness.

Thus far, we have been looking at human dignity from a philosophical point of view, without reference to revelation, which confirms and enhances human dignity. As a theologian, John Paul II draws initially on the creation narratives of Genesis. Man, he holds, was created to the image and likeness of God and destined to have dominion over the rest of creation (Gen. 1:26-28). But the full meaning of human life cannot be grasped except in the light of Christ, who, in revealing God, reveals humanity to itself (*Redemptor Hominis,* Nos. 8-9). There is no more impressive evidence for the value that God sets upon the human than God's gift of His own Son as the price of our redemption (No. 20). Every human being is intended by God to be redeemed and to come through Christ to final self-realization.

Some philosophers, influenced by Feuerbach and his school, have contended that God must die in order for man to attain his full stature. The present Pope, like Henri de Lubac (*The Drama of Atheist Humanism*), argues just the contrary. The world must be reminded, he says, that while men and women can organize the world without God, without God it will always in the last analysis be organized against humanity. In denying the transcendent source and goal of our being, we would deprive man of the source of his true dignity (*Centesimus Annus* [1991], No. 13). Without God as creator there would be no inviolable human rights. Without Christ as saviour, human hope would no longer extend to everlasting union with the divine. In this connection John Paul II quotes from Augustine the famous sentence, "You have made us for yourself, O Lord, and our hearts cannot find rest until they rest in you" (*Confessions,* 1.1).

3. Human Existence as Communal

Against excessive individualism John Paul II insists that human existence is essentially communal. He writes: "Man's resemblance to God finds its basis, as it were, in the mystery of the most holy Trinity. Man resembles God not only because of the spiritual nature of his immortal soul but also by reason of his social nature, if by this we understand that he 'cannot fully realize himself except in an act of pure self-giving'" (*Sources of Renewal,* 1981). The Pope then goes on to explain that human beings are intended to exist not only side by side, but in mutuality, for the sake of one another. The Latin term *communio* indicates the reciprocal giving and receiving that goes on within this relationship.

Human community is realized on many different levels, from the family to the state and the international community. Vatican II, in its "Pastoral Constitution on the Church in the Modern World," had four separate chapters dealing with family, culture, economy and political community. On each of these levels conscience obliges us to transcend the narrow limits of our own self-enhancement and to contribute to the good of others. In a small unit such as the family, the members act primarily for the individual good of their partners, but in larger groups the primary objective is the well-being of the group as such. As distinct from the "I-thou" community, the "we"-society comprises a group who exist and act together for the sake, primarily, of the common good.

4. The Family

The family, according to John Paul II, is the basic cell of society and for that reason the primary locus of humanization (*Christifideles Laici* [1988], No. 40). The Pope's doctrine of the family, adumbrated in his early work *Love and Responsibility* (1960), is amplified in several documents from his papacy. He sees the family in a state of crisis, especially because of the reigning consumerist mentality that leads to false concepts concerning freedom and sexual fulfillment (*Familiaris Consortio* [1981], Nos. 6, 32). He draws on the traditional Catholic teaching regarding conjugal morality, divorce and remarriage in

order to protect the family as a stable community of generous love. Sexuality, he asserts, is realized in a truly human way only if it is an integral part of the loving communion by which a man and a woman commit themselves to one another until death. The sexual relationship between married persons should always promote human dignity. The unitive meaning of marriage cannot be separated from the procreative. The deliberate exclusion of procreation, according to the Pope, is detrimental to the unitive relationship between the couple.

Although Christian preachers have often proclaimed that wives should be subject to their husbands, John Paul II goes to some pains to point out that the domination of the husband is a sign and effect of original sin. In the Christian order there should be an equality of mutual service between wives and husbands (*Mulieris Dignitatem* [1988], No. 10). In this connection the Pope sets forth a doctrine of women's rights based on the complementarity and communion between male and female.

5. The Order of Culture

Culture has been a major concern of John Paul II from his early days, when he developed his talents for music, poetry and drama. Between 1977 and 1980 he published several important papers on the philosophy of culture. In 1982, when establishing the Pontifical Council for Culture, he wrote in a letter to Cardinal Agostino Casaroli: "Since the beginning of my pontificate I have considered the church's dialogue with the cultures of our time to be a vital area, one in which the destiny of the world at the end of the 20th century is at stake."

The Pope's theory of culture is thoroughly humanistic. "Man lives a really human life thanks to a culture" (address to UNESCO, Paris, 1980). Man is the subject of culture, its object and its term. Culture is of man, since no other being has culture; it is from man, since man creates it; and it is for man, since its prime purpose is human advancement. Everyone lives according to some culture, which determines the mode of one's existence.

Culture, as a human achievement, involves our capacity for self-creation, which in turn radiates into the world of products. Culture is a materialization of the human spirit and at the same time a spiritualization of matter. It thus serves to render our world more human.

We should not imagine that every culture, just because it is a culture, is above criticism. John Paul speaks of a dialogue between faith and culture. Like everything human, culture needs to be healed, ennobled and perfected through Christ and the Gospel (*Redemptoris Missio* [1991], No. 54). Because culture is a human creation, it is also marked by sin. The church must prophetically oppose what the Pope, at his visit to Denver last August, called "the culture of death." On another occasion (1984) he said: "More than ever, in fact, man is seriously threatened by anti-culture which reveals itself, among other ways, in growing violence, murderous confrontations, exploitation of instincts and selfish interests." In technologically advanced societies, people tend to value everything in terms of production and consumption, so that man is reduced to an epiphenomenon. Authentic culture, on the contrary, resists the reduction of man to the state of an object. "It signifies the march towards a world where man can achieve his humanity in the transcendence proper to him, which calls him to truth, goodness and beauty."

One aspect of the contemporary crisis of culture is the crisis in education. To an alarming degree education has become focused on having rather than being. All too often it turns people into instruments of the economic or political system. In the alienated society, education is in danger of becoming a form of manipulation (UNESCO Address, 1980).

The term "alienation," which the Pope borrows from Marxist literature, is central to his social philosophy. For him it is the opposite of participation. In the good society all the members contribute to the common good and share in its benefits. Alienation arises when the society does not serve the dynamism of its own members, but unfolds at their expense, so that they, or some of them, feel cut off. The neighbor becomes the stranger, even the enemy.

6. The Economic Order

The dynamics of participation and alienation, which are the key to John Paul II's theory of culture and education, are also central to his economic analysis. While he does not purport to give lessons in economics, he insists that any sound economy must accept the primacy of the human person and the common good as guiding principles. His teaching on this subject is set forth in three important encyclicals.

In the first of these, ***Laborem Exercens*** (1981), he concentrates on the theological meaning of work, as a fulfillment of the biblical mandate to subdue the earth (Gen. 1:28). He protests against systems in which man is treated as an instrument of production rather than as the effective subject of work. By transforming nature, says the Pope, man can achieve greater fulfillment as a human being. All too often labor is regarded as a mere means to the production of capital and property, to the detriment of workers themselves. As a champion of human dignity, the church has a duty to speak out in defense of the rights of labor.

In his second encyclical on economics, ***Sollicitudo Rei Socialis*** (1987), John Paul II recognizes personal economic initiative as a fundamental human right, stemming from the image of the Creator in every human being. Does not the denial of the right to take initiatives in economic matters, he asks, "impoverish the human person as much as, or more than, the deprivation of material goods?" Drawing, no doubt, on his experience behind the Iron Curtain, he castigates systems in which citizens are reduced to passivity, dependence and submission to the bureaucratic apparatus. He likewise criticizes consumerist societies in which things take priority over persons. "To 'have' objects and goods," he writes, "does not in itself perfect the human subject unless it contributes to the maturing and enrichment of that subject's 'being,' that is to say, unless it contributes to the realization of the human vocation as such."

In ***Centesimus Annus*** (1991), his third social encyclical, John Paul II returns to many of the same themes. He points out that while the natural fruitfulness of the earth was once the primary source of wealth, today the principal resource is rather the initiative and skill of human persons. He defends private property, profit and the free market as against the socialist alternatives. At the same time he cautions against consumerism, "in which people are ensnared in a web of false and superficial gratifications rather than being helped to experience their personhood in an authentic and concrete way." He speaks at some length of the alienation that can arise in capitalist as well as in socialist societies.

From the beginning of his pontificate, the present Pope has shown a constant concern for the environment. Unlike some creationists, he bases this concern less on the inherent goodness of nature than on what is genuinely good for humanity. In ***Redemptor Hominis*** (1979) he noted that the power of humanity to subdue the earth seems to be turning against humanity itself. Many seem to see no other meaning in the natural environment than its immediate use and consumption. Such exploitation, however, instead of making our life on earth more human, carries with it the threat of an "environmental holocaust." At the root of our senseless destruction of the natural environment, he observes, lies a prevalent anthropological error, further described in ***Centesimus Annus.*** We are often driven by a desire to possess things rather than respect their God-given purpose. We lack the disinterested attitude, born of wonder, that would enable us to find in nature the message of the invisible God. We also violate our obligations toward future generations.

7. The Political Order

The thinking of John Paul II about politics and the state is closely intertwined with his reflections about culture and economics. Emphasizing the human dimension, he consistently speaks of the personalist values of participation, dialogue and solidarity. The common good, he maintains, is threatened on the one hand by selfish individualism and on the other hand by totalitarian systems that trample on the fights of the individual person. No single group may be allowed to impose itself by power upon the whole of society. The enormous increase of social awareness in our day requires that the citizens be allowed to participate in the political life of the community (***Redemptor Hominis,*** No. 17). The Pope accordingly praises the democratic system "inasmuch as it ensures the participation of citizens in making political choices, guarantees to the governed the possibility both of electing and of holding accountable those who govern them and of replacing them through peaceful means when appropriate" (*Centesimus Annus,* No. 46). Yet even his endorsement of democracy contains a warning against certain popular misunderstandings. Too often our contemporaries assume that agnosticism and skeptical relativism are the philosophy and basic attitude that best correspond to democratic forms of political life. John Paul II replies that, on the contrary, a democracy without objective values and ethical responsibility can easily turn into open or thinly disguised totalitarianism. The rights of the human person must be acknowledged as inviolable.

The Pope has repeatedly praised the Universal Declaration of Human Rights that was adopted by the United Nations in 1948. In his address to the United Nations in 1979 he enumerated, among the human rights that are universally recognized, "the right to life, liberty and security of person; the right to food, clothing, housing, sufficient health care, rest and leisure; the right to freedom of expression, education and culture; the right to freedom of thought, conscience and religion." This list (too long to be repeated here) ended with the "right to political participation and the right to participate in the free choice of the political system of the people to which one belongs." In speaking of human rights, the Pope frequently alludes to the evils of abortion and euthanasia, which he regards as scandalous violations of human dignity (address to the United Nations, 1979).

All these declarations of human rights are abstract. The Pope clearly recognizes that philosophical and theological principles cannot be automatically translated into positive law or judicial practice. The talents of statesmen and jurists are needed to determine the extent to which a given right— for example, the right to education or free expression—can be implemented in a given situation.

8. The Church

Thus far, we have been speaking of essentially natural societies, whose existence does not rest on the Gospel and on faith. In dealing with them, John Paul II speaks primarily as a philosopher. As a theologian and teacher of the people of God, he extends his theory of personal action, participation and community into the order of revealed truth, where it becomes the basis of an ecclesiology.

John Paul II's ecclesiology is not a simple corollary from his general doctrine of society. The church has a unique status and mission. In a memorable phrase he calls it "the social subject of responsibility for divine truth" (*Redemptor Hominis,* No. 19). The Gospel, he reminds us, does not spring spontaneously from any cultural soil. It always has to be transmitted by apostolic dialogue, because it comes to the church through the apostles. The message is that of Christ, who declared, "The word that you hear is not mine but is from the Father who sent me" (Jn. 14:24).

The idea of the Gospel as a word coming down from above might appear to conflict with the view that the human vocation is to active self-realization. John Paul II is aware of this difficulty, and he replies that God's redeeming action in Christ comes to meet the deepest longings of the human heart for truth, freedom, life and community. The gift of divine adoption enables us to fulfill our deepest identity in a surpassing manner. The church as communion is the locus of this personal and communal participation in the divine. It reflects and shares in the trinitarian communion of the divine persons among themselves.

Thanks to the presence of the Holy Spirit in the hearts and minds of the faithful, the people of God experience a unique awareness of their divine adoption. "The Christian bears witness to Christ not 'from outside' but on the basis of participation" (*Sources of Renewal,* 1981). The entire people of God shares in the threefold office of Christ as prophet, priest and king (*Christifideles Laici,* No. 14). Each individual member is called to share in the life-giving mystery of redemption, to make a perfect gift of self and thereby to achieve definitive self-realization. For it is always in giving that one finds one's true self.

The members of the church share in the threefold office of Christ in differentiated ways. All the ministries, whether hierarchical or charismatic, serve to build up the one community in unity. The Holy Spirit gives the church a corporate "sense of the faithful" to discern the meaning of God's word. This "supernatual sense of the faith," however, is not a matter of majority opinion. It is a consensus achieved through the collaboration of the various orders in the church. In this process "pastors must promote the sense of the faith in all the faithful, examine and authoritatively judge the genuineness of its expressions, and educate the faithful in an ever more mature evangelical discernment" (*Familiaris Consortio,* No. 5).

The special role of the hierarchy within the church is reiterated by John Paul II. Instituted by Christ, the episcopal order, together with the pope as successor of Peter, has an irreplaceable responsibility for assuring the unity of the church in the truth of the Gospel (*Sources of Renewal,* 1981). Like charismatic gifts, hierarchical office is essentially a service toward the community. Its whole task is to build up the community of the people of God. The Pope warns against a laicism that denies the proper role of the hierarchy. The contrary error is clericalism, which arises either when the clergy usurp the competence of the laity or when the laity shirk their responsibilities and throw them on the clergy.

In his Christology and ecclesiology, John Paul II frequently appeals to the category of prophetic testimony. Jesus Christ, he says, is the great prophet, the one who proclaims divine truth. The church and all its members are called to share in His prophetic mission. The transmission of the sacred heritage of saving truth can be an extremely demanding task. When asked to preach a retreat to the papal curia, Cardinal Wojtyla chose as his title *Sign of*

Contradiction (1979). After describing the burdensome vocation of ancient prophets such as Jeremiah, he went on to say that the church and the pope himself are often called to be signs of contradiction in our day. Secular society exerts heavy pressures on the church and its hierarchy to relax moral norms and permit unbridled self-indulgence.

The then cardinal's answer was typically firm: "In recent years there has been a striking increase in contradiction, whether one thinks of the organized opposition mounted by the anti-Gospel lobby or of the opposition that springs up in apparently Christian and 'humanistic' circles linked with certain Christian traditions. One has only to recall the contestation of the encyclical *Humanae Vitae,* or that provoked by the latest declaration by the Sacred Congregation for the Doctrine of the Faith, *Personae Humanae.* These examples are enough to bring home the fact that we are in the front line in a lively battle for the dignity of man. . . . It is the task of the church, of the Holy See, of all pastors to fight on the side of man, often against men themselves!"

In an important speech on Catholic universities, John Paul II made a special appeal to them to be a "critical and prophetic voice" in confronting the increasingly secularized society of our day. It would be a mistake, he says, for such universities to attenuate or disguise their Catholic character. They must take full cognizance of their responsibility to affirm a truth that does not flatter but is absolutely necessary to safeguard the dignity of the human person (see John Paul II's apostolic constitution on Catholic higher education, *Ex Corde Ecclesiae* [1990], No. 32).

In the end, therefore, authentic humanism is compelled, for the sake of its own integrity, to become prophetic. Conscious that the dignity of the person rests both upon freedom of conscience and upon a transcendent order of truth most perfectly revealed in Christ, the faithful Christian must protest against dehumanizing forces, whether collectivistic or individualistic, whether absolutistic or relativistic. The testimony of the church, like that of Christ, must be against the world for the world. By courageously taking up this task, John Paul II has made himself, in my estimation, the leading prophet of authentic humanism in the world today.

Douglas Johnston (review date 6 November 1994)

SOURCE: "Asking the Really Big Questions," in *Los Angeles Times Book Review,* November 6, 1994, pp. 1, 11.

[In the following review, Johnston offers favorable analysis of Crossing the Threshold of Hope.*]*

One wonders what the College of Cardinals though it was getting when it elected Karol Wojtyla the first non-Italian pope in 455 years. That will remain an eternal secret, but there can be little doubt that Pope John Paul II has surprised everyone with his vitality and political shrewdness.

Now he surprises again with this book—the first ever written by a sitting pope for a general audience. Reading what may be the last testament of this extraordinary but ailing man is an enriching experience, as he presents his views on a range of difficult moral and spiritual questions.

Readers need not be steeped in Catholic theology to appreciate the insight and energy which *Crossing the Threshold of Hope* brings to questions of the sort that have troubled many of us at one time or another: Why does God tolerate suffering? Why does He not reveal himself more clearly? Why should one believe in Him if it is possible to live an honest life without the Gospel? How does one reconcile the right to life of the unborn with the humanitarian arguments of those who practice contraception on who seek to legalize abortion?

For the politically inclined, the pope comments on the reasons underlying the demise of communism, the continuing problems of capitalism, the needs of the developing world, human rights, Middle East peace (including the establishment of ties with Israel), and the Catholic Church as a force in world politics and international organizations.

Although some of the arguments posed and explanations offered are highly technical and require a close reading, most of the book is conversational; almost rambling in style. On balance, its thrust is pastoral; there are no doctrinal surprises here.

For the pope's purposes, the book is timely. Throughout the 15 years of his papacy, Pope John Paul II's dynamism has inspired admiration and respect, as has his role on the international stage. Gorbachev himself credits the pope with having made possible the recent transformation not only of Poland, but of all Eastern Europe. With the pope's health failing, though, there is concern that his moral authority in the world is also in decline. At this point in his tenure, John Paul II is generally perceived to be engaged in a holding pattern, seeking to stem the tide of moral relativism while avoiding new debates. His traditional stands on issues of church authority and sexuality are viewed as being unresponsive to the realities of women's rights and the population explosion. All but totally lost in this perception are his earlier, genuinely counter-cultural teachings on social justice and reform.

Thus, this book comes at a critical time and provides him a valuable tool for further outreach. Its simultaneous release in 35 countries now makes available to millions his current thinking across a broad spectrum of inquiry. With the obvious need to curtail his extensive travels—62 trips at last count—the book becomes a surrogate for personal presence as he continues his quest to revitalize the 600 million Catholics in local churches the world over.

Especially relevant in this regard is the pope's ecumenical treatment of other religious traditions. He pays homage to their contributions to morality and culture and notes certain commonalities as well as some of their differences with Christianity. In the final analysis, his description suggests that it is the unique balance between involvement and detachment that sets Christianity apart. Both Hinduism and Buddhism, in their different ways, seek a state of detached liberation from the anguish of the human condition. Christianity, on the other hand, acknowledges the world as God's creation "redeemed by Christ" and teaches that it is in the world that man meets God. This, in turn, translates to a positive attitude toward creation and a constant striving toward transformation and perfection.

As a Christian, the pope most closely identifies with the monotheistic religions of Islam and Judaism. He expresses deep respect in this book for the "religiosity" of Muslims and refers to Jews as "our elder brothers in the faith." In Islam, however, he sees divine revelation reduced to the point where the God of the Koran is essentially a "God outside of the world . . . *only Majesty, never Emmanuel,* God-with-us." Conspicuous by its absence is any comparable treatment of what sets Judaism apart from Christianity, but that may be assumed.

The pope also makes interesting reference to the ancestor worship of the primitive or animistic religions: Here he draws a parallel between veneration of ancestors and the Christian concept of the Communion of Saints; in which all believers—"whether living or dead"—form a single body. Perhaps this accounts for the fact that the fastest rates of growth of the Catholic Church today are among the animists of Africa and Asia. Referring to the church's ever-renewing vitality, the pope recalls the words of Cardinal Hyacinth Thiandoum, who "foresaw the possibility that the Old World might one day be evangelized by black missionaries. "Indeed, there is some speculation that this pope's successor may be either Cardinal Francis Arinze of Nigeria or Cardinal Bernadin-Gantin of Benin.

Ironically, a number of countries in Africa, where most of the church membership growth is taking place, face enormous population problems that seem to make some form of birth control a matter of national survival. Here the pope's treatment falls short of what a policy-maker would need for taking effective action. In defending the rights of the unborn, he indicates that "what is at stake is the commandment Do not Kill!" Whatever the pope's views on war and capital punishment, his treatment of abortion allows for no exceptions because "a child conceived in its mother's womb is never an unjust aggressor, it is a defenseless being that is waiting to be welcomed and helped." This defense ties to a more pervasive theme that celebrates the dignity of man, the joy of creation, and the concept of "person" as representing the center of the human ethos.

Where the gruel gets thin is in the book's prescription for the problem of overpopulation, suggesting that the answer is "responsible parenthood." As early as 1932, T. S. Eliot, writing as a high-church Episcopalian, suggested in an es-

say entitled "Thoughts After Lambeth" that if Catholic doctrine requires unlimited procreation up to the limit of the mother's strength," then the church should be "obliged to offer some solution to the economic questions raised by such a practice: for surely if you lay down a moral law which leads, in practice, to unfortunate social consequences—such as overpopulation or destitution—you make yourself responsible for providing some resolution of these consequences." (Until the Lambeth conference of 1930, no Christian denomination viewed contraception as acceptable.)

At the recent International Conference on Population and Development in Cairo, the issue assumed something of a North-South context as the Holy See delegation advocated economic development, health care and education as appropriate remedies. As expressed by the Rev. Diarmuid Martin, deputy head of the delegation, "wealthy states must realize that it is only by helping poor countries raise their living standards that they will solve the population problem, not by forcing them to adopt Western attitudes toward abortion and contraception."

If *Crossing the Threshold of Hope* is weak in providing constructive alternatives for population control, it is anything but weak in its criticisms of the inequities and excesses of capitalism. The flaws in the practice of capitalism that initially attracted people to socialism are seen as continuing unabated, a theme the pope has been espousing for some time. In an earlier work titled *Sign of Contradiction,* he suggested that Western consumerism and communist collectivism both share materialistic utilitarianism as their common philosophical root. It is this consumerism without transcendental ends that ultimately undermines the spirituality and dignity of man.

But here again, the book's prescriptions are weak. The fate of the authoritarian alternatives to capitalism that have wreaked such havoc for most of the 20th century suggests there are limits to what human nature can accommodate. Undeniably, excessive consumerism has contributed to moral indifference and an unhealthy focus on what one has rather than what one is. Many people seem to be losing their sense of balance between individual freedom and discipline, between liberty and justice, between the temporal and the eternal—becoming insensitive to what the pope calls "the Last Things." Reigning in the excesses of consumerism and individual liberty so that spiritual values can be recaptured and reflected in daily behavior is a very tall order. Enlightened approaches are in woefully short supply and, regrettably, this book offers few clues.

If Pope John Paul II seems unduly conservative in his strong-minded adherence to Catholic doctrine, it is because he takes seriously the words of the Apostle Paul (2 Tim 4:3): "Proclaim the message; be persistent whether the time is favorable or unfavorable . . . For the time is coming when people will not put up with sound doctrine, but having itching ears, they will accumulate for themselves teachers to suit their own desires, and will turn away from listening to the truth." Whether or not we are at that time, Pope John Paul II certainly is not a teacher who caters to the itching ears of modernity, telling us what we want to hear. As the pope further notes, "Christ forewarned us, telling us that the road to eternal salvation is not broad and comfortable, but narrow and difficult. We do not have the right to abandon that perspective, nor to change it."

Perhaps it is unfair to impose upon the pope the task of providing workable solutions to intractable problems, but that is the sort of expectation this inspiring man invites. Whatever else one might think, the pope deserves our respect as a bastion of uprightness and integrity in a world that is undergoing a crisis of moral leadership. Just as man and the divine merge in the figure of Christ, so too do Karol Wojtyla, long-time social revolutionary and champion of human rights, and Pope John Paul II, arch-defender of the faith, come together in this book. It is very worth reading.

Peter Hebblethwaite (review date 11 November 1994)

SOURCE: "Professor in Slippers," in *Times Literary Supplement,* November 11, 1994, p. 32.

[*In the following review, Hebblethwaite examines John Paul's religious and political views in* Crossing the Threshold of Hope.]

Librarians will have problems cataloguing this work. The author appears on the title-page as "His Holiness Pope John Paul II". Perhaps the easiest thing would be to put it under Messori, Vittorio, ed. Then it would join the celebrated interviewer's other books like *The Ratzinger Report*—which had their fifteen minutes of fame.

Pope John Paul has been interviewed before. In 1984, André Frossard (author of *God Exists, I've Met Him*) published ***"Be Not Afraid!": André Frossard in conversation with John Paul II.*** Frossard's is the better book for penetrating the Pope's Polish mind. He was allowed to probe away through supplementaries. Messori, though at one point claiming to be a gadfly, fails to buzz and is totally overawed by his subject.

This is partly because he has such an exalted view of the papacy that he makes the ordinary ultramontane look positively liberal: "The Pope is considered", Messori announces with false confidence, "the man on earth who represents the Son of God, who 'takes the place' of the Second Person of the Omnipotent God of the Trinity." That is why, he concludes, Catholics call the Pope "Vicar of Christ", "Holy Father", or "Your Holiness". "You are either", says Messori, addressing John Paul and evoking Blaise Pascal's wager, ". . .the mysterious living proof of the Creator of the universe or the central protagonist of a millennial illusion." More bluntly put: You either prove the existence of God, or you are a fraud. Is he trying to make Protestants of us all?

Now John Paul responds to this hype with skilful dialectic. "Vicar of Christ" is indeed dangerous language, going to the very edge of blasphemy. But as Vatican II teaches, every bishop is the "Vicar of Christ" for his diocese. And "in a certain sense" every Christian is a "vicar of Christ". Just imagine: Let me introduce my wife, a vicar of Christ. A new order: the VCs. But the point is: he remains *the* Vicar of Christ. So that shimmy doesn't quite work.

On the less significant titles, "Holy Father" and "Your Holiness", John Paul quotes the powerful words of Jesus himself: "Call no one father on earth; you have but one father in heaven. Do not be called 'Master'; you have but one Master, the Christ" (Matthew 23:9-10). That is one of the clearest statements of the New Testament, and an express command of the Lord. Yet, having reminded us of it, John Paul simply sweeps it aside: "These expressions, nevertheless, have evolved out of a long tradition, becoming part of common usage. One must not be afraid of these words either." John Paul saves the day with the magnificent phrase of St Augustine: "Vobis sum episcopus, vobiscum christianus." ("For you I am a bishop, with you I am a Christian"), adding that "*christianus* has far greater significance than *episcopus,* even if the subject is the bishop of Rome".

John Paul does not speak of death, but admits to feeling old. So he reminisces. In his day, young people's idealism was expressed in the form of *duty;* today, it takes the form of *criticism*. Today, positivism prevails; in his day, "romantic traditions" still persisted. No native English-language speaker could ever say that.

John Paul tells the story of the brilliant engineer, Jerzy Ciecielski, who decided after much prayer that he should get married. What to do? Instead of going to the local disco or the parish ball, "he sought a companion for his life and sought her on his knees, in prayer". That is the difference between the Polish "romantic traditions" in which John Paul II was brought up, and not only our Western societies but today's Poland too. But how hard he tries to bridge the gap. His message to youth is always: "What I am going to say to you is much less important than what you are going to say to me."

He may really believe that. But no one about him does. Hence the *Time*-magazine epithets, "hard-nosed", "hard-line", "inflexible". But he can't lower the bar or mitigate moral demands that are not his but the Church's. That is why, in *Veritatis Splendor,* the only form of holiness he knows is heroism. He has often quoted Georges Bernanos: "The Church doesn't need reformers; it need saints."

Maybe so. But when, in *Crossing the Threshold of Hope,* he talks of martyrs as the true heroes of the faith, he lists only the victims of Communism, starting with the politically uncorrect "martyrs" of the Spanish Civil War. Yet nearly all the martyrs in his pontificate have been the victims of Latin American dictators who went to Mass every Sunday. But he simply *cannot* see that. It is his Polish blind spot. Like any Catholic, he starts out from a national culture which provides a strong sense of identity, and then tries to rise to the level of the universal Church. With his knowledge of languages, he has succeeded better than most of us in this enterprise.

But when he comes to talk of human rights, he has two paradigms unknown to the rest of the world. The Kraków Theological Faculty, he tells Messori, "condemned the violence perpetrated against the Baltic peoples" at the Council of Constance in 1414. They condemned, in other words, forced conversions. Later, he adds, the Spanish theologians of the Salamanca school condemned the forcible conversion of the native Americans on the same grounds. And so on to wartime Croatia, no doubt. But Poland scored a first Bravo.

You may never have heard of Father Kasamierz Klósak, a Kraków theologian of immense erudition. Neither had I, a student of such things. For John Paul, Klósak is a major figure, since in him "Marxist natural philosophy was challenged by an innovative approach that allowed for the discovery of the *Logos*—creative thought and order—in the world". I must confess that I have not the faintest idea what this means.

What picture of John Paul the man emerges? He is like an elderly professor in carpet slippers, with a passionate interest in comparative linguistics. (I once heard him discussing whether Portuguese had a word for "nostalgia".) He has thought deeply and prayed about every question that Messori can bowl at him. His reading is a little out of date—he introduces Albert Camus to illustrate a "bleak vision" of the world. But he has read Emmanuel Levinas.

This "conversation with every home" implies a very sophisticated household, expected to know the difference between the young and the mature Ludwig Wittgenstein. Such households may appreciate the truth that "man's existence is always coexistence". But they will make heavy weather of John Paul's remark that "it is not possible to affirm that when something is trans-empirical, it ceases to be empirical".

A question of more general interest is "Was God at work in the Fall of Communism?" After a ramble through God-at-work in the "new movements" and another vote of confidence in youth, he says that if people do not hear the voice of God in history, that is partly because they have blocked their ears and partly because they have been deafened by society, the mass media and the ideological foes who, since the eighteenth century, have led "the struggle against God". That is another swipe at the Enlightenment. John Paul reduces it to an anti-God movement whose aim is "the systematic elimination of all that is Christian". Marxism appears as a cut-price version of this scheme. Now Marxism has gone, "a similar plan is revealing itself in all its danger and, at the same time, in all its faultiness". Moreover, there was some merit in Marxism. It began as "part of the history of protest in the

face of injustice", a genuinely justified workers' protest which was then, alas, turned into an ideology. Fortunately, this "protest" seeped into the life of the Church. It led to *Rerum Novarum* in 1891. Indeed, Leo XIII "in a certain sense predicted the fall of Communism, a fall which would cost humanity and Europe dearly, since the medicine could prove more dangerous than the disease itself".

John Paul next exploits the Fátima story, claiming that the three children could not have invented the predictions that "Russia will convert". They simply "did not know enough about history for that". The attempt on John Paul II's life was "necessary", which is another way of saying it was "providential". It occurred in 1981, on the feast of Our Lady of Fátima, "so that all could become more transparent and comprehensible, so that the voice of God which speaks in human history through the 'signs of the times' could be more easily heard and understood". This comes close to disclosing the "providential meaning" of his pontificate.

It would, however, be "simplistic to say that Divine Providence *caused* the fall of Communism". It crumbled under the weight of its own mistakes and abuses. The causes of its collapse were internal: "It fell by itself, because of its own inherent weaknesses." He dealt more fully with this theme in his interview with Jas Gawronski in the *Guardian* and in his address to Latvian intellectuals in Riga in September 1993. In the preparation for the Euro-Synod, he acutely remarked that "now that Communism has gone, the Church has to be on the side of the poor, otherwise they will go undefended". This upset those who regarded him as the sole victor in the duel with Marxism. You cannot please all men all the time. Or, as Messori says, in an "inclusive" translation of St Paul: "I have become all things to all, to save at least some" (1 Corinthians 9:22).

Garry Wills (review date 22 December 1994)

SOURCE: "The Tragic Pope?," in *New York Review of Books,* December 22, 1994, pp. 4, 6-7.

[*In the following review, Wills discusses John Paul's Christian theology in* Crossing the Threshold of Hope. *Though noting contradictions and evasions, Wills writes, "It is a relief to see the Pope talk of the truths of faith with the excitement they deserve (whether true or false)."*]

Was the Pope subjecting us to a Great Wu routine? It seemed so. Let Orson Welles, always a bit of a Wu himself, explain:

> *Mister Wu* is a classic example [of theatrical hype]— I've played it once myself. All the other actors boil around the stage for about an hour shrieking. "What will happen when Mister Wu arrives?" "What is he like, this Mister Wu?" and so on. Finally, a great gong is beaten, and slowly over a Chinese bridge comes Mr. Wu himself in full mandarin robes. Peach Blossom (or

whatever her name is) falls on her face and a lot of coolies yell, "Mister *Wu!!!*" The curtain comes down, the audience goes wild, and everybody says, "Isn't that guy playing Mr. Wu a great actor!" *That's* a star part for you!

The release of the Pope's multimillion-dollar project had clear marks of Wu upon it. The books and tapes were warehoused, embargoed, surrounded with the hush-hush of great revelations withheld. Then the drumbeat of anticipation ended in a clash of publicity's cymbals. The books came sluicing out, in twenty-one languages, with television cameras recording their arrival in the stores, their opening, their (disappointing) sales.

In other cases, there would have been an explosion of disapproval if readers found there was nothing new in a book so wrapped in conspiratorial trappings. One looks silly striving to hide a thing that is not there. But for a pope of dogma and tradition, there is no shame in saying nothing new. He is not supposed to make reckless additions to the "deposit of faith." Only God can issue new commandments, a new revelation.

The promoters of the book seem hard put to justify their exercise in mystification. Vittorio Messori, the journalist whose questions form the basis of the book, claims that the new thing is the format—the Pope promised to comply (but ultimately did not) with a request to be interviewed at length on television. John Paul II, who required that the questions be submitted beforehand, wrote his answers at leisure and sent them back to the journalist through his press representative. This is what Messori calls "a conversation."

A snake-oil salesman has to think his audience obtuse in order to keep up his act. So Messori boasts that the Pope answered all his questions "without avoiding one of them"—though anyone who turns the page will find that the Pope avoided the very first one. After a long deferential windup, Messori asked: "Haven't you ever had, not doubts certainly, but at least questions and problems (as is human) about the truth of this *Creed?*" Despite the tuckings and bowings (not *doubts, as is human*), he was asking a personal question. The Pope gave an institutional answer: even Peter had trouble with the idea that God could suffer. Nothing about the Pope's own doubts (if any). Yet the "candor" of the new book was supposed to set it aside from all the Pope's earlier (non-multimillion-dollar) publications. The Pope sidestepped another question (Number 22) when Messori asked about the "decisions by the Anglican Church [that] have created new obstacles" to church union. He was clearly referring to ordination of women priests. The Pope answered by saying high-minded things about the ecumenical movement; he never addressed the specific Anglican decisions.

Messori is not a dogged questioner (though he apologizes for being "provocative"). He butters up the Pope at all opportunities: "Allow me to observe that your very clear words once again demonstrate the partiality, the short-sightedness of those who have suspected you of pushing for a 'restoration,' of being a 'reactionary' with regard to the Council." So certain questions begging to be asked were not asked—e.g., about the Pope's partiality to the secretive and authoritarian Opus Dei movement. Messori is friendly with the papal press agent who arranged the "conversation" in the first place, Dr. Joaquin Navarro-Valls, who is himself a member of Opus Dei.

There seems to be something of the Great Wu in the Pope's own attitude toward himself. Asked about the role of a Polish pope in the downfall of communism, he answers: "Perhaps this is why it was necessary for the assassination attempt [on John Paul's life] to be made in St. Peter's Square precisely on May 13, 1981, the anniversary of the first apparition [of Mary] at Fátima." That reminds me of James I's belief that two plots on his life were providentially arranged to fall on a Tuesday, both of them the fifth in their month.

Actually, many people see something providential in John Paul's strengthening of Polish resistance to communism. It is the tie-in with Fátima that puzzles. And though Catholics believe that God's providence embraces all the world, as well as their Church's leadership, Bernhard Schimmelpfennig's analytical history, *The Papacy,* reminds us that providence has also provided mankind with murderer-popes, perjurer-popes, and even heretic-popes.

As an apologist for the faith, John Paul II seems to be giving rote answers. When Messori asks how one can tell that Jesus is the Son of God, John Paul answers that this is what Peter called him at Matthew 16:16. When Messori asks why God seems to hide his existence, the Pope answers that this question is just a result of Cartesian rationalism—which is not much comfort to those who see the problem very clearly but have never heard of Descartes.

But it is worth persevering with the book. As he goes along, the Pope seems to loosen up, to become more personal, to go back continually to his Polish experience, as if clamoring to get out of the restraints of his office. If there are no new doctrines, there are new approaches to doctrine. The Pope labors to say what *he* believes, not (only) what the office demands him to pronounce. Asked about eternal life—about heaven and hell—John Paul says that hell exists, but no man, not even Judas, can be said to be there. He repeats the text of 1 Timothy 2:4, that God wants everyone to be saved. It is an open question, he maintains whether man *can* be rejected by a God who saves. This goes far beyond what the new Catholic catechism says about hell. The Pope even quotes a favorite author of his, Saint John of the Cross, on *interior* hell and purgatory existing during one's lifetime.

On the subject of salvation in general, the Pope says that the Church once placed too much emphasis on individual salvation, whereas God came to save the whole world, even to "divinize" it. Teilhard de Chardin got into trouble with the Vatican for holding those views. Yet the new catechism, by returning to old mysteries, unearths a vision of universal salvation in the teaching of the Creed. The dead Jesus "descended into hell" to reclaim the whole of history since Adam's time. The catechism quotes an ancient homily saying. "He has gone to search for Adam, our first father, as for a lost sheep," so that none shall be lost.

The Pope's ecumenism is also less grudging than that of his predecessors. John Paul admits that Rome has things to learn from other churches; that truths emerge from other religions, including Buddhism, which might lie hidden but for the "dialectic" process of interaction between the various faiths. Elsewhere he gives an example of this by referring with approval to Cardinal Newman's famous words, "I shall drink to the Pope, if you please; still, to Conscience first, and to the Pope afterwards." Newman was criticized for talking like a Protestant—and he had, indeed, learned of the primacy of conscience from the Reformation. Now the Pope has learned it, too. (The Catholic catechism quotes Newman on conscience, but from a less pointed text.)

As his book becomes more personal, the Pope goes back to his own history in Poland, to his first experiences of piety, to his study of phenomenology. One Catholic philosopher has criticized the Pope for speaking out of a specific philosophical school, as if people had to study Husserl in order to be Catholics. The same objections were raised to Saint Augustine's Neoplatonic background, or to Saint Thomas's Aristotelianism. But one must use refined language to approach divine mysteries, and it is bracing to see the Pope grappling with the most basic doctrines in fresh ways—especially for us Catholics who must listen to the sermons preached these days. For most priests in the pulpit, the basic doctrines of the Church—the Trinity, the Incarnation—are "mysteries" in the sense that they are technical points of theology not "relevant" to Catholics' modern concerns. Sermons become therapeutic and empathetic, leveling farther down every day toward the *Oprah Winfrey Show.*

The sermons of Saint Augustine tried to take Christians into the heart of the faith—and so do John Paul's reflections on the meaning of Jesus as the entry point for human beings into the inmost self-communication of God: "Man is saved in the Church by being brought into the Mystery of the Divine Trinity." By reflecting on the Trinity, Saint Augustine developed a whole new view of human personality—that we are selves, not a self; that even God must exist in dialogue; that he is not only a unity (as Plato thought) but a community. It is in this vein that John Paul uses the insights of Martin Buber (the "I" is a relation, not a substance) or of the Jewish philosopher Emmanuel Lévinas (identity cannot be constituted without a sense of other beings to talk of man's relation to God). Saint Augustine would find something trinitarian in these views.

When a newspaper article of the 1920s called the conciliar "quibbles" about the dual nature of Christ a sign of the degenerate Greek intellect (Gibbon's view), Chesterton wrote a poetic answer that showed the reaching of two Greek myths toward complementarity—the eagle of Zeus imposing order on the world, the vulture of Zeus feeding on Prometheus. At the end, a "simple" combination, the centaur, reacts in fear to a greater monster, who cries:

> I am Prometheus. I am Jupiter.
> In ravening obedience down from heaven,
> Hailed of my hand and by this sign alone,
> My eagle comes to tear me.

The idea of the Incarnation may be monstrous. It is hardly dull, or irrelevant to the way people think of themselves and their world. In Jesus, the Pope writes, God does not answer Job from on high, but comes down to join him in "the tragedy of redemption." It is a relief to see the Pope talk of the truths of faith with the excitement they deserve (whether true or false). The new catechism offers some of the same stimulation.

But when I am asked whether I am a church-going Catholic and answer yes, no one inquires whether I really believe in such strange things as the Trinity, the Incarnation, the Resurrection. I am asked about ovaries and trimesters. The great mysteries of faith have become, for many inside the church as well as outside, the "doctrines" on contraception and abortion. These are hardly great concerns in the gospels and the letters of Saint Paul, which never mention them. But they crowd out most other talk of Catholic beliefs in modern conversation.

For this the current Pope must bear some of the blame. He tells us, in this book, that he is not obsessed with abortion; but he certainly encourages that obsession in others. His fine Husserlian talk of personality degenerates, at second hand, to hairsplitting on the difference between all the fertilized ova that fail to attach themselves to the uterine wall and those few that *do*. It's a wonder some of the Pope's followers, with this view of the fertilized egg as a person, do not stand by to baptize every uterine flux as well as every aborted fetus. (The Church did not baptize even fully formed fetuses in the past). Talk of the degeneration of intellect into quibbles.

The real mysteries of the faith are easier to believe than the supposedly rational condemnation of contraceptives based on "natural law." According to the Pope, the sex act must always be ordinated toward procreation, and never to pleasure alone. By that logic, eating and drinking must always be ordinated toward self-preservation, never to pleasure. The toast of fellowship among well-fed people is ruled out, all the symbolic and extraordinary uses of feasting and drink that find their highest expression in the *agape* feast and the Eucharist. The body does not physically need the eucharistic bread or cup, so they are unnatural.

The Pope attacks biblical fundamentalism in this new book. But his approach to women's ministry is absurdly fundamentalist. Jesus chose only men apostles, in the context of his own culture, so there is something essentially *male* about priesthood. Yet he also chose only Jews, who spoke Aramaic, who were married, who had not read the (nonexistent) gospels; and those requirements are not imposed in modern conditions. The Pope, of course, claims that no denigration of women is intended in this "divisions of labor." But his view of the superior dignity of males slips out when the Pope speaks of the father-hood of God: "The father-son paradigm is ageless. It is older than human history." The "rays of fatherhood" are divine. We hear of no mother-daughter paradigm for the divine-human relationship. No wonder the Pope can write, without any sense of irony: "Not only abortion, but also contraception, are *ultimately bound up with the truth about man.*"

How can the Pope be so intellectually probing and honest, yet so closed and simplistic on certain matters (all having to do with sex)? That is a conundrum his biographers will have a hard time reading. The answer may lie in his Polish experience at a time of crisis—as his own frequent references backward show. A church under persecution holds to all signs and rituals as acts of resistance. The piety of John Paul was embattled and sacrificial—he often refers to the benefits of persecution and laments the failure of "heroism" in a pampered age. Furthermore, he lost his mother at the age of nine (she died in childbirth!) and he seems to have shifted his love for the missing woman over to the Virgin Mary.

The Pope's piety toward Mary is almost scary. She is the subject of more entries in the collected *Prayers and Devotions* than any other aspect of God or religion. The Pope can say the biblically correct things about Mary, as First Disciple and symbol of the church, but he is also interested in all the supposed apparitions of Mary in modern times—not only in Fátima, Guadalupe, and Lourdes, but in dubious events like that which occurred at Knock in Ireland (where the Pope went to pay homage to "Our Lady of Knock"). The Pope's emphases on Mary verge on those in a sermon I heard an Italian priest give in Verona last September: "Our Protestant brothers—I say this with infinite sorrow—do not honor the Madonna, so they cannot understand the Faith, since she is at the center of it."

It may seem odd that the Pope should honor Mary so, yet have a constricted view of women's role in the church. But his image of Mary is one of submission. As a replacement for the mother who died early in Wojtyla's life, she is a guardian of chastity, inhibiting sexual expression. The minatory role of celibacy shows up in the Pope's odd argument that married people will not stay faithful to each other if they do not have the model of celibate fidelity near at hand. As he puts it in *Prayers and Devotions:* "Consecrated celibacy helps married couples and family members to keep the conscience and the practice of the loftiest ideals of their union alive . . . Virginity keeps consciousness of the mystery of matrimony alive in the Church and defends it from being reduced in any way and from all impoverishment." By this standard, Jews or Protestants lacking a celibate priesthood, would be incapable of marital fidelity.

After his initial evasions, the Pope has invited us into his psyche with his own reflections on his early life. The challenge to biographers is very great. They will find important clues in his poems. His best-known poem deals with his experience working in a quarry, where comradeship and anger mix in ways more explosive than the blasting powder. He deals with alienation in **"The Car Factory Worker."** But his other experience was as an actor and playwright. **"Actor"** begins:

> So many grew around me, through me, from my self, as it were,
> I became a channel, unleashing a force called man.
> Did not others crowding in, distort the man that I am?

As a prelate under Communist rulers, Wojtyla had to maneuver, be strong but flexible. No wonder we read paradoxical lines like "truth must be hurtful, must hide" (from **"Gospel"**) or that Jesus must "walk behind the heart" (from **"Development of Language"**). The man who recognizes Jerusalem yet confers knighthood on Kurt Waldheim, who is open himself yet harbors those who hide in the Opus Dei, is one of the more complex and fascinating figures of the twentieth century. We do not know, yet, whether he will be one of the more tragic. If so, he will be repeating the pattern of one of the most fascinating and tragic figures of the nineteenth century, a man he very much admires and tries to imitate—Pope Pius IX.

Paul Gray (essay date 26 December 1994)

SOURCE: "Empire of the Spirit," in *Time,* December 26, 1994, pp. 48-57.

[*In the following essay, Gray discusses John Paul's significance as an international moral leader.*]

People who see him—and countless millions have—do not forget him. His appearances generate an electricity unmatched by anyone else on earth. That explains, for instance, why in rural Kenyan villages thousands of children, plus many cats and roosters and even hotels, are named John Paul. Charisma is the only conceivable reason why a CD featuring him saying the rosary—in Latin—against a background of Bach and Handel is currently ascending the charts in Europe. It also accounts for the dazed reaction of a young woman who found herself, along with the thousands around her in a sports stadium in Denver, cheering and applauding him: "I don't react that way to rock groups. What is it that he has?"

Pope John Paul II has, among many other things, the world's bully-est pulpit. Few of his predecessors over the past 2,000 years have spoken from it as often and as forcefully as he. When he talks, it is not only to his flock of nearly a billion; he expects the world to listen. And the flock and the world listen, not always liking what they hear. This year he cast the net of his message wider than ever: *Crossing the Threshold of Hope,* his meditations on topics ranging from the existence of God to the mistreatment of women, became an immediate best seller in 12 countries. It is an unprecedented case of mass proselytizing by a Pontiff—arcane but personal, expansive but resolute about its moral message.

John Paul can also impose his will, and there was no more formidable and controversial example of this than the Vatican's intervention at the U.N.'s International Conference on Population and Development in Cairo in September. There the Pope's emissaries defeated a U.S.-backed proposition John Paul feared would encourage abortions worldwide. The consequences may be global and—critics predict—catastrophic, particularly in the teeming Third World, where John Paul is so admired.

The Pontiff was unfazed by the widespread opprobrium. His popular book and his unpopular diplomacy, he explained to *Time* two weeks ago, share one philosophical core: "It always goes back to the sanctity of the human being." He added, "The Pope must be a moral force." In a year when so many people lamented the decline in moral values or made excuses for bad behavior, Pope John Paul II forcefully set forth his vision of the good life and urged the world to follow it. For such rectitude—or recklessness, as his detractors would have it—he is *Time*'s Man of the Year.

The Pope is, in Catholic belief, a direct successor of St. Peter's, the rock on whom Jesus Christ built his church. As such, John Paul sees it as his duty to trouble the living stream of modernity. He stands solidly against much that the secular world deems progressive: the notion, for example, that humans share with God the right to determine who will and will not be born. He also lectures against much that the secular world deems inevitable: the abysmal inequalities between the wealthy and the wretched of the earth, the sufferings of those condemned to lives of squalor, poverty and oppression. "He really has a will and a determination to help humanity through spirituality," says the Dalai Lama. "That is marvelous. That is good. I know how difficult it is for leaders on these issues."

John Paul's impact on the world has already been enormous, ranging from the global to the personal. He has covered more than half a million miles in his travels. Many believe his support of the trade union Solidarity in his native Poland was a precipitating event in the collapse of the Soviet bloc. After he was nearly killed in 1981, he visited and pardoned his would-be assassin in jail. Asked an awed Mehmet Ali Agca: "Tell me why it is that I could not kill you?" Even those who contest the words of John Paul do not argue with his integrity—or his capacity to forgive those who trespass against him.

His power rests in the word, not the sword. As he has demonstrated throughout the 16 years of his papacy, John Paul needs no divisions. He is an army of one, and his empire is both as ethereal and as ubiquitous as the soul. In a slum in Nairobi, Mary Kamati is dying of AIDS. In her mud house hangs a portrait of John Paul. "This is the only Pope who has come to this part of the world," she says. During his most recent visit, he sprinkled her with holy water. "That," she says, eyes trembling, "is the way to heaven."

In 1994 the Pope's health visibly deteriorated. His left hand shakes, and he hobbles with a cane, the result of bone-replacement surgery. Asked about his health, he offered an "Oh, so-so" to *Time.* It is thus with increased urgency that John Paul has presented himself, the defender of Roman Catholic doctrine, as a moral compass for believers and nonbelievers alike. He spread through every means at his disposal a message not of expedience or compromise but of right and wrong; amid so much fear of the future, John Paul dared to speak of hope. He did not say what everyone wanted to hear, and many within and beyond his church took offense. But his fidelity to what he believes people need to hear remained adamant and unwavering. "He'll go down in history as the greatest of our modern Popes," says the Rev. Billy Graham. "He's been the strong conscience of the whole Christian world."

And then there was the sorry state of the globe he proposed to save. Patches of the Third World sank further into revolutionary bloodshed, disease and famine. The developed nations began to resemble weird updatings of Hieronymous Bosch: panoramas of tormented bodies, lashed, flailed and torn by the instruments of material self-gratification. Secular leaders dithered and disagreed and then did nothing about the slow death of Bosnia, the massacres in Rwanda.

Private behavior appeared equally adrift. People trained to know better showed that they did not, notably the younger members of Britain's royal family, who energetically pursued self-implosion, with TV documentaries and books their detonators of choice. In Los Angeles two separate juries could not agree on a verdict in the trials of Lyle and Erik Menendez, young men who admitted killing their parents, at close range, with shotguns. The nightly news became a saraband of sleaze: Tonya, Lorena, Michael, O. J.; after 10 days of claiming to have been the victim of a car-jacking, a South Carolina mother confessed she pushed the vehicle into a lake with her two tiny sons strapped inside.

The secular response to the tawdriness of contemporary life was not uplifting; it largely amounted to a mingy, mean spirited vindictiveness, a searching for scapegoats. Many interpreted the Republican sweep in the November elections as a sign that voters were as mad as hell and ready for old-fashioned verities. That seemed to be the view of incoming House Speaker Newt Gingrich, who called for a constitutional amendment allowing voluntary school prayer in public schools. He also suggested it might be a good idea to fill orphanages with the children of welfare mothers.

John Paul was personally affected by the turmoil of 1994. He could not make planned visits to Beirut and Sarajevo because enmities on the ground were too volatile. Rwanda dealt him particular grief: an estimated 85% of Rwandans are Christians, and more than 60% of those Roman Catholics. Some priests were accessories to massacre. The new faith was unable to overcome tribal conflict.

But when circumstances allowed him to act, John Paul did so decisively. His major goals have been to clarify church doctrine—believers may experience doubt but should be spared confusion—and to reach out to the world, seek contacts with other faiths and proclaim to all the sanctity of the individual, body and soul.

He made advances on all of these fronts in 1994. The Catechism of the Catholic Church appeared in English translation, the first such comprehensive document issued since the 16th century. It clearly summarizes all the essential beliefs and moral tenets of the church. Some Catholics believe it will be the most enduring landmark of John Paul's papacy. In June, John Paul oversaw the establishment of diplomatic relations between the Holy See and Israel, ending a tense standoff that had existed ever since 1948.

In May the Pope released an apostolic letter in which he set to rest, for the foreseeable future, the question of the ordination of women. His answer, in brief, was no. The document disappointed and outraged many Catholic women and men; even some sympathetic to the Pope felt that his peremptory tone, his strict argument from precedent, i.e., that Christ appointed only males as his Apostles, represented a missed opportunity to teach, to explain an exclusionary policy that contemporary believers find outmoded or beyond understanding.

The high or the low point of the Pope's year, depending on who did the reporting, came in September. The U.N. population conference convened in Cairo, with representatives from 185 nations and the Holy See in attendance. On the table was a 113-page plan calling on governments to commit $17 billion annually by the year 2000 to curb global population growth. About 90% of the draft document had been approved in advance by the participants, but the remaining 10% contained some bombshells John Paul had seen coming. The most explosive was Paragraph 8.25, which owed its inclusion in part to a March 16 directive from the Clinton Administration to all U.S. embassies; it stated that "the United States believes access to safe, legal and voluntary abortion is a fundamental right of all women" and insisted the Cairo conference endorse that policy.

John Paul was not in Cairo, but he kept in constant touch with his delegation. Vatican spokesman Joaquin Navarro-Valls recalls the Pope's reaction to Paragraph 8.25: "He feared that for the first time in the history of humanity, abortion was being proposed as a means of population control. He put all the prestige of his office at the service of this issue." For nine days the Vatican delegates, under his direction, lobbied and filibustered; they kept their Latin

American bloc in line and struck up alliances with Islamic nations opposed to abortion. In the end, the Pope won. The Cairo conference inserted an explicit statement that "in no case should abortion be promoted as a method of family planning"; in return the Vatican gave partial consent to the document.

In public relations terms, it was a costly victory. There he goes again, the standard argument ran, imposing his sectarian morality on a world already hungry and facing billions of new mouths to feed in the coming decades. One Spanish critic said the Pope had "become a traveling salesman of demographic irrationality." Says dissident Swiss theologian Hans Kung: "This Pope is a disaster for our church. There's charm there, but he's closed-minded." The British Catholic weekly the *Tablet* summed up Cairo, "Never has the Vatican cared less about being unpopular than under Pope John Paul II."

Cairo perfectly crystallized reciprocal conundrums: the problem of the Pope in the modern world and the problem the Pope has with the modern world. The conflict boils down to different paths of reason and standards of truth. In ***Crossing the Threshold of Hope,*** John Paul locates the source of the great schism between faith and logic in the writings of the 17th century French philosopher Rene Descartes, particularly his assertion "Cogito ergo sum" (I think; therefore I am). The Pope points out that Descartes's formulation turned on its head St. Thomas Aquinas' 13th century pronouncement that existence comes before thought—indeed, makes thought possible. Descartes could presumably have written "Sum ergo cogito," but then the history of the past 300 years might have been profoundly different.

Although not the only one, Descartes was a major inspiration for the scientific revolution and the Enlightenment. Truth became a matter not of doctrine or received traditions but of something materially present on earth, accessible either through research or sound reasoning. "Know then thyself, presume not God to scan," Alexander Pope wrote in 1733-34. "The proper study of Mankind is Man."

The human intellect, thus liberated, proved prodigious; the fruits of its accomplishments are ever present in the developed world and tantalizingly seductive to those peering in from outside the gates. John Paul is not a fundamentalist who wants to repeal the Enlightenment and destroy the tools of technology; the most traveled, most broadcast Pope in history knows the advantages of jet airplanes and electronics. Instead he argues that rationalism, by itself, is not enough: "This world, which appears to be a great workshop in which knowledge is developed by man, which appears as progress and civilization, as a modern system of communications, as a structure of democratic freedoms without any limitations, this world is not capable of making man happy."

In essence, the Pope and his critics are talking at cross-purposes, about different universes. His reaffirmations of the church's doctrines on sexual matters actually form a small part of his teachings, but they have drawn most of the attention of troubled Catholics and the Pope's critics in the West. The conviction is widespread that sexual morality and conduct are private concerns, strictly between individuals and their consciences. But who guides those consciences? the Pope would ask. Many population experts see a future tide of babies as a problem to be solved; the Pope sees these infants-in-waiting as precious lives, the gifts of God. The church's doctrine that condoms should not be used under any circumstances has provoked, in the age of AIDS, deep anger. Henri Tincq, who writes on religious subjects for Paris' *Le Monde,* sums up this reaction, "The church's refusal of condoms even for saving lives is absolutely incomprehensible. It disqualifies the church from having any role in the whole debate over AIDS." As heartless as John Paul's position may seem, it is consistent with his view of the world: the way to halt the effects of unsafe sexual practices is to stop the practices.

Those who will never agree with the Pope on birth control, abortion, homosexuality and so on may nonetheless have benefited from hearing him speak out. Says Father Thomas Reese of the Woodstock Theological Center in Washington: "He's the one keeping these issues alive, things people should reflect on morally. He can't force them to do things, but he provides a constant reminder that these are moral questions, not simply medical or economic ones."

John Paul has never stepped back from difficulties, and he looks forward to an arduous 1995 agenda. First up is a scheduled 10-day trip in January to Papua New Guinea, Australia, Sri Lanka and the Philippines, where the Archbishop of Manila is in open conflict with the country's Protestant President over population control. The Pope is also laying strategy for the 1995 U.N. World Conference on Women in Beijing, which figures to be a replay of Cairo. In June, he plans to meet with Ecumenical Patriarch Bartholomew I, the leader of the Eastern Orthodox Church. John Paul has long spoken of mending the breach between the Roman and Eastern churches that became final in 1054. The Berlin Wall, put up in 1961, came down 11 years into his papacy; undoing the effects of a millennium may take him a little longer.

The Man of the Year's ideas about what can be accomplished differ from those of most mortals. They are far grander, informed by a vision as vast as the human determination to bring them into being. After discovering the principle of the lever and the fulcrum in the 3rd century B.C., Archimedes wrote, "Give me where to stand, and I will move the earth." John Paul knows where he stands.

Camille Paglia (review date 26 December 1994)

SOURCE: "Pope Fiction," in *New Republic,* December 24, 1994, pp. 24-5.

[*In the following review, Paglia offers positive evaluation of* Crossing the Threshold of Hope. *According to Paglia,* "Crossing the Threshold of Hope *comes as a stunning display not of Catholic autocracy but of the ideological flexibility and rueful insight of the modern mind.*"]

The pope speaks. But ***Crossing the Threshold of Hope*** is a peculiar document. Each chapter opens with the journalist Vittorio Messori's questions, sometimes bold and querulous, sometimes obsequious and honorific in the Italian way—"Allow me to play, although respectfully, the gadfly." The pope then replies at length, his reflections moving impressionistically from the philosophical and theological to the historical and autobiographical. The didactic structure of Catholic catechism is thus reversed. During preparation for the sacrament of confirmation, for example, the preceptor asks, and the novice answers. But in John Paul II's book, the ultimate authority figure of church hierarchy submits to interrogation, a warping of tradition typical of a man whose kissing of airport tarmacs has dramatized his conviction that the pope is the servant of humanity.

I approached the pope's book as an atheist for whom Italian Catholicism is a rich ethnic identity rather than a religion. Catholic doctrine, particularly regarding sexuality and obedience to authority, has been troublesome to many members of my generation in America, and John Paul's reputation has become increasingly conservative. Thus, ***Crossing the Threshold of Hope*** comes as a stunning display not of Catholic autocracy but of the ideological flexibility and rueful insight of the modern mind. Its complex sequence of wide-ranging meditations—on prayer and salvation, the existence of God, the uniqueness of Jesus, the permanence of suffering, the overcoming of fear through faith—establishes John Paul as an eloquent and erudite intellectual, struggling to bridge the gap between universal human longings and the bitter political realities of the twentieth century.

In literary terms, the voice of the book is intense and powerful, yet peculiarly distant and exalted. All hierarchs suffer the isolation of power. Reaching us from stone walls of the labyrinthine Vatican, ***Crossing the Threshold of Hope*** resembles prison literature, in which physical immobility and sensory deprivation seem to intensify an author's power of language and originality of imagination. John Paul's captivity by rigid, royal protocol gives this book a distinct and affecting air of loneliness.

The former Karol Wojtyla, whose name honors his predecessor, John Paul I (who fused the names of *his* predecessors, John XXIII and Paul VI), has suffered an obliteration of personal identity in his higher function, the almost unimaginable burden of his election as pope, whom millions regard as the single living human closest to God. Hence the text oscillates between the first and third persons, sometimes in the same paragraph. "I," who privately takes pen in hand, had a father and homeland, but "he," the Supreme Pontiff on public view, is a nearly abstract being, the successor to Saint Peter, whose apostolic mission came from the lips of Jesus himself. It is a harrowing, mutilating privilege. Take this surreal example:

> As a young priest and pastor I came to this way of looking at young people and at youth, and it has remained constant all these years. It is an outlook which allows me to meet young people wherever I go. Every parish priest in Rome knows that my visits to the parish must conclude with a meeting between the Bishop of Rome and the young people of the parish. And not only in Rome, but anywhere the Pope goes, *he seeks out the young and the young seeks him out. Actually, in truth, it is not the Pope who is being sought out at all. The one being sought out is Christ* who knows "that which is in every man" (cf Jn 2:25), especially in a young person, and who can give true answers to his questions!

Wojtyla, the long-ago aspiring priest, melts into John Paul, the venerable Bishop of Rome, commander of many priests, who in turn swells into the world-traversing pope. But like a ghost, the latter suddenly vanishes into the Divine Being, Christ, whose vicar he is on earth and whom like all celebrants of Mass he literally impersonates in the Communion service (hence the ban on female priests). The passage is eerily chameleonic.

After the nihilism of poststructuralism and game-playing postmodernism, it is a relief to find the history of ideas treated in so respectful, cohesive and luminous a way. Studded with emphatic italicized phrases, the pope's book radiates with passion. Its central plot line, sketched with disarming simplicity, is a "struggle for the soul of the contemporary world." The dramatis personae in this Faustian combat are both living and dead. On one side is René Descartes and his modern progeny, Kant, Hegel and Heidegger. One hundred years after Descartes, John Paul asserts, European Christianity was already defeated: the French Revolution "tossed crucifixes in the street" and introduced "the cult of the goddess Reason." Today's Cartesians are the atheists and moral relativists of the "intellectual elite" who rule "the worlds of science, culture and media." On the other side are the warriors for Christ, beginning with Saint Paul, whose failed missionary visit to Athens illustrated the resistance of those trained in Greek "philosophical speculation" to the faith-based rigor of Christian "mystery." On the eternal battlefield of Western thought, Descartes' greatest opponent is Saint Thomas Aquinas, the medieval theologian John Paul believes to be unjustly neglected by the contemporary Church. He groups with Thomas other members of the Scholastic tradition, leading to John Henry Cardinal Newman, nineteenth-century Catholicism's most glamorous convert. With each recitation of the Nicene Creed at Mass, Catholics align themselves with this ancient lineage, for the words of the Creed are "nothing other than the reflection of Paul's doctrine."

The young are John Paul's hope. He writes feelingly of their needs and desires, of their "searching for the meaning of life." Remembering the "heroism" of his contempo-raries, who "laid down their young lives" in the Warsaw uprising of 1944, he laments the predicament of today's young. "They live in freedom, which others have won for them, and have yielded in large part to the consumer culture." He asks, "What is youth?"—implicitly opposing the soul-centered Christian view to the pagan one. The Hellenophile Oscar Wilde, for example, celebrated the beauty of youth quite differently. It is this carnal strain in the West, heterosexual as well as homosexual, that John Paul protests when defining as unethical, and inconsistent with true love, the use of any person as "an object of pleasure."

And yet his own style is remarkably in tune with '60s sensibility. With its slow, trancelike rhythms and breathtaking vision, *Crossing the Threshold of Hope* is nearly psychedelic. Its floating fantasia of ideas has the hallucinatory vividness of '60s expanded consciousness, calm, contemplative and psychologically disassociated. Its theater is hugely multicultural: John Paul makes Jesus confront Buddha and Muhammad and celebrates African and Asian animists for their sympathy to Christianity. Reopening staid establishment theology toward superstitious "populist piety," he accepts testimony about mystic coincidences and apparitions, particularly of Mary at Fatima and Jasna Góra. He rightly praises Mircea Eliade for showing how world anthropology has healed the break made by the Enlightenment between intellect and religion. True multiculturalism reveres the sacred.

The pope's persona is beyond sex, as conveyed by the dazzling purity of his white cassock and skull cap. He is a father-mother of shamanistic androgyny, a caring, contemplative, emanating being whose inconvenient body is merely a sensual entrapment or, as now, a living proof of human vulnerability to disease and death. As with worshipers of Plato's male-favoring Uranian Aphrodite, the pope's ancestry and affiliations are of the spirit rather than the flesh. Hence in this book he seems on charmingly intimate terms with the evangelists Luke and John and with Jesus himself, whom he calls, in a nearly Protestant way, "the only Friend" who walks beside us and will not disappoint. Real women, unfortunately, exist for John Paul only as celibate heroic saints or as dimly hallowed mothers in the obedient image of Mary. *Crossing the Threshold of Hope* is a book of transitions and new directions, but like much of current Catholic policy, it remains confounded by the pagan paradox of gender.

Kevin Wildes (essay date 26 December 1994)

SOURCE: "In the Name of the Father," in *New Republic*, December 26, 1994, pp. 21-5.

[In the following essay, Wildes examines the importance of phenomenology as the philosophical framework of John Paul's Christian theology and teachings. According to Wildes, "Pope John Paul II has grounded the authority of

Karol Wojtyla's modern phenomenology in the ancient authority of God."]

Since the close of the Second Vatican Council, the Roman Catholic Church has struggled, in public, about how it should move: forward into the modern world or backward to the austere certitude of the past. In 1979, when an obscure Polish cardinal was elected pope, it seemed as if a decision had been made in favor of the past. And in the years since, the former Karol Wojtyla has been portrayed—with some reason—as an arch-reactionary. But he is, in fact, something far more complex than that. His theology, as it emerges in his life's writings, is strikingly modern, more rooted in nineteenth-and twentieth-century philosophy than anything else. Indeed, it may even be the very modernism of his theology that has led him into the ecclesiastical authoritarianism for which he is more renowned.

How this happened is an interesting twentieth-century story. Wojtyla's central philosophical identity is rooted in what is known as the method of "phenomenology." This off-putting term translates into a relatively simple idea: it is that one can come to understand the truth of something not simply by reference to the authority of science, or revelation, or dogma, but by "moving around" it, experiencing it from different perspectives and letting the reflections of each perspective communicate the truth of the object.

The central metaphor of such philosophy is "walking around." It is in this way that Wojtyla has consistently understood the Church. Amid dramatic changes, he has led it around and around its identity, traditions, central practices and beliefs. Hence also his constant travel around the world: it is part of his attempt to circle human experience, in the belief that there is an essential core that is normative for being human. That core is, for him, what defines authentic human existence. It is not a subjective matter, but a mission of objective discovery. In *Veritatis Splendor,* John Paul's recent encyclical on morality, he wrote, "The splendor of truth shines forth in all the works of the Creator and in a special way in man, created in the image and likeness of God." The splendor of that truth can be found by a form of traveling, observing and circling. Theologically, in fact, Wojtyla hasn't led the Church forward or backward. He has led it in circles.

Wojtyla's philosophical interests began in his earlier priestly formation and doctoral work in theology. In his pre-seminary years, as a worker and university student in Krakow, Wojtyla came under the spell of the underground priest Jan Tyranowski, a hero of the Polish church during the Nazi occupation. It was Tyranowski who, in his bid to revive a deeper spirituality among Poland's persecuted Catholics, introduced Wojtyla to the work of Spanish mystics such as John of the Cross, a sixteenth-century Carmelite monk who, with Teresa of Avila, led the Carmelite order in reform.

Steeped in this spirituality, Wojtyla presented himself in 1942 to Archbishop Sapieha of Krakow as a candidate for the seminary. Four years later, he was ordained as a priest and immediately packed off to Rome for a doctoral studies in theology. The decision by Archbishop Sapieha to send Wojtyla was part of a plan to rebuild the Polish church intellectually after so many of its priests—more than 2,000—had been killed by the Nazis. In Rome, Wojtyla studied at the Angelicum, a college now called the Pontifical University of St. Thomas, and wrote his dissertation under the direction of Reginald Garrigou-Lagrange. Perhaps sensing the young priest's background, Lagrange directed Wojtyla to write on the problem of faith in the writings of John of the Cross.

The problem Wojtyla dealt with was that, in John's writings, faith seemed to lack any cognitive content. It was all mystical spirituality, no hard knowledge. But Wojtyla found both categories unsatisfying. Perhaps influenced by his early years in the political turmoil of occupied Poland, Wojtyla argued that faith was, above all, rooted in *experience.* In the experience of faith, the human being is transformed and participates in divine life. First highlighted in this 1950 treatise, **The Question of Faith in St. John of the Cross,** the importance of the category of experience came to be critical in all of Wojtyla's thought.

After his return to Poland, Wojtyla worked for a time in a parish. But in 1951, Sapieha, then a cardinal, insisted he work on a second doctorate, in order to qualify as a university teacher. This time, the thesis was on a less traditional subject. Completed in 1957, the dissertation's title is **An Evaluation of the Possibility of Constructing Christian Ethics on the Assumptions of Max Scheler's Philosophical System.**

Scheler was a phenomenologist who deployed Edmund Husserl's intuitive philosophy to discover a basis for ethics. Here, Wojtyla began to pin down exactly what "experience" could really mean. Scheler argued it was possible objectively to describe "ethical" states of consciousness. He claimed that many emotions—including those of moral values—had an objective basis, and that it was the objective attraction to the good—not the imposition of an "ought"—that moves us to moral action. But Wojtyla felt that Scheler's account of moral experience was insufficient, since moral experience is more than the experience of values: it is *acting* upon them. For Wojtyla, it was in the choice of action that all the various aspects of the moral life came together, that internal, philosophical experience and external moral experience intersected.

This concentration on action was in turn influenced by the work of Maurice Blondel, a turn-of-the-century Catholic philosopher who was best known, in his book *l'Action,* for exalting the role of the will. Blondel argued that philosophy must give an account of action rather than pure thought, an idea that recurs throughout Wojtyla's later work. In linking together the observation of objective moral values (Scheler) and the centrality of action in human morality (Blondel), Wojtyla had constructed the foundation of his ethics: the authentic, acting human person. This understanding of the person suggested not only how people ought not to be treated but also how they ought to be treated.

In his new book, ***Crossing the Threshold of Hope,*** Wojtyla explains his development this way: "So the development of my studies centered on man—on the human person—can ultimately be explained by my pastoral concern." But it was also affected by his political experience. His emphasis on the person is, in part, a reaction to totalitarian regimes that impoverished the mystery of the person in order to control people by the mechanisms of mass, centralized societies. In the face of first Nazi and then Soviet tyrannies, Wojtyla stressed the unique richness of each person. But he also emphasized that the person becomes a person because of community. In an address in Canada in 1984 he argued that "the human person lives in a community. . . . And with the community he shares hunger and thirst and sickness and malnutrition and misery. . . . In his own person the human being is meant to experience the needs of others." He refused to counter totalitarianism with the liberal individualism of the West.

An account of his view of the authentic nature of personhood came in his 1960 book, ***Love and Responsibility,*** in which Wojtyla deployed his phenomenonlogical method to pastoral ends. He argued that in the matter of love there are natural sexual desires and that "the natural direction of the sexual urge is toward a human being of the other sex." The moral order builds upon the natural order and transcends it. He writes that "the commandment to love is, as has been said, a form of the personalistic norm. We start from the existence of the person." The personalist norm "leads to the recognition of the principle of monogamy and the indissolubility of the marriage tie."

In defending this position, he later wrote: "I formulated the concept of a *personalist principle.* This principle is an attempt to translate the commandment of love into the language of philosophical ethics. *The person is a being for whom the only suitable dimension is love.* We are just to a person if we love him. . . . Love for a person *excludes the possibility of treating him as an object of pleasure.* . . . It requires more; it requires the *affirmation of the person as person.*" He goes on to say, "Above all, the principle that a person has value by the simple fact that he is a *person* finds very clear expression: man, it is said by Vatican II, "is the only creature on earth that God has wanted for his own sake.'" "Personhood" subsequently became a fixation. Wojtyla's next book, ***Osoba i Czyn,*** written in 1969 and republished and revised ten years later as ***The Acting Person,*** is devoted to the subject.

Throughout Wojtyla's intellectual development, the phenomenological framework is clear. Wojtyla as a theologian had not responded to modernity by retreating into reactionary certitude, or by reasserting dogma or a simple elaboration of Thomist natural law. He had explored belief with all the modern philosophical tools available. He brought to his faith the mysticism of John of the Cross,

but had developed this with the thought of such modern thinkers as Blondel, Scheler and Husserl. Throughout, he was responding, as the Church was, to the fundamental problem of faith in a rationalist, amoral, scientific age. And like the Second Vatican Council, he did not seek to escape these facets of modernity, but to understand more fully their unique challenges to faith.

Truth was not simply a matter of revelation, or a blind leap of faith, or a self-evident product of nature. It was, according to Wojtyla, found by observation, observation as a reflection on *all* experience. It could be conducted from all sorts of angles; what seemed like contradictions—say the contradiction between faith and science—were actually different ways of looking at the same thing. Take the question of science's challenge to religious belief. Wojtyla, in a 1987 letter to Father George Coyne, director of the Vatican Observatory, saw science and religion forming "a *community of interchange.* Such a community of interchange encourages its members to expand their partial perspectives and form a unified vision." What's more, "science can purify religion from idolatry and false absolutes. Each can draw the other into the wider world, a world in which both can flourish."

But this remarkable openness had its problems, too. By relying on phenomenology, Wojtyla also suffered from some of its more obvious difficulties. What if the different appearances of something don't fit together? What if, instead of coherence and connection, we get chaos and disjunction? What if science actually contradicts faith? What, to take another example, if the Church had changed its own doctrines, contradicting itself? One strategy is to gloss over the dissonance. In ***Redemptor Hominis,*** the 1979 encyclical on changes in Church doctrine, John Paul simply asserts the continuity of the Church yesterday and today. In ***Dives in Misericordia,*** written about the mercy of God, there is no struggle between the teachings of the Old and the New Testaments, merely the statement that "Christ reveals the Father within the framework of the same perspective and on ground already prepared, as many pages of the Old Testament demonstrate."

While Wojtyla *assumes* there is continuity, what happens when there is real conflict? In a world that is culturally diverse and morally pluralistic, it is not clear why men and women outside the community of believers should accept certain understandings of "authenticity" over others. Indeed, the development of practices such as free markets, limited democracies and informed consent are responses to pluralistic conceptions of authentic human experience. They are practices that convey moral authority when people hold different moral views. What did Wojtyla have in his arsenal to counter them? More important, what resources did John Paul have?

In the letter on ordination and women, ***Ordinatio Sacerdotalis,*** for example, John Paul was forced to address an issue that Wojtyla the theologian had few resources to solve. Here, authenticity wasn't a good enough argument. After all, who was to say which notion of the priesthood was more authentic than another? A phenomenologist might look at priestly roles in the Church and in society, observe how other cultures and churches have found sacerdotal roles for women; or notice the correlation between some theological views of the symbolism of women and the pastoralism of the priesthood. But none of this is evident in John Paul's edict. He quotes Pope Paul VI who wrote, "The real reason [for not ordaining women] is that, in giving the Church her fundamental constitution, her theological anthropology—thereafter always followed by the Church's tradition—Christ established things in this way." He simply lays down the law, arguing, it seems, that tradition is the primary way to decide what is authentic or inauthentic, what is true and what is false.

The truth is, phenomenology can only get you so far. A description of any phenomenon, no matter how objective, must start from somewhere. All descriptions embody certain presuppositions, biases and values of the observer. A visitor to a city may get two very different tours of the city from two separate friends. One friend may highlight the artistic centers of the city while the other may highlight the sporting attractions. Another still may notice its industry, or its architecture. The visitor is left with a question of how to determine which tour of the city reveals its authentic nature.

Wojtyla is aware of the problem, of course. His own writing provides an explanation of why there are such divergent interpretations of authenticity: human reason is limited while the phenomena of human existence are complex and rich. Without a common framework, accounts of authenticity will move in very different directions and reach very different conclusions. But who is to provide the common framework? The answer is not a surprise. When all else fails, Wojtyla appeals to the authority of revelation to pick out the normative account of humanity. And the arbiter of that authority turns out to be Wojtyla himself, in the person of the pope.

When talking to the world at large, John Paul II has simply invoked the authority of the Scriptures as interpreted by himself. This is certainly the strategy in his latest book. But the strategy was clear as early as 1979 in Puebla, Mexico, on a trip to meet with the bishops of Central America. In that meeting, John Paul proclaimed: "Faced with so many other forms of humanism that are often shut in by a strictly economic, biological or psychological view of man, the Church has the right and duty to proclaim the truth about man that she has received from her Teacher, Jesus Christ."

Of course, this assertion of authority is not an innovation. But its stridency is notable. The irony is that when the phenomenologist Karol Wojtyla became pope, he simply asserted that the papacy's "authenticity" lay in its fiats. This turned out to be particularly true when the papacy addressed the internal matters of the Church itself. In these affairs, to be sure, the papacy has always exercised

considerable authority. But this always has been in the context of many different levels of authority in its magisterial teachings. There are those teachings when the pope or Church council speaks ex cathedra or infallibly. This is the extraordinary teaching authority of the Church. There is also the ordinary papal magisterium, which, in principle, is open to development, change and reform.

But John Paul II seems to have created a new category of authentic papal teaching in both *Veritatis Splendor* and the letter on ordination. The claims made in those letters are not said to be infallible in a technical sense. Yet they are said to be regarded as definitive for all the faith and for all time. In the letter on ordination John Paul wrote that "in some places it [the ban on women's ordination] is nonetheless considered still open to debate, or . . . to have merely disciplinary force." The implications of such views is that the ban can be changed. He goes on to write:

> In order that all doubt may be removed regarding a matter of great importance, a matter which pertains to the Church's divine constitution itself, in virtue of my ministry of confirming the brethren (cf Luke 22:32) I declare that the Church has no authority whatsoever to confer priestly ordination on women and that this judgment is to be definitively held by all the Church's faithful.

The theologian Francis Sullivan had perhaps the most succinct response to this innovation: "I can only conclude that claims are being made which, to my knowledge, have never been made about any document of ordinary papal teaching."

Anyone who deploys a phenomenological method must address at some point the problem of the circularity of the method. Every description is contextualized and relies on prior assumptions made by the describer. The describer must assume what is important to describe. Wojtyla's work does not escape this fundamental problem of phenomenology. It is particularly problematic for him when he encounters the pluralism and multiculturalism of many secular societies. Differences in cultures frequently signal different accounts over others. How can he break out of the circle? He does so simply by appealing to authority. And the more circular the reasoning, the cruder the authoritarianism.

In a public, pluralistic forum John Paul II has appealed to the authoritative content of God's revelation to say why some accounts are authentic and others are inauthentic. But *within* the Church, he has done something more radical. Throughout its life, the Church has contained a pluralism of spiritualities and interpretations of what it is to be authentically human and Christian. One has only to think of the different religious orders of the Church to find examples of different views of authenticity. In this context, John Paul II cannot rely on the authority of content since the revelation is shared by all believers. Instead he must appeal to the authority of office. It is by appeal to juridical authority that he must move to break the circle. Perhaps this is why, in what seems almost desperate fashion, the current pope has been making new and radical claims for papal authority, sometimes, it seems, each day. It is, after all, only God who enjoys the view from nowhere: the view without context or particularity. Only God escapes the circle of interpretation. In the last resort, perhaps, Pope John Paul II has grounded the authority of Karol Wojtyla's modern phenomenology in the ancient authority of God.

Peter Steinfels (review date 13 January 1995)

SOURCE: "Surprising, Demanding, Impressive," in *Commonweal*, January 13, 1995, pp. 21-2.

[*In the following review, Steinfels offers positive assessment of* Crossing the Threshold of Hope.]

Millions of people scarcely able to understand this book will purchase and peruse it. Other millions who could appreciate and benefit from its insights will spurn it out of hand. The reason is the same in both cases: the author is the pope.

Behind the widespread interest and best-seller status of **Crossing the Threshold of Hope** is the belief that it will reveal a "real pope" behind the official Vicar of Christ, a down-home Karol Wojtyla who will relax, invite us into his Vatican apartments, and tell us what he really believes, how he really prays, what really makes him tick, all in terms at once more intimate, more accessible, and yet more oracular than those of papal documents or Catholic theology generally.

The book utterly defies these expectations. In a world of precooked, nearly predigested, thought, the pope's performance is uncompromising. Although he knowingly set out to write for masses of devout or curious readers, by page 22 he is discussing "cognitive realism." On that page and the three that follow, he cites Ludwig Wittgenstein, Aristotle, Plato, Kant, Aquinas, Paul Ricoeur, Emmanuel Levinas, Mircea Eliade, Martin Buber, and the Polish archbishop and thinker, Marian Jaworski, as well as the Gospel of John, the Book of Wisdom, and Saint Paul's Letters to the Romans and to the Ephesians.

My favorite passage of this sort occurs on page 51 where John Paul explains how Descartes "inaugurated the great anthropocentric shift in philosophy" and brought the world to "the threshold of modern immanentism and subjectivism":

> The author of *Meditationes de Prima Philosophia* with his ontological proofs, distanced us from the philosophy of existence, and also from the traditional approaches of Saint Thomas which lead to God who is "autonomous existence," *Ipsum esse subsistens.* By making subjective consciousness absolute, Descartes moves instead toward pure consciousness of the Absolute, which is pure thought.

There may be a snobbish, morally dubious glee in imagining the impact of that passage on the kind of reader who picks up the pope's book from the "inspiration" shelf at the airport bookstore, where it was grouped with *The Celestine Prophecy,* Robert Fulghum, and Marianne Williamson. Yet it is justiably satisfying that the current successor of Peter takes it for granted that serious answers to serious questions demand not just piety and good will but also knowledge and intellectual effort.

However, those prepared and willing to make such an effort may find other obstacles blocking their appreciation of John Paul's book. One is the temptation to read it not for itself but as a source of clues to his papacy, its successes or shortcomings. Another is the obsequious manner in which Italian journalist Vittorio Messori frequently poses the questions that John Paul II answers in each of the thirty-five brief chapters that move from discussions of God's existence, the divinity of Jesus, and the problem of evil to non-Christian religions, contemporary youth, the fall of communism, immortality, human rights, women, and other topics.

Catholics honor and respect the pope primarily because of the office he holds, one firmly anchored in accountability to the church and its tradition. Only secondarily do Catholics focus on the pope's personal holiness, which may not equal that of the widow down the street (or, in some historical periods, the pickpocket down the street).

But Messori oils every difficult question with verbal prostrations that seem more suited to addressing an Eastern potentate or Hindu holy man. Messori's notion of "Vicar of Christ" seems closer to the popular Tibetan understanding of the Dalai Lama than to the Catholic theology of the Petrine ministry. In this respect, the conservative journalist is probably representative, as is the commercial success of this volume, of a reborn "pope cult" that flourished from Pius IX to Pius XII and that John XXIII and the Vatican Council had temporarily eclipsed.

John Paul, it should be added, adroitly parries much of what is most theologically offensive about Messori's abject and ingratiating exaltation of the papacy. He steers the journalist's evocation of papal titles back to a discussion of collegiality and ultimately of the calling of all baptized Christians.

The pope of this volume is not "inspirational," although at times his observations are inspiring. His voice is very much the one heard in his encyclicals. It is the voice of a high-strung Polish intellectual, abstract, romantic, steeped in history, tempered by modern tragedy. His view of Christianity is heroic and baroque, dwelling not on the "little way" but on the grandeur and misery of humanity, on the extremes of joy and suffering, which are never far apart from one another in his reflections.

This is not the voice of John XXIII; it lacks the peasant calm, the sweetness, the earthy, self-deprecating humor. But who is to say that this is not a voice at least equally valid for the century of gulags and genocide, of global communication and probes into space?

Obviously *Crossing the Threshold of Hope* is not to be read as a treatise. When John Paul II is asked, "Does God really exist?" he is not going to say no, nor is he going to close the question definitively in a few pages. This is a book to be read for insights, perspectives, connections, formulations that spark meditation and enrich our understanding.

There is no shortage of these. In reply to the question, "If God exists why is he hiding?" John Paul, after a typical circling of the issue by way of Descartes, Aquinas, Catherine of Siena, the Book of Proverbs, Ludwig Feuerbach, the Gospel of John, and First Corinthians, proposes that the real problem may not be the hiddenness but the visibility of God. In taking on humanity and revealing himself in Jesus, God

> could go no further. In a certain sense, God has gone too far! Didn't Christ perhaps become "a stumbling block to Jews and foolishness to Gentiles" (1 Cor. 1:23). Precisely because he called God his Father, because he revealed him so openly in himself, he could not but elicit the impression that it was too much. . . . Man was no longer able to tolerate such closeness, and thus the protests began.

For me that does not close the discussion. Maybe the problem is that God is both too hidden and too visible, the divine revelation in Jesus too obscured by confusing and contradictory human witness in both the Scriptures and the historical church. But the pope's formulation altered my framework of thinking.

In some cases, the interplay of question and answer is fascinating in itself. In one of Messori's more challenging moments, with a minimum of groveling ("Taking advantage of the freedom you have granted me . . ."), the interviewer asks, "did a God who is a loving Father really need to sacrifice cruelly his own Son?"

John Paul opens his response with what looks like apologetic intellectualism at its worst: "Let's begin by looking at the history of European thought after Descartes." By the time the next question is posed, it seems that the pope, like a good politician, has completely evaded what has long haunted Jewish commentary on Abraham's sacrifice of Isaac as well as Christian soteriology.

Then, ten pages later, John Paul reintroduces the apparently evaded question himself in the context of the "great mystery of suffering." His brief answer will not settle doubts, but it demonstrates his unwillingness to set aside the embarrassing and intractable paradoxes of faith.

Likewise, John Paul's comments on other religions, including animism, are at once frank and generous, highlighting both what divides and unites. One wonders, of course, whether his treatment of Buddhism and Islam would be different if it were informed by the personal contacts and experience that warms his understanding of Judaism.

He affirms many of the themes of Vatican II, of *Gaudium et spes,* of the *Declaration on Religious Liberty,* of ecu-menism, of the church as a reality greater than its visible structure and organization.

John Paul's thought, whatever one may think of it, has always been profoundly Christocentric, and so is his reading of Vatican II: "The council is far from proclaiming any kind of ecclesiocentrism. Its teaching is Christocentric in all of its aspects."

It is legitimate to ask how these views, expressed with passion, accord with the policies of John Paul's papacy. Historians may someday explore the oddity that a pope of romantic, heroic, Christocentric outlook should preside over the triumph of authoritarian, bureaucratic, and centralizing forces in the church.

But that would hardly be the greatest of ironies historians confront. Seldom in fact can one read recognized masterpieces of Christian thought without finding unpalatable opinions or recalling inconsistencies between the texts' profound sentiments and the more earthbound actions or circumstances that shadowed the lives of their authors.

It would be a shame if unhappiness with current Vatican actions, irritation at inflated claims of papal authority, suspicion of a gap between the pope's views and his policies, or simply impatience with the hoopla surrounding its publication kept readers from *Crossing the Threshold of Hope.*

Leo D. Lefebure (essay date 15 February 1995)

SOURCE: "John Paul II: The Philosopher Pope," in *Christian Century,* February 15, 1995, pp. 170-6.

[*In the following essay, Lefebure examines John Paul's intellectual development and the philosophical underpinnings of his Christian theology. Lefebure contends that John Paul's rigid demand for Catholic obedience is tempered by his affinity for modern philosophical thought and belief in the sanctity of individual conscience.*]

During World War, Karol Wojtyla was a member of the underground Rhapsodic Theater. He was in the middle of performing one of the most patriotic plays in Polish literature when the sound of the Nazi radio interrupted with news of a German victory on the Russian front. While loudspeakers proclaimed the triumph of Hitler's armies, the young actor intoned his lines all the more forcefully: "The night was passing over the milky sky, the rosy beams of dawn began to fly."

At a time when some of his contemporaries fought in the Polish underground or joined in the uprising in Warsaw in 1944, Wojtyla pursued the quieter path of a seminarian. He was convinced, however, that literature, philosophy, theology and religious service could be weapons in the struggle for freedom. He would later look back on the war years and the sacrifices of his contemporaries: "I was a part of that generation and I must say that *the heroism of my contemporaries helped me to define my personal vocation.*"

Nazis and communists might be defeated, but threats to human rights and life remained. The sacred dignity of the human person has remained at the center of Wojtyla's concerns. He has brought to successive struggles a deep religious fervor rooted in traditional Polish Catholicism, an intellectual background that includes two doctorates, and experience in a wide variety of roles. Before becoming pope he had been a poet, playwright, philosopher, parish priest, university professor and ecclesiastical prelate.

Wojtyla's life has never been free from conflict and controversy He has described his role as pope as that of being a "sign that will be contradicted . . . . a challenge." He has been criticized by liberal Catholics and Protestants for demanding strict loyalty to traditional positions on ordination and sexual ethics, and he has been hailed by conservatives as the pope of "the Catholic restoration." He has disappointed Protestant ecumenical leaders for his uncompromising stances, and he has aroused the ire of Orthodox Christians for his efforts to establish the Catholic Church in Eastern Europe after the fall of communism. John Paul is a complex figure whose thought escapes stereotypes; the effects of his pontificate will be many-sided. His recent writings—***Crossing the Threshold of Hope,*** responses to the questions of Italian journalist Vittorio Messori, and ***As the Third Millennium Draws Near,*** his Apostolic Letter for the jubilee of the Year 2000—reflect his lifelong intellectual journey and his hopes for the future of Christianity. Whether one agrees with his positions or not, he is one of the few world leaders to possess a deeply considered religious and philosophical perspective on human existence.

As a theology student in Rome, under the guidance of one of the leading Thomist theologians of the day, Reginald Garrilou-LaGrange, Wojtyla a wrote his first doctoral dissertation on the meaning of faith in St. John of the Cross. St. John, the Mystical Doctor, taught the young doctoral candidate that the journey to God leads through the dark night of the soul, a time of deprivation and suffering. The dark night takes both active and passive forms. In this experience every natural ability of the person must be emptied so that God can accomplish a supernatural transformation of grace. Faith guides one through the painful process, even though this faith, in Wojtyla's words, "lacks all consolation and is without any light from above or below." Faith continues to trust in God despite its inability to see. Wojtyla conceded that this is better understood by experience than by concepts. The dark night is also the time of love, and perseverance leads to rapturous union with God.

Though embracing the mystical theology which assumed faith in divine revelation and spoke to the community of believers, Wojtyla and his mentors knew that philosophical analyses of human action and ethics were of the utmost importance in the confrontation with communist theoreticians. To prepare for a university career in a communist society, Wojtyla studied the foundations of ethics in modern Western philosophy, writing his second dissertation on the phenomenology of Max Scheler (1874-1928). Scheler, who was for a time a convert to Catholicism, warned that moral relativism could lead modern culture into a barbarism made more dreadful because of technology. In response to this threat, Scheler adopted the descriptive approach of phenomenology. He proposed that ethics be based on the intuition of values as the objects of feeling. Scheler's style of thought was intuitive and introspective. He excelled at describing subtle states of consciousness such as sympathy, resentment, repentance, love and joy Scheler argued that these states of consciousness put us in touch with objective values. Defending the objectivity of values has absorbed Wojtyla throughout his career.

Phenomenology never displaced the Thomistic structure of Wojtyla's thought, but it has had a lasting influence on his way of thinking. The young Wojtyla doubted that Scheler's proposal could serve as a basis for Catholic ethics because the emotional intuitions of value lack the objectivity of revelation. Nonetheless, Wojtyla admired Scheler's ability to clarify lived experience, and he suggested that one could apply the phenomenological method of reflection to the experience of the believer in attending to revelation. Wojtyla's approach to the human person has been shaped by Scheler's emphasis on human personality and his intuitive style of reflecting on experience and values. The pope's recent encyclical, ***The Splendor of Truth*** (***Veritatis Splendor***), returns to some of these concerns and defends the objectivity of values against the threat of moral relativism.

As bishop, archbishop and eventually cardinal of Krakow, Wojtyla continued to lecture and write, and he became well known in phenomenological circles. While auxiliary bishop and docent at the Catholic University of Lublin, he authored a philosophical study, ***Love and Responsibility*** (Polish edition, 1960; English translation, 1981), that explores the ethical dimension of human love and sexuality. The work arose from concerns he encountered in his pastoral ministry, especially his work with married couples and with university students preparing for married life or celibate religious vocations. He sought to confront Catholic ethical teachings with concrete experience, and he insisted on the responsibility and dignity of the human person as the norm for sexual behavior: "The mill loves only when a human being consciously commits his or her freedom in respect of another human being seen as a person, a person whose value is fully recognized and affirmed." Wojtyla warned against the self-deceptions of subjectivism and argued that self-giving love is the only dimension in which humans can truly affirm themselves and realize their full identity. Love is "the reciprocated gift of the self," and it is genuine only if it includes responsibility for the beloved.

The conclusions that Wojtyla drew for sexual ethics were among the most controversial of his career. He argued that in human sexuality there is a complex, interdependent synthesis of two orders: the order of nature, in which sexual relations aim solely at procreation, and the personal order, which seeks the full expression of the love of persons. Wojtyla asserted that it would violate both the order of nature and the order of personal love to use artificial methods of contraception, and he cited Gandhi's *Autobiography* as a supporting witness. Precluding the possibility of conception, Wojtyla feared, would shift the focus of sexual expression to enjoyment, thereby violating the personal order as well.

The book attracted attention in Europe and was translated into Italian, French and Spanish. Pope Paul VI read the work while he was awaiting the report of the Papal Commission on Problems of Birth and the Family. Wojtyla's arguments against artificial contraception influenced Paul VI's decision to reject the recommendation of the commission, and Pope Paul used Wojtyla's thought in writing his encyclical *Of Human Life* (*Humanae Vitae*, 1968), which rejected artificial contraception. A growing bond between the pope and the cardinal of Krakow led to Cardinal Wojtyla's being invited to conduct a Lenten retreat for Pope Paul VI and the papal household in 1976.

Wojtyla continued to ponder the philosophical foundation of ethics, and became increasingly interested in understanding the human person who acts. His most important philosophical book, **The Acting Person,** appeared as Volume 10 of the *Analecta Husserliana,* the Yearbook of Phenomenological Research (Polish edition, 1969; revised and translated into English, 1979). Acknowledging his debt to Scheler, Wojtyla explored the meaning of conscience and the process of human integration and self-fulfillment in action. Through analyses of consciousness, conscience, will, subjectivity and self-determination, he argued that we realize ourselves most profoundly through our sense of obligation and our decision to love. While most of the discussion remains philosophical, the closing pages of the book probe the significance of the evangelical commandment to love one's neighbor as oneself in a world of alienation and dehumanization. In a world in which individuals are too often submerged in collective systems, Wojtyla insisted that love of the neighbor is the reference point and norm for participation in any community that is truly human.

As archbishop of Krakow during the 1960s and '70s, Wojtyla learned to act on the national stage, and he became adept at mobilizing the resources of the Polish Catholic tradition and the faith and enthusiasm of millions of Polish people in the struggle against communism. He honed the skills of confrontation and negotiation, being careful not to push the communist government too far but demanding concessions each time the communists desperately sought the Catholic Church's support for the struggling economy. The church in Poland grew strong through policies of strict discipline and determined opposition. Undergirding the political maneuvering was a profound philosophical and theological struggle over the meaning and value of human existence.

As pope, John Paul II's impact on the world stage has been enormous, and *Time* magazine's selection of him as the 1994 Man of the Year is only one mark of his influence. He has been called the most powerful pope in the political arena since Innocent III in the 13th century, and it has been estimated that he has been seen face to face by more people than anyone else in the history of the human race. The very presence of a pope from Poland changed the dynamics of power throughout communist Europe. In 1981 Jaroslav Pelikan commented on the significance of a Slav being the visible head of Catholic Christianity: "Remember Stalin asking how many battalions the pope had? Now the Russians know. What would Kosygin—may he rest in peace—or Brezhnev or any of those guys give to go into a East European country and have a million people spontaneously turn out to cheer? It must blow their minds. . . . Whatever the Russians do will be wrong. . . . Whatever they do, they're going to lose."

But victory over established communism has not brought peace to Eastern Europe or the world. The new assaults on human dignity are in some ways even more painful for Pope John Paul II than the old: it was not Nazis or atheistic communists but Catholics in Croatia and Rwanda who actively participated in atrocities against persons of other ethnic groups.

The coming of the third millennium of Christianity has given a special focus to the pope's concerns, and he has declared that "preparing for the year 2000 has become as it were a hermeneutical key of my pontificate." This sense of anticipation is reflected in **Crossing the Threshold of Hope** and **As the Third Millennium Draws Near.** While the two publications are very different in form—**Crossing the Threshold** is conversational, wandering from topic to topic; the Apostolic Letter is a focused call to action—they express a single purpose: to infuse new vigor into the age-old mission of the church to proclaim Christ to the world.

Central to the pope's preparation for the new millennium is the "new evangelization." What is "new" in the task of evangelization involves both the contemporary context of the Catholic Church and a changed attitude toward those outside the church. In John Paul II's view, proclamation of the gospel demands both maintaining Catholic Christian identity and fostering dialogue with the world. While the concerns for identity and dialogue at times appear to move in different directions and give rise to certain tensions of thought and practice, they are inseparable in the pontiff's program.

In the pope's eyes, the greatest threat to Christian identity arises from the subjectivism, rationalism, relativism and indifferentism of much of modern Western culture as expressed by its philosophers and lived by millions of people who never read philosophy. Moral relativism is but one aspect of a broader relativizing trend which undermines the quest for the truth in any form. Cut off from metaphysical and religious foundations, all forms of culture risk being dissolved into forms of competition fueled by the will to power. In the struggle for the soul of modern culture, the dialogue with modern Western philosophy takes on a critical importance. The former philosophy professor is extremely critical of Descartes for seeking to ground philosophy in the human subject; he sees the fruit of this strategy in the later rationalism of the Enlightenment, which abandoned metaphysics, banished God from the world, and left humans to follow their own reason. In the French Revolution reason presided over the reign of terror. The search for freedom and pleasure divorced from responsibility has led to a culture of death in which the most vulnerable are made the victims.

While harshly critical of modern rationalism and positivism, John Paul is nonetheless warmly appreciative of philosophers who have a more complex relationship to modern thought. He cites with approval such philosophers as Emmanuel Levinas and Paul Ricoeur, both of whom have a more positive relation to the major figures of modern philosophy than the pope's teacher, Garrigou-LaGrange, would ever have tolerated. Ricoeur, for example, has a profound respect for the philosophy of limits of Immanuel Kant and for Kant's retrieval of the role of the symbol. Ricoeur invites Christians and secularists alike to a deeper appreciation of religious symbols as evoking more than can be captured in concepts. In welcoming Levinas's and Ricoeur's theories of interpretation as authentic retrievals of the profound meaning of religious metaphors and symbolic language, John Paul is at least implicitly opening the path to a more positive relationship to major elements in modern thought.

In *As the Third Millennium Draws Near,* the pope reaffirms the church's preferential option for the poor and commitment to work for justice, and proposes that the biblical tradition of the jubilee year be revived: the year 2000 could become a time of reducing or canceling the international debt that burdens poorer nations. He also welcomes broader movements in society that seek scientific, technological and especially medical progress, as well as efforts on behalf of the environment, peace and justice.

Within the Catholic Church, the pope's concern for safeguarding identity has led to strict discipline, an insistence on fidelity to received understandings of the truth of the gospel. John Paul II is acutely aware that many Catholics do not follow all papal teachings, especially in matters of sexual ethics. He publicly laments a "crisis of obedience" in relation to the church's teaching office. He has relentlessly demanded loyalty to papal and conciliar teaching and has been firm in rejecting alternative visions of Catholic belief and practice—as the censures of theologians Hans Kung, Leonardo Boff and Charles Curran have indicated. Even bishops are not secure. Last month Bishop Jacques Gaillot of Evreux in northern France was dismissed from his responsibilities as bishop because of his open challenge to the pope's teaching on abortion, the use of condoms, married priests and homosexual couples.

Nonetheless, the pope also shares the modern concern for religious freedom, and he is unequivocal in rejecting coercion of the conscience. His early philosophical studies deepened his conviction concerning the inviolability of conscience and the necessity of drawing people to the truth through their own free inquiry and judgment. In *Crossing the Threshold of Hope,* John Paul cites Aquinas: even an erroneous conscience that forbids one to profess faith in Jesus Christ must be followed. John Henry Newman once raised a famous toast: "To the pope, if you please—still to conscience first, and to the pope afterwards." Newman insisted that conscience is the "aboriginal Vicar of Christ," and that the pope cannot replace its role.

John Paul notes with approval that Newman placed conscience above authority. Quietly ignoring that in 1832 Gregory XVI condemned freedom of conscience as the "most pestilential error," John Paul says that in exalting conscience "Newman is not proclaiming anything new with respect to the constant teaching of the Church." The pope recalls with pride the Polish heritage of toleration of religious differences, at least among Christians. Passing over the country's history of anti-Semitism, he notes that in the late 16th century, when heretics were being burned at the stake, the last Polish king of the Jagiellonian dynasty refused to use violence, saying: "I am not the king of your consciences."

Respect for conscience means that the "new evangelization" cannot proceed according to methods used in earlier centuries. Indeed, for John Paul II, Christians preparing for the new millennium need to acknowledge and repent for the many crimes committed in the name of Christ throughout Christian history. In his Apostolic Letter, he challenges Christians to mourn the past actions of Christians who suppressed the opinions of others, at times using violence "in the service of truth." Even in recent years, he laments, Christians have supported totalitarian regimes that brutally violated fundamental human rights. The pope urges Christians to learn a lesson from such painful memories and cites the principle of Vatican II's *Declaration on Religious Freedom:* "The truth cannot impose itself except by virtue of its own truth, as it wins over the mind with both gentleness and power."

The pope's concern for dialogue has opened up encounters unprecedented in the history of the papacy. Though he yields to no one in his insistence upon the centrality of Jesus Christ in the economy of salvation (he proclaims that Jesus Christ is "absolutely unique" among the religious leaders of the world), he also asserts "the *common fundamental element* and the *common root*" of the world's religions. Moreover, he cites with admiration and respect the work of the late Romanian historian of religions, Mircea Eliade, who argued that there are common patterns shared by the world's religions.

The pope recognizes that the struggle for human dignity and world peace challenges the world's religions to come together in prayer and dialogue. He has sought better relations with the Jewish community, and he may be the first bishop of Rome since Peter to visit a synagogue in Rome. In October 1986 John Paul II invited religious leaders from a wide range of traditions to come to Assisi, Italy, to pray for world peace. Jews and Muslims, Buddhists, Sikhs and Hindus, representatives of traditional African and Native American religions, Shintoists and Jains all participated. Many popes have censured and condemned the teachings of theologians, often in far harsher terms and with more dire consequences for life and limb than Pope John Paul II has. No pope in the history of the papacy ever invited religious leaders from the world's religions, including the Dalai Lama, a figure traditionally revered by Buddhists as the reincarnation of the bodhisattva of compassion, to come to Assisi and pray.

Proclaiming Jesus Christ as the unique Savior of the world while also respecting the values of other religious traditions presents a difficult challenge, and the pope's comments on other religious traditions have not always been well received. This past December a conference of Buddhist monks in Sri Lanka protested against John Paul's description of their tradition as being "in large measure an *'atheistic' system*" and offering an "almost exclusively negative soteriology." In *Crossing the Threshold of Hope,* John Paul II ignores the central Buddhist virtues of generosity and compassion, as well as the long history of constructive Buddhist engagement in the world. Neglecting the positive signification of nirvana as the ultimate, the pope interprets nirvana as simply "a state of perfect indifference with regard to the world," and presents Buddhist practice as solely a path of negative detachment from the world. He sees it as a first step that leads to the point where the Carmelite mysticism of love proposed by John of the Cross begins. Buddhist monks in Sri Lanka were angered by the pope's remarks and threatened to boycott his visit unless the remarks were withdrawn. Shortly before embarking for Asia the pope suggested there had been a misunderstanding, and he denied that he intended to portray Buddhism in a derogatory manner. But leading Buddhist monks were not satisfied, and they boycotted the meeting of the pope with Hindu and Muslim leaders.

While he clearly proclaims Jesus Christ as the one mediator through whom all salvation comes, John Paul also acknowledges that the prayers of other religions are genuine worship and are welcomed by God. In his remarks at Assisi, the pontiff commented on both the difficulty and the importance of diverse traditions coming together: "Certainly we cannot pray together, namely, to make a common prayer, but we can be present while others pray." The presence of the pope at the prayers of other religious people expressed a profound respect for the genuine, grace-filled experience of God in other religious traditions. In his Apostolic Letter he expresses the hope of holding joint meetings with Jews and Muslims at sites of significance for all three traditions.

John Paul also admits that there are profound reasons that can hinder sincere persons from conversion to Christianity.

In *Crossing the Threshold,* the pope praises the "deeply evangelical manner" of Mahatma Gandhi, a Hindu, and acknowledges the situation facing Gandhi: "Could a man who fought for the liberation of his great nation from colonial dependence accept Christianity in the same form as it had been imposed on his country by those same colonial powers?"

In considering the divisions among Christians themselves, the pope has firmly defended the traditional claims of Catholic Christianity, often to the frustration of partners in ecumenical dialogue. Nonetheless, he has also on occasion expressed a rather different perspective on those who directly reject his authority. In response to Messori's question about why the Holy Spirit permitted the historical divisions in Christianity, John Paul notes that sin was a factor in the divisions, and that the historical causes are well known; but he then speculates on "a metahistorical reason" for the differences. He wonders whether the full wealth of meaning of the gospel and of redemption in Christ could have come to light if it were not for such diverse paths. "For human knowledge and human action a certain *dialectic* is present. Didn't the Holy Spirit, in His divine 'condescendence,' take this into consideration? It is necessary *for humanity to achieve unity through plurality, to learn to come together in the one Church, even while presenting a plurality of ways of thinking and acting, of cultures and civilizations.*" This metahistorical perspective, the pope suggests, would be more in accord with the wisdom of God's providence. Thus the pope admits that the painful oppositions among Christians, including the rejection of papal authority itself, may well make an indispensable contribution to the unfolding of the gospel under the guidance of the Spirit.

As *Time* acknowledged, John Paul's is one of the strongest and clearest moral voices in the world. The strength of his convictions is clear, as is his will to lead a united Catholic Church in evangelizing the world. His own demand for respect for conscience and his invitations to dialogue call the church to a posture not only of proclaiming but also of listening. The pope remains a sign that will be contradicted. For one who follows a dialectical path of knowledge and action open to the unpredictable role of the Holy Spirit, differences of perspective may not be simply obstacles to be lamented but may be invitations to deeper reflection and prayer and hope for a unity in the Spirit that no one can foresee.

J. Bryan Hehir (essay date 19 May 1995)

SOURCE: "Get a (Culture of) Life," in *Commonweal,* May 19, 1995, pp. 8-9.

[*In the following essay, Hehir offers analysis of John Paul's* The Gospel of Life *encyclical.*]

John Paul II's eleventh encyclical, *The Gospel of Life* (March 25, 1995) is yet another testimony to a central conviction of this papacy, namely, that words and ideas are the crucial determinants of history. The reception accorded the most recent text demonstrates John Paul II's continuing ability to gain a hearing for his ideas, however different they are from prevailing cultural convictions. The *New York Times* devoted almost a quarter of the front page to a photo and story about the encyclical; *Newsweek* made it the cover story; European colleagues tell me the coverage there was extensive. All this occurred before the religious community began its detailed analysis in weekly and monthly journals.

The encyclical bears the pope's distinctive style, a biblically based meditation and argument about a broad range of controversial issues. The text exhibits the discursive, sometimes repetitive character of earlier encyclicals. The four chapters logically admit of a different order than one finds in the text. It seems to me that the first chapter, on threats to life, leads directly to chapter 3, a detailed argument about the defense of life in different circumstances. Chapter 2, the positive Christian vision of life, leads directly to chapter 4, building a culture of life.

Embedded in these four long chapters are a variety of arguments. The dominant character of the encyclical is its overarching moral vision. Cast in the cosmic categories of a "culture of death" contending with a "culture of life," *The Gospel of Life* seeks to galvanize the witness of the church and to challenge ideas, laws, and policies which threaten human life in different but deadly ways.

The pope's classification of these threats to life can be divided into ancient, modern, and postmodern categories. The ancient threats, well-known, are rooted in the worst instincts of human nature and persist with a virulence which defies any conception that history is a constant march toward improvement. The ancient threats are poverty and hunger, war and genocide. From Central Europe to Sub-Saharan Africa, the ancient scourges— some the product of nature, others the result of human hatred—number their victims today in the millions.

The modern threats are more complex in origin and character. They are often rooted in the best instincts of human nature, in the quest for knowledge, the development of modern science, the expanding reach of technology. The modern threats characteristically are rooted in the qualitatively new power which modern science and technology have placed in human hands.

In the past fifty years, American society has split the atom, cracked the genetic code, and pierced the veil of space. We have also dramatically expanded our capacity for medical intervention in the final stages of life. Each of these developments has produced major advances in human knowledge, in applied technology, and in creating the culture of postindustrial society. Each of them also has demonstrated that technological innovation is not always accompanied by moral wisdom. Churchill's comment that the Balkans produced more history than they could

consume finds an analogous application here. Technology—nuclear, genetic, medical—has its own logic, but it does not have its own ethic. From the first encyclical of his pontificate, *The Redeemer of Man,* John Paul II has focused on the issue of providing moral direction for science and technology as a dominant challenge for church and society. The pope never assumes a position of fundamental opposition to either scientific research or technological change; his concern is to place both within the identifiable limits of the moral universe.

This abiding interest in maintaining traditional restraints in the face of contemporary developments in science, technology, and politics reaches a new level of intensity and detail in *The Gospel of Life* when the pope turns to the "postmodern" threats to life. These are rooted not in what we can do but in how we think. Peter Steinfels (*New York Times,* April 1, 1995) accurately identified the principal objective of this encyclical: it is the pope's address to the culture of advanced technological societies. In one sense it is an attempt at dialogue, in the spirit of Vatican II's *Gaudium et spes.* But the tone is not entirely dialogical; in many passages it is a declaration, a lecture to the culture of societies which John Paul believes have lost their moral moorings. The postmodern threats are the pope's principal concern; they are well represented in two passages of the encyclical: "Choices once unanimously considered criminal and rejected by the common moral sense are gradually becoming socially acceptable. . . . no less grave and disturbing is the fact that conscience itself, darkened as it were by such widespread conditioning, is finding it increasingly difficult to distinguish between good and evil in what concerns the basic value of human life."

This is the heart of the issue. The fundamental purpose of *The Gospel of Life* is to project a moral vision and to provide a structure of moral reasoning that will illuminate a direction for personal conscience, professional ethics, and public policy on questions threatening human life in this final decade of a very violent century. Neither the vision (chapter 2) nor the moral argument (chapter 3) breaks new ground; the power and value of the encyclical lie in its synthetic quality, bringing together broad themes and specific conclusions in the style of a Brandeis brief, projecting a definite viewpoint on a multiplicity of issues which are usually treated in isolation in our civil debates.

The pope's opposition to abortion reaffirms what has been said at every level of Catholic teaching; his case against euthanasia and assisted suicide is carefully drawn and summarizes traditional and recent teaching on topics which will be increasingly the focus of the "life debate" in American society. Even the well-publicized section on capital punishment amounts to a change in emphasis; the pope raises substantially the presumption against the state's right to take life in the name of domestic security. It is an important and welcome authoritative statement, but continues a pattern of reasoning used by the American bishops and others for the past fifteen years.

The encyclical combines, therefore, a powerful moral vision, a traditional moral argument, and an urgent call to personal and social conscience. How will it be received? The answer depends on three large arguments which the pope enters and which can only be identified here and must await further commentary. First, an internal issue in Catholic social teaching; John Paul II addresses his case to the church and civil society, but it is a case made almost exclusively in terms of biblical imagery and theological reflection. Unlike John XXIII's moral appeal to civil society in *Peace on Earth,* John Paul calls upon all to enter the rich symbolic discourse of the Scriptures to find direction for moral choice. There is a tension here between this vision and secular pluralistic culture which the encyclical never acknowledges.

Second, the heart of the pope's appeal to civil society is his discussion of law and morality. His position is a classical statement that civil law and policy must reflect moral law, even if they cannot simply replicate it. But John Paul's vision of how much civil law can do in postindustrial societies is very expansive. In many ways his proposals are exactly what one would expect from a magisterial document. But they do not struggle with the conditions which Catholic politicians, administrators, and professionals face even if they are wholly convinced of the moral vision of *The Gospel of Life.* We will need to hear from the practitioners on this topic.

Third, John Paul continues in this letter a theme found in *Centesimus annus* (1991) and *Veritatis splendor* (1993). He distinguishes the political institutions of democracy from the cultural context of democratic societies. He endorses the first more decisively than any pope in the Catholic tradition. He finds much less to support in the culture. There is much to criticize in the cultural presuppositions of postindustrial society, but the dynamic of politics and culture requires more attention than even this long, welcome encyclical provides.

John O'Neill (essay date June 1995)

SOURCE: "Intrinsic Evil, Truth, and Authority," in *Religious Studies,* Vol. 31, No. 2, June, 1995, pp. 209-19.

[*In the following essay, O'Neill examines the argument for intrinsic evil and moral authority in* Veritatis Splendor. *Though supporting John Paul's view that some acts are intrinsically evil, O'Neill objects to the pope's claim to "epistemological authority."*]

Pope John Paul's recent encyclical, *Veritatis Splendor,* addresses itself beyond its immediate audience in the Catholic Church to 'all people of good will'. While my Catholic friends assure me that the Catholic Church is one club that once entered can't be left, I assume myself to be in the wider audience: I write here as an atheist and one still happy to be called a Marxist, both condemned in the document. The paper is not written, however, from a position of hostility to all in the document. My aim in the first part of the paper is to defend one claim in *Veritatis Splendor,* that some human acts are intrinsically evil, and to relate that claim to another central thought of the document, that one should live in truth. I outline two versions of the idea of living in truth and suggest why the Thomist position defended in the encyclical is to be preferred. In defending the claim that some acts are intrinsically evil, I am not endorsing the specific claims about which acts are intrinsically evil, in particular that claim which, in media coverage of *Veritatis Splendor,* was construed to be one of its main messages, namely that contraceptive practices which intentionally render the sexual act infertile are intrinsically evil. Indeed one problem with that claim is that it trivializes the otherwise *prima facie* plausible Vatican II list of intrinsically evil acts that precedes it. Even contentious members of that list, for example abortion and euthanasia, have a recognizable moral seriousness that the question of contraception lacks. However, the problem with John Paul's reaffirmation of Paul IV's teaching on contraception is that it misdescribes a particular act, not with the claim that there are intrinsically evil acts. More generally, the claim that some acts are intrinsically evil can be defended independently of any theological position. The first part of the paper provides such a defence of the position.

In the second section of the paper I outline where, as a part of the wider audience addressed, I have difficulties with the encyclical. I refer here to the authoritarianism of the document. The problem lies not with the concept of 'authoritative teaching' as such. All teaching presupposes some form of epistemological authority. It lies rather in the way that the document defines such authority in a way which is incompatible with one precondition of it, that is, reasoned dialogue.

I

To assert that some acts are intrinsically evil is to affirm the Pauline principle, that it is not permissible to do evil that good might come of it (Romans 3:8). To affirm that principle is to deny consequentialism: there are acts one ought not to perform even if their consequences are good or even the best. That denial of consequentialism is quite independent of how what is intrinsically good is characterized: it rules out for example not just classical utilitarianism, and its modern ideal and preference-based versions, but consequentialist reasoning employing traditional Christian characterizations of the good. One reason that Catholic teaching remains influential especially in the sphere of medical ethics is that it offers a theoretically grounded opposition to the consequentialism that dominates discussion. What I want to do here is link it with another powerful set of objections to consequentialism which might at first sight seem distant from the Catholic tradition.

An objection to consequentialism which has informed a great deal of recent discussion of the doctrine is that it fails to respect personal integrity. The objection is developed by Bernard Williams, in part, through the example of George, an unemployed chemist of poor heath, with a family who are suffering in virtue of his being unemployed. An older chemist, knowing of the situation tells George he can swing him a decently paid job in a laboratory doing research into biological and chemical warfare. George is deeply opposed to biological and chemical warfare, but the older chemist points out that if George does not take the job then another chemist who is a real zealot for such research will get the job, and push the research along much faster than would the reluctant George. Should George take the job? For the consequentialist, given any plausible account of the good, the right thing to do is obvious: George should take the job. That will produce better consequence both for his family and the world in general. However, to do that would be to undermine George's integrity. He must treat his own projects and commitments as just so many desires to be put into the calculus with others.

> It is absurd to demand of such a man, when the sums come in from the utility network which the projects of others have in part determined, that he should just step aside from his own project and decision and acknowledge the decision which the utilitarian calculation requires. It is to alienate him in a real sense from his actions and the source of his action in his own convictions. It is to make him into a channel between the input of everyone's projects, including his own, and an output of optimific decision; but this is to neglect the extent to which his actions and his decisions have to be seen as the actions and decisions which flow from the projects and attitudes with which he is most closely identified. It is thus, in the most literal sense, an attack on his integrity.

This objection to consequentialism, that it fails to respect an individual's integrity, has import outside any merely theoretical arguments of philosophers. It has its counterpart in the practical world of political conflict, most notably in Havel's defence of living in truth in his essay 'The Power of the Powerless'. Thus, to take Havel's example, a greengrocer puts up in his window each day a slogan 'Workers of the World Unite', not because it expresses an ideal he holds and which he wants others to know and share, but for a quiet life, because if he refuses he and his family will be in trouble. In doing so he lives a lie, and Havel argues that what he calls 'post-totalitarianism' (I'm not sure why the 'post' is pre-fixed, but then it's a rather vacuous pre-fix in all its recent uses) is a society whose foundation lies in its members colluding in acts in which they live a lie. Hence, for Havel, its vulnerability to those who live in truth: 'Let us now imagine that one day something in our greengrocer snaps and he stops putting up the slogans merely to ingratiate himself . . . His revolt is an attempt to live within the truth.' While Havel's justification for this revolt occasionally slips into a consequentialist mode, it is a gamble to produce desired results, the thrust of his argument is anti-consequentialist. The prevalence of utilitarian modes of thought represents one of the ideological buttresses of living a lie. Against it Havel invokes an ethic of integrity. To live within the truth is to live in accordance with one's basic beliefs, to refuse

the unwillingness of the consumer-orientated 'to sacrifice some material certainties for the sake of their own spiritual and moral integrity', to refuse to be 'alienated from themselves', to live an 'authentic existence'. The concepts invoke a picture of the individual who refuses in her acts to live against her own commitments, even if the consequences are for the worst. To have integrity is to live in accordance with that one believes to be true. It is to live in truth.

How might the consequentialist respond? Both chemist and greengrocer are open to a consequentialist temptation that might undermine the claim that there is in consequentialism something incompatible with integrity. Consider the chemist. Surely, like the older chemist, the consequentialist might tempt the agent in terms of his or her own commitments: 'Look, if you are really opposed to chemical weapons, you want to do all you can to stop their development, and that's best achieved by your taking the job. That is what it is to be committed to opposition to them.' What can George say? I think if he is to retain his integrity he has to resist the consequentialist temptation: he has to say something like: 'Even if that is true, I don't want to be the kind of person that could do that. Regardless of the consequences, I won't collude with that with which I am opposed. I refuse to engage in making chemical weapons. There are some things I simply won't do.' The consequentialist temptation is corrupting of integrity because it will not allow an agent to refuse to perform some acts, in virtue of the kind of act it is alone, an act of doing research on chemical weapons, of murder, of torture, and so on, regardless of actual consequences or the desire to realize such consequences. But to say that, that there acts of a kind that one simply won't perform, is to affirm the Pauline principle: there are acts I cannot permit myself to do, even though I believe, in my own terms, that they will produce the best outcome. The Pauline principle is built into the concept of integrity. If integrity is to be possible then the Pauline principle has to be accepted.

Why should integrity be of such basic value that it can override consequentialist reasoning? There are two influential, but very different forms of justification that might be offered. One justification of that position is that of the virtues ethic. Both integrity and its Pauline presupposition have their basis in an ethic of virtues. Integrity is of basic value, which cannot be overridden by consequentialist considerations, since one believes that primitives of ethical appraisal include about the excellences of character, the virtues. There are acts I cannot do as such, because I do not want to be the kind of person that can do them. To hold a virtues ethic is to take the question 'what kind of person should I be?' to be primitive in ethical deliberation. Integrity is a central virtue, because it is a condition of having others. As Williams notes, it is closely related to the Socratic concept of courage as the virtue concerned with having a sense of what is important and staying firm to it.

A second and very different justification is that of a pure ethic of authenticity which is based on a strong sense of individual moral autonomy, a sense that individuals are the authors of their own values. There is no moral authority beyond the individual, each individual is the author of her ethical beliefs, and, given that this is true, the only basic value one can assert, true of every agent from her own perspective, is that they have integrity. One demands that individuals live authentic lives, that they be true to their own beliefs and desires, whatever they be, that they refuse to engage in acts of 'bad faith'.

Veritatis Splendor is of interest in part because it represents an encounter of the older virtues tradition with the modern ethic of authenticity. And I think the latter is rightly characterized in the encyclical as a modern variant on the Romantic version of an ethic of conscience. And again, while one might differ on specific ethical claims, the position of the Thomist virtues ethic does provide a well-founded criticism of any pure ethic of authenticity. Whatever the general truth of the doctrine of the unity of the virtues, it is true that integrity is only a virtue amidst virtues. Thus, consider the story told by Williams re-written from the perspective of the zealot for the chemical weapon. Would integrity or authenticity be a virtue? Authenticity is the last quality one would hope the zealot possessed. The sooner he is tempted to betray his beliefs for a comfortable job in advertising the better. Likewise, if Havel's greengrocer is an unrepentant fascist, who since 1945 has been untrue to his convictions for the sake of a quiet life, one might hope he continued to do so, that he live a lie, that he eschew an authentic existence, that anti-semitic slogans fail to appear in his window in place of those required of him and he does not refuse to serve Jewish customers. While a lack of integrity or failure of authenticity might be a fault, it does not follow that integrity or authenticity is a good; and inauthenticity and a lack of integrity might save both agent and victims from much worse. Integrity or authenticity is a virtue only in good company, in particular the company of good ethical judgement.

To live in truth is not merely to live in accordance with what one believes to be true, but involves a responsibility to discover what is true. Authenticity is a virtue only given good ethical judgement, and that concept presupposes it makes sense to distinguish what I believe is good and what is. The subjectivist foundations of the pure ethic of authenticity needs to be rejected.

> [I]t is always from the truth that the dignity of conscience derives. In the case of the correct conscience, it is a question of the *objective truth* received by man; in the case of the erroneous conscience, it is a question of what man, mistakenly *subjectively* considers to be true. It is never acceptable to confuse a 'subjective' error about the moral good with the 'objective' truth rationally proposed to man in virtue of his end, or to make the moral value of an act performed with a true and correct conscience equivalent to the moral value of an act performed by following the judgement of erroneous conscience.

With this rejection of a subjectivist account of ethical reasoning, I have no disagreement.

II

Where then does disagreement exist? It exists over different kinds of claim: (1) on substantive claims about what it is for a person to lead a good life; (2) on epistemological claims about the proper criteria for accepting the truth or falsity of propositions about what it is to live a good life. Differences on the first set of claims would require a book unto itself. Differences on the second set of issues do warrant further comment.

The defence of moral realism in *Veritatis Splendor,* and the corresponding rejection of 'relativism, pragmatism and positivism', is associated with a reassertion of hierarchical authority:

> While exchanges and conflicts of opinion may constitute normal expressions of public life in the representative democracy, moral teaching cannot depend simply upon respect for a process: indeed, it is in no way established by following rules and deliberative procedures typical of democracy. *Dissent,* in the form of carefully orchestrated protests and polemics carried on in the media, is *opposed to ecclesiastic communion and to a correct understanding of the hierarchical constitution of the People of God.* Opposition to the teaching of the Church's Pastors cannot be seen as a legitimate expression either of Christian freedom or the diversity of the Spirit's gifts. When this happens, the Church's Pastors have the duty to act in conformity with their apostolic mission, insisting that *the right of the faithful* to receive Catholic doctrine in its purity and integrity must always be respected.

That passage is worth quoting in length in virtue of the strength of the anti-enlightenment view of reason in moral matters that it expresses. The passage is not aimed against anti-realism about ethics, but against an account of the right epistemological criteria for the acceptance or rejection of a putative ethical truth. It is instructive to set beside it Kant's classic statement of the nature of the enlightenment:

> *Enlightenment is man's emergence from his self-incurred immaturity. Immaturity* is the inability to use one's own understanding without the guidance of another. The immaturity is *self-incurred* if its cause is not lack of understanding, but lack of resolution and courage to use it without the guidance of another. The motto of the enlightenment is therefore: *Sapere aude!* Have courage to use your *own* understanding . . . For enlightenment of this kind, all that is needed is *freedom*. And the freedom in question is the most innocuous form of all—freedom to make *public use* of one's reason in all matters. But I hear on all sides the cry: *Don't argue!* The officer says: Don't argue, get on parade! The tax-official: Don't argue, pay! The clergyman: Don't argue, believe!

Kant in thus defining the enlightenment is not here claiming that every individual is the author of their morality. His concern is rather with the epistemological conditions under which an individual can be said to have good grounds for a moral belief. Right moral belief emerges from the public use of reason, and an individual's grounds for a belief must be that it has been tested against public argument. John Paul, by contrast, asserts an epistemological authority of a hierarchical kind, in which public argument is rejected, and the believer's right is that of receiving doctrine untainted by controversy. While public controversy is allowable outside of the church, it is understood simply as political principle required for 'representative democracy'. It is not a necessary epistemological condition for right moral belief: the proper process is a hierarchical one.

Is there anything to be said for the epistemological authoritarianism defended by John Paul? A case might be made of a negative kind. There is a problem with the Enlightenment view defended by Kant that forms the strong epistemological core of conservative political thought. The problem is that any person who relied simply on his own understanding would understand very little. Any process of education, be it in the sciences, the arts, in language or in morals depends on the acceptance of the authority of others. There is a sense in which all teaching is authoritative and all learning requires some deference to an authority:

> The acceptance of authority is not just something which, as a matter of fact, you cannot get along without if you want to participate in rule-governed activities; rather, to participate in rule-governed activities is, in a certain way to accept authority. For to participate in such an activity is to accept that there is *a right and a wrong way of doing things,* and the decision as to what is right and wrong in a given case can never depend *completely* on one's own caprice.

Take science, the model of rational activity for the enlightenment. One learns science from school to university by practising standard cases of good experiment, adopting exemplars of good inference and theory, and accepting correction from an authority when one goes wrong. Such epistemological authority is not a luxury that one could do without, preferring one's own understanding: one can only exercise one's own understanding given authoritative education. Failure to do so when one enters some practice like science involves no lack of courage: it is a requirement which must be followed if one is ever to be in a position to exercise epistemological courage against received opinion. To dare to refuse to believe any opinion on authority takes not courage but foolhardiness. It is only when equipped with good judgement and belief born of authoritative education that the question of courage arises, and enlightenment could conceivably be its result. Moreover, the conservative notes that acceptance of epistemological authority is not something that can be done in abstract: the authoritative way of doing something is necessarily embodied in the practice and teaching of other human persons, who, for all their fallibility, are the only way into a practice. Thus goes the conservative argument, and the case is a powerful one.

Let us grant that conservative case. Does epistemological authority thereby rest in a hierarchical form of organisation, as John Paul assumes? Or is there something that can be rescued from Kant's enlightenment view? I believe that a more sophisticated version of the Enlightenment position can be rescued, and it is not clear indeed that the Kantian passage quoted above is not compatible with that position. Consider the imperatives discussed by Kant: 'I hear on all sides the cry: *Don't argue!* The officer says: Don't argue, get on parade! The tax-official, Don't argue, pay! The clergyman: Don't argue, believe!' Even given the conservative's defence of epistemological authority there is a powerful point to be made here. Given an imperative 'Do X' there are two kinds of answer that might be made to a response 'Why?': (1) because I am your officer, your tax collector, your clergyman, paying you, etc.; (2) because it would be the right thing to do, the best thing to do, because it is a valid inference, etc. The first set of responses make essential reference to the individual's occupancy of a particular institutional position or status. If it turned out that the individual did not have that position, or that the addressee was not within the range of the person's institutional authority, that for example the officer was addressing a civilian or a general, then the imperative is infelicitous. On its own terms there is no backing for its authority. The second set of responses are not of this kind. They make no essential call on institutional positions of authority, but, rather, on standards independent of institutional positions and status. The felicity of the speech act calls only on impersonal standards. A feature of the imperatives that Kant criticises is that they are the first institutional kind. Their felicity is essentially founded upon institutional authority, not on any standards independent of those positions. I take it that part of Kant's point here is that to defer to the beliefs of another, to believe simply in virtue of a person's institutional position is never defensible. A person's status, wealth or power is never good reason to defer to their judgements: to do so is mere sycophancy. The only good grounds a mature individual has for deferring to the judgements of other persons is that there are good reasons to believe that they meet standards independent of those persons.

This is true even where, as in the case of a teacher, their institutional authority is called upon. Consider, a mathematics teacher who in an exasperated moment in the classroom, when faced with students who argue with what she says: 'Look this isn't the time for argument; for the moment take it on authority, and later you'll be able to see why your objections can be met.' In all teaching there is a time and place for making a claim on authority, for saying something like 'Don't argue, believe'. However, the grounds for the deference to authority in that context will be one that is independent of the institutional position of the individual as such. It is because she has the position she has in virtue of publicly recognized competences that one has good reasons for the temporary silencing of one's dissent.

The root of a great deal of modern relativism lies in a refusal to recognize the difference between authority grounded solely in institutional position and authority grounded in standards independent of such positions. There is a widespread anti-enlightenment view that all epistemological authority is simply a disguised way of enforcing social power. That view cannot be sustained. The very statement of it is difficult, since on its own terms it must itself be interpreted as an act of power: it denies the very conditions for there to be utterances critical of unjustified social power. However, reading **Veritatis Splendor** it is possible to detect a similar identification of epistemological authority and social authority. The distinction between social authority and epistemological authority is nowhere clearly drawn and the defence of epistemological authority often appears to be primarily aimed at the reassertion of hierarchical authority. To the question 'why should I believe P?' the answer looks like 'because I, the pope/church pastor, tell you so': hence the rejection of dissent.

It might be objected that this judgement is too harsh. The Catholic tradition in which the papal letter is written does recognize the distinction between authority that is backed by standards of reason and authority that is not. Both the distinction and the use to which it is put are ancient ones that are, for example, recognized by Augustine: 'with regard to the acquiring of knowledge, we are of necessity led in a twofold manner: by authority and by reason. In point of time, authority is first; in order of reality, reason is prior.' While in learning sometimes one must first accept a proposition on authority since that is a condition for coming to a position to understand it, reason is ultimately prior. The object of learning is to arrive at propositions justifiable by standards of reason, and which the learner can recognize as such. Nothing in the papal defence of '*the right of the faithful* to receive Catholic doctrine in its purity' entails a conflation of epistemological and social authority.

This response does not yet fully resolve the differences between the revised Kantian and papal perspectives on epistemological authority, although it does clarify where the differences ultimately lie. They concern the conditions a community of inquiry must possess in order that authority be accepted at all. The point is again one that is recognized by Augustine: 'Authority demands faith, and prepares man for reason. Reason leads on to knowledge and understanding. But reason is not entirely useless to authority; it helps in considering what authority is to be accepted.' A mature individual needs reason to decide to which authority deference is justifiable. This point provides I believe a way of rescuing the core of Kant's position.

The sophisticated defender of the enlightenment position might accept that the public use of one's reason might not always and everywhere be appropriate: there may be occasions in which deference to authority is justifiable. However, one needs some reason to believe that the practice in which authoritative teaching is made is itself in order. Justifiable deference to epistemological authority is possible only if one has grounds for believing the authority in question could be redeemed in public argument. Deference would be quite improper if no public use of reason is possible even at level of those competent and, hence, that the doctrines in question could not be subject

to the scrutiny of competent peers. Where the possibility of public dialogue and argument is absent one has good reason to believe something is amiss. A practice that allows only opinion untainted by dissent is not one in which authoritative utterances could be redeemed, and hence is not one in which deference to authoritative judgments is justifiable.

It is at this point that the Kantian defence of public reason does have power against the position asserted by Pope John Paul. The encyclical defends a silencing of internal dissent, and insists on 'the right of the faithful' to receive doctrine without the stain of controversy. Now whatever one thinks of modern theologians—and I find it difficult to take seriously those among them who combine anti-realism with religious belief—an institution that insists on a hierarchical power to silence dialogue and to state what is to be the 'pure' doctrine which the faithful are to receive lacks those marks which would make deference to authority rational. Here of course problems arise in particular for those 'people of good will' outside of the Catholic church to whom the document addresses itself. Specific problems of religious authority are at stake. The papal position relies on the possibility of authority beyond reason—that of revelation—and the claim to represent that authority. In Augustinian terms 'the authority of the mysteries' overrides 'the circumlocution of disputation'. However, even given that specific background, which is unlikely itself to move the outsider, there is a problem. Augustine adds a qualification that the papal document lacks: 'but human authority is often deceiving'.

Human authority is never more deceiving than when it is self-deceptive, and self-deception is never more likely than when an authority fails to admit the possibility that it is sometimes in error. A central virtue of moral realism is that it is a condition for accepting one's own views can be mistaken—that one's beliefs about the good may be wrong. Hence, combined with the virtue of intellectual humility, it allows space for being corrected. Correction, however, requires openness to public dissent. The strong social authoritarianism of the papal document undermines the conditions for correction of belief. Hence, it undermines the grounds for claims on others to defer to its putative epistemological authority. The document defines its epistemological authority in a way that is incompatible with one necessary condition of any proper instance of it, that is, reasoned dialogue.

Desmond Sullivan (essay date September 1996)

SOURCE: "The Pope and Christian Unity," in *Contemporary Review*, Vol. 269, No. 1568, September, 1996, pp. 135-8

[*In the following essay, Sullivan examines John Paul's advocacy for reconciliation within the Christian Church. "While proclaiming, fearlessly, his office as successor of*

Peter," writes Sullivan, "John Paul II has personally . . . shattered most of the post-Reformation arguments and obstacles to Christian unity."]

There was considerable disappointment among many ecumenical Christians that the Pope did not use the occasion of his visit to Germany—where the Reformation began—to make any memorable pronouncement on Christian unity. Yet three letters did come out of Rome last year from, I think, the personal pen of John Paul II, which have astonishingly contradicted our media-controlled view of the triumphalism and superstar quality of the present Pope. Such is the potential impact of these documents that it seems that the present Pope has used his unique position to release ecumenism and lay wide open the future role and position of the historic papacy.

The three documents are: a letter on Christian unity called *Ut Unum Sint;* a letter to the Churches of the East called *Orientale Lumen;* and the third his famous millenium letter *Tertio Millenio Adveniente.* (Their texts can be found in *L'Osservatore Romano* of 2 May, 25 May and 10 November 1995.)

While proclaiming, fearlessly, his office as successor of Peter, John Paul II has personally with gentleness and precision shattered most of the post-Reformation arguments and obstacles to Christian unity. The best way to picture this breakthrough is the image of the Bishop of Rome, in penitential stance, kneeling at the threshold of the new millenium trying to lead his own to become a church in need of reform—'*semper reformanda*'—facing the rest of the churches with the plea that 'Peter' being 'once converted could confirm his brethren'. He, in the name of Peter, may once again in truth and love no longer be an obstacle to the dying wish of the Saviour 'that they may be one'.

The approach of the millenium seems to exercise his mind, for he too has not many years left. In his letter on unity he stresses that the final wish of Jesus at the Last Supper was to pray to the Father that they may be one. His life so far has not achieved much here, perhaps; this urges him to risk all to break down the barriers to unity.

Martyrdom too has a fascination for the current successor of Peter. He has himself shed his blood in an attempted assassination in 1981. He writes that martyrs, in the East and in the West, were believers in Christ; united in following his footsteps, the martyrs cannot remain divided, and he asks for the churches to have a common list of martyrs to celebrate in unity so that we will respect each other's martyrs for a change, for 'they profess together the same truth about the Cross'.

In a similar way he expresses love and veneration for the fidelity, example of Christian teaching, integrity and spiritual heritage of the Churches of the East. Recalling the many mutual exchanges of visits with those in communion with Constantinople, with Moscow, and with the Oriental churches he rejoices that this unity in faith and sacraments and friendship proves the reality of diversity within unity as a hallmark of catholicity.

Often the world-wide tours of John Paul II, as seen on television, appeared to be embarrassingly populist and almost un-Christ-like. The Pope reveals that behind all the public fuss there has been very direct and serious meeting of Christian minds. For he shows in his letter on unity that he has made it his duty to visit, in friendship and in real dialogue, the leaders of churches and other religions in every one of the countries he has visited.

It is quite touching for us in England to read, in this regard, of his visit to Canterbury in May 1982. For it was an earlier bishop of Rome who called on the young Augustine to go to that far away land and bring into the fold of Christ the Angels of those lands and to found the see of Canterbury. John Paul II recalls, with some emotion and affection, his visit to Canterbury, his prayer for unity with the Archbishop and the love and respect for 'those elements of grace and truth and the work of the Holy Spirit in the Church of England'. He was, I believe, the first Bishop of Rome to visit this see founded at the request of his own predecessor.

Travelling has certainly broadened the mind of John Paul II for he lists the positive fruits which he has observed over the years of the Ecumenical Movement. He wisely notes that this, as a modern Movement, stems directly from the missionaries of the 'Churches of the Reformation', and humbly affirms how his own Church came only very late to the movement. He wants to make up for lost time. He therefore enumerates some very real lessons for his own Church.

For example, he says his own Church must get rid of some of the pet ideas of 'Church', some of the false impressions left with them by their ancestors in the faith. Such notions that outsiders have no hope; that we must be hostile to dissenters: many of these ideas have become ingrained as a result of the hostilities arising from the Reformation period or from the fortress mentality of recent years. John Paul affirms that the Catholic Church has preserved unity for two thousand years, and most of the Church was united for the first thousand years, when East and West, Celts and Romans, all were in one Church. However, recently we seem to have rejoiced in our dividedness, and in so doing have hidden the face of Christ like a smashed church window. From this perspective, towards the end of this millenium, 'both sides are to blame'. He cites the infidelity of some Church leaders, of some priests, the faults of members, the sins and betrayals, weaknesses and mediocrity of her children. Even so there are many shared values, beliefs and areas of co-operation.

These kinds of remarks and the tone of sorrow, the asking for forgiveness and the mood of penitence has got the ageing Pope into trouble. The Catholic press, so 'loyal', has not much reported these kinds of statements. Even

Cardinals have expressed in public their rejection of the mood of admission of guilt, or of any faults from the past!

From all his experience of travel, of looking at history and an awareness of the urgency of his age and of the age of the world, John Paul II has tried to charter a new way through on his own initiative in an area that few others would dare to go.

Then, after bravely recognising the shared common heritage of many things in the churches, he calls for 'honesty, truth and integrity'. Fancy words, phrases and grand statements of doctrinal committees must not risk ambiguity and false irenicism. Each of us must approach dialogue as a move to our own personal 'conversion'. The fruits of dialogue must also become the common heritage of all Christians and not remain remote theological propositions. There are, he writes, five major problems at the present time:

1. the relationship between Scripture and tradition,

2. the Eucharist as a sacrament, as a sacrificial memorial and the Real Presence,

3. the ordination to the threefold ministry,

4. the magisterium of Pope and bishops as properly understood in relation to Christ,

5. the Virgin Mary, as Mother of God and as Icon of the Church.

But there is one other problem. This brings us to the nub of the question of unity and to the core of this letter from the Bishop of Rome. During his many travels and visits John Paul has been hit by a paradox: people of all churches, faiths, religions and countries have shown him great respect and have affirmed his undoubted world-wide influence. At the same time these very people have made it very clear that for many Christians his very office 'constitutes a great difficulty: it has, over the centuries, built up many painful and hurtful recollections, stemming sometimes from personal sins, from structural sins and many non-religious factors.'

In his letter on unity John Paul says we must re-examine our painful past, purify past memories, the mistakes made, the factors involved in our deplorable divisions and we must pray for each other and seek our own personal conversion and repentance and the reformation that is necessary for achieving mutual respect for the diversity of our different spiritual heritages, both in the East and in the West.

As a first step John Paul wishes to give a lead and in a spirit of repentance on behalf of his own church he personally asks, in this letter and during his visits, for forgiveness from those countries he visits. The traditional stance of Rome in this matter has been to refrain from any admission of mistakes. John Paul has abolished this stance. The

traditional view in Rome was for strict uniformity. John Paul, following the second Vatican Council, has on the contrary, affirmed true Catholicity is diversity—diversity of culture and of spiritual heritage. The old stance was against structural change—or any change. John Paul has refused any change in teachings, but wants to examine the way we express our teachings. He has affirmed that: 'reading the signs of the time' he sees a 'new situation' has arisen. He tells us that he has received many requests from the churches begging him to find a new way of exercising his personal office as a successor of Peter, a way which is open to this new situation in his own and in all the churches. He realises that often in the past 'for a great variety of reasons and against the will of all concerned what should have been a service sometimes manifested itself in a very different light'. The Pope then says 'To the extent that we are responsible for these, I join with my predecessor Paul VI in asking forgiveness.'

He goes on to say 'After centuries of bitter controversies, the other Churches and Ecclesial Communities are more and more taking a fresh look at this ministry of unity'.

Here, I think, we have a clear contemporary example of Newman's teaching about the development of doctrine. A new situation with pressure from below and above has given rise to the development of aspects, in this case of the role of Peter, which have been obscured and lay for so long hidden, but are now appearing as an authentic interpretation of Scripture and tradition. The old doctrine is then seen in a new light.

So it is that John Paul says: I want as Pope to start this re-examination of the role of Peter. I want this to be done in the light of Christ's word, his wish and prayer for unity. Many aspects need to be examined: doctrinal, disciplinary, social, historical and political considerations surround this task. The Bishop of Rome says 'I cannot do this by myself'. He wants to accede to the many requests from around the world and from different churches. As unity cannot be achieved by one church alone, he calls on the bishops and theologians of all the churches to set about this examination. He hints that the turn of the millenium would be a good target!

Such a profound declaration from a Pope carries one's mind back over the centuries in search of such a precedent in the history of the papacy. No wonder commentators have been shy about it. They seem to have chosen to ignore it. John Paul, in a very moving remark, writes: 'This is an immense task, which we cannot refuse and which I cannot carry out by myself.' He proposes that 'leaving all useless controversies behind, keeping only the will of Christ before us let church leaders engage with me in a patient dialogue on this subject and be moved only by that plea of Christ "that they may be one so the world may believe that you sent me".'

As St Luke records the role of Peter is not 'the exercise of power over people as the rulers of the Gentiles and their great men do but as leading them to new pastures.' He sees the new idea, or the original idea of the Bishop of Rome with all the other bishops (he calls them too vicars of Christ) as a college of pastors keeping watch so the true voice of Christ may be heard in all the particular Churches.

For these reasons he says 'I insistently pray to the Holy Spirit to shine His light upon us, enlighten all the Pastors and theologians of our Churches, that we may—together, of course—seek new forms in which this ministry may accomplish a service of love recognised by all concerned.'

The challenge to all the Churches is really put clearly. Are we willing to give up our pet ideas, our inherited prejudices, even our concept of church in order to become that church which Christ so earnestly prayed for? The Pope quotes, significantly (and perhaps biographically) the words in Luke's Gospel about Peter that he will have to 'strengthen his brethren when he has been converted' (Luke 22, 32). Of this, Peter's conversion, Pope John Paul II writes: 'It is as though the Master especially concerned Himself with Peter's conversion as a way of preparing him for the task he was about to give him in his Church.'

In a final plea Pope John Paul prays that at the dawn of the new millenium we will not refuse to implore the grace to prepare ourselves, together, to offer this sacrifice of unity.

Jonathan Kwitny (essay date 10 October 1997)

SOURCE: "Neither Capitalist Nor Marxist: Karol Wojtyla's Social Ethics," in *Commonweal,* October 10, 1997, pp. 17-21.

[*In the following essay, Kwitny examines John Paul's contradictory affinity for Marxist revolution and free market principles as delineated in* Catholic Social Ethics. *According to Kwitny, John Paul endorses "class-conscious revolution," though objects to "Marxism's subjugation of the individual human spirit . . . after the revolution."*]

Romuald Kukolowicz, now in his seventies, is the son of Polish Catholic intellectuals. In 1953, he was working as a clerk. At the time, Poland was firmly part of Stalin's Soviet empire. During World War II, Kukolowicz had done work as an underground printer. Some friends from those days, now students at the Jagiellonian University in Krakow, approached him, raving about a young professor whose lectures on Catholic ethics and communism were inspiring and ought to be published. Did Kukolowicz know anyone who could do it?

Kukolowicz found an underground printer in Lublin. His friends arranged for him to pick up the manuscript from the professor—Father Karol Wojtyla—at a convent in Krakow. As the manuscript was typed, edited, and published, there were more meetings between Kukolowicz and Wojtyla, but little small talk. "When I saw him it was always

[to discuss] what to publish and how," Kukolowicz remembers. "It was a very strict conspiracy."

Some 250 reams of printing paper were stolen by the members of this "conspiracy" from the state institutions where they worked. A World War II press was used that required each page be rolled by hand over a typed matrix. Kukolowicz calculates that his friends had to press some 112,750 sheets of paper separately to make the book. It was published in two volumes, the first in 1953, the second the following year, with only 200 to 250 copies in each edition—loose pages in an envelope, to be bound, if desired, by the recipient. Copies went to priests who taught students in all the major cities of Poland. "They weren't given [directly] to students because of the need for secrecy," Kukolowicz says. "Police agents infiltrated the classes. If the security forces found such a book in your apartment, you would be subject to ten years in prison."

The work, called *Catholic Social Ethics,* is nowhere described in *Kalendarium* (the official diary of John Paul II's life up to his pontificate) or any other available literature; Kukolowicz's is the only copy I have encountered. The Vatican confirms his story. To my knowledge, this is the book's first public disclosure, and it belies much that has been written in the West about Wojtyla in recent years portraying the pope as an ally of free-market Western politicians.

Bishop Tadeusz Pieronek, now secretary of the Polish episcopate but in 1954 a student in Wojtyla's social ethics course at the Jagiellonian, remembers being stunned to learn that Father Wojtyla had written a manual, several copies of which were passed around at the school. "It was impossible to publish a manual in those days," Bishop Pieronek explains. "All printers were registered by the government. Even typewriters were registered, but authorities allowed you to type. The university had a library, but the books were not accessible to the average reader. You can't imagine how libraries looked. Till the 1980s, whole lists of books were banned."

As a priest in the 1970s, Pieronek visited Cardinal Wojtyla for dinner and found parts of that old manual on a bookshelf in the dining room. "We learned about capitalism for the first time from Wojtyla's text," Bishop Pieronek recalls. "He tried to explain each system."

Catholic Social Ethics reinforces the notion that Wojtyla was a Thomist rather than a phenomenologist; it asserts at its inception that Aquinas's natural law "allows theories of ethics" to be stated with "scientific" precision. It also shows that by age thirty-three, Wojtyla had adopted unreservedly both the welfare-state economic ideas and the courage of Cardinal Stefan Wyszynski, the Polish primate. No longer a novice or small-parish priest, Wojtyla instead marked himself in this book as a serious, innovative thinker with his eye on the world.

"The main task of the Catholic social ethic is to introduce the principles of justice and love into social life," Wojtyla wrote in the first volume, on politics. Tracing economic history from feudalism to the industrial age, he endorsed the Marxist notions of a working class and a class struggle. But he stressed that class should be among a person's secondary loyalties. Primary was the family, the success of which depended on its "close cooperation" with the church and the state. "The nation, as the natural society, must be respected," he wrote, but "the common good demands" a balance between "loyalty to the nation . . . and, on the other hand, avoidance of overzealous nationalism."

Government had "a superior function" that was "very useful in achieving the common good of society." Its power "comes directly from society, indirectly from God." Wojtyla condemned "individualism," a word that he and other European scholars used to refer to unregulated capitalism. "Individualism and totalitarianism," he declared, "remain opposed to the principle of correlating the individual good and the social good, which Catholic ethics accepts."

"Justice and love" must govern international relations as well, he wrote: "War is evil. It should be avoided even as a last resort to restore justice between countries, because it may result in even greater evil and injustice than it combats." His statement on war went significantly beyond other current Catholic teaching, which allowed war if all else failed. Although many anti-Communists would later try to co-opt Wojtyla into their military policies, he condemned war unequivocally in 1953, even as a means to correct injustice, because he believed it tended only to create new injustice. (He did not, however, dispute Catholic teaching that violence could be used to repel violent attacks.)

In a chapter on Marxism, Wojtyla saw beyond the system that tyrannized his own life and into the issues that would later present themselves to him as pope. He wrote:

> The relentless materialism in Marxism contradicts Catholicism, [which] sees man as spirit and matter in one, [and which] proclaims the superiority of the spirit. . . . Ethics is . . . the science of spiritual good, such as justice or love, that provides the material activities of human beings with specifically human values. This gives ethics primacy [over materialism] in economics or biology.

But, he added, "the goal of these thoughts is not to criticize Marxism entirely." He explicitly embraced Marx's essential theory that "the economic factor . . . explains, rather substantially, the different facts of human history. . . . Criticism of capitalism—the system of exploitation of human beings and human work—is the unquestionable 'part of the truth' embodied in Marxism."

In 1993, John Paul II would provoke mocking headlines when he criticized Poland and other post-Communist countries for accepting pure market economics from the West and thus abandoning the "grain of truth" in Marxism. Although many thought the pope was reversing himself, he was in fact using almost the same words he had used

forty years before in class lectures and in his book, and had been using ever since.

Wojtyla separated Marx's *analysis* of economic exploitation, which he largely accepted, from Marx's *solutions,* which he rejected. "The Catholic social ethic," he wrote in 1953, "agrees that in many cases a struggle is the way to accomplish the common good. Today . . . a class struggle . . . is the undeniable responsibility of the proletariat." Not only is class conscious revolution compatible with Christianity, he argued; it is sometimes *necessary* to Christianity. What is incompatible is Marxism's subjugation of the individual human spirit to a grand economic design *after* the revolution.

In *Catholic Social Ethics,* Wojtyla set down rules for social struggle that are strikingly similar to those that would be enunciated less than a decade later by the Reverend Martin Luther King, Jr., in the United States. Wojtyla and King each believed the struggle should be aimed at persuasion, not at violent, Marxist-style upheaval. Wojtyla wrote:

> Demonstrations, protests, strikes, and passive resistance—all these are means of class struggle that need to be considered appropriate. The struggle for rights, after exhausting all peaceful means . . . is a necessary act of justice that leads only to the achievement of the common good, which is the goal of social existence. . . .
>
> It is clear that from the view of the ethical assumptions of the Bible, such a struggle is a necessary evil, just like any other human struggle. . . . It is also evident from the Bible that struggle itself is not the opposite of love. The opposite of love is hate.
>
> A struggle in a specific case does not have to be caused by hate. If it is caused by social and material injustice, and if its goal is to reinstate the just distribution of goods, then such a struggle is not [hatred]. . . . Social justice is the necessary condition for realization of love in life. . . .
>
> Many times Jesus Christ has proven that God's kingdom cannot be achieved in man without a struggle. . . . Achievement of social justice in one element of achieving God's kingdom on earth.

Wojtyla made a major distinction between revolution within a country and international war—though in some ways, the distinction seems paradoxical:

> Revolution causes much more damage than war, because the unity of the natural society—the nation or state—is much greater than the international unity of humanity that gets torn in war. . . . Hatred for those who are close to us is much more dangerous and inflicts much more damage than hatred for people who are further removed.

Yet, war, he said, isn't permissible and isn't likely to improve conditions. Revolution, though best avoided, *is* permissible and *can* improve conditions:

> Can the opposition that brings down [an unjust] government surpass all the damage that was caused by an

armed struggle, and thus make the revolution ethically justified? The answer is yes. . . .

It can be accepted that the majority of the people who have taken part in revolutions—even violent ones—have acted on their convictions, in accordance with their consciences. . . .

Such a struggle is a necessary evil. Although it does not have to be an act of hatred . . . such a struggle undoubtedly provides an opportunity for acts of hatred. . . . One can hate negative characteristics of human beings. But one cannot hate the human being himself. . . .

Marxism . . . does not see any other way to solve the burning social issues. . . . Catholicism sees the possibility of solving . . . social issues by evolutionary means. The struggle of the oppressed classes against their oppressors becomes the stimulus for the evolution to proceed faster. . . .

The class struggle . . . grows stronger when it meets resistance from the economically privileged classes. Pressure from the class struggle should bring appropriate changes in the socioeconomic system.

Although Marxism saw struggle as inevitable and desirable, Wojtyla goes on, "Catholicism cannot accept struggle as the principal ethical dictate. . . . Regardless of all the factors that set people apart in society . . . there exist deeper factors that foster unity and solidarity."

Wojtyla's biggest problem with Marxism, though, wasn't its advocacy of struggle but its opposition to the institution of private property. Grappling with this forced him to think through, perhaps for the first time in print, what Saint John of the Cross had said about material wealth. The question must have crossed Wojtyla's mind before: If Saint John, about whom Wojtyla had written a dissertation in Rome in 1948, had been right about abandoning physical property, why weren't the Communists right about it? The answer, Wojtyla decided, lay in distinguishing worthy ideals from practical possibilities. Marxism, he wrote, sought

a classless society. To achieve this order, one must get rid of private property because it is the only source of class opposition. . . .

While the church clearly sees and proclaims the need for reform of the socioeconomic system, it does not consider necessary a radical upheaval in attitude toward property. . . . The re-creation of the socioeconomic system may be achieved while maintaining the institution of private property, and should be based on the enfranchisement of the proletariat.

Wojtyla's rationale for private property differed from that of free-market theorists, and what he wrote about it makes for fairly explosive reading in the 1990s: "The church realizes that the bourgeois mentality, and capitalism with its material spirit, are contradictions of the Bible. According to the tradition of . . . monastic/religious life, the church also can appreciate the idea of communism. . . . Communism, as a higher ethical rule of ownership, demands from people higher ethical qualifications."

After a subsection headed "The Objective Superiority of the Communist Ideal" (the text of which I was unable to obtain), Wojtyla noted,

At the present state of human nature, the universal realization of this [Communist] ideal . . . meets with insurmountable difficulties. Private property is suited to human nature. The goal that should be pursued is to achieve, in the system based on private property, such reforms as will lead to the realization of social justice. The class struggle leads to this. . . .

Revolution is not the doom of society, but at most a punishment for specific offenses in socioeconomic life.

Wojtyla wrote that "ethical evil is caused" not by those wishing to rebel but "by those factors of the socioeconomic system that have spawned the need for a radical movement."

The second volume of *Catholic Social Ethics* was more specifically concerned with "rebuilding the economic system [and] defining the many moral obligations of owning and using property." Its premise was: "Because private ownership of property is ethically good if the property is used appropriately, individual owners and especially the state should carefully watch its use." Regarding labor, Wojtyla again rejected strict free-market doctrine, returning instead to the ideal of the Polish poet Cyprian Norwid (1821-83), that "work cannot be treated as merchandise." Regarding capitalism, Wojtyla said,

An economic enterprise based on capital is ethically justified if it contributes to social prosperity. But if its main goal is to maximize the profit of the owner, then it is ethically wrong. . . .

The entire tradition and teaching of the church is clearly opposed to capitalism as the socioeconomic system of life, and as a general value system.

The exchange of goods complements the economic process. . . . Therefore it is ethically justified, like production, so long as it does not lead to unjustified, speculative profits. . . . A just profit depends on a just price for merchandise, which is determined by using an appropriate value theory. Determination of the price is a function of society. . . .

[Because] money . . . is very important in the socioeconomic process . . . the state should supervise monetary and credit policies for the good of the whole society.

Wojtyla said that collecting interest on loans "is ethically justified, given the current state of the world's economy." But he said interest rates should be limited not by what the market will bear but by ethical considerations.

Wojtyla was very concerned with pay. "The profit gained from work in the form of compensation is the main factor in the just division of the income of society," he wrote. And "the just solution to the problem of pay is the principle of family pay." He has championed the "family pay" concept ever since, arguing that the size and needs of a worker's family should influence the amount of wages or salary. While this idea was somewhat Marxist (Marx said, "From each according to his abilities, to each according to his needs"), Wojtyla rejected the determination of compensation by need alone. "In determining family pay," he wrote, one should consider the economic state of the enterprise and of the whole country. An entrepreneur has a right to a reasonable, moderate profit, considering both his own work and his financial investment . . . for example, for renting land. . . .

The common good is best achieved when individual members of society evenly attain material prosperity. So we must strive to limit luxury and excessive wealth.

The society must use all ethical means to save its members from poverty and lead them to prosperity. Society should take special care of those in poverty.

Rather than allying him with market capitalists, these views ring closer to those of supporters of "liberation theology," a Catholic movement that Wojtyla would later encounter in Latin America, which sought to redistribute capital. After several years of close reading of Wojtyla's published words as both priest and pope, I cannot cite an instance of his saying anything to contradict what he wrote in *Catholic Social Ethics.*

Michael Sean Winters (essay date 9 February 1998)

SOURCE: "Old Faithful: John Paul v. Modernity," in *New Republic,* February 9, 1998, pp. 16, 18.

[*In the following essay, Winters discusses John Paul's opposition to Marxism, capitalism, and modern technological societies.*]

In a country accustomed to one message and one messenger, the Pope's visit to Cuba is the stuff of high political drama, certainly a more provocative threat to Castro's regime than the Helms-Burton Act. For weeks now, the U.S. press has been buzzing with speculation as to whether the Pope may precipitate the fall of communism in Cuba—finally succeeding where generations of U.S. policy-makers have failed. After all, as *Newsweek* cheerfully notes, "this well-traveled Pope has crusaded with fervor against his old Communist foes."

But make no mistake: while the Pope is happy to praise democracy, he is no champion of capitalist values out to slay the last defender of Marxism. In fact, as Castro has gleefully observed, the Pope "has done all his criticisms of communism. Now he's criticizing capitalism." That's because John Paul is guided by a theological vision that is as hostile to capitalism as it is to communism. And while some high-profile neoconservative Catholics are content to celebrate the collapse of communism—and bask in the capitalist afterglow—John Paul is already retrofitting the arguments he used against Marxism and the Marxist-tinged liberation theologians of the 1970s for use against advocates of U.S.-style capitalism during the 1990s.

Though always more popular on U.S. campuses than in the barrios of Latin America, liberation theology was an ideological threat to John Paul's Christian vision. It borrowed heavily from Marxism in an attempt to equate the Christian gospels with the socioeconomic struggles of the poor. But John Paul's objection to the movement was never based on economic or geostrategic considerations. (The Catholic Church can live with shoddy economics and confused politics—the Vatican, after all, is in Italy.) Rather, John Paul argued that the "liberation" promised by liberation theology was inadequate because its conception of the human person was too limited. Marxism reduced the human person to a *homo economicus.* So, as Monsignor Lorenzo Albacete, a key theological ally of John Paul's in the attack on liberation theology, puts it: "What do we say to a man who is dying? That he should place his hope in the end of economic exploitation? When the Church ceases to be concerned with eternity, it ceases to be the Church."

To the Pope, the capitalist, consumerist ethic of the West is just as unsatisfactory an alternative, since it also entails a reduction of the human person to its economic dimension. Thus, John Paul and his followers within the Church view capitalism's cold war victory over Marxism with ambivalence. They're glad to be rid of an alarming threat to Catholic principles, but unenthusiastic about the strengthening of what they perceive as a different—but equally serious—menace.

At a synod of bishops from North and South America held in Rome last autumn, a prevailing theme was anxiety over the extension of U.S.-style capitalism into the traditionally Catholic cultures of Latin America. Some bishops even used the term "invasion." While praising the restoration of democracy throughout Latin America and acknowledging the free market's ability to break up the often corrupt oligarchies that dominate many Latin American economies, the bishops expressed dismay at capitalism's general disregard for individual suffering in the name of overall economic progress. They condemned economic models that ignore the needs of the poor. (After all, it's as dehumanizing to reduce a poor person to a mere statistic in an IMF austerity program as it is to lump him into the ranks of the faceless proletariat.) And most of the Latin American bishops at the synod endorsed John Paul's call for a severe reduction—if not outright cancellation—of the debt burden of poor developing countries.

The bishops' concern for the human impact of free-market policies also shapes their pronouncements in the United States. Recently, in both St. Louis and Los Angeles, the local bishops strongly opposed the selling of Catholic hospitals to for-profit conglomerates. As Roger Cardinal Mahony of Los Angeles explained, "the primary goal of health care delivery is not to generate a profit for shareholders; rather, it is a public asset to be directed toward the common good of the society." Bernard Cardinal Law of Boston was even more blunt: "Business considerations should not take precedence over mission." This may seem a naïve and ultimately unworkable position, but as Archbishop Daniel Pilarczyk of Cincinnati explains: "We are pastors. We ask, 'How does this affect the poor?' Whatever the economic presuppositions, this is a question we can't stop asking."

Despite its economic implications, John Paul and his bishops' critique of U.S. capitalism is fundamentally centered on cultural concerns. Specifically, the Pope worries about the free market's power to break familial and social bonds that may not be profitable but are nonetheless humane. In a recent statement, U.S. bishops pronounced this withering critique of modern culture:

> In our country, the modern, technological, functional mentality creates a world of replaceable individuals incapable of authentic solidarity. In its place, society is grouped by artificial arrangements created by powerful interests. The common ground is an increasingly dull, sterile consumer conformism, so visible especially among too many of our young people, created by artificial needs promoted by the advertising media to support powerful economic interests.

How to rescue mankind from this bleak new world? A recurrent theme of John Paul's writings is the need for a new humanism to serve as the foundation of a new post-modern culture. This new humanism should not be confused with the humanism of post-Enlightenment philosophy. In fact, to John Paul, it is precisely the rationalist approach that is at the heart of the problem. For the "technological, functional" mentality he decries is rooted not just in capitalist or Marxist materialism, but in all modern, post-Enlightenment thought. The culprit here is not Karl Marx or Adam Smith but René Descartes! In short, the Pope's visit to Cuba is part not of a battle against communism but of a lifelong crusade against modernity itself. And that's a good deal more challenging than confronting Fidel Castro.

FURTHER READING

Biography

Kwitny, Jonathan. *Man of the Century: The Life and Times of Pope John Paul II.* New York: Henry Holt, 1997, 754 p.
> Examines John Paul's life, career, and complex religious, political, and philosophical perspective.

Malinski, Mieczyslaw. *Pope John Paul II: The Life of Karol Wojtyla.* Translated by P. S. Falla. New York: Seabury Press, 1979, 283 p.
> A personal recollection of John Paul's early parish activities, writings, and tenure as archbishop in Krakow.

Criticism

Czerwinski, E. J. Review of *The Collected Plays and Writings on Theater. World Literature Today* 62, No. 3 (Summer 1988): 477-8.
> A positive review of *The Collected Plays and Writings on Theater.*

Doerr, Edd. "Church and State." *Humanist* 51, No. 2 (March-April 1991): 31-2.
> Discusses John Paul's contradictory statements regarding religious freedom and civil liberties.

Donahue, Charles, Jr. "Theology, Law and Women's Ordination: 'Ordinatio Sacerdotalis' One Year Later." *Commonweal* (2 June 1995): 11-6.
> Examines the papal argument against female ordination as put forth in "Ordinatio Sacerdotalis."

Dulles, Avery. "John Paul II and the Advent of the New Millennium." *America* (9 December 1995): 9-15.
> Discusses John Paul's writings on the significance of the nearing millennium as a call for ecumenism and reexamination of personal faith.

Escurra, Ana Maria. "Pope's View of Capitalism Troublesome for Have-Nots." *National Catholic Reporter* (5 December 1997): 12-3.
> Examines John Paul's writings on capitalism after the fall of communism in Eastern Europe.

Frazier, Kendrick. "Pope's Affirmation of Evolution Welcomed by Scientists, Educators." *Skeptical Inquirer* 21, No. 1 (January-February 1997): 5-6.
> Provides editorial commentary on John Paul's official acceptance of evolutionary theory as compatible with biblical interpretation of the origin of life.

Garvey, John. "The Pope's Two Voices: Notes on an Asian Journey." *Commonweal* (27 March 1981): 165-7.
> Discusses social and religious controversies within the Catholic church upon John Paul's 1981 visit to Asia.

Hehir, J. Bryan. "A New Era of Social Teaching." *Commonweal* (23 October 1981): 585, 607.
> Offers analysis of *On Human Work.*

Lernoux, Penny. "Opus Dei and the 'Perfect Society': The Papal Spiderweb—I." *Nation* (10 April 1989): 469, 482, 484-7.
> Examines John Paul's relationship to the secretive Catholic movement known as Opus Dei.

Maneli, Mieczyslaw. "John Paul II: The Universal Pole." *Humanist* 47, No. 5 (September-October 1987): 26-7, 38.
> Discusses John Paul's political perspective, social consciousness, and role as a world leader.

Marton, Kati. "The Imperial Pope." *New Republic* (1 January 1981): 16-9.
> Discusses John Paul's conservatism and resistance to internal dissent concerning issues of sexuality and women's rights.

Negri, Maxine. "Pope John Paul II and Freedom." *Humanist* 47, No. 5 (September-October 1987): 23-5.
> Examines John Paul's attitudes toward personal and religious freedom within the Catholic church.

Safire, William. "Structures of Sin." *New York Times* (22 February 1988): A19.

    Offers editorial response to John Paul's criticism of capitalism in *The Social Concerns of the Church.*

"Sollicitudo rei socialis." *Commonweal* (11 March 1988): 131-2.

    Provides editorial commentary on *Sollicitudo Rei Socialis.*

Stanford, Peter. "Madonna Fan Steals Show." *New Statesman & Society* (11 November 1994): 36-7.

    A negative review of *Crossing the Threshold of Hope.*

Review of *Veritatis splendor. Commonweal* (22 October 1993): 3-5.

Provides an overview and analysis of *Veritatis Splendor.*

Weigel, George. "John Paul II and the Priority of Culture." *First Things* 80 (February 1998): 19-25.

    Discusses John Paul's political, historical, and cultural perspective.

Williams, George Huntston. *The Mind of John Paul II: Origins of His Thought and Action.* New York: Seabury Press, 1981, 396 p.

    A book-length study of John Paul's intellectual development, including his phenomenological investigations, religious studies, and writings from his student days forward.

Additional coverage of Pope John Paul II's life and career is contained in the following sources published by the Gale Group: *Contemporary Authors,* **Vols. 106, 133.**

Marge Piercy
1936-

American novelist, poet, essayist, and editor.

The following entry presents an overview of Piercy's career through 1998. For further information on Piercy's life and works, see *CLC*, Volumes 3, 6, 14, 18, 27, and 62.

INTRODUCTION

Among the most distinguished contemporary feminist writers, Marge Piercy is recognized as a trenchant poet and novelist whose work is infused with explicit political statement and social critique. Her direct, highly personal writing, informed by her experiences as a radical political activist during the 1960s and 1970s, condemns the victimization—both physical and psychological—of women and other marginalized individuals under the patriarchal, capitalist ideologies of mainstream American society. Piercy's best known novels, including *Woman on the Edge of Time* (1976), *Braided Lives* (1982), and *Gone to Soldiers* (1987), reveal her ability to convey such themes in genres ranging from science fiction to social realism and historical fiction. An outspoken feminist and humanitarian, Piercy emphasizes the utilitarian aspect of her work as a vehicle for effective communication, evident in the colloquial, polemical tone of her fiction and free verse.

BIOGRAPHICAL INFORMATION

Born in Detroit, Michigan, Piercy was raised by her Welsh father, a machinist, and Jewish mother in a working-class neighborhood of the city; Piercy also had an older half-brother, her mother's child from a previous marriage. While Piercy's creativity was inspired by her mother's curiosity and maternal grandmother's storytelling, her political consciousness was forged by the repressive social climate and economic disparities she experienced during her formative years. Piercy won a scholarship to attend the University of Michigan, becoming the first member of her family to receive a college education. While at Michigan she won Hopwood Awards in poetry and fiction and became involved in radical politics. She traveled to France after completing her A.B. in 1957, then enrolled at Northwestern University where she earned her M.A. degree in 1958. While living in Chicago, Piercy worked odd jobs to support her writing and taught at the Gary extension of Indiana University from 1960-62. Her first marriage to a French-Jewish physicist was short-lived; she remarried in 1962, though this unconventional, open relationship deteriorated by the mid-1970s.

During the 1960s, Piercy became active in the civil rights and antiwar movements as an organizer for the left-wing political organization Students for a Democratic Society (SDS), though shifted her allegiance to the women's movement by the end of the decade. She published her first volume of poetry, *Breaking Camp* (1968), and first novel, *Going Down Fast* (1969), during this period. Piercy won the Borestone Mountain Poetry award in 1968 and 1974. She worked as a writer-in-residence and visiting lecturer at various colleges during the 1970s, and held professorships at the State University of New York, Buffalo, and the University of Cincinnati. After moving between Boston, San Francisco, and New York, Piercy finally settled in rural Cape Cod, where she has made her home since 1971. Piercy married writer Ira Wood, her third husband, in 1982, with whom she has collaborated on several works. She won a grant from the National Endowment for the Arts in 1978 and many additional honors, including the Orion Scott Award in the Humanities, the Carolyn Kizer Poetry Prize in 1986 and 1990, a Shaeffer Eaton-PEN New England award in 1989, the Golden Rose Poetry Prize in

1990, the May Sarton Award in 1991, and the Arthur C. Clarke Award in 1993 for *He, She, and It* (1991).

MAJOR WORKS

Piercy's fiction and poetry is a direct expression of her feminist and leftist political commitments. In language that is alternately realistic, didactic, and poetic, Piercy repeatedly draws attention to the suffering of the socially persecuted—women, the poor, racial minorities, lesbians—and the mercenary ethics of their oppressors—the government, corporations, technocrats, abusive men, repressive gender roles—often incorporating multiple narrators to this end. Her first novel, *Going Down Fast,* exposes the injustice of urban gentrification as callous city planners move to raze an existing low-income neighborhood to build upscale residences. Drawing upon her experiences as an SDS activist, *Dance the Eagle to Sleep* (1971) involves a small band of young political agitators and idealists who abandon the city to organize an alternative, utopian community based on Native American culture. *Small Changes* (1973), set in Boston during the 1960s, relates the parallel struggles of two young women—a middle-class Jew and working-class lesbian—whose experiences reveal the effects of female subjugation across class lines. *Woman on the Edge of Time* (1976) portrays the state's manipulation and control of the individual through the horrific experiences of a young Chicano woman who is institutionalized in an insane asylum. There she is anesthetized, stripped of her identity, sterilized, and detained against her will, prompting her to experience hallucinatory leaps into an egalitarian future world where, in stark contrast to the dystopic near present, there are no class, race, or gender divisions among its inhabitants.

The High Cost of Living (1978) relates the dilemmas faced by a lesbian graduate student in Detroit who struggles to reconcile her literary aspirations, financial needs, and self-respect within the demoralizing structure of the academic establishment. *Vida* (1980), also based on Piercy's involvement with the SDS, features protagonist Davida Asch, a beautiful, renegade political radical whose revolutionary activities during the 1960s have forced her underground. Through flashbacks Vida's recollections document the rise and fall of the "Network," the militant antiwar faction that she once headed, her long period of hiding and desolation, and newfound love with another fugitive. *Braided Lives* (1982), Piercy's most autobiographic novel, portrays the cultural oppression of women during the 1950s. The protagonist, a scholarship student and aspiring writer from humble origins in Detroit, struggles to define herself against the social humiliations of her milieu—particularly those surrounding sexuality, marriage, abortion, and rape—while she watches her friends succumb to the conventional roles of their mothers. *Fly Away Home* (1984), set amid the exclusionary prosperity of Reaganomics, traces the growing awareness of protagonist Daria Walker, a traditional wife who becomes liberated and politically engaged after discovering her husband's dark dealings as a white-collar slum lord and arsonist who victimizes the poor. *Gone to Soldiers* (1987), a work of historical fiction, follows the lives of ten main characters—six women, four men—on the home front and abroad during the Second World War. Their various experiences as civilians, soldiers, Resistance fighters, and refugees illustrate the personal disruptions, despair, and harrowing realities of the war, especially among women.

Returning to small-scale interpersonal drama in her next novel, *Summer People* (1989) revolves around real estate dealings on Cape Cod and the deterioration of a long-term love triangle involving a married couple and their female neighbor. *He, She, and It,* a work of science fiction that borrows from the cyberpunk novels of William Gibson, involves a Jewish woman's relationship with an illegal cyborg, Yod, in a dystopic twenty-first century world. Yod, like a golem of the Hebrew folklore, is designed to protect her Jewish community from danger—in this case, the evils of the corporate state and criminal underworld—raising ethical questions about the creation and destructive potential of technology. *The Longings of Women* (1994) juxtaposes the precarious lives of three very different women—a sixty-one-year-old homeless housekeeper, an unhappily married college professor, and a young wife accused of murdering her husband—each of whom seek, on their own separate terms, the keys to emotional and physical security. *City of Darkness, City of Light* (1996), an extensively researched work of historical fiction, is a reinterpretation of events surrounding the French Revolution that parallels the vicissitudes of American leftist politics during the 1960s and 1970s. Presented through the perspective of six historical personages, both male and female, Piercy traces the formative events in each characters' life and their involvement in the radical politics, murderous rampages, and fractious alliances of their time.

In *Storm Tide* (1998), written in collaboration with husband Ira Wood, Piercy returns to a Cape Cod setting where the protagonist, a divorced, former professional baseball player, becomes entangled in a web of sexual intrigue, small-town politics, and guilt over a deadly accident. *Three Women* (1999), which centers upon strained mother-daughter relationships, involves a successful lawyer whose midlife contentment is suddenly shattered when she must take in her unemployed, emotionally scarred daughter and demanding, stroke-afflicted mother. As in her novels, Piercy's poetry reveals her effort to merge literature and political engagement. Her socially and ecologically conscious verse, influenced by the poetry of Walt Whitman and Muriel Rukeyser, is characterized by its informality, autobiographic content, striking imagery, depiction of everyday life and objects, and political message. Her first several volumes, *Breaking Camp, Hard Loving* (1969), and *To Be of Use* (1973), composed while active in the civil rights, peace, and women's movements, contain some of her most polemical verse. *Living in the Open* (1976) marks a shift in focus from urban to rural environments following her move from New York to Cape Cod. Nature themes are also present in *The Twelve-Spoked Wheel Flashing* (1978) and *The Moon Is Always Female* (1980), which explore personal and feminist concerns in relation to the archetypal cycles of Mother Earth and the moon. *Circles on the Water* (1982) contains selections from her six previous volumes along with several new poems. Piercy's subsequent volumes—*Stone, Paper, Knife* (1983), *My Mother's Body* (1985), *Available Light* (1988), *Mars and Her Children* (1992), and *What Are Big Girls Made Of?* (1997)—are less overtly political, though continue to focus on her private struggles with love, sexuality, family relationships, female self-identity, domestic life, and the redemptive pleasures of the natural world. *The Art of Blessing the Day* (1999) contains previous and new poems in which Piercy explores her Jewish heritage and religious faith. *Early Grrrl* (1999), another collection of new and previous poems, is dedicated to the new generation of fringe feminists behind the small magazine and Internet-based "Grrrl" movement. Piercy has also published a collection of her articles, book reviews, and interviews in *Parti-Colored Blocks for a Quilt* (1982).

CRITICAL RECEPTION

Piercy is widely recognized as a major contemporary feminist poet and novelist. Her writing in both genres is praised for its intensity, clarity, and important social message. While some critics disapprove of her emotional tenor and propagandistic condemnation of social, economic, and environmental ills, others praise the passion and immediacy of her depictions of injustice and exploitation. "Piercy has always seemed to be ahead of her time in dealing with contemporary social and political issues," writes Sue Walker, "and she has done this with some risk to popular acclaim, but with an authenticity that should merit more lasting critical recognition and attention." Critics also appreciate Piercy's insight into the aspirations and shortcomings of organized activism and her ability to present compelling, multidimensional characters whose individual complexity often rises above the socially malignant stereotype they are intended to illustrate. "If Piercy is accused of being preachy," Joyce R. Ladenson explains, "it is because her characters are struck by pain which they need to explain and about which they are enraged once they examine its social sources." Among her many novels *Woman on the Edge of Time* is generally regarded as her most original and important, considered by many a classic of feminist science fiction. *Small Changes, Braided Lives,* and *Gone to Soldiers* have also attracted favorable reviews and continued critical interest, though other novels such as *Summer People, Fly Away Home,* and *He, She, and It* have been deemed less successful. As Judith Wynn comments in a review of *The Longings of Women,* "Piercy is not an elegant writer. Interesting, swift-moving plots and careful social observation are her main strengths." Despite the bleak circumstances she often describes, Piercy's fiction and poetry is noted for its essentially optimistic outlook which, in keeping with her artistic commitment to political action, continually presents alternatives to the status quo and inspires the possibility of communal solidarity and meaningful change.

PRINCIPAL WORKS

Breaking Camp (poetry) 1968
Going Down Fast (novel) 1969
Hard Loving (poetry) 1969
Dance the Eagle to Sleep (novel) 1971
4-Telling [with Bob Herson, Emmet Jarrett, and Dick Lourie] (poetry) 1971
Small Changes (novel) 1973
To Be of Use (poetry) 1973
Living in the Open (poetry) 1976
Woman on the Edge of Time (novel) 1976
The High Cost of Living (novel) 1978
The Twelve-Spoked Wheel Flashing (poetry) 1978
The Moon Is Always Female (poetry) 1980
Vida (novel) 1980
Braided Lives (novel) 1982
Circles on the Water: Selected Poems (poetry) 1982
Parti-Colored Blocks for a Quilt (prose) 1982
Stone, Paper, Knife (poetry) 1983
Fly Away Home (novel) 1984
My Mother's Body (poetry) 1985
Gone to Soldiers (novel) 1987
Available Light (poetry) 1988
Early Ripening: American Women Poets Now [editor] (poetry) 1988
Summer People (novel) 1989
He, She, and It (novel) 1991
Mars and Her Children (poetry) 1992
The Longings of Women (novel) 1994
City of Darkness, City of Light (novel) 1996
What Are Big Girls Made Of? (poetry) 1997
Storm Tide [with Ira Wood] (novel) 1998
The Art of Blessing the Day: Poems with a Jewish Theme (poetry) 1999
Early Grrrl: The Early Poems of Marge Piercy (poetry) 1999
Three Women (novel) 1999

CRITICISM

Jack Hicks (essay date 1981)

SOURCE: "Fiction from the Counterculture: Marge Piercy, Richard Brautigan, Ken Kesey," in *In the Singer's Temple: Prose Fictions of Barthelme, Gaines, Brautigan, Piercy, Kesey, and Kosinski,* University of North Carolina Press, 1981, pp. 138-76.

[*In the following excerpt, Hicks provides analysis of* Dance the Eagle to Sleep, *noting flaws in the novel's overt political rhetoric and characterization. Hicks writes, "I believe the fiction's weaknesses, perhaps even more than its virtues, are instructive and exemplary."*]

> Every soul must become a magician; the magician is
> in touch.
> The magician connects: the magician helps each thing
> to open into what it truly wants to utter.
> The saying is not the magic: we have drunk words
> and eaten
> manifestoes and grown bloated on resolutions
> and farted winds of sour words that left us weak.
> It is in the acting with the strength we cannot
> really have till we have won.
>
> —Marge Piercy

Marge Piercy has published extensively in the twelve years since her first book, **Breaking Camp** (poems) in 1968. Five more collections of poems have followed. An excerpt from **"Maude Awake"** (an unpublished novel) appeared in a feminist anthology in 1966, her first published fiction. Since then, she has published six novels, from **Going Down Fast** (1969)—a very solid first work—to **The High Cost of Living** (1978) and **Vida** (1979). Her most balanced and impressive work to date is **Woman on the Edge of Time** (1976), in which she successfully blends techniques of social realism and prophetic science fiction. I focus on her second prose work, the "cautionary tale" **Dance the Eagle to Sleep.**

Because of her involvement in Students for a Democratic Society during the early 1960s, Piercy has defined herself as "a committed radical artist." Her work has grown increasingly sympathetic to the plights of women in a capitalist, sexist culture, but her earlier comments on **Dance the Eagle to Sleep** still serve as a personal, artistic, and political credo:

> I wanted to examine alternatives and choices and daydreams and accepted mythologies and tendencies of behavior in the New Left. I am a revolutionary, my work is all committed and engaged writing. I make poems for people as people bake bread for people and people grow corn for people and people make furniture for people. This novel, like my poems and other writing, is intended to be useful: I live in a situation of feedback. I articulate what I perceive needs to be articulated out of me, out of those around me, out of those I work with, out of those who push on me, out of those who are trying to kill me . . . . I am involved in showing people changing through struggle, becoming, always in process. I am concerned with drawing characters who are full and able to be identified with, but not heroes or heroines of impeccable revolutionary virtue.
>
> I get a lot of flak for that. But the people I love and thus the characters I can make out of my life and those around me are mixtures, products of a society that socializes through guilt and competition and fear and repression.

I work with Piercy's cautionary tale for several reasons. First, it was written in the midst of radical dissent in the late 1960s, examining, as she explains, "alternatives and choices and daydreams and accepted mythologies and tendencies of behavior in the New Left." Second, I wish to examine flaws in the work. Its considerable narrative powers are diluted by long stretches of a "saying" and by a wide streak of rhetorical preaching and posing of the sort criticized by Piercy herself in the epigraph, "The Aim." I believe the fiction's weaknesses, perhaps even more than its virtues, are instructive and exemplary.

Dance the Eagle to Sleep is set in an indefinite future, a time when a small army of alienated and oppressed youths band together to create an alternate culture. As Piercy explains, "the emphasis is on significant episodes of a collective action. There are five major characters, four of them viewpoint characters and one seen only from the other's eyes. Her major characters are familiar "youth culture" types: Corey is half-Indian, an outlaw, a strongly mystical figure given to fasting and seeking visions in which America is redeemed by her tribal children:

> They could turn away from the ways of metal to the ways of the flesh. They could learn the good ways of being in harmony, of cooperating, of sane bravery in defense of each other, to be one with their bodies and their tribe and each other and the land. The children would turn away from being white. For the whites were crazy. The whites were colonizers and dominators and enslavers. They came to rob and steal and develop and conquer. Already the children wore beads and headbands and smoked ritually. They were awaiting the coming of the real tribes.

Closest to Corey is Shawn, cooler and more aristocratic, the leader of a rock band and a youth culture hero. Through Shawn's summarized experiences, Piercy relates her unsettling vision of "The Nineteenth Year of Servitude," brainchild of a "Task Force on Youth Problems." Implemented by a liberal president, The Nineteenth Year seems to be the ultimate in social programming:

> Most guys still ended up in the Army, and a great many went into street patrols and the city militia. But a number were channeled into overseas aid and pacification corps, the rebuilding programs in the bombed-out ghettoes, and pollution clean-up corps. Girls who weren't rushed into the nursing corps worked in the pre-school socialization programs in the ghettoes, or as teachers' aides or low-level programmers for the array of teaching machines. Of course, students in medicine, engineering and the sciences just kept trotting through school.
>
> School records, grades, and counselors determined some of the channeling, but the prime tools were the mass exams everyone took, separating out levels of skill and verbal intelligence, and locating potential troublemakers. . . . For two years now, The Nineteenth Year had bottled up the so-called Youth Revolution.

Shawn's involvement with the rebels is much more uncertain than Corey's. He drifts through life, and his only strong interests are his music and the passion it compels. Channeled as a musician for The Nineteenth Year, he finds his talents being used to manipulate his peers; he rebels, is arrested and court-martialed. Befriended by Corey, Shawn joins the commune and lends his music to serve the ends of the Revolution.

Bill Batson is a third major figure. Named for the human weakling in which comic book superhero Captain Marvel hid, Billy is a scientific genius, cynical and dispossessed. He joins The Indians when they occupy his high school—their first act of secession. Billy's mind and skills are quickly assimilated; even more than Corey, he comes to argue for militant, violent face-offs with the government. Piercy's rhetorical excesses are especially blatant in her descriptions of Billy:

> Born twisted, born warped, born in the center of the empire, he could only pride himself that they had not succeeded in using him. They had come close. But he had escaped them and turned. For the society, the system was mad: it caused the people in it to go slowly mad. They could not care for each other. They could only hate and fear and compete and fantasize; they could only rub against each other and try to use each other and suck on their own anxieties.

> He would never live to be human. Nobody like him or these people could imagine what it might be like to be human, in a society people ran for the common good instead of the plunder of the few. . . . Tenderness swept his body. He could almost imagine. Someday there would be people. But that coming would not be gentle. It would sprout from struggle and death. Someday there would be human people.

Joanna is the major female character. Like the other four, she is virtually a sociological type: an army child, an inveterate runaway, she finally attaches herself to The Indians at their lower East Side commune. Sleeping her way through the tribe, she finally settles as Corey's woman. Joanna is the most static of the cast, revealed to us in skeletal form; indeed, her "brainwashed" character remains unconvincing throughout the novel. She too serves as a handy mouthpiece for the preachiest of political lectures:

> It depressed her that she could only define herself in negatives. She was not like her mother. She was not like her father. The conventional masculine and the conventional feminine roles were for shit. The primary business of base ladies was to talk about each other. What her mother knew could be contained in a greeting card and consisted of You're Supposed To's and Don't You Dare's. It could be summed up as, "Don't sit with your knees apart, Jill, you're a big girl now."

> She did not want to be somebody's wife or somebody else's mother. Or somebody else's servant or somebody else's secretary. Or somebody else's sex kitten or somebody else's keeper. She saw no women around who seemed to be anybody in themselves. They all wore some man's uniform. She wanted to be free, and free meant not confined, not forced to lie, not forced to pretend, not warped, not punished, not tortured.

After the initial rounds of this sort of crude exposition, *Dance the Eagle to Sleep* picks up markedly. Her characters swing into action: after occupying a school, forming a sizeable youth commune in New York, directing the formation of the Warriors (their guerrilla wing under Billy's leadership), and setting similar movements off throughout the country, The Indians move to a rural New Jersey commune, where they hope to build a serious land base.

Although her central characters share a marionette-like quality early in the novel, they become less wooden and more convincing in action. Drawing directly on her own movement experiences, Piercy does indeed "examine alternatives and choices and daydreams and accepted mythologies and tendencies of behavior in the New Left." As The Indians work hard to establish a revolutionary base, take "bread" (a kind of psychedelic sacrament), and dance out their visions in tribal gatherings, personal and political relationships become strained and factions develop. Corey and his "water people" argue for continuing the commune farms and tribal families: "Creating something better is struggling, too. We need to keep it up on both fronts: making real, visible alternatives, and confronting the system. . . . Here they're all the way out of the system. That's the biggest trouble we can make. . . . But we have to gather all the tribes. Everybody can't make it on the streets. We have to grow or we perish. The tribe is the core. The whole tribe."

His brother-antagonist Billy Batson is more urban directed, insisting on militant, confrontation-provoking tactics. Modeled closely after several of the Weathermen, most violent of the New Left factions in the late 1960s, Billy scorns tribes and farm communes: "If you had bothered with nineteenth-century history, you'd know that this whole farm business is a throwback, Brook Farm-utopian cranks off in the woods to start the good society, and at each other's throats in six months. . . . So we set up a summer camp in the Jersey hills for wayward adolescents. The man can let us get away with that. What would it matter to General Motors if we set up twenty?" Factions flourish: faced with revolutionary paradoxes—the need to murder and to create, for example—The Indians drain their energies by squabbling. The liberal American government is replaced by a harder line, and "The System" methodically and harshly eliminates their numbers. Billy's warriors use bombings and terrorism to force a showdown and are quickly crushed. The authorities move into the farm commune; after a time lapse at the end of the tenth chapter, we see what is left: Billy is dead, Joanna captured, Corey crushed by a bulldozer.

Driven west by the government, the remnants of The Indians gather with the shreds of other tribes; in a familiar historical parallel, almost all are annihilated. By the end of ***Dance the Eagle to Sleep,*** only Shawn, a scruffy female named Ginny, and a badly scarred black (Marcus) remain alive. It remains for the pregnant Ginny, who is politically naive, to issue final judgments of her male revolutionaries: "She was gentle with them both and angry with them both. She would not love them, because they had not been willing to escape. She told them they were in love with apocalypse, like all men, more in love with machomyths than any woman." The tale ends on the tiniest of glimmers. Shawn, Ginny, and Marcus have come through the fire with few illusions left. At the end, somewhat sentimentally, they are prepared to make a start. The fiction closes with the difficult birth of Ginny's child: "The baby lived and she lived and it was day for Marcus and for him, it was day for them all."

The political import of Marge Piercy's cautionary tale was seized by most reviewers. Her strongest messages are delivered mainly to her fellow leftists:

> I regard the politics of Apocalypse as dangerous to our success in taking the control of the world away from those who own it and us, and I was trying to exorcise that fascination with a struggle viewed as final, fatal, sudden, and complete in *Dance.* The end is trying to suggest, So you get your Armageddon, so? What do you do then? You still have to go on, if you survive, trying to change things. The enemy is very real, real as Rockefeller ordering the murders at Attica, but so is the fact that our course is long and slow and this revolution, for all that we win or die, will never be finished.

Praised by left liberal critics in *Nation, Commonweal,* and *New Republic* (John Seelye, Linda Kuehl, Todd Gitlin), *Dance the Eagle to Sleep* is politically informed and convincing. The force and detail of Marge Piercy's analyses are valuable—the liberal undermining and cooptation of the radical left, the roots of radical divisiveness, the agonizing self-criticism and dialectical examinations—these are astute observations. But I have basic reservations about the work and dwell on the question of how art may most effectively move people to share or act upon a political belief. More exactly, how can fiction best convey a political vision? How can political concepts, values, and judgments be submerged in fictional forms, be translated into compelling patterns of character in action with which people can identify?

John Updike seems right in suggesting that Piercy's tale is less persuasive than it might have been and therefore politically inefficient. She has a tendency to indulge in "saying" rather than "showing." Individual characters are offered in exposition as case studies rather than as individuals *in actions* with which we can empathize. Although large segments of *Dance the Eagle to Sleep* are told through the viewpoints of Shawn, Corey, Joanna, and Billy, the language and rhythms of their flashbacks, dreams, or monologues are undifferentiated and incessantly editorial. Updike is correct in saying that Piercy is "not fastidious about cliches, resorts to a hurried sociological tone, makes people talk like press handouts, and declines to linger upon sensual details."

"The emphasis is on the significant episodes of a collective action": although Piercy's comment suggests a purposeful lack of individual focus, it cannot excuse the weaknesses of the tale. Adults, parents, indeed most of the human components of "The System" are never seen in action. Rather, they are offered as a vast, monolithic repression-machine, and their corporate heinousness is finally difficult to accept. Psychological aberration forms

the nucleus of each of her characters, but neither aberrations nor their causes are accounted for beyond this sort of general rhetorical posturing:

> For years the culture has been telling everybody through every boob tube that only youth was sexual and beautiful, and that all an over-twenty-five schmuck like you could do was buy Brand X to look a little more youthful. Schmuck, schmuck, the boob tube said all evening long, you're powerless, sexless, fumbling, clumsy, mindless, unable to decide. Average man=schmuck. Average woman=bag. Buy our product once, and maybe nobody will notice what a drag you are. . . . Thus is a people conditioned to hate its young and focus its frustrations down upon them in a vast dream of those half-dependent, half-independent children demanding and rebelling and threatening. . . . They were different, alien. You were warned that you could not hope to communicate with them or understand their ways without the guidance of certified experts who had degrees in studying them, like biologists, specializing in tree monkeys or fighting fish. Them Versus Us: the first step in the psychological conditioning for war.

Only later, when Piercy is more patient in depicting the involvements of her characters, especially the sexual ones, and in coiling the springs of their actions, does the fiction engage one's attentions and belief. Although *Dance the Eagle to Sleep* is finally impressive, it only partially fills its promise. Judging from Piercy's other recent writings, she is fully aware of the main requisite of political fiction:

> Now I get coarse when the abstract nouns start flashing.
> I go out to the kitchen to chat about cabbages and habits.
>
> I try hard to remember to watch what people do.
> Yes, keep your eyes on the hands, let the voice go buzzing.
>
> Economy is the bone, politics is the flesh,
> Watch who they beat and who they eat,
> Watch who they relieve themselves on, watch who they own.
>
> The rest, the rest, the rest is decoration.

Brina Caplan (review date 6 March 1982)

SOURCE: "Not So Happy Days," in *The Nation*, March 6, 1982, pp. 280-2.

[*In the following review, Caplan offers tempered analysis of* Braided Lives.]

The 1950s may not seem long ago, but they are long ago enough to have become history, the object of academic speculation and commercial nostalgia. On campus, scholars revise Eisenhower's Presidential reputation. On television, loops of tape endlessly reincarnate *Happy Days* and bring us, in prime time, the joys of Elvis and the sorrows of Marilyn. But anyone who came of age during the

McCarthy-Eisenhower era is likely to need neither revision nor television. Simple recall suffices: the way we were is not a way we want to be again.

As Marge Piercy's seventh novel, **Braided Lives,** reminds us, growing up female in the 1950s hurt. Even the fashions were punitive—shoes with pencil-point toes, skirts as tight as mummy windings or flared so as to require lofting by layers of starched, scratchy crinolines. Thirty years later, the then-fashionable distortions of female anatomy must seem comic. "A decent bra in 1953," Piercy's narrator, Jill Stuart, reports, "is nearer to an armor breastplate than to a silky froth of lingerie. It holds the breasts apart, forward and out as if setting up a couple of moon shots." Yet what Jill finds in recollection unlaughable still is the distortion of women's ambitions, impulses and self-regard. At 43, she wonders how she managed to live through ages 16 to 22. Her remembrance of a working-class childhood in Detroit, college years in Ann Arbor and a writer's life in New York City is, in fact, a survivor's retrospective. Like all narratives of survival, **Braided Lives** affects us by contrast—by distinction made between then and now, between those who have and have not survived and, most important, between the subtleties of individual development and the more general movement of history.

In 1953, sex is for marriage, not because, as the Victorians saw it, the act is so deeply profane that only sanctification makes it endurable. Instead, in the utilitarian 1950s, sexuality gives women their one legitimate hold on power. They are expected, with the goad of pleasure, to herd men into families. This herding ritual, as Jill observes it, is a blind-end game. A too-early marriage transforms her childhood best friend from a street-wise adventurer into "a housewife padding around in slip and feather mules, a permanent whine in her voice and a puzzled frown pulling at her wide mouth." At her home, the power derived from earning belongs to Jill father; her industrious, beleaguered mother "works for free." And so Mr. Stuart battles for control of family affairs through bluster and the surreptitious scheming of the weak. Although a child of her time, by age 16 Jill is already planning an escape into the future.

Her own efforts pay for four years, at the University of Michigan, where thoughtfulness, disparaged at home, proves an asset, and friendly voices help her articulate her own native radicalism. But there is other tuition to be paid, at a different price. The same destructive ambivalence that caused high school boys to pursue—and then to scorn—"girls who do" infects every male-female relationship of Jill's college years. Men bully and wheedle, disregard women's pain and ignore the gravity of childbearing. Once discovered, sex nonetheless remains a sweet release—no other contemporary novelist writes about women's sexual pleasures with Piercy's good-humored, unmuddied sensuality—and Jill does enjoy an almost easy relationship with a factory worker in Ann Arbor. His respect for her independence, however, is offset both by his line of night work, burglary, and by his exploitative

racism. In Jill's experience, men want not "just one thing" from the women they love; they want a soul-eviscerating everything.

The great passions of her life become her poetry, her politics and her friendships. She has discovered "the core of falsity in the search for love: a woman gives herself to a man as if that got rid of the problem of making an identity." But most women she knows, including those with whom she shares political opinions, do not agree. Indeed, the woman she most loves, her cousin and sometime roommate, Donna, is haunted by a despair that she believes only marriage can alleviate. Although their intimacy provides them both with safe harbor during troubled times, its intensity inevitably frightens Donna, who then cools and resumes cruising for a husband. Her coolness, Jill's fervor; her self-loathing, Jill's self-sufficiency are played off against each other in a counterpoint of crises—the last of which is the unwanted pregnancy that ends Donna's life.

Of the lives that intertwine with Jill's to produce **Braided Lives,** her own is virtually the one unbroken strand: Howie, her New York lover and former high school friend, dies in a Ku Klux Klan ambush; Donna's death is fated by her marriage to a woman-hater; women friends disappear into prison, asylums, the insularity of serial baby-bearing. "I do not know a girl who does not say," Jill remarks early in her story, "'I don't want to live like my mother'. . . . Is it our mothers, ourselves or our men who mold us?" Jill alone has escaped to tell us, and her answers implicate all three agents. Certainly, this account of women's lives during the 1950s does not relieve them of responsibility for preserving the status quo. Jill recounts with bemusement, for example, how in dormitory confessions her college friends, preferring contest to mutuality, claimed themselves virginities that could appear and disappear and reappear to suit competitive moment.

If, in **Braided Lives,** Piercy's humor has satiric bite, her dialogue achieves a more vicious edge. Jill's mother and lovers tend to go at her in butchering arguments that appear to aim at total annihilation. "'You poor blind ugly slut! You dirty little gutter worm living on your own shit!'" screams the mother at the daughter who has confronted her about repainting a room. Despite their compelling momentum, such scenes transport a puzzling excess, too particular and too poisoned to be explained away by a generalized feminist vision. Indeed, excess may be the one fault of this energetic novel, which in the course of nearly 450 pages manages to accommodate almost every humiliation to which women are liable: there are rapes, memories of childhood seduction, psychological manipulation, verbal and physical abuse, the agony of illegal abortion and exploitation on and off the job. Although, given Piercy's accuracy of eye and ear, any one incident is likely to be absorbing, the total catalogue is somehow numbing. Piercy might well have kept in mind Jill's weary reaction to her friend Stephanie's rendition of a childhood of horrors. Stephanie's story, Jill remarks, "has beaten me into a submission of the imagination."

Elizabeth Wheeler (review date 12 August 1984)

SOURCE: "It's Her Life and Welcome to it," in *Los Angeles Times Book Review,* August 12, 1984, p. 7.

[*In the following review, Wheeler offers unfavorable assessment of* Fly Away Home.]

Fly Away Home is a novel I much wanted to like, and there is much in the novel to admire. It's a novel that says much without taking a preachy tone, and it's a novel that has something to say. It's also a novel of human experience and human scale, one that takes problems of our age and time and domesticates them. It is written by a woman, about a woman and for women, and there's certainly nothing wrong with that.

In fact, its virtues may do this novel in. For example, there's author Marge Piercy's obvious skill in the creation of a detailed fictional world. She not only knows every inch of the house her heroine, Daria Walker, occupies and loves, she also knows every piece of underwear in her drawer and every thought in her head.

Each detail Piercy presents has behind it the richness of a thousand others. The result is an enormous strength of the parts but also a weakness of the whole. The details are perfect, but they add up to one woman's life rather than a fully realized novel.

Here again Piercy's virtues point up her failings. Daria Walker is a wonderful character. She's essentially good without being perfect, perceptive without being preternaturally wise, gentle without being mushy, she is, in fact, extraordinary enough to be interesting yet average enough to be representative. She is also, unfortunately, the only complete character in the book. There's some real humanity in her two daughters, her secretary and some of the tenants of the buildings her husband owns, but these characters seem cardboard when compared to Daria.

There are also some characters who would seem cardboard if compared to a box at a checkout counter. The husband who discards her, for example, is not only guilty of bad taste. He turns out to have the charm of bubble gum on the bottom of a shoe and about the same amount of intrinsic merit. Piercy is making a point about how two individuals can grow apart in a marriage, but it could have been made without turning one of those individuals into a snob, a bully and a vicarious pyromaniac with homicidal tendencies.

The problem of Daria's husband brings up, quite naturally, the greatest of this novel's vices of virtue. Piercy has points to make, several of them. She is not only writing about estrangement in a long marriage and what the 1980s can do to a man and a woman who seemed to have much in common in the 1960s, she's also writing about how money can corrupt the weak, how evil can be seen as necessary and how times of crisis can turn into times of self-discovery and, therefore, self-fulfillment.

Now these are all valid concerns for a novelist and merit thoughtful exploration. Piercy, however, doesn't give them one. Long before Daria and her new lover—younger, stronger, bigger, sexier and infinitely more sensitive than that creep who was her husband—have fantastic sex, this novel may seem more an exercise in wish-fulfillment than self-fulfillment. The line between the two is subtle, but many readers will have little doubt that Piercy has crossed it.

Elaine Tuttle Hansen (essay date 1985)

SOURCE: "Marge Piercy: The Double Narrative Structure of *Small Changes,*" in *Contemporary American Women Writers: Narrative Strategies,* edited by Catherine Rainwater and William J. Scheick, University Press of Kentucky, 1985, pp. 209-23.

[*In the following essay, Hansen examines Piercy's mistrust of language, narrative strategies, and appropriation of dominant male discourse in* Small Changes.]

"This is the oppressor's language / yet I need it to talk to you." Speaking thus of the equivocal relationship between women and language, Adrienne Rich in the earliest days of the women's movement addressed the central question that female writers and feminist critics still seek to answer. Is the dominant discourse a male construct that women cannot use to represent their experience, or can women control or escape this discourse to speak of and for themselves? In *Small Changes,* more explicitly than in any of her other six novels so far published, Marge Piercy confronts this troubling question. The novel reflects at various levels a profound suspicion of "the oppressor's language," but like Rich, Piercy finally wants to appropriate—with certain modifications—the dominant discourse. Her aim as a writer, she claims, is to communicate, and after all how else to do so: "I need it to talk to you." Affirming that women must simultaneously mistrust and use language, Piercy goes on to explore in *Small Changes,* through its narrative structure, the possibilities and limitations of two different ways in which the female artist can use "the oppressor's" words, as well as his conventional narrative modes, to write—and perhaps even rewrite—female experience.

In *Small Changes,* a profound and pervasive suspicion of the dominant discourse is explicitly articulated by one of the two main characters, Beth Walker. Beth both recognizes and suspects the power of words. In the opening chapter, she tries to suppress her own discomfort and misgivings, as she stands at the altar with Jim, by invoking "magic words that made things happen or go away, recipes like I Love You, and I'm Sorry, and I Pledge Allegiance, and God Bless Mommy and Daddy, and Will You Marry Me, and Fine, Thank You, and I Do." But she cannot hear these soothing formulas "over the roaring in her ears," the sound of an apparently instinctive, inner pulse that prefigures the roars of an anger she gradually learns, in the course of the novel, to acknowledge and express. In the same scene we find that Beth, although untrained in Speech Act Theory, fully understands the performative power of "magic words," as she hears what the clichés really say and demystifies those old recipes. So, for example, she translates her sister's description of her wedding dress, written for a newspaper that will never print it: "Nancy had written 'the train comes away.' That meant the thing that dragged could be taken off, with a little timely help." Beth's debunking revision frankly emphasizes the oppression of women that the formulaic words conceal: the conventional train of the white wedding gown is in fact a useless burden, "the thing that dragged," symbolizing not elegance—or pretensions to elegance—but woman's lack of power, her need for "a little timely help" to rid herself of obstacles to comfort and freedom of action. Beth's revisionist insight into the way words both reflect and hide the oppression of women continues throughout the novel: again, when Dorine laments her loneliness—"I feel sometimes as if I'll go through life and never belong to anyone"—Beth responds: "But you aren't a dog, why do you want to be owned?" On her wedding night, "going all the way" with Jim for the first time, she is left completely unsatisfied by his rapid defloration: "they had made love finally, but where was the love they had made?"

Beth's mistrust of magic words extends to the written word as well. Reflecting on her past, as she tries to find out what is going wrong in her marriage, she notes that she was once an avid reader, first consuming adventure stories for boys and later "a lot of Frank Yerby and Galsworthy," and "all of Aldous Huxley and Iris Murdoch." But she stopped reading as she began to feel the gap between "reality" and fiction: "The books had betrayed her, leading her to want what she could not approach." She finds the diary she kept in high school and discovers that she, too, wrote words that misrepresented life, lying to herself in order to cover up painful experience with a story of "how it was all supposed to be." Even "Jim," she comes to believe, is "a character made up as she used to make over her daily life for her diary." To escape her depressing marriage to the real Jim, she once again turns to books—to Hemingway and Colette, among others—and to daydreaming. Beth finds something "shameful," however, about this retreat to a fantasy world, "something second rate about an imaginary life." Later, after her first actual escape from Jim and Syracuse, at a point at which she no longer needs to imagine herself taking part in fictional adventures, she picks up some magazines from an old friend's coffee table. With clear sight she analyzes the way they prescribe and distort female life, but she can still feel their power: "The effect of reading them was to feel discontented and sad and vaguely stirred up, as if lacking, as if something were wrong with her. Quickly she put down the magazine."

On her own for the first time, in Boston and on the fringes of academe, Beth learns about another (ab)use of words.

The educated men she now meets play a "verbal game," while the women "sat on the sidelines and watched the words go by." Talking for these men is "a kind of playing," like Jim's car races and football games, but this game has serious consequences. Men have the power to name women: just as Jim called Beth "Little Girl," the men in the apartment on Pearl Street call Dorine "Chlorine"; Beth is "Peter Rabbit" and Miriam is "Venus." (Later male epithets for Miriam are even more offensive and destructive: Jackson identifies her with his ex-wife—"You're both cunts"—and Neil criticizes her for her failure to behave as "my wife"—even "a professor's wife"—should.) Dorine consoles Beth for her inability to play the verbal game by arguing that it is just a little harmless sport—"It's jaw exercise. It's Indian wrestling." But Beth sees more: "I think it's their way of putting things in their place and people in their place and keeping them there. . . . They're making a pecking order."

In her suspicion of words and the ways they are used to keep people, especially women, in their places, Beth explores alternative ways of understanding and expressing herself and of communicating with others. She turns first to music, where "sometimes it was people saying things sharper and cleaner than people ever talked to each other in her life . . . great charges of feeling, someone and then someone else talking to her with power." Through music she joins "the heart of feeling" she cannot otherwise enter, and she hears the vague but powerful promise of "something, something" that "hung out there in music and birds, wheeling against the dusk and crickets chirping in the weeds." She also thinks in images; she studies herself as a turtle in an attempt to understand what she feels and believes. Later she finds alternative outlets for her creativity, first in the children's story that she and the women of the commune collectively invent, and ultimately in the women's theater group. She also continues to talk and listen and write, but always with a marked effort to be honest, to say what she means, and to hear what other people are saying. She replaces magic words that distort, falsify, and oppress with the mottoes she writes on the walls of her room in Back Bay, sayings that use language itself, as Beth always does, to demystify, debunk, and deconstruct the dominant discourse and replace it with words that speak of and for women: "NOBODY LOVES A DOORMAT, THEY JUST WALK ON OVER. THE MIRROR IS THE FIRST DAILY TRAP. CHICK—small, fuzzy, helpless, stupid, cute, lays eggs and in the end gets eaten. CAT—predator, active, alert, tough, independent, mean, quick. The language says one is predator and the other is prey. LOVE IS WHAT WOMEN DO INSTEAD OF KNOWING OR FIGHTING OR MAKING OR INVENTING."

Beth even writes a poem, a self-help piece that ends with a chant of defiance and self-affirmation—"Yes, Beth! Yes, Beth! / Yes"—whose chief virtue is that it makes her feel better. Miriam's perceptive analysis of Beth's surprisingly strong sense of her identity underscores Beth's escape from the dominant discourse that (mis)directs and (dis)figures most women's lives: "She seemed to have her own cry that she uttered through the confusions they all lived in."

But Beth herself understands that "her own cry" is not enough for a woman, and despite her strong distrust of their uses of language, she wants to engage with men in the verbal game. She articulates to Dorine the reason for her apparently contradictory desire to play a game she hates and in which she has no confidence: "I want to be better with words. I want to be able to answer them back. But I don't believe that's how you do anything. I only want to use words as weapons because I'm tired of being beaten with them. Tired of being pushed around because I don't know how to push back." When Beth says that words, as men use them, are inadequate to "do anything," she is not denying the potency of words; she is voicing, rather, her political belief in action as opposed to a hollow rhetoric that is not useful to women, or to anyone else who wants to change the world. As she puts it later, explaining her distrust of Phil: "He talks too much. He turns everything into words and makes it change in words, but nothing changes." Without relinquishing this insight into the insufficiency of words, she acknowledges their real power to oppress and wants access to that power, not to join in the dominant discourse, not to play the game as men play it, but to protect herself against oppression. In *Small Changes* Piercy expresses her mistrust of language but does not advocate or sentimentalize silence on the part of women. While women need to seek alternatives and to reject language and literature when they are used to keep women in their place, they cannot allow themselves to be muted; inarticulateness is not a useful weapon.

Other characters and events in the novel support Beth's explicit stance on the troubled question of women and language. Miriam, for instance, who has had more formal education than Beth has had, is always talking and has less suspicion of the dominant discourse, perhaps because she is better at playing the verbal game herself. But while she is seldom at a loss for words, she is also the most oppressed woman in the novel, or at least the one who is most damaged by the epithets and plots assigned to her by men. She uses words to hide—chiefly from herself—the truth about her relationships with men. Her lovers and her husband repeatedly shut her out from their games and refuse to speak, while she tries in vain to understand and communicate: "Still she watched him for a sign, any sign." Fittingly, like so many women, Miriam has a special facility for language, which is manifest in her interest as a computer scientist in the problems of artificial language. She begins work on a project that will facilitate communication between people and computers and between various incompatible computer languages, but when she marries the director of the project, she is transferred to work on a missile contract. Only Phil ever really talks with Miriam, but then Phil is an unusual man, the exception that proves the rule. A hustler with words—as are women—Phil is beaten down by the establishment, undergoes a conversion, and in the end recants his old

phallogocentrism. He gives up writing poetry—whose eternal status he earlier celebrated—drops out of graduate school, and even distances himself from his friend Jackson because "being with him pushes me into my old way of using words." He chooses to withdraw from the dominant discourse and becomes a carpenter: "I want to do simple useful things with my hands and keep my rotten fucked-up head out of it. I don't trust how I use words."

The pervasive and fundamental suspicion of words that separates the sheep from the goats in *Small Changes* may also serve, self-reflexively, to explain and defend Piercy's own characteristic use of language. Critics have repeatedly faulted her novels for their stylistic lapses, their failure to display "the felicities of a decent prose style." A reader might be reminded, however, when reading such criticism, of Virginia Woolf's self-mocking critique of *Life's Adventure,* the imaginary novel by Mary Carmichael analyzed in *A Room of One's Own:* "She had broken up Jane Austen's sentence," Woolf complains, "and thus given me no chance of pluming myself upon my impeccable taste, my fastidious ear." Piercy, in *Small Changes,* as did Mary Carmichael in *Life's Adventure,* insists that we question our standards of taste, our fastidious assumptions about stylistic decency, that we see the political *indecency* of "very very literary literature," and that we recognize Piercy's effort to communicate with a "popular" audience, specifically one that includes men and women "who don't go into bookstores," as she puts it. There are dangers, of course, in this insistence and this effort. There is a danger, for instance, that Piercy will go unread, or unappreciated, by people who do go into bookstores—people whom she also wants to reach, or so she says. And there is the more serious danger, perhaps, that Piercy's mistrust of language and literature can radically undercut the political message of the novel for any reader. If literature falsifies experience, why should anyone believe what *Small Changes* says about women's lives? If words change nothing, can a novel be "of use," as Piercy wants hers to be?

Such are the questions raised in *Small Changes,* crucial questions for many women writers today, and to my mind they make this novel a particularly exciting document for both the feminist critic and the student of contemporary narrative. This is not the conventional novel or the "merely" popular work that so many critics have plumed themselves on criticizing. Whether it succeeds or fails in the attempt to set new standards and say new things, it raises questions that are on the cutting edge of feminist aesthetics and feminist theory, and it repays critical analysis. One type of analysis, to which some of Piercy's other novels—especially *Woman on the Edge of Time*— might more obviously give occasion, is examination of her narrative technique as a kind of literary manifesto for contemporary women writers. From this perspective, *Small Changes* suggests several by now almost commonplace strategies and principles, including the subversion of conventional narrative openings and closings; the intentionally didactic, oversimplified, even allegorical nature of the work and its characters; the use of what DuPlessis has called "multi-personed or cluster protagonists" to affirm the "feminine" values of "collectivity" and "interdependence"; the rich, even "exhaustive" and "obsessively observed"—details, often associated with stereotypically female interests such as the way space is arranged in various domiciles, or the way "life support" activities are managed.

Along these lines, I want to suggest that the narrative structure of **Small Changes,** built on the stories of two women, can be seen as an experiment, not in "the variety of lifestyles that women in our time are adopting," but in two alternative ways in which the woman writer can write, can represent the experience of women while using the only language available and the traditional forms and myths available to any writer. I want to suggest, that is, that Piercy, wary like Beth of language, investigates the possibilities and the limitations of two prominent ways in which the woman writer can appropriate the dominant discourse: either by inverting the classic male plot, as in Beth's story; or by revitalizing and perhaps "legitimating" a conventional female form of narrative, as in "the ongoing soap opera" of Miriam's life. **Small Changes** is in this regard not an optimistic novel; it reveals in both modes the difficulties as well as the possibilities of appropriation, the price that women pay, the resistance of the dominant discourse—a system that is not user-friendly, as Miriam might put it, when the user is a woman writing for women and hoping to "do" something with words.

The plot of Beth's story represents an example of the first possibility that is available to the feminist writer: the revolutionary use of a classic male narrative structure to portray a radical female experience. Beth's story is a version—and an inversion—of both the *Bildungsroman* (or even the *Kunstlerroman,* in which Beth is the artist as a young woman, unable to speak) and the melodrama. Endowed only with her seemingly innate feminist sensitivity—"She bruises easily," her mother says—Beth miraculously escapes imprisonment in the perpetual childhood of the married woman. She begins to educate herself, is recaptured, escapes again, and finally after many adventures meets the perfect woman and finds her true identity, both sexual and social, as a lesbian feminist. This plot is clearly presented as a romantic journey from darkness to light, a narrative of revolution and rebirth into a new and higher state. Appropriately, the climax of the story comes when the hero explicitly breaks the law she has already transgressed in private and escapes as nearly as possible, not just from her personal patriarchs, but from the patriarchal state as a whole. At the end of the novel, Beth goes underground, literally creating a new identity and renaming herself and her family. The maleness of this plot, despite its feminist twist, is underscored by the characterization of Beth. The name Jackson gives her—Peter Rabbit—is shown to be apt; although she loves women and is abused by men, she has few traditionally feminine traits and tastes. She is cool and dry, flat-chested and narrow-hipped; she hates to cook, travels light, and refuses to be caught in the reproductive cycle: "I can't be mothered and

I won't mother," she tells Miriam. Tellingly—and with the homoerotic overtones characteristic of the central male-male and female-female relationships in the novel—Miriam likes Beth because she seems, like Phil or Neil, more an equal than other women. At the same time, however, Beth's feminine capacity to love and care for others—for Wanda and her sons, in particular, and for the hypothetical patients she will treat if she becomes, as she plans, a paramedic—is validated by the ending of her story. Piercy may be attempting to suggest here what Lee Edwards has recently argued: that the woman hero challenges stereotypical associations of sex and behavior. "Permitted, like others of her sex, to love and nurture, to comfort, to solace, and to please," Edwards argues, "the heroic woman specifies these impulses as human, not just female, and endows them with a value that counters their usual debasement."

Where Beth and her plot, like the classic male story of education and adventure upon which it is built, are basically "simple and contained," Miriam and her story are "vast and yeasty," hopelessly complicated and archetypally feminine. The characters themselves suggest to us the specific genre of Miriam's story: as she herself says and as Jackson later repeats, she is the heroine of a soap opera. Closer analysis confirms and clarifies the significance of this point, as we see how Piercy manipulates narrative structure, point of view, and thematic elements so that Miriam's story corresponds in critical respects to the shape and style of the soaps, and is in sharp contrast to the story of the woman hero. The novel begins, for instance, with "The Book of Beth," in which we are introduced to the protagonist as she learns about herself, and thus we are given a sense, as in the typical *Bildungsroman,* of the freedom and capacity of the central character to grow, to make choices, and to take action. Miriam, by contrast, is first introduced in Beth's book as just one of a group of people with complex histories and relationships, a small but complete cast of characters whose lives are already—and only, and always—in progress when Beth tunes in. We later see Miriam and Phil but know no more than Beth does about their relationship at this point; in the penultimate chapter and narrative climax of "The Book of Beth," set on the day of the Street Fair, Dorine and Lennie and Beth walk in on Miriam and Jackson, who are in bed.

In "The Book of Miriam," which begins shortly thereafter, we are offered the testimony of Miriam's childhood, college days, and affairs with Phil and Jackson, in a lengthy reprisal that appears to introduce us to Miriam in the same way in which we were introduced to Beth. But when we have finally come again to that same point in narrative time where we were in Beth's Book—the day of the Street Fair—we already know what is going to happen. Our knowledge makes us perceive Miriam's experience much differently from the way we perceive Beth's: the soap-opera heroine is caught in predetermined circumstances, unable to choose or to act on her own. She is constrained by the narrative structure, and hence by the reader's foreknowledge, as much as by her own all too predictable desires.

Furthermore, as is that of any character in a good soap opera, Miriam's story is interrupted by other characters in a way that Beth's is not. In "The Book of Miriam," two chapters are in fact written from Phil's point of view; Miriam, who sometimes feels as if she is Phil's product—or his poodle—relinquishes control to him even in her titular story. In the third and longest section of the novel, "Both in Turn," the reader is farther from Miriam, especially in crucial scenes such as the party she gives, where we see her first through Beth's eyes, just as, in the last chapter, we see her through Helen's. The effect is that in general we *see with* Beth, where we often merely *see* Miriam.

Like a soap opera, and unlike Beth's evolutionary plot, Miriam's story is also one of continual and unfulfilled anticipation, obsessive and ungratified desire, and formless repetition. Miriam repeatedly thinks her dreams have at last come true—first when she meets Phil, then when she succumbs to Jackson, then when she marries Neil—but we soon see how blind she is and how little progress she makes. Again, the narrative structure highlights her self-deception: when Beth returns to Boston, finds Miriam married to Neil, and asks how it happened, Miriam clearly represses the all-important meeting in Washington with Wilhelm Graben; only later does she reveal to us how much this episode influences her decision to marry Neil and to have a baby. Her life is presented as a series of defeats, as her story moves relentlessly from one predictable scene to the next. Phil gets stoned and lets Miriam down, but makes Miriam feel that she has let him down; Jackson wins the chess game; Tom Ryan—or Wilhelm Graban, or Phil, or Neil—has sex with her while she is drunk, or unable to object, or too sleepy to use her diaphragm; Neil humiliates her for smoking marijuana when she is carrying "his" child, or for talking to the wrong people, or for spilling her drink, or for spoiling or neglecting Ariane. Occasionally Miriam even sees the predictability and shapelessness of her narrative. With Jackson, she feels unable to "shatter the web of myth," and toward the end of the novel, comments on the ironic exchange of roles that she and Dorine have undergone: "It's strange, Beth. As if our lives had no inner shape."

Contrast the exhausting, repetitious, shapeless series of defeats that Miriam experiences with the functional repetition in Beth's plot. When, for example, Jim's detective takes Beth back to Syracuse, and she has to escape from him all over again, what might look like a frustration, even a regression, of her development serves to demonstrate how Beth has in fact grown in moral stature and in heroic resolve. Juxtaposed in this way, the two escapes reveal Beth's development from passive resistance—before, she simply lied and evaded confrontation—to active, even aggressive self-defense, as she now takes up the bread knife and gets herself a lawyer. Whereas she simply boards a plane to Boston the first time she runs away—"She thought she would be less frightened to get on a plane and be in Boston in an hour and a half"—after her second escape she hitchhikes to California and back,

exercising her new self-reliance and earning her stripes (she has her first lesbian affair on the way) before returning to the women's house. Literally as well as figuratively the heroine covers much more space—"what a distance she had traveled beyond what she has been raised to"—than does the soap-opera heroine, who stays in the same small world—within easy range of Route 128—for the central part of the action.

And as in the soap operas, the predominant concern within Miriam's small world is the life of the emotions. She earns a Ph.D. in computer science from M.I.T. and speaks of the joys of work, but when "she understood that she was in love" with Jackson, she forgets everything else, "plans and projects and curiosities and relationships and speculations." She is not really committed to her career even in the beginning; she dreams of saving half her first year's salary, then taking a leave of absence or quitting to travel with Phil. By the time her second child is born—only three years after her "leave of absence" from Logical Systems Development—she feels totally unmarketable. Rationalizing her professional failure, Miriam might speak for all soap opera characters when she says "People are the most important thing to me." Again and again, in long stretches of dialogue or interior monologue, we hear of her obsessive desire to be loved, and we also hear the simple Freudian psychologizing that guides her—and most of the characters—in her thinking about love and sex.

The final and most emphatic similarity between Miriam's narrative and the genre of soap opera is its open-endedness. We do not know exactly what will become of Beth and Wanda, but the effect of the final two-page narrative of "Cindy" and "Marie," and their sons, and their dog Dean, is to seal off Beth's story. Our brief glimpse of this happy family sitting down to a meal of potato soup and discussing Cindy and Marie's plan to train as paramedics is as idealized and romantic as the happy ending of the most conventional novel. In our last view of Miriam, on the other hand, we witness yet another fight with Neil, who is already having an affair— soon to be revealed to us, unbeknown to Miriam—with his secretary. He leaves Miriam, and she sits alone in the dark house, thinking about her dreams, her love, her children, and her connections with Beth, Wanda, Dorine, Phil, Sally—the principal players in the cast. Although we know Miriam is still deceiving herself in her hope that she can regain Neil's love, we are—at least momentarily—invited to believe that the strength of her connections will enable her to survive, to recover her energy, and perhaps even to break the cycle of repeated defeat, not as Beth does in one fell revolutionary swoop, but through "the slow undramatic refounding, single thought by small decision by petty act, of a life: her life." This all-but-final vision of Miriam crouched in the dark, looking out at the streetlights, could encourage the reader to invent a future that takes the character out of a world of endless repetition without insisting that she become a heroine, a superwoman, or a lesbian separatist.

But *Small Changes* does not end with this plausible if limited optimism: instead, underscoring its affinities with the constitutionally endless soap operas, the last brief chapter of the novel—"Another Desperate Soprano (Helen)"—introduces a new heroine, mentioned in passing by Neil in the preceding chapter, and a new point of view. The story, however, is depressingly familiar: Helen is on the verge of taking Miriam's place in the plot, repeating her error, and fleeing gratefully from a hard, lonely life into the deceptive protection of Neil Stone's petrifying embrace. The final word in *Small Changes* implies that for every woman who manages to escape even a little, as Miriam might, there is another soprano waiting in the wings, doomed to reenact a plot that offers no relief from oppression, no freedom from endless anticipation and frustration of desire.

Piercy thus uses the double narrative in *Small Changes* to explore both the possibilities and the limitations of two available narrative structures, one male and one female, for speaking the unspoken and perhaps unspeakable story of women's lives. The feminist *Bildungsroman*, built on a culturally male model, facilitates the representation of a certain kind of revolutionary change, of individual growth and development in a woman's life; the soap opera more accurately presents and records ordinary women's experience. Each genre, as used in *Small Changes,* can be deployed to expose the oppression of women and to write stories that diminish the gap, for women, between reality and fiction, stories that do not betray the woman reader as Beth was betrayed by the fiction she once devoured, and stories that enable women to play the verbal game without turning into the oppressors. But neither mode is yet adequate to communicate a truly satisfactory vision of the as yet unrealized future in which no one is oppressed. *Small Changes* does not ask us to trust language and its present forms fully, but to remain wary of the ways in which literary conventions, like the world that produces and is shaped by them, "push women around"; and so from a late-twentieth-century feminist point of view each of the two characters and her story serves as a critique of the other.

Beth's story, the classic male narrative, works for women only if it is inverted to show the radical feminist's escape from rather than reintegration into society; in this way it may also reprivilege individual over collective values and cannot easily accommodate heterosexual relationships. At the same time that Beth's narrative thematically supports female bonding, Beth's individual heroism of necessity implies a rejection of traditional women's culture and, most problematical, of motherhood. Wanda breaks the law in order to keep her children; but if Beth had children, could she sacrifice them to her love for Wanda? Again, only because Beth will not be a mother is she free to act in a heroic plot. Miriam takes as much of a risk as she can to help Wanda because both are mothers—"Suppose they were my children? Of course she has to get them back." But she cannot go underground with her friends. She articulates precisely the limitations of Beth's career, the elitism that radical feminism can seem to perpetuate: "Come on, you call it the women's movement, but what

do you have for an ordinary woman? . . . What have you got for me? I love my kids and I don't burn banks down or run around the streets with picket signs."

In response to Miriam's indictment, Beth has no easy answer, but her thoughtful advice in turn exposes the inadequacies of soap opera from a feminist perspective. Above all Beth blames the isolation of woman that is the result of an excessively private life, a total investment of self in the male object of desire, and a mistaken belief that she is solely responsible for, and hence chained to, her children. The soap opera, as others have argued, could be said to affirm the collective character, the community, that the male narrative subordinates to the individual hero, but such a possibility is unrealized as long as the love of a man is the primary source of narrative action, and hence of meaning, in women's lives. Soap operas give narrative space to the experience of women in a way that the male plot cannot, but by replicating the web of myth they also serve to deny an ordinary woman the chance to escape its constraints.

Edith J. Wynne (essay date 1985)

SOURCE: "Imagery of Association in the Poetry of Marge Piercy," in *Publications of the Missouri Philological Association,* Vol. 10, 1985, pp. 57-63.

[*In the following essay, Wynne discusses emotional and psychological motifs associated with the imagery of Piercy's poetry.*]

Under the title, *Circles on the Water,* Marge Piercy published, in 1982, a collection of more than one hundred and fifty poems selected from seven of her previously published volumes. In the introduction to *Circles on the Water,* Piercy remarks,

> One of the oldest habits of our species, poetry is powerful in aligning the psyche. A poem can momentarily integrate the different kinds of knowing of our different and often warring levels of brain, from the reptilian part that recognizes rhythms and responds to them up through the mammalian centers of the emotions, from symbolic knowing as in dreams to analytical thinking, through rhythms and sound and imagery as well as overt meaning. A poem can momentarily heal not only the alienation of thought and feeling Eliot discussed, but can fuse the different kinds of knowing and for at least some instants weld mind back into body seamlessly.

Piercy's allusion to T. S. Eliot in her discussion of what poetry can do to integrate our ways of knowing is significant. While Piercy gives some attention to the relatively new psychological theory of opposing brain hemisphere functions, she also recalls the old debate between the functions of logic and emotion in the metaphysical poets, a group with which Piercy has some commonality in her imagistic techniques. Piercy's collected poems contain a startling array of images which, in their variety and number, in their apparently haphazard distribution, in their wide-ranging sensuousness, and in their seemingly antithetical juxtaposition of thought and feeling, create that kind of *discordia concors* so often associated with the metaphysical tradition. On the surface, Piercy's poems might aptly be described by Samuel Johnson's observation on the poet, Cowley:

> The most heterogeneous ideas are yoked by violence together; nature and art are ransacked for illustrations, comparisons, and allusions; their learning instructs, and their subtilty surprises.

Yet, Piercy's poetry does more than merely surprise and instruct. Eliot and other theorists have made commonplace the critical edict that the metaphysicals were able to express experience both emotionally and intellectually at the same instance. Piercy contends that, in her poems, the richness of thought and feeling possessed by all human beings informs her choice of images and brings a kind of unity out of chaos for us:

> That the poems may give voice to something in the experience of a life has been my intention. To find ourselves spoken for in art gives dignity to our pain, our anger, our lust, our losses. . . . We have few rituals that function for us in the ordinary chaos of our lives.

Piercy speaks directly to her readers in her own voice although she reminds us that the experiences she recounts are not always her own, nor are the poems confessional. She states that when she is writing she is not aware of any distinction between her own and other people's experiences, but that she is "often pushing the experience beyond realism." In this sense, Piercy creates a vortex of images which are often paradoxical but "reader-friendly." As Cleanth Brooks noted in his discussion of the language of paradox,

> The poet must work by analogies, but the metaphors do not lie in the same plane or fit neatly edge to edge. There is continual tilting of the planes; necessary overlappings, discrepancies, contradiction. Even the most direct and simple poet is forced into paradoxes far more often than we think, if we are sufficiently alive to what he is doing.

Piercy is such a direct and simple poet as Brooks describes, particularly in diction, tone, and form. She writes, she tells us, as a social animal and intends her poems not for other poets, but to be "of use" to the reader; she says, "I am not a poet who writes primarily for the approval or attention of other poets. . . . Poetry is too important to keep to ourselves." She admits to occasional didacticism and to conscious feminist politics; she believes that her poems "coax, lecture, lull, seduce, exhort, denounce." Her poetry reminds us in several ways of the metaphysical tradition but stripped of the intellectual pyrotechnics of that tradition.

Piercy's use of imagery is one of the major assets of her poetic technique. The title of the volume *Circles on the Water* provides a descriptive metaphor for the recurrent,

intertwined, echoic use of images so characteristic of her work. A few of her poems are built upon a single, extended metaphor; among these are "A work of artifice" in which a bonsai tree is compared throughout the poem to the stunted growth of a stereotyped female, and "The best defense is offensive" in which the actions of a turkey vulture are equated with a useful political stance. Much more typical of her work, however, is a lyrical, almost free-flowing series of images, built upon emotional and psychological associations rather than upon logical paradox or metaphysical conceit. Like circles on water created when a pool's surface tension is disturbed, her images form concentric, ever-widening patterns linked only by the energy and force of the precipitating experience. Usually, we are made fully aware of the initial event, for Piercy often begins with a narrative and maintains a strong sense of time and place. The force and energy of the image patterns is, therefore, one of the most exciting and unique qualities of the poems, but a quality not easily analyzed.

One of the poems which most clearly and dramatically displays the image-by-association artistry through which Piercy constructs an organic whole is **"Sign,"** written in 1967 and included in her first published volume, ***Breaking Camp.*** As in the majority of her poems, Piercy provides a dramatic narrative structure; an event in the present precipitates contemplation. In **"Sign,"** this event is quite commonplace—the poet discovers an emblem of aging:

> The first white hair coils in my hand,
> more wire than down.
> Out of the bathroom mirror it glittered at me.
> I plucked it, feeling thirty creep in my joints,
> and found it silver. It does not melt.

This brief opening stanza contains four images which are interwoven throughout the remainder of the poem in a carefully orchestrated, psychological point counter-point. The hair itself is the focal object, but one made up of several different sense impressions. The hair has color (white, then silver), texture (more "wire" than "down"), and substance (unlike quicksilver, it does not "melt" at body warmth). Furthermore, the hair is seen in a mirror, glitters, and is "plucked." Then, the poet feels thirty "creep" in her joints.

These visual, tactile, and kinaesthetic impressions of the hair are repeated in the next stanza, but within a completely different time and place:

> My twentieth birthday lean as glass
> spring vacation I stayed in the college town
> twangling misery's electric banjo offkey.
> I wanted to inject love right into the veins
> of my thigh and wake up visible:
> to vibrate color
> like the minerals in stones under black light.
> My best friend went home without loaning me money.
> Hunger was all of the time the taste of my mouth.

This shift to past time is perfectly natural; finding a white hair at thirty precipitates a realistic and commonplace reaction; the subject remembers her twentieth birthday. What is not so commonplace is the subtle, almost incremental, repetition of images from the first stanza, given new meaning in this different context. The mirror in which she first sees the hair is now transformed into her body, for she is "lean as glass." She spends time "twanging" an electric banjo "offkey," as in the first stanza she "plucked" the offending wire-like hair. Both actions call up misery, an emotion. At twenty, she twangs "misery's" banjo; at thirty, she experiences the misery of awareness of aging. The hair is, in its natural state, white or silver, almost colorless; at twenty, she had wanted to "vibrate color," but as minerals do, under "black" light. In both stanzas, the parts of the body receive attention. At twenty, she wished to inject love directly into "veins" and "thigh." At thirty, age is felt creeping into her "joints." Finally, in the second stanza, a new sense impression is added to the catalogue of recurrent images; "hunger" and "taste" provide a gustatory dimension which will be repeated in the third stanza, as the poet returns to present time:

> Now I am ripened and sag a little from my spine.
> More than most I have been the same ragged self
> in all colors of luck dripping and dry,
> yet love has nested in me and gradually eaten
> those sense organs I used to feel with.
> I have eaten my hunger soft and my ghost grows
> stronger.

The love which the subject wished to inject into thigh and vein in her twentieth year, when she was lean, constantly hungry, and eager for an awakening to visible self, has now "nested" in her and gradually "eaten" her sense organs. The aging process of which she has become dramatically aware causes her spine to sag, as a parallel to the creeping of age into her joints in stanza one. The hunger of her college vacation now consumes itself, but her "ghost" grows stronger although she is the "same ragged self" with "all colors of luck" within her. The word "ghost" appears intentionally ambiguous, open to several interpretations, all of which may best be treated after examination of the final stanza which brings together again the colors, textures, and motions of the opening lines:

> Gradually, I am turning to chalk,
> to humus, to pages and pages of paper,
> to fine silver wire like something a violin
> could be strung with, or somebody garroted,
> or current run through: silver truly,
> this hair, shiny and purposeful as forceps
> if I knew how to use it.

Once again, the color motif returns to become central to the message. Chalk and paper are white or colorless, as is the found hair. Humus is dark, as is black light, and as are youthful tresses. With these colors, attention to the ambiguity of aging is further disclosed. Darkness (or blackness) is both life-giving and death-dealing. Black light brings up colors in minerals; humus is fertile loam; dark hair is abundantly youthful growth. On the other hand, humus is soil, black soil, the earth to which we return in death. Black light is an artificial means which uncovers natural

mineral beauty hidden to the naked eye, just as death perhaps transforms the soul (or "ghost"), or as a mirror brings attention to the sign of aging. White is played upon equally paradoxically. Now the subject becomes white chalk and colorless paper, inert, yet potentially productive. The coarse white hair of the opening stanza has become "fine silver wire" strung into a violin, in sharp contrast to the wire strung into an offkey electric banjo in her twentieth year. Paradoxically, however, this same fine silver wire is associated with death by garroting or by electrocution. Finally, the hair shines as purposefully and usefully as forceps, instruments commonly associated with birth rather than death. The poet ultimately perceives in the silver wire-hair a power as ambiguous as the images employed to re-tell the experience. Life or death, creativity or repression, growth or stagnation—the meaning lies not within the discovered object itself, the emblem of aging, but within the human spirit. The ghost which grows stronger within the poet may be death or life; the outcome depends upon the qualifying clause, "If I knew how to use it."

This intensive study of the images in **"Sign"** demonstrates the intricate networking and intertwining of seemingly disparate elements which is one of the great strengths of Piercy's poetic vision. While not every poem in her canon is so full of leit-motifs as is **"Sign,"** patterns of psychological association appear in many other places in her work. A brief glance at three other pieces can identify the pattern. In **"Erasure"** from the volume *Hard Loving,* the poet's subject is the loss of a lover. Images of light, vision, and a mouse graphically convey the emotional impact of the experience. The poet moves from "blood turned grey," to a burning out of the "glittering synapses of the brain," to "stars fading in the galaxy," and on to a picture of the imaginary animal figures of the constellations that "would photograph more like a blurry mouse." Falling out of love she then defines as a "correcting vision" which nevertheless damages the optic nerve. The final lines of the poem powerfully unite all these loosely connected images:

> To find you have loved a coward and a fool
> is to give up the lion, the dragon, the sunburst
> and take away your hands covered with small fester-
> ing bites
> and let the mouse go in a grey blur
> into the baseboard.

A further example of Piercy's technique is found in the poem **"Some collisions bring luck"** which is from her third volume, *To Be of Use.* A chance meeting with a lover during the month of October provides the poem's speaker with momentary relief from the state of mind with which she opens the narrative:

> I had grown invisible as a city sparrow.
> My breasts had turned into watches.
> Even my dreams were of function and meeting.

The chance encounter is reported in the ten lines of the next stanza. The setting is a "pumpkin afternoon"; the lover is "bright rind carved into a knowing grin." The couple run upstairs, and at the lover's sexual touch, the poet "flew open." Soon, "orange and indigo feathers" break through her skin and she rolls in the lover's "coarse rag-doll hair." She sucks the lover "like a ripe apricot down to the pit." The images circle around the visions and colors of fall, orange and apricot, like the hair of a Raggedy-Ann doll. Once again, the concluding lines of the stanza switch from objects to emotions:

> Sitting crosslegged on the bed we chattered
> basting our lives together with ragged stitches.

In the closing stanza, the stitches do not hold, yet the warmth of the chance encounter in the October afternoon replaces the mechanical self expressed in the opening lines:

> Of course it all came apart
> but my arms glow with the fizz of that cider sun.
> My dreams are of mating leopards and bronze waves.
> We coalesced in the false chemistry of words
> rather than truly touching
> yet I burn cool glinting in the sun
> and my energy sings like a teakettle all day long.

One final example from the volume *The Twelve-Spoked Wheel Flashing,* a poem entitled **"The window of a woman burning"** will underscore what Piercy accomplishes with her rich imagery. The poem opens with what appears to be the realistic description of a woman caught up in a fire, her hair a "cone of orange snakes," as she writhes in flames. Quickly, however, the burning woman is differentiated from other martyrs; she is neither a Joan at the stake nor a crucified madonna or saint. She is, instead, "the demon of a fountain of energy," energy which flows from her brain, from her fiery hair:

> flickering lights from the furnace in the solar
> plexus, lush scents from the reptilian brain,
> river that winds up the hypothalamus
> with its fibroids of pleasure and pain
> twisted and braided like a rope,
> firing the lanterns of the forebrain
> till they glow blood red.

The next stanza emphasizes the strong fire-woman's dance, in "beauty that crouches / inside like a cougar in the belly / not in the eyes of others measuring." This transformed woman leaps through a green forest. In the final stanza, she becomes "the icon of woman sexual," who is "with the cauldrons of her energies / burning red, burning green." From the opening images of death by fire and sacrifice to the concluding image of red and green as life and growth in the sexual cycle, Piercy bombards the senses with quick, agile turns of impression that somehow hold together. What Marge Piercy accomplishes with her circling, concentric, seemingly disparate images is exciting, fresh, and flexible poetry as demanding of the reader as any metaphysical performance by Donne. With Piercy, as with Donne, we are always in touch with the human elements, body and mind, flesh and spirit. Piercy's purposeful and powerful use of images is perhaps most clearly stated in her own words. Introducing a series of poems based upon the Tarot deck, she says:

> We must break through the old roles to encounter our own meanings in the symbols we experience in dreams, in songs, in vision, in meditation. . . . What we use we must remake. Then only are we not playing with dead dreams but seeing ourselves more clearly, and more clearly becoming.

Piercy is, then, constructing a poetic vehicle through which old ways of seeing, old ways of knowing, are wrenched out of old contexts to be given new meaning. True to the feminist movement which she claims changed her life, she intends to break with linear, patriarchal patterns in favor of circles, moons, emotions superior to logic. These form a dialectic which teaches us, as she says in her recent poem **"Digging in":**

> You are learning to live in circles
> as well as straight lines

Sandra M. Gilbert (review date December 1985)

SOURCE: A review of *My Mother's Body,* in *Poetry,* Vol. CXLVII, No. 3, December, 1985, pp. 159-61.

[*In the following review, Gilbert offers tempered assessment of* My Mother's Body.]

It is hard to believe that the determinedly literary Amy Clampitt and the programmatically anti-literary Marge Piercy share a publisher. Rough-hewn and "realistic," preferring politics to poetics, Piercy has always presented herself as a raw-boned working-class woman, a woman whose name, as she comically observes in *My Mother's Body,* sounds "like an oilcan, like a bedroom / slipper, like a box of baking soda, / useful, plain. . . ." When I say that Piercy is anti-literary, I should note, I don't mean that she is in any sense against *writing,* but rather that she often seems to feel more strongly about what she says than she does about how she says it. Perhaps inevitably, therefore, she lapses at times into clumsiness, into editorializing, even into sloganeering.

"What Remains," the elegiac sequence for the poet's mother which opens this collection, is marred now and then by such lapses. Finding "a bottle-cap flower: the top / from a ginger ale / into which had been glued / crystalline beads from a necklace" among her dead mother's things, Piercy is moved in **"Out of the Rubbish"** to awkward (though socially accurate) meditation:

> A receding vista opens
> of workingclass making do:
> the dress that becomes
> a blouse that becomes
> a doll dress, potholders,
> rags to wash windows.

Similarly, in **"Why Marry at All?,"** one of the poems in the wedding sequence called **"The Chuppah,"** she becomes earnest and flat-footed in her eagerness to communicate key ideas—

> Why encumber our love with patriarchal
> word stones, with the old armor
> of husband and the corset stays
> and the chains of wife? Marriage
> meant buying a breeding womb
> and sole claim to enforced sexual service

—and the opening of her final stanza embarrassingly recalls those Sixties weddings where barefoot girls and boys swore groovy oaths of allegiance to each other on Vermont or California mountaintops:

> This is a public saying to all our friends
> that we want to stay together. We want
> to share our lives.

Again, the obviously heartfelt **"Homage to Lucille, Dr. Lord-Heinstein,"** seems almost parodic in its use of feminist and counterculture jargon. The heroine of this piece is a gynecologist who has "gently, carefully and slowly" opened "our thighs and our vaginas / and show[n] us the os smiling / in the mirror like a full rising moon." Enthuses Piercy:

> Your language was as gentle and caring
> as your hands. On the mantel
> in the waiting room the clippings hung,
> old battles, victories, marches.
> You with your flower face, strong
> in your thirties in the thirties,
> were carted to prison for the crime
> of prescribing birth control
> for workingclass women in Lynn.

I too admire "caring" women, but I care enough about their heroism to wish it could be more imaginatively recorded.

Luckily, despite some of these linguistic lapses, Piercy does—though sometimes, it seems, almost in spite of herself—produce a number of poems in *My Mother's Body* which offer more imaginative and vivid records of female heroism, of the joys of wedded love, and of the pleasures of daily life. As a whole, for instance, the elegiac **"What Remains"** is gravely moving in its expression of grief for the lost mother's hard and wasted life—for "the ugly things / that were" in this women's world "sufficient for every / day and the pretty things for which / no day of hers was ever good enough." And the sequence is poignantly impassioned, too, in its hope for transfiguration of the dead woman's ashes: ". . . just as I knew when you / really died, you know I have brought / you home. Now you want to be roses."

Perhaps less dramatically but just as vividly, the wedding ceremony of **"The Chuppah"** transcends the poet's intermittent proclivity for jargon when, in "Words plain as pancakes. / Simple as potatoes, homely as cottage cheese," she celebrates the ordinary pains and pleasures out of

which the extraordinary house of marriage is built. That this new volume ends with a careful but exuberant exploration of **"Six Underrated Pleasures"** (**"Folding Sheets," "Picking Pole Beans," "Taking a Hot Bath," "Sleeping with Cats," "Planting Bulbs,"** and **"Canning"**) suggests that Piercy's sometimes aesthetically problematic political commitment may ultimately arise from an aesthetically energizing talent for attention to the work and play of dailiness, a talent for understanding what is "useful, plain"— and frequently delightful.

Carmen Cramer (essay date Summer 1986)

SOURCE: "Anti-Automaton: Marge Piercy's Fight in *Woman on the Edge of Time,*" in *Critique: Studies in Modern Fiction,* Vol. XXVII, No. 4, Summer, 1986, pp. 229-33.

[*In the following essay, Cramer examines the female protagonist's struggle for autonomy and individuality in* Woman on the Edge of Time.]

Marge Piercy in ***Woman on the Edge of Time*** presents a classic American conflict based on the notion of *e pluribus unum.* In the United States' traditional ideal, the individual, capable of heroic action, forms society. In reality, that ideal is often eclipsed by society failing to recognize the individual. Connie, the main character in Piercy's 1976 novel, is such a negated individual due to her status as a woman, a Mexican-American, and a poor person, as well as a mental patient. ***Woman on the Edge of Time*** dramatizes the struggle between society and the individual by presenting the present culture in which the society controls the individual and a possible future culture in which individuals control society.

In the present culture, Connie is an "invisible" person. She speaks, and literally, no one hears. For instance, Connie tries to explain to a nurse that she does not feel well enough to stand in line for an half hour: "The medication makes me dizzy. I'll wait here," to which the nurse replies, "You're very confused [Connie]. It's time to line up for your lunch." Due to her invisibility, she is imprisoned in a state mental institution; a pimp commits her in an unconscious state and the doctors never listen to her explanation later. Connie is nonexistent because she is "merely" a woman, overpowered by Geraldo physically, and by both him and her brother Luis societally when she is institutionalized. Because her labels mean more to society than she does—abuser, Mexican, woman—no one hears what Connie says.

Connie is allowed no dignity in the present society that Piercy displays. This is partly because she is "not allowed"; she has no control over her own life. Constantly, important life decisions are made for Connie: a man forces her to abort her baby; medical students decide to sterilize her; the law takes away her two loves, Angelina and Claud;

and of course, a pimp commits her. Connie says of her lack of power: "All my life I been pushed around by my father, by my brother Luis, by schools, by bosses, by cops, by doctors and lawyers and case-workers and pimps and landlords. By everybody who could push." Only when she goes to college to learn what she wants does she feel vital and self-directed. This, too, though, is cut short by an "Anglo boy." With forced passivity of choice, Connie feels herself worthless, with nothing upon which to base self-respect. Likewise, in an ironic but realistic cycle, society—which has removed all of her choices—offers her no respect because she does not control her own life.

Even Connie's privacy is eliminated in her present society, privacy which is the hallmark of the individual heart and mind in a "free" society: "She was never alone, not even in the toilets without doors, never away from surveillance." This lack of privacy reinforces Connie's lack of choice, lack of power. She has no chance to think quietly, to move privately; therefore, she has no chance to take action. Without independent action, individuality does not exist, as illustrated by Gildina, the futuristic version of women controlled by society: "everybody's implanted. What's the good them knowing who, if they don't know where and how?" Gildina is watched and monitored for use by "them," the society's power-wielders, a terrifyingly similar situation to Connie's, especially as Piercy cleverly lets Connie meet Gildina only after the "electronic monitoring/controlling device" is implanted by men into her mind.

A societal automaton—whether mechanical or human—is no individual, and obviously cannot be a hero since heroism requires self-control, independent decisions, and action. Connie is being turned into an automaton, perhaps more quickly than the rest of the people in her culture because she is institutionalized; however, Piercy suggests that the rest of the people in the United States are not far behind Connie in losing identity to the society. Dolly, Luis, Claud, even the nurses, doctors, and social workers, each in his/her way is institutionalized and categorized rather than individualized.

Piercy provides an alternative of individualism, though, when she presents Mattapoisett, in the year 2137. Whether this future time and place are supposed to be fictionally real or are hallucinations in Connie's mind does not matter. What matters is the possibility—in Connie's understanding as well as in Piercy's—of a return to the ideal that individuals can form and control a society, rather than the other way around. The American tradition of *e pluribus unum* seems a paradox: that strong individuals do not negate a strong society. Mattapoisett, like the original concept of the United States, proves this paradox true.

In Mattapoisett, no person (and no "category" of persons) is invisible. Luciente, for instance, is seen and heard as the strong individual that she is. Even Connie respects Luciente, which causes her to assume that Luciente is a man: "she moved with that air of brisk unselfconscious authority Connie associated with men." Contrary to Connie's

cultural training, women and men in Mattapoisett are individuals rather than members of a class of people. In the present, Connie's mother tells her, "You'll do what women do," but in Luciente's world, each woman is educated (like any other "person") to know and be whatever is possible. Each Mattapoisett person is individualized by education which operates on personal choice: "But after naming, we go wherever we must to learn. . . . Where you go depends on what you want to study." Small children are encouraged to make independent decisions about their preferences.

Each person is treasured by the society, during childhood and adulthood, because each person's work is considered valuable: "To plant beans correctly is important. To smoke fish so it doesn't rot. To store food in vacuum. To fight well. . . . To make good decisions in meeting. To be kind to each other." This Mattapoisett attitude gives each individual dignity. Once children have been individually educated and encouraged to make decisions, they grow into self-determined adults. People in Mattapoisett control their individual lives and are also capable of controlling their collective lives through decision making. They gather to argue out their preferences, each knowing his/her mind well enough to express it, because of experience with personal preferences. As Luciente—the plant geneticist— illustrates, such choices are not hindered by class or economic status or sex.

To encourage both equality and individualism, a difficult combination, Mattapoisett people have redefined their population. Their test tube babies are from a genetic pool which eliminates generations of fixed race, creed, color. And these babies are nurtured by both men and women, allowing a society without fixed expectation for the sexes. As the man Barbarossa breast-feeds a child, Luciente explains that "at least two of the three [parents] agree to breast-feed. . . . We suspect loving and sensual enjoyment are rooted in being held and sucking and cuddling" for both men and women. Likewise, "poor" and "rich" as categories do not exist because Mattapoisett does not use money, but rather collective ownership is their economic mode, a mode that is repeated in the lack of ownership and power of people over others. Such equality is reflected in the language: pronouns have been revised to eliminate sex differentiation; Luciente is curious about the word "poor" in Connie's culture; and the citizens of Mattapoisett have no names which imply possession of people, such as Connie has always known with her identifying Consuelo (Connie) Camacho Alvarez Ramos.

People in Mattapoisett enjoy community because they have preserved privacy. Each person has his/her personal space: "We each have our own space!" Luciente exclaims, amazed that Connie would think otherwise. This privacy encourages personal dignity and self-respect which is essential if people are to respect each other: "How could one live otherwise? How meditate, think, compose songs, sleep, study? . . . We live *among* our family." Mattapoisett has developed a society of independent people who can be interdependent, rather than Connie's present society which encourages dependence. Luciente's people know that they must struggle together to preserve each person's privacy and individuality to keep their society healthy. This is reflected in their constant war with overly mechanized, overly masculinized cultures: "Technology is imbalanced. Too few have too much power. . . . We must fight to come to exist, to remain in existence."

Piercy's conflict in *Woman on the Edge of Time* arises out of Connie's new awareness from her visits to Mattapoisett that she too can struggle against a Gildina-world, a present-world: "The war raged outside her body now, outside her skull, but the enemy would press on and violate her frontiers again as soon as they chose their next advance. She was at war." Her war is to win back her individuality, lost to the "flacks of power." In Mattapoisett, Connie feels self-respect; she is reminded of unclassified love; Connie experiences action. She takes these with her back to Rockover State Hospital and begins her fight. Piercy gives Connie "the rich fictional possibilities inherent in the struggle of women."

Connie finds that she is capable of independence, of individual choice, and of action when she poisons the doctors at Rockover. She consciously strikes out at her captors, despite their probable retaliation:

> I just killed six people. . . . Because *they* are the violence-prone. Theirs is the money and the power, theirs the poisons that slow the mind and dull the heart. Theirs are the powers of life and death. I killed them. Because it is war. . . . I'm a dead woman now too. I know it. But I did fight them. I'm not ashamed. I tried.

Through her action against the power-wielders, Connie makes an independent action in order to protect a worthwhile society. Even though death—in one form or another—may be the outcome of her choice, Connie would have a worse death if she had not acted; she would have continued in invisibility in a society overwhelmed with itself. Through her decision to struggle, Connie saves individuality and in doing that she is helping to save her society, *e pluribus unum.*

The conflict on which *Woman on the Edge of Time* is based is the same as Connie and Luciente's conflict: can the individual be preserved? Connie, against all odds, takes independent action, and Piercy writes a novel in which a hero exists. In modern American novels, the anti-hero, the entropic and passive person, generally looms central, because authors forget to struggle with possibility, forget that there may still be a future." Piercy looks to possibility and dares to create a modern hero. A hero, by definition, must be an individual more powerful—due to her will—than society itself. Marge Piercy gives her protagonist exposure to the hopeful future in Mattapoisett, so that Connie conquers her society heroically.

Hilma Wolitzer (review date 10 May 1987)

SOURCE: "Women at War," in *The New York Times Book Review,* May 10, 1987, p. 11.

[*In the following review, Wolitzer offers qualified praise for* Gone to Soldiers, *citing flaws in the novel's excessive length and lack of focus.*]

The battlefront has historically been the literary province of men and the home front that of women. Of course there have been exceptions, notably Virginia Woolf's "Mrs. Dalloway," a slender novel in which she covered both fronts brilliantly in a single domestic postwar day. Now Marge Piercy attempts the same synthesis, but on a vast scale and with varying degrees of success.

Gone to Soldiers, Ms. Piercy's most ambitious novel to date, follows the lives of 10 main characters, their families, friends and lovers throughout World War II. The extensively researched book gives the reader a strong sense of the war's events and locations, with sustained sections set in both the European and Pacific theaters as well as the United States. The disruption of civilian life and the weariness and terror of battle are shown in great detail. Occasionally, there is a distracting pedantic tone, as when the acronyms and full names of various organizations are given consecutively, or the action is halted for exposition.

The war is the focus for the novel's various characters, some of whose lives will converge before it is over. The most memorable are two larger-than-life heroines, a French-Jewish teen-ager named Jacqueline Lévy-Monot and an American bomber pilot named Bernice Coates. Though they never meet, there is a vital connection between them: Bernice's brother, Jeff, becomes Jacqueline's colleague in the Jewish underground and her lover. The two women have other things in common, especially their need to escape domineering fathers. The widowed Professor Coates is oppressive in his control of Bernice, whom he has appointed his permanent housekeeper. Her long-dead mother, whose "Latin and Greek were far superior to The Professor's," is only a vague role model; it is the war and Bernice's talent and love of flying that finally free her.

As the war progresses, Jacqueline becomes less antagonistic toward her Zionist Papa, partly because they are allied in their resistance work. We also learn, eventually, that Jacqueline's mother and her younger sister Rivka have both perished in the Dora-Nordhausen concentration camp. (Rivka's twin, Naomi, had been sent while it was still possible to live with relatives in Detroit.) Their father is implicated in the twins' disparate destinies through a tragic decision, reminiscent of "Sophie's Choice."

In all novels, but especially in a war novel, the writer makes godlike choices, and it is to Ms. Piercy's credit that the casualties in *Gone to Soldiers,* except in the concentration camps, seem as random as in real life. She does not kill off her less interesting characters, as she might have done, as a matter of convenience, but gives them equal space, which made this reader impatient to return to the more interesting ones. Neither Louise Kahan, a popular-fiction writer; her former husband, Oscar; nor his young lover, Abra Scott, held my attention long. Despite their varied involvement in America's defense work, their self-involvement seems to overshadow the war.

The other major characters are more engrossing, but none so much, to my mind, as Jacqueline and Bernice. Most of Jacqueline's chapters are (in the tradition of Anne Frank and Etty Hillesum) diary entries. We watch her evolve from a rather vain and anti-Semitic young woman to a courageous worker for the Jewish underground. The wrenching account of her experiences in Auschwitz and on the Polish death march is the most powerful section of the book.

Bernice has a quirky charm. She is an ungainly and uncertain young woman who becomes graceful and self-assured at the controls of a plane: "The things that mattered . . . she was good at." The rendering of her sexual confusion, and its resolution in her love for another woman, is convincing and moving.

Most of Marge Piercy's work, both poetry and fiction, has been concerned with feminist issues, and *Gone to Soldiers* is no exception. Jacqueline's and Bernice's struggles with their fathers, and Bernice's search for her sexual identity, are important elements of the book, as are the imposed and chosen war-time roles of men and women. In many male war novels character development is sacrificed; the "woman's touch" here is excellent. The battlefront is not all blood and guts—there is also the grief of separation from family and the mitigating solace of friendship. On the home front there are race riots as well as ration books, and the heartbreak of shattered families.

I very much admire the ambition and heart of *Gone to Soldiers,* an enormous, well-meaning novel, but I wish it were shorter and more concentrated, less exhaustively thorough and more focused.

Judith Wynn (review date 10 May 1987)

SOURCE: "Piercy's Big War: 'Soldiers' is Not the 'Good' Fight Nostalgia Recalls," in *Chicago Tribune Books,* May 10, 1987, p. 3.

[*In the following essay, Wynn offers praise for* Gone to Soldiers.]

Intricately braided plots, salt-of-the-earth characters, hearty cuisine and copulation down among the counterculture—these are a few of Marge Piercy's favorite things.

Then there's her civil rights and women's liberation activism—as well as her regularly voiced conviction that the United States is steering a rocky, vainglorious course to disaster. In *Fly Away Home,* the heroine's once-idealistic slumlord husband tried to obtain his goals by burning down his own house. *Woman on the Edge of Time* posited a hellish futuristic America run entirely by and for the

"Rockemellons" and the "DukePonts." Piercy has been accused of writing didactic potboilers yet, for her, art is always political.

Her latest, *Gone To Soldiers*—which answers the musical question, "Where have all the young men gone?"—is Piercy's most gripping, ambitious work to date. Although the story gets off to a ponderous start as the author erects her complex superstructure and limns the historical background in passages that are occasionally redolent of the research stacks, all in all she's done a skillful job interweaving the adventures of six young women and four young men caught up in the military/political cataclysm of World War II.

Unlike Herman Wouk's World War II epic, "Winds of War," there are no portraits herein of the Great: Roosevelt, Churchill, etc. Instead, Piercy studs her narrative with cameos of little-known movers and shakers: aviatrix Jacqueline Cochran, founder of the Women's Air Force Service Pilots (WASP); cryptanalyst William Friedman, who broke Japan's diplomatic code in 1940.

As the story opens, the Great Depression has given way to wartime boom. The United States is fighting for survival, its eastern coast littered with debris from American casualties to German U-boats. But even this worthy conflict, our last "good" war, is full of contradictions. And Piercy misses few of them. Although at war with racist Nazis, Washington, D.C., of the early 1940s is an overgrown Southern town, segregated down to its last toilet and drinking fountain. Race riots rage in Detroit. Jew-baiting divides U.S. soldiers in the Pacific theater.

As for American women—yes, the war transforms their lot for the duration; millions enter the mainstream labor force though most of them will be sluffed off after VJ Day by a postwar economy that no longer needs them.

It's against this strife-torn background of social upheaval that Piercy turns to what she does best: unleashing a diverse cast of characters to ricochet off one another in various unexpected ways.

First come the New York intellectuals and think-tank specialists. Energetic Louise Kahan writes popular romances and leftwing journalism. As a government propagandist, she reluctantly uses guilt and glamor images to sell the war to American women. In between assignments, Louise wrangles with her ex-husband (Imagine "His Girl Friday" with a Jewish Rosalind Russell and Cary Grant), rides hard on her bobby-soxer daughter, and beds down a young decoder who works for the OSS, a CIA forerunner. She will eventually cover the liberation of Paris for Colliers magazine and view the Nazis' grisly treasure-horde of Jewish plunder in defeated Germany.

Meanwhile, out in the American heartland, another sexual triangle develops among spinster Bernice and her secret-agent brother's lover, Zach, who helps supply the French

Resistance. Zach teaches Bernice to fly planes and considers her a pretty good lay for a woman; she runs off to join the WASPs, concluding that, on the whole, she'd rather be a man, too.

And finally, there's the Parisian Jewish Levy-Monot family who are scattered—some into concentration camps, some into hiding—when the Nazis enter France. Rebellious teenager Jacqueline becomes a hero of the Pyrenees-based Jewish Resistance before she's abducted to Germany. Her little sister Naomi is smuggled past hostile U.S. immigration authorities to live with working class relatives in Detroit.

Piercy is boldly incisive, whether depicting Auschwitz savagery or domestic terrorism in the "normal" American household. Margaret Atwood once observed that Piercy's vigorous, occasionally awkward diction suggests that she has never taken a creative writing class. If not, that lapse may partly account for her unselfconscious, forward-thrusting narrative pace, which steadily accelerates through *Gone To Soldiers* as cliffhanger follows riveting cliffhanger. Capture, escape, exhilaration and despair and brutal holocaust follow in masterful order, capped by a disturbing picture of Americans fighting their way—first and foremost—to a higher living standard, into "an advertisement full of objects they had coveted but never owned and seldom even touched."

Gone To Soldiers presents aspects of a World War II that are antithetical to late-show movie nostalgia. Piercy's war may not be the "good" fight one prefers to remember, but it happened, too, and *Gone To Soldiers* brings it vividly home.

Ron Grossman (review date 5 July 1989)

SOURCE: "'Summer People' Ideal for Season," in *Chicago Tribune Books*, July 5, 1989, p. 3.

[*In the following review, Grossman offers favorable assessment of* Summer People.]

Whatever Marge Piercy's other virtues—and her literary ones are considerable—she is shamelessly disrespectful of the commandment against fouling one's own nest.

In her 10th novel, Piercy has set the ultimate summer romance on Cape Cod, where she herself lives. Resort towns, Piercy says, operate on a Manichean morality that divides the human race in two. "Summer people" are always strangers, no matter how many seasons they keep coming back. Year-round residents, though, are forgiven virtually any transgression.

So it is with Dinah, Susan and Willie. They have been on the Cape of Piercy's novel for so long that the community has virtually forgotten that each was born someplace else. Scarcely noticed, too, is that they are a menage a trois.

"They were an old and respected public scandal," Piercy observes.

Willie and Susan came first. He a sculptor, she a clothing designer, they fled New York so their kids could have a healthier place to grow up. They also needed to get away from Manhattan rents. Susan doesn't like to work too hard, and Willie's personal muse is always a few years behind or ahead of the current interest of cutting-edge collectors.

"Willie liked to create humanoid figures trying to crawl out of coffins, reaching through barbed wire or slats," Piercy reports. "Some of them involved tapes of unpleasant noises like screaming and gunfire."

Dinah, an avant-garde composer, bought the next cottage over from Willie and Susan as a place to tend her poet husband through his final battle with cancer. After his death she, Willie and Susan rediscovered Euclid's proposition that a triangle is the stablest configuration.

For Susan and Willie, their separate but equal involvement with Dinah has kept their own marriage alive. Without it, they, like many couples, would have inflated each other's shortcomings, discounted their strengths.

For Dinah, the arrangement lets her put out of mind nagging questions about who she is and/or ought to be. For the sake of her music, she always wanted a life unencumbered by family responsibilities, an attitude that was only reinforced by her short, tragic marriage. But her father, a Holocaust survivor, argued that it was her duty to help restore the Jews by having children.

Fortunately for her sanity, Dinah discovered that when you go to bed with the man next door in the morning and his wife in the evening, there isn't much energy left for debating your own identity.

Alas, after 10 years, their three-way tranquillity dissolves, and each becomes entangled in the vacation-time involvements of summer people. Writing about sex isn't particularly difficult, especially since recent court decisions have greatly increased authors' erotic vocabulary. The tradition of analyzing what makes the heart tick goes back to Ovid and Sappho.

This reviewer, though, knows no other writer with Piercy's gifts for tracing the emotional route that two people take to a double bed, and the mental games and gambits each transacts there.

Accordingly, there are many hours of beach-reading pleasure in Piercy's novel. My guess is that, from Martha's Vineyard to Malibu, readers will take their eyes off her pages only long enough to try guessing which of the local summer people might be doing what with whom this season.

Judith Wilt (essay date 1990)

SOURCE: "'We Are Not Dying': Abortion and Recovery in Four Novels by Women," in *Abortion, Choice, and Contemporary Fiction: The Armageddon of the Maternal Instinct,* University of Chicago Press, 1990, pp. 67-100.

[*In the following excerpt, Wilt examines feminist themes surrounding reproduction, maternity, and Piercy's explicit argument for abortion rights in* Braided Lives.]

The decade which saw the institutionalization of the right not to become a mother saw many women writers affirming daughterhood more powerfully than ever. If, as George Eliot says, every limit is a beginning as well as an ending, so also the response to a removal of limits may be an instinctive grasp at an anchor—mother, or motherhood.

In Joan Didion's *Play It as It Lays* (1970) and Margaret Atwood's *Surfacing* (1972), the abortion on which the plot hinges is an encounter with nonbeing, which threatens the extinction of female personality. The plot conflates the imaginary recovery of the lost child with the recovery of the mother and of the self. In Didion's existential romance the aborted fetus was quite simply "the point" of being itself, the winning point in the game, key point in the argument, a point tragically and stupidly conceded to the philosophical nothingness and cultural emptiness which encroach at every level. In Atwood's Hemingwayan quest the empty space of the protagonist's womb acquires grim personification as death itself until the lost child surfaces in vision as the protagonist's mother, god, grail, self. Mary Gordon's Felicitas, protagonist of *The Company of Women* (1980), suffers in vision this same presence: abortion is her death, death itself. She averts it, but only the many mothers of the company, recovered to her by her crisis, make the birth and survival of the new child and the new Felicitas possible.

Not until 1982, as the pro-life movement gathers momentum, do we find a full-throated cry for abortion rights in Marge Piercy's *Braided Lives.* This novel's stern and vulnerable poet-protagonist, undergoing at seventeen a nearly ruinous home abortion prepared by her fearful mother, lays the key on the table about the dark side of maternal desire: "Only I will know how I sometimes dream of that small changeling dribbling love on my breasts and how sick is that dream quivering with power. It would love me, poor bastard; it would have to." The chapter in which this morally strict choice is made is called "The Agon."

All these novels are set in those prelegal days when abortion itself meant an intimacy with death for the woman as well as the fetus. The heroines mostly experience both the choice that ends in birth and the choice that ends in abortion as male plots, part of the network of "sick arrangements," as Didion's protagonist calls them, by which patriarchy manipulates women, coming or going, into the structures of its normalcy. The female counterplot inevitably turns on some kind of outlawry. Didion's Maria Wyeth and Atwood's nameless narrator skirt the edges of madness. Piercy's Jill Stuart forms an illegal abortion referral service. Even Gordon's Felicitas Taylor, who chooses against the abortion plot and makes a determined effort to adjust to "ordinary life. . . . the daughter of my mother, the mother of my daughter, caretaker of the property, soon to be a man's wife," wears that camouflage of the ordinary uneasily, afflicted still with a noble and "specific hunger" for an as yet still alienated relationship with the absolute, with the sacred, with God.

The female counterplot also strives to transform the deaths of ordinary life, aborted fetus, aborted woman, into life. "We are not dying" is the elated final judgment of Felicitas's once-endangered daughter on her once-endangered and still not fully-actualized mother. "Take my death inside. Give birth to me!" cries the specter of Jill's beloved cousin, Donna, dead in a self-induced abortion, and "I will," Jill answers. *Sine qua non,* the value of not dying, of giving birth, survives in these novels, whether attached to blood motherhood or not. . . .

Braided Lives: Women Giving Birth to Women

Mary Gordon, though she can see the possibility of "a radical life," does not depict one. Marge Piercy does. ***Braided Lives*** is a flat-out feminist analysis of the fight for women's freedom and a call, in the face of the conservative rollback of the 1980s, for confirmation of the first article in that feminist bill of rights, reproductive freedom. The objects of the several abortions which braid the novel's plot are never understood to be babies, as in the other three books studied here. Pregnancy always symbolizes possession by one of the three forces—male lovers, the myth of motherhood, the truths of the female body itself—which in this society seek dominance over, instead of harmony with, the fourth force in life, the drive for female selfhood. The book is unashamed of its existence as argument but succeeds as a human story because of the passion of its argument, and because the protagonist sustains in the end a love for all humans: man and child as well as woman, for mother as well as self, for the body as integral with, and to, the will.

But Jill Stuart bears no children. Her fertility and creativity takes the form of seven books of poems (Piercy herself had written seven volumes at the time of ***Braided Lives***), and her human empathy takes the form of an increasingly confident participation in the right-to-life issues of the 1950s and 1960s: save the Rosenbergs, ban the bomb, feed the black children of Mississippi. And give life to women dying from botched abortions. Placed tellingly at the climax of the description of the self-induced abortion Jill barely survived at age seventeen in 1954 is this flashforward to a birth differently chosen, fiercely wanted:

> Brooklyn, 1963. The doctor botched the abortion. She is hemorrhaging. I am one of a group of women who help other women secure abortions. . . . Now this woman, fat, gentle, in her late 30's and the mother of

5, is bleeding like a slaughtered pig—like I did. I pack her vagina with ice. I hold her against me, a woman twice my size and twice my body weight, and rock her like a baby. . . . Live, live, I whisper to her, dear one, sweetheart, angel darling, live. Only live.

In her forties, a successful poet and lecturer, in the 1980s a feminist activist, Jill Stuart looks back on a life "braided," and abraded, with the lives of two key women, her mother and her cousin, Donna Stuart. "Were I pointing out a different pattern in the weave," the poet says, other women's lives would stand out as strands in the braid. But in this pattern the unifying topos is abortion; the central figures are the mother, who "is scared of the world and thinks if she punishes me first, I will be broken down enough to squeak through," and the pretty blond cousin, "like negative and photo—me dark and you light," who, like Jill's mother a generation before, tries to have her freedom within the complicit terms of, under the cover of, conformity to feminine stereotypes.

In the eight years of the novel's main focus—Jill's adolescence in Detroit, college in Ann Arbor, and early adulthood in New York City—classic battles between mother and daughter break all but one thread of that strand. Her own birth, Jill speculates, both cause and result of that "love, cannibal love," which is the other side of maternal self-denial, initiated the war. But the narrative of the forty-three-year-old Jill is rich with slowly surfacing insight about the unbreakable last thread, the desire between women, especially between mother and daughter, for a final non-cannibal form of love. The daughter's understanding of the mother increases: "She is a figure shaped by troubles I will never have to know. Sometimes I do listen, even if what I hear isn't what she is trying to tell me." As time goes on, understanding offers both a warning and a healing.

> A year goes by while she never takes a cigarette out. Then one evening after supper on a day that feels no more unusual than any other, she appears with a slender brown cylinder cupped elegantly between her fingers, acting in her own movie. Then I see in her the young beauty from the slums, studying seductive graces in darkened theaters. All she had to save herself was encompassed in being female.

Having thus internalized "femininity" from the movies, from American culture of the thirties and forties, Jill's mother sensed the danger as her daughter grew up rough, self-motivated, ambitious for education, mysteriously committed to the uncertain life of a writer, and desirous of the rich and sometimes dangerous experiences that feed a writer's omnivorous imagination. The battle to "break" her daughter to the accepted female stereotype emerges from fear for her. What it bred in Jill was a ferocious desire to make her own choices: "I will escape you all. I will choose what I do." Mother and motherhood, even daughterhood, become the enemy of choice-defined self. Rejecting all such ready-made roles, Jill nevertheless wins the beauty with the cigarette—the fear-ridden, punishing mother, the woman born into troubles—with the rock-bottom identity of poet and lover she creates for herself.

My mother; the miracle is that in middle age we are friends. . . . Why did she stop disapproving of me? She likes the row of books. . . . Now that I am in my forties, she tells me I'm beautiful . . . and we have the long, personal, and even remarkably honest phone calls I always wanted so intensely I forbade myself to imagine them. . . . I am deeply grateful. With my poems, I finally won even my mother. The longest wooing of my life.

This relationship ends in lifegiving friendship, though its adult phase began with the devouring mother, witchlike and deadly, fearing the silent, destroying force of the father but complicit with his values, enforcing on the pregnant, seventeen-year-old daughter a home made abortion which nearly killed her.

The other key relationship in the braid ends in tragedy, though it began with physical and emotional love making between the thirteen-year-old cousins, Donna and Jill. Meeting again at college, the two women form a nonsexual, a metaphysical bond: "We strike against each other, chipping off the useless debris of our childhood. What one of us bites into, the other chews and swallows. . . . We define each other." Donna, the bond, "negative" female image, anxious to move into the schizophrenic world of 1950s femininity, rushes into secret sex and forces herself into "love" and towards marriage with Jim, with Lennie, finally with Peter. Jill, Piercy's "positive" female image, reluctantly follows, imitating, with Mike, with Peter, with Kemp, finally with Howie. Donna fits her body into "iron-maiden bras" and high-heeled shoes, brightly and consciously seeking freedom through "accepting my destiny as a woman," while inexplicable rages of resentment and self-loathing overpower her regularly: one of them results in her death by self-induced abortion. Jill, seeking to center life "on some good work you want to do," experiences obsessions, loneliness, failures, but survives as the "scavenger," the "alley cat," finally the artist that she wants to be.

In this leapfrogging, braiding, finally diverging relationship between women, abortion is the key symbol for both Donna's and Jill's kind of "freedom." First to enter a sexual relationship, Donna is first to fear pregnancy and seek money for an abortion. Trying to borrow money from her lover for this project, Jill finds him truculently "siding with the fathers . . . who say no to women" on the basis of sweeping generalizations about the sacredness of life. She responds, "That's just words. A fancy position for a man to take. I mean it. I care about Donna. I'm willing for chickens and cows to die to feed her, and this embryo to keep her free."

Donna's plight turns out to be a false alarm this time, but later that summer Jill takes Donna's place in the female predicament for real, because she gave in to her lover's desire (he cited, poet to poet, man to woman, the dictums about "the natural" from D. H. Lawrence) to stop using condoms, "that damn armor." Remembering his earlier attitude, knowing he won't marry her and won't free her for an abortion, Jill hides the fact from her lover, but her mother uncovers the truth. Obliquely hating/protecting her daughter, siding with the father—"If you go roaming around to doctors, and you can't trust a one of them, only in it for the money, I'll tell your father and he'll make you have it"—Jill's mother puts her through several harrowing home remedies. Finally, while gunshots from the father's TV western echo from the living room (the representation of pregnancy as gun appears again) and her mother holds her mouth to keep her silent, Jill carries out her choice in its enforced primitive mode: "Now I will go to work attacking my body in earnest . . . by force I open my womb."

The rhetoric of attack Piercy uses here is carefully limited. It is not herself or her life, or a fetal life identified with hers, or even with her lover's that Jill feels she needs to attack. Rather it is the unruly body, cells subdividing without her volition, which she needs to confront, cherish, and rule, so that it can bear her free self. Jill had considered suicide, but a powerful will to live and to experience the variety of life dissolved that desire. After the abortion she lives a sexless life for a time—"sex . . . seems to me a device for converting will and energy into passivity and flesh"—but that kind of self-mutilation does not last either.

She makes friends with her body again through two simple expedients: she buys a diaphragm—"my first passport, something magical that permits passage out"—and she begins to collect the names of, and the personal funds for, competent abortionists for herself and any other woman in danger. The following year, ready to contract her upper-class dream marriage, Donna becomes pregnant after a rape from a lower-class hoodlum she had dated in one of her self-condemning fits of rage at herself and at that very dream. And Jill, deploring the feminine dream but steadfastly preserving Donna's freedom to pursue it, takes all necessary steps, even thievery, to procure money for an illegal but medically safe abortion.

It is interesting to note the ambiguous and important role of "the doctor" in this novel. He is cleanliness and training; he is safety, sought more heatedly than the lover, he is a necessary third presence in the procedure. Self-induced abortion, as represented here, seems much too close to suicide, not only pragmatically (the woman is untrained) but symbolically (the woman is deeply at odds with her own body). Yet he is still a man, not, finally, to be trusted.

This ambiguity locates itself in a metaphorical displacement, at a few key moments, of "the doctor" by "the dentist." At virtually the same time that she is helping Donna with the abortionist, Jill provides the money and the energy to get her mother to the dentist for work on her bad teeth. To the family's shock and rage, the dentist simply extracts all Mrs. Stuart's teeth, sound ones and decaying ones alike. The dire image of "dark blood welling" in the mouth here recapitulates and anticipates the abortion motif. Both procedures, necessary to health yet associated with damage, performed by men for money on

the bodies of women who submit not exactly from choice but to keep open the possibility of choice, combine elements of woe and success for the women who rage at them while desiring them. Jill helps a friend rob a dental supply store for Donna's abortion money. Later, fetus successfully aborted, engagement back on track, Donna persuades the wealthy, intelligent, handsome, and faintly sinister Peter Crecy to marry her quickly: "Fast is painless. Like pulling a tooth."

Marriage for Donna is growing up, accepting womanhood, giving order to life. Her "work," she thinks, is her husband, Peter, a man in rebellion against his father and yet in training to be a junior patriarch just like him. Helpless to prevent it, sliding in her cousin/alter ego's wake towards marriage with Howie, her friend and lover, Jill watches Donna plan the compromises, engage in the psychic denials, of modern "femininity." She defines health as love and domesticity and the career in television news she clearly desires and thrives on as merely a temporary expedient until "the relationship" and its finances settle down. Peter has agreed, she thinks, to postpone children indefinitely, so when she finds a tiny hole in her diaphragm she responsibly buys a new one, celebrating at the same time the "instant respectability" that Jill attains when she announces her engagement to Howie.

Donna believes, genuinely, that Howie will "save" Jill, as Peter "saved" her, through marriage, from the "bad patterns," the disorderly-looking life—"Destroying myself. Ending up alone and crazy. Winding up a two-bit whore"—which is the only alternative society can envision for unmarried women. The major break-through in Jill's artistic life, a new, personal, poetic voice freed by an encounter with the poetry of Allen Ginsberg, goes by unrecognized by anyone but herself as she leaves Donna, her "negative" twin, the bright but self-denied woman she wanted to truly save, in New York while she goes to Detroit to be inspected by prospective in-laws.

When Jill returns the novel's tragic climax has occurred. The death by abortion that has lain in the braided lives of women since the novel's opening, fended off at seventeen by Jill, is taken instead by the conflicted, compromised, self-loathing, twenty-three-year-old Donna, "grown up" to her schizophrenic and finally deadly destiny as a woman. The novel's last "rose of blood" blooms under Donna's body on the sheets of Jill's apartment. And Jill, notifying Peter of a death whose nature he somehow knows before he is told, remembering the "small hole, like a pinprick" in Donna's diaphragm, grows "cold, cold through," like the corpse on the bed. She believes he has pricked a hole in the diaphragm, deliberately made Donna pregnant without her consent or knowledge, killed her.

At the funeral it is all Jill can do to resist signing her name "Donna" in the visitors' book, so sunk is she in guilty identification with the lost twin, with the deadly archetype of femininity which Donna represents: the ancient fatality of women who either make a dead life bearing children to a betraying man, or who would rather die than give birth.

Separation from this archetype of femininity has been the struggle of Jill's life. A period of dreams and madness not unlike that undergone by the protagonist of Atwood's *Surfacing* climaxes at the novel's end with the mythic birth of a new and redeeming Donna. While Jill walks the night streets a bloody and ghostly Donna, "sharp ivory doppelganger," wails for entrance like some frail indestructible Catherine Earnshaw.

> "Leave me alone! Take me with you! It's cold and it hurts. It's getting colder. Mother. Make it stop! Momma! Momma!" "I will take you with me. I will!" "Take my death inside. Give birth to me!" "I will."

Donna's voice, ambiguously that of child to mother, of aborting woman, or more deeply, of aborted woman, to self-saved woman, uses the ancient language of birth. Jill's "I will," unlike Heathcliff's, which signals his final obliterating immersion in his demon, represents not possession but parturition, the erasure of abortion as death, the inauguration of a wider motherhood. It crystallizes at the end the early image of woman giving birth to woman that rode under the enactment of Jill's abortion at seventeen. Its material embodiment is an underground network of safe abortion referrals called "Donna." This network functioned through the 1960s as that "small female government [of] conspirators and mutual advisors" that Jill and Donna lived out in college together before Donna's choices, programmed by male lovers and her own entrapment in the myths of femininity, estranged them somewhat. Its spiritual legacy is a simple pledge in the teeth of mortality "to express my caring all the time" to women and to men, and ultimately to the readers of her poems. Its practical result for Jill is a diffused and fractious loving which precludes traditional marriage and children of the blood, to spend itself on all the worthy human encounters of her life (at novel's end Jill is living, working, amiably quarreling with a long-term lover named Josh, and mothering Howie's daughter by another woman, as well as producing books and lectures).

As for the abortion freedom which paradoxically grounds this elliptical motherhood, this "death inside me" which makes births possible, both the narrator and the narrative structure argue forcefully for it. The bloody abortion that kills the protagonist's doppelganger at the climax does not contradict this. As a procedure which failed because its illegality made help impossible during the complications of aftermath, it stands starkly at one of the no exit gates—the other is death by immersion in unchosen maternity—of patriarchally-constructed "destiny as a woman." As an accident of nature which proved fatal to a woman who had cast her lot with a "femininity" which makes no room for a fully trusting relationship with a husband or with other women, the episode speaks to the self-destructive quality of that myth. Some force in the world—woman's own complicit desire for the maternity of the myth, the disorderly energies of sex and the body, the malice of

individual and collective men—stands ready to prick a hole in the diaphragm, to close down the freedom of the passage out. To define that force as "life" and condemn the counterforce, the diaphragm, the abortion, as death, is too simple, Piercy's narrative says. In fact, to women in patriarchal culture, "a society we do not control and scarcely influence, [in which] we survive and perish both by taking lovers," the opposite may be true.

"With my poems I finally won even my mother. The longest wooing of my life." It is interesting to consider that the mother wooed and won by the poem-producing but childless Jill Stuart is the only one of the protagonists' mothers alive and in good health at the end of these four novels. Maria Wyeth's mother, dead in an "accidental" car crash, surfaces along with Maria's repressed, aborted self as the memory of a figure yearning to "fly the ocean in a silver plane." The mother of the narrator of *Surfacing*, dead years before, returns along with the repressed memory of her aborted self both as the human mother who broke her ankles thinking she could fly from the roof of a barn and as the visionary maternal guide to the experience in the woods which exorcised "the old belief that I am powerless." Felicitas Taylor's mother is included with her daughter in her granddaughter's vatic, final speech-act, "we are not dying," but Felicitas has before this affirmed that her acceptance of her own maternity was precisely the signal that allowed her mother, and the others of that generation of mothers, to begin to grow old and die, since now "They could leave things to me."

The mothers of the protagonists in these novels, in various degrees complicit with patriarchy, powerless and fearful, cannot keep their daughters free or themselves alive. When their daughters become biological mothers they are marked as mortal, but the imaginary child—the ghost children of Didion's and Atwood's abortion protagonists, the haunting Donna, and the other poetic fictions of Piercy's Jill—somehow restores the mother, the original "lover," original home, the "imaginary" itself. The novels that close on an achieved biological motherhood—Maria "playing" for Kate, Felicitas protecting Linda—must accept some element of entrapment in that closing. Like Drabble's Rosamond these mothers are embedded in time, plotted into a game. They must look to an end, begin to die.

The novels that culminate in a meeting with ghosts, strive against closure. In these opened worlds, *Surfacing*'s protagonist still follows her dead mother and father, harboring the mystic "baby in the bottle" of her womb, a kind of third eye. And ***Braided Lives***'s Jill still carries the ghost child "Donna" as the undeliverable source for her poems. And *The Middle Ground*'s Kate Armstrong sees in the fairy tale windings of London's rivers and streets the "little sister" who was her mother, her child self and her aborted child, her full being, "always decaying yet always renewed . . . unplanned . . . intricate, enmeshed . . . the old and the new side by side."

Joyce R. Ladenson (essay date 1991)

SOURCE: "Political Themes and Personal Preoccupations

in Marge Piercy's Novels," in *Ways of Knowing: Essays on Marge Piercy,* edited by Sue Walker and Eugenie Hamner, Negative Capability, 1991, pp. 111-9.

[*In the following essay, Ladenson discusses the dominant political and autobiographic features of Piercy's fiction.*]

> My existence in the English Department at Michigan was exceedingly perilous and bumpy. . . . I was a garlic among the Anglican-convert lilies. I felt the wrong shape, size, sex, volume level, class, and emotional coloration. I fought, always with a sense of shame, for I could never define what I felt was being throttled in me.

> Marge Piercy, *Parti-Colored Blocks for a Quilt*

> In the fifties when I got pregnant I couldn't get an abortion, had to do it myself at eighteen and almost bled to death. In the fifties I was at the mercy of a male culture terrified of sex and telling me I was either frigid, a nymphomaniac, an earth mother, or stunted with penis envy, and there were no women's experiences available to compare with mine. In the fifties nowhere could I find images of a life I considered good or useful or dignified. Nowhere could I find a way to apply myself to change the world to one I could live in with more joy and utility. Nowhere could I find a community to heal myself to in struggle. Nowhere could I find space in which affluent white men were not the arbiters of all that was good and bad. I could not grow anywhere but through the cracks.

> Marge Piercy, *Parti-Colored Blocks for a Quilt*

Marge Piercy's painful memories of what life was like for her as a young woman in the fifties, recorded in *Parti-Colored Blocks for a Quilt,* are metaphorically recounted in her novel *Braided Lives;* both personal confession and fictional analog comprise radical documents which critique her times and the role of women in them. Indeed, *Braided Lives,* Piercy's most self-revelatory novel thus far, represents a backward glance at the roots of her abiding social and political involvement and provides something of a personal and critical perspective on her five preceding novels, which, in rough chronological sequence, mirror her perceptions of and experiences with radical American movements of the sixties and seventies. Personally involved in the Civil Rights, anti-Vietnam War and Feminist Movements, Piercy reflects political themes in all her work, charging her novels with authenticity and vitality, rendering her characters and situations highly complex, and successfully engaging the reader in her female and male characters, most of whom are specifically identified as activists, revolutionists or would-be politicoes.

Piercy's interest in radical politics, especially feminism, is also significant from a comparative perspective because it places her already prodigious canon together with women novelists who share similar concerns— namely such writers as Agnes Smedley, Tillie Olsen, Zora Neal Hurston, Harriet Arnow, Meridel Le Seur, Grace Paley, and Alice Walker, among others. In "From the Thirties: Tillie Olsen and the Radical Tradition," Deborah Rosenfelt raises questions about Olsen's "relationships of writing to political commitment; the circumstances of class and sex and their

effect on sustained creative activity, literary or political; and the strengths and weaknesses of the radical cultural tradition in this country." These concerns in addition to the dimension of Jewish ethnicity describe Piercy's themes and characterize her as a novelist whose relationship between political vision, personal commitment, and the creative process, like Olsen's, et al., is intimately linked.

A brief review of Piercy's novels up to *Braided Lives* helps locate her themes and concerns. In her first two novels, *Going Down Fast* (1969) and *Dance the Eagle to Sleep* (1971), Piercy records, through the lives of working class women and men, a resistance to the pressures of mid-sixties urban economic expansion with its concomitant social dislocation and disorganization, and to the trials and tribulations within the Civil Rights and burgeoning anti-Vietnam War Movements. While there is implicit and strong criticism of the dehumanizing values associated with American political culture, Piercy also records the painful ways resisting women and men exploit each other while trying to work collectively toward change. Living the revolution is harder than fantasizing about or planning it. Thus, her vision, from the beginning, is unrelentingly honest, avoiding romanticization of the larger ideological currents and of the relationships among those on the edge of change.

Personally active in the Women's Movement since the mid-sixties, Piercy reflects this involvement in all her succeeding novels while maintaining a persistent sympathy with working class ethnic and racial minorities. In *Small Changes* (1973), for instance, the personal evolutions of her two main characters, Miriam, a New York Jewish middle-class woman, and Beth, a working class, small town Protestant woman, are central to an understanding of the way they are molded by the first stirrings of Second Wave Feminism. Both torn and enabled by her New York Jewish family roots, which include political commitments and blacklisting during the McCarthy era, Miriam tries to balance her personal life against her strong, intellectual abilities in computer science and math. As an undergraduate in the Boston-Cambridge era, she becomes involved in three consuming relationships with men, the first two outside marriage—tumultuous, frustrating, and complex— and the last to Neil, the cad whom she marries and who leaves her and their two children for his secretary. Her personal life in pieces, she rebounds when she integrates again into the movement, teaching computer technology in an alternative educational setting.

Beth, Miriam's lesbian-feminist counterpart—strengthened by separatism, rebellious, painfully coming to terms with her abused childhood—dedicates herself to the feminist movement in Boston-Cambridge and finally goes underground to help her lover, Wanda, escape the Grand Jury and its judgment to separate Wanda from her children. As a committed rebel-feminist, willing to take great personal risks to fight the system, she somewhat prefigures the later Vida.

The men in this novel are complex political and social rebels who are sympathetic because they exist outside the

Establishment and work to change it; in their personal lives, especially in their relationships with Miriam, they are, with one exception, archetypically patriarchal, dominating to greater or lesser degrees the women they live with. Yet this is not a political tract, with characters and plot lines serving the didactic purposes of their author; the characters are skillfully developed, the plot engaging and not melodramatic. Devoted to social realism, Piercy recreates, in detail, the uneven rhythms of her uncommon and common rebels.

A remarkable novel for its breadth and vision, **Woman on the Edge of Time** (1976) is Piercy riding the last great crest of the New Left before it recedes into underground paranoia and disguise, or is co-opted by the realities of late seventies politics. Piercy's vision here is part utopian-socialist, part seventies feminist extended to its ideological and imaginative limits. A future world, Mattapoisett, is an androgynous, collective society where gender, race, ethnicity and sexual orientation are truly chosen; indeed the prevailing, consummate ethos of choice, combined with a nostalgia for a lost variety in human culture, is realized through public policy in which humane multi-cultural laboratory birthing helps newly evolved persons realize a harmony and nirvana of body and soul: e.g., through freely chosen families with multiple mothers; egalitarian political structures; individuated art, not confined by the market-place or state-imposed standards; freely chosen racial and ethnic identities; ecological harmony with nature, etc.

Piercy's hypothesizing and fantasizing in this quasi-utopian, quasi-science-fiction and half-realistic novel, is appropriate to the mid-seventies when radical and socialist-feminism reached its own apotheosis of mind and spirit, and feminist theory stretched to often romantic extremes. Thus, with her double vision of the utopian, of what a human and womanly possibility could be, Piercy also sees the present as unacceptable by comparison. Reality is harsh, phantasmagoric, and morally and spiritually hideous; it is so beyond redemption, with particular reference to women, that it allows for no other alternative but violent rebellion. Thus Consuelo Ramos, her Chicana heroine, a woman pushed to extremes, has no choice but to murder her oppressors, in this case psychiatrists who are the most powerful killers of women's minds and souls.

Piercy returns to a thoroughgoing realism in 1979, with **Vida,** and to the last remains of the New Left, in her fugitive heroine whose long period of hiding from the FBI comprises another of Piercy's glimpses at the culture, the loves and the conflicts of the Left's protagonists and the insular way in which it turns on itself (cf. **Dance the Eagle to Sleep**); yet there is a continuing vitality associated with a radical critique, with all its failures.

Piercy takes a closer look at women's personal lives, those caught in a complex political web, often a repressive social and sexual one, in **Braided Lives** (1982), and in the novel somewhat resembling it in theme and focus, **The High Cost of Living** (1978). Here are women and men more put-upon than triumphant, confined by society yet without a movement as a counter-balance, and significantly, both novels take place in Michigan. **The High Cost of Living** is about lesbian and gay identity in an academic, Wayne State setting, with the major theme being the compromise of one's values and principles when faced with the pressures of succeeding as a graduate student, or as an aspiring writer or professional bound by a patronage system. Piercy's pen draws the academy's flaws, while uncovering as well the desperate and manipulative personal relations within a lesbian-gay community. Here personal relations mirror, to a large degree, the values of the Establishment. Society wins in this novel as Piercy lapses into an unprecedented cynicism.

Yet, if repression wins in **The High Cost of Living,** it loses in **Braided Lives.** This is encouraging since it appears to resemble Piercy's life closer than any of her other novels, and perhaps bodes well for the novelist. Jill Stuart, her fictional persona, is a sixteen year old Detroit high school senior at the novel's beginning—the same age Piercy was, growing up in Detroit in the fifties—of Eastern European, Jewish descent, possibly with some mixture of Tartar and Karan, anxious but wary about leaving her working class neighborhood for the status-conscious, elitist University of Michigan—again following Piercy's biography. This novel is about the emerging personality of a young Jewish woman yearning to be recognized as a beginning writer, looking for but not finding that recognition from an entrenched literary-academic establishment or from her young lover- confidants.

Ann Arbor in the fifties harbors its own Beat and Existential generation with literary heroes such as Allen Ginsberg, Aldous Huxley, John Dos Passos, Albert Camus (his novel, *The Stranger,* always pronounced in French), George Orwell and Jean Paul Sartre. A part of this milieu Jill finds fascinating; another part she rejects or is rejected by because it is a male club. Jill is an outsider to the New Critical, high culture style of which Ann Arbor is a bastion, and to the social and political culture represented by Joseph McCarthy and the Korean War, by cashmere sweaters and being "preppy" before it became "neo," by *The Wild One* and *Rebecca of Sunnybrook Farm.* She is an economic outsider as well since in order to remain in school, she must steal her texts, supplies and incidental clothing. Jill is clearly a class apart in multiple ways.

Jill's distance from the norm as a young writer is reflected in a wonderful scene where she reads from her own poetry for the first time. The setting is an auditorium on the University of Michigan campus, and she feels anxious about appearing not only before an audience of her peers but of her instructors, who hope she has learned her lessons properly and can objectify her personal experiences, making them spare, unsentimental, unromantic, unemotional, in short, masculinized and New Critical. Interjecting her view from the present when she is in her mid-forties—the book is a reflection on the fifties and uses the same extended flashback technique as *Vida*—Jill recalls the critics' hostile comments toward a Mrs. Starini, a middle-aged poet and another reader on the program, "for her domestic themes and for being dumpy. She was punished for lacking appeal to their gonads." Clearly, Starini's self-disclosing poems are the antithesis of the fashionably satiric, distanced, cynical works read by Jill's lover, Mike, another English major and aspiring poet, and by others that night. Indeed, Mike's complaint to Jill is that her poem is "'soft, pumpkin. Too soft to waste on those jerks. . . . Of course it's formless and silly. It isn't art, naturally.'" Jill's struggle is to affirm her talent, the authenticity of her feelings, and her role as political rebel against McCarthyism with her men friends, and finally to rebel against that aspect of fifties repression which affected women most dramatically: the laws against abortion. She is as yet an artist and a lover without a movement.

The conflict between her emerging literary talents and the conservative academy is one of several Jill experiences. Two other important dimensions of Jill's identity, her ethnicity and working-class origins, compound the stress she experiences around her emerging sexuality, and she collides with the repressive and conforming fifties ethos. Again in *Braided Lives,* Jill's late teens and early twenties seem close to her creator's: she is a street-wise sophisticate whose obsessive relationship with her mother is at once cloying and tender especially when, after her father's death, emotion is less frozen, less formed by convention and the past; it is also central to her sexuality. For instance, her first clandestine (at least to her parents), heterosexual affair—with Mike, by whom she becomes pregnant—is so disapproved of by both Jill's parents that they have her followed and force a false confession and promise of marriage from him. Finally Jill's pregnancy is ended by her mother's insistence that she perform the abortion, a violent act which brings her very close to death and causes an unbridgeable distance between her and Mike.

Men and their laws are the villains of this piece as Jill's father is shielded from any knowledge of her abortion for fear that he will harm both Jill and Mike; as Jill's mother supervises the abortion instead of going to a physician for fear of being apprehended; and as her lover Mike, uneasy and inexperienced, relinquishes responsibility. The development of Jill's sexuality comes at a terrible price to her body, her perception of self and her relations with men. Here is a real sense of what political and social repression in the fifties meant to women, how women like Jill were victimized but managed to survive and love again, and how men who were champions of social and political justice against McCarthy nevertheless gleaned the rewards of gender privilege, largely uncritical of conforming fifties sexual politics.

Astonishingly, Jill not only survives but prevails. Her last love in the novel, Howie, her gentle, warm Jewish childhood friend, wants to marry her yet finally cannot abide her independent spirit; her love for Howie lingers, but she is able to leave him, herself intact. Jill's recollection of her survival through a crucible of fifties' torment also reminds her that she has passed another danger zone—that moment between thirty-eight and forty-four when her mother, also the neighborhood fortune teller, predicted she would die. Via her persona Jill, Piercy revisits "that burned-over district where [she] learned to love—in friendship and in passion—and to work." This is a novel distinguished by its honesty and commitment to personal and social justice. The closeness of friendship, especially with women, the love on which she must have drawn to recover her mother's and her own heritage, and the general lack of cynicism and high degree of emotional engagement mark this as her most personal and self-revelatory work of fiction. *Braided Lives* is an explanation Piercy wrote both to herself and to the reader of her coming to maturity: it expands the feminist dictum that the personal is political in depth and dimension.

If Piercy is accused of being preachy, it is because her characters are struck by pain which they need to explain and about which they are enraged once they examine its social sources. So, when Donna, Jill's college roommate and closest friend, dies of an illegal abortion toward the novel's end, Jill's words are angry and pointed in their rage against the law which, in its false morality, kills innocent women and which almost kills her earlier. The brief political commentaries and up-to-date news inserts, italicized and set apart in Dos Passos fashion, inform the reader of the bedrock of reality on which this fiction is grounded. *Braided Lives* successfully draws the reader into its web of pain, compassion, and love. Piercy has written another moving novel in her continuing quest for personal and political knowledge.

Sue Walker (essay date 1991)

SOURCE: "Marge Piercy: An Overview (31 March 1936-)," in *Ways of Knowing: Essays on Marge Piercy,* edited by Sue Walker and Eugenie Hamner, Negative Capability, 1991, pp. 132-47.

[In the following essay, Walker provides a survey of Piercy's literary career and the central themes and feminist perspective of her poetry and fiction.]

Although Marge Piercy—poet, novelist, playwright, and essayist—describes herself as a political writer and a feminist, her works move beyond the causes she supports to incorporate an overall thematic interest in the struggle between freedom and oppression. Most of her creative energies are devoted to fiction and poetry, and she writes both with amazing productivity—a novel published one year, a book of poems the next. Her first publication was a book of poems entitled *Breaking Camp* (1968); *Going Down Fast,* her first published novel appeared in 1969, though she had written six other novels prior to its publication and feels that her difficulty in breaking into print stemmed from the fact that her work was too political and too feminist for publication in the 1950's and 1960's.

Marge Piercy was born in Detroit, Michigan, the daughter of Robert and Bert Bunnin Piercy. She has one half-brother thirteen years her senior, the son from her mother's former marriage. Her father worked for Westinghouse and repaired machinery; her mother, named Bert because Piercy's grandfather wanted a boy instead of a girl, was the oldest daughter of nine children. It was she who had to help raise the younger siblings, the four girls and five boys who survived childhood. Forced to leave school before finishing the tenth grade, Bert grew up in poverty, but later taught Marge to observe closely, value curiosity, and to love books. This legacy became a major theme in Piercy's work, as *Parti-Colored Blocks for a Quilt* (1982) attests:

> My mother taught me to observe. A woman who had not been allowed to finish the tenth grade, she had some extraordinary ideas about how to raise very young children. . . . She had contempt for people who did not observe, who did not notice, and would require me to remember the houses we passed going to the store, or play mental hide-and-seek in other people's houses that we had visited. We would give each other three random words to make stories around. We would try to guess the stories of people we saw on the bus and would argue to prove or disprove each other's theories.

A writer's childhood, Piercy believes, often stimulates the muse. "You learn to sink roots into your childhood and feed on it," she says, "twist it, wring it, use it again and again. Sometimes one daub of childhood mud can set a whole poem right or save a character." And it is childhood, growing up within a typical patriarchal working-class family in inner-city Detroit that Piercy describes with Proustian fidelity in *Parti-Colored Blocks for a Quilt.* Blacks and whites fought; husbands cheated on and beat their wives, drug abuse, drunkenness, rape, and child-molestation were common. Little tolerance was given to Jews, and yet, in the midst of ugliness and violence, Piercy finds beauty in her own backyard. She writes of a garden rampant with tomatoes, beans, lettuce, onions, and Swiss chard. She notes the pansies, iris, mock oranges, wisteria, hollyhocks along the alley fence, the black-eyed susans and the goldenglow, its stems red with spider mites. "Nothing," Piercy writes, "will ever be more beautiful than the flowers in that yard, except my mother when I was young."

Two things illumine this reflection. First, Piercy's method of observation and commentary. She dredges the ugly for social utterance and never spares the ways it limits and destroys human growth and development. Yet simultaneously she sees beauty that thrives in the midst of and in spite of oppression, violence, internal and external disruptions; Second, the role of the mother is a major theme that occurs throughout her work. In *My Mother's Body* (1985), written after her mother's death, an entire section is devoted to elucidating the mother-daughter relationship. It is one fraught with ambivalence, with love and with the less tolerated feelings of hate. "A woman must reconcile herself to her mother and to the mother within her, if she is not to become her," Piercy remarked in a discussion of her poem **"Crescent moon like a canoe,"** a poem that appeared in the 1980 volume of *The Moon Is Always*

Female. It deals with how the poet and her mother "fought like snakes, biting / hard at each other's spine to snap free," and in an angry accusation directed to her mother, she rails that "You burned my paper armor, rifled my diaries, / sniffed my panties looking for smudge of sex, / so I took off and never came back." Leaving home, however, was more geographical than psychological, and the poet reflects:

> My muse, your voice on the phone wavers with tears.
> The life you gave me burns its acetylene
> of buried anger, unused talents, rotted wishes,
> the compost of discontent, flaring into words
> strong for other women under your waning moon.

My Mother's Body reiterates the old concerns, but it seems that death has brought a reconciliation and buried the long years of ambivalence that were often voiced in earlier poetry and prose. The final poem of the section **"What Remains"** addresses the mother's body, and asks:

> What is it we turn from, what is it we fear?
> Did I truly think you could put me back inside?
> Did I think I would fall into you as into a molten
> furnace and be recast, that I would become you?
> · · ·
>
> This body is your body, ashes now
> and roses, but alive in my eyes, my breasts,
> my throat, my thighs. You run in me
> a tang of salt in the creek waters of my blood,
> you sing in my mind like wine. What you
> did not dare in your life you dare in mine.

It is from this core that individuation occurs, that a woman moves beyond the concerns of the mother to the self and to other human relationships, to the significance of sex, to political concerns, to the world beyond the confines of family and geographical location.

An overview of Piercy's work chronologically gives the reader insight into sociological interests and recurring psychological themes. Piercy's first published book, significantly entitled *Breaking Camp,* is a compilation of the best of her early poems. It lacks the cohesion, the synthesis, of her later work but establishes the pattern of political concern that will reoccur in later poetry and fiction.

Going Down Fast, a first novel written from 1965-1967, followed the publication of *Breaking Camp.* It shows the least women's consciousness of any Piercy novel and reflects her Chicago experience. Concern with the ruthlessness of urban renewal, police brutality, and university politics made it difficult for a woman to establish herself as a writer. *Going Down Fast* features a male rather than a female protagonist. Piercy explains that at the time of the book's publication in 1969, feminist concerns were not popular. Editors would return manuscript after manuscript with comments such as "I don't believe in these people," and "I don't want to read about people like these." Serious fiction about being a woman was hard to place, and the five novels written prior to *Going Down Fast* were rejected because of their stance, it seems, not because of any lack of quality.

In *Hard Loving,* also published in 1969, political themes merge with female consciousness and with the difficulty of forging relationships. The poems were written at a time when Piercy was involved in SDS activities, with the antiwar movement, and with living in a matrix of four relationships that united her political and personal concerns. Walking slowly into love rather than falling in love marks the initial sequence of six poems. It is followed by "The death of the small commune" which marks the disintegration of SDS and what Piercy feels to be one of the best schools of political organizers that existed in twentieth-century America. "What we wanted to build," she says in the title poem, "was a way station for journeying to a new world, / but we could not agree," and nothing remains "but a hole in everything." The poems in *Hard Loving,* represent a "learning experience," a time when the author was teaching at the Gary extension of Indiana University. A boy sits in her classroom "in boredom thick and greasy as vegetable shortening," and Piercy has come out on the train from Chicago to talk / about dangling participles." The poet says "I am supposed / to teach him to think a little on demand," but:

> The boy yawns and does not want to be in the classroom in Gary
> where the furnaces that consumed his father seethe rusty smoke
> and pour cascades of nerve-bright steel
> while the slag goes out in little dumpcars smoking,
>
> but even less does he want to be in Today's Action Army
> in Vietnam, in the Dominican Republic, in Guatemala,
> in death that hurts.
> In him are lectures on small groups, Jacksonian democracy,
> French irregular verbs, the names of friends
> around him in the classroom in Gary in the pillshaped afternoon
> where tomorrow he will try and fail his license to live.

Dance the Eagle to Sleep (1970) continues to explore the bewilderment and rebellion of youth in their attempt to build a visionary new society. Piercy was driving herself hard at the time she was working on this novel— getting up at 6:30 A.M. in order to find time to write. She was living in New York with her second husband, Robert Shapiro, and writing came second to political activities. Although she would often give poetry readings for SDS benefits and cultural events, life revolved around the concerns and activities of the movement. In the autobiographical commentary Piercy wrote for *Contemporary Authors,* she describes the years in New York as "extremely intense, full, densely populated times" and says:

> Rarely did Robert and I stay alone in the big sunny rent-controlled apartment on 98th and Broadway. At least fourteen other people lived there at various times for various lengths of time, and every night for supper I was cooking for up to twelve people. I have never been quite so fully involved with numerous people as I was during those years. For Robert and I to be alone, we had to make appointments with each other and arrangements with the others living with us.

It is not surprising that Piercy's health broke and that she became critically ill. Lungs damaged by habitual smoking since the age of twelve gave way to chronic bronchitis, to illness, and a physician's death sentence if she did not stop. An accidental fall complicated earlier back injuries derived from a beating by American Nazi men during an antiwar demonstration in Central Park and from injuries received during a demonstration against the Foreign Policy Association. "A body can grow used / to a weight, / used to limping / and find it hard / to learn again / to walk straight," Piercy asserts in *4-Telling* (1971).

In both the novel *Small Changes* and *To Be of Use,* a book of poems published in the same year, Piercy returns to predominant feminist concerns and begins an exploration of women's struggle to achieve autonomy. *Small Changes,* Piercy says, is "the equivalent of a full experience in a consciousness-raising group for many women who would never go through that experience." The issue of what it means to be a "real woman" is revealed in the liberation of the novel's protagonist, Beth Phail. The novel begins with Beth preparing for her wedding as she looks in the mirror of her mother's vanity and becomes the image of her mother's pride, her mother's attitudes, expectations that shape her identity, and vision of herself. "This is the happiest day of your life!" her mother exclaims, "the happiest day!" The way that language functions to preserve stereotypes on one hand and to liberate on the other is an essential feature of *Small Changes.* The issue is one of definition, that is what it means to be a real woman. Mrs. MacRae, who lived upstairs during Beth's childhood, was not really a woman, Mrs. Phail said, because she had had her organs removed, and that was why she did not have children like everybody else. Although having females organs is an essential qualification for being a real woman, men assert that there are additional requirements. A real woman must be available when a man wants her, and Beth's husband insists that she make herself available or he will end their relationship. Finally Beth is able to define herself according to her own standards and to forge a different kind of relationship, a lesbian involvement with another woman.

The poems in *To Be of Use* continue to address the evolution of women's social and political consciousness. The first section, "A Just Anger," begins in exploitation and dependence and works through the difficult task women have in bonding with other women, a necessary prerequisite to fuller consciousness and deliberate action. The use of such consciousness is the concern of "The Spring Offensive of the Snail," part two of the book. It addresses the issue of what to do after feminine consciousness is raised, and finally, in "Laying Down the Tower," Piercy takes a feminist perspective in interpreting the symbolism of the ancient Tarot. Myth, history, and politics are united in these poems to examine womanness, its mystery, power, and capacity for growth and change.

With *Woman on the Edge of Time* Piercy moves into futuristic feminist fiction and creates a different utopia. Masculine visions of the time have dealt with governmental concerns, with economics, and with social classes. Piercy instead sets up a feminist revolution. No longer is childbirth the procreative inheritance of a woman; test-tube babies have arrived. Child bearing is done in brooders for the community, and Luciente, the woman who reaches across time from the future, explains it thus:

> It was part of women's long revolution. When we were breaking all the old hierarchies. Finally there was that one thing we had to give up too, the only power we ever had, in return for more power for everyone. The original production: the power to give birth. Cause as long as we were biologically enchained, we'd never be equal. And males never would be humanized to be loving and tender. So we all became mothers. Every child has three. To break the nuclear bonding.

Piercy seeks to create a future that is free from the stereotypes of gender, but she is not fooled that Connie can be a savior; she is poor, speaks Spanish, has lost her daughter to a foster home, and has been involved in taking drugs. What's more she is held against her will in a mental institution and must fight her way to a future that promises more than oppression. But Piercy shows that there is hope for individuation, a hope that becomes personal in *Living in the Open* (1976).

For the first time Piercy gives an autobiographical account of her life. She tells how she came to live on the edge of a fresh-water marsh on Cape Cod, of how it came to be a particular place to be healed. "Finally I have a house / where I return," she says, a "House half into the hillside, / wood that will weather to the wind's gray, / house built on sand / drawing water like a tree from its roots / where my roots are set / and I return." It is a place where she is "Kneeling and planting," "making fertile," and putting some of herself back in the soil. But it is not utopia, and there are "rough times." "Those who speak of good and simple / in the same sandwich of tongue and teeth / inhabit some other universe."

The personal and the political, the emotional and intellectual are inseparable in Piercy's life, and *The Twelve-Spoked Wheel Flashing* (1978) exemplifies this synthesis. The poetry is organized around the sequence of a year, the diurnal turn from winter to spring, the ease of summer into fall. The seasons of political ferment and activity are joined with the seasons of love and friendship, the seasons of the land. *The Twelve-Spoked Wheel Flashing* is a solar book with cosmic significance. Everything takes place under the wheel of the sun, including the twelve-spoked microcosmic wheel flashing its earthly seasons. The wheel with its twelve monthly spokes turns year after year but never returns the same way to the same place.

The High Cost of Living, also published in 1978, is a book that deals specifically with the dead-end desperation of some lesbian relationships, and it may be classed as Piercy's least successful novel. Even a critic as positive as Joanna Russ posits reservations. Perhaps it is a too stark and authentic rendition of female homosexuality and as such lacks the humor, the play, of Rita Mae Brown's *Rubyfruit Jungle,* which was well received despite the similarity of its thematic content. Piercy has always seemed to be ahead of her time in dealing with contemporary social and political issues, and she has done this with some risk to popular acclaim, but with an authenticity that should merit more lasting critical recognition and attention.

In *Vida* (1979), the underground world of the 1960's and 1970's is probed through the eyes of a female protagonist. Vida, in an attempt to work out her political commitments to SAW (Students Against the War) and a fierce separatist group called the Little Red Wagon, comes to terms with an untenable marriage and attempts to establish a more viable relationship, one in which sex is mutual satisfaction instead of supply and demand. Her lifestyle is portrayed in contrast to her sister's more traditional orientation toward marriage, family, and mothering. Vida is in pursuit of individual interests, political commitments, and social awareness. Two aspects of womanhood are thus surveyed in *Vida,* and the novel is a commentary on how difficult it is to set aside the indoctrination of past attitudes, behavioral patterns, and psychological conditioning in order to establish a new order of feminine integration into a political, often violent, and dangerous world.

This world is rent by revolution and war on one hand and by a refusal to change, by clinging to a dead past on the other. In *The Moon Is Always Female* (1980), Piercy recognizes, as did Anna Freud, that the voice of the intellect is a soft one. Intellectual claims to gain insight and transform experience fail to right the wrongs of the world, set order against chaos, or provide an easy means of dealing with fear, pain, anger, lust, or loss. There must be another way of knowing, and the numinous poems of *The Moon is Always Female* open a doorway to comprehending the nonrational aspects of being a woman. "There is knowing with the teeth as well as knowing with the tongue," Piercy says, "and knowing with the fingertips / as well as knowing with words and with all / the fine flickering hungers of the brain." Women are the first healers; they are the gatherers of herbs and roots, the dispensers of foxglove, thyme, valerian and poppy, of herbs that cure. Harking back to the lunar calendar, the natural evolution of time's turning, the history of woman moves with tidal ebb and flow into a kind of negative capability, the capacity or ability to tolerate, in Keat's definition, uncertainties, mysteries, and doubts, without any irritable reaching after fact and reason. In the title poem, **"The Moon is Always Female,"** Piercy phrases the concept thus:

> I am waiting for the moon to rise. Here
> I squat, the whole country with its steel
> mills and its coal mines and its prisons
> at my back and the continent tilting

up into mountains and torn by shining lakes
all behind me on this scythe of straw,
a sand bar cast on the ocean waves, and I
wait for the moon to rise red and heavy
in my eyes. Chilled, cranky, fearful
in the dark I wait and I am all the time
climbing slippery rocks in a mist while
far below the waves crash in the sea caves;
I am descending a stairway under the groaning
sea while the black waters buffet me
like rockweed to and fro.

Earth is the archetypal mother who generates birth and whose seasons typify a girl's development into a woman. It ushers in a bloom of life when a woman is able to choose who will become the flesh of her flesh, a time when "life is a non-negotiable demand." It is not an easy achievement Piercy notes in **"The wrong anger";** there is "infighting," "gut battles," "carnage in the fish tank." There are "Alligators wrestling in bed. / Nuclear attack / across the breakfast table. Duels in the women's center. The fractioning faction fight." Women face their failing again and again; they grow out of and beyond their mothers and strive toward reconciliation. The poems of *The Moon Is Always Female* reveal a woman who is secure in her sexuality, a mature woman whose energy and vision are in harmony with her nature.

In 1982 Piercy's career took on new momentum with the publication of two significant works: *Circles on the Water* and *Parti-Colored Blocks for a Quilt. Circles on the Water* is a composite selection of poems from previous works: *Breaking Camp, Hard Loving, 4-Telling, To Be of Use, Living in the Open, The Moon is Always Female,* plus an addition of seven new poems. This collection provides an overview of Piercy's poetry in a volume that may serve as a text for an integrated study of her major poetic works. The University of Michigan's "Poets on Poetry" edition of Marge Piercy's *Parti-Colored Blocks for a Quilt,* adds a critical approach through a collection of articles, interviews, book reviews, and commentary.

Braided Lives, also published in 1982, is set in the 1950's and in it Piercy again demonstrates her ability to reveal American conscience and consciousness. Strictures on women place strictures on an age that needs to move beyond such narrow confines. *Braided Lives* shows how divisions of class and gender shape future generations.

It is obvious by 1983 that the discipline of art has relegated any polemic to secondary significance, and the question asked in *Stone, Paper, Knife*—"Who shall bear hope back into the world?"—places Piercy among those active women writers who would like to see man, woman, and the earth joined in warm, interdependent relationships. "Poetry is an utterance that heals on two levels," Piercy says in *Parti-Colored Blocks for a Quilt.* It heals the psyche by blending ways of knowing:

> Poetry is a saying that uses verbal signs and images, sound and rhythm, memory and dream images. Poetry blends all different kinds of knowing, the analytical and the synthetic, the rational and the prerational and the gestalt grasping of the new or ancient configuration, the separate and fused hungers and satisfaction and complaints and input of the senses, the knotted fibrous mass of pleasure and pain, the ability to learn and to forget. . . . Poetry has a healing power because it can fuse for the moment all the different kinds of knowing in its saying.

Poetry can also heal as a communal activity, and *Stone, Paper, Knife* is a statement of faith that follows an attack on the destructive power of bombs, the pollution of water, the waste of disease. How can we "open our hands and let go / the old dangerous toys we clutch hard," she asks. "How can we with only stone and paper and knife build with imagination a better game?" Piercy answers that human beings, male and female, need to accept the burden of responsibility. "We must begin with the stone of mass / resistance, and pile stone on stone, / begin cranking out whirlwinds of paper."

The tone of hope represents several changes in Piercy's personal life, a move to Wellfleet, putting down roots, and finding sustenance and strength in the establishment of home and a marriage to Ira Wood.

The novel, *Fly Away Home* (1984), also marks Piercy's turn to bearing hope back into the world. The protagonist of her story, Daria Walker, divorces, establishes her independence, moves toward a more creative and fulfilling relationship and recognizes, at the end of the book, that she is a better woman than she used to be before she was on her own.

It seems that both Piercy's marriage and the death of her mother have marked a period of growth and development in her work. *My Mother's Body* resolves old dilemmas and affirms an outlook of hope, a capacity for joy. The first series of poems concerns burial and resurrection. A body is put to rest, but what transcends that body lives—in memory, in giving, in being and becoming. The second half of the book represents a new union, a marriage, a going forth.

The lyrics of the 1960's song "Where Have All The Flowers Gone" provide a touchstone for examining Marge Piercy's World War II novel, *Gone to Soldiers.*

Although the song lyrics differ among various recordings, the major questions and answers are: "Where have all the flowers gone?" Answer: Young girls pick them, every one. "When will they ever learn?" This question is never answered. It is followed by another question: "Where have all the young girls gone?" The answer: Gone to young men—or gone to husbands. "When will they ever learn?" "Where have all the young men gone?" Answer: They have gone for soldiers. The reason for picking flowers is clear with an additional question: "Where have all the graveyards gone?" Answer: Gone to flowers the young girls pick. But the terrible abiding question is left unanswered still. When will they ever learn?

Although World War II was "the war to end all wars," mankind has not learned its lessons. The Sixties song attests to the terrible cycle of repetition—to the fact that history repeats itself. The final words of Piercy's novel are haunting and prophetic: "The End of One Set of Troubles Is But the Beginning of Another." Will we ever learn? *Gone to Soldiers* is a lesson on the consequences of failure. It defines what our failures have been and reinforces the stark refrain—"will we ever learn?"

Because Marge Piercy is a major American poet as well as novelist, it is fitting that the preface to this epic work on war should be a poem about the past carried into the present, about ancestors. Piercy writes:

> The survivors have written their own books
> and those who perished are too many and too hungry
> for this to do more than add a pebble to the cairn
>
> So this is for my grandmother Hannah
> who was a solace to my childhood
> and who was a storyteller even in the English
> that never fit comfortably in her mouth
>
> for the moment when she learned that of her
> village, none and nothing remained
>
> for her weak eyes, strong stomach and the tales
> she told, her love of gossip, of legend
> her incurable romantic heart
> her gift for making the past
> walk through the present

Marge Piercy, like Grandmother Hannah, is a story-teller, but her audience is not just a granddaughter, the members of her immediate family; it is, instead, the world. And far more than entertainment is involved. Survival is at stake; lessons must be learned—lessons about the consequences of war and violence, lessons about prejudice and religious intolerance and interpersonal relationships. In our humanness, we fail others, and we fail ourselves. Wars are external and internal too.

In reviews of *Gone to Soldiers,* critics stress the fact that "A woman writer treads on male turf," that Marge Piercy, in writing about war, has entered into an area reserved for Men. But Piercy, in all of her novels and poems, has seen the world as whole. Her world is one inhabited by women AND men, and its violence affects everyone regardless of gender, age, or race.

Marge Piercy is a humanitarian and as such, there should be no question of gender, of male or female turf. War kills—male and female, adult and child, on the front line, in a classroom or factory, in a residence or a department store. The "Who" that is involved names every human being that inhabits the earth. The "Where" is the United States; it is Germany, Russia, England, Iran, Japan, the World. What have we learned? Will we ever learn?

In 1941, the International Institute of Intellectual Cooperation was instructed by the Permanent Committee for Literature and the Arts of the League of Nations to arrange for exchanges of letters between representative intellectuals on subjects deemed of common interest; they asked Albert Einstein to pick a topic for discussion and to choose a person with whom to exchange letters. Einstein chose "Why War?" and in a letter written at Caputh near Potsdam, the 30th of July, 1932, to Professor Sigmund Freud, he asked:

> Is there any way of delivering mankind from the menace of war? It is common knowledge that, with the advance of modern science, this issue has come to mean a matter of life and death for civilization as we know it; nevertheless, for all the zeal displayed, every attempt at its solution has ended in a lamentable breakdown. (*Sigmund Freud,* ed., James Strachey, 1964)

Einstein's letter is long, but it is worth quoting, at least in part, because it not only illumines Piercy's theme that the end of one set of troubles, namely war, is but the beginning of another, it also explores the seemingly unanswerable question that Einstein raised: "Why War?".

The lack of success in solving the problem, Einstein wrote, "Leaves us no room to doubt that strong psychological factors are at work, which paralyze these efforts." He explains:

> The craving for power which characterizes the governing class in every nation is hostile to any limitation of the national sovereignty. This political power-hunger is wont to batten on the activities of another group, whose aspirations are on purely mercenary lines. I have specially in mind that small but determined group, active in every nation, composed of individuals who, indifferent to social considerations and restraints, regard warfare, the manufacture and sale of arms, simply as an occasion to advance their personal interests and enlarge their personal authority.

The question follows of how a seemingly small clique can bend the will of the majority when they stand to lose and suffer by a state of war, and Einstein comments that he does not exclude "soldiers of every rank who have chosen war as their profession, in the belief that they are serving to defend the highest interests of their race and that attack is often the best defense." The obvious answer, he says, "would seem to be that the majority, the ruling class . . . has the schools and press, usually the Church as well, under its thumb." This enables the clique "to organize and sway the emotions of the masses, and make its tool of them."

In exploring the cause of this situation, Einstein believes that there is only one explanation as to what would rouse "men to such wild enthusiasm, even to sacrifice their lives" and that is "because man has within him a lust for hatred and destruction."

"Is it possible," Einstein asks Freud, "to control man's mental evolution so as to make him proof against the psychoses of hate and destructiveness?" And he concludes by saying he had been speaking of wars between nations—

international conflicts—but that he was aware also that the aggressive instinct operates under other forms and circumstances. He names "the persecution of racial minorities" as an example.

Piercy's *Gone to Soldiers* might well be called a 1987 answer to Einstein's question. It is a monumental work of ten novels woven into one collection. Its base is World War II, but individual wars between man and man, woman and woman, between woman and man, between families, within the self, are all played out in the lives of ten major characters, each one presenting his or her own individual point of view. Yet each part becomes integrated into the larger anatomy of war. *Gone to Soldiers* is a hard lesson. But will we ever learn? Perhaps, if we make use of the past, and perhaps part of the lesson could be reading Piercy's important masterpiece of craft and design. *Gone to Soldiers* should establish Piercy as one of the leading novelists of our time.

Available Light, published by Knopf in 1988, is Piercy's tenth book of poetry. It celebrates political, religious, seasonal, and personal revolutions. Again themes of coming into selfhood, forgiving one's parents, and growing into love are displayed with celerity. The poet, at 50, assesses her life. She examines and affirms her Jewish identity and in doing so, seeks to reconcile religion with her embrace of the ancient earth goddess. She confronts her ambivalence toward her father in "Burial by salt" and says "What was between us was history, not love. / I have striven to be just to you, / stranger, first cause, old man, my father, / and now I give you over to salt and silence."

In *Available Light,* Piercy confronts problems of aging, menopause, making love, her own Detroit childhood, society's concern with being forever young, even the annoyance of answering machines. Though she extols country pleasures, Piercy asserts that "life makes women crazy." "We lose and we go on losing as long as we live," she says. Yet Piercy's vision is a clear and available light that informs a triumph of understanding one's self, one's relationships, and one's place in the world.

Piercy's *Summer People,* published in 1989, moves from the political arena of *Gone to Soldiers* to the social set of summer people on fashionable Cape Cod. The focus is a ten-year-old *menage a trois* and its tortuous disintegration. It examines the bonds of love that exist between Dinah, a 38 year-old Jewish musician and her bisexual lover, Susan. Dinah is also involved with Susan's husband, Willie, and an avant-garde composer, Itsak Raab. The novel explores, through triangular and one-sided relationships, the difficulty involved in becoming a separate person who is able to fulfill his or her own needs while establishing a healthy reciprocal relationship with another person. Stephen Schiff, in his review of the novel in *The New York Times Book Review,* calls the novel a "red-hot pastorale" and questions if amid the novel's painful lurching, "we ever begin to understand how a happy, bisexual triangle might work?" Although the bisexual triangle of Dinah and Susan, Dinah

and Willie, Willie and Susan, is central to the novel, other relationships are explored as well: Dinah and Raab, Susan and Tyrone Burdock, the wealthy New York art speculator who summers on the other side of the pond; Jimmy and Tyrone's daughter, Laurie. *Summer People* is a study of codependency. It does not intend to address itself to how a happy bisexual triangle might work—for if such a relationship works and is happy, why explore it further? A primary psychological issue in 1989 is codependency, and Piercy is right on target in showing how addictive relationships destroy the love they intend to nurture.

Throughout her career as novelist and poet, Piercy addresses the hard issues that affect the way people live and love. In the 60's and early 70's this was the issue of feminism and women's rights. In the 80's, it is codependency, but Piercy has not limited herself to the vicissitudes of love. She has addressed issues of religion and culture, and in particular how a Jewish heritage directs one's life. She addresses the psychology of mother-daughter and father-daughter relationships, attitudes toward youth and aging, and on a global scale, Einstein's question of "Why War?" The canon of Piercy's work is impressive in both poetry and fiction. Piercy is a literary force with which to reckon.

Malcolm Bosse (review date 22 December 1991)

SOURCE: "A Cyborg in Love," in *The New York Times Book Review,* December 22, 1991, p. 22.

[*In the following review, Bosse offers negative assessment of* He, She, and It.]

Her highly praised novel *Gone to Soldiers* and her other works of fiction, essays and poetry attest to Marge Piercy's achievement. But her ambitious new novel, *He, She and It,* is not likely to enhance her reputation.

In the high-tech world of A.D. 2059, people live under protective domes because of an ecological disaster and plug into computers through sockets located in their foreheads. This society, although it is described in the lingo of science fiction (gruds, stimmies, security apes, fused user syndrome), still has a familiar assortment of domestic problems. The brilliant young scientist Shira battles her former husband for custody of their son, Art, but unfortunately for Shira the despotic, male-dominated multinational corporation that employs her—and administers justice—rules against her. She moves to a "free town" where she stays with her grandmother and works on an artificial-intelligence project concerned with the construction of cyborgs.

Malkah, Shira's grandmother, opens a second narrative line by explaining to Yod, a newly created cyborg, what life for oppressed Jews was like in 16th-century Prague. Malkah's narrative includes complex disquisitions on astrology, the cabala, medieval science and the intellectual fervor of Central Europe during the Renaissance. But her tale focuses on Judah Loew, the head rabbi of Prague, who creates a golem, a man made from clay and invested with life, "as tall and broad as the strongest soldier." The rabbi names his creation Joseph and charges it with protecting the city's Jews (gathered together in a walled ghetto) from intruders.

Malkah has been recruited to work with the cyborg by its creator, her old lover Avram. Yod is unique, far superior to any other cyborg. Much like the golem in Malkah's tale, he has been created to protect an endangered community—in this case the town to which Shira flees. As Yod explains to Shira, "I am not a robot. . . . I'm a fusion of machine and lab-created components." He is dark-haired, "of medium height, with a solid compact build," and, he explains to an astonished Shira, "anatomically male."

Shira is given the job of civilizing the cyborg. And—much as in Malkah's tale of 16th-century Prague, in which a young woman takes pity on the golem and his "beautiful hunger" for knowledge and teaches him to read—she finds herself fascinated by Yod.

Assassins from an enemy coalition, Yakamura-Stichen (recalling the Axis of World War II), who can strike through a computer to kill its user, attack Malkah. She is saved by Yod. Shira and Yod begin a steamy love affair. Because the free town is now under siege, Shira's mother, Riva, returns to help out. Riva is an information pirate ("She finds hidden knowledge," Malkah explains to Shira, "and liberates it") who brings with her a formidable accomplice, Nili, a Ninja-like woman warrior who comes from an underground cave beneath Israel, where a community of Jewish and Palestinian women live together in harmony. From this complex and rather funky domestic setting, a plot emerges to rescue Shira's child from her former husband.

Both Joseph the golem and Yod face violence and must kill to protect their charges. The golem fights off the forces threatening the Jews of the Prague ghetto: Yod first helps the women penetrate an enemy base through its computer to track down Shira's son, then proves essential in saving the boy.

Once Joseph has heroically saved the Prague ghetto from a vicious mob, the rabbi, through ritual chanting, returns the golem to inanimate clay. The fate of Yod is similar, although it is he who destroys himself, along with the laboratory in which he was created, so that enslaved machines won't be made to act as weapons against their will.

Shira is initially determined to create a new lover from a data base, but she finally decides that enough tampering with free will has already been done, so she destroys the records that would allow the creation of more cyborgs like Yod.

Marge Piercy confronts large issues in this novel: the social consequences of creating anthropomorphic cyborgs, the dynamics of programming both humans and machines, the ethical question of our control of machines that might feel as well as think.

At the present time, virtual reality experiments promise many startling changes in society. But Ms. Piercy's high-tech world of the near future is filled with wonders that stretch credulity. People transform their looks within a computer program, then emerge with their shapes permanently changed. Or they are zipped physically by some kind of teleportation from one place to another.

Perhaps one problem is that the details of *He, She and It* are cribbed, as Ms. Piercy acknowledges in an afterword, from the genre of science fiction known as cyberpunk, without the introduction of believable characters, men and women acutely aware of the extraordinary possibilities of a computer-mediated world. Most of the figures in this novel are described as being brilliant, their scholarship great, their minds superior, yet they behave like rather ordinary characters, exhausted by domestic and romantic problems, in a plot that is intermittently frenetic and weird and that is frequently reminiscent of a video game. Surprises abound, though the rationale behind them is often contrived and only too familiar. Shira's mother, killed before Shira's eyes in a raid, surfaces again; someone else's corpse had been substituted for hers. Love affairs develop easily and quickly in a game of musical beds that fails to engage our interest.

Some of the prose belies Ms Piercy's reputation as a poet: "Her heart collapsed like a crushed egg"; "She felt a roiling hot mixture of emotions, like a pot of thick fudge about to boil over"; "Nili cracked her knuckles sensually"; "It is a torment like fire in his mind."

The parallel stories of the golem and the cyborg, both created by men to serve humankind, initially offer a welcome strategy for varying the book's time and setting. Yet the heavy symbolism, unrelieved by humor, retards the pace of both narratives until *He, She and It,* despite its complicated plot and use of Buck Rogers fantasy, often reads more like an extended essay on freedom of conscience than a full-rigged work of fiction.

Billie Maciunas (essay date March 1992)

SOURCE: "Feminist Epistemology in Piercy's *Woman on the Edge of Time,*" in *Women's Studies,* Vol. 20, Nos. 3-4, March, 1992, pp. 249-58.

[*In the following essay, Maciunas relates Sandra Harding's delineation of feminist epistemology and scientific bias to Piercy's vision of society in* Woman on the Edge of Time.]

Sandra Harding's view of science as a social activity leads her to propose critical interpretation as a mode of knowledge-seeking, useful in particular for theorizing "the effects on the natural sciences of gender symbolism, gender structure, and individual gender." Early in her book, *The Science Question in Feminism,* she suggests that novelists and poets may provide an "intuitive grasp" of the emancipatory theory needed to get beyond the categories of "science-as-usual," which she regards as indistinguishable from bad science. Harding names Marge Piercy and Anne McCaffrey as two such visionaries whose respective work explores a culture without gender institutionalization and the ambiguous relation between human and machine. Accordingly, I have chosen Piercy's novel, **Woman on the Edge of Time,** with a view toward discovering how a contemporary American feminist writer envisions a non-gendered society. Specifically, I will examine some of the ways in which Piercy's imaginary culture relates to Harding's discussion of feminist epistemologies that are emerging as a response to sexist, classist and racist policies in science.

For Harding, science-as-usual, while functioning under cover of a supposed value-neutral ethics, is inherently sexist, racist and classist. She identifies three types of feminist epistemologies whose nascent practice has the potential for producing "a politics of knowledge-seeking that would show us the conditions necessary to transfer control from the 'haves' to the 'have-nots.'" Harding labels these epistemologies *feminist empiricism,* the *feminist standpoint,* and *feminist postmodernism.*

Feminist empiricism, working for the reform of "bad science," reveals the incoherencies of empiricist epistemologies by subverting the notion that the social identity of the observer is irrelevant to the results of the research. Harding points out, for example, that women in science are "more likely than men to notice androcentric bias." In spite of their commitment to empiricist principles, feminist empiricists argue that "as a group [they] are more likely to produce unbiased and objective results than are men (or nonfeminists) as a group."

The second type of feminist epistemology, the feminist standpoint, is based in Hegelian "thinking about the relationship between the master and the slave" as elaborated in the writings of Marx, Engels, and G. Lukács. The proposal of the feminist standpoint is that subjugated knowledge provides the grounds for unravelling the "partial and perverse understandings" of a science based on the interests of dominant groups. Unlike feminist empiricism, the feminist standpoint regards the social identity of the inquirer as a variable.

The third type of feminist epistemology, feminist postmodernism, would begin from the perspective of inevitable fragmentation. As a part of the general postmodernist movement, feminist postmodernism would seek a solidarity of oppositions to the myth of an essential human being, a being conceptualized in fact by historical males. Feminist postmodernism shares with the feminist standpoint the view that the fiction of the "uniquely human" has gener-

ated distorted and exploitative policies. However, postmodern suspicion of holistic epistemologies precludes acceptance of a single feminist standpoint.

For Harding, the epistemological foundations of our present science practices are history-specific. She divides the emergence of the "New Science Movement" of the fourteenth century into stages. The final stage the "moment of mythologizing," coincides with the development of Descartes' method for the production of a "value-neutral" science. Instrumentalist in its outlook, Cartesian science "compromised the political goals of the New Science Movement," whose organization of social labor stood in opposition to church dogma. As Harding herself points out, her argument follows that of Thomas Kuhn in *The Structure of Scientific Revolution* in which Kuhn shows how "normal science" and its methods are merely the after-effects of revolutionary paradigm shifts. Moreover, defenders of normal science "rewrite its history in a way that often hides the nature of its early struggles."

Harding compares the practices of women scientists (presumably feminist empiricists) to the practices of those artisans of the New Science Movement. Their "new kind of labor made possible the ensuing widespread appreciation of the virtues of experimental observation." She lists five kinds of critiques which have helped in forming an emancipators theory in response to normal science. They are:

1) equity studies that identify and document the ways that *de facto* discrimination is maintained even after formal barriers have broken down. Motivation studies, for example, show a difference between boys' and girls' interest in excelling in such subjects as science, engineering, and mathematics. To the point, Harding asks why women would want to be "just like men" in interesting themselves in questions "skewed toward men's perception of what they find puzzling."

2) studies documenting the abuses of scientific technologies in biology and the social sciences. Such abuses include the perpetration of reproductive policies that are oppressive to women (doubly so in the case of poor women, including women of color). As an example of such abuse Harding mentions

> the resuscitation of scientifically supported sentimental images of motherhood and nuclear forms of family life for some at the same time that social supports for mothers and nonnuclear families are systematically withdrawn for others.

3) challenges to the idea of the possibility of a "pure science." Harding relates this challenge to the process of selection of problems to be solved by science. The hierarchical structure of the science profession assures that a white male elite ("less than 0.01 percent of scientific workers") is privileged with decision-making, while the technicians and domestic staff who carry out the work are composed for the most part of white middle class women

(in the upper ranks of technicians) and minority men and women (among the lower ranks of technicians and domestic staff). The case for value-neutral results is damaged when one considers the gap in knowledge between "the scientist" in his search for truth and the workforce that implements the research into problems deemed worthy of inquiry.

Harding questions whether the selection of problems to be solved will not always reflect the interests of dominant groups. But given this necessarily value-laden bias she considers whether some value-laden research projects may not be "maximally objective" within the structure of an already existing overtly sexist, racist, and classist program. For example, would not self-consciously anti-sexist and/or anti-racist inquiries be more objective than "sex-blind" ones?

4) "[T]he related techniques of literary criticism, historical interpretation and psychoanalysis" have unveiled the social meanings of metaphors used in the founding of modern science. In addition, the familiar dichotomies, reason vs. emotion, mind vs. body, etc., are related to masculinity and femininity, especially in the context of a supposed necessity to control emotions, the body, and "the feminine" in the interest of human progress

5) Finally, as mentioned, feminist epistemologies have emerged that reflect more accurately "shifting configurations of gender, race, and class. . . ."

Marge Piercy's novel, published in 1976, offers contrasting visions between the present world view (perhaps the early 1960's) and a "possible" future (2137) in which the feminist epistemologies described by Harding help to form the world view. This possible future can emerge only through the imagination and intentional actions of Connie, a 37 year old Chicana mental patient. Connie's visions take her into the world of Luciente, who may be imagined as a possible version of Connie herself, given a world in which gender socialization and the concurrent division of labor along gender and/or class lines is abolished. Luciente is a plant geneticist whose work involves reconstructing species of plants that have been destroyed by pollution, as well as creating plants that are useful for food and other human needs. Most of the other characters in Piercy's novel also mirror each other in terms of present and future. For example, Sybil, who is confined to the hospital for being a witch, is mirrored by Erzulia, a black woman in the future who practices both witchcraft and traditional surgery.

When Luciente first appears to Connie she is mistaken for a man. The narrator says

> Luciente spoke, she moved with that air of brisk unselfconscious authority Connie associated with men. Luciente sat down, taking up more space than women ever did. She squatted, she sprawled, she strolled, never thinking about how her body was displayed.

By contrast, women in Connie's world are absurdly socialized according to men's conceptions of their reality. Con-

nie's niece, Dolly, for example, is a prostitute who changes her appearance so that she will look more like the white male's idea of a beautiful woman. She says

> I got to stay skinny, carita. The money is with the Anglos and they like you skinny and American-looking. It pays more if you look Anglo, you know.

The nightmare of such a reality is glaringly shown in Piercy's image of another possible world into which Connie stumbles by accident while trying to contact Luciente. In the near future Connie encounters Gildina, Dolly's exaggerated double. Gildina is "a built-up contracty . . . [c]osmetically fixed for sex use."

Piercy shows, too, the contradiction inherent in the socialization of women strictly for motherhood. Connie and her niece can afford to raise their children only at the cost of dependence on men who are for the most part abusive. At the same time, the women in Connie's world are subject to the abusive technology connected with reproductive policies that deny them the achievement of the ideal of motherhood. Both Connie and her mother, for example, after being admitted to the hospital for other reasons, were given hysterectomies "because the residents wanted practice." Connie's sister is given sugar pills instead of birth control pills after her sixth child because of an experiment. Her seventh child is then born with deficiencies that require costly treatment, "All because Inez thought she had a doctor, but she got a scientist."

For Piercy, egalitarianism necessitates women giving up their exclusive right to bear children, in order that men may participate in the community as mothers (children are laboratory created; men are administered hormones so that they can nurse their children). Luciente explains

> It was part of women's long revolution. When we were breaking all the old hierarchies. Finally there was that one thing we had to give up too, the only power we ever had, in return for no more power for anyone. The original production: the power to give birth. Cause as long as we were biologically enchained, we'd never be equal. And males never would be humanized to be loving and tender. So we all became mothers.

In this instance, Piercy imagines a future whose grounding is in feminist postmodernism. Feminist postmodernism does not ostensibly seek to reform science or to raise subjugated forms of knowledge to higher status. Rather, like postmodernist theories in general, it seeks an end to globalizing discourses in which an elite avant-garde is empowered to define and administer the tenets of "truth." One type of feminist postmodernist theory is object-relations theory. Object-relations theory considers philosophy to be the site of the problematization of "the relationships between subject and object, mind and body, inner and outer, reason and sense. . . ." It proposes that men's preoccupation with objectivity stems from infantile separation from the mother. Men, more than women, remain "frozen in a defensive infantile need to dominate and/or repress others in order to retain . . . individual identity."

Women's experience thereby becomes the opposite pole of the duality by which men "take their own experience as paradigmatically human rather than merely as typically masculine." Mothering (caring work), then, must be incorporated as a human experience and located at the center of culture, rather than remaining at the margins of culture as "women's work," under-valued and/or sentimentalized.

Feminist postmodernism, as Harding notes, proposes reciprocity as a more desirable way of knowing than defensive gendering. In **Woman on the Edge of Time** Piercy imagines a world in which interpersonal relations are valued as a form of community activity. Members of this intentional community participate in "wormings" in order to discover and eliminate the sources of hostility between individuals. Connie, visiting from the past, complains, "Don't you people have nothing to worry about besides personal stuff?" One of the community members then points out the connection between individual and national warfare:

> [W]e believe many actions fail because of inner tensions. To get revenge against someone an individual thinks wronged per, individuals have offered up nations to conquest.

Thieves in this society are given presents to relieve feelings of neglect and poverty (there is no private property). Likewise, crimes of violence are regarded as treatable by healing. However, if a person commits such a crime for a second time, they are executed. Parra, the Hispanic woman who is selected as referee (judge) for a worming explains, "We don't want to watch each other or to imprison each other. We aren't willing to live with people who choose to use violence. We execute them."

Piercy's valuation of interpersonal relations (to the point of an absolute intolerance for violence) reflects the feminist standpoint epistemology in which relational forms of knowing are regarded as morally preferable to the objectification of individuals and groups. In opposition to Cartesian dualisms, interpersonal caring as community work unites the "manual, mental, and emotional ('hand, brain, and heart') activity characteristic of women's work. . . ." It also recalls the craft labor necessary for the emergence of the "New Science Movement" of the fourteenth century. As Harding points out

> The organizational forms of the women's movement, unlike those of capitalist production relations and its science, resist dividing mental, manual, and caring activity among different classes of persons. And its project is to provide the knowledge women need to understand and manage our own bodies: subject and object of inquiry are one.

The intolerance of violence in the possible future can be read as Piercy's reaction to the disproportionate number of violent crimes committed by men in our present society, particularly when many of the most violent are committed as a matter of course by men *against women*. Piercy shows

a parallel between violent crimes against women and the practices of science-as-usual. The white male doctors privileged to define Connie's reality on the ward label her as violent. The description, however, is ironic since Connie's violence consists in her defending herself against physical abuse by her niece's pimp, referred to as the niece's "fiance" by the doctors. The interpretation of Connie's actions as "violent" is used to justify forms of research into behavior control, called "treatment," such as forced isolation, administration of soporific drugs, shock therapy, and brain implants for the control of "patient's" emotions by electrical impulses administered from outside.

In order to avoid "treatment" Connie tries to prove her normalcy by volunteering to do housework on the ward. Likewise, in order to persuade her brother (who has committed her) to let her visit him, Connie must agree to do the housework for him and his Anglo wife. Thus Connie's labor is extracted on the basis of definitions of normalcy for women that posit a natural genesis for women's caring, as opposed to a social one. These definitions of women and their reality help to naturalize their victimization. In Piercy's book, Connie is aware of the connection:

> [T]he pressure was to say please and put on lipstick and sit at a table playing cards, to obey and work for nothing, cleaning the houses of the staff. To look away from graft and abuse. To keep quiet as you watched them beat other patients. To pretend that the rape in the linen room was a patient's fantasy.

Reading the above passage from a feminist standpoint, it is easy to see that the rape fantasy is that of the white male doctors. The parallel drawn earlier between the division of labor in the sciences and in society makes clear that ruling conceptual schemes do not include categories adequate for defining women's reality, although the attempt is nevertheless made, with an arrogance that is both ignorant and invasive. Regarding women's work of personal maintenance Harding says,

> Men who are relieved of the need to maintain their own bodies and the local places where they exist can . . . see as real only what corresponds to their abstracted mental world.

Piercy's novel is hopeful in its images of a possible future in which the revolutionary feminist epistemologies described by Harding are instrumental in creating a more egalitarian world. As Harding suggests, change is a labor intensive activity. The emergence of the "New Science Movement" in the early Renaissance required a new type of individual who was both educated and willing to perform manual labor: "artisans, shipbuilders, mariners, miners, foundrymen, and carpenters." When Connie imagines revolution as "Honchos marching around in imitation uniforms," she is informed that

> It's the people who worked on the labor-and-land intensive farming we do. It's all the people who changed how people bought food, raised children, went to school!

Sybil, the mental ward image of Erzuha, the healer, manages to make contact with the future in such a concrete way. Near the conclusion of the book Sybil notes that some of the college girl volunteers on the ward are interested in the healing properties of herbs. Although Sybil could not go to college, much less study witchcraft there, she is told by the college girls about "a class in a women's school" where they learned, among other things, to cure infections with lovage compresses. Thus, Sybil can be seen as a "foremother" of the emerging movement in which forms of medicine that have been suppressed as "voodoo" and "witchcraft" are practiced along with surgery and genetic engineering. One of the most renowned "healers" in Piercy's possible future is a black woman, Erzulia, who is famous for developing a method of setting bone fractures in the aged and who practices mental telepathy in the control of physical processes. Connie asks, "How can anybody be into voodoo and medicine? It doesn't make sense!" Luciente, her guide, responds, "Each makes a different kind of sense, no?" Piercy's vision reflects the emergence of feminist epistemologies in that forms of subjugated knowledge stemming from suppressed practices are accepted in her future world. In addition, the valorization of a black woman as a professional healer indicates an interest in redressing the imbalance of the division of labor discussed by Harding as the position of feminist empiricists. In this instance, Piercy is imagining a reform of science such that the presence of women scientists works to eliminate androcentric bias that prohibits useful forms of medicine. Further, the character of Erzulia addresses the issue of the absence of black women (and men) in the upper strata of the science profession's hierarchy and the forms of knowledge consequently lacking in science for any sort of "objective" knowledge about the world we inhabit.

Piercy's novel reveals the emergence of the three feminist epistemologies as detailed by Harding. It does not, however, offer a Utopian vision, nor does it show an "intuitive grasp" of any emancipatory theory. Piercy simply imagines a possible world given the intentionality of people receptive to change. Connie's "receptivity" in contacting Luciente is a metaphor for the ability to comprehend and implement change for those whose ways of knowing and forms of knowledge have been denied reality. Piercy's metaphor for implementing these changes, however, is war. She concludes her book with the certainty that Connie will be forced to undergo a brain implant in spite of her model behavior. Such an event bodes the emergence of Gildina's world and the possibility of melding human and machine for use and control by the empowered.

At the conclusion of Piercy's story, as at the beginning, Connie's choice is to defend herself against violence with violence. After losing her appeal to the doctors that she be allowed to forego the brain implant, Connie poisons four of the doctors with a pesticide that she has stolen from her brother's nursery. Her method of murder underscores the tragedy of her being thwarted in her potential development as a member of a caring community. As mentioned, her mirror image in the future, Luciente, is a plant geneticist who is concerned to create and use plants for the growth of the community, not its destruction. Moreover, Sybil and her future counterpart, Erzulia, show how the development of their knowledge of plants can lead to cures. Connie's solution of murder with the very tools that could be used for good reflects the dominant culture's own misuse of technology in its objectifying view of the environment.

As soon as Connie has poisoned the doctors, she understands that she is no longer receptive to Luciente's world. Piercy thus seems to conclude that the possibility of the world that she imagines is closed off by violence. Although Connie was receptive to change, she could not escape the confines of the reality defined for her by the dominant white male culture. But neither was she active in the political struggles (like Sybil, for example) that would have created a more ambiguous relationship with that culture than definitions of mother and/or mental patient could provide. Instead, Connie's resistance is confined to conforming to her doctors' expectations of her in order to buy time and gain privileges, attempting to escape, and finally committing murder.

While this paper is unable to address in detail all of the issues raised in Harding's and Piercy's books, it is hoped that it nonetheless demonstrates the relationship between sexist, classist, and racist policies in science and in society at large. For Harding, such policies are not a result of bad science as much as they are a consequence of science-as-usual, whose epistemological foundation of value-neutral, objective inquiry is skewed toward the needs of a white male elite. As both Harding's and Piercy's texts argue, feminist epistemologies indicate revolutionary changes in knowers, ways of knowing, and the world to be known. They ought to and do show us "the conditions necessary to transfer control from the 'haves' to the 'have-nots.'"

Patricia Volk (review date 20 March 1994)

SOURCE: "The Three of Them," in *The New York Times Book Review*, March 20, 1994, p. 23.

[*In the following review, Volk offers tempered praise for* The Longings of Women.]

Why is it that women who think they can't survive without a man invariably pick the wrong one? In her 12th novel, ***The Longings of Women,*** Marge Piercy explores the tragic female myth—"I'm nothing without him"— and how lives get trapped by it. Alternating chapters focus on three wildly different people who intersect, bounce off one another and dramatically change course.

Divorced by her husband, at 61 Mary Burke has spiraled down from tennis at the country club to the nightmare of homelessness. She is a chilling reminder that having no place to live can happen to anybody. On bad winter nights in Boston she sweeps leftovers from the food court at the mall into her shopping bag and winds mufflers around her thighs so she won't freeze to death.

A good night is not much better. Mary squats at homes where she does day work, having rifled her employers' desks, dressers and appointment calendars to check when they'll be out of town. You may think twice about leaving a cleaning lady the key when you learn that Mary knew "Mr. Douglas coddled an ulcer and liked dirty movies of women together. . . . Mrs. DeMott had had liposuction. . . . Mrs. Anzio was on tranquilizers. . . . Mr. Landsman was unfaithful to his wife."

Mary is a world-class snoop but she's admirable, too, nurturing her self-respect by wearing found lipsticks and caring about homeless women even worse off than she is.

On Wednesdays Mary cleans for Leila Landsman, an associate professor at Lesley College in Boston whose work with incest survivors is "only marginally respectable academically." Self-probing yet myopic, Leila suspects that her husband, an actor turned director, is cheating on her for the 16th time. Still, she calls Nick "Beloved" and doesn't worry about AIDS. Terrified of feeling anger, she believes "love was not a constant. It swelled and shrank. It grew weak and recovered into vigor."

That's a good observation because it's true. It becomes pivotal to the novel when Ms Piercy lets Leila use it to deceive herself.

Becky Burgess enters the picture when Leila gets a contract to write a book about her. Details of Becky's character appear to be based on Pamela Smart, the New Hampshire high school teacher who was convicted of conspiring with a student to murder her husband and sentenced to life imprisonment in 1991.

Becky also torments her adolescent lover until he kills her husband. She even puts the dead man's clothes in a garbage bag and drops it off at the in-laws', just as Pamela Smart reportedly did. If you're familiar with the case, co-opting details so specific might break the fictional spell, but I got right back under it as Becky's grisly single-mindedness steered her toward the slammer.

Marge Piercy can seat 15 strangers around a Thanksgiving table, and by the time dessert is served you'll know all of them. Her paragraph on Leila's interview techniques for talking with battered women is a miniature master class. These characters are so authentic, you'll want to shake them: "Leave that creep!"; "Get a shrink!"; "Work at Legal Seafood!"

But do we really need to be told, "Leila aimed to be a good woman and a dependable human being"? A novel this generous requires no work, but robs the reader of those participatory moments when a truth is discovered on its own. Yet Ms Piercy's take on victimization is deliber-

ate: these women engineer the terrible things that happen to them. They don't happen to them because they are women.

Fiction doesn't have to have a message, but *The Longings of Women* throbs with one. Nobody's security should depend on somebody else. Ladies, are you listening? Get a job. Never long for men who long for other women. And if, God forbid, you're ever homeless, get out of the Snow Belt, fast.

Constance Casey (review date 27 March 1994)

SOURCE: "Yearning for a Home," in *Washington Post Book World,* March 27, 1994, p. 5.

[*In the following review, Casey offers qualified praise for* The Longings of Women.]

If this tale of three heroines is to be believed, then the answer to the question "What do women want?" is, simply, a house. According to Marge Piercy, what women long for is shelter with an affordable mortgage. If this doesn't sound particularly literary or inspiring, you should understand that Piercy doesn't give a damn about literary or inspiring. Harsh truths are what Piercy cares for; she has no taste or talent for what John Updike calls "fiction's shapely lies." The plot—for each of Piercy's heroines—is: Woman Meets House. Woman Loses House. Woman Gets House. (In one case, perhaps The Big House.)

Piercy's three heroines appear in descending order of net worth and ascending order of interest. The most well-off and least engaging is Leila, 45, who teaches sociology and writes about women in prison. Her husband is a theater director who has affairs—close to one a year over the course of 20 years of marriage—which Leila tolerates.

Piercy's second heroine, Becky, 25, was one of seven children growing up in a poor New Bedford household with one bathroom. The first in her family to go to college, Becky marries a dull man (with well-heeled parents) to gain respectability—specifically, a sunny shingled condo on the Cape, where with joyful proprietariness she cleans the bathroom grout with a toothbrush. A Becky Sharp for our era, this Becky, derives her values from the Shopping Channel and inane motivational tapes. She is certainly calculating and self-centered (her brother's death at sea makes her feel like a celebrity) but we're not so sure she's capable of plotting with her teen lover to kill her husband. Becky and Leila meet when Leila begins a book about the case; Piercy keeps Leila and the reader in suspense for a while about Becky's guilt.

The poorest of the novel's characters is Piercy's star. Mary, 61, has been house-cleaning for Boston families, including Leila's, since she was left by her husband and lost her clerical job. She's dependable, respectably dressed and hard working. So hard-working that she can finish a six-hour cleaning job in three hours and lie down for the rest of her time alone in the house. A necessity because Mary is homeless, burned out of her apartment. Her clients think she lives with her daughter somewhere in Boston. In fact, her daughter lives with spouse and children in Chevy Chase and sends the occasional check to Mary's post-office box.

When concentrating on Mary, Piercy's militant sympathy and her eye for concrete detail are used to best effect. Mary usually sleeps at Logan Airport or in a church basement. She takes care always to keep her few possessions in an unwrinkled bag (crumpled shopping bags draw police attention). She subsists on spoonfuls of cornflakes or granola or leftover soup from clients' cupboards. A few nights a month she can afford a motel room; mostly she bathes with paper towels in restrooms.

Most vividly rendered is the tedium of having to kill time by walking around, of never being able to sit down for long. One of Mary's airport tactics is to seek out a delayed flight so that she can rest surrounded by other tired, dejected-looking people.

How did she end up homeless? It's a question many women ask themselves when they see women begging on the street, fearing that some misfortune could land them there, too. A college graduate, Mary was married to a civil-servant, and entertained his colleagues in her Bethesda Home. Her husband now lives comfortably with his third wife and second set of children; the injustice of the situation is not lost on Mary.

Marry a professional man, older women had advised Mary in her youth. Now, she thinks, "They should have said, be a caterer, buy a property and pay it off fast. Never mind the rest."

With all the timely power of Mary's story, why should we care about the gracelessness of Piercy's writing? There are popularisms like, "Being married and having his own life and his own home were just not priorities." There are Judith Krantzisms like, "She put on the red silk Victoria's Secret nightgown he had given her for her birthday two years before, rather than the flannel Eileen West she usually wore." And there are even saccharine cute cat-isms. Of Leila's newly adopted tom, Piercy writes, "He did not feel it was too soon to begin that vital training that lubricated the loving relationship between the cat and the person he owned." And there are chats we doubt ever got chatted. Establishing her credentials to a source, Leila explains: "I believe I've had a small influence in legislation concerning the rights of women in prison vis-a-vis their children in three states." When the author's voice is this artless and humorless, it shakes the reader's faith in her judgment, especially her sense of proportion. (Not to mention that Piercy seems to lack sympathy for 49 percent of the human race. The lovable cat has been fixed.)

Piercy has always been an unapologetic ideologue. Her first popular book, *Small Changes,* brought to life the discontents outlined in Betty Friedan's *The Feminine Mystique.* Interestingly, the best of her 11 novels is a work of science fiction, *Woman on the Edge of Time,* in which Piercy was freed from realism. Then her heroine was a mental patient who could escape forward in time. Reading Piercy's descriptions of Mary's life in *The Longings of Women* is like reading science fiction. In this case, science fiction about time travel to some nearly unthinkable future in which people have no homes and have to live on the streets. More than unhappily, this does occur in our present and is no fiction. *The Longings of Women* is not a book for the ages, but it is a book for this exact moment.

Judith Wynn (review date 17 April 1994)

SOURCE: "Marge Piercy Tells a Cautionary Tale of Women on the Edge," in *Chicago Tribune Books,* April 17, 1994, p. 3.

[*In the following review, Wynn offers favorable evaluation of* The Longings of Women.]

What do women want? Freud—for one—pondered the question. In *The Longings of Women* novelist-poet Marge Piercy gives a clear, ringing answer: A woman wants some space all her own-ask any bag lady. And Piercy does. Or, to be accurate, Mary Burke, one of the three heroines of this lively, densely textured novel, is almost a bag lady.

Mary started out a "normal girl from Normal, Illinois," and spent 20-some years tending her husband and her two spoiled children in posh suburbia. But as Piercy knows—and most other women at least suspect—the stay-at-home housewife can be just one husband away from poverty.

Divorced in her mid-40s and then moved to Boston by her boyfriend/employer, who dumped her a few years later, Mary has joined the ranks of the homeless as *Longings* begins. Her life is a succession of semi-legal sleepovers in the houses she cleans for a living. Whenever one of her clients goes out of town, Mary lets herself in with her cleaning-lady key for a few precious nights of peace and shelter. If her client returns unexpectedly, Mary retreats to the garage. If the garage is locked, she sleeps in church basements or sitting up in the international terminal at Logan Airport. Institutionalized shelters for the homeless would destroy the feisty independence that Mary must maintain in order to fool both herself and her clients: "Her class drop would transfix and repel them at once."

Mary's most baffling client is 40ish Leila Landsman, a professor at a small college next door to Harvard. Leila tolerates her theater-director husband's many affairs even though she pays most of the household bills. Mary can't figure it.

Leila, meanwhile, is writing a scholarly book about a young woman named Becky Burgess, who has murdered her husband for the insurance money. This, Mary can understand: "Thinking of doing violence to someone who was hurting you could be soothing in a minor way."

The author's more political-minded, class-conscious fans will no doubt be pleased to see that Piercy has returned from the cyberpunk realms of her most recent novel—the sci-fi dystopia fantasy *He, She & It*—to the nitty-gritty, present-day struggle between the haves and the have-nots. Harking back to the Cambridge, Mass., of Piercy's first big feminist hit, *Small Changes, The Longings of Women* is a feminist cautionary tale—although its message is somewhat dated now that the economic realities of family life have put full-time housewifery well beyond the reach of the average family-and-career-juggling American woman.

What makes *Longings* such an arresting work, nevertheless, is the way Piercy yokes the homeless issue to the disturbing phenomenon of women who murder their spouses for cash. Becky is the fictitious counterpart of New Hampshire's true-crime villainess Pamela Smart, who drew a life sentence in 1991 for persuading her teenage boyfriend to murder her husband.

Piercy does a fine job of digging beneath the sleazy surface of the boy-seducing vamp to the blue-collar murderess' yearnings for respect and for a nicer, more spacious home than her overburdened parents were able to provide for her. Though Piercy supplies some hot and heavy sex scenes, she makes it clear that Becky's real love affair is with the pretty condo that comes with her unhappy marriage.

"I won't lie down and let you shovel me off the porch," Becky silently promises her scornful, philandering husband. "This is war."

Leila is the most stable and analytical of the novel's three main characters. A solid career and a few loyal friends are her hedges against the misfortunes that hobble Mary and Becky.

Dismayed by her own collapsing marriage, Leila considers love "a long and tedious delusion . . . a one-person brainwashed cult." But love eventually finds Leila, even though it's a more provisional, autumnal love than the victorious unions of such earlier Piercy novels as *Fly Away Home* and *Summer People.*

Piercy shrewdly traces her three protagonists' small, crucial changes and their ambivalent triumphs. Cool and self-possessed in jail, Becky trims her ambitions to suit her new circumstances. Mary gets a new chance, too. Although she appears to be setting herself up for the same old letdowns, it's heartening to see that the women-centered options created by quiet feminists like Leila may make a difference after all.

Piercy is not an elegant writer. Interesting, swift-moving plots and careful social observation are her main strengths.

Although she has been criticized for writing didactic potboilers, *The Longings of Women* gives its characters plenty of space to play out their truest instincts, right or wrong.

M. Keith Booker (essay date November 1994)

SOURCE: "Woman on the Edge of a Genre: The Feminist Dystopias of Marge Piercy," in *Science-Fiction Studies,* Vol. 21, Part 3, November, 1994, pp. 337-50.

[*In the following essay, Booker discusses Piercy's fusion of utopian and dystopian literary conventions to present a distinct feminist perspective in* Woman on the Edge of Time *and* He, She, and It.]

Marge Piercy's science-fiction visions of the future have made important in-roads into what has been a traditionally masculine territory. *Woman on the Edge of Time* has become a contemporary classic, and the recent *He, She, and It* (winner of the 1992 Arthur C. Clarke Award) is already gaining considerable attention as well. These works, similar in their imaginative power and political commitment, are otherwise quite different, and Piercy's move from the first to the second can be taken as indicative of the increasingly complex intermixture of utopian and dystopian moods that has informed feminist imaginative fiction in the last few decades. *Woman on the Edge of Time* was written in the mid-1970s and reflects some of the utopian optimism of the women's movement of that era, though it has a significant grim side as well. *He, She, and It,* meanwhile, was written at the end of the 1980s, for many a decidedly dark decade for women's causes. As might be expected, the latter book contains a much larger portion of dystopian images than does the former. At the same time, and curiously, the overall mood of *He, She, and It* is in many ways far more positive than that of its predecessor. Still, both texts include a mixture of positive and negative imaginative projections of the future. Indeed, they gain much of their energy precisely from the dialogic combination of these perspectives, a combination that acknowledges the complexity of history itself while at the same time suggesting important generic interrelationships between utopian and dystopian fiction.

In some ways dystopian fiction would seem to be a natural genre for feminist writers, despite the fact that such writers have more typically been associated with *utopian* fiction. Centrally concerned with the clash between individual desire and societal demand, dystopian fiction often focuses on sexuality and relations between the genders as elements of this conflict. For example, the governments of dystopian societies like those described in *We, Brave New World,* and *1984* all focus on sexuality as a crucial matter for their efforts at social control. And it is also clear that this focus comes about largely because of a perception on the part of these governments that sexuality is a potential locus of powerful subversive energies.

On the other hand, despite this consistent focus on sexuality in dystopian fiction, the major works of the genre have done relatively little to challenge conventional notions of gender roles. Despite giving frequent lip service to equality of the genders, literary dystopias (and utopias, for that matter) have typically been places where men are men and women are women, and in relatively conventional ways. As in many other ways, More's original *Utopia* sets the tone for this trend. In contrast to his belief that social and economic inequality is the source of most of the ills of his contemporary European society, More's Raphael Hythloday describes an ideal Utopian society where equality is emphasized above all else, even to the point of suppression of individual liberty and imposition of a potentially oppressive conformity. However, despite this demand for complete social homogeneity, More's Utopia is still a strongly patriarchal society. The principal political unit is the family household, and households are generally ruled by the eldest male member of the family. Upon marriage women transfer to the household of their husband's family, while males remain members of their own family for life. Within the household, meanwhile, the hierarchy of authority is clearly defined: "Wives are subject to their husbands, children to their parents, and generally the younger to their elders."

It is important, however, to recognize that More is not unusual in his vision of the subservience of women in his otherwise homogeneous society. Indeed, it seems clear that More sought to include women in the egalitarian basis of his society—women have opportunities for education and employment in his Utopia that far outstrip those available in early-16th-century England. That More was unable to imagine a society in which women were genuinely the equals of men thus stands as a reminder of the profound embeddedness of gender prejudice in Western society. The idea that men should be regarded as inherently superior to women was apparently for More such an obvious and natural one that it never occurred to him that gender inequality should be among the various other social hierarchies leveled in his ideal society.

Most of the literary utopias that followed in the next four centuries after More similarly failed to make the imaginative leap required to envision true equality for women, even though utopian thought itself is centrally concerned with the imagination of alternative societies that surmount the prejudices and conventions of the status quo. But some prejudices and conventions are more difficult to overcome than others, and the lack of genuine attention to gender issues in so many utopian and dystopian works right up to the present day suggests that patriarchal habits are among the most ingrained of all of the characteristics of Western civilization. Feminist thinkers of the last century or so have been well aware of this fact, of course, and among other things they have responded with their own alternative utopian tradition that has been centrally concerned with demonstrating the possibility of thinking beyond thousands of years of patriarchy. Women like Elizabeth Stuart Phelps and Mary E. Bradley wrote late-19th-century utopian works with feminist affinities, and the early-20th-century work of Charlotte Perkins Gilman (*Moving the Mountain, Herland,* and *With Her in Ourland*) can be regarded as the beginning of a full-blown feminist utopian tradition.

This tradition gained considerable energy with the feminist movement of the late 1960s and the 1970s. Indeed, during this period writers like Piercy, Ursula K. Le Guin, Samuel Delany, and Joanna Russ produced works that reenergized the utopian genre as a whole, moving toward an open-endedness that sought to overcome the tendency toward monological stagnation that had long haunted conceptualizations of utopia. Tom Moylan argues that such writers attempted to create in their works what he calls "critical utopias," retaining an "awareness of the limitations of the utopian tradition, so that these texts reject utopia as blueprint while preserving it as dream." Such utopias are able to function effectively as critiques of the status quo, while maintaining a self-critical awareness that prevents them from descending into empty utopian cliché.

On the other hand, in the context of a 1980s America dominated by Reagan-Bush conservative politics and highlighted (if that is the word) by the defeat of the Equal Rights Amendment, feminist writers found it more and more difficult to see better times ahead. Of course, the writers of feminist utopias have always been aware that their positive visions were imperiled by the existing patriarchal order and have thereby often included dystopian warnings within their utopian texts. Suzy McKee Charnas, for example, sets up her utopian *Motherliness* with *Walk to the End of the World,* an earlier dystopian fiction. Meanwhile, both Piercy and Joanna Russ (*The Female Man*) present alternative futures that suggest multiple possibilities, some utopian, some decidedly dystopian. And by the mid-1980s Margaret Atwood produces *The Handmaid's Tale,* a feminist text that is almost purely dystopian. Indeed, as Fitting notes, feminist visions of the future tended in general to show a dark turn in the 1980s, probably due to political reverses that damped the feminist optimism of the 1970s: "More recent fictions no longer give us images of a radically different future, in which the values and ideals of feminism have been extended to much of the planet, but rather offer depressing images of a brutal reestablishment of capitalist patriarchy."

Piercy's work is particularly interesting because of its ability to maintain clear links to the tradition of feminist utopias while at the same time opening important dialogues with the masculine utopian classics and with the traditionally masculine dystopian genre. For example, ***Woman on the Edge of Time*** closely parallels More's *Utopia* in form. More's book includes two parts, the first of which describes the social ills of early-16th-century England and the second of which outlines an alternative society in which the problems of Part One have been solved. Indeed, the book's satirical and critical effect derives largely from the contrast between these two societies, which in essence casts More's England as a sort of dystopia. Similarly,

Woman on the Edge of Time presents Piercy's contemporary America as a society that is already a dystopia for marginal members of society like her protagonist Connie Ramos, then contrasts this dystopian America with an ideal 22nd-century utopia based on tolerance, nurturing, communality, ecological responsibility, and the complete effacement of conventional gender differences.

Piercy's Ramos is a 37-year-old Chicana woman who has been a victim of the white male power structure in America throughout her life. Her status as an outsider to mainstream American society thus places her in much the same position as the protagonists of numerous dystopian fictions. And her victimization becomes particularly vivid when she is wrongly diagnosed as a violent paranoid schizophrenic and incarcerated in a nightmarish mental institution that serves as a sort of microcosm of the oppressively carceral society in which she lives. Meanwhile, Ramos's telepathic trips to the future utopian community of Mattapoisett place her very much in the vein of the classic visitor to utopia, and what she encounters there is an idealized vision that clearly grows out of a number of political movements in Ramos's (and Piercy's) own time, including feminism, socialism, and environmentalism. This utopian community manages successfully to integrate advanced technology, social planning, individual liberty, and a close connection to nature, based on Third World cultures and the culture of the Wamponaug Indians. All citizens of Mattapoisett are valued and loved, and all are treated equally regardless of race, gender, or other differences. In short, this society accepts and even welcomes precisely the differences that have marginalized Ramos in her own world.

The contrast between Mattapoisett and 1970s America is reinforced by the presentation of a second possible future, a dystopian one that grows out of an intensification of the already-existing problems of oppression, environmental destruction, class difference, and sexual exploitation. Piercy's dystopian alternative occupies only one chapter (the fifteenth) of *Woman on the Edge of Time,* but it is a striking vision that ranks in power with the classic dystopias of Zamyatin, Huxley, and Orwell. In its treatment of gender issues (as in the depiction of the woman Gildina as a mutilated sexual object), it goes well beyond any of these predecessors in power. In this society women function only as the property of men and the men themselves are little more than machines. The message seems clear: we can continue the way we are going until we reach this dystopian state, or we can change our ways and work toward utopia.

In *Woman on the Edge of Time* Piercy draws the lines between utopia and dystopia quite clearly, and the resultant dialogue between the two is an important source of energy for her book. Indeed, recalling Mikhail Bakhtin's emphasis on the importance of generic heterogeneity as a source of dialogic energy in the novel, a great deal of the power of *Woman on the Edge of Time* arises from confrontations among genres and the worldviews they imply. In addition to the opposition of utopian and dystopian genres, Piercy's vivid depiction of the present-day experiences of Connie Ramos introduces the genre of realistic fiction into this dialogue. And the book ends with a supposed reproduction of some of Ramos's medical records from various mental institutions, thus introducing still another genre. This last genre involves a direct statement of the official ideology of the medical establishment and of the social values it represents. Meanwhile, the content of the realistic passages in the novel conducts an explicit critique of this official ideology, even as the realistic form itself is in constant danger of being co-opted by that ideology. After all, realistic fiction involves a relatively straightforward reproduction of official reality that tacitly acknowledges conventional assumptions about the nature of that reality. By attacking the mental health system through what appears to be a transparent, "rational" narration of its treatment of Ramos, Piercy runs the risk of subtly reinforcing the ideology of rationalism that makes it possible safely to contain Ramos's potentially subversive energies simply by declaring her mad. But Piercy's mixture of realism with fantasy of both utopian and dystopian kinds is clearly designed to challenge that ideology by presenting explicit defamiliarizing alternatives. In particular, she projects a utopia based on fundamentally different principles than those which inform her contemporary society, then depicts a nightmarish dystopia whose principles are in fact recognizably similar to those of present-day America.

There are, of course, pitfalls in this procedure. In particular, as Bakhtin points out, dialogue in the novel is greatly influenced by the perspective of the reader. Though Piercy's position in *Woman on the Edge of Time* is clear, the line between utopia and dystopia can be a fine one. Many of the practices of the society of Mattapoisett are rather extreme, and some readers may not find conditions there ideal at all. Indeed, Mattapoisett shares many characteristics with classic *dystopias.* And it is always possible that a given reader will focus on the realistic portions of Piercy's text, which might then undermine the fantasy sections rather than the other way around. Among other things, the book leaves open the possibility that both the utopian and the dystopian futures are merely projections of Ramos's fantasies. A doggedly literal reader might then conclude that the alternative futures presented in the book are nothing more than hallucinations which prove that Ramos is indeed mad.

Piercy, in short, avoids a repetition of oppressive practices by refusing to demand that her book, however didactic, be interpreted in any given way. The ending of the book is similarly ambiguous. Ramos fatally poisons several members of the hospital staff, which might be (and has been, by most critics) taken as Piercy's endorsement of necessary political violence. But there is certainly some question as to the political effectiveness of this multiple murder, though it might be read as an indictment of a system that insists so blindly on defining Ramos as violent and dangerous that it eventually makes her that way. As

Carol Farley Kessler suggests, Ramos's eventual violent reaction to the violence that has been done to her might be taken as a comment on the way violence in our society triggers more violence, showing "the violence that our dystopian present perpetrates upon the innocent and sensitive powerless in our midst." But one could also read this ending simply as a demonstration that the diagnosis of Ramos was in fact right all along.

Such ambiguity in what is primarily a didactic work is obviously risky, but on balance the openness of *Woman on the Edge of Time* to variant readings is a point in its favor that allows the text to escape the finality and stasis that have traditionally been associated with utopian thought. Moreover, if Piercy's novel gains a certain dynamism from its internal dialogue among different genres and styles, it also picks up considerable energy from dialogues with other related texts. For example, the openness of Piercy's text can trace its genealogy back to H. G. Wells's *A Modern Utopia,* which set the tone for many modern utopian works with its insistence that the ideal society of the future "must be not static but kinetic, must shape not as a permanent state but as a hopeful state, leading to a long ascent of stages." Indeed, Wells's modern utopia, like Piercy's Mattapoisett, is highly open to diversity and difference, and one of its central characteristics is its dynamism. Moreover, Wells's text itself is structurally and rhetorically complex, including different and sometimes contradictory voices that tend to keep interpretation of the text from being finalized.

Of course, *Woman on the Edge of Time* shows much more awareness of feminist issues than does Wells's text, though Wells does include a chapter entitled "Women in a Modern Utopia." However, while Wells pays lip service to the notion of equality between men and women, his solution to the "woman problem" would mostly involve programs of planned parenthood and of the payment to women of maternity benefits, projects that might ease the suffering of individual women but that do not seem to address the fundamental attitudes toward gender that underlie that suffering. Indeed, that Well's discussion of marriage and childhood dominates the "Women in a Modern Utopia" section of his book indicates his acceptance of the fact that such issues are the principal ones with which women are concerned.

In fairness, it should be pointed out that Wells is writing in a turn-of-the-century climate far different from the one in which Piercy writes, and many of his ideas are firmly rooted in that context. In terms of its contemporary historical context, *Woman on the Edge of Time* clearly has more in common with modern "open" or "critical" utopias by writers like Russ, Delany, and Le Guin than with the earlier work of Wells. As Peter Ruppert notes, such open utopias typically achieve their openness through increased reader participation. In particular, he suggests that "in making the reader aware of his or her own role in shaping what the future will be, Piercy shows that the struggle for utopia depends on our actions in an open-ended historical process." In this sense, the works of writers like Russ, Le Guin, Delany, and Piercy also have much in common with the plays of Brecht, which similarly employ complex literary strategies to engage their audiences in a critical examination of their roles in the historical process and which also avoid simplistic and unequivocal statements of any single ideology in favor of numerous voices that complicate, but enrich their messages. Indeed, an understanding of the resonances between Piercy's text and those of predecessors like More, Wells, and Brecht greatly enriches the reading of *Woman on the Edge of Time,* as does an appreciation of the similarities between Piercy and contemporaries like Russ, Le Guin, and Delany.

Interestingly, the intertextual dialogues that constitute such an important part of Piercy's text are later extended by Piercy herself, who rethinks many of the principles of Mattapoisett in her later *He, She, and It.* Like the earlier *Woman on the Edge of Time, He, She, and It* is considerably enriched by dialogues with other texts, including sf predecessors like Russ's *The Female Man* and the cyberpunk fiction of William Gibson—as well as *Woman on the Edge of Time* itself. However, far from derivative, *He, She, and It* manages to effect a fascinating dialogic combination of these various sources to emerge with a voice all its own. Less angry (or formally innovative) than either *Woman on the Edge of Time* or *The Female Man, He, She, and It* differs from both in the patience with which it details a credible vision of the future, à la Gibson. However, where Gibson's postmodernist bricolage style is a highly visible element of his work, Piercy almost seems intentionally to present her future in a straightforward, matter-of-fact prose style that avoids intruding into the believability of her imaginative vision of the future. Meanwhile, this realistic prose style combines with the sf content to generate some of the same kinds of generic dialogues that inform *Woman on the Edge of Time.* In addition, Piercy's feminist sensibilities obviously contrast strongly with Gibson's, and she goes well beyond Gibson's high-tech cyberpunk world by drawing upon other genres and realms (like Jewish mysticism) that greatly enrich the dialogic power of her text.

Among other things, Piercy's later book undoes much of the antitechnologism of the earlier one. Granted, Piercy's Mattapoisett is actually quite high-tech, but its technology is decidedly kinder, gentler, and more biodegradable than that of the Western patriarchal tradition. Moreover, the contrast between the utopian and dystopian futures of *Woman on the Edge of Time* comes dangerously close to being a version of the opposition between nature and technological culture that has informed a number of feminist arguments in recent years. Acknowledging that technology has been a central tool through which the white male power structure has perpetuated its power, this argument in its purest form would suggest that those opposed to this power structure should reject technology altogether and attempt to escape its clutches by moving back to nature.

But the political wisdom of ceding something as powerful as technology to one's opponents is questionable in the extreme. As Donna Haraway argues in her now-famous essay "A Manifesto for Cyborgs," feminists and other oppositional groups would probably do better to contest the realm of technology rather than simply surrender technology and all the power that goes with it to the white-male-capitalist establishment. Piercy takes this suggestion to heart in *He, She, and It* by depicting a future oppositional culture that is if anything more technologically adept than the official society, much like the Mephis of Zamyatin's *We.* Indeed, Piercy has identified Haraway's essay as a major influence on *He, She, and It.* In particular, Haraway places special emphasis on the sf notion of cyborgs as an image of transgression of conventional boundaries (especially between human and machine) the problematic status of which challenges essentialist models of identity upon which the power structure of Western society has traditionally been based. And *He, She, and It* includes cyborgs as a central part of its dual utopian/dystopian message.

He, She, and It describes a mid-21st century society that has much in common with the dystopian vision put forth in Chapter 15 of *Woman on the Edge of Time,* liberally spiced with details taken almost verbatim from sources like *The Female Man* and the cyberpunk future of Gibson. For example, the feminist message of *He, She, and It* is enhanced and clarified through numerous parallels with *The Female Man,* while Piercy's challenge to the conventional traditions of dystopian fiction and science fiction is most specific in her appropriation of Gibson's high-tech masculinist fiction very much along the lines of the appropriation of conventionally masculine technology outlined in Haraway's cyborg manifesto.

Piercy's overt adoption of so many images and motifs from Gibson's work represents both a congratulatory nod to the power of Gibson's imaginative vision and a powerful reminder of certain gaps in that vision. In particular, Gibson has been criticized by numerous critics for the apparent masculine bias of his work. For example, Andrew Ross presents an extensive discussion of the rejection of the feminine in the work of Gibson and other cyberpunk writers, arguing that this work is centrally informed by typical white male fantasies and anxieties. Piercy's use of so much of Gibson's vision of the future as a framework for her own feminist fiction calls attention to the lack of attention to feminist concerns in Gibson's work and in that sense reinforces the critiques of Ross and others. At the same time, Piercy's demonstration that Gibson's vision is not necessarily inimical to feminist thought can be seen as a valuable supplement to Gibson's work. Indeed, Piercy's suggestion that feminists can make productive use of Gibson's ideas rather than simply rejecting them can be read as a literary equivalent of Haraway's argument that women should attempt to use technology for their own purposes rather than simply abandoning it as a masculine preserve.

In the future America of *He, She, and It* environmental degradation has left much of the continent virtually uninhabitable, while the population has been devastated by famines, wars, plagues, and other disasters. Conventional nations have ceased to exist, and most political power lies in the hands of the "multis," large multi-national corporations (much like Gibson's zaibatsus) whose employees live and work either in domed cities on earth or on space stations. In addition to the corporate domes, there are a few "free towns" that have managed to remain independent of control by any one multi, usually because they produce some product in demand by several different multis. The rest of North America is covered by either barren wasteland or the "Glop"—a violent, dirty, crime-ridden, gang-ruled Megalopolis that stretches from what had been Boston to what had been Atlanta.

This Glop, like Gibson's "Sprawl," is a sort of dystopian projection of contemporary urban problems. Drugs are rampant, conventional law and order have broken down almost completely, and masses of people live in abject poverty. In the anarchic atmosphere of the Glop, even the powerful multis have little direct political control, though they do exercise a subtle influence, especially through the workings of an Adornian Culture Industry (again re-calling *Brave New World*) that keeps the populace in thrall to a constant flow of images designed to avert critical thought. The staple of this industry is the drug-like "stimmie," which—like Huxley's feelies and even more like Gibson's simstims—produces a wide range of artificial sensations that replace real experience with simulation and divert energy and attention from the real world.

But Piercy's vision is more hopeful than Huxley's or Gibson's. The anarchy of the Glop leads to a great deal of crime and violence, but the Glop's relative independence from direct domination by the multis makes it a potential source of social and cultural revival. This hope of revival is symbolized in the name of "Lazarus," leader of the "Coyote Gang," a rebel group that is actively working to unify the Glop work force in order to oppose exploitation by the multis. The Coyote Gang is a locus of utopian energies as its members seek, through education and cooperation, to build a better world within the dystopian climate of the Glop. And the gang's racial mix (recalling that of Mattapoisett) indicates the diversity from which the Glop draws much of its potential for cultural rebirth: "Most of the people were black-or-brown-skinned, but almost every combination was represented: red hair, brown eyes and black skin; light skin, black hair, blue eyes; and other permutations. Most people in the Glop were of mixed race nowadays." This diversity is also inherent in the language of the Glop, whose inhabitants speak their own "patois, language rich and gamy with constantly changing slang." This language, in short, is a sort of literalization of Bakhtinian heteroglossia that incorporates diversity and genuine historical change, both of which are anathema to the multis.

In contrast, the multis employ a sterile technical/business language that leaves little room for the expression of ideas contrary to official corporate policy. Their domed enclaves are clean, well-lighted places in which corporate employees live in material comfort, relatively safe from crime, disease, and the ravages of environmental devastation. But for Piercy it is the very orderliness of these enclaves—as opposed to the mess of the Glop—that represents the real dystopia, because this orderliness is indicative of a rigid corporate structure that leaves no room either for individual freedom or for the possibility of eventual change. Within a given class, individuals dress alike, live in identical housing, and even have themselves surgically altered to have similar physical appearances according to standardized models provided by their own Culture Industry, "faces as much like the one on the view screen as each could afford." And this emphasis on physical sameness echoes the demand for ideological conformity in which all employees are expected to think and act in accordance with official prescribed corporate policies and goals. As in 20th-century corporations, employees of the multis occupy strictly-defined places in the corporate hierarchy. But the multi hierarchies extend beyond the workplace to include every element of social and cultural life, including sex: "Which persons you might make love to was as defined by your place in the hierarchy as the people to whom you bowed and the people who bowed to you. Sexual privileges depended upon your rank and place." Such privileges also depend upon gender, with males enjoying decidedly more advantages than females. For example, while there are women professionals, there are also large numbers of "cosmetically recreated" women (à la Gildina of *Woman on the Edge of Time,* though less extreme) who serve purely as sexual perquisites for successful men. Corporate success dictates that positions within the hierarchy be determined to a certain extent by merit, but one of the greatest "merits" that one can have from the perspective of the multis is to be a white male.

The strongest utopian energies of *He, She, and It* are concentrated in Piercy's depiction of Tikva, a free town in New England that maintains its political and economic independence by producing high-quality security software that is very much in demand by the multis. Tikva echoes the Mattapoisett of *Woman on the Edge of Time* in many ways, though its citizens are oriented much more overtly toward technology and less toward nature, perhaps reflecting the influence of Haraway's warnings against the romanticization of nature as a locus of resistance to white male power. Indeed, the Tikvans prove more than able to hold their own in the high-tech future. When the giant Yakamura-Stichen (Y-S) multi launches a war against the town, it is the multi that suffers disastrous consequences, including damage to its crucial computer data base and the death of most of its top executives. Still, Tikva's inhabitants respect nature and keep in touch with it as much as possible, though environmental conditions dictate that the town itself remain inside an electronic "wrap" that wards off the killing rays of the sun in a world with no ozone layer and with a runaway greenhouse effect. Tikva is a mostly Jewish community (though it is characterized by tolerance in religious and other matters) whose strong communal spirit draws much from Jewish tradition. It is also highly democratic, with all citizens having an equal voice in the affairs of the town. In particular, Tikva is characterized by complete equality between the genders and by tolerance for all forms of non-exploitative sexuality.

As indicated by the title, gender issues are preeminent in *He, She, and It.* For one thing, the book features a number of strong female characters who avoid conventional stereotypes (both patriarchal and feminist) by contesting traditionally male areas of technology and warfare. Malkah, a brilliant software designer now in her seventies, has led an active heterosexual life with numerous lovers but has always insisted on remaining emotionally and intellectually independent of the men with whom she has been involved. Malkah's daughter Riva is an internationally-renowned Robin Hood-like data pirate who steals information from the rich (usually the multis) and gives it to the poor (usually in the Glop). Riva is intelligent, resourceful, and skilled in both computer science and martial arts. Her partner (and lover) Nili is a Jewish woman from a community founded in the ruins of an Israel destroyed by nuclear war. Recalling both Gibson's Molly Millions and Russ's Jael, Nili is a formidable warrior whose artificially-enhanced muscles and reflexes make her more than a match for the security forces of the multis. Finally, the book's central character is computer specialist Shira Shipman, the daughter of Riva and granddaughter of Malkah. As the book begins Shira has led a relatively conventional life as a wife, mother, and employee of the Y-S multi. Though as talented as her illustrious mother and grandmother, Shira has thus far been unable to fulfill her professional potential because of the patriarchal structure of the Y-S world and because Y-S considers her suspect due to the terrorist activities of Riva, activities of which Shira is entirely unaware.

Much of the plot of *He, She, and It* involves Shira's gradual declaration of independence from her conventional past and exploration of her own emotional and intellectual capabilities. A major element of this exploration concerns Shira's relationship with Yod, an android created by the Tikvan scientist Avram to aid in the defense of the town against the powerful multis. As a result Yod is a deadly weapon, programmed by Avram to be a master of both physical and computerized violence. Yod is also strictly illegal, weapons in general being legal only for the multi security forces and humanoid robots having been universally banned after early experiments led to violent demonstrations on the part of a human population afraid of being rendered obsolete. But, despite his status as an illegal weapon, Yod is also endowed with a very human-like capacity for abstraction and even for emotion. He has been programmed by Avram according to the masculine ideology of the Enlightenment. But he is intellectually androgynous, also programmed by Malkah with a "feminine" ability to feel and to share that counters the masculine drive for power and domination. Malkah explains:

> "Avram made him male—entirely so. Avram thought
> that was the ideal: pure reason, pure logic, pure

violence. The world has barely survived the males we have running around. I gave him a gentler side, starting with emphasizing his love for knowledge and extending it to emotional and personal knowledge, a need for connection."

Yod thus transgresses not only the conventional boundary between human and machine, but between male and female as well. Yod's duality is also enhanced by his participation in both the high-tech tradition of science fiction and in the kabbalistic traditions of Jewish mysticism, to which he is linked through Piercy's inclusion of the parallel story of the "golem" Joseph in early-17th-century Prague. This story, told to Yod by Malkah in segments that run throughout the text, helps him to gain a sense of his own identity and background. Meanwhile, the invited comparison between Yod and Joseph adds to our understanding of the multiple traditions in which Yod participates while at the same time connecting the oppressive conditions of Piercy's future dystopian America (and, by extension, Piercy's contemporary America) with a history of past barbarisms that include the medieval and early modern pogroms and the twentieth-century Holocaust. Moreover, by linking Joseph and Yod, whose stories separately participate in the generic traditions of Jewish mysticism and science fiction, Piercy is able to effect a dialogic interaction between two ostensibly very different genres, enriching the dialogic texture of her book while at the same time suggesting that these two genres may have more in common than is immediately obvious.

But Yod's most important "dialogic" characteristic is his androgyny. In a reverse response to the notorious question of Alan Jay Lerner, in Yod Piercy has created a man who can indeed be more like a woman. Physically male, Yod is so human that he is able to engage in a torrid sexual relationship with Shira, who had previously thought herself incapable of sexual passion after a series of unfortunate experiences with sexually insensitive men. But the relationship between Shira and Yod is continually informed by gender role reversals in which she finds herself occupying the aggressive role that she has traditionally associated with males. Sex for Yod is a matter of intimacy rather than conquest or possession, and he derives his pleasure primarily from pleasing his partner, which he has been programmed by Malkah to do with considerable skill: "Yod was really a beautiful instrument of response and reaction. The slightest touch of pressure on his neck, and he understood what she wanted and gave it to her." As a lover he is tender, considerate, and indefatigable. His penis becomes erect on command and stays so as long as necessary for Shira's satisfaction, even after his "small discharge" of innocuous fluid. Moreover, this marvelous organ is scrupulously clean, with "no tang of human or animal scent." Yod's entire body is free of the kind of physical imperfections that characterize human men:

> His tongue was a little smoother than a human tongue but moist. Everything was smoother, more regular, more nearly perfect. The skin of his back was not like the skin of other men she had been with, for always there were abrasions, pimples, scars, irregularities. His skin was sleek as a woman's but drier to the touch.

Yod is, in short, an "ideal" man, and in that sense he resembles Haraway's notion of the cyborg as a product of both "social reality" and fictional expectations. However, in his conformance to a variety of stereotypes of the ideal sensitive male, Yod differs substantially from Haraway's notion that the problematic gender of the cyborg is considerably more "dangerous" than that of the sensitive male, whose very androgyny may in fact involve an attempt subtly to appropriate power. Read literally as an idealization, Piercy's Yod is certainly a less interesting figure than Haraway's cyborg. It seems clear, however, that Yod can usefully be read not as an ideal figure but as a parodic reversal of traditional Western fantasies of the "ideal" woman. For example, his lack of any sort of physical messiness can be read as a comment on the traditional male fear and loathing of the physicality of women—a phenomenon embodied, for example, in the distaste for "meat things" shown by many of Gibson's male characters. And Yod is clearly a sort of male parody of those artificially-created ideal women who, from Galatea forward, have functioned as central images of the objectification of women in Western civilization. In the end, however, Piercy eschews such fantasies and thereby declines to reproduce in reverse the tradition of attempting to define women according to masculine specifications. When Yod is destroyed during a mass assassination of Y-S executives, Shira has all of the necessary data and material to recreate him (maybe even with a little fine tuning of her own), but she declines to do so, recognizing that no one has the right to create sentient beings according to one's own specifications. Rather than seek fulfillment in an ideal man, Shira learns to find fulfillment in her own emotional and intellectual capabilities.

In general, Piercy's book gains a great deal of energy from its dialogue with masculine texts and traditions of the past. The specific content of her utopian and dystopian visions directly confronts a number of masculine stereotypes (most specifically the science fiction of Gibson), and her deft use of the genres of dystopian fiction and science fiction contests traditionally masculine territory much in the way Haraway suggests marginal groups should contest the control of technology. Piercy also emphasizes the presentation of utopian alternatives to complement her dystopian vision, and in this she continues to participate in the modern tradition of women's utopias. But her dystopian fictions claim a place for feminist statement in that traditionally male genre as well, demonstrating that utopian and dystopian visions need not be incompatible. The recent feminist appropriation of dystopian fiction indicates that the genre is extremely flexible as a mode of social commentary. Moreover, the mixture of utopian and dystopian energies that characterizes much recent feminist imaginative writing shows that dystopian warnings in no way require the complete surrender of any hope of a better future.

Elham Afnan (essay date Winter 1996)

SOURCE: "Chaos and Utopia: Social Transformation in

Woman on the Edge of Time," in *Extrapolation,* Vol. 37, No. 4, Winter, 1996, pp. 330-40.

[*In the following essay, Afnan discusses parallels between utopian fiction and chaos theory in* Woman on the Edge of Time, *particularly the significance of nonlinearity and indeterminacy surrounding social change.*]

The existence of utopia is based on a pun: it is at once "eutopia" (good place) and "outopia" (no place). Thomas More exploited the contradiction inherent in the term when he chose the title for his account of the imaginary island that enjoyed perfection in laws, politics, and economy. However, this paradox has also helped create a dichotomy with far-reaching consequences for modern readers for whom utopia is often synonymous either with totalitarian social engineering or with impractical wishful thinking. Utopian works are often denigrated or dismissed as unrealistic and dull because readers insist on approaching them as either blueprints for creating a perfect, and therefore static, society or as purely fictive works of imagination that can be realized "nowhere."

A common usage of the term equates utopia with impractical idealism. This is probably the dominant view of utopia as something illusory, unrealistic, and ineffective. In a world struggling with overwhelming social, political, economic, environmental, and moral problems, "utopian" is more often than not a derogatory epithet suggesting naiveté and escapism. Given this view, the enemies of utopia fall into two main categories: those who scorn utopia because it is an unattainable dream and those who fear that it can be attained and will turn out to be a nightmare. The polemical attacks of Marx and Engels on "utopian" as opposed to "scientific" socialism were an example of the first response. They viewed non-Marxist socialists as utopians because "they reject all political, and especially all revolutionary, action. . . . They endeavour . . . to deaden the class struggle and to reconcile the class antagonisms. They still dream of experimental realization of their social Utopias." Their main objection to utopian thought was that it diverted revolutionary energy into fantasy and escapism. Much of the satire directed against utopianism also arises out of this same impulse. *Gulliver's Travels* and Samuel Butler's *Erewhon,* to name two of the better known utopian satires concern themselves with the futility of utopian aspirations in the face of human absurdity and inconsistency.

The second response, fear of utopia realized, can be discerned in the widespread identification of utopia with such twentieth-century phenomena as social engineering and totalitarian government. Utopia has to a large extent "become synonymous with totalitarianism . . . [it] has become anathema, a nightmare of political repression and total uniformity to be avoided at all costs" (Ruppert). Where at one time it was a vision of an alternative far removed in time or space, an ideal to strive for, utopia in the modern world has become a real possibility looming ahead of us and around us. The result has been a preoc-cupation with dystopia, the "bad place." The dystopian nightmare takes different shapes, of course, depending on the version of utopia against which it is reacting. Some writers, such as George Orwell, warn against the dehumanization and enslavement that result from rigid centralization and bureaucratic behavior control. Others, like Aldous Huxley, fear the deadening effects of materialism and hedonistic excess on human creativity and endeavor.

Variations on this kind of pessimism characterize many of the attitudes toward utopia in this century to the extent that it has become a commonplace to proclaim the death of utopia. As Peter Ruppert puts it, "two world wars, Hiroshima, Auschwitz, and Vietnam, . . . the failure of socialism . . . the emergence of consumer capitalism . . . have produced political situations in which inertia, complacency, and a general satisfaction with things as they are have repressed the desire to contemplate any kind of significant social change." The faith in progress implied by utopia is hard to sustain in the face of such developments. With the perceived failure of utopia as concept, utopia as narrative has become "a residual literary form" (Tom Moylan).

Perhaps all of these various criticisms of the literary utopia have arisen because readers generally insist on approaching it from one of two diametrically opposed viewpoints. Those whose primary interest is in the "sociopolitical function of these texts . . . tend to read all utopias as proposals for social reform"; those whose interests are primarily literary "tend to read utopias first and foremost as fictions, as products of the imagination that may or may not be intended for realization" (Ruppert). However, as blueprints for social action, utopias are usually vague, reductive, and impractical. As fictive works of imagination, they can be static, stereotypical, and dull. There is little in either description to recommend the genre. The general view has been that the utopian impulse is at best naive and at worst dangerous and that utopian writing is irrelevant and of limited practical or literary value.

And yet the last two centuries have witnessed a burgeoning of utopian literature. The problem lies not in the utopias themselves, but in the binary logic that many readers apply to them. By always defining utopias in opposition to something else, they suppress their true value as agents of transformation. This is an unproductive approach to works that in fact require a more creative response from the reader. This realization has led critics to explore new ways of approaching utopia that suggest that utopian literature can indeed be relevant to the human effort to understand the world and change it for the better. Interestingly, it is H. G. Wells, one of the most prolific of utopian writers, who suggests a new approach to the topic. In *A Modern Utopia,* Wells writes, "Utopia must be not static but kinetic, must shape not as a permanent state but as a hopeful stage, leading to a long ascent of stages."

Darko Suvin provides a useful starting point for exploring the dynamic qualities inherent in utopia: "Neither prophecy nor escapism, utopia is, as many critics have remarked, an 'as if,' an imaginative experiment. . . . a heuristic device for perfectibility, an epistemological and not an ontological entity. . . . If utopia is, then, philosophically, a method rather than a state, it cannot be realized or not realized—it can only be applied." There are two ideas here that are important to my approach to the topic. First is the recognition that the most important question to ask about utopia is not what shape it will take when realized or even whether or not it can be realized, but rather what processes of change it entails. In Suvin's terms, what is significant is utopia as method, not utopia as state. Secondly, as a heuristic device, the literary utopia can be achieved—or "applied"—only through the reader's participation.

A number of critics, for instance Chris Ferns, have argued that utopian fiction has an "essentially hybrid nature" since "its aspirations are both political . . . and aesthetic." I would argue that for this reason it makes sense that the critical approach used to analyze utopia should also be hybrid. The field of science and literature, which locates in both discourses the need for multivalence, provides the basis for just such an approach. A new understanding of utopia requires a move from the static to the dynamic. Chaos theory, the site of a major paradigm shift in modern science, can suggest a way of discerning a similar paradigm shift in literature because of its concern with process and method. Like utopia, which is "a method rather than a state" (Suvin), so too chaos theory is "a science of process rather than state, of becoming rather than being" (Gleick). Clearly, there is a point of intersection between utopian fiction and chaos theory that promises new insights into both.

The work of Marge Piercy provides a good example of this intersection. In a lecture on her conception of "politically conscious" writing, Piercy said, "If we view the world as static, if we think ahistorically, we lack perspective on the lives we are creating. . . . We must be able to feel ourselves active in time and history." Such activity is at the center of Piercy's vision as expressed in *Woman on the Edge of Time,* a novel that has become a classic of feminist utopian writing since its publication in 1976. In its emphasis on the process of social transformation, Piercy's novel affirms the didactic, social function of utopian writings: it "acknowledges the power of the word to move an audience to action" (Carol Farley Kessler). The novel begins with the first contact between Connie, a mental patient and the time traveler of the title, and Luciente, her guide to the utopian future she visits. Luciente's role is analogous to that of the author: both of them not only present the distinguishing features of a new society, but they also try to stimulate in their auditor/reader the activism that will bring that society into being.

The most obviously relevant aspect of chaos theory in relation to *Woman on the Edge of Time* is the concept of nonlinearity. In mathematics, nonlinear equations are those that express relationships that are not strictly proportional; non-linear systems generally cannot be solved. But nonlin-

earity may be more broadly defined: in James Gleick's words, "[it] means that the act of playing the game has a way of changing the rules." Piercy's notion of historical "cruxes" is clearly akin to this concept, for it implies that history is nonlinear: it does not have one solution, one necessary outcome. One of the inhabitants of the utopian world of the year 2137 tells Connie, "at certain cruxes of history . . . forces are in conflict. Technology is imbalanced. Too few have too much power. Alternate futures are equally or almost equally probable . . . and that affects . . . the shape of time."

In physical systems, nonlinearity translates into a high degree of unpredictability. There is often great incongruity between cause and effect such that a small cause can give rise to a large effect. Sensitive dependence on initial conditions is thus another characteristic of nonlinear or chaotic systems. In such systems, small uncertainties, even at the subatomic level, are quickly brought up to macroscopic expression. By stressing the methods of nonlinear dynamics, chaos researchers have observed that "a small change in one parameter . . . could push . . . [a physical] system across a bifurcation point into a qualitatively new behaviour" (Gleick). Piercy seems to apply a similar principle to social systems. At crucial points in time, small acts can have great repercussions that will change the course of history. This is the reason why the utopians of the future have perfected a method of time travel that enables them to reach receptive individuals in the "crux time" of the late twentieth century. They believe that it is not the powerful who make revolutions, but rather ordinary people who "changed how people bought food, raised children, went to school. . . . who made new unions, withheld rent, refused to go to wars, wrote and educated and made speeches" (*Woman*). They repeat again and again that their very existence is precarious because Connie and those of her time may fail to engage in the struggle that will bring about the necessary changes.

Mattapoisett, the utopia depicted in *Woman on the Edge of Time,* is based on principles of community and equality. The people work together to provide the necessities of life for everyone, but they have no money and no concept of ownership. They have their own private spaces, but most of their activities are communal. Their government is highly decentralized and based on consensus decision making in local and regional councils. Their education combines study and work and involves a system of mentorship that makes learning personal. They are profoundly conscious of their place in "the web of nature," and their sense of responsibility toward the environment is heightened by their awareness of the damage done to it by the excesses of the twentieth century. They believe in cultural diversity and, above all, in gender equality. Women and men are equal in all things: education, work, sexual expression ("all coupling, all befriending goes on between biological males, biological females, or both") and even parenting. Children are grown in "brooders" and upon birth are given three "mothers," of either sex and biologically unrelated to them, who share all responsibilities, including breast-feeding. As Luciente puts it, "It was part of women's long revolution. When we were breaking up all the old hierarchies. Finally there was that one thing we had to give up too, the only power we ever had, in return to no more power for anyone . . . the power to give birth." The revolution has also included the reform of language so that the pronouns "he" and "she" are now replaced by "person" or "per."

However, unlike many of its utopian predecessors, Mattapoisett is not a static, finished object. Its inhabitants are still in the process of determining its laws and engage in controversies about matters of public policy, such as social engineering. But even more importantly, they are constantly fighting to protect their way of life against the dystopian alternative that exists side by side with them. Their enemies are the remnants of the old multinational corporations (with names like Texaroyal and Mobilgulf) who have taken twentieth-century consumerism and technological excess to their logical conclusion. They consist "mostly of androids, robots, cybernauts, partially automated humans" and their weapons are those of "the biological sciences. Control of genetics. Technology of brain control. Birth-to-death surveillance. Chemical control through psychoactive drugs and neurotransmitters." It would seem that their biggest victims are women, whose only choice is between becoming surgically altered prostitutes or turning into "duds," who are nothing more than "walking organ banks" to be used by the "richies" wanting to prolong their lives indefinitely.

Having introduced us to the salient features of an ideal society in the first half of the novel, Piercy goes on in the second half to develop the idea that we must fight to make this society real. Utopia will win over dystopia only "if history is not reversed." In the war to achieve utopia, "the past is a disputed area." After accidentally visiting the dystopian territory, Connie realizes that "that was the other world that might come to be. That was Luciente's war, and she was enlisted in it." The rest of the novel is concerned with how Connie becomes involved in this "war." Back in her own time, her final act, which she considers a necessary act of war, is to poison the doctors and psychologists who have been experimenting on her with drugs and brain implants. The ending of the novel has, understandably, been controversial, since Connie's solution seems hardly utopian. And yet there is something fitting about it, particularly if we keep in mind the idea suggested by chaos theory that a small cause can give rise to a large effect. Connie's act is one whose ramifications will alter the future. Her success in averting one particular form of biological engineering will retard or even halt the development of the dystopian world populated by automated beings and will thus contribute to the emergence of the utopian Mattapoisett where human potential is valued.

Also present is the element of unpredictability inherent in the concept of nonlinearity. As Ferns puts it, "in Piercy's hands, the normally static utopia has become kinetic with a vengeance," and in order to remain so, it must remain open to change and motion. Once she has committed the murders, Connie can no longer reach over to Mattapoisett: "She had annealed her mind and she was not a receptive woman. She had hardened." Her inability to see the future any longer underscores the personal cost of committing an act of violence, even if is for a good cause. Symbolically, however, the loss of contact with the future also emphasizes the unpredictability of the utopian project. The openness of the ending discourages us from trying to reduce utopia to something fixed and permanent.

The idea of nonlinearity is not only a central theme of **Woman on the Edge of Time,** but it also determines its structure. Though fairly obvious, it bears pointing out that Piercy's narrative, "unlike the traditional guided tour format of earlier utopias, proceeds by alternating utopian episodes and a narrative set in something resembling contemporary reality" (Ferns). Ferns observes that the alternating format is significant because it shows that "the utopian ideal is itself a product of the present, and that it changes as the nature of the present changes." The nature of Connie's initial visit to each of the two alternative futures is determined by what she is going through in her own time immediately before-hand.

The first encounter between Connie and Luciente takes place at Connie's apartment, before she is committed to the psychiatric hospital. At this point, however, it is Luciente who comes to Connie's time. Connie travels to the future only some time after her admission to the hospital when she is locked in seclusion because she resists taking the numbing drugs given to her. The world she steps into is in every way the opposite of the confined place she inhabits. The initial description of Mattapoisett emphasizes its rural, natural setting: a river, vegetable gardens, animals. Even the buildings are compared to "long-legged birds with sails that turned in the wind." A little later, Connie visits Luciente's "space," which contracts with both the crowdedness and the isolation of Connie's life. As a member of a poor Chicano family, Connie has grown up living with many siblings in a crowded home. In the hospital, she oscillates between two extremes: she is either denied all privacy in the general ward or denied any human contact in the seclusion cell. The utopian alternative, as Luciente explains it, combines personal freedom with a sense of community: "We each have our own space! . . . How could one live otherwise? How meditate, think, compose songs, sleep, study? . . . We live *among* our family."

Connie's visit to dystopia is also related to her experiences in her own time. After a dialytrode—a device for administering psychoactive drugs directly—has been implanted in her brain, she travels to the future, only to find herself not in Mattapoisett but in the other part of the future where everyone is mechanically enhanced. The link between what she sees in the future and her own experience of being controlled by a machine is obvious. As more and more people on the ward are subjected to the same procedure, Connie begins to fight back so that they will remove her implant. At this point, she visits a third place in the future: the front where the two sides are fighting their war. As she joins Luciente and others in the battle, she seems to recognize among the enemies of Mattapoisett the faces of "all the caseworkers and doctors and landlords and cops, the psychiatrists and judges and child guidance counsellors . . . who had pushed her back and turned her off and locked her up." Interestingly, Luciente later tells her that she had not been at the front. Connie's experience thus points to the uncertainty and precariousness of the future and its sensitive dependence on her present condition.

The link between present and future also extends to what Libby Falk Jones calls a "web of character relationships radiating from Connie." Parallels between sets of characters in the novel indicate that ultimately utopia is about fulfilling individual potentials that are denied and suppressed in contemporary society. There are a number of pairs or groups of characters that represent the utopian/dystopian versions of the same person. One example is the parallel between Connie's daughter, Angelina, and Luciente's daughter, Dawn. After an incident of child abuse, Angelina has been taken from Connie and placed in a foster home, forever beyond her mother's reach. Dawn, beautiful, happy, and well loved, reminds Connie of her lost daughter and thinks of her as what Angelina would be if she lived in utopia: "Suddenly she assented with all her soul to Angelina in Mattapoisett, to Angelina hidden forever one hundred fifty years into the future. . . . She will be strong there, well fed, well housed, well taught, she will grow up much better and stronger and smarter than I." Dawn thus becomes the fulfillment not only of Angelina's but also of Connie's own potential.

Another parallel is that between Skip and Jackrabbit. Skip is one of Connie's fellow patients in the hospital, committed after several botched attempts at suicide. He is intelligent and witty but has been in mental institutions since he was thirteen because he is homosexual and, as he says, "My parents thought I didn't work right, so they sent me to be fixed." Jackrabbit, who lives in Mattapoisett, is about the same age as Skip, and he represents the fruition of all that has been blighted in Skip's life. Jackrabbit is a highly respected artist and a fully integrated member of his family and his community. He, like most of the others around him, has sexual relations with both women and men and is beginning to prepare for his mothering duties. But the two are also linked in that they struggle against a common enemy, that of dehumanizing technology. Skip finally kills himself after receiving the brain implant. Shortly thereafter, Jackrabbit, who has gone on defense duty, is killed in the war against the robots. They are both casualties, but both die fighting. At Jackrabbit's wake, Connie's mourning explicitly joins the two young men: "Slowly tears coursed down her face, perhaps more for Skip than for Jackrabbit, perhaps for both."

The most significant parallels, however, are between several of the characters and Connie herself. Connie and Luciente are obviously closely linked, as together they create the bridge between the two times. Luciente's child reminds Connie of her own daughter; Luciente's two lovers remind Connie of the two men she has loved in her own life. She thinks of Luciente "as a fraction of her mind, as a voice of an alternate self." She also sees herself in Parra, a woman who is people's judge for Mattapoisett. They are "roughly the same size and complexion" and come from the same place. As they talk, Connie feels increasingly fascinated by Parra: "She was serving as people's judge. Doctor of rivers. She herself could be such a person here. . . . Then she would be useful. She would like herself." She would become what she cannot be in her own time.

Significantly, however, Connie also meets an alternate self when she visits the dystopian side of the future. Gildina, the woman she talks to there, is "a cartoon of femininity," surgically altered and implanted to conform to the fantasies of the men to whom she is contracted for sex. But underneath the cosmetic surgery, she too is a Chicana like Connie. And like Connie, she has potentials of which she is unaware. Connie recognizes that "Gildina has a special mental power, even if she doesn't know it," because it is her receptivity that has enabled Connie to travel to her time and place. Connie's relationship to Gildina is similar to Luciente's relationship to Connie. Connie initially mistakes Luciente for a man because she moves with "that air of brisk unselfconscious authority Connie associated with men . . . taking up more space than women ever did." Similarly, the guard who finds Connie with Gildina tells her, "You look me in the eyes, unlike a fem." The people of Mattapoisett are, as one of them tells Connie, "potentialities in [your loved ones] that could not flourish in your time." Witnessing the fulfillment of these potentialities transforms Connie and enables her to start fulfilling them herself and thereby influencing the future.

The shifts back and forth between the present and the future, between utopia and dystopia, and between different versions of the same character suggest that Connie is a "woman on the edge" in more ways than one. Her life, as depicted in the novel, has been chaotic in the conventional sense of the term. She has been exploited and abused, raped and beaten, deprived of education and meaningful work. She has lost the men she has loved to violence and her child to a harsh, uncaring system. She has finally lost her freedom and control over her life by being confined to one mental institution after another. But seen from another perspective, Connie's life is also filled with chaos in its new, positive sense.

The traditional opposition between chaos and order is being reevaluated by chaos theory. Katherine Hayles attributes the negative valuation of chaos in the Western tradition to "the predominance of binary logic in the West" and invokes instead the four-valued logic of Taoist thought where "not-order is . . . distinct from and valued differently than anti-order." Chaos is no longer synonymous with disorder in the traditional sense. It is rather, to quote Gleick, "order *masquerading* as randomness." There are two main approaches in the scientific community to the relationship between chaos and order. One approach, which is the focus of Gleick's book, finds order hidden in chaos. Physicist Doyne Farmer sees chaos theory as an operational way of defining free will in a way that reconciles it to determinism: a chaotic system is "deterministic, but you can't say what it is going to do next." Nonlinearity is what combines determinism with unpredictability. It also accounts for the spontaneous emergence of self-organization in the world, which is at the center of the second approach to chaos. Ilya Prigogine and Isabelle Stengers, the best-known proponents of this idea, redefine chaos as a space of creation where being and becoming are reconciled.

Clearly concepts of order, particularly order concealed within or arising out of disorder, are central to the creation of a utopian society. Chaos theory offers an understanding of the dynamics of emergent order that is applicable not only to physical systems but also, analogically, to cultural situations. Of particular relevance to **Woman on the Edge of Time** is the idea of the boundary between order and chaos. Gleick describes a computer program that generates fractal shapes by saying that "the boundary is where [it] spends most of its time and makes all of its compromises." The boundary serves as a threshold where the system "chooses between competing options" (Gleick). Connie spends much of her time in the novel in a similar region as she crosses and recrosses the "edge of time" separating her from utopia.

Frances Bartkowski observes that "Piercy's novel is narratively structured through a process of gaining and losing consciousness." The mechanism whereby Connie travels to the future involves her letting go of her own consciousness and receiving that of Luciente. Luciente explains that she is "a super-strong sender" and Connie "a top catcher" and that this is what enables them to communicate. "If I was knocked on the head and fell unconscious," she says, "you'd be back in your time instantly." The novel begins with Connie's dawning awareness of the boundary between her world and utopia, but at this point her awareness is passive. She attributes it to dreams or the hallucinatory effects of the drugs she has to take. Initially, her movement across this boundary depends entirely on Luciente. Gradually, however, she becomes more adept at tapping into Luciente's consciousness and crossing the boundary to the future at will. At one point Luciente tells her, "you could be a sender too. What a powerful and unusual mix!" As the novel progresses, Connie travels to different parts of the future increasingly independently. The merging of her consciousness with that of the utopians is a process of empowerment whose direct outcome is Connie's ability to take control of her actions at the end, to decide not merely to visit the future but to take part in creating it.

Writing about her fiction, Piercy has said, "I am involved in showing people changing through struggle, becoming, always in process." Connie's experience of "becoming" il-

lustrates that the realization of utopia can be understood as a chaotic process. The movement, within the novel, from contemporary reality to utopian ideal is in one sense deterministic: Connie, and the reader, witness the final achievement and so it must exist. At the same time, however, they are told that this is only one possible future and that they must make the choices that will lead to its attainment. The paradox can be resolved only in that boundary between consciousness and reality, between chaos and order, where the process of change occurs. Jones describes this process well when she writes, "Interacting with the future allows Connie to rescue her present as well as to preserve and even reinvent her past. Rather than establish past, present, and future as a logical continuum, the novel blends them in Connie's consciousness. The movement is not linear, but spiralling." By integrating her memories of the past, her present experience, and her expectation of the future, Connie succeeds in recreating her own—and, by extension, her society's—reality. The emphasis on consciousness reminds us that the primary locus of utopia is in the mind. Once we are conscious of utopian possibilities, we can then realize them in the world, but their greatest significance remains in the conception rather than the execution.

In discussing Piercy's fiction, critics generally focus on her feminism. It is of course entirely appropriate to do so since Piercy herself says that she is "writing politically, writing as a feminist, writing as a serious woman." This paper has not dealt with this issue in detail because my concern has been with **Woman on the Edge of Time** as a utopian novel. However, I agree with Frances Bartkowski that "utopian thinking is crucial to feminism" in that both "declare that which is not-yet as the basis for . . . practice, textual, political, or otherwise." The 1970s and 1980s witnessed a burgeoning in both utopian fiction and criticism. The best of the fiction has been written by women: Marge Piercy, Ursula Le Guin, Joanna Russ. A feature of particular interest in these works is that while strongly critical of contemporary society, and particularly of the prevalent patriarchal ideology, their outlook is generally positive. Russ and Bartkowski both note "the predominance of pessimism in contemporary science fiction, which is not, however, shared by women writing in this genre" (Bartkowski). Another characteristic of these works, related to the first, is their use of utopia and dystopia together in the same work. Like **Woman on the Edge of Time,** LeGuin's *The Dispossessed* and Russ's *The Female Man* depict two or three parallel worlds, each of which embodies some of the potentialities present in contemporary society. Their purpose is not to give the reader the blueprint for a new society but to engage her in the activity of bringing about social change by making a choice between utopia and dystopia. For these writers and, as we have seen, especially for Piercy, the transformation of existing society into utopia is a precarious enterprise attainable only through a process of making choices and crossing boundaries.

Elayne Rapping (review date February 1997)

SOURCE: "Les Ms.," in *Women's Review of Books,* Vol. XIV, No. 5, February, 1997, pp. 5-6.

[*In the following review, Rapping offers positive evaluation of* City of Darkness, City of Light.]

Marge Piercy writes a lot of novels. Each is refreshingly political, in the most blatant (as opposed to subtly subtextual) sense. Each is passionately feminist. Each—most remarkably—is written, and successfully marketed, for a mainstream audience.

I am, I confess, a Piercy admirer and fan. But I read each new novel with my fingers crossed. For as admirable as her efforts are, she doesn't always hit the mark. Works like **Woman on the Edge of Time, Small Changes** and her recent **The Longings of Women** are to me classics of feminist fiction which can open a reader's heart and mind to radically new views of the world. But others simply fail to catch fire. Their characters remain abstractions, their ideas prosaic and preachy

As I read **City of Darkness, City of Light**—an ambitious, dense and demanding rewriting of the history of the French Revolution which includes and integrates the roles and perspectives of some of the many women involved—I could not decide, for quite some time, which category it belonged in. Was it a work that large numbers of readers would find engrossing enough to stick with and learn from, or a misfire, doomed to be put aside in frustration and confusion—as I was tempted to do more than once? But one hundred or so pages into the book, I found myself, finally, riveted.

Piercy centers her narrative on six historical figures, from whose rotating points of view the revolution—and what precipitated and ensued from it—is seen. Pauline Léon is a Parisian chocolate shop owner who, as a child, witnesses the torture and execution of those who riot for bread, and goes on to become a leader of the radically feminist Revolutionary Republican Women. Beautiful Claire Lacombe escapes provincial poverty by joining a theatre group, and works with Pauline to make the voices of women and the poor heard during the Revolution. Manon Philipon—better known as Madame Roland—is a worshipper of Rousseau and the life of the mind who marries an aging bureaucrat and becomes a political force as his ghost-writer, strategist and salon hostess.

The men's names are more familiar: Maximilien Robespierre, the utopian idealist who, once in power, becomes the author of the bloodbath called the Terror; Georges Danton, opportunist and compromiser, Robespierre's comrade and sometime opponent; and Nicolas Condorcet, aristocrat, feminist and intellectual, who believes in the principle of constitutional law above all. Through these six characters, diverse in class, gender and political perspective, Piercy brings the blood and guts, the ideas and passions, of the

revolution to life, with all its idealism, its contradictions and its ultimately horrifying failures.

The narrative begins with key incidents from each character's childhood. The earliest chapter is dated 1765, and the last 1812, some eighteen years after the story proper ends. Some events are familiar from the history books: the women's march on Versailles; the brief period of the Paris Commune, before the tragic decline of the revolution into the Terror; the execution of the radical Marat by the Girondin Charlotte Corday. Other incidents are personal, often marking formative moments in key characters' lives. We see the child Manon, taken to the home of an aristocratic lady, feeling shock and contempt at the superficiality of this supposedly superior being. We share young Max's disappointment and disillusion when he is chosen to represent his school at a celebration for Louis XVI and his queen, only to be sprayed with mud as the royal carriage, hours late, speeds past the waiting crowd without stopping. We listen in at the salon of the Condorcets, where such notables as Lafayette and Tom Paine gather, and on meetings of the radical Cordeliers and Jacobins, where political liaisons and strategies are hammered out. Each episode is clearly intended to reveal the characters' developing political agendas, as well as the human traits, values and flaws that drove them.

Every major and minor character, event and document has been prodigiously researched and portrayed in factual detail; Piercy even translates (with uneven success) actual speeches into contemporary English. As she explains in her "Author's Note," she has imagined dialogue, thoughts and feelings with the help of diaries and letters from the period. A lengthy appendix summarizes key details about each character and organization.

Piercy has chosen to present this mass of emotional, historical and philosophical material in brief—three-to four-page—chronologically overlapping chapters of rotating personal narrative, a structural device that is often cumbersome and confusing. So much detail is stuffed into so limited a space that the reader must concentrate mightily to keep track of it all. It is particularly difficult, until far into the narrative, to get a sense of the key characters themselves, and the textures and intricacies of their relationships. One longs to linger on the emotional and dramatic meat of each situation, to see the nuances of political and emotional conflict and contradiction spun out into deeper, richer dramatic patterns.

These are the novel's flaws. But they are largely, if gradually, compensated for by Piercy's masterful employment of shifting points of view. We see and hear each event, often several times, from different characters' perspectives, revealing the nuances of class and gender difference that are the meat of the story.

Danton, for example, portrayed as an uncouth sensualist used to manipulating and conquering women of his own circle, is thwarted in his attempts upon both Manon and

Claire. Recognizing Manon as the political force behind her increasingly conservative Girondin husband, he sets out to seduce her in order to win her over politically. "She has a gorgeous bosom. Nice arms. Nice eyes. Her husband doesn't fuck her, I can tell. I'll get her on our side," he tells a more radical Cordelier comrade. But Manon's version of their relationship is very different: "She could hardly bear to look at him. . . . Several times he put his huge hot hands on her shoulder, her arm. Once he dared touch her posterior, giving her a pat as though she were a pack animal. She almost slapped him but political considerations . . . prevented her. Instead she glared and he withdrew at once, looking, she could swear, slightly puzzled."

With the sexually independent Claire, Danton manages a night in bed, but again is left unsatisfied and puzzled. "She was sensual without being jaded, accomplished without a hint of whorishness," he thinks. "But she did not admire him as he liked to be admired . . . She had a critical eye he disliked in a woman . . . She was good at sex, but he did not think she would be good at loving." And, to further his bewilderment, "She left early in the morning, not lingering for breakfast or expecting a present."

Piercy dwells on the subtleties and contradictions of this revolution, in which women and the working classes, participants for the first time in politics, continuously confound and finally enrage the male leaders—aristocrats as well as those, like Robespierre and Danton, who have risen to power from the middle class.

Social and political differences become emotionally concrete through Piercy's use of these rotating points of view. The gulf between the relatively elitist, anti-feminist Manon, who dislikes all women's groups and prefers to wield power from behind the office of a man, and the independent, necessarily self-sufficient working-class Pauline and Claire, is dramatic. So are the shortcomings of the aristocrat Condorcet: a true feminist in his own marriage and a believer in equality for all in the abstract, he nonetheless cannot fathom the rage, nor stomach the uncouth style, of those for whom bread and price controls mean so much more than the linguistic elegance of his painstakingly written constitution.

Piercy, here as always, remains true to the ideals which drove her as a feminist and New Left activist in the sixties. "Why write about the French Revolution?" she asks in her "Author's Note." "For me, modern politics, the modern left began there as did the women's movement . . . I have been passionately involved in left and women's politics," she writes, "and I knew all of these characters very well, under other names of course. What went wrong, personally and politically, is thus fascinating to me, and I hope to you." For "women have fought again and again for causes that, when won, have not given us the freedom, the benefits we expected."

As Piercy sees the revolution, it is at once heroic and tragic. Committed to an abstract belief in radical democ-

racy, it is nonetheless flawed by its leaders' inability to see beyond their own class and gender interests, and by the propensity of those in power—like the despots they overturn—to resort to brutality in the interest of maintaining their own position.

Each of the major male characters, and Manon among the women, is viewed by Piercy with a mixture of respect, admiration and growing disdain, as youthful idealism gives way to hypocrisy, self-aggrandisement and a narrowing of vision. Manon, for example, is a model of what present-day feminists would call a token woman, content to serve a male order as long as she herself prospers and rises to power and influence. Only the radical women, Pauline and Claire, represent what seems to be Piercy's own position on the revolution and on democratic politics generally. Only they fight unreservedly for true democracy as it would be practiced in a world in which both male and class privilege disappeared, but not at the price of committing random, inhuman violence.

It is not only the past that Piercy hopes to illuminate, but also the present. "Americans live in an increasingly violent society that is inured to violence (as eighteenth-century France was) and one in which the top is growing ever richer and further in every way from the vast bulk of the population," she writes. "I thought looking at a society in crisis so very strange in some ways and so familiar in others might illuminate our own situation." Thus while gender issues are highlighted in the book, they, like everything else, are seen and understood most dramatically through the lens of class and in the context of violence—its roots, its dynamic and its results—as practiced by those in power and those permanently disempowered. For it is the failure of the middle and upper-class revolutionaries to hear and respond to the demands of the women and the poor that fuels the downward spiral of mass violence, turning the ideals and hopes for democracy into a massive bloodbath of uprisings and executions.

Piercy understands the frustrations of the poor and voiceless, and why they turn, inexorably, to violence. But she also documents the hopelessness of such desperate measures. There is something truly terrifying in her incessant, graphic chronicling of one bloodbath after another, one brutal execution after another. So fully does violence ultimately take over the narrative that the famously symbolic death of Marie Antoinette is barely given a moment's notice, so inconsequential is it among the multitude of executions of the lesser-known. Instead, it is the guillotining of Manon Roland, and then of Robespierre, whom we have come to know intimately and view with shifting emotions of admiration, affection, contempt and compassion, that is most shocking and unforgettable.

It is not on this note of tragedy and defeat that Piercy chooses to end her narrative, however, but one of feminist idealism and hope. For in the coda, we find Claire and her longtime female lover, now retired to a farm, entertaining Pauline, now the conventional wife of the radical comrade she has married. "We did make a new world," says Claire. "Just not exactly the one we intended. It's a bigger job than we realized, to make things good and fair. It won't be us who finish it. But we gave it a pretty good start before we lost our way." And Pauline agrees. "I remember and I make sure my daughters know, it was old biddies like we are now and young women who brought the King down. We are the Revolution, ladies, and we carry it in our blood to the future."

Having come to the end of the narrative, the reader is struck by a methodological, or perhaps ethical, problem. Piercy has constructed out of the stuff of eighteenth-century history a story which is meant to say something about our own time—something which may or may not be true. Is hers a fair reading of the French Revolution? Unlike her other historical fictions—*Gone to Soldiers* comes to mind immediately—this book portrays real people, not fictional constructs. What are the sources for Piercy's ambitious, perhaps presumptuous, reconstructions of so many events and ideas and motivations, experienced by so many historical personages? Whose reading of the period is she drawing upon? Where are the footnotes?

As a reviewer who is in no sense an expert on the French Revolution, I confess to feeling somewhat uncomfortable about this. *City of Darkness*, *City of Light* presents a version of history that reads and feels— intentionally—like a reading of our own 1960s history as told by a militant Left feminist, which of course Piercy was. Is it good history? Is Piercy justified in giving radical feminism so early and clearly articulated a life? Are the various factions and leaders of the time really as similar to those of our own recent past as she portrays them? I admit that I don't know.

But putting those thorny issues aside, one may still ask if Piercy has written a good novel. I think for the most part she has. If it is fair to use a past age, and the lives of those who created it, to make a statement about the politics of the present, then Piercy has done well by her material. She has illuminated and dramatized the failure of our own radical history, even as she has reminded us—at a time when it is difficult to recall such realities—of the truly idealistic and visionary impulses that fueled our activism, and especially of the centrality of feminism to that vision.

John Taylor (review date January 1998)

SOURCE: A review of *What Are Big Girls Made Of?*, in *Poetry*, Vol. CLXXI, No. 3, January, 1998, pp. 221-4.

[*In the following review, Taylor provides positive assessment of* What Are Big Girls Made Of?.]

Marge Piercy is a versatile poet with broad interests, and *What Are Big Girls Made Of?*—her thirteenth collection—invokes several public and private issues that have long haunted or angered her. Opening with seven intimate "Brother-Less Poems," Piercy draws us inside a "family snapshot" in which she hugs "the two pillars" of her "cracked world": her "cold father" and her "hot brother," the latter also described as "the dark pulsating sun of [her] childhood, / the man whose eyes could give water / instead of ice." Graphic evocations of this half-brother (who has recently died) follow, beginning with flashbacks to the end of the Second World War, when he returns stateside, "still a Marine, crazy on experimental / drugs for malaria." Piercy delves further into their common past, recalling their coming-of-age within a family that resembles "a pit lined with fur and barbed wire; / roast chicken and plastique, warmth / and bile, a kiss and a razor in the ribs."

Later, as the half-brother passes from divorces and real-estate speculations through troubled relationships with his estranged stepchildren (and an inability to communicate with his half-sister), a fragmentary portrait emerges of a tormented man in whom collide the desperate impulses of his innermost will and the violent outside forces of history. This theme in fact characterizes the entire collection. "We both felt the world as a great pain," remarks Piercy, ". . . and we each / set out to change it: our separate ways." Yet after formulating this insight, the poet must admit, in the final poem, that she lacks a real hold on the man whom her half-brother became. "It is hard // to say goodbye to nothing / personal," she concludes, "mouthfuls bitten off / of silence and wet ashes." While constructing his portrait, Piercy has likewise sought to deconstruct his myth (in her eyes); and her words trouble us because, as she herself confesses, she fails in both endeavors. Yet in her failing are disclosed truths. It is paradoxically the poet's inability to define her half-brother and the exact borders of their relationship—whence the interpretative openness of these verses—that is sincere and moving.

Her half-brother's "self" is half-authentic—"built of forged documents, / stories lifted from magazines, / charm, sweat and subterfuge"—and Piercy's postulate (here and elsewhere) is that these chaotic intersections of the public and the private constitute what all "big girls" (and boys) are made of. From a number of vantage points, she tries to perceive how these perilous, if inevitable, crossroads arise in our bodies and minds. After dissecting her family background (tenderness for her parents manifests itself in later poems, although even soft feelings can be offset by bluntness), she draws back—in the second section—from her own self's preoccupations. Engaging poems on current topics ensue, the most memorable of which narrates in unadorned sextains the everyday routines of an abortion-clinic receptionist. The woman's day begins at four a.m. with a telephone call: "Of course she does not / pick up, but listens / through the answering machine / to the male voice promising / she will burn in hell."

Other committed poems poke fun at administrators, describe looming mortgages (in the form of birds "with heavy hunched shoulders / nesting in shredded hundred dollar bills"), and bring out the banal gruesomeness of a talk show in which the speaker's voice "roars . . . / like a freight from a tunnel," every car carrying "the same / coke load of fury." Piercy also takes a stand on a woman's right to "choose" ("to be pregnant / . . . childless / . . . lesbian / . . . to have two lovers or none") and satirizes men's views of sexual harassment.

These feminist poems may stir listeners who hear them read aloud ("Stand up now and say No More. / Stand up now and say We will not / be ruled by crazies and killers"), yet their language resembles that of rallying cries. It is a language confident in its power to designate and deplore, which is to say that Piercy no longer pushes language, haltingly, to its fragile, uncertain limits so as to more genuinely interrogate, speculate on, and explore the equally uncertain frontiers of the perceptible and imaginable worlds with which she challenges herself. These engaging verses are unsubtle when compared to the half-brother sequence, the evocative erotic poems (in the section entitled "Salt in the Afternoon"), and especially the metaphysically rich nature poems collected in "A Precarious Balance."

This latter group reveals Piercy to be a precise, sensitive observer, a quality that disappears whenever her diction waxes ideological. Poems here describe a blizzard, several different does, morning moths, and, most originally, grackles whose "cries are no more melodious / than the screech of unadjusted / brakes, and yet I like their song / of the unoiled door hinge creaking, / the rusty saw grating, the squawk / of an air mattress stomped on." Two arresting poems depict the same early-morning car accident when "a doctor with Georgia plates / [comes] roaring over the hill far too fast" and kills one of two young deer darting across the road. Piercy, who has witnessed the accident, must close her hands over the windpipe of the dying deer in order to put it out of its suffering. Elsewhere, meditating on garter snakes, the poet observes that "we see everything except that swift / archaic beauty brushing over the earth." Yet Piercy has indeed grasped this beauty, and her nature writing consistently seeks such aeon-spanning glimpses, yearns for a cosmic wholeness, and—thereby rejoining her political concerns—suggests that our fundamental duty is to care. This responsibility is well summed-up in her last lines, from a long-poem entitled **"The art of blessing the day":**

> What we want to change we curse and then
> pick up a tool. Bless whatever you can
> with eyes and hand and tongue. If you
> can't bless it, get ready to make it new.

Fred Moramarco and William Sullivan (essay date 1998)

SOURCE: "'A Whole New Poetry Beginning Here': The Assertion of Gender," in *Containing Multitudes: Poetry in the United States Since 1950,* Twayne, 1998, pp. 163-94.

[*In the following excerpt, Moramarco and Sullivan provide an overview of the central themes and preoccupations in Piercy's poetry.*]

> I am an instrument in the shape of a woman trying to translate pulsations into images for the relief of the body and the reconstruction of the mind.
>
> —Adrienne Rich

Although many of the central poets of the modernist movement were women, including Amy Lowell, Gertrude Stein, H. D., and Marianne Moore, for many male writers, the idea of a "women's poetry" in the late 1950s and early 1960s still conjured visions of genteel lyricism by what were then called "poetesses," such as Sara Teasdale, Josephine Preston Peabody, or Edna St. Vincent Millay. Some of it was skillfully crafted and memorably expressed, but it did not seem to embody the realities of many women's situation in life. Not until poets like Muriel Rukeyser, Adrienne Rich, Sylvia Plath, Anne Sexton, Audre Lorde, and Marge Piercy and, more recently, emergent writers like Sharon Olds, Olga Broumas, Louise Glück, and Marilyn Hacker became established did the phrase "women's poetry" come to imply resistance to the social limitations placed on women's lives.

Rukeyser, Brooks, Rich, and Plath opened new worlds for a whole generation of women who became empowered to speak what had previously been unspeakable. The dissatisfactions of motherhood, the stifling conformity of suburban housewifery, the dominance of male intellectuality, the dismissal of female perceptions of reality, the objectification of women's bodies, the social tolerance of rape and sexual harassment of all kinds, the politics of abortion, the blatant economic inequality of the sexes, and many other subjects previously ignored or actively repressed began to be dealt with openly and in depth. Ironically, "women's poetry" became in some ways the opposite of what it had previously been. No longer genteel and lyrical, it began to carry a political edge. Much of this poetry was controversial and rejected, especially by male critics, who often viewed it as self-indulgent and artless. But as its body began to gather heft and momentum throughout the sixties, seventies, and eighties, it could no longer be ignored as a dominant force in contemporary poetry.

Women were demonstrating that gender is an important component of poetic value, although many writers, both men and women, continued to resist that idea. Elizabeth Bishop, for example, refused to be anthologized in any women-only poetry anthology because she believed that the art of poetry transcends gender. And although Diane Wakoski clearly writes a "woman-centered" poetry that focuses especially on relationships between men and women, she believes that any gender adjective that precedes the word *poet* diminishes it. But to say that gender is a component of poetic value is not to argue that it is the only component. Writing is related to life experience, and the experiences of men and women in our society are significantly different in many respects: childbearing, childrearing, domestic responsibilities, military experience (until recently), and economic opportunities are just a few differences that create the foundation for a poetry influenced by gender.

Some women take the gender issue a step further and talk about a "female poetics" that informs the women's poetry of note in our time. In her important revisionist history of women's poetry in America, Alicia Suskin Ostriker writes about "an assertive desire for intimacy" that she believes characterizes this poetics: "As the poet refuses to distance herself from her emotion, so she prevents us [as readers] from distancing ourselves." For Ostriker and for other feminist writers like Adrienne Rich, Suzanne Juhasz, and Audre Lorde, a woman-centered poetry has emerged that has as its project the definition of a "female self" unmitigated by the assumptions and cultural priorities of male writers. This poetry intends to transform literary culture as well as the social culture it both grows out of and affects. Consequently, much of the women's poetry of our time is involved in revising traditional myths, whether explicitly, as in Anne Sexton's *Transformations,* or implicitly, as in Marge Piercy's reconstruction of male-female relationships. In addition, Adrienne Rich sees "a passion for survival" as one of the great themes of women's poetry today and finds it ironic "that male critics have focused on our suicidal poets, and on their 'self'-destructiveness rather than their capacity for hard work and for staying alive as long as they did." Combining a desire for intimacy with the shaping of a new female identity based on revising the myths of the past and transforming the realities of the present has produced an intensely personal poetry that is also pointedly political. In fact, the distinctive contribution of contemporary women's poetry is that the personal and political are identified with each other and conjoined.

In addition to the women mentioned above, many other writers have been instrumental in creating this new kind of "woman-centered" poetry that departs from the constricted sensibility often associated (usually by men) with feminine norms. These include Sonia Sanchez, Gloria Anzaldúa, Paula Gunn Allen, Wendy Rose, and others who are creating what Adrienne Rich calls "a whole new poetry beginning here." Those women who also broadened the context of writing in the United States by underscoring their ethnic and cultural heritages will be explored more fully in chapter 7. Here we will look at how the assertion of gender reshaped American poetry in the seventies and eighties. . . .

Born to a working-class family in Detroit, Marge Piercy now lives on two acres in Wellfleet, Massachusetts, and both her midwestern urban roots and her New England village present are important factors in her poetry. A prolific writer, she has published more than a dozen collections of poetry as well as many works of fiction, including *Woman on the Edge of Time* (1976), an important feminist work that influenced a generation of women and encouraged their involvement in the women's movement. Piercy also edited an anthology of American women's poetry in 1987 called *Early Ripening,* in which she argues that women's poetry in late twentieth-century America is characterized by a fused rather than "dissociated" sensibility—emotion and intellect working together rather than at

war with each other. Women's poetry in our time, according to Piercy, tends also to be a poetry of "re-invention" that is often confrontational vis à vis traditional social institutions and structures. There is in much of the work included in *Early Ripening* "a remaking, a renewing, a renaming, a re-experiencing, and then recasting."

This understanding of contemporary women's poetry permeates nearly all of Piercy's own work. Though that work is diverse and reflects different stages of her life, it is important to her that poetry be *useful,* particularly to other women who will recognize themselves in various aspects of her life journey. Several kinds of poem make up the bulk of Piercy's canon. First there are feminist-oriented poems on topics like rape, abortion, abused women, and working-class women that tend to speak directly to other women with the idea of enrolling them in the "we" of the poem. Second, there are poems of social criticism that deal with issues other than those exclusively concerned with women: automation, technology, war, inhumanity, indifference to suffering, and many others that constitute the "cancers" of modern life that need to be exposed and rooted out. Third, there are poems about Piercy's Detroit working-class childhood, especially family poems about her troubled relationship with her mother and father. Fourth, there are love poems, especially apparent in the later work, either celebrating the renewal of love or lamenting its demise. A persistent theme that crosses the boundaries of several of these subjects is the need for transformation, particularly the transformation of relationships between men and women.

Piercy's best work through 1980 is collected in *Circles on the Water: Selected Poems* (1982). Most of these poems were written in the sixties and seventies phase of the contemporary feminist movement and are predominantly political in orientation and militant in tone, although they also deal with the status of male/female relationships in the period. In **"Doing it differently,"** Piercy makes a dramatic attempt to alter the status quo. She wants to reconstruct male-female relationships and move them out of the wasteland that many have inhabited. Although the poem is preachy, it is also affecting, and very much a document of its time. The lovers in the poem are "bagged in habit," but the woman feels they have the power to choose their destiny and not simply accept the conventions handed down to them. The woman appears vulnerable as she crawls into the man "as a bee crawls into a lily," but while the woman is always vulnerable, the man is vulnerable only when he is making love. The narrator asks if men and women can ever be free of the roles of dominance and submission. Sounding surprisingly apolitical, Piercy evokes the image of a rose as a symbol of male-female union.

> I am a body beautiful only when fitted with yours.
> Otherwise, it walks, it lifts packages, it spades.
> It is functional or sick, tired or sturdy. It serves.
> Together we are the rose, full, red as the inside
> of the womb and head of the penis,
> blossoming as we encircle, we make that symmetrical

fragrant emblem,
then separate into discrete workday selves.

Can this rosy picture actually become the norm? Can there be a "new man and woman" committed to this kind of beautiful union? The woman in the poem feels powerless to make it happen because her inferiority is encased in the language, laws, institutions, and traditions of society. To create this kind of equal union, men need to take positive steps toward change:

> We are equal only if you open too on your heavy hinges
> and let your love come freely, freely, where it will never be safe,
> where you can never possess.
>
>   (*Circles*)

In the books published since *Circles on the Water,* Piercy's poetry is even less politically programmatic, more complex. *Stone, Paper, Knife* (1983), *My Mother's Body* (1986), and *Available Light* (1988) contain some of her strongest work. The central elements of these books are an insistence on dealing with the specifics of her experience; a willingness to see both men and women as individual, real people rather than as stereotypical role models; an introspective sense of self-discovery; and an attempt to understand the roots of the anger that permeates so much of her life and work. For like Audre Lorde and Adrienne Rich, Piercy values anger as a spur for her muse and almost fears its dissipation. In a poem called **"How divine is forgiving?"** from *Available Light,* she sees forgiveness as a weakness—a recognition of our imperfections rather than a large, magnanimous gesture:

> We forgive because we too have done
> the same to others easy as a mudslide;
> or because anger is a fire that must be fed
> and we are too tired to rise and haul a log.
>
>   (*Circles*)

My Mother's Body, written shortly after her mother's death, locates the source of that anger very specifically:

> The anger turned inward, the anger
> turned inward, where
> could it go except to make pain?
> It flowed into me with her milk.
>
>   (*Circles*)

Rummaging through her mother's things after her death, she finds artifacts that connect her to her mother's experience. Piercy, a middle-class woman, a successful writer, looks back at her mother's working-class life with a feminist eye, venting what she believes were her mother's repressed feelings of anger. She notices that her mother, like so many women of her generation, used "ugly" things for everyday and kept her beautiful things locked in storage. They were never used because "no day of hers was ever good enough" to use them, and so they become an emblem of the repressed beauty and creativity of the women of her mother's generation.

In the lovely title poem of this collection, mother and daughter become interchangeable:

> My mother is my mirror and I am hers.
> What do we see?
>
>   (*Circles*)

Looking back from the vantage point of a mature and seasoned life, the narrator realizes that the two women are less mother and daughter than twin sisters who happen to live in different times. Her feelings of youthful rebellion and resentment give way to mature self-recognition as the narrator takes on her mother's anger as her own:

> I will not be the bride you can dress,
> the obedient dutiful daughter you would chew,
> a dog's leather bone to sharpen your teeth.
>
> You strike me sometimes just to hear the sound.
> Loneliness turns your fingers into hooks
> barbed and drawing blood with their caress.
>
> My twin, my sister, my lost love,
> I carry you in me like an embryo
> as once you carried me.
>
>   (*Circles*)

My Mother's Body is also notable for its sequence of love poems called **"Chuppah,"** after the canopy used in Jewish wedding ceremonies. These poems were written for Piercy's marriage to writer Ira Wood, and she includes two poems by Wood in the sequence.

Available Light continues in this vein of self-discovery and retrospection. More than any of her books it chronicles the transformation of a "bad girl" from the inner city into a successful woman and widely respected writer. The poem **"Joy Road and Livernois,"** though clearly feminist in its depiction of the lot of working-class women, is also a very personal poem about Piercy's Detroit upbringing and the grim fate of some of her girlfriends, dead from accidents or drug overdoses, dying of cancer, or trapped in a mental institution. Offering short biographical sketches of each of these women—Pat, Evie, Peggy, Theresa, Gladys—in the vein of Edgar Lee Masters's *Spoon River Anthology*—Piercy emerges as a survivor of a world nearly impossible to transcend.

In a poem called **"I see the sign and tremble,"** inspired by a "Self Storage" sign glimpsed from the highway advertising a company offering storage lockers, Piercy creates a metaphor for the evolution of her poetry. She thinks of her poems as places where she has stored her various "selves" at different parts of her life. The poem itself is a catalog of Piercy's various identities, from "the gang girl running over the tarred / roofs sticky under her sneakers" through "the New York femme fatale dancing through a maze of mirrors" to "the woman alone / in the Midwest of a rented room sent into exile."

Available Light is also a very sensuous book, containing some of Piercy's best love poems, rich in the physicality of an opulent sexuality yet also tempered by the actual ups and downs of a long-term relationship. She chronicled the end of one love affair and the beginning of another in *Stone, Paper, Knife,* and here she writes about both the abundance of a happily married sex life as well as the bumpy road to reconciliation after horrendous arguments:

> Eat, drink, I am your daily bread
> and you are mine made every morning fresh
> In the oven of the bed we rise and bake
> yeasty, dark, full of raisins and seeds
>
> . . . .
>
> You have come back from your hike
> up the sandblasted mountains of ego
> and I have crawled out from my squat
> in the wind caves of sulk
>
> (*Circles*)

Finally, a poignant poem, **"Burial by Salt,"** is an important landmark in Piercy's work, representing her attempt to let go of her anger about her father's distant silence and lack of personal support. The iciness of the father-daughter relationship is captured in two lines that underscore the tragedy of too many American families:

> To you I made no promises. You asked none.
> Forty-nine years we spoke of nothing real
>
> (*Circles*)

Although desperate for her father's love, Piercy never felt it. The two have between them, as Piercy sees it, only "history / not love," and as she scatters his ashes to the wind (as she did with her mother's ashes, recorded in an earlier poem, **"What remains"**), she tries finally to come to terms with that limitation.

Her poetry published in the 1990's, *Mars and Her Children* (1992) and *What Are Big Girls Made Of?* (1997) carry on her lifetime concerns, showing a growing awareness of the "precarious balance" between the social and natural worlds. A poem like **"The ark of consequence,"** which organizes the sections of the former volume according to the colors of the rainbow, deals with ecological issues (the consequences of an oil spill). The title poem of that book, **"For Mars and her children returning in March,"** laments the threat humanity poses to the humpback whale. Animal rights issues surface as well in the latter book. **"Death of a doe on Chequesset Neck"** projects the narrator into the pain of a dying animal, and **"Crow babies"** sees the society of crows as superior to our own.

Piercy's poetry is uneven, often raw and unfiltered by a concern for formalist constraints. One critic even describes her poetry as seeming "for the most part to have been poured out and then cut up into lines." That assessment does capture something of the "I must get all of this down" quality of Piercy's work. Yet despite the unedited feel of many of the poems, they also contain what Marianne Moore called "a place for the genuine."

FURTHER READING

Criticism

Carnes, Pauli. "Chasing Their Tales." *Los Angeles Times Book Review* (3 April 1994): 5.
    A positive review of *The Longings of Women.*

Gould, Jean. "Marge Piercy." In her *Modern American Women Poets,* pp. 297-305. New York: Dodd, Mead, and Company, 1984.
    Provides an overview of Piercy's life, literary career, and poetry.

Hansen, Elaine Tuttle. "Mothers Yesterday and Mothers Tomorrow, But Never Mothers Today: *Woman on the Edge of Time* and *The Handmaid's Tale.*" In *Mother Without Child: Contemporary Fiction and the Crisis of Motherhood,* pp. 158-83. Berkeley, CA: University of California Press, 1997.
    Examines the significance of maternal loss and the ideology of reproduction, motherhood, and female identity in Piercy's *Woman on the Edge of Time* and Margaret Atwood's *The Handmaid's Tale.*

Lauret, Maria. "Seizing Time and Making New: Marge Piercy's *Vida.*" In her *Liberating Literature,* pp. 144-64. London and New York: Routledge, 1994.
    Provides analysis of the narrative presentation, historical context, and radical political and feminist themes of *Vida.*

Mesic, Penelope. Review of *Stone, Paper, Knife,* by Marge Piercy. *Poetry* CXLIII, No. 5 (February 1984): 299-300.
    Provides unfavorable assessment of *Stone, Paper, Knife.*

Orr, Elaine Neil. "Negotiated Motherhood: Contradictory Leanings in Marge Piercy's *Woman on the Edge of Time.*" In her *Subject to Negotiation: Reading Feminist Criticism and American Women's Fictions,* pp. 105-26. Charlottesville, VA: University Press of Virginia, 1997.
    Examines conflicting feminist interpretations of motherhood, biological identity, and female social experience in *Woman on the Edge of Time.*

Pacernick, Gary. "Interview with Marge Piercy." *Prairie Schooner* 71, No. 4 (Winter 1997): 82-6.
    Piercy discusses the craft of poetry and the Jewish, mythological, and personal themes in her work.

Rapping, Elayne. "Vintage Piercy." *Women's Review of Books* XI, Nos. 10-11 (July 1994): 46.

A review offering qualified praise for *The Longings of Women.*

Redding, Arthur F. "The Fantasy Life of the Movement: The Rhetoric of Violence on the New Left and After." In his *Raids on Human Consciousness: Writing, Anarchism, and Violence,* pp. 160-212. Columbia, SC: University of South Carolina Press, 1998.

Discusses the failure of leftist political radicalism during the 1970s, drawing upon Piercy's *Vida* as a fictional illustration.

Rodden, John. "A Harsh Day's Light: An Interview with Marge Piercy." *Kenyon Review* XX, No. 2 (Spring 1998): 132-43.

Piercy discusses her personal life and related political, feminist, and autobiographic aspects of her poetry.

Shands, Kerstin W. *The Repair of the World: The Novels of Marge Piercy.* Westport, CT: Greenwood Press, 1994.

A comprehensive, book-length critical study of Piercy's novels.

Sizemore, Christine W. "Masculine and Feminine Cities: Marge Piercy's *Going Down Fast* and *Fly Away Home.*" *Frontiers: A Journal of Women Studies* XIII, No. 1 (1992): 90-110.

Examines Piercy's presentation of female characters and their relationship to urban settings in *Going Down Fast* and *Fly Away Home.*

Additional coverage of Piercy's life and career is contained in the following sources published by the Gale Group: *Contemporary Authors,* **Vols. 21-24R,** *Contemporary Authors Autobiography Series,* **Vol. 1;** *Contemporary Authors New Revision Series,* **Vols. 13, 43, 66;** *Dictionary of Literary Biography,* **Vol. 120;** and *Major 20th-Century Writers.*

Anne Rice
1941-

(Also wrote under pseudonyms Anne Rampling and A. N. Roquelaure) American novelist.

The following entry presents an overview of Rice's career. For further information on her life and works, see *CLC*, Volume 41.

INTRODUCTION

Anne Rice is the best-selling author of mainstream gothic fiction that centers on the alluring subjects of vampirism, occult demonology, and the supernatural. Her debut novel, *Interview with the Vampire* (1976), attracted a large popular audience and established her as a foremost contemporary author of horror fiction. Subsequent installments in the "Vampire Chronicles" series, including *The Vampire Lestat* (1985) and *The Queen of the Damned* (1988), fortified her reputation as a highly imaginative writer of macabre fantasy. Rice's engaging novels are distinguished for their richly descriptive settings, provocative eroticism, and looming metaphysical concerns that reflect the precarious nature of religious faith and truth in the postmodern world. Her vampires, demons, and historical personages are typically dispossessed or alienated individuals who wrestle with existential questions of morality, religion, sex, and death. Though best known for her "Vampire Chronicles" and "Mayfair Witches" series, Rice has also published several successful historical novels, *The Feast of All Saints* (1980) and *Cry to Heaven* (1982), both of which feature exotic historical settings and social outcasts.

BIOGRAPHICAL INFORMATION

Born Howard Allen O'Brien in New Orleans, Louisiana, Rice was named after her postal worker father, Howard O'Brien, and mother, Katherine Allen O'Brien. As a child she disliked her first name so much that she changed it to Anne in grade school. The second of four sisters, Rice grew up in the blue-collar "Irish Channel" neighborhood of New Orleans. The Irish Channel borders the affluent Garden District of the city, and Rice mentions walking by the neighborhood's opulent homes, conscious of her status as an outsider, as an influence on her life and work. Rice attended a Catholic church throughout her childhood, though eventually rejected organized religion as a teenager. After her mother's death from alcoholism when Rice was fourteen, the family moved to Texas, where Rice met her high-school sweetheart and husband, poet Stan Rice. They married in 1961 and shortly afterward moved to San Francisco, where their daughter, Michelle, was born.

Rice initially attended Texas Women's University but transferred to San Francisco State University, where she earned a bachelor's degree in political science in 1964 and a Master of Arts in creative writing in 1971. She also took graduate classes at the University of California, Berkeley. When Michelle, then five years old, died of leukemia in 1972, Rice and her husband sought solace in alcohol, a destructive pattern that lasted several years. Rice found some measure of relief by writing *Interview with the Vampire* in only five weeks; the novel's child-vampire character, Claudia, resembles Michelle in age and appearance. Two works of historical fiction, *The Feast of All Saints* and *Cry to Heaven* followed during the early 1980s before Rice returned to vampires. Her popularity soared with the 1985 publication of the second book in the "Vampire Chronicles" series, *The Vampire Lestat,* followed by *The Queen of the Damned,* a Literary Guild main selection, in 1988, *The Tale of the Body Thief* (1992), *Memnoch the Devil* (1995), and *The Vampire Armand* (1998). The popular "Mayfair Witches" series, comprised of *The Witching Hour* (1990), a Book-of-the-Month selection, *Lasher* (1993), and *Taltos* (1994), added to her popularity and incredible commercial success. Rice also adapted *Interview with the Vampire* into the screenplay for the Hollywood film version of the novel, starring Tom Cruise and Brad Pitt, which appeared in 1994. Rice returned to New Orleans in 1988, purchasing a mansion in the Garden District, which serves as the setting for her books about the Mayfair Witches. She lives there today with her husband and son, Christopher.

MAJOR WORKS

Rice's fiction revolves around the situations of outsiders and misfits in society, questions of atheism and agnosticism, and themes of power and submission. Often including supernatural characters and plotting, Rice's work is noted for its darkness, eroticism, and evocation of setting and historical detail. In *Interview with the Vampire* a vampire named Louis relates his life story and adventures to a reporter who tape-records their session. Recalling his transformation as a vampire in 1790 at age twenty-five, Louis describes his first kill and evolving relationships with Lestat, his maker, and Claudia, a child-vampire whom they have created together. Unlike Claudia and Lestat who revel in murderous bloodshed, Louis is tormented by a moral dilemma—he believes it is wrong to kill, but he must kill to eat. An ensuing power struggle between Louis and Lestat results in Lestat's second death, for which Louis is imprisoned in the Theatre des Vampires, a coven of vampires in Paris. After burning the Theatre and escaping with Armand, an older vampire who mentors him, Louis returns to New Orleans where he is an outcast. As in much gothic fiction, underlying themes of homoeroticism and incest are prevalent throughout the novel. Rice also examines religious beliefs by comparing Louis, who tries and fails to construct his own moral framework, to his brother, a devout Roman Catholic. In the sequel, *The Vampire Lestat,* Lestat awakes from a moribund slumber in the year 1980, upon which he becomes a leather clad rock star. Presented as an autobiographic account, the novel traces the origins and history of vampirism through ancient, medieval, and modern history. The story concludes as Lestat performs in San Francisco to an audience of vampires who prepare to kill him for revealing their secrets in his published autobiography and lyrics. A continuation of the previous novel, *The Queen of the Damned* involves Akasha, mother of all vampires, whose scheme to institute world peace involves exterminating most of the male population and founding an empire governed by women.

In *The Tale of the Body Thief* Lestat contemplates suicide and eventually agrees to exchange his body with a mortal to temporarily escape his relentless ennui. Lestat must relearn mortal habits and a desperate chase follows after his counterpart disappears with his immortal body. Rice grapples with a shift in her personal philosophy from atheism to uncertainty about God's existence in *Memnoch the Devil,* in which Lestat converses with God and the Devil and tours Hell before deciding whether to join forces with the Devil. In *The Vampire Armand,* the sixth installment of the "Vampire Chronicles," Rice resurrects the title character, who earlier succumbed to a lethal dose of sunlight. Armand recollects his apprenticeship to Marius De Romanus in sixteenth-century Venice and subsequent rise as head of a Parisian vampire clan.

The "Mayfair Witches" series features Rowan Mayfair, scion of a matrilineal old New Orleans family whose members possess supernatural gifts and have been shadowed through time by a mysterious entity named Lasher. These books are characterized by intricate plotting, cliffhanger endings, and frequent flashbacks that tell the story of the Mayfair family's entanglement with Lasher over hundreds of years. *The Mummy* (1992) takes place in London, where young Julie Stratford falls in love with the reanimated mummy of Pharaoh Ramses III, who possesses the secret elixir of life. Julie and Ramses travel to Egypt where Ramses revives a murderous Cleopatra. In *Servant of the Bones* (1996), the genie Azriel fights the attempts of a demented millionaire to commit genocide on the population of the Third World.

Rice combined her interest in history with her exploration of social exiles by writing two historical novels. *The Feast of All Saints* enters the world of the *gens de couleur,* the group of free mulattoes who lived in antebellum New Orleans. The story focuses on the experiences of siblings Marcel and Marie, whose distinctive golden skin prohibits their full acceptance within either black or white society. *Cry to Heaven* centers upon the life of an eighteenth-century Italian castrati, a male singer who is castrated as a boy to preserve his high voice. The protagonist, Tonio Treschi, attempts to fulfill his desire to become one of the greatest opera singers in Europe while plotting revenge on his brother for treacherously having him castrated and exiled. Both books focus on characters who, like Rice's vampires and witches, exist on the fringes of mainstream society without being accepted by it. Rice also explored her fascination with sadomasochism by writing a pseudonymous series of pornographic novels—*The Claiming of Sleeping Beauty* (1983), *Beauty's Punishment* (1984), and *Beauty's Release* (1985) as A. N. Roquelaure and *Exit to Eden* (1985) and *Belinda* (1986) as Anne Rampling.

CRITICAL RECEPTION

Most critics recognize Rice's remarkable talent for constructing page-turning plots, evoking a sense of place—particularly when writing about her native New Orleans—and creating whole new universes peopled by supernatural characters. She is widely praised for rejuvenating the hackneyed genre of vampire fiction with her intelligent, ambitious novels. Rice's novels are also noted for their appealing eroticism and have attracted the interest of gay readers who identify with the themes of alienation depicted in the underground culture of vampiric society. However, Rice's major goal—acceptance as a serious writer by the literary fiction world—has so far eluded her. Though some critics appreciate Rice's philosophical musings on immortality and incorporation of occult history in her novels, others find her writing verbose, implausible, and clichéed. Some dismiss her otherworldly subject matter and frequent erotic descriptions as unworthy of serious literary effort. Reviewers have criticized Rice's later work, notably *Servant of the Bones* and *Memnoch the Devil,* for frequent and lengthy digressions from plot and description to use her characters as mouthpieces for Rice's ideas of philosophy and life. Despite such criticism, Rice remains one of the United States's best-selling authors. Her weird casts of characters and fantastic storylines hold a terrific appeal for readers and have broken new ground in contemporary literature. As Susan Ferraro writes in *New York Magazine:* "Rice's vampires are loquacious philosophers who spend much of eternity debating the nature of good and evil. Trapped in immortality, they suffer human regret. They are lonely, prisoners of circumstance, compulsive sinners, full of self-loathing and doubt. The are, in short, Everyman Eternal."

PRINCIPAL WORKS

Interview with the Vampire (novel) 1976
The Feast of All Saints (novel) 1980
Cry to Heaven (novel) 1982
The Claiming of Sleeping Beauty [as A. N. Roquelaure] (novel) 1983

CRITICISM

Pat Hilton (review date 19 December 1982)

SOURCE: "The Alienated World of the Mutilated Men," in *Los Angeles Times Book Review,* December 19, 1982, p. 11.

[*In the following review, Hilton offers qualified praise for* A Cry to Heaven.]

Guido Maffeo was castrated when he was 6 years old. Born the 11th child in a peasant family, where hunger and cruelty were routine, the boy was taken gently, petted and fed; even the knife was not used unkindly. Although the memory of the surgery never left him, he had exchanged what he would not experience for a profession that afforded him a passion some men might envy.

Tonio Treschi was not so fortunate with his memories. At 15 he had already tasted the joys of sex; he had a strong sense of manhood, pride and heritage. The knife was applied violently, a shocking act of brutality and misplaced revenge. The mutilation stripped him of his family, of his position in the culture, of his masculinity and pride. He was thrust into a profession for which he was qualified by virtue of talent, but of which he was an unwilling and humiliated member.

Once again author Anne Rice delves into a society of the alienated. Her provocative first novel. *Interview With the Vampire,* was followed by *The Feast of All Saints,* a tale of the quadroons of New Orleans in the 19th Century. Now eunuchs. The 18th-Century castrati were usually selected because of their beautiful voices, and the determining surgery was only the first step in a disciplined schedule of study for the male soprano, whose greatest glory was to perform in the opera.

In that time the opera had some of the same sense of public excitement currently associated with the World Series or the Super Bowl. Who would sing at the opera was on the tip of every tongue, the tradespeople as well as the noble families. Performers vied on stage, personally competing as well as seeking to win the favor of the audiences, who were not above shouting down a newcomer if he posed a threat to an old favorite.

Eunuchs fortunate enough to reach the opera were rewarded richly. Indeed, as it turns out, eunuchs are not necessarily sexually deprived. Capable of intercourse but not procreation, they could find loving relationships with one another and were highly sought after by many women—and men. As their popularity grew, so did their opportunities for sexual activity.

For Guido, who would otherwise have been condemned to an existence of squalor and deprivation, loss of sexual identity in exchange for security, position, popularity and an opportunity to nourish his musical abilities was not something worth contemplating or regretting.

Tonio was unable to be as philosophical. Determined to revenge himself for the mutilation, he dealt daily in his mind with the meaning of his castration. Although talented, touted, able to enjoy sexual pleasures and desirable to women, he felt set apart and he had suffered great humiliation. He was not a man.

As he begins to grow taller, he asks Guido in anguish. "What is happening to me?" "You will continue to grow tall." Guido tells him. "Your arms and legs will increase in length . . . it is this flexibility of bone which gives you such power with your voice. Every day that you practice you increase the size of your lungs, and the elastic bones let those lungs grow. So that very soon you will have power in the upper register that no woman could ever possess. No boy, for that matter. No other man."

"But your hands will hang low on your body, and your feet will flatten out. And you will be weak in the arms as a woman is weak. You will not have the natural muscularity of a man."

Tonio's greatest dread is that one day he will be forced to appear on stage as a woman, an act he despises even though its refusal might cost the greatest satisfaction still open to him—that of performing. Tonio's question is contemporary: What does it mean to be a man? Will taking revenge on the perpetrator of the crime restore some sense of his masculinity to him? Can the power and satisfaction of winning audiences and becoming the darling of society compensate for unfulfilled sexuality? Rice's themes are particularly suited to our own culture—attempting to put new faces on old roles.

Cry to Heaven is satisfying. Only in conclusion does the writing fail to sustain the power of the action, a failure to be forgiven.

E. F. Bleiler (review date 6 November 1988)

SOURCE: "The Night Has a Thousand Eyes," in *Washington Post Book World,* November 6, 1988, pp. 8-9.

[*In the following excerpt, Bleiler evaluates* The Queen of the Damned *in relation to previous volumes of "The Vampire Chronicles."*]

I did things backwards when I approached Anne Rice's *The Queen of the Damned,* the third volume in her "Vampire Chronicles." I read it first, then the second volume (*The Vampire Lestat*) and, last of all, *Interview with the Vampire,* the first book in the series. In one way this turned out to be an advantage, since I could see the latest book as an independent work, as a new reader might see it and not as a book sustained by others. As a disadvantage, I first thought, there might be a problem coming in cold on situations, events, and personalities all based on the past.

It turned out, when I read the other two novels, that the problem wasn't a large one. The carry-over from *The Vampire Lestat* is not great, and *Interview with the Vampire* is not only irrelevant, but somewhat misleading to later developments. The author seems to have replanned her work after writing the interview.

Rice's vampire world was easily picked out from *The Queen of the Damned,* and it is very different from the classical pattern that J. M. Rymer, J. S. Le Fanu, and Bram Stoker established. For Rice a vampire's victim does not automatically become a vampire; making a new vampire is a fairly complicated process, almost a rite, that involves exchanging blood. Nor do vampires have any of the remarkable abilities or disabilities that Count Dracula had, like transforming himself into a bat, sliding around as a mist through keyholes, not showing on mirrors, or worrying about stakes and garlic. But Rice's vampires are abnormally strong, immortal except for fire and total destruction, and with advanced age they apparently pick up some paranormal abilities like thought reading, levitation, etc. All take their daily blood, animal as well as human, and all are photophobic.

They are also a very mixed-group. Some, like Lestat, enter life with high spirits and brio, and with small disguise pass for mortals. They enjoy music, the theater, and are immortal hedonists, wealthy and cultured. Others live as outlaws, mad dogs whose hand is against everyone. And still others carry on strange cults with elaborate superstitions, like avoidance of crosses. But there is one general pattern: Even more than mortals, they can be violently hostile to one another, and it takes very little to set them against one another with fire and scythe.

The Vampire Lestat, which is the best of the three books, despite divagations was basically a quest for meaning in the life of a vampire. Lestat wanted to find out what it was all about. He eventually learned a historical point of view, but it didn't seem to make much difference to him. In *The Queen of the Damned* Lestat sets things in motion with a new project: He wants vampires to go public, and initiate a dialogue/war with mortals. Why? This is not entirely clear, but it seems to be for the excitement and thrills involved, for vampires get very bored over the centuries. His mode: setting himself up as a rock star and on record and in rock concerts revealing the mythic secrets of the vampires as far as he knows them. But more happens than he expects when the living dead come to-life.

But then Lestat lapses into the background, only poking a canine tooth out occasionally, as the book shifts around a succession of characters, some with the same names as those in the earlier volumes (though not with good characterization), some new. About the time that one grows used to a character, the story shifts. To carry on the plot, which is complex, Rice adds three new elements to the vampire situation: a synthetic creation myth that is revealed in fragments to account for the existence of vampires; a feminist approach, which shifts to woman characters and a female responsibility for vampirism; and a world peril, both threatened and averted by women vampires. In this last, unless the force that Lestat has awakened can be stopped, not only vampires but roughly half of all mortals will die. This, of course, is descending to the pulp level of decades ago.

All in all, if one wants to read a member of the Vampire Chronicles, *The Vampire Lestat,* despite some problems, is worthwhile.

Laurence Coven (review date 6 November 1988)

SOURCE: "A History of the Undead," in *Los Angeles Times Book Review,* November 6, 1988, p. 13.

[*In the following review, Coven offers favorable assessment of* The Queen of the Damned.]

In *Interview With the Vampire,* the first volume of the "Vampire Chronicles," Anne Rice ushers us into the eerily succulent, yet refined world of Louis de Pointe du Lac, a man who became a vampire in late-18th-Century New Orleans.

The second book, *The Vampire Lestat,* explodes with fury into the world of high-tech 20th-Century San Francisco. Lestat, the charismatic iconoclast of the undead, relates his tale from his human youth as a French nobleman of the early 1700s to his ascension to rock superstardom and cult hero worship as a modern-day vampire.

With *The Queen of the Damned,* Anne Rice has created universes within universes, traveling back in time as far as ancient, pre-pyramidic Egypt and journeying from the frozen mountain peaks of Nepal to the crowded, sweating streets of southern Florida.

In all truth, the epic scope of this novel is mandated by the profound mysteries and timeless questions which Rice seeks to answer. What lies beyond death? What is the nature of goodness? Is there meaning to life? But here these age-old enigmas are mulled over, puzzled through and furiously attacked, not by mere mortals, but by the blood-sucking undead. Rice's vampires are natural philosophers. Their immortality serves to heighten those concerns which have beguiled and befuddled humans for centuries.

One of Rice's many splendid characters is Armand, a beautiful boy-vampire who has walked the Earth since the early Renaissance. He becomes enamored of Daniel, a lovely young human lad and the "interviewer" of the first novel. Their relationship, though unnatural in the extreme, is both breathlessly erotic and heart-breakingly sad. Daniel, who cannot bear his own aging, implores Armand for the "dark gift," to be made immortal, but Armand desperately needs to hold onto Daniel who is his last link to the humanity he has forever lost.

"More and more they argued philosophy. . . . Pulling Daniel out of a theatre in Rome, Armand had asked what did Daniel really think that death was? People who were still living knew things like that! Did Daniel know what Armand truly feared?"

When a creature of potential immortality ponders the nature of death, or when a being who must drink the blood of the living to survive, consciously seeks the high moral ground, the irony is inevitable, yet their futility is no less agonizing than man's. Enormously old, incredibly powerful, and constantly questing, many of Rice's vampires remain, like humans, incurably neurotic.

Much of *The Queen of the Damned* is devoted to the actual resolution of one arcane mystery. How and when were vampires first created? The more sensitive of the undead share a common need to know the nature of their origins. They also share a kind of vampiric Jungian universal subconscious. They find flashing through their collective minds visions of an incredibly ancient legend about two red-haired sisters who are brutally attacked while engaged in the holy tradition of eating their dead mother. Simultaneously there is also a common knowledge that Akasha, the mother of all vampires, once again roams the Earth.

Akasha, however, is no nurturer. Bent on world conquest, she embarks on an apocalyptic journey of bloodcurdling slaughter and destruction. For her companion and co-ruler she chooses Lestat, whom she seduces through fear and lust. Yet the Young Lestat (not yet three centuries old) is hideously torn between the seditious lure of Akasha's charms and his crying, if vestigial need to be embraced by the love of mortals:

"Why did my heart come up in my throat now? Why was I crying inside, like something dying myself?"

"Maybe some other fiend could have loved it; some twisted and conscienceless immortal could have sneered at her visions, yet slipped into the robes of a god as easily as I had slipped into that perfumed bath."

Occasionally, Rice can become repetitive and overly instructional in her need to recount every detail of the vampires' ancient beginnings. More often she provides an exhilarating blend of philosophic questing and pure, wondrous adventure.

Rice's vampiric world is a continually unfolding one, a tapestry too enormous to be hung on any wall. And just when we begin to think we can see its borders, she leaves us with a tantalizing final chapter that promises us weavings we never even suspected.

Eric Kraft (review date 27 November 1988)

SOURCE: "Do Not Speak Ill of the Undead," in *New York Times Book Review,* November 27, 1988, pp. 12-3.

[*In the following review, Kraft offers tempered assessment of* The Queen of the Damned. *According to Kraft, Rice's "enormous ability" as a novelist is "wasted on vampires."*]

When last we saw him, in the second book of Anne Rice's vampire chronicles, the vampire Lestat was a rock star, flaunting his evil ways before a horde of screaming mortal fans in San Francisco, sweating blood under hot lights. Then suddenly he was being attacked—not by Tipper Gore and her committee for cleaner language in popular music, but by a gang of the undead, bent on destroying him because his lyrics and autobiography named names and revealed secrets. Just in the nick of time, though, Lestat hopped into his Porsche and fled into a gap between installments.

The Queen of the Damned opens before the concert, with angry blood drinkers plotting to destroy the rogue spiller of the vampire beans. A Lestat cult has arisen among young mortals, so the real vampires don't have much trouble mixing with the fans, who emulate vampire style and hang out at a bar called Dracula's Daughter. Lestat has some supporters among the undead, including Akasha, the original vampire, mother of all the others, queen of the damned. She's been catatonic for centuries, seated on a throne in a crypt deep in the earth, but she's up and about now, roused by Lestat. She's got big ideas, this one, including a plan for world peace, starting with a nice bloodbath.

The first book in the chronicles belonged to the vampire Louis and his immortal angst, the second to Lestat and his life's story. *The Queen of the Damned* is told from many points of view, by a big cast of vampires. They're a diverse bunch, some elders, others mere fledglings, some wise, others naïve. Louis and Lestat are back, and so is Armand, former head of the Paris coven, who builds a huge pleasure island off Miami, open all night—but only at night. There's

Khayman, an ancient Egyptian who loves our times, when he can drive fast cars and pick up beautiful women, when "princesses sallied forth onto the Champs Elysées in carefully faded rags." A fledgling, Baby Jenks, brings the liveliest voice in the book to a chapter that rips along as fast and tough as her Harley. She's mean, cute, dead and a little dumb: "She'd tried to read the Vampire Lestat's book—the whole history of Dead guys back to ancient times and all—but there were just too many big words and konk, she was asleep."

A pair of twin sisters, Maharet and Mekare, support the overarching plot. Long ago, Akasha commanded their rape and mutilation; now Mekare wants revenge. All the other vampires are troubled by a disturbing dream, an image of that ancient outrage visited on the twins. They aren't sure what the dream means, but they sense that it portends a great struggle. Since none of them knows the whole story, we learn it as they come to know it, mostly through long talks. These vampires love talk as much as blood; they go on about what may happen, has happened, may have happened or may be going to happen, about why they are as they are and what the point of it all is. They tell tales, and they tell tales within tales. In the course of all this talk a complex story emerges—vast, spanning centuries, continents and thousands upon thousands of words, in which a set of vampire myths is most artfully linked and nicely fitted into other mythologies, reality, and the plots of the earlier books.

Though the story unfolds in many vampire voices, two other voices pop up throughout, regardless of which vampire holds the stage. One, used for chronicling vampire lore and legend, sounds like an official history—pompous and impersonal. Whenever a vampire employs it, all individuality is lost. The other, used for describing the messy pleasure of the nightly kills, is prurient: teeth pierce, lips suck, blood spurts, victims swoon and lassitude follows the passion of feeding. With each kill, these images of sex and chicken Kiev are repeated—another silken neck, more piercing, sucking and spurting, another swooning victim.

Ms. Rice can't seem to decide how she feels about all this killing, which goes far beyond simple bloodsucking. In one orgy of butchery, Lestat really runs amok, exploding heads, "rupturing brains and hearts and arteries," while Akasha cheers him on: "Yes, kill them. Strike for the tender organs; rupture them; make the blood flow." But this slaughter is committed in the name of peace. Akasha means to end the bloody history of the human race by killing most of the mortal males, the real monsters.

The other vampires oppose her hypocrisy with their own. They anticipate a new enlightenment, a rejection of the superstitions that have inspired the killing Akasha claims to deplore, and they want to give the mortals time to change. Of course, they'll go on killing. They can't help themselves; it's in their blood, and Ms. Rice's lush imagery invites us to enjoy it, to share their bloodlust, smell the blood, yearn for it as they do, feel the luscious rush when they drink it hot. But nearly every bloody scene is followed by a repudiation of it—some vampires hate themselves for what they do, others echo Akasha's outrage at humankind's horrors. This juxtaposition of righteous indignation and salacious slaying doesn't elevate the vampires; it debases the noble sentiments. The book itself wallows in gore while preaching peace.

Perhaps the trouble lies with the vampires themselves. They're fit characters for a writer of horror tales, but maybe they're just not good enough for one who seems to aim for something more than being the greatest living American author of vampire novels. Anne Rice is a writer of enormous ability. She has a masterly way with language, works on a broad canvas, has a vast range of knowledge, brings exotic settings vividly to life and is wonderfully clever, but these gifts are wasted on vampires. May she find subjects worthy of her talents before these dead guys suck her dry.

Frank J. Prial (review date 11 June 1989)

SOURCE: "Undead and Unstoppable," in *New York Times Book Review,* June 11, 1989, p. 9.

[*In the following review, Prial offers qualified praise for* The Mummy, *though finds fault in Rice's prose. "If you liked her vampires," Prial concludes, "you'll love her mummies."*]

In George Axelrod's Hollywood spoof of a generation back, "Will Success Spoil Rock Hunter?," a veteran hack explains to a young writer that film lovers can't just meet—"They gotta meet cute."

"How about this?" the neophyte replies. "He's a shrink, she's a hooker, and they meet at the upholsterer's getting their couches fixed."

In her latest novel, ***The Mummy, or Ramses the Damned,*** Anne Rice gives new meaning to meeting cute. Julie Stratford has soft brown eyes, porcelain cheeks, a guileless mouth and is 20 years old. Ramses II, a k a Ramses the Great and, to close friends, Ramses the Damned, is manly, stalwart and, oh, around 3,000 years old, give a dynasty or two.

They meet in London, in Julie's home. It's 1914.

> The face, my God, the face. There were eyes there, great shining blue eyes under the thin wrappings. It reached up suddenly and tore loose the bandages . . . from its skull and released a soft mop of brown hair.
>
> Then it rose on its knees with quiet grace and reached down into the fountain with its bandaged hands, scooping up the sparkling water to its lips. It drank and drank the water, with deep sighing gulps. Then it stopped and turned towards her, wiping away more of the thick ashen layer of linen from its face.

A man looking at her! A blue-eyed man with intelligence looking at her! . . .

She backed into the Egyptian room, legs trembling; her body moist all over, her hands clawing at her lace peignoir.

Lawrence Stratford, Egyptologist—father to Julie and heir to a shipping fortune—had just discovered Ramses in a tomb near Cairo. Better he hadn't. No sooner had he uncovered his Pharaoh than he met with what they used to call an untimely death, right there in the tomb. He'd barely time to order the mummy shipped to the British Museum.

Well, not directly to the museum; the lovers still have to meet. Breathing his last, Lawrence directed that the mummy be dropped off for a few days at his London home with innocent Julie. Doing what young things always do when someone delivers a mummy, Julie throws a party. All Mayfair turns up, but the scene is pure Irish wake: guests mingling while Ramses, the center of attraction, stands propped in a corner.

Soon after the guests leave (prompted by what, I won't say), Ramses, who has been stirring for days, comes to life. Julie, as we have seen, does likewise. In a matter of hours, Ramses is speaking pure Oxbridge and, caparisoned in the late Lawrence's Savile Row best, becomes Reginald Ramsey, also an Egyptologist.

That he wears his hair in a shoulder-length page-boy, sports a George Hamilton tan and eats with his fingers doesn't seem to bother anyone but, hey, Edwardian London was always a funky town.

Ramses ruled Egypt 3,000 years ago but, Ms. Rice tells us, instead of dying like any normal Pharaoh, he discovers the secret of immortal life, a kind of super-Geritol he mixes up himself. Stuffing a common soldier into his sarcophagus, he disguises himself and for hundreds of years travels the ancient world, returning to Egypt every century or so to counsel whoever happens to be running the place at the time. Eventually, bored with existence, he settles into a long sleep, leaving word at the front desk, so to speak, that sunlight can wake him but that he'd prefer to sleep in.

A few centuries along, someone does wake him: Cleopatra—the Cleopatra—who had heard the old legends and was curious. She learns of the elixir and tries to get it, first for herself, later for Mark Antony. Ramses, who loves her, refuses. When she does herself in with the asp, he goes back into hibernation—until Lawrence Stratford comes along 2,000 years later.

Once Julie and Ramses get to Egypt (How did they get to Egypt? Don't ask), Ramses heads for the Cairo Museum, where—purely by chance—he finds, stretched in a glass case, Cleopatra herself. Out comes the elixir and, shriveled and moth-eaten, out of the glass case comes Cleopatra:

"Dear God, man, what have you done! What have you awakened! . . . It's not whole. You've raised a thing which is not whole."

Cleopatra comes to much the same conclusion after her first glimpse of herself in a thousand years and before she's had a chance to do anything with her hair. But that doesn't stop her. Two pastimes she missed during the dead years were sex and murder; she quickly makes up for lost time.

One victim is—no, really—a Ford dealer from Hannibal, Mo., who seems to have driven one of his cars to Egypt. Cleopatra knocks him off when he ungallantly remarks that one of her legs appears to be just skeleton. Clever empress that she is, she masters the stick shift, an innovation in 1914, and drives off.

In Ms. Rice's world, there is no true line between the living and the, er, unliving. Ramses, who loves to play around with his elixir, rejuvenates a mummy's hand. It scuttles around until he juliennes it with paring knife but, even then, the pieces hop about like animated hamburger.

In fact, the only thing really dead here is much of Ms. Rice's prose. She favors a mock-epic style that went out with Rafael Sabatini. She evokes Conan Doyle and H. Rider Haggard, but when they wrote this way, they were serious. When Cleopatra cries "Okaaaay! Super!" the mood slips away quickly.

With her past efforts and now with Ramses, Anne Rice has pretty much cornered the literary market on the undead. If this sort of thing didn't appeal to you before, there isn't much reason to start. On the other hand, if you liked her vampires, you're going to love her mummies.

Angela Carter (review date 1 September 1989)

SOURCE: "The Curse of Ancient Egypt," in *New Statesman & Society,* September 1, 1989, pp. 31-2.

[*In the following review, Carter offers favorable assessment of* The Mummy.]

According to Franco Morretti (*Dialectic of Fear*), the tale of terror relies for its specific *frisson* on repression. "The repressed returns . . . but disguised as a monster." The horror novels of Anne Rice comprehensively trash this theory; she lets the repressed return in splendour. When the crumbling bandages at last fall from the eponymous mummy of this, her latest novel, young Julie Stamford, the shipping heiress, reels back, but not in horror.

"Dear God, she thought, this is not merely a man gifted with beauty; this is the most beautiful man I've ever seen."

Ramses III, former Pharoah of Egypt, is, admittedly, not so much one of the undead as an immortal. He may make his entrance in a manner characteristic of a fifties movie ghoul but he is also an intellectual giant and a formidable sexual athlete, to boot. This is the return of the repressed, not as Dracula but as Rhett Butler. What *is* going on?

More than meets the eye, probably. Anne Rice is a writer of great scope, invention, imaginative energy and sexual daring who has opted to work in mass market genre fiction. Her work in the "tale of terror" is also a kind of commentary on the idea of the tale of terror, and a working through of how much you can get away with in it.

Anne Rice is self-conscious in a way that antique masters of the genre—Bram Stoker, Lovecraft, even Poe—were not, and contemporaries such as Clive Barker and Stephen King are, well, too repressed to be. Among the dedicatees of **The Mummy** is Rider Haggard, who "created the immortal *She*". But the unacknowledged tension behind the psychosexual geography of that extraordinary novel, with its insane depiction of Africa and resplendent S-M heroine, are resolved in Anne Rice's work.

No gruff hinting at homo-erotic bonding here. True to the spirit, rather than the letter, of such friendships as Allan Quartermain's with Sir Henry Curtis (*King Solomon's Mines*) Julie's father and his best friend have indeed been lovers, once upon a time. The villainous Henry's attempts at blackmail follow a liaison with elements of the relationship between Uncle Holly and young Leo before they went off together to look for She-Who-Must-Be-Obeyed.

This self-consciousness extends to individual horrors. A severed hand in **The Mummy,** posthumously reanimated, hops and skips around, recalling Freud's equation between the imagery of severed limbs and castration anxiety. This glimpse of the machinery behind the effect doesn't diminish the shudder it provokes; it increases it, because it indicates the nature of the fear for which the paraphernalia of the horror narrative provides a screen of consolation.

In the Anne Rice trilogy collectively known as "The Vampire Chronicles" (**Interview with the Vampire, The Vampire Lestat** and **The Queen of the Damned**), the undead are perfectly aware they are not performing elaborate metaphors for tabooed acts. They know that what they *do* is just what is taboo. For them, to suck is transcendent bliss; the cannibal tenderness of the mother-child relation is Anne Rice's sexual paradigm here, more Kleinian than Freudian. When the vampire Lestat turns his beloved mother into a vampire with a deal of passionate and reciprocal sucking in a glorious triumph of polymorphous perversity, Anne Rice seems to be suggesting that it is straight sex itself that is the metaphor for some more atavistic and savagely intimate form of congress.

So it comes as something of a disappointment to discover that, in spite of the enticingly ambiguous element in its title, **The Mummy** is, give and take the youthful indiscretions of old men, straightforwardly heterosexist. Ramses III is a man, after all, and Julie a woman; a 5,000 year age difference is no insuperable barrier to a consummation of a kind the ravishing, sexy vampires of the earlier books would find exceedingly tame: ". . . and she felt his delicious weight come down upon her, crushing her. The tears had sprung to her eyes, tears of relief. A soft moan escaped her lips."

Admittedly, even though it weighs in at a hefty 436 pages, Anne Rice promises that "the Adventures of Ramses the Damned Shall Continue", so we can confidently expect another two volumes, at least, and she may well be writing herself in. What seem at first to be signs of a certain carelessness, especially in the early part of the novel, may be part of a plan. Certainly her evocation of Edwardian London is barely plausible—a dining room, ready for breakfast, smells of "coffee, cinnamon and freshly baked muffins"; a singer lives in a flat over the music hall at which she performs. Then we realise that this is a studio-bound London like that briefly glimpsed in *Gone with the Wind.*

When Ramses mixes up his *elixir vitae,* Anne Rice borrows directly from B-movies: "Within seconds the change had taken place. The raw ingredients, already quite potent in their own right, had been changed into a bubbling liquid full of vague phosphorescent lights." It is as if we are seeing with the innocent eye we once took to Saturday morning pictures. Even when Ramses returns to Egypt with his new friends, there is still a clean, bright simplicity to everything, which recalls Hollywood in the early days of technicolour. Cleopatra herself, soon reanimated as a homicidal nymphomaniac, has this kind of dimensionless brio. This world is far away from the *maudit* midnights, the mean streets, the guilt-lacerated and existentially complex vampires of the "Chronicles", as if Anne Rice had decided to relocate herself beyond the polymorphously perverse stage—in the latency period, perhaps. And **The Mummy** probably isn't a tale of terror at all, though it retains elements of the form, but a narrative in the process of mutating into some other form—supernatural romance, perhaps—that indicates a tale of terror can only really exist in a state of unknowing, that the writer of tales of terror must, first of all, terrify him or herself.

Yet what fresh *frissons* can volume two hold? Impossible not to look forward to it! And let us hope Anne Rice escapes the strange curse that hangs over all writers who deal with Ancient Egypt. Most recently it struck down Norman Mailer, whose *Ancient Evenings* contained, evidently with no facetious intent, dialogue such as: "Would you like my obelisk in you?" and "I am known as the degenerate who sups on bat shit"—both lines Anne Rice must wish she'd thought of first.

Patrick McGrath (review date 4 November 1990)

SOURCE: "Ghastly and Unnatural Ambitions," in *New York Times Book Review,* November 4, 1990, p. 11.

[*In the following review, McGrath offers unfavorable assessment of* The Witching Hour, *citing weak characterization and repetitiousness as the novel's major flaws.*]

The evil that blights the pages of **The Witching Hour,** Anne Rice's new novel, has an intriguing origin. In the

1600's, in Scotland, a naïve young woman called Suzanne Mayfair learns for a lark how to summon demons. Later she's burned at the stake, but the demon she summons, Lasher by name, goes on to bedevil her descendants down to the present day, apparently seeing in them the means of fulfilling his ghastly and unnatural ambitions. In the process he turns them into a "witch family," a witch here being "a person who can attract and manipulate unseen forces."

But what's interesting about poor Suzanne's fate is that it's a *witch judge,* an inquisitor, who teaches her how to rouse Lasher in the first place—as if the law, in its zeal, actually foments transgression, the better to serve its function. It's this sort of complex intertwining of antagonistic forces—moral, psychological and finally biological—that forms the basic structural principle of this huge and sprawling tale of horror.

Lasher is really the protagonist of *The Witching Hour.* Possibly he's Satan; possibly he's an old Celtic god turned demon after the collapse of that civilization. Certainly the strongly Irish flavor of the novel would reinforce this notion. What is sure is that down the centuries, in Scotland, in Haiti, finally in New Orleans, he appears to members of the Mayfair family, mainly the women, as a slim, pale, elegant figure with dark eyes and dark hair and a hypnotically seductive power over any of them reckless enough to entertain him.

And, over time, through Lasher's offices, the family becomes enormously wealthy, though to sustain itself it relies rather heavily on incestuous unions and tends to deal harshly with inquisitive outsiders. One chap is found rolled up in a carpet in the attic 60 years after being murdered there; we know that he died in the carpet because he'd started to chew through it.

This is the sort of book in which one sees a lot of the undertaker. Mayfairs often come to bad ends, generally either burning to death or falling from high places, and we meet many members of many generations of them in the long second section: Julien, for instance, the genial dandy who can be in two places at once and start fires with his mind; Stella, the flapper, wildly dancing the Charleston; the witch who just wants to have fun; her granddaughter Deirdre, whose sexual passion for Lasher is so intense that terrible old Aunt Carlotta keeps her doped to the eyeballs on Thorazine all her adult life; and lots more, all vividly sketched, all gloriously weird.

Latest and strongest of the Mayfair witches, and inheritor of the fantastic Mayfair legacy, is Rowan, who's a brilliant neurosurgeon in San Francisco when the novel opens, never having returned to the family home in New Orleans since the day of her birth. But she is a Mayfair, so we soon must ask whether she's truly a healer, as her profession would suggest—or a destroyer. It becomes clear that she has the potential for both, and the question as to which will triumph when, at last, she comes to grips with Lasher

is one with which Ms. Rice tantalizes us to the very last page of the book, and beyond.

But despite its tireless narrative energy, despite its relentless inventiveness, the book is bloated, grown to elephantine proportions because more is included than is needed. Repetition is a problem: the same stories are told several times, accruing more detail with each telling. Also, the principal characters have a way of regurgitating what they've learned, even though the reader was with them when they learned it. At times the prose, which for the most part is solid and workmanlike, even lyrical in its evocation of the architecture and vegetation of Haiti and New Orleans, collapses into grinding cliché; editorially, rigor of excision is sadly wanting.

A further, allied problem is in the characterization. Rowan and her lover, the robust hunk Michael Curry, are the central human characters here and must play complicated parts in the moral equation that finally issues from the vast tonnage of narrative material. The problem is, they have both been so constructed that they hardly for a moment live or breathe except as structural elements serving specific design functions in the grand scheme. And while this sort of caricatural sketchiness works fine for the huge army of bit players, Rowan and Michael make claims to be taken seriously as moral actors in the drama.

Those who demand a measure of depth and plausibility in the characters with whom they're asked to identify, and who value formal elegance and compression in their fiction, will find *The Witching Hour* too shallow, and too ungainly, to provide much more than pleasantly creepy entertainment. Big, generous and energetic though it is, finally the novel fails to say anything substantial about its theme, beyond making the dubious suggestions that evil is transmitted through heredity rather than environment and flourishes best in large, odd, matrilineal families like the Mayfairs.

Rita Mae Brown (review date 18 November 1990)

SOURCE: "The Queen of Darkness," in *Los Angeles Times Book Review,* November 18, 1990, pp. 1, 8.

[*In the following review, Brown offers enthusiastic praise for* The Witching Hour, *which she hails as "[Rice's] best novel yet."*]

The Witching Hour unfolds like a poisonous lotus blossom redolent with luxurious evil. Or so it would seem to a Medieval or "born-again" Christian. For those Christians and non-Christians not fearful of stories about unearthly powers, witches and secular resurrections, this novel will delight the senses.

Author Anne Rice uses her beloved New Orleans to good effect. Of all American cities, it is the least Puritan and the most resistant to English priggishness.

Michael Curry, the primary male character and an impoverished native of this delicious city, dies and is brought back to life by Rowan Mayfair, a woman of science who happens to have magical powers. However, the price of resurrection comes very high, and Michael is drawn into an ancient web spun for more than three centuries by a dynasty of witches and a demon named Lasher—souls, undead, yet not alive either. They need Michael and Rowan for their purposes.

Rice thoroughly enjoys herself as she slides through 17th-Century France, the fetid plantations in Port-au-Prince, the pain of the Civil War South and the seeming "normalcy" of today's San Francisco and New Orleans.

The multiple generations of Mayfair women in the house on First Street are strange. Generation after generation, since the first Mayfair woman landed on American soil after fleeing a slave insurrection in Haiti, these women have had incredible power. At least one female per generation, the one who wears the Mayfair emerald, has exercised this power in worldly ways and has come to a tragic, mournful end.

Rice must be wearing the Mayfair emerald herself, since she writes with hypnotic power. In *The Witching Hour,* as in her vampire chronicles, she attacks the idea that good and evil are polar opposites. Renewal through destruction and regeneration through violence drive the plots of Rice's "supernatural" novels. This is a concept repellent and alien to Christians, but something Hindus always have known. This idea allows Rice to create vampires, witches and demons who can be figures that excite our compassion, most especially in their deaths.

The execution of Comtesse Deborah Mayfair de Montclève in September, 1689, in the town of Montclève, France, is one such scene. This beauty (the witches always are beautiful) is accused by her mother-in-law of sleeping with Satan and murdering her husband. The doomed Deborah at least enjoys melancholy exaltation as she destroys her accusers by unleashing a storm upon their heads.

It's a scene that satisfies emotionally because the "bad guys" die. In the hands of a less-skilled writer that's all this scene would have accomplished, but Rice uses it to spur on a witness to this disaster, a former lover of Deborah's, one Petyr van Abel. A student of witchcraft, he follows Deborah's 20-year-old daughter Charlotte (*his* daughter as it happens) to Port-au-Prince, where she flees to escape a charge of witchcraft against herself.

Conveniently, Abel keeps a file on the Mayfair witches, which he sends to his comrades in the Talamasca, an order formed in the 14th Century for the study of the supernatural and whose members often possessed supernatural powers themselves—white witches, if you will.

Breaking up the time sequence of a novel always is a risky device. Using epistles to advance the story is another volatile invention, because if the reader does not like the first-person voice of the letter the thread is broken. To Rice's credit, she makes the epistolary interruption work. The fact that the letters are packed with sexual scrimmages (and incest, no less) helps. Americans can swallow anything if sex is the lure.

What we're asked to swallow is a fascinating look at our ability to change ourselves and those around us: Just how much free will do we really have? And, are there intelligent spirits who share the Earth with us?

What we can't explain, we declare irrational or evil. What we can't understand, we dismiss. What we can't control, we kill. And when we kill. we assign evil to our victims, goodness to ourselves. Our victims can be Jews, homosexuals, African-Americans; fill in the blanks. They are in some way seen as bad, as devils, as subhuman or superhuman; either extreme is frightening.

The Devil in Western thought really represents responsibility. Polarizing human behavior into a flat struggle between God and the Devil, good and evil, is an elaborate rationalization for our infantilism, for the refusal to take responsibility for our actions.

What makes Rice so fascinating is her obsession with this theme and her great good sense never to discuss it in terms of nonfiction. It's hard to imagine a Protestant writing in her ornate style. Her cherubims and seraphims of lust, her incubi of desire, seem as gilded and sensual as baroque cathedrals, buildings of exquisite sensuality dedicated to eradicating that same sensuality in the flesh.

When she brings the story to our century, she uses a frail child, Deirdre Mayfair, to confess to Father Mattingly that she sees a tall, dark, handsome man. Years later this disturbed woman gives birth to an illegitimate child who is packed away to California. This daughter, Rowan, has inherited all the unholy power of the Mayfair women, although she knows nothing of Deborah Montcleve's death in 1689, the New Orleans coven, the stories about her great-grandmother as a voodoo queen, who had a purse of gold wherein each spent coin returned to the purse by nightfall. But Rowan suffers premonitions—or are they ancestral memories? When she revives Michael and falls in love with him, she is drawn back to her ancestors, back to the sweltering secrets of the centuries, of the demon and the witches.

As the novel hurtles toward its conclusion, all of the characters from the various epochs begin to interweave. There is even a character named Rita Mae, which this reviewer found quite gratifying. Each character, sharply drawn, has a card to play, a card that must be thrown at exactly the right time for someone to hit the zygotic jackpot.

For that's what this novel is really about: putting flesh around our dreams, flesh around our fears.

As Michael Curry, the hero, sits alone re-reading *Great Expectations* or writing to make sense of his insane, or unsane, experiences with the witches, he calms the reader, a necessary medication for this most uncalming book.

He says near the end: "Life must be founded upon the infinite possibility for choice and accident. And if we cannot prove that it is, we must believe that it is. We must believe that we can change, that we can control, that we can direct our own destinies."

It is questionable whether Curry had a snowball's chance in hell of directing his own destiny, but you can. Run right out to the bookstore and buy *The Witching Hour.* Rice has written her best novel yet. But I warn you: There's the Devil to pay.

Barbara Frey Waxman (essay date Summer 1992)

SOURCE: "Postexistentialism in the Neo-Gothic Mode: Anne Rice's *Interview with the Vampire,*" in *Mosaic,* Vol. 25, No. 3, Summer, 1992, pp. 79-97.

[*In the following essay, Waxman explores the confluence of existential philosophy, postmodernism, and gothic fiction in* Interview with the Vampire *and subsequent Rice novels. According to Waxman, "Rice presents with fervor a profound exploration of freedom, moral constraints and contingency in order to prepare us for the philosophical issues that face us on the darkling plain of the twenty-first century."*]

Serious philosophical questioning, ethical inquiry, struggles of individuals to shape their identity and create a meaningful existence are not uncommon in twentieth-century American literature. Recently, however, a writer of "popular" fiction, Anne Rice, has carried these philosophical themes into a seemingly unusual genre: Gothic vampire fiction. In such novels as *Interview with the Vampire* (1976), Rice is not only chilling readers' spines but drawing their minds into the angst of twentieth-century philosophical inquiry. According to Rice—who has been an enthusiastic reader of such existentialist philosophers as Kierkegaard, Camus and Sartre since her college days—the intensely emotional moods, strange atmospheres and supernatural elements of Gothic fiction are "the most powerful means . . . for writing about real life."

In this essay, I wish to explore the "real life" issues of our postmodern world that Rice addresses in *Interview with the Vampire,* the first of her three Vampire Chronicles. Specifically, my purpose is threefold: to note the way that existentialist themes have characterized Gothic fiction from its beginnings; to demonstrate the way that Rice's "postmodernist" reinterpretation of these themes gives *Interview with the Vampire* a distinctly "neo-Gothic" character and "postexistentialist" perspective; to suggest the variety of ways in which Rice has explored these

concerns in her fiction after *Interview with the Vampire* and the reasons for these later modulations in genre and philosophy.

From its beginnings as a subgenre emerging with the development of Romanticism in the later eighteenth century, Gothic fiction has always been more than mere "thrills and chills" sensationalism and escapist entertainment. In its probing of forbidden realms and occult experiences, it has been hospitable to philosophical ideas and quests: to speculations about ontology; to analysis of the nature of reality and surrealistic states; to investigation of the constituents of moral behavior; and to determination of the meanings of human existence. As G. R. Thompson has noted, Gothic literature, which represents the darker side of the Romantic movement, expresses "an existential terror generated by a schism between a triumphantly secularized philosophy of evolving good and an abiding obsession with the Medieval conception of guilt-laden, sinridden man. . . . [It] is the drama of the mind engaged in the quest for metaphysical moral absolutes in a world that offers shadowy semblances of an occult order but withholds final revelation and illumination."

Challenged by the ambiguity of the universe and the complexity of human nature, these "dark Romantics" attempted to interpret humankind's moral capacities and to discover reasons for our existence. To Mark M. Hennelly, Jr., therefore, the existential philosophizing of Maturin's *Melmoth the Wanderer* and other Gothic novels links them to the later tradition of such novelists as Dostoevsky and Kafka (665, 669). Similarly, Robert D. Hume has described the heroes of writers like Beckford and Byron as suffering from "existential agony" because they cannot have what they long for: "solutions . . . absolutes, ontological certitude." Hume, echoing Jean-Paul Sartre, notes that these Gothic heroes suffer a pattern of "pain, No Exit, and damnation."

Maturin's Melmoth is an early example of the Gothic supernatural hero who prefigures the existential seeker. His insatiable thirst for forbidden knowledge—God's knowledge about the origins and meaning of human existence—locks him into a hellish existence that transcends time and space; he "lives" and witnesses horrible events centuries apart and flies over the earth, like Satan and vampires, acting as eternal witness "to the truth of gospel amid fires that shall burn for ever and ever." Melmoth's destiny alienates him from the human beings who must become his victims, denying him human joys and the solace of human religions, both of which he cynically interrogates. His existence becomes the fruitless search for a person who would change places with him; he continually seeks vulnerable individuals who wish to escape from a desperate situation into which their own passions and weaknesses have placed them. Seeing these flaws of human nature, Melmoth can believe in no one, even though Immalee, the child of nature who becomes his wife, begins to revive his religious faith. One of his near-victims, Moncada, sums up the frustrating nature of the quest for meaning and belief: "we ask with the desponding and rest-less scepticism of Pilate, 'What is truth?' but the oracle that was so eloquent one moment, is dumb the next, or if it answers, it is with that ambiguity that makes us dread we have to consult again—again—and for ever—in vain."

Despite Melmoth's blasting of humankind for its "malig-nity and hostility," Maturin's narrator hopes to establish a moral framework for the world: "Such, perhaps, will be the development of the moral world. We shall be told why we suffered, and for what; but a bright and blessed lustre shall follow the storm, and all shall yet be light." Although this passage sounds optimistic, light and certitude do not prevail in Maturin's novel. As Elizabeth R. Napier has observed, in works like *Melmoth the Wanderer* we experi-ence the existentialist quester's "exhaustion at being tantalized by meaning and finally being denied it."

The prefiguring of existentialism in *Melmoth* is apparent not only in the novel's quest motif, but also in its emphasis on issues of entrapment, escape and individual moral agency. Such issues, within a Christian framework, are raised in Moncada's tale of his imprisonment in the monastery and his escape with the aid of his brother and a man who had committed parricide. Moncada describes the pressure of moral responsibility and our occasional desire to relinquish it: "I was like a clock whose hands are pushed forward, and I struck the hours I was impelled to strike. When a powerful agency is thus exercised on us,—when another undertakes to think, feel, and act for us, we are delighted to transfer to him, not only our physical, but our moral responsibility. We say, with selfish cowardice, and self-flattering passiveness, 'Be it so—you have decided for me,'—without reflecting that at the bar of God there is no bail."

The will to freedom and Immalee's choice to wed Mel-moth are also analyzed existentially by the narrator of Im-malee's tale: "When a mind strong by nature, but weakened by fettering circumstances, is driven to make one strong spring to free itself, it has no leisure to calculate the weight of its hindrances, or the width of its leap,—it sits with its chains heaped about it, thinking only of the bound that is to be its liberation—." Maturin ponders the individual's capacity for moral choices while being hampered by vices that can turn her/him into Satan's agent: he concludes bleakly that we are our own worst enemies.

Victor Frankenstein, protagonist of Mary Shelley's classic Gothic novel, is another Romantic quester, the personifica-tion of the scientific researcher-hero who seeks knowledge about human existence, answers to ontological questions and understanding of our moral nature. Although he thinks that by creating human life he has found one answer, the result is that he is left with more problems, with "pain, No Exit, and damnation." Even family ties as a source of meaningful existence, the spiritual satisfactions of nature, romantic love and domestic happiness are interrogated by Shelley: none offer Victor permanent solace or refuge in his morally ambiguous, post-creature world. The frozen

wastelands of the North are a fit emblem of the existential void surrounding Victor at the end of his life.

Concern with moral choice and speculation about the nature and origins of evil are also evident in Bram Stoker's vampiric Gothic novel *Dracula*. Through the character of Professor Van Helsing, who has analyzed the facets of evil, Stoker suggests that evil is not an isolatable force, but is inextricably linked to good. The two moral absolutes, as bipolar opposites, define each other, according to Van Helsing: "For it is not the least of its terrors that this evil thing [Dracula] is rooted deep in all good; in soil barren of holy memories it cannot rest." Van Helsing postulates that evil originates in good, that it develops as a radical rebel-lion against goodness. Stoker implies that Dracula could not have seduced the virtuous Lucy were it not for the lustful impulses growing in the soil of her virtuous soul. Conversely, Dracula himself might have had some "train-ing" in good that led to his rebellious alienation or satanic leap into the realm of evil.

Dracula moves beyond Maturin's and Shelley's existential concerns by blending "modern" scientific thinking with theology in the moral project of Van Helsing. By focusing on the seductive nature of evil and the human psyche's vulnerability to it, *Dracula* offers a quasi-Freudian investigation of the way that the amoral human uncon-scious and its pleasure-seeking impulses conflict with societal taboos and moral codes. With its interweaving of good and evil, and in its illustration of the amoral nature of human sexuality in a world no longer supported by a framework of faith, Stoker's novel heralds the perspective of a twentieth-century existentialist.

Like Stoker, Shelley, Maturin and other Romantic writers, Anne Rice embraces the Gothic, and in particular the vampire, as a vehicle for philosophic speculation. While vampires have historically been considered an image "of anthropomorphized evil," Rice's vampires become what Susan Ferraro calls "loquacious philosophers who spend much of eternity debating the nature of good and evil." They are also vehicles to explore the *tabula rasa* condition of twentieth-century human existence, as well as the quest for truths, moral rules and a purposeful existence.

Interview with the Vampire is structured in four parts, beginning and ending as an interview between a young journalist and the vampire Louis, set in New Orleans in the present (1970s). In the middle sections, Louis mostly narrates his past, with questions and reactions occasionally interjected by the journalist. The interview is being recorded on a cassette player, as Louis describes how he became a vampire in 1791 at the age of 25 and how he developed relationships with other vampires, particularly Lestat, his maker, and Claudia, the child-vampire whom he and Lestat have created. The plot offers traditional Gothic love triangles and power struggles, as in Louis's alliance with Claudia to "kill" Lestat and rid themselves of his domination, and in Claudia's withdrawal from Louis to be with Madeleine, the vampire that Louis had created for her. After the "death" of Lestat, the scene shifts to Paris, home of an old "coven" of vampires, the Théâtre des Vampires.

In the Théâtre lives an ancient vampire, Armand, to whom Louis is attracted mentally and physically: as is typical of Gothic fiction, incest and homoeroticism are prominent in the book. Armand acts as his teacher, warning Louis against killing the other vampires. Despite his wisdom, Armand's world-weariness pushes Louis toward desperate action, a war with the Théâtre des Vampires in which Louis is imprisoned (the conventional entrapment imagery). He is rescued by Armand. Claudia is burnt to ashes in these wars, Louis torches the Théâtre, and Lestat returns from the "undead," seeking reunion. Finally, Louis and Armand, now outcasts from vampiric society, return to New Orleans. At the end of the novel, despite having learned of Louis's ordeals as a vampire, the young interviewer asks to be turned into a vampire and to join the search for Lestat.

In many respects *Interview*—despite or by way of its popular Gothic plot of power struggles—contains Rice's most complete existentialist and postexistentialist philosophizing. Ferraro captures its philosophical spirit when she calls it "a brooding meditation on good and evil, immortality and death." According to Ferraro, the novel's comparison of mortal death to versions of immortality implies that sometimes mortal death is preferable. This may be because of Rice's view of the prevalence of human evil in her godless world. Her paralleling of evil vampirism with immoral human behavior is suggested when one of the Parisian vampires declares that "men [are] capable of far greater evil than vampires," but that vampires "strive to rival men in kills of all kinds." In the aftermath of the Nazi Holocaust, which has greatly expanded philosophy's and literature's conceptualizing of human evil, this statement is acceptable to many thoughtful readers. With evil a given, then, Rice offers existentialist paths to meaningful action. She also posits some postexistentialist conditions and ideas about moral choice.

In his study of *Melmoth the Wanderer*, Hennelly has observed that existentialism comes in many varieties, but in all of them there is a "revolt against any authority—Church, State, Society—that places a synthetic, abstract system between the individual and real life experience." In other words, he sees the existentialist, isolated from all institutions, as confronting a universe devoid of moral absolutes, where the individual must construct his/her own system of authority. The existentialist's "ontological insecurity" is an angst about the universe's "relativism, meaninglessness, and even nihilism."

There is, however, a component of existentialism that pulls the individual back from the edge of suicidal despair: the freedom of choice and the ethic of responsibility. These empower one to choose actions, to shape a meaningful moral life, to judge oneself, and to take responsibility for the consequences of one's actions. The difference between existentialism and postexistentialism, as I use the terms, is that the postexistentialist cynically notes the relativity not only of morality, but also of freedom and choice. Postexistentialism recognizes that there are internal and external constraints on the individual's ability to build a good life. The vampire Louis is like that still-hopeful existentialist who must confront the compelling postexistentialist outlook which fears that freedom itself may be a chimera.

Rice's novel places Louis in a life which Kierkegaard would identify as pure existence. Helmut Kuhn describes this rarified existence as "that passionately intensified form of human life which makes the mind susceptible to experiencing a crisis, and through crisis, existence." Rice explores the complexities of human nature by analyzing Louis's life-crisis and by highlighting his differences from humans. As Elizabeth MacAndrew has noted, Rice's novel "uses the supernatural, as the Gothic tradition has always done, to present new views of human nature ambiguously, so we are forced to ask questions about it."

Rice's novel is unique, however, because in it the vampire's conduct is self-condemned. Even after rejecting God's law, Louis accepts responsibility for the consequences of his evil acts, including his killings. He sees his evil conduct as resembling Sartre's acts of "bad faith," behaviors whereby the existentialist "lapses" and temporarily rejects both responsibility for acts and freedom of choice. In other words, when he kills, Louis temporarily believes that his vampiric nature forces him to kill; after the kill, he struggles against any notion of having a fixed nature that dictates his conduct and thus reaffirms his moral responsibility. In addition, Louis is repelled by his objectification of each victim as Other and by his efforts to make his victims' surrender of their freedom the means by which he fulfills his own goals.

Persistent in spite of his compulsion to kill, then, is Louis's urge to embrace ethical behavior, which according to philosopher Hazel E. Barnes involves "recognition of the need to justify one's life," as well as acceptance of "responsibility for others and for one's own past and future." Louis's ethical stance provokes the derision of Lestat and Claudia, who revel in their killings. His alienation from them by these moral promptings suggests the existentialist's condition: "an isolated individual," he "is not compelled to acknowledge his involvement with others unless he cares to do so." Suffering from this loneliness, Louis parries his ethics and does seek reunion with them, despite their egocentrism and amorality.

Through Louis, Rice's novel displays a twentieth-century ethical relativism more complex than Stoker's. Presenting the vampire as a metaphor for the ambiguities of human nature and of our moral energies, Rice extends Stoker's notion that evil is rooted in good: as she presents it, evil encompasses a profound knowledge of and longing for good. *Interview* thus explores what Judith Wilt describes as the "tempting proposition that the killer obtains special knowledge and special sensitivity to life, and the vampire, whose life *is* death, has supreme comprehension and sensitivity." Rice gives this proposition an existentialist framework by positing that the morally sensitive Louis lacks supreme comprehension of the meaning of his life, even as he struggles to obtain gnosis or to create an explanation for his existence. Rice's postexistentialist addendum is to emphasize the naivete of the existentialist assumption that one can obtain supreme comprehension and shape his/her own fate.

There are three ways, in particular, that Rice encourages readers to rethink good and evil and to analyze the human condition, first as existentialists and then as postexistentialists.

The first way involves the depiction of Louis's feelings about religion and ethics. At the beginning of the novel, Louis describes his own indirect contact with religious fervor and ethical commitment through his brother Paul's visionary religion and fanatical devotion to God's work. He describes his initial tolerance of Paul's holiness, even building him an oratory for his prayers. Yet out of his own vicious egotism, "which could not accept the presence of an extraordinary human being in its midst," he disbelieves in Paul's prophetic visions. After his brother's death, Louis expresses a new awe at Paul's sanctity and appreciates the contrast between good and evil: "Evil is always possible. And goodness is eternally difficult." In retrospect, the awesome challenge of doing good impresses Louis. He finally appreciates his brother's moral fiber and commitment to God. At the same time, Louis also recognizes his own moral laziness, his shallow "lip service to God and the Virgin."

Still half-believing in Christian humility, Louis chastises his own egotism and attributes to it all his evil impulses; egotism is central to the evil characters of Lestat, Gabrielle and Armand as well. Perhaps the paradigm for vampiric egotism is Milton's Satan; he is propelled by an egotism, "Pride and worse Ambition" that makes him think he can challenge God's authority in heaven. Because of his egotism, he tumbles to hell. There he declares, "Evil be thou my Good," thus redefining through its polar opposite the evil egotism which he must endlessly feed.

Louis's egotism, however, is undermined when he meets Lestat. While traditional Christianity might applaud this change, existentialism—because it values the energetic ego—would not see it as positive. When they meet, Lestat's aura crushes Louis's ego, reduces him to nothing, so that "[he] completely forgot [himself]"; yet at the same moment he "knew totally the meaning of possibility." An existentialist would see this reaction as problematic. To the existentialist, Louis's insight into the meaning of possibility would be a cause for celebration, since the individual must choose a future from among infinite possible futures and must be able to diverge from past choices. An existentialist, however, might begin to worry about whether Louis could fulfill the rich possibilities for his future without an alert ego to make and implement decisions.

With traces of Christian belief remaining in him, then, Louis feels guilty about his egotism. In turn, as his existential outlook develops, he views with alarm Lestat's ego-crushing impact on him, the existentialist equivalent of a cardinal sin: Lestat objectifies Louis (the Other) and makes of Louis's freedom "the instrument of [his] own project." Lestat's egocentric project is to turn Louis into a vampire, even if he does not freely choose to become one, in order to secure Louis's plantation for his ailing father.

Looking back on his transformation from man into vampire, Louis cannot say how or whether he decided on this fateful step in his life. The ambiguity of his language reflects his crushed ego, his repressed self-consciousness, his confusion about the determining factors behind this choice, all of which traits are uncharacteristic of the existentialist:

> "And so you decided to become a vampire?" [the interviewer] asked. . . .
>
> "Decided. It doesn't seem the right word. Yet I cannot say it was inevitable from the moment that the [Lestat] entered the room. . . . Let me say that when he'd finished speaking, no other decision was possible for me."

Katherine Ramsland points out that these themes of "choice and limitation" pursued by Sartre and Camus had always fascinated Rice, even if she did not consciously intend to set forth an existential outlook in *Interview*. Thus, while Lestat's charismatic presence offers Louis liberating possibilities for existential action, his presence simultaneously becomes the mechanism for a postexistential, "sinful" diminishment of his consciousness and freedom.

Through Lestat's influence, Louis finds it increasingly difficult to distinguish between good and evil. Perhaps this conflation of good and evil makes it easier for Louis to slip into the role of the vampire, to see good in its evil. In persuading Louis to become a vampire, Lestat consciously chooses language that blurs Judeo-Christian distinctions between good and evil and thus moves the disoriented Louis closer to existentialism's relativism. Lestat's pseudo-religious linguistic games are evident in his claim that vampires' acts of killing enable them to "see a human life in its entirety" and to have "a hand in the divine plan." Sounding like a parody of Van Helsing, Lestat equates the Master with the anti-Master, sophistically positing resemblances between vampires and God: "Evil is a point of view . . . God kills, and so shall we; indiscriminately He takes the richest and poorest, and so shall we; for no creatures under God are as we are, none so like him as ourselves. . . ."

By seeing evil as a concept defined according to one's perspective, by implicitly criticizing God's decision-making as random and indiscriminate, and hence by subverting the concept of a God who sanctions moral beliefs and conduct, Lestat is articulating existentialism's central tenet, as philosopher Robert G. Olson puts it: "each man will tend to become a law unto himself [and] . . . choose for himself" (515). Louis gradually moves toward creation of his own moral laws. Yet by weakening Louis's ability to choose, Lestat also makes him question human responsibility for ethical behavior, without which the universe is empty and chaotic. Caught between existentialist and postexistentialist views of life, Louis suffers moral paralysis.

Ironically, the very fact of his philosophical quest places Louis among the morally and spiritually earnest citizens of our century. Unlike the anti-religious Undead in *Dracula,* Louis does not shrink from the crucifix after he becomes a vampire and in fact "rather likes looking on crucifixes." Early in his vampiric life, he even visits a church, wistfully seeking a priest for confession. He also seeks some theological answers to his questions about God's mercy toward killers and His reason for the sacrilege of allowing Louis to exist. That he winds up at the end of this scene killing the priest in frustration and rage—a Nietzschean act confirming that God is dead—does not lessen the intensity of his quest for a meaningful life and for confirmation of the presence of good and evil principles in the universe. By killing the priest, however, Louis relinquishes the Victorian vestiges of his belief in a God and embraces the modern existential tenet of individual moral responsibility. Like Nietzsche, Louis "thinks a human life triumphant just insofar as it escapes from inherited descriptions of the contingencies of its existence and finds new descriptions"; until the end of the novel, Louis believes he can "create himself" and make his life meaningful despite the constraints of his circumstances.

Louis's spiritual impulses are in contrast to those of Armand. Armand denies the existence of gods and devils, calling Satan and God "these old fantastical lies, these myths, these emblems of the supernatural." Like existentialist philosophers, Armand cites the self as the true repository of authority: "the only power that exists is inside ourselves." This power includes the freedom to do good and evil and the responsibility to distinguish one from the other. Knowing of this condition, Armand is able to offer Louis no incentive for ethical conduct, only cynicism. Armand's deepening cynicism is what assures his survival and makes him the world's oldest vampire; Hennelly has suggested the same reason for Melmoth's survival: "In the topsy-turvy world of existentialism . . . it is not the discoverers of some good in the universe who survive, as much as it is the guardians against such self-restricting delusion who fully choose not to be blinded by the mere appearance of cosmic benevolence or divine providence."

At first Louis denies this "loss of absolutes," which according to Ramsland had been a painful loss for Rice herself. When the ethical optimism of Louis fades after Armand's lesson, however, readers expect that his quest for meaning and hope of good will end and that he will completely abandon himself to evil. Yet he has enough moral scruples and moral urgency left to hesitate to fulfill Claudia's request that he turn her friend Madeleine into a

vampire. He resists performing this act of Sartreian "bad faith," that of reifying Madeleine by trapping her in the vampiric role, which abolishes her freedom. Claudia's angry response to Louis's refusal is also that of an existentialist, as she points out that Louis is attempting to curb their right to choose another path: "How dare you make this decision for both of us!" Her anger also prompts her to malign Louis's vampiric "virility" and his claim to freedom: "Your evil is that you cannot be evil." Her allusion here is to Louis's conflicting existences in the human and vampiric worlds, to his persistent yearning for good, and to the impairment of his freedom: his postexistentialist condition.

Although Louis is beginning to recognize that this conflicted condition will doom him, even when he ultimately transforms Madeleine and gives up the last traces of his humanness, he is still yearning to justify his existence; he is still clinging tenuously to the notion that he has the freedom to do so, and still actively probing into the heart of evil through Armand. He sees in Armand "the only promise of good in evil of which I could conceive" even though Armand has taught him all the subtle gradations of evil and the phenomenon of evil without guilt. Almost to the end, when his life has virtually been destroyed, Louis resists with rueful self-derision Armand's lesson on the absence of goodness, calling his resistance "that refusal to compromise a fractured and stupid morality." Eventually, however, even a vampire becomes exhausted by the futility of the struggle and must acknowledge irreducible restrictions on his freedom. With that acknowledgment, Louis becomes a postexistentialist.

Louis achieves the detached wisdom and moral indifference of the pure vampire when he ends the quest and separates himself from those he has cared for: Claudia (who has died) and Armand (who is dying). This is his parting message to Armand: "I wanted love and goodness in this which is living death. . . . It was impossible from the beginning, because you cannot have love and goodness when you do what you know to be evil. . . . You can only have the desperate confusion and longing and the chasing of phantom goodness in its human form." He had created a moral code in his life, but attempts to follow it were futile; he cannot justify his life, as Barnes would observe, because he cannot say that "he has freely chosen the values by which he has guided and judged his life." Surrendering moral responsibility for his actions, this erstwhile existentialist accepts the constraints of his nature.

Because he knows that he is constrained by his compulsion to kill, Louis is now closer to postexistentialist Maurice Merleau-Ponty's ethic of contingency, which acknowledges that one's ethics are related to the given of one's situation. In contrast to some earlier existentialists, Merleau-Ponty says that "no one by himself is subject nor is he free, that freedoms interfere with and require one another, that history is the history of their dispute, which is inscribed and visible in institutions, in civilizations, and in the wake of important historical actions." While Sartre claims that only *men* and *things* exist, Merleau-Ponty suggests that there is also "the interworld, which we call history, symbolism, truth-to-be-made"; all actions in this interworld are symbolic and are constrained by other actions. American philosopher Richard Rorty also recognizes the constraints of one's historical situation, sees freedom "as the recognition of contingency [and] . . . insist[s] on the sheer contingency of individual existence." Louis finally sees the operation of contingency on his life, realizes that he is being acted upon by a world that condemns killing and by his internal world of vampiric cravings, while at the same time he acts upon the world both to satisfy these cravings and to perform ethical deeds. With these conflicts hampering his freedom, he is more likely to act unethically, to fail as an existentialist. Louis finally understands the problematic nature of freedom and thereby names his postexistential condition.

Readers who interpret philosophically and metaphorically Louis's final statement about love, goodness and vampirism are left with nagging questions about the statement's applications to the human condition. Is human morality stupid, or a mere phantom? Can we define good or evil? Is our striving for morality as outmoded for us in our postexistential condition as it is for Louis, since we may, like him, be circumscribed by our natures? Louis's quest may not provide unequivocal answers to important metaphysical questions, but Rice does show readers how simplistic are their usual conceptions of human nature and good and evil. She also demonstrates a postmodern mode of thinking by addressing questions about ethical conduct in a more fluid and situational manner.

The second aspect of *Interview with the Vampire* that encourages an existential interpretation of Louis's strivings and a postexistential perspective on the human condition involves Rice's blurring of the distinctive character traits of the human and the vampire in Louis, so that he experiences guilt about killing, divided allegiances, and alienation from both humans and vampires. Unlike Stoker's vampires, who can move down the Great Chain of Being, turning into wolf, bat or elemental dust, Louis remains a vampire tied to humans and nostalgic about sunrises. He burns "with the questions of [his] divided nature," like so many conflicted human beings; as Ferraro puts it, he is "full of self-loathing and doubt . . . in short [he is] Everyman Eternal." Louis retains a human aversion to killing and asserts his freedom to make an esthetic and moral decision when he determines to satisfy his cravings by killing only animals. In such decision-making, Louis enacts the human being who strives to repress his baser impulses in order to perform higher intellectual and ethical tasks. He behaves in accordance with the existential belief articulated by Alasdair MacIntyre that peoples' freely made choices "bring whatever nature they have into being." Louis believes that he *can* determine the kind of vampire he will become. We see him struggle to avoid the basic impulses of vampiric nature, the characteristic detachment and the parasitical killing instinct, in order to live a more human life.

Yet Louis's conception of humanity may be naive; postmodern philosophers like Rorty point out the parasitical nature of human life and its incapacity to be independently willed: "one may say that there can be no fully Nietzschean lives, lives which are pure action rather than reaction, no lives which are not largely parasitical on an un-redescribed past and dependent on the charity of unborn generations." Confused in his definition of human nature, yet yearning to be human, Louis experiences an identity crisis which puts him in what Karl Jaspers calls a "boundary situation," an intense, unchangeable situation—such as endurance of suffering or guilt—that we "cannot see through as a whole" and that we can avoid "only by closing our eyes to [it]"; boundary situations are "like a wall we run into, a wall on which we founder. We cannot modify them; all that we can do is to make them lucid." In his boundary situation, Louis accepts responsibility for being a flawed vampire because he thinks and feels too much: he is too human.

His human longings draw Louis to human culture and specifically to the arts because they promise him "a deeper understanding of the human heart." Like Sartre, who in his earlier years was drawn to a literature yoked to ethics, Louis turns to the young journalist to help him shape his life's story and extrapolate its moral significance. According to Paul Jude Beauvais, Sartre sees the writer as "a unique volitional agent" who dwells in a particular historical context and who desires to observe and record his or her life and times; Sartre's writer is also shaped by membership in a social class. Thus the writer embodies both existential possibility and the prison of circumstances, a combination that reflects Louis's existential/postexistential conflict and explains his attraction to the journalist. As he speaks to the young writer, the otherness of Louis is dispelled. MacAndrew has observed that this narrative arrangement encourages readers to give "imaginative assent" to the vampire's tale "of passions that we can recognize," to identify with Louis as if he were a human being.

Louis also turns to other human arts, especially drama, when he visits the Théâtre des Vampires in Paris. It is fitting that Rice brings Louis on a pilgrimage to Paris, a major center both of art and of existentialist thought, to seek justification of his existence. Although Louis kills, one of the few acts that even Sartre would see as irredeemably evil, he still maintains this human cultural framework, which encourages him to hope in his future goodness. Surely goodness can grow in this rich soil, even though it has been sown with the vampire's evil. Rice, until near the end of the novel, leads readers to believe, with Louis, in such a possibility.

This possibility seems especially viable when readers consider the third aspect of Rice's novel: the concepts of community and love, vampiric and human, that Louis affirms and seeks. As MacAndrew points out, Rice "explores the forms of human love and the nature of its relationships" through Louis and the others. Ramsland also notes that through Louis she depicts "the impetus in the human heart to seek others." In contrast to Stoker's Dracula, whom Wilt calls an *isolato,* Louis actively seeks to end his painful isolation, the given condition of the existentialist. He forges relationships, although ultimately unsatisfactory ones, first with the woman Babette, then with Claudia, and finally with Armand. He also experiences community both when he and Lestat live with Claudia, a curiously incestuous triangle, and when Madeleine forms a new triangle with Claudia and Louis. Finally, he visits the vampire "commune" in Paris, which enacts the negative traits of the extended nuclear family: unified by kinship and conformity, it is also ravaged by jealousy, mistrust and power struggles.

As Hennelly notes in his study of Melmoth, alienation and the failure of love are common existential themes in Gothic literature: "Love does not usually provide the needed release from the universal *Angst;* rather it frustratingly highlights the failure of real communication." His words would also apply to the love life of Louis, on which he had hoped to build a life of goodness. The frustration and disillusionment about love which Hennelly describes become Louis's postexistential condition.

Louis's loneliness is most alleviated by Armand, for whom he feels a deepening love: "it was as if the great feminine longing of my mind were being awakened again to be satisfied." Later he says, "I felt a longing for him so strong that it took all my strength to contain it." While Rice uses sexual language to describe this love, sexual passion may also be a metaphor for Louis's impassioned philosophical and intellectual searching: he feels the deep love and admiration of an apprentice-philosopher for a wise master and his stores of knowledge. For this love, however, Claudia and Madeleine must eventually be sacrificed. This love between vampires—a reflection of love between human beings—can destroy those who experience it. So-called humanizing love becomes the impetus for inhumanity, for acts of existential bad faith, for murder. All that the wise Armand can, ultimately, teach Louis is the complexity of evil, just as Rice leads us to realize that no good can emerge from the vampire.

Despite his initial hopes and longings, then, Louis finally confronts the nothingness of the universe. When his relationship with Armand fails, Louis understands that he is alone. His intention of creating a valuable pattern for his life, which had included loving relationships, has not been fulfilled; so, as Barnes would conclude, his existence has not been "worthwhile." He recognizes that he will never "grow warm again and filled with love." There comes a Kierkegaardian moment of "generalized dread . . . of nothing in particular . . . [of] this nothing, this void we confront." Then he takes up the vampire's stoic detachment, rejecting the option of reaching out to others in love. He acknowledges his postexistential condition, letting his vampirism now dictate his actions.

Louis's last hope is in reaching out, not in love but in despair, to the journalist who might be able to make mean-ing out of his life's story for other human beings. By speaking to the journalist, Louis hopes to warn humans not to seek the eternal life of the vampire and to dispel the illusion that they are free to shape their own destinies and to eschew evil. This reaching out to the young writer also fails, it may be argued, since the journalist's response to the story is to ask to be turned into a vampire too. He would not have made this request if he had really understood Louis's portrayal of the vampire's enslavement to his own nature.

Love and community have actually been Louis's downfall, not his salvation. Formerly Louis had mirrored the Victorian age in which he was born, an age, Walter Houghton has observed, that replaced God with love as the source of salvation. Louis had looked to love with great hope. Now, however, having seen into the essence of love, he experiences a crushing fall from "grace and faith [that] is the fall of a century." This fall propels him, philosophically speaking, into the postmodern world, where Rice destabilizes Louis's and readers' usual categories of good and evil by aligning love with eternal damnation.

Just before her death, Claudia is clear-eyed about the love between vampires—love among the ruins of a moral structure. She teaches Louis about vampiric love's quintessential evil, and he gives it a philosophical dimension: "that is the crowning evil, that we can even go so far as to love each other . . . and who else would show us a particle of love, a particle of compassion or mercy? Who else, knowing us as we know each other, could do anything but destroy us?" As one vampire peers into the soul of another, he sees absolute evil and, if ethically motivated like Louis, he must judge that soul as harshly as he judges himself. Barnes says of the existentialist's vision, "my own judgments cannot move outward without an accompanying inward movement. Consequently, I am always before the Bench. The eye of Judgment is ever there." Louis has, nevertheless, loved two vampires, thereby denying his ability to judge himself or others and surrendering his power to choose what is good over what is evil. Such postexistentialist moral tolerance, needed for vampires' love, is defined by Claudia and Louis as the vampires' permanently damning evil: it seems inhuman, a tolerance of which humans would be incapable.

Or would they? Readers of Rice's novel have been drawn into this postmodern world of the vampire so powerfully and have had their simplistic moral sensibilities so thoroughly "drained" that in their disorientation they might be receptive to new objects of love and compassion, open to more complex categorizings of good and evil and to new ways of explaining the universe. Through the interview format, Rice has swayed us to suspend our aversion toward the vampire, and in so doing leads us to question assumptions about human nature and to re-envision the repositories of good and evil in the world. Moreover, because Rice morally energizes the vampire Louis, we are inclined to reject the traditional compartmentalizing of good and evil. Louis emerges as an appealing, remorseful, though obsessive, killer: his obsessive need to kill makes him a victim of his nature, but he struggles against this restriction of his freedom.

Under Rice's tutelage, therefore, persuaded by Louis's eloquence and the poignancy of his struggle, we begin to recognize the legitimacy of the vampire's quest for good in evil in good. Yet by witnessing the futility of Louis's struggle, we are also forced to surrender our naivete about individual freedom. Ultimately we come to tolerate a postexistentialist world view that emphasizes the relativity of morality, freedom and choice in a universe wherein the only meaning is that which we ourselves must construct, but which also vitiates our power to do so.

Rice's later vampiric fiction reveals the consistency of her interest in the major philosophical questions of modern and postmodern times. In *The Vampire Lestat,* especially, the protagonist from the beginning is a vampire with a conscience, repelled by "the stories of the ugly nihilistic men of the twentieth-century" and seeking guidelines for moral choices, even in selecting for his kills only remorseless evildoers. As Lestat's mentor the ancient vampire Marius says, even seventeen-hundred years ago vampires were "questing . . . rejecting the answers given us"; but Lestat is unique among mortals and immortals in his commitment to the quest for knowledge: "To really ask is to open the door to the whirlwind. . . . But you have been truly asking." Lestat, decrying the placelessness of the vampire's evil nature and actions in the world, moves beyond the despairing conclusion of Rice's earlier novel. He finds a function for his evil condition, which is to create "the art that repudiates evil," the music of rock stars that "dramatize[s] the battles against evil that each mortal fights within himself." Louis had had hopes for the efficacy of art, but his hopes had been dashed by the failure of his relationship with Armand.

Through art and beauty Lestat in Rice's second novel takes up where Louis leaves off. The work begins with his despairing observation that on their deathbed people "probably don't find out the answer as to why [they] were ever alive. . . . We pass into nonexistence without ever knowing a thing." Then, however, he turns to the beauty that humankind creates, cultivating an amoral wilderness that he calls the Savage Garden, "an uncharted land where one could make a thousand fatal errors, a wild and indifferent paradise without signposts of evil or good." He suggests that meanings and guiding laws, derived from the esthetic, do exist. The Master painter-vampire Marius becomes his role model, because Marius "found a way to imitate mortal life.. . . He created good things . . . he believed more in the vistas of heaven that he painted than in himself." Both Lestat and Marius believe in the beauty and goodness of the world, and Lestat admires Marius's efforts to stem the chaos that threatens to destroy the world: as he sees it, this is a way for a vampire to achieve some good—to become a little more lovable.

Lestat's amoral esthetic framework has a drawback, however: it encourages the Théâtre of the Vampires in Paris to "make a mockery of all things sacred" and it sanctions Lestat's plans to wage war against mortals as the novel ends. Lestat uses his "Satanic powers to simulate the actions of a good man!" In other words, Lestat has the moral conscience of an existentialist, but he redefines the conscience as something that prompts the individual to do whatever he or she wants. Since art has limited redemptive force, Lestat also considers the salvational powers of love. Like some of Rice's other vampires, he believes in and longs for love, even while declaring that "it's a concept born out of moral idiocy, this idea of love!" A vampire seeks companionship and love because he cannot stand being alone as a killer, because he cannot accommodate death easily or name a place for evil in the world. Yet even with his impulse for love and goodness fighting his evil instincts, he emerges at the end of the novel without a system of ethics and, like Louis, with a postexistentialist sense that his freedom to choose is circumscribed by his thirst for blood and the vagaries of history. In her second novel Rice is more optimistic about the value of art and love than in the first novel, but she still does not fully trust that they will offer a meaningful life.

Lestat, nevertheless, continues his existential quest and asserts his freedom to break the rules of vampires; as Ferraro has observed, "in Lestat's search for the meaning of existence, he gleefully breaks them all." There is a comedic quality to his outlook that is missing from Louis's view. Even though Lestat knows that vampires, like mortals, are "prisoners of circumstance," he is not as burdened by such knowledge as Louis had been. With a satirist's humor, he describes his mission to create new evil in rock music, with its "images of evil, not evil . . . [its] image of death, not death": "So let us take on a new meaning . . . I crave the divine visibility. I crave war [with mortals] . . . the new evil . . . the twentieth-century evil." In seeing evil as shaped by the historical moment that makes rock music its fit vehicle, Lestat mirrors Sartre's post-World War II blend of Marxism and existentialism which, as Beauvais has observed, leaves "a margin of freedom . . . for individuals to act in ways that contradict their social conditioning"; Beauvais suggests that for Sartre, "self and society are mutually determining: history makes man, but man makes history." More than Louis, Lestat in Rice's second novel persists in his existentialist quest, despite his postexistentialist recognition of constraints.

Whatever tentative conclusions Lestat reaches at the end of his tale about the conditions of individual freedom, purposes of evil, and influences of history on existence, the vampiric quest for meaning and philosophical questioning continues in the ensuing Vampire Chronicles. In Rice's 1988 novel, *The Queen of the Damned,* which revisits the power struggles of the vampires and depicts Queen Akasha's efforts to defeat Lestat, Ramsland observes the existentialist concern with "paradox, free will, personal choice." Moreover, Rice's metaphysical speculations are even present in her nonvampiric erotic novels, such as *Exit to Eden* (1985) and *Belinda* (1986), written under the pen name of Anne Rampling, and *The Claiming of Sleep-*

ing Beauty (1983), written under the name A. N. Roquelaure. In these works Rice uses a less supernatural but still fantastical medium and continues to explore issues of freedom and moral choice. Indeed, in these works, she suggests that intimate sexual relations and vampirism have many things in common.

In *Exit to Eden,* for example, instead of describing vampires who create and possess mortals through the Dark Trick, Rice depicts mortals who possess one another by fuelling sexual fantasies and desires and who obtain sexual fulfillment through pain and pleasure. A sadomasochistic fantasy island of the Club-Med variety is the site of the elaborate slave/master sex games that transform patrons and employees of the Club into uncivilized, almost supernatural, creatures. Like the vampires who feel their victims' hearts beating as they suck their blood, the participants in the Club's sadomasochistic rituals experience an intimacy in which "you reached out and touched the beating heart of the person."

This context prompts the "head sex-manager" Lisa to question her own morality and the objectives of the other island "Professionals," as well as to explore philosophical alienation and the degree of freedom available to the individual. Lisa confesses to having felt like a freak, a sexual outlaw, as a younger woman because of her sexual feelings and fantasies. Every bit as lost and marginalized as Rice's vampires, Lisa suggests that perhaps "we are all outsiders, we are all making our own unusual way through a wilderness of normality that is just a myth." Questioning her mentor Martin about her creation of an "Outsider Heaven" on the island, she echoes the questions about identity and earthly purpose raised by vampires and existentialists: "Is what we do right, Martin? Or is it evil? Are we the good thing that we tell ourselves we are, are we the healthy thing we say we are to others? Or are we some evil, twisted thing that never should come to be?" The tentative conclusion she reaches before the book's romantic, love-affirming ending is that by channeling aggressive, violent feelings into harmless sexual fantasizing and game-playing, the Club people may save the world from war.

Lisa's quest leading to this conclusion begins with an episode that suggests the existentialist's sensation of exile, fear of the borders of freedom, and interrogation of the meaning of work and life. Returning from a vacation, Lisa's plane has to circle for a long time before landing; that is, she has psychic and literal difficulty re-entering the island—"no entry" instead of "no exit"—and feels as if as she is experiencing "an existentialist play. There is my world down there but I cannot get into it. Maybe it is all something I've imagined." As the narrative progresses, however, the nightmare recedes. The search for love by Lisa and her lover Elliott recalls the yearning for companionship of Louis, Lestat and Armand; their exploration of freedom is similar to the rebellious paths that were taken by Louis (as autobiographer) and Lestat (as rock star). Whereas the vampires failed in their quest, however, Lisa and Elliott ultimately succeed.

The clue to their success is suggested by Martin, who encourages Lisa to claim both freedom AND love: "very few of us anymore get through life without a dramatic bid for freedom. . . . But most of us never really reach our goal. We get stuck halfway between the morass of myth and morality we left behind and the utopia on which we've set our sights. . . . You've scored your victories [freedom in sexual behavior without beings denounced for sinfulness] . . . but if you think you cannot love Elliott, you've paid an awfully high price at the same time." This couple eventually enjoy their freedom together, in contrast to the vampires, who make the victim/lover's surrender of freedom the necessary condition for fulfilling their own goals. Lisa and Elliott carve out a utopian world of love for themselves under their own rules of moral behavior.

In certain ways, therefore, *Exit to Eden* is a philosophically naive throwback to pre-nihilist impulses of the earlier nineteenth century, whereas Rice's vampiric fiction is a provocative harbinger of more complex postmodern philosophizing. Although Rice may have tried to write a conceptually sophisticated novel in *Exit to Eden* and failed, it is likely, instead, that she has simply taken a brief respite from her bleak vision of our condition on this planet. Her overall artistic mission and greatest intellectual energies seem directed toward the metaphysical questions and grim answers of her Vampire Chronicles. In *Interview with the Vampire,* especially, Rice presents with fervor a profound exploration of freedom, moral constraints and contingency in order to prepare us for the philosophical issues that face us on the darkling plain of the twenty-first century.

Carolyn See (review date 25 October 1992)

SOURCE: "Vampire Tans! News at 11," in *Los Angeles Times Book Review,* October 25, 1992, pp. 1, 9.

[*In the following review, See offers praise for* The Tale of the Body Thief.]

Anne Rice's elegant smoothie, the Vampire Lestat, is back, and up to all his old immortal tricks [in *The Tale of the Body*]. He's the same charmer, dressing in black velvet, meandering through museums to admire the Rembrandts, restoring a lovely crumbling mansion in New Orleans (that he himself lived in 100 years before). He's the same inveterate, starry-eyed tourist, zooming from London to Paris to Miami to New Orleans to South American jungles to Caribbean resorts, still absolutely gaga over each and every new excursion.

What a *refined* vampire! How given to nostalgia; his memories of the filthy 18th-Century French castle he grew up in, his recurring visions of little Claudia, the orphan he rescued from a plague-infested novel and played the "Dark Trick" on, turning her into an immortal, quintessential, ungrateful child, trying, as she did, to do away with him, but failing—of course. It's possible, in theory, to kill a vampire, but the vampire *Lestat*? Get serious.

For as Lestat himself announces, "No one out-shines this figure you see before you—no one! . . . I am not time's fool, nor a god hardened by the millennia; I am not the trickster in the black cape, nor the sorrowful wanderer. I have a conscience. I know right from wrong. I know what I do, and yes, I do it. I am the Vampire Lestat. That's your answer. Do with it what you will."

Lestat, this vampire of fine feeling, occupies himself at the novel's opening as a kind of transfusion social worker: He scours city streets for serial killers and destroys them by charitably draining them of their blood. (Every once in a while he gets carried away and kills their intended victims too.) But Lestat is lonely and bored, distressed, sick of his vampiric life. He decides to do away with himself and flies as high as he can above the Gobi Desert, waiting at the edge of the Earth's atmosphere for the blinding, destructive sun to come up.

This should kill him, but it doesn't. A couple of days of this strenuous and painful suicide attempt leaves him with nothing more than a very bad sunburn that mellows to a becoming tan.

The trouble is, what's the point of living—as a human or a vampire—if there's no meaning to existence? As Lestat insists repeatedly, he's "the miracle" without "the revelation." He knows there are spirits aplenty shuffling and bumping along through the air, but he can't get at the stuff behind it. He can't make himself believe in God; he certainly can't believe in the Devil.

But during these past years Lestat has made friends with an erudite and compassionate mortal, David Talbot, the head of a secret metaphysical society that keeps track of spirits, vampires and all manner of occult lore. David is getting just a little bit old—he's 74 now, and every time Lestat sees his friend, he can't help but get anxious about him. With preternatural hearing, Lestat can hear David's heart speeding up and getting weaker. Repeatedly, Lestat asks David to come on over! Take a ticket for the Dark Trick, get a vampire transfusion, and live on the Dark Side, forever. David, facing human death, steadfastly refuses.

David, unlike his immortal friend, believes in God *and* in the Devil, because he heard them chatting once in a Paris cafe. From these overheard fragments (spoken in an unknown but understandable language), David was able to intuit that God is far from perfect and still in the process of exploration (how like Gregg Easterbrook's hypothesis in his novel *This Magic Moment*), and that the Devil is smart enough by now to be fed up with his own thankless job.

Why David didn't stroll over to the table right then and ask those Big Guys what they were up to is not adequately explained here, but it remains a beguiling subtext for the "real" plot of this book, which is this: Lestat is tempted by a low-life "body thief" who offers him the chance to switch bodies for a couple of days—so that Lestat will have the chance of being human again for at least a while. Lestat takes this scoundrel up on his offer. The scoundrel promptly disappears, leaving Lestat with a body—bad cold and all—and "the abysmal struggle and trivia and fear" of being human.

There's a lot of fun to all this: good sex, great food, sunshine seen a hundred ways, and even a cruise on the QEII—a perfect place for a vampire, incidentally, since all the elderly passengers are one step away from death anyway and serve as perfect snack food for ravenous blood drinkers.

No one seems to have as much fun as Anne Rice as she takes us through these crazy fictional settings. She notices everything—the heavy silver coffee pots you find in first-class hotels, the buttery grits from fine Southern restaurants, exotic plants in unexplored jungles, and of course, blood, described in 132 possible ways. People love these books, and not, I think, for only this delicious sensuality. Reading Anne Rice is like sneaking by the back door into God's mansion. There He is, chatting with the Devil. Is that how It works, then? For many people of education, "God," "Religion," "good-and-evil" are subjects far more forbidden and iffy than sex. You can't talk about these things! Anne Rice opens the door to all that, suavely and charmingly. Beyond the blood, the food, the sex, and *beignets,* you can glimpse the Divine.

Elizabeth Hand (review date 10 October 1993)

SOURCE: "The Demon Seed," in *Washington Post Book World,* October 10, 1993, pp. 4-5.

[*In the following review, Hand offers praise for* Lasher.]

Is there a madder, badder, braver bestselling writer than Anne Rice? Maybe so—but it's hard to imagine anyone else being able to pull off the literary legerdemain that Rice manages in her new novel. With *Lasher* she concocts heady and potent salmagundi of contemporary witchcraft, Caribbean voodoo, aristocratic decadence and good old-fashioned Celtic paganism, and makes what should be an unpalatable mess as wickedly irresistible as a Halloween stash of Baby Ruths.

At the heart of all this is the Mayfair clan, the impossibly wealthy New Orleans dynasty of witches first encountered in her 1990 *The Witching Hour.* For centuries the fate of the Mayfairs has been entwined with that of *Lasher's* eponymous anti-hero, an androgynous being of dubious spiritual provenance who has been haunting family members since way back when they were getting burned at the stake. Now Lasher has been given corporeal being through the unwitting agency of Rowan Mayfair and her husband, Michael Curry. Rowan, a brilliant neurosurgeon who by virtue of her psychic abilities has been named chief witch of the Mayfair clan, is kidnapped and brutalized by Lasher. He seeks to impregnate her and so ensure the propagation of his kind—whatever his kind may be. His efforts leave Rowan in a coma and Lasher himself at large in New Orleans and beyond, preying on the Mayfair women in a desperate attempt to find the one who will give birth to his children. Lest serious readers find this all veering too much down the shadowy side of the street, it should be pointed out that **Lasher** also contains several heads in jars, a skeleton wrapped in a rug, numerous apparitions, cross-dressers and psychic investigators, as well as ancient stone circles, arcane Catholic rites, incestuous pairings, clairvoyant children, gray-suited attorneys, The Little People and Anne Boleyn.

What all of the above have in common is, of course, the beautiful and innocently corrupt Lasher. Much of this book involves speculation by various characters as to his true nature. Is he a ghost? A demon? A saint? The late-20th century incarnation of that ancient pagan harvest deity popularized in *The Golden Bough* and certain enduring Western religions? Malevolent and childlike by turns, Lasher acts the seductive incubus and brutal rapist with equal facility. Over the centuries, he has harmed as many people as he's charmed, although he remains enduringly faithful to one thing: the Mayfair clan itself, which through Lasher's agency has become expansive and successful and glamorously wealthy—a sort of Kennedy dynasty filtered through "Dark Shadows." But now that Lasher's sexual depredations are laying waste the Mayfair women, the future of the family itself is at stake. Not only that, but one of Lasher's precocious spawn manages to get herself born. She starts walking towards New Orleans, just as her demonic *pere* is making his own way back to the Mayfair family homestead, where the entire clan has gathered to mourn their murdered women. Can anyone, or anything, stop Lasher and his daughter?

Anne Rice, nee O'Brien, has a Celtic flair for ritual and melancholy and dark beauty, be it the way the sun strikes a Scottish ruin or the elegantly twisted erotic pairings of her characters. The novel gets off to a slow and somewhat confusing start, and the author strikes a few jangling notes: a silly 13-year-old nymphet-witch-cum-computer-whiz; some anachronistic musings by a Civil War era ghost; several unnecessary efforts to shore up a ghost story with scientific folderol. And the breathtakingly bizarre turnings of her plot defy close scrutiny.

But who cares? As Oscar Wilde (another moody Gael) remarked, "To have a style so gorgeous that it conceals the subject is one of the highest achievements." Rice's descriptive writing is so opulent it almost begs to be read in a seraglio by candlelight—though the morning Metro from East Falls Church will do.

Ultimately, though, what makes **Lasher** so compelling is its refreshingly traditional stance. Behind all the velvet drapes and gossamer winding sheets, this is an old-fashioned family saga. Rice's Mayfairs are as gorgeous and doomed and steeped in the South as Scarlett O'Hara, and bound by the same things—"Our world is about to perish . . . we are a small valley, a small glen, only one tiny part of the north country. But we have endured and we would live on. And that is all the world is, finally, small valleys, groups of people who pray and work and love together as we do. . . . And what you were—and what your mother and father did—these things do not matter one whit."

It's comforting to know that even in the most ancient covens, family values still have a place.

Paul West (review date 24 October 1993)

SOURCE: "Witchcraft Is Their Science," in *New York Times Book Review,* October 24, 1993, p. 38.

[*In the following review, West offers tempered evaluation of* Lasher.]

If you have read **The Witching Hour,** you will understand who's who among the horde of names unleashed in Anne Rice's new novel; *Lasher.* Reading the novel is often like hearing someone mumble on in a monotone about famous cricketers of the 19th-century when you, the reader, are a baseball fan or a fan of nothing at all.

Lasher, about the branches and generations of a witch matriarchy called Mayfair, evokes part of London once given over to a hospital for leprous women. In their complex comings and goings, the Mayfair witches wangle themselves into the fabric of New Orleans society with experienced ease; they are a subversive class that has risen and prospered over the centuries without always doing what they were best at: sorcery with malign intent, traffic with the Devil and the exercise of supernatural powers. Ms. Rice's witches are not broomstick riders, as in the old days, but Mafia wives encased in brainwashed daintiness. Witchcraft is the savviest science at least for them, and irresistible power is the book's focus: power passed on and made new, power grafted from nature and upturned against it. A strong theme, to be sure, but here tacked onto a silly vehicle.

Ms. Rice evokes a type of person we have all met: the ectoplasmic orator who says aloud everything he or she thinks—in this case, writes it down. I could take all the monofilamentous, monotone rambling about this or that branch of the Mayfair family tree, and every witch bird roosted in it, if we were getting Jamesian amplification or (as in the novels of C. P. Snow, even) new doors opening on familiar personages. But Ms. Rice repeats herself, never for stylistic felicity, only to confirm some kind of ritual, to tell readers they have been here before.

As it is, most well-educated readers will not get beyond the first chapter, done with a faux-naif folklorish touch:

"Father was waiting for her. She had to grow fast and grow strong for Father. When the time came, Mother had to help her. She had to drink Mother's milk." It goes on: "Mother slept. Mother cried. Mother dreamed. Mother was sick. And when Father and Mother quarreled, the world trembled. Emaleth knew dread." The prose picks up and does a better job of recording the detail of phenomena, though there are no sentences so beautiful they dare you to go past them without savoring them several times.

The novel has several aspects, the most powerful and arresting of which is the character of the brilliant neurosurgeon witch-mother, who gives birth to an extraordinary not-quite-human being who comes out of the womb and rapes her on the spot—more or less. He impregnates her with a being similar to himself. Potentially this is vigorous stuff, limning a Mother Courage of obstetrics, otherwise known as Rowan Mayfair, queen of the coven.

Unfortunately, though dramatically mentioned and suggestively evoked, this character does not appear in the first 200 pages, no doubt because she is familiar to readers of **The Witching Hour,** which introduced the Mayfair dynasty of witches. Once Rowan at last turns up (thinking, "Have I done this to myself? Is this how it ends for me, because of my own selfishness, my own vanity?"), the novel convulses into an almost orgasmic pageant of miscegenation—its horrors, its marvels, its sheer biological hubris. We have to make our own way through the thicket of implication, wondering exactly how we stand with mutants, how we would cope with them, where human self-interest leaves off and enlightened interest in cosmic variety begins.

Ms. Rice seems much more at home with such a tornado of ideas than with traditional witchcraft. Indeed, she is more a writer of science or speculative fiction than she is a purveyor of Gothic or whimsy. Amid the blather of names, few of whom surge up as characters, and the roughhouse sexual coupling, poignant images begin to form: Rowan breast-feeding her mutant, getting into X-ray departments to run a brain scan on him, hemorrhaging time and again and scraping up the "tiny gelatinous mass at the core of her hemorrhage. . . . There was something here, and it-had limbs!" She asks him what he knows of prehuman history and notes that his sexual organ is thick and slightly curved.

Ms. Rice tells all this in plodding prose, but she does tell it as if it interested her, as does literature, at least if we heed the roll-call of authors grafted onto the mutant child Julien, who tells a story within this story, citing Terence, Ovid, George Chapman and others.

Eponymous Lasher, 6 feet 6 inches tall, blue-eyed with luxuriant black hair, sometimes resembling "an acolyte of the rock-music star David Bowie," can speak Latin and Gaelic, sings menus aloud and brings to mind Dürer's representations of Jesus. As far as he goes he's an imposing energumen, but Ms. Rice sometimes calls him "the creature," gently stereotyping until he almost becomes a prop. He has little private life, and little interior, at least until toward the end, when Ms. Rice lets him begin to narrate. He rises to a dutiful perfunctoriness when he might have become a voice both stylish and cantankerous.

The Talamasca, a foundation devoted to historical research, addresses itself to the hypothesis that Lasher possesses a unique genome, is desperate to reproduce and needs witches with whom to do it. Lasher nags at the mind. More's the pity that Ms. Rice did not delve into him as Nathalie Sarraute might have, probing with deviant finesse yet another-man unknown.

Douglas E. Winter (review date 9 October 1994)

SOURCE: "Son of a Witch," in *Washington Post Book World,* October 9, 1994, p. 4.

[*In the following review, Winter offers qualified assessment of* Taltos. *"Certain to please the many fans of Anne Rice,"* writes Winter, Taltos *"is not likely to gain her any new readers."*]

It seems natural that new novels by Stephen King and Anne Rice should be linked with the seemingly unavoidable word "horror." Yet King writes from a decidedly populist perspective; he is a Faulkner by way of Jim Thompson, Don Robertson and Richard Matheson, with a lot of B movies and episodes of "Twilight Zone" and "Outer Limits" thrown in for good measure. The essence of his fiction is the disruption of everyday life by the outre: a funfair for the common man. Anne Rice, on the other hand, finds her roots in fairy tales; medieval romances and gothic novels—particularly the decadent "yellow gothics" that closed down the 19th century. Her perspective is patrician; the fundamental icon of her work is the elevated Outsider, the one person among us who is fated to a life that cannot be mundane—not everyman, but neverman.

Nowhere is this more apparent than in her new novel, **Taltos,** a romantic fantasy populated almost entirely by superhuman characters. Virtually devoid of the emotional aesthetics of horror—save for one skillfully enacted comeuppance—the novel is a curious amalgam of gothic, glamour fiction, alternate history and high soap opera.

Taltos is the third, and perhaps final, book in a series known as the "Lives of the Mayfair Witches," and it is written with a rather firm expectation that its predecessors have been read. For the uninformed, it is enough to know that the members of the Mayfair family—women and men—are blessed and cursed by genetics with witchery. There is neither double double nor toil and trouble; indeed, the witches here seem adept only at mind-reading and psychokinesis, talents which are too easily manipulated for plot convenience. Their haunted heritage has brought the family great wealth, which is exercised from a New

Orleans manse with Southern gentility; but of course such power cannot escape notice . . . or challenge.

The Mayfair saga unfolded laboriously in **The Witching Hour,** but then seemed to find its stride with last year's **Lasher,** a deliciously decadent triumph that centered on the revelation that the mating of two Mayfairs could produce a genetic aberration from a legendary race of giants known as Taltos. Such a creature, called Lasher, wreaked havoc before dying in the second book; in **Taltos,** another member of the breed, Ashlar, takes center stage.

Ashlar, as his very name suggests, is the inverse of Lasher—a gentle giant who hides his monstrosity through Howard Hughes like seclusion and philanthropy, making dolls for the masses. He is also the consummate Rice creation; an immortal who yearns for integration into humanity and yet recognizes his aristocracy, which is symbolized strikingly by his height above the masses.

Ashlar is brought into contact with the Mayfairs through the antics of certain members of the Talamasca, a secret society devoted to the pursuit of the weird. The confrontation of giant and witch is enacted in a heady hyper-reality: from its settings—limousines and private jets, penthouses and bayou mansions, Claridge's in London—to its often luxurious prose, this novel grapples literally with the haunts of the very rich.

The story of Ashlar slowly intertwines with that of 13-year-old Mona Mayfair, a precocious nymphet who makes Lolita look like Doris Day. Mona manages a mutual fund, tosses off words like "approbation," seduces her cousin's husband and becomes pregnant by him without a care in the world. Neither the cousin nor anyone else seems to mind; indeed, every major player lusts after each other at some point in this book—even our pregnant 13-year-old ponders a lesbian tryst with yet another cousin.

Ironically, none of these sexual shenanigans seems particularly lurid or shocking; certainly we have seen them before in Rice's fiction. And that suggests the more fundamental problem confronting the reader of **Taltos:** the dire feeling of deja vu, of not moving forward but covering old ground. It is a problem amplified by a story that advances less through action than through the discussion and dissection of events, with characters talking each plot development into near-stasis.

At one juncture, Rice has her elegant Ashlar lament the modern corruption of language, dismissing "realism in fiction, and journalism which is filled with colloquialisms. . . . It has lost all formality, and instead abides by an intense compression. When people write now, it is sometimes like the screech of a whistle compared to the songs they used to sing." If **Taltos** is meant to invoke some older and better style of storytelling, then its song of choice is a dirge. There are passages of intense lyricism here—particularly in the stories of ancient days told by Ashlar—yet too often Rice's style lingers and, on occasion, malingers.

This is a novel that demands both a taste—and a patience—that has been refined by prior experience. **Taltos** is thus certain to please the many fans of Anne Rice, but it is not likely to gain her any new readers. And this is a shame, because Rice is a formidable talent among writers of the fantastique.

Ken Gelder (essay date 1994)

SOURCE: "Vampires in the (Old) New World: Anne Rice's Vampire Chronicles," in *Reading the Vampire,* Routledge, 1994, pp. 108-23.

[*In the following essay, Gelder explores Rice's portrayal of vampire characters, family structures, and homoeroticism in* Interview with the Vampire, The Vampire Lestat, The Queen of the Damned, *and* The Tale of the Body Thief.]

The 'vampire chronicle'—where the life and fortunes of a vampire are mapped out through a number of novels—is a recent development in popular horror fiction. Chelsea Quinn Yarbro's *Hotel Transylvania* (1978) was the first of a sequence of novels about le Comte de Saint-Germain, an aristocratic (and, as it happens, ambidextrous) vampire who effortlessly glides through history. She has also written a trilogy about a female vampire, Olivia, Saint-Germain's one and only true love. Patricia Nead Elrod's 'vampire files' series, which began with *Bloodlist* (1990), traces the fortunes of a vampire detective, Jack Fleming, in his search for the woman he loves— who, again, is another vampire. Yarbro in particular has sold well, marketed at one point as the 'Queen of Horror'—although *Hotel Transylvania* has been out of print now for some time. But the best-known contemporary chronicler of vampires is without question Anne Rice.

Her first novel in the 'Vampire Chronicles', **Interview with the Vampire** (1976), was not an immediate best-seller because Rice at this time was unknown—she had not been published before. Her biographer, Katherine Ramsland, reports that Ballantine made the book into an 'event' the following year, however (with an extensive tour, coffin-shaped book displays, T-shirts, and so on), ensuring its success through heavy promotion. The second novel in the sequence, **The Vampire Lestat** (1985), was published almost ten years later; but Rice's reputation as a horror novelist was secure by this time, and it became a best-seller the first week it was released. **The Queen of the Damned** (1988) went to the top of *The New York Times* best-seller lists during its first week of publication, and stayed in the lists for seventeen weeks, far outselling (at 400,000 copies) the previous novels in the series. None of these novels has since been out of print. Hollywood has at last been successful in negotiating with Rice for the film rights of **Interview** (she was reportedly unhappy at the decision to cast Tom Cruise as Louis, however); there was talk of producing a Broadway musical (the pop singer

Sting had apparently been involved in discussions); the Vampire Lestat Fan Club launched itself in 1988; in 1990 Innovation, an art production outfit, had begun to serialise *The Vampire Lestat* in comic book form; and—to give an idea of her reach into other kinds of markets—the hip New York music magazine *Reflex* took Anne Rice as the topic of its first non-music cover story. The fourth novel in the chronicles, *The Tale of the Body Thief,* was published at the end of 1992.

We should note that Yarbro, Elrod and Rice are women writers, although for the most part their vampire heroes are male. Their chronicles share a number of characteristics usually associated with women's romance—notably, the tracing out of the vampire's search for fulfilment, for a 'complete' love relationship. But, under the umbrella of the vampire genre, romance themes may be dispersed or channelled through other topics or interests—an involvement with criminality, for instance (Elrod's 'vampire files' are a variation on the hardboiled detective fiction genre), or a detailed recreation of historical events (Yarbro and Rice's novels are well researched, historically speaking), or a kind of macro-presentation of occult or mythological activity which is shown to control the narrative in certain ways (as in Rice's later novels). That is, these novels are not *just* romances. Some differences can be noted between Elrod and Yarbro on the one hand, and Rice on the other, by way of introduction. The former novelists' vampires are solitary figures, rarely coming into contact with their own kind. Rice's vampire chronicles, however, have something in common with the family saga genre. Her vampires often cohabit with one another in familial relationships; and in *The Queen of the Damned,* this is opened up to an extended 'great family' with an original set of vampire parents from which all the others are descended. Consequently, her novels are more genealogical than the others. This may seem to characterise Rice's fiction as conservative, essentially grounded in a coherent family structure. But that claim is complicated by the fact that her male vampire protagonists—Louis, Lestat and Armand—are decidedly 'queer'. Rice flaunts the gayness of her male vampires; they cohabit together as 'queer' parents, with vampire children; at other times, they may be bisexual or sexually 'polymorphous'. We would need to think about what it means for Rice, a reputedly heterosexual wife and mother, to write 'as' a queer male vampire. And here is another reason for Rice's importance as a vampire novelist: she was possibly the first writer to narrate her stories in the first person from the vampire's point of view.

INTERVIEW WITH THE VAMPIRE

Rice's first vampire novel took an unorthodox approach to the genre by having its vampire protagonist, Louis, interviewed by a boy (presumably in late adolescence) with a tape-recorder. This narrative strategy emphasises disclosure (through confession or revelation) and publicity, topics which become increasingly important in Rice's vampire chronicles. The reader hears the 'other' speaking first-hand; the vampire comes out of the closet and makes himself known; he gives us 'the real story' (at last) about vampires. Moreover, the boy is the perfect listener, hooked by the narrative to such an extent that, at the end, he wants to be *like* Louis, a vampire. That is, the novel builds its own ideal reception—where the interviewer is thoroughly passified, standing as an image for the converted reader, the fan—into its structure. Yet even as the 'truth' of Louis-as-a-vampire is taken for granted—to be believed—the novel sets into motion a complicated version of the dialectic between belief and disbelief, illusion and disillusion, that, as we have seen, has preoccupied so many of the vampire narratives so far discussed. *Interview with the Vampire* maintains the illusion of vampires at one level, since Louis 'exists'; at another level, it disillusions its own investment in 'real' vampires almost entirely, turning vampirism into something akin to a posture or style, a *simulation* of the real. This novel seeks the 'truth' about vampires, and comes back empty-handed; it does, however, make a significant conversion (namely, the interviewer/ reader) along the way.

The novel opens in 1791, with Louis—actually, Louis de Pointe du Lac—as the son of a plantation owner in New Orleans, Louisiana, the setting for much of Rice's horror fiction. This Southern American city becomes a powerful, occult site for events—a place in the New World which is nevertheless somehow older and more decadent than Europe, simultaneously 'primitive' and sophisticated, a 'mixture' of all kinds of peoples:

> There was no city in America like New Orleans. It was filled not only with the French and Spanish of all classes who had formed in part its peculiar aristocracy, but later with migrants of all kinds, the Irish and the German in particular. Then there were not only the black slaves, yet unhomogenised and fantastical in their garb and manners, but the great growing class of free people of colour, those marvellous people of our mixed blood and that of the islands, who produced a magnificent and unique caste of craftsmen, artists, poets, and renowned feminine beauty. Then there were the Indians, who covered the levee on summer days selling herbs and crafted wares. And drifting through all, through this medley of languages and colours, were the people of the port, the sailors of ships, who came in great waves to spend their money in the cabarets, to buy for the night the beautiful women both dark and light, to dine on the best of Spanish and French cooking and drink the imported wines of the world.

We can easily note how this passage naturalises pre-Civil War New Orleans as—somewhat against the odds—a place where different ethnicities interact 'freely' with one another, where class differences are dissolved (everyone is suitably 'aristocratic') and so on. But this utopian image of what might be termed the 'global exotic' is important as a background to Rice's vampire fiction—and perhaps to vampire fiction in general. This genre tends to override class and ethnic differences at one level by emphasising mobility and movement. As I have already noted in previous chapters, the vampire was consciously constructed as a 'citizen of the world', a figure to whom boundaries (national boundaries in particular) meant very little. To recall Wolfgang Schivelbusch's phrase, utilised in Chapter 1, this fiction tends to offer a 'panoramic perception' of the world—a perception which is intimately related to travel in its broader manifestations. Indeed, as we shall see in the next chapter especially, contemporary vampire fiction is 'panoramic' in both space and *time.* It visits as many moments in history as it does countries, and each moment is as freely interactive in terms of class and ethnicity as the next one.

Louis is a lapsed Catholic, a *disillusioned* Catholic—perhaps he has seen too much of the 'world' which circulates through New Orleans. His brother, by contrast, is a religious zealot who has visions; that is, he believes wholeheartedly in the illusions of the Catholic Church. This juxtaposition of illusion and disillusion—belief and disbelief—is important in Rice's novel. Louis does not 'believe' (in) his saintly brother; yet precisely because of this traumatic disillusion, he is allowed to see the 'reality' of vampires. His subsequent belief in vampires, in other words, is a kind of modern, secular replacement for his lost Catholic faith. Because Louis has 'no illusions', he is, then, both less than Catholic—and more than Catholic. That is, he both believes in nothing, and is (therefore) able to believe in *anything,* including the unbelievable—vampires. As he says to Armand much later in the novel,

> you ask me how I could believe I would find a meaning in the supernatural! I tell you, after seeing what I have become, I could damn well believe anything! Couldn't you? And believing thus, being thus confounded, I can now accept the most fantastical truth of all: that there is no meaning to any of this!

Rice's novel plays with this folding together of illusion and disillusion in a number of ways. It takes the form of a quest, primarily to find out the 'truth' about vampires. Louis, a 'Creole' American vampire with a French accent, feels 'shaped by Europe more deeply and keenly than the rest of Americans'. The girl-vampire Claudia encourages Louis to return there, to 'see where it had all begun': 'It was her idea most definitely that we must go to central Europe, where the vampire seemed most prevalent. She was certain we could find something there that would instruct us, explain our origins'. But in Transylvania, the vampires are simply 'mindless, animated corpse[s]', offering no answers to Louis and Claudia. The novel rejects Eastern Europe as a source: it is too 'primitive' (not 'aristocratic' enough? not glamorous enough?) to be of any use; it only disillusions. Louis and Claudia travel instead to Paris, 'the mother of New Orleans'—the city which 'had given New Orleans its life'. They are led to the Théâtre des Vampires, a theatre in which real vampires *act* as vampires for a mesmerised audience. The troupe presents the audience with an illusion (theatricality) of an illusion ('real' vampires); far from leading Louis and Claudia to the 'origins' of vampirism, they show it to have been (always?) a mode of representation, a *sign* of vampirism, a style or a posture. To be a vampire is, in other words, to *act* like a vampire. This is vampirism at its most *disillusioned,* a rejection of all the European traditions and

superstitions. In the same spirit, Louis tells the boy interviewer that vampire lore—crosses, garlic, stakes through the heart and so on—is 'bullshit'.

Yet the novel allows the illusion of vampirism to flourish at the level of representation itself. There is no reality or meaning behind vampirism, as Louis realises—and this is 'the most fantastical truth of all'. But one can still 'be' a vampire because—since there is no reality behind it—acting and being collapse into each other. The reality of vampirism lies precisely in this point. And for Rice, a new kind of faith is subsequently produced, one that is aligned with popular fiction rather than with the Catholic religion. Her audience at the Théâtre des Vampires is mesmerised by the performance. They are a 'titillated crowd', under the 'spell' of theatre. A highly erotic, somewhat disturbing scene unfolds on the stage—where a young woman is stripped naked and killed by the troupe of vampires. Louis, who is watching, can actually 'taste' her; his involvement with the performance is entirely sensual. That is, he is 'carried away' with what he sees. The scene anticipates Rice's later sketches of mesmerised audiences at Lestat's rock concerts in *The Vampire Lestat;* the erotics of the event (illusory as it may be) produce real effects (excitement, arousal) at the mass level. I have noted that being and acting are collapsed into each other to make vampires 'real' in this novel. But Rice also attempts to collapse the boundaries—we might say, the 'critical distance'—between audience and performance, reader and text, outside and inside. In this context, the boy interviewer's desire to become a vampire at the end of the novel (he reappears, in fact, as the vampire Daniel in *The Queen of the Damned*) is not entirely surprising. It is, as he expresses it, a way of rejecting 'despair'—where one's faith, having lapsed in the modern world, is recuperated through a closing conversion (in) to the fiction itself. It is hard to imagine a more effective way of accounting for fandom, in this closing image of the converted reader/listener.

Louis himself is given the 'Dark Gift'—that is, converted into a vampire—by Lestat, in the first of a number of 'queer' scenes. Lestat is like a 'lover', and Louis is 'taken', in a drawn-out ecstatic moment which has them mingling their fluids together. Rice emphasises the differences between these two male vampires, with Louis as delicate and sensitive (i.e. feminised) and Lestat as aggressive and impetuous (i.e. masculinised). It is worth noting, given my use of Bennett and Woollacott in the previous chapter, that in both *The Queen of the Damned* and *The Tale of the Body Thief* Lestat in fact refers to himself as 'the James Bond of vampires', emphasising his recklessness and his lack of concern about killing. He also emphasises his loner identity; in spite of this, however, he helps Louis to pass the Dark Gift on to a 5-year-old girl, Claudia, and the three of them coexist for a while as a family. But this is a 'queer' family: Claudia's persistent questioning of how she was 'created' by two men—'How was it done?'—resonates in this context. Louis and Lestat are a kind of demonic (but not demonised) gay couple, queer male parents competing with each other for 'our daughter' Claudia. At the same time, they are Claudia's 'lovers': the queerness of their relationship lies partly in the folding together of gay love with heterosexual incest/paedophilia.

This way of representing parent-child relations is certainly unconventional, to say the least. But it is 'normalised' through Louis's search for what is missing in the relationship: the mother. Claudia's actual mother had died of the plague shortly before Claudia was 'taken' by Louis and Lestat. The journey to Paris—'the mother of New Orleans'—is, then, also a kind of Oedipal return, an attempt to recover a lost maternity. Indeed, it is triggered by Claudia's two attempts to kill Lestat, the most fatherly (i.e., patriarchal) of the two male vampire parents. But, as already indicated, Paris ultimately offers no 'meaning' to Claudia—and she expresses her 'inevitable disillusionment' to a distraught Louis. He responds by trying to create a surrogate mother for her, turning the dollmaker Madeleine into a vampire. In the meantime, he is drawn to Armand, an older male vampire; and, to complicate matters, Lestat has also journeyed to Paris to look for them.

The result is a variation on Eve Kosofsky Sedgwick's 'erotic triangle', where a struggle 'between men' ensues over a woman. In this case, the struggle 'between men' (Lestat and Armand) takes place over another *man*, Louis. Claudia and Madeleine, far from being crucial to this arrangement, are apparently its most disposable features— soon afterwards, they are both burnt to death. But they become all the more important after they have gone; Claudia in fact comes to haunt the later novels in the chronicles, as a kind of absent presence. Louis—an immortal vampire—now realises that everything, even great art, is transient: 'The magnificent paintings of the Louvre were not for me intimately connected with the hands that had painted them. They were cut loose and dead like children turned to stone. Like Claudia, severed from her mother'. He joins Armand, his 'companion', on a trip around the world. Returning to New Orleans at last, he finds Lestat set up in a 'domestic' scene with another 'smart, gay' male vampire—and a baby. The scene is, in part, a parody of the moment in Stoker's novel when Dracula throws a baby to the hungry vampire women. Rice's vampires are hungry, too—they may feed on the child—but they are also maternalised. Louis rocks the baby and finally returns it safely to its crib—but in his despair he leaves New Orleans soon afterwards, wishing to be somewhere 'where there was nothing familiar to me. And nothing mattered'.

Thus the novel moves back and forth between the recuperation of a mother-and-child relationship (the familiar relationship: home) and the unfamiliarity of one's separation from the mother (away from home). In this sense it is nostalgic; but it recognises that the return to the mother (like the return to Paris) is ultimately an illusion— that such a pre-Oedipal moment can never be completely recovered. It recognises, too, that to be disillusioned— separated—is nevertheless to require that such illusions exist—the illusion that vampires are real, the illusion of a return to the pre-Oedipal mother. Since the novel puts this dialectic between illusion and disillusion into play, Rice's authorial relations to her imagined audience might be figured in exactly these terms. In its most disillusioned moments—like the magnificent paintings of the Louvre, and like Claudia—Rice's novel is a kind of orphan, 'cut loose' from the mother and set adrift in an unfamiliar, even hostile, world. At the same time, the illusory metaphor of author-as-mother is maintained: Rice's audience (like the boy interviewer at the end) is eventually converted through a pre-Oedipal relation to the novel, working at the level of sense and arousal and desire.

In an interview with Rice, Greg Fasolino asked, 'You now have a rather large cult of fans—people obsessed with your work. Does that excite you?' Rice admitted that it is 'a little frightening', but emphasised her commitment to *them:* 'The thing they really want from me is the most extreme and true and personal stuff I have to give, and I'm gonna keep doing it, as long as I have breath in my body'. It is difficult to avoid reading this as an image of the author-as-mother, feeding her fans—her children. The image of author-as-vampire might also be invoked, and the two images in this context are not inconsistent with each other. Conversely, the image of fans-as-vampires is also apparent in her comment to Fasolino ('The thing they really want from me'). Rice's own Dark Gift is the novel itself; she writes the exchange between author and fan into the novel in terms of two vampires, parent and child— lovers—mingling their fluids together and sharing the ecstasy, but nevertheless wondering afterwards how it was done.

The Vampire Lestat and *Queen of the Damned*

Rice's second and third novels in the Vampire Chronicles opened up the vampire's search for his origins on an epic scale. *The Vampire Lestat* is in fact structured as a series of narratives which begin in the present day—the modern age—and then move further and further back through history to an original moment, to a moment of Genesis for vampires. Lestat de Lioncourt is older than Louis, and he gives an account of his own conversion in pre-Revolutionary Paris at the hands (or teeth) of the alchemist-turned-vampire, Magnus. We should note that Lestat in turn converts his own mother, Gabrielle, in an obviously incestuous scene—she is, he confesses, '[t]he only woman I had ever loved'. In the next narrative sequence, Lestat describes his meeting with Armand, an even older vampire who still lives according to 'the Rules of Darkness'. He takes these Rules as a means of verifying his own authenticity—whereas Lestat, by contrast, is seen as inauthentic, a modernised, sceptical vampire who does not abide by traditionally sanctioned vampire lore. Armand himself was converted by Marius in Renaissance Venice—in another gay scene which connects Marius to the painter Caravaggio, with Armand as his willing apprentice. Lestat then searches for Marius and the origins of the Dark Gift. Interestingly enough, given the discussion in Chapter 2, he finds Marius in Greece—and learns all about Marius's conversion to vampirism hundreds of years ago in classical Rome. Marius and Lestat identify with each other because, as the novel has it, their respective epochs had undergone the same kind of crisis. That is, religious faith was declining in 'the years of Augustus Caesar', just as it is in decline in the modern age. Both characters thus stand 'on the cusp of the old way of doing things', living without faith (without illusions) and yet not entirely 'cynical' (disillusioned) either. As Marius notes, 'We sprang up from a crack between faith and despair'— precisely the crack occupied and empathetically exploited by Rice's fiction.

But there are older vampires than Marius. The novel turns to Egyptian mythology as a source for the oldest kind of magic, imagining two original vampire 'parents', the father Enkil and the mother Akasha—to whom all other vampires are ultimately connected, as a kind of extended family. Marius has the task of minding these parents, 'Those Who Must Be Kept', who are almost inanimate—appearing like statues to Lestat. Given the Oedipal and pre-Oedipal structures in Rice's fiction, it is not surprising to see Lestat attracted to Akasha. (Her name, and her role as the 'original' mother, clearly recalls H. Rider Haggard's 'She', Ayesha.) He feeds from her ('My mother, my lover'), and incurs Enkil's rage. But in Rice's fiction, the mother is always more powerful and more *present* than the father, and in fact Enkil is later easily destroyed in *The Queen of the Damned.* The novel closes with Lestat, resurrected in 1984, preparing for his rock concert, his ultimate act of self-disclosure—and aware of Akasha's presence.

In *The Queen of the Damned,* Akasha returns as a vengeful mother, who claims Lestat as her son and her lover— but begins to destroy her other 'children', the vampires she had originally 'animated', in order to create a matriarchy, a world ruled entirely by women. Rice introduces a second narrative alongside this one, however, juxtaposing them against one another. This second narrative involves Jesse, an orphaned girl adopted by a formidable woman, Marahet. Marahet keeps extensive records of her family chronicles on computer files, and Jesse soon realises that she is part of a 'Great Family' which stretches back, matrilinearly, into the distant past. Jesse joins the Talamasca, a secret, Masonic organisation which has been observing and documenting supernatural activity—and which believes, as a matter of course, that vampires are real. This organisation is also matrilineal: it is administered from a 'Motherhouse', and in fact constitutes 'another "Great Family"' through its own extensive records and files. The two 'Great Families'— whose histories are recorded in Marahet's and the Talamasca's chronicles—are in fact one and the same: both provide matrilineal genealogies of vampires. Akasha, on the other hand, wishes to wipe these genealogies clean and start again, like an exterminating angel. The novel traces out the battle between Marahet, who is productive vampire—she produces genealogies, writes family histories, adopts children—and Akasha, who has none of these

interests and sees history as, instead, destructive. Rice polarises the two positions in terms of gender, allowing her two female characters to argue that history is productive when maternalised, and destructive when patriarchal—an argument which makes Akasha herself patriarchal, since she, too, wishes to destroy in order to (re)create a new matrilineal order. In response to this, Marahet empathetically invokes the 'Great Family' once more, demonstrating on a huge electronic map of the world that vampires have been everywhere in place and time, appealing to the others through an image of global multiculturalism:

> No people, no race, no country does not contain some of the Great Family. The Great Family is Arab, Jew, Anglo, African; it is Indian; it is Mongolian; it is Japanese and Chinese. In sum, the Great Family is the human family.

This image carries the day: Marahet's twin sister Mekare, an earth-Mother figure, arrives soon afterwards and dispatches Akasha, cutting off her head and consuming her brain and heart.

In their article 'Undoing Feminism in Anne Rice's Vampire Chronicles', Devon Hodges and Janice L. Doane offer a powerful criticism of Rice's investment in this kind of narrative structure. They note the shift from Oedipal structures in *Interview with the Vampire,* to pre-Oedipal structures in *The Vampire Lestat* and *The Queen of the Damned*—since the latter novels recover the 'archaic' mother and (in Lestat's case) represent the pleasure of the pre-Oedipal return. Hodges and Doane focus on Claudia in *Interview,* suggesting that—through this 5-year-old girl vampire, the 'daughter' of Louis and Lestat—Rice shows how a woman's attempt to resist 'her position as an infantilised object of desire' is 'eventually contained by being redefined as an object of exchange between men'. Because this novel is concerned with Oedipal struggles—focussing around Claudia and her 'parents'—it is able, at least, to show how culture 'devalues women'. As I had noted above, Claudia—and Madeleine—are in one sense the most disposable characters in this novel; at another level, of course, Claudia in particular is the most *disturbing* character, unsettling the 'homosocial' and essentially 'patriarchal' bond 'between men', that is, between Louis and Lestat, and later, Louis and Armand (who helps to destroy Claudia in order to make that bond more secure). In the later novels, however, this kind of feminist critique is lost. The shift into pre-Oedipal 'pleasures', usually associated with a conversion to vampirism, certainly places the mother 'in a more privileged position'; but it also colonises this otherwise unconscious realm, turning it into an idealised or utopian space which ultimately overrides or 'precedes' sexual difference. Hodges and Doane look at the relationship between Lestat and his mother Gabrielle in these terms. Lestat has a tyrannical father; he identifies instead with his mother, and she helps him to realise his masculinity by turning him into a wolf-hunter. Or rather, she helps him to realise *her* masculinity: 'She spoke in an eerie way of my being a secret part of her anatomy, of my being an organ for her which women do not really have.

"You are the man in me," she said'. Gabrielle is masculinised through her relations with her son (she dresses as a young man after her conversion). Lestat, on the other hand, is feminised—that is rendered 'effeminate'—through his relations with Gabrielle. Hodges and Doane rightly note the 'regressive' representation of homosexuality here, that is, that it is related to a son's overidentification with his mother. But this pre-Oedipal, utopian exchange of gender roles has another implication:

> The return to the mother that seems to disrupt gender boundaries by feminising the son who embraces the maternal, and by lending to the mother the son's phallic power, is also the path to postfeminism. Ironically, the return to the mother is what allows Rice to kill off and transcend feminist politics . . . sexual difference is a dead issue.

This is a persuasive argument; but I would note at least two problems with its direction. The first lies in the way Hodges and Doane smooth over the 'queer' aspects of Rice's vampires. A certain 'normalisation' of parental relationships occurs as a consequence—for example, they are able to speak confidently about 'patriarchy' in *Interview with the Vampire*—which is at odds with the later claims that Rice kills off the issue of 'sexual difference'. More importantly, they never explore the realm of 'queerness' in all its contradictory splendours. Their article is worth contrasting to Sue-Ellen Case's 'Tracking the Vampire', discussed in Chapter 3. While Case celebrates the possibilities inherent in the 'queer' vampiric realm (in Rice's case, this might involve the peculiar folding together of parenthood and paedophilia, or reproduction and gay love), Hodges and Doane see it as a 'postfeminist' form of neutralisation. (It would be worth teasing out the connections between this claim and metaphors of sterility in their article—as if 'queer' sexuality is not (re)productive for feminists, as if it doesn't get them anywhere.) Certainly Rice's fiction is oriented towards the fantasy of maternal origins; but it also occupies the kind of 'in-between' state explored by Case in her article, which sees the vampirish mingling of bodily fluids as something in *excess* of the 'normalised' mother-child relation. Case had described the non-normative pleasures to be derived from 'queer' vampires in positive terms; Hodges and Doane, on the other hand, speak disapprovingly—for example—of Rice's fascination with sado-masochism, of her 'fantasies of power and surrender'. We should note, however, that Case focuses primarily on the 'lesbian vampire'—whereas Rice's 'queer' vampires are always male.

The second problem concerns their view of mass or popular cultural forms. Hodges and Doane's (unsuccessful) search for 'an emancipatory maternal rhetoric' leads them to critique the 'conservative, postfeminist narratives of mass culture' so 'greedily ingested by American readers'. We can certainly entertain the notion that Rice's fans 'ingest' their vampire narratives. I have developed an image above of Rice herself as Mother Vampire, lovingly 'colonising' her readers; but I have also noted that the image can work the other way, with the fans in turn 'colonising'—or vampirising—the novels. That is—to use

the description a second time—a *mingling* of fluids occurs: the relationship between mass or popular cultural narratives and their readers, in other words, is not simply one-way. Rice's novels have at least two kinds of readerships—her 'gay audience' and her 'mainstream readers'—which, by her own account at least, are barely aware of each other. To regard these readerships as 'colonised' by mass culture is both to collapse them together (to erase their own 'sexual differences') and to disempower them—to refuse the possibility of an active engagement with the narratives, to refuse readers of popular fiction the kind of 'productive consumption' described in Chapter 4.

Hodges and Doane do away with this dynamic altogether: these readers are nothing more than passive (but insatiable) consumers. Worse, for these critics they must also be *bored* consumers—Rice's readers 'can only be bored' by the fiction, they claim, because of its 'repetitive structure'. (We could again tease out the metaphor of sterility here: Rice's fiction, like mass culture itself, doesn't get us anywhere; it offers only un(re)productive pleasures.) Hodges and Doane also claim that, through their 'repetitive' returns to an original moment, Rice's novels are thus essentialist, preferring 'truth' over 'lies': 'Not for Rice an avant-garde modernism that would play on the undecidability of representation'. This claim returns us to the kind of polarity we have seen before, in which high culture is privileged and popular or mass culture is disparaged. The former, according to this argument, defamiliarises us, while the latter is all *too* familiar. Hodges and Doane want Rice to write avant-garde, modernist novels because it is here that 'representation' becomes problematic; instead, she writes popular fiction where everything is apparently straightforward. It is not difficult to deconstruct this polarity, however—by attending, in particular, to Rice's play with illusion and disillusion, belief and disbelief, discussed above.

FLANEURIAN VAMPIRES: *THE TALE OF THE BODY THIEF*

The kind of polarity just described—which privileges high culture (complex) over popular culture (simple)—divides its readers along similar lines. Most commonly, the high cultural reader is imagined as contemplative; by contrast, the reader of popular fiction, the fan, is distracted— and, for Hodges and Doane, easily bored, experiencing either dubious or unproductive pleasures. (This particular polarity—juxtaposing contemplation and distraction—has already been noted in relation to Polidori's 'The Vampyre', discussed in Chapter 2.) It could well be argued, however, that Rice's vampire fiction enables both reading positions to be occupied, again making this polarity difficult to maintain. The novels may well be distractive, taking readers 'out of themselves'. But, passing over the question of the kinds of pleasures this then enables (productive or otherwise), the novels do in fact also encourage philosophical contemplation. Fasolino calls them 'metaphysical'; Rice is seen as an *intellectual* writer of popular fiction. Her novels unfold as meditations; their moments of ecstasy puncture long passages of inquiry amongst vampires into a range of 'classical' topics—faith, art, humanity, purpose. The vampire is itself, of course, a contemplative creature who is *subject* to distractions—a philosopher and a sensualist, a frequenter of libraries and galleries who must regularly surrender to an uncontrollable appetite. For Lestat, this appetite is also a topic to be contemplated: he ceaselessly wonders about the kinds of distractions (the urges, the pleasures) that make him what he is. In the meantime, he watches the world go past and discourses about it at great length; he collects works of art, wears fine clothes, and refines his sensibilities. In this sense, he is, in effect, an aesthete—a dandy.

Rice's fiction actually flaunts its high cultural orientations, drawing in particular on Italian Renaissance and Baroque iconography—where high culture is also at its most sensual. (Not untypically, for example, the cover of *The Tale of the Body Thief* (1992) shows a fragment from Giovanni da Bologna's *The Rape of the Sabines*.) Her vampires are familiar with the kind of 'magnificent paintings' Louis had described in *Interview with the Vampire;* they have enough time on their hands to contemplate them at length. Indeed, to be a vampire is to be 'cultured'— that is, to have 'aristocratic' tastes—and also (these points are related) to be idle. Louis, Lestat and the other vampires do not work, although they do have investments and, with the help of financial advisers, are able to accumulate large amounts of capital. Their 'job' is, instead, to find out who they are and where they came from. In *Interview with the Vampire,* this is an entirely recreational procedure—making this novel more of a 'distraction' than the others, perhaps. But in *The Vampire Lestat, The Queen of the Damned* and *The Tale of the Body Thief,* self-discovery becomes part of a much larger process—involving, as I have noted above, the establishment of extensive computer files and archives. That is, self-discovery is no longer personal (or familial), but organisational. Lestat has to negotiate with the Talamasca to access his archives; he realises, in the meantime, that he has come into contact with an organisation which knows more about him that he knows about it. That is, he realises that he has been all this while under surveillance.

Yet this is also a feature of the vampires themselves, which constantly monitor each other's movements and read each other's thoughts (or, conversely, try to 'cloak' their thoughts from each other). In *The Queen of the Damned* they are likened to radio receivers. A tension is worked out in the novels between the vampires' need for anonymity or privacy, and their nagging sense that someone— another vampire, usually—is watching them, that they are part of a larger network of 'airwaves'. Lestat tries to break out of this predicament by making himself as visible as possible, by making his vampirism public—as a rock star playing to a mass audience. This only upsets the other vampires and the Talamasca, however, since no one else believes him (although his human fans may believe in him—a distinction Lestat entertains in *The Tale of the Body Thief*). By the beginning of *The Tale of the Body*

Thief, Lestat is disillusioned with publicity and has returned to the anonymous world of the city—but he is still being watched.

The Tale of the Body Thief opens in Miami, rather than New Orleans—a city of 'desperation' and 'risk', full of murderers and therefore 'perfect . . . for the vampire'. Here, Lestat operates as a kind of solitary vigilante, pursuing serial killers with the help of his own computer and the extensive files he has 'purloined' from the Police Department. Lestat is himself, of course, a serial killer with 'style'; his quarry, on the other hand, is 'filthy' and 'sloppy', a bad dresser, someone of no interest whatsoever at the level of individuality (he is never named by Lestat). The vampire's dandy-like posture distinguishes him from the urban jungle—a place which would seem to do away with individuality altogether. Lestat is essentially *different;* he has 'style'; he breaks the 'rules'; and he has the means to negotiate the otherwise anonymous city through his extensive surveillance systems. With his Parisian background and his refined sensibilities, he might in fact be viewed as a kind of *flâneur*—that is, a city stroller, an urban spectator, someone with leisure enough to watch the world go past and skill enough to read its various 'commonplace' signs. The word has been given a particular currency by Walter Benjamin, who utilised it—in a discussion of Charles Baudelaire as a nineteenth-century urban lyric poet—to speak about crime fiction, taking the *flâneur* as a kind of prototype of the detective. The *flâneur*—a Parisian dandy, in this case—puts his idleness to good use: 'He only seems to be indolent for behind this indolence there is the watchfulness of an observer who does not take his eyes off a miscreant'. Benjamin noted a contradiction at work in the figure of the *flâneur,* however—that, while he subjected the urban world to an 'individualising' gaze (i.e., his own), he simultaneously assisted in the erasure of individuality by reducing what he saw to a series of statistical points.

Taking up Benjamin's thesis in the context of a discussion of the crime fiction of Edgar Allan Poe, Dana Brand has noted that in effect the *flâneur* 'domesticates' the world, rendering it manageable and thus reassuring himself of his mastery over it. But reassurance at one level produces anxiety at another—knowing that there is 'deep crime' out there which is beyond the flâneurian gaze and therefore cannot be managed or domesticated. Brand suggests that Poe's detective, Dupin, is an attempt to engage this deeper level of activity, to move beyond the flâneurian level. He is, in other words, 'capable of mastering the urban environment *without* inhibiting its capacity to produce anxiety and terror'. He 'focuses, rather than denies, the city's power to produce shock and dislocation'. We can note in passing that Brand's description of Dupin, Poe's aristocratic and cynical detective, makes him sound very much like a vampire: 'Secluding himself by day in a mansion with closed shutters, Dupin explores the Paris streets by night . . . distanced from and invisible to the inhabitants of the city through which he moves'. When Dupin solves his crimes, however, this 'distance' is collapsed and, vampire-like again, he actually *inhabits* those inhabitants—that is, he occupies their consciousness (in order to get at the truth they are concealing). Brand quotes a passage from Baudelaire himself, which expresses the vampiric aspect of the detective's inhabitation of others as he goes about solving their crimes: 'like those wandering souls who go looking for a body, he enters as he likes into each man's personality'. This kind of detective fiction, then, both focuses on the production of 'shock and dislocation' in the city—and indulges in panoptic 'fantasies of control' over the city's radical 'otherness'.

Rice's *The Tale of the Body Thief* is precisely about the inhabitation of someone else's body—an inhabitation which causes (rather than does away with) 'shock and dislocation'. While he monitors his serial killers, Lestat is aware that he, too, is being watched. The Talamasca have a benign interest in Lestat and follow his movements carefully in order to protect him from unnecessary publicity. Their motto is, 'We watch and we are always there'—a version, perhaps, of the famous Pinkerton's detective agency motto, 'we never sleep'. But Lestat is also monitored by someone less benign (and once associated with the Talamasca), the mysterious Raglan James—the 'body thief'—who spies on Lestat through computer surveillance networks and, more archaically, through out-of-body travel. James finally convinces Lestat to exchange bodies, to give Lestat his longed-for experience of being human again. The homoeroticism of the exchange is emphasised. James, a young man, 'wants' Lestat's body—and Lestat in turn confesses, 'I couldn't take my eyes off him, off this body which might soon become mine'. But the exchange, for Lestat, is profoundly disillusioning—and to reflect this disillusion, the novel shifts out of the fantastic mode and into a kind of 'dirty realism'. That is, the kind of 'shock and dislocation' Brand had described above also operates at a generic level; the novel literally 'dislocates' *itself*. The vampire's flâneurian distance from the inhabitants of Miami is now entirely collapsed; but the inhabitation of one of those inhabitants by no means supports the panoptic 'fantasy of control'. Lestat's engagement with the real world makes him *more* anxious, not less—as if to be a vampire is to keep anxiety at bay. He becomes sickly and downtrodden, and all his money is stolen. However, a particular kind of 'fantasy of control' *does* become available to him. Losing his vampire's body, Lestat is 'no longer one of them'—that is, no longer 'queer'. The mingling of fluids associated with vampirism—which emphasises mutual attraction and consent, and produces sublime pleasures—is replaced, for Lestat, by heterosexist power. In fairly graphically described scenes, he rapes a young woman, and later deflowers a somewhat masochistic nun. To be human (that is, male), he thus considers at one point, is 'monstrous'; it triggers off an overwhelming desire to escape from this particular radical 'otherness' and return to the 'queer' flâneurian realm of the vampire.

The novel thus inverts the conventional perception of realism-as-real and horror-as-fantasy—since, here, realism takes Lestat 'out of himself' and the experience is unexpectedly disturbing. He returns, instead, to a conception of *fantasy*-as-real, noting sardonically that the desire to be 'human' (to be 'real') is in fact based on an 'illusion'. Lestat, with the help of David Talbot, an ageing ex-leader of the Talamasca, tracks Raglan James to—of all places—the *Queen Elizabeth II*, as it cruises around the Caribbean. Here, he regains his vampire's body in a rebirthing scene that represents the *QEII* as a kind of womb, a 'sad and tawdry' mother. The exchange enables Lestat to leave the realist mode behind and re-enter the 'queer' realm of horror fantasy. David, it turns out, has also exchanged his body for the one vacated by Lestat—becoming a young man again. Lestat is ambivalent about this exchange, however, and decides to leave. He travels to Asia and then to Europe, reasserting his vampirish role as a 'citizen of the world': 'the old cliché was true—*the world was mine*'. In Barbados, he sees David again—who tells Lestat that he, too, would like to be a part of the grand tour: 'There are places I want to go—lands and cities I always dreamt I would visit'. For Lestat, this amounts to saying that he would like to become a vampire—not least because travel is viewed by David precisely as he views it, that is, as a means of contemplation: 'There has to be a period of traveling, of learning, of evaluation. . . . And as I engage in my studies, I write. I write everything down. Sometimes the record itself seems the goal'. Lestat then 'takes' David in a passionately homoerotic scene and, with Louis, they begin the first part of their travels, to the Rio carnival.

The novel thus returns to the connection between the vampire and what I had called earlier in this chapter the 'global exotic'—where the vampire functions as a kind of internationalised, cosmopolitan tourist, mobile (and leisured) enough to make the world 'my own'—and channelling that world through the kind of 'panoramic perception' discussed elsewhere in this book. The point is taken up by Dana Brand in relation to the *flâneur* and the detective: 'The viewpoint of the detective is, like that of the *flâneur*, panoramic. . . . Like the *flâneur*, he distances himself from what he observes in order to achieve his panoramic perspective'. In Stoker's *Dracula*, Jonathan Harker had travelled by train to Transylvania, reproducing the panoramic perspectives of late nineteenth-century travelogues. In Rice's *The Tale of the Body Thief*, Lestat and David cruise around the Caribbean on a luxury ocean liner and then make their way to South America—elevating tourism to the global level, and so turning the entire world into a place without borders—a place without 'otherness', a place with which one is, then, already *familiar*. This is certainly a 'fantasy of control'—but it is also a fragile fantasy which, in *The Tale of the Body Thief*, at least, is 'dislocated' through Lestat's disturbing encounter with the unfamiliarity of the 'real'.

Anne Rice with Mikal Gilmore (interview date 13-27 July 1995)

SOURCE: "The Devil and Anne Rice," in *Rolling Stone*, July 13-27, 1995, pp. 92-4, 97-8.

[*In the following interview, Rice discusses her literary career, critical reception, supernatural themes in her fiction, and* Memnoch the Devil.]

For nearly 20 years now, Anne Rice has been telling stories that share secrets—secrets of life and death, of sex and the soul, of monsters and humans. In particular, though, it is with her series of novels known as *The Vampire Chronicles* that Rice has created her most binding mix of mystery and meaning as well as what may prove her most enduring body of literature. *Interview With the Vampire* (1976)—the first of the *Vampire Chronicles* and Rice's first published novel—is a horror narrative unlike any other. It is the story of Louis de Pointe du Lac, an 18th-century New Orleans plantation owner who has lost faith in his life and in God. Seeking death one night, Louis instead finds a vampire and a cruel paradox. This broken man who wanted to die must now endure lifetimes of no meaning, and he must murder daily to do so. *Interview* is also the story of the French-born Lestat de Lioncourt, the smart, mean aristocrat who made Louis a vampire, and Claudia, the child immortal who unites Louis and Lestat in a bitter kinship and eventually separates them at an awful price. Mostly, though, *Interview With the Vampire* is a haunting meditation on loss, mortality and the uncertain purposes of faith. By the book's end, Rice's vampires have come to understand a terrible but emboldening truth: There is no God, no ultimate meaning to life's anguish. The vampires are finally left alone, wandering through the turbulence of time and history, killing others so that they themselves might evade the oblivion of death.

With *Memnoch the Devil* (excerpted in this issue), the fifth and perhaps final volume of *The Vampire Chronicles*, the fates of the vampires change radically and irrevocably. Narrated by Rice's most cherished character, the vampire Lestat, *Memnoch* tells a tale as old as Scripture's legends and as modern as today's religious strife. In *Memnoch,* Lestat comes face to face with his most feared supernatural counterpart, the devil, and hears the devil's dreadful, fascinating secret: It is God who has made human history so murderous, and it is God from whom the world must be saved. With Lestat's help, the devil claims, he might just be able to accomplish the task.

I meet Anne Rice at her large, Greek revival-style home, which she shares with her husband, Stan, and their son, Christopher, in the aged Garden District of New Orleans. Rice was born and raised not far from this grand house. At 15 she left New Orleans and eventually settled in the San Francisco Bay area with Stan, a poet, painter and, at the time, professor at San Francisco State University. After some 30 years in California, Rice missed her hometown and extended family and, with her husband and son, moved back to New Orleans. In 1989 she purchased the First Street house where she now lives and writes. It is a richly atmospheric place, and it is little wonder that Rice has used it as the haunted central setting of *The Witching Hour, Lasher* and *Taltos*—the first three volumes of her *Lives of the Mayfair Witches* series. The house is crammed with the stuff of Rice's obsessive imagination: showcases of valuable 19th-century French porcelain Bru dolls (utterly spooky with their humanlike eyes), walls of books on ancient mythology and religious theory, rooms of religious statuary and even the odd skeleton or two, outfitted in century-old bridal or ballroom gowns and sporting flowing blond wigs. ("But they aren't real skeletons," says Rice as she gives me a tour of the upstairs. "I couldn't live with a real one.")

As we talk, Rice and I sit in a glassed-in side porch overlooking a large, lush lawn not far from the site where the fictional demon Lasher lies fictionally buried under a vast and ancient oak tree. Rice is dressed in a white, high-collared, billowy blouse with frilly cuffs and a long, black skirt, and she wears her trademark owlish glasses. At age 53, Rice is direct, plain-spoken and intellectually passionate. These days, she says, when she isn't sequestered in her upstairs office writing she is busy researching matters related to religious history and mythology—the same subject matter that she says preoccupied her in *Memnoch the Devil* and will be at the thematic core of her next few books.

[Mikal Gilmore:] **Memnoch the Devil** *strikes me as perhaps your most passionate and inventive work since* **Interview With the Vampire.** *Obviously you've taken considerable risks with this story—not only risks for your vampire characters and their secretive, immortal world but also risks that given the story's shock points might even affect your career. I also couldn't help wondering if the risks might run deeper—if perhaps there's something personal at stake for you in this parable about God and the devil.*

[Anne Rice:] If there was any book that ever beat me up, it was **Memnoch.** I had been thinking about it for more than two years—swimming in the ideas of it, going back and forth between its various scenes in my head. I had even made false starts and then thrown them away. Finally, early last year I sat down and thought, "I'm either going to write this, or it's going to kill me." So I took the month of February, wrote it and then collapsed. It nearly *did* kill me. I mean, there was something so dark in writing this book. I remember lying in bed one night thinking. "All right, Lestat's got to go to hell today. There's no putting this off any longer—it's time." And it was like . . . it was like going there with him, I guess. Toward the end, when he ran up the stairs of hell to escape, I was right with him. It was not a pleasure, writing those scenes. It was real agony, because I'm as close to Lestat as any character that I've been able to imagine and write.

Like **Interview With the Vampire,** *much of* **Memnoch** *has a half-maddened, fever-pitch intensity to it, plus it takes some wildly unpredictable turns. Did you ever find yourself surprised by what you were writing?*

Basically, I knew what I wanted: Lestat was going to meet the devil and God, and they were going to talk. And I knew that the devil was going to present certain arguments to Lestat, but I didn't know how *well* he was going to make them until I got into making them for him.

But you're right. This book was just as instinctively written as *Interview With the Vampire,* and there's been no book in between that's been that instinctively written. With all the others there was more thought, more doubt, more hesitation—some more so than others. Now I've come full circle. I write now like I did when I wrote *Interview*—all night long. *Interview With the Vampire* was written in five weeks, this was written in about four weeks, and it was the same sort of experience—just surrendering to the process. And I found myself asking the same kinds of questions. I kept saying, "How *dare* you write these things!"

Where did your interest in writing a novel about the argument between God and the devil come from?

I had a teacher in comparative literature at San Francisco State back in the 1960s. I remember him once saying in a class in Goethe, "What would God and the devil have to talk about if it weren't for men?" I never forgot that, and I think I have always been going at that idea in one form or another in my writing, though behind masks, you could say. I mean, when I wrote *The Vampire Lestat,* and I talked about ancient Egypt, I was going at it in a less direct way. Now I'm going right into my own heritage. I'm spending hours and hours reading every translation of the Bible that I can find as well as other religious histories and texts, and I'm fascinated by it all. It's an obsession, a passion. I see things now about my own religion and my own religious upbringing that I never could have seen in my 30s. I certainly couldn't have seen them in this way when I wrote *Interview With the Vampire* or *The Vampire Lestat.*

So how would you describe your view of religion now?

When I wrote *Interview With the Vampire,* I didn't think there was any question: There was no God. What was terribly important was to live in spite of that fact. Now I think it's terribly important that there *might* be. And it's not detached from life. It's right in the neutrinos and the atoms and the explosion in Oklahoma City.

But my obsession is more than that. I'm trying to stand back, and understand, as if I were one of my characters, why this age—which has come so far in so many ways—why is this age obsessed with near-death experiences and angels and gods, and why are movies showing people coming back from the dead over and over again as a common image? Why are the movies flooded with images of people who can fly? What does it all mean? What *does* it mean? Things are not getting simpler to me. They're getting more and more complicated, and the questions are multiplying. I was more sure there was no God when I was younger. I still suspect there isn't, that there isn't anything. That's my suspicion: that there is nothing. But I'm just not so *sure* anymore. It's all I want to talk about, all I want to think about, all I want to deal with—and I see this book and the next one as a new path for me.

By the end of **Memnoch the Devil,** *Lestat would seem to have few questions about the matter: He's seen God and the devil face to face, and he's heard their debate.*

Actually, I think that at the end, Lestat really hasn't been given any more direct sign from heaven than anybody is ever given. Maybe that's part of what I'm trying to say. That it can't make sense. You just can't have a God that cares that little. You *can't.* Either he doesn't know, or he's stupid, or he's a bad person. And if it is all true, then it certainly is a horror novel. That's part of what I'm trying to say.

The basic premise of **Memnoch** *is so strong, it seems it could just as easily have been a non-vampire book—and may even have reached a different or broader audience than "The Vampire Chronicles."*

I *tried* to make it a non-vampire book. I tried to write it with immortal men, to take immortal men through the same experiences, and it simply could not get going. And I finally gave it back to Lestat. It's almost like he laughed and said, "You know you need *me* to go there." And, of course, he was right: His going there did make quite a bit of difference. But I'm afraid my relationship with him is over. He left me when I finished reading the page proofs for this book. That same night, I put a message on my answering machine—I have a listed number for people to call—and I said: "Lestat is gone. He left me as he was standing in front of a Mercedes-Benz dealership on St. Charles Avenue, in New Orleans. This is a very strange feeling, but it's happened."

It was like after all the things we'd gone through together—I'd survived Tom Cruise, I'd survived the [*Interview With the Vampire*] movie, even though **Memnoch** was written before the film was released—I'd gotten through all of that, and, *still,* he left me. It was like he was saying. "This is it—we've done it. You've done it. We've said what we have to say with each other. If you go on now, you've got to go on in another way."

What will you do next?

The current book I'm writing is called *Servant of the Bones.* The only thing I'd like to say about it is that it's about a very old ghost who is made for a particular purpose and decides after thousands of years just not to do what he's supposed to do. This book will be more similar to **Memnoch** than anything else. **Memnoch** put me right up against where I want to be—where I can write about ghosts and spiritual forces as something that may be real. I know I run a certain risk. My audience might say, "She's flipped out," you know? But it's very exciting to me to be writing about this ghost in the 20th-century and what he sees in something like the Oklahoma bombing.

You've written vampire and witch chronicles and a mummy yarn, and now you're undertaking an epic ghost series. In the course of writing these stories, you're become known as one of the pre-eminent authors of supernatural literature. What is it about that story form that has attracted you so?

I think all my writing has been part of a battle with my fears. When I write, I explore my worst fears and then take my protagonist right into awful situations that I myself am terrified by. And I think that the act of putting all that fear and terror and confusion into an orderly, plotted story has been very therapeutic for me. It definitely helps me to continue through life.

Obviously I'm obsessed with death. I'm not obsessed, *per se,* with pain and suffering. I actually try not to write about it, surprisingly enough. And so even though my books are supposed to be bloody and horrible, there is a shrinking from this. Or at least there's a terrible moral dilemma there. I mean, I have to write about pain, obviously—the pain that other people have suffered and pain I'd be afraid to suffer myself. I feel very driven to do it, and it clearly helps me. I only hope that it's in such a framework that it does not simply add to the horror of someone else.

You mention your obsession with death. It has seemed that in some ways your best work has been a rage against death. Vampires achieving immortality and spirits seizing human life amount to a fantasized overcoming of death and all its sheer horrors and unfairness.

I think that since moving back here to New Orleans, I've begun to find some way I can accept the fact that we're going to die. But it is true that for a long time I found it just horrifying. I found it horrifying not so much because my life will be extinguished but because of the possibility that the Holocaust might mean nothing. Or the suffering of my daughter might mean nothing. [Anne and Stan Rice's daughter, Michelle, died in 1972, a few weeks before her 6th birthday, of a rare form of leukemia. Anne Rice has since said that in part *Interview With the Vampire*—and particularly its haunting vampire-child character, Claudia—was an unconscious way of expressing grief over her daughter's death.] That's the part that bothers me: the meaninglessness of it. The utter meaninglessness of it. And I'm still fascinated by the way people convince themselves that things have to have meaning. Every time you turn on a TV, you see a reporter talking to the parent of a retarded child or somebody who's been hit by a ton of bricks, and they say. "There *has* to be a meaning for this." And I'm always thinking: "No. There really doesn't have to be any at all." Despite that I now think atheism might be a bit naive and cocky, I still believe there is possibly no meaning to anything. There's *nothing* that can't be swept off the face of the earth. Nothing.

I remember going through that time when life was just unendurable. It lasted about three months. I was literally quivering. I would grab people and say, "Do you believe that there's a God? Do you believe we're all here for

nothing?" I put it in **The Vampire Lestat.** I had Lestat do it, but actually it was me.

It's changed for me now. I just don't feel the same suffocating horror. I don't feel resigned. . . . It's hard to describe what I feel. Maybe what I feel is a capacity, finally, to enjoy everything, even though there may be no meaning. I was talking to a woman whose son recently committed suicide. He was a teen-ager here. I had lost a child, and this woman had lost a child. I was talking to her, and I said that what I honestly thought was, when the lights go out, and when that darkness comes, it never really goes away. The darkness never is really going to go away, but you just somehow learn to see the light also. And you know something other people don't know. You meet them, and you don't know whether they're better off or not, but you know something that they don't know. Because those lights have gone off for you.

Did you find that time provides a means of healing?

Well, it must, but I have a suspicion of that. I truly believe it's ruthless to be healed. You know what I mean?

Let me tell you a story. I've been scared of the dark all my life. I've been scared to be alone. I've spent very few nights of my life alone in any house—and I never stay in this house alone. But recently I have been losing my fear of the dark, and it is one of the most wonderful things. Just a week or so ago I was sitting up in my office. It was about 1:10 a.m., and I'd been thinking for a while about getting up and writing something on my wall. I write all over my office walls in felt pen. I was going to get up and write, "Someday I will die, and it will all be over." But before I could do that the lights went out. There was a power shortage in the neighborhood, and it was as black as it is in the country. So I got up from my desk and woke my sister, because I knew she would have a lighter so that I could light a candle.

The lights were out for about 20 minutes, and it was *beautiful.* I remember walking through the house with my poor little sister, who was half-asleep. We came downstairs, and I thought: "This is what this house was like in 1857. It was this dark. This is a rare moment." I remember feeling absolutely euphoric, thinking how much I loved to walk through this house in the dark and how great it was not to be afraid anymore. At 1:30 the lights came back on, and I went upstairs. And then something occurred to me. I went and checked a memorial clipping on my bulletin board, and I realized it had been a year earlier to the day and hour that my best friend, John Preston [a social critic and author of gay pornography], had died.

What lingered from that whole experience, more than anything else, was the *euphoria*. When I walked around in the dark, I didn't feel absolute horror that John Preston had died at 48 years of age, at the height of his talent, of AIDS, in a coma. I didn't feel a trembling horror. I felt a euphoria—an ability to tolerate *everything* at that moment.

That was a great feeling, and so I'm calling that ruthless. Somehow, in spite of all the cruelty and absurdity of life, I was not afraid that night. I will die someday, and I will share that with everyone else. But I felt a fearlessness in those minutes, rather than the panic that used to clutch at me—for years—in the face of darkness and death.

That's the whole purpose, I think, of what people call fantasy writing. You can put the most horrible things into a frame, and you can go into that frame safely and talk about those things. You can go into the world of Louis and Lestat and Claudia and be able to talk about grief or loss or survival and then come back safely. That, to me, is the reason for all the artifice—the obvious high style of my books and their use of the supernatural. I would find it *much* harder to write a realistic novel about my life. I would find it too raw. I just wouldn't be able to get the doors open, I wouldn't be able to go deep enough.

Obviously, though, for many readers you have gone deep enough. Your books are not only terrifically popular, but they have also attracted the kind of fervent following more commonly associated with that of pop stars.

I did not expect books as eccentric as mine to have that kind of appeal or that kind of commercial momentum. I knew enough about publishing just to know what that meant, and I was astonished. I remember thinking that a book like **Interview With the Vampire** was just flat-out too weird. I thought at best it would become some sort of underground best seller. I had no idea that it would have the great commercial life it's had as well.

But I've always had good luck, or good breaks, compared with many authors. And in the last few years the audience has spread out in an enormous way. If I lack any reader, if there's any audience I've failed to reach in America, it's the elite, literary audience. If there's been a failure to communicate, it's at the top—at the so-called top.

Well, judging from some of the reviews you've received over the years from literary quarters, that may well be true. What do you think accounts for much of the critical disdain that your work has received?

The subject matter. Scorn for the idea that anyone would write seriously about vampires. And then a secondary thing sets in once you become No. 1—that if you are the No. 1 best seller, you must be an illiterate idiot. Those are two prejudices that I fight.

I also think there's a cynical tendency in modern literary values to dismiss books that take on huge questions or issues, because nobody with any true sophistication could possibly do that. It's a sort of by-product of the post-World War II aesthetic of existential nihilism that says you cannot have heroes and heroines in novels. There are those who say that the great art of today is about nothing at all—that to be *about* something is pretentious and old-fashioned and limited. And my writing is filled with a kind

of naive, dead seriousness about: Why are we here? How do we lead a good life? How do we keep believing fervently in love, and how do we make our lives not only good but heroic?

In a way I've been blessed in that I can ask those questions, and I'm blessed that I have the vision I have—a belief that one sensible person can study the world and learn something of God through the world.

Has that critical dismissal been hard for you?

Oh, yeah. In the very early days, definitely. People would practically come up to me and say, "I know you've written this calculated potboiler best seller about a vampire. Well, it's not something I want to read." I wanted terribly to be taken seriously. I wanted to say, "Look, this is not about what you think. Give this a chance!" I was horrified by some of the reviews my work received.

But let me tell you something: I have a real problem with much of the so-called literary fiction of these times. I have not read John Updike or Anne Tyler. I can't. I try. I just don't get into it. I think that there's a real arrogance to the pedestrian realism of the 20th-century novel. Not only are books about ordinary people and ordinary lives and ordinary events and little-bitty epiphanies, not only are they *not* worth reading most of the time, they're simply garbage. I think our literature is at a low ebb right now, and there's a lot of reasons we came to this point where we turned away from the incredible power of Nathaniel Hawthorne or Herman Melville or Edgar Allan Poe and have chosen instead to write a diluted version of Henry James over and over again.

The reasons are, I think, more economic than the elite would like to face. It's an outgrowth of industrialization, really. It's the literature of quiet desperation or contentment—a literature that tells you that to try to attempt anything great in your life is unrealistic to the point of being irresponsible and dangerous. It tells you that any novel of substance is going to be about a normal couple in Connecticut or Berkeley and their quarrel over the custody of the children and how they both work it out, each in her or his own way.

The truth is that is not the only story we have to tell. That is not even what our world is about. Our world is in fact filled with abnormal people and outrageous people and cataclysmic events and extremely romantic stories and acts of incredible heroism, and yet for some reason the upper-middle-class literary writers have decided that that's not worthy subject matter for their books. And they're dogmatic and nasty about it.

Clearly you're a writer who doesn't hedge your feelings. A couple of years ago that outspokenness landed you in a public controversy when you protested Neil Jordan's casting of Tom Cruise for the film version of **Interview with the Vampire.** *Looking back on all that now, do you ever* *regret any of the things you said? Do you feel that possibly you were a bit too hasty in your criticisms?*

My frank feeling is that it turned out so well that I can't think too much about doing anything differently. That's not to say that everything I did was wise or kind or constructive or that everything they did was wise or kind or constructive. I think they were very, very unkind to me and my readers in many respects—the people associated with the making of that movie—and they were very unwise. At the same time, I'm not sure that if I had been on the team whether anybody would have paid any attention to anything I had to say. Whereas when I wasn't on the team—when I was public enemy No. 1—there was a lot of attention paid to the things I said. I don't think people should be rewarded for saying angry and negative things, but in some ways I don't see how the movie could have turned out better. I think it's an absolutely unique film, and I'm very happy with it. I spend almost no time at all regretting anything that happened, and I don't want to hold any grudges, either.

Do you remember at which moment the film won you over?

When I saw Tom Cruise walking past the mosquito netting around the bed, and I heard his voice, and I saw that he was Lestat. I knew it instantly. He had gotten it. And I do credit him. That actor, for some reason, really made a contact with that character, and he produced a fabulous version of him. He made Lestat his own without taking my Lestat from me, and I feel tremendous love for Tom as a result. Now, to what degree I hurt him with my personal comments, or to what degree I spurred him on, that will always be open to debate. I don't want anyone to be hurt, especially not someone as nice as he is. In fact, I don't want anyone to be hurt, even if they're not nice [*laughs*]. But what I said, I said from my heart, and the feeling I got was that he understood. And in my conversations with him, I found him to be just a completely loving person, and I think his take on the books is right-on. He knows the character and understands the character perfectly. I'm not so sure about other people involved in the production, you know. I really don't know Brad Pitt at all. I'm not in any way connected with him. I know the readers loved him. They felt that he captured the guilt in Louis, and they were very pleased with him.

I couldn't help laughing when I read your statement: "I think we should nickname [Brad Pitt] the Barbie Doll From Hell because of the way he behaves toward us 'Vampire Chronicle' people."

Oh, yes, in my newsletter. Oh, I do think he looks like that [*laughs*], but I meant that lovingly. He's cute, you know? He is cute. But I have to confess, when he was declared the sexiest man in the world, I nearly fell over dead, because he does look to me like the Barbie Doll From Hell. He looks cute and young and like a kid. He looks like he's about 14. That was a teasing comment.

It is possible, of course, that you may be in for a whole new round of controversy when **Memnoch the Devil** *hits*

the bookstores. You're written a book that questions the validity of God's ethos in a time when a powerful segment of American Christianity has become an increasingly intolerant, even violent, political force. Plus, the book has a couple of rather inflammatory scenes—particularly the moment when the vampire Lestat meets Jesus Christ on the road to his Crucifixion.

It was inflaming to *me*. I didn't find it an easy thing to do, and yet it had the wonderful feeling of something absolutely inevitable and something that *should* happen. I was confronting there the Christ in whom I had believed totally as a young girl when I used to sit in church on Good Friday and imagine his wounds. I was really standing there with that Christ at that moment, and it was an excruciatingly difficult thing to write.

Yes, sometimes I'm afraid for this book. The public is very hard to inflame and very hard to wake up, but when they do notice or take offense at something, they can turn their fury with considerable bad effect, and I'm a bit afraid they may do that with this book. I never felt that way before. At the same time, I don't really think it's true. I think we'd be lucky if people notice that there's book slated to be a best seller that actually cares about God and the devil.

This book is so much about God, it's so much about compassion, it's so anti-violence and so anti-blood sacrifice that, to me, it's a wonderful book. I'm very proud of it. I don't really think it's going to draw to itself a lot of opposition, but I could be completely wrong. I'm certainly ready to defend it. I'm ready to stand there and talk about what I think is good in it and to defend it against people who would criticize it and defend the importance of us being able to talk about God and the devil in our work. I mean, we're living in the most amazing times. Amazing and horrible. It's a very exciting time to be a writer.

Kevin Allman (review date 6 August 1995)

SOURCE: "The Last of Lestat," in *Washington Post Book World*, August 6, 1995, p. 2.

[*In the following review, Allman offers favorable assessment of* Memnoch the Devil.]

When it comes to fervent fandom, Anne Rice's partisans are up there with the Star Trek brigade. They love her dark imagination, her Gothic prose, her wry sense of humor and especially Lestat—the handsome, vain vampire who's become her signature character. Lestat and Rice are each the focus of a fan club, 'zines and an Internet group; Rice herself even pens a newsletter, "Commotion Strange," full of Lestat-related news and views.

The latest issue of "Commotion Strange" brings the news that's broken the hearts of Lestatians everywhere: Rice has decided that **Memnoch the Devil,** the fifth installment in her *Vampire Chronicles,* will be the last Lestat story. That might be a wise decision, because Rice has painted herself into quite a corner with this one. By the end of *Memnoch,* there's not much for her favorite vampire to do but hop back in the box.

The book begins in modern Manhattan. Lestat is stalking his latest victim, Roger, a drug kingpin who has amassed a vast hoard of religious treasures in a private reliquary. Equally intriguing to the vampire is Roger's daughter Dora, a New Orleans televangelist with a soul as pure as her father's is corrupt. But Lestat himself is being stalked. He's hearing voices. Feeling footsteps. Sensing presences. And they're getting closer.

Enter Memnoch, a fellow so very ordinary-looking that Lestat calls him "generic." But the devil isn't offended: "It's the form I prefer in every age and place, because it doesn't attract very much attention. Going about with black wings and goat's feet, you know—it overwhelms mortals instantly." Memnoch, it seems, has been watching Lestat, and he thinks the vampire would make a dandy sidekick, kind of a Boy Wonder to the Prince of Darkness.

Having never believed in God or the devil, Lestat is nonplussed, outraged and rather snippy: "Well, let me tell you, Your Royal Highness of Darkness. I'm not helping you with anything! I don't serve you!." But Memnoch makes him one of those diabolical offers he can't refuse. "I'll take you to Hell and to Heaven, if you like, you can talk to God for as long as He allows, and you desire." After this cosmic tour, Lestat can decide whom he'll serve—and in what capacity.

With the stage thus set, the book transmogrifies into a modern *Paradise Lost,* The Universe According to Rice. Many, many pages of **Memnoch** are devoted to her personal cosmology and angelology, to her versions of creation, evolution and the Crucifixion. It's a tour that's interesting at times and poky at others. True Lestatians might lap this stuff up; for others, it'll be leaden sledding.

Not that there aren't a few of Rice's trademark eyebrow-raisers along the way. Lestat resolves his contradictory impulses toward Dora by drinking her menses. And in a scene unlikely to be duplicated on-screen by Tom Cruise any time soon, Lestat meets Jesus on the road to Calvary and is invited by Him to taste His blood. As the crowd goes wild, Lestat absconds with the veil of Veronica and returns with it to the 20th-century, where its display at St. Patrick's Cathedral enflames a worldwide religious revival.

As one might suspect, Rice is full of sympathy for the devil, who in her version spends his days trying to move souls out of Sheol (Purgatory) and into Heaven. Compared to the furious, anguished Memnoch, God is drawn as a pretty dull character, an Almighty surrounded by a sycophantic chorus of angels, virtues and the rest. It's a portrait of God that will be familiar to anyone who's browsed the life-after-life books on the bestseller list.

Better is Rice's evocation of New Orleans. The city has always been a character unto itself in the *Vampire Chronicles,* and there's no better guide than Rice when it comes to describing the Blakean splendor and rot behind the city's mansard roofs and tatwork balconies. Of particular interest to her fans will be the descriptions of the immense old Garden District mansion that becomes Lestat's new home; its nonfictional counterpart is St. Elizabeth's, the 19th-century convent/orphanage that Rice is remodeling for her own residence.

Perhaps it's for the best that the Lestat saga is over. With a new Christian millennium sweeping the world at the end of the book, it's hard to imagine where Lestat could go next—unless all of **Memnoch the Devil** turns out to be one of those elaborate "Dallas" type dreams. As it stands, Rice has penned an ambitious close to this long-running series, as well as a classy exit for a classic horror character. Hardcore fans will no doubt devour this last visit with Lestat, although casual readers might close the book wishing for a little more blood sucking and a lot less speechifying.

Daniel Mendelsohn (review date 11 August 1996)

SOURCE: "All This and Heaven Too," in *New York Times Book Review,* August 11, 1996, p. 5.

[*In the following review, Mendelsohn offers unfavorable assessment of* Servant of the Bones.]

Anne Rice's latest supernatural melodrama, **Servant of the Bones,** is dedicated to God, and if God has any commercial savvy whatsoever, He'll dedicate His next book to her. The creator of **Interview with the Vampire** and its numerous best-selling sequels is bringing out her new book (part of which is set in an Old Testament milieu) in a first print run of one million copies; the Creator, on the other hand, has more than once had to resort to samizdat, distributing His work in tiny hand-copied editions that took centuries to find the right marketing niche, even after He'd achieved name recognition. You wonder when God will get a clue and move to Knopf.

Far more interesting to the student of commercial publishing are the striking similarities between God and Anne Rice. Both have cannily stuck throughout their careers to the Big Themes: good versus evil, mortality and immortality, that sort of thing. Both, moreover, have presented those themes accessibly enough to have won vast and occasionally fanatical international followings. And both, as a result, have become critic-proof. In Ms. Rice's case, her popularity seems, if anything, to have grown in inverse proportion to the readability of each new and ever more unwieldy novel.

To say that Anne Rice's strengths—most evident in her earliest work—are essentially the slender ones of a Gothic novelist is not at all to condescend. She has a real gift for rendering psychically charged mood and melancholy atmosphere, and an old-fashioned penchant for chiaroscuro characterization and intricate if sometimes improbable plotting. All this stands in stark contrast to much of what you find in today's affectedly affectless "literary" fiction, and goes a long way to explaining her immense popularity among an astonishingly diverse reading public, which has snapped up vast numbers of the five "Vampire Chronicles" novels, the three "Mayfair Witches" books, one mummy fiction and assorted soft-core erotica.

When deployed, Ms. Rice's stylistic strengths have admirably served her compulsively recurrent subject: a quest for the meaning of mortality and suffering, undertaken by outsiders—either angst-ridden immortals, like the soulful vampires in *Interview,* or mortal freaks exiled from the community of the "normal," like the libidinous castrati in her richly atmospheric novel of 18th-century Italian opera, *Cry to Heaven,* or the half-castes in her historical fiction of old New Orleans, *The Feast of All Saints.* At her best, she skillfully balances lush and occasionally overripe descriptions of these alien characters in their exotic milieus with a sense of their underlying troubled humanity. *Interview* was so successful precisely because its sensitive-esthete vampire narrator, the melancholy New Orleans aristocrat Louis, was a nice Byronic departure from your garden-variety Nosferatu with his unkempt nails and bad table manners.

Yet Ms. Rice has always seen herself as much more than the kudzu-crowned, fog-caped Queen to Stephen King's King. In a recently published series of interviews with the film historian and author Michael Riley, she recalls being "deeply hurt" when people called her a Gothic writer at the beginning of her career. Her subsequent books seem intended to demonstrate that she's much more than the mistress of "escapist" chain-store fantasy-romance or historical fiction—that she can transform her increasingly farfetched supernatural story lines into vehicles for the themes of serious fiction: "people seeking to be good, perversity, incest, the feelings of the damned, whatever."

There's certainly nothing wrong with ambition, but the recent books—especially the new one—suggest that Ms. Rice's reach has seriously exceeded her grasp. She has taken to literalizing, often with numbing clunkiness, the metaphysical conflicts that lately preoccupy both her and her increasingly long-winded characters; and the more she does so, the less persuasive are her attempts to say something important about it all. That would probably be bearable if the books weren't getting progressively less readable; but she's the Ayn Rand of the spirit realm. Even faithful fans who succeeded in hacking their way through the Amazonian densities of *The Queen of the Damned* or *Taltos* probably gave up before getting to the part in *Memnoch the Devil* where Ms. Rice brings on God as a character.

Servant of the Bones is the unfortunate culmination of this trend. A main selection of the Book-of-the-Month Club and the Quality Paperback Book Club, and likely to become a huge best seller, it's the clearest demonstration yet of the way that Ms. Rice's pretensions are crushing her prose. Although it mocks you with parallels to her earlier better books—its eponymous protagonist, the dark angel Azriel, is, like Louis, a kind of outcast spirit—its garrulous gods, horny angels and "Dr. Strangelove" climax aren't anchored to any convincing psychological or even supernatural reality. These self-indulgences make for reading that is neither enlightening nor entertaining.

The first of the book's four wildly disjointed parts ostensibly serves to relate how Azriel was transformed from your standard-issue Ricean mortal—a wealthy and sensuously beautiful aristo—into your standard-issue Ricean immortal, a sensuously beautiful spirit with a cosmic chip on his shoulder. He begins life as a Hebrew teen-ager, circa 600 B.C., whose captive weeping by the water of his hometown, Babylon, is alleviated by considerable wealth and frequent tête-à-têtes with the pagan deity Marduk; but after nobly consenting to be sacrificed in order to free his people, he is betrayed and placed under a spell that turns him into the powerful genie called the Servant of the Bones. If all this takes a rambling and repetitive 120 pages to get through, it's probably because Ms. Rice wants you to appreciate the convincing period touches ("Call on Yahweh to stop this sandstorm, you fool!").

In the book's brief second part, Azriel describes the first and the last of the many masters whom he served before bedding down for 600 years and waking up in time for the plot to begin on page 188. The first master, Zurvan the Wise Man, is not (as you may think at first) an attraction at Ringling Brothers, but an important ancient Greek thinker who explains the Purpose of Life to a grateful Azriel, who returns the favor by flying Zurvan all around the globe. The last, Samuel of Strasbourg, is a wealthy Jew just trying to get by during the Black Death.

Ms. Rice reserves the actual story line for the third part; given the plot's rococo improbabilities, this seems wise. Here Azriel finds redemption by foiling the evil design of a deranged renegade billionaire Hasid named Gregory Belkin. Belkin heads a powerful worldwide cult called, rather optimistically, the Temple of the Mind. Between painstakingly hiding his Jewish origins and delivering himself of computer-generated New Age axioms, he's found time to develop a deadly virus with which he plans to wipe out the entire population of the third world. After unsuccessfully attempting to clue Belkin in to the wonders of multiculturalism ("The West isn't the world, Gregory"), Azriel resorts to more forceful and permanent forms of persuasion—but not before conducting an energetic adulterous fling in Miami Beach with Belkin's wife, Rachel, who is suffering from a nameless but terminal ailment that by this point in the narrative could well be boredom.

All this may have looked like the bare bones of a big novel about God and Man and betrayal and salvation, but it turns out to be little more than an excuse for Ms. Rice to write about interesting stuff she's recently boned up on: Babylon, the Middle Ages, New York Jews. Anyway, what *could* it have added up to? The metaphysical payoff here is hardly bone-rattling. It's difficult to take the author as seriously as she takes herself when the book's crowning insight, which she puts in the mouth of her fictional Greek philosopher, is that the purpose of life is "to love and to learn"—surely more Hallmark than Heraclitus.

The book's structural weaknesses and aromatherapy metaphysics wouldn't grate so much if you were at least getting the sense of mood and locale at which Ms. Rice used to excel, but her big ideas have pulverized the tiny details that can make or break the verisimilitude of supernatural fiction. It's odd that someone who prides herself on the historical accuracy of her period characters' speech has her ancient Greeks and Babylonians oscillating between archaisms like "Ye gods" and nails-on-the-blackboard anachronisms such as "Like hell, great King"; in a similar vein, you can't help wondering why, after re-awakening in the late 20th century after 600 years, Azriel instinctively knows what filoviruses are but is relatively clueless about plastic. Four hundred pages of this kind of sloppiness can get on your nerves if there's no narrative to distract you.

It's possible that the soft-focus, New Age *faux* spirituality that suffuses *Servant of the Bones* is precisely what gives Ms. Rice's recent work its huge appeal in this millennial decade, lousy as it is with angels. (The new book even describes the "stairway to heaven," which is likely to elicit a wince from readers who went to their high school proms in the 70's.). But you miss her writing. The grandiose self-indulgences of this latest Anne Rice blockbuster make you wish she'd forget heaven and plant her feet back on the fog-wreathed ground where she started. With any luck, her next book will be about—and maybe even dedicated to— mere mortals.

Sandra Tomc (essay date 1997)

SOURCE: "Dieting and Damnation: Anne Rice's *Interview with the Vampire*," in *Blood Read: The Vampire as Metaphor in Contemporary Culture,* edited by Joan Gordon and Veronica Hollinger, University of Pennsylvania Press, 1997, pp. 95-113.

[*In the following essay, Tomc explores the cultural significance of female body image, androgyny, and self-abnegation in* Interview with the Vampire. *According to Tomc, "Rice modeled the vampire's transformation on one of the most powerful narratives of gender metamorphosis available to 1970s culture: the story of successful dieting."*]

At one point in Anne Rice's *Interview with the Vampire,* the vampires Louis and Claudia journey to Eastern Europe on a quest to find others like themselves. Elegant, intelligent, and beautiful, Louis and Claudia are shocked to find that the fabled vampires of Romania are little more than zombies, rotten half-eaten corpses who suffer the fate of being animated. "I had met the European vampire, the creature of the Old World," Louis pronounces as he kills the last of these. "He was dead."

Although literally a comparison of monsters, Louis's words might just as well describe a generic as a narrative twist. In 1975, the year before Rice published *Interview with the Vampire,* Stephen King published his only vampire novel, *Salem's Lot,* a novel that featured vampires who resembled, to a remarkable degree, the kind that would repulse Louis. King's vampires were, of course, the norm. They partook of an ancestry that threads its way from the works of Polidori, Le Fanu, and Stoker in the nineteenth century to those of Theodore Sturgeon, Robert Aickman, and Paul Morrissey in the twentieth, an ancestry whose members, even the most illustrious, are manifestly sub-human. They were clever, they might be attractive, but their bodies were too hairy, their sense of smell too acute. When the chic and beautiful Louis met the vampires of Eastern Europe, he was, as Rice well knew, meeting one hundred and fifty years of monster stereotype.

It was, of course, the pattern of Rice's chic vampire rather than Stephen King's bestial one that became the focus of such absorbed and wild popularity in the 1980s and 1990s. From Rice's own sequels, *The Vampire Lestat* (1985), *Queen of the Damned* (1988), *The Tale of the Body Thief* (1992), and *Memnoch the Devil* (1995), to such films as *The Lost Boys, Innocent Blood,* and Francis Ford Coppola's *Bram Stoker's Dracula,* the vampire of enviable looks and inspiring ambitions—not sub-human so much as ultra-human—reigned. But the vampire's transformation had its corollary in a process of domestication, a process that seemed to be cemented with the casting of Tom Cruise, a squeaky-clean icon of normative masculinity, in the role of the amoral, sexually ambiguous Lestat for the 1994 film version of *Interview with the Vampire.* Vampirism, says Joan Copjec, "presents us with a bodily double that we can neither make sense of nor recognize as our own." But with Cruise playing Lestat—a piece of casting that Rice herself bitterly opposed and then enthusiastically supported—the vampire had ceased to be unrecognizable. Once a menace to the conclaves of average America, he was now an honorary resident.

The journey of the vampire from monster to yuppie may not have been predicted in *Interview with the Vampire,* but it is, I would suggest, encoded there. In order to separate her own vampires from those indigenous to the genre, Rice borrowed heavily from 1970s discourses of gender mutability and bodily transformation, finding in the twin paradigms of androgyny and weight loss an articulation appropriate to her generically radical aims. But if the then-revolutionary potential of gender and corporeal metamorphosis liberated Rice's vampires from the stocks of their heritage, it also, I would suggest, facilitated their bland domestication. The following essay examines the mechanisms of that domestication, with, I might add, as much an eye to using Rice's text to read 1970s discourses of bodily alteration as the reverse. In the 1970s upheaval around bodies and weight, particularly women's bodies, we can trace the means by which the very process of becoming ultra-human—of becoming a new person, a new monster, a new woman—could realize itself in confinement and limitation.

When Rice set out to make the "animal" vampire a new person, she imagined the process as part of a larger program of what the 1970s called "liberation," whether sexual, gay, or women's. The icons of this program were already figures of ambiguous signification, bodied forth by the beautiful-boy stars of glam rock or the "unisex" fashions launched by designers like Rudi Gernreich. For Rice, trying to unsettle "clichés" and to imagine her way out of the ossified categories of human and monster, self and other, gender uncertainty provided an exemplary metaphor. But what emerged as the sexual ambiguity of Rice's vampires was finally more than just a flouting of generic conventions. Rice told her biographer, "I've always loved the images of androgyny . . . whether it's a beautiful woman in the opera dressed as a man or rock stars changing and shifting. . . . I see the androgynous figure as the ideal figure." That ideal was consonant with the egalitarian aims of 1970s' liberalism: Rice wanted to image "erotic scenes . . . that take place between totally equally franchised human beings."

While perhaps startling to us today, it would have come as no surprise to anyone thinking about bodies in 1975 that Rice modeled the vampire's transformation on one of the most powerful narratives of gender metamorphosis available to 1970s culture: the story of successful dieting. With its promised dissolution of female secondary sex characteristics, the story of successful dieting forcefully projected an androgynous body, one whose challenge to traditional gender roles would lie in its exclusion of their physical signifiers. The intersections of slimness, androgyny, and liberation are encapsulated in the (to many of us) memorable series of ads run by Virginia Slims. Tagged by the copy "You've come a long way, baby," these ads featured a sepia-tinted inset of "our grandmothers" laboring over some archaic domestic task. They were laced into late-Victorian S-shaped corsets, their bosoms and hips enormous, their figures patently maternal. Striding over the inset in full color, by contrast, was the modern Virginia Slims woman. Long-legged, flat, and hipless, the Virginia Slims woman had been unburdened of her woman's body—and, concomitantly, of her domestic chores. For American middle-class women of this period who were leaving behind nearly two decades of post-war domesticity and entering the labor force in unprecedented numbers, such icons articulated their abandonment of women's conventional nurturing and reproductive functions. By the same token, narratives of dieting provided for women authors an apt means of contemplating the socio-sexual alternatives available through corporeal alteration.

Now *Interview with the Vampire* incorporates the liberatory model of radical weight loss, but it does so in a striking and uncharacteristic way. Although the novel contains all the signal features of the diet narrative—its characters are preoccupied throughout with hunger and food and with the manipulation of their bodies—it also contains no significant women characters. Rice's impulse here complements her utopian agenda in a particularly extreme way. In its pursuit of a kind of pure and ultimate androgyny, *Interview with the Vampire* takes the Virginia Slims story to its ultimate conclusion by fantasizing a community of beings from which all signs of female sexuality and its traditional limitations have been erased. And here, curiously, is where the model of revised and liberated personhood begins to break down. If the erasure of the female body is precisely what enables Rice to transform the monster vampire into a free and equal "franchised being," it is also, paradoxically, the gap around which her utopian project undoes itself.

Perhaps nowhere is Rice's dissociation of traditional woman and ideal being more evident than in the fact that her community of vampires is populated by men and children only. Theoretically, Rice's supernatural beings are not meant to be read as either men or children. Although the erotic interactions among the male vampires in this novel led many to praise Rice for her daring presentation of homosexuality, the sexuality of her vampires, in fact, bears little resemblance to the forms of gratification conventionally associated with the interactions of men's bodies. Rather, the vampire's body is something entirely new. It represents a type of polymorphousness and androgyny founded on the disappearance of the markers of sexual and reproductive difference. No matter what his or her residual sexual organs denote, both the vampire's experience of erotic pleasure and its ability to reproduce are located orally, not genitally; sucking blood is the vampire's way of feeding, of gratifying itself, and of making other vampires. This "gender-free" ideal does not of necessity exclude vampires who are residually women, but it is powerfully associated in the novel with an absence of women's characteristics. Not only are all Rice's central vampires residually male, her only significant female vampire, Claudia, is a little girl permanently arrested in her physical development at the age of five.

While Claudia's little-girlishness signals the exclusion of adult female sexuality from the vampire's body, the scene of her creation emphasizes the extent to which that exclusion predicates vampire existence generally. When Louis and Lestat make a vampire out of Claudia, they do so quite literally over her mother's dead body. Discovering the still-human little girl alone in a house and crying over the corpse of her mother, Louis is at first aware of some mysterious maternal power that emanates from the mother and challenges his own claims to Claudia. But this "natural" maternity is soon exposed as the inferior stuff of mortal frailty. In a fit of humor, Lestat grabs the mother's "stinking body" from the bed and dances with her while her decaying head "snaps" back and "black fluid" pours out of her mouth. This violent demystification of maternal power, centered as it is on the mother's body as something dead and obsolete, then opens the conceptual space for the alternative represented by vampire sexuality. Having traduced conventional motherhood, Lestat takes over the mother's role: "I want a child tonight," he tells Louis. "I am like a mother . . . I want a child!" Claudia's birth in turn inaugurates an expansion of socio-sexual options for the vampires, who now play through an almost dizzying variety of roles. Louis is variously Claudia's lover, father, and mother; he is Lestat's wife and son, Armand's gay paramour, Madeleine's father and husband. And their radical diversity is what makes the vampires, as Louis says, all "equal."

That the demystification of traditional maternal power is the founding moment of this equality underlines Rice's reliance on the refusal of female sexuality to legitimate the alternatives her vampires represent. Yet, strangely enough, Rice's exclusion of the feminine body from her descriptions of vampire life and physiology seems to demand a similar, and less explicable, exclusion at the level of representation. Not only does Rice purge her vampire community of all signs of women's sexuality, she avoids representing women characters, even human women characters, in her novel. In part, this strategy operates as a metaphor for the anomaly that women represent in Rice's gender-free economy. Accordingly, when women characters do appear for brief moments—when the women vampires kiss Armand, for instance, and Louis is overcome with jealousy—they function metaphorically as a threat to the seamlessness of the androgyne order. However, more interesting than these metaphoric moments is the fact that Rice apparently *can't* introduce women characters as significant players in the drama without her own representation of androgyny showing signs of dismantling itself. Witness what happens, for example, when at the end of her novel she introduces the provocative and motherly Madeleine. Confronted with having to make Madeleine a vampire, which means enjoying her sexually, the till now thoroughly feminized Louis admits: "Desire her I did, more than she knew. . . . And with a *man's* pride I wanted to prove that to her" (my emphasis). Women characters, in other words, are not absent in this novel just to make a metaphoric point. They present a problem, and to avoid confronting that problem in ways that could compromise the gender-free ideal, Rice simply gets rid of them.

Now what is interesting about this lack of women characters is the way in which it replicates one of the central fantasies of dieting, albeit a fantasy that is not entirely compatible with dieting's projection of an androgynous body. On the one hand, dieting extremists, those with eating disorders like anorexia nervosa, wish for exactly the kind of body that Rice imagines, one that has been purged of the signs of being a woman. As one anorexic puts it, "I have a deep fear of having a womanly body, round and fully developed. I want to be tight and muscular and thin"; another asserts, "I want to stay slender because I look more like a man," while another, fantasiz-

ing a Claudia-like stasis, says: "not wanting to mature as a female body is a child's way of looking at it. I never wanted to grow up." On the other hand, the absence of women characters in *Interview with the Vampire* illustrates how closely bound this revision of the body is to another related desire on the part of compulsive slimmers not just to revise the body but to disown it—to go the route of 1970s icon Karen Carpenter and diet until you disappear. This is a fantasy Rice inadvertently expressed about her own body. Having gained a worrisome amount of weight just before she started writing *Interview with the Vampire*, Rice began to "defend" herself by telling friends "that the extra pounds weren't really her." She would "acknowledge only the parts from the wrist down and the neck up." In other words, if *Interview with the Vampire* locates its revision of gender categories in an equally radical revision of gendered bodies, its lack of women characters also indicates how dependent this model is on a fantasy of "disownership." To assure the success of her radical bodily ideal, Rice premises its representation on the logical extreme of the diet narrative: that the ever-diminishing substance of the female body, far from producing a new kind of body, will simply conclude with the body vanishing.

To ascertain the effect of this disappearance it is useful to compare *Interview with the Vampire* to two novels also published in the mid-1970s but more overtly concerned with women and dieting: Margaret Atwood's *Lady Oracle* (1976) and Judith Krantz's *Scruples* (1978). Both novels recapitulate the narrative we saw in the Virginia Slims ad: the heroine begins the story as an overweight, unhappy individual and through rigorous dieting sheds her unwanted flesh and discovers both personal empowerment and an abrupt proliferation of social options. But the crucial thing in both novels is that no matter how much weight the heroine loses her body never stops being a problem— either for the heroine, who must now contend with the bewildering pressures of being an object of male desire, or in the text itself as a problematic site of competing cultural values. Atwood's heroine Joan Foster may, like Rice, wish to end her dilemmas by turning "invisible," and may indeed stage a series of "disappearances" by faking her own death, but that wish remains a fantasy; her woman's body, no matter how thin, remains a bulk to be reconciled with the ideal of its own disappearance. Indeed, Joan's and Krantz's heroine Billy's changing yet ever-present flesh forces an ongoing reevaluation in both texts of the female body's relationship as a material entity to the material conditions of its subordination.

In *Interview with the Vampire,* however, this is not the case. The disownership of a problematic womanhood may enable Rice to posit the purity of her androgynous vampires, but Rice's paradigm of disownership, while it fantasizes the absence of the feminine body, does not at the same time incorporate the logical terms for a dismantling of the feminine as a frame of gender reference. What *Interview with the Vampire* accentuates, rather, is that in the economy formulated by dieting the idea of the womanly body remains untouched in the imagination of the dieter where it resides as the symbolic focus of hunger. As such, its power is felt in a degree proportional to its negation. That is, the less you eat and the more thin and immaterial you become, the hungrier you get and the more you long for the state of feminine fullness and bodily plenitude that eating represents. Thus, while Rice effects the disappearance of women's bodies, according to the logic made legible in her text the hypothetical point at which the feminine body disappears completely is also, paradoxically, the point at which it reaches the height of its power and desirability over the hungering self—or in this case, over the hungering text.

One of the first things we notice about *Interview with the Vampire* is that, while the feminine body is effectively purged from the narrative, it is nevertheless systematically reinscribed in other areas of the text where it functions as a kind of disembodied counterpoint to its own erasure. So on the one hand we have the dead body of Claudia's mother, reviled, horrifying, a thing to be discarded and left behind, while on the other we have the eulogy to abstract motherhood that accompanies Louis's rebirth: he wanders through the forest enamored of his new condition, hearing the night "as if it were a chorus of whispering women, all beckoning me to their breasts." During this same scene, while taking blood from Lestat, Louis rediscovers "for the first time since infancy the special pleasure of sucking nourishment." Such metaphors not only re-present an erased maternal body through a complex of disembodied symbols, they also, through their conventional equation of the mother's body and food, obliquely identify femininity itself as an object of hunger, as a thing that fulfils.

The synonymy of female bodies and food suggested here is even more pointedly manifested in the several spectacular scenes in this novel in which women literally form the meals on which the vampires feast. Memorable among these is Louis's visit to the Théâtre des Vampires where the vampire Armand, before an audience of rapt humans, feeds on a young woman of "heartbreaking beauty." Rice's description here highlights the special allure, the promise of the body being consumed: "And slowly he [Armand] drew the string from the loose gathers of her blouse. I could see the cloth falling, see the pale, flawless skin pulsing with her heart and the tiny nipples letting the cloth slip precariously, the vampire holding her right wrist tightly. . . . And now, turning her slowly to the side so that they [the audience] could all see her serene face, he was lifting her, her back arching as her naked breasts touched his buttons, her pale arms enfolded his neck. She stiffened, cried out as he sank his teeth . . . the nape of her neck as enticing as the small buttocks or the flawless skin of her long thighs." The erotic quality of this description modulates into an equally charged presentation of the girl as an object of gastronomic desire. Watching the performance, Louis says, "I felt weak, dazed, hunger rising in me, knotting my heart, my veins. . . . The air seemed fragrant with her salted skin, and close and hot and sweet. . . . I was sitting back in my chair, my mouth full of the taste of her, my

veins in torment." Unlike the scene with Claudia's dead mother, there is no attempt here to demystify the allure of the feminine body. On the contrary, when the show is over and the lights come up, Louis still "tastes" the girl on his lips. "It was as though on the smell of the rain came her perfume still, and in the empty theater I could hear the throb of her beating heart." It is worth noting that the power of the girl resides in the fact that she doesn't last, that she is immediately dissolved into the amorphous rain and converted into the "emptiness" of the theater. Beginning as an unreachable, distant object of a hunger that Louis, sitting in the audience, is unable to satisfy, the girl's body exerts an attraction proportional to its unavailability, an attraction that reaches its crescendo at the moment the girl disappears as a physical entity.

The relevance of this scene to Rice's gender polemic, moreover, lies not only in its reinscription of the feminine as an object of desire but in its simultaneous staging of conventional heterosexual concourse—the "seduction" of the girl by Armand—a concourse the text is subsequently unable to challenge precisely because one of its terms, the feminine, has already been established as *not there*. Although this is surely one of the most striking scenes in the novel, it intrudes not at all on any of the events that follow. In the next scene the androgyne order is reestablished, the erotic concourse reasserted as an energy among residual males only. Yet the more conventional sexual possibilities implied in the scene with the girl, identified as they are with hunger, linger as something unsatisfied.

To the extent that Rice's vampires are the subjects on whose bodies is written the novel's excision of womanhood, they tend to behave in the same way that the text behaves, incorporating its agendas and, particularly in Louis's case, replicating its contradictions. Much like the text itself, Louis is preoccupied with the purity and freedom available to the body that refuses food. Ostensibly, Louis's refusal to eat is framed as a metaphysical and moral issue. Because for vampires eating involves killing people, Louis, who cannot discard his human moral sensibilities, who associates killing with damnation, is engaged in a constant struggle to keep his soul and his body morally pure. But that this desire for purity mirrors Rice's similar attempts to purify the gendered body is made evident by the fact that Louis's refusal of food is not simply described as a reluctance to commit murder. It resembles a constant vigil to keep from gaining weight. Subsisting for the most part on a diet of small animals— the vampiric counterpart, one supposes, of celery sticks and Rykrisp crackers—Louis describes over and over again how he is "Torn apart by the wish to take no action—to starve, to wither in thought on the one hand" or to give in to his "craving," his "vile insupportable hunger" on the other. When Louis does break down and indulge his craving, he describes it as a "sin," an illicit gorging, like eating a whole chocolate cake. Coming upon Claudia when she is still a human child and he is in one of his fits of self-starvation, he says: "You must understand that by now I was burning with physical need to drink. I could not have made it through another day without feeding. But there were alternatives: rats abounded in the streets, and somewhere very near a dog was howling hopelessly. . . . But the question pounded in me: Am I damned? . . . If I am damned I must want to kill her, I must want to make her nothing but food for a cursed existence. . . . [A]nd I felt, yes, damned and this is hell, and in that instant I had bent down and driven hard into her soft, small neck. . . . For four years I had not savored a human; for four years I hadn't really known . . . the rich blood rushing too fast for me, the room reeling."

If Louis is the anorexic produced in this novel's extremist association of freedom and physical attenuation, his problems with eating also reflect back on the apparatus that determines him. What is significant about the passage I just quoted is not Louis's understandable reluctance to commit murder but his attraction to the object of his self-denial, his choice of Claudia above the dog and the rats not because he needs humans to survive but because Claudia in his perception is more delicious; she exerts a power over him. The source of this power lies not in Claudia herself but in Louis's idea of his own body. Because Louis's sense of integrity is bound up with his control over the needs of his body, with his affirmation of finer spirit over base substance, his power over himself increases in proportion not only to his hunger but to the allure of the food that he keeps refusing. The greater his temptation, that is, the more pious and empowering his self-denial. Such syllogisms invest food with a power that paradoxically intensifies as Louis's control of his own body grows, for, of course, that control is always predicated on a fairly equal contest between the power of food and the power of self. Given that Rice's idea of the androgyne's freedom is founded on a similar notion of conquest and manipulation, it contains the same kind of paradox. In other words, it isn't that the text represses the feminine body at the level of narrative only to have it inadvertently reinscribed elsewhere, but that its model of androgyny depends on that reinscription. It depends on the desirability in abstract form of the body through whose recurring conquest the dieting self acquires power and viability.

It is perhaps no surprise that this repetitive conquest, by which one's power over body or soul diminishes as it increases, should finally end in the self's dissolution. This is the fate of Rice's androgynes, all of whom by the end of the novel are engaged in acts of self-destruction. Claudia, on whose body is most radically written the absence of femininity, spends the novel affirming her freedom by searching for the mother she lost and the mature maternal body from which she has been barred. Like Louis's pursuit of self-determination, Claudia's is articulated as hunger, her desire for the plenitude that both sustains and relentlessly undermines her identity: "I kill humans every night. I seduce them, draw them close to me, with an insatiable hunger, a constant, never-ending search for something . . . something, I don't know what it is." That this desire for satiation is paradoxically both the fulfillment and the end of her freedom is underlined by the fact that as soon

as Claudia gets the mother she wants in the form of Madeleine, she dies. Her death literalizes the identities among satiation, womanhood, and vacancy. In a grisly echo of the paradigm of the vanishing woman's body, nothing is left of Claudia when Louis finds her but her hair and her empty clothes. The journeys of Louis, Lestat, and Armand, similarly self-destructive, are also similarly determined by the logic of attenuation. At the novel's end, the gormandizing Lestat, deprived of food for his soul, ends his existence by starving himself on a diet of alley-cats. Armand, who tells Louis that when an old vampire "goes out to die" he will leave nothing of his body—"He will vanish"—finally performs this trick on himself and disappears. Although knowing that eating "threaten[s] consciousness," Louis eventually succumbs to his craving for humans. But within the logic that equates plenitude with vacancy, the result of Louis's eating is not that he gets fuller but that the more he eats the emptier he feels until at last he thinks of himself as "nothing."

By the end of *Interview with the Vampire,* the absence that was supposed to guarantee the success of Rice's radical gender alternative has assured its dissolution. With their androgyny in the first place anchored in their hunger for a lost womanhood, the vampires can only achieve their ideal status through an ongoing process of self-sabotage, becoming more radical only as their hunger for traditionalism intensifies. And yet for all that this novel's utopian agenda folds in on itself and finally collapses, it would be inaccurate to ascribe to its politics of hunger an inherent or inevitable conservatism. When Rice, almost ten years after she published *Interview with the Vampire,* returned to the topic of vampirism in a series of novels she called *The Vampire Chronicles,* she abandoned hunger as a central component of vampire life. These later novels feature the same characters we met in *Interview,* but they purport to tell a "truer" version of their story, one in which appetite, significantly, plays no part. For this purpose, Rice invents a new feature of vampire physiology: when vampires become ancient enough—as her protagonists quickly do—they no longer need nourishment to survive. Thus unburdened of their problematic desire for food, Louis, Lestat, and Armand return from nothingness to take their place in a bucolic "Great Family" of vampires, a circle of gender renegades whose members live their lives with precisely that grace and success that had eluded the vampires in *Interview.*

There is much to suggest, however, that ridding the vampire of his desire and self-deprivation is at the heart of his eventual domestication. In their continued pursuit of utopian alternatives, Rice's later novels do away with the equation of hunger and emancipation that had proved so debilitating in her first; but, as Janice Doane and Devon Hodges point out, Rice's later novels are also considerably more tentative in their critique of accepted norms: "In *Interview with the Vampire* . . . a decidedly angry woman [Claudia] does battle with men in her hopes to rewrite the script for femininity. She fails, though the precariousness of male bonds at the end of the novel suggests that patriarchy has been nonetheless weakened." By the time we get to *Queen of the Damned,* the angry little girl has given way to the primal, "post-feminist" "good mother," a figure who fights her battles not with patriarchy but with the man-hating Akasha, a woman turned "feminist monster." In some sense, the differences between *Queen of the Damned* and *Interview* are a product of the time that separates them, a decade of "backlashing," "postfeminism," New Right agitation, and the rise of New Age women's cults. But it remains significant that the victory of the "good mother" in *Queen of the Damned* is secured through the recasting of women's relationship to food. Unlike the eternally tiny and voracious Claudia, the "good mother" Mekare is a figure in whom hunger and skinniness have given way to appeasement and expansion. In their roles as matriarchs, nurturers, primal origins, Mekare and her twin sister Maharet could well be the vanishing mother from *Interview* restored to her material embodiment. The manner of her triumph is instructive. Mekare succeeds against the rabidly feminist Akasha by cannibalizing her, by literally gobbling up her heart and brain in order to appropriate her considerable powers. Whereas the absent mother in *Interview* left "precariousness" in her wake, the fully present "good mother" in *Queen of the Damned,* who consumes without guilt, is the means by which dissent is incorporated into a unitary anatomy.

Rice's manipulation of appetite illuminates the trajectory of the vampire from tortured anorexic to guiltless consumer; but it also clarifies the complexity of the relationship between dieting and women's liberation in 1970s culture. On one level, that relationship is clearly recuperative. The massive entry of middle-class women into the North American labor force between 1970 and 1980 required a female body whose iconography would specify its productivity in the workplace rather than its traditional reproductivity and nurturance in the home. But as the yearnings of Rice's vampires suggest, it was precisely by dissolving the material signifiers of women's domesticity that dieting withdrew an economically obsolete femininity from the "real" world of material relations in order to constitute it elsewhere as an object of fantasy. Organizing hunger around an untenable and disappearing womanhood, dieting effectively assured the continued centrality of traditional femininity psychically in an economy that had ceased to have need of it materially. It is this process of internalization that *Interview with the Vampire* inadvertently uncovers. Within the logic manifested in Rice's text, the starving away of archaic women's flesh results only in the displacement of traditional gender norms from their depiction on the body to their invisible operation on desire.

On another level, however, *Interview with the Vampire* also suggests how the displacement of femininity, even as it sabotages the meaningful realization of alternative gender standards, might simultaneously generate the conditions for a heightened political awareness. The key to this possibility is to be found in the richer, more fully individuated and fully aware self acquired by Louis as he fetishizes and refuses food. If traditional womanly plenitude is symbolically contained in the food the dieter desires, Louis's situation indicates that the very act of staying hungry, the choice of keeping gratification at bay, consolidates the self around acts of resistance, producing an expansion of consciousness that is proportional to the diminishment of the body. The stakes in this game of resistance are high. "Today," *Vogue* informed its readers in 1976, "many women are wondering if it is possible to be fully human and still remain feminine." For Rice the answer is no. The process of self-enrichment through starvation may finally annihilate both Claudia and Louis, but it also anchors their status as "equally franchised beings." As a direct result of their hunger, that is, both Louis and Claudia experience a dilation of consciousness that makes them, in the idiom of 1970s feminism, more "fully human"—and thus more fully deserving of their "human rights."

In Louis's case, his physical transformation from human being to vampire overtly marks the start of what the novel repeatedly refers to as his development of a richer "humanity." "My vampire nature has been for me the greatest adventure of my life," he tells Lestat. "[A]ll that went before was confused, clouded; I went through mortal life like a blind man groping from solid object to solid object. It was only when I became a vampire that I respected for the first time all of life. I never saw a living pulsing human being until I was a vampire; I never knew what life was until it ran out in a red gush over my lips, my hands!" The continual war that Louis wages with the needs of his body in order to preserve life, precisely because it affirms the power of spirit over substance and respect over abuse, enhances his "soul," producing his exquisite moral sensibilities, his "passion," his "sense of justice." From the "vicious egotism" of his former self, Louis expands through self-denial to represent, despite his vampirism, what is best about "humanity." The other vampires, Armand tells him, "reflect the age in cynicism. . . . You reflect your age differently. You reflect its broken heart." Louis's expansion, constituted as it is through his refusal of normative categories, produces not just a richer humanity but a political awareness of the inequity of his circumstances. It is while trying to convince Lestat, the "Father," of the value of self-starvation that Louis understands the true nature of their relationship: "I realized I'd been his slave all along."

For Claudia, whose tiny body signifies her more fundamental resistance to womanly plenitude, the result of her famine is a kind of tragic over-development of the inner self. As Claudia gets hungrier and hungrier without ever getting physically "full," her soul keeps expanding until her minuscule shape harbors an "eerie and powerful seductress" and a mature "woman's" mind too ambitious for its girlish confines. "To give me immortality in this hopeless guise," she cries to Louis, "this helpless form!" Louis thinks of her as empty: cold, detached, devoid of the "humanity" he so cherishes in himself. But he discovers that her diminutive shape has filled her to the brim with "rage" and "pain" and "suffering," the very elements that constitute Louis's own claims to humanity. As with Louis, the expansion of Claudia's self generates a radicalized consciousness—a more radicalized consciousness, since her hunger for plenitude is greater. In the process of her "growth," Claudia acquires an awareness of her own potential and integrity that culminates in the recognition that she has been "enslaved" by her "fathers." As Louis tells Lestat, she "sees herself as equal to us now, and us as equal to each other." Her decision to murder Lestat, which Doane and Hodges call "a protest against the kind of femininity offered to women in a patriarchal culture," is also a radical decision to demand the father's power for herself: "Such blood, such power. Do you think I'll possess his power and my own power when I take him?"

Of course, the idea that dieting might generate the conditions for political awareness is radically at odds with what the vast majority of feminist scholars and researchers have concluded. For them dieting is inimical to feminist agendas because, by forcing women to concentrate so completely on their bodies, it diverts them from the more politically constructive cultivation of their minds. Susan Bordo says of anorexia: "Paradoxically—and often tragically—these pathologies of female 'protest' . . . actually function as if in collusion with the cultural conditions that produced them. . . . Women may feel themselves deeply attracted by the aura of freedom and independence suggested by the boyish body ideal of today. Yet, each hour, each minute that is spent in anxious pursuit of that ideal . . . is *in fact* time and energy diverted from inner development and social achievement. As a feminist protest, the obsession with slenderness is hopelessly counterproductive." Similarly, Kim Chernin equates the starvation of women's bodies with the starvation of their "souls" and recommends as "food" for these souls a "reentry into the positive knowledge of women's experience," "our capacity to think, to act, to struggle, to cry out, to express."

Worth noting, however, is that various discourses of dieting concur with Rice in emphasizing an expansion of the "soul" as a crucial consequence of slimming. Anorexics almost unanimously report on the increased feelings of independence, confidence, self-worth, pride, and power that accompany their compulsive weight-watching. Many equate their shrinkage with individuation. Hilda Bruch recalls one patient who "explained that losing weight was giving her power, that each pound lost was like a treasure that added to her power. This accumulation of power was giving her another kind of 'weight,' the right to be recognized as an individual." The theme of individuation, which features so centrally in the language of anorexia, appears with equal force in 1970s diet advice, which invariably insists on the power, independence, and self-esteem available to those who discipline their bodies. In a 1976 article explaining the function of metabolism, *Cosmopolitan* advised its readers: "Now consider again the girl who blames metabolism for her inability to lose weight. The truth is she probably wasn't *born* with a sluggish metabolism, but rather cultivated a lazy one. Consider all

she can do to pep up her metabolism so calories are pressed into *service* rather than just turning into fat! Sweet to know *you're* the one in control, isn't it?"

For Judith Krantz, as for Rice, the result of such exercises of self-control is the self's consolidation. When her heroine Billy's new svelte figure gives her the confidence to speak aloud in French, her spirit expands: "It opened all the doors of Billy's mind, destroyed all her hesitations, vanquished her timidity." As for Atwood's heroine Joan Foster, who after years of being overweight has trouble learning to *think* like a thin person, Billy's former "Freakish" self stays with her, leaving her with "scars that no amount of outward physical change could ever erase." But her resistance to this ghost, played out in her constant hunger, at once expands her soul and, by extension, sustains her rejection of traditional feminine roles. Following the abysmal end of her first love affair, Billy realizes, "She was thin and she was beautiful. . . . Those were the important things. The rest she would have to get for herself. She had no intention of dying for love of a man, like one of the nineteenth-century women in the books she had read. She was no Emma Bovary, no Anna Karenina, no Camille—no spineless, adoring, passive creature who would let a man take away her reason for living by taking away his love. The next time she loved, she promised herself, it would be on her terms."

Claudia's evaporation, Louis's nothingness, Billy's hedgings and compromises, and the anorexic's hospitalization are less than salutary ends to their ecstatic burgeoning of selfhood. But in these individual manifestations of consciousness expansion and "raising" we can see how women's diet fads might have encouraged the emancipatory energies they also curtailed. The paradox of this process is illuminated by Michel Foucault's description of a not-dissimilar congruence of self-discipline and humanistic self-enrichment that occurred in the evolution of the "soul" of modern prisoners. In *Discipline and Punish* Foucault addresses the historical moment at which the state's punitive strategies shift focus from the prisoner's body, which had earlier been the object of public spectacles of torture and execution, to his inner conscience, "a punishment that acts in depth on the heart, the thoughts, the will, the inclinations." As Foucault sees it, this shift of focus does not address a consciousness that already exists. Rather, the new "technology of power over the body," the forms of supervision, training, and moral correction that replace corporal punishment, themselves produce a "soul," a "psyche, subjectivity, personality, consciousness," on which reformed punitive methods can act. We could say, in effect, that the development of more "humane" and "liberal" forms of punishment produces a more "human" subject, one whose newly constituted "soul" is capable of fulfilling liberalist ideals of justice and reform.

While it would be misleading to map Foucault's explication wholesale onto the synchrony of diet fads and women's liberation, his insights are instructive. As a significant change in the political technology of women's bodies, dieting helped to generate the spirit of a modernized woman-hood—savvy, political, sexually emancipated, and newly formed for what Stuart Ewen calls a migration into "the social structures of industrial discipline." Although women's thinness had come into fashion in the 1960s, it is in the 1970s, the decade whose midpoint is marked by the International Year of the Woman, that weight-watching acquires the proportions of an obsession and the rigors of a "technology." According to Roberta Pollack Seid, "Between 1968 and 1969, twenty-five diet articles were listed in the *Reader's Guide.* By 1978-79, the number had leapt to eighty-eight—a deceptively low figure, since the *Guide* did not include the diet columns that were now regular magazine features nor the myriad diets that routinely appeared in more popular publications." Hillel Schwartz reports that Weight Watchers' revenues jumped from $8 million in 1970 to $39 million in 1977. This flowering of interest in slimming was accompanied by a growing rationalization of the methods by which pounds were to be shed. Calorie counters, fat farms, clinics, injections, surgery, jaw-wiring, stomach-stapling, regimens of jogging, programs of fasting, hundreds of books offering the wisdom of doctors and psychologists (like Atkins, Tarnower, and Cott), now augmented the relatively simple appetite suppressants popular in the 1960s.

That this immense apparatus reorganized women's bodies for the paths of emancipation is made apparent by the change in the prevailing ideals identified with women's thinness. In the 1960s women's thinness was associated with little-girlishness. Waifs and adolescents, bodied forth by models like Twiggy and the young Jean Shrimpton, or the "daddy's girl" who could never quite manage anything on her own, played by Marlo Thomas in the TV series *That Girl,* were the hallmarks of feminine style. In the 1970s, by contrast, women's thinness began to be associated with women's ambition, strength, and self-control. The heroine of the decade was the slim, independent, emphatically single Mary Richards on *The Mary Tyler Moore Show,* who, unlike Marlo, didn't need daddy's help; she was going to "make it on her own." Whereas 1960s fashions in women's dress sought to recapture infancy—baby-doll dresses, Mary Jane shoes—1970s fashions aimed at a rangy mannishness, with designers producing pinstriped suits, man-tailored shirts, hacking jackets, and stacked-heel loafers as part of the new working woman's "uniform."

Like the punitive reforms of the early nineteenth century, the rigors of dieting at once re-located women's bodies ideologically and addressed a consciousness they themselves helped to construct. It is concomitantly not without reason that Foucault shares with Rice, Chernin, and Krantz an emphasis on the term "soul." Discussing this same propensity in anorexics, who obsess about the expansion and purity of their spirits, Susan Bordo characterizes the "metaphysics" of dieting as an extension and "crystallization" of Western culture's privileging of spirit over flesh. But Rice, whose characters search for the "soul"'s grace,

or Chernin (a former anorexic) who speaks of the "soul"'s nourishment, might agree with Foucault that the mind/body split encouraged by dieting is more than merely symptomatic of a long-entrenched preference for the ephemeral. Its generation of a psyche is real. As Foucault says of the prisoner, "A 'soul' inhabits him and brings him into existence"; "It would be wrong to say that the soul is an illusion, or an ideological effect. On the contrary, it exists, it has a reality." When modern women collectively converted to what Krantz calls the "religion of thinness," they perforce found at its altars the constituents of their own empowerment as politicized subjects.

But the "soul" doubtless gets ample space in the discourses of dieting not just because it blooms as the flesh disintegrates, but because it is an area of contending energies. Where the traces of dieting as a political technology—a strategy by which power is negotiated and exercised—reveal themselves is in the armature that originates and supports the "soul" of liberated womanhood—the soul's dependence, that is, on an ongoing, and therefore unwinnable, battle with the ghosts of mothering and domesticity. The insight of novels like *Lady Oracle* and *Scruples* lies in their sensitivity to the negotiations this battle requires. Although Atwood and Krantz pay tribute to slenderness as the key to personal development, they also realize that the heroine's selfhood hinges on her simultaneous acceptance of and resistance to traditional roles. Thus Billy's choice of marriage weirdly provokes a fresh bout of independence—"if she wanted to stay married to Vito . . . she had to establish an abiding interest in life that did not depend on him in any way." The end of Atwood's novel finds Joan trapped in a maze and locked in permanent solidarity and contention with all her old "tenuous bodies," the see-through women on whom her liberation depends: the Fat Lady, the Mother, the demure Good Girl, her enemies, her cohorts.

For Rice, of course, the conflicted terrain of the self is figured—indeed, allegorized—as the zone of war between good and evil, salvation and damnation, between compromised survival and all-out annihilation. It is a testimony to the extremity of her project in *Interview with the Vampire* that she dismisses the negotiations that characterize Billy's and Joan's development and forces a victory in the battle between emancipated self-hood and its vaporous domestic Other. The results may not be inspiring. Whether in Claudia's case, where, like a little balloon inflated with too much selfhood, she just explodes, or in Louis's where the allure of plenitude wins over resistance, "nothingness" is equally the victor. With their subjectivity constituted by the conflict itself, Rice's vampires obliterate themselves at the instant they either win or lose. The delicacy of this equilibrium is illustrated by the aftermath of its upset. If Rice's later novels abandon the radical extremes of her first, they also suggest how closely the domestication of her vampires was tied to a larger defeat. Like the dieting iconoclasts of the 1970s who were reedified for 1980s consumerism and corporate culture, the vampire succumbed to the recuperative energies that were all along inherent in the strategies of abstinence.

And yet despite the pitfalls, the fits of hunger and longing that are too easily conscripted for mandates of self-indulgence, *Interview with the Vampire* insists on the wisdom of self-abnegation. In the end Louis gives up on "humanity" and starts eating his fill. His parting words to the journalist who is interviewing him speak eloquently of the choice he has made: "I drank of the beauty of the world as a vampire drinks. I was satisfied. I was filled to the brim. But I was dead." Rice would go on in her other novels to rewrite this death as a necessary fact of vampire life, but her first novel acknowledges the bitter pressure exerted by plenitude on the self that will only find sustenance through resistance and loss.

FURTHER READING

Criticism

Conway, Anne-Marie Conway. Review of *The Tale of the Body Thief,* by Anne Rice. *Times Literary Supplement* (11 December 1992): 20.

A favorable review of *The Tale of the Body Thief.*

Kendrick, Walter. "Better Undead Than Unread: Have Vampires Lost Their Bite?" *New York Times Book Review* (18 October 1992): 55.

Offers a summary of the "The Vampire Chronicles" and comments on Rice's significance as a leading author of contemporary vampire fiction.

Korn, Eric. "The Devil's Own Job." *Times Literary Supplement* (17 November 1995): 8.

A review of *Memnoch the Devil.*

Leithauser, Brad. "Fear of Horror." *New York* (24 July 1995): 44-5.

Discusses the supernatural fiction of Rice and Stephen King, with a brief review of *Memnoch the Devil.*

Morrison, Patt. "All Souls." *Los Angeles Times Book Review* (31 October 1993): 3, 12.

A favorable review of *Lasher.*

Alain Robbe-Grillet
1922-

French novelist, screenplay writer, short story writer, essayist, and autobiographer.

The following entry presents an overview of Robbe-Grillet's career through 1996. For further information on his life and works, see *CLC*, Volumes 1, 2, 4, 6, 8, 10, 14, and 43.

INTRODUCTION

A provocative literary experimenter, theoretician, and filmmaker, Alain Robbe-Grillet is one of the most influential and vigorously disputed French literary figures of the postwar period. As a leading proponent of the *nouveau roman,* or New Novel, during the 1950s and 1960s, Robbe-Grillet was instrumental in the formulation of avant-garde literary techniques that challenged basic assumptions about the possibility of truth, the function of literature, and the integrity of plot, character, and chronology in the conventional novel. Drawing attention to the indefinite, disconcerting quality of human experience and imagination, Robbe-Grillet's trademark fiction features the use of ambiguous narrators, surreal temporal dislocations and juxtapositions, sadoerotic imagery, and *chosisme,* a literary style involving meticulous description of external objects and activities. His groundbreaking novels *Le Voyeur* (1955; *The Voyeur*), *La Jalousie* (1957; *Jealousy*), and *Dans le labyrinthe* (1959; *In the Labyrinth*) became important models for subsequent antinovels and foreshadowed the literary theories of postmodernism.

BIOGRAPHICAL INFORMATION

Born in Brest, France, Robbe-Grillet was raised in the coastal region of Brittany by his eccentric mother and father, an engineer and former soldier; both parents were atheists with extreme right-wing sympathies. As a young reader Robbe-Grillet was captivated by Lewis Carroll's Alice stories and the exotic settings of Rudyard Kipling's novels. After receiving a secondary education at lycées in Paris and Brest, he won admittance to the Institut National d'Agronomie in 1942. However, his studies were interrupted by the Second World War, during which, under the terms of the Nazi Occupation of France, he was forced into compulsory labor service in Nuremberg, Germany, where he worked as a lathe operator in a Nazi tank factory from 1943 to 1944. Eventually graduating in 1945, Robbe-Grillet found employment at the National Institute for Statistics in Paris. He visited Bulgaria in 1948 to help

rebuild railways as a volunteer member of the International Reconstruction Brigade. From 1948 to 1951 he worked as an agronomist for the Institute des Fruits et Agrumes Coloniaux, a position that included posts in Morocco, Guinea, Guadelope, and Martinique. He completed a first novel, *Un Régicide,* in 1948, but it was rejected by publishers and remained in manuscript until 1978. In 1951 Robbe-Grillet abandoned his scientific career to devote himself to full-time writing. His first published novel, *Les Gommes* (1953; *The Erasers*), received the Fénéon prize in 1954. He also contributed essays on literature to the newspaper *L'Express* and literary journal *Critique.* Many of these articles were reprinted in *Pour un nouveau roman* (1963; *For a New Novel*) along with his polemical writings on the New Novel. With the 1955 publication of *The Voyeur,* Robbe-Grillet received the Prix des Critiques award and became the center of critical controversy. Robbe-Grillet fortified his reputation as the leading representative of the New Novel movement with *Jealousy* in 1957 and *In the Labyrinth* in 1959. In 1955 he was employed as literary director at Editions de Minuit, the publisher of his books as well as those of Samuel Beckett and other New Novelists, including Claude Simon, Nathalie Sarraute, and Michel Butor. Robbe-Grillet married Catherine Rstakian in 1957.

During the 1960s, he produced a volume of short fiction, *Instantanés* (1962; *Snapshots*), and the novel *La Maison de rendez-vous* (1965; *The House of Assignation*). He also turned to filmmaking with screenplays for *L'Anneé dernière à Marienbad* (1961; *Last Year at Marienbad*), directed by Alain Resnais, *L'Immortelle* (1963; *The Immortal One*), *Trans-Europ-Express* (1967), and *L'Homme qui ment* (1968). With the exception of the first, Robbe-Grillet wrote and directed all of his films; several won awards at European film festivals. Over the next two decades Robbe-Grillet continued to alternate between cinema and fiction, producing films such as *L'Eden et aprés* (1970) and *Glissements progressifs du plaisir* (1973) and the novels *Projet pour une révolution à New York* (1970; *Project for a Revolution in New York*), *Topologie d'une cité fantôme* (1976; *Topology of a Phantom City*), and *Souvenirs du triangle d'or* (1984; *Recollections of the Golden Triangle*). The novel *Djinn* (1981) was written as a textbook for intermediate French language students. He also published three volumes of unconventional autobiography—*Le Miroir qui revient* (1984; *Ghosts in the Mirror*), *Angélique ou L'Enchantement* (1988), and *Les Derniers Jours de Corinthe* (1994). A guest lecturer at conferences throughout the world, Robbe-Grillet has also taught literature and film as a visiting professor at New York University and Washington University in St. Louis.

MAJOR WORKS

Robbe-Grillet's fiction is guided by the theoretical principles of the New Novel, a literary mode characterized by the deconstruction of narrative authority, metafictional techniques, and *chosisme*. In *For a New Novel*, Robbe-Grillet delineates his project to purify the novel of verisimilitude, tragedy, and the pathetic fallacy, the practice of attributing human emotions to the natural world, through the creation of objective, nonrepresentational texts that depict man's neutral relationship to the universe. Reacting against the philosophical outlooks of nineteenth-century realism and postwar existentialism, Robbe-Grillet asserts, "the world is neither meaningful nor absurd. It quite simply *is*." *The Erasers* introduces many of the narrative devices found in his fiction, particularly the use of flashbacks, time lapses, and the obsessive repetition of events and observations. Drawing upon tropes and stereotypes of the detective thriller, a recurring aspect of Robbe-Grillet's work, the novel revolves around a perplexing murder investigation headed by special agent Wallas. No body is found at the crime scene and, as the reader soon learns, the reported victim, Daniel Dupont, has actually survived his attacker and is in hiding. Clues in the narrative begin to suggest that real Wallas is Dupont's murderer, a paradoxical suspicion that becomes when Wallas fatally shoots a man he assumes to be Dupont's returning assailant, but is Dupont himself. Resembling the structure of a Greek tragedy, the novel includes underlying allusions to the Oedipus myth, as the slain Dupont may also be Wallas's father. *The Voyeur* similarly involves a violent death and gradual unfolding of clues that reveal the identity of the perpetrator. The story's protagonist is Mathias, an itinerant watch salesman who arrives by ferry to an island community to make his rounds. While unsuccessfully peddling his wares to the local inhabitants, Mathias learns that a young girl, Jacqueline Leduc, has disappeared. When her body washes ashore, it is assumed that she has simply slipped and fallen into the ocean. However, as Mathias compulsively calculates the time expended on his sales route, he is unable to account for a lost hour. This computational anomaly and a panic-stricken sense of guilty lead Mathias to suspect that he has raped, tortured, and murdered Jacqueline himself and pushed her into the sea. The only possible witness, a young man named Julien Marek, does not implicate him and Mathias leaves the island with impunity. The voyeur of the title is ultimately uncertain, as either Mathias or Julien may have killed Jacqueline while the other watched. Along with themes of repressed memory and aberrant sexuality, the novel is permeated by the imagery of figure eights, represented by the double loops of rope, a pair of watching eyes, and Mathias's circuitous route on the island.

Jealousy, set on a banana plantation in the tropics, involves an untrusting husband who spies on his wife, referred to as A, in an effort to confirm his suspicion that she is having an affair with a neighboring man, Franck. The French word "jalousie" means both jealousy and slatted shutters, a double reference that alludes to the blinds through which the husband peers. Though the unnamed narrator's surreptitious observation of A. and her interactions with Franck reveal nothing conclusive, his preoccupation with her imaginary infidelity suggests a voyeuristic indulgence. The husband's detached description of events and objects, including the image of a crushed centipede—a symbol of his jealousy—underscores his emotional alienation and maddening inability to ascertain truth. *In the Labyrinth* involves a lost soldier who wanders the desolate streets of a wartime city in search of a man to whom he has agreed to deliver the personal effects of a fallen comrade. As the enemy army advances on the city, the soldier is wounded and eventually dies in an apartment occupied by a young woman and her small son. An attempt by Robbe-Grillet to produce a self-generating text based on neutral "signs" or "triggers," the novel functions primarily around description of key objects in the room, including a bayonet, the undelivered box, and an engraved picture of a military debacle entitled "The Defeat of Reichenfels."

Robbe-Grillet's subsequent experiments with the novel, which he has distinguished as *nouveau, nouveau roman*, draw increasingly upon themes of sexual fantasy and sadomasochism, blurring distinctions between art and pornography. *The House of Assignation*, set in Hong Kong, features sexual obsession and criminal dealings in a Chinese brothel, and *Project for a Revolution in New York*, only nominally a story of political intrigue, exploits pornographic motifs and the imagery of sexual violence. Likewise, *Topology of a Phantom City* and *Recollections of a Golden Triangle* portray apocalyptic future worlds in which sexual transgression and perversity is ubiquitous. His three autobiographical works—*Ghosts in the Mirror, Angélique ou L'Enchantement,* and *Les Derniers Jour de Corinthe*—represent an attempt to develop a new form of personal memoir, dubbed "new autobiography," based on the free interplay of biographical fact, memory, and imagination.

CRITICAL RECEPTION

Widely acclaimed as an iconoclastic literary innovator, Robbe-Grillet is considered among the most important French novelists of the 1950s and 1960s. His first four novels—*The Erasers, The Voyeur, Jealousy,* and *In the Labyrinth*—established him as one of the most original writers of his generation and remain his best known works. *The Voyeur* and *Jealousy* are still considered his most accomplished ventures in the New Novel form that he pioneered. Though many reviewers initially rejected his novels as incomprehensible and esoteric, important early critics such as Roland Barthes praised Robbe-Grillet and legitimized his theoretical principles. Critics often note similarities between Robbe-Grillet's work and that of Franz Kafka, Beckett, Albert Camus, and Jean-Paul Sartre, as well as Robbe-Grillet's intellectual debts to surrealism and phenomenology. While critics continue to appreciate his challenging textual puzzles and compelling treatment of human perception and the relativity of truth and individual experience, some note that his conceptual approach to art embodies its own limitations. In particular, his attempt to strip language and fiction of metaphor, allegory, and psychological associations is considered an ambitious though ultimately impossible and self-defeating task. As evidence, critics cite elements of humanism, existential anxiety, and symbolism in his work, all of which contradict his claims to pure objectivity or dispassionate description of the human condition. Ben Stoltzfus writes: "As a creator of fictions, he is asking his readers to believe in them, yet at the same time he negates the right to believe. He builds the reality of his fiction then he destroys it." Consequently, many critics regard his novels and films after *In the Labyrinth* as repetitions of previous inventions rather than fresh developments. In addition, Robbe-Grillet has received unfavorable attention for his preoccupation with pornographic images, especially those including adolescent girls and sexual violence against women, which some consider a dehumanizing aestheticization of sexual desire. Despite such criticism, Robbe-Grillet is highly regarded as a major intellectual force whose radical literary enterprises exerted an indelible influence on contemporary experimental writing.

PRINCIPAL WORKS

Les Gommes [*The Erasers*] (novel) 1953
Le Voyeur [*The Voyeur*] (novel) 1955
La Jalousie [*Jealousy*] (novel) 1957
Dans le labyrinthe [*In the Labyrinth*] (novel) 1959
L'Anneé dernière à Marienbad [*Last Year at Marienbad*] (screenplay) 1961
Instantanés [*Snapshots*] (short stories) 1962
L'Immortelle [*The Immortal One*] (screenplay) 1963
Pour un nouveau roman [*For a New Novel: Essays on Fiction*] (essays) 1963
La Maison de rendez-vous [*The House of Assignation*] (novel) 1965
Trans-Europ-Express (screenplay) 1967
L'Homme qui ment (screenplay) 1968
L'Eden et aprés (screenplay) 1970
Projet pour une révolution à New York [*Project for a Revolution in New York*] (novel) 1970
Rêves de jeunes filles [with photographs by David Hamilton; translated as *Dreams of a Young Girl* and *Dreams of Young Girls*] (text and photographs) 1971
Les Demoiselles d'Hamilton [with photographs by David Hamilton; translated as *Sisters*] (text and photographs) 1972
Glissements progressifs du plaisir (screenplay) 1973
La Belle Captive (novel) 1975
Construction d'un temple en ruines à la déesse Vanadé [with engravings by Paul Delvaux] (text and engravings) 1975
La Jeu avec le feu (screenplay) 1975
Topologie d'une cité fantôme [*Topology of a Phantom City*] (novel) 1976
Temple aux miroirs [with photographs by Irina Ionesco] (text and photographs) 1977
Un Régicide (novel) 1978
Djinn: Un trou rouge entre les pavés disjoints [*Djinn*] (novel) 1981
Souvenirs du triangle d'or [*Recollections of the Golden Triangle*] (novel) 1984
La Belle Captive (screenplay) 1983
Le Miroir qui revient [*Ghosts in the Mirror*] (autobiography) 1984
Angélique ou L'Enchantement (autobiography) 1988
Les Derniers Jours de Corinthe (autobiography) 1994

CRITICISM

H. A. Wylie (essay date 1967)

SOURCE: "Alain Robbe-Grillet: Scientific Humanist," in *Bucknell Review,* Vol. XV, No. 2, 1967, pp. 1-9.

[*In the following essay, Wylie discusses the combination of humanist concerns and scientific observation in Robbe-Grillet's fiction. Noting the influence of Surrealism and existential philosophy on his work, Wylie writes, "For Robbe-Grillet the cosmos is neither absurd nor tragic; it simply is."*]

A return to stylistic experimentation sets Robbe-Grillet and the *nouveau roman* apart from their predecessors, the existentialists. Early criticism preoccupied itself with these technical innovations, with Robbe-Grillet's visual images and his striking use of language and vocabulary. This analysis seemingly considered subject matter of lesser importance or irrelevant. The truth is probably that early critics were unable to find a connecting link between Robbe-Grillet's themes and his literary technique. My description of the novelist as a "scientific humanist" is an attempt to provide this link.

By "humanist" I mean to describe any writer who concerns himself primarily with man and with those basic, unchanging problems which traditionally have been the province of literature, themes such as faith and despair, love, madness and war, freedom and creativity. The term "humanist" seems to have been first applied to various Renaissance scholars and philologists (Petrarch, Boccaccio, Erasmus, Luther, Montaigne) who sought to arrive at a comprehension of man through intensive analysis of language and elucidation of the basic texts of their civilization: the Bible and the "Classics." These and later attempts to define man's essence by scholarly efforts unaided by recourse to revelation and dogma have given the term "humanist" the further implication of secular thought, of independence from any preconceived religious or political system.

By "science" I mean not only a certain attitude toward truth and knowledge but also a particular vision of reality and nature, even an emotional set toward matter and energy, toward the correspondence between mental and physical phenomena. Science as science is marked, usually, by a materialistic bias, by the implicit belief that man's frame of reference is the bio-physical world of matter and motion. Science may also be defined through its detachment and objectivity, by its desire to know through systematic and sustained observation, while humanism suggests a pursuit of human values and goals.

Trained as a plant pathologist and having spent several years in the patient study of the diseases of banana trees in the tropics, Robbe-Grillet as writer manifests both attitudes and approaches. He may be added to the company of notable figures to whom the label "scientific humanist" has been applied: Alfred North Whitehead, C. P. Snow, Teilhard de Chardin. He shares with them the belief characteristic of the scientific humanist that the hidden mainsprings of the material world are of critical importance to the understanding of our human condition, and that the relation of physical reality to our mental processes—perception and thought—is the key to knowledge and truth.

What then are the primary manifestations of this humanistic concern? It must be made clear at the outset that Robbe-Grillet's continuing interest in the natural sciences is an integral part of this humanism. For Robbe-Grillet the ultimate metaphysical problems are those of epistemology and ontology, of how can we have true knowledge of ourselves and our world. Robbe-Grillet has said that science is an essential instrument of our comprehension and has implied that the arts should make use of the latest scientific discoveries and techniques. Quantum theory, which demonstrates the dependence of physical phenomena on their observer, seems to interest the author particularly. Its definition of science is inclusive and fluid, allowing a vital communication between science and the arts. But the intellectual detachment of the scientist and his quest for objectivity are responsible for that stylistic precision and sharpness which set Robbe-Grillet apart from much that is shoddy in twentieth-century thought. Perhaps it would be fair to say that like Théophile Gautier and the Parnassians, Robbe-Grillet has bothered to master the technical problems of his craft and hence has attained the impersonal validity of the scientist. He prefers to remain silent rather than voice a half-truth or a provisionary truism.

The first problem attacked was the fundamental one of the nature of existence: the existence of man in his surroundings. This ontological problem was found to be inseparable from the problem of knowledge: how can man know his fellows and his environment? Thus in *Les gommes* Robbe-Grillet studies one man's attempt to penetrate misleading appearances and circumstances in order to arrive at a true understanding of a relatively simple situation. With irony the author depicts the two hermetic realms of material reality and the related mental processes which twist the exterior reality into a new entity. Especially important in this study of the nature of the mind and its dependence or independence of the material world is the typical "object"; in *Les gommes* this is often a clue. Robbe-Grillet is fascinated with clues, and probably for this reason cast his first novel, *Le voyeur*, as a detective story. A material clue is for Robbe-Grillet closely related to the surrealist object as defined by Maurice Nadeau: "tout objet dépaysé" or "sorti de son cadre habituel." A clue is no longer a mere gum eraser or piece of chalk but takes on a heightened existence, an immediacy, a human relevance. It serves as a link between man and the inert surroundings, as a *correspondance* in the Baudelairean sense. Perhaps this humanizing factor explains some of the continued popularity of Simenon, Ellery Queen and Agatha Christie.

Critics have realized the importance of these clues but have been at a loss to explain their value, since in the light of Robbe-Grillet's critical writings they have been hesitant to view them as symbols. The eraser, the famous quarter of tomato, the drawbridge serve to focus our awareness, to channel our psychic energy. A repeated image in Robbe-Grillet's works is that of a man rapt in meditation before a poster, a painting or a statue. It would seem that the individual is attempting to penetrate to ultimate reality through complete comprehension of even one banal, everyday object.

The natural scientist was soon forced to admit that both the problems of being and of knowing were essentially psychological. In the surrealist sense, in the sense proclaimed by Rimbaud, man's mind creates the universe around it, particularly the modern technological cityscape. So Robbe-Grillet broadened his perspective to take in the area of human creativity, especially as expressed in the labyrinthian architecture of modern life. Bruce Morrissette has noted that in *Dans le labyrinthe* it is the narrator and not the author who is the creator of this involved, convolute fiction: "le narrateur est occupé à l'élaboration d'une fiction destinée à composer une harmonie en soi, une sorte de 'roman pur.'" We might say that Robbe-Grillet has given us an unusual illustration of existential man in the act of self-creation.

Now turning outward again we can see that the typical protagonist of Robbe-Grillet creates his own environment by his observation, his response to and interaction with it. This is most apparent at the beginning of *Dans le labyrinthe*, where, as James Lethcoe has remarked, the conflicting detail and the hesitancy in choice of tense represent either the narrator's fumbling attempts at imagining his tale or his difficulty in recounting a previous event. The mutual interaction and interdependence of man and his surroundings are also responsible for the baffling "false scenes" of which Robbe-Grillet is so fond. Perhaps *Les gommes* provides the best example; here the variant passages are most characteristically the detective's projections of various possible solutions to the 'givens' furnished by the clues.

Robbe-Grillet has insisted that his novels are not non-human and has pointed to the central presence of a perceiving, thinking protagonist in each of his works. This human presence is responsible not only for its own being and for the particular existence of its surroundings, as we have seen, but also for the action which ensues and for the evaluation of both the present situation and the future outcome. Time for Robbe-Grillet, as for Proust, is a living, changing thing; even the past is not fixed, dead. But increasingly Robbe-Grillet has turned toward the future. As we will see, hope has become an important element in the author's outlook.

Most of Robbe-Grillet's critics have refused to treat thematic or "philosophic" content in his works. Is it true, as Robbe-Grillet once seemed to say, that we can make no generalization about the discrete entities which surround us? Recurring images and themes, ideas repeated by his characters and key statements of his own in *Pour un nouveau roman* would indicate that certain objects, certain modes of action and perception, certain ideas are "privileged" in the Proustian sense or have an aura which detaches them from the purely meaningless. We have already noted the themes of contemplation and of creation, both involving the problem of comprehension. We might now briefly enumerate two other themes.

Foremost among those subjects which are given sustained treatment are love and sexual passion. Since Baudelaire and Proust few writers have presented such a polyvalent description of human affection and desire or have probed so deeply into their related motives and thoughts. Always the "realist" seeking a true understanding of a human phenomenon, Robbe-Grillet has not falsified what his observation has told him, has not evoked a sentimental or romantic picture of love. Instead he gives us without comment descriptions of passion, with all the bewildering complexity and demonic intensity of the emotion of Racine's Phèdre or Baudelaire's madonna. This love is often tormented or twisted, as in *Le voyeur* and *La jalousie*; but *L'Anneé dernière à Marienbad* is more full of hope in its suggestion that through the surrealist linking of love and revolt the lovers can win through to freedom.

The sustained analysis of love, transforming scientific case history into the archetypal patterns of art, reveals several humanistic implications. Love, for Robbe-Grillet, is often illusory or obsessive, the result of Freudian displacement of psychic energies caused by free association. Robbe-Grillet condemns self-deceit and hypocrisy in our efforts to picture romantic love. But he also seems to suggest—in the lovers of *Marienbad* and the spontaneous relation between the soldier and the boy of *Dans le labyrinthe*—that disinterested affection is possible and worth striving for.

A second major object of attention is the technological landscape with which man has surrounded himself. The traditional humanist has tended to look upon the modern with a biased eye, yearning to return to a simpler, sweeter, mythical past. Even Camus showed considerable prejudice in his hostility toward science and technology, a view which tends to falsify his analysis of what Lewis Mumford has termed "neotechnic" civilization. Robbe-Grillet accepts this new world as a given and projects his characters into it; the task of judging and evaluating both what is viable and what is harmful in it is largely left to the reader. The author, however, intimates that the joys and artifacts of the modern world are as valid for it as were other cultural manifestations for past societies. Perhaps a new humanism, in harmony with neotechnic science, engineering and art, is evolving to bring new order and meaning into our lives and our environment.

One example will illustrate both Robbe-Grillet's handling of the imagery of the neotechnic world and his characteristic "technological" lyricism:

> Un groupe, immobile, tout en bas du long escalier gris-fer, dont les marches l'une après l'autre affleurent, au niveau de la plate-forme d'arrivée, et disparaissent une à une dans un bruit de machinerie bien huilée, avec une régularité pourtant pesante et saccadée en même temps, qui donne l'impression d'assez grande vitesse à cet endroit où les marches disparaissent l'une après l'autre sous la surface horizontale, mais qui semble au contraire d'une lenteur extrême. . . .

This evocation of the *métro* escalator is followed by the description of a corridor and a man:

> En dépit de la taille énorme du dessin et du peu de détails dont il s'orne, la tête du spectateur se penche en

avant, comme pour mieux voir. Les passants doivent s'écarter un instant de leur trajectoire rectiligne afin de contourner cet obstacle inattendu. . . .

In dispassionate understatement the author muses on the perversity and freedom of man. Only one of these scurrying Dantesque voyagers of the underworld has stopped to reflect, to contemplate the modern Beatrice; but who knows? If Brunetto Latini, the poet Dante acknowledged as master, could sing in Hell, this solitary figure, disrupting the flow of harried souls, may resist even the subway.

The attempt, not to pigeonhole the author but rather to put him in the context of his age in relation to his predecessors, is difficult but important. The comparison with Camus and with the Surrealists is particularly rewarding. Robbe-Grillet undoubtedly studied at great length the work of Albert Camus, perhaps the leading French humanist and moralist of the past generation. In a detailed analysis of Camus' *L'étranger*, Robbe-Grillet points out the stylistic progression from a simple declarative prose at the beginning to increasingly involved and metaphoric language in the portrayal of the murder of the Arab: "La scène capitale du roman nous présente l'image parfaite d'une solidarité douloureuse: le soleil implacable est toujours 'le même,' son reflet sur la lame du couteau que tient l'Arabe 'atteint' le héros en plein front et 'fouille' ses yeux." These subjective anthropomorphic metaphors, according to Robbe-Grillet, falsely humanize nature, and Camus' famed *absurde* becomes a form of tragic humanism. Its multiple symbols will be Meursault the innocent victim, Sisyphus the plaything of the gods, and the rats of La peste. But Robbe-Grillet rejects, like André Breton, this acquiescence in a tragic view of man, this seeming conquest of the absurd by a new linking of man and nature through this *solidarité douloureuse*. For Robbe-Grillet the cosmos is neither absurd nor tragic; it simply is. With the Surrealists, Robbe-Grillet looks toward the future and hopes for an ultimate harmony with nature.

Thus it is up to man to impose both order and meaning on his surroundings. Although some of Robbe-Grillet's protagonists may seem passive, the most important—Wallas in **Les gommes**, the hunted soldier of **Dans le labyrinthe**, and X, the lover in **Marienbad**—are persistent in their effort to uncover or to create a moral and human truth. To Camus, who felt at home in the primitive culture of Algeria, man's state is fixed and unchanging, whereas to Robbe-Grillet man is constantly modifying the essence of his life through technological and cultural evolution. For Robbe-Grillet history is neither cyclical nor static.

Robbe-Grillet also rejects the existentialist idea of *engagement* in art, since he sees in Sartre's definition of commitment only the peril of didacticism. In the context of our definition of humanism, we might say that the artist directs his energies to creating forms or new "myths" which have only an indirect moral influence. The artist, like the scientist, must strive to maintain a certain detachment and impartiality in order, precisely, to function as artist. The artist or writer as humanist is neither partisan nor preacher.

Robbe-Grillet's revival of the disinterested dedication, the intensity, of the art-for-art's-sake movement of the nineteenth century has been a fresh wind in our times.

The boldest and most sustained effort mounted in our own century to know ourselves and nature through art is that of the Surrealists: of Guillaume Apollinaire, André Breton, Paul Eluard, Max Ernst, Joan Miró, Alberto Giacometti, Picasso. In rejecting traditional definitions and limitations of reality, they strove, in varying ways, to find new freedom, new strength for man in liberating the subconscious and creating a new mental and intellectual "super-reality." This would be accomplished by reconciling the subconscious and conscious mind with our inanimate, indifferent world. Breton states in the *Manifesto of Surrealism* that the channel and form for this new harmony would be a fusion of art and science.

Robbe-Grillet is close to the Surrealists in his interest in artistic form and technique; he too is a literary technician and experimenter, a *magicien ès lettres*. His formal innovations lend a haunting musicality to his prose, the product of a characteristic density and texture closely related to those of the atonal serial music he describes in **Marienbad**. This musicality, however, is far from that of Verlaine. Here the *volupté* is that of the gnarled and twisted tree: sharp and hard consonants replace the rather gooey vowels of Verlaine. The words are precise, objective, scientific and have a cerebral sensuality; typical are *scrutigère, centimètre, rectiligne, périphérique, homogène, imperceptiblement*.

Robbe-Grillet is close to the Surrealists too in his interest in Freud, in the subconscious and in dreams. Several critics have pointed out the presence of multiple layers of consciousness and the important roles played by the subconscious in both the observation and description of objects and in the cross-relations among them. It is really the subconscious which provides the missing links between scenes in a work by Robbe-Grillet. Kafka is one of the non-French writers to whom Robbe-Grillet turned for inspiration; the latter's work shows the influence of the fantastic, non-Aristotelian logic of his precursor. The dream-atmosphere of a Robbe-Grillet novel has been often noticed, particularly in **Marienbad**. There is always an aura of mystery, of strangeness, awakened by the immanence of obsessive images and by encantatory language. The surrealist force of the quarter tomato of **Les gommes** derives perhaps from the synthesis of these elements, whose essence is represented by the *gelée verdâtre*.

The last major bond between Robbe-Grillet and the Surrealists is their common rebellion against all forms of servitude and their quest for total freedom. For Robbe-Grillet the labyrinth is a recurring image of man's imprisonment; but the possibility of escape exists, and at times Robbe-Grillet suggests that his characters do or will escape from the enclosure of the room, the hotel, or the maze of city streets. Especially at the end of **Marienbad** is the hope of a definitive departure strong. Robbe-Grillet refuses any resignation and often returns to the potentiality of man finally breaking out of those restraints and frontiers which bind him. The true life will be fluid, an eternal flux, a life always looking forward: "vous étiez maintenant déjà en train de vous perdre, pour toujours, dans la nuit tranquille, seule avec moi."

The open world of Robbe-Grillet is infinitely complex, a plenitude in which the reader can plumb the depths, can lose himself in the labyrinthian passages of this watery timeless realm. There is an addictive quality to these works; one runs the same danger of being engulfed here as in Proust's *Combray*. But like Theseus, we will emerge from the maze with new understanding and increased vigor.

Bruce Morrissette (essay date Fall 1967)

SOURCE: "The Evolution of Narrative Viewpoint in Robbe-Grillet," in *Novel*, Vol. 1, No. 1, Fall, 1967, pp. 24-33.

[*In the following essay, Morrissette examines the development of narrative perspective in Robbe-Grillet's fiction and films. According to Morrissette, Robbe-Grillet's "ingenious and constantly varying narrative modes cover almost the entire spectrum of current experimentation and practice."*]

1. EMERGENCE OF THEORIES OF "JUSTIFIED" VIEWPOINT

Two decades ago the question of narrative viewpoint seemed quite amenable to critical analysis; yet today it appears one of the most ambiguous and unresolved aspects of fictional structure. The elimination of the omniscient narrator and his replacement by posts of observation within the fictional field are steps in a well-known history: first, in the English tradition of narrative analysis, James and Lubbock argued on esthetic grounds for observers located within the framework of the novel; then, in the French tradition, Sartre offered a systematic philosophical defense of internal viewpoints, holding that Einsteinian relativity and existential views of knowledge justify relative "frames of reference" in fiction and the restriction of content to that present in a "framing" consciousness. But the apparent stability of a fictional geometry based on internally justified viewpoints proved illusory, and the prospect of rational coherence was of short duration. Indeed, we can see in retrospect that the novel had already rejected such tidy consistency. Soon it would proliferate with new narrative modalities, to return, astonishingly and unpredictably, to a kind of "omniscient" stance in which the reader himself is placed at the—often shifting—narrational focus.

Some of the main factors of instability that led to the abandonment of the novel of justified viewpoint lay, paradoxically, in the novel of the first person which had always seemed to call for little if any structural defense,

because its straight-forward and automatically justified recital of events is given by a single character, a central or peripheral observer of the action, whose thoughts, observations, and other direct testimony constitute an unassailably coherent text. When the mode was further justified by the *cadre* of a diary, letters, or other pretexts of written documents it seemed to produce the maximum illusion of reality or authenticity, if not with respect to outer reality or the real universe, at least with respect to the fictional field. But already in the case of Proust, the *"je"* or first-person mode had revealed unsuspected ambiguities (see Marcel Muller's recent study identifying as many as nine separate modes of "je" in the "narrative voices" of *A la recherche du temps perdu*); and André Gide in *Les Faux-monnayeurs* had played mirror tricks with the first person by introducing an inner novel or journal, while ironically reserving to himself the supposedly outmoded privilege of intervening as the "real" author. Meanwhile, the urgent claims of interior psychology had led to wide acceptance of interior monologue and stream of consciousness techniques which in most cases found no place within the logical schema of the novel of justified viewpoint.

To complicate matters further, the example of films and cinematic construction, which seemed at one time to strengthen the case for the objective novel (see the classic chapter on "Roman et cinéma" in Claude-Edmonde Magny's *L'Age du roman américain*), underwent an abrupt change. With the advent of what Raymond Borde calls the "cinéma de la vérité intérieure," subjective viewpoints appeared on the screen with spectacular results, as in *Hiroshima mon amour* and ***L'Anneé dernière à Marienbad*** (not to mention the long prehistory of cinematic flashbacks, camera scenes shot from the viewpoint of a single character, contrapuntal soundtrack monologues, and the like). When mental content was projected on the screen, the last bulwarks of justified, pseudo-objective cinematic structure began to crumble. Both films and novels were entering a phase of *ad hoc* framing and *découpage* wherein each new work would create its own narrative perspective.

No contemporary author's works illustrate these tendencies and techniques more brilliantly than those of Alain Robbe-Grillet, whose ingenious and constantly varying narrative modes cover almost the entire spectrum of current experimentation and practice.

2. ROTATION OF VIEWPOINT IN LES GOMMES (1953)

In this pseudo-detective story of a protagonist who repeats, without realizing it, an inverted and semi-parodied version of the myth of Oedipus, as he murders the "victim" whose death he is investigating, Robbe-Grillet sets out deliberately to destroy clock time (which he calls "linear and without surprises") in favor of human time, the time that each man "secretes about himself like a cocoon, full of flashbacks, repetitions, and interferences." Consequently, the author seeks also to present the contradictory versions of the same events that exist in a world of observational perspectives which he compares, following Sartre's lead, to Einstein's universe of multiple frames of reference. Such an intention explains, indeed almost necessitates, the use of a wide range of viewpoints in *Les Gommes*. The characters see the same décor from different angles, observe each other, witness and interpret according to their *situations*. (Robbe-Grillet's own comments on *Les Gommes* are preserved in a rare pamphlet, never republished.)

The specific narrative mode in most cases is a third-person pronoun, but one deepened and extended by use of Flaubertian indirect discourse and passages of interior monologue, as well as pseudo-objectification of conjectures, memories, and even hallucinations. The characters who "see" the scenes number about a dozen; they are, in order of their "appearance," the following: the owner of the Café des Alliés, a focal point in the action; Garinati, the hired assassin; Juard, a shady abortionist who ministers to the "victim"; Marchat, a fearful friend of the intended victim; Laurent, the police chief; Wallas, the "special agent" who has been sent to solve the crime; Anna, the victim's maid; "Bona," Jean Bonaventure, the ring leader of the band of political assassins; Mme. Bax, whose apartment overlooks the house of the crime; the drunkard who recites distorted versions of the riddle of the Sphinx; Mme. Jean, a postal employee; and Dupont himself, the intended and eventual victim of murder. Some of these "observe" only one or two scenes, but the principal characters, such as Wallas, Garinati, and Laurent, are interwoven into a complex design of different viewpoints.

In the case of Wallas especially, radically new techniques of objectifying the character's imaginings cause the ostensibly realistic framework of the third-person mode to collapse suddenly into visionary subjectivity. At times, pure inventions or speculations, such as Laurent's theory of the crime, are described as if actually occurring, as might befit the visualized hypothesis of a trained police chief. Along with the general pattern of rotating viewpoints there exist, consequently, the special techniques of mixed objectivity and subjectivity which Robbe-Grillet will in later novels employ apart from any arrangement involving multiple viewpoints.

One question of theoretical difficulty arising in *Les Gommes* is the following: if, in the novel, everything is seen or described from some particular character's viewpoint, how can such hidden allusions as those to the Oedipus myth, or to the Tarot cards, be communicated to the reader, if all the characters remain ignorant thereof? More importantly, how can such "metafictional" elements be tolerated at all? The answer must lie close to the basic paradox of all fiction. Reflection will show that the universe "observed" by the characters cannot be their own creation, in any real sense, but must emanate from the novelist, whether he "intervenes" visibly or not to make his presence known. It is he who determines what kind of universe will be observed by his characters; he can therefore hide, or partially reveal, at will, features recognizable by the reader but not by the characters. This intentionality is essential to the creation of any fictional field, since an opposing theory would necessarily fall into the realistic fallacy of a Zola, who tried to persuade himself and his readers that the fictional world he had created was somehow real, and subject to the same "scientific" laws as nature or society itself.

One additional narrative mode remains to be identified in *Les Gommes*. At first it appears to be an anomaly, if not a regression to outmoded omniscience or at least direct authorial intervention. It is the impersonal mode that appears here and there in passages that seem to come from nowhere or no one ("Un bras machinal remet en place le décor. Quand tout est prêt, la lumière s'allume . . ." etc.). The explanation, which does not justify the passages in the sense of fitting them into the pattern of observational viewpoints, shows them nevertheless to be structurally related to the conception of the particular novel. They are passages attributable to a "chorus." The work, with its five chapters (acts), prologue, and epilogue parallels in form the divisions of a Greek tragedy, such as *Oedipus the King*, whose plot is also paralleled. In this regard, Robbe-Grillet has allowed formal, esthetic considerations to outweigh philosophical or metaphysical ideas concerning the relativity of time or viewpoint. Thus at the outset of his career, he reassumes authorial privileges which should be theoretically excluded.

3. SINGLE AND DUAL VIEWPOINT IN LE VOYEUR (1955)

Point of view in *Le Voyeur* has a paradoxical quality which analysis shows to be related to the theme and structure of the novel. Some critics have found in the work only a single focus, that of the protagonist Mathias, the traveling salesman who lands on an island to sell wristwatches to its inhabitants and departs several days later, after murdering, in a "suppressed" scene whose content is only gradually revealed, a young girl whose (probably) tortured body is thrown over a cliff into the sea. According to the unified view, the whole text (written in the third person) describes only Mathias' perceptions and outlook on the surrounding world. But, as I have tried to demonstrate elsewhere, there are large blocks of text wherein Mathias is very definitely seen from the outside, long, "neutral" passages and developments incompatible with the single viewpoint theory. It is from these scenes that the paradox or ambiguity of narrative mode arises, and not from the mixing of real and imagined scenes in the sections of the text which do render the world and mind of Mathias through techniques of objectified subjectivity.

Assuming the correctness of this analysis (see my study *Les Romans de Robbe-Grillet* for a full treatment of the point), one may discover, on probing more deeply into the problem, the reason for the paradox as well as its solution. The fundamental structural intention served by the narrative mode of pseudo-objective third person is indeed that of incarnating the world of Mathias, a character "out of phase with himself," a sadistic schizophrenic obsessed with visions of erotic violence. But to present this deformed universe, the author has need of an undeformed background against which the distortions, alterations, and other psychic projections of Mathias may be discriminated, measured, and judged. It is for this reason that Mathias is frequently observed and described from a *point d'optique* that cannot be his own (as, for example, when he is depicted looking downward) and that he is seen against a décor presented in a "style Robbe-Grillet" whose objects and other consistent elements (geometrical terms, scientific precisions, deceptive qualifiers, and the like) mark the general "manner" of the author (as, for example, in those descriptive portions of the scenario of *Marienbad* designed primarily for the director), and are not a style specifically adapted to the character's mentality. Moreover, when—in a fashion comparable to that of Faulkner when he presents the world through idiot Benjy's eyes—Robbe-Grillet creates a vision of the world distorted by Mathias' psychopathology, it is this neutral, background universe that is distorted, and the style takes on a deformed, hallucinatory quality only by its relationship to the primary décor.

The well-known figure-of-eight object series of *Le Voyeur* illustrates how the two worlds, that of the stylized universe in which the protagonist exists and that of the visionary erotic sadist's mind, are linked. In the "background" world, the coiled cord, the marks of the iron rings on the quay, the pattern of eyes on the doors, the spirals of cigarette smoke, the adjacent rings left on the bar by wet glasses, and all the other 8's are coincidental forms such as any attentive observer, with an eye for geometrical patterns, might discern about him. But as they enter Mathias' mind they become charged with morbid psychological tensions and sinister associations, and the reader begins to feel the upsurge of violent emotion, to recognize in these objects cords that may bind wrists, rings that could hold young limbs apart, bonds, watching eyes, and the whole repertory of obsessive objects found in the novel.

After a certain critical resistance, recent studies of Robbe-Grillet have come to agree with the analysis that finds *Le Voyeur* "organisé selon deux perspectives," as Jean Alter has expressed it. What is important is to perceive that this dual perspective, that of the author and that of the protagonist, coincides perfectly with the novelist's intention to make the reader experience as directly as possible the disorientation of the schizoid mind, including a "blackout" or period of amnesic repression during which the crime is committed, a "hole" in the text during which the viewpoint entirely ceases to exist.

As the novel progresses, the point of view of Mathias (or his mental content) occupies more and more the volume of the text, so that the latter sections function in an almost pure single viewpoint mode. Even before that, as we have seen, when we speak of a dual viewpoint in *Le Voyeur* we do not mean one belonging to two narrators or fictional characters, but rather the opposition described between the author's "nominal," stylized décor, and the personalized view of that world as apprehended in the mind of the protagonist. In a sense, the remarks made earlier concerning certain details of the author's world in *Les Gommes*, as opposed to the world of the characters themselves, apply to *Le Voyeur*.

4. SUPPRESSED FIRST-PERSON NARRATION IN LA JALOUSIE (1957)

Seeking a term to describe the innovation in narrative viewpoint invented by Robbe-Grillet in La Jalousie, I called the new mode that of the *"je-néant,"* or absent-I. Without entering into the metaphysics of Sartrean *néantisation* and its relationship to the perceiving consciousness, the *je-néant* may be defined as a technique of the suppressed first-person in which all pronouns or forms associated with it (such as I, me, my, mine, and the like) are eliminated. The perceptions of the protagonist of the novel, a jealous husband who exercises an intense surveillance over his wife, constitute the "narrative," which is expressed without perceptible self-reference. A central focus of vision is created, in a style related to that of the cinematic subjective camera, but lacking the first-person commentary on the sound track which typically accompanies the subjective sequences of films made in this mode, such as *Lady in the Lake*. A hole (Robbe-Grillet calls it a *"creux"*) is created at the core of the narrative, and the reader installs himself therein, assuming the narrator's vision and performing, without verbal clues, all the unspoken and implicit interpretation of scenes and events that, in the conventional novel of psychological analysis and commentary, would normally be spelled out by the author or his character. Not only does the text embody the naked dynamics of the husband's perceptions of external events and objects; it also, as the incarnation of the magma of his mental content, contains secondary, associative materials, such as memories more or less deformed by emotional tensions, exaggerated visions of an erotic or paranoid nature (such as the paroxysmal image of the enlarged *mille-pattes* or centipede whose crushing carries the weight of the husband's dread of his wife's possession by another), and even purely hypothetical scenes of murderous wish fulfillment, such as the crash and burning of the car containing his wife and her presumed lover.

This esthetically fascinating and quite powerful effect, arising almost entirely through the special narrative mode employed, seems extraordinarily appropriate to a novel about jealousy. The husband's preoccupation is not with himself; he has, therefore, little reason for self-reference. What obsesses him is what his wife "A . . ." is doing, is planning to do, or has done, with the virile and aggressive Franck. He returns constantly to past scenes, reexamining them for clues as he visualizes them, and simultaneously transforming them and distorting them in line with his mounting suspicions. Sharing these visions through the technique of the *je-néant*, the reader feels, rather than thinks, jealousy. The wiping away of the conventional vocabulary of jealousy, as one would find it in Proust, for example, allows nothing to intervene between the phenomena that give rise to jealousy and the emotion itself. The reader's psychophysical responses take over. We may compare in this sense the text of **La Jalousie** and the essays in the "simulation" of psychopathological states, including paranoia, written by Breton and Eluard in *L'Immaculée Conception* during the surrealist period. The contrast between a novel like **La Jalousie** and a traditional novel of psychological analysis is paralleled by the contrast between the poetic texts of simulation of abnormal mental states and the texts found in conventional manuals of psychopathology, including Freud's and Stekel's, which embed the pathological experience and its visions in the rational context of an explanatory commentary.

Other writers of the *nouveau roman*, especially Claude Ollier and Jean Ricardou, have used the suppressed first-person mode to good effect. It would seem that the *je-néant* will enter the repertory of techniques of point of view (along with Michel Butor's "narrative you") destined for future exploitation by many novelists. Looking back, one may now discern a link between Robbe-Grillet's *je-néant* and the partially suppressed first-person mode of the *je* in Camus' *L'Etranger*. While there is in Camus' novel no suppression whatever of the pronoun *je* (on the contrary, it becomes even obtrusive in its proliferation), Meursault's "I" appears as a pronoun of surfaces only, oddly lacking in depth or interiority. The protagonist of *L'Étranger* almost never "thinks," or analyzes, and, like the husband of **La Jalousie**, he communicates his sense impressions at a more or less objective level. The reader quickly passes over Meursault's repeated *je*, so weightless is it. Suppression takes place *behind* the pronoun. It remained for Robbe-Grillet to erase the pronoun itself, and to create a wholly new mode.

5. *The Hidden Author within the Narrative Framework:* Dans le labyrinthe (1959)

In the first sentence of **Dans le labyrinthe**, a "je" speaks. No further first-person form appears until near the end, in the phrase "à ma dernière visite," and in the last sentence a departing narrator closes his text with the word "moi." Thus, having announced himself at the outset, the narrator has retired from view (though we sense his presence in passages employing a type of *je-néant* mode), to reappear—but not fully, even then—as the novel closes. Yet as we become sensitive to his presence, we feel near him, in his small author's room, even when the action is taking place outside, in the labyrinthine streets where the soldier protagonist, ill or wounded, makes his way, from café to barracks to ambiguous apartments, carrying his box to the recipient whose identity he cannot remember, towards some forgotten rendezvous.

What has Robbe-Grillet gained by this narrative structure, involving the interior duplication of an author composing a novel? One could easily imagine another version of the novel in which the wanderings of the soldier, described more or less in the third-person style used here, would alone form the text. Even brief reflection should show that such a simplification would not only impoverish the novel;

it would, in fact, negate its meaning. The author is obviously concerned less with the adventures of the soldier, pathetic as they may be, than with the relationship between the soldier's feverish story and the concealed inner author whose struggles in the labyrinth of novelistic creation form the real "subject" of the book.

The title is not "The Labyrinth," but "*In the Labyrinth.*" Once the inner author, whose voice creates the novel, is seen as the real protagonist, the narrative viewpoint becomes clear, and the first-person frame is justified. As this writer attempts to build from the materials in his room (a steel engraving of a soldier in a café, a shoe box, a bayonet, etc.) a coherent novel, his stops and starts, revisions and alterations, give rise to the image of the labyrinth, an image not only of the maze of identical perpendicular streets in the story, but also of the labyrinthine verbal style of the text itself. The fact that towards the end of the work this narrator merges with the doctor who treats the dying soldier may be viewed as an effort finally to push the narrator himself into the story, in a fashion somewhat analogous to the re-entrant line in certain drawings of Steinberg, which, having emerged from the pen of an artist depicted in the sketch, rejoins eventually the figure of the artist himself. The effect is the opposite of that employed by Camus in *La Peste*, wherein Doctor Rieux, hitherto seen only as a third person, suddenly emerges as the first-person narrator, abandoning "il" for an unambiguous "je."

In **Dans le labyrinthe**, Robbe-Grillet appears to adopt a kind of Mallarméan esthetics in which the creation of the literary work itself becomes the primary theme, lying beneath the fictional incarnation which may have its own anecdotal or pseudo-anecdotal value, as in *L'Apres-midi d'un faune*, or more strikingly, in *Un Coup de dés jamais n'abolira le hasard*. Like Mallarmé's "*ptyx*" sonnet, which the poet termed "allégorique de lui-même," **Dans le labyrinthe** is in a sense analogical of itself. Since the intention was to devise a structure appropriate to a *self-contained* novel, the inner author and inner subject (duplicated in the engraving) seem perfectly justified, as do the pages lying on the table at the end, as the narrative voice leaves the room at last, uttering the final phrase, "derrière moi."

Of particular interest to the study of the evolution of techniques of mode and viewpoint in Robbe-Grillet is the creation in **Dans le labyrinthe** of a new type of authorial intervention that permits, by means of an author placed within the fictional field, the use of free modalities of narration that would be impossible in the system of existentially justified viewpoints. Whereas the passages of abstract intervention in Les Gommes had to be explained in terms of formal imitation of the Greek dramatic chorus, such intervention now becomes part of the activities of a "creator" whose operations and maneuvers are at once the subject and the text of the novel itself. The relative "realism" of **Le Voyeur** and **La Jalousie** begins to disappear, in favor of a new constructionalism.

6. *Point of View in the Films:* L'Anneé
dernière à Marienbad *(1961) and*
L'Immortelle *(1963)*

The prefaces to these two films, as well as their structure
and the camera angles which they employ, show them to
be closely related, as far as viewpoint is concerned, to the
novels of Robbe-Grillet's middle period, *Le Voyeur* and
La Jalousie. (His latest film, *Trans-Europ-Express*, has
not yet been shown in this country, or viewed by the
present writer.) In the preface to *Marienbad*, Robbe-Grillet
states that when two people converse, for example, what is
present in their minds, as counterpart to the actual words
of their dialogue, can only be visual or sensory images
related to the topic under discussion. Thus mental content,
which is primarily visual, becomes a natural narrative
mode for the cinema, which can show the characters' imaginings while retaining the same degree of "realism" in the
décor and photography as that used in the "normal" scenes,
if indeed any scenes may be thought of as existing apart
from the characters' perceptions.

Consequently, if a character in a film remembers or
imagines something, especially under the influence of emotion, the scene appears before us as it does in the
character's own mind. Sometimes subtle alterations mark
such an imaginary scene, but not as a clue to permit the
discrimination between the real and the imaginary. The
alterations must result from the tensions exerted by the
character's emotions: thus the heroine's bedroom in
Marienbad, recalled in great stress, appears in a heightened
baroque style. When recalled scenes recur in *L'Immortelle*,
they are deformed in accordance with the "narrator's" jealous scrutiny, in a technique exactly comparable to that
employed in the written, rather than visual, text of *La
Jalousie*.

Neither *Marienbad* nor *L'Immortelle*, however, uses a
consistently justified system of viewpoint in the manner
just described. In *Marienbad*, in addition to some scenes
taken from an imaginary and "impossible" angle high in
the air, there are shots wherein the mingling of two
viewpoints occurs, as when the lover X "intervenes"
(verbally) in the vision he evokes in the heroine's mind of
the seduction scene, and which we see through her eyes.
In both *Marienbad* and *L'Immortelle* two or more
characters appear twice in different parts of a panoramic
camera movement, creating a strange effect of continuity
between two moments of time and two spatial locations
which on a realistic level could not be proximate. Nor is it
always possible to "linearize" such shots by assuming
them to consist of memories or imaginings within a single
mind. As with the "chronological impasses" of *La Jalousie*,
one senses in Robbe-Grillet an impatience with the limitations of the justified system and a tendency to reclaim
authorial rights over point of view, to replace the old
doctrine of the omniscient author by a new but in a sense
similar one that would place the point of view not necessarily within a given character, but in the spectator (or
author) himself. The novelist demands a creative freedom
not possible within the theoretical limits of the James-
Sartre system.

The extent to which Robbe-Grillet's ideas and practices
had changed by 1963 may be measured by referring to the
short article he published in 1958 bearing the long title,
"Notes sur la localisation et les déplacements du point de
vue dans la description romanesque." Therein we find
almost complete support for the visually justified viewpoint, and the cinema is held up as an example to the
novel, since the film, "whether or not there is a person
from whose viewpoint the scene is shot, must absolutely
be shot from some precise point," and this post of observation must be that of a *man*, either one within the fictional
frame, or one placed at a possible vantage point. But within
a few years the new novelist-deity of Robbe-Grillet will
compensate in creative freedom for what the old Balzacian
author-god had lost in omniscience and protean viewpoint.
The justification will move from within the characters to
the form or structure of the novel itself.

7. *Interplay and Entanglement of Narrative
Viewpoint:* La Maison de rendez-vous *(1965)*

In his latest novel, Robbe-Grillet employs a number of apparently new techniques, not only of viewpoint but also of
plot structure. These may, however, be shown to be
developments and intensifications of practices already
discernible in his earlier works, and represent outgrowths
of tendencies whose evolutionary possibilities may be
identified retrospectively, even if they were not clearly
predictable.

The common principle uniting these innovations is what
may be termed reentry or infolding, a procedure which
causes both point of view and story line to turn in upon
themselves, with metamorphoses and transfers occurring
not only backward and forward in time, but also between
characters. Though the closest anticipation of the technique
is the inner author's assumption of the role of the doctor
mentioned above in *Dans le labyrinthe*, the origins of the
mode may be traced back as early as *Les Gommes*, where
the transitions, however, appear easily detectable, as the
viewpoint moves from person to person, and where the
temporal junctions, when non-linear, involve no serious
"dechronology." With *La Jalousie* the viewpoint never
changes, but the temporal reversals and impasses, with the
altered reiterations of scenes, create something of the
contradictory quality of the structure of *La Maison de
rendez-vous*. An example in *La Jalousie* is the passage in
which Franck replaces on an adjacent table a drinking
glass in which the ice has completely melted. A few lines
further, we read that one melting ice cube remains. We
soon realize that two different moments of time have
merged in the narrator's mind, linked by associative tensions, and the apparent impossibility is resolved. In *La
Maison de rendez-vous* no such resolutions will exist for
such non-linear transitions. Thus the fleeing protagonist
Johnson, escaping the police by going through a hotel and
out the back way, continues on to commit the very crime
for which he was being pursued. Not only this—the crime
itself occurs more than once, and each time under different
circumstances: not theoretically, as in *Les Gommes* (where

several characters visualize the same crime according to their separate hypotheses), or through imaginary projections, like those of Mathias in *Le Voyeur* (as he creates *fantomatique* scenes of selling watches to the same clients, etc.), but literally, or, at least, textually.

Accompanying this change is an extension of the device of the "initial I" used in *Dans le labyrinthe*. A first person appears and reappears, but its accounts of events merge with virtually verbatim repetitions attributed to another character, such as Johnson. Robbe-Grillet progressively establishes what amounts to a state of *viewpoint*; justification is not only abandoned, but distorted and negated so violently that the reader acquires or shares a kind of omnipresence similar to that of certain dreams. If, as its author has stated, *La Maison de rendez-vous* is indeed the house of our imagination, it is a domain in which the reader, with the novelist, feels free to create whatever structures of space, time, and action he wishes.

In her excellent analysis of the non-linear aspects of this novel (see *Etudes*, March 1966), Mme. Mireille Latil-Le Dantec quotes from one of my articles my formulation (here translated) of the "eternal question of the novel": "What justifies or explains the existence of a narrative text, this deceitful text which pretends to be plausible, which comes to us from somewhere, from someone who speaks from a hidden or ambiguous place, and who presents us with an ever stranger novelistic universe, structured according to the perspectives of his evermore polymorphous point of view?" Mme. Latil-Le Dantec replies that *La Maison de rendez-vous* seems to offer to this basic question of the justification of viewpoint, "the proudest of replies," namely, that "Nothing justifies the narrative text other than itself. It seeks no *vraisemblance*, deriving its truth only from itself. It comes from nowhere. It is a mental space, the rendezvous of viewpoints successively adopted or abandoned by an *imaginaire* who has no support other than himself, and who creates his own world."

Must we admit, then, that the omniscient author of Balzac, driven from the house of fiction by a score of novelists from Flaubert and James to Sartre, has returned through the back door of *La Maison de rendez-vous*? Are dechronology, entangled and shared viewpoints, and non-linear structures only a modern form of the older mode? Careful reflection and analysis will show, I believe, that it is not a case of *Plus ça change, plus c'est la même chose*. The Balzacian omniscient author played his god-like role in a world of characters offered as Aristotelian imitations of life. Even the scientific pretensions of a Zola implied a transfer from fiction to reality itself. But in Robbe-Grillet's latest work we enter a domain of psycho-fiction, akin to that of Mallarméan poetry or the invented novelistic world of Raymond Roussel, with its formal schematics and its principles of self-generating content and self-contained structure. It remains to be seen whether Robbe-Grillet's future novels and films will evolve further in this direction, and to what extent these new developments will be accepted as authentic fictional techniques, or regarded as over-elaborate, byzantine projects of concern to only a small group of specialized readers. At present, *La Maison de rendez-vous* leads all of Robbe-Grillet's novels in sales and public acclaim. Even if some of this popularity may be attributed to erotic elements in the book, or to its pseudo-James Bond atmosphere and plot, we may still detect a willingness to accept, in fiction, some of the same formal liberties and absence of conventional justifications that prevail in modern pictorial styles (from abstract to op) and musical compositional methods (from serial to chance). A McLuhanite or a disciple of George Steiner might argue that the phenomenon is related to the breakdown of language, or at least the breakdown of the old rhetoric of fiction in the direction of the non-rational, if not the non-verbal. To so argue would be in one sense a paradox, since works like *La Maison de rendez-vous* have a stylistic intricacy and polish that set them apart from the "revolution of the word" syntax of lettrism, beat poetry, post-Joycean free association, syllabic interplay, mangled texts à la William Burroughs, or other symptoms of that retreat from reality which now, according to Steiner, "begins outside the verbal language." One thing at least seems assured: the *nouveau roman*, in the hands of Robbe-Grillet and other experimentalists, continues to promise evolutionary surprises.

George H. Szanto (essay date 1972)

SOURCE: "Internalized Reality: The Subjective Point of View," in *Narrative Consciousness: Structure and Perception in the Fiction of Kafka, Beckett, and Robbe-Grillet*, University of Texas Press, 1972, pp. 134-48.

[*In the following essay, Szanto examines the presentation of character and narrative perspective in Robbe-Grillet's fiction. According to Szanto, "Robbe-Grillet is not telling stories as much as he is creating characters—not really creating characters, either, as much as creating an atmosphere for a character."*]

There are a number of ways in which the narrator of a tale can present himself to a reader. Robbe-Grillet's first three novels, *The Erasers*, *The Voyeur*, and *Jealousy* are told in the third person, yet the importance of each novel lies in its capacity to produce the immediate presence of a narrator. In each novel the narrator exists at every point only within the character relevant to that particular narrative. There is no gratuitous description, no gratuitous object; everything is linked to the central character. Of *The Voyeur*, Bruce Morrissette remarks, ". . . even the most 'neutral' and innocent-seeming description of natural objects may contain, imperceptible at first glance but beyond a doubt fully intentional, some formal theme or coincidence of vocabulary that relates the object to the plot, or to the personality of Mathias, or to some aspect of a later action."

In the novels the narrational voice, a unified source of information, becomes the theoretical basis for an image of the world; the voice seems to speak in absolutes. Each voice's primary relevance is to the fiction itself, but the situation of the narrator is analogous to that of the chief of police in *The Erasers*: "He dares not reject his assistant's hypothesis out of hand, for you never know: suppose that happened to be what happened, what would he look like then? Then too the obscurities and contradictions of the case have to be interpreted one way or another." All obscurities and contradictions must be forced into a mold so that they make sense to a perceiving consciousness; the only mold capable of holding the incidents in proper relation to each other is the one formed by the narrating mind.

The first three novels interchange normal characteristics of first- and third-person narration. Although each novel maintains a first person point of view, the pronoun itself is in the third person; each "I" character (except A . . .'s husband) designates himself with his own proper name. In *The Erasers*, although the point of view is distributed among several characters, each in his turn follows this rule of self-objectification—the manager of the Café des Alliés, Laurent the chief of police, Garinati, Wallas.

Snatches of conversation, in their banality, record the undecorated sounds of the human voice immediately, as they are perceived. Wallas's uncertainty in the matter of a simple question is recorded together with the exchanged words. His uncertainty in this trivial matter is the weak echo of his far greater uncertainty and one of the novel's structuring motifs, his Oedipal search for his (probable) father (Dupont).

Maison de rendez-vous (1965) in a sense returns to the multi-narrational technique of *The Erasers*; with the apparent exception of the "I" character, who begins the book and returns to its pages at odd intervals, the several "narrators" each see themselves in the third person. Kim, for example, enters the building of Manneret's apartment; with her is one of Madame Ava's dogs. "Kim has only to follow the dog: in her turn she climbs the steep, narrow, wooden steps, a little more slowly of course, . . . the absence of light constituting a further obstacle for eyes accustomed to the bright sun outside." The difference here is that the novel is dominated by one character alone, the narrator "I" is creating the conflicting snatches of narrative as he sits in his room. The reader knows that it is probably in an apartment house also, for in the quarters above the narrator's room a man is rocking in a chair, to the great irritation of the narrator. The narrator later gives the rocking chair to Manneret when Kim visits him.

Much more remains of the room in which the narrator/doctor of In the Labyrinth writes the story of the soldier returning from the war, who carries a box filled with irrelevancies to be given to someone whose name he has forgotten at a place and time he does not remember. The narrator's room contains all the elements from which the story of the soldier grows: a bayonet, a box, tracks in the dust (which become tracks in the snow), filaments in the light bulb, and, most of all, a picture, titled *The Defeat at*

Reichenfels, in which the soldier, the boy, and the bartender figure as principles. The narrator weaves a story from these elements, a story almost fulfilling Flaubert's attempts to conceive a *roman pur*, a novel created from nothing. *Maison de rendez-vous* is, in this sense, purer; only a rocking chair links the created events with the narrator's reality.

Like the created characters of *Maison de rendez-vous*, the soldier attains his own point of view, but it is granted him by a narrator who is constantly in the process of forming his hero. Robbe-Grillet's narrator puts himself in the midst of the situation being described. Whereas the events of the first three novels are actually occurring at a single remove—they are the fictions of Robbe-Grillet (everything happens to the narrator)—In the Labyrinth and *Maison de rendez-vous* are operating at a further remove. Robbe-Grillet is writing the story of a narrator who is creating the events he is describing. In this respect the structural development of the two latter novels approaches that of the later novels of Samuel Beckett. A story is told by a narrator within the novel who plays little active part in the story being created. But whereas Beckett's narrator would say, "I am now going to create a narrative," or, "No, no, this won't do, this is badly written," Robbe-Grillet's narrator omits the step; the reader is not certain whether Robbe-Grillet or his narrator is telling the story.

The inability to differentiate between "real" and "imaginary" events is not limited to the later novels. Mathias of *The Voyeur* is quite capable of imagining what could happen as he goes out to sell his watches. In his thoughts he has visited a house, has sold several watches, and starts to go. "As he was leaving he wanted to say a few words of farewell, but none came out of his mouth. He noticed this at the same moment he realized the whole scene had been a stupidly worthless one [*sic*]. Once on the road, behind the closed door, his suitcase unopened in his hand, he understood that it all still remained to be done." Here is a further remove, a further frame: first person interplay between imagination and immediate reality is disguised behind what appears to be a third-person narrative. The interplay itself is presented from the single point of view, Mathias's mind. Robert Champigny notes that

> the technique of *Le Voyeur* is the result of an attempt to present everything that occurs (gestures, perceptions, projects, images, memories, calculations) on the same plane. This search for flatness means a reduction of the conditional mood (the alibi) to the indicative, of the unreal to the real: the alibi is unreal, but the images in Mathias' mind are real. It also leads to a reduction of the past and future to an eternal present: Mathias' memories and projects may point toward the past or the future, but they themselves are present. The thoughts and images which crop up in Mathias' mind are thus assimilated to perception.

A . . .'s husband in *Jealousy* also mixes imagination with past incident and projected possibility. But the element deleted from Robbe-Grillet's third novel is an objectification, at any point in the narrative, of the narrator himself.

The narrating voice must be relevant to the story; context forces the realization that it is A . . .'s husband. He never refers to himself, either with adjective or with proper noun, or with "I" or "he"; his single device for self-reference is the generalizing "one" or the passive voice. The tone of jealousy itself demands the conclusion that no one living in the house with A . . . other than her husband would be jealous of Franck, with whom, to the narrator's mind, A . . . spends too much time and to whom she pays too much attention. The narrator could be another lover, but the possibility is eliminated by the propriety of circumstances in which the events take place; and A . . . does speak of her husband, who can be present only in the person of the narrator—never more than three chairs are occupied. The husband will not admit to himself what he strongly suspects is happening between his wife and Franck. "In order to avoid the danger of upsetting the glasses in the darkness, A . . . has moved as near as possible to the armchair Franck is sitting in, her right hand carefully extending the glass with his drink in it. She rests her other hand on the arm of the chair and bends over him, so close that their heads touch. He murmurs a few words: [she is] probably thanking him." "Probably" forces the reader to doubt the explanation. The husband fools no one but himself.

In a sense, elimination of the personal pronoun in reference to oneself is an honest fictionalized description of the relation between a subjective conception and the objectification of oneself. In speaking, one does say "I." In thinking, such pronouns are rare. Nor does one use the label of a name (with which the external world objectifies all the qualities compounded to describe an individual) for oneself in personal thoughts. Since memory and imagination do not reach a stage of symbolization demanding words, and pictures suffice (much as they suffice to describe what one sees at a given moment), the need of a pronoun or any label for self-reference is not necessary. A . . .'s husband finds need neither for this nor for labels other than the most simple (A . . .) in referring to his wife; whether he has reduced their relationship to this single letter or whether the letter suffices to bring to his mind all associations of their life together is not important.

Contrary to Robbe-Grillet's pronouncements that characters no longer exist in fiction, he has created, as thoroughly as most authors can, characters who may be spoken of as real and full people; one learns about them as they expose their consciousness to the reader. And they are each sufficiently conscious to display themselves not only in the functioning of their minds, but also in their ability to watch themselves as they act out given situations. For example, Kim, seeking out M. Tchang, locates him; but he, for a reason at that point unknown, will not make contact with her. She then transports herself in her mind out of the situation and begins over. The second beginning belongs to the narrator. (To claim it belongs merely to Robbe-Grillet would be to beg the question; it is Robbe-Grillet who is creating the mind of an author/narrator whose several attempts at writing a story are all described.) The juxtaposi-

tion belongs to the narrator and as much explains his inability to work out a facet of the plot as it explicates the character of Kim. What the reader of *Maison de rendez-vous* has before him are, in effect, notebooks of the imagination for a novel about an evening in Hong Kong. It has been said that watching the evolution of characters in Gide's notebooks for *The Counterfeiters* is as interesting as reading the novel itself. Robbe-Grillet accepts such a sentiment literally and writes a novel about the psychological movement expressed almost completely in the episodes invented by a writer carrying on his occupation. The changing situations of characters in relation to each other, and in relation to time sequences, is nothing more than a shift in the author's conception of characters with which his mind is working. As the shifts and changes proceed, a novel comes into being.

This experiment relates most completely to Robbe-Grillet's first novel: the process of an examination into the death of Dupont changes constantly as new evidence is introduced. Each new hypothesis is a corrective to previous explanation, an improvement that brings complete explanation (of the case and of the novel) closer. Each incorrect analysis clarifies something not only about the case but also about Wallas, for *The Erasers* is primarily his story. The process of the novel, the constant process of change, is a correction by erasure of those "facts" previously assumed correct. As new information is accumulated, both by the novel's investigators and by the reader, earlier information is edited and events are given more valid explanations. What is incorrect is, so to speak, erased.

Because the reality of each of Robbe-Grillet's novels changes under one's eyes, it becomes essential for the reader to find one point in the novel that remains steady. The point of view of the narrator alone will suffice. Of *Jealousy*, Morrissette says, "The point of view, with its rotations, emerges from a consciousness inside the text which the reader must assume, thus placing himself at the observational center." The reader must, in effect, become the jealous husband, thereby himself experiencing pangs of jealousy for this beautiful woman, his wife, a sensuous female with beautiful hair brushing her bare shoulders and back, who wears tight-fitting dresses so that Franck's wife herself becomes jealous and suggests that A . . . wear something loose there in the tropics. This place for the reader Robbe-Grillet calls a "hollow" in the text. The same kind of missing factor, this time called a "hole," must be recognized in *The Voyeur*. The time during which Mathias kills Jacqueline is a blank both in the book and in Mathias's mind; the latter position must be assumed by the reader for him to realize the existence of this empty space. Only from within does Mathias's avoidance of the events, even silently in his mind, become evident.

The demands of In the Labyrinth and *Maison de rendez-vous* are more stringent. The early novels contain events with which memory and imagination can be linked; the later novels are moving so quickly toward the *roman pur* that very little landscape remains. The reader must submit himself so rigorously to the flexibilities of the author/narrator's mind that imagining events on the snow-covered streets of the city in In the Labyrinth and sensing the smells of Hong Kong in *Maison de rendez-vous* become the only conscious reality. The narrative implicates the imagination, even though it consists only of generalizations and clichés about Hong Kong. Yet, when related to each other in Robbe-Grillet's carefully structured descriptions, the pictures and images evoke complicity and force the reader into the chair behind the writer's desk, making him a part of the novel.

Robbe-Grillet is not telling stories as much as he is creating characters—not really creating characters, either, as much as creating an atmosphere for a character. An atmosphere remains for only a limited period of time; Robbe-Grillet's novels never take place over a period of more than a day or two. The period of *Maison de rendez-vous* covers one late afternoon and the subsequent evening. The narrator's recorded episodes attempt to evoke the exoticism of Hong Kong, an exoticism of the city as well as an exoticism of pleasure. Carnal pleasure is present from the beginning, from the moment the narrator characterizes himself with his opening statement, "Women's flesh has always played, no doubt, a great part in my dreams." A crude interpretation of the intent of the narrator could be paraphrased in Genêt's words, that he wrote *Our Lady of the Flowers* merely to maintain an erection. But the intent here is far more complex, for it makes of a possible Genêt-like author merely another character to serve Robbe-Grillet's fiction-making process. The success of exoticism in *Maison de rendez-vous* is achieved without the use of exotic language or unnatural description; the inventive juxtaposition of clichés suffices.

Robbe-Grillet's methods for presenting a scene or situation are relatively simple. That his artist's mind's eye is no camera should by now be obvious. His descriptions edit too completely; they do not begin with panoramas that a camera's image could embrace; rather they choose microscopic details of large scenes and landscapes. When describing the rows of banana trees, for example, Robbe-Grillet omits not only the foreground of the picture but also the spaces between the trees themselves; furthermore, to differentiate between trees is impossible. The importance of Camus's experiments is discernible here: as Meursault tries to recall, "en imagination," the details of his room, he lets his mind's eye wander from one wall to another, cataloguing, enumerating everything he can recall, the objects as well as the wall's imperfections, and though he carries on this procedure many times he finds that each repeated survey of the same image reveals more details than had the previous. Without verbalizing this difficulty, as did Camus's narrator, Robbe-Grillet leaves to the reader's discovery the incomplete picture before him. Not even a six-page description of *The Defeat at Reichenfels* suffices to describe all the elements the picture contains.

Of course, Robbe-Grillet is partly responsible for the confusion. He has quite deliberately called the published form of both *Last Year at Marienbad* and *The Immortal* "ciné-roman," and his collection of brief prose narratives he has named *Instantanées* (*Snapshots*). Since, aside from his theoretical pieces, these represent his only publication besides his novels, it is not difficult to conclude that Robbe-Grillet is merely applying the techniques of one medium to the presentation of another. But the evidence of his fictional heritage stands opposed to carrying the supposition too far; Robbe-Grillet has, of course, utilized techniques from the film, but artists have always sought new forms in neighboring disciplines. It is his ability to edit language, to keep the narrative relevant, that retains his identity as fabulator. What is not relevant is never absorbed, either by narrator or by protagonist. Like Mathias, Robbe-Grillet is trying to sell his product. Mathias hears from the sailor all the details about the family of the sailor's sister: "Mathias, who expected to put them to good use soon, added all these facts to the inquiries he had made the day before. In work like this, there was no such thing as a superfluous detail." Nor must Robbe-Grillet allow superfluous details.

The point of view of narrative consciousness is capable of a great deal. It can, for example, converse, as does the husband in *Jealousy*:

> The conversation has returned to the story of the engine trouble: in the future Franck will not buy any more old military *materiel*; his latest acquisitions have given him too many problems; the next time he replaces one of his vehicles, it will be with a new one.
>
> But he is wrong to trust modern trucks to the Negro drivers, who will wreck them just as fast, if not faster.
>
> "All the same," Franck says, "if the motor is new, the driver will not have to fool with it."

Franck's words are reported as direct or indirect discourse, the words of the narrator/husband appear as generalized thoughts, a pedestal to which only "objectively" true statements are usually elevated. Such a technique is successful in its re-emphasis of the feeling that one's own utterances are always valid.

Even in description that might otherwise be deemed purely "objective," Robbe-Grillet's narrators manage to inject a note of doubt. The usual technique is to overstress otherwise innocent situations. So A . . .'s husband speaks of A . . . and Franck in town: "It is only natural that they will meet there, especially for dinner, since they must start back immediately afterwards. It is also natural that A . . . would want to take advantage of this present opportunity to get to town, which she prefers to the solution of a banana truck." All this is so natural that there seems little need for the narrator to mention it; yet he does, and implies that much is going on below the surface of his reports. Much the same effect is gained with such words as *no doubt, probably, certainly*, and *perhaps*. Knowing it not to be true, the husband nevertheless notes: "The table is set for three. A . . . has probably just had the boy add Franck's place, since she was not to be expecting any guest for lunch today." To show the complicity between A

. . . and Franck, the narrator describes by concealment the reaction of one to another in a certain situation: "A . . . is humming a dance tune whose words remain unintelligible. But perhaps Franck understands them, if he already knows them, from having heard them often, perhaps with her. Perhaps it is one of her favorite records." Whether the two ever heard it together is uncertain; only the narrator's suspicions are clear. The narrator chooses ambiguity partly in order to avoid accusing A . . . and Franck without absolute evidence; partly, however, he does not wish to admit to himself the possibility that his wife is having an affair. Evasion on the part of the narrator plays a large role in Robbe-Grillet's early novels. Wallas is unaware that his search is leading him into a situation in which he will have to kill his (possible) father, and so the evasion is perpetrated by the author on the reader only; but Mathias is capable of, and completely involved in, doing so by himself. The last two parts of his narrative involve nothing but evasion: he will not even admit to his own conscious mind what he has done, and the reader must piece the information together from the images that do come to his mind, for not everything appearing in print can be accepted as "truth," not even very limited truth. Mathias's refusal to admit his acts to himself is based in a conscious desire to establish an alibi for himself to cover the time of Jacqueline's rape and murder.

The narrator, seeing A . . . leaning through the car window to kiss Franck, describes the scene as geometrically as possible. The fact of passion is absent. In much the same way the husband takes his mind off A . . .'s late return from her trip to town with Franck by considering with almost paranoid exactness the details of the house; the more control he can retain over his mind the greater will be his ability to withstand his jealousy. In much the same way the narrator will shift his glance from A . . . and Franck to something irrelevant if he believes he may see some hint of tenderness that transcends the relationship of neighbors, or if he already has seen more than he wishes. The description of A . . .'s hair gives away the narrator's attitude to the scene; since the sensation of jealousy usually corresponds to the realization of imminent (or already determined) loss, the husband must be shown admiring his wife. This is not to say that Robbe-Grillet portrays in the husband a love of A . . . ; love is not necessary for, although it probably deepens, the imagined oncoming loss. At any rate, Robbe-Grillet is content to portray A . . . , to her husband's eyes, as a sensual, desirable woman—at least her sensuality is prime in the husband's mind. It is difficult to determine if A . . . is beautiful. One can assume she is attractive to Franck, who visits her even when his own wife is ill, and she obviously arouses her husband, even though he apparently never considers more of her than her hair, her lips, her shoulder and her figure in a tight dress, which suffices.

Much the same technique is used to establish sensuality in *Maison de rendez-vous*. Once the narrator has avowed his partiality for women's flesh, his always incomplete hints at possible perversions are sufficient to retain the sensation of sensuality, which becomes a major element in the tone of exoticism dominant in the novel. Even his obsession for the very tight dresses worn by Chinese women, slit to the thigh, suggests the constant presence of exotic pleasure.

Sensuality is not the only tone, though it is one of the most prominent, that Robbe-Grillet attempts to create in his novels. All atmospheres can be determined by the external (and externalized) "things" chosen by the mind's eye. Although related to T. S. Eliot's objective correlatives, such objects cannot achieve any immediate evocation of parallel emotions; the blue cigarette package, the figure eight, and the piece of rope in no way add up to Mathias's crime, but they do point to the obsessive nature of his mind. Robbe-Grillet's success lies in his ability to lead one toward the necessary background that will explain the crime, much as Camus makes it obvious that sun, sand, and sky forced Meursault to kill the Arab. The choice of the "things" the eye of the narrating consciousness perceives is based in their ability to suggest rather than in their power to equate and define.

The choice of objects most relevant to the perceiving mind and the manner in which those objects are described establish the state of mind that controls the point of view in Robbe-Grillet's fiction. The subconscious mind is projected onto an external world, but this never becomes a conscious process; the conscious mind merely reports what it is driven to view. Such a formula allows an identification between Franck's killing the centipede and his probable affair with A . . . : "A . . . seems to be breathing a little faster, but this may be an illusion. Her left hand gradually closes over her knife. The delicate antennae accelerate their alternate swaying." As when A . . .'s hand came too close to Franck's, the narrator looks away, fearing the overdisplay of emotion to which he might be a witness. The implicit comparison comes almost to the surface when Franck's attack on the centipede is described again later: "A . . . moves no more than the centipede while Franck approaches the wall, his napkin wadded up in his hand." This motif reaches its climax when the husband is awaiting the return of Franck and A . . . ; it combines with the sense of loss to give the centipede enormous proportions: "The pantry door is closed. Between it and the doorway to the hall is the centipede. It is enormous: one of the largest to be found in this climate. With its long antennae and its huge legs spread on each side of its body, it covers the area of an ordinary dinner plate. The shadow of various appendages doubles their already considerable number on the light-colored paint." Every ounce of objective hatred is expended on the centipede Franck has destroyed just as he has defiled, in the husband's mind, the purity of his beautiful wife and the sanctity of their marriage.

In the same way the eraser and the girl in the shop (who may be his stepmother) combine to arouse in Wallas the beginnings of sensuality, essential for the novel's structure in which the son kills his (possible) father. "Once out in the street, Wallas mechanically fingers the little eraser; it is obvious from the way it feels that it is no good at all. It would have been surprising, really, for it to be otherwise in so modest a shop. . . . That girl was nice. . . . He rubs his thumb across the end of the eraser. It is not at all what he is looking for." Wallas and A . . .'s husband have a confederate in Mathias, who establishes his own lustful nature in the cafe after leaving the ferry; he sees a natural action of the waitress: "She held her head to one side, neck and shoulders bent, in order to observe more closely the rising level of liquid in the glass. Her black dress was cut low in back. Her hair was arranged so that the nape of her neck was exposed." A much more generalized object of sensual thought than A . . . , the waitress helps explain how to Mathias's mind his perversion and crime become possible. All females, even thirteen-year-olds (perhaps especially thirteen-year-olds, who are less capable of resistance—lack of resistance becomes a motif in **Maison de rendez-vous**), can arouse Mathias's lust.

Emphasis of a narrator's glance also plays its part. A . . .'s husband watches Franck and remarks: "He drinks his soup in rapid spoonfuls. Although he makes no excessive gestures, although he holds his spoon quite properly and swallows the liquid without making any noise, he seems to display, in this modest task, a disproportionate energy and zest. It would be difficult to specify exactly in what way he is neglecting some essential rule, at what particular point he is lacking in discretion." Having in effect stared at Franck as he eats, the narrator seems surprised that A . . . has finished her soup without drawing attention to herself; but the attention to be caught is that of the husband, and he was too busy being irritated at Franck to notice. Franck is not actually lacking in discretion; because the husband is bothered by something far more basic than seeing Franck eat his soup, he expresses his irritation within the context of the incident of the moment. In much the same way and for similar reasons Franck apparently grew sufficiently angry at his own wife when Christiane criticised A . . . for wearing so tight-fitting a dress.

Having limited his glance only to Franck, the narrator (under the author's control) edits his point of view until he forgets completely the presence of A . . . . Obliquely this may begin to explain possible causes for A . . .'s probable infidelity, but since that path of inquiry is both impossible to follow and not relevant to the obsession of jealousy that remains the novel's subject, Robbe-Grillet draws the attention back to the narrator's point of view. Only the fact that A . . .'s plate is stained lets one (the narrator) realize that she has indeed been eating all the time. The matter, as Bernard Pinguad points out, is not that the glance of the jealous husband deforms what he sees so much as it is that he chooses and sees in a limited way. Mathias's eyes, for example, fall only on a limited number of kinds of things; even in a village shop his eye can find the appropriate object—a mutilated naked mannequin.

> In one corner, at eye level, stood a window mannequin: a young woman's body with the limbs cut off—the arms just below the shoulder and the legs eight inches from the trunk—the head slightly to one side and

forward to give a "gracious" effect, and one hip projecting slightly beyond the other in a "natural" pose. The mannequin was well proportioned but smaller than normal as far as the mutilations permitted her size to be estimated. Her back was turned, her face leaning against a shelf filled with ribbons. She was dressed only in a brassiere and a narrow garter-belt popular in the city.

The extreme subjectivity of a narrator's glance defines his nature. But a descriptive narrative needs more than an atmosphere if it is to succeed as fiction; it needs a relevant interrelation of its parts. It is already apparent that all images in these novels emanate from the mind of the narrator; their sources—the glance of the moment, a picture from the memory, the image of a hoped for or feared future event—are totally interconnected. Stoltzfus notes that Robbe-Grillet unites the several imaginative processes. What Robbe-Grillet "seems to be saying is that dream, day-dream, fantasy, imagination, the creative process, are all related; that the factor which differentiates dreams from imaginative creation or fiction is a matter of volition, direction, or perhaps even coherent organization." Precisely this organization is the artist's domain; more than simply searching for new experiences, the act of structuring uses atmosphere-creating words and shapes them into the beginnings of fiction.

George H. Szanto (essay date 1972)

SOURCE: "Toward a New Novel: A Theory for Fiction," in *Narrative Consciousness: Structure and Perception in the Fiction of Kafka, Beckett, and Robbe-Grillet,* University of Texas Press, 1972, pp. 123-33.

[*In the following essay, Szanto discusses Robbe-Grillet's philosophical perspective and concept of the "new novel" as delineated in* Towards a New Novel. *Szanto notes that Robbe-Grillet's theoretical writings have "contributed to the rampant misunderstanding about his fiction."*]

Alone among the novelists discussed here, Alain Robbe-Grillet has published a volume of purposely theoretical writing. Kafka's diaries and letters, certainly not meant for publication, deal with the events, the day-to-day trivialities of his personal life; any information about his art must be carefully culled from them, and then it usually appears as its own kind of parable. Beckett's essays on Joyce and on Proust and his three dialogues with Georges Duthuit, all written before his presently published novels, these ostensibly deal with subjects other than himself; they explain what Beckett has discovered in the works of Joyce, Proust, and several modern painters but do not allow him to elaborate on what he adds to the innovations of those from whom he learned. On the other hand, although Robbe-Grillet's Towards a New Novel (**Pour un nouveau roman**) contains essays he has written about other people—understanding the tradition is essential if an author wishes to grow from it—the book's primary force arises from its apparently heretical outline for a new kind of novel.

And yet the program the book demands is often little more than a description of fiction already written by Robbe-Grillet's predecessors, Kafka and Beckett. Certainly it contains something more—it contains passages lending themselves to interpretations that infuriated and impressed critical thinking for more than ten years. Perhaps only in retrospect can one see how Robbe-Grillet's essays could be misunderstood while at the same time they presented a plan for novels unrelated to interpretations of his theories by others. For just as each of his novels shows an increased subtlety and comprehension of technique, his theory too develops to a point where it eliminates the confusion imposed on it by such critics as Roland Barthes, who, himself linguistically and scientifically oriented, saw Robbe-Grillet's first two novels (**The Erasers** [1953] and **The Voyeur** [1955]) as representing worlds void of human beings except insofar as humans were viewed, much like all objects within the narrative, as things. In the beginning, Robbe-Grillet did not deny this analysis. He could write the novels and sense their importance, but he could not yet abstract and define the theory. So in 1956 he wrote:

> Even the least conditioned observer can't manage to see the world around him with an unprejudiced eye. Let us make it quite clear before we go any further that we are not here concerned with that naive preoccupation of subjectivity which so amuses the analysts of the (subjective) soul. Objectivity, in the current meaning of the term—a completely impersonal way of looking at things—is only too obviously a chimera. But it is *liberty* which ought at least to be possible—but isn't, either. Cultural fringes (bits of psychology, ethics, metaphysics, etc.) are all the time being attached to things and making them seem less strange, more comprehensible, more reassuring. Sometimes the camouflage is total: a gesture is effaced from our minds and its place taken by the emotions that are supposed to have given rise to it . . .

Although the argument appears to develop into a plea for objectivity in viewing the world, at the same time it admits that such a project is impossible; the inescapability of subjective vision is a dominant note from the beginning. Yet Robbe-Grillet is not talking about his way of seeing the world, but about the world itself; the distinction has become blurred for many of those who follow Barthes's comprehension of Robbe-Grillet's novels and theories.

To no small extent Robbe-Grillet himself has contributed to the rampant misunderstanding about his fiction; at the beginning he was more interested in considering the nature of the external world than he was in discussing the techniques he utilized in viewing that world. His bent led him to adapt to literature the dictum that "the world is neither meaningful nor absurd. It quite simply is . . . All around us, defying our pack of animistic or domesticating adjectives, things *are there*." An explanation about the nature of the world from a novice writer is only natural if, as Robbe-Grillet does, he considers himself to be writing "realistically." It is even more natural if he is only in the process of developing his theories about art and its relationship to that world: one must first understand what one is describing before finding the tools for that description. In this respect, a writer's theories about his art begin only after he has begun to write novels; the novels must, by definition (even if not in their stress), be about the world. The theory follows the fact of creation despite an author's possible understanding of the theory before he began to write.

Therefore, when Robbe-Grillet maintained the *presence* of things to be their primary importance, he gave strong argument to those who believed he was going to be working with things in and of themselves. In this early essay, Robbe-Grillet justly claims that the nineteenth-century fictional tradition sees literature as a mode of expression in which the writer defined and delineated his relation to the external world (called by Robbe-Grillet "tragic complicity") by explaining the world in terms of himself, by finding in the external world correspondences to his own moods and sensibilities. By carefully using the adjective to anthropomorphize and domesticate his environment (a countryside is "austere" or "calm," depending on the mood to be established), the writer made of it an accomplice for his hero, as well as an accomplice for himself in his attempt to explain his hero. Robbe-Grillet the theorist wished to eliminate such complicity, since ultimately it must eliminate the possibility of any relationship between man and a universe already by definition nonhuman; only the nonrelationship remains, what existentialism calls the gap of absurdity. Robbe-Grillet, not believing that the simple fact of non-connection between man and his environment should be seen pejoratively (absurdly), claimed that a new kind of fiction could develop if the unbridgeable distance between man and his world was accepted as a neutral fact.

Between taking the world as a series of surfaces, which exist in complete freedom from man's domesticating adjectives and have little relevance for man, and taking the world as a unified projection of man's inmost subjective nature (when the heart is clouded so is the sky, the sun comes out when love is rediscovered—or vice versa, if irony is intended), there is the middle ground upon which Robbe-Grillet attempts to stand. But by arguing forcibly against the nineteenth-century complicity between man and his universe, Robbe-Grillet sounds as if he is embracing the view expounded by Barthes's *chosisme*, and evidence for Robbe-Grillet's possible *chosiste* leanings can be garnered from his 1958 article, "Nature, Humanism and Tragedy," to which he prefixes a quotation from Barthes. The article itself, however, is thoroughly denied by both his previous and his subsequent fictions, which, although they do take as fact the equality of everything external, cannot free his heroes from a complicity with the external world. No human can perceive the world in a nonhuman way; no center other than a living eye, or at least a perceiving mind, can validly explain its environment.

The complicity between man and the universe need not be tragic, and if it is not it differs already from any view within the novels of the past. The fiction of Robbe-Grillet dismisses, as his theories demand, the old myths of depth whose fictions describe at great length what lies beneath the world's surfaces. Robbe-Grillet makes it clear that for him there is no (human) depth in the external world. But there is a depth to man, a psychology man does not understand, which governs much of his life; that psychology is defined analytically by the manner in which the governing psychology sees the external world and by what it finds appropriate to its glance. Whereas nineteenth-century writers of fiction anthropomorphized the universe, Robbe-Grillet allows his heroes their delineations according to what segments of their universe they choose to see and according to the manner in which they see and understand the segments. The universe remains an accomplice of the consciousness that views it. It is still a humanist's universe; the viewer is no less a victim of his own complicity than he is in the novels of Balzac or of Camus. The great difference, however, and the great contribution of phenomenological fiction, lies in immediacy, in its ability to implicate the reader in the situation of the hero without ever explaining what the situation is. Far from being a scientistic literature, a *chosiste* fiction, Robbe-Grillet's novels display a relevant realism that keeps them in the tradition of that fiction which is altogether descriptive of human experience.

The shame is that, in his enthusiasm to formulate the boundaries of a new novel, Robbe-Grillet attempted to begin with too much of a clean slate, and, for the earlier critics, everything was erased. In his essay of 1957, "On Some Outdated Notions," he states that such trappings of the novel as character and plot must be eliminated in the new attempt at writing fiction. Although he claims that plot and character are outdated notions, he himself is working with precisely those two elements of fiction, in a modified form, as were Beckett and Kafka before him; merely his method of approach to these problems has differed from that of the nineteenth-century authors. In Robbe-Grillet's fiction, the emphasis has shifted to a tone that describes the character obliquely by engulfing the whole series of events (plot) within the mood established by the narrative; the whole of a novel is completely relevant to the character about whom the events take place.

Even in the article dealing with tragic complicity, "Nature, Humanism, and Tragedy," Robbe-Grillet undercuts his theory of man's non-involvement with nature: ". . . it must be added that the characteristic of humanism, whether Christian or otherwise, is precisely to incorporate *everything*, including things that may be trying to limit it, or even totally reject it. This may even be said to be one of the most reliable mainsprings of its action." Here he is, in effect, admitting what he discovers later in his theory and knows already after the appearance of *The Voyeur*, that one consciousness narrates only what is relevant to itself—nothing else is incorporated. The unity lies in the human consciousness itself, which can relate details relevant only to its own humanity; everything considered by that consciousness is dependent upon it for the kind of existence it will be allowed. Each man is an internalized

universe who considers the external world in accordance with his own nature. In this sense, Robbe-Grillet practices precisely what he condemns: his dismissal of the contemporary relevance of nineteenth-century fiction is so broad that he denounces techniques of his own that differ greatly from those of Balzac. Yet, whereas Balzac sought unified external correlatives to explain his characters, Robbe-Grillet's characters pick tiny segments of the external world, which they draw to themselves; these segments give the only available clues to their natures and obsessions. And this is the distinction Robbe-Grillet does not draw.

The difficulty from the beginning lies in a distinction between the consideration of things themselves and the *presence* of these things. For the presence of a thing is relevant only to the mind that grasps that presence. If this is the distinction Robbe-Grillet was attempting to make, he allowed himself to be misled by the intriguing ideas of Roland Barthes and the praises of Barthes's followers. It would be too much to say that the *chosiste* critics misinterpreted what Robbe-Grillet was writing about (in his theories), since a sufficient base existed for their attitudes. But ***Towards a New Novel***, as a volume of critical essays, cannot be viewed as base for *chosiste* interpretations. Robbe-Grillet claims, quite rightly, that the volume presents a collection of essays, thoughts about the novel that have evolved over a period of years. Such a description is quite valid, provided an attempt is not made to draw parallels between the chronological development of his art and of his theory. A further danger lies in forcing his novels into the mold of previous theoretical statements. Robbe-Grillet points out the writer's difficulty in knowing precisely where he is going before he gets there; the work of art evolves as the attitude to it evolves, as the writer works with it. To take a ten-page theory and attempt to fit into it a three-hundred-page novel is a dangerous business; some aspects of the theory will fit the novel, but the novel must, if it is to be of value, contain far more than the theory itself. In his novels themselves Robbe-Grillet warns, indirectly, against the danger of any immediate parallels between objective, that is, theoretical, statements and the "meaning" of the fiction. In ***The Erasers***, Wallas interrogates the concierge and concludes that in his story, filled with details, "It is apparent that the author only reproduces all those trifling remarks out of a concern for objectivity; and despite the care he takes to present what follows with the same detachment, he obviously regards it as much more important." The words of the concierge, as well as the techniques of the novel, must be seen in their subjective unity.

In the evolution of Robbe-Grillet's theories, there is mounting emphasis on the need for absolute subjectivity to dominate the form and the description of the world perceived. In his 1961 essay, **"New Novel, New Man,"** he openly proclaimed this subjectivity:

> As there are many objects in our books, and as people thought there was something unusual about them, it didn't take long to decide on the future of the word

"objectivity," which was used by certain critics when referring to those objects, but used in very particular sense, i.e. oriented towards the object. In its usual sense which is neutral, cold and impartial, the word becomes an absurdity. Not only is it a man who, in my novels, for instance, describes everything, but he is also the least neutral, and the least impartial of men; on the contrary, he is *always* engaged in a passionate adventure of the most obsessive type—so obsessive that it often distorts his vision and subjects him to phantasies bordering on delirium. It is also quite easy to show that my novels . . . are even more subjective than those of Balzac . . ."

Even if the objects seen appear with hard-edged objectivity, they will be the subjective choices of a psychology enforcing its obsessions onto a conscious and recording mind, and they will be colored by the needs of that mind. For example, the paperweight in the office of Dupont in *The Erasers* is a harmless object when it is first described: "A kind of cube, but slightly misshapen, a shiny block of gray lava, with its faces polished as though by wear, the edges softened, compact, apparently hard, heavy as gold, looking about as big around as a fist; a paperweight?" But, when Wallas arrives at the end of the narrative to kill Dupont, there is murder in his mind and the same paperweight appears other than it was: "The cube of vitrified stone with its sharp edges and deadly corners, is lying harmlessly between the inkwell and the memo-pad."

This kind of subjectivity was already present in Robbe-Grillet's first novel. Perhaps as a counterargument, the example of the tomato can be considered. Geometrically described, this slice appears totally objective:

> A quarter of tomato that is quite faultless, cut up by the machine into a perfectly symmetrical fruit.
>
> The periphereal flesh, compact, homogeneous, and a splendid chemical red, is of an even thickness between a strip of gleaming skin and the hollow where the yellow, graduated seeds appear in a row, kept in place by a thin layer of greenish jelly along a swelling of the heart. This heart, of a slightly grainy, faint pink begins—toward the inner hollow—with a cluster of white veins, one of which extends toward the seeds—somewhat uncertainly.
>
> Above, a scarcely perceptible accident has occurred: a corner of the skin, stripped back from the flesh for a fraction of an inch, is slightly raised.

But its neither appetizing nor disgusting nature underlines merely what has been made clear earlier, that Wallas is not really hungry, that eating is merely one of the functions he pursues as automatically as the automat where he has chosen to eat carries on its preparation of the food: all the dishes offered, for example, are variations of the basic marinated herring. There is a unified, totally objective center controlling all objects and scenes that appear, binding them to a dominating structure; that point of view of narrating consciousness is human from the first of Robbe-Grillet's novels. Roland Barthes in his introduction to Morrissette's *Les Romans de Robbe-Grillet* asks the question, "Between the two Robbe-Grillets, Robbe-Grillet no. 1, the 'chosiste,' and Robbe-Grillet no. 2, the humanist,

between the one portrayed by all the early analysis [established by Barthes himself] and the one portrayed by Bruce Morrissette, must one choose?" The answer must be an emphatic yes.

The link between Robbe-Grillet and the phenomenological theory of Merleau-Ponty especially is constant; in a parallel, rather than influential, relationship, the philosopher and the novelist are working at the same kind of problem with differing tools. In *Jealousy*, the manner in which A . . .'s husband sees his wife writing at her desk and the assumptions he must make are filtered through his narrative consciousness: "The shiny black curls tremble slightly on her shoulders as the pen advances. Although neither the arm nor the head seems disturbed by the slightest movement, the hair, more sensitive, captures the oscillations of the wrist, amplifies them, and translates them into unexpected eddies which awaken reddish highlights in its moving mass." Only the surface is visible, only the details of the surface, and one is not interested in what lies beneath it; the perceiving mind alone establishes the mood. Perhaps A . . . is terrified, perhaps she is nervous, perhaps impatient—the husband can merely guess, and his mood decides for him. *Jealousy*, for example, follows the movements of the eye of the narrator, the husband. If he closes his eyes for a moment and an object or a person changes position, then, when his eyes turn back to it, it will seem to have appeared or disappeared suddenly. Robbe-Grillet underscores this movement with the image of a lizard that fascinates the husband: "On the column itself there is nothing to see except the peeling paint and, occasionally, at unforeseeable intervals and at various levels, a greyish-pink lizard whose intermittent presence results from shifts of position so sudden that no one could say where it comes from or where it is going when it is no longer visible." Or, in *The Erasers*, when Juard is waiting for Wallas, the apparently confused echoes and re-echoes that will dominate the surface of the later novels are present in the train station: "A tremendous voice fills the hall. Projected by invisible loudspeakers, it bounces back and forth against the walls covered with signs and advertisements, which amplify it still more, multiply it, reflect it, baffle it with a whole series of more or less conflicting echoes and resonances, in which the original message is lost—transformed into a gigantic oracle, magnificent, indecipherable, and terrifying." With Robbe-Grillet, narrative consciousness is complete. The uncertainty and fear of Kafka have disappeared, the doubts and improbabilities of Beckett have been all but forgotten (they still do hide below the surfaces, disguised beneath such adverbs as *doubtless, perhaps*, and *probably*): but experiments with the purity of narrative consciousness, with a fiction in which the central interest is the narrating voice, have begun to bear fruit.

It is obvious that writers other than Kafka and Beckett have left their influence on Robbe-Grillet; both Sartre and Camus work with objects and situations, especially in their respective novels *Nausea* and *The Stranger*. As Bruce Morrissette reminds one, *Nausea* makes constant use of object descriptions. "Roquentin's depiction of a chestnut-tree root was also an object lesson in the '*être-là* des choses.'" But thereafter comes the difference: ". . . where Sartre freely employs metaphor and draws intellectual conclusions, Robbe-Grillet rigorously restricts himself to the external object." With Robbe-Grillet, there is no reflection. Camus, even in Robbe-Grillet's eyes, removes some of the anthropomorphism from fiction; but, though a purer narrative emerges, the domesticating complicity continues to persist. It remains for Robbe-Grillet to cleanse fiction of arbitrary anthropomorphism before he can bring to it description of an external world that delineates the viewer rather than the world. When he speaks of a need to liberate the human glance from the categories that limit its value, he knows he demands the impossible; everything is linked to the entire psychology of the viewer. Therefore all preconditions symptomized by his fiction must be based in a comprehension of this basic limitation; but the proper response must also rise from an awareness of an extremely precise reanthropomorphization with which Robbe-Grillet purposely mars his purified fiction. Robbe-Grillet's heroes undergo exactly that Rorschach test in which most critics of Kafka indulge: among generally geometric (objective) descriptions, edges of cubes that are "murderous" appear. But these descriptions no longer dominate the narrator; they are instead his creation. Complicity still exists between man and the world, but, because the descriptions have become humanly controlled, a great part of the liberation Robbe-Grillet demanded has taken place. Certainly the relation is "humanistic," and because all distance between himself and the world is controlled by man (as theorist or narrator), the complicity need no longer be tragic. "It can in any case quite obviously only be a question of the world as my *point of view* orientates it; I shall never know any other. The relative subjectivity of my look serves precisely to define *my situation in the world*. I simply avoid making common cause with those who turn this situation into a kind of slavery."

Ben Stoltzfus (essay date Winter 1976)

SOURCE: "Alain Robbe-Grillet: The Reflexive Novel as Process and Poetry," in *Symposium: A Quarterly Journal in Modern Foreign Literatures,* Vol. XXX, No. 4, Winter, 1976, pp. 343-57.

[*In the following essay, Stoltzfus examines the artistic, literary, and theoretical influences behind the creative process in Robbe-Grillet's fiction. "According to Robbe-Grillet," writes Stoltzfus, "every fiction is the story of a gamesman in a quicksand world who is continuously reinventing himself."*]

The inner need that structures Alain Robbe-Grillet's novels and films seems to stem from the same creative source: his epistemology and the ontological imagination that surrounds it. His art as well as his essays have the precise optics of the scientist mingling with the sensibility of the

artist, thus forming a kind of binocular vision: one form of perception seemingly canceling out the other, and the two together giving a view of the world that is existentially absurd.

The realism of Robbe-Grillet's novels and films belies an antirealism that is forever questioning the reality this realism is supposed to elicit. This process gives his art a rhythm that builds and at the same time destroys; it is a systole and a diastole whose expansions and contractions regulate the artistic flow of ideas. This metaphoric breathing implies two simultaneous and seemingly contradictory levels: the objective and the subjective. The chiseled style of Projet pour une révolution à New York, for instance, controls a sado-eroticism that, at any moment, threatens to break through the shell of his quasi-scientific detachment. In this sense Robbe-Grillet's work probably embodies Gide's dictum that classicism (the objective level) is no more than a vanquished romanticism (the subjective level).

Such phenomenology raises interesting and provocative questions concerning the novel as object, the novel as nonobjective art, and ultimately the novel as poetry. To speak of the novel as an object, or for that matter of any art form using language nonobjectively (i.e., with no referents in external reality), must seem anomalous, since until the twentieth century, the novel as a genre, like painting, was, or was thought to be a window on the world, a realistic "hole in the wall" (as art historians call landscape painting) through which the artist let his viewers, or his listeners, or his readers see "reality" in a truer light. Painters, however, at the turn of the twentieth century, with the Impressionists' discoveries to guide them on the one hand, moved toward nonobjective art and Kandinsky is often credited with having rendered the first abstract painting around 1910. Music, on the other hand, has always been more or less abstract. In painting, the first thing to disappear was perspective. In the novel, particularly since Proust, plot, like perspective, has been disappearing. *Les Fauxmonnayeurs*, with its mirrored levels of self-consciousness, was also instrumental in moving the novel closer to reflexiveness as an art form. In painting, objects and people were replaced, gradually, by line, color, and pure composition. We need only think of a Mondrian to perceive a total abstraction in design, while Kandinsky, in the 1930's, among other goals, claimed to be painting the sounds of music. But without words, music is unable to connote anything but the vaguest feelings: its message, like recent experiments of the "nouveau nouveau roman," is itself and only itself.

Traditional, objective paintings, like words, were signs: they stood for something else. However, as soon as painting became abstract, it stopped signifying in order to become the signified, or perhaps, more accurately, simultaneously signifier and signified. A nonobjective painting represents only itself and nothing else, except perhaps by indirect allusion to a body of work by other, earlier nonobjective painters.

Music, even more than painting, has been the purest of art forms; so pure in fact that in order to communicate ideas about love, religion, death, or patriotism, the score required accompanying words. It was the words, inevitably, that imposed the meaning the music was supposed to elicit. Without words, even with the familiar conventions of church, martial, or popular music, the sounds never evoked specific meanings. Music, by its very nature, has been and is nonobjective. Sound is its content and its form. But painting was different and it changed radically when the technical precision of photography replaced the painstaking accuracy of landscape or portrait painters. Photography interiorized painting, making it aware that its uniqueness lay not in realism, but in color, line, and form. In short, the materials of the painter, like notes or sounds for music, became the subject matter of painting: art became reflexive.

Unlike painters, novelists were or are relative latecomers to the non-representational world of art. It was, comparatively speaking, easy for painters to "purify" their art by substituting line and color for recognizable objects. Words, no matter how nonsensically arranged, always seem to mean something in spite of themselves. In this context, the purpose of reflexive writing is not to express a vision of the world, but to obtain a universe which obeys the specific laws of writing. Gérard Genette is probably right in saying that man's contemporary ideas on art, unlike man's thinking from Aristotle to La Harpe, no longer stress art's mimetic role. Whereas the classicists strove for resemblance between art and nature, we moderns, on the contrary, are looking for radical originality with an absolutely new creative dimension. Like Genette, Roland Barthes, in his *Essais critiques*, speaks of the freedom that man has to make things mean something. Objects signify themselves (i.e., have no external referents), and a work of art which signifies itself or becomes self-reflexive is part of a general twentieth century trend toward "abstraction." In painting we speak of nonobjective or abstract art, whereas in literature the term that seems to have emerged is "self-reflexive."

Reflexive novels are formal structures in which the signs are not primarily Freudian or Marxist or social or religious or human, but essentially literary. In this sense, *Finnegans Wake* is a reflexive work. A sentence like "The Mookse and the Gripes," combining the "Fox and the Grapes" with the "Mock-turtle and the Gryphon" does not speak of God, or the class struggle, or beauty. It points instead to the imagination and the creative spirit of its author and is, by extension, an invitation to the reader to participate in the recreation of its meaning. It signifies itself, and as such, is pure literature. But what, if anything, is its message? It refers us, to be sure, to one of Aesop's *Fables* in which the fox, unable to reach the grapes, says they are too green. The same sentence also invokes *Alice in Wonderland* in which the Mock Turtle sings of "Beautiful Soup, so rich and green." The fox is frustrated while the Mock Turtle is not. The fox goes hungry while the Mock Turtle will eat. The word "green" is the point of contact for both experiences. As a signifier within a mythical realm, it signifies two contradictory reactions that cancel each other out.

While the moral significance of such a construct is, at best, ambiguous, it points undeniably to the author's inventive spirit, to his ability to put words, melds, neologisms and the like into new, original, and startling combinations, to recreate perhaps, the consciousness of his race. Such compression of language takes it out of the realm of ordinary discourse by emphasizing its literary, self-reflexive, ambiguous, and hence poetic qualities.

Except for Joyce and Roussel, the "nouveau roman" of the 1950's and the "nouveau nouveau roman" of the 1960's and 1970's is a relative newcomer to the nonobjective or self-reflexive realm. In the nineteenth century a number of artists wished to transmute reality, thereby to transform life which was base into art which was sublime, believing that Art, like the touch of Midas, affecting all those who came in contact with it, made life, if not better, at least bearable. Through Art, Flaubert and Baudelaire and Mallarmé and eventually Proust wished to lift the veil of this imperfect world, thereby providing us with glimpses of a higher perfection. I am not prepared to argue the merits or demerits of their varying degrees of Platonism; that is another matter. Of interest here is the fact that they did seek to achieve varying degrees of self-contained, hermetic structures in order to give their individual utterances a perfection and a durability capable of transcending nature as well as their own, particular, finite lives.

Even though *A la recherche du temps perdu* is a vast panoramic view of French life and society at the turn of the century, art, Proust's art, like a flying carpet, transports us as though in a dream, a waking dream, toward those privileged places, such as Martinville, where metaphor, imagery, metonymy, and "les anneaux d'un beau style," may work their magic. The voyage, perhaps inevitably, was toward an art and a language in which the artist's *parole*, his trademark, made the novel an increasingly self-conscious art. Nevertheless, Proust seems traditional when compared with the recent writings of Philippe Sollers or Jean-Pierre Faye. Proust's artistic method relies on the well-established use of metaphor and comparative imagery. He transforms Charlus into a drone, Jupien into an orchid, valets into greyhounds, and Guermantes into birds. The wild rose has a red bodice, while the apple trees of Normandy are wearing rose-colored satin evening gowns. Such reciprocal imagery is for Proust one of the first conditions of style. Thus the role of metaphor is to give the reader insight into an unknown quantity and, in order to evoke feelings that are difficult to describe, it claims a similarity between two different but familiar objects. But by describing the brief flowering season of the human plant, the passages "within a budding grove" communicate a true and meaningful reciprocity. In admiring the girls' freshness, the narrator distinguishes those imperceptible tell-tale signs that already indicate the full growth of the fruit that will lead to its ripeness, its seeding, and its final dessication. But the use of metaphor, while reciprocal in function, is objective in purpose. The imagery signifies, and the comparisons refer the reader to a familiar, identifiable world of things signified.

As for poetry in the novel, Hemingway, in speaking of *The Old Man and the Sea*, said that he wished to write a prose that would be so dense and so charged with latent meaning, that it would be harder to write than poetry. The message, like an iceberg that is seven-eighths below the surface, was to remain hidden. Only one eighth would be visible to the profane eye. While Proust and Hemingway are stylistically and temperamentally galaxies apart, each writer's *parole* and imagination gives his art the stamp of his individuality and, perhaps, the independence of a new, necessary, and created object. If Proust and Hemingway have anything in common it is a need, verging on compulsion, to create something that will resist death. Like these two living artists, Sartre's fictional Roquentin, feeling "de trop" in a contingent world, believes that only music and eventually the writing of novel can dispel the fear of a nauseous, viscous, natural world of things that is only one step away from the disintegration of being and self.

Nevertheless, in contrast to Roquentin or Hemingway or Proust or Baudelaire or Flaubert, as one of the strongest proponents of the committed artist, Sartre insists that art should have social or political relevance; that the artist who writes and the reader who reads must not ignore the realities of world hunger, suffering, and injustice. Ives Buin in *Que peut la littérature* has traced the debate between Sartre and other committed novelists like him, and the defenders of the "nouveau roman" of 1965 who, like Faye, Sollers, and Ricardou are among the current crop of "nouveaux nouveaux romanciers." It is possible for both kinds of art to coexist. Robbe-Grillet, for all his disavowals, writes novels and films that are simultaneously useful and useless. Like the *Tel Quel* group, he rejects Sartre's insistence that the artist be committed to a cause beyond art. Art for the "nouveaux romanciers" is, in and of itself, a sufficient cause, and the artist, they feel, need not search for political or social involvement beyond his work. But unlike that of the "nouveaux nouveaux romanciers" Robbe-Grillet's art, even though it is reflexive and does explore the ramifications of the creative process, is, in spite of itself, rooted in reality. It is not a pure exercise in language or optics or structure. While the proponents of non-objective art may claim him, death and eroticism, as two of Robbe-Grillet's main themes, relate too strongly to the world (even though they may not be intended to mirror it), not to involve us in a relationship which postulates interaction. Robbe-Grillet's art occupies a middle ground somewhere between Sartre's extreme commitment of words to reality and the equally extreme linguistic hermeticism of the *Tel Quel* group.

Robbe-Grillet's art serves as a point of contact for Ricardou's solipsism and Sartre's "words." Each of these positions explains the ambivalent relationship between Robbe-Grillet the author and the willfulness of his characters. In *Le Voyeur* Robbe-Grillet imagines Mathias; Mathias imagines the seduction of Jacqueline. Robbe-Grillet imagines the doctor in *Dans le labyrinthe*; the doctor imagines the city maze of Reichenfels through which the soldier endlessly walks. Robbe-Grillet imagines *Marien-*

bad and his male lead invents a meeting "last year." Robbe-Grillet puts his characters on the Trans-Europ-Express where they invent their roles and adapt them to the continuously shifting demands of each hour, each new encounter, and each new complicating circumstance. Hence all the contradictions, which are not contradictions because everything is imaginary to begin with. L'Homme que ment is about a man who may or may not be telling the truth. It really does not matter and ultimately we do not care whether the things he says or imagines are true or not. What does interest us, if it interests us at all, is the process itself, since we are being asked to watch the imagination build its own reality and then destroy it. In *Pour un nouveau roman* Robbe-Grillet writes that "the *true*, the *false*, and the *make believe* have become, more or less, the subject matter of every modern work which, instead of claiming to be a fragment of reality, evolves as a reflexion on reality (or what little reality there is, which ever you wish)." The "nouveau roman" is a reflexion on the role of the artist's imagination in relation to the real and the non-real, thus casting doubt on Sartre's emphasis on the necessary correspondence between words and the reality for which are alleged to stand. Words no longer signify another reality, they create it, and in this role—argues Philippe Sollers in *Logique*—language, like music and nonobjective painting, is autonomous: supremely independent. Language is now free to signify itself.

Before delving further into this fascinating topic, we should note in passing that Sartre's ideas on freedom and choice have provided an indispensable magma for the gestation of Robbe-Grillet's work: since there is no *a priori* morality and all values are relative, the artist, like other men, is free to invent the world in which he lives or writes; he manifests this freedom in his choices and these choices, in turn, confer their authenticity on his behavior. My intention then is to move into that "secret room" (the title of one of Robbe-Grillet's short stories), from which and through which all art is possible. It is as though he had modified Descartes and Sartre by saying "j'invente, donc je suis." This premise has given Robbe-Grillet poetic license. His *parole* has even renewed Roussel's imaginary worlds which, to many, were purely decadent, but which now seem like the necessary and preliminary exercises of an important precursor. Beckett's characters also invent new lives and new fictions as they lie dying of old age or boredom or decrepitude.

Robbe-Grillet's novels of the 1950's, innovative as they were, evolved from a literary tradition which, for the most part, had gone unnoticed, and which only now, within the last decade, has been defining itself. Robbe-Grillet's work has obliged us to revalue earlier writers going as far back as Flaubert and Diderot's *Jacques le fataliste*. It must seem paradoxical to some to speak of Sartre and Flaubert as exerting a seminal influence on Robbe-Grillet. Many would no doubt argue that the offspring of such a forced marriage could only produce an "idiot in the family." Indeed, writers and critics like Jean-Bertrand Barrère, Romain Gary, and Kléber Haedens see Robbe-Grillet's fiction as, if anything, cretinous, a mentally retarded child, wearing Charles Bovary's pointed hat, and wandering around like the soldier of *Dans la labyrinthe*, going nowhere. But since poetry, like the dance, as Valéry so nicely puts it, was never meant to go anywhere (whereas prose was), we should probably not be offended by a type of fiction that seems to lack direction, that seems aimless, that seems to go around in circles, that is primarily interested in itself. If it behaves like compulsive Viennese waltzers, it is perhaps because dancing is more pleasurable than walking and poetry more satisfying to the mind than prose.

Valéry's poetry, much of which was about the creative process—hence a poetry that by definition is reflexive—anticipates some of the pronouncements by the "nouveaux romanciers" on the novel as object and the novel of the future as "process." Robbe-Grillet's *Dans le labyrinthe* is a novel of process because it stands, in part, for the novelist's exploration of the creative act. Butor defines his own endeavors as "le roman comme recherche." *La Nausée*, for example, is an early novel of process, a novel in search of meaning, because, among other things, it is a study of nausea, its effects, and its causes. Characterization, plot, interaction among characters, like the disappearance of perspective in painting, are secondary to nonexistent. As much can be said for *L'Étranger*, a novel which traces Meursault's evolution from his intuitive, animal reaction to the world, to his human, intellectualized understanding of the absurd. Butor's *L'Emploi du temps* gives the reader the substance, the very process of self-discovery which enables his protagonist, Jacques Revel, to escape from the labyrinth of Bleston that threatens to destroy him. Significantly, Butor's novel, like *La Nausée*, is written in diary form. Such contemporary writing is the mythical equivalent of Ariadne's thread, looping back on itself so as to enable the protagonists to isolate the objects, understand the events, and escape from the monster threatening their sanity.

The fever-wracked soldier of *Dans le labyrinthe*, who wanders hopelessly lost in search of somebody's father, unlike the protagonists of the three novels just mentioned, does succumb to things, places, and events. He becomes trapped in the labyrinth of history, war, mythology, language (there are so many possible interpretations), the victim of that "tragic complicity" Robbe-Grillet referred to in his famous essay entitled **"Nature, Humanisme, Tragédie."** But the message or meaning of this novel, unlike the above three, does not seem to concern the lost soldier. Instead, everything in the novel, as Morrissette, Alter, and others have demonstrated, points to the novelist's exploration of the creative process *per se*, so that the subject matter of the work becomes not existentialism, or the absurd, or the alienation of self, or the hero in search of meaning, but is, instead, a novel about the writing of a novel. Essentially, it is a novel in search of itself.

The internal signs of the three transitional novels just mentioned are still part of the signifier/signified aspect of a phenomenological world. Roquentin's reaction to the

chestnut tree root is intended to be "real." Meursault's reactions to the sky one fateful day on the beach, when it rains fire down upon him, are intended to be "real." Revel's map of Bleston also, in this sense, is intended to remind us of all such similar city maps. The signs of *La Nausée*, *L'Étranger*, and *L'Emploi du temps* have familiar, identifiable, referents in the outside world. The signs of *Dans le labyrinthe* also seem to signify familiar things, but in doing so they serve only to entrap the wandering soldier. He becomes lost in a maze of familiar things which he expects to mean something, but which in fact are disorienting, as the author-protagonist explores one street after another, one dead-end after the next, opens doors that lead nowhere, ascends, descends staircases that, as in a Kafka novel, will never lead him to the place where he is supposed to meet the father. In spite of the fact that the messenger has forgotten the name of the street, the time of the rendezvous, and the name of the man he seeks, he walks compulsively in search of that elusive something that will provide him and the reader with some shred or thread of continuity out of the labyrinth of confusion. The soldier wanders through the city of Reichenfels in which necessary points of reference have vanished. Something is being signified, but the signifiers have disappeared. In due course the trapped soldier dies trying to deliver the enigmatic shoebox.

What has happened? It is as though the eternal minotaur has become the "connivence tragique" of language and things, a metaphoric alienation that would humanize an inhuman world in which objects and signs are merely "there" signifying nothing. The signs of this novel, therefore, have a double purpose and carry a double meaning. They refer the soldier and the reader to a seemingly familiar world of objects, streets, and places. However, when these are perceived as false, the novel turns back upon itself so that its conative, emotive, metalingual message, to use Jakobson's terminology, becomes reflexive, a structured internal meaning whose code orients the receiver, i.e., the reader, toward internal referents which seem to be either linguistic or affective. Language, says Robbe-Grillet, more specifically, metaphors which humanize and anthropomorphize our environment are responsible for its contamination and man's alienation.

In *Le Voyeur*, for example, the figure-eight imprint on the levy, in the center of which is the piton with its rusty excrescence, assumes significant sexual overtones for Mathias. He is fascinated with a crumpled blue cigarette wrapper floating on the water and the long detailed descriptions of its motions reveal the importance Mathias attributes to it. The wrapper—or more precisely cigarettes—is Mathias' image of violent sexual fantasy and desire. His eyes roam selectively and subjectively from the figure eight to the cigarette wrapper to sensual configurations of seaweed revealed when the water recedes from the rocks, back to the blue paper wrapper which emerges from the waves with the sound of a slap and is associated with the blue pack of cigarettes seen that morning in a bedroom of imagined violence. Figure eights are multiplied in their associations to include knots on doors, eyeglasses, cigarette holes in paper, the black holes of eyes, and presumably the burns on the genitalia of past, present, and imaginary fictions. Robbe-Grillet has insisted that objects have no inherent symbolism, but he does not exclude their catalytic impact on an imagination that may precipitate actual or imagined crimes.

To say that waves "slap" against the rocks is an example of linguistic contamination, the type of tragic complicity Robbe-Grillet denounces. How then does he purify language, fumigate it, decontaminate it? Robbe-Grillet's ambiguous answer is to write novels like *Le Voyeur* and *La Jalousie* in which metaphor has been replaced by metonymy, novels in which language seems cleansed of metaphors, but is in fact as contaminated as ever, since contiguous descriptions of objects, in due course, begin to "ooze" violence or jealousy. Another answer is to write purely self-reflexive novels—novels in which language, as with Ricardou's *La Prise de Constantinople*, transforms itself into *La Prose de Constantinople*. The author's parole becomes repetitive, convoluted, solipsistic, self-contained. There is no "histoire" as such. Nor is it history, since it has nothing to do with the fall of Constantinople in 1453. The title of Claude Simon's *Histoire* is, in this sense, appropriately ambiguous. Are we not again dealing with process, but a process this time which, instead of being metaphysical or creative, as it was in *Dans le labyrinthe*, is now linguistic? Are the novels of Ricardou, Faye, and Sollers real? Yes, of course. They are as real as objects, they exist as books. We touch them, we read them, we talk about them, even write about them, but their code is different. Like "The Mookse and the Gripes" they speak not of life but of literature. They refer not to things, but to language. They use the materials of the poet—words—and these words have intentionally become part of a new system whose code is primarily linguistic. Whereas the referents of works like *Nombres, L'Écluse, Imaginez la nuit* are primarily internal, language-oriented, dehumanized, *Dans le labyrinthe* belongs to both worlds, the internal and the external, hence its hypnotic mood and extraordinary power. It can be read as a metaphysical allegory or as a self-reflexive novel.

In *La Maison de rendez-vous* the narrative voice moves back and forth in time: it remembers, imagines, observes, and most frequently, "plays" with different and contradictory possibilities. Is it Johnson or Jonestone. Lauren or Loraine, Marchat or Marchand? Was there a murder or was it an accident? Does the telephone number 1-234-567 belong to the Blue Villa, "The South Liberation Soviet," or the Society for War on Narcotics? Is Johnson a Peking agent? Symbolic labyrinth or brothel, *La Maison de rendez-vous* is more than a place of encounter for clandestine relationships. It may be also the house of the author's imagination, or ours, or everybody's. It may well be the spot where objective and subjective reality meet, where illusion creates its own reality, where the play within the play's the thing. This novel is a house of encounter for many people and many things, not the least of which is the exploration of the artist's creative process.

Robbe-Grillet's exploration of the creative process reveals, as a corollary, a profound distrust of reality. Nor is it merely a reality that is in a constant state of flux. As a creator of fictions, he is asking his readers to believe in them, yet at the same time he negates the right to believe. He builds the reality of his fiction and then he destroys it. The unwary reader, like the soldier of *Dans le labyrinthe*, is now lost in the maze of the city. False streets, false doors, and false stairways are the labyrinth through which the creative process struggles to assert itself. But this game bears a strange resemblance to life because in the final analysis it is also a mirror of uncertainty, chaos, flux, and violence—those frequent reminders of the harsh world we are so well acquainted with. Any attempt to give Robbe-Grillet's art a solipsistic independence is bound to fail. Or perhaps it succeeds too well. Because if his art is only a game, a game which in spite of itself mirrors the sublimity of the absurd, or a game which the creator and his characters are free to play at will, and whose parts are interchangeable (as *Trans-Europ-Express* demonstrates so neatly), then language, words, or pictures are never only just what they are, but forever, in spite of "pure" intentions, will involve man in the world from which they claim to be autonomous.

Nevertheless, Robbe-Grillet's fiction casts doubt, not only on the world which claims our attention, but also on itself as signifying something. In the second part of *Le Voyeur*, for example, Mathias "sur le double-circuit" spends most of his time trying to destroy the evidence of rape and murder that he has left behind. But in the third part Robbe-Grillet, the author, seems to be erasing the reality of the first two in order to focus our attention on the novel as pure creation—on the novel as object. If this is "the age of suspicion," as Nathalie Sarraute claims it is, then the only dimension of Robbe-Grillet's fiction that is not in doubt is the language itself. It is this indirect emphasis on the novelist's individual *parole* which, after *process*, makes the work of art reflexive, and in Robbe-Grillet's case, ultimately, poetic.

We have been concerned mainly with recent historical patterns of the self-conscious novel. Implicit in the discussion has been the idea that in Robbe-Grillet's fiction, particularly, there is a link between poetry and the reflexive process. We should perhaps look more closely at this aspect of his work in order to determine its poetic content and structure. In his *Structuralism in Literature* Robert Scholes defines poetry as a message for which the receiver has to "supply the missing elements in an act of communication." This definition is, no doubt, vague enough to be accurate. Its usefulness, however, stems from the fact that it distinguishes between a poetic image, such as for example Mallarmé's "les rails de l'infini," and a prosaic equivalent in daily discourse such as "bicycle tracks in the snow," whose meaning is obvious and requires no interpretation. What happens if we apply Scholes' definition to Robbe-Grillet's *La Jalousie*? Since *La Jalousie*, in keeping with Robbe-Grillet's novelistic technique, confines itself for the most part to situating, describing and defining objects and events in space, we may wonder how such a technique, which seems to have cleansed objects, which has killed the adjective, restored to objects, as Barthes says, their "maigreur essentielle," and to writing, as Genette says, a cathartic dimension, how such writing could ever become poetry.

Perhaps the answer lies in distinguishing between metaphor and metonymy as different aspects of poetic language. Scholes believes, as do Jakobson and Saussure, that "metaphorical substitution is based on a likeness or *analogy* between the literal word and its metaphorical replacement (as when we substitute *den* or *burrow* for *hut*), while metonymical substitution is based on an association between the literal word and its substitute." Things that are related by cause and effect in a logical way (*wealth* and *mansion*) or whole and part (mansion and veranda) as well as things that are customarily found together in familiar contexts (*plantation* and *millionaire*) are in metonymic relationship to one another. For Jakobson, in any work of literature, the discourse may move from topic to topic according to relationships of similarity, i.e., metaphor, or of contiguity, i.e., metonymy.

To reflect on the novel *La Jalousie* is to see it primarily in metonymic terms. Whenever the husband sees, imagines, or describes a centipede and its corollary, the stain, the reader, in due course, appropriately, substitutes the word or the feeling "jealousy." There is a signifier, *centipede*, and a signified concept, *jealousy*: this is its denotation. But since the word *centipede* or the descriptive paragraph identifying it has been substituted for the idea of *jealousy*, the relationship between the signifier and the signified can be defined as a *figure*. According to Genette, such a figure within a rhetorical code clearly identifies it as belonging to a poetic category. It functions as the signifier of something newly signified, poetry, on a second semantic level, which is its rhetorical connotation. Since to connote is to imply, to signify in addition to the primary meaning, by using the first meaning as a form with which to designate the second concept, the hermeneutics of a novel, like *La Jalousie* implies the following diagram: centipede-jealousy-poetry.

Why do we have metonymy instead of metaphor? The answer depends on interpreting (i.e., providing the missing link) the contiguous metonymic signs: centipede-jealousy; sportscar-woman; driving-the sex act; car crashing into tree and bursting into flames-sexual climax, etc. Associations that move us from topic to topic according to relationships of contiguity may be auditory as well as visual: sound of centipede mandibles, A . . . combing her hair, tree burning. Jealousy, like fire, has become a passion that consumes. The protagonist's mind, his "temps mental," which is also the reader's "temps mental," filters all "reality" through the emotion of jealousy. Jealousy, then provides the *gestalt* for the sexual connotation of the images and the events described.

Everything that is seen, heard, imagined, and remembered is part of the poem which, like the song of the native

squatting by the river, meanders, stops, starts, retraces itself according to its own, invisible, yet for us clearly identifiable laws—laws of jealousy whose signs Robbe-Grillet has posted along the way: objects, descriptions, juxtapositions, associations that seem to define a process at work—the jealous mind objectified, rendered visible. The subjectivity of the mind has been exteriorized, as though a subconscious process had been identified and labeled. Thus, Hemingway's definition of prose poetry, like the iceberg being seven-eighths below the surface, applies to *La Jalousie*. The reader provides the missing links and in so doing, recreates not only the jealous process which is the consciousness of the husband, but also the intention of the novelist himself. Once again the novel turns in upon itself and, like *Finnegans Wake*, has become reflexive. *La Jalousie* is a reflexive novel of process that is now also a poem.

As for the objects of *La Jalousie*, contrary to Robbe-Grillet's theoretical pronouncements, they have not been cleansed. The centipede, a blue piece of paper, a calendar on the wall, the sound of a car at night, like rusty pitons, blue cigarette wrappers, and slapping waves in *Le Voyeur*, act as catalysts to the husband's sensitized and susceptible mind. In this sense the husband, Mathias, Meursault, and Roquentin are kindred souls. The chestnut tree root brings on waves of nausea not unlike the waves of jealousy that overwhelm the husband at the sight of a centipede or the waves of heat and molten metal that blind Meursault before he shoots the Arab. Where Sartre and Camus use metaphor to define tragic complicity ("la connivence tragique"), Robbe-Grillet uses metonymy. Nevertheless, like its predecessors, La Jalousie is a novel of process, only more so. Names disappear, faces disappear, characterization is even sketchier, and time circular. Jakobson observes, in *Fundamentals of Language*, that "following the path of contiguous relationships, the realist author metonymically digresses from the plot to the atmosphere and from the characters to the setting in space and time." On the realistic level (since this novel, like all of Robbe-Grillet's fiction, has an unrealistic dimension) the atmosphere of Robbe-Grillet's book is jealousy, while characters and things, in keeping with Jakobson's definition, are functions of the protagonist's mind. Time is a function of space visualized in the present tense: the real and the unreal, the seen and the unseen, the imagined and the remembered function with equal intensity and a mobility that casts doubt on the novel's verisimilitude.

This implied doubt about Robbe-Grillet's realism draws attention to the creative process, to his artistic imagination. Robbe-Grillet's *parole*, the structure of *La Jalousie*, as in all his novels, focuses on its formal properties, away from referential significance. Nevertheless, the fascinating aspect of his work is that it can always be read on at least two levels. The descriptions are realistic (though not always—the seagull in *Le Voyeur* is one of many exceptions), but the novels themselves, in their total effect, call attention to their lack of realism, to their imaginary, self-willed dimension, to the fact that they signify the mind at work, the imagination, the creative process as pure invention, as poetry.

The meaning of Robbe-Grillet's books, and particularly his first, **Les Gommes**, is now much clearer than it used to be. All the contradictions of the novel: the detective who is a murderer; Wallas who has a double, named V. S.; the murder which is not a murder and which, although it apparently occurred at the beginning, occurs at the end; all the minute contradictions of reality—a reality which is at first constructed and then destroyed—are abolished by the creative process which effaces one possibility after another. Hypothetical possibilities also represent the artist's alternate choices. Since the work of art is, for the moment, the only admissible reality, many choices are possible, even contradictory ones.

Projet pour une révolution à New York presents similar ambiguities and contradictory realities in a city in which Laura, Joan Robeson (who is perhaps Robertson), Ben Said, and others are characters in a state of continuing metamorphosis. There is for instance a locksmith, who is so nearsighted a voyeur that he cannot tell whether the picture of a nude girl on the other side of a keyhole is real or false. Projet is a novel in which everything is possible, a novel in which the certainty of events is negated finally by the creative imagination of the author. The author lies because perception itself is suspect.

In the film, **L'Homme qui ment** the central character "plays" with the past, the present and the future which he invents, reinvents, and then negates, because reality functions exactly like that. According to Robbe-Grillet, every fiction is the story of a gamesman in a quicksand world who is continuously reinventing himself. Robbe-Grillet's art is, in fact, the mirror of constantly shifting and contradictory realities. The "man who lies" is therefore the main character and metaphor of such fiction. Not only is reality suspect, but all art as well, particularly that conventional art which is supposed to mirror a stable reality. But a novel which constructs itself and then questions its right to exist, abolishes itself, leaving us with the ontological void described in Sartre's *L'Etre et le néant*.

The worst fears of the "nouveau roman" critics may now have been realized, since the "nouveau roman" has destroyed, in effect, the traditional nineteenth-century novel with its plot, story line, and well-developed characters. Process has been substituted for the old conventions. Michel Butor's novel *La Modification*, though it may seem to describe a husband who is going to leave his wife in Paris for his mistress in Rome, is not so much about the husband, as it is an analysis of that "change of heart" which prompts a return to his wife. The novel is an exploration of this "change." Such writing about process, this *Emploi du temps*, as Butor calls it in his novel of the same name, is the "murder of Bleston," the symbolic killing of the traditional novel form with its well-defined plot and characters and its linear chronological development in time and space.

It may be useful, finally, to distinguish between the traditional novel which depicts "life," the "nouveau roman" which pictures life and the novel itself, alternately, and the "nouveau nouveau roman" which is completely reflexive, picturing only itself. While Robbe-Grillet's novels may be self-reflexive, and like the non-objective paintings of Mondrian, Pollock, or Frank Stella be on the verge of abstraction, they always somehow, in spite of themselves, by virtue of their ambiguity, do finally signify more than themselves. Robbe-Grillet's *parole* is not purely formal and its referents are not exclusively within the work of art, as they are, I believe, with Faye, Ricardou, and Sollers. The silence of Robbe-Grillet's dream-like constructions is, after all, our silence. The hesitant, circuitous patterns of his novels and of his protagonists' desires, lies, and imaginings are in large measure our own. The voyeurism of his early works and the sado-eroticism of his recent ones gives us a variety of "glissements progressifs du plaisir" between life and art, the real and the unreal, prose and poetry, bondage and freedom. Such is the ambiguity of Robbe-Grillet's Art as it objectifies itself while defining its essence, subjectively.

John J. Clayton (essay date Spring 1977)

SOURCE: "Alain Robbe-Grillet: The Aesthetics of Sado-Masochism," in *Massachusetts Review,* Vol. XVIII, No. 1, Spring, 1977, pp. 106-19.

[*In the following essay, Clayton discusses Robbe-Grillet's presentation of eroticism, degradation, and cruelty in his fiction. According to Clayton, Robbe-Grillet's "precise, unemotional description" represents a distancing technique employed to "protect the writer against his own full experiencing of his fantasy life."*]

I enjoy Robbe-Grillet's fiction for its ability to bring me inside the process of line-by-line creation. In their very different ways Burroughs does this and Kerouac does it. I am drawn into the energy of image exploding into image. Coover works in the same mode—blatantly: "I wander the island, inventing it. I make a sun for it, and trees—pines and birch and dogwood and fir—and cause the water to lap the pebbles of its abandoned shores." Nabokov does it through his madly unreliable narrators, like Hermann (*Despair*):

> How should we begin this chapter? I offer several variations to choose from. Number one (readily adopted in novels where the narrative is conducted in the first person by the real or substitute author). . . .

But in Robbe-Grillet no narrator whom we can see indicates the experience—so that it seems to occur "nowhere else except in the mind of the invisible narrator, in other words of the writer, and of the reader." I become the invisible narrator.

Here is the opening passage from **La Maison de rendez-vous**:

Women's flesh has always played, no doubt, a great part in my dreams. Even when I am awake, its images constantly beset me. A girl in a summer dress exposing the nape of her bent neck—she is fastening her sandal—her hair, fallen forward, revealing the delicate skin with its blond down, I see her immediately subject to some command, excessive from the start. The narrow hobble skirt, slit to the thighs, of the elegant women of Hong Kong is quickly ripped off by a violent hand, which suddenly lays bare the rounded, firm, smooth, gleaming hip, and the tender slope of the loins. The leather whip, in the window of a Parisian saddle-maker, the exposed breasts of wax mannequins, a theater poster, advertisements for garters or a perfume, moist parted lips, an iron manacle, a dog collar, generate around me their provocative, insistent setting. A simple canopied bed, a piece of string, the glowing tip of a cigar, accompany me for hours, as I travel for days. In parks, I organize celebrations. For temples, I establish ceremonies, command sacrifices. Arabian or Mogul palaces fill my ears with screams and sighs. On the walls of Byzantine churches, the slabs of marble sawed in symmetrical patterns suggest, as I stare, vaginas parted wide, forced open. Two rings set into the stone, in the depths of an ancient Roman prison, are enough to conjure up the lovely captive chained there, doomed to long tortures, in secrecy, solitude, and at leisure.

Often I linger to stare at some young woman dancing, at a party. I like her to have bare shoulders and, when she turns around, to be able to see her cleavage. The smooth skin glistens softly, under the light from the chandeliers. She performs, with a graceful diligence, one of those complicated steps in which she remains a certain distance from her partner, a tall, dark, almost recessive figure, who merely indicates the movements in front of her, while her lowered eyes seem to watch for the slightest sign the man's hand makes, in order to obey him at once while continuing to observe the complicated laws of the ritual. Then, at an almost imperceptible command, smoothly turning around, again she offers her shoulders and the nape of her neck.

Now she has stepped back, a little to one side, to fasten the buckle of her sandal, made of slender gold straps which criss cross several times around the bare foot. Sitting on the edge of a sofa, she is leaning over, her hair, fallen forward, revealing more of the delicate skin with its blond down. But two people step forward and soon conceal the scene, a tall figure in a dark tuxedo listening to a fat, red-faced man talking about his travels.

Everyone knows Hong Kong, its harbor, its junks, its sampans, the office buildings of Kowloon, and the narrow hobble skirt, split up the side to the thigh, worn by the Eurasian women, tall, supple girls, each in her clinging black silk sleeveless sheath with its narrow upright collar, cut straight at the neck and armpits. The shiny, thin fabric is worn next to the skin, following the forms of the belly, the breasts, the hips, and creasing at the waist into a sheaf of tiny folds when the stroller, who has stopped in front of a shop-window, has turned her head and bust toward the pane of glass where, motionless, her left foot touching the ground only with the toe of a very high-heeled shoe, ready to continue walking in the middle of the interrupted stride, her right hand raised forward, slightly away from the body, and her elbow half bent, she stares for a moment at the wax girl wearing an identical white silk dress, or else at her own reflection in the glass, or else at the braided leather leash the mannequin is holding in her left hand, her bare arm away from the body and her elbow half bent in order to control a big black dog with shiny fur walking in front of her.

It is an obscene, sexist, sadistic imagination I have entered. The light image of a girl in a summer dress evokes a fantasy out of a sado-masochistic novel with all its paraphernalia. Delicate parts of the body are "exposed," "forced open," "laid bare." The whip, the cigar, the manacle—and the imagining become the fantasies of ceremonial sadism. Then a scene of "civilized" control, the dance, which contains the earlier imaginings as a sinister undertone.

At "Now she has stepped back . . ." the fiction takes off. The imagined girl or remembered girl becomes present. Suddenly we cut—apparently to the talk or thought of two men. The image of the hobble skirt comes into sharper and sharper focus until—presto—a scene begins in which man-controlling-dancer becomes mannequin-controlling-dog. In the passage immediately following the excerpt I've quoted, the stuffed dog in the still life turns alive—the girl and dog are moving through the streets. Then we return to the two men at the party.

What is real? Is there a party? Is the girl alive or a mannequin? The questions are obviously absurd. What is real is the process of creation itself, the flow of images. Are they reflections of any external reality? Is (for example) *La Maison* a spy novel in which the narrator is pondering his actions and formulating possible alibis and alternative explanations? That is one way to read the novel. But better—all the action is real and its locale is the page—which is to say, the imagination shared by narrator and reader. There is only that imagination—there are no characters who have any status more real than the image of a hobble skirt. What is real is the ongoing act of fictionalizing.

> At this point in the narrative, Johnson stops: he thinks
> he has heard a scream. . . .

But it is only *in the narrative*, in the ongoing process of talking, that Johnson stops. It is *in the narrative* that he hears a scream. The novel is like an author's notebook of possibilities—fragments of scenes are "tried on," altered, discarded, shuffled into new combinations. As Robbe-Grillet puts it, ". . . the image is jeopardized as it is created. A few paragraphs more and, when the description comes to an end, we realize that it has left nothing behind it: it has instituted a double movement of creation and destruction. . . ." Alternative explanations, alternative chronologies, alternative characters. An author's notebook of possibilities—or the consciousness of a nearly mad narrator: in his consciousness but without his advantage of knowing what is imaginary, what is real. So we struggle to *make sense* out of his world—what happens, how, in what order. In *Jealousy*, when do A . . . and Franck go off to town? When, and how, is the centipede killed? Robbe-Grillet says, "any attempt to reconstruct an external chronology would lead, sooner or later, to a series of contradictions, hence to an impasse." But it is not just chronology that is undercut. The images mix, dissolve, contradict like a moving collage-like abstract cinematic montage. The reader can't help putting the images together in meaningful ways—putting them into causal patterns or psychological relationships. But he is led into a *labyrinth*; until finally he gives up the attempt to make a coherent picture of reality. He is left with *this* on the page, then this on the page, then *this*. And he recognizes that he is free to play with any number of patternings—they are all there— but, in another sense, they are all a product of his engagement with the images. It is a perfect analogue to life in the world. Just as the reader gives up his search for a novel *under* the existent novel—for a novel which correlates with an external reality, so in our ordinary lives we can see the uselessness of a search for a substratum of reality.

Indeed, we see nothing of "reality" in this novel. Robbe-Grillet would smile at the word. *La Maison de rendezvous* or *Project for a Revolution in New York* have the same relation to ordinary reality as an early cubist work which pastes a real piece of newspaper over newspaper painted in *trompe l'oeil*. It is a playful construction obeying only its own laws of organization. But more than the cubist painter, Robbe-Grillet is interested in playing with motifs out of the popular imagination—out of *la série noire* (detective thrillers often set in exotic locales), out of popular fantasies of Hong Kong as a city of sin, out of sado-masochistic fantasies of hidden violence and sexuality. Robbe-Grillet is not mistaking these fantasies for "reality"; he is using them as highly charged material to play with, so as to demonstrate the workings of the creative imagination—*the workings, therefore, of our everyday lives*, which, he would insist, are also literature, are precisely as "literary" as his fictions or the fictions he uses as material for his games.

Ultimately, he wants to give us back a world in which we are not betrayed by our fantasies; he wants to give us back the world of sheer presences by first removing us from the world we have been taught to call real.

And so the critique of a Lukacs, who speaks of the attenuation of reality in modernist literature, is both applicable and beside the point. Certainly reality is attenuated in modernist literature; and surely Robbe-Grillet tries to dissolve it completely. But Lukacs is working from nineteenth-century assumptions about reality and about fiction. That is, simply, he believes that there is a way of accurately reporting the social world; that subjectivity is acceptable as a deviation from a norm or as a way of recording reflections of reality. But he complains about the "flight from reality" in modernist literature (in contrast to the literature of contemporary realism). The modernist writer, according to Lukacs, does not understand that the loss of reality he reports is the condition of a particular class in a particular society; incorrectly he sees it as a universal *condition humaine*. His understanding, and his art, are false.

But Robbe-Grillet is working from a different set of assumptions about reality—modernist assumptions, and if he

is to be attacked, it should be in the light of those assumptions: 1) The perceiving of reality is an activity, a process of creation—it is not the mere recording of something *out there*. 2) The officially approved version of reality taught to us is only a version—and not a particularly interesting one. 3) The writer's job is to imitate not any version of reality but the process of encountering/creating reality.

Robbe-Grillet would argue that the reality which is being "attenuated" is (like the world Jesus says one must die to) not the reality of things existing in their own right, but a manageable, humanized reality given us by our culture. Then to undermine this version of reality would be an act of subversion, an act of liberation.

Is Robbe-Grillet a liberator, then? He believes that his fiction is dedicated to freedom—"seeking new forms for the novel, forms capable of expressing (or of creating) new relations between man and the world. . . ." He is teaching us how to play with our culturally derived fantasies which we have confused with reality; how to see our own engagement in the process of the creation of reality (we are all novelists). Robbe-Grillet believes that the conventionally humanized world is a prison and that 1) his stripping bare of the conventional humanist trappings of reality and 2) his encouragement to the reader to share in the process of creation are ways of unlocking that prison.

> Freedom of observation should be possible, yet it is not. At every moment, a continuous fringe of culture (psychology, ethics, metaphysics, etc.) is added to things, giving them a less alien aspect, one that is more comprehensible, more reassuring.

Robbe-Grillet is insistent on ridding us of this cultural screen of meaning. He recognizes that even the writers of meaninglessness assert one final form of tragic humanism. He insists—"But the world is neither significant nor absurd. It is, quite simply." Robbe-Grillet wants us to regain the freedom to reinvent the world beyond the screen of "literary," cultural meanings.

This concern explains the contradiction that critics have accused Robbe-Grillet of falling prey to: this writer who wishes to give us the world free of its incrustations brings us novels narrated by compulsives, madmen, perhaps murderers—characters—or rather eyes—who are certainly imprisoned by *their* perceptive screens. But it is not—at least in an obvious way—a contradiction: Robbe-Grillet says, "Man is present on every page, in every line, in every word."

> Even if many objects are presented and are described with great care, there is always, and especially, the eye which sees them, the thought which reexamines them, the passion which distorts them . . . Not only is it a *man* who, in my novels . . . describes everything, but it is the least neutral, the least impartial of men: always engaged, on the contrary, in an emotional adventure of the most obsessive kind, to the point of distorting his vision and of producing imaginings close to delirium.

Then, Robbe-Grillet would argue, the difference from the conventional novel is this: in an ordinary novel the filter—the projective mechanisms, the perceptual grid—is treated as if it were a transparent window on *the* world. The desolate room, the melancholy hill, the broken tree—we are handed a pre-humanized world as if it were simply the world. In the "new" novel the filter is seen for what it is. And so the reader is *invited to understand the process of projective distortion in perception by putting on the severely distorted lenses of a Robbe-Grillet narrator.* Further, to free the reader of the pre-packaged humanization of reality, Robbe-Grillet creates eyes that see without much metaphor of a traditional sort; that see outlines, that watch the warp in a window pane or the shadow of a column enter into a scene; eyes that see the way a director intentionally sees when he sets up camera shots. I could argue that the tradition of modern fiction—and of modern epistemology—has made it impossible to take a "naïve" relation to reality. Point of view is *always* taken into account. The "world" is always a character's world. The desolate room is the desolation of a character or a persona—and we are not ever meant to forget that. And in first person narratives the perception is always biased, distorted—we are expected to see in a bifurcated way—to find a second world set off against the narrator's distorted one. It is the tension between the two worlds that creates the excitement of the modern first-person form. But Robbe-Grillet goes further. On the one hand, we *become* the compulsive, perhaps lying schizophrenic eye, we experience his world very directly, experience his ongoing act of imagining. On the other hand, we are not given any familiar landmarks, are not given the comfort of a metaphorical, humanized world. And so the world we experience is ours—yet clearly alien. We are thrust away from our comfortable, unrecognized subjectivity into a comparable subjectivity which makes us sweat—and makes us recognize for what it is our own process of making up a comfortable, culturally derived world. He is attempting to give us back the world of presence in exchange for a world of worn meaning: and therefore he is offering us the freedom to reinvent the world.

The freedom to create a different work of art, a different *play*. In Robbe-Grillet, as in so much modernist literature, the core metaphor is THEATRE.

Inevitably we are taken, in *La Maison*, "behind the narrative" to examine the paraphernalia of what we have been through. It all turns to stage props:

> I stand up furtively and reach the little exit door, which I find by groping my way. . . . It is a kind of filthy courtyard, lit by huge oil lamps, which must be used to store props, for parts of the sets are strewn here and there in great confusion.

And now, in the form of "props" we are shown again the iron rings, the mannequin, the black dog on a leash.

> I also discover some pieces of furniture which must belong to the opium den scene. . . .

Robbe-Grillet wants to let us behind the scenes. We are introduced to the mystery of the human creation of reality;

we take part in that creation. We see a scene repeated, erased, rewritten; see it as belonging inside another scene, see the other scene inside the first. Life becomes a haunting dream in which we are imprisoned and from which we *can* choose to awaken.

And it is very very beautiful, very haunting: the poetry of objects turned into images, seen first as part of one *assemblage*, then another; seen as literal, "real," then as photographic image, then as statuary, then as surmise. Objects in our real lives tend to vibrate differently after we've read Robbe-Grillet; which means that we begin to experience the objects freed from their ordinary contexts—begin to experience their *magic*. We are liberated from our own mental sets.

It is the realm of what Nabokov calls "aesthetic bliss." Aestheticization involves two complementary ways of seeing: the work of art is seen as a self-contained world, not referential to any prior reality; life is seen as no different from the work of art—it also is seen as a work of imagination and can be viewed with aesthetic principles as a human creation. To enter into this way of seeing is to become free for a time of the world of change, of chaos.

But what kind of liberation is this? When I give up the search for meaning, for a novel which correlates with an external reality, to what extent do I really receive from Robbe-Grillet the gift of creative freedom? I want to argue that even on the basis of his own assumptions, Robbe-Grillet is more jailor than liberator.

Robbe-Grillet tells us that his fiction expresses the consciousness of a compulsive. But of course that changes utterly the meaning of the style's objectivity. Even if Robbe-Grillet would like to dismiss "psychology" from fiction, it is hard not to be aware of the psychological dynamics of his style. For in the context of this very special consciousness it is not the world of things-in-their-presence which I enter. I feel, in the use of quantitative description (the arrangement of banana trees in *Jealousy*, the construction of a room in In The Labyrinth), in the use of precise detail ("When the blinds are open to the maximum the slats are almost horizontal and show their edges. Then the opposite slope of the valley appears in successive, superimposed strips separated by slightly narrower strips")—I feel not so much contact with an existent world as avoidance of a reality the examining consciousness cannot face. It is examining banana trees because it cannot examine the relationship between A . . . and Franck. It is not engagement with a strange world but avoidance of a familiar world that I am haunted by. In the more recent and stranger *La Maison*, the compulsion is more diffuse—but still intense in the precise description of scenes of torture, manipulation, and life frozen into sculpture. The *examining eye* turns out to be one more metaphor—one more way of humanizing the world—humanizing it by abstracting its emotional tone. We are no closer to "reality."

Precise, unemotional description—the objective style which has become the trademark of Alain Robbe-Grillet.

He speaks of his "adjectival complacency." He is interested in *the facts*—beautifully crafted assertions of fact; occasional questions about fact; wonderfully precise descriptions which turn surreal by the very intensity of focus. But just as surely as the hard-nosed look at *the facts* on a TV show like *Dragnet* represents a masking of emotional subjectivity and permits the program's simplistic authoritarian attitudes, so Robbe-Grillet's objectivity is a disguised armoring against feelings the narrator—and writer—can't let himself experience. Sado-masochistic fantasies are pleasurable when dealt with aesthetically—when you don't have to face the pain and degradation which are part of the experience. Then perhaps Robbe-Grillet's theories are a complicated form of rationalization, their purpose to protect the writer against his own full experiencing of his fantasy life. Against its *meaning*. **Project for a Revolution in New York** seems the extreme case of a consciousness armoring itself against its own fantasy life by using a style that keeps fantasy defused. The imagery for the novel comes, once again, from sado-masochistic fiction and spy "thrillers," but the tone is detached, methodical. First, the narrative is forced in upon itself. The S & M imagery, its language, is—far from being mistaken for reality—framed in the way a pop artist might frame a Coca-Cola ad. We are never permitted to forget that we are reading a fictional narrative—again and again an unnamed interrogator interrupts to ask the narrator about contradictions or obscurities in the text.

> "I must stop you once again. You have several times employed, in your narrative, expressions such as 'unformed little breasts,' 'charming buttocks,' 'cruel operation,' 'fleshy pubic area,' 'splendid red-haired creature,' 'luxuriant plentitude,' and once even 'voluptuous curves the hips.' Don't you think you're exaggerating?"
>
> "From what point of view would that be an exaggeration?"
>
> "From the lexicological point of view."
>
> "You regard such things as inexactitudes?"
>
> "No, not at all!"
>
> "Material errors?"
>
> "That is not the question."
>
> "Lies, then?"
>
> "Still less!"
>
> "In that case, I must say I do not see what it is you mean. I am making my report, that's all there is to it. . . ."

Neither lies nor material errors, the language exemplifies the kind of humanized description that Robbe-Grillet rejects, a description infused with popular imagination, with *fiction*. The effect of the questioning is to remove the narrative from the passionate fantasies of erotic literature.

Second, the tone is kept cool by describing horrors with the exactitude of a technical manual: "In order to get on with the tearing-out of the toenails, then of the nipples, according to the regulation scenario recorded in the descrip-

tion, I must now go get the pliers. . . ." Hardly the tone of an inflamed sexual pervert. "I shall begin by raping you," an agent says to JR. "I shall doubtless do so again during the course of the interrogation, as is recommended in our instructions." *Regulation scenario . . . recommended in our instructions*—or, as they put it at Nuremberg: Don't blame me, I was just following orders. The torturers, the narrators, are not responsible. "The whole scenario is articulated like a piece of machinery," says the narrator. Over and over these comparisons to theatre and machinery create distance. The emotional, even erotic elements, are continually ignored in favor of exact description—for example, ". . . a young woman who is entirely naked appears in a three quarters view, astride a sawblade with very sharp teeth, her legs pulled wide apart by chains attached to two rings, which hold her legs about eight inches above the stone-paved ground."

Such language turns the victims of cruelty into objects of art or experiment. It routinizes cruelty and defuses the torturer-narrator's pain and guilt. Stanley Milgrim, in his brilliant studies of obedience, has shown that as you increase emotional distance you increase the likelihood of one person torturing another. The Nazis were able with little remorse to murder millions of people in the camps by depersonalizing and routinizing the process. The language of Robbe-Grillet is not far from Pentagonese, which talks of "body count" and "megakill," which programmed a computer at the Institute of Defense Analysis to print out a bombing run for the use of ordinary men who could never hold a cigarette lighter to the body of even a single child they could see.

I am reminded of the mad projector in Swift's *Modest Proposal*, who masks the human meaning of killing and eating children by turning them into statistics and speculating about economic advantages or describing them with incredible exactitude as meat, gloves and boots—as animal carcasses, not human beings. Swift's projector, unlike the consciousness in Project, salves his conscience by an unctuous, self-serving moralizing; Robbe-Grillet's "projector" never moralizes. But both are able to indulge themselves in fantasies of cruelty without any accompanying empathy, responsibility, or guilt.

Is Robbe-Grillet, like Swift, satirizing the consciousness of *his* "projector"? Is he satirizing a prose style which, aestheticizing cruelty, anesthetizes the psyche against responsibility? If we ignore Robbe-Grillet's own theories, which reject any meaning that transcends the text, we *can* read the novel in this way. Then, the approach of daylight towards the end of the novel and the thump of police boots that make the narrator hurry—"Faster, faster, faster!"—indicates the arousal of daylight consciousness, the emergence of the superego. At the end, ". . . Morgan, who then looks up from the papers accumulated on the table, recognizes with amazement the narrator's features. Without hesitating, realizing I have been discovered . . . Cut." *Consciousness revealed to itself*, breaking through the disguises of multiple narrators and a distancing prose style.

The question is: Is Robbe-Grillet *writing* this novel or is *he* this novel? At a recent conference in Wisconsin many women attacked him for torturing and murdering women in his fiction. His defense was not that they were confusing him with the central consciousness in his novels, nor that he meant to confront us with our own voyeuristic imaginations; instead, he replied, "you wouldn't want to deprive me of my fantasies, would you?" It is true that in this novel we see the mad fantasist, like Swift's projector, keeping his fantasies aestheticized, cerebral. But it appears that the fantasist is Robbe-Grillet himself. He may be aware of the games that consciousness plays with itself to avoid the implications of its fantasy life, but they seem to be his own games, and he is merely dazzled, charmed, by the playing.

In a sense, what Robbe-Grillet's theories permit him to do is to keep his fantasies purely mental. In a recent essay Robbe-Grillet says, "Man is fully human only if everything passes through his head, even (and especially) sex. We recall the famous remark of the mathematician Henri Poincaré: an adult needs pornography as a child needs fairy tales." I remember D. H. Lawrence's detestation of "sex in the head," of "the dirty little secret," of pornography. He wanted to return sex to the body and treat it as sacred mystery. Lawrence believes—and I think he's right—that sexual feelings, dangerous feelings of all kinds, are intellectualized to permit one to stay safely in control, in charge. It is one more defense against full experiencing. And so Robbe-Grillet's fantasy is in the realm of King Boris. The novelist not as humble responder to the voices of his life, but as king over his aesthetic empire.

There is no freedom in this dreaming. A kingdom under the rule of King Boris, a figure who recurs with increasing insistence in *La Maison*. There is the loud rapping of the tip of a cane on the floor upstairs:

> The old mad king has an iron tipped cane. . . . Have I said that this old king was named Boris? He never goes to bed, since he no longer manages to fall asleep. Sometimes he merely stretches out in a rocking chair and rocks for hours, banging the floor with the tip of his cane at each oscillation, to maintain the pendulum movement.

King Boris is always there, his cane rapping, insisting, demanding. The old mad king upstairs—a figure of compulsive command, like the narrative imagination itself, one of "command, excessive from the start." The kingdom of the totalitarian imagination. Totalitarian in its insistence on unemotional objectivity, totalitarian in its aesthetic control.

For as we submit to the ongoing process of creation, as we delight in the repeating motifs of the controlling consciousness, we find that in fact the freedom of engagement is illusory too. We *do* have to submit; the consciousness *is controlling*. In direct contrast to the work of Brecht, who wants us to be aware that we are watching a fiction *just so that we can examine the questions it raises and make up our minds*, Robbe-Grillet wants to turn us into hypnotized

spectators. We become the sadistic voyeur watching the half naked girl about to be ripped apart by a tiger. We are absorbed into the voyeuristic imagination of the work—in *La Maison* and *Project* as much as in *Le Voyeur* or *Jealousy*.

> This piece of music which has come on for some time, perhaps even since the beginning of the evening, is a kind of cyclically repeated refrain in which the same passages can always be recognized at regular intervals.
>
> (*La Maison*)

Precisely. We are locked inside a carefully organized aesthetic construction. The ordering is not that of conventional reality; but it is an ordering. And the ordering, the emphasis on ordering, on control, on domination, on command, is much more insistent in Robbe-Grillet than in any traditional novelist.

The world is aestheticized. Is turned into an art object. Our relation to it, however, is not so much that of the connoisseur as of an element in the design. And the design is, for all Robbe-Grillet's insistence on freedom, frozen, like the life on Keats' urn. The narrative consciousness kills what it examines, turns it—in *La Maison* into a still life, a statuary, a window display of mannequins. *This aestheticization of reality is simply another aspect of the imagination of control*—of white slavery, prostitution, control by drugs, sadism—a totalitarian imagination that has to stop the world dead!

To stop the world dead: the "wax girl," the life-sized statuary, the scene which becomes a photograph or a theatrical tableau, an insistence on motionlessness, repetition, petrifaction. Robbe-Grillet takes us into an aestheticized world outside of change—not a world of human creativity at all. We participate in the way of being The Artist—but it is the artist as creator of a wax museum, glass flowers.

Robbe-Grillet knows, of course, that the reality on his page is both fluid—in the sense of alterable—and frozen. Both fluidity and frozenness are part of his vision of a life alien to pre-packaged human meaning. Is he also aware that the aestheticized frozen quality of the life in his novels is deeply analogous to the human meaning of contemporary Western life—I mean life reified, life turned into a snapshot or the collage of snapshots in the Spectacle (as the French Situationists term our society)? Of course, Robbe-Grillet's fiction is in some ways the enemy to the Spectacle, because the Spectacle demands that we accept unthinkingly its images while Robbe-Grillet shows us how to make images appear and disappear. But he is the magician, we are the stunned spectators. And in the same way, his "characters" are puppets in the artist's hands. They are merely images, enacting, in their somnambulistic compulsiveness, the deadened life of subjects of the Spectacle.

But finally, just as an absorption into the totalitarianism of the Spectacle is not enough to utterly deaden us, just as somehow we remember our powerlessness and in response take part in terrible rituals of violence and control to deal ritually—but only ritually—with that powerlessness, in a similar way the frozen life of the aesthetic vision in Robbe-Grillet has murder, sadism, and manipulation as its undergrowth. Under a modernist aesthetic which proclaims the human invention of reality, we find again and again a tendency towards a totalitarian politics. Aestheticization involves the imposition of totalitarian order on the world. It is a covert exercise of power in the midst of a world in which the writer experiences powerlessness. No wonder then that in elaborate form Robbe-Grillet rather recites the fantasies of our enslavement than liberates us from them. No wonder, then, that he confuses the fantasies of sado-masochistic violation with liberation, arguing that he wants the kind of socialism that "dares claim the right to pleasure for all, the right to a voluptuous tomorrow." But the voluptuous tomorrow we look forward to is not one of sado-masochism. It will not have to be. The fantasies Robbe-Grillet plays with are the poisonous results of a false life. To what extent do they make evident the falsity of that life; to what extent do they reinforce that falsity? I am not sure.

The writer as liberator of consciousness? How should the writer help in our liberation? First, by establishing, largely by means of style, a realm of grace and power that offers us a model for life lived in its spirit. Beyond this, the writer has the responsibility to return to us the reality of our experience—not "objective" reality but the reality of our ongoing lives, reality we are made to deny and forget. Insofar as that reality is drenched in destructive fantasy the writer must not simply pander to our enslavement but undermine the fantasies we secretly live by as well as those we are told to live by. The writer may create a world, but that world must encounter the one we share—either to challenge it or to plumb its depths. Robbe-Grillet is enamoured of his own fictional worlds. And so his work is, finally, a brilliant exercise in conceptual art, an exercise which has opened up fiction to new possibilities, but is narrow and life-denying in its spirit.

Bruce Morrissette (essay date 1985)

SOURCE: "Games and Game Structures in Robbe-Grillet," in *Novel and Film: Essays in Two Genres,* University of Chicago Press, 1985, pp. 157-64.

[*In the following essay, Morrissette discusses the significance of game patterns and allusions in the novels of Robbe-Grillet. According to Morrissette, Robbe-Grillet employs the formal structure of games to create a forum for new possibilities.*]

Along with mathematics, games have come to play a considerable role in contemporary literary works and criticism. From the outset, the proliferation of game structures in the works of Alain Robbe-Grillet identifies him as a notable example of *artifex ludens.* Almost all the tendencies that are termed "aspects ludiques" in his novels and films may be uncovered by careful scrutiny of his earliest productions. It is even possible to reduce the numerous game structures to a few basic models, such as the circular or winding path of individual *cases* or rectangles (like those found on board games played with dice and pawns), the maze or labyrinth, and the multiple-solution type of game, such as Clue, in which shuffling the cards or figures representing characters and places allows each separate *partie*, although created out of identical elements, to produce a totally different outcome.

The conception of a fundamentally gamelike structure of the novel would also make specific games mentioned in the works, or specifically played by the characters therein, examples of mise en abyme or interior duplication, functioning with respect to the overall structure in some what the same way as an "inner novel" (cf. *La Jalousie*) or play (cf. *L'Anneé dernière à Marienbad*) that duplicates, at the level of the characters and within the fictional field, the general pattern of the novel or film. This integrative principle constitutes one type of "justification" of an actual game (as in *Marienbad*) as coherently incorporated into the aesthetic structure. The literal game may be minimized or may not appear at all, but the "metaphysical" aspect of general game structure cannot, since it is part of the novelistic technique, be avoided. It is in turn this metaphysical implication that protects the work from falling into the gratuity of a neo-Kantian "free play of the faculties" conception of fictional art that might, if pushed to the limit, reduce the creative process to a kind of aesthetic billiard game or acrobatic display. It is also evident that the problem of formalism in the use of game structures in novels and films has its parallels in painting (from abstract expressionism to pop art) and the other arts, especially contemporary music. In order to tie the discussion to the specifics of fiction, however, I will set aside these tempting analogies.

If, as Hjelmslev declares, language itself is "put together like a game," with a large but finite number of underlying structures that permit a vast repertory of combinations representing the totality of actual practice or usage in all given cases, then by the principle of analogous extension all fiction may be said to be put together like a game, with each specific story or novel constituting merely one of the possible *parties* or individual playings of the game of fictional composition. However, such a broad view, though perhaps sound in theory, fails to distinguish between a novel whose structure bears no identifiable or obvious resemblance to any known *game* (in the usual sense), such as *Madame Bovary*, and one that closely parallels or imitates a known game structure, such as Robbe-Grillet's ***Dans le labyrinthe*** (1959). Here I am concerned with the latter type of novel, as well as with the playing of games or execution of gamelike patterns by characters in the novel, and with specific or hidden allusions to games in novelistic contexts of which the characters (and sometimes the readers themselves) remain unaware.

Puzzles, mathematical games, riddles, paradoxes, topological curiosities (like the Möbius strip), optical illusions (like the pinhole fly image in **Dans le labyrinthe**), and all such pararational phenomena have fascinated Robbe-Grillet since his childhood. I recall his once calculating rapidly and precisely the number of times a single sheet of paper would have to be folded to make it thick enough to reach from the earth to the moon (it is a mathematical possibility). I have described elsewhere his first project for a novel, whose pertinence here justifies repeating the following essentials: this novel, which he never gave a title, was to have its plot organized according to the hermetic series of 108 scales on drawings made by medieval alchemists of the legendary snake Ouroboros. Note that we are dealing from the outset with the combination of an archetype or traditional symbolic representation (the Gnostic snake biting its own tail, symbolizing the Universe in Horapollo's *Hieroglyphics*, Time in Plotinus, and the repeated cycles of metempsychosis among the Ophites) and a mathematical game, depending on the properties of a unique series of the numbers from 1 to 108 (108 being also, Mircea Eliade informs me, a sacred number among certain Hindu sects). If one constructs a mandalalike wheel or circle with 108 spaces around the circumference (a pattern suggestive of board-and-dice games), it is possible, according to a certain formula, to arrange the numbers 1 to 108 in such a way that at any given point the sum of the two numbers on opposite sides of the circle will be 108. No other number will permit such an arrangement. What the "prenovelist" Robbe-Grillet proposed to do was divide his plot chronologically into 108 narrative elements or narremes and put them textually in the order of the spaces around the Ouroboros diagram. "Dechronology" would thus be introduced artificially into the novel's time structure, in a manner directly comparable to the use of external forms or models in determining the order of musical elements in certain compositions of John Cage and others. Also, the novel, however random in apparent structure, would in reality be constructed upon secret inner principles of organization left unrevealed to the reader or critic, a procedure the author was shortly to follow in his first published novel. The effect of such chronological juggling would no doubt have been to some extent comparable to that produced by the ordering of plot elements in such later works as **La Maison de rendez-vous** (1965), especially if Robbe-Grillet, having rearranged his 108 plot elements into his hermetic series, had then established *liaisons de scène* to articulate the whole into an apparent continuity, in defiance of the obvious nonlinearity of the intrigue. At any rate, two fundamental compositional principles, circularity and series, may be seen in their earliest form in the gamelike project for the Ouroboros novel.

In **Les Gommes** (1953) Robbe-Grillet employs myth as hidden structure and establishes ingenious correspondences between myth and the semioccult "game" of tarot cards. Neither the myth (that of Oedipus) nor the tarot is specifically mentioned in the text, and the general recognition now of their presence may be attributed to the publication of various critical essays, beginning with my own. It is now possible to reinforce and extend my original findings, thanks to the unexpected and welcome collaboration of the distinguished surrealist critic Jacques Brunius. I had limited myself to studying more or less separately the systematic correspondences between the Oedipus myth and the plot of Les Gommes (in which Wallas, the protagonist, seeks a murderer only to *become* that murderer in the end), reflected in references to an abandoned child, Thebes, the riddle of the Sphinx, Apollo's oracle, Laïus's chariot, and the like, and to separate parallels between traditional readings of certain tarot cards and the fictional situations in which they occur (in hidden form) in the novel. The reader may recall that the tarot references first appear as the "other protagonist," Garinati, climbs the stairs to Dupont's study, intending to murder him. This stairway consists of twenty-one wooden steps plus one nonconforming stone step at the bottom that "bears a brass column . . . ending in a fool's head capped with a three-belled bonnet." This detail, together with the picture on the wall at the sixteenth step, described exactly in terms of the sixteenth tarot card, the *Maison Dieu*, establishes the parallel without revealing it explicitly: the *Mat* or Fool, which may be card one or twenty-two, has no number in the tarot pack, while the remaining *arcanes majeurs* correspond to the twenty-one wooden steps. I have pointed out that the Fool "upside down" (or in the bottom position) stands in the tarot manuals for the sudden stopping of progress, thus forming a subtle support for the first "frozen" scene in **Les Gommes**, Garinati's motionless pause on these steps. The resonances of the Maison Dieu card are more complicated, since what is merely announced in the first stairway passage recurs later with more explicit allusions to the death of a king (Laïus), with the card (or rather its picture image) contributing its traditional meaning of *coup de théâtre, choc inattendu* to reinforce the novel's surprising final twist.

What Jacques Brunius proposed to me, in his letters, was the possibility of discerning in the novel certain cross-correspondences between the Oedipus myth and the tarot pack that would "bring out a troubling parallelism between the two perspectives on Destiny represented by Oedipus and the tarot." The effect of these would be to further integrate the "game" aspect of the tarot into the novel's total structure. For example, Brunius points out that the café where the protagonist Wallas tries to answer the riddles posed by the drunkard (riddles composed of various distorted versions of the Sphinx's riddle about man in Sophocles' play) is at 10, rue des Arpenteurs, and that the major tarot card ten, called the Wheel of Fortune, shows a sphinx seated on the wheel. Moreover, the chariot statue on the square (which I had seen only as a reference to the chariot of Laïus in the scene of the murder at the crossroads in *Oedipus the King*) recalls card seven, showing a king (father image) on such a chariot, cubical like the *gomme* eraser and the basalt cube in Dupont's (the father's?) study; and the Hanged Man of card twelve is suspended by one foot like the infant Oedipus on the mountain. These findings do indeed create a new parallelism within the novel, and they demonstrate conclusively that the notion of game, in the sense of purely formal diversion, carries with it implications reaching all the way into the domains of archetypes and myths. True, the tarot is rarely if ever played as a "pure" game, since it is used for fortune-telling and prophecy. Yet its structure and interpretative systems are gamelike in their organization, and from its minor *arcanes* the pack of cards used in contemporary "empty" games has been derived.

While there are no outright or hidden references to games in *Le Voyeur* (1955) and *La Jalousie* (1957)— if we except such offhand allusions as that to pinball machines in the café scenes of *Le Voyeur*—both novels show serial patternings with analogies to the general conception of game structure referred to earlier. One might, *à la rigueur*, compare some of these patterns to the "game of resemblances" familiar to readers of magazines and Sunday supplements. The entire series of eight-shaped objects and forms in *Le Voyeur* is a case in point, as is the more subtle series of Y-shaped objects and designs that can be discerned in a minute reading of the text, and which are organized around the Y of the pubis and thus brought into the erotosadistic gestalt of the eight-shaped bonds, rings, and the like associated with Mathias's rape and murder of his victim Jacqueline. Similarly, the V series of *La Jalousie*, from the parquet floors to the "accidental" arrangement of logs waiting to be used on the footbridge, as well as the "spot" series (centipede, oil spot, grease spot at Franck's place at the table, defective spot on the window, and the like), may all be seen as an extension of a high-order game of "find the resemblance." Needless to say, this aspect of the novel is subordinated to less gamelike and more "serious" matters; but the games "people play," like Mathias's burning holes side by side in paper (and perhaps a girl's flesh) with his cigarette, or like the husband's testing the mathematical regularity of his trapezoidal banana fields, have easily recognizable psychic meanings and readily find their place in novelistic structures that are far from constituting "mere" games.

It is *Dans le labyrinthe* (1959), which offers, for the first but not the last time in Robbe-Grillet's production, outright analogies with those board games that depend for their effect on multiple attempts, with advances and retreats, with side excursions into dead ends, with repeated efforts to find the "right" path to the center and win the game (in the case of the soldier in the novel, to deliver the box). The title of the work invites the comparison, and the paragraphs of the text itself often give the effect of a throw of the dice permitting no movement ("Non. Non.") or of frantic turnings from right to left (the scenes in the corridor), of arrivals at hopeless impasses. I have suggested that this whole pattern is a metaphor of the problem of writing this or any novel; in this view the "game" aspect of randomness, multiplicity, and alternatives becomes an allegory of the creative process, somewhat in the Mallarméan sense. Every narrative effort, to paraphrase the poet, is a throw of the dice and will never abolish chance.

We now come to *L'Anneé dernière à Marienbad* (1961), which could well serve as a model of game structure in novel and film. Readers and viewers of the film may recall

the worldwide reaction to this game, ranging from articles setting forth its basis in binary mathematics (or contesting this basis) to the distribution in movie houses, in New York and elsewhere, of matchbooks bearing the rules of the game. Alain Resnais, the director, announced after the release of the film that the "Marienbad game" was a variant of the ancient "Chinese" game of Nim; it was also learned that Robbe-Grillet thought that he himself had invented it, and at least one angry French citizen, claiming to have invented and patented the game, threatened to sue the producer, director, and scenarist. *Cinéma 61* and *62* carried a learned debate on the mathematics of Nim, and I myself appended to my study of *Les Romans de Robbe-Grillet* (1963) an explanation with examples of the binary calculations necessary to win in any situation. Following the general impression, I also spoke of Nim as "Chinese" in origin; but later a mathematician, D. W. Bushaw, sent me an article, "On the Name and History of Nim," arguing convincingly that the name derives from German *nimm*, a form of *nehmen*, meaning to take. Aside from the incidental interest of the game itself, the important point suggested by the existence of a mathematical theory is that Nim, both in reality and in the film, is not a "game" in the open sense, but the execution of a predetermined certainty by one familiar with its system. Obviously, only M, the husband figure, is privy to Nim's secrets in the film, and the various remarks heard among the spectators (such as "It must be a logarithmic series," etc.) reflect the surrounding ignorance on which the power of M's play depends. (In a sense, the "native song" of *La Jalousie*, described as incoherent only to one not familiar with its "rules," is an analogous structure.) The antagonists X and M confront each other in two ways: in the struggle of passion to possess A, and in the duel of the mind to win at Nim (or at poker, dominoes, etc.). A certain tonality of playing dice with the devil is sounded in these encounters at the gaming table. M always wins, but he "can lose," as he says, and in the end he does. Is it deliberately?

It is perhaps unnecessary to do more than refer briefly to the integration of Nim into the visual series of the film, and thus into the implicit psychology of the characters, especially A: the broken glass, the slippers, the photographs, the torn pieces of a letter, even the final oblique reference in the pattern of the lighted windows along the facade of the château as the film ends. All the games of the film, including that of the shooting gallery, reinforce the themes of contest, domination, imposition of one's will upon another, even violence, that form the basis of the main action of *Marienbad*. Like the play on the château stage, the games of the film are forms of interior duplication, of *mise en abyme* in the Gidian sense, which serve not only to permit the characters themselves to take cognizance of their situations (as the dialogue on the statue does, for example), but also to let the spectator or reader plunge deeper into the "vertical" significance of the work.

When in the summer of 1967 I mentioned to Robbe-Grillet that I planned to do a piece on *le jeu* in relation to his work, he replied, "Ah, il faut parler de *Trans-Europ-*

Express. C'est fait comme le *jeu de l'oie*." Indeed, this film (1967) carries to great lengths the "duck game" principle of starts, retreats, and new starts. A novelist-scenarist on a luxury train begins to "imagine" a scenario suitable for filming on the train; his first conjectures, objectified into actual sequences, are broad caricatures of spy movies and are almost immediately "erased" and replaced by more "serious" attempts. As this game of improvisation continues, the reality of the game, though retaining its tendency to proliferate into alternatives, begins to overwhelm the ostensible reality of the character of the writer, and his imaginings. In this sense *Trans-Europ-Express* is closer to *Dans le labyrinthe* than to *La Maison de rendez-vous*, in which the "alternatives" (such as the various forms taken by the murder of Manneret) are spliced together in an "impossible" topology in which events can occur in reverse or double order: for example, as I have pointed out in this connection, the protagonist Johnson, fleeing the police who are seeking to arrest him for Manneret's murder, evades them and proceeds to commit the murder for which he is being sought. (Note a certain similarity here to the plot of *Les Gommes*.) As for the other "games" of *La Maison de rendez-vous*—the erotic sketches, the garden of statues—these are mostly examples of interior duplications linked in typically complicated ways to other elements in this work as well as in previous works of the author.

Is the predilection for games and game structures evidence of excessive formalism in Robbe-Grillet? It would be possible to argue that since Raymond Roussel the creation of novels on game premises has given rise to certain tendencies in fiction leading away from the "serious" thematics (such as Sartrian *engagement*, the depiction of contemporary alienation, and the like) associated with the novel in the mind of the public. These tendencies appear not only increasingly in Robbe-Grillet, but also in such works as Jean Ricardou's *La Prise de Constantinople* (1965), one of the most significant and "serious" novels-as-game yet to appear. Meanwhile, game for Robbe-Grillet has come to mean structural freedom, absence of traditional rules of transition, viewpoint, chronology, and other parameters of previous fiction, and, on the constructive side, an invitation to create new models, to develop new combinations, to push ahead even further the aptly termed *nouveau roman*.

Alain Robbe-Grillet (essay date 1986)

SOURCE: "Alain Robbe-Grillet," in *Three Decades of the French New Novel*, edited by Lois Oppenheim, translated by Lois Oppenheim and Evelyne Costa de Beauregard, University of Illinois Press, 1986, pp. 21-30.

[*In the following essay, Robbe-Grillet discusses his literary career, artistic concerns, critical reception, and the development of the New Novel.*]

I am going to try to say why I write and to specify, perhaps with some difficulty, what my present concerns are and how they may be situated in relation to those of the 1950s. It is true that the Nouveau Roman is already a quarter-of-a-century old and this word "nouveau" [new] is therefore somewhat comical. It is comical, however, in a way which, all in all, suits me rather well and, aside from the fact that the New Novel has continually renewed itself, as Tom Bishop pointed out, it may be said that its novelty remains intact since the revolution which it started in the 1950s never really materialized. Contrary to what I naively hoped as a young man, all of literature was not really turned upside down by the Nouveau Roman and, here again, I am interested in knowing why.

First, why did I start writing? At the end of the 1940s and the beginning of the 1950s I was already thirty years old. I was not at all a novelist by profession; I was not even trained in literature. I was a scientist and suddenly I wanted to write novels, not then knowing that they would be the Nouveau Roman. I wanted, in other words, to write a certain kind of novel, but it was the way the critics received it that made me understand that what I was writing was not what was expected of a *true good* novelist. This, of course, surprised me, as I was under the impression that the criteria by which I was being judged had not been applicable to literature for a very long time and that after Proust, Kafka, Faulkner, Joyce, and so on, literature no longer bore any resemblance to the model which French academic criticism continued to impose on it. It was in reading the reviews which my first books received, reviews which opposed what I was doing with what was expected of me, that little by little I had a clearer idea of what I wanted to do. These reviews, as you know, were unfavorable at the beginning. I have in no way built my career on public acclaim, but rather on its rejection, and on an almost universal critical condemnation, at least by the academic critics in authority: those who rule in the papers and magazines. Among those who supported me at the beginning were Roland Barthes, Georges Bataille, and Maurice Blanchot, but at that time they were not as renowned as they were to be later. Barthes, in particular, who was about my age, was no more famous than I. The major critics, on the other hand, seemed to continually expect of us novelists that we copy those models which had made the nineteenth century so glorious, but which I naively believed to have been old-fashioned for a long time.

How shall I characterize this literature which I was reproached for not writing? All the novels of the nineteenth century, and later those of the twentieth century which followed in their footsteps, manifested a kind of hiatus between the narrator's speech and the characters' consciousness. This was apparent to both French and American critics. It was as if in Balzac or in Zola, as well as in a lot of others, the novelist had to render an account of something that was a change in the world. This change in the world was a splitting apart, a fragmentation: there were cracks in the world, there were rifts, and the fragmentation of the world went so deep as to touch the characters' very consciousness. Fragmentation, scattering, dissemination, these were the evils of which the characters suffered, so to speak, while it was the calm voice of the novelist which recounted these difficulties, these sufferings, and the characters' ultimate expulsion from society—for almost all the great nineteenth-century novels are ceremonies of expulsion. Fabrice del Dongo, Madame Bovary, and even Nana are people whom society expels because they do not conform to the established order.

Thus what is curious is precisely the opposition which exists between these characters, those consciousnesses which are aware of being fragmented, cracked, full of holes and contradictions, and the narration itself which is a completely reconciled story, continuous, causal, univocal. This is to say that the narrator seems not to suffer from the same troubled awareness, as he himself is perfectly coherent and competent. The coherence and competency of the narrator are fundamental in the nineteenth-century novel. That is why, as Leo Bersani has pointed out in one of his most remarkable essays, this novel, in claiming to criticize a society which fragments, scatters, and separates, seems, all in all, to denounce an evil while, in fact, it does the very opposite. As the language of the novelist is completely coherent and reassuring, the established order of society is, in a sense, reinforced by the novel. All of Zola's work, like that of Balzac, is more or less built on this model of a story whose functioning is completely vulnerable to its meaning. From beginning to end, everything has a meaning, the same meaning, while the character dies because the world lacks meaning or because its meaning is too fragmented and contradictory.

This divorce between the character's situation in the world and the writer's account of this situation is quite remarkable, for the novel is a game which both disturbs, for a considerable number of pages, and reassures, particularly at the end since, in the last analysis, if the novelist can be a coherent voice, it is precisely that the world itself is just, that God exists, and so on. And thus there is no problem of consciousness: those characters suffering from a clash either with themselves or with society are only maladjusted people whom we would do well to cure.

Every reading of a nineteenth-century and later of a twentieth-century novel—which is to say for the French novel, Mauriac, Montherlant, Maurois, and others—is based on this opposition between two possible routes. Either one tries to be in the character's consciousness and thereby feel this fragmentation of the world, this fragmentation of the self, this fragmentation of the work, and this fragmentation of society or, on the other hand, one sides with the text, with the reading, and in this case one is perfectly calm and reassured. Constantly ambivalent in this sense, the novel, though seeming to criticize the established order of society, is ultimately reinforcing it.

It was in the twentieth century that, little by little, novels appeared where the narrative rules were progressively diluted. I will not recount its entire history, but well before the appearance of the New Novel as a so-called school, there were the novels of Faulkner, for example, where, as

in *As I Lay Dying*, the fragmentation of the world and the fragmentation of consciousness were enacted within the very text. The famous Benjy of *The Sound and the Fury* is also to be mentioned, for he is the typical incompetent narrator, the narrator, in other words, who does not understand anything of his own story. In the context of "knowing one's own story," there is a progression to be followed in the evolution of the novel. In the medieval novel, an author who knows a story tells it to a public who already knows it as well. During the nineteenth century, an author who knows a story relates it to a public who does not yet know it. Finally, in the twentieth century, the situation has developed that gave rise to the Nouveau Roman: that of an author who does not know a story recounting it to a public who does not know it either.

When I started writing and was thus criticized, I suddenly felt that I was not being accused of having characters who suffered from this fragmentation and from this severing or separation from the world—after all, Roquentin in *La Nausée* [*Nausea*] or Mersault in *L'Etranger* [*The Stranger*] were in the same situation—but rather, that I myself was being accused of being deficient and full of contradictions. I was reproached, in short, for not being comprehensible, which meant that I, as an author, was supposed to have made clearly understandable that which the character did not understand. And I realized that it was precisely there that a characteristic of newness in modern times occurred, a characteristic which might even be one of the fundamental elements of modernity: things must take place within the text itself. It is impossible to write a text which, as a narration, is based on the old established order when its purpose is to show that this order is wavering. On the contrary. Everything must happen within the text so that severances, faults, ambiguities, mobilities, fragmentation, contradictions, holes must be enacted. It is the text which must display them.

I began at that time to find equivalent preoccupations among the novelists whose works were to be classified as "Nouveau Roman," those novelists who had in many cases been writing for a long time when I began publishing my own work. I found these preoccupations in *Tropismes* by Nathalie Sarraute, for instance, of which Tom Bishop spoke, and in the essays on literature by Nathalie Sarraute that were published in *Les Temps modernes* (and later in *L'Ere du soupçon*) and which, in effect, rendered account of the same experience of the novelist grappling with a substance—the text—which itself had to be the arena for these fights between order and disorder. I found them as well when I read *Mahu ou le matériau* by Robert Pinget. *Mahu* was published in 1952, before my first published novel, **Les Gommes**, which appeared in 1953. *Mahu* is for me a kind of premonitory text where already—though Pinget claims not to have a strong theoretical awareness—there is in the text itself a kind of theoretical formalization of these problems through the character's difficulty with words. (Mahu is a character whose adventures I really advise you to read. I would not dare to try to evoke them here in a mere few minutes.) Somewhat later, I had in my possession the manuscript of Claude Simon's Le Vent, a manuscript whose title was then much longer and which is now a subtitle: *Tentative de restitution d'un retable baroque d'aprés les restes trouvés dans une chapelle en ruines* [*The attempt to restore a baroque altarpiece according to the remains found in the ruins of a chapel*], which is quite a program! A narrator of questionable competence, grappling with scattered fragments! And there again, it was the text itself which staged this attempt, one which was like that of trying to exist today, to have an awareness today, to be a free consciousness today.

Nevertheless, as far as my first novels are concerned, *Les Gommes*, *Le Voyeur*, and *La Jalousie*, I noticed that in spite of an extremely hostile reception at the beginning, they were recouped rather quickly. The efforts of Bruce Morrissette, for example, who was supposed to be at this colloquium but who was unable to come, were very interesting for he showed that, in a way, even *La Jalousie* worked as a readable novel. This book had been considered unreadable by all the French critics. I believe that there was not even one favorable review when the book was published. And then, shortly thereafter, an American professor, unknown in France at the time, explained that this book was perfectly readable. He explained it very clearly, but he explained it according to the standards of a psychological coherence which, in fact, the book challenged. It must have also existed within the book, but Morrissette reconstituted, as it were, this coherent speech which the narrator had not been able to adopt.

I remember, apropos of this, that on the back of the book there was a blurb which began: "Le narrateur de ce récit: un mari qui surveille sa femme" [The narrator of this story: a husband keeping watch on his wife]. Though it is never said in the book that it is a husband keeping watch on his wife, I was the one who had written this introductory notice, and thus it would seem that at that moment I myself was starting to overstep the text by furnishing more or less fake keys which would allow the reader to enter the book. They would not allow it immediately, unfortunately, but Morrissette helped people to enter the story with this false key and the book again became the story of jealousy, the story, in other words, of a crisis, of a passion, with birth, development, and downfall. At the same time, we received a letter from Maurice Blanchot complaining about the jacket blurb. As it was signed "The Editors," Maurice Blanchot had sent a vehement letter to the editor saying that it was shameful to limit the scope of the book so stupidly with "The narrator: a husband keeping watch on his wife." "It is not a husband speaking in La Jalousie," claimed Blanchot, "but a pure anonymous presence." And, of course, Blanchot was right. I wrote to him that he was right, but that it was I who had written this blurb and that, in fact, it was not intended for him, but for those hurried critics who do not have time to read the books they have to write about in the papers. The blurb was, of course, not addressed to Maurice Blanchot who, in the cell of his tower, actually reads the books.

But what was disturbing in this affair? It was that I myself had written that blurb and thus, to a degree, I myself was a nineteenth-century novelist who had made clear and coherent a world of uncertainties, of struggles, and of contradictions. Though coherence was no longer in the book, it was now beside it. And I think that this was a very important discovery for me, a very productive discovery, as it made me understand that there is no pure revolutionary consciousness. No one can be a free consciousness: The ideology of the society in which I live is not in front of me, as though I were a kind of archangel who had escaped this ideology and who would write New Novels fallen from heaven into a world refusing of them. No, not at all! The ideology is in me, too, and consequently this longing for order and coherence, this struggle against incoherence, exists in me as well and probably, therefore, in my text, too.

Starting with *La Jalousie*, something became clear to me: this experience had to be generalized, books had to become the fighting ground. Blanchot said, "Le livre est le lieu où le monde a lieu" [Books are where the world takes place]. I would say, even more precisely, that books are where the fight of the world takes place because it is in the text that the world creates itself in the form of a fight between irreconcilable forces—forces, let us say, like the prevailing ideology and revolution, to simplify and to use stereotypes, and more generally, order and disorder. Or, to relate to the topic as I considered it at the beginning, since it is inadmissible to speak of the fragmentation without trying to remedy it, books must be, on the one hand, the site of this fragmentation and, on the other, the site of the incessant struggle to try to put these fragments in order.

For me, the turning point in my work is *Dans le labyrinthe* where, for the first time in my books, there appears a kind of rupture within the narrative word. *Le Voyeur* and *La Jalousie* are, in fact, strongly centered novels which, in the case of *La Jalousie*, means that whether called "husband" or "pure anonymous presence," there is something which is an organizing center of the whole text. This is true of *Le Voyeur* as well. Starting with *Dans le labyrinthe*, however, we have the impression of being in the presence of two distinct voices; without ever knowing which voice we are penetrating, we nevertheless feel, from time to time, their antagonism. On the one hand, there is the doctor, the one who says "me" at the end and "I" at the beginning. Yes, it is probably the doctor. I say probably the doctor because I do not have any clearer ideas about my books than those any good reader might have. And, on the other hand, there is the soldier, the central character in *Dans le labyrinthe*, who is also completely fragmented and incessantly in search of his self.

Starting with *Dans le labyrinthe*, books like *La Maison de rendez-vous*, Projet pour une révolution à New York, *Topologie d'une cité fantôme*, and *Souvenirs du triangle d'or* (the only one not yet translated into English) represent a clearer and clearer tendency to refuse that someone take over in the text: The text is a fight for power between irreconcilable forces. In *La Maison de rendez-vous*, one might already have the impression—and I think that this would be a good reading of the text—that there are numerous narrative forces, one of which is called Johnson, another Lady Ava, a third Edouard Manneret, and there are a lot of others. It is not only characters but also *places* (the theater of the Blue Villa, the park of the villa with its statues) which tell a story, as if each element of the narration tended at each moment to seize the narrative power. And it is this fight between the different powers which, in fact, is the subject of the book.

As I must not take up the whole session with my lecture, I will tell you very quickly how far I have come. I will say something, in other words, about my last book, *Djinn*, which was published in France in 1982 and here, in the United States, by Grove Press three or four months ago [also in 1982].

Djinn was a very old project of mine which, specifically, consisted of using as the prescribed order of the story the fundamental order which every writer faces: his language. The French language—French vocabulary and grammar—constitutes a kind of established order. Even if, in *La Jalousie*, I turned the narration upside down—let us say chronology, for example—or even a bit later, space, as in *Projet pour une révolution à New York*, there is one thing which I have always rigorously and even maniacally respected, and that is French grammar. I refer constantly to a grammar book and dictionaries when I write. I take great care to use words in their true meaning. This grammar, this vocabulary, this French language are for me, in a way, law. And this law is extremely important for the writer, for every novel is more or less generated by the language in which it was written, that which makes the difficulty, the unsolvable problems, of translation. One does not write the same novels if one writes in Japanese or in Hebrew. These are two languages which function differently, and it is the functioning of a language which produces the narrative standards and, consequently, the discrepancies in relation to the ruling discourse.

Thus I had the idea of using grammar, the French language, and of even writing a text for teaching French to foreign students. I had on hand Yvonne Lenard's books, in particular *Parole et Pensée*, where a certain number of texts were written to demonstrate the increasing difficulties of language and vocabulary. And here is what appeared to me to be a very interesting generative outline: the first chapter would consist of verbs in the present indicative, ending in -er, and this would be followed by other conjugations, other tenses, other moods, and so on, from chapter to chapter, with pronominal verbs, reflexive pronouns, complex relative clauses. It was this order that was to generate the text of the novel which was simultaneously an exercise in learning the language. It was, in fact, published by Holt, Rinehart and Winston as a textbook to study French at the intermediate college level. At the same time, however, the book is an experience in human

freedom: How can a free consciousness live within a language already representing a law which cannot be circumvented?

Of course, I had a good time reproducing a few stereotypes of this kind of book: a young American woman arrives in Paris to learn French, she meets a young Frenchman. There is the shock of two civilizations and whatever else you wish. At the same time, however, this convention of the shock of two foreign consciousnesses, a man and a woman, was of particular interest to me by virtue of the very notion of strangeness.

What do I call strangeness? Almost the same thing as Freud called strangeness, or Heidegger called strangeness: *Unheimlichkeit*, the fact that the individual feels his nature to be different from that of the things and people which are before him. In the familiar world, our relations with things seem happy, without problems, and consequently coherence between the world and us is constantly preserved until, suddenly, in everyday life, in the life of every moment, we abruptly feel something else which is the strangeness of the world. All at once, we no longer understand. And it is precisely at that moment that things start to be fascinating. It is at that moment, says Heidegger, that one begins to experience freedom, for as long as a thing is understandable, it belongs to meaning and therefore to the established order. It is precisely at that moment when a thing becomes incomprehensible that the liberating shock is born within the awareness and body of man. And, indeed, this strangeness is to be found in *Djinn*: in the dual form of what may be called, on the one hand, simply a love story, and, on the other, a science-fiction novel.

In the shock of being in love, as described by the Romantics, there is something very remarkable, something which I have felt, which everybody has felt, and that is that the other is extraordinary. A young man meets a young woman, and this young woman is not the same as others. When Fabrice del Dongo suffers from never having been in love and he suddenly encounters Clélia, he has a revelation: she is different from the others. This is to say that there is the rest of the world, which is the familiar world, and then, suddenly, there is a strange being who is precisely the other. This young woman is an extraordinary being, a being who seems to have fallen from another planet. It is something that we have all experienced and that we still experience very often. The inexplicable is fascinating. And this is probably also what is found in what we today call science-fiction novels, which I pronounce the French way, of course, as in *Djinn*.

What is science fiction? It is two worlds that should not communicate one with the other, but which suddenly start communicating, which means that there is a fault in the quotidian world and through it, another world is suddenly visible. This other world functions differently and thus we are thrown into a functioning (both of consciousness and of the world) which is not the one with which we were familiar. *Djinn* has a subtitle in French: "Un trou rouge entre les pavés disjoints" [A red hole between loose cobblestones]. This subtitle was deleted in the American edition, though I do not know why. It probably is a mistake to be corrected in the next printing. It really was quite important to me: in an ordinary, familiar city, we suddenly enter a street we do not know, the cobblestones of this street are loose, and between them we can see another world. There is another world there. This is also one of the great revolutionary myths, isn't it? The revolution in May, 1968, in Paris, found a nice slogan: "sous les pavés, la plage" [under the cobblestones, the beach]. This meant that under the established order, grey and made of concrete, there is freedom which insists on emerging.

I think I have spoken longer than I was supposed to. We will have the opportunity to speak of these things again, particularly at the roundtable, so for the moment I will stop here.

Michel Rybalka (essay date 1986)

SOURCE: "Alain Robbe-Grillet: At Play with Criticism," in *Three Decades of the French New Novel*, edited by Lois Oppenheim, translated by Lois Oppenheim and Evelyne Costa de Beauregard, University of Illinois Press, 1986, pp. 31-43.

[*In the following essay, Rybalka provides an overview of Robbe-Grillet's critical reception, the development of his fiction, and the interrelationship between theory and criticism in his work.*]

In attempting to take an overall look at the work of Alain Robbe-Grillet, one cannot avoid being struck by both the attention which he has always paid to criticism and theory and by the distinct difference which exists between his creative work (both novels and film) and his critical work. Considering the complexity of the task, I wish to limit myself to two principal goals: on the one hand, a retrospective consideration of the different critical evaluations which have been associated with Robbe-Grillet's work for these last thirty years and, on the other hand, a determination of how much Robbe-Grillet has internalized these critical judgments and constituted for himself an ideological double of unquestionable originality. There is a third aspect which I will only indirectly consider but which must be evident for those who attend his classes here at New York University. It is that Robbe-Grillet is one of our best critics and lecturers and that his critical work is among that which demands our serious consideration. As Olivier Veillon rightly noticed, Robbe-Grillet has played and continues to play two simultaneous roles: "celui d'un incitateur permanent à la recherche théorique" [that of a permanent initiator of theoretical research] and "celui d'un prophète de la déception théorique qui annonce 'la faillite de tout ordre présenté comme *vrai*'" [that of a prophet of theoretical disillusionment which announces "the failure of any order presented as *true*"].

To situate more clearly the remarks that follow, I must point out that I am writing a documentary work on Robbe-Grillet, one that is similar in scope to the *Ecrits de Sartre*. My aim, therefore, is to list and analyze systematically everything related to him, with a distinct preference for his first writings and the unpublished works. I will save for another occasion, however, a detailed lecture on the twenty-odd critical reviews which Robbe-Grillet published even before *Les Gommes* came out and on his very early writings which include many poems (of which one, "Le Jugement des juges," still unpublished, would be particularly appropriate here), a short story on a thwarted love affair, and an account of a journey, "Quatre jours en Bulgarie," published in 1947 in an industrial journal.

In his 1963 preface to Bruce Morrissette's book, Roland Barthes already distinguished between a first "thingist" Robbe-Grillet and a second "humanist" Robbe-Grillet. Later, at the Cerisy colloquium on the Nouveau Roman in 1971, Morrissette, in a lecture entitled "Robbe-Grillet nø 1, 2, . . . X," showed this kind of distinction to be arbitrary and simplifying. It would no doubt be risky to compare Robbe-Grillet's first published text, "Application de la méthode de la pyramide des âges à l'évolution du cheptel bovin français à la Libération" (1945), to his last novel, *Djinn*, or his last film, *La Belle Captive*. Nevertheless, in retrospect, Robbe-Grillet's work appears to be of an extraordinary continuity. In his preface to the videographic edition of the films, Dominique Château rightly speaks of the "persistence d'une oeuvre mobile" [persistence of a moving work]. My own methodological prejudices, stemming from Sartre and his notion of totality as well as from my knowledge of the work, lead me to see in all that Robbe-Grillet has done an extreme coherence rather than a discontinuity, though we should perhaps say with Raymond Queneau: "Au fil des ans au fil des ans / Il est pareil et non le même" [Throughout the years throughout the years / He is alike and not the same].

This continuity, which is visible in the novels and in the films, is not found in the criticism which has accompanied Robbe-Grillet's work since 1953. As thirty years of Robbe-Grillet are being evaluated here, thirty years of Nouveau Roman, I think it useful, providing limits of this enterprise are marked, to adopt and update the periodization delineated by Roland Barthes. Another reason impels such an Aristotelian exercise, one that is provided by Tom Bishop when he characterizes, as follows, the classes given by Alain Robbe-Grillet at New York University: "Il est professeur de Robbe-Grillet, mais il professe aussi autre chose. D'ailleurs, s'il parle de lui-même, il parle simultanément de tout un entourage culturel, philosophique, romanesque, etc." [He teaches Robbe-Grillet, but he also teaches something else. If he speaks of himself, he simultaneously speaks of an entire cultural, philosophical, and novelistic background]. Sartre would appeal here, as he did with regard to Flaubert in *L'Idiot de la famille*, to the notion of *programming*. To review the different critical moments which have marked Robbe-Grillet's work is, up to a certain point, to review our own history and to redefine the routes of modernity.

I intend, therefore, in evoking memories and generally accepted ideas rather than a rigorous archeology of criticism, to distinguish five periods in Robbe-Grillet's work and in its reception. The first period, that which Barthes qualifies as "thingist" and apropos of which he speaks of objective and even objectal literature, includes the first three novels (*Les Gommes*, *La Jalousie*, *Le Voyeur*), in part Dans le labyrinthe (published in 1959), and the texts of *Instantanés* [*Snapshots*]. The first interview with Robbe-Grillet, which was conducted by Jacques Brenner in March, 1953, was entitled "Alain Robbe-Grillet, géomètre du temps." The scientific training of the writer and his taste for long and precise geometric descriptions were strongly emphasized then, as was later the case with Boris Vian. The Nouveau Roman was then defined as "le roman policier pris au sérieux" [the detective story taken seriously] and as "l'école du regard" [the school of the gaze]. Robbe-Grillet claimed to be very influenced by Raymond Roussel, and many critics appealed to phenomenology to explain his books.

Robbe-Grillet was then appreciated and backed by the best of the French intelligentsia: Bataille, Blanchot, Goldmann, Sartre. It was also at that time, however, that he was most attacked by the traditional critics, to whom he responded with several polemical texts (such as "Nature, humanisme, tragédie"), later collected in *Pour un nouveau roman* [*For the New Novel*]. It might be noted that this book, which as a manuscript was entitled "Pro Domo: Plaidoyer pour la littérature de demain," begins with the sentence "Je ne suis pas un théoricien du roman" [I am not a theoretician of the novel]. Interviewed in 1970, Robbe-Grillet confirmed:

> Je n'ai pas de théorie. Historiquement j'ai commencé par écrire des romans. Les critiques que m'ont adressées les spécialistes de la littérature m'ont montré qu'eux avaient une théorie sur ce que devait être le roman. Moi, je ne savais pas ce qu'il devait être. J'avais seulement l'idée qu'il fallait l'inventer. J'ai voulu répondre à ces critiques. J'essayais de détruire la conception théorique périmée qu'ils se faisaient du roman. A ce moment-là, on m'a accusé d'être un théoricien. . . . [Je suis] très opposé à toute idée de théoriser la littérature avant de l'écrire.
>
> [I have no theory. Historically, I started by writing novels. The reviews addressed to me by specialists in literature showed me that they were the ones who had a theory of what the novel should be. I only had the idea that it was to be invented. I wanted to respond to those critics. I tried to destroy the old-fashioned theoretical conception they had of the novel. At that time, I was accused of being a theoretician. . . . [I am] very opposed to any idea of theorizing literature before writing it.]

In retrospect, this period appears similar to that of the Epiphanies, to use Renato Barillo's phrase. The Nouveau Roman did not have a large following—only 500 copies of *La Jalousie* were sold the year it was published—but it had the wind in its sails: Robbe-Grillet believed in its future, though later he did not hesitate to speak of a dead end, a dead end not only endured but also sought. This period when the Nouveau Roman was on the rise may be considered the classical period, the period when, in spite of the emphasis placed on novelty and avant-garde, the most assimilated works were produced. I think that the forthcoming school editions of *La Jalousie*, *Le Voyeur*, and *Les Gommes* are proof of this.

In 1959, *Dans le labyrinthe* was published. This was a turning point constituting a transition toward the second period, that which Barthes called "humanist" but which I consider to be that of the fantastic, of mental realism, and of symbolism. Through works such as *Dans le labyrinthe*, the film-story *L'Anneé dernière à Marienbad* [*Last Year at Marienbad*], and above all, Robbe-Grillet's first movie, *L'Immortelle* [*The Immortal One*], the objectivism of the preceding period was entirely reevaluated. It was discovered that "la précision conduit en définitive au fantastique" [precision leads in fact to the fantastic]. The roundtable dedicated to the film *L'Immortelle* in *Cahiers internationaux du symbolisme* may be cited as a mark of this reversal which, as Barthes noticed, was due at once to the author, the critics, and the public.

This was the time of greatest public acclaim, although some, like Roland Barthes, no longer took part in it, preferring to follow what I would consider a purist route. For them, there was a return to meaning, and Robbe-Grillet was too open to the comeback of humanism. Bruce Morrissette's book, published in 1963, toward the end of this period, seemed to confirm this presence of meaning in proposing what are essentially rather traditional keys to Robbe-Grillet's different works. It is noted that this book, the first one devoted to Robbe-Grillet, was written by an American: the Nouveau Roman was very quickly becoming famous in the United States and, ultimately, it would become more appreciated and analyzed there than in France.

Bruce Morrissette is absent from this colloquium for reasons of health, so I wish to emphasize the essential role played by him in Robbe-Grilletian criticism. It is he who, internationally, followed most closely the work of Robbe-Grillet, and it is he who constituted from it a critical corpus which, by its perspicacity and its unclassifiability, goes well beyond the "humanist" qualification of 1963, thereby revealing itself to be of an unmatched, and undoubtedly unmatchable, richness.

The third period began after 1963, when the Nouveau Roman became the Nouveau Nouveau Roman, although this was not really perceived before the Cerisy colloquium in 1971. It includes *La Maison de rendez-vous*, Projet pour une révolution . . . New York [Project for a Revolution in New York], and the films *Trans-Europ-Express* and *L'Homme qui ment*, though in the case of the films it is less clear than in that of the novels. This was the period of Jean Ricardou, which corresponds to the structuralist wave. In an approach paradoxically smacking of narcissism, the notion of author was then almost entirely eliminated in favor of the concepts of generator, sequence, and play.

Exploiting, serially, erotic clichés, Robbe-Grillet wanted to shed light on the phantasms, on the dull and decadent mythology of the society in which we live. He described *Projet pour une révolution à New York* as "une tentative de construction formelle mobile à partir de matériaux populaires" [an attempt to make a mobile formal construction out of popular materials]. He advocated a society of play where he wanted us to learn "`jouer avec les oeuvres" [how to play with the works].

In a recent interview, Robbe-Grillet defined his position as follows: "La liberté humaine est faite de morceaux. La société sans cesse me parle et me fournit des stéréotypes que ma liberté se limite à réarranger de façon personnelle. La liberté de la parole ne consiste pas du tout en une liberté essentielle des contenus, mais dans une combinatoire" [Human freedom is made of pieces. Society always speaks to me and provides me with stereotypes which my freedom confines itself to rearranging in a personal way. Freedom of speech is not at all composed of an essential freedom of content; rather, it consists of a combinational freedom]. And Robbe-Grillet even qualified this freedom as a "liberté de réarrangement" [freedom of rearranging]. This position, on the whole, is not so far removed from that adopted by Sartre in *La Nausée*, which, as I have demonstrated elsewhere, was conceived as a "roquentin," a speech made of parts of other speeches, quotations, fragments of songs, rearranged in a structure which allows a certain discontinuity. This freedom of rearranging may be understood in terms of the distinction made by Sartre, in *L'Idiot de la famille*, between constitution and personalization.

Textualism, formalism, and eroticization of speech characterize the works produced at that time. The Nouveau Nouveau Roman provoked theoretical texts of the highest order but, considered too abstruse, it could not manage to attract a wide enough public. Works by Robbe-Grillet were no longer of use in school and, for many, they appeared condemned to repetition and a dead end.

The fourth period, beginning around 1971, retained many characteristics of the previous one, but its originality came from Robbe-Grillet's growing interest in the avant-garde of the visual arts, painting and photography. Robbe-Grillet was then writing on Magritte (to give us the splendid book *La Belle captive*), and he was working with David Hamilton, Delvaux, and Rauschenberg to produce pictonovels, like *Topologie d'une cité fantôme* [*Topology of a Phantom City*], and films, such as *L'Eden et aprés, Glissements progressifs du plaisir*, and *La Jeu avec le feu*. The intertextual assemblages, the polyfictions created by Robbe-Grillet, who was then combining the most important elements of his previous works with circumstantial texts generated by the painting and photography of others, defined a new writing technique and impressed us with startling beauty. This transformation was remarkably perceived and analyzed by Bruce Morrissette in his latest book.

As early as the beginning of the 1970s, another change occurred in Robbe-Grillet's image: having already accumulated an abundant corpus of works which were both original and linked to his time, he was from then on to be considered a historical figure. He was led, in particular in his lectures and in the courses he has given since 1971, to teach Robbe-Grillet and to respond to the biographical curiosity which has begun to emerge about him.

On a deeper level, he felt the need to recover without any pathos or sentimentality what had marked his childhood and determined his vocation as a writer. Thus he entered his fifth period, which can be called, without hesitation, autobiographical.

By 1960, Robbe-Grillet had already planned an autobiography, and he had even promised a text to the journal *Tel Quel*. This project, however, was constantly postponed for ideological reasons: Robbe-Grillet was so strongly opposed to the notion of author, the times were so unfavorable to the notion of subject, that he did not dare to be drawn to a genre which his intellectual peers disparaged. It was only around 1976 that he decided to undertake a *Robbe-Grillet par lui-même*, probably inspired by Roland Barthes, who was then publishing a similar book at the Editions du Seuil. The entire book has not yet been completed, resistance to autobiography still being very strong, but some fascinating excerpts were published in *Minuit* in 1978 and in *Nota Bene* in 1981. Moreover, a novel such as **Djinn** owes, it seems to me, a large part of its value to the fact that it is a return to the source of Robbe-Grillet's imagining and, specifically, to the fact that, under the guise of grammar, Robbe-Grillet yields the fragments of a phantasmic autobiography. He himself confirms this in the text published in *Minuit*:

> Je n'ai jamais parlé d'autre chose que de moi. Comme c'était de l'intérieur, on ne s'en est guère aperçu. Heureusement. Car je viens là, en deux lignes, de prononcer trois termes suspects, honteux, déplorables, sur lesquels j'ai largement concouru à jeter le discrédit et qui suffiront, demain encore, à me faire condamner par plusieurs de mes pairs et la plupart de mes descendants: "moi," "intérieur," "parler de."
>
> [I have never spoken of anything other than myself. As it was from within, it was not really noticed. Fortunately, because I have just pronounced, in two lines, three suspicious, shameful, deplorable terms to whose disrepute I myself have largely contributed and which will be sufficient, tomorrow still, to have me condemned by many of my peers and most of my descendants: "myself," "within," "speak of."]

Referring then to the notion of author, he added:

> J'ai moi-même beaucoup encouragé ces rassurantes niaiseries. . . . Elles me paraissent avoir fait leur temps: elles ont perdu en quelques années ce qu'elles pouvaient avoir de scandaleux, de corrosif, donc de révolutionnaire, pour se ranger dorénavant parmi les idées reçues.
>
> [I myself have greatly encouraged these reassuring foolishnesses. . . . They appear to me to have seen their better days: they have lost in a few years what was scandalous, corrosive, and therefore revolutionary about them to be classified now among generally accepted ideas.]

One may wonder of what Robbe-Grillet's autobiographic project, his current work, consists. It will no doubt be very different from the autofiction which Serge Doubrovsky gave us in *Fils* and the remarkable *Un Amour de soi*, very different from books such as *Amer Eldorado* by Raymond Federman or *Le Testament amoureux* by Rezvani. Robbe-Grillet is discreet: he has never described in his books people making love. His aims above all at a phantasmic autobiography which would allow him to rewrite his own story and to return to his origins. It is in this context, I think, that he finally agreed, in 1978, to publishing his first novel, *Un Régicide. Autobiography*, and it has never been emphasized enough, is a text made out of other texts and it implies a textualization of that which has been lived by the writer. In a recent essay, Dominique Château clearly characterizes this process. For him, there is "dialectisation de l'auteur par ses personnages" [dialectization of the author by his characters] while the intrusion of the imaginary in autobiography transforms "l'habituelle reconstitution pseudo-réaliste en une poétique du souvenir" [the habitual pseudorealistic reconstitution in a poetics of memory]. Château concludes: "Robbe-Grillet entreprend aujourd'hui avec lui-même cette lutte pour la reconnaissance qu'il menait amoureusement avec Violette dans L'Eden ou avec Alice dans Glissements. Non seulement il persiste, mais il signe." [Robbe-Grillet undertakes with himself this battle for recognition which he lovingly fought with Violette in L'Eden or Alice in Glissement. He not only persists in this, but also adds his personal signature to it.]

This autobiographical period is marked by numerous interviews where Robbe-Grillet abundantly disseminates biographemes and where he provides us with information on his childhood and his literary start. It is beginning to be possible to write Robbe-Grillet's biography; ten years ago it would have been absolutely out of the question.

I also notice in this period a marked comeback to the Sartrian issues. Sartre as a writer, that of *La Nausée* and *Situations I*, but not of *Les Chemins de la liberté* [*The Roads to Freedom*], considerably interests Robbe-Grillet. He took part in the colloquia on Sartre in Los Angeles and Cerisy and he even gave a lecture on *Situations I* in Brussels. There is more and more use of a Sartrian vocabulary in his critical writings. He has come back to the notion of person and project, the work as a calling, and so on. Almost as much as Sartre, he thinks against himself and advocates change against prevailing ideology. In fact, Sartre, Barthes, Robbe-Grillet, these are three figures of modernity who, in the future, will have to be considered together.

Finally, the autobiographical period is interesting because it is both a return to past history and a new direction for writing. It is without a doubt in this perspective that Robbe-Grillet's last novel, *Djinn*, is to be situated. As Jacqueline Piatier (who, incidentally, is probably the best literary journalist there is) has rightly noticed, *Djinn* offers us an "excellent synthàse de l'univers romanesque de

Robbe-Grillet" [excellent synthesis of Robbe-Grillet's novelistic universe] and furthermore, Robbe-Grillet has "jamais allé aussi loin dans ses angoisses" [never gone so far in his anguish].) This period has not yet found its theoretician but, in a more general context, Philippe Lejeune's excellent works may, of course, be cited.

The summary periodization which I have outlined here leaves numerous unresolved difficulties. Robbe-Grillet's works are similar to the banana plantation which he describes in *La Jalousie*: "Tous les éléments du cycle ont lieu en même temps chaque jour, et les menus incidents périodiques se répètent aussi, tous à la fois, ici ou là, quotidiennement" [All the elements of the cycle occur at the same time every day, and the periodical trivial incidents also repeat themselves simultaneously, here and there, daily]. Overlappings, cross-checkings, opaque or blind points can all be observed. And the phenomenon of hysteresis, by which I mean the phenomenon of delay in the conception or reception of a work, comes into play as well. Criticism has always discovered after the fact what there was in a fiction. When first published, Robbe-Grillet's books generally have a rather limited success, but thereafter they are read regularly and constantly. Robbe-Grillet himself is convinced that there is a deferred appreciation of him. The main difficulty is that of programming Robbe-Grillet's works on the sociohistorical level. I leave this problem posed.

In conclusion, I would like to propose three or four topics for reflection concerning the status of critical discourse in relation to fiction. In the first place, it seems to me that Robbe-Grillet is a unique case in recent literature. With the possible exception of Butor, I do not know of any other writer of such notoriety who has had so close a link with criticism and theory. As Oliver Veillon wrote:

> L'écrivain se doit d'être son premier théoricien, sans que le rapport de la théorie à la pratique soit réglé extérieurement mais toujours de "l'intérieur," dans une contamination réciproque et permanente de la théorie et de la fiction qui, bien que constitutivement différentes, voire contradictoires, sont deux éléments d'une même stratégie.
>
> [The writer owes it to himself to be his own first theoretician, with the link between theory and practice being governed not from the outside, but always from "within," in a reciprocal and permanent contamination of theory and fiction which, though being of two different, even contradictory, constitutions, are two elements of a single strategy.]

In spite of his protests, Robbe-Grillet appears a true critic. It is even more to his credit that he does not "pratiquer la théorie par théoriciens interposés" [practice theory through intermediary theoreticians]. The accusation made by Ricardou at the Cerisy colloquium in 1971—that Robbe-Grillet was still at a pretheoretical point—can be justified only insofar as one can say, with Barthes, that precriticism is always being written.

Moreover, the extreme continuity which characterizes Robbe-Grillet's creative works has already been stressed.

These works constantly play on the same elements. They remain secure and without compromise, while Robbe-Grillet as a critic is amazingly malleable. With him, the critic is like Proteus: he makes the most of everything, he promises marriage to every theory enamored of him (though without ever fulfilling this promise), he does not hesitate to contradict himself, and he even exults in his contradictions. The creative works, however, are inherently linked to a project, to a truth whose presence is so strong from beginning to end that it resists the theories of others, and even those of Robbe-Grillet himself. To speak in Sartrian terms, it seems that in this respect there is a total commitment to literature, one that is comparable to that of Flaubert or Joyce. This commitment, however, is significantly tempered by criticism: Robbe-Grillet internalizes criticism while keeping it at a distance—a distance which, though close to empathy, can also be qualified as pathaphysical.

At the Cerisy colloquium, I questioned Robbe-Grillet about the part played by criticism in the elaboration of his works and he answered:

> C'est pour moi un apport extrêmement enrichissant, dans la mesure où le critique qui a mis en lumière une signification, dans mes oeuvres, ne m'indique pas une voie à suivre mais une voie à abandonner. . . . A chaque fois qu'à propos d'un de mes films ou d'un de mes romans j'ai développé moi-même un fragment théorique (quoique je n'aie pas, en général, la tête délibérément théorique, comme peut l'avoir Ricardou), à chaque fois, ce que j'ai eu envie de faire (contre moi, comme j'ai envie de le faire contre les critiques), c'est précisément *autre* chose.

> [It is for me an extremely enriching contribution to the extent that the critic who sheds light on meaning in my work does not show me a path to follow, but a path to leave. Each time that I developed for myself a theoretical fragment concerning one of my films or one of my novels (though, in general, I do not have a resolutely theoretical mind, such as Ricardou may have), each time, what I wanted to do (against myself, as I want to do it against the critics) was precisely something *else*.]

An essential difference between Sartre and Robbe-Grillet is noticed here. Sartre practically disregarded what the critics could offer him, which is a paradox for a philosopher who placed such importance on relations with others. When he thought against himself, it was from an internal point of view, distinctly his own. Robbe-Grillet, on the other hand, weighs more heavily the image people have of him: a clearly more narcissistic writer than Sartre, he internalizes in a different way, but also in a deeper way, the opinions of others. This functioning, as has been seen, does not implicate the coherence and continuity of his creative works. It affects, above all, his critical attitude and implies a kind of splitting in two.

Sartre used to say that there was the true Sartre, the one who was living and writing and whom nobody really knew, and the Other one, the one who had been created by public opinion and over whom he had no control, for he defined himself on a purely social level. The same distinction,

with different investments, may undoubtedly be applied to Robbe-Grillet. On the level of interest here is the notion of *ideological double* which Olivier Veillon evoked in speaking of Robbe-Grillet as a critic, a notion which may be supplemented by another, once again Sartrian, that of *ideological interest*.

The Robbe-Grillet heard here is not the true one; he was his double, his ideological mutant. Truth and its double, this merits stopping here.

Michael Wood (review date 4 November 1988)

SOURCE: "Mirror, Mirror . . . ," in *New Statesman & Society,* November 4, 1988, p. 31.

[*In the following review, Wood offers tempered assessment of* Ghosts in the Mirror. *"Fortunately," writes Wood, "the writing itself is better than the pompous theory."*]

The New Novel in France was a lingering cross-channel stab at modernism, hampered in many ways by the assumptions it thought it was toppling. But it understood very well the interest of reported obsessions, and the way the wildest obsessions can hide in the tidiest, most rational-seeming of discourses.

In this book Alain Robbe-Grillet mentions a painting by Marc Tansey, held in the Museum of Modern Art in New York, which shows the writer in a desert of cultural rubble. It's called *Robbe-Grillet cleansing everything in sight.* Robbe-Grillet likes the picture, accepts the charge. He does collect details, miniatures, miscellaneous objects, does long for the order which will result from their classification. Yet he also recognises that this is not an antidote to obsession, but is itself obsessive; and he wants us to see the monsters and the ghosts which lurk in the ascetic landscapes of his novels and films.

This work is a "modest autobiography", Robbe-Grillet says, a "sidelong look" at himself over his (then) 62 years. Those are his terms when he is feeling relaxed about the enterprise. He remembers Roland Barthes with admiration and affection; recalls very precisely a number of Kipling stories read long ago. He evokes his eccentric, right-wing parents without nostalgia but with amusement and evident fondness. His father, for example, put up a picture of Pétain when everyone else was taking theirs down; his mother read *Le Voyeur* in manuscript and liked it, though she said she "would have preferred it not to be written by my son".

The family lived in Paris when the writer was small, but also spent much time in an old house on the outskirts of Brest, and the most memorable parts of this book concern Robbe-Grillet's Breton childhood, full of fears of the sea, and flooded with folklore and legend. The book itself included a quest for a shadowy aristocrat, Henri de Corinthe—"Who was Henri de Corinthe?" we read on the first page. We are not much wiser at the end, but we have been well haunted. De Corinthe was a friend of Robbe-Grillet's father, rider of a mythical white horse, founder of an abortive right-wing political party, hero of a Breton rumour involving the reappearance in a floating mirror of a long-drowned fiancée.

This rumour—the story locals have made of this rumour and which Robbe-Grillet recounts—is the source of the book's title, very deftly translated into English. *Le Miroir qui revient* literally means the mirror which returns, but a "returner" is also a ghost, a revenant. There is another mirror in the book, too, but that occurs when modesty gets left behind, when the relaxed writer becomes fussy and starts posing. This mirror is that of ideology, favorite buzzword of the disaffected of the eighties: "It's a hydra-headed mirror: whenever one head is cut off it soon springs up again, presenting the adversary with his true face in the mirror, which he believed he had defeated."

It is a little messy that Robbe-Grillet, who insists that he doesn't believe in Truth—"Truth, in the final analysis, has only ever served oppression"—should be so confident about what Truth is, but we are in the realm of fading oppositional chic here—Robbe-Grillet's own version of the untimely portrait of Pétain. He sees this clearly enough himself, but doesn't seem disposed to do anything about it, and the book is full of lordly scorn for what he supposes other people like and need. "For whoever's interested I affirm my objection to the autobiography that claims to assemble a whole life . . . making it into a closed book with no gaps . . ."

"For whoever's interested" is just nervous bravado—he'll be in a fine fix if no one cares. Only the dimmest autobiographer thinks he can tell the whole story, and very few autobiographers even want to. Robbe-Grillet's defence of the fragmentary nature of his own work is meant to reassure us about how up to date he is, but has the reverse effect. Fortunately, the writing itself is better than the pompous theory.

When he says, for example, that characters in novels and films are phantoms, it's a truism of which only the most naive realist can remain unconvinced. But when he says *his* characters are phantoms, "desperately trying to gain access to a fleshly existence which is denied them, trying to enter a veracious world which is closed to them", we come very close to what is happening i n *Last Year at Marienbad* and other works, and we see that his characters hanker for Truth even if he doesn't believe in it.

What seems dated here, then, is the sturdy commitment to a very narrow version of the modern. "Reality begins at the precise moment when meaning becomes uncertain." The good guys know this, and the rest are "moved by the comforting familiarity of the world" and "write like the Sagans . . . make film like the Truffauts." "Why not?" Robbe-Grillet says, lending condescension the mask of tolerance. But I'm afraid reality is even more uncertain than he thinks. Not even uncertainty and unfamiliarity are to be counted on all the time.

Paul West (review date 27 January 1991)

SOURCE: "A Phenomenologist Bares His Heart," in *The New York Times Book Review,* January 27, 1991, p. 24.

[*In the following review, West offers favorable evaluation of* Ghosts in the Mirror.]

Recently, during a panel discussion on Parisian television, a French novelist plucked out the earpiece of his headset and tossed it across the set at me; of course, being tethered, the earpiece merely rebounded.

Such antics seemed a long way from my no doubt severe notion of a French novelist, at least one of the 20th century. Consider, for example, Alain Robbe-Grillet, deviser and austere high priest of the French "new novel" that emerged in the 1950s, who used such works as *The Voyeur* (1955) and *Jealousy* (1957) to reveal the novel as a form in search of itself, emerging in his version as objective and non-psychological, rather like an inventory or timetable of plot-refuting and character-denying images of hard, inscrutable, untragic things.

Mr. Robbe-Grillet, the epitome of rational poise and calibrated steadiness, would never have tried such a stunt; instead, a voluminously described raspberry would have arrived in my mail, inviting me to respond with even more relentless philatelic finality, as if truth were a feat of exhaustion.

Scrupulously impersonal, in his novels at least, Mr. Robbe-Grillet won a reputation for meticulous, patient accuracy by cultivating sheer indefatigability of the eye, as if to imply that fiction cannot be based upon, cannot be, anything slovenly or vague. Mr. Robbe-Grillet maintains that the novelist has nothing to say and might as well make a good job of describing the world instead. He sees the novelist as a top-notch phenomenologist, untouched by the egotistical sublime.

Here, however, comes Mr. Robbe-Grillet baring his heart, exposing the lyrical and rather lilting soul we suspected was there all along, behind those solemn and strict nouveaux romans of his. Surprisingly enough, the means of this revelation is the first volume of a projected three-book memoir, which ranges from Brest to the Rue Gassendi in Paris, from New York's Bleecker Street to the Jura Mountains to Istanbul.

The prose manner is controlled, of course, but almost voluptuous and, throughout, lush, ripe and luminously intuitive. Mr. Robbe-Grillet still disdains metaphor, but he revels in sensuous describing, as if the people of his own life had conferred upon him license to plumb and guess, to sample their interior lives with eclectic fondness, not as copiously as Nathalie Sarraute, an other but very different pioneer of the French new novel, does in her books of "sub-conversation," yet much more than is usual with him.

Mr. Robbe-Grillet still mistrusts "adjectivity," as he calls it, after Roland Barthes, and the thick prose of Zola, but he does allow one phobia into view: from the beginning of the 1940's, he "couldn't listen to 'Pelléas' or 'Tristan' without feeling instantly uplifted by the insidious, perilous surge of the sea, then sucked reluctantly into the heart of an unknown, unstable, irrational liquid universe ready to engulf me." Look at the adjectives there.

Without laboring it, Mr. Robbe-Grillet makes the point on every page that good prose must be at least as detailed as the world it seeks to evince or supplant, whether the writer is guessing or just reporting. Take this passage about a 1951 trip to Turkey, for example—mauve if not purple, and essentially celebrational: "Caïques sailing up the Golden Horn through the lengthening rays of the setting sun; the main street of Pera already lit by signs for dancing girls in the soft twilight and the floods of silent men in dark robes; the Galatasaray lycée where sugary, nostalgic melodies *alla turca* throbbed, lulling us to sleep in the big white marble dormitories."

Nevertheless, Mr. Robbe-Grillet remains the detached observer who began writing his first novel in 1948 while working at a biology laboratory, "taking vaginal smears every eight hours from hundreds of sterile rats injected with urine from mares in foal." But he seems to be mellowing his effects, ushering in sentence after sentence in a procession that resembles a conga of gorgeous animals.

The most vivid and moving writing in this relaxed, well-tempered book is about Mr. Robbe-Grillet's parents. Although they lived in Paris, the author's father and mother shuttled regularly between the Jura (his father's home ground) and the countryside near Brest (to the home of his maternal family, where he was born in 1922).

Mr. Robbe-Grillet pays devout attention to both parents, but most of all to his mother, who once kept an ailing bat for several weeks under her blouse "in what she called her pouch," to the horror of visitors, who watched it emerge from her white collar and spread its wings over her breast and neck. Myopic, big-nosed, she doted on tiny things (Japanese figurines made from grains of rice, for instance) and so loved all forms of animal life that, when washing watercress, she became completely sidetracked by the aquatic insects she found among the stems. She had no sense of time and, like her husband, was both anti-Semitic and an Anglophobe.

Without knowing a word of German, Mr. Robbe-Grillet's "Papa" translated Schiller's plays with gusto; he also resoled the family's shoes, worked in a cardboard box factory, had a passion for making porridge and, like his wife, subscribed to "an almost visceral atheism."

The book evolves by sentimental convection as Mr. Robbe-Grillet drops themes only to pick them up later, creating a wafty, haphazard atmosphere. With so many good things to get to, he sometimes tries to attend to them all at the same time; the effect is of a book long resisted and then allowed to burst forth, ebullient and chiming.

In addition to plenty of crackling gunfire about the stodginess of the 20th-century novel, Mr. Robbe-Grillet offers commentary on Barthes, Camus and Sartre; memories of starting out as a fiction writer; and a dispersed portrait of Henri de Corinthe—a nebulous, mythic family visitant, a Wagnerian Nazi, sometimes a mummy stripped of its wrappings, sometimes a Breton horseman out of legend who lived alone in an old gun emplacement and bore a double puncture on the back of his neck.

This is all solid material, required reading for Robbe-Grillet buffs, but the nonspecialist reader, whose awareness of the nouveau roman may by now have waned, is going to remember the family, the seagoing forebears; the scene of Mr. Robbe-Grillet and his father renting a wheelbarrow to haul a sack of coal across wartime Paris the affectionate sketch of Mr. Robbe-Grillet's uncannily young-looking wife, Catherine, who, along with the author, survived the crash of an Air France Boeing 707 in 1961; and the days of Mr. Robbe-Grillet's forced labor during World War II in Nuremberg, Germany, where he worked as a lathe operator in an armaments factory and began to make his own steel chess set.

Several times Mr. Robbe-Grillet reminds us that language, that uniquely human thing, is subjective to begin with and can never with utter authority reveal the nature of anything. There is fiction among the facts of this memoir, as he admits. Breastfed until the age of 2, playing with china dolls bound hand and foot for sexual rituals, he comes across as a dreamer, a conjurer, an uncontriving eccentric.

Mr. Robbe-Grillet's latest book has all the amenity of *For a New Novel: Essays on Fiction*, and some other qualities too, once latent and implicit in his work but now in the open for amazement and study. When his novel *La Maison de rendez-vous* appeared in 1965, *The Times Literary Supplement* of London observed that Mr. Robbe-Grillet had become a gifted pornographer; *Ghosts in the Mirror* also shows him in a new role, that of gifted rhapsodist, akin to the Albert Camus of the North African essays.

Jo Levy's translation is winning and artistic. I wonder why this book, which was originally published in France in 1984, has taken so long to appear in English.

Tony Chadwick and Virginia Harger-Grinling (essay date 1992)

SOURCE: "Alain Robbe-Grillet and the Fantastic," in *State of the Fantastic: Studies in the Theory and Practice of Fantastic Literature and Film,* edited by Nicholas Ruddick, Greenwood Press, 1992, pp. 91-6.

[*In the following essay, Chadwick and Harger-Grinling examine elements of fantasy in Robbe-Grillet's fiction. According to the critics, "Robbe-Grillet takes his reader into a fantastic world whose closeness to everyday existence prompts the kind of anxiety that he feels characterizes life in the late twentieth century."*]

The novels and films of Alain Robbe-Grillet were originally decried as too objective by those critics who had not studied this author in depth, or who took at surface value Robbe-Grillet's own pronouncements on his work. The two volumes of what may be his autobiography, *Le Miroir qui revient* (1984) and *Angélique* (1987), testify to the irony implicit in all the artist's creations. If these volumes are indeed autobiographical (Robbe-Grillet gives them the generic title *"romanesques"*), then they are autobiographies in which it is the mind that is depicted, an inner reality, one that bears little resemblance to anything external. These *romanesques* are concerned with memory, both individual and collective, and are inspired by a world of the fantastic, associated in Robbe-Grillet's case with the inner world of childhood and the obsessional world of adulthood. The autobiographies reinforce the intended confusions that mark his novels and films, and they force the reader to see that the world of fantasy, illusion, and nightmare has always been the real subject matter and the central interest of Robbe-Grillet's work.

Robbe-Grillet, speaking in *Towards a New Novel* (1962) of the so-called objective descriptions in his works, emphasizes the importance of the reader's being aware of "the little detail that strikes a *false note*." This concept has affinities with Riffaterre's notion—borrowed from Russian formalism—of literariness [*littérarité*], according to which the distinction between the language of everyday and that of literature is frequently a question of the difference of a minor detail. The presence of the detail creates a new pattern (in Riffaterre's terms, offers a new grammar) in order to guide the reader to realms that are far from that of the real. In this way, Robbe-Grillet is warning the reader to avoid oversimplification and is answering those critics who seem to him merely to have skimmed the surface of his books, if indeed they can be said to have read them at all. He is stating that all is not as it seems, that in fact the novels he writes, far from being simply about things and containing mere descriptions of things, are about a way of seeing, and to the reader are an invitation to interpretation.

Similarly in stories of the *merveilleux* [marvelous], as distinct from the fantastic, it is these small details, or slips one might say, that indicate that all is not as it seems. In this genre, moreover, they invite the reader to see *beyond*— not necessarily beyond the text but beyond what is presented as reality, and indeed to question one's assumptions about that reality. It might be added here that if Robbe-Grillet has a mission in his art, it is exactly that of questioning the tenets of the establishment, while extending the boundaries of what might be defined as art.

In the 1950s and 1960s Robbe-Grillet was first accused of writing difficult books about nothing but objects, then of writing difficult books about nothing. In the 1970s and even the 1980s, he was variously accused of writing about women as sex objects, about violence (particularly sexual violence), and of being a pornographic writer and voyeur. While all this criticism does contain certain elements of truth, the insightful reader and critic will realize that it is by no means the whole truth.

Robbe-Grillet seems to take a malicious delight in confounding readers and critics. In his essays collected in *Towards a New Novel*, for example, he refuses the concept of metaphor in his work. It is now obvious, after an examination of *Le Miroir qui revient* and *Angélique*, that he was simply refusing the accepted definition of metaphor and was indeed once again playing with his readers. He admits in these two volumes that he has always used metaphor and imagery of various kinds. These two works testify to the inherent lie in all his writings. Nothing could be so unlike an autobiography and yet contain so much truth. Elements from the fantastic abound in these books; whether they originate from legends springing from his family's past, from Breton folklore, or from his own fertile imagination is left to the reader to ascertain.

Similarly, Robbe-Grillet's apparent rejection of previous schools of thought and writing in *Towards a New Novel* is underscored by a perverse deconstructing of these modes of thought and expression in nearly all his writings. In sometimes very evident ways, even classical myths and legends abound, from the Oedipus of *Les Gommes* [*The Erasers*] (1953), where the mythical element is only too obvious, to the legends of Theseus and Pandora more subtly hinted at in *Dans le labyrinthe* [*In the Labyrinth*] (1959). The labyrinth features in both the form and content of many modern works and is prevalent throughout the work of Robbe-Grillet. More obscure elements from past stories and beliefs are also present, such as the Tarot symbolism, which first appeared in the figure of the hanged man in *Les Gommes*, but was also suggested in many of the earlier works.

A good example is one of Robbe-Grillet's earliest published novels, *Le Voyeur* [*Le Voyeur*] (1955), superficially a tale of obsession and repressed violence. The main character wanders in ever more confused figure-eight patterns around the island at which he has, or perhaps has not yet, arrived. These wanderings can be seen as an inner journey through obsession and memory. Moreover the cyclic journey, like the cyclic nature of the story itself, adds an element of horror—and of humorous frustration to the reader who can stand aside from the content and view the text as an exercise in interpretation, or in frustration and impotence.

Yet the nightmare quality of the true horror story exists here as the impression of being trapped in a situation from which there is no escape and of endless repetition—an internalized, Sisyphean hell. There are in fact constant references to the devil and his disciples, overt ones in the case of the young girl Jacqueline/Violette: she is at once a victim of rape and murder, and a devil's advocate who violates the protagonist's (and perhaps the reader's) mind. In the case of young Julien Marek, the allusions are more covert: he is a doppelgänger figure whose fixed stare fascinates and repels Mathias, as would his own mirror image. Even the sea, first suggested as murkily reflecting the turgid depths of Mathias's mind, is later referred to as the home of a Leviathan-like monster who demands the sacrifice of nubile young women.

While all this can be interpreted as another form of Mathias's obsession, it must still be admitted that this text is a long way from being a simple series of objective descriptions. The protagonist has become immersed in spite of himself in an enclave-like aspect of Breton culture; it is easy to imagine that atavistic elements of the Celtic past still rule the lives and minds of the inhabitants of this island. If, as is suggested but never verified, Mathias himself was born on the island and had once left it, he has obviously not succeeded in really leaving it and its legends behind him. One tends to think of Robbe-Grillet himself here, a native of Brittany whose writings in their vocabulary and concise images reflect the agronomist and scientist he became. Yet in spite of the modernist, avant-garde, and even postmodern aspects of his writings, the seas and skies of ancient Brittany—not to mention the author's mother who used to wander around with a bat clutched to her bosom—are ever present within them.

Running through the preceding comments is a common thread, which may provide a key to the importance of the fantastic in Robbe-Grillet's work. The denial of an authoritative view of the real, the deconstruction or negation of classical myth and Breton legend (especially those that contain an oedipal figure), and the conscious rejection of literary avatars point to a dynamic that Harold Bloom drew to the attention of critics of the fantastic at the Second Eaton Conference in 1980. His "formula" is phrased as follows:

> *Fantasy, as a belated version of romance, promises an absolute freedom from belatedness, from the anxieties of literary influence and origination, yet this promise is shadowed always by a psychic over-determination in the form itself of fantasy, that puts the stance of freedom into severe question.* What promises to be the least anxious of literary modes becomes much the most anxious.

Bloom's notion offers a rich vein of ideas. On the one hand, it suggests that fantasy represents a pull away from the dominant literary models that constitute the canon (in particular that of realism), at the same time as it manifests a fear of freedom from such models. On the other hand, freedom itself is thrown into question by the form of fantasy itself, since it cannot take comfort in the representation of the real. By posing fundamental questions, fantasy is able to hold out the possibility of creation without fear of the father and anxiety because of the lack of the father.

As the leading theoretical exponent of the *nouveau roman* (new novel) in France, Robbe-Grillet could be seen as

striking the (literary) father dead, and thereby assuring his own artistic freedom. Yet in a move that is at the same time perverse and aesthetically defensible, Robbe-Grillet moves his fictional world as close to the objective reality of the everyday as he possibly can, separating it from the real by the thickness of a mirror or the play of light on a surface that may be the exterior of a mannequin or the skin of a human being. This psychological strategy intensifies the aesthetic impact of the writing by undermining its purely referential qualities and by offering a new poetics. If one considers for a moment Pierre Reverdy's concept of the metaphor in poetry, the extent of Robbe-Grillet's aesthetic revolution becomes clearer. For Reverdy, the greater the distance between two terms of a metaphor, the greater the impact of the metaphor on the reader. This theory had a great influence on the Surrealists and could thus be considered an important factor accounting for the nature of much of the fantasy of the modernist period. It is this kind of fantasy that Bloom probably had in mind when he formulated his definition. But for Robbe-Grillet, as for many contemporary makers of horror films, it is the closeness of the fantasy world, its barely disguised absence, that marks the revolution in thinking about the nature of the literary experience.

The desire to be free of literary influence, of a spiritual father, does not mean that Robbe-Grillet thinks that he can write in a void. Indeed he has admitted to several major influences on his work. One that is obvious and has been already studied and discussed by ourselves and other critics is that of the Alice books (1865, 1872) by Lewis Carroll. The Alice story as interpreted by Robbe-Grillet presents an adolescent accompanied by a repressed sexuality seen as an invitation to imagination and violence. This is not of course to say that Carroll was not portraying a similar figure. His sexual preferences have been well noted in literary and psychoanalytic circles. Whereas the original Alice would have read fairy stories or other similar material, and have converted and integrated these tales into her own wonderland, Robbe-Grillet's young girls and women have been assailed by a far more violent imagery—of the cinema and television, of the newspaper and radio—so that their passage through a sometimes painful adolescence would elicit a different imagery. But the wonderland that Alice explores in her rite of passage is in the mirror, no further away from the real than the thickness of the glass.

As a literary father for Robbe-Grillet, Carroll offers a minimal threat, at least for a French writer in postwar France. Faced with the giant figures of Sartre, Malraux, Gide and Camus, all of whom were writing in the realist mode, it is not surprising that Robbe-Grillet should choose a forefather who elicited less anxiety than these fellow countrymen—namely Carroll, the English fantasist.

Robbe-Grillet has often been accused of portraying women as victims. A close examination of his novels and films, however, reveals that the acts of violence against the young women are never actually realized—to the gratification or frustration of the audience—but presented in such a way that they can only be conceived of as internalized images of obsession. It would seem to be the male characters who are haunted by these images and the young women who engender them. The few adult female characters in the novels and films are never victims, but indeed they are depicted as being in total control of themselves and others, including men; unlike the male characters, they are also in control of the world around them. One has only to think of A in *La Jalousie* [*Jealousy*] (1957) or the female figures in *La Maison de rendez-vous* (1965), or *Vanadé* in *Topologie d'une cité fantôme* (1976). The male protagonists, conversely, are caught in the web of their own obsessions and compulsions. They are afraid and lost in the external, physical world, and whether in the imagined or real world around them, they seem to need the relationship, sadistic or otherwise, that they attempt to establish with the female characters in order to allow them contact with their own reality.

An important part of the Alice scenario is the mirror or looking glass. The mirror is a constant motif in Robbe-Grillet's work, as is suggested by the title of the first volume of his autobiography, *Le Miroir qui revient*. With its multiple possibilities of signification, for its association with both the female figure and the fantastic, it is the ideal Robbe-Grillet motif. As the mirror is specifically associated in the Alice books with the entry into the fantastic realm, the world of multiple mirrors suggested in *Djinn* (1981) continues this theme and adds to it the ideas of the confusion, untrustworthiness, and distortion of reality, an integral part of the Robbe-Grillet thesis as presented in his writings. The multiple Simon Lecoeurs in *Djinn*, the very title of which suggests both magic and, in the echo of "Jean," the banality of the everyday, are simultaneously figures in a hall of mirrors and multiple versions of the Self. The indecipherable writing can quite easily be dismissed as mirror writing or seen as an invitation to mystery. Presence is underlined as absence in a hall of mirrors; yet at the same time it suggests another presence beyond.

Starting from elements of the modern world—billboards, the architecture of large urban agglomerations, glass, and steel—Robbe-Grillet takes his reader into a fantastic world whose closeness to everyday existence prompts the kind of anxiety that he feels characterizes life in the late twentieth century. By emphasizing the proximity of the two worlds, he denies the reader a route to easy escapism while simultaneously offering a critique of his realist predecessors. For his refusal to accept realism's validation of the real, Robbe-Grillet deserves to be considered a writer of the fantastic.

Yoseph Milman (essay date January 1994)

SOURCE: "Absurdist Estrangement and the Subversion of Narrativity in 'La Plage,'" in *Modern Language Review*, Vol. 89, No. 1, January, 1994, pp. 50-60.

[*In the following essay, Milman provides analysis of Robbe-Grillet's metaphysical concerns and narrative presentation in the short story "La Plage." Milman notes strong similarities between Robbe-Grillet's "absurd view of man" and the philosophical tenets of Albert Camus and Jean-Paul Sartre.*]

In the 'snapshots' he wrote at the beginning of his career as a writer Robbe-Grillet established a new subgenre of the short story, a kind of 'story-picture' in which he radically actualized the poetic approach of 'Chosisme'. These story-pictures, including **'La Plage'** which is the subject of this study, are thus not some immature experiment heralding Robbe-Grillet's innovative writing as it has been regularly scrutinized and publicized by critics (basing themselves on his novels). The time perspective allows one to see these apparent 'études' as the fullest realization, in both philosophical and aesthetic respects, of the unique writing of one of the major theoreticians of the French 'Nouveau Roman'. It is therefore surprising that in contrast to his novels, which aroused and continue to arouse much critical response, Robbe-Grillet's short stories have been scarcely studied (not even in the fairly numerous monographs on his work appearing from time to time). **'La Plage'** is no exception, in that the critical response to it has been limited and confined to very general or narrow aspects of the work. In the present study, however, an attempt will be made to examine in detail how in **'La Plage'** Robbe-Grillet managed to realize, by meticulous application of his pictorial narrative technique, a work which patently expresses the basic metaphysical premises as well as the fundamental poetic principles of 'Chosisme'.

The reality depicted in **'La Plage'** consists of a quite small number of motifs. Three children walk along a deserted beach, to their right an expanse of sea stretching away, only a single wave rising and breaking close to the shore to disturb the stillness; to their left a steep cliff with no apparent egress. At the water's edge, just in front of the children, approaches a flock of sea-birds whose star-like tracks are being washed away by the recurrent waves. In contrast, the children, slightly away from the edge, leave three close lines of footprints which bisect the beach along its entire length. From time to time the chime of a distant bell elicits brief snatches of conversation among the children. The three children, the flock of birds, the divided strip of beach, the tracks, the sea, the wave, the cliff, the sounds of the bell and the occasional talk are the basic motifs of the story. Their description, repeated each time with some slight variation, constitutes the whole 'plot'.

Compared with 'Le Mannequin', another of Robbe-Grillet's 'snapshots', this story is much easier to accept as a simple, direct description of 'a piece of reality' appropriate to a realistic story (of course, only as a part of it, since it is difficult to imagine a whole story devoted to such a scene). The first reason is that a landscape description such as the one presented here (for itself and from a purely 'aesthetic' point of view) is far more common in real life than a detailed account of ordinary household items like those depicted in 'Le Mannequin'. Whoever tells about a landscape which has made an impression on him needs no additional justification. Nor does the angle of vision from which the description is presented in **'La Plage'** depart from the normal view of a landscape: there is no unusual close-up or atomization of the described scene, and the perception of common objects (the cliff, the wave, the birds, the tracks, and so on) appears here in a more or less ordinary way. Moreover, the narrative convention more readily admits the description of landscape as a means of creating the effect of the real (with no additional signifying intention) than a thorough description of domestic objects. The choice of materials as well as the perspective from which they are presented therefore construct a quite convincing realistic scene. In contrast to 'Le Mannequin', there is nothing estranging or distancing in the depicted objects themselves, which allows emphasis to be placed upon different estranging factors such as characters, plot, space, and time.

While 'Le Mannequin', for example, is outstanding in the complete absence of any human protagonist (except, perhaps, the implicit presence of an observer's point of view), the children in **'La Plage'**, who appear right at the beginning of the story and remain there until the end, are clearly not only a human component among the other components of the described world but also major characters who make up the central object of the plot (if one can call their walking and brief exchanges of conversation 'plot'). In addition they are the major object of the description, whereas everything else is presented and located in relation to them: the beach stretching before and behind them, the sea to their right, the cliff to their left, the birds proceeding in front of them, the bells heard at a great distance from them, and so on. In fact, because of their central role in the described reality, a role which suits the traditional function of the characters in realistic fiction, the children in the story become a major factor in the de-familiarization and the alienating effect of that same reality.

In contrast to what is expected in a characteristically realistic description, the characters in **'La Plage'** are not given names, and moreover the readers in no way make their acquaintance. The sentence which opens with 'Trois enfants marchent le long d'une grève', by giving no information about the subject and place, actually avoids endowing the characters, even indirectly, with that specific identity which acts as one of the central characteristics of realism in literature. The only information supplied is that which might be given by a passing witness: the external appearance of the children, their movements, and their words. This information, however, despite the fact that it presents the reader with these characters' 'stage presence', separates this presence from any link with a wider context, which is necessary for a complete picture of reality. We know nothing about the children beyond their 'être-là' in that place, in the state and time-frame given in the story. Even the minimal information we might expect from this particular situation is missing: we do not know where the

children come from, what beach they are strolling along, where they are heading, and why they have to get there. The brief exchanges which take place among them and which might, eventually, fill in the gaps, only increase the obscurity. Here is their dialogue, presented in full, but taken out of the descriptive narrative continuum into which it is placed in the original:

> 'Voilà la cloche', dit le plus petit des garçons [. . .]
>
> 'C'est la première cloche', dit le plus grand [. . .]
>
> 'C'est peut-être pas la première', reprend le plus petit, 'si on n'a pas entendu l'autre avant [. . .]
>
> 'On l'aurait entendue pareil', répond son voisin [. . .]
>
> 'Tout à l'heure, on n'était pas si près', dit la fille [. . .]
>
> 'On est encore loin'. [. . .]
>
> Le plus grand des garçons dit alors: 'Voilà la cloche'.

This is the whole dialogue, but the spaces of time between the brief comments (the narrated time of the fictional reality as well as the narration real time) provide it with relative importance (one of the four pages over which the story is spread). And they undermine the continuity and connection between the children's statements. In any case, rather than replying to the questions that the situation raises, this type of dialogue directs attention to those unanswered questions, thereby increasing the atmosphere of obscurity: the remaining distance between the children and their destination, for example, only directs our attention to the fact that we do not know what the objective of the walk is, where it is situated, even whether it is close or far away, and why the children want to get there.

The structure and development of the dialogue also contribute to the obfuscation of things. The opening sentence spoken by the smallest child ('Voilà la cloche') only mentions a fact that the readers, and probably the other children, are already aware of, since it has already been mentioned ('de très lointains coups de cloche résonnent dans l'air calme'). This same sentence, however, also closes the argument, the only difference being that now it is spoken by the biggest child. This emphasizes the circular nature of the conversation and paucity of information it contains.

But this is not all. The second sentence, 'C'est la première cloche', expresses a vague claim. This is not only because it is disconnected from the context of the wider conversation, or because the children's statements are factual and do not reveal any emotional involvement, but also because of the ambiguity of the formulation. 'Bell' here might be a metonym for the sound of the bell, indicating time priority, but it might also be a metonym for the belfry, in which case we are dealing with priority from the point of view of place. The continuation of the dialogue ('C'est peut-être pas la première [. . .]') is not conclusive regarding this question, or regarding the point of statement of the speaker, whose explanation is cut off from the start: 'si on n'a pas entendu l'autre avant [. . .].' His companion's answer,

'On l'aurait entendue pareil [. . .]', is thus incomprehensible, since again we do not know what it refers to nor what argument it intends to contradict. The girl's words, 'Tout à l'heure, on n'était pas si près [. . .]', might in fact express the smaller boy's interrupted assertion, but this is not certain, and anyway the answer precedes the formulation of the claim which it perhaps answers. If nevertheless some small piece of information remains in the girl's words that might be a key to understanding the dialogue (suggesting that the children are already close to their destination), the next brief comment, 'On est encore loin', contradicts this information undermining further the communicative value of the whole conversation. In addition, considering the large intervals between the replies, which raise doubts about the connection between them, it is not surprising that this dialogue ultimately returns to its starting-point, the establishment of the fact that a bell is ringing, and that is all.

In the end, the whole dialogue, by its disconnection from the circumstances, its lack of continuity, the paucity of information in it, the circular nature of its argument, and its semantic vagueness, not only fails to shed light upon the scene (the characters' intentions, the point of their action and so on) but even adds the element of linguistic opacity to the opacity of the described reality. In this regard it clearly contradicts Jean-Paul Sartre's claim that 'le dialogue [. . .] est le moment de l'explication, de la signification' and that to give it a place of honour would be to admit that meanings exist. A dialogue such as the one in **'La Plage'** apparently demonstrates the opposite: how the dialogue can blend into the narration as part of the totality of factors which blur the significance of the text. Of course, this only emphasizes the basic agreement that exists between Robbe-Grillet and Sartre about the traditional explanatory or 'rationalizing' role of the dialogue in the narrative, and the need to undermine this tradition if one wishes to undermine the meaning of the work. Robbe-Grillet only demonstrates that it is possible to do this in different ways and not necessarily, as suggested by Sartre's claim, by abolishing the dialogue's *place privilégiée or privilège typographique* in the text.

The explicit description of the characters, however, acts to estrange the presented reality no less than the opacity of the action and the dialogue does. In the first place, the fact that the three children are hardly distinguishable stands out. Their lack of individual identifying names is complemented by their almost identical appearance: all three are almost the same height and age, and have the same complexion, similar faces, the very same look, and identical clothing. Their movements, obviously, are exactly alike: all three walk along the beach holding hands and looking straight ahead. If so far reference has been made only to their external appearance, we now see that the dialogue (which because the description is purely of the surface remains the only possible way of hinting at some internal quality) also lacks any individual uniqueness. On the one hand it is reduced to impersonal, factual content; on the other, it ends with another child repeating the

sentence that began the conversation, 'Voilà la cloche', as if to suggest that in this way, through an exchange of roles, another round of the same exchange of words has opened. Ultimately it seems that the only purpose of the slight differences among the children (one is smaller than his companion, one is a girl, and their places in the line are different) is to emphasize the similarity between them. Yet this slight difference imparts a trace of human uniqueness to the characters, without which they would be perceived as almost mechanical duplications of indistinguishable individual portraits very like the dressmaker's dummies of 'Le Mannequin'.

The humanity (and with it the realistic level) of the characters is undermined not only by the absence of discrimination but also by the nature of the description, which is identical to the mode of presentation of lifeless objects. Indeed, in regard to the characters also, the narrator adheres to the purely observational approach, avoiding any analytical or evaluative comments and any emotional involvement. In fact, he limits himself to essentially visual impressions: sights, shapes, colours. Even if one of the children's voices intervenes here or there, the description still remains essentially external (the privilege of relating to an auditory phenomenon, which the narrator occasionally allows himself, does not go beyond what he allows himself in regard to the lifeless universe, for instance, when 'un bruissement de graviers roulés' or 'de très lointains coups de cloche' are mentioned). The mathematical element in the description (expressed in the relatively large number of measurements: size, quantity, angles, directions), as well as the geometrical terminology and the geometrical nature of the division of space, are directed equally to natural objects and human beings. The impression finally achieved is not only of 'dehumanization' of the natural world but also of 'reification' of the human universe. The purely observational, and quantitative approach applied to the characters transforms them into material bodies devoid of any psychological dimension and perceived only through their external physical features (just like lifeless objects).

This analogy between the human world and the world of objects becomes even stronger because of the similarities between the characters and the other components of the landscape: the children's skin is of a yellowish hue, like the sand; their clothes are blue, like the sea; in their walk they form a straight line and produce a rhythmical movement, similar to the wave. In contrast to 'the romantic analogy' rejected by Robbe-Grillet, which 'personifies' objects, we have here 'objectivation' of human beings. The lack of distinction between the different children, which, as I have shown, depersonalizes the characters, is compounded by the basic lack of distinction between man and object, bringing about an almost complete 'reification' of the whole reality presented, including its living and its lifeless components. All in all the characters of **'La Plage'** quite clearly recall the picture of man drawn by Albert Camus in *Le Mythe de Sisyphe*, when he discusses the 'inhumanity' which sometimes men themselves exude, the 'mechanical' aspect of their gestures, and the 'pantomime privée de sens' which their deeds resemble when seen at certain moments of awareness. This characterization, especially because it extends over the whole work, is undoubtedly linked with Camus's fundamental claim that each individual 'nous demeure à jamais inconnu', and that the only possible recognition that exists in such a case is 'practical' recognition, which limits itself to recognizing men and women by their behaviour, 'à l'ensemble de leurs actes, aux conséquences que leur passage suscite dans la vie'.

Nevertheless, I am not merely referring to behaviouristic relativism. Although in *Le Mythe de Sisyphe* a phenomenological description can certainly be found which fits the characters that appear in Robbe-Grillet, as can a theoretical expression suiting the espistemological assumption upon which the characterization of these same characters is based, there is nothing in Camus to explain more specifically the almost pure 'objectal' nature with which the human world adorns itself in a story such as **'La Plage'**. This type of explanation can be more easily found in an analysis of Sartre's concept of *être-pour-autrui*, in which there is a phenomenological description of 'the Other' as he exists for us, which is likely to reflect the fundamental ontological assumptions upon which Robbe-Grillet's conception of character is based.

In his attempt to counter the realist approach (in the philosophical sense of the term) to the Other, as it is expressed in the positivistic psychology of the nineteenth century, Sartre discusses in *L'Etre et le Néant* the fact that the conclusion we tend to draw from the presence of the Other's body in regard to the existence of a consciousness similar to ours is in no way certain recognition (despite its being a reasonable hypothesis). 'Il reste toujours probable qu'autrui ne soit qu'un corps', claims Sartre. Thus the first appearance of the Other, according to him, is essentially 'objective'. 'Object-ness' is the basic condition of the Other's being-for-me, and 'objectivation' is the fundamental relation between the self (that is the 'me-as-subject') and the Other. 'Cette femme que je vois venir vers moi', writes Sartre, 'cet homme qui passe dans la rue [. . .] sont pour moi des *objets*, cela n'est pas douteux'. He even stresses the basic analogy which exists between this kind of presence of the Other and the way lifeless objects exist.

> Je vois cet homme, je le saisis comme un objet, à la fois et comme un homme. Qu'est-ce que cela signifie? [. . .] Si je devais penser qu'il n'est rien d'autre qu'une poupée, je lui appliquerais les catégories qui me servent ordinairement à grouper les 'choses' temporo-spatiales. C'est à dire que je le saisirais comme étant 'à côté des chaises, à 2m.20 de la pelouse, comme exerçant une certaine pression sur le sol, etc.

'Cet homme', of course, is not a puppet. Yet being 'Other' he is not essentially different from any puppet or other similar 'thing', and that, at least in regard to 'une, du moins, des modalités de la présence à moi d'autrui'. And referring to this same 'modality' (*l'être-pour-autrui*) Sartre adds:

> Mais *autrui* est encore objet *pour moi*. Il appartient *à mes* distances: l'homme est là, à vingt pas de moi, il me tourne le dos. En tant que tel, il est de nouveau à deux mètres vingt de la pelouse, à six mètres de la statue [. . .]. Au milieu du monde, je peux dire 'homme-lisant' comme je dirais 'pierre froide', 'pluie fine'; je saisis une 'gestalt' close dont la *lecture* forme la qualité essentielle et qui, pour le reste, aveugle et sourde, se laisse connaître et percevoir comme une pure et simple chose temporo-spatiale.

It is difficult to miss the clear similarity that exists between the human character as drawn in Robbe-Grillet's work and Sartre's 'object-ness' or temporal-spatial 'thingness' of the other (or Camus's mechanical 'inhumanity' exuded by men). Moreover, what in Sartre is nothing but *one* of the modalities of the other's 'presence to me' becomes in Robbe-Grillet virtually the *only* presence of the human character for the reader. The other modality of the Other's presence, his *être-sujet* (or *pour-soi*) whose threatening presence that apprehends me as *être-vu-par-autrui* (or *être-objet-pour-autrui*, that is as an 'object' or 'thing') manifests itself according to Sartre in the Other's look, is entirely absent in the characters of **'La Plage'**. This mode of presence, to the extent that it exists in Robbe-Grillet's work, is almost always situated in the point of view from which the reader is lead to observe things, while the observed characters are tied to the same objectal characterization upon which the total picture of reality is fashioned.

In Robbe-Grillet's theoretical writings, collected in **Pour un nouveau roman**, there is explicit evidence for the connection between his objectal approach to the world and the world-view held by Sartre and Camus, as well as express support for the link between his 'objectified' approach to the character and the existentialist-absurdist view of man. This is so, for instance, when he asks, in his defence of the identity-lacking characters of modern literature: 'Combien de lecteurs se rappellent le norm du narrateur dans *La Nausée* ou dans *L'Étranger*?' This is also the case when he bases himself on Heidegger ('La condition de L'Homme, dit Heideger, c'est d'être là'), in his attempt to explain 'le théme essentiel de la *présence*' which manifests itself in the 'being there' of Beckett's characters and which needs no significance beyond itself. It is thus impossible to doubt that the fashioning of the characters in Robbe-Grillet is in some way connected to the absurd view of man held by Camus and Sartre. It is also obvious that the method of characterization in a story such as **'La Plage'** greatly corresponds to several of the central stylistic-poetic basic positions of the Absurd (the pure descriptive approach, for instance, 'cognitive humility' and so on).

One should not draw the conclusion that the characters in this story constitute part of the picture of an explicit absurd world and that they therefore play some part in constructing the experience of encounter with such a world. A condition for this would be the existence of minimal thematic direction in the story towards existential problematics (something completely absent here), and there should, at least, be some minimal realistic credibility for the world presented, which would posit its opacity as an analogy for the opacity of the actual world, and the feeling of estrangement it arouses as a significant ontological experience. Instead, in **'La Plage'** there are various factors which undermine both the sense of reality and the referential, absurdist significance connected with it.

First, belief in the 'reality' drawn is increasingly undermined throughout the reading in regard both to the characters and to the background, and, following this, belief in the referential dimension of the text as a whole is diminished. This undermining of the meaning of the work, on both the fictional world and the language levels, is caused by the prominent emphasis given to the aesthetic nature of the description. On the diegetic level, the more unreal the nature of the descriptions becomes, the more we become conscious of the aesthetic point of their existence. This is the case, for example, with the characters: if the children's walking hand-in-hand along the beach might have been acceptable at the beginning of the story as a 'realistic' description of a momentary situation, its verisimilitude is later reduced. Actually, the longer this walking continues, the more its mechanical character becomes conspicuous. Moreover, the gradual negation of any link between the children and the surrounding reality (for example, the children never glance at the cliff or at the distance they have covered, they are indifferent to the waves as well as to the flock of birds advancing before them) cancels all the 'realistic' justifications which might have given credibility to the situation. In the absence of any significant relation of contiguity (causal, practical, purposeful) between the characters and the other components of reality, attention is drawn to the formal-pictorial analogy between them: the blue of the children's clothes and the sea, the hue of their skin which corresponds to the colours of the sand, the straight line of their footsteps which is parallel to the sea and to the cliff, and the steady rhythm of the movement of both the children and the waves. The description of the figures, which at first one tends to accept as an act of significant estranging of some basic aspects of human reality, increasingly becomes a component of a demonstratively aesthetic composition of a stylized picture, whose correlation with actual reality, and even perhaps its very relationship with such a reality, is doubtful.

Just as one can find in **'La Plage'** an aesthetic estrangement of the human world, one can also find a similar estrangement of the non-human universe. While this estrangement (unlike that of 'Le Mannequin', for instance) is not applicable to the objects depicted in the story's fictional world *per se* (the sea, the wave, the beach, the birds), whose presentation more or less matches the general impression one gets in reality, it is certainly applicable to the links which join the objects and establish the general character of the reality described. Thus all causal linkage among the objects is absent in the text (that is, from the linguistic presentation of the reality, not from the 'reality' presented itself), and this is so even when these objects appear in a realistic context which obviously invites such linkage: for example, when mention is made of the wave

which suddenly rises *when* there is neither cloud nor wind (and not *despite* this fact), or of the sudden flight of the birds, *when* the children seem just about to catch up with them (and not *because* of this). Clearly these phenomena may have a simple realistic explanation whose implicit presentation in the text might have created the connection between them. It is the way things are presented, however, with synchronism being the only basis for linking the phenomena, which creates the estranging effect, deriving not from the objects themselves but from the space in which they appear as a whole and from the picture of reality they ultimately constitute.

A similar estranging effect takes place with regard to movement and time. If the movement appears to be an attempt to change the location of something in relation to something else, such a change does not occur in any of the movements presented in this story. The different stages of the wave's movement (its rise, breaking, dispersal) appear in fixed places. Similarly, there is no stable point of reference (a distinct exit point, intermediary position, or final destination) against which the movements of the children (or of the birds) can be measured, nor are these movements accompanied by any visible change of location in relation to their surroundings. If the varying distance between the children and the birds still creates some kind of change in the arrangement of the space, the periodicity (or circularity) of this change, by removing the progress forward from movement and realizing in this way Zeno's well-known paradox of Achilles and the Tortoise, finally cancels the point and purpose of this movement. What emerges is a movement which does not come close to any place, does not move off from any place, does not bring about any significant change in space, and which thus represents some kind of marking time that on the one hand emphasizes the static and mechanistic nature of the described reality, and on the other hand, by virtue of its stylized artificiality, undermines the actual character (and realistic credibility) of that very reality.

Movement, however, imagined from experience, occurs not only on the spatial continuum but also on the temporal, and the method of its description in **'La Plage'** is therefore significant regarding the nature of the time no less than the nature of space. An obvious example can be seen in the last description of the flock of birds:

> Les oiseaux, qu'ils étaient sur le point de rattraper, battent des ailes et s'envolent, l'un d'abord, puis deux, puis dix [. . .].
>
> Puis toute la troupe est de nouveau posée sur le sable, progressant le long du rivage, à cent mètres environ devant les enfants.

From the moment the birds take off until they land upon the sand, the flight of the flock is divided here into almost static situations which are presented one after the other and whose actualization in the mind's eye might be more or less like this: first we visualize the birds beating their wings; later we see one bird in the air at the beginning of its flight, after that two, then (there appears to be a leap in time here) ten birds flying in the air; finally (this time definitely after a leap in time) the whole flock is 'seen' again, as it rests on the sand after landing.

On this occasion it is the continuum of time which is undermined because of the method of describing the movement. If earlier I discussed a kind of realization of the paradox of Achilles and the Tortoise which, as it were, divided space into non-continuous sections, the present description is an even more explicit realization of another of Zeno's paradoxes, that of the Flying Arrow. Like the flight of the arrow in Zeno, the movement of the birds also breaks down into almost static non-continuous parts of the present. Together with the cancellation of the movement (or at least its freezing in the spirit of Zeno's paradox) and the undermining of the continuity of time, the duration of time itself is thus undermined. The fragmentation of the action into separate moments of (the) present, situated next to each other, cancels the various possible connections between the different units of time upon which continuity, change, and the concept of 'action' itself are based. In Robbe-Grillet's language one can say that in such a case 'L'instant nie la continuité'. This time, which, as Robbe-Grillet put it, has been 'cut off from its temporality' and which neither flows nor supports any action, thus joins the other components of reality (characters, space, movement) to establish a static, atomistic, and mechanical world which is essentially objectal. The human dimension contributed by time to this 'world' is illusory and its only purpose is to emphasize the human continuity it lacks, just as the presence of the characters and the action only emphasizes the absence of both the emotional involvement and purposeful intention expected in human deeds. This temporality-severed time in the end only strengthens the feeling of confusion and estrangement which anyway alienates the reader, because of the mechanistic 'thingness' of the whole reality presented to him.

It is hard, however, to accept unequivocally this treatment of fictional reality as a significant estrangement of the real world. Because of the remoteness of this time from experienced time (whether it be Bergson's internal 'concrete duration' or the practical time of physics), attention is necessarily drawn to the aesthetic function it fulfils: by the fact that the static character of time combines with the pictorial nature of the work, for example, or by the fact that its atomism and mechanical nature combine with the demonstratively aesthetic functioning of the other components of the described reality.

The reality formed in **'La Plage'** may thus be approached from different directions. It can, at first, be mimetically read as a direct and accurate reflection of reality. Yet the objectal estrangement of this picture of reality undermines its illusory realistic appearance and directs us towards an absurdist realization. None the less, the aesthetic estrangement which is consistent with neither the realistic nor absurdist realizations leads towards an aesthetic approach. Since every one of the three approaches can be justified,

we are finally left with a picture of reality open to different possible interpretations. The three approaches and the three corresponding dimensions of the text remain open, to one degree or another: two of them, the realistic and 'objectal' (or absurdist), constructing a referential, meaningful text, inviting interpretation, while the third establishes a 'literal' text, devoid of any significance, which has a purely aesthetic character.

The openness to the various interpretations, however, also acts as a sealant against any of them. While such interpretations can separately constitute a coherent explicative model which might cope successfully with the opacity of the text, they cannot simultaneously co-exist in a meaningful realization of the story, because of their contradictory approaches. It thus appears likely that it is, in fact, the openness of the work to different meanings which is likely to undermine the meaningful nature of the text, while it is the actual 'blocking of meanings' (achieved through the opacity of different elements in the story) which constitutes a central factor in its establishment as a meaning-bearing text. If the whole of Robbe-Grillet's art lies essentially in his ability to 'decevoir le sens dans le temps même qu'il l'ouvre', or to 'provoquer le sens pour l'arrêter', as Roland Barthes put it, then it is no less true that the uniqueness of Robbe-Grillet's writing consists essentially in producing the meaning of the text by the very act of withholding it. One of the most striking expressions of the poetic heritage of the Absurd in Robbe-Grillet, as it is realized in **'La Plage'**, is the tension which exists in the text between the 'meaning-creating' vector and the vector which negates (or 'decreates') it, both of which grow out of the very same elements. Such a paradoxical, self-undermining text (which negates its own meanings by establishing them and establishes its meaning by negating it) indeed manifests Robbe-Grillet's attempt both to realize and transcend one of the most essential principles of the Absurd poetics: the obligation of the work to express the absurdity of existence while paying strict heed not to deviate from the basic lack of meaning which, from the Absurd viewpoint, characterizes all human action.

None the less, Robbe-Grillet's story, goes beyond the self-abnegation that a consistently absurd work must demand of itself. Indeed, a story such as this not only raises doubts about its message or significance but also undermines the very concept of narration, the 'eidos' of the narrative which defines it both as a story and literary work. In an article devoted to Baudelaire's prose poems, Barbara Johnson raises the possibility of regarding such poems 'as ironic reflections on the nature of poetic language as such'. Robbe-Grillet's stories are not prose poems, despite their prevalently cold and alienated poetic atmosphere, since prose poems, as Suzanne Bernard claims, must, first and foremost, be poems. In contrast, the realistic materials and the narrative patterns which make up **'La Plage'** clearly identify it as prose. If it undermines the narrativity and realism which are considered to be basic attributes of traditional prose fiction, then this type of story does so from within the narrative itself, paradoxically achieving this by implanting them there in the first place.

It is this which allows us to see Robbe-Grillet's *Instantanés* as what Barbara Johnson would call an ironic statement which relates to the very nature of narrative language as such. The revolt of the mid-nineteenth-century prose poem against the generic conventions of the time (primarily against the verse lyric) aimed at exposing the limitations of such conventions and creating a new poetics which would both extend the limits of poetic language and undermine it. Similarly, and in line with the most subversive manifestations of the modernistic twentieth-century prose poem (Jacob, Tzara, Breton, Michaud), Robbe-Grillet's use of narrative elements is supposed to deconstruct the narrative and, even, negate the possibility of narration itself. The conception of time and action implied in Robbe-Grillet's stories thus has a fundamental aesthetic significance, in addition to the metaphysical significance discussed throughout this essay, and the anti-narrative 'nouveau conte', which Robbe-Grillet created, ultimately embodies a new generic poetics of the short fiction, which complements the metaphysical view to which it is linked.

Michael Sheringham (review date 7 October 1994)

SOURCE: "Corinthian Casual," in *Times Literary Supplement,* October 7, 1994, p. 12.

[*In the following review, Sheringham offers tempered criticism of* Les Derniers Jours de Corinthe. *"If not for the pinch of irony which still enlivens Robbe-Grillet's writing, and his authentic merit as a stylist (often self-consciously paraded),"* writes Sheringham, *"few readers . . . would be likely to stay the course."*]

Not as quick off the mark in the autobiography stakes as some of his fellow nouveaux romanciers, Alain Robbe-Grillet has compensated for this by a higher rate of productivity. *Les Derniers Jours de Corinthe* is the third and apparently final instalment of a series called "Romanesques", a label designed, presumably, to make it clear that straight autobiography is not the name of the game. The eponymous figure of Henri de Corinthe is once again used to make the same point. In *Le Miroir qui revient* (1985), Corinthe featured in a number of patently fictional passages which, from time to time, interrupted Robbe-Grillet's otherwise fairly conventional account of his background and early life. A composite figure—now a friend of the narrator's father, with traces of Proust's Swann, now a First World War soldier in scenarios deriving partly from the works of Claude Simon, now a legendary figure on a white charger—Corinthe was less an *alter ego* than an ever-changing cipher for the powerful currents of fantasy and creativity which, for Robbe-Grillet, are a vital part of his curriculum vitae.

In *Angélique ou L'Enchantement* (1985). Robbe-Grillet took Corinthe a stage further by making him a second author-narrator, and then blurring the boundaries and

transitions between narrative levels. At any point the narrating "I" could turn out to be Corinthe attempting to make sense of some event in his rather lurid past, rather than Robbe-Grillet doing likewise. But since the fabric of Corinthe's "past" consisted entirely of Robbe-Grillet's fabrications, these passages into fiction were autobiography by another means, a point the author of *La Jalousie* had been driving home since his combative assertion, at the beginning of his autobiographical project, that, however, forbiddingly self-contained they seemed, his novels had always been all about their writer.

This new book is in the same vein, full of state-of-the-art postmodernist undecidabilities, neo-baroque excrescences and *trompe-l'oeil* surfaces. The Corinthe material, now dominated by sado-masochistic goings on and obscure political rumblings in a comic-strip Uruguay, is more prominent than ever, particularly since the lack of any strong autobiographical motivation or focus is now more acute than ever. *Angélique* was theoretically centered on the relationship between writing and erotic fantasy. *Les Derniers Jours de Corinthe* reverts to some sort of chronology, and gives patchy coverage to the 1950s, the decade which saw the publication of Robbe-Grillet's first few novels and the constitution of the *nouveau roman* group with the author of *Les Gommes* as its ringleader. Robbe-Grillet has little to say about all this, except when he sounds off about the touchy ingratitude of Marguerite Duras and Claude Simon (who are both now more famous than the man who is convinced that he gave them their first break).

If Robbe-Grillet seems disinclined to notice, or to worry about, how hopelessly petty and unilluminating he is being, it's partly because it suits his attempt to discredit the whole genre of what he sees as conventional autobiography. "Serious" autobiography is dismissed as "un bavardage public" which artificially arrests the perpetual motion of memory and fantasy that makes up our authentic, unstable identities. Robbe-Grillet sees himself as the exponent of "New Autobiography"—critically self-conscious, mobile, subversive, committed to plurality and proliferation rather than fixity and form. As in *Angélique*, he makes Corinthe the mouthpiece for some of his ideas, thus achieving a little ironic distance from what might otherwise seem a rather rigid, not to say platitudinous, set of allegedly new prescriptions. Well-worn analogies with particle physics and chaos theory are accompanied by frequent invocations of Mallarmé and Nietzsche. Robbe-Grillet's "enterprise auto-hétéro-biographique" is placed under the patronage of Zarathoustra, dancer on tightropes and reveller in ruins. The absence of fixed identity, the recognition that we postmoderns must deal with the debris of past systems, is seen not as a cause for lamentation but for rejoicing, and as a spur to anarchic creativity.

Robbe-Grillet gets good mileage out of this freewheeling credo, and his "vacillante aventure polymorphe" certainly has its moments, particularly when the constant switches of narrative level, the melting and merging of contexts, the variable geometries of real and imaginary experience work together to induce a pleasurably vertiginous state in the reader's mind. But vertigo has its drawbacks, and were it not for the pinch of irony which still enlivens Robbe-Grillet's writing, and his authentic merits as a stylist (often self-consciously paraded), few readers of **Les Derniers Jours de Corinthe** would be likely to stay the course.

It is one thing to push against the limitations of conventional narrative autobiography in the name of a compelling desire to articulate selfhood or its abeyance. But Robbe-Grillet seems to lack such a desire, and this probably accounts for his failure to establish any real dialogue between the well-rounded public persona, with opinions about everything, who features in the more prosaic passages, and the fantasized subject for whom Corinthe is one of the vehicles. Some key issues are broached in original ways, for example the risk that autobiographical recollection destroys the very material it raises into consciousness. But **Les Derniers Jours de Corinthe**, like its predecessors, tends to evade the challenges of authentic autobiography, new or otherwise, and to settle for the safer ground of purely textual dislocation.

Raylene Ramsay (essay date December 1996)

SOURCE: "Writing on the Ruins in *Les Derniers Jours de Corinthe:* From Reassemblage to Reassessment in Robbe-Grillet," in *French Review*, Vol. 70, No. 2, December, 1996, pp. 231-44.

[*In the following essay, Ramsay examines Robbe-Grillet's pastiche of autobiography, myth, memory, literary text, and history in* Les Derniers Jours de Corinthe. *According to Ramsay, "The text sets out to consciously stage, deconstruct, indeed to 'ruin,' both its own generative mechanisms and the monsters and the sirens lurking in the writer's subconscious."*]

> *Nous écrivons, désormais, joyeux, sur des ruines*
> —Alain Robbe-Grillet, **Les Derniers Jours de Corinthe**, 1994.

In this "new autobiography," a writing of the self characterized by self-consciousness about the "impossibility" of any such definitive self-reconstitution, according to Robbe-Grillet, the reader is embarked, once again, on a ludic, intertextual journey through the ruins of humanist enlightenment, of tragedy, and of autobiography. Guided/lured by the pure and false Ariadne (alternatively, Mina, Marianic and Marie-Ange) along now familiar passageways strewn with the debris of Western culture and Robbe-Grillet's own earlier texts, the reader stumbles across artefacts inspired by images of cruelty in Lautréamont or Delacroix or "decadent" refinement in Moreau, or again, by flat material objects of the everyday represented in the paintings of Jasper Johns or the sculptures of George Segal. Enchanted by an intoxicated story-telling ("la folie fabulante"), we follow the narrator via the disconnected pages of his

singular history ("ces feuillets décousus de souvenires") to investigate the secret rooms of a cliched, yet particularized sado-erotic imagination. The text sets out to consciously stage, deconstruct, indeed to "ruin," both its own generative mechanisms and the monsters and the sirens lurking in the writer's subconscious.

The artefacts that serve in the re-constitution of underground stories and memories, the bloodstained high-heeled shoe, the entwining seaweed as feminine hair and the devouring sea as female vulva, the provocative, punished child-woman, like the fairy-tale search for the fountain of youth, bring together both ready-made collective myths and their self-conscious personal reference. The blue shoe, a variant of Cinderella's fur/glass slipper, used in the film **Glissements progressifs du plaisir**, for example, is conspicuously showcased in the living room of Robbe-Grillet's Paris apartment. Tales of the fear and fascination of drowning that is also a stereotyped Freudian metaphor for fear of being consumed/castrated by the mother/the feminine, proliferate in realistic and precise detail in this third set of autobiographical "memories." The incident at "Le Minou" ["Pussy"] in Brittany where the young child is carried off by a freak wave (another of those stories not remembered directly but perhaps "recounted" by his parents, notes the narrator), or the accident in Martinique where the young agronomist working on the diseases of banana plants capsizes while out sailing, appear to observe the conventions of autobiographical truth telling. Yet, such anecdotes are also clearly ironic as they invert, for example, the traditional autobiographical use of the present to mark the time of the narration and of the past to indicate the event narrated: "Je vois déjà ma fin venue, ce que je trouve bête par un si beau temps, avec encore toute mon oeuvre à faire." This passage makes an indirect comment on the arbitrariness and artifice of autobiographical conventions: their double perspective presented as unified (the mature self in the present and the child it claims to have been) and their pretence at recapture of the past. For, any capture can only be effected in the present and the perception of the past is necessarily modified by what has happened in the intervening period. The apparently real or lived memories recall figures from Robbe-Grillet's earlier fictional texts, the sailor lost at sea (péri en mer/mère), whose portrait appears in the novel **Djinn** (1981) and the fear of being caught and enveloped by the rising tide on childhood beaches in the short story **"Le Chemin du retour"** (*Instantanés* 1962). The other face of this fear of drowning or of the feminine sea/mother (mère/mer), and of the lure of the song of the very young sirens, that is, the numerous fantasies of capture of the seductive and dangerous child-woman present throughout Robbe-Grillet's work, is related by the writer to a description of his first encounter and subsequent imaginative relation with his ice-cream eating "Lolita" wife, Catherine, a still present and very real companion despite some complicated sexual arrangements in the intervening years, but seen as his little girl or child.

In the course of iterative journeys through the underground passageways of the dungeons of the Breton cliff fortress that echo the fantasy of the return through the inner organs to the womb, we encounter Henri de Corinthe, also a product of history and story, of the past and of the present, of text and experience and an avatar of the writer since the first volume of this autobiographical trilogy. This fictional character and figure of the autobiographical writer, alone in the writing cell with the disordered pages of his manuscript, is a prey to the anxiety that his third person narrative concerns some distant person who is not himself. Indeed, on the South American frontier between Brasilia and Uruguay, another Henri de Corinthe, insinuating himself into the plot at every opportunity, finds a further double sitting in his chair in the exotic beach cafe already described in earlier texts. This imposter is concealing his erotic interest in the ball-game of a young adolescent girl, spying from behind the mobile screen and alibi of the newspaper, *Le Globe*, familiar from *Souvenirs du triangle d'or* (1978) where it recounts a sexual crime. Other curiously recognizable encounters follow between this proliferating hero-villain and his accusers—or are they perhaps his accomplices in crime? He is interrogated by the Professor of parapsychology, Van der Reeves, father or manager of the seductive very young call-girl Marie-Ange who offers his daughter for Corinthe's suspect purposes and by a quixotic and comic police Inspector. Both of these male characters figured in the film, *La Belle Captive*.

The reader is lead to dance light-heartedly on the ruins of earlier characters and texts, uncertain memories, and pseudo-confessions. She/he is asked to negotiate the truths behind the fictionality of familiar yet new re-tellings of fragmented tales of wild adolescent gangs and their acts of sexual enslavement and cruel punishment of their more beautiful captives during a conflict to the death with the army. The soldiers, more brutal even than the adolescents, intern their victims in the Lyric Theater, transformed to a prison, where the criminal passions of the austere ruling class (magistrates, police, archbishops, business men and women) find a secret outlet. These violent futuristic scenarios recall both the stories of Robbe-Grillet's assemblage novels, *Topologie d'une cité fantôme* and *Souvenirs*, and the hypothesis of hidden passions beneath the surface of civilization exploited in the popular holocaust or catastrophe genre—comparable to the cruelty, and orgiastic freedom of certain Fellini films, *City of Women*, for example, or even feminist fables of the will to power over others such as Atwood's *The Handmaid's Tale*. However, power over the threat of feminine seduction and disorder in Robbe-Grillet's stories is not exerted through the more standard methods of ritualized insemination and the control of reproduction as in Margaret Atwood's feminist critique of power struggles latent in society. Rather, order is reestablished through the "specialized" and less generally practised sexual control manifested in the bondage, torture, and suppression of the feminine body or through female pain and domination in a game of master and slave, defined as pleasure.

The twelve young girls in various stages of filmy white (un)dress for their first communion, mannequins that

Robbe-Grillet claims to have seen in a shop-window in General Franco's very Catholic Spain before they found their way into *Souvenirs*, may conceal-reveal a sexual symbolism as the writer suggests. Their self-giving as brides of Christ can be read in terms of a certain form of "feminine" ecstasy experienced in self-loss or self-sacrifice and resembling the passionate physical experience of divine possession of the "feminized" mystics. In *La Violence et le sacré*, René Girard argues that the cathartic cleansing of collective guilt by the violent ritual shedding of the sacrificial blood of an innocent victim is characteristic of classical and modern societies. Self-reflexive and ironic, pointing insistently at the violent sexual underpinnings of sacrifice and the sacred, Robbe-Grillet's free-thinking tableaux are not essentialist in Girard's sense. In what was clearly deliberate sacrilegious excess, pastiche, and confessional pirouette, his previous texts had depicted the dresses stained at the groin with blood and the communicants nailed to crosses upside down with candles in their vaginas, victims of the nefarious priest/alias Dr Morgan, an early avatar of Corinthe. Yet, although close to those of Sade, Robbe-Grillet's representations remain distinctive. Young boys, for example, do not share the cruel fates of the fair angels in a work where the beautiful captive and victim is invariably a pubescent girl or a very young beautiful woman. I suggest that Robbe-Grillet's claim to be exploiting "the richness of popular fantasies in this [sado-erotic] domain" ("la richesse des fantasmes populaires dans ce domaine") is at least as much a screen and an alibi for the self-centered confessional and investigative staging of the ruins of his own personal mythologies as it is the pretended moral crusade to open the reader's eyes to the true nature of our shared sexual phantasies in freedom and subversion.

The real personally familiar hotel Lutetia on the Boulevard Raspail and the fictive hotel Lutetia d'Heropolis in South America where Herod and Salome play out their erotic scenarios, are products of a particular if dimming memory, of an unconscious, and of the "folie fabulante" that embodies the exploration of the links between the collective and the individual subconscious. The "fabulations" of *Les Derniers Jours de Corinthe* are generated from the mixed fragments of the ageing Robbe-Grillet's memories, imagination, and an eclectic range of existing texts, including the pornographic and the underground (Sade in particular has interested Robbe-Grillet) as the writer attempts to choreograph a distinctive dance on the ruins—of popular mythologies, of the recent history of France and of Western civilisation, of the old coherent ego, of narrative and autobiographical convention, and of his own past selves.

If Man is a Heideggerian tightrope or Nietzschean bridge, stretched out over an abyss, as Robbe-Grillet writes in *Les Derniers Jours de Corinthe*, in mortal danger that the past will crumble to ashes if he looks back (or be absorbed into a liquid universe of the swelling feminine if he looks down), his salvation appears to lie less in a return journey than in a lucid Heideggerian "ab-bau" or deconstruction of his situation with "mocking self-awareness" ("une conscience rieuse"). This is neither to accept the long sleep of a defeated "Grand Architect" and to resign oneself to offering only unrelated fragments, broken columns, and systems in collapse, claims Robbe-Grillet, nor to return, repentant, to some rational and stable entity. It is, rather, to "weave proliferating structures" that vanish as they are put in place. The ruins are to be envisioned not with existential despair but with the pleasure and knowledge afforded by these active processes of deconstruction and reconstruction that are the effects of lucidity and liberty.

For Kafka, there was a goal but no path. For Robbe-Grillet, there appears to be a path but no goal. Is Robbe-Grillet's narrator, then, simply a slightly more determinedly joyous Sisyphus still pushing a barely post-Camusian rock and evoking, if not man's destiny or tragedy, at least the aleatory character or absurdity of his condition? There are some new elements in the existential scenario—the "grilling" (Robbe-Grilling) or sceptically self-consuming process and the passionate character of the fire devouring the new structures even as they take form. Fire illuminates the background threads that configure the canvas. Playing with fire is exciting, dangerous.

The writer is both product and producer of art in ruins in Robbe-Grillet. His hybrid, sceptical work is generated from disparate visual images—from Delacroix, Moreau, and the contemporary Americans Mark Tansey and George Segal—and from literary texts, selected for the detail that captures the heart and mind (Barthes' "punctum") and with transforming purpose. There are, once again, a number of unacknowledged "quotations" from Baudelaire ("O Mort, vieux capitaine . . .") and from Mallarmé ("Vierge, cette écume . . .") and Marguerite Duras' luxury liner, casting light and waltz music over a phosphorescent sea cradling the young drowned lover, makes a provocative entrance, somewhere between pastiche and "homage." These link the marine universe once again with femininity, bliss, and death.

Les Derniers Jours de Corinthe similarly re-collects Robbe-Grillet's own earlier emblems and texts and again, re-assembles these in new autobiographical configurations. The oedipal tale of *Les Gommes* is re-called, but re-read here more particularly as a story of Dr. Juard's elitist politico-economic movement ("Synarchie"), close to Robbe-Grillet's pirouetting "confession" of his own right-wing political positions. Or does the eraser derive, as the text later perversely hypothesizes, from the need to erase the "stains" ("taches") or "suspect traces" on the smooth surfaces, the white robing ("robe blanche") of the Gallimard books found in formative years in Macrez's book shop on the Boulevard Raspail—to erase guilt? The voyeuristic sexual crime against a precocious young girl concealed at the heart of *Le Voyeur*, the meticulously ordered banana plants of *La Jalousie* that hide a second face as symbols of an unstable, shifting world organized by sexual jealousy and by a potential crime and evoked by fissures and suspect surface traces, or undulating feminine

tresses are reread in this more introspective work. Despite being turned completely towards the outside world, claims Robbe-Grillet, these novels express a consciousness imprisoned in its own void. From the autobiographical perspective of *Les Derniers Jours de Corinthe*, Corinthe-Robbe-Grillet can identify the early vertigo in his work as the piercing and still present terror of having disappeared from within oneself, the fear of inner void and the paranoia of take over by the other ("cette expérience fondamentale d'une désertion par l'intérieur, face à l'ennemi qui a investi la place").

The underground passages and the imprisoned female captives recalled from *Souvenirs* begin to signify as cliche by their very repetition, along with the assemblage of other familiar and suspect sea-changed objects from the first two autobiographical fictions. These include the magic mirror cast up by the sea in which Corinthe sees not himself but the victim Angélique and the white horse (principle of virility) sees his own death, the writer's desk made out of a block of wood, out of the ruins from a shipwreck, and the "lavandeuses de nuit," the fairy washer-women of Breton legend and Robbe-Grilletian sado-erotic transformations, sirens drying their bloodstained gossamer underclothing in the moonlight on the sexualized curve of the beach.

The "ruins" are the products of the deconstruction of an *imaginaire*. This is, in part, the collective and popular imaginary of the sadomasochistic "confrérie" that Robbe-Grillet here claims to avoid; in part, Robbe-Grillet's particular and self-confessed story of sadistic phantasies of commerce with the fair *Angélique* and preference for very young girls. Self-conscious figures of the writer, the self-deconstructing Narcissus-narrators are at risk of falling into the water and drowning in their reflection, confused with that of the nymph Echo, the dangerous (feminine) other, Mina, Manrica, *Angélique* or the feminine in the self. At the same time, the sceptical and suspicious "new autobiographical" enterprise is conscious of the greater perils of any single image or self-constitution, aware that certain forms of truth-telling may be less "true" than certain forms of fabulation or "lying"—selecting or constituting one's preferred or imaginatively productive images of self, for example. A self from fragments and in ruins may be "truer" than a monolithic edifice, less coherent and complete but more authentic than the "identity" constructed by traditional self-representation.

The "ruining" of traditional autobiographical conventions—identity between character, narrator and writer (or between the "I" who writes, the "I" of the story, and the "I" of history)—of the autobiographical pacts of sincerity, and of the chronological and causal continuities and coherence of narrative serve a critical and deconstructionist enterprise similar to the deconstruction of an *imaginaire*. Along with unified and self-identical, self-present, authorial self and conventional story, the myths of the coherence and knowability of twentieth-century French history, particularly those of resistance and collaboration, also undergo a similar process of deconstruction. Corinthe, the military man of Heropolis, Resistance fighter or Nazi collaborator and later South American exile or trafficker, embodies the French difficulties in deciding who was the hero and traitor in and after the wars with Germany. These questions have become particularly acute with the recent trials of Klaus Barbie and the first charges brought against Frenchmen (Bousquet and Touvier) for crimes against humanity. The revelation of Mitterrand's connections with Bousquet and with the Pétain government, and the revisionist backlash that would contest the existence of the gas chambers suggest the complexity of the situation. At the same time as he stages the French myths of resistance and the more recent myths of general collaboration, Corinthe corresponds to Robbe-Grillet's personal concern to explain his own apparently blameworthy political past (right-wing and Germanophile) and present positions to his reader. His belief in the failure of both liberal democracy and communist dictatorship; his predilection for a strong, elitist, (paternalistic?) form of government and pessimistic recognition of failure are reflected in the comi-tragic end of the aristocratic Corinthe, implicated in shadowy movements resembling the nationalistic Croix du feu or the Action Française to which Robbe-Grillet's parents were close. Corinthe will die solitary and immured in his Breton stone fortress on that "ancient soil" ("vieux sol d'argile") of Celtic-Germanic strength, long under siege, his belongings seized, and nostalgic for a lost order.

More generally, the mise en scène of the past indicates the impossibility of acceding to any absolute vantage point from which to know or judge history and its heroes. In *Les Derniers Jours de Corinthe*, the past can only be looked at from the relative standpoint of a specific (and changing) present. The political and the personal, inner and outer event cannot be separated; the hero is also potentially the villain. The cavalry officer, knight in shining armor, or war hero comes upon his double lying dead on the ground and (shades of *Angélique ou L'Enchantement*) discovers the latter's participation in a sexual crime against a captured young woman enemy agent.

The ruins of the imaginary, of autobiography, of history and of the rational taxonomies and ordered knowledge to which Robbe-Grillet admits a very considerable attachment become the material of a rebuilding undermined in its turn by phantasies dismantled in self-critical irony—Salomé dancing before Herod (by the "decadent" painter Moreau and so many other artists before and after him), the already too well-known Robbe-Grilletian erotic description of the young girl ("Ici prendrait place une description érotisée ordinaire de la jeune Allemande . . . Insistance habituelle sur les charmes intimes, abus des adjectifs interdits, cruauté latente"). The ruined material proliferates and functions to construct open, variable new geometries and mobile architectures, invisible cities and virtual realities, characteristic of the "post-modern," the "post-modern" being defined here as what comes out of and after modernism. At the same time, this material is chosen by a particular, situated, writer. Indeed, the nature

of the reassembled material in this final "romanesque" or autofictional text by Robbe-Grillet makes it evident that his writing also concern his personal experience. As the story-teller is doubled by an experiential subject of the history of his period, so, alongside the theorist stands the libertine who may have sought the anonymity of text to disown a particular face and body while revelling in displaying it. Paradoxically, then, writing although intellectually exigent, and on the hunt to deconstruct the ready-thought, in its refusal of fixed and single identity, may be as much a will to self-effacement or to epitaph as to self-knowledge.

In the literary traditions of Europe, ruins have most often been symbols of the glories of past civilizations and of humankind's achievements. For the Romantic intellectuals of the eighteenth century, the tour of classical sites was a source at once of inspiration and of the melancholy that accompanied the post-Napoleonic generation's feelings of loss of power and of decline, their subsequent world-weariness, and emotionally intense longing for a lost absolute. Ruins for the Romantics become a catalyst for intense emotions that create a feeling of existence. Camus, for his part, writing of the Roman ruins at Tipasa in the essays "Noces" and "Retour à Tipasa," sees their glory less in their character as symbols of the lost grandeur of human civilization than in their return to unpolished natural stone, to the fierce beauty and innocence of the elements, part of the intense marriage of the sensual feminine earth and the fierce masculine sun, and indifferent to human affairs. Despite the existence of the "absurd" (lack of transcendental meaning and his own inevitable death), his duty as a "Man" is to accept happiness in his physical body, in sensual harmony with the elemental beauty of the natural world of sun and sea that constitutes the origins of the Mediterranean race to which he belongs. Camus' recognition is that without such a return to the body and the elemental natural world, lucidity and commitment to the abstract fight for justice against all the "plagues" that diminish humankind remain arid and unsustainable. This formulation of the symbolism of ruins as return to a nature that has little in common with man, although at opposite poles from the Romantic pathetic fallacy (a sentient nature in sympathy with human emotions), nonetheless rejoins the latter in its affirming of the primacy of the emotional or sentient body. While Camus' body is assimilated to nature by the outside world's assault on the senses—the fierce heat of the sun, the velvet enclosing and sharp salt sting of the sea—romantic (and even realist) sensibility projects the inner emotions onto nature.

In Robbe-Grillet's work, there is a breaking down of such binary oppositions between inside and the outside, humankind and nature. The ruins of Western culture represent less a melancholy sense of the loss of human grandeur, less a return to and renewal in the earth/sea from which one's body comes, than the freedom to reconstruct just such constitutive dichotomies. Outside comes to coexist with inside, culture with nature, without clear boundaries or mutual exclusion as in the figure of the Moebius strip. In a conventional autobiographical frame (outside), the evocation of ruins in Robbe-Grillet's last autobiography would be linked to a sense of time running out. Ruins would connote the approach of death. In Corinthe's besieged fortress, Robbe-Grillet indeed regrets that the golden naiads have disappeared along with the sun, pleasure, and the dangerous song of the sirens. Accompanying the sense of increasing cold, the decline in desire, and feelings of loss and anguish is the strong sense of decomposition and catastrophe that has, in fact, always been a distinctive characteristic of both post-modern thematics (outside) and Robbe-Grillet's own personal preoccupations (inside). The date groves in the Persian gulf, ruined by the destruction of millenary irrigation canals in an absurd, bloody, eight-year war, the ominous and alien unpredictable patterns of the boiling mud pools in Rotorua that are all that Robbe-Grillet's autobiography retains of his 1986 lecture tour of New Zealand, re-collected in **Les Derniers Jours de Corinthe**, are further outer signs of the inner obsession with decay and the strangeness of the universe. The autobiographical anguish occasioned by the uprooting of the one hundred and fifty year old trees on his property at Mesnil-au-Grain in a violent storm, and the recall, once again, of the war-time bombing of his house of birth at Brest on the Kerangoff plain echo a fictionalized fear of disorder and catastrophe present in the writer's work since the earliest text, **Un Régicide**. Such fears are projected, ruined, transferred from inside to outside into the play of eroticized text that, like irony, is an ever-present antidote. Untouched by the storm, the statue in the fountain, Angélique, young and beautiful for eternity, arms raised gracefully, protects her delicate features against the trees that bend threateningly towards her. Dancing on the ruins may be a conscious strategy, an attempt to preempt or at least negotiate with inner or unconscious fears; it may be sufficient to temporarily neutralize the sea-monster, Corinthe, who in Robbe-Grillet's autofictions is characterized by his hidden predilection for devouring very young (and dangerous) girls to preempt his own demise.

Beyond the elucubrations of Corinthe in his cliff fortress or in Uruguay, however, back at Mesnil-au-Grain, Robbe-Grillet's stately eighteenth-century mansion in Normandy, the reader has also been following a more traditional and sedentary autobiographical itinerary whose monsters are relatively domesticated and where the ruins of the park are cleared away and the strangeness (the Unheimliche or the uncanny other or the "feminine") of scenes of unexplained night bells ringing or an extraordinary fall of snow is assimilated into the fabric of the homely and everyday. Motivated by the approaching end of the "great writer," the latter records the genesis and history of his writing for posterity with as much precision as possible. Footnotes add the corrections or clarification of certain details contributed by his editor and friend, Jérôme Lindon (the owner of the Editions de Minuit). In this recapitulation of the minutiae of the origins and trajectory of his work, Robbe-Grillet "constitutes himself as a great writer" much as Roland Barthes describes such traditional autobiographical endeavors in the first "new autobiography," *Barthes par Roland Barthes*. In anecdotes about his adventurous and studious life as Visiting Professor of literature at NYU and Washington University of St. Louis until his still rankling exclusion from the latter by what he depicts with rancour (only partially concealed by his usual ironic camouflage) as "rabid feminists," Robbe-Grillet defines himself as a teacher and literary critic. Accounts of his relations with other French men and women of letters, including Sartre, Sarraute, Simon and Duras, and some pejorative remarks about the detested Simone de Beauvoir complete this portrait of the artist as a not so young man. Memories here are no longer subverted by irony, or the intrusive processes of writing. Robbe-Grillet's autofiction may dance on some ruins of the autobiographical genre. Nonetheless, traditional autobiography constitutes an appreciable part of the material of the new autographics.

In this respect, it cannot be said that what Robbe-Grillet, autobiographer, has dared to look back on has turned to dust. On the contrary, his early work is framed very traditionally by the present autobiography as great art, initially unrecognized by the establishment (in particular, by Gallimard). Robbe-Grillet, critic, is set up to share the laurels with Jérôme Lindon as he who was able to detect and encourage genius—in Marguerite Duras' *Moderato Cantabile* or Claude Simon's Nobel prize-winning work, for example. To the fury of Nathalie Sarraute and a number of others among his fellow "new novelists," Robbe-Grillet in his own person is at pains to set the record of his leadership of that critical movement straight for posterity. There is little irony (self-irony, in any case) and indeed, relatively little self-consciousness in these passages. No splitting of this narrator, no evocation of a ruined country prevents a literary history and self-portrait (a monument to self) being set in prose for posterity. Similarly, Robbe-Grillet's critical reflections that function to interrupt, to fragment or ruin the unfolding of story or anecdote are often simply repeated from his earlier public conference performances, their import further weakened by autobiographical self-indulgence or need for self-vindication. Presenting the case for sexual liberation, for example, he notes the omnipresence of phantasies of sexual cruelty in Japan and the Far East where freedom is limited and the lesser frequency of these cruel phantasies in more sexually open societies. But the writer's very respectable case for greater openness towards taboo sexual practices is then "proven" by the example of the young part-Vietnamese woman who, after the filming of **Trans-Europ-Express**, left her loving American boyfriend, unwilling to tie her to the iron bedpost, for Robbe-Grillet, more open to variations on the bonds of love.

It is nonetheless the writing and not the writer that is situated at the center of this work. "La chair des phrases a toujours occupé, sans doute, une grande place dans mon travail" claims the introductory sentence. This multiform flesh or body of the text shifts from personal anecdote, to literary reflection or theory, or to the extended fable of the elixir of life or death to be found behind one of three doors. Occasionally progressing by linguistic analogy (between, for example, such different sounds and referents as "flacon" and "flocon"), it is self-aware, as Robbe-Grillet puts it, of the fictions that thread through it and the lacks and aporias that, as in life, undermine any possible stability of meaning. Although, like Camus, Robbe-Grillet speaks of his personal experience of the beauty of the natural world and the colors of the lichens, his writing, with its attention to sonorities, rhythm, regularity, and unpredictability, echoes and ruptures presents itself as a work on language rather than on the world. It is the movements of the prose that models the non-mutually exclusive contradictions of the "monotony and violence" of Robbe-Grillet's landscapes and sea-scapes, the alternating of caressing flow and sudden violent eddies of inner sexual phantasies, and of the movements of the sea, in textual play. This text is multilayered in its reference: the opening sentence, for example, is at once textual, sexual, and intertextual as it reconstructs the first sentence of *La Maison de rendez-vous* (1965), "La chair des femmes a toujours occupé, sans doute, une grande place dans mes rêves."

Robbe-Grillet's creative work, his "temple in ruins" is dedicated to the future divinity named "Construction." I would suggest that where the traditional autobiographical edifice is not sufficiently reduced to ruins to permit these new constructions, where traditional autobiographical "truth-telling" predominates and selected anecdotes of the origins of a work, Parisian literary quarrels and the incidents of a day at Mesnil-au-Grain hold the stage, the death of Corinthe (that is, the establishing of his genius for posterity) can appear longwinded, egocentric, self-indulgent and less than intellectually mobilising or linguistically enchanting. This particular style, present in all three autofictions and of varying but generally limited degrees of interest for all but the most devoted of Robbe-Grillet's readers, leaves the reader nostalgic for the creative tightness, the distanced, and artistically controlled self-exploration through the staging of another consciousness already both empty and full, both inner and outer, of the always inventive early fictions—*Les Gommes* (1955), *Le Voyeur* (1955), *La Jalousie* (1957). The interest of the exploration of the processes of textual generation in *Dans le labyrinthe*, of the myths of violence in contemporary urban society and in Robbe-Grillet's own imaginary society in Projet pour une révolution à New York (1970), again constitute threads in this latest work but are no longer novel or subversive.

This third work of the autobiographical trilogy also lacks the originality of the interrogation of the confessional autobiographical genre introduced by the first autofiction, *Le Miroir qui revient* (1985). Its explicit and detailed taboo erotic scenarios no longer have the shock value and provocation of the weaving of sado-eroticism into medieval and knightly legend that cast a spell of fascination on the reader in the pirouetting "confession" of *Angélique ou L'Enchantement* (1988). While Les Derniers Jours de Corinthe does specialize in the Lolita/Salomé phantasies in elaborate detail, and appears to probe yet more deeply into the "true" heroism and lonely courage or

"false" villainy of Corinthe, it does not develop a form that introduces a noticeably new figuration into the auto fictional textual dance. Although the use of visual art as generator of the diegesis is striking, particularly the narration of Robbe-Grillet's encounter and identification with Segal's ashen, frozen life-like sculptures of ordinary people, this is again a continuation of the experiments of the picto-novels whose assembled and interconnected texts largely constitute *Topologie d'une cité fantôme* (1976) and *Souvenirs du triangle d'or* (1978). The constant movements between representation and real simply continue to refine the now familiar practice of mise en abyme or interior duplication that feeds into the self-conscious reflexivity or metatextual level of textual functioning.

However, where the narrators represent both the collective and the particularized unconscious in contradictory but not mutually exclusive mobile architectures, and to the extent that the heterogeneous styles that clash and set up oppositions are also organized in new "complementary" and "chaotic" constructions, this third autobiography is again a "new autobiography." The unexpected narrative movements of the text, the recognition of inter texts, the creative and critical play of its multiple layers of meaning, make the reading of this less than strikingly original third new autobiography an intellectual pleasure. There is interest in its reassemblage and rewriting on the ruins of the span of a life and work and in the exploration of the links between the collective and the individual unconscious; some interest in Robbe-Grillet's own critical and philosophical reflections. The configurations of the dance of the text on the ruins of the imaginary, history and genre in *Les Derniers Jours de Corinthe* are critical, dynamic and constructive, not those of a writing in ruins.

On the other hand, Robbe-Grillet's self-deconstruction is rendered suspect, once again, by his inability to reduce the conventional binary oppositions of gender to ruins, and to envision the traditional "feminine" sacrificial victim and "masculine" aggressor, the siren and the deviant sailor as interchangeable and "complementary" pairs in their turn. The refusal to deconstruct further the intact scenarios of her pain and loss of power, as his (and indeed her) pleasure limits the revolutionary potential of the staging and examination of the significant and repressed psychological complex of sado-masochism. Paradoxically, it is to the extent that the text is not able to engage fully with the "ruins" of self, tragedy, and history or with the "ruin(ing)" of Robbe-Grillet that this joyous autofictional writing on the ruins fails.

FURTHER READING

Criticism

Bogue, Ronald. "Roland Barthes, Alain Robbe-Grillet, and

the Paradise of the Writerly Text." *Criticism: A Quarterly for Literature and the Arts* XXII, No. 2 (Spring 1980): 156-71.

Examines the interrelationship between the novelist and critic in the development of Robbe-Grillet's fiction and the formulation of Barthes's literary theories.

Brown, Royal S. "An Interview with Alain Robbe-Grillet." *Literature-Film Quarterly* 17, No. 2 (1989): 74-83.

Robbe-Grillet comments on the major themes, creative influences, and production of his films.

————"Serialism in Robbe-Grillet's *L'Eden et aprés:* The Narrative and Its Double." *Literature-Film Quarterly* 18, No. 4 (1990): 210-20.

Provides analysis of the narrative and thematic structure of *L'Eden et aprés.*

DuVerlie, Claud. "Beyond the Image: An Interview with Alain Robbe-Grillet." *New Literary History* XI, No. 3 (Spring 1980): 527-34.

Robbe-Grillet discusses the relationship between text and image in his novels and his artistic concerns in *La Belle Captive* and *Topologie d'une cité fantôme.*

Hayman, David. "An Interview with Alain Robbe-Grillet." *Contemporary Literature* 16, No. 1 (Winter 1975): 273-85.

Robbe-Grillet discusses his fiction, literary influences, and the development of the New Novel.

Morrissette, Bruce. "The Case of Robbe-Grillet." In *Novel and Film: Essays in Two Genres,* pp. 40-58. Chicago: University of Chicago Press, 1985.

Offers discussion of Robbe-Grillet's overlapping creative ventures in literature and film.

Ramsay, Raylene L. "The Sado-Masochism of Representation in French Texts of Modernity: The Power of the Erotic and the Eroticization of Power in the Work of Marguerite Duras and Alain Robbe-Grillet." *Literature and Psychology* XXXVII, No. 3 (1991): 18-28.

Provides comparative analysis of sadoerotic imagery and themes in the work of Robbe-Grillet and Marguerite Duras.

Stoltzfus, Ben. "Toward Bliss: Barthes, Lacan, and Robbe-Grillet." *Modern Fiction Studies* 35, No. 4 (Winter 1989): 699-706.

Offers a Lacanian reading of Robbe-Grillet's *Le Miroir qui revient* and Barthes's autobiography, *Roland Barthes.*

Sturrock, John. "The Frisky and the Unfriendly." *Times Literary Supplement* (17 June 1988): 671.

A review of *Angélique ou L'Enchantement.*

Szanto, George H. "Structure as Process: The Temporal Point of View." In *Narrative Consciousness: Structure and Perception in the Fiction of Kafka, Beckett, and Robbe-Grillet,* pp. 149-56. Austin: University of Texas Press, 1972.

Examines the presentation of psychological time and narrative consciousness in Robbe-Grillet's fiction.

Additional coverage of Robbe-Grillet's life and career is contained in the following sources published by the Gale Group: *Contemporary Authors,* **Vols. 9-12R;** *Contemporary Authors New Revision Series,* **Vol. 33;** *Dictionary of Literary Biography,* **Vol. 83; and** *Major 20th-Century Writers,* **Eds. 1 and 2.**

How to Use This Index

Literary Criticism Series
Cumulative Author Index

Amis, Martin (Louis) 1949- .... **CLC 4, 9, 38, 62, 101**
See also BEST 90:3; CA 65-68; CANR 8, 27, 54, 73; DA3; DLB 14, 194; INT CANR-27; MTCW 1

Ammons, A(rchie) R(andolph)
1926- ...... **CLC 2, 3, 5, 8, 9, 25, 57, 108; DAM POET; PC 16**
See also AITN 1; CA 9-12R; CANR 6, 36, 51, 73; DLB 5, 165; MTCW 1, 2

Amo, Tauraatua i
See Adams, Henry (Brooks)

Amory, Thomas 1691(?)-1788 .... **LC 48**

Anand, Mulk Raj 1905- .. **CLC 23, 93; DAM NOV**
See also CA 65-68; CANR 32, 64; MTCW 1, 2

Anatol
See Schnitzler, Arthur

Anaximander c. 610B.C.-c.
546B.C. .... **CMLC 22**

Anaya, Rudolfo A(lfonso) 1937- ...... **CLC 23; DAM MULT, NOV; HLC 1**
See also AAYA 20; CA 45-48; CAAS 4; CANR 1, 32, 51; DLB 82, 206; HW 1; MTCW 1, 2

Andersen, Hans Christian
1805-1875 .... **NCLC 7, 79; DA; DAB; DAC; DAM MST, POP; SSC 6; WLC**
See also CLR 6; DA3; MAICYA; SATA 100; YABC 1

Anderson, C. Farley
See Mencken, H(enry) L(ouis); Nathan, George Jean

Anderson, Jessica (Margaret) Queale 1916-
CLC 37
See also CA 9-12R; CANR 4, 62

Anderson, Jon (Victor) 1940- . **CLC 9; DAM POET**
See also CA 25-28R; CANR 20

Anderson, Lindsay (Gordon)
1923-1994 .... **CLC 20**
See also CA 125; 128; 146; CANR 77

Anderson, Maxwell 1888-1959 .... **TCLC 2; DAM DRAM**
See also CA 105; 152; DLB 7; MTCW 2

Anderson, Poul (William) 1926- .... **CLC 15**
See also AAYA 5; CA 1-4R, 181; CAAE 181; CAAS 2; CANR 2, 15, 34, 64; CLR 58; DLB 8; INT CANR-15; MTCW 1, 2; SATA 90; SATA-Brief 39; SATA-Essay 106

Anderson, Robert (Woodruff)
1917- .... **CLC 23; DAM DRAM**
See also AITN 1; CA 21-24R; CANR 32; DLB 7

Anderson, Sherwood 1876-1941 ..... **TCLC 1, 10, 24; DA; DAB; DAC; DAM MST, NOV; SSC 1; WLC**
See also AAYA 30; CA 104; 121; CANR 61; CDALB 1917-1929; DA3; DLB 4, 9, 86; DLBD 1; MTCW 1, 2

Andier, Pierre
See Desnos, Robert

Andouard
See Giraudoux, (Hippolyte) Jean

Andrade, Carlos Drummond de ...... **CLC 18**
See also Drummond de Andrade, Carlos

Andrade, Mario de 1893-1945 .... **TCLC 43**

Andreae, Johann V(alentin)
1586-1654 .... **LC 32**
See also DLB 164

Andreas-Salome, Lou 1861-1937 ... **TCLC 56**
See also CA 178; DLB 66

Andress, Lesley
See Sanders, Lawrence

Andrewes, Lancelot 1555-1626 .... **LC 5**
See also DLB 151, 172

Andrews, Cicily Fairfield
See West, Rebecca

Andrews, Elton V.
See Pohl, Frederik

Andreyev, Leonid (Nikolaevich) 1871-1919
TCLC 3
See also CA 104

Andric, Ivo 1892-1975 .... **CLC 8; SSC 36**
See also CA 81-84; 57-60; CANR 43, 60; DLB 147; MTCW 1

Androvar
See Prado (Calvo), Pedro

Angelique, Pierre
See Bataille, Georges

Angell, Roger 1920- .... **CLC 26**
See also CA 57-60; CANR 13, 44, 70; DLB 171, 185

Angelou, Maya 1928- .... **CLC 12, 35, 64, 77; BLC 1; DA; DAB; DAC; DAM MST, MULT, POET, POP; WLCS**
See also AAYA 7, 20; BW 2, 3; CA 65-68; CANR 19, 42, 65; CDALBS; CLR 53; DA3; DLB 38; MTCW 1, 2; SATA 49

Anna Comnena 1083-1153 .... **CMLC 25**

Annensky, Innokenty (Fyodorovich)
1856-1909 .... **TCLC 14**
See also CA 110; 155

Annunzio, Gabriele d'
See D'Annunzio, Gabriele

Anodos
See Coleridge, Mary E(lizabeth)

Anon, Charles Robert
See Pessoa, Fernando (Antonio Nogueira)

Anouilh, Jean (Marie Lucien Pierre)
1910-1987 .... **CLC 1, 3, 8, 13, 40, 50; DAM DRAM; DC 8**
See also CA 17-20R; 123; CANR 32; MTCW 1, 2

Anthony, Florence
See Ai

Anthony, John
See Ciardi, John (Anthony)

Anthony, Peter
See Shaffer, Anthony (Joshua); Shaffer, Peter (Levin)

Anthony, Piers 1934- .... **CLC 35; DAM POP**
See also AAYA 11; CA 21-24R; CANR 28, 56, 73; DLB 8; MTCW 1, 2; SAAS 22; SATA 84

Anthony, Susan B(rownell)
1916-1991 .... **TCLC 84**
See also CA 89-92; 134

Antoine, Marc
See Proust, (Valentin-Louis-George-Eugene-) Marcel

Antoninus, Brother
See Everson, William (Oliver)

Antonioni, Michelangelo 1912- .... **CLC 20**
See also CA 73-76; CANR 45, 77

Antschel, Paul 1920-1970
See Celan, Paul
See also CA 85-88; CANR 33, 61; MTCW 1

Anwar, Chairil 1922-1949 .... **TCLC 22**
See also CA 121

Anzaldua, Gloria 1942-
See also CA 175; DLB 122; HLCS 1

Apess, William 1798-1839(?) .... **NCLC 73; DAM MULT**
See also DLB 175; NNAL

Apollinaire, Guillaume 1880-1918 .. **TCLC 3, 8, 51; DAM POET; PC 7**
See also Kostrowitzki, Wilhelm Apollinaris de CA 152; MTCW 1

Appelfeld, Aharon 1932- .... **CLC 23, 47**
See also CA 112; 133; CANR 86

Apple, Max (Isaac) 1941- .... **CLC 9, 33**
See also CA 81-84; CANR 19, 54; DLB 130

Appleman, Philip (Dean) 1926- .... **CLC 51**
See also CA 13-16R; CAAS 18; CANR 6, 29, 56

Appleton, Lawrence
See Lovecraft, H(oward) P(hillips)

Apteryx
See Eliot, T(homas) S(tearns)

Apuleius, (Lucius Madaurensis)
125(?)-175(?) .... **CMLC 1**
See also DLB 211

Aquin, Hubert 1929-1977 .... **CLC 15**
See also CA 105; DLB 53

Aquinas, Thomas 1224(?)-1274 ..... **CMLC 33**
See also DLB 115

Aragon, Louis 1897-1982 .. **CLC 3, 22; DAM NOV, POET**
See also CA 69-72; 108; CANR 28, 71; DLB 72; MTCW 1, 2

Arany, Janos 1817-1882 .... **NCLC 34**

Aranyos, Kakay
See Mikszath, Kalman

Arbuthnot, John 1667-1735 .... **LC 1**
See also DLB 101

Archer, Herbert Winslow
See Mencken, H(enry) L(ouis)

Archer, Jeffrey (Howard) 1940- ...... **CLC 28; DAM POP**
See also AAYA 16; BEST 89:3; CA 77-80; CANR 22, 52; DA3; INT CANR-22

Archer, Jules 1915- .... **CLC 12**
See also CA 9-12R; CANR 6, 69; SAAS 5; SATA 4, 85

Archer, Lee
See Ellison, Harlan (Jay)

Arden, John 1930- .... **CLC 6, 13, 15; DAM DRAM**
See also CA 13-16R; CAAS 4; CANR 31, 65, 67; DLB 13; MTCW 1

Arenas, Reinaldo 1943-1990 . **CLC 41; DAM MULT; HLC 1**
See also CA 124; 128; 133; CANR 73; DLB 145; HW 1; MTCW 1

Arendt, Hannah 1906-1975 .... **CLC 66, 98**
See also CA 17-20R; 61-64; CANR 26, 60; MTCW 1, 2

Aretino, Pietro 1492-1556 .... **LC 12**

Arghezi, Tudor 1880-1967 .... **CLC 80**
See also Theodorescu, Ion N. CA 167

Arguedas, Jose Maria 1911-1969 .... **CLC 10, 18; HLCS 1**
See also CA 89-92; CANR 73; DLB 113; HW 1

Argueta, Manlio 1936- .... **CLC 31**
See also CA 131; CANR 73; DLB 145; HW 1

Arias, Ron(ald Francis) 1941-
See also CA 131; CANR 81; DAM MULT; DLB 82; HLC 1; HW 1, 2; MTCW 2

Berry, Chuck .... **CLC 17**
See also Berry, Charles Edward Anderson
Berry, Jonas
See Ashbery, John (Lawrence)
Berry, Wendell (Erdman) 1934- ... **CLC 4, 6, 8, 27, 46; DAM POET; PC 28**
See also AITN 1; CA 73-76; CANR 50, 73; DLB 5, 6; MTCW 1
Berryman, John 1914-1972 ... **CLC 1, 2, 3, 4, 6, 8, 10, 13, 25, 62; DAM POET**
See also CA 13-16; 33-36R; CABS 2; CANR 35; CAP 1; CDALB 1941-1968; DLB 48; MTCW 1, 2
Bertolucci, Bernardo 1940- .... **CLC 16**
See also CA 106
Berton, Pierre (Francis Demarigny) 1920- **CLC 104**
See also CA 1-4R; CANR 2, 56; DLB 68; SATA 99
Bertrand, Aloysius 1807-1841 .... **NCLC 31**
Bertran de Born c. 1140-1215 .... **CMLC 5**
Besant, Annie (Wood) 1847-1933 ..... **TCLC 9**
See also CA 105
Bessie, Alvah 1904-1985 .... **CLC 23**
See also CA 5-8R; 116; CANR 2, 80; DLB 26
Bethlen, T. D.
See Silverberg, Robert
Beti, Mongo . **CLC 27; BLC 1; DAM MULT**
See also Biyidi, Alexandre CANR 79
Betjeman, John 1906-1984 ...... **CLC 2, 6, 10, 34, 43; DAB; DAM MST, POET**
See also CA 9-12R; 112; CANR 33, 56; CDBLB 1945-1960; DA3; DLB 20; DLBY 84; MTCW 1, 2
Bettelheim, Bruno 1903-1990 .... **CLC 79**
See also CA 81-84; 131; CANR 23, 61; DA3; MTCW 1, 2
Betti, Ugo 1892-1953 .... **TCLC 5**
See also CA 104; 155
Betts, Doris (Waugh) 1932- ...... **CLC 3, 6, 28**
See also CA 13-16R; CANR 9, 66, 77; DLBY 82; INT CANR-9
Bevan, Alistair
See Roberts, Keith (John Kingston)
Bey, Pilaff
See Douglas, (George) Norman
Bialik, Chaim Nachman 1873-1934 .... **TCLC 25**
See also CA 170
Bickerstaff, Isaac
See Swift, Jonathan
Bidart, Frank 1939- .... **CLC 33**
See also CA 140
Bienek, Horst 1930- .... **CLC 7, 11**
See also CA 73-76; DLB 75
Bierce, Ambrose (Gwinett) 1842-1914(?) **TCLC 1, 7, 44; DA; DAC; DAM MST; SSC 9; WLC**
See also CA 104; 139; CANR 78; CDALB 1865-1917; DA3; DLB 11, 12, 23, 71, 74, 186
Biggers, Earl Derr 1884-1933 .... **TCLC 65**
See also CA 108; 153
Billings, Josh
See Shaw, Henry Wheeler
Billington, (Lady) Rachel (Mary) 1942- .... **CLC 43**
See also AITN 2; CA 33-36R; CANR 44
Binyon, T(imothy) J(ohn) 1936- .... **CLC 34**
See also CA 111; CANR 28

Bioy Casares, Adolfo 1914-1999 ... **CLC 4, 8, 13, 88; DAM MULT; HLC 1; SSC 17**
See also CA 29-32R; 177; CANR 19, 43, 66; DLB 113; HW 1, 2; MTCW 1, 2
Bird, Cordwainer
See Ellison, Harlan (Jay)
Bird, Robert Montgomery 1806-1854 .... **NCLC 1**
See also DLB 202
Birkerts, Sven 1951- .... **CLC 116**
See also CA 128; 133; 176; CAAE 176; CAAS 29; INT 133
Birney, (Alfred) Earle 1904-1995 .. **CLC 1, 4, 6, 11; DAC; DAM MST, POET**
See also CA 1-4R; CANR 5, 20; DLB 88; MTCW 1
Biruni, al 973-1048(?) .... **CMLC 28**
Bishop, Elizabeth 1911-1979 ..... **CLC 1, 4, 9, 13, 15, 32; DA; DAC; DAM MST, POET; PC 3**
See also CA 5-8R; 89-92; CABS 2; CANR 26, 61; CDALB 1968-1988; DA3; DLB 5, 169; MTCW 1, 2; SATA-Obit 24
Bishop, John 1935- .... **CLC 10**
See also CA 105
Bissett, Bill 1939- .... **CLC 18; PC 14**
See also CA 69-72; CAAS 19; CANR 15; DLB 53; MTCW 1
Bissoondath, Neil (Devindra) 1955- .... **CLC 120; DAC**
See also CA 136
Bitov, Andrei (Georgievich) 1937- ... **CLC 57**
See also CA 142
Biyidi, Alexandre 1932-
See Beti, Mongo
See also BW 1, 3; CA 114; 124; CANR 81; DA3; MTCW 1, 2
Bjarme, Brynjolf
See Ibsen, Henrik (Johan)
Bjoernson, Bjoernstjerne (Martinius) 1832-1910 .... **TCLC 7, 37**
See also CA 104
Black, Robert
See Holdstock, Robert P.
Blackburn, Paul 1926-1971 .... **CLC 9, 43**
See also CA 81-84; 33-36R; CANR 34; DLB 16; DLBY 81
Black Elk 1863-1950 .... **TCLC 33; DAM MULT**
See also CA 144; MTCW 1; NNAL
Black Hobart
See Sanders, (James) Ed(ward)
Blacklin, Malcolm
See Chambers, Aidan
Blackmore, R(ichard) D(oddridge) 1825-1900 .... **TCLC 27**
See also CA 120; DLB 18
Blackmur, R(ichard) P(almer) 1904-1965 **CLC 2, 24**
See also CA 11-12; 25-28R; CANR 71; CAP 1; DLB 63
Black Tarantula
See Acker, Kathy
Blackwood, Algernon (Henry) 1869-1951 **TCLC 5**
See also CA 105; 150; DLB 153, 156, 178
Blackwood, Caroline 1931-1996 .... **CLC 6, 9, 100**
See also CA 85-88; 151; CANR 32, 61, 65; DLB 14, 207; MTCW 1
Blade, Alexander
See Hamilton, Edmond; Silverberg, Robert

Blaga, Lucian 1895-1961 .... **CLC 75**
See also CA 157
Blair, Eric (Arthur) 1903-1950
See Orwell, George
See also CA 104; 132; DA; DAB; DAC; DAM MST, NOV; DA3; MTCW 1, 2; SATA 29
Blair, Hugh 1718-1800 .... **NCLC 75**
Blais, Marie-Claire 1939- .... **CLC 2, 4, 6, 13, 22; DAC; DAM MST**
See also CA 21-24R; CAAS 4; CANR 38, 75; DLB 53; MTCW 1, 2
Blaise, Clark 1940- .... **CLC 29**
See also AITN 2; CA 53-56; CAAS 3; CANR 5, 66; DLB 53
Blake, Fairley
See De Voto, Bernard (Augustine)
Blake, Nicholas
See Day Lewis, C(ecil)
See also DLB 77
Blake, William 1757-1827 .... **NCLC 13, 37, 57; DA; DAB; DAC; DAM MST, POET; PC 12; WLC**
See also CDBLB 1789-1832; CLR 52; DA3; DLB 93, 163; MAICYA; SATA 30
Blasco Ibanez, Vicente 1867-1928 .... **TCLC 12; DAM NOV**
See also CA 110; 131; CANR 81; DA3; HW 1, 2; MTCW 1
Blatty, William Peter 1928- .... **CLC 2; DAM POP**
See also CA 5-8R; CANR 9
Bleeck, Oliver
See Thomas, Ross (Elmore)
Blessing, Lee 1949- .... **CLC 54**
Blish, James (Benjamin) 1921-1975 . **CLC 14**
See also CA 1-4R; 57-60; CANR 3; DLB 8; MTCW 1; SATA 66
Bliss, Reginald
See Wells, H(erbert) G(eorge)
Blixen, Karen (Christentze Dinesen) 1885-1962
See Dinesen, Isak
See also CA 25-28; CANR 22, 50; CAP 2; DA3; MTCW 1, 2; SATA 44
Bloch, Robert (Albert) 1917-1994 .... **CLC 33**
See also AAYA 29; CA 5-8R, 179; 146; CAAE 179; CAAS 20; CANR 5, 78; DA3; DLB 44; INT CANR-5; MTCW 1; SATA 12; SATA-Obit 82
Blok, Alexander (Alexandrovich) 1880-1921 **TCLC 5; PC 21**
See also CA 104; 183
Blom, Jan
See Breytenbach, Breyten
Bloom, Harold 1930- .... **CLC 24, 103**
See also CA 13-16R; CANR 39, 75; DLB 67; MTCW 1
Bloomfield, Aurelius
See Bourne, Randolph S(illiman)
Blount, Roy (Alton), Jr. 1941- .... **CLC 38**
See also CA 53-56; CANR 10, 28, 61; INT CANR-28; MTCW 1, 2
Bloy, Leon 1846-1917 .... **TCLC 22**
See also CA 121; 183; DLB 123
Blume, Judy (Sussman) 1938- .. **CLC 12, 30; DAM NOV, POP**
See also AAYA 3, 26; CA 29-32R; CANR 13, 37, 66; CLR 2, 15; DA3; DLB 52; JRDA; MAICYA; MTCW 1, 2; SATA 2, 31, 79

Bradley, Marion Zimmer 1930- ...... **CLC 30;
DAM POP**
See also AAYA 9; CA 57-60; CAAS 10;
CANR 7, 31, 51, 75; DA3; DLB 8;
MTCW 1, 2; SATA 90

Bradstreet, Anne 1612(?)-1672 ...... **LC 4, 30;
DA; DAC; DAM MST, POET; PC 10**
See also CDALB 1640-1865; DA3; DLB
24

Brady, Joan 1939- .... **CLC 86**
See also CA 141

Bragg, Melvyn 1939- .... **CLC 10**
See also BEST 89:3; CA 57-60; CANR 10,
48; DLB 14

Brahe, Tycho 1546-1601 .... **LC 45**

Braine, John (Gerard) 1922-1986 . **CLC 1, 3,
41**
See also CA 1-4R; 120; CANR 1, 33; CD-
BLB 1945-1960; DLB 15; DLBY 86;
MTCW 1

Bramah, Ernest 1868-1942 .... **TCLC 72**
See also CA 156; DLB 70

Brammer, William 1930(?)-1978 ...... **CLC 31**
See also CA 77-80

Brancati, Vitaliano 1907-1954 .... **TCLC 12**
See also CA 109

Brancato, Robin F(idler) 1936- .... **CLC 35**
See also AAYA 9; CA 69-72; CANR 11,
45; CLR 32; JRDA; SAAS 9; SATA 97

Brand, Max
See Faust, Frederick (Schiller)

Brand, Millen 1906-1980 .... **CLC 7**
See also CA 21-24R; 97-100; CANR 72

Branden, Barbara .... **CLC 44**
See also CA 148

Brandes, Georg (Morris Cohen) 1842-1927
TCLC 10
See also CA 105

Brandys, Kazimierz 1916- .... **CLC 62**

Branley, Franklyn M(ansfield)
1915- .... **CLC 21**
See also CA 33-36R; CANR 14, 39; CLR
13; MAICYA; SAAS 16; SATA 4, 68

Brathwaite, Edward (Kamau)
1930- ...... **CLC 11; BLCS; DAM POET**
See also BW 2, 3; CA 25-28R; CANR 11,
26, 47; DLB 125

Brautigan, Richard (Gary)
1935-1984 .... **CLC 1, 3, 5, 9, 12, 34, 42;
DAM NOV**
See also CA 53-56; 113; CANR 34; DA3;
DLB 2, 5, 206; DLBY 80, 84; MTCW 1;
SATA 56

Brave Bird, Mary 1953-
See Crow Dog, Mary (Ellen)
See also NNAL

Braverman, Kate 1950- .... **CLC 67**
See also CA 89-92

Brecht, (Eugen) Bertolt (Friedrich)
1898-1956 .... **TCLC 1, 6, 13, 35; DA;
DAB; DAC; DAM DRAM, MST; DC
3; WLC**
See also CA 104; 133; CANR 62; DA3;
DLB 56, 124; MTCW 1, 2

Brecht, Eugen Berthold Friedrich
See Brecht, (Eugen) Bertolt (Friedrich)

Bremer, Fredrika 1801-1865 .... **NCLC 11**

Brennan, Christopher John
1870-1932 .... **TCLC 17**
See also CA 117

Brennan, Maeve 1917-1993 .... **CLC 5**
See also CA 81-84; CANR 72

Brent, Linda
See Jacobs, Harriet A(nn)

Brentano, Clemens (Maria)
1778-1842 .... **NCLC 1**
See also DLB 90

Brent of Bin Bin
See Franklin, (Stella Maria Sarah) Miles
(Lampe)

Brenton, Howard 1942- .... **CLC 31**
See also CA 69-72; CANR 33, 67; DLB 13;
MTCW 1

Breslin, James 1930-1996
See Breslin, Jimmy
See also CA 73-76; CANR 31, 75; DAM
NOV; MTCW 1, 2

Breslin, Jimmy .... **CLC 4, 43**
See also Breslin, James AITN 1; DLB 185;
MTCW 2

Bresson, Robert 1901- .... **CLC 16**
See also CA 110; CANR 49

Breton, Andre 1896-1966 .. **CLC 2, 9, 15, 54;
PC 15**
See also CA 19-20; 25-28R; CANR 40, 60;
CAP 2; DLB 65; MTCW 1, 2

Breytenbach, Breyten 1939(?)- .. **CLC 23, 37,
126; DAM POET**
See also CA 113; 129; CANR 61

Bridgers, Sue Ellen 1942- .... **CLC 26**
See also AAYA 8; CA 65-68; CANR 11,
36; CLR 18; DLB 52; JRDA; MAICYA;
SAAS 1; SATA 22, 90; SATA-Essay 109

Bridges, Robert (Seymour)
1844-1930 ... **TCLC 1; DAM POET; PC
28**
See also CA 104; 152; CDBLB 1890-1914;
DLB 19, 98

Bridie, James .... **TCLC 3**
See also Mavor, Osborne Henry DLB 10

Brin, David 1950- .... **CLC 34**
See also AAYA 21; CA 102; CANR 24, 70;
INT CANR-24; SATA 65

Brink, Andre (Philippus) 1935- . **CLC 18, 36,
106**
See also CA 104; CANR 39, 62; INT 103;
MTCW 1, 2

Brinsmead, H(esba) F(ay) 1922- ...... **CLC 21**
See also CA 21-24R; CANR 10; CLR 47;
MAICYA; SAAS 5; SATA 18, 78

Brittain, Vera (Mary) 1893(?)-1970 . **CLC 23**
See also CA 13-16; 25-28R; CANR 58;
CAP 1; DLB 191; MTCW 1, 2

Broch, Hermann 1886-1951 .... **TCLC 20**
See also CA 117; DLB 85, 124

Brock, Rose
See Hansen, Joseph

Brodkey, Harold (Roy) 1930-1996 ... **CLC 56**
See also CA 111; 151; CANR 71; DLB 130

Brodskii, Iosif
See Brodsky, Joseph

Brodsky, Iosif Alexandrovich 1940-1996
See Brodsky, Joseph
See also AITN 1; CA 41-44R; 151; CANR
37; DAM POET; DA3; MTCW 1, 2

Brodsky, Joseph 1940-1996 ..... **CLC 4, 6, 13,
36, 100; PC 9**
See also Brodskii, Iosif; Brodsky, Iosif Alexandrovich MTCW 1

Brodsky, Michael (Mark) 1948- .... **CLC 19**
See also CA 102; CANR 18, 41, 58

Bromell, Henry 1947- .... **CLC 5**
See also CA 53-56; CANR 9

Bromfield, Louis (Brucker)
1896-1956 .... **TCLC 11**
See also CA 107; 155; DLB 4, 9, 86

Broner, E(sther) M(asserman)
1930- .... **CLC 19**
See also CA 17-20R; CANR 8, 25, 72; DLB
28

Bronk, William (M.) 1918-1999 .... **CLC 10**
See also CA 89-92; 177; CANR 23; DLB
165

Bronstein, Lev Davidovich
See Trotsky, Leon

Bronte, Anne 1820-1849 .... **NCLC 4, 71**
See also DA3; DLB 21, 199

Bronte, Charlotte 1816-1855 ...... **NCLC 3, 8,
33, 58; DA; DAB; DAC; DAM MST,
NOV; WLC**
See also AAYA 17; CDBLB 1832-1890;
DA3; DLB 21, 159, 199

Bronte, Emily (Jane) 1818-1848 ... **NCLC 16,
35; DA; DAB; DAC; DAM MST, NOV,
POET; PC 8; WLC**
See also AAYA 17; CDBLB 1832-1890;
DA3; DLB 21, 32, 199

Brooke, Frances 1724-1789 .... **LC 6, 48**
See also DLB 39, 99

Brooke, Henry 1703(?)-1783 .... **LC 1**
See also DLB 39

Brooke, Rupert (Chawner)
1887-1915 .... **TCLC 2, 7; DA; DAB;
DAC; DAM MST, POET; PC 24; WLC**
See also CA 104; 132; CANR 61; CDBLB
1914-1945; DLB 19; MTCW 1, 2

Brooke-Haven, P.
See Wodehouse, P(elham) G(renville)

Brooke-Rose, Christine 1926(?)- ...... **CLC 40**
See also CA 13-16R; CANR 58; DLB 14

Brookner, Anita 1928- .... **CLC 32, 34, 51;
DAB; DAM POP**
See also CA 114; 120; CANR 37, 56, 87;
DA3; DLB 194; DLBY 87; MTCW 1, 2

Brooks, Cleanth 1906-1994 . **CLC 24, 86, 110**
See also CA 17-20R; 145; CANR 33, 35;
DLB 63; DLBY 94; INT CANR-35;
MTCW 1, 2

Brooks, George
See Baum, L(yman) Frank

Brooks, Gwendolyn 1917- ..... **CLC 1, 2, 4, 5,
15, 49, 125; BLC 1; DA; DAC; DAM
MST, MULT, POET; PC 7; WLC**
See also AAYA 20; AITN 1; BW 2, 3; CA
1-4R; CANR 1, 27, 52, 75; CDALB 1941-
1968; CLR 27; DA3; DLB 5, 76, 165;
MTCW 1, 2; SATA 6

Brooks, Mel .... **CLC 12**
See also Kaminsky, Melvin AAYA 13; DLB
26

Brooks, Peter 1938- .... **CLC 34**
See also CA 45-48; CANR 1

Brooks, Van Wyck 1886-1963 .... **CLC 29**
See also CA 1-4R; CANR 6; DLB 45, 63,
103

Brophy, Brigid (Antonia)
1929-1995 .... **CLC 6, 11, 29, 105**
See also CA 5-8R; 149; CAAS 4; CANR
25, 53; DA3; DLB 14; MTCW 1, 2

Brosman, Catharine Savage 1934- ..... **CLC 9**
See also CA 61-64; CANR 21, 46

Brossard, Nicole 1943- .... **CLC 115**
See also CA 122; CAAS 16; DLB 53

Brother Antoninus
See Everson, William (Oliver)

Burns, Tex
  See L'Amour, Louis (Dearborn)
Burnshaw, Stanley 1906- .... **CLC 3, 13, 44**
  See also CA 9-12R; DLB 48; DLBY 97
Burr, Anne 1937- .... **CLC 6**
  See also CA 25-28R
Burroughs, Edgar Rice 1875-1950 . **TCLC 2, 32; DAM NOV**
  See also AAYA 11; CA 104; 132; DA3; DLB 8; MTCW 1, 2; SATA 41
Burroughs, William S(eward) 1914-1997
  CLC 1, 2, 5, 15, 22, 42, 75, 109; DA; DAB; DAC; DAM MST, NOV, POP; WLC
  See also AITN 2; CA 9-12R; 160; CANR 20, 52; DA3; DLB 2, 8, 16, 152; DLBY 81, 97; MTCW 1, 2
Burton, SirRichard F(rancis) 1821-1890
  NCLC 42
  See also DLB 55, 166, 184
Busch, Frederick 1941- .... **CLC 7, 10, 18, 47**
  See also CA 33-36R; CAAS 1; CANR 45, 73; DLB 6
Bush, Ronald 1946- .... **CLC 34**
  See also CA 136
Bustos, F(rancisco)
  See Borges, Jorge Luis
Bustos Domecq, H(onorio)
  See Bioy Casares, Adolfo; Borges, Jorge Luis
Butler, Octavia E(stelle) 1947- .... **CLC 38, 121; BLCS; DAM MULT, POP**
  See also AAYA 18; BW 2, 3; CA 73-76; CANR 12, 24, 38, 73; DA3; DLB 33; MTCW 1, 2; SATA 84
Butler, Robert Olen (Jr.) 1945- .... **CLC 81; DAM POP**
  See also CA 112; CANR 66; DLB 173; INT 112; MTCW 1
Butler, Samuel 1612-1680 .... **LC 16, 43**
  See also DLB 101, 126
Butler, Samuel 1835-1902 . **TCLC 1, 33; DA; DAB; DAC; DAM MST, NOV; WLC**
  See also CA 143; CDBLB 1890-1914; DA3; DLB 18, 57, 174
Butler, Walter C.
  See Faust, Frederick (Schiller)
Butor, Michel (Marie Francois)
  1926- .... **CLC 1, 3, 8, 11, 15**
  See also CA 9-12R; CANR 33, 66; DLB 83; MTCW 1, 2
Butts, Mary 1892(?)-1937 .... **TCLC 77**
  See also CA 148
Buzo, Alexander (John) 1944- .... **CLC 61**
  See also CA 97-100; CANR 17, 39, 69
Buzzati, Dino 1906-1972 .... **CLC 36**
  See also CA 160; 33-36R; DLB 177
Byars, Betsy (Cromer) 1928- .... **CLC 35**
  See also AAYA 19; CA 33-36R, 183; CAAE 183; CANR 18, 36, 57; CLR 1, 16; DLB 52; INT CANR-18; JRDA; MAICYA; MTCW 1; SAAS 1; SATA 4, 46, 80; SATA-Essay 108
Byatt, A(ntonia) S(usan Drabble)
  1936- ..... **CLC 19, 65; DAM NOV, POP**
  See also CA 13-16R; CANR 13, 33, 50, 75; DA3; DLB 14, 194; MTCW 1, 2
Byrne, David 1952- .... **CLC 26**
  See also CA 127
Byrne, John Keyes 1926-
  See Leonard, Hugh
  See also CA 102; CANR 78; INT 102

Byron, George Gordon (Noel) 1788-1824
  NCLC 2, 12; DA; DAB; DAC; DAM MST, POET; PC 16; WLC
  See also CDBLB 1789-1832; DA3; DLB 96, 110
Byron, Robert 1905-1941 .... **TCLC 67**
  See also CA 160; DLB 195
C. 3. 3.
  See Wilde, Oscar
Caballero, Fernan 1796-1877 .... **NCLC 10**
Cabell, Branch
  See Cabell, James Branch
Cabell, James Branch 1879-1958 .... **TCLC 6**
  See also CA 105; 152; DLB 9, 78; MTCW 1
Cable, George Washington
  1844-1925 .... **TCLC 4; SSC 4**
  See also CA 104; 155; DLB 12, 74; DLBD 13
Cabral de Melo Neto, Joao 1920- ... **CLC 76; DAM MULT**
  See also CA 151
Cabrera Infante, G(uillermo) 1929- . **CLC 5, 25, 45, 120; DAM MULT; HLC 1**
  See also CA 85-88; CANR 29, 65; DA3; DLB 113; HW 1, 2; MTCW 1, 2
Cade, Toni
  See Bambara, Toni Cade
Cadmus and Harmonia
  See Buchan, John
Caedmon fl. 658-680 .... **CMLC 7**
  See also DLB 146
Caeiro, Alberto
  See Pessoa, Fernando (Antonio Nogueira)
Cage, John (Milton, Jr.) 1912-1992 . **CLC 41**
  See also CA 13-16R; 169; CANR 9, 78; DLB 193; INT CANR-9
Cahan, Abraham 1860-1951 .... **TCLC 71**
  See also CA 108; 154; DLB 9, 25, 28
Cain, G.
  See Cabrera Infante, G(uillermo)
Cain, Guillermo
  See Cabrera Infante, G(uillermo)
Cain, James M(allahan) 1892-1977 .. **CLC 3, 11, 28**
  See also AITN 1; CA 17-20R; 73-76; CANR 8, 34, 61; MTCW 1
Caine, Hall 1853-1931 .... **TCLC 99**
Caine, Mark
  See Raphael, Frederic (Michael)
Calasso, Roberto 1941- .... **CLC 81**
  See also CA 143
Calderon de la Barca, Pedro
  1600-1681 .... **LC 23; DC 3; HLCS 1**
Caldwell, Erskine (Preston)
  1903-1987 .. **CLC 1, 8, 14, 50, 60; DAM NOV; SSC 19**
  See also AITN 1; CA 1-4R; 121; CAAS 1; CANR 2, 33; DA3; DLB 9, 86; MTCW 1, 2
Caldwell, (Janet Miriam) Taylor (Holland)
  1900-1985 .. **CLC 2, 28, 39; DAM NOV, POP**
  See also CA 5-8R; 116; CANR 5; DA3; DLBD 17
Calhoun, John Caldwell
  1782-1850 .... **NCLC 15**
  See also DLB 3
Calisher, Hortense 1911- ..... **CLC 2, 4, 8, 38; DAM NOV; SSC 15**
  See also CA 1-4R; CANR 1, 22, 67; DA3; DLB 2; INT CANR-22; MTCW 1, 2

Callaghan, Morley Edward
  1903-1990 ...... **CLC 3, 14, 41, 65; DAC; DAM MST**
  See also CA 9-12R; 132; CANR 33, 73; DLB 68; MTCW 1, 2
Callimachus c. 305B.C.-c.
  240B.C. .... **CMLC 18**
  See also DLB 176
Calvin, John 1509-1564 .... **LC 37**
Calvino, Italo 1923-1985 .... **CLC 5, 8, 11, 22, 33, 39, 73; DAM NOV; SSC 3**
  See also CA 85-88; 116; CANR 23, 61; DLB 196; MTCW 1, 2
Cameron, Carey 1952- .... **CLC 59**
  See also CA 135
Cameron, Peter 1959- .... **CLC 44**
  See also CA 125; CANR 50
Camoens, Luis Vaz de 1524(?)-1580
  See also HLCS 1
Camoes, Luis de 1524(?)-1580
  See also HLCS 1
Campana, Dino 1885-1932 .... **TCLC 20**
  See also CA 117; DLB 114
Campanella, Tommaso 1568-1639 .... **LC 32**
Campbell, John W(ood, Jr.)
  1910-1971 .... **CLC 32**
  See also CA 21-22; 29-32R; CANR 34; CAP 2; DLB 8; MTCW 1
Campbell, Joseph 1904-1987 .... **CLC 69**
  See also AAYA 3; BEST 89:2; CA 1-4R; 124; CANR 3, 28, 61; DA3; MTCW 1, 2
Campbell, Maria 1940- .... **CLC 85; DAC**
  See also CA 102; CANR 54; NNAL
Campbell, (John) Ramsey 1946- ..... **CLC 42; SSC 19**
  See also CA 57-60; CANR 7; INT CANR-7
Campbell, (Ignatius) Roy (Dunnachie)
  1901-1957 .... **TCLC 5**
  See also CA 104; 155; DLB 20; MTCW 2
Campbell, Thomas 1777-1844 .... **NCLC 19**
  See also DLB 93; 144
Campbell, Wilfred .... **TCLC 9**
  See also Campbell, William
Campbell, William 1858(?)-1918
  See Campbell, Wilfred
  See also CA 106; DLB 92
Campion, Jane .... **CLC 95**
  See also CA 138; CANR 87
Camus, Albert 1913-1960 ...... **CLC 1, 2, 4, 9, 11, 14, 32, 63, 69, 124; DA; DAB; DAC; DAM DRAM, MST, NOV; DC 2; SSC 9; WLC**
  See also CA 89-92; DA3; DLB 72; MTCW 1, 2
Canby, Vincent 1924- .... **CLC 13**
  See also CA 81-84
Cancale
  See Desnos, Robert
Canetti, Elias 1905-1994 .. **CLC 3, 14, 25, 75, 86**
  See also CA 21-24R; 146; CANR 23, 61, 79; DA3; DLB 85, 124; MTCW 1, 2
Canfield, Dorothea F.
  See Fisher, Dorothy (Frances) Canfield
Canfield, Dorothea Frances
  See Fisher, Dorothy (Frances) Canfield
Canfield, Dorothy
  See Fisher, Dorothy (Frances) Canfield
Canin, Ethan 1960- .... **CLC 55**
  See also CA 131; 135
Cannon, Curt
  See Hunter, Evan

Caxton, William 1421(?)-1491(?) .... **LC 17**
See also DLB 170

Cayer, D. M.
See Duffy, Maureen

Cayrol, Jean 1911- .... **CLC 11**
See also CA 89-92; DLB 83

Cela, Camilo Jose 1916- .... **CLC 4, 13, 59, 122; DAM MULT; HLC 1**
See also BEST 90:2; CA 21-24R; CAAS 10; CANR 21, 32, 76; DLBY 89; HW 1; MTCW 1, 2

Celan, Paul .... **CLC 10, 19, 53, 82; PC 10**
See also Antschel, Paul DLB 69

Celine, Louis-Ferdinand ... **CLC 1, 3, 4, 7, 9, 15, 47, 124**
See also Destouches, Louis-Ferdinand DLB 72

Cellini, Benvenuto 1500-1571 .... **LC 7**

Cendrars, Blaise 1887-1961 ...... **CLC 18, 106**
See also Sauser-Hall, Frederic

Cernuda (y Bidon), Luis
1902-1963 .... **CLC 54; DAM POET**
See also CA 131; 89-92; DLB 134; HW 1

Cervantes, Lorna Dee 1954-
See also CA 131; CANR 80; DLB 82; HLCS 1; HW 1

Cervantes (Saavedra), Miguel de 1547-1616
LC 6, 23; DA; DAB; DAC; DAM MST, NOV; SSC 12; WLC

Cesaire, Aime (Fernand) 1913- . **CLC 19, 32, 112; BLC 1; DAM MULT, POET; PC 25**
See also BW 2, 3; CA 65-68; CANR 24, 43, 81; DA3; MTCW 1, 2

Chabon, Michael 1963- .... **CLC 55**
See also CA 139; CANR 57

Chabrol, Claude 1930- .... **CLC 16**
See also CA 110

Challans, Mary 1905-1983
See Renault, Mary
See also CA 81-84; 111; CANR 74; DA3; MTCW 2; SATA 23; SATA-Obit 36

Challis, George
See Faust, Frederick (Schiller)

Chambers, Aidan 1934- .... **CLC 35**
See also AAYA 27; CA 25-28R; CANR 12, 31, 58; JRDA; MAICYA; SAAS 12; SATA 1, 69, 108

Chambers, James 1948-
See Cliff, Jimmy
See also CA 124

Chambers, Jessie
See Lawrence, D(avid) H(erbert Richards)

Chambers, Robert W(illiam) 1865-1933
TCLC 41
See also CA 165; DLB 202; SATA 107

Chamisso, Adelbert von
1781-1838 .... **NCLC 82**
See also DLB 90

Chandler, Raymond (Thornton) 1888-1959
TCLC 1, 7; SSC 23
See also AAYA 25; CA 104; 129; CANR 60; CDALB 1929-1941; DA3; DLBD 6; MTCW 1, 2

Chang, Eileen 1920-1995 .... **SSC 28**
See also CA 166

Chang, Jung 1952- .... **CLC 71**
See also CA 142

Chang Ai-Ling
See Chang, Eileen

Channing, William Ellery
1780-1842 .... **NCLC 17**
See also DLB 1, 59

Chao, Patricia 1955- .... **CLC 119**
See also CA 163

Chaplin, Charles Spencer
1889-1977 .... **CLC 16**
See also Chaplin, Charlie CA 81-84; 73-76

Chaplin, Charlie
See Chaplin, Charles Spencer
See also DLB 44

Chapman, George 1559(?)-1634 .... **LC 22; DAM DRAM**
See also DLB 62, 121

Chapman, Graham 1941-1989 .... **CLC 21**
See also Monty Python CA 116; 129; CANR 35

Chapman, John Jay 1862-1933 .... **TCLC 7**
See also CA 104

Chapman, Lee
See Bradley, Marion Zimmer

Chapman, Walker
See Silverberg, Robert

Chappell, Fred (Davis) 1936- ..... **CLC 40, 78**
See also CA 5-8R; CAAS 4; CANR 8, 33, 67; DLB 6, 105

Char, Rene(-Emile) 1907-1988 .... **CLC 9, 11, 14, 55; DAM POET**
See also CA 13-16R; 124; CANR 32; MTCW 1, 2

Charby, Jay
See Ellison, Harlan (Jay)

Chardin, Pierre Teilhard de
See Teilhard de Chardin, (Marie Joseph) Pierre

Charlemagne 742-814 .... **CMLC 37**

Charles I 1600-1649 .... **LC 13**

Charriere, Isabelle de 1740-1805 .. **NCLC 66**

Charyn, Jerome 1937- .... **CLC 5, 8, 18**
See also CA 5-8R; CAAS 1; CANR 7, 61; DLBY 83; MTCW 1

Chase, Mary (Coyle) 1907-1981 .... **DC 1**
See also CA 77-80; 105; SATA 17; SATA-Obit 29

Chase, Mary Ellen 1887-1973 .... **CLC 2**
See also CA 13-16; 41-44R; CAP 1; SATA 10

Chase, Nicholas
See Hyde, Anthony

Chateaubriand, Francois Rene de 1768-1848
NCLC 3
See also DLB 119

Chatterje, Sarat Chandra 1876-1936(?)
See Chatterji, Saratchandra
See also CA 109

Chatterji, Bankim Chandra 1838-1894
NCLC 19

Chatterji, Saratchandra .... **TCLC 13**
See also Chatterje, Sarat Chandra

Chatterton, Thomas 1752-1770 ..... **LC 3, 54; DAM POET**
See also DLB 109

Chatwin, (Charles) Bruce
1940-1989 . **CLC 28, 57, 59; DAM POP**
See also AAYA 4; BEST 90:1; CA 85-88; 127; DLB 194, 204

Chaucer, Daniel
See Ford, Ford Madox

Chaucer, Geoffrey 1340(?)-1400 .... **LC 17; DA; DAB; DAC; DAM MST, POET; PC 19; WLCS**
See also CDBLB Before 1660; DA3; DLB 146

Chavez, Denise (Elia) 1948-
See also CA 131; CANR 56, 81; DAM MULT; DLB 122; HLC 1; HW 1, 2; MTCW 2

Chaviaras, Strates 1935-
See Haviaras, Stratis
See also CA 105

Chayefsky, Paddy .... **CLC 23**
See also Chayefsky, Sidney DLB 7, 44; DLBY 81

Chayefsky, Sidney 1923-1981
See Chayefsky, Paddy
See also CA 9-12R; 104; CANR 18; DAM DRAM

Chedid, Andree 1920- .... **CLC 47**
See also CA 145

Cheever, John 1912-1982 ..... **CLC 3, 7, 8, 11, 15, 25, 64; DA; DAB; DAC; DAM MST, NOV, POP; SSC 1, 38; WLC**
See also CA 5-8R; 106; CABS 1; CANR 5, 27, 76; CDALB 1941-1968; DA3; DLB 2, 102; DLBY 80, 82; INT CANR-5; MTCW 1, 2

Cheever, Susan 1943- .... **CLC 18, 48**
See also CA 103; CANR 27, 51; DLBY 82; INT CANR-27

Chekhonte, Antosha
See Chekhov, Anton (Pavlovich)

Chekhov, Anton (Pavlovich) 1860-1904
TCLC 3, 10, 31, 55, 96; DA; DAB; DAC; DAM DRAM, MST; DC 9; SSC 2, 28; WLC
See also CA 104; 124; DA3; SATA 90

Chernyshevsky, Nikolay Gavrilovich
1828-1889 .... **NCLC 1**

Cherry, Carolyn Janice 1942-
See Cherryh, C. J.
See also CA 65-68; CANR 10

Cherryh, C. J. .... **CLC 35**
See also Cherry, Carolyn Janice AAYA 24; DLBY 80; SATA 93

Chesnutt, Charles W(addell) 1858-1932
TCLC 5, 39; BLC 1; DAM MULT; SSC 7
See also BW 1, 3; CA 106; 125; CANR 76; DLB 12, 50, 78; MTCW 1, 2

Chester, Alfred 1929(?)-1971 .... **CLC 49**
See also CA 33-36R; DLB 130

Chesterton, G(ilbert) K(eith) 1874-1936
TCLC 1, 6, 64; DAM NOV, POET; PC 28; SSC 1
See also CA 104; 132; CANR 73; CDBLB 1914-1945; DLB 10, 19, 34, 70, 98, 149, 178; MTCW 1, 2; SATA 27

Chiang, Pin-chin 1904-1986
See Ding Ling
See also CA 118

Ch'ien Chung-shu 1910- .... **CLC 22**
See also CA 130; CANR 73; MTCW 1, 2

Child, L. Maria
See Child, Lydia Maria

Child, Lydia Maria 1802-1880 .. **NCLC 6, 73**
See also DLB 1, 74; SATA 67

Child, Mrs.
See Child, Lydia Maria

Child, Philip 1898-1978 .... **CLC 19, 68**
See also CA 13-14; CAP 1; SATA 47

Cooper, J(oan) California (?)- .... **CLC 56; DAM MULT**
See also AAYA 12; BW 1; CA 125; CANR 55; DLB 212

Cooper, James Fenimore
1789-1851 .... **NCLC 1, 27, 54**
See also AAYA 22; CDALB 1640-1865; DA3; DLB 3; SATA 19

Coover, Robert (Lowell) 1932- ...... **CLC 3, 7, 15, 32, 46, 87; DAM NOV; SSC 15**
See also CA 45-48; CANR 3, 37, 58; DLB 2; DLBY 81; MTCW 1, 2

Copeland, Stewart (Armstrong)
1952- .... **CLC 26**

Copernicus, Nicolaus 1473-1543 .... **LC 45**

Coppard, A(lfred) E(dgar)
1878-1957 .... **TCLC 5; SSC 21**
See also CA 114; 167; DLB 162; YABC 1

Coppee, Francois 1842-1908 .... **TCLC 25**
See also CA 170

Coppola, Francis Ford 1939- ... **CLC 16, 126**
See also CA 77-80; CANR 40, 78; DLB 44

Corbiere, Tristan 1845-1875 .... **NCLC 43**

Corcoran, Barbara 1911- .... **CLC 17**
See also AAYA 14; CA 21-24R; CAAS 2; CANR 11, 28; CLR 50; DLB 52; JRDA; SAAS 20; SATA 3, 77

Cordelier, Maurice
See Giraudoux, (Hippolyte) Jean

Corelli, Marie 1855-1924 .... **TCLC 51**
See also Mackay, Mary DLB 34, 156

Corman, Cid 1924- .... **CLC 9**
See also Corman, Sidney CAAS 2; DLB 5, 193

Corman, Sidney 1924-
See Corman, Cid
See also CA 85-88; CANR 44; DAM POET

Cormier, Robert (Edmund) 1925- ... **CLC 12, 30; DA; DAB; DAC; DAM MST, NOV**
See also AAYA 3, 19; CA 1-4R; CANR 5, 23, 76; CDALB 1968-1988; CLR 12, 55; DLB 52; INT CANR-23; JRDA; MAICYA; MTCW 1, 2; SATA 10, 45, 83

Corn, Alfred (DeWitt III) 1943- .... **CLC 33**
See also CA 179; CAAE 179; CAAS 25; CANR 44; DLB 120; DLBY 80

Corneille, Pierre 1606-1684 ..... **LC 28; DAB; DAM MST**

Cornwell, David (John Moore)
1931- .... **CLC 9, 15; DAM POP**
See also le Carre, John CA 5-8R; CANR 13, 33, 59; DA3; MTCW 1, 2

Corso, (Nunzio) Gregory 1930- .... **CLC 1, 11**
See also CA 5-8R; CANR 41, 76; DA3; DLB 5, 16; MTCW 1, 2

Cortazar, Julio 1914-1984 ... **CLC 2, 3, 5, 10, 13, 15, 33, 34, 92; DAM MULT, NOV; HLC 1; SSC 7**
See also CA 21-24R; CANR 12, 32, 81; DA3; DLB 113; HW 1, 2; MTCW 1, 2

CORTES, HERNAN 1484-1547 .... **LC 31**

Corvinus, Jakob
See Raabe, Wilhelm (Karl)

Corwin, Cecil
See Kornbluth, C(yril) M.

Cosic, Dobrica 1921- .... **CLC 14**
See also CA 122; 138; DLB 181

Costain, Thomas B(ertram)
1885-1965 .... **CLC 30**
See also CA 5-8R; 25-28R; DLB 9

Costantini, Humberto 1924(?)-1987 . **CLC 49**
See also CA 131; 122; HW 1

Costello, Elvis 1955- .... **CLC 21**

Costenoble, Philostene
See Ghelderode, Michel de

Cotes, Cecil V.
See Duncan, Sara Jeannette

Cotter, Joseph Seamon Sr.
1861-1949 ...... **TCLC 28; BLC 1; DAM MULT**
See also BW 1; CA 124; DLB 50

Couch, Arthur Thomas Quiller
See Quiller-Couch, SirArthur (Thomas)

Coulton, James
See Hansen, Joseph

Couperus, Louis (Marie Anne) 1863-1923 **TCLC 15**
See also CA 115

Coupland, Douglas 1961- ..... **CLC 85; DAC; DAM POP**
See also CA 142; CANR 57

Court, Wesli
See Turco, Lewis (Putnam)

Courtenay, Bryce 1933- .... **CLC 59**
See also CA 138

Courtney, Robert
See Ellison, Harlan (Jay)

Cousteau, Jacques-Yves 1910-1997 .. **CLC 30**
See also CA 65-68; 159; CANR 15, 67; MTCW 1; SATA 38, 98

Coventry, Francis 1725-1754 .... **LC 46**

Cowan, Peter (Walkinshaw) 1914- .... **SSC 28**
See also CA 21-24R; CANR 9, 25, 50, 83

Coward, Noel (Peirce) 1899-1973 . **CLC 1, 9, 29, 51; DAM DRAM**
See also AITN 1; CA 17-18; 41-44R; CANR 35; CAP 2; CDBLB 1914-1945; DA3; DLB 10; MTCW 1, 2

Cowley, Abraham 1618-1667 .... **LC 43**
See also DLB 131, 151

Cowley, Malcolm 1898-1989 .... **CLC 39**
See also CA 5-8R; 128; CANR 3, 55; DLB 4, 48; DLBY 81, 89; MTCW 1, 2

Cowper, William 1731-1800 . **NCLC 8; DAM POET**
See also DA3; DLB 104, 109

Cox, William Trevor 1928- ... **CLC 9, 14, 71; DAM NOV**
See also Trevor, William CA 9-12R; CANR 4, 37, 55, 76; DLB 14; INT CANR-37; MTCW 1, 2

Coyne, P. J.
See Masters, Hilary

Cozzens, James Gould 1903-1978 . **CLC 1, 4, 11, 92**
See also CA 9-12R; 81-84; CANR 19; CDALB 1941-1968; DLB 9; DLBD 2; DLBY 84, 97; MTCW 1, 2

Crabbe, George 1754-1832 .... **NCLC 26**
See also DLB 93

Craddock, Charles Egbert
See Murfree, Mary Noailles

Craig, A. A.
See Anderson, Poul (William)

Craik, Dinah Maria (Mulock) 1826-1887 **NCLC 38**
See also DLB 35, 163; MAICYA; SATA 34

Cram, Ralph Adams 1863-1942 ..... **TCLC 45**
See also CA 160

Crane, (Harold) Hart 1899-1932 .... **TCLC 2, 5, 80; DA; DAB; DAC; DAM MST, POET; PC 3; WLC**
See also CA 104; 127; CDALB 1917-1929; DA3; DLB 4, 48; MTCW 1, 2

Crane, R(onald) S(almon)
1886-1967 .... **CLC 27**
See also CA 85-88; DLB 63

Crane, Stephen (Townley)
1871-1900 .... **TCLC 11, 17, 32; DA; DAB; DAC; DAM MST, NOV, POET; SSC 7; WLC**
See also AAYA 21; CA 109; 140; CANR 84; CDALB 1865-1917; DA3; DLB 12, 54, 78; YABC 2

Cranshaw, Stanley
See Fisher, Dorothy (Frances) Canfield

Crase, Douglas 1944- .... **CLC 58**
See also CA 106

Crashaw, Richard 1612(?)-1649 .... **LC 24**
See also DLB 126

Craven, Margaret 1901-1980 .... **CLC 17; DAC**
See also CA 103

Crawford, F(rancis) Marion 1854-1909 **TCLC 10**
See also CA 107; 168; DLB 71

Crawford, Isabella Valancy
1850-1887 .... **NCLC 12**
See also DLB 92

Crayon, Geoffrey
See Irving, Washington

Creasey, John 1908-1973 .... **CLC 11**
See also CA 5-8R; 41-44R; CANR 8, 59; DLB 77; MTCW 1

Crebillon, Claude Prosper Jolyot de (fils)
1707-1777 .... **LC 1, 28**

Credo
See Creasey, John

Credo, Alvaro J. de
See Prado (Calvo), Pedro

Creeley, Robert (White) 1926- .. **CLC 1, 2, 4, 8, 11, 15, 36, 78; DAM POET**
See also CA 1-4R; CAAS 10; CANR 23, 43; DA3; DLB 5, 16, 169; DLBD 17; MTCW 1, 2

Crews, Harry (Eugene) 1935- ..... **CLC 6, 23, 49**
See also AITN 1; CA 25-28R; CANR 20, 57; DA3; DLB 6, 143, 185; MTCW 1, 2

Crichton, (John) Michael 1942- .... **CLC 2, 6, 54, 90; DAM NOV, POP**
See also AAYA 10; AITN 2; CA 25-28R; CANR 13, 40, 54, 76; DA3; DLBY 81; INT CANR-13; JRDA; MTCW 1, 2; SATA 9, 88

Crispin, Edmund .... **CLC 22**
See also Montgomery, (Robert) Bruce DLB 87

Cristofer, Michael 1945(?)- ... **CLC 28; DAM DRAM**
See also CA 110; 152; DLB 7

Croce, Benedetto 1866-1952 .... **TCLC 37**
See also CA 120; 155

Crockett, David 1786-1836 .... **NCLC 8**
See also DLB 3, 11

Crockett, Davy
See Crockett, David

Crofts, Freeman Wills 1879-1957 .. **TCLC 55**
See also CA 115; DLB 77

Croker, John Wilson 1780-1857 .... **NCLC 10**
See also DLB 110

Crommelynck, Fernand 1885-1970 .. **CLC 75**
See also CA 89-92

Davies, Rhys 1901-1978 .... **CLC 23**
See also CA 9-12R; 81-84; CANR 4; DLB 139, 191

Davies, (William) Robertson
1913-1995 .... **CLC 2, 7, 13, 25, 42, 75, 91; DA; DAB; DAC; DAM MST, NOV, POP; WLC**
See also BEST 89:2; CA 33-36R; 150; CANR 17, 42; DA3; DLB 68; INT CANR-17; MTCW 1, 2

Davies, Walter C.
See Kornbluth, C(yril) M.

Davies, William Henry 1871-1940 ... **TCLC 5**
See also CA 104; 179; DLB 19, 174

Davis, Angela (Yvonne) 1944- .... **CLC 77; DAM MULT**
See also BW 2, 3; CA 57-60; CANR 10, 81; DA3

Davis, B. Lynch
See Bioy Casares, Adolfo; Borges, Jorge Luis

Davis, B. Lynch
See Bioy Casares, Adolfo

Davis, H(arold) L(enoir) 1894-1960 . **CLC 49**
See also CA 178; 89-92; DLB 9, 206

Davis, Rebecca (Blaine) Harding 1831-1910
TCLC 6; SSC 38
See also CA 104; 179; DLB 74

Davis, Richard Harding
1864-1916 .... **TCLC 24**
See also CA 114; 179; DLB 12, 23, 78, 79, 189; DLBD 13

Davison, Frank Dalby 1893-1970 ..... **CLC 15**
See also CA 116

Davison, Lawrence H.
See Lawrence, D(avid) H(erbert Richards)

Davison, Peter (Hubert) 1928- .... **CLC 28**
See also CA 9-12R; CAAS 4; CANR 3, 43, 84; DLB 5

Davys, Mary 1674-1732 .... **LC 1, 46**
See also DLB 39

Dawson, Fielding 1930- .... **CLC 6**
See also CA 85-88; DLB 130

Dawson, Peter
See Faust, Frederick (Schiller)

Day, Clarence (Shepard, Jr.) 1874-1935
TCLC 25
See also CA 108; DLB 11

Day, Thomas 1748-1789 .... **LC 1**
See also DLB 39; YABC 1

Day Lewis, C(ecil) 1904-1972 . **CLC 1, 6, 10; DAM POET; PC 11**
See also Blake, Nicholas CA 13-16; 33-36R; CANR 34; CAP 1; DLB 15, 20; MTCW 1, 2

Dazai Osamu 1909-1948 .... **TCLC 11**
See also Tsushima, Shuji CA 164; DLB 182

de Andrade, Carlos Drummond 1892-1945
See Drummond de Andrade, Carlos

Deane, Norman
See Creasey, John

Deane, Seamus (Francis) 1940- ...... **CLC 122**
See also CA 118; CANR 42

de Beauvoir, Simone (Lucie Ernestine Marie Bertrand)
See Beauvoir, Simone (Lucie Ernestine Marie Bertrand) de

de Beer, P.
See Bosman, Herman Charles

de Brissac, Malcolm
See Dickinson, Peter (Malcolm)

de Campos, Alvaro
See Pessoa, Fernando (Antonio Nogueira)

de Chardin, Pierre Teilhard
See Teilhard de Chardin, (Marie Joseph) Pierre

Dee, John 1527-1608 .... **LC 20**

Deer, Sandra 1940- .... **CLC 45**

De Ferrari, Gabriella 1941- .... **CLC 65**
See also CA 146

Defoe, Daniel 1660(?)-1731 .... **LC 1, 42; DA; DAB; DAC; DAM MST, NOV; WLC**
See also AAYA 27; CDBLB 1660-1789; CLR 61; DA3; DLB 39, 95, 101; JRDA; MAICYA; SATA 22

de Gourmont, Remy(-Marie-Charles)
See Gourmont, Remy (-Marie-Charles) de

de Hartog, Jan 1914- .... **CLC 19**
See also CA 1-4R; CANR 1

de Hostos, E. M.
See Hostos (y Bonilla), Eugenio Maria de

de Hostos, Eugenio M.
See Hostos (y Bonilla), Eugenio Maria de

Deighton, Len .... **CLC 4, 7, 22, 46**
See also Deighton, Leonard Cyril AAYA 6; BEST 89:2; CDBLB 1960 to Present; DLB 87

Deighton, Leonard Cyril 1929-
See Deighton, Len
See also CA 9-12R; CANR 19, 33, 68; DAM NOV, POP; DA3; MTCW 1, 2

Dekker, Thomas 1572(?)-1632 . **LC 22; DAM DRAM**
See also CDBLB Before 1660; DLB 62, 172

Delafield, E. M. 1890-1943 .... **TCLC 61**
See also Dashwood, Edmee Elizabeth Monica de la Pasture DLB 34

de la Mare, Walter (John)
1873-1956 ..... **TCLC 4, 53; DAB; DAC; DAM MST, POET; SSC 14; WLC**
See also CA 163; CDBLB 1914-1945; CLR 23; DA3; DLB 162; MTCW 1; SATA 16

Delaney, Franey
See O'Hara, John (Henry)

Delaney, Shelagh 1939- .... **CLC 29; DAM DRAM**
See also CA 17-20R; CANR 30, 67; CD-BLB 1960 to Present; DLB 13; MTCW 1

Delany, Mary (Granville Pendarves)
1700-1788 .... **LC 12**

Delany, Samuel R(ay, Jr.) 1942- .. **CLC 8, 14, 38; BLC 1; DAM MULT**
See also AAYA 24; BW 2, 3; CA 81-84; CANR 27, 43; DLB 8, 33; MTCW 1, 2

De La Ramee, (Marie) Louise 1839-1908
See Ouida
See also SATA 20

de la Roche, Mazo 1879-1961 .... **CLC 14**
See also CA 85-88; CANR 30; DLB 68; SATA 64

De La Salle, Innocent
See Hartmann, Sadakichi

Delbanco, Nicholas (Franklin)
1942- .... **CLC 6, 13**
See also CA 17-20R; CAAS 2; CANR 29, 55; DLB 6

del Castillo, Michel 1933- .... **CLC 38**
See also CA 109; CANR 77

Deledda, Grazia (Cosima) 1875(?)-1936
TCLC 23
See also CA 123

Delgado, Abelardo B(arrientos) 1931-
See also CA 131; CAAS 15; DAM MST, MULT; DLB 82; HLC 1; HW 1

Delibes, Miguel .... **CLC 8, 18**
See also Delibes Setien, Miguel

Delibes Setien, Miguel 1920-
See Delibes, Miguel
See also CA 45-48; CANR 1, 32; HW 1; MTCW 1

DeLillo, Don 1936- ..... **CLC 8, 10, 13, 27, 39, 54, 76; DAM NOV, POP**
See also BEST 89:1; CA 81-84; CANR 21, 76; DA3; DLB 6, 173; MTCW 1, 2

de Lisser, H. G.
See De Lisser, H(erbert) G(eorge)
See also DLB 117

De Lisser, H(erbert) G(eorge) 1878-1944
TCLC 12
See also de Lisser, H. G. BW 2; CA 109; 152

Deloney, Thomas 1560(?)-1600 .... **LC 41**
See also DLB 167

Deloria, Vine (Victor), Jr. 1933- ...... **CLC 21, 122; DAM MULT**
See also CA 53-56; CANR 5, 20, 48; DLB 175; MTCW 1; NNAL; SATA 21

Del Vecchio, John M(ichael) 1947- .. **CLC 29**
See also CA 110; DLBD 9

de Man, Paul (Adolph Michel) 1919-1983
CLC 55
See also CA 128; 111; CANR 61; DLB 67; MTCW 1, 2

De Marinis, Rick 1934- .... **CLC 54**
See also CA 57-60; CAAS 24; CANR 9, 25, 50

Dembry, R. Emmet
See Murfree, Mary Noailles

Demby, William 1922- .... **CLC 53; BLC 1; DAM MULT**
See also BW 1, 3; CA 81-84; CANR 81; DLB 33

de Menton, Francisco
See Chin, Frank (Chew, Jr.)

Demetrius of Phalerum c.
307B.C.- .... **CMLC 34**

Demijohn, Thom
See Disch, Thomas M(ichael)

de Molina, Tirso 1580-1648
See also HLCS 2

de Montherlant, Henry (Milon)
See Montherlant, Henry (Milon) de

Demosthenes 384B.C.-322B.C. ...... **CMLC 13**
See also DLB 176

de Natale, Francine
See Malzberg, Barry N(athaniel)

Denby, Edwin (Orr) 1903-1983 .... **CLC 48**
See also CA 138; 110

Denis, Julio
See Cortazar, Julio

Denmark, Harrison
See Zelazny, Roger (Joseph)

Dennis, John 1658-1734 .... **LC 11**
See also DLB 101

Dennis, Nigel (Forbes) 1912-1989 ...... **CLC 8**
See also CA 25-28R; 129; DLB 13, 15; MTCW 1

Dent, Lester 1904(?)-1959 .... **TCLC 72**
See also CA 112; 161

De Palma, Brian (Russell) 1940- ...... **CLC 20**
See also CA 109

De Quincey, Thomas 1785-1859 .... **NCLC 4**
See also CDBLB 1789-1832; DLB 110; 144

Donleavy, J(ames) P(atrick) 1926- .... **CLC 1, 4, 6, 10, 45**
See also AITN 2; CA 9-12R; CANR 24, 49, 62, 80; DLB 6, 173; INT CANR-24; MTCW 1, 2

Donne, John 1572-1631 .... **LC 10, 24; DA; DAB; DAC; DAM MST, POET; PC 1; WLC**
See also CDBLB Before 1660; DLB 121, 151

Donnell, David 1939(?)- .... **CLC 34**

Donoghue, P. S.
See Hunt, E(verette) Howard, (Jr.)

Donoso (Yanez), Jose 1924-1996 ... **CLC 4, 8, 11, 32, 99; DAM MULT; HLC 1; SSC 34**
See also CA 81-84; 155; CANR 32, 73; DLB 113; HW 1, 2; MTCW 1, 2

Donovan, John 1928-1992 .... **CLC 35**
See also AAYA 20; CA 97-100; 137; CLR 3; MAICYA; SATA 72; SATA-Brief 29

Don Roberto
See Cunninghame Graham, R(obert) B(ontine)

Doolittle, Hilda 1886-1961 . **CLC 3, 8, 14, 31, 34, 73; DA; DAC; DAM MST, POET; PC 5; WLC**
See also H. D. CA 97-100; €ANR 35; DLB 4, 45; MTCW 1, 2

Dorfman, Ariel 1942- ...... **CLC 48, 77; DAM MULT; HLC 1**
See also CA 124; 130; CANR 67, 70; HW 1, 2; INT 130

Dorn, Edward (Merton) 1929- ... **CLC 10, 18**
See also CA 93-96; CANR 42, 79; DLB 5; INT 93-96

Dorris, Michael (Anthony)
1945-1997 .... **CLC 109; DAM MULT, NOV**
See also AAYA 20; BEST 90:1; CA 102; 157; CANR 19, 46, 75; CLR 58; DA3; DLB 175; MTCW 2; NNAL; SATA 75; SATA-Obit 94

Dorris, Michael A.
See Dorris, Michael (Anthony)

Dorsan, Luc
See Simenon, Georges (Jacques Christian)

Dorsange, Jean
See Simenon, Georges (Jacques Christian)

Dos Passos, John (Roderigo)
1896-1970 ... **CLC 1, 4, 8, 11, 15, 25, 34, 82; DA; DAB; DAC; DAM MST, NOV; WLC**
See also CA 1-4R; 29-32R; CANR 3; CDALB 1929-1941; DA3; DLB 4, 9; DLBD 1, 15; DLBY 96; MTCW 1, 2

Dossage, Jean
See Simenon, Georges (Jacques Christian)

Dostoevsky, Fedor Mikhailovich 1821-1881
NCLC 2, 7, 21, 33, 43; DA; DAB; DAC; DAM MST, NOV; SSC 2, 33; WLC
See also DA3

Doughty, Charles M(ontagu) 1843-1926
TCLC 27
See also CA 115; 178; DLB 19, 57, 174

Douglas, Ellen .... **CLC 73**
See also Haxton, Josephine Ayres; Williamson, Ellen Douglas

Douglas, Gavin 1475(?)-1522 .... **LC 20**
See also DLB 132

Douglas, George
See Brown, George Douglas

Douglas, Keith (Castellain)
1920-1944 .... **TCLC 40**
See also CA 160; DLB 27

Douglas, Leonard
See Bradbury, Ray (Douglas)

Douglas, Michael
See Crichton, (John) Michael

Douglas, (George) Norman
1868-1952 .... **TCLC 68**
See also CA 119; 157; DLB 34, 195

Douglas, William
See Brown, George Douglas

Douglass, Frederick 1817(?)-1895 .. **NCLC 7, 55; BLC 1; DA; DAC; DAM MST, MULT; WLC**
See also CDALB 1640-1865; DA3; DLB 1, 43, 50, 79; SATA 29

Dourado, (Waldomiro Freitas) Autran 1926-
CLC 23, 60
See also CA 25-28R; 179; CANR 34, 81; DLB 145; HW 2

Dourado, Waldomiro Autran 1926-
See Dourado, (Waldomiro Freitas) Autran
See also CA 179

Dove, Rita (Frances) 1952- .... **CLC 50, 81; BLCS; DAM MULT, POET; PC 6**
See also BW 2; CA 109; CAAS 19; CANR 27, 42, 68, 76; CDALBS; DA3; DLB 120; MTCW 1

Doveglion
See Villa, Jose Garcia

Dowell, Coleman 1925-1985 .... **CLC 60**
See also CA 25-28R; 117; CANR 10; DLB 130

Dowson, Ernest (Christopher) 1867-1900
TCLC 4
See also CA 105; 150; DLB 19, 135

Doyle, A. Conan
See Doyle, Arthur Conan

Doyle, Arthur Conan 1859-1930 .... **TCLC 7; DA; DAB; DAC; DAM MST, NOV; SSC 12; WLC**
See also AAYA 14; CA 104; 122; CDBLB 1890-1914; DA3; DLB 18, 70, 156, 178; MTCW 1, 2; SATA 24

Doyle, Conan
See Doyle, Arthur Conan

Doyle, John
See Graves, Robert (von Ranke)

Doyle, Roddy 1958(?)- .... **CLC 81**
See also AAYA 14; CA 143; CANR 73; DA3; DLB 194

Doyle, Sir A. Conan
See Doyle, Arthur Conan

Doyle, Sir Arthur Conan
See Doyle, Arthur Conan

Dr. A
See Asimov, Isaac; Silverstein, Alvin

Drabble, Margaret 1939- ...... **CLC 2, 3, 5, 8, 10, 22, 53; DAB; DAC; DAM MST, NOV, POP**
See also CA 13-16R; CANR 18, 35, 63; CDBLB 1960 to Present; DA3; DLB 14, 155; MTCW 1, 2; SATA 48

Drapier, M. B.
See Swift, Jonathan

Drayham, James
See Mencken, H(enry) L(ouis)

Drayton, Michael 1563-1631 ..... **LC 8; DAM POET**
See also DLB 121

Dreadstone, Carl
See Campbell, (John) Ramsey

Dreiser, Theodore (Herman Albert)
1871-1945 .... **TCLC 10, 18, 35, 83; DA; DAC; DAM MST, NOV; SSC 30; WLC**
See also CA 106; 132; CDALB 1865-1917; DA3; DLB 9, 12, 102, 137; DLBD 1; MTCW 1, 2

Drexler, Rosalyn 1926- .... **CLC 2, 6**
See also CA 81-84; CANR 68

Dreyer, Carl Theodor 1889-1968 ...... **CLC 16**
See also CA 116

Drieu la Rochelle, Pierre(-Eugene)
1893-1945 .... **TCLC 21**
See also CA 117; DLB 72

Drinkwater, John 1882-1937 .... **TCLC 57**
See also CA 109; 149; DLB 10, 19, 149

Drop Shot
See Cable, George Washington

Droste-Hulshoff, Annette Freiin von
1797-1848 .... **NCLC 3**
See also DLB 133

Drummond, Walter
See Silverberg, Robert

Drummond, William Henry
1854-1907 .... **TCLC 25**
See also CA 160; DLB 92

Drummond de Andrade, Carlos 1902-1987
CLC 18
See also Andrade, Carlos Drummond de CA 132; 123

Drury, Allen (Stuart) 1918-1998 .... **CLC 37**
See also CA 57-60; 170; CANR 18, 52; INT CANR-18

Dryden, John 1631-1700 .... **LC 3, 21; DA; DAB; DAC; DAM DRAM, MST, POET; DC 3; PC 25; WLC**
See also CDBLB 1660-1789; DLB 80, 101, 131

Duberman, Martin (Bauml) 1930- ..... **CLC 8**
See also CA 1-4R; CANR 2, 63

Dubie, Norman (Evans) 1945- .... **CLC 36**
See also CA 69-72; CANR 12; DLB 120

Du Bois, W(illiam) E(dward) B(urghardt)
1868-1963 ... **CLC 1, 2, 13, 64, 96; BLC 1; DA; DAC; DAM MST, MULT, NOV; WLC**
See also BW 1, 3; CA 85-88; CANR 34, 82; CDALB 1865-1917; DA3; DLB 47, 50, 91; MTCW 1, 2; SATA 42

Dubus, Andre 1936-1999 ..... **CLC 13, 36, 97; SSC 15**
See also CA 21-24R; 177; CANR 17; DLB 130; INT CANR-17

Duca Minimo
See D'Annunzio, Gabriele

Ducharme, Rejean 1941- .... **CLC 74**
See also CA 165; DLB 60

Duclos, Charles Pinot 1704-1772 .... **LC 1**

Dudek, Louis 1918- .... **CLC 11, 19**
See also CA 45-48; CAAS 14; CANR 1; DLB 88

Duerrenmatt, Friedrich 1921-1990 ... **CLC 1, 4, 8, 11, 15, 43, 102; DAM DRAM**
See also CA 17-20R; CANR 33; DLB 69, 124; MTCW 1, 2

Duffy, Bruce 1953(?)- .... **CLC 50**
See also CA 172

Duffy, Maureen 1933- .... **CLC 37**
See also CA 25-28R; CANR 33, 68; DLB 14; MTCW 1

Ehrenbourg, Ilya (Grigoryevich)
See Ehrenburg, Ilya (Grigoryevich)
Ehrenburg, Ilya (Grigoryevich) 1891-1967
CLC 18, 34, 62
See also CA 102; 25-28R
Ehrenburg, Ilyo (Grigoryevich)
See Ehrenburg, Ilya (Grigoryevich)
Ehrenreich, Barbara 1941- .... **CLC 110**
See also BEST 90:4; CA 73-76; CANR 16,
37, 62; MTCW 1, 2
Eich, Guenter 1907-1972 .... **CLC 15**
See also CA 111; 93-96; DLB 69, 124
Eichendorff, Joseph Freiherr von 1788-1857
NCLC 8
See also DLB 90
Eigner, Larry .... **CLC 9**
See also Eigner, Laurence (Joel) CAAS 23;
DLB 5
Eigner, Laurence (Joel) 1927-1996
See Eigner, Larry
See also CA 9-12R; 151; CANR 6, 84; DLB
193
Einstein, Albert 1879-1955 .... **TCLC 65**
See also CA 121; 133; MTCW 1, 2
Eiseley, Loren Corey 1907-1977 .... **CLC 7**
See also AAYA 5; CA 1-4R; 73-76; CANR
6; DLBD 17
Eisenstadt, Jill 1963- .... **CLC 50**
See also CA 140
Eisenstein, Sergei (Mikhailovich) 1898-1948
TCLC 57
See also CA 114; 149
Eisner, Simon
See Kornbluth, C(yril) M.
Ekeloef, (Bengt) Gunnar
1907-1968 ... **CLC 27; DAM POET; PC
23**
See also CA 123; 25-28R
Ekelof, (Bengt) Gunnar
See Ekeloef, (Bengt) Gunnar
Ekelund, Vilhelm 1880-1949 .... **TCLC 75**
Ekwensi, C. O. D.
See Ekwensi, Cyprian (Odiatu Duaka)
Ekwensi, Cyprian (Odiatu Duaka) 1921-
CLC 4; BLC 1; DAM MULT
See also BW 2, 3; CA 29-32R; CANR 18,
42, 74; DLB 117; MTCW 1, 2; SATA 66
Elaine .... **TCLC 18**
See also Leverson, Ada
El Crummo
See Crumb, R(obert)
Elder, Lonne III 1931-1996 .... **DC 8**
See also BLC 1; BW 1, 3; CA 81-84; 152;
CANR 25; DAM MULT; DLB 7, 38, 44
Elia
See Lamb, Charles
Eliade, Mircea 1907-1986 .... **CLC 19**
See also CA 65-68; 119; CANR 30, 62;
MTCW 1
Eliot, A. D.
See Jewett, (Theodora) Sarah Orne
Eliot, Alice
See Jewett, (Theodora) Sarah Orne
Eliot, Dan
See Silverberg, Robert
Eliot, George 1819-1880 ...... **NCLC 4, 13, 23,
41, 49; DA; DAB; DAC; DAM MST,
NOV; PC 20; WLC**
See also CDBLB 1832-1890; DA3; DLB
21, 35, 55
Eliot, John 1604-1690 .... **LC 5**
See also DLB 24

Eliot, T(homas) S(tearns)
1888-1965 ...... **CLC 1, 2, 3, 6, 9, 10, 13,
15, 24, 34, 41, 55, 57, 113; DA; DAB;
DAC; DAM DRAM, MST, POET; PC
5; WLC**
See also AAYA 28; CA 5-8R; 25-28R;
CANR 41; CDALB 1929-1941; DA3;
DLB 7, 10, 45, 63; DLBY 88; MTCW 1,
2
Elizabeth 1866-1941 .... **TCLC 41**
Elkin, Stanley L(awrence)
1930-1995 .. **CLC 4, 6, 9, 14, 27, 51, 91;
DAM NOV, POP; SSC 12**
See also CA 9-12R; 148; CANR 8, 46; DLB
2, 28; DLBY 80; INT CANR-8; MTCW
1, 2
Elledge, Scott .... **CLC 34**
Elliot, Don
See Silverberg, Robert
Elliott, Don
See Silverberg, Robert
Elliott, George P(aul) 1918-1980 .... **CLC 2**
See also CA 1-4R; 97-100; CANR 2
Elliott, Janice 1931- .... **CLC 47**
See also CA 13-16R; CANR 8, 29, 84; DLB
14
Elliott, Sumner Locke 1917-1991 ..... **CLC 38**
See also CA 5-8R; 134; CANR 2, 21
Elliott, William
See Bradbury, Ray (Douglas)
Ellis, A. E. .... **CLC 7**
Ellis, Alice Thomas .... **CLC 40**
See also Haycraft, Anna DLB 194; MTCW
1
Ellis, Bret Easton 1964- ..... **CLC 39, 71, 117;
DAM POP**
See also AAYA 2; CA 118; 123; CANR 51,
74; DA3; INT 123; MTCW 1
Ellis, (Henry) Havelock
1859-1939 .... **TCLC 14**
See also CA 109; 169; DLB 190
Ellis, Landon
See Ellison, Harlan (Jay)
Ellis, Trey 1962- .... **CLC 55**
See also CA 146
Ellison, Harlan (Jay) 1934- ... **CLC 1, 13, 42;
DAM POP; SSC 14**
See also AAYA 29; CA 5-8R; CANR 5, 46;
DLB 8; INT CANR-5; MTCW 1, 2
Ellison, Ralph (Waldo) 1914-1994 .... **CLC 1,
3, 11, 54, 86, 114; BLC 1; DA; DAB;
DAC; DAM MST, MULT, NOV; SSC
26; WLC**
See also AAYA 19; BW 1, 3; CA 9-12R;
145; CANR 24, 53; CDALB 1941-1968;
DA3; DLB 2, 76; DLBY 94; MTCW 1, 2
Ellmann, Lucy (Elizabeth) 1956- ..... **CLC 61**
See also CA 128
Ellmann, Richard (David)
1918-1987 .... **CLC 50**
See also BEST 89:2; CA 1-4R; 122; CANR
2, 28, 61; DLB 103; DLBY 87; MTCW
1, 2
Elman, Richard (Martin)
1934-1997 .... **CLC 19**
See also CA 17-20R; 163; CAAS 3; CANR
47
Elron
See Hubbard, L(afayette) Ron(ald)
Eluard, Paul .... **TCLC 7, 41**
See also Grindel, Eugene

Elyot, Sir Thomas 1490(?)-1546 .... **LC 11**
Elytis, Odysseus 1911-1996 .... **CLC 15, 49,
100; DAM POET; PC 21**
See also CA 102; 151; MTCW 1, 2
Emecheta, (Florence Onye) Buchi
1944- .. **CLC 14, 48, 128; BLC 2; DAM
MULT**
See also BW 2, 3; CA 81-84; CANR 27,
81; DA3; DLB 117; MTCW 1, 2; SATA
66
Emerson, Mary Moody
1774-1863 .... **NCLC 66**
Emerson, Ralph Waldo 1803-1882 . **NCLC 1,
38; DA; DAB; DAC; DAM MST,
POET; PC 18; WLC**
See also CDALB 1640-1865; DA3; DLB 1,
59, 73
Eminescu, Mihail 1850-1889 .... **NCLC 33**
Empson, William 1906-1984 ... **CLC 3, 8, 19,
33, 34**
See also CA 17-20R; 112; CANR 31, 61;
DLB 20; MTCW 1, 2
Enchi, Fumiko (Ueda) 1905-1986 ..... **CLC 31**
See also CA 129; 121; DLB 182
Ende, Michael (Andreas Helmuth)
1929-1995 .... **CLC 31**
See also CA 118; 124; 149; CANR 36; CLR
14; DLB 75; MAICYA; SATA 61; SATA-
Brief 42; SATA-Obit 86
Endo, Shusaku 1923-1996 ..... **CLC 7, 14, 19,
54, 99; DAM NOV**
See also CA 29-32R; 153; CANR 21, 54;
DA3; DLB 182; MTCW 1, 2
Engel, Marian 1933-1985 .... **CLC 36**
See also CA 25-28R; CANR 12; DLB 53;
INT CANR-12
Engelhardt, Frederick
See Hubbard, L(afayette) Ron(ald)
Enright, D(ennis) J(oseph) 1920- .. **CLC 4, 8,
31**
See also CA 1-4R; CANR 1, 42, 83; DLB
27; SATA 25
Enzensberger, Hans Magnus
1929- .... **CLC 43; PC 28**
See also CA 116; 119
Ephron, Nora 1941- .... **CLC 17, 31**
See also AITN 2; CA 65-68; CANR 12, 39,
83
Epicurus 341B.C.-270B.C. .... **CMLC 21**
See also DLB 176
Epsilon
See Betjeman, John
Epstein, Daniel Mark 1948- .... **CLC 7**
See also CA 49-52; CANR 2, 53
Epstein, Jacob 1956- .... **CLC 19**
See also CA 114
Epstein, Jean 1897-1953 .... **TCLC 92**
Epstein, Joseph 1937- .... **CLC 39**
See also CA 112; 119; CANR 50, 65
Epstein, Leslie 1938- .... **CLC 27**
See also CA 73-76; CAAS 12; CANR 23,
69
Equiano, Olaudah 1745(?)-1797 .... **LC 16;
BLC 2; DAM MULT**
See also DLB 37, 50
ER .... **TCLC 33**
See also CA 160; DLB 85
Erasmus, Desiderius 1469(?)-1536 ...... **LC 16**
Erdman, Paul E(mil) 1932- .... **CLC 25**
See also AITN 1; CA 61-64; CANR 13, 43,
84

Erdrich, Louise 1954- .... **CLC 39, 54, 120;
DAM MULT, NOV, POP**
See also AAYA 10; BEST 89:1; CA 114;
CANR 41, 62; CDALBS; DA3; DLB 152,
175, 206; MTCW 1; NNAL; SATA 94

Erenburg, Ilya (Grigoryevich)
See Ehrenburg, Ilya (Grigoryevich)

Erickson, Stephen Michael 1950-
See Erickson, Steve
See also CA 129

Erickson, Steve 1950- .... **CLC 64**
See also Erickson, Stephen Michael CANR
60, 68

Ericson, Walter
See Fast, Howard (Melvin)

Eriksson, Buntel
See Bergman, (Ernst) Ingmar

Ernaux, Annie 1940- .... **CLC 88**
See also CA 147

Erskine, John 1879-1951 .... **TCLC 84**
See also CA 112; 159; DLB 9, 102

Eschenbach, Wolfram von
See Wolfram von Eschenbach

Eseki, Bruno
See Mphahlele, Ezekiel

Esenin, Sergei (Alexandrovich) 1895-1925
TCLC 4
See also CA 104

Eshleman, Clayton 1935- .... **CLC 7**
See also CA 33-36R; CAAS 6; DLB 5

Espriella, Don Manuel Alvarez
See Southey, Robert

Espriu, Salvador 1913-1985 .... **CLC 9**
See also CA 154; 115; DLB 134

Espronceda, Jose de 1808-1842 ..... **NCLC 39**

Esquivel, Laura 1951(?)-
See also AAYA 29; CA 143; CANR 68;
DA3; HLCS 1; MTCW 1

Esse, James
See Stephens, James

Esterbrook, Tom
See Hubbard, L(afayette) Ron(ald)

Estleman, Loren D. 1952- ..... **CLC 48; DAM
NOV, POP**
See also AAYA 27; CA 85-88; CANR 27,
74; DA3; INT CANR-27; MTCW 1, 2

Euclid 306B.C.-283B.C. .... **CMLC 25**

Eugenides, Jeffrey 1960(?)- .... **CLC 81**
See also CA 144

Euripides c. 485B.C.-406B.C. .... **CMLC 23;
DA; DAB; DAC; DAM DRAM, MST;
DC 4; WLCS**
See also DA3; DLB 176

Evan, Evin
See Faust, Frederick (Schiller)

Evans, Caradoc 1878-1945 .... **TCLC 85**

Evans, Evan
See Faust, Frederick (Schiller)

Evans, Marian
See Eliot, George

Evans, Mary Ann
See Eliot, George

Evarts, Esther
See Benson, Sally

Everett, Percival L. 1956- .... **CLC 57**
See also BW 2; CA 129

Everson, R(onald) G(ilmour) 1903- . **CLC 27**
See also CA 17-20R; DLB 88

Everson, William (Oliver)
1912-1994 .... **CLC 1, 5, 14**
See also CA 9-12R; 145; CANR 20; DLB
212; MTCW 1

Evtushenko, Evgenii Aleksandrovich
See Yevtushenko, Yevgeny (Alexandrovich)

Ewart, Gavin (Buchanan)
1916-1995 .... **CLC 13, 46**
See also CA 89-92; 150; CANR 17, 46;
DLB 40; MTCW 1

Ewers, Hanns Heinz 1871-1943 ..... **TCLC 12**
See also CA 109; 149

Ewing, Frederick R.
See Sturgeon, Theodore (Hamilton)

Exley, Frederick (Earl) 1929-1992 .... **CLC 6,
11**
See also AITN 2; CA 81-84; 138; DLB 143;
DLBY 81

Eynhardt, Guillermo
See Quiroga, Horacio (Sylvestre)

Ezekiel, Nissim 1924- .... **CLC 61**
See also CA 61-64

Ezekiel, Tish O'Dowd 1943- .... **CLC 34**
See also CA 129

Fadeyev, A.
See Bulgya, Alexander Alexandrovich

Fadeyev, Alexander .... **TCLC 53**
See also Bulgya, Alexander Alexandrovich

Fagen, Donald 1948- .... **CLC 26**

Fainzilberg, Ilya Arnoldovich 1897-1937
See Ilf, Ilya
See also CA 120; 165

Fair, Ronald L. 1932- .... **CLC 18**
See also BW 1; CA 69-72; CANR 25; DLB
33

Fairbairn, Roger
See Carr, John Dickson

Fairbairns, Zoe (Ann) 1948- .... **CLC 32**
See also CA 103; CANR 21, 85

Falco, Gian
See Papini, Giovanni

Falconer, James
See Kirkup, James

Falconer, Kenneth
See Kornbluth, C(yril) M.

Falkland, Samuel
See Heijermans, Herman

Fallaci, Oriana 1930- .... **CLC 11, 110**
See also CA 77-80; CANR 15, 58; MTCW
1

Faludy, George 1913- .... **CLC 42**
See also CA 21-24R

Faludy, Gyoergy
See Faludy, George

Fanon, Frantz 1925-1961 ... **CLC 74; BLC 2;
DAM MULT**
See also BW 1; CA 116; 89-92

Fanshawe, Ann 1625-1680 .... **LC 11**

Fante, John (Thomas) 1911-1983 ..... **CLC 60**
See also CA 69-72; 109; CANR 23; DLB
130; DLBY 83

Farah, Nuruddin 1945- ...... **CLC 53; BLC 2;
DAM MULT**
See also BW 2, 3; CA 106; CANR 81; DLB
125

Fargue, Leon-Paul 1876(?)-1947 .... **TCLC 11**
See also CA 109

Farigoule, Louis
See Romains, Jules

Farina, Richard 1936(?)-1966 .... **CLC 9**
See also CA 81-84; 25-28R

Farley, Walter (Lorimer)
1915-1989 .... **CLC 17**
See also CA 17-20R; CANR 8, 29, 84; DLB
22; JRDA; MAICYA; SATA 2, 43

Farmer, Philip Jose 1918- .... **CLC 1, 19**
See also AAYA 28; CA 1-4R; CANR 4, 35;
DLB 8; MTCW 1; SATA 93

Farquhar, George 1677-1707 ... **LC 21; DAM
DRAM**
See also DLB 84

Farrell, J(ames) G(ordon)
1935-1979 .... **CLC 6**
See also CA 73-76; 89-92; CANR 36; DLB
14; MTCW 1

Farrell, James T(homas) 1904-1979 . **CLC 1,
4, 8, 11, 66; SSC 28**
See also CA 5-8R; 89-92; CANR 9, 61;
DLB 4, 9, 86; DLBD 2; MTCW 1, 2

Farren, Richard J.
See Betjeman, John

Farren, Richard M.
See Betjeman, John

Fassbinder, Rainer Werner
1946-1982 .... **CLC 20**
See also CA 93-96; 106; CANR 31

Fast, Howard (Melvin) 1914- .... **CLC 23;
DAM NOV**
See also AAYA 16; CA 1-4R, 181; CAAE
181; CAAS 18; CANR 1, 33, 54, 75; DLB
9; INT CANR-33; MTCW 1; SATA 7;
SATA-Essay 107

Faulcon, Robert
See Holdstock, Robert P.

Faulkner, William (Cuthbert) 1897-1962
**CLC 1, 3, 6, 8, 9, 11, 14, 18, 28, 52, 68;
DA; DAB; DAC; DAM MST, NOV;
SSC 1, 35; WLC**
See also AAYA 7; CA 81-84; CANR 33;
CDALB 1929-1941; DA3; DLB 9, 11, 44,
102; DLBD 2; DLBY 86, 97; MTCW 1, 2

Fauset, Jessie Redmon
1884(?)-1961 .... **CLC 19, 54; BLC 2;
DAM MULT**
See also BW 1; CA 109; CANR 83; DLB
51

Faust, Frederick (Schiller) 1892-1944(?)
TCLC 49; DAM POP
See also CA 108; 152

Faust, Irvin 1924- .... **CLC 8**
See also CA 33-36R; CANR 28, 67; DLB
2, 28; DLBY 80

Fawkes, Guy
See Benchley, Robert (Charles)

Fearing, Kenneth (Flexner)
1902-1961 .... **CLC 51**
See also CA 93-96; CANR 59; DLB 9

Fecamps, Elise
See Creasey, John

Federman, Raymond 1928- .... **CLC 6, 47**
See also CA 17-20R; CAAS 8; CANR 10,
43, 83; DLBY 80

Federspiel, J(uerg) F. 1931- .... **CLC 42**
See also CA 146

Feiffer, Jules (Ralph) 1929- ..... **CLC 2, 8, 64;
DAM DRAM**
See also AAYA 3; CA 17-20R; CANR 30,
59; DLB 7, 44; INT CANR-30; MTCW
1; SATA 8, 61, 111

Feige, Hermann Albert Otto Maximilian
See Traven, B.

Feinberg, David B. 1956-1994 .... **CLC 59**
See also CA 135; 147

Feinstein, Elaine 1930- .... **CLC 36**
See also CA 69-72; CAAS 1; CANR 31,
68; DLB 14, 40; MTCW 1

Feldman, Irving (Mordecai) 1928- ..... **CLC 7**
See also CA 1-4R; CANR 1; DLB 169

Froude, James Anthony
1818-1894 .... **NCLC 43**
See also DLB 18, 57, 144

Froy, Herald
See Waterhouse, Keith (Spencer)

Fry, Christopher 1907- .... **CLC 2, 10, 14; DAM DRAM**
See also CA 17-20R; CAAS 23; CANR 9, 30, 74; DLB 13; MTCW 1, 2; SATA 66

Frye, (Herman) Northrop
1912-1991 .... **CLC 24, 70**
See also CA 5-8R; 133; CANR 8, 37; DLB 67, 68; MTCW 1, 2

Fuchs, Daniel 1909-1993 .... **CLC 8, 22**
See also CA 81-84; 142; CAAS 5; CANR 40; DLB 9, 26, 28; DLBY 93

Fuchs, Daniel 1934- .... **CLC 34**
See also CA 37-40R; CANR 14, 48

Fuentes, Carlos 1928- .. **CLC 3, 8, 10, 13, 22, 41, 60, 113; DA; DAB; DAC; DAM MST, MULT, NOV; HLC 1; SSC 24; WLC**
See also AAYA 4; AITN 2; CA 69-72; CANR 10, 32, 68; DA3; DLB 113; HW 1, 2; MTCW 1, 2

Fuentes, Gregorio Lopez y
See Lopez y Fuentes, Gregorio

Fuertes, Gloria 1918- .... **PC 27**
See also CA 178, 180; DLB 108; HW 2

Fugard, (Harold) Athol 1932- . **CLC 5, 9, 14, 25, 40, 80; DAM DRAM; DC 3**
See also AAYA 17; CA 85-88; CANR 32, 54; MTCW 1

Fugard, Sheila 1932- .... **CLC 48**
See also CA 125

Fuller, Charles (H., Jr.) 1939- .... **CLC 25; BLC 2; DAM DRAM, MULT; DC 1**
See also BW 2; CA 108; 112; CANR 87; DLB 38; INT 112; MTCW 1

Fuller, John (Leopold) 1937- .... **CLC 62**
See also CA 21-24R; CANR 9, 44; DLB 40

Fuller, Margaret .... **NCLC 5, 50**
See also Fuller, Sarah Margaret

Fuller, Roy (Broadbent) 1912-1991 ... **CLC 4, 28**
See also CA 5-8R; 135; CAAS 10; CANR 53, 83; DLB 15, 20; SATA 87

Fuller, Sarah Margaret 1810-1850
See Fuller, Margaret
See also CDALB 1640-1865; DLB 1, 59, 73, 83

Fulton, Alice 1952- .... **CLC 52**
See also CA 116; CANR 57; DLB 193

Furphy, Joseph 1843-1912 .... **TCLC 25**
See also CA 163

Fussell, Paul 1924- .... **CLC 74**
See also BEST 90:1; CA 17-20R; CANR 8, 21, 35, 69; INT CANR-21; MTCW 1, 2

Futabatei, Shimei 1864-1909 .... **TCLC 44**
See also CA 162; DLB 180

Futrelle, Jacques 1875-1912 .... **TCLC 19**
See also CA 113; 155

Gaboriau, Emile 1835-1873 .... **NCLC 14**

Gadda, Carlo Emilio 1893-1973 .... **CLC 11**
See also CA 89-92; DLB 177

Gaddis, William 1922-1998 ... **CLC 1, 3, 6, 8, 10, 19, 43, 86**
See also CA 17-20R; 172; CANR 21, 48; DLB 2; MTCW 1, 2

Gage, Walter
See Inge, William (Motter)

Gaines, Ernest J(ames) 1933- ...... **CLC 3, 11, 18, 86; BLC 2; DAM MULT**
See also AAYA 18; AITN 1; BW 2, 3; CA 9-12R; CANR 6, 24, 42, 75; CDALB 1968-1988; CLR 62; DA3; DLB 2, 33, 152; DLBY 80; MTCW 1, 2; SATA 86

Gaitskill, Mary 1954- .... **CLC 69**
See also CA 128; CANR 61

Galdos, Benito Perez
See Perez Galdos, Benito

Gale, Zona 1874-1938 .... **TCLC 7; DAM DRAM**
See also CA 105; 153; CANR 84; DLB 9, 78

Galeano, Eduardo (Hughes) 1940- . **CLC 72; HLCS 1**
See also CA 29-32R; CANR 13, 32; HW 1

Galiano, Juan Valera y Alcala
See Valera y Alcala-Galiano, Juan

Galilei, Galileo 1546-1642 .... **LC 45**

Gallagher, Tess 1943- ...... **CLC 18, 63; DAM POET; PC 9**
See also CA 106; DLB 212

Gallant, Mavis 1922- .. **CLC 7, 18, 38; DAC; DAM MST; SSC 5**
See also CA 69-72; CANR 29, 69; DLB 53; MTCW 1, 2

Gallant, Roy A(rthur) 1924- .... **CLC 17**
See also CA 5-8R; CANR 4, 29, 54; CLR 30; MAICYA; SATA 4, 68, 110

Gallico, Paul (William) 1897-1976 ..... **CLC 2**
See also AITN 1; CA 5-8R; 69-72; CANR 23; DLB 9, 171; MAICYA; SATA 13

Gallo, Max Louis 1932- .... **CLC 95**
See also CA 85-88

Gallois, Lucien
See Desnos, Robert

Gallup, Ralph
See Whitemore, Hugh (John)

Galsworthy, John 1867-1933 .... **TCLC 1, 45; DA; DAB; DAC; DAM DRAM, MST, NOV; SSC 22; WLC**
See also CA 104; 141; CANR 75; CDBLB 1890-1914; DA3; DLB 10, 34, 98, 162; DLBD 16; MTCW 1

Galt, John 1779-1839 .... **NCLC 1**
See also DLB 99, 116, 159

Galvin, James 1951- .... **CLC 38**
See also CA 108; CANR 26

Gamboa, Federico 1864-1939 .... **TCLC 36**
See also CA 167; HW 2

Gandhi, M. K.
See Gandhi, Mohandas Karamchand

Gandhi, Mahatma
See Gandhi, Mohandas Karamchand

Gandhi, Mohandas Karamchand 1869-1948 **TCLC 59; DAM MULT**
See also CA 121; 132; DA3; MTCW 1, 2

Gann, Ernest Kellogg 1910-1991 ..... **CLC 23**
See also AITN 1; CA 1-4R; 136; CANR 1, 83

Garcia, Cristina 1958- .... **CLC 76**
See also CA 141; CANR 73; HW 2

Garcia Lorca, Federico 1898-1936 . **TCLC 1, 7, 49; DA; DAB; DAC; DAM DRAM, MST, MULT, POET; DC 2; HLC 2; PC 3; WLC**
See also CA 104; 131; CANR 81; DA3; DLB 108; HW 1, 2; MTCW 1, 2

Garcia Marquez, Gabriel (Jose)
1928- .... **CLC 2, 3, 8, 10, 15, 27, 47, 55, 68; DA; DAB; DAC; DAM MST, MULT, NOV, POP; HLC 1; SSC 8; WLC**
See also AAYA 3; BEST 89:1, 90:4; CA 33-36R; CANR 10, 28, 50, 75, 82; DA3; DLB 113; HW 1, 2; MTCW 1, 2

Garcilaso de la Vega, El Inca 1503-1536
See also HLCS 1

Gard, Janice
See Latham, Jean Lee

Gard, Roger Martin du
See Martin du Gard, Roger

Gardam, Jane 1928- .... **CLC 43**
See also CA 49-52; CANR 2, 18, 33, 54; CLR 12; DLB 14, 161; MAICYA; MTCW 1; SAAS 9; SATA 39, 76; SATA-Brief 28

Gardner, Herb(ert) 1934- .... **CLC 44**
See also CA 149

Gardner, John (Champlin), Jr. 1933-1982 **CLC 2, 3, 5, 7, 8, 10, 18, 28, 34; DAM NOV, POP; SSC 7**
See also AITN 1; CA 65-68; 107; CANR 33, 73; CDALBS; DA3; DLB 2; DLBY 82; MTCW 1; SATA 40; SATA-Obit 31

Gardner, John (Edmund) 1926- ...... **CLC 30; DAM POP**
See also CA 103; CANR 15, 69; MTCW 1

Gardner, Miriam
See Bradley, Marion Zimmer

Gardner, Noel
See Kuttner, Henry

Gardons, S. S.
See Snodgrass, W(illiam) D(e Witt)

Garfield, Leon 1921-1996 .... **CLC 12**
See also AAYA 8; CA 17-20R; 152; CANR 38, 41, 78; CLR 21; DLB 161; JRDA; MAICYA; SATA 1, 32, 76; SATA-Obit 90

Garland, (Hannibal) Hamlin 1860-1940 **TCLC 3; SSC 18**
See also CA 104; DLB 12, 71, 78, 186

Garneau, (Hector de) Saint-Denys 1912-1943 **TCLC 13**
See also CA 111; DLB 88

Garner, Alan 1934- ..... **CLC 17; DAB; DAM POP**
See also AAYA 18; CA 73-76, 178; CAAE 178; CANR 15, 64; CLR 20; DLB 161; MAICYA; MTCW 1, 2; SATA 18, 69; SATA-Essay 108

Garner, Hugh 1913-1979 .... **CLC 13**
See also CA 69-72; CANR 31; DLB 68

Garnett, David 1892-1981 .... **CLC 3**
See also CA 5-8R; 103; CANR 17, 79; DLB 34; MTCW 2

Garos, Stephanie
See Katz, Steve

Garrett, George (Palmer) 1929- .. **CLC 3, 11, 51; SSC 30**
See also CA 1-4R; CAAS 5; CANR 1, 42, 67; DLB 2, 5, 130, 152; DLBY 83

Garrick, David 1717-1779 .... **LC 15; DAM DRAM**
See also DLB 84

Garrigue, Jean 1914-1972 .... **CLC 2, 8**
See also CA 5-8R; 37-40R; CANR 20

Garrison, Frederick
See Sinclair, Upton (Beall)

Garro, Elena 1920(?)-1998
See also CA 131; 169; DLB 145; HLCS 1; HW 1

Glaspell, Susan 1882(?)-1948 . **TCLC 55; DC 10**
   See also CA 110; 154; DLB 7, 9, 78; YABC 2

Glassco, John 1909-1981 .... **CLC 9**
   See also CA 13-16R; 102; CANR 15; DLB 68

Glasscock, Amnesia
   See Steinbeck, John (Ernst)

Glasser, Ronald J. 1940(?)- .... **CLC 37**

Glassman, Joyce
   See Johnson, Joyce

Glendinning, Victoria 1937- .... **CLC 50**
   See also CA 120; 127; CANR 59; DLB 155

Glissant, Edouard 1928- . **CLC 10, 68; DAM MULT**
   See also CA 153

Gloag, Julian 1930- .... **CLC 40**
   See also AITN 1; CA 65-68; CANR 10, 70

Glowacki, Aleksander
   See Prus, Boleslaw

Gluck, Louise (Elisabeth) 1943- .. **CLC 7, 22, 44, 81; DAM POET; PC 16**
   See also CA 33-36R; CANR 40, 69; DA3; DLB 5; MTCW 2

Glyn, Elinor 1864-1943 .... **TCLC 72**
   See also DLB 153

Gobineau, Joseph Arthur (Comte) de 1816-1882 .... **NCLC 17**
   See also DLB 123

Godard, Jean-Luc 1930- .... **CLC 20**
   See also CA 93-96

Godden, (Margaret) Rumer 1907-1998 .... **CLC 53**
   See also AAYA 6; CA 5-8R; 172; CANR 4, 27, 36, 55, 80; CLR 20; DLB 161; MAI-CYA; SAAS 12; SATA 3, 36; SATA-Obit 109

Godoy Alcayaga, Lucila 1889-1957
   See Mistral, Gabriela
   See also BW 2; CA 104; 131; CANR 81; DAM MULT; HW 1, 2; MTCW 1, 2

Godwin, Gail (Kathleen) 1937- ..... **CLC 5, 8, 22, 31, 69, 125; DAM POP**
   See also CA 29-32R; CANR 15, 43, 69; DA3; DLB 6; INT CANR-15; MTCW 1, 2

Godwin, William 1756-1836 .... **NCLC 14**
   See also CDBLB 1789-1832; DLB 39, 104, 142, 158, 163

Goebbels, Josef
   See Goebbels, (Paul) Joseph

Goebbels, (Paul) Joseph 1897-1945 .... **TCLC 68**
   See also CA 115; 148

Goebbels, Joseph Paul
   See Goebbels, (Paul) Joseph

Goethe, Johann Wolfgang von 1749-1832 **NCLC 4, 22, 34; DA; DAB; DAC; DAM DRAM, MST, POET; PC 5; SSC 38; WLC**
   See also DA3; DLB 94

Gogarty, Oliver St. John 1878-1957 .... **TCLC 15**
   See also CA 109; 150; DLB 15, 19

Gogol, Nikolai (Vasilyevich) 1809-1852 **NCLC 5, 15, 31; DA; DAB; DAC; DAM DRAM, MST; DC 1; SSC 4, 29; WLC**
   See also DLB 198

Goines, Donald 1937(?)-1974 . **CLC 80; BLC 2; DAM MULT, POP**
   See also AITN 1; BW 1, 3; CA 124; 114; CANR 82; DA3; DLB 33

Gold, Herbert 1924- .... **CLC 4, 7, 14, 42**
   See also CA 9-12R; CANR 17, 45; DLB 2; DLBY 81

Goldbarth, Albert 1948- .... **CLC 5, 38**
   See also CA 53-56; CANR 6, 40; DLB 120

Goldberg, Anatol 1910-1982 .... **CLC 34**
   See also CA 131; 117

Goldemberg, Isaac 1945- .... **CLC 52**
   See also CA 69-72; CAAS 12; CANR 11, 32; HW 1

Golding, William (Gerald) 1911-1993 ..... **CLC 1, 2, 3, 8, 10, 17, 27, 58, 81; DA; DAB; DAC; DAM MST, NOV; WLC**
   See also AAYA 5; CA 5-8R; 141; CANR 13, 33, 54; CDBLB 1945-1960; DA3; DLB 15, 100; MTCW 1, 2

Goldman, Emma 1869-1940 .... **TCLC 13**
   See also CA 110; 150

Goldman, Francisco 1954- .... **CLC 76**
   See also CA 162

Goldman, William (W.) 1931- ...... **CLC 1, 48**
   See also CA 9-12R; CANR 29, 69; DLB 44

Goldmann, Lucien 1913-1970 .... **CLC 24**
   See also CA 25-28; CAP 2

Goldoni, Carlo 1707-1793 .... **LC 4; DAM DRAM**

Goldsberry, Steven 1949- .... **CLC 34**
   See also CA 131

Goldsmith, Oliver 1728-1774 . **LC 2, 48; DA; DAB; DAC; DAM DRAM, MST, NOV, POET; DC 8; WLC**
   See also CDBLB 1660-1789; DLB 39, 89, 104, 109, 142; SATA 26

Goldsmith, Peter
   See Priestley, J(ohn) B(oynton)

Gombrowicz, Witold 1904-1969 .... **CLC 4, 7, 11, 49; DAM DRAM**
   See also CA 19-20; 25-28R; CAP 2

Gomez de la Serna, Ramon 1888-1963 .... **CLC 9**
   See also CA 153; 116; CANR 79; HW 1, 2

Goncharov, Ivan Alexandrovich 1812-1891 **NCLC 1, 63**

Goncourt, Edmond (Louis Antoine Huot) de 1822-1896 .... **NCLC 7**
   See also DLB 123

Goncourt, Jules (Alfred Huot) de 1830-1870 **NCLC 7**
   See also DLB 123

Gontier, Fernande 19(?)- .... **CLC 50**

Gonzalez Martinez, Enrique 1871-1952 **TCLC 72**
   See also CA 166; CANR 81; HW 1, 2

Goodman, Paul 1911-1972 ..... **CLC 1, 2, 4, 7**
   See also CA 19-20; 37-40R; CANR 34; CAP 2; DLB 130; MTCW 1

Gordimer, Nadine 1923- ...... **CLC 3, 5, 7, 10, 18, 33, 51, 70; DA; DAB; DAC; DAM MST, NOV; SSC 17; WLCS**
   See also CA 5-8R; CANR 3, 28, 56; DA3; INT CANR-28; MTCW 1, 2

Gordon, Adam Lindsay 1833-1870 .... **NCLC 21**

Gordon, Caroline 1895-1981 . **CLC 6, 13, 29, 83; SSC 15**
   See also CA 11-12; 103; CANR 36; CAP 1; DLB 4, 9, 102; DLBD 17; DLBY 81; MTCW 1, 2

Gordon, Charles William 1860-1937
   See Connor, Ralph
   See also CA 109

Gordon, Mary (Catherine) 1949- .... **CLC 13, 22, 128**
   See also CA 102; CANR 44; DLB 6; DLBY 81; INT 102; MTCW 1

Gordon, N. J.
   See Bosman, Herman Charles

Gordon, Sol 1923- .... **CLC 26**
   See also CA 53-56; CANR 4; SATA 11

Gordone, Charles 1925-1995 .... **CLC 1, 4; DAM DRAM; DC 8**
   See also BW 1, 3; CA 93-96, 180; 150; CAAE 180; CANR 55; DLB 7; INT 93-96; MTCW 1

Gore, Catherine 1800-1861 .... **NCLC 65**
   See also DLB 116

Gorenko, Anna Andreevna
   See Akhmatova, Anna

Gorky, Maxim 1868-1936 ..... **TCLC 8; DAB; SSC 28; WLC**
   See also Peshkov, Alexei Maximovich
   MTCW 2

Goryan, Sirak
   See Saroyan, William

Gosse, Edmund (William) 1849-1928 .... **TCLC 28**
   See also CA 117; DLB 57, 144, 184

Gotlieb, Phyllis Fay (Bloom) 1926- .. **CLC 18**
   See also CA 13-16R; CANR 7; DLB 88

Gottesman, S. D.
   See Kornbluth, C(yril) M.; Pohl, Frederik

Gottfried von Strassburg fl. c. 1210- .... **CMLC 10**
   See also DLB 138

Gould, Lois .... **CLC 4, 10**
   See also CA 77-80; CANR 29; MTCW 1

Gourmont, Remy (-Marie-Charles) de 1858-1915 .... **TCLC 17**
   See also CA 109; 150; MTCW 2

Govier, Katherine 1948- .... **CLC 51**
   See also CA 101; CANR 18, 40

Goyen, (Charles) William 1915-1983 .... **CLC 5, 8, 14, 40**
   See also AITN 2; CA 5-8R; 110; CANR 6, 71; DLB 2; DLBY 83; INT CANR-6

Goytisolo, Juan 1931- . **CLC 5, 10, 23; DAM MULT; HLC 1**
   See also CA 85-88; CANR 32, 61; HW 1, 2; MTCW 1, 2

Gozzano, Guido 1883-1916 .... **PC 10**
   See also CA 154; DLB 114

Gozzi, (Conte) Carlo 1720-1806 .... **NCLC 23**

Grabbe, Christian Dietrich 1801-1836 .... **NCLC 2**
   See also DLB 133

Grace, Patricia Frances 1937- .... **CLC 56**
   See also CA 176

Gracian y Morales, Baltasar 1601-1658 .... **LC 15**

Gracq, Julien .... **CLC 11, 48**
   See also Poirier, Louis DLB 83

Grade, Chaim 1910-1982 .... **CLC 10**
   See also CA 93-96; 107

Graduate of Oxford, A
   See Ruskin, John

Grafton, Garth
   See Duncan, Sara Jeannette

Graham, John
   See Phillips, David Graham

Graham, Jorie 1951- .... **CLC 48, 118**
See also CA 111; CANR 63; DLB 120
Graham, R(obert) B(ontine) Cunninghame
See Cunninghame Graham, R(obert)
B(ontine)
See also DLB 98, 135, 174
Graham, Robert
See Haldeman, Joe (William)
Graham, Tom
See Lewis, (Harry) Sinclair
Graham, W(illiam) S(ydney)
1918-1986 .... **CLC 29**
See also CA 73-76; 118; DLB 20
Graham, Winston (Mawdsley)
1910- .... **CLC 23**
See also CA 49-52; CANR 2, 22, 45, 66;
DLB 77
Grahame, Kenneth 1859-1932 ...... **TCLC 64;
DAB**
See also CA 108; 136; CANR 80; CLR 5;
DA3; DLB 34, 141, 178; MAICYA;
MTCW 2; SATA 100; YABC 1
Granovsky, Timofei Nikolaevich 1813-1855
NCLC 75
See also DLB 198
Grant, Skeeter
See Spiegelman, Art
Granville-Barker, Harley
1877-1946 .... **TCLC 2; DAM DRAM**
See also Barker, Harley Granville CA 104
Grass, Guenter (Wilhelm) 1927- ... **CLC 1, 2,
4, 6, 11, 15, 22, 32, 49, 88; DA; DAB;
DAC; DAM MST, NOV; WLC**
See also CA 13-16R; CANR 20, 75; DA3;
DLB 75, 124; MTCW 1, 2
Gratton, Thomas
See Hulme, T(homas) E(rnest)
Grau, Shirley Ann 1929- . **CLC 4, 9; SSC 15**
See also CA 89-92; CANR 22, 69; DLB 2;
INT CANR-22; MTCW 1
Gravel, Fern
See Hall, James Norman
Graver, Elizabeth 1964- .... **CLC 70**
See also CA 135; CANR 71
Graves, Richard Perceval 1945- .... **CLC 44**
See also CA 65-68; CANR 9, 26, 51
Graves, Robert (von Ranke)
1895-1985 ... **CLC 1, 2, 6, 11, 39, 44, 45;
DAB; DAC; DAM MST, POET; PC 6**
See also CA 5-8R; 117; CANR 5, 36; CD-
BLB 1914-1945; DA3; DLB 20, 100, 191;
DLBD 18; DLBY 85; MTCW 1, 2; SATA
45
Graves, Valerie
See Bradley, Marion Zimmer
Gray, Alasdair (James) 1934- .... **CLC 41**
See also CA 126; CANR 47, 69; DLB 194;
INT 126; MTCW 1, 2
Gray, Amlin 1946- .... **CLC 29**
See also CA 138
Gray, Francine du Plessix 1930- ..... **CLC 22;
DAM NOV**
See also BEST 90:3; CA 61-64; CAAS 2;
CANR 11, 33, 75, 81; INT CANR-11;
MTCW 1, 2
Gray, John (Henry) 1866-1934 ...... **TCLC 19**
See also CA 119; 162
Gray, Simon (James Holliday)
1936- .... **CLC 9, 14, 36**
See also AITN 1; CA 21-24R; CAAS 3;
CANR 32, 69; DLB 13; MTCW 1

Gray, Spalding 1941- ..... **CLC 49, 112; DAM
POP; DC 7**
See also CA 128; CANR 74; MTCW 2
Gray, Thomas 1716-1771 .... **LC 4, 40; DA;
DAB; DAC; DAM MST; PC 2; WLC**
See also CDBLB 1660-1789; DA3; DLB
109
Grayson, David
See Baker, Ray Stannard
Grayson, Richard (A.) 1951- .... **CLC 38**
See also CA 85-88; CANR 14, 31, 57
Greeley, Andrew M(oran) 1928- ..... **CLC 28;
DAM POP**
See also CA 5-8R; CAAS 7; CANR 7, 43,
69; DA3; MTCW 1, 2
Green, Anna Katharine
1846-1935 .... **TCLC 63**
See also CA 112; 159; DLB 202
Green, Brian
See Card, Orson Scott
Green, Hannah
See Greenberg, Joanne (Goldenberg)
Green, Hannah 1927(?)-1996 .... **CLC 3**
See also CA 73-76; CANR 59
Green, Henry 1905-1973 .... **CLC 2, 13, 97**
See also Yorke, Henry Vincent CA 175;
DLB 15
Green, Julian (Hartridge) 1900-1998
See Green, Julien
See also CA 21-24R; 169; CANR 33, 87;
DLB 4, 72; MTCW 1
Green, Julien .... **CLC 3, 11, 77**
See also Green, Julian (Hartridge) MTCW
2
Green, Paul (Eliot) 1894-1981 .... **CLC 25;
DAM DRAM**
See also AITN 1; CA 5-8R; 103; CANR 3;
DLB 7, 9; DLBY 81
Greenberg, Ivan 1908-1973
See Rahv, Philip
See also CA 85-88
Greenberg, Joanne (Goldenberg)
1932- .... **CLC 7, 30**
See also AAYA 12; CA 5-8R; CANR 14,
32, 69; SATA 25
Greenberg, Richard 1959(?)- .... **CLC 57**
See also CA 138
Greene, Bette 1934- .... **CLC 30**
See also AAYA 7; CA 53-56; CANR 4; CLR
2; JRDA; MAICYA; SAAS 16; SATA 8,
102
Greene, Gael .... **CLC 8**
See also CA 13-16R; CANR 10
Greene, Graham (Henry)
1904-1991 .... **CLC 1, 3, 6, 9, 14, 18, 27,
37, 70, 72, 125; DA; DAB; DAC; DAM
MST, NOV; SSC 29; WLC**
See also AITN 2; CA 13-16R; 133; CANR
35, 61; CDBLB 1945-1960; DA3; DLB
13, 15, 77, 100, 162, 201, 204; DLBY 91;
MTCW 1, 2; SATA 20
Greene, Robert 1558-1592 .... **LC 41**
See also DLB 62, 167
Greer, Richard
See Silverberg, Robert
Gregor, Arthur 1923- .... **CLC 9**
See also CA 25-28R; CAAS 10; CANR 11;
SATA 36
Gregor, Lee
See Pohl, Frederik
Gregory, Isabella Augusta (Persse)
1852-1932 .... **TCLC 1**
See also CA 104; DLB 10

Gregory, J. Dennis
See Williams, John A(lfred)
Grendon, Stephen
See Derleth, August (William)
Grenville, Kate 1950- .... **CLC 61**
See also CA 118; CANR 53
Grenville, Pelham
See Wodehouse, P(elham) G(renville)
Greve, Felix Paul (Berthold Friedrich)
1879-1948
See Grove, Frederick Philip
See also CA 104; 141, 175; CANR 79;
DAC; DAM MST
Grey, Zane 1872-1939 . **TCLC 6; DAM POP**
See also CA 104; 132; DA3; DLB 212;
MTCW 1, 2
Grieg, (Johan) Nordahl (Brun) 1902-1943
TCLC 10
See also CA 107
Grieve, C(hristopher) M(urray) 1892-1978
CLC 11, 19; DAM POET
See also MacDiarmid, Hugh; Pteleon CA
5-8R; 85-88; CANR 33; MTCW 1
Griffin, Gerald 1803-1840 .... **NCLC 7**
See also DLB 159
Griffin, John Howard 1920-1980 ..... **CLC 68**
See also AITN 1; CA 1-4R; 101; CANR 2
Griffin, Peter 1942- .... **CLC 39**
See also CA 136
Griffith, D(avid Lewelyn) W(ark)
1875(?)-1948 .... **TCLC 68**
See also CA 119; 150; CANR 80
Griffith, Lawrence
See Griffith, D(avid Lewelyn) W(ark)
Griffiths, Trevor 1935- .... **CLC 13, 52**
See also CA 97-100; CANR 45; DLB 13
Griggs, Sutton Elbert
1872-1930(?) .... **TCLC 77**
See also CA 123; DLB 50
Grigson, Geoffrey (Edward Harvey)
1905-1985 .... **CLC 7, 39**
See also CA 25-28R; 118; CANR 20, 33;
DLB 27; MTCW 1, 2
Grillparzer, Franz 1791-1872 .... **NCLC 1;
SSC 37**
See also DLB 133
Grimble, Reverend Charles James
See Eliot, T(homas) S(tearns)
Grimke, Charlotte L(ottie) Forten
1837(?)-1914
See Forten, Charlotte L.
See also BW 1; CA 117; 124; DAM MULT,
POET
Grimm, Jacob Ludwig Karl 1785-1863
NCLC 3, 77; SSC 36
See also DLB 90; MAICYA; SATA 22
Grimm, Wilhelm Karl 1786-1859 .. **NCLC 3,
77; SSC 36**
See also DLB 90; MAICYA; SATA 22
**Grimmelshausen, Johann Jakob Christoffel
von** 1621-1676 .... **LC 6**
See also DLB 168
Grindel, Eugene 1895-1952
See Eluard, Paul
See also CA 104
Grisham, John 1955- .... **CLC 84; DAM POP**
See also AAYA 14; CA 138; CANR 47, 69;
DA3; MTCW 2
Grossman, David 1954- .... **CLC 67**
See also CA 138
Grossman, Vasily (Semenovich) 1905-1964
CLC 41

Hamburger, Michael (Peter Leopold) 1924-
CLC **5, 14**
See also CA 5-8R; CAAS 4; CANR 2, 47;
DLB 27

Hamill, Pete 1935- .... **CLC 10**
See also CA 25-28R; CANR 18, 71

Hamilton, Alexander
1755(?)-1804 .... **NCLC 49**
See also DLB 37

Hamilton, Clive
See Lewis, C(live) S(taples)

Hamilton, Edmond 1904-1977 .... **CLC 1**
See also CA 1-4R; CANR 3, 84; DLB 8

Hamilton, Eugene (Jacob) Lee
See Lee-Hamilton, Eugene (Jacob)

Hamilton, Franklin
See Silverberg, Robert

Hamilton, Gail
See Corcoran, Barbara

Hamilton, Mollie
See Kaye, M(ary) M(argaret)

Hamilton, (Anthony Walter) Patrick
1904-1962 .... **CLC 51**
See also CA 176; 113; DLB 191

Hamilton, Virginia 1936- ...... **CLC 26; DAM
MULT**
See also AAYA 2, 21; BW 2, 3; CA 25-28R;
CANR 20, 37, 73; CLR 1, 11, 40; DLB
33, 52; INT CANR-20; JRDA; MAICYA;
MTCW 1, 2; SATA 4, 56, 79

Hammett, (Samuel) Dashiell
1894-1961 .... **CLC 3, 5, 10, 19, 47; SSC
17**
See also AITN 1; CA 81-84; CANR 42;
CDALB 1929-1941; DA3; DLBD 6;
DLBY 96; MTCW 1, 2

Hammon, Jupiter 1711(?)-1800(?) . **NCLC 5;
BLC 2; DAM MULT, POET; PC 16**
See also DLB 31, 50

Hammond, Keith
See Kuttner, Henry

Hamner, Earl (Henry), Jr. 1923- ...... **CLC 12**
See also AITN 2; CA 73-76; DLB 6

Hampton, Christopher (James)
1946- .... **CLC 4**
See also CA 25-28R; DLB 13; MTCW 1

Hamsun, Knut .... **TCLC 2, 14, 49**
See also Pedersen, Knut

Handke, Peter 1942- ... **CLC 5, 8, 10, 15, 38;
DAM DRAM, NOV**
See also CA 77-80; CANR 33, 75; DLB 85,
124; MTCW 1, 2

Handy, W(illiam) C(hristopher) 1873-1958
TCLC 97
See also BW 3; CA 121; 167

Hanley, James 1901-1985 ..... **CLC 3, 5, 8, 13**
See also CA 73-76; 117; CANR 36; DLB
191; MTCW 1

Hannah, Barry 1942- .... **CLC 23, 38, 90**
See also CA 108; 110; CANR 43, 68; DLB
6; INT 110; MTCW 1

Hannon, Ezra
See Hunter, Evan

Hansberry, Lorraine (Vivian) 1930-1965
**CLC 17, 62; BLC 2; DA; DAB; DAC;
DAM DRAM, MST, MULT; DC 2**
See also AAYA 25; BW 1, 3; CA 109; 25-
28R; CABS 3; CANR 58; CDALB 1941-
1968; DA3; DLB 7, 38; MTCW 1, 2

Hansen, Joseph 1923- .... **CLC 38**
See also CA 29-32R; CAAS 17; CANR 16,
44, 66; INT CANR-16

Hansen, Martin A(lfred)
1909-1955 .... **TCLC 32**
See also CA 167

Hanson, Kenneth O(stlin) 1922- .... **CLC 13**
See also CA 53-56; CANR 7

Hardwick, Elizabeth (Bruce)
1916- .... **CLC 13; DAM NOV**
See also CA 5-8R; CANR 3, 32, 70; DA3;
DLB 6; MTCW 1, 2

Hardy, Thomas 1840-1928 .. **TCLC 4, 10, 18,
32, 48, 53, 72; DA; DAB; DAC; DAM
MST, NOV, POET; PC 8; SSC 2; WLC**
See also CA 104; 123; CDBLB 1890-1914;
DA3; DLB 18, 19, 135; MTCW 1, 2

Hare, David 1947- .... **CLC 29, 58**
See also CA 97-100; CANR 39; DLB 13;
MTCW 1

Harewood, John
See Van Druten, John (William)

Harford, Henry
See Hudson, W(illiam) H(enry)

Hargrave, Leonie
See Disch, Thomas M(ichael)

Harjo, Joy 1951- ...... **CLC 83; DAM MULT;
PC 27**
See also CA 114; CANR 35, 67; DLB 120,
175; MTCW 2; NNAL

Harlan, Louis R(udolph) 1922- .... **CLC 34**
See also CA 21-24R; CANR 25, 55, 80

Harling, Robert 1951(?)- .... **CLC 53**
See also CA 147

Harmon, William (Ruth) 1938- .... **CLC 38**
See also CA 33-36R; CANR 14, 32, 35;
SATA 65

Harper, F. E. W.
See Harper, Frances Ellen Watkins

Harper, Frances E. W.
See Harper, Frances Ellen Watkins

Harper, Frances E. Watkins
See Harper, Frances Ellen Watkins

Harper, Frances Ellen
See Harper, Frances Ellen Watkins

Harper, Frances Ellen Watkins 1825-1911
**TCLC 14; BLC 2; DAM MULT, POET;
PC 21**
See also BW 1, 3; CA 111; 125; CANR 79;
DLB 50

Harper, Michael S(teven) 1938- ... **CLC 7, 22**
See also BW 1; CA 33-36R; CANR 24;
DLB 41

Harper, Mrs. F. E. W.
See Harper, Frances Ellen Watkins

Harris, Christie (Lucy) Irwin
1907- .... **CLC 12**
See also CA 5-8R; CANR 6, 83; CLR 47;
DLB 88; JRDA; MAICYA; SAAS 10;
SATA 6, 74

Harris, Frank 1856-1931 .... **TCLC 24**
See also CA 109; 150; CANR 80; DLB 156,
197

Harris, George Washington
1814-1869 .... **NCLC 23**
See also DLB 3, 11

Harris, Joel Chandler 1848-1908 ... **TCLC 2;
SSC 19**
See also CA 104; 137; CANR 80; CLR 49;
DLB 11, 23, 42, 78, 91; MAICYA; SATA
100; YABC 1

**Harris, John (Wyndham Parkes Lucas)
Beynon** 1903-1969
See Wyndham, John
See also CA 102; 89-92; CANR 84

Harris, MacDonald .... **CLC 9**
See also Heiney, Donald (William)

Harris, Mark 1922- .... **CLC 19**
See also CA 5-8R; CAAS 3; CANR 2, 55,
83; DLB 2; DLBY 80

Harris, (Theodore) Wilson 1921- ..... **CLC 25**
See also BW 2, 3; CA 65-68; CAAS 16;
CANR 11, 27, 69; DLB 117; MTCW 1

Harrison, Elizabeth Cavanna 1909-
See Cavanna, Betty
See also CA 9-12R; CANR 6, 27, 85

Harrison, Harry (Max) 1925- .... **CLC 42**
See also CA 1-4R; CANR 5, 21, 84; DLB
8; SATA 4

Harrison, James (Thomas) 1937- ...... **CLC 6,
14, 33, 66; SSC 19**
See also CA 13-16R; CANR 8, 51, 79;
DLBY 82; INT CANR-8

Harrison, Jim
See Harrison, James (Thomas)

Harrison, Kathryn 1961- .... **CLC 70**
See also CA 144; CANR 68

Harrison, Tony 1937- .... **CLC 43**
See also CA 65-68; CANR 44; DLB 40;
MTCW 1

Harriss, Will(ard Irvin) 1922- .... **CLC 34**
See also CA 111

Harson, Sley
See Ellison, Harlan (Jay)

Hart, Ellis
See Ellison, Harlan (Jay)

Hart, Josephine 1942(?)- .... **CLC 70; DAM
POP**
See also CA 138; CANR 70

Hart, Moss 1904-1961 .... **CLC 66; DAM
DRAM**
See also CA 109; 89-92; CANR 84; DLB 7

Harte, (Francis) Bret(t)
1836(?)-1902 ... **TCLC 1, 25; DA; DAC;
DAM MST; SSC 8; WLC**
See also CA 104; 140; CANR 80; CDALB
1865-1917; DA3; DLB 12, 64, 74, 79,
186; SATA 26

Hartley, L(eslie) P(oles) 1895-1972 ... **CLC 2,
22**
See also CA 45-48; 37-40R; CANR 33;
DLB 15, 139; MTCW 1, 2

Hartman, Geoffrey H. 1929- .... **CLC 27**
See also CA 117; 125; CANR 79; DLB 67

Hartmann, Eduard von
1842-1906 .... **TCLC 97**

Hartmann, Sadakichi 1867-1944 ... **TCLC 73**
See also CA 157; DLB 54

Hartmann von Aue c. 1160-c.
1205 .... **CMLC 15**
See also DLB 138

Hartmann von Aue 1170-1210 ...... **CMLC 15**

Haruf, Kent 1943- .... **CLC 34**
See also CA 149

Harwood, Ronald 1934- .... **CLC 32; DAM
DRAM, MST**
See also CA 1-4R; CANR 4, 55; DLB 13

Hasegawa Tatsunosuke
See Futabatei, Shimei

Hasek, Jaroslav (Matej Frantisek)
1883-1923 .... **TCLC 4**
See also CA 104; 129; MTCW 1, 2

Hass, Robert 1941- ... **CLC 18, 39, 99; PC 16**
See also CA 111; CANR 30, 50, 71; DLB
105, 206; SATA 94

Hastings, Hudson
See Kuttner, Henry

Heppenstall, (John) Rayner
1911-1981 .... **CLC 10**
See also CA 1-4R; 103; CANR 29

Heraclitus c. 540B.C.-c. 450B.C. ... **CMLC 22**
See also DLB 176

Herbert, Frank (Patrick)
1920-1986 .... **CLC 12, 23, 35, 44, 85;
DAM POP**
See also AAYA 21; CA 53-56; 118; CANR
5, 43; CDALBS; DLB 8; INT CANR-5;
MTCW 1, 2; SATA 9, 37; SATA-Obit 47

Herbert, George 1593-1633 ..... **LC 24; DAB;
DAM POET; PC 4**
See also CDBLB Before 1660; DLB 126

Herbert, Zbigniew 1924-1998 ..... **CLC 9, 43;
DAM POET**
See also CA 89-92; 169; CANR 36, 74;
MTCW 1

Herbst, Josephine (Frey)
1897-1969 .... **CLC 34**
See also CA 5-8R; 25-28R; DLB 9

Heredia, Jose Maria 1803-1839
See also HLCS 2

Hergesheimer, Joseph 1880-1954 ... **TCLC 11**
See also CA 109; DLB 102, 9

Herlihy, James Leo 1927-1993 .... **CLC 6**
See also CA 1-4R; 143; CANR 2

Hermogenes fl. c. 175- .... **CMLC 6**

Hernandez, Jose 1834-1886 .... **NCLC 17**

Herodotus c. 484B.C.-429B.C. .... **CMLC 17**
See also DLB 176

Herrick, Robert 1591-1674 .... **LC 13; DA;
DAB; DAC; DAM MST, POP; PC 9**
See also DLB 126

Herring, Guilles
See Somerville, Edith

Herriot, James 1916-1995 ..... **CLC 12; DAM
POP**
See also Wight, James Alfred AAYA 1; CA
148; CANR 40; MTCW 2; SATA 86

Herrmann, Dorothy 1941- .... **CLC 44**
See also CA 107

Herrmann, Taffy
See Herrmann, Dorothy

Hersey, John (Richard) 1914-1993 .... **CLC 1,
2, 7, 9, 40, 81, 97; DAM POP**
See also AAYA 29; CA 17-20R; 140; CANR
33; CDALBS; DLB 6, 185; MTCW 1, 2;
SATA 25; SATA-Obit 76

Herzen, Aleksandr Ivanovich 1812-1870
NCLC 10, 61

Herzl, Theodor 1860-1904 .... **TCLC 36**
See also CA 168

Herzog, Werner 1942- .... **CLC 16**
See also CA 89-92

Hesiod c. 8th cent. B.C.- .... **CMLC 5**
See also DLB 176

Hesse, Hermann 1877-1962 ... **CLC 1, 2, 3, 6,
11, 17, 25, 69; DA; DAB; DAC; DAM
MST, NOV; SSC 9; WLC**
See also CA 17-18; CAP 2; DA3; DLB 66;
MTCW 1, 2; SATA 50

Hewes, Cady
See De Voto, Bernard (Augustine)

Heyen, William 1940- .... **CLC 13, 18**
See also CA 33-36R; CAAS 9; DLB 5

Heyerdahl, Thor 1914- .... **CLC 26**
See also CA 5-8R; CANR 5, 22, 66, 73;
MTCW 1, 2; SATA 2, 52

Heym, Georg (Theodor Franz Arthur)
1887-1912 .... **TCLC 9**
See also CA 106; 181

Heym, Stefan 1913- .... **CLC 41**
See also CA 9-12R; CANR 4; DLB 69

Heyse, Paul (Johann Ludwig von) 1830-1914
TCLC 8
See also CA 104; DLB 129

Heyward, (Edwin) DuBose
1885-1940 .... **TCLC 59**
See also CA 108; 157; DLB 7, 9, 45; SATA
21

Hibbert, Eleanor Alice Burford 1906-1993
CLC 7; DAM POP
See also BEST 90:4; CA 17-20R; 140;
CANR 9, 28, 59; MTCW 2; SATA 2;
SATA-Obit 74

Hichens, Robert (Smythe)
1864-1950 .... **TCLC 64**
See also CA 162; DLB 153

Higgins, George V(incent) 1939- ... **CLC 4, 7,
10, 18**
See also CA 77-80; CAAS 5; CANR 17,
51; DLB 2; DLBY 81, 98; INT CANR-
17; MTCW 1

Higginson, Thomas Wentworth 1823-1911
TCLC 36
See also CA 162; DLB 1, 64

Highet, Helen
See MacInnes, Helen (Clark)

Highsmith, (Mary) Patricia
1921-1995 .... **CLC 2, 4, 14, 42, 102;
DAM NOV, POP**
See also CA 1-4R; 147; CANR 1, 20, 48,
62; DA3; MTCW 1, 2

Highwater, Jamake (Mamake)
1942(?)- .... **CLC 12**
See also AAYA 7; CA 65-68; CAAS 7;
CANR 10, 34, 84; CLR 17; DLB 52;
DLBY 85; JRDA; MAICYA; SATA 32,
69; SATA-Brief 30

Highway, Tomson 1951- .... **CLC 92; DAC;
DAM MULT**
See also CA 151; CANR 75; MTCW 2;
NNAL

Higuchi, Ichiyo 1872-1896 .... **NCLC 49**

Hijuelos, Oscar 1951- .... **CLC 65; DAM
MULT, POP; HLC 1**
See also AAYA 25; BEST 90:1; CA 123;
CANR 50, 75; DA3; DLB 145; HW 1, 2;
MTCW 2

Hikmet, Nazim 1902(?)-1963 .... **CLC 40**
See also CA 141; 93-96

Hildegard von Bingen 1098-1179 . **CMLC 20**
See also DLB 148

Hildesheimer, Wolfgang 1916-1991 .. **CLC 49**
See also CA 101; 135; DLB 69, 124

Hill, Geoffrey (William) 1932- ...... **CLC 5, 8,
18, 45; DAM POET**
See also CA 81-84; CANR 21; CDBLB
1960 to Present; DLB 40; MTCW 1

Hill, George Roy 1921- .... **CLC 26**
See also CA 110; 122

Hill, John
See Koontz, Dean R(ay)

Hill, Susan (Elizabeth) 1942- .... **CLC 4, 113;
DAB; DAM MST, NOV**
See also CA 33-36R; CANR 29, 69; DLB
14, 139; MTCW 1

Hillerman, Tony 1925- . **CLC 62; DAM POP**
See also AAYA 6; BEST 89:1; CA 29-32R;
CANR 21, 42, 65; DA3; DLB 206; SATA
6

Hillesum, Etty 1914-1943 .... **TCLC 49**
See also CA 137

Hilliard, Noel (Harvey) 1929- .... **CLC 15**
See also CA 9-12R; CANR 7, 69

Hillis, Rick 1956- .... **CLC 66**
See also CA 134

Hilton, James 1900-1954 .... **TCLC 21**
See also CA 108; 169; DLB 34, 77; SATA
34

Himes, Chester (Bomar) 1909-1984 .. **CLC 2,
4, 7, 18, 58, 108; BLC 2; DAM MULT**
See also BW 2; CA 25-28R; 114; CANR
22; DLB 2, 76, 143; MTCW 1, 2

Hinde, Thomas .... **CLC 6, 11**
See also Chitty, Thomas Willes

Hine, (William) Daryl 1936- .... **CLC 15**
See also CA 1-4R; CAAS 15; CANR 1, 20;
DLB 60

Hinkson, Katharine Tynan
See Tynan, Katharine

Hinojosa(-Smith), Rolando (R.) 1929-
See Hinojosa-Smith, Rolando
See also CA 131; CAAS 16; CANR 62;
DAM MULT; DLB 82; HLC 1; HW 1, 2;
MTCW 2

Hinojosa-Smith, Rolando 1929-
See Hinojosa(-Smith), Rolando (R.)
See also CAAS 16; HLC 1; MTCW 2

Hinton, S(usan) E(loise) 1950- .... **CLC 30,
111; DA; DAB; DAC; DAM MST,
NOV**
See also AAYA 2; CA 81-84; CANR 32,
62; CDALBS; CLR 3, 23; DA3; JRDA;
MAICYA; MTCW 1, 2; SATA 19, 58

Hippius, Zinaida .... **TCLC 9**
See also Gippius, Zinaida (Nikolayevna)

Hiraoka, Kimitake 1925-1970
See Mishima, Yukio
See also CA 97-100; 29-32R; DAM DRAM;
DA3; MTCW 1, 2

Hirsch, E(ric) D(onald), Jr. 1928- .... **CLC 79**
See also CA 25-28R; CANR 27, 51; DLB
67; INT CANR-27; MTCW 1

Hirsch, Edward 1950- .... **CLC 31, 50**
See also CA 104; CANR 20, 42; DLB 120

Hitchcock, Alfred (Joseph)
1899-1980 .... **CLC 16**
See also AAYA 22; CA 159; 97-100; SATA
27; SATA-Obit 24

Hitler, Adolf 1889-1945 .... **TCLC 53**
See also CA 117; 147

Hoagland, Edward 1932- .... **CLC 28**
See also CA 1-4R; CANR 2, 31, 57; DLB
6; SATA 51

Hoban, Russell (Conwell) 1925- . **CLC 7, 25;
DAM NOV**
See also CA 5-8R; CANR 23, 37, 66; CLR
3; DLB 52; MAICYA; MTCW 1, 2; SATA
1, 40, 78

Hobbes, Thomas 1588-1679 .... **LC 36**
See also DLB 151

Hobbs, Perry
See Blackmur, R(ichard) P(almer)

Hobson, Laura Z(ametkin)
1900-1986 .... **CLC 7, 25**
See also CA 17-20R; 118; CANR 55; DLB
28; SATA 52

Hochhuth, Rolf 1931- .. **CLC 4, 11, 18; DAM
DRAM**
See also CA 5-8R; CANR 33, 75; DLB 124;
MTCW 1, 2

Hochman, Sandra 1936- .... **CLC 3, 8**
See also CA 5-8R; DLB 5

Hochwaelder, Fritz 1911-1986 .... **CLC 36; DAM DRAM**
See also CA 29-32R; 120; CANR 42; MTCW 1

Hochwalder, Fritz
See Hochwaelder, Fritz

Hocking, Mary (Eunice) 1921- .... **CLC 13**
See also CA 101; CANR 18, 40

Hodgins, Jack 1938- .... **CLC 23**
See also CA 93-96; DLB 60

Hodgson, William Hope
1877(?)-1918 .... **TCLC 13**
See also CA 111; 164; DLB 70, 153, 156, 178; MTCW 2

Hoeg, Peter 1957- .... **CLC 95**
See also CA 151; CANR 75; DA3; MTCW 2

Hoffman, Alice 1952- ... **CLC 51; DAM NOV**
See also CA 77-80; CANR 34, 66; MTCW 1, 2

Hoffman, Daniel (Gerard) 1923- . **CLC 6, 13, 23**
See also CA 1-4R; CANR 4; DLB 5

Hoffman, Stanley 1944- .... **CLC 5**
See also CA 77-80

Hoffman, William M(oses) 1939- ..... **CLC 40**
See also CA 57-60; CANR 11, 71

Hoffmann, E(rnst) T(heodor) A(madeus)
1776-1822 .... **NCLC 2; SSC 13**
See also DLB 90; SATA 27

Hofmann, Gert 1931- .... **CLC 54**
See also CA 128

Hofmannsthal, Hugo von
1874-1929 ...... **TCLC 11; DAM DRAM; DC 4**
See also CA 106; 153; DLB 81, 118

Hogan, Linda 1947- .. **CLC 73; DAM MULT**
See also CA 120; CANR 45, 73; DLB 175; NNAL

Hogarth, Charles
See Creasey, John

Hogarth, Emmett
See Polonsky, Abraham (Lincoln)

Hogg, James 1770-1835 .... **NCLC 4**
See also DLB 93, 116, 159

Holbach, Paul Henri Thiry Baron 1723-1789 **LC 14**

Holberg, Ludvig 1684-1754 .... **LC 6**

Holden, Ursula 1921- .... **CLC 18**
See also CA 101; CAAS 8; CANR 22

Holderlin, (Johann Christian) Friedrich
1770-1843 .... **NCLC 16; PC 4**

Holdstock, Robert
See Holdstock, Robert P.

Holdstock, Robert P. 1948- .... **CLC 39**
See also CA 131; CANR 81

Holland, Isabelle 1920- .... **CLC 21**
See also AAYA 11; CA 21-24R, 181; CAAE 181; CANR 10, 25, 47; CLR 57; JRDA; MAICYA; SATA 8, 70; SATA-Essay 103

Holland, Marcus
See Caldwell, (Janet Miriam) Taylor (Holland)

Hollander, John 1929- .... **CLC 2, 5, 8, 14**
See also CA 1-4R; CANR 1, 52; DLB 5; SATA 13

Hollander, Paul
See Silverberg, Robert

Holleran, Andrew 1943(?)- .... **CLC 38**
See also CA 144

Holley, Marietta 1836(?)-1926 ...... **TCLC 100**
See also CA 118; DLB 11

Hollinghurst, Alan 1954- .... **CLC 55, 91**
See also CA 114; DLB 207

Hollis, Jim
See Summers, Hollis (Spurgeon, Jr.)

Holly, Buddy 1936-1959 .... **TCLC 65**

Holmes, Gordon
See Shiel, M(atthew) P(hipps)

Holmes, John
See Souster, (Holmes) Raymond

Holmes, John Clellon 1926-1988 ...... **CLC 56**
See also CA 9-12R; 125; CANR 4; DLB 16

Holmes, Oliver Wendell, Jr.
1841-1935 .... **TCLC 77**
See also CA 114

Holmes, Oliver Wendell
1809-1894 .... **NCLC 14, 81**
See also CDALB 1640-1865; DLB 1, 189; SATA 34

Holmes, Raymond
See Souster, (Holmes) Raymond

Holt, Victoria
See Hibbert, Eleanor Alice Burford

Holub, Miroslav 1923-1998 .... **CLC 4**
See also CA 21-24R; 169; CANR 10

Homer c. 8th cent. B.C.- .. **CMLC 1, 16; DA; DAB; DAC; DAM MST, POET; PC 23; WLCS**
See also DA3; DLB 176

Hongo, Garrett Kaoru 1951- .... **PC 23**
See also CA 133; CAAS 22; DLB 120

Honig, Edwin 1919- .... **CLC 33**
See also CA 5-8R; CAAS 8; CANR 4, 45; DLB 5

Hood, Hugh (John Blagdon) 1928- . **CLC 15, 28**
See also CA 49-52; CAAS 17; CANR 1, 33, 87; DLB 53

Hood, Thomas 1799-1845 .... **NCLC 16**
See also DLB 96

Hooker, (Peter) Jeremy 1941- .... **CLC 43**
See also CA 77-80; CANR 22; DLB 40

hooks, bell .... **CLC 94; BLCS**
See also Watkins, Gloria Jean MTCW 2

Hope, A(lec) D(erwent) 1907- .... **CLC 3, 51**
See also CA 21-24R; CANR 33, 74; MTCW 1, 2

Hope, Anthony 1863-1933 .... **TCLC 83**
See also CA 157; DLB 153, 156

Hope, Brian
See Creasey, John

Hope, Christopher (David Tully)
1944- .... **CLC 52**
See also CA 106; CANR 47; SATA 62

Hopkins, Gerard Manley
1844-1889 .... **NCLC 17; DA; DAB; DAC; DAM MST, POET; PC 15; WLC**
See also CDBLB 1890-1914; DA3; DLB 35, 57

Hopkins, John (Richard) 1931-1998 .. **CLC 4**
See also CA 85-88; 169

Hopkins, Pauline Elizabeth
1859-1930 ...... **TCLC 28; BLC 2; DAM MULT**
See also BW 2, 3; CA 141; CANR 82; DLB 50

Hopkinson, Francis 1737-1791 .... **LC 25**
See also DLB 31

Hopley-Woolrich, Cornell George 1903-1968
See Woolrich, Cornell
See also CA 13-14; CANR 58; CAP 1; MTCW 2

Horatio
See Proust, (Valentin-Louis-George-Eugene-) Marcel

Horgan, Paul (George Vincent O'Shaughnessy) 1903-1995 . **CLC 9, 53; DAM NOV**
See also CA 13-16R; 147; CANR 9, 35; DLB 212; DLBY 85; INT CANR-9; MTCW 1, 2; SATA 13; SATA-Obit 84

Horn, Peter
See Kuttner, Henry

Hornem, Horace Esq.
See Byron, George Gordon (Noel)

Horney, Karen (Clementine Theodore Danielsen) 1885-1952 .... **TCLC 71**
See also CA 114; 165

Hornung, E(rnest) W(illiam) 1866-1921 **TCLC 59**
See also CA 108; 160; DLB 70

Horovitz, Israel (Arthur) 1939- ...... **CLC 56; DAM DRAM**
See also CA 33-36R; CANR 46, 59; DLB 7

Horvath, Odon von
See Horvath, Oedoen von
See also DLB 85, 124

Horvath, Oedoen von 1901-1938 ... **TCLC 45**
See also Horvath, Odon von CA 118

Horwitz, Julius 1920-1986 .... **CLC 14**
See also CA 9-12R; 119; CANR 12

Hospital, Janette Turner 1942- .... **CLC 42**
See also CA 108; CANR 48

Hostos, E. M. de
See Hostos (y Bonilla), Eugenio Maria de

Hostos, Eugenio M. de
See Hostos (y Bonilla), Eugenio Maria de

Hostos, Eugenio Maria
See Hostos (y Bonilla), Eugenio Maria de

Hostos (y Bonilla), Eugenio Maria de
1839-1903 .... **TCLC 24**
See also CA 123; 131; HW 1

Houdini
See Lovecraft, H(oward) P(hillips)

Hougan, Carolyn 1943- .... **CLC 34**
See also CA 139

Household, Geoffrey (Edward West)
1900-1988 .... **CLC 11**
See also CA 77-80; 126; CANR 58; DLB 87; SATA 14; SATA-Obit 59

Housman, A(lfred) E(dward) 1859-1936
TCLC 1, 10; DA; DAB; DAC; DAM MST, POET; PC 2; WLCS
See also CA 104; 125; DA3; DLB 19; MTCW 1, 2

Housman, Laurence 1865-1959 .... **TCLC 7**
See also CA 106; 155; DLB 10; SATA 25

Howard, Elizabeth Jane 1923- ..... **CLC 7, 29**
See also CA 5-8R; CANR 8, 62

Howard, Maureen 1930- .... **CLC 5, 14, 46**
See also CA 53-56; CANR 31, 75; DLBY 83; INT CANR-31; MTCW 1, 2

Howard, Richard 1929- .... **CLC 7, 10, 47**
See also AITN 1; CA 85-88; CANR 25, 80; DLB 5; INT CANR-25

Howard, Robert E(rvin)
1906-1936 .... **TCLC 8**
See also CA 105; 157

Howard, Warren F.
See Pohl, Frederik

Howe, Fanny (Quincy) 1940- .... **CLC 47**
See also CA 117; CAAS 27; CANR 70; SATA-Brief 52

Ilf, Ilya .... **TCLC 21**
    See also Fainzilberg, Ilya Arnoldovich

Illyes, Gyula 1902-1983 .... **PC 16**
    See also CA 114; 109

Immermann, Karl (Lebrecht) 1796-1840
    NCLC 4, 49
    See also DLB 133

Ince, Thomas H. 1882-1924 .... **TCLC 89**

Inchbald, Elizabeth 1753-1821 ...... **NCLC 62**
    See also DLB 39, 89

Inclan, Ramon (Maria) del Valle
    See Valle-Inclan, Ramon (Maria) del

Infante, G(uillermo) Cabrera
    See Cabrera Infante, G(uillermo)

Ingalls, Rachel (Holmes) 1940- .... **CLC 42**
    See also CA 123; 127

Ingamells, Reginald Charles
    See Ingamells, Rex

Ingamells, Rex 1913-1955 .... **TCLC 35**
    See also CA 167

Inge, William (Motter) 1913-1973 ..... **CLC 1,
8, 19; DAM DRAM**
    See also CA 9-12R; CDALB 1941-1968;
    DA3; DLB 7; MTCW 1, 2

Ingelow, Jean 1820-1897 .... **NCLC 39**
    See also DLB 35, 163; SATA 33

Ingram, Willis J.
    See Harris, Mark

Innaurato, Albert (F.) 1948(?)- ... **CLC 21, 60**
    See also CA 115; 122; CANR 78; INT 122

Innes, Michael
    See Stewart, J(ohn) I(nnes) M(ackintosh)

Innis, Harold Adams 1894-1952 .... **TCLC 77**
    See also CA 181; DLB 88

Ionesco, Eugene 1909-1994 ... **CLC 1, 4, 6, 9,
11, 15, 41, 86; DA; DAB; DAC; DAM
DRAM, MST; WLC**
    See also CA 9-12R; 144; CANR 55; DA3;
    MTCW 1, 2; SATA 7; SATA-Obit 79

Iqbal, Muhammad 1873-1938 .... **TCLC 28**

Ireland, Patrick
    See O'Doherty, Brian

Iron, Ralph
    See Schreiner, Olive (Emilie Albertina)

Irving, John (Winslow) 1942- ... **CLC 13, 23,
38, 112; DAM NOV, POP**
    See also AAYA 8; BEST 89:3; CA 25-28R;
    CANR 28, 73; DA3; DLB 6; DLBY 82;
    MTCW 1, 2

Irving, Washington 1783-1859 . **NCLC 2, 19;
DA; DAB; DAC; DAM MST; SSC 2,
37; WLC**
    See also CDALB 1640-1865; DA3; DLB 3,
    11, 30, 59, 73, 74, 186; YABC 2

Irwin, P. K.
    See Page, P(atricia) K(athleen)

Isaacs, Jorge Ricardo 1837-1895 ... **NCLC 70**

Isaacs, Susan 1943- .... **CLC 32; DAM POP**
    See also BEST 89:1; CA 89-92; CANR 20,
    41, 65; DA3; INT CANR-20; MTCW 1, 2

Isherwood, Christopher (William Bradshaw)
    1904-1986 .. **CLC 1, 9, 11, 14, 44; DAM
DRAM, NOV**
    See also CA 13-16R; 117; CANR 35; DA3;
    DLB 15, 195; DLBY 86; MTCW 1, 2

Ishiguro, Kazuo 1954- . **CLC 27, 56, 59, 110;
DAM NOV**
    See also BEST 90:2; CA 120; CANR 49;
    DA3; DLB 194; MTCW 1, 2

Ishikawa, Hakuhin
    See Ishikawa, Takuboku

Ishikawa, Takuboku
    1886(?)-1912 ... **TCLC 15; DAM POET;
PC 10**
    See also CA 113; 153

Iskander, Fazil 1929- .... **CLC 47**
    See also CA 102

Isler, Alan (David) 1934- .... **CLC 91**
    See also CA 156

Ivan IV 1530-1584 .... **LC 17**

Ivanov, Vyacheslav Ivanovich 1866-1949
    TCLC 33
    See also CA 122

Ivask, Ivar Vidrik 1927-1992 .... **CLC 14**
    See also CA 37-40R; 139; CANR 24

Ives, Morgan
    See Bradley, Marion Zimmer

Izumi Shikibu c. 973-c. 1034 .... **CMLC 33**

J. R. S.
    See Gogarty, Oliver St. John

Jabran, Kahlil
    See Gibran, Kahlil

Jabran, Khalil
    See Gibran, Kahlil

Jackson, Daniel
    See Wingrove, David (John)

Jackson, Jesse 1908-1983 .... **CLC 12**
    See also BW 1; CA 25-28R; 109; CANR
    27; CLR 28; MAICYA; SATA 2, 29;
    SATA-Obit 48

Jackson, Laura (Riding) 1901-1991
    See Riding, Laura
    See also CA 65-68; 135; CANR 28; DLB
    48

Jackson, Sam
    See Trumbo, Dalton

Jackson, Sara
    See Wingrove, David (John)

Jackson, Shirley 1919-1965 . **CLC 11, 60, 87;
DA; DAC; DAM MST; SSC 9; WLC**
    See also AAYA 9; CA 1-4R; 25-28R; CANR
    4, 52; CDALB 1941-1968; DA3; DLB 6;
    MTCW 2; SATA 2

Jacob, (Cyprien-)Max 1876-1944 .... **TCLC 6**
    See also CA 104

Jacobs, Harriet A(nn)
    1813(?)-1897 .... **NCLC 67**

Jacobs, Jim 1942- .... **CLC 12**
    See also CA 97-100; INT 97-100

Jacobs, W(illiam) W(ymark) 1863-1943
    TCLC 22
    See also CA 121; 167; DLB 135

Jacobsen, Jens Peter 1847-1885 .... **NCLC 34**

Jacobsen, Josephine 1908- .... **CLC 48, 102**
    See also CA 33-36R; CAAS 18; CANR 23,
    48

Jacobson, Dan 1929- .... **CLC 4, 14**
    See also CA 1-4R; CANR 2, 25, 66; DLB
    14, 207; MTCW 1

Jacqueline
    See Carpentier (y Valmont), Alejo

Jagger, Mick 1944- .... **CLC 17**

Jahiz, al- c. 780-c. 869 .... **CMLC 25**

Jakes, John (William) 1932- . **CLC 29; DAM
NOV, POP**
    See also AAYA 32; BEST 89:4; CA 57-60;
    CANR 10, 43, 66; DA3; DLBY 83; INT
    CANR-10; MTCW 1, 2; SATA 62

James, Andrew
    See Kirkup, James

James, C(yril) L(ionel) R(obert) 1901-1989
    CLC 33; BLCS
    See also BW 2; CA 117; 125; 128; CANR
    62; DLB 125; MTCW 1

James, Daniel (Lewis) 1911-1988
    See Santiago, Danny
    See also CA 174; 125

James, Dynely
    See Mayne, William (James Carter)

James, Henry Sr. 1811-1882 .... **NCLC 53**

James, Henry 1843-1916 ..... **TCLC 2, 11, 24,
40, 47, 64; DA; DAB; DAC; DAM
MST, NOV; SSC 8, 32; WLC**
    See also CA 104; 132; CDALB 1865-1917;
    DA3; DLB 12, 71, 74, 189; DLBD 13;
    MTCW 1, 2

James, M. R.
    See James, Montague (Rhodes)
    See also DLB 156

James, Montague (Rhodes)
    1862-1936 .... **TCLC 6; SSC 16**
    See also CA 104; DLB 201

James, P. D. 1920- .... **CLC 18, 46, 122**
    See also White, Phyllis Dorothy James
    BEST 90:2; CDBLB 1960 to Present;
    DLB 87; DLBD 17

James, Philip
    See Moorcock, Michael (John)

James, William 1842-1910 .... **TCLC 15, 32**
    See also CA 109

James I 1394-1437 .... **LC 20**

Jameson, Anna 1794-1860 .... **NCLC 43**
    See also DLB 99, 166

Jami, Nur al-Din 'Abd al-Rahman
    1414-1492 .... **LC 9**

Jammes, Francis 1868-1938 .... **TCLC 75**

Jandl, Ernst 1925- .... **CLC 34**

Janowitz, Tama 1957- .. **CLC 43; DAM POP**
    See also CA 106; CANR 52

Japrisot, Sebastien 1931- .... **CLC 90**

Jarrell, Randall 1914-1965 .... **CLC 1, 2, 6, 9,
13, 49; DAM POET**
    See also CA 5-8R; 25-28R; CABS 2; CANR
    6, 34; CDALB 1941-1968; CLR 6; DLB
    48, 52; MAICYA; MTCW 1, 2; SATA 7

Jarry, Alfred 1873-1907 . **TCLC 2, 14; DAM
DRAM; SSC 20**
    See also CA 104; 153; DA3; DLB 192

Jawien, Andrzej
    See John Paul II, Pope

Jaynes, Roderick
    See Coen, Ethan

Jeake, Samuel, Jr.
    See Aiken, Conrad (Potter)

Jean Paul 1763-1825 .... **NCLC 7**

Jefferies, (John) Richard
    1848-1887 .... **NCLC 47**
    See also DLB 98, 141; SATA 16

Jeffers, (John) Robinson 1887-1962 .. **CLC 2,
3, 11, 15, 54; DA; DAC; DAM MST,
POET; PC 17; WLC**
    See also CA 85-88; CANR 35; CDALB
    1917-1929; DLB 45, 212; MTCW 1, 2

Jefferson, Janet
    See Mencken, H(enry) L(ouis)

Jefferson, Thomas 1743-1826 .... **NCLC 11**
    See also CDALB 1640-1865; DA3; DLB
    31

Jeffrey, Francis 1773-1850 .... **NCLC 33**
    See also DLB 107

Jelakowitch, Ivan
    See Heijermans, Herman

Jellicoe, (Patricia) Ann 1927- .... **CLC 27**
    See also CA 85-88; DLB 13

Jovine, Francesco 1902-1950 .... **TCLC 79**

Joyce, James (Augustine Aloysius)
    1882-1941 .. **TCLC 3, 8, 16, 35, 52; DA;
    DAB; DAC; DAM MST, NOV, POET;
    PC 22; SSC 3, 26; WLC**
    See also CA 104; 126; CDBLB 1914-1945;
    DA3; DLB 10, 19, 36, 162; MTCW 1, 2

Jozsef, Attila 1905-1937 .... **TCLC 22**
    See also CA 116

Juana Ines de la Cruz 1651(?)-1695 .... **LC 5;
    HLCS 1; PC 24**

Judd, Cyril
    See Kornbluth, C(yril) M.; Pohl, Frederik

Juenger, Ernst 1895-1998 .... **CLC 125**
    See also CA 101; 167; CANR 21, 47; DLB
    56

Julian of Norwich 1342(?)-1416(?) . **LC 6, 52**
    See also DLB 146

Junger, Ernst
    See Juenger, Ernst

Junger, Sebastian 1962- .... **CLC 109**
    See also AAYA 28; CA 165

Juniper, Alex
    See Hospital, Janette Turner

Junius
    See Luxemburg, Rosa

Just, Ward (Swift) 1935- .... **CLC 4, 27**
    See also CA 25-28R; CANR 32, 87; INT
    CANR-32

Justice, Donald (Rodney) 1925- .. **CLC 6, 19,
    102; DAM POET**
    See also CA 5-8R; CANR 26, 54, 74;
    DLBY 83; INT CANR-26; MTCW 2

Juvenal c. 60-c. 13 .... **CMLC 8**
    See also Juvenalis, Decimus Junius DLB
    211

Juvenalis, Decimus Junius 55(?)-c. 127(?)
    See Juvenal

Juvenis
    See Bourne, Randolph S(illiman)

Kacew, Romain 1914-1980
    See Gary, Romain
    See also CA 108; 102

Kadare, Ismail 1936- .... **CLC 52**
    See also CA 161

Kadohata, Cynthia .... **CLC 59, 122**
    See also CA 140

Kafka, Franz 1883-1924 . **TCLC 2, 6, 13, 29,
    47, 53; DA; DAB; DAC; DAM MST,
    NOV; SSC 5, 29, 35; WLC**
    See also AAYA 31; CA 105; 126; DA3;
    DLB 81; MTCW 1, 2

Kahanovitsch, Pinkhes
    See Der Nister

Kahn, Roger 1927- .... **CLC 30**
    See also CA 25-28R; CANR 44, 69; DLB
    171; SATA 37

Kain, Saul
    See Sassoon, Siegfried (Lorraine)

Kaiser, Georg 1878-1945 .... **TCLC 9**
    See also CA 106; DLB 124

Kaletski, Alexander 1946- .... **CLC 39**
    See also CA 118; 143

Kalidasa fl. c. 400- .... **CMLC 9; PC 22**

Kallman, Chester (Simon)
    1921-1975 .... **CLC 2**
    See also CA 45-48; 53-56; CANR 3

Kaminsky, Melvin 1926-
    See Brooks, Mel
    See also CA 65-68; CANR 16

Kaminsky, Stuart M(elvin) 1934- ..... **CLC 59**
    See also CA 73-76; CANR 29, 53

Kandinsky, Wassily 1866-1944 .... **TCLC 92**
    See also CA 118; 155

Kane, Francis
    See Robbins, Harold

Kane, Paul
    See Simon, Paul (Frederick)

Kanin, Garson 1912-1999 .... **CLC 22**
    See also AITN 1; CA 5-8R; 177; CANR 7,
    78; DLB 7

Kaniuk, Yoram 1930- .... **CLC 19**
    See also CA 134

Kant, Immanuel 1724-1804 ..... **NCLC 27, 67**
    See also DLB 94

Kantor, MacKinlay 1904-1977 .... **CLC 7**
    See also CA 61-64; 73-76; CANR 60, 63;
    DLB 9, 102; MTCW 2

Kaplan, David Michael 1946- .... **CLC 50**

Kaplan, James 1951- .... **CLC 59**
    See also CA 135

Karageorge, Michael
    See Anderson, Poul (William)

Karamzin, Nikolai Mikhailovich 1766-1826
    NCLC 3
    See also DLB 150

Karapanou, Margarita 1946- .... **CLC 13**
    See also CA 101

Karinthy, Frigyes 1887-1938 .... **TCLC 47**
    See also CA 170

Karl, Frederick R(obert) 1927- .... **CLC 34**
    See also CA 5-8R; CANR 3, 44

Kastel, Warren
    See Silverberg, Robert

Kataev, Evgeny Petrovich 1903-1942
    See Petrov, Evgeny
    See also CA 120

Kataphusin
    See Ruskin, John

Katz, Steve 1935- .... **CLC 47**
    See also CA 25-28R; CAAS 14, 64; CANR
    12; DLBY 83

Kauffman, Janet 1945- .... **CLC 42**
    See also CA 117; CANR 43, 84; DLBY 86

Kaufman, Bob (Garnell) 1925-1986 . **CLC 49**
    See also BW 1; CA 41-44R; 118; CANR
    22; DLB 16, 41

Kaufman, George S. 1889-1961 ...... **CLC 38;
    DAM DRAM**
    See also CA 108; 93-96; DLB 7; INT 108;
    MTCW 2

Kaufman, Sue .... **CLC 3, 8**
    See also Barondess, Sue K(aufman)

Kavafis, Konstantinos Petrou 1863-1933
    See Cavafy, C(onstantine) P(eter)
    See also CA 104

Kavan, Anna 1901-1968 .... **CLC 5, 13, 82**
    See also CA 5-8R; CANR 6, 57; MTCW 1

Kavanagh, Dan
    See Barnes, Julian (Patrick)

Kavanagh, Julie 1952- .... **CLC 119**
    See also CA 163

Kavanagh, Patrick (Joseph)
    1904-1967 .... **CLC 22**
    See also CA 123; 25-28R; DLB 15, 20;
    MTCW 1

Kawabata, Yasunari 1899-1972 ..... **CLC 2, 5,
    9, 18, 107; DAM MULT; SSC 17**
    See also CA 93-96; 33-36R; DLB 180;
    MTCW 2

Kaye, M(ary) M(argaret) 1909- .... **CLC 28**
    See also CA 89-92; CANR 24, 60; MTCW
    1, 2; SATA 62

Kaye, Mollie
    See Kaye, M(ary) M(argaret)

Kaye-Smith, Sheila 1887-1956 .... **TCLC 20**
    See also CA 118; DLB 36

Kaymor, Patrice Maguilene
    See Senghor, Leopold Sedar

Kazan, Elia 1909- .... **CLC 6, 16, 63**
    See also CA 21-24R; CANR 32, 78

Kazantzakis, Nikos 1883(?)-1957 .... **TCLC 2,
    5, 33**
    See also CA 105; 132; DA3; MTCW 1, 2

Kazin, Alfred 1915-1998 ..... **CLC 34, 38, 119**
    See also CA 1-4R; CAAS 7; CANR 1, 45,
    79; DLB 67

Keane, Mary Nesta (Skrine) 1904-1996
    See Keane, Molly
    See also CA 108; 114; 151

Keane, Molly .... **CLC 31**
    See also Keane, Mary Nesta (Skrine) INT
    114

Keates, Jonathan 1946(?)- .... **CLC 34**
    See also CA 163

Keaton, Buster 1895-1966 .... **CLC 20**

Keats, John 1795-1821 ...... **NCLC 8, 73; DA;
    DAB; DAC; DAM MST, POET; PC 1;
    WLC**
    See also CDBLB 1789-1832; DA3; DLB
    96, 110

Keene, Donald 1922- .... **CLC 34**
    See also CA 1-4R; CANR 5

Keillor, Garrison .... **CLC 40, 115**
    See also Keillor, Gary (Edward) AAYA 2;
    BEST 89:3; DLBY 87; SATA 58

Keillor, Gary (Edward) 1942-
    See Keillor, Garrison
    See also CA 111; 117; CANR 36, 59; DAM
    POP; DA3; MTCW 1, 2

Keith, Michael
    See Hubbard, L(afayette) Ron(ald)

Keller, Gottfried 1819-1890 .... **NCLC 2; SSC
    26**
    See also DLB 129

Keller, Nora Okja .... **CLC 109**

Kellerman, Jonathan 1949- .. **CLC 44; DAM
    POP**
    See also BEST 90:1; CA 106; CANR 29,
    51; DA3; INT CANR-29

Kelley, William Melvin 1937- .... **CLC 22**
    See also BW 1; CA 77-80; CANR 27, 83;
    DLB 33

Kellogg, Marjorie 1922- .... **CLC 2**
    See also CA 81-84

Kellow, Kathleen
    See Hibbert, Eleanor Alice Burford

Kelly, M(ilton) T(errence) 1947- ...... **CLC 55**
    See also CA 97-100; CAAS 22; CANR 19,
    43, 84

Kelman, James 1946- .... **CLC 58, 86**
    See also CA 148; CANR 85; DLB 194

Kemal, Yashar 1923- .... **CLC 14, 29**
    See also CA 89-92; CANR 44

Kemble, Fanny 1809-1893 .... **NCLC 18**
    See also DLB 32

Kemelman, Harry 1908-1996 .... **CLC 2**
    See also AITN 1; CA 9-12R; 155; CANR 6,
    71; DLB 28

Kempe, Margery 1373(?)-1440(?) .... **LC 6**
    See also DLB 146

Kempis, Thomas a 1380-1471 .... **LC 11**

Kendall, Henry 1839-1882 .... **NCLC 12**

Keneally, Thomas (Michael) 1935- ... **CLC 5, 8, 10, 14, 19, 27, 43, 117; DAM NOV**
See also CA 85-88; CANR 10, 50, 74; DA3; MTCW 1, 2

Kennedy, Adrienne (Lita) 1931- ..... **CLC 66; BLC 2; DAM MULT; DC 5**
See also BW 2, 3; CA 103; CAAS 20; CABS 3; CANR 26, 53, 82; DLB 38

Kennedy, John Pendleton 1795-1870 .... **NCLC 2**
See also DLB 3

Kennedy, Joseph Charles 1929-
See Kennedy, X. J.
See also CA 1-4R; CANR 4, 30, 40; SATA 14, 86

Kennedy, William 1928- .. **CLC 6, 28, 34, 53; DAM NOV**
See also AAYA 1; CA 85-88; CANR 14, 31, 76; DA3; DLB 143; DLBY 85; INT CANR-31; MTCW 1, 2; SATA 57

Kennedy, X. J. .... **CLC 8, 42**
See also Kennedy, Joseph Charles CAAS 9; CLR 27; DLB 5; SAAS 22

Kenny, Maurice (Francis) 1929- ..... **CLC 87; DAM MULT**
See also CA 144; CAAS 22; DLB 175; NNAL

Kent, Kelvin
See Kuttner, Henry

Kenton, Maxwell
See Southern, Terry

Kenyon, Robert O.
See Kuttner, Henry

Kepler, Johannes 1571-1630 .... **LC 45**

Kerouac, Jack .... **CLC 1, 2, 3, 5, 14, 29, 61**
See also Kerouac, Jean-Louis Lebris de AAYA 25; CDALB 1941-1968; DLB 2, 16; DLBD 3; DLBY 95; MTCW 2

Kerouac, Jean-Louis Lebris de 1922-1969
See Kerouac, Jack
See also AITN 1; CA 5-8R; 25-28R; CANR 26, 54; DA; DAB; DAC; DAM MST, NOV, POET, POP; DA3; MTCW 1, 2; WLC

Kerr, Jean 1923- .... **CLC 22**
See also CA 5-8R; CANR 7; INT CANR-7

Kerr, M. E. .... **CLC 12, 35**
See also Meaker, Marijane (Agnes) AAYA 2, 23; CLR 29; SAAS 1

Kerr, Robert .... **CLC 55**

Kerrigan, (Thomas) Anthony 1918- .. **CLC 4, 6**
See also CA 49-52; CAAS 11; CANR 4

Kerry, Lois
See Duncan, Lois

Kesey, Ken (Elton) 1935- ..... **CLC 1, 3, 6, 11, 46, 64; DA; DAB; DAC; DAM MST, NOV, POP; WLC**
See also AAYA 25; CA 1-4R; CANR 22, 38, 66; CDALB 1968-1988; DA3; DLB 2, 16, 206; MTCW 1, 2; SATA 66

Kesselring, Joseph (Otto) 1902-1967 .... **CLC 45; DAM DRAM, MST**
See also CA 150

Kessler, Jascha (Frederick) 1929- ...... **CLC 4**
See also CA 17-20R; CANR 8, 48

Kettelkamp, Larry (Dale) 1933- .... **CLC 12**
See also CA 29-32R; CANR 16; SAAS 3; SATA 2

Key, Ellen 1849-1926 .... **TCLC 65**

Keyber, Conny
See Fielding, Henry

Keyes, Daniel 1927- ...... **CLC 80; DA; DAC; DAM MST, NOV**
See also AAYA 23; CA 17-20R, 181; CAAE 181; CANR 10, 26, 54, 74; DA3; MTCW 2; SATA 37

Keynes, John Maynard 1883-1946 .... **TCLC 64**
See also CA 114; 162, 163; DLBD 10; MTCW 2

Khanshendel, Chiron
See Rose, Wendy

Khayyam, Omar 1048-1131 .... **CMLC 11; DAM POET; PC 8**
See also DA3

Kherdian, David 1931- .... **CLC 6, 9**
See also CA 21-24R; CAAS 2; CANR 39, 78; CLR 24; JRDA; MAICYA; SATA 16, 74

Khlebnikov, Velimir .... **TCLC 20**
See also Khlebnikov, Viktor Vladimirovich

Khlebnikov, Viktor Vladimirovich 1885-1922
See Khlebnikov, Velimir
See also CA 117

Khodasevich, Vladislav (Felitsianovich) 1886-1939 .... **TCLC 15**
See also CA 115

Kielland, Alexander Lange 1849-1906 .... **TCLC 5**
See also CA 104

Kiely, Benedict 1919- .... **CLC 23, 43**
See also CA 1-4R; CANR 2, 84; DLB 15

Kienzle, William X(avier) 1928- ..... **CLC 25; DAM POP**
See also CA 93-96; CAAS 1; CANR 9, 31, 59; DA3; INT CANR-31; MTCW 1, 2

Kierkegaard, Soren 1813-1855 ..... **NCLC 34, 78**

Kieslowski, Krzysztof 1941-1996 .... **CLC 120**
See also CA 147; 151

Killens, John Oliver 1916-1987 .... **CLC 10**
See also BW 2; CA 77-80; 123; CAAS 2; CANR 26; DLB 33

Killigrew, Anne 1660-1685 .... **LC 4**
See also DLB 131

Kim
See Simenon, Georges (Jacques Christian)

Kincaid, Jamaica 1949- .... **CLC 43, 68; BLC 2; DAM MULT, NOV**
See also AAYA 13; BW 2, 3; CA 125; CANR 47, 59; CDALBS; DA3; DLB 157; MTCW 2

King, Francis (Henry) 1923- .... **CLC 8, 53; DAM NOV**
See also CA 1-4R; CANR 1, 33, 86; DLB 15, 139; MTCW 1

King, Kennedy
See Brown, George Douglas

King, Martin Luther, Jr. 1929-1968 .... **CLC 83; BLC 2; DA; DAB; DAC; DAM MST, MULT; WLCS**
See also BW 2, 3; CA 25-28; CANR 27, 44; CAP 2; DA3; MTCW 1, 2; SATA 14

King, Stephen (Edwin) 1947- .... **CLC 12, 26, 37, 61, 113; DAM NOV, POP; SSC 17**
See also AAYA 1, 17; BEST 90:1; CA 61-64; CANR 1, 30, 52, 76; DA3; DLB 143; DLBY 80; JRDA; MTCW 1, 2; SATA 9, 55

King, Steve
See King, Stephen (Edwin)

King, Thomas 1943- ... **CLC 89; DAC; DAM MULT**
See also CA 144; DLB 175; NNAL; SATA 96

Kingman, Lee .... **CLC 17**
See also Natti, (Mary) Lee SAAS 3; SATA 1, 67

Kingsley, Charles 1819-1875 .... **NCLC 35**
See also DLB 21, 32, 163, 190; YABC 2

Kingsley, Sidney 1906-1995 .... **CLC 44**
See also CA 85-88; 147; DLB 7

Kingsolver, Barbara 1955- .... **CLC 55, 81; DAM POP**
See also AAYA 15; CA 129; 134; CANR 60; CDALBS; DA3; DLB 206; INT 134; MTCW 2

Kingston, Maxine (Ting Ting) Hong 1940- **CLC 12, 19, 58, 121; DAM MULT, NOV; WLCS**
See also AAYA 8; CA 69-72; CANR 13, 38, 74, 87; CDALBS; DA3; DLB 173, 212; DLBY 80; INT CANR-13; MTCW 1, 2; SATA 53

Kinnell, Galway 1927- ..... **CLC 1, 2, 3, 5, 13, 29; PC 26**
See also CA 9-12R; CANR 10, 34, 66; DLB 5; DLBY 87; INT CANR-34; MTCW 1, 2

Kinsella, Thomas 1928- .... **CLC 4, 19**
See also CA 17-20R; CANR 15; DLB 27; MTCW 1, 2

Kinsella, W(illiam) P(atrick) 1935- . **CLC 27, 43; DAC; DAM NOV, POP**
See also AAYA 7; CA 97-100; CAAS 7; CANR 21, 35, 66, 75; INT CANR-21; MTCW 1, 2

Kinsey, Alfred C(harles) 1894-1956 .... **TCLC 91**
See also CA 115; 170; MTCW 2

Kipling, (Joseph) Rudyard 1865-1936 .... **TCLC 8, 17; DA; DAB; DAC; DAM MST, POET; PC 3; SSC 5; WLC**
See also AAYA 32; CA 105; 120; CANR 33; CDBLB 1890-1914; CLR 39; DA3; DLB 19, 34, 141, 156; MAICYA; MTCW 1, 2; SATA 100; YABC 2

Kirkup, James 1918- .... **CLC 1**
See also CA 1-4R; CAAS 4; CANR 2; DLB 27; SATA 12

Kirkwood, James 1930(?)-1989 .... **CLC 9**
See also AITN 2; CA 1-4R; 128; CANR 6, 40

Kirshner, Sidney
See Kingsley, Sidney

Kis, Danilo 1935-1989 .... **CLC 57**
See also CA 109; 118; 129; CANR 61; DLB 181; MTCW 1

Kivi, Aleksis 1834-1872 .... **NCLC 30**

Kizer, Carolyn (Ashley) 1925- ... **CLC 15, 39, 80; DAM POET**
See also CA 65-68; CAAS 5; CANR 24, 70; DLB 5, 169; MTCW 2

Klabund 1890-1928 .... **TCLC 44**
See also CA 162; DLB 66

Klappert, Peter 1942- .... **CLC 57**
See also CA 33-36R; DLB 5

Klein, A(braham) M(oses) 1909-1972 . **CLC 19; DAB; DAC; DAM MST**
See also CA 101; 37-40R; DLB 68

Klein, Norma 1938-1989 .... **CLC 30**
See also AAYA 2; CA 41-44R; 128; CANR
15, 37; CLR 2, 19; INT CANR-15; JRDA;
MAICYA; SAAS 1; SATA 7, 57

Klein, T(heodore) E(ibon) D(onald) 1947-
CLC 34
See also CA 119; CANR 44, 75

Kleist, Heinrich von 1777-1811 ...... **NCLC 2,
37; DAM DRAM; SSC 22**
See also DLB 90

Klima, Ivan 1931- .... **CLC 56; DAM NOV**
See also CA 25-28R; CANR 17, 50

Klimentov, Andrei Platonovich 1899-1951
See Platonov, Andrei
See also CA 108

Klinger, Friedrich Maximilian von
1752-1831 .... **NCLC 1**
See also DLB 94

Klingsor the Magician
See Hartmann, Sadakichi

Klopstock, Friedrich Gottlieb 1724-1803
NCLC 11
See also DLB 97

Knapp, Caroline 1959- .... **CLC 99**
See also CA 154

Knebel, Fletcher 1911-1993 .... **CLC 14**
See also AITN 1; CA 1-4R; 140; CAAS 3;
CANR 1, 36; SATA 36; SATA-Obit 75

Knickerbocker, Diedrich
See Irving, Washington

Knight, Etheridge 1931-1991 . **CLC 40; BLC
2; DAM POET; PC 14**
See also BW 1, 3; CA 21-24R; 133; CANR
23, 82; DLB 41; MTCW 2

Knight, Sarah Kemble 1666-1727 .... **LC 7**
See also DLB 24, 200

Knister, Raymond 1899-1932 .... **TCLC 56**
See also DLB 68

Knowles, John 1926- . **CLC 1, 4, 10, 26; DA;
DAC; DAM MST, NOV**
See also AAYA 10; CA 17-20R; CANR 40,
74, 76; CDALB 1968-1988; DLB 6;
MTCW 1, 2; SATA 8, 89

Knox, Calvin M.
See Silverberg, Robert

Knox, John c. 1505-1572 .... **LC 37**
See also DLB 132

Knye, Cassandra
See Disch, Thomas M(ichael)

Koch, C(hristopher) J(ohn) 1932- .... **CLC 42**
See also CA 127; CANR 84

Koch, Christopher
See Koch, C(hristopher) J(ohn)

Koch, Kenneth 1925- .... **CLC 5, 8, 44; DAM
POET**
See also CA 1-4R; CANR 6, 36, 57; DLB
5; INT CANR-36; MTCW 2; SATA 65

Kochanowski, Jan 1530-1584 .... **LC 10**

Kock, Charles Paul de 1794-1871 . **NCLC 16**

Koda Shigeyuki 1867-1947
See Rohan, Koda
See also CA 121; 183

Koestler, Arthur 1905-1983 ... **CLC 1, 3, 6, 8,
15, 33**
See also CA 1-4R; 109; CANR 1, 33; CD-
BLB 1945-1960; DLBY 83; MTCW 1, 2

Kogawa, Joy Nozomi 1935- .. **CLC 78; DAC;
DAM MST, MULT**
See also CA 101; CANR 19, 62; MTCW 2;
SATA 99

Kohout, Pavel 1928- .... **CLC 13**
See also CA 45-48; CANR 3

Koizumi, Yakumo
See Hearn, (Patricio) Lafcadio (Tessima
Carlos)

Kolmar, Gertrud 1894-1943 .... **TCLC 40**
See also CA 167

Komunyakaa, Yusef 1947- .... **CLC 86, 94;
BLCS**
See also CA 147; CANR 83; DLB 120

Konrad, George
See Konrad, Gyoergy

Konrad, Gyoergy 1933- .... **CLC 4, 10, 73**
See also CA 85-88

Konwicki, Tadeusz 1926- .... **CLC 8, 28, 54,
117**
See also CA 101; CAAS 9; CANR 39, 59;
MTCW 1

Koontz, Dean R(ay) 1945- .... **CLC 78; DAM
NOV, POP**
See also AAYA 9, 31; BEST 89:3, 90:2; CA
108; CANR 19, 36, 52; DA3; MTCW 1;
SATA 92

Kopernik, Mikolaj
See Copernicus, Nicolaus

Kopit, Arthur (Lee) 1937- ..... **CLC 1, 18, 33;
DAM DRAM**
See also AITN 1; CA 81-84; CABS 3; DLB
7; MTCW 1

Kops, Bernard 1926- .... **CLC 4**
See also CA 5-8R; CANR 84; DLB 13

Kornbluth, C(yril) M. 1923-1958 .... **TCLC 8**
See also CA 105; 160; DLB 8

Korolenko, V. G.
See Korolenko, Vladimir Galaktionovich

Korolenko, Vladimir
See Korolenko, Vladimir Galaktionovich

Korolenko, Vladimir G.
See Korolenko, Vladimir Galaktionovich

Korolenko, Vladimir Galaktionovich
1853-1921 .... **TCLC 22**
See also CA 121

Korzybski, Alfred (Habdank Skarbek)
1879-1950 .... **TCLC 61**
See also CA 123; 160

Kosinski, Jerzy (Nikodem)
1933-1991 .... **CLC 1, 2, 3, 6, 10, 15, 53,
70; DAM NOV**
See also CA 17-20R; 134; CANR 9, 46;
DA3; DLB 2; DLBY 82; MTCW 1, 2

Kostelanetz, Richard (Cory) 1940- .. **CLC 28**
See also CA 13-16R; CAAS 8; CANR 38,
77

Kostrowitzki, Wilhelm Apollinaris de
1880-1918
See Apollinaire, Guillaume
See also CA 104

Kotlowitz, Robert 1924- .... **CLC 4**
See also CA 33-36R; CANR 36

Kotzebue, August (Friedrich Ferdinand) von
1761-1819 .... **NCLC 25**
See also DLB 94

Kotzwinkle, William 1938- ..... **CLC 5, 14, 35**
See also CA 45-48; CANR 3, 44, 84; CLR
6; DLB 173; MAICYA; SATA 24, 70

Kowna, Stancy
See Szymborska, Wislawa

Kozol, Jonathan 1936- .... **CLC 17**
See also CA 61-64; CANR 16, 45

Kozoll, Michael 1940(?)- .... **CLC 35**

Kramer, Kathryn 19(?)- .... **CLC 34**

Kramer, Larry 1935- .. **CLC 42; DAM POP;
DC 8**
See also CA 124; 126; CANR 60

Krasicki, Ignacy 1735-1801 .... **NCLC 8**

Krasinski, Zygmunt 1812-1859 .... **NCLC 4**

Kraus, Karl 1874-1936 .... **TCLC 5**
See also CA 104; DLB 118

Kreve (Mickevicius), Vincas 1882-1954
TCLC 27
See also CA 170

Kristeva, Julia 1941- .... **CLC 77**
See also CA 154

Kristofferson, Kris 1936- .... **CLC 26**
See also CA 104

Krizanc, John 1956- .... **CLC 57**

Krleza, Miroslav 1893-1981 .... **CLC 8, 114**
See also CA 97-100; 105; CANR 50; DLB
147

Kroetsch, Robert 1927- .... **CLC 5, 23, 57;
DAC; DAM POET**
See also CA 17-20R; CANR 8, 38; DLB
53; MTCW 1

Kroetz, Franz
See Kroetz, Franz Xaver

Kroetz, Franz Xaver 1946- .... **CLC 41**
See also CA 130

Kroker, Arthur (W.) 1945- .... **CLC 77**
See also CA 161

Kropotkin, Peter (Aleksieevich) 1842-1921
TCLC 36
See also CA 119

Krotkov, Yuri 1917- .... **CLC 19**
See also CA 102

Krumb
See Crumb, R(obert)

Krumgold, Joseph (Quincy)
1908-1980 .... **CLC 12**
See also CA 9-12R; 101; CANR 7; MAI-
CYA; SATA 1, 48; SATA-Obit 23

Krumwitz
See Crumb, R(obert)

Krutch, Joseph Wood 1893-1970 ..... **CLC 24**
See also CA 1-4R; 25-28R; CANR 4; DLB
63, 206

Krutzch, Gus
See Eliot, T(homas) S(tearns)

Krylov, Ivan Andreevich
1768(?)-1844 .... **NCLC 1**
See also DLB 150

Kubin, Alfred (Leopold Isidor) 1877-1959
TCLC 23
See also CA 112; 149; DLB 81

Kubrick, Stanley 1928-1999 .... **CLC 16**
See also AAYA 30; CA 81-84; 177; CANR
33; DLB 26

Kumin, Maxine (Winokur) 1925- ..... **CLC 5,
13, 28; DAM POET; PC 15**
See also AITN 2; CA 1-4R; CAAS 8;
CANR 1, 21, 69; DA3; DLB 5; MTCW
1, 2; SATA 12

Kundera, Milan 1929- . **CLC 4, 9, 19, 32, 68,
115; DAM NOV; SSC 24**
See also AAYA 2; CA 85-88; CANR 19,
52, 74; DA3; MTCW 1, 2

Kunene, Mazisi (Raymond) 1930- ... **CLC 85**
See also BW 1, 3; CA 125; CANR 81; DLB
117

Kunikida Doppo 1871-1908 .... **TCLC 100**

Kunitz, Stanley (Jasspon) 1905- .. **CLC 6, 11,
14; PC 19**
See also CA 41-44R; CANR 26, 57; DA3;
DLB 48; INT CANR-26; MTCW 1, 2

Kunze, Reiner 1933- .... **CLC 10**
See also CA 93-96; DLB 75

Laurent, Antoine 1952- .... **CLC 50**
Lauscher, Hermann
   See Hesse, Hermann
Lautreamont, Comte de
   1846-1870 .... **NCLC 12; SSC 14**
Laverty, Donald
   See Blish, James (Benjamin)
Lavin, Mary 1912-1996 . **CLC 4, 18, 99; SSC 4**
   See also CA 9-12R; 151; CANR 33; DLB 15; MTCW 1
Lavond, Paul Dennis
   See Kornbluth, C(yril) M.; Pohl, Frederik
Lawler, Raymond Evenor 1922- .... **CLC 58**
   See also CA 103
Lawrence, D(avid) H(erbert Richards)
   1885-1930 .... **TCLC 2, 9, 16, 33, 48, 61, 93; DA; DAB; DAC; DAM MST, NOV, POET; SSC 4, 19; WLC**
   See also CA 104; 121; CDBLB 1914-1945; DA3; DLB 10, 19, 36, 98, 162, 195; MTCW 1, 2
Lawrence, T(homas) E(dward) 1888-1935 **TCLC 18**
   See also Dale, Colin CA 115; 167; DLB 195
Lawrence of Arabia
   See Lawrence, T(homas) E(dward)
Lawson, Henry (Archibald Hertzberg)
   1867-1922 .... **TCLC 27; SSC 18**
   See also CA 120; 181
Lawton, Dennis
   See Faust, Frederick (Schiller)
Laxness, Halldor .... **CLC 25**
   See also Gudjonsson, Halldor Kiljan
Layamon fl. c. 1200- .... **CMLC 10**
   See also DLB 146
Laye, Camara 1928-1980 ... **CLC 4, 38; BLC 2; DAM MULT**
   See also BW 1; CA 85-88; 97-100; CANR 25; MTCW 1, 2
Layton, Irving (Peter) 1912- .... **CLC 2, 15; DAC; DAM MST, POET**
   See also CA 1-4R; CANR 2, 33, 43, 66; DLB 88; MTCW 1, 2
Lazarus, Emma 1849-1887 .... **NCLC 8**
Lazarus, Felix
   See Cable, George Washington
Lazarus, Henry
   See Slavitt, David R(ytman)
Lea, Joan
   See Neufeld, John (Arthur)
Leacock, Stephen (Butler)
   1869-1944 . **TCLC 2; DAC; DAM MST**
   See also CA 104; 141; CANR 80; DLB 92; MTCW 2
Lear, Edward 1812-1888 .... **NCLC 3**
   See also CLR 1; DLB 32, 163, 166; MAI-CYA; SATA 18, 100
Lear, Norman (Milton) 1922- .... **CLC 12**
   See also CA 73-76
Leautaud, Paul 1872-1956 .... **TCLC 83**
   See also DLB 65
Leavis, F(rank) R(aymond)
   1895-1978 .... **CLC 24**
   See also CA 21-24R; 77-80; CANR 44; MTCW 1, 2
Leavitt, David 1961- ..... **CLC 34; DAM POP**
   See also CA 116; 122; CANR 50, 62; DA3; DLB 130; INT 122; MTCW 2
Leblanc, Maurice (Marie Emile) 1864-1941 **TCLC 49**

   See also CA 110
Lebowitz, Fran(ces Ann) 1951(?)- ... **CLC 11, 36**
   See also CA 81-84; CANR 14, 60, 70; INT CANR-14; MTCW 1
Lebrecht, Peter
   See Tieck, (Johann) Ludwig
le Carre, John .... **CLC 3, 5, 9, 15, 28**
   See also Cornwell, David (John Moore) BEST 89:4; CDBLB 1960 to Present; DLB 87; MTCW 2
Le Clezio, J(ean) M(arie) G(ustave) 1940- **CLC 31**
   See also CA 116; 128; DLB 83
Leconte de Lisle, Charles-Marie-Rene
   1818-1894 .... **NCLC 29**
Le Coq, Monsieur
   See Simenon, Georges (Jacques Christian)
Leduc, Violette 1907-1972 .... **CLC 22**
   See also CA 13-14; 33-36R; CANR 69; CAP 1
Ledwidge, Francis 1887(?)-1917 .... **TCLC 23**
   See also CA 123; DLB 20
Lee, Andrea 1953- ... **CLC 36; BLC 2; DAM MULT**
   See also BW 1, 3; CA 125; CANR 82
Lee, Andrew
   See Auchincloss, Louis (Stanton)
Lee, Chang-rae 1965- .... **CLC 91**
   See also CA 148
Lee, Don L. .... **CLC 2**
   See also Madhubuti, Haki R.
Lee, George W(ashington)
   1894-1976 .... **CLC 52; BLC 2; DAM MULT**
   See also BW 1; CA 125; CANR 83; DLB 51
Lee, (Nelle) Harper 1926- . **CLC 12, 60; DA; DAB; DAC; DAM MST, NOV; WLC**
   See also AAYA 13; CA 13-16R; CANR 51; CDALB 1941-1968; DA3; DLB 6; MTCW 1, 2; SATA 11
Lee, Helen Elaine 1959(?)- .... **CLC 86**
   See also CA 148
Lee, Julian
   See Latham, Jean Lee
Lee, Larry
   See Lee, Lawrence
Lee, Laurie 1914-1997 .... **CLC 90; DAB; DAM POP**
   See also CA 77-80; 158; CANR 33, 73; DLB 27; MTCW 1
Lee, Lawrence 1941-1990 .... **CLC 34**
   See also CA 131; CANR 43
Lee, Li-Young 1957- .... **PC 24**
   See also CA 153; DLB 165
Lee, Manfred B(ennington)
   1905-1971 .... **CLC 11**
   See also Queen, Ellery CA 1-4R; 29-32R; CANR 2; DLB 137
Lee, Shelton Jackson 1957(?)- .... **CLC 105; BLCS; DAM MULT**
   See also Lee, Spike BW 2, 3; CA 125; CANR 42
Lee, Spike
   See Lee, Shelton Jackson
   See also AAYA 4, 29
Lee, Stan 1922- .... **CLC 17**
   See also AAYA 5; CA 108; 111; INT 111
Lee, Tanith 1947- .... **CLC 46**
   See also AAYA 15; CA 37-40R; CANR 53; SATA 8, 88

Lee, Vernon .... **TCLC 5; SSC 33**
   See also Paget, Violet DLB 57, 153, 156, 174, 178
Lee, William
   See Burroughs, William S(eward)
Lee, Willy
   See Burroughs, William S(eward)
Lee-Hamilton, Eugene (Jacob) 1845-1907 **TCLC 22**
   See also CA 117
Leet, Judith 1935- .... **CLC 11**
Le Fanu, Joseph Sheridan
   1814-1873 ..... **NCLC 9, 58; DAM POP; SSC 14**
   See also DA3; DLB 21, 70, 159, 178
Leffland, Ella 1931- .... **CLC 19**
   See also CA 29-32R; CANR 35, 78, 82; DLBY 84; INT CANR-35; SATA 65
Leger, Alexis
   See Leger, (Marie-Rene Auguste) Alexis Saint-Leger
Leger, (Marie-Rene Auguste) Alexis
   Saint-Leger 1887-1975 .. **CLC 4, 11, 46; DAM POET; PC 23**
   See also CA 13-16R; 61-64; CANR 43; MTCW 1
Leger, Saintleger
   See Leger, (Marie-Rene Auguste) Alexis Saint-Leger
Le Guin, Ursula K(roeber) 1929- ..... **CLC 8, 13, 22, 45, 71; DAB; DAC; DAM MST, POP; SSC 12**
   See also AAYA 9, 27; AITN 1; CA 21-24R; CANR 9, 32, 52, 74; CDALB 1968-1988; CLR 3, 28; DA3; DLB 8, 52; INT CANR-32; JRDA; MAICYA; MTCW 1, 2; SATA 4, 52, 99
Lehmann, Rosamond (Nina)
   1901-1990 .... **CLC 5**
   See also CA 77-80; 131; CANR 8, 73; DLB 15; MTCW 2
Leiber, Fritz (Reuter, Jr.)
   1910-1992 .... **CLC 25**
   See also CA 45-48; 139; CANR 2, 40, 86; DLB 8; MTCW 1, 2; SATA 45; SATA-Obit 73
Leibniz, Gottfried Wilhelm von 1646-1716 **LC 35**
   See also DLB 168
Leimbach, Martha 1963-
   See Leimbach, Marti
   See also CA 130
Leimbach, Marti .... **CLC 65**
   See also Leimbach, Martha
Leino, Eino .... **TCLC 24**
   See also Loennbohm, Armas Eino Leopold
Leiris, Michel (Julien) 1901-1990 ..... **CLC 61**
   See also CA 119; 128; 132
Leithauser, Brad 1953- .... **CLC 27**
   See also CA 107; CANR 27, 81; DLB 120
Lelchuk, Alan 1938- .... **CLC 5**
   See also CA 45-48; CAAS 20; CANR 1, 70
Lem, Stanislaw 1921- .... **CLC 8, 15, 40**
   See also CA 105; CAAS 1; CANR 32; MTCW 1
Lemann, Nancy 1956- .... **CLC 39**
   See also CA 118; 136
Lemonnier, (Antoine Louis) Camille
   1844-1913 .... **TCLC 22**
   See also CA 121

Marques, Rene 1919-1979 ..... **CLC 96; DAM MULT; HLC 2**
See also CA 97-100; 85-88; CANR 78; DLB 113; HW 1, 2

Marquez, Gabriel (Jose) Garcia
See Garcia Marquez, Gabriel (Jose)

Marquis, Don(ald Robert Perry) 1878-1937 **TCLC 7**
See also CA 104; 166; DLB 11, 25

Marric, J. J.
See Creasey, John

Marryat, Frederick 1792-1848 .... **NCLC 3**
See also DLB 21, 163

Marsden, James
See Creasey, John

Marsh, Edward 1872-1953 .... **TCLC 99**

Marsh, (Edith) Ngaio 1899-1982 .... **CLC 7, 53; DAM POP**
See also CA 9-12R; CANR 6, 58; DLB 77; MTCW 1, 2

Marshall, Garry 1934- .... **CLC 17**
See also AAYA 3; CA 111; SATA 60

Marshall, Paule 1929- .. **CLC 27, 72; BLC 3; DAM MULT; SSC 3**
See also BW 2, 3; CA 77-80; CANR 25, 73; DA3; DLB 157; MTCW 1, 2

Marshallik
See Zangwill, Israel

Marsten, Richard
See Hunter, Evan

Marston, John 1576-1634 .... **LC 33; DAM DRAM**
See also DLB 58, 172

Martha, Henry
See Harris, Mark

Marti (y Perez), Jose (Julian) 1853-1895 **NCLC 63; DAM MULT; HLC 2**
See also HW 2

Martial c. 40-c. 104 .... **CMLC 35; PC 10**
See also DLB 211

Martin, Ken
See Hubbard, L(afayette) Ron(ald)

Martin, Richard
See Creasey, John

Martin, Steve 1945- .... **CLC 30**
See also CA 97-100; CANR 30; MTCW 1

Martin, Valerie 1948- .... **CLC 89**
See also BEST 90:2; CA 85-88; CANR 49

Martin, Violet Florence
1862-1915 .... **TCLC 51**

Martin, Webber
See Silverberg, Robert

Martindale, Patrick Victor
See White, Patrick (Victor Martindale)

Martin du Gard, Roger
1881-1958 .... **TCLC 24**
See also CA 118; DLB 65

Martineau, Harriet 1802-1876 .... **NCLC 26**
See also DLB 21, 55, 159, 163, 166, 190; YABC 2

Martines, Julia
See O'Faolain, Julia

Martinez, Enrique Gonzalez
See Gonzalez Martinez, Enrique

Martinez, Jacinto Benavente y
See Benavente (y Martinez), Jacinto

Martinez Ruiz, Jose 1873-1967
See Azorin; Ruiz, Jose Martinez
See also CA 93-96; HW 1

Martinez Sierra, Gregorio
1881-1947 .... **TCLC 6**
See also CA 115

Martinez Sierra, Maria (de la O'LeJarraga)
1874-1974 .... **TCLC 6**
See also CA 115

Martinsen, Martin
See Follett, Ken(neth Martin)

Martinson, Harry (Edmund)
1904-1978 .... **CLC 14**
See also CA 77-80; CANR 34

Marut, Ret
See Traven, B.

Marut, Robert
See Traven, B.

Marvell, Andrew 1621-1678 .. **LC 4, 43; DA; DAB; DAC; DAM MST, POET; PC 10; WLC**
See also CDBLB 1660-1789; DLB 131

Marx, Karl (Heinrich) 1818-1883 . **NCLC 17**
See also DLB 129

Masaoka Shiki .... **TCLC 18**
See also Masaoka Tsunenori

Masaoka Tsunenori 1867-1902
See Masaoka Shiki
See also CA 117

Masefield, John (Edward)
1878-1967 ..... **CLC 11, 47; DAM POET**
See also CA 19-20; 25-28R; CANR 33; CAP 2; CDBLB 1890-1914; DLB 10, 19, 153, 160; MTCW 1, 2; SATA 19

Maso, Carole 19(?)- .... **CLC 44**
See also CA 170

Mason, Bobbie Ann 1940- ... **CLC 28, 43, 82; SSC 4**
See also AAYA 5; CA 53-56; CANR 11, 31, 58, 83; CDALBS; DA3; DLB 173; DLBY 87; INT CANR-31; MTCW 1, 2

Mason, Ernst
See Pohl, Frederik

Mason, Lee W.
See Malzberg, Barry N(athaniel)

Mason, Nick 1945- .... **CLC 35**

Mason, Tally
See Derleth, August (William)

Mass, William
See Gibson, William

Master Lao
See Lao Tzu

Masters, Edgar Lee 1868-1950 .... **TCLC 2, 25; DA; DAC; DAM MST, POET; PC 1; WLCS**
See also CA 104; 133; CDALB 1865-1917; DLB 54; MTCW 1, 2

Masters, Hilary 1928- .... **CLC 48**
See also CA 25-28R; CANR 13, 47

Mastrosimone, William 19(?)- .... **CLC 36**

Mathe, Albert
See Camus, Albert

Mather, Cotton 1663-1728 .... **LC 38**
See also CDALB 1640-1865; DLB 24, 30, 140

Mather, Increase 1639-1723 .... **LC 38**
See also DLB 24

Matheson, Richard Burton 1926- .... **CLC 37**
See also AAYA 31; CA 97-100; DLB 8, 44; INT 97-100

Mathews, Harry 1930- .... **CLC 6, 52**
See also CA 21-24R; CAAS 6; CANR 18, 40

Mathews, John Joseph 1894-1979 .. **CLC 84; DAM MULT**
See also CA 19-20; 142; CANR 45; CAP 2; DLB 175; NNAL

Mathias, Roland (Glyn) 1915- .... **CLC 45**
See also CA 97-100; CANR 19, 41; DLB 27

Matsuo Basho 1644-1694 .... **PC 3**
See also DAM POET

Mattheson, Rodney
See Creasey, John

Matthews, (James) Brander
1852-1929 .... **TCLC 95**
See also DLB 71, 78; DLBD 13

Matthews, Greg 1949- .... **CLC 45**
See also CA 135

Matthews, William (Procter, III) 1942-1997 **CLC 40**
See also CA 29-32R; 162; CAAS 18; CANR 12, 57; DLB 5

Matthias, John (Edward) 1941- .... **CLC 9**
See also CA 33-36R; CANR 56

Matthiessen, F. O. 1902-1950 .... **TCLC 100**
See also DLB 63

Matthiessen, Peter 1927- ... **CLC 5, 7, 11, 32, 64; DAM NOV**
See also AAYA 6; BEST 90:4; CA 9-12R; CANR 21, 50, 73; DA3; DLB 6, 173; MTCW 1, 2; SATA 27

Maturin, Charles Robert
1780(?)-1824 .... **NCLC 6**
See also DLB 178

Matute (Ausejo), Ana Maria 1925- .. **CLC 11**
See also CA 89-92; MTCW 1

Maugham, W. S.
See Maugham, W(illiam) Somerset

Maugham, W(illiam) Somerset 1874-1965 **CLC 1, 11, 15, 67, 93; DA; DAB; DAC; DAM DRAM, MST, NOV; SSC 8; WLC**
See also CA 5-8R; 25-28R; CANR 40; CDBLB 1914-1945; DA3; DLB 10, 36, 77, 100, 162, 195; MTCW 1, 2; SATA 54

Maugham, William Somerset
See Maugham, W(illiam) Somerset

Maupassant, (Henri Rene Albert) Guy de
1850-1893 . **NCLC 1, 42, 83; DA; DAB; DAC; DAM MST; SSC 1; WLC**
See also DA3; DLB 123

Maupin, Armistead 1944- ..... **CLC 95; DAM POP**
See also CA 125; 130; CANR 58; DA3; INT 130; MTCW 2

Maurhut, Richard
See Traven, B.

Mauriac, Claude 1914-1996 .... **CLC 9**
See also CA 89-92; 152; DLB 83

Mauriac, Francois (Charles)
1885-1970 .... **CLC 4, 9, 56; SSC 24**
See also CA 25-28; CAP 2; DLB 65; MTCW 1, 2

Mavor, Osborne Henry 1888-1951
See Bridie, James
See also CA 104

Maxwell, William (Keepers, Jr.)
1908- .... **CLC 19**
See also CA 93-96; CANR 54; DLBY 80; INT 93-96

May, Elaine 1932- .... **CLC 16**
See also CA 124; 142; DLB 44

Mayakovski, Vladimir (Vladimirovich)
1893-1930 .... **TCLC 4, 18**
See also CA 104; 158; MTCW 2

Mayhew, Henry 1812-1887 .... **NCLC 31**
See also DLB 18, 55, 190

Mayle, Peter 1939(?)- .... **CLC 89**
See also CA 139; CANR 64

Maynard, Joyce 1953- .... **CLC 23**
See also CA 111; 129; CANR 64

Mayne, William (James Carter)
1928- .... **CLC 12**
See also AAYA 20; CA 9-12R; CANR 37,
80; CLR 25; JRDA; MAICYA; SAAS 11;
SATA 6, 68

Mayo, Jim
See L'Amour, Louis (Dearborn)

Maysles, Albert 1926- .... **CLC 16**
See also CA 29-32R

Maysles, David 1932- .... **CLC 16**

Mazer, Norma Fox 1931- .... **CLC 26**
See also AAYA 5; CA 69-72; CANR 12,
32, 66; CLR 23; JRDA; MAICYA; SAAS
1; SATA 24, 67, 105

Mazzini, Guiseppe 1805-1872 .... **NCLC 34**

McAlmon, Robert (Menzies) 1895-1956
TCLC 97
See also CA 107; 168; DLB 4, 45; DLBD
15

McAuley, James Phillip 1917-1976 .. **CLC 45**
See also CA 97-100

McBain, Ed
See Hunter, Evan

McBrien, William Augustine 1930- .. **CLC 44**
See also CA 107

McCaffrey, Anne (Inez) 1926- .... **CLC 17;
DAM NOV, POP**
See also AAYA 6; AITN 2; BEST 89:2; CA
25-28R; CANR 15, 35, 55; CLR 49; DA3;
DLB 8; JRDA; MAICYA; MTCW 1, 2;
SAAS 11; SATA 8, 70

McCall, Nathan 1955(?)- .... **CLC 86**
See also BW 3; CA 146

McCann, Arthur
See Campbell, John W(ood, Jr.)

McCann, Edson
See Pohl, Frederik

McCarthy, Charles, Jr. 1933-
See McCarthy, Cormac
See also CANR 42, 69; DAM POP; DA3;
MTCW 2

McCarthy, Cormac 1933- ...... **CLC 4, 57, 59,
101**
See also McCarthy, Charles, Jr. DLB 6, 143;
MTCW 2

McCarthy, Mary (Therese)
1912-1989 .. **CLC 1, 3, 5, 14, 24, 39, 59;
SSC 24**
See also CA 5-8R; 129; CANR 16, 50, 64;
DA3; DLB 2; DLBY 81; INT CANR-16;
MTCW 1, 2

McCartney, (James) Paul 1942- . **CLC 12, 35**
See also CA 146

McCauley, Stephen (D.) 1955- .... **CLC 50**
See also CA 141

McClure, Michael (Thomas) 1932- ... **CLC 6,
10**
See also CA 21-24R; CANR 17, 46, 77;
DLB 16

McCorkle, Jill (Collins) 1958- .... **CLC 51**
See also CA 121; DLBY 87

McCourt, Frank 1930- .... **CLC 109**
See also CA 157

McCourt, James 1941- .... **CLC 5**
See also CA 57-60

McCourt, Malachy 1932- .... **CLC 119**

McCoy, Horace (Stanley)
1897-1955 .... **TCLC 28**
See also CA 108; 155; DLB 9

McCrae, John 1872-1918 .... **TCLC 12**
See also CA 109; DLB 92

McCreigh, James
See Pohl, Frederik

McCullers, (Lula) Carson (Smith) 1917-1967
**CLC 1, 4, 10, 12, 48, 100; DA; DAB;
DAC; DAM MST, NOV; SSC 9, 24;
WLC**
See also AAYA 21; CA 5-8R; 25-28R;
CABS 1, 3; CANR 18; CDALB 1941-
1968; DA3; DLB 2, 7, 173; MTCW 1, 2;
SATA 27

McCulloch, John Tyler
See Burroughs, Edgar Rice

McCullough, Colleen 1938(?)- .... **CLC 27,
107; DAM NOV, POP**
See also CA 81-84; CANR 17, 46, 67; DA3;
MTCW 1, 2

McDermott, Alice 1953- .... **CLC 90**
See also CA 109; CANR 40

McElroy, Joseph 1930- .... **CLC 5, 47**
See also CA 17-20R

McEwan, Ian (Russell) 1948- .... **CLC 13, 66;
DAM NOV**
See also BEST 90:4; CA 61-64; CANR 14,
41, 69, 87; DLB 14, 194; MTCW 1, 2

McFadden, David 1940- .... **CLC 48**
See also CA 104; DLB 60; INT 104

McFarland, Dennis 1950- .... **CLC 65**
See also CA 165

McGahern, John 1934- ... **CLC 5, 9, 48; SSC
17**
See also CA 17-20R; CANR 29, 68; DLB
14; MTCW 1

McGinley, Patrick (Anthony) 1937- . **CLC 41**
See also CA 120; 127; CANR 56; INT 127

McGinley, Phyllis 1905-1978 .... **CLC 14**
See also CA 9-12R; 77-80; CANR 19; DLB
11, 48; SATA 2, 44; SATA-Obit 24

McGinniss, Joe 1942- .... **CLC 32**
See also AITN 2; BEST 89:2; CA 25-28R;
CANR 26, 70; DLB 185; INT CANR-26

McGivern, Maureen Daly
See Daly, Maureen

McGrath, Patrick 1950- .... **CLC 55**
See also CA 136; CANR 65

McGrath, Thomas (Matthew) 1916-1990
CLC 28, 59; DAM POET
See also CA 9-12R; 132; CANR 6, 33;
MTCW 1; SATA 41; SATA-Obit 66

McGuane, Thomas (Francis III)
1939- .... **CLC 3, 7, 18, 45, 127**
See also AITN 2; CA 49-52; CANR 5, 24,
49; DLB 2, 212; DLBY 80; INT CANR-
24; MTCW 1

McGuckian, Medbh 1950- .... **CLC 48; DAM
POET; PC 27**
See also CA 143; DLB 40

McHale, Tom 1942(?)-1982 .... **CLC 3, 5**
See also AITN 1; CA 77-80; 106

McIlvanney, William 1936- .... **CLC 42**
See also CA 25-28R; CANR 61; DLB 14,
207

McIlwraith, Maureen Mollie Hunter
See Hunter, Mollie
See also SATA 2

McInerney, Jay 1955- .... **CLC 34, 112; DAM
POP**
See also AAYA 18; CA 116; 123; CANR
45, 68; DA3; INT 123; MTCW 2

McIntyre, Vonda N(eel) 1948- .... **CLC 18**
See also CA 81-84; CANR 17, 34, 69;
MTCW 1

McKay, Claude . **TCLC 7, 41; BLC 3; DAB;
PC 2**
See also McKay, Festus Claudius DLB 4,
45, 51, 117

McKay, Festus Claudius 1889-1948
See McKay, Claude
See also BW 1, 3; CA 104; 124; CANR 73;
DA; DAC; DAM MST, MULT, NOV,
POET; MTCW 1, 2; WLC

McKuen, Rod 1933- .... **CLC 1, 3**
See also AITN 1; CA 41-44R; CANR 40

McLoughlin, R. B.
See Mencken, H(enry) L(ouis)

McLuhan, (Herbert) Marshall 1911-1980
CLC 37, 83
See also CA 9-12R; 102; CANR 12, 34, 61;
DLB 88; INT CANR-12; MTCW 1, 2

McMillan, Terry (L.) 1951- .... **CLC 50, 61,
112; BLCS; DAM MULT, NOV, POP**
See also AAYA 21; BW 2, 3; CA 140;
CANR 60; DA3; MTCW 2

McMurtry, Larry (Jeff) 1936- .. **CLC 2, 3, 7,
11, 27, 44, 127; DAM NOV, POP**
See also AAYA 15; AITN 2; BEST 89:2;
CA 5-8R; CANR 19, 43, 64; CDALB
1968-1988; DA3; DLB 2, 143; DLBY 80,
87; MTCW 1, 2

McNally, T. M. 1961- .... **CLC 82**

McNally, Terrence 1939- ... **CLC 4, 7, 41, 91;
DAM DRAM**
See also CA 45-48; CANR 2, 56; DA3;
DLB 7; MTCW 2

McNamer, Deirdre 1950- .... **CLC 70**

McNeal, Tom .... **CLC 119**

McNeile, Herman Cyril 1888-1937
See Sapper
See also DLB 77

McNickle, (William) D'Arcy
1904-1977 .... **CLC 89; DAM MULT**
See also CA 9-12R; 85-88; CANR 5, 45;
DLB 175, 212; NNAL; SATA-Obit 22

McPhee, John (Angus) 1931- .... **CLC 36**
See also BEST 90:1; CA 65-68; CANR 20,
46, 64, 69; DLB 185; MTCW 1, 2

McPherson, James Alan 1943- .. **CLC 19, 77;
BLCS**
See also BW 1, 3; CA 25-28R; CAAS 17;
CANR 24, 74; DLB 38; MTCW 1, 2

McPherson, William (Alexander)
1933- .... **CLC 34**
See also CA 69-72; CANR 28; INT
CANR-28

Mead, George Herbert 1873-1958 . **TCLC 89**

Mead, Margaret 1901-1978 .... **CLC 37**
See also AITN 1; CA 1-4R; 81-84; CANR
4; DA3; MTCW 1, 2; SATA-Obit 20

Meaker, Marijane (Agnes) 1927-
See Kerr, M. E.
See also CA 107; CANR 37, 63; INT 107;
JRDA; MAICYA; MTCW 1; SATA 20,
61, 99; SATA-Essay 111

Medoff, Mark (Howard) 1940- ... **CLC 6, 23;
DAM DRAM**
See also AITN 1; CA 53-56; CANR 5; DLB
7; INT CANR-5

Medvedev, P. N.
See Bakhtin, Mikhail Mikhailovich

Meged, Aharon
See Megged, Aharon

Meged, Aron
See Megged, Aharon

Megged, Aharon 1920- .... **CLC 9**
See also CA 49-52; CAAS 13; CANR 1

Olyesha, Yuri
   See Olesha, Yuri (Karlovich)
Ondaatje, (Philip) Michael 1943- .... **CLC 14, 29, 51, 76; DAB; DAC; DAM MST; PC 28**
   See also CA 77-80; CANR 42, 74; DA3; DLB 60; MTCW 2
Oneal, Elizabeth 1934-
   See Oneal, Zibby
   See also CA 106; CANR 28, 84; MAICYA; SATA 30, 82
Oneal, Zibby .... **CLC 30**
   See also Oneal, Elizabeth AAYA 5; CLR 13; JRDA
O'Neill, Eugene (Gladstone) 1888-1953
   TCLC 1, 6, 27, 49; DA; DAB; DAC; DAM DRAM, MST; WLC
   See also AITN 1; CA 110; 132; CDALB 1929-1941; DA3; DLB 7; MTCW 1, 2
Onetti, Juan Carlos 1909-1994 ... **CLC 7, 10; DAM MULT, NOV; HLCS 2; SSC 23**
   See also CA 85-88; 145; CANR 32, 63; DLB 113; HW 1, 2; MTCW 1, 2
O Nuallain, Brian 1911-1966
   See O'Brien, Flann
   See also CA 21-22; 25-28R; CAP 2
Ophuls, Max 1902-1957 .... **TCLC 79**
   See also CA 113
Opie, Amelia 1769-1853 .... **NCLC 65**
   See also DLB 116, 159
Oppen, George 1908-1984 ...... **CLC 7, 13, 34**
   See also CA 13-16R; 113; CANR 8, 82; DLB 5, 165
Oppenheim, E(dward) Phillips 1866-1946
   TCLC 45
   See also CA 111; DLB 70
Opuls, Max
   See Ophuls, Max
Origen c. 185-c. 254 .... **CMLC 19**
Orlovitz, Gil 1918-1973 .... **CLC 22**
   See also CA 77-80; 45-48; DLB 2, 5
Orris
   See Ingelow, Jean
Ortega y Gasset, Jose 1883-1955 ... **TCLC 9; DAM MULT; HLC 2**
   See also CA 106; 130; HW 1, 2; MTCW 1, 2
Ortese, Anna Maria 1914- .... **CLC 89**
   See also DLB 177
Ortiz, Simon J(oseph) 1941- . **CLC 45; DAM MULT, POET; PC 17**
   See also CA 134; CANR 69; DLB 120, 175; NNAL
Orton, Joe .... **CLC 4, 13, 43; DC 3**
   See also Orton, John Kingsley CDBLB 1960 to Present; DLB 13; MTCW 2
Orton, John Kingsley 1933-1967
   See Orton, Joe
   See also CA 85-88; CANR 35, 66; DAM DRAM; MTCW 1, 2
Orwell, George .... **TCLC 2, 6, 15, 31, 51; DAB; WLC**
   See also Blair, Eric (Arthur) CDBLB 1945-1960; DLB 15, 98, 195
Osborne, David
   See Silverberg, Robert
Osborne, George
   See Silverberg, Robert

Osborne, John (James) 1929-1994 .... **CLC 1, 2, 5, 11, 45; DA; DAB; DAC; DAM DRAM, MST; WLC**
   See also CA 13-16R; 147; CANR 21, 56; CDBLB 1945-1960; DLB 13; MTCW 1, 2
Osborne, Lawrence 1958- .... **CLC 50**
Osbourne, Lloyd 1868-1947 .... **TCLC 93**
Oshima, Nagisa 1932- .... **CLC 20**
   See also CA 116; 121; CANR 78
Oskison, John Milton 1874-1947 .. **TCLC 35; DAM MULT**
   See also CA 144; CANR 84; DLB 175; NNAL
Ossian c. 3rd cent. - .... **CMLC 28**
   See also Macpherson, James
Ostrovsky, Alexander 1823-1886 .. **NCLC 30, 57**
Otero, Blas de 1916-1979 .... **CLC 11**
   See also CA 89-92; DLB 134
Otto, Rudolf 1869-1937 .... **TCLC 85**
Otto, Whitney 1955- .... **CLC 70**
   See also CA 140
Ouida .... **TCLC 43**
   See also De La Ramee, (Marie) Louise DLB 18, 156
Ousmane, Sembene 1923- ... **CLC 66; BLC 3**
   See also BW 1, 3; CA 117; 125; CANR 81; MTCW 1
Ovid 43B.C.-17 . **CMLC 7; DAM POET; PC 2**
   See also DA3; DLB 211
Owen, Hugh
   See Faust, Frederick (Schiller)
Owen, Wilfred (Edward Salter) 1893-1918
   TCLC 5, 27; DA; DAB; DAC; DAM MST, POET; PC 19; WLC
   See also CA 104; 141; CDBLB 1914-1945; DLB 20; MTCW 2
Owens, Rochelle 1936- .... **CLC 8**
   See also CA 17-20R; CAAS 2; CANR 39
Oz, Amos 1939- ...... **CLC 5, 8, 11, 27, 33, 54; DAM NOV**
   See also CA 53-56; CANR 27, 47, 65; MTCW 1, 2
Ozick, Cynthia 1928- .... **CLC 3, 7, 28, 62; DAM NOV, POP; SSC 15**
   See also BEST 90:1; CA 17-20R; CANR 23, 58; DA3; DLB 28, 152; DLBY 82; INT CANR-23; MTCW 1, 2
Ozu, Yasujiro 1903-1963 .... **CLC 16**
   See also CA 112
Pacheco, C.
   See Pessoa, Fernando (Antonio Nogueira)
Pacheco, Jose Emilio 1939-
   See also CA 111; 131; CANR 65; DAM MULT; HLC 2; HW 1, 2
Pa Chin .... **CLC 18**
   See also Li Fei-kan
Pack, Robert 1929- .... **CLC 13**
   See also CA 1-4R; CANR 3, 44, 82; DLB 5
Padgett, Lewis
   See Kuttner, Henry
Padilla (Lorenzo), Heberto 1932- ..... **CLC 38**
   See also AITN 1; CA 123; 131; HW 1
Page, Jimmy 1944- .... **CLC 12**
Page, Louise 1955- .... **CLC 40**
   See also CA 140; CANR 76
Page, P(atricia) K(athleen) 1916- ...... **CLC 7, 18; DAC; DAM MST; PC 12**
   See also CA 53-56; CANR 4, 22, 65; DLB 68; MTCW 1

Page, Thomas Nelson 1853-1922 .... **SSC 23**
   See also CA 118; 177; DLB 12, 78; DLBD 13
Pagels, Elaine Hiesey 1943- .... **CLC 104**
   See also CA 45-48; CANR 2, 24, 51
Paget, Violet 1856-1935
   See Lee, Vernon
   See also CA 104; 166
Paget-Lowe, Henry
   See Lovecraft, H(oward) P(hillips)
Paglia, Camille (Anna) 1947- .... **CLC 68**
   See also CA 140; CANR 72; MTCW 2
Paige, Richard
   See Koontz, Dean R(ay)
Paine, Thomas 1737-1809 .... **NCLC 62**
   See also CDALB 1640-1865; DLB 31, 43, 73, 158
Pakenham, Antonia
   See Fraser, (Lady) Antonia (Pakenham)
Palamas, Kostes 1859-1943 .... **TCLC 5**
   See also CA 105
Palazzeschi, Aldo 1885-1974 .... **CLC 11**
   See also CA 89-92; 53-56; DLB 114
Pales Matos, Luis 1898-1959
   See also HLCS 2; HW 1
Paley, Grace 1922- .... **CLC 4, 6, 37; DAM POP; SSC 8**
   See also CA 25-28R; CANR 13, 46, 74; DA3; DLB 28; INT CANR-13; MTCW 1, 2
Palin, Michael (Edward) 1943- .... **CLC 21**
   See also Monty Python CA 107; CANR 35; SATA 67
Palliser, Charles 1947- .... **CLC 65**
   See also CA 136; CANR 76
Palma, Ricardo 1833-1919 .... **TCLC 29**
   See also CA 168
Pancake, Breece Dexter 1952-1979
   See Pancake, Breece D'J
   See also CA 123; 109
Pancake, Breece D'J .... **CLC 29**
   See also Pancake, Breece Dexter DLB 130
Panko, Rudy
   See Gogol, Nikolai (Vasilyevich)
Papadiamantis, Alexandros
   1851-1911 .... **TCLC 29**
   See also CA 168
Papadiamantopoulos, Johannes 1856-1910
   See Moreas, Jean
   See also CA 117
Papini, Giovanni 1881-1956 .... **TCLC 22**
   See also CA 121; 180
Paracelsus 1493-1541 .... **LC 14**
   See also DLB 179
Parasol, Peter
   See Stevens, Wallace
Pardo Bazan, Emilia 1851-1921 .... **SSC 30**
Pareto, Vilfredo 1848-1923 .... **TCLC 69**
   See also CA 175
Parfenie, Maria
   See Codrescu, Andrei
Parini, Jay (Lee) 1948- .... **CLC 54**
   See also CA 97-100; CAAS 16; CANR 32, 87
Park, Jordan
   See Kornbluth, C(yril) M.; Pohl, Frederik
Park, Robert E(zra) 1864-1944 ..... **TCLC 73**
   See also CA 122; 165
Parker, Bert
   See Ellison, Harlan (Jay)

Rattigan, Terence (Mervyn)
1911-1977 .... **CLC 7; DAM DRAM**
See also CA 85-88; 73-76; CDBLB 1945-1960; DLB 13; MTCW 1, 2

Ratushinskaya, Irina 1954- .... **CLC 54**
See also CA 129; CANR 68

Raven, Simon (Arthur Noel) 1927- .. **CLC 14**
See also CA 81-84; CANR 86

Ravenna, Michael
See Welty, Eudora

Rawley, Callman 1903-
See Rakosi, Carl
See also CA 21-24R; CANR 12, 32

Rawlings, Marjorie Kinnan
1896-1953 .... **TCLC 4**
See also AAYA 20; CA 104; 137; CANR 74; DLB 9, 22, 102; DLBD 17; JRDA; MAICYA; MTCW 2; SATA 100; YABC 1

Ray, Satyajit 1921-1992 .. **CLC 16, 76; DAM MULT**
See also CA 114; 137

Read, Herbert Edward 1893-1968 ..... **CLC 4**
See also CA 85-88; 25-28R; DLB 20, 149

Read, Piers Paul 1941- .... **CLC 4, 10, 25**
See also CA 21-24R; CANR 38, 86; DLB 14; SATA 21

Reade, Charles 1814-1884 .... **NCLC 2, 74**
See also DLB 21

Reade, Hamish
See Gray, Simon (James Holliday)

Reading, Peter 1946- .... **CLC 47**
See also CA 103; CANR 46; DLB 40

Reaney, James 1926- .. **CLC 13; DAC; DAM MST**
See also CA 41-44R; CAAS 15; CANR 42; DLB 68; SATA 43

Rebreanu, Liviu 1885-1944 .... **TCLC 28**
See also CA 165

Rechy, John (Francisco) 1934- ...... **CLC 1, 7, 14, 18, 107; DAM MULT; HLC 2**
See also CA 5-8R; CAAS 4; CANR 6, 32, 64; DLB 122; DLBY 82; HW 1, 2; INT CANR-6

Redcam, Tom 1870-1933 .... **TCLC 25**

Reddin, Keith .... **CLC 67**

Redgrove, Peter (William) 1932- . **CLC 6, 41**
See also CA 1-4R; CANR 3, 39, 77; DLB 40

Redmon, Anne .... **CLC 22**
See also Nightingale, Anne Redmon DLBY 86

Reed, Eliot
See Ambler, Eric

Reed, Ishmael 1938- .. **CLC 2, 3, 5, 6, 13, 32, 60; BLC 3; DAM MULT**
See also BW 2, 3; CA 21-24R; CANR 25, 48, 74; DA3; DLB 2, 5, 33, 169; DLBD 8; MTCW 1, 2

Reed, John (Silas) 1887-1920 .... **TCLC 9**
See also CA 106

Reed, Lou .... **CLC 21**
See also Firbank, Louis

Reese, Lizette Woodworth 1856-1935 . **PC 29**
See also CA 180; DLB 54

Reeve, Clara 1729-1807 .... **NCLC 19**
See also DLB 39

Reich, Wilhelm 1897-1957 .... **TCLC 57**

Reid, Christopher (John) 1949- .... **CLC 33**
See also CA 140; DLB 40

Reid, Desmond
See Moorcock, Michael (John)

Reid Banks, Lynne 1929-
See Banks, Lynne Reid
See also CA 1-4R; CANR 6, 22, 38, 87; CLR 24; JRDA; MAICYA; SATA 22, 75, 111

Reilly, William K.
See Creasey, John

Reiner, Max
See Caldwell, (Janet Miriam) Taylor (Holland)

Reis, Ricardo
See Pessoa, Fernando (Antonio Nogueira)

Remarque, Erich Maria
1898-1970 ... **CLC 21; DA; DAB; DAC; DAM MST, NOV**
See also AAYA 27; CA 77-80; 29-32R; DA3; DLB 56; MTCW 1, 2

Remington, Frederic 1861-1909 ..... **TCLC 89**
See also CA 108; 169; DLB 12, 186, 188; SATA 41

Remizov, A.
See Remizov, Aleksei (Mikhailovich)

Remizov, A. M.
See Remizov, Aleksei (Mikhailovich)

Remizov, Aleksei (Mikhailovich) 1877-1957 **TCLC 27**
See also CA 125; 133

Renan, Joseph Ernest 1823-1892 .. **NCLC 26**

Renard, Jules 1864-1910 .... **TCLC 17**
See also CA 117

Renault, Mary .... **CLC 3, 11, 17**
See also Challans, Mary DLBY 83; MTCW 2

Rendell, Ruth (Barbara) 1930- . **CLC 28, 48; DAM POP**
See also Vine, Barbara CA 109; CANR 32, 52, 74; DLB 87; INT CANR-32; MTCW 1, 2

Renoir, Jean 1894-1979 .... **CLC 20**
See also CA 129; 85-88

Resnais, Alain 1922- .... **CLC 16**

Reverdy, Pierre 1889-1960 .... **CLC 53**
See also CA 97-100; 89-92

Rexroth, Kenneth 1905-1982 .... **CLC 1, 2, 6, 11, 22, 49, 112; DAM POET; PC 20**
See also CA 5-8R; 107; CANR 14, 34, 63; CDALB 1941-1968; DLB 16, 48, 165, 212; DLBY 82; INT CANR-14; MTCW 1, 2

Reyes, Alfonso 1889-1959 .. **TCLC 33; HLCS 2**
See also CA 131; HW 1

Reyes y Basoalto, Ricardo Eliecer Neftali
See Neruda, Pablo

Reymont, Wladyslaw (Stanislaw)
1868(?)-1925 .... **TCLC 5**
See also CA 104

Reynolds, Jonathan 1942- .... **CLC 6, 38**
See also CA 65-68; CANR 28

Reynolds, Joshua 1723-1792 .... **LC 15**
See also DLB 104

Reynolds, Michael Shane 1937- .... **CLC 44**
See also CA 65-68; CANR 9

Reznikoff, Charles 1894-1976 .... **CLC 9**
See also CA 33-36; 61-64; CAP 2; DLB 28, 45

Rezzori (d'Arezzo), Gregor von 1914-1998 **CLC 25**
See also CA 122; 136; 167

Rhine, Richard
See Silverstein, Alvin

Rhodes, Eugene Manlove
1869-1934 .... **TCLC 53**

Rhodius, Apollonius c. 3rd cent.
B.C.- .... **CMLC 28**
See also DLB 176

R'hoone
See Balzac, Honore de

Rhys, Jean 1890(?)-1979 ...... **CLC 2, 4, 6, 14, 19, 51, 124; DAM NOV; SSC 21**
See also CA 25-28R; 85-88; CANR 35, 62; CDBLB 1945-1960; DA3; DLB 36, 117, 162; MTCW 1, 2

Ribeiro, Darcy 1922-1997 .... **CLC 34**
See also CA 33-36R; 156

Ribeiro, Joao Ubaldo (Osorio Pimentel)
1941- .... **CLC 10, 67**
See also CA 81-84

Ribman, Ronald (Burt) 1932- .... **CLC 7**
See also CA 21-24R; CANR 46, 80

Ricci, Nino 1959- .... **CLC 70**
See also CA 137

Rice, Anne 1941- .. **CLC 41, 128; DAM POP**
See also AAYA 9; BEST 89:2; CA 65-68; CANR 12, 36, 53, 74; DA3; MTCW 2

Rice, Elmer (Leopold) 1892-1967 ...... **CLC 7, 49; DAM DRAM**
See also CA 21-22; 25-28R; CAP 2; DLB 4, 7; MTCW 1, 2

Rice, Tim(othy Miles Bindon)
1944- .... **CLC 21**
See also CA 103; CANR 46

Rich, Adrienne (Cecile) 1929- ... **CLC 3, 6, 7, 11, 18, 36, 73, 76, 125; DAM POET; PC 5**
See also CA 9-12R; CANR 20, 53, 74; CDALBS; DA3; DLB 5, 67; MTCW 1, 2

Rich, Barbara
See Graves, Robert (von Ranke)

Rich, Robert
See Trumbo, Dalton

Richard, Keith .... **CLC 17**
See also Richards, Keith

Richards, David Adams 1950- .... **CLC 59; DAC**
See also CA 93-96; CANR 60; DLB 53

Richards, I(vor) A(rmstrong)
1893-1979 .... **CLC 14, 24**
See also CA 41-44R; 89-92; CANR 34, 74; DLB 27; MTCW 2

Richards, Keith 1943-
See Richard, Keith
See also CA 107; CANR 77

Richardson, Anne
See Roiphe, Anne (Richardson)

Richardson, Dorothy Miller
1873-1957 .... **TCLC 3**
See also CA 104; DLB 36

Richardson, Ethel Florence (Lindesay)
1870-1946
See Richardson, Henry Handel
See also CA 105

Richardson, Henry Handel .... **TCLC 4**
See also Richardson, Ethel Florence (Lindesay) DLB 197

Richardson, John 1796-1852 .... **NCLC 55; DAC**
See also DLB 99

Richardson, Samuel 1689-1761 ...... **LC 1, 44; DA; DAB; DAC; DAM MST, NOV; WLC**
See also CDBLB 1660-1789; DLB 39

Richler, Mordecai 1931- ...... **CLC 3, 5, 9, 13, 18, 46, 70; DAC; DAM MST, NOV**
See also AITN 1; CA 65-68; CANR 31, 62; CLR 17; DLB 53; MAICYA; MTCW 1, 2; SATA 44, 98; SATA-Brief 27

Richter, Conrad (Michael) 1890-1968 .... **CLC 30**
See also AAYA 21; CA 5-8R; 25-28R; CANR 23; DLB 9, 212; MTCW 1, 2; SATA 3

Ricostranza, Tom
See Ellis, Trey

Riddell, Charlotte 1832-1906 .... **TCLC 40**
See also CA 165; DLB 156

Ridge, John Rollin 1827-1867 ...... **NCLC 82; DAM MULT**
See also CA 144; DLB 175; NNAL

Ridgway, Keith 1965- .... **CLC 119**
See also CA 172

Riding, Laura .... **CLC 3, 7**
See also Jackson, Laura (Riding)

Riefenstahl, Berta Helene Amalia 1902-
See Riefenstahl, Leni
See also CA 108

Riefenstahl, Leni .... **CLC 16**
See also Riefenstahl, Berta Helene Amalia

Riffe, Ernest
See Bergman, (Ernst) Ingmar

Riggs, (Rolla) Lynn 1899-1954 ..... **TCLC 56; DAM MULT**
See also CA 144; DLB 175; NNAL

Riis, Jacob A(ugust) 1849-1914 ..... **TCLC 80**
See also CA 113; 168; DLB 23

Riley, James Whitcomb 1849-1916 .... **TCLC 51; DAM POET**
See also CA 118; 137; MAICYA; SATA 17

Riley, Tex
See Creasey, John

Rilke, Rainer Maria 1875-1926 .. **TCLC 1, 6, 19; DAM POET; PC 2**
See also CA 104; 132; CANR 62; DA3; DLB 81; MTCW 1, 2

Rimbaud, (Jean Nicolas) Arthur 1854-1891 **NCLC 4, 35, 82; DA; DAB; DAC; DAM MST, POET; PC 3; WLC**
See also DA3

Rinehart, Mary Roberts 1876-1958 .... **TCLC 52**
See also CA 108; 166

Ringmaster, The
See Mencken, H(enry) L(ouis)

Ringwood, Gwen(dolyn Margaret) Pharis 1910-1984 .... **CLC 48**
See also CA 148; 112; DLB 88

Rio, Michel 19(?)- .... **CLC 43**

Ritsos, Giannes
See Ritsos, Yannis

Ritsos, Yannis 1909-1990 .... **CLC 6, 13, 31**
See also CA 77-80; 133; CANR 39, 61; MTCW 1

Ritter, Erika 1948(?)- .... **CLC 52**

Rivera, Jose Eustasio 1889-1928 ... **TCLC 35**
See also CA 162; HW 1, 2

Rivera, Tomas 1935-1984
See also CA 49-52; CANR 32; DLB 82; HLCS 2; HW 1

Rivers, Conrad Kent 1933-1968 .... **CLC 1**
See also BW 1; CA 85-88; DLB 41

Rivers, Elfrida
See Bradley, Marion Zimmer

Riverside, John
See Heinlein, Robert A(nson)

Rizal, Jose 1861-1896 .... **NCLC 27**

Roa Bastos, Augusto (Antonio) 1917- .... **CLC 45; DAM MULT; HLC 2**
See also CA 131; DLB 113; HW 1

Robbe-Grillet, Alain 1922- .... **CLC 1, 2, 4, 6, 8, 10, 14, 43, 128**
See also CA 9-12R; CANR 33, 65; DLB 83; MTCW 1, 2

Robbins, Harold 1916-1997 .... **CLC 5; DAM NOV**
See also CA 73-76; 162; CANR 26, 54; DA3; MTCW 1, 2

Robbins, Thomas Eugene 1936-
See Robbins, Tom
See also CA 81-84; CANR 29, 59; DAM NOV, POP; DA3; MTCW 1, 2

Robbins, Tom .... **CLC 9, 32, 64**
See also Robbins, Thomas Eugene AAYA 32; BEST 90:3; DLBY 80; MTCW 2

Robbins, Trina 1938- .... **CLC 21**
See also CA 128

Roberts, Charles G(eorge) D(ouglas) 1860-1943 .... **TCLC 8**
See also CA 105; CLR 33; DLB 92; SATA 88; SATA-Brief 29

Roberts, Elizabeth Madox 1886-1941 .... **TCLC 68**
See also CA 111; 166; DLB 9, 54, 102; SATA 33; SATA-Brief 27

Roberts, Kate 1891-1985 .... **CLC 15**
See also CA 107; 116

Roberts, Keith (John Kingston) 1935- .... **CLC 14**
See also CA 25-28R; CANR 46

Roberts, Kenneth (Lewis) 1885-1957 .... **TCLC 23**
See also CA 109; DLB 9

Roberts, Michele (B.) 1949- .... **CLC 48**
See also CA 115; CANR 58

Robertson, Ellis
See Ellison, Harlan (Jay); Silverberg, Robert

Robertson, Thomas William 1829-1871 **NCLC 35; DAM DRAM**

Robeson, Kenneth
See Dent, Lester

Robinson, Edwin Arlington 1869-1935 ... **TCLC 5; DA; DAC; DAM MST, POET; PC 1**
See also CA 104; 133; CDALB 1865-1917; DLB 54; MTCW 1, 2

Robinson, Henry Crabb 1775-1867 .... **NCLC 15**
See also DLB 107

Robinson, Jill 1936- .... **CLC 10**
See also CA 102; INT 102

Robinson, Kim Stanley 1952- .... **CLC 34**
See also AAYA 26; CA 126; SATA 109

Robinson, Lloyd
See Silverberg, Robert

Robinson, Marilynne 1944- .... **CLC 25**
See also CA 116; CANR 80; DLB 206

Robinson, Smokey .... **CLC 21**
See also Robinson, William, Jr.

Robinson, William, Jr. 1940-
See Robinson, Smokey
See also CA 116

Robison, Mary 1949- .... **CLC 42, 98**
See also CA 113; 116; CANR 87; DLB 130; INT 116

Rod, Edouard 1857-1910 .... **TCLC 52**

Roddenberry, Eugene Wesley 1921-1991
See Roddenberry, Gene

See also CA 110; 135; CANR 37; SATA 45; SATA-Obit 69

Roddenberry, Gene .... **CLC 17**
See also Roddenberry, Eugene Wesley AAYA 5; SATA-Obit 69

Rodgers, Mary 1931- .... **CLC 12**
See also CA 49-52; CANR 8, 55; CLR 20; INT CANR-8; JRDA; MAICYA; SATA 8

Rodgers, W(illiam) R(obert) 1909-1969 .... **CLC 7**
See also CA 85-88; DLB 20

Rodman, Eric
See Silverberg, Robert

Rodman, Howard 1920(?)-1985 .... **CLC 65**
See also CA 118

Rodman, Maia
See Wojciechowska, Maia (Teresa)

Rodo, Jose Enrique 1872(?)-1917
See also CA 178; HLCS 2; HW 2

Rodriguez, Claudio 1934- .... **CLC 10**
See also DLB 134

Rodriguez, Richard 1944-
See also CA 110; CANR 66; DAM MULT; DLB 82; HLC 2; HW 1, 2

Roelvaag, O(le) E(dvart) 1876-1931 .... **TCLC 17**
See also CA 117; 171; DLB 9

Roethke, Theodore (Huebner) 1908-1963 **CLC 1, 3, 8, 11, 19, 46, 101; DAM POET; PC 15**
See also CA 81-84; CABS 2; CDALB 1941-1968; DA3; DLB 5, 206; MTCW 1, 2

Rogers, Samuel 1763-1855 .... **NCLC 69**
See also DLB 93

Rogers, Thomas Hunton 1927- .... **CLC 57**
See also CA 89-92; INT 89-92

Rogers, Will(iam Penn Adair) 1879-1935 **TCLC 8, 71; DAM MULT**
See also CA 105; 144; DA3; DLB 11; MTCW 2; NNAL

Rogin, Gilbert 1929- .... **CLC 18**
See also CA 65-68; CANR 15

Rohan, Koda .... **TCLC 22**
See also Koda Shigeyuki

Rohlfs, Anna Katharine Green
See Green, Anna Katharine

Rohmer, Eric .... **CLC 16**
See also Scherer, Jean-Marie Maurice

Rohmer, Sax .... **TCLC 28**
See also Ward, Arthur Henry Sarsfield DLB 70

Roiphe, Anne (Richardson) 1935- .. **CLC 3, 9**
See also CA 89-92; CANR 45, 73; DLBY 80; INT 89-92

Rojas, Fernando de 1465-1541 .... **LC 23; HLCS 1**

Rojas, Gonzalo 1917-
See also HLCS 2; HW 2

Rojas, Gonzalo 1917-
See also CA 178; HLCS 2

Rolfe, Frederick (William Serafino Austin Lewis Mary) 1860-1913 .... **TCLC 12**
See also CA 107; DLB 34, 156

Rolland, Romain 1866-1944 .... **TCLC 23**
See also CA 118; DLB 65

Rolle, Richard c. 1300-c. 1349 ...... **CMLC 21**
See also DLB 146

Rolvaag, O(le) E(dvart)
See Roelvaag, O(le) E(dvart)

Romain Arnaud, Saint
See Aragon, Louis

Romains, Jules 1885-1972 .... **CLC 7**
See also CA 85-88; CANR 34; DLB 65;
MTCW 1

Romero, Jose Ruben 1890-1952 .... **TCLC 14**
See also CA 114; 131; HW 1

Ronsard, Pierre de 1524-1585 . **LC 6, 54; PC 11**

Rooke, Leon 1934- . **CLC 25, 34; DAM POP**
See also CA 25-28R; CANR 23, 53

Roosevelt, Franklin Delano
1882-1945 .... **TCLC 93**
See also CA 116; 173

Roosevelt, Theodore 1858-1919 ..... **TCLC 69**
See also CA 115; 170; DLB 47, 186

Roper, William 1498-1578 .... **LC 10**

Roquelaure, A. N.
See Rice, Anne

Rosa, Joao Guimaraes 1908-1967 ... **CLC 23; HLCS 1**
See also CA 89-92; DLB 113

Rose, Wendy 1948- .. **CLC 85; DAM MULT; PC 13**
See also CA 53-56; CANR 5, 51; DLB 175;
NNAL; SATA 12

Rosen, R. D.
See Rosen, Richard (Dean)

Rosen, Richard (Dean) 1949- .... **CLC 39**
See also CA 77-80; CANR 62; INT
CANR-30

Rosenberg, Isaac 1890-1918 .... **TCLC 12**
See also CA 107; DLB 20

Rosenblatt, Joe .... **CLC 15**
See also Rosenblatt, Joseph

Rosenblatt, Joseph 1933-
See Rosenblatt, Joe
See also CA 89-92; INT 89-92

Rosenfeld, Samuel
See Tzara, Tristan

Rosenstock, Sami
See Tzara, Tristan

Rosenstock, Samuel
See Tzara, Tristan

Rosenthal, M(acha) L(ouis)
1917-1996 .... **CLC 28**
See also CA 1-4R; 152; CAAS 6; CANR 4,
51; DLB 5; SATA 59

Ross, Barnaby
See Dannay, Frederic

Ross, Bernard L.
See Follett, Ken(neth Martin)

Ross, J. H.
See Lawrence, T(homas) E(dward) ·

Ross, John Hume
See Lawrence, T(homas) E(dward)

Ross, Martin
See Martin, Violet Florence
See also DLB 135

Ross, (James) Sinclair 1908-1996 ... **CLC 13; DAC; DAM MST; SSC 24**
See also CA 73-76; CANR 81; DLB 88

Rossetti, Christina (Georgina) 1830-1894
NCLC 2, 50, 66; DA; DAB; DAC; DAM MST, POET; PC 7; WLC
See also DA3; DLB 35, 163; MAICYA;
SATA 20

Rossetti, Dante Gabriel 1828-1882 . **NCLC 4, 77; DA; DAB; DAC; DAM MST, POET; WLC**
See also CDBLB 1832-1890; DLB 35

Rossner, Judith (Perelman) 1935- . **CLC 6, 9, 29**
See also AITN 2; BEST 90:3; CA 17-20R;
CANR 18, 51, 73; DLB 6; INT CANR-
18; MTCW 1, 2

Rostand, Edmond (Eugene Alexis)
1868-1918 .... **TCLC 6, 37; DA; DAB; DAC; DAM DRAM, MST; DC 10**
See also CA 104; 126; DA3; DLB 192;
MTCW 1

Roth, Henry 1906-1995 ..... **CLC 2, 6, 11, 104**
See also CA 11-12; 149; CANR 38, 63;
CAP 1; DA3; DLB 28; MTCW 1, 2

Roth, Philip (Milton) 1933-... **CLC 1, 2, 3, 4, 6, 9, 15, 22, 31, 47, 66, 86, 119; DA; DAB; DAC; DAM MST, NOV, POP; SSC 26; WLC**
See also BEST 90:3; CA 1-4R; CANR 1,
22, 36, 55; CDALB 1968-1988; DA3;
DLB 2, 28, 173; DLBY 82; MTCW 1, 2

Rothenberg, Jerome 1931- .... **CLC 6, 57**
See also CA 45-48; CANR 1; DLB 5, 193

Roumain, Jacques (Jean Baptiste) 1907-1944
TCLC 19; BLC 3; DAM MULT
See also BW 1; CA 117; 125

Rourke, Constance (Mayfield) 1885-1941
TCLC 12
See also CA 107; YABC 1

Rousseau, Jean-Baptiste 1671-1741 ...... **LC 9**

Rousseau, Jean-Jacques 1712-1778 .... **LC 14, 36; DA; DAB; DAC; DAM MST; WLC**
See also DA3

Roussel, Raymond 1877-1933 .... **TCLC 20**
See also CA 117

Rovit, Earl (Herbert) 1927- .... **CLC 7**
See also CA 5-8R; CANR 12

Rowe, Elizabeth Singer 1674-1737 ..... **LC 44**
See also DLB 39, 95

Rowe, Nicholas 1674-1718 .... **LC 8**
See also DLB 84

Rowley, Ames Dorrance
See Lovecraft, H(oward) P(hillips)

Rowson, Susanna Haswell 1762(?)-1824
NCLC 5, 69
See also DLB 37, 200

Roy, Arundhati 1960(?)- .... **CLC 109**
See also CA 163; DLBY 97

Roy, Gabrielle 1909-1983 .... **CLC 10, 14; DAB; DAC; DAM MST**
See also CA 53-56; 110; CANR 5, 61; DLB
68; MTCW 1; SATA 104

Royko, Mike 1932-1997 .... **CLC 109**
See also CA 89-92; 157; CANR 26

Rozewicz, Tadeusz 1921- .. **CLC 9, 23; DAM POET**
See also CA 108; CANR 36, 66; DA3;
MTCW 1, 2

Ruark, Gibbons 1941- .... **CLC 3**
See also CA 33-36R; CAAS 23; CANR 14,
31, 57; DLB 120

Rubens, Bernice (Ruth) 1923- .... **CLC 19, 31**
See also CA 25-28R; CANR 33, 65; DLB
14, 207; MTCW 1

Rubin, Harold
See Robbins, Harold

Rudkin, (James) David 1936- .... **CLC 14**
See also CA 89-92; DLB 13

Rudnik, Raphael 1933- .... **CLC 7**
See also CA 29-32R

Ruffian, M.
See Hasek, Jaroslav (Matej Frantisek)

Ruiz, Jose Martinez .... **CLC 11**
See also Martinez Ruiz, Jose

Rukeyser, Muriel 1913-1980 . **CLC 6, 10, 15, 27; DAM POET; PC 12**
See also CA 5-8R; 93-96; CANR 26, 60;
DA3; DLB 48; MTCW 1, 2; SATA-Obit
22

Rule, Jane (Vance) 1931- .... **CLC 27**
See also CA 25-28R; CAAS 18; CANR 12,
87; DLB 60

Rulfo, Juan 1918-1986 ...... **CLC 8, 80; DAM MULT; HLC 2; SSC 25**
See also CA 85-88; 118; CANR 26; DLB
113; HW 1, 2; MTCW 1, 2

Rumi, Jalal al-Din 1297-1373 .... **CMLC 20**

Runeberg, Johan 1804-1877 .... **NCLC 41**

Runyon, (Alfred) Damon
1884(?)-1946 .... **TCLC 10**
See also CA 107; 165; DLB 11, 86, 171;
MTCW 2

Rush, Norman 1933- .... **CLC 44**
See also CA 121; 126; INT 126

Rushdie, (Ahmed) Salman 1947- .... **CLC 23, 31, 55, 100; DAB; DAC; DAM MST, NOV, POP; WLCS**
See also BEST 89:3; CA 108; 111; CANR
33, 56; DA3; DLB 194; INT 111; MTCW
1, 2

Rushforth, Peter (Scott) 1945- .... **CLC 19**
See also CA 101

Ruskin, John 1819-1900 .... **TCLC 63**
See also CA 114; 129; CDBLB 1832-1890;
DLB 55, 163, 190; SATA 24

Russ, Joanna 1937- .... **CLC 15**
See also CANR 11, 31, 65; DLB 8; MTCW
1

Russell, George William 1867-1935
See Baker, Jean H.
See also CA 104; 153; CDBLB 1890-1914;
DAM POET

Russell, (Henry) Ken(neth Alfred)
1927- .... **CLC 16**
See also CA 105

Russell, William Martin 1947- .... **CLC 60**
See also CA 164

Rutherford, Mark .... **TCLC 25**
See also White, William Hale DLB 18

Ruyslinck, Ward 1929- .... **CLC 14**
See also Belser, Reimond Karel Maria de

Ryan, Cornelius (John) 1920-1974 ..... **CLC 7**
See also CA 69-72; 53-56; CANR 38

Ryan, Michael 1946- .... **CLC 65**
See also CA 49-52; DLBY 82

Ryan, Tim
See Dent, Lester

Rybakov, Anatoli (Naumovich) 1911-1998
CLC 23, 53
See also CA 126; 135; 172; SATA 79;
SATA-Obit 108

Ryder, Jonathan
See Ludlum, Robert

Ryga, George 1932-1987 .... **CLC 14; DAC; DAM MST**
See also CA 101; 124; CANR 43; DLB 60

S. H.
See Hartmann, Sadakichi

S. S.
See Sassoon, Siegfried (Lorraine)

Saba, Umberto 1883-1957 .... **TCLC 33**
See also CA 144; CANR 79; DLB 114

Sabatini, Rafael 1875-1950 .... **TCLC 47**
See also CA 162

Sabato, Ernesto (R.) 1911- .... **CLC 10, 23;**
DAM MULT; HLC 2
See also CA 97-100; CANR 32, 65; DLB
145; HW 1, 2; MTCW 1, 2
Sa-Carniero, Mario de 1890-1916 . **TCLC 83**
Sacastru, Martin
See Bioy Casares, Adolfo
Sacastru, Martin
See Bioy Casares, Adolfo
Sacher-Masoch, Leopold von 1836(?)-1895
NCLC 31
Sachs, Marilyn (Stickle) 1927- .... **CLC 35**
See also AAYA 2; CA 17-20R; CANR 13,
47; CLR 2; JRDA; MAICYA; SAAS 2;
SATA 3, 68; SATA-Essay 110
Sachs, Nelly 1891-1970 .... **CLC 14, 98**
See also CA 17-18; 25-28R; CANR 87;
CAP 2; MTCW 2
Sackler, Howard (Oliver)
1929-1982 .... **CLC 14**
See also CA 61-64; 108; CANR 30; DLB 7
Sacks, Oliver (Wolf) 1933- .... **CLC 67**
See also CA 53-56; CANR 28, 50, 76; DA3;
INT CANR-28; MTCW 1, 2
Sadakichi
See Hartmann, Sadakichi
Sade, Donatien Alphonse Francois, Comte
de 1740-1814 .... **NCLC 47**
Sadoff, Ira 1945- .... **CLC 9**
See also CA 53-56; CANR 5, 21; DLB 120
Saetone
See Camus, Albert
Safire, William 1929- .... **CLC 10**
See also CA 17-20R; CANR 31, 54
Sagan, Carl (Edward) 1934-1996 .... **CLC 30,**
112
See also AAYA 2; CA 25-28R; 155; CANR
11, 36, 74; DA3; MTCW 1, 2; SATA 58;
SATA-Obit 94
Sagan, Francoise .... **CLC 3, 6, 9, 17, 36**
See also Quoirez, Francoise DLB 83;
MTCW 2
Sahgal, Nayantara (Pandit) 1927- .... **CLC 41**
See also CA 9-12R; CANR 11
Saint, H(arry) F. 1941- .... **CLC 50**
See also CA 127
St. Aubin de Teran, Lisa 1953-
See Teran, Lisa St. Aubin de
See also CA 118; 126; INT 126
Saint Birgitta of Sweden c.
1303-1373 .... **CMLC 24**
Sainte-Beuve, Charles Augustin 1804-1869
NCLC 5
Saint-Exupery, Antoine (Jean Baptiste
Marie Roger) de 1900-1944 .... **TCLC 2,**
56; DAM NOV; WLC
See also CA 108; 132; CLR 10; DA3; DLB
72; MAICYA; MTCW 1, 2; SATA 20
St. John, David
See Hunt, E(verette) Howard, (Jr.)
Saint-John Perse
See Leger, (Marie-Rene Auguste) Alexis
Saint-Leger
Saintsbury, George (Edward Bateman)
1845-1933 .... **TCLC 31**
See also CA 160; DLB 57, 149
Sait Faik .... **TCLC 23**
See also Abasiyanik, Sait Faik
Saki .... **TCLC 3; SSC 12**
See also Munro, H(ector) H(ugh) MTCW 2

Sala, George Augustus .... **NCLC 46**
Saladin 1138-1193 .... **CMLC 38**
Salama, Hannu 1936- .... **CLC 18**
Salamanca, J(ack) R(ichard) 1922- .. **CLC 4,**
15
See also CA 25-28R
Sale, J. Kirkpatrick
See Sale, Kirkpatrick
Sale, Kirkpatrick 1937- .... **CLC 68**
See also CA 13-16R; CANR 10
Salinas, Luis Omar 1937- ..... **CLC 90; DAM**
MULT; HLC 2
See also CA 131; CANR 81; DLB 82; HW
1, 2
Salinas (y Serrano), Pedro 1891(?)-1951
TCLC 17
See also CA 117; DLB 134
Salinger, J(erome) D(avid) 1919- .. **CLC 1, 3,**
8, 12, 55, 56; DA; DAB; DAC; DAM
MST, NOV, POP; SSC 2, 28; WLC
See also AAYA 2; CA 5-8R; CANR 39;
CDALB 1941-1968; CLR 18; DA3; DLB
2, 102, 173; MAICYA; MTCW 1, 2;
SATA 67
Salisbury, John
See Caute, (John) David
Salter, James 1925- .... **CLC 7, 52, 59**
See also CA 73-76; DLB 130
Saltus, Edgar (Everton) 1855-1921 . **TCLC 8**
See also CA 105; DLB 202
Saltykov, Mikhail Evgrafovich 1826-1889
NCLC 16
Samarakis, Antonis 1919- .... **CLC 5**
See also CA 25-28R; CAAS 16; CANR 36
Sanchez, Florencio 1875-1910 .... **TCLC 37**
See also CA 153; HW 1
Sanchez, Luis Rafael 1936- .... **CLC 23**
See also CA 128; DLB 145; HW 1
Sanchez, Sonia 1934- .... **CLC 5, 116; BLC 3;**
DAM MULT; PC 9
See also BW 2, 3; CA 33-36R; CANR 24,
49, 74; CLR 18; DA3; DLB 41; DLBD 8;
MAICYA; MTCW 1, 2; SATA 22
Sand, George 1804-1876 ..... **NCLC 2, 42, 57;**
DA; DAB; DAC; DAM MST, NOV;
WLC
See also DA3; DLB 119, 192
Sandburg, Carl (August) 1878-1967 . **CLC 1,**
4, 10, 15, 35; DA; DAB; DAC; DAM
MST, POET; PC 2; WLC
See also AAYA 24; CA 5-8R; 25-28R;
CANR 35; CDALB 1865-1917; DA3;
DLB 17, 54; MAICYA; MTCW 1, 2;
SATA 8
Sandburg, Charles
See Sandburg, Carl (August)
Sandburg, Charles A.
See Sandburg, Carl (August)
Sanders, (James) Ed(ward) 1939- ... **CLC 53;**
DAM POET
See also CA 13-16R; CAAS 21; CANR 13,
44, 78; DLB 16
Sanders, Lawrence 1920-1998 .... **CLC 41;**
DAM POP
See also BEST 89:4; CA 81-84; 165; CANR
33, 62; DA3; MTCW 1
Sanders, Noah
See Blount, Roy (Alton), Jr.

Sanders, Winston P.
See Anderson, Poul (William)
Sandoz, Mari(e Susette) 1896-1966 .. **CLC 28**
See also CA 1-4R; 25-28R; CANR 17, 64;
DLB 9, 212; MTCW 1, 2; SATA 5
Saner, Reg(inald Anthony) 1931- .... **CLC 9**
See also CA 65-68
Sankara 788-820 .... **CMLC 32**
Sannazaro, Jacopo 1456(?)-1530 .... **LC 8**
Sansom, William 1912-1976 .... **CLC 2, 6;**
DAM NOV; SSC 21
See also CA 5-8R; 65-68; CANR 42; DLB
139; MTCW 1
Santayana, George 1863-1952 .... **TCLC 40**
See also CA 115; DLB 54, 71; DLBD 13
Santiago, Danny .... **CLC 33**
See also James, Daniel (Lewis) DLB 122
Santmyer, Helen Hoover 1895-1986 . **CLC 33**
See also CA 1-4R; 118; CANR 15, 33;
DLBY 84; MTCW 1
Santoka, Taneda 1882-1940 .... **TCLC 72**
Santos, Bienvenido N(uqui)
1911-1996 .... **CLC 22; DAM MULT**
See also CA 101; 151; CANR 19, 46
Sapper .... **TCLC 44**
See also McNeile, Herman Cyril
Sapphire
See Sapphire, Brenda
Sapphire, Brenda 1950- .... **CLC 99**
Sappho fl. 6th cent. B.C.- ..... **CMLC 3; DAM**
POET; PC 5
See also DA3; DLB 176
Saramago, Jose 1922- ..... **CLC 119; HLCS 1**
See also CA 153
Sarduy, Severo 1937-1993 .... **CLC 6, 97;**
HLCS 1
See also CA 89-92; 142; CANR 58, 81;
DLB 113; HW 1, 2
Sargeson, Frank 1903-1982 .... **CLC 31**
See also CA 25-28R; 106; CANR 38, 79
Sarmiento, Domingo Faustino 1811-1888
See also HLCS 2
Sarmiento, Felix Ruben Garcia
See Dario, Ruben
Saro-Wiwa, Ken(ule Beeson)
1941-1995 .... **CLC 114**
See also BW 2; CA 142; 150; CANR 60;
DLB 157
Saroyan, William 1908-1981 ... **CLC 1, 8, 10,**
29, 34, 56; DA; DAB; DAC; DAM
DRAM, MST, NOV; SSC 21; WLC
See also CA 5-8R; 103; CANR 30;
CDALBS; DA3; DLB 7, 9, 86; DLBY 81;
MTCW 1, 2; SATA 23; SATA-Obit 24
Sarraute, Nathalie 1900- . **CLC 1, 2, 4, 8, 10,**
31, 80
See also CA 9-12R; CANR 23, 66; DLB
83; MTCW 1, 2
Sarton, (Eleanor) May 1912-1995 ..... **CLC 4,**
14, 49, 91; DAM POET
See also CA 1-4R; 149; CANR 1, 34, 55;
DLB 48; DLBY 81; INT CANR-34;
MTCW 1, 2; SATA 36; SATA-Obit 86
Sartre, Jean-Paul 1905-1980 . **CLC 1, 4, 7, 9,**
13, 18, 24, 44, 50, 52; DA; DAB; DAC;
DAM DRAM, MST, NOV; DC 3; SSC
32; WLC
See also CA 9-12R; 97-100; CANR 21;
DA3; DLB 72; MTCW 1, 2

Seelye, John (Douglas) 1931- .... **CLC 7**
See also CA 97-100; CANR 70; INT 97-
100

Seferiades, Giorgos Stylianou 1900-1971
See Seferis, George
See also CA 5-8R; 33-36R; CANR 5, 36;
MTCW 1

Seferis, George .... **CLC 5, 11**
See also Seferiades, Giorgos Stylianou

Segal, Erich (Wolf) 1937- . **CLC 3, 10; DAM POP**
See also BEST 89:1; CA 25-28R; CANR
20, 36, 65; DLBY 86; INT CANR-20;
MTCW 1

Seger, Bob 1945- .... **CLC 35**

Seghers, Anna .... **CLC 7**
See also Radvanyi, Netty DLB 69

Seidel, Frederick (Lewis) 1936- .... **CLC 18**
See also CA 13-16R; CANR 8; DLBY 84

Seifert, Jaroslav 1901-1986 .. **CLC 34, 44, 93**
See also CA 127; MTCW 1, 2

Sei Shonagon c. 966-1017(?) .... **CMLC 6**

Séjour, Victor 1817-1874 .... **DC 10**
See also DLB 50

Sejour Marcou et Ferrand, Juan Victor
See S

Selby, Hubert, Jr. 1928- .... **CLC 1, 2, 4, 8; SSC 20**
See also CA 13-16R; CANR 33, 85; DLB 2

Selzer, Richard 1928- .... **CLC 74**
See also CA 65-68; CANR 14

Sembene, Ousmane
See Ousmane, Sembene

Senancour, Etienne Pivert de 1770-1846
NCLC 16
See also DLB 119

Sender, Ramon (Jose) 1902-1982 ...... **CLC 8; DAM MULT; HLC 2**
See also CA 5-8R; 105; CANR 8; HW 1;
MTCW 1

Seneca, Lucius Annaeus c. 1-c.
65 .... **CMLC 6; DAM DRAM; DC 5**
See also DLB 211

Senghor, Leopold Sedar 1906- .... **CLC 54; BLC 3; DAM MULT, POET; PC 25**
See also BW 2; CA 116; 125; CANR 47,
74; MTCW 1, 2

Senna, Danzy 1970- .... **CLC 119**
See also CA 169

Serling, (Edward) Rod(man)
1924-1975 .... **CLC 30**
See also AAYA 14; AITN 1; CA 162; 57-
60; DLB 26

Serna, Ramon Gomez de la
See Gomez de la Serna, Ramon

Serpieres
See Guillevic, (Eugene)

Service, Robert
See Service, Robert W(illiam)
See also DAB; DLB 92

Service, Robert W(illiam) 1874(?)-1958
TCLC 15; DA; DAC; DAM MST, POET; WLC
See also Service, Robert CA 115; 140;
CANR 84; SATA 20

Seth, Vikram 1952- .... **CLC 43, 90; DAM MULT**
See also CA 121; 127; CANR 50, 74; DA3;
DLB 120; INT 127; MTCW 2

Seton, Cynthia Propper 1926-1982 .. **CLC 27**
See also CA 5-8R; 108; CANR 7

Seton, Ernest (Evan) Thompson 1860-1946
TCLC 31
See also CA 109; CLR 59; DLB 92; DLBD
13; JRDA; SATA 18

Seton-Thompson, Ernest
See Seton, Ernest (Evan) Thompson

Settle, Mary Lee 1918- .... **CLC 19, 61**
See also CA 89-92; CAAS 1; CANR 44,
87; DLB 6; INT 89-92

Seuphor, Michel
See Arp, Jean

Sevigne, Marie (de Rabutin-Chantal)
Marquise de 1626-1696 .... **LC 11**

Sewall, Samuel 1652-1730 .... **LC 38**
See also DLB 24

Sexton, Anne (Harvey) 1928-1974 ..... **CLC 2, 4, 6, 8, 10, 15, 53; DA; DAB; DAC; DAM MST, POET; PC 2; WLC**
See also CA 1-4R; 53-56; CABS 2; CANR
3, 36; CDALB 1941-1968; DA3; DLB 5,
169; MTCW 1, 2; SATA 10

Shaara, Jeff 1952- .... **CLC 119**
See also CA 163

Shaara, Michael (Joseph, Jr.)
1929-1988 .... **CLC 15; DAM POP**
See also AITN 1; CA 102; 125; CANR 52,
85; DLBY 83

Shackleton, C. C.
See Aldiss, Brian W(ilson)

Shacochis, Bob .... **CLC 39**
See also Shacochis, Robert G.

Shacochis, Robert G. 1951-
See Shacochis, Bob
See also CA 119; 124; INT 124

Shaffer, Anthony (Joshua) 1926- ..... **CLC 19; DAM DRAM**
See also CA 110; 116; DLB 13

Shaffer, Peter (Levin) 1926- .. **CLC 5, 14, 18, 37, 60; DAB; DAM DRAM, MST; DC 7**
See also CA 25-28R; CANR 25, 47, 74;
CDBLB 1960 to Present; DA3; DLB 13;
MTCW 1, 2

Shakey, Bernard
See Young, Neil

Shalamov, Varlam (Tikhonovich)
1907(?)-1982 .... **CLC 18**
See also CA 129; 105

Shamlu, Ahmad 1925- .... **CLC 10**

Shammas, Anton 1951- .... **CLC 55**

Shange, Ntozake 1948- .... **CLC 8, 25, 38, 74, 126; BLC 3; DAM DRAM, MULT; DC 3**
See also AAYA 9; BW 2; CA 85-88; CABS
3; CANR 27, 48, 74; DA3; DLB 38;
MTCW 1, 2

Shanley, John Patrick 1950- .... **CLC 75**
See also CA 128; 133; CANR 83

Shapcott, Thomas W(illiam) 1935- .. **CLC 38**
See also CA 69-72; CANR 49, 83

Shapiro, Jane .... **CLC 76**

Shapiro, Karl (Jay) 1913- . **CLC 4, 8, 15, 53; PC 25**
See also CA 1-4R; CAAS 6; CANR 1, 36,
66; DLB 48; MTCW 1, 2

Sharp, William 1855-1905 .... **TCLC 39**
See also CA 160; DLB 156

Sharpe, Thomas Ridley 1928-
See Sharpe, Tom
See also CA 114; 122; CANR 85; INT 122

Sharpe, Tom .... **CLC 36**
See also Sharpe, Thomas Ridley DLB 14

Shaw, Bernard .... **TCLC 45**
See also Shaw, George Bernard BW 1;
MTCW 2

Shaw, G. Bernard
See Shaw, George Bernard

Shaw, George Bernard 1856-1950 .. **TCLC 3, 9, 21; DA; DAB; DAC; DAM DRAM, MST; WLC**
See also Shaw, Bernard CA 104; 128; CD-
BLB 1914-1945; DA3; DLB 10, 57, 190;
MTCW 1, 2

Shaw, Henry Wheeler 1818-1885 .. **NCLC 15**
See also DLB 11

Shaw, Irwin 1913-1984 .... **CLC 7, 23, 34; DAM DRAM, POP**
See also AITN 1; CA 13-16R; 112; CANR
21; CDALB 1941-1968; DLB 6, 102;
DLBY 84; MTCW 1, 21

Shaw, Robert 1927-1978 .... **CLC 5**
See also AITN 1; CA 1-4R; 81-84; CANR
4; DLB 13, 14

Shaw, T. E.
See Lawrence, T(homas) E(dward)

Shawn, Wallace 1943- .... **CLC 41**
See also CA 112

Shea, Lisa 1953- .... **CLC 86**
See also CA 147

Sheed, Wilfrid (John Joseph) 1930- . **CLC 2, 4, 10, 53**
See also CA 65-68; CANR 30, 66; DLB 6;
MTCW 1, 2

Sheldon, Alice Hastings Bradley
1915(?)-1987
See Tiptree, James, Jr.
See also CA 108; 122; CANR 34; INT 108;
MTCW 1

Sheldon, John
See Bloch, Robert (Albert)

Shelley, Mary Wollstonecraft (Godwin)
1797-1851 ..... **NCLC 14, 59; DA; DAB; DAC; DAM MST, NOV; WLC**
See also AAYA 20; CDBLB 1789-1832;
DA3; DLB 110, 116, 159, 178; SATA 29

Shelley, Percy Bysshe 1792-1822 .. **NCLC 18; DA; DAB; DAC; DAM MST, POET; PC 14; WLC**
See also CDBLB 1789-1832; DA3; DLB
96, 110, 158

Shepard, Jim 1956- .... **CLC 36**
See also CA 137; CANR 59; SATA 90

Shepard, Lucius 1947- .... **CLC 34**
See also CA 128; 141; CANR 81

Shepard, Sam 1943- .... **CLC 4, 6, 17, 34, 41, 44; DAM DRAM; DC 5**
See also AAYA 1; CA 69-72; CABS 3;
CANR 22; DA3; DLB 7, 212; MTCW 1,
2

Shepherd, Michael
See Ludlum, Robert

Sherburne, Zoa (Lillian Morin) 1912-1995
CLC 30
See also AAYA 13; CA 1-4R; 176; CANR
3, 37; MAICYA; SAAS 18; SATA 3

Sheridan, Frances 1724-1766 .... **LC 7**
See also DLB 39, 84

Sheridan, Richard Brinsley
1751-1816 .. **NCLC 5; DA; DAB; DAC; DAM DRAM, MST; DC 1; WLC**
See also CDBLB 1660-1789; DLB 89

Sherman, Jonathan Marc .... **CLC 55**

Sherman, Martin 1941(?)- .... **CLC 19**
See also CA 116; 123; CANR 86

Sherwin, Judith Johnson 1936-
See Johnson, Judith (Emlyn)
See also CANR 85

Sherwood, Frances 1940- .... **CLC 81**
See also CA 146

Sherwood, Robert E(mmet)
1896-1955 .... **TCLC 3; DAM DRAM**
See also CA 104; 153; CANR 86; DLB 7,
26

Shestov, Lev 1866-1938 .... **TCLC 56**

Shevchenko, Taras 1814-1861 .... **NCLC 54**

Shiel, M(atthew) P(hipps)
1865-1947 .... **TCLC 8**
See also Holmes, Gordon CA 106; 160;
DLB 153; MTCW 2

Shields, Carol 1935- .... **CLC 91, 113; DAC**
See also CA 81-84; CANR 51, 74; DA3;
MTCW 2

Shields, David 1956- .... **CLC 97**
See also CA 124; CANR 48

Shiga, Naoya 1883-1971 ..... **CLC 33; SSC 23**
See also CA 101; 33-36R; DLB 180

Shilts, Randy 1951-1994 .... **CLC 85**
See also AAYA 19; CA 115; 127; 144;
CANR 45; DA3; INT 127; MTCW 2

Shimazaki, Haruki 1872-1943
See Shimazaki Toson
See also CA 105; 134; CANR 84

Shimazaki Toson 1872-1943 .... **TCLC 5**
See also Shimazaki, Haruki DLB 180

Sholokhov, Mikhail (Aleksandrovich)
1905-1984 .... **CLC 7, 15**
See also CA 101; 112; MTCW 1, 2; SATA-
Obit 36

Shone, Patric
See Hanley, James

Shreve, Susan Richards 1939- .... **CLC 23**
See also CA 49-52; CAAS 5; CANR 5, 38,
69; MAICYA; SATA 46, 95; SATA-Brief
41

Shue, Larry 1946-1985 .... **CLC 52; DAM DRAM**
See also CA 145; 117

Shu-Jen, Chou 1881-1936
See Lu Hsun
See also CA 104

Shulman, Alix Kates 1932- .... **CLC 2, 10**
See also CA 29-32R; CANR 43; SATA 7

Shuster, Joe 1914- .... **CLC 21**

Shute, Nevil .... **CLC 30**
See also Norway, Nevil Shute MTCW 2

Shuttle, Penelope (Diane) 1947- .... **CLC 7**
See also CA 93-96; CANR 39, 84; DLB 14,
40

Sidney, Mary 1561-1621 .... **LC 19, 39**

Sidney, Sir Philip 1554-1586 .... **LC 19, 39; DA; DAB; DAC; DAM MST, POET**
See also CDBLB Before 1660; DA3; DLB
167

Siegel, Jerome 1914-1996 .... **CLC 21**
See also CA 116; 169; 151

Siegel, Jerry
See Siegel, Jerome

Sienkiewicz, Henryk (Adam Alexander Pius)
1846-1916 .... **TCLC 3**
See also CA 104; 134; CANR 84

Sierra, Gregorio Martinez
See Martinez Sierra, Gregorio

Sierra, Maria (de la O'LeJarraga) Martinez
See Martinez Sierra, Maria (de la
O'LeJarraga)

Sigal, Clancy 1926- .... **CLC 7**
See also CA 1-4R; CANR 85

Sigourney, Lydia Howard (Huntley)
1791-1865 .... **NCLC 21**
See also DLB 1, 42, 73

Siguenza y Gongora, Carlos de 1645-1700
LC 8; HLCS 2

Sigurjonsson, Johann 1880-1919 ... **TCLC 27**
See also CA 170

Sikelianos, Angelos 1884-1951 ...... **TCLC 39; PC 29**

Silkin, Jon 1930- .... **CLC 2, 6, 43**
See also CA 5-8R; CAAS 5; DLB 27

Silko, Leslie (Marmon) 1948- .... **CLC 23, 74, 114; DA; DAC; DAM MST, MULT, POP; SSC 37; WLCS**
See also AAYA 14; CA 115; 122; CANR
45, 65; DA3; DLB 143, 175; MTCW 2;
NNAL

Sillanpaa, Frans Eemil 1888-1964 ... **CLC 19**
See also CA 129; 93-96; MTCW 1

Sillitoe, Alan 1928- ... **CLC 1, 3, 6, 10, 19, 57**
See also AITN 1; CA 9-12R; CAAS 2;
CANR 8, 26, 55; CDBLB 1960 to Present;
DLB 14, 139; MTCW 1, 2; SATA 61

Silone, Ignazio 1900-1978 .... **CLC 4**
See also CA 25-28; 81-84; CANR 34; CAP
2; MTCW 1

Silver, Joan Micklin 1935- .... **CLC 20**
See also CA 114; 121; INT 121

Silver, Nicholas
See Faust, Frederick (Schiller)

Silverberg, Robert 1935- .... **CLC 7; DAM POP**
See also AAYA 24; CA 1-4R; CAAS 3;
CANR 1, 20, 36, 85; CLR 59; DLB 8;
INT CANR-20; MAICYA; MTCW 1, 2;
SATA 13, 91; SATA-Essay 104

Silverstein, Alvin 1933- .... **CLC 17**
See also CA 49-52; CANR 2; CLR 25;
JRDA; MAICYA; SATA 8, 69

Silverstein, Virginia B(arbara Opshelor)
1937- .... **CLC 17**
See also CA 49-52; CANR 2; CLR 25;
JRDA; MAICYA; SATA 8, 69

Sim, Georges
See Simenon, Georges (Jacques Christian)

Simak, Clifford D(onald) 1904-1988 . **CLC 1, 55**
See also CA 1-4R; 125; CANR 1, 35; DLB
8; MTCW 1; SATA-Obit 56

Simenon, Georges (Jacques Christian)
1903-1989 .... **CLC 1, 2, 3, 8, 18, 47; DAM POP**
See also CA 85-88; 129; CANR 35; DA3;
DLB 72; DLBY 89; MTCW 1, 2

Simic, Charles 1938- ... **CLC 6, 9, 22, 49, 68; DAM POET**
See also CA 29-32R; CAAS 4; CANR 12,
33, 52, 61; DA3; DLB 105; MTCW 2

Simmel, Georg 1858-1918 .... **TCLC 64**
See also CA 157

Simmons, Charles (Paul) 1924- .... **CLC 57**
See also CA 89-92; INT 89-92

Simmons, Dan 1948- ... **CLC 44; DAM POP**
See also AAYA 16; CA 138; CANR 53, 81

Simmons, James (Stewart Alexander) 1933-
CLC 43
See also CA 105; CAAS 21; DLB 40

Simms, William Gilmore
1806-1870 .... **NCLC 3**
See also DLB 3, 30, 59, 73

Simon, Carly 1945- .... **CLC 26**
See also CA 105

Simon, Claude 1913-1984 . **CLC 4, 9, 15, 39; DAM NOV**
See also CA 89-92; CANR 33; DLB 83;
MTCW 1

Simon, (Marvin) Neil 1927- ... **CLC 6, 11, 31, 39, 70; DAM DRAM**
See also AAYA 32; AITN 1; CA 21-24R;
CANR 26, 54, 87; DA3; DLB 7; MTCW
1, 2

Simon, Paul (Frederick) 1941(?)- ..... **CLC 17**
See also CA 116; 153

Simonon, Paul 1956(?)- .... **CLC 30**

Simpson, Harriette
See Arnow, Harriette (Louisa) Simpson

Simpson, Louis (Aston Marantz)
1923- ...... **CLC 4, 7, 9, 32; DAM POET**
See also CA 1-4R; CAAS 4; CANR 1, 61;
DLB 5; MTCW 1, 2

Simpson, Mona (Elizabeth) 1957- .... **CLC 44**
See also CA 122; 135; CANR 68

Simpson, N(orman) F(rederick)
1919- .... **CLC 29**
See also CA 13-16R; DLB 13

Sinclair, Andrew (Annandale) 1935- . **CLC 2, 14**
See also CA 9-12R; CAAS 5; CANR 14,
38; DLB 14; MTCW 1

Sinclair, Emil
See Hesse, Hermann

Sinclair, Iain 1943- .... **CLC 76**
See also CA 132; CANR 81

Sinclair, Iain MacGregor
See Sinclair, Iain

Sinclair, Irene
See Griffith, D(avid Lewelyn) W(ark)

Sinclair, Mary Amelia St. Clair 1865(?)-1946
See Sinclair, May
See also CA 104

Sinclair, May 1863-1946 .... **TCLC 3, 11**
See also Sinclair, Mary Amelia St. Clair CA
166; DLB 36, 135

Sinclair, Roy
See Griffith, D(avid Lewelyn) W(ark)

Sinclair, Upton (Beall) 1878-1968 ..... **CLC 1, 11, 15, 63; DA; DAB; DAC; DAM MST, NOV; WLC**
See also CA 5-8R; 25-28R; CANR 7;
CDALB 1929-1941; DA3; DLB 9; INT
CANR-7; MTCW 1, 2; SATA 9

Singer, Isaac
See Singer, Isaac Bashevis

Singer, Isaac Bashevis 1904-1991 .. **CLC 1, 3, 6, 9, 11, 15, 23, 38, 69, 111; DA; DAB; DAC; DAM MST, NOV; SSC 3; WLC**
See also AAYA 32; AITN 1, 2; CA 1-4R;
134; CANR 1, 39; CDALB 1941-1968;
CLR 1; DA3; DLB 6, 28, 52; DLBY 91;
JRDA; MAICYA; MTCW 1, 2; SATA 3,
27; SATA-Obit 68

Singer, Israel Joshua 1893-1944 .... **TCLC 33**
See also CA 169

Singh, Khushwant 1915- .... **CLC 11**
See also CA 9-12R; CAAS 9; CANR 6, 84

Singleton, Ann
See Benedict, Ruth (Fulton)

Sinjohn, John
See Galsworthy, John

Sinyavsky, Andrei (Donatevich) 1925-1997
CLC 8
See also CA 85-88; 159

Sirin, V.
See Nabokov, Vladimir (Vladimirovich)

Sissman, L(ouis) E(dward)
1928-1976 .... **CLC 9, 18**
See also CA 21-24R; 65-68; CANR 13;
DLB 5

Sisson, C(harles) H(ubert) 1914- .... **CLC 8**
See also CA 1-4R; CAAS 3; CANR 3, 48,
84; DLB 27

Sitwell, Dame Edith 1887-1964 ..... **CLC 2, 9,**
67; DAM POET; PC 3
See also CA 9-12R; CANR 35; CDBLB
1945-1960; DLB 20; MTCW 1, 2

Siwaarmill, H. P.
See Sharp, William

Sjoewall, Maj 1935- .... **CLC 7**
See also CA 65-68; CANR 73

Sjowall, Maj
See Sjoewall, Maj

Skelton, John 1463-1529 .... **PC 25**

Skelton, Robin 1925-1997 .... **CLC 13**
See also AITN 2; CA 5-8R; 160; CAAS 5;
CANR 28; DLB 27, 53

Skolimowski, Jerzy 1938- .... **CLC 20**
See also CA 128

Skram, Amalie (Bertha)
1847-1905 .... **TCLC 25**
See also CA 165

Skvorecky, Josef (Vaclav) 1924- ...... **CLC 15,**
39, 69; DAC; DAM NOV
See also CA 61-64; CAAS 1; CANR 10,
34, 63; DA3; MTCW 1, 2

Slade, Bernard .... **CLC 11, 46**
See also Newbound, Bernard Slade CAAS
9; DLB 53

Slaughter, Carolyn 1946- .... **CLC 56**
See also CA 85-88; CANR 85

Slaughter, Frank G(ill) 1908- .... **CLC 29**
See also AITN 2; CA 5-8R; CANR 5, 85;
INT CANR-5

Slavitt, David R(ytman) 1935- ..... **CLC 5, 14**
See also CA 21-24R; CAAS 3; CANR 41,
83; DLB 5, 6

Slesinger, Tess 1905-1945 .... **TCLC 10**
See also CA 107; DLB 102

Slessor, Kenneth 1901-1971 .... **CLC 14**
See also CA 102; 89-92

Slowacki, Juliusz 1809-1849 .... **NCLC 15**

Smart, Christopher 1722-1771 .. **LC 3; DAM**
POET; PC 13
See also DLB 109

Smart, Elizabeth 1913-1986 .... **CLC 54**
See also CA 81-84; 118; DLB 88

Smiley, Jane (Graves) 1949- ...... **CLC 53, 76;**
DAM POP
See also CA 104; CANR 30, 50, 74; DA3;
INT CANR-30

Smith, A(rthur) J(ames) M(arshall)
1902-1980 .... **CLC 15; DAC**
See also CA 1-4R; 102; CANR 4; DLB 88

Smith, Adam 1723-1790 .... **LC 36**
See also DLB 104

Smith, Alexander 1829-1867 .... **NCLC 59**
See also DLB 32, 55

Smith, Anna Deavere 1950- .... **CLC 86**
See also CA 133

Smith, Betty (Wehner) 1896-1972 .... **CLC 19**
See also CA 5-8R; 33-36R; DLBY 82;
SATA 6

Smith, Charlotte (Turner)
1749-1806 .... **NCLC 23**
See also DLB 39, 109

Smith, Clark Ashton 1893-1961 .... **CLC 43**
See also CA 143; CANR 81; MTCW 2

Smith, Dave .... **CLC 22, 42**
See also Smith, David (Jeddie) CAAS 7;
DLB 5

Smith, David (Jeddie) 1942-
See Smith, Dave
See also CA 49-52; CANR 1, 59; DAM
POET

Smith, Florence Margaret 1902-1971
See Smith, Stevie
See also CA 17-18; 29-32R; CANR 35;
CAP 2; DAM POET; MTCW 1, 2

Smith, Iain Crichton 1928-1998 .... **CLC 64**
See also CA 21-24R; 171; DLB 40, 139

Smith, John 1580(?)-1631 .... **LC 9**
See also DLB 24, 30

Smith, Johnston
See Crane, Stephen (Townley)

Smith, Joseph, Jr. 1805-1844 .... **NCLC 53**

Smith, Lee 1944- .... **CLC 25, 73**
See also CA 114; 119; CANR 46; DLB 143;
DLBY 83; INT 119

Smith, Martin
See Smith, Martin Cruz

Smith, Martin Cruz 1942- .... **CLC 25; DAM**
MULT, POP
See also BEST 89:4; CA 85-88; CANR 6,
23, 43, 65; INT CANR-23; MTCW 2;
NNAL

Smith, Mary-Ann Tirone 1944- .... **CLC 39**
See also CA 118; 136

Smith, Patti 1946- .... **CLC 12**
See also CA 93-96; CANR 63

Smith, Pauline (Urmson)
1882-1959 .... **TCLC 25**

Smith, Rosamond
See Oates, Joyce Carol

Smith, Sheila Kaye
See Kaye-Smith, Sheila

Smith, Stevie .... **CLC 3, 8, 25, 44; PC 12**
See also Smith, Florence Margaret DLB 20;
MTCW 2

Smith, Wilbur (Addison) 1933- .... **CLC 33**
See also CA 13-16R; CANR 7, 46, 66;
MTCW 1, 2

Smith, William Jay 1918- .... **CLC 6**
See also CA 5-8R; CANR 44; DLB 5; MAI-
CYA; SAAS 22; SATA 2, 68

Smith, Woodrow Wilson
See Kuttner, Henry

Smolenskin, Peretz 1842-1885 .... **NCLC 30**

Smollett, Tobias (George) 1721-1771 ... **LC 2,**
46
See also CDBLB 1660-1789; DLB 39, 104

Snodgrass, W(illiam) D(e Witt)
1926- .... **CLC 2, 6, 10, 18, 68; DAM**
POET
See also CA 1-4R; CANR 6, 36, 65, 85;
DLB 5; MTCW 1, 2

Snow, C(harles) P(ercy) 1905-1980 ... **CLC 1,**
4, 6, 9, 13, 19; DAM NOV
See also CA 5-8R; 101; CANR 28; CDBLB
1945-1960; DLB 15, 77; DLBD 17;
MTCW 1, 2

Snow, Frances Compton
See Adams, Henry (Brooks)

Snyder, Gary (Sherman) 1930- . **CLC 1, 2, 5,**
9, 32, 120; DAM POET; PC 21
See also CA 17-20R; CANR 30, 60; DA3;
DLB 5, 16, 165, 212; MTCW 2

Snyder, Zilpha Keatley 1927- .... **CLC 17**
See also AAYA 15; CA 9-12R; CANR 38;
CLR 31; JRDA; MAICYA; SAAS 2;
SATA 1, 28, 75, 110; SATA-Essay 112

Soares, Bernardo
See Pessoa, Fernando (Antonio Nogueira)

Sobh, A.
See Shamlu, Ahmad

Sobol, Joshua .... **CLC 60**

Socrates 469B.C.-399B.C. .... **CMLC 27**

Soderberg, Hjalmar 1869-1941 ...... **TCLC 39**

Sodergran, Edith (Irene)
See Soedergran, Edith (Irene)

Soedergran, Edith (Irene)
1892-1923 .... **TCLC 31**

Softly, Edgar
See Lovecraft, H(oward) P(hillips)

Softly, Edward
See Lovecraft, H(oward) P(hillips)

Sokolov, Raymond 1941- .... **CLC 7**
See also CA 85-88

Solo, Jay
See Ellison, Harlan (Jay)

Sologub, Fyodor .... **TCLC 9**
See also Teternikov, Fyodor Kuzmich

Solomons, Ikey Esquir
See Thackeray, William Makepeace

Solomos, Dionysios 1798-1857 .... **NCLC 15**

Solwoska, Mara
See French, Marilyn

Solzhenitsyn, Aleksandr I(sayevich) 1918-
CLC 1, 2, 4, 7, 9, 10, 18, 26, 34, 78; DA;
DAB; DAC; DAM MST, NOV; SSC 32;
WLC
See also AITN 1; CA 69-72; CANR 40, 65;
DA3; MTCW 1, 2

Somers, Jane
See Lessing, Doris (May)

Somerville, Edith 1858-1949 .... **TCLC 51**
See also DLB 135

Somerville & Ross
See Martin, Violet Florence; Somerville,
Edith

Sommer, Scott 1951- .... **CLC 25**
See also CA 106

Sondheim, Stephen (Joshua) 1930- . **CLC 30,**
39; DAM DRAM
See also AAYA 11; CA 103; CANR 47, 68

Song, Cathy 1955- .... **PC 21**
See also CA 154; DLB 169

Sontag, Susan 1933- .... **CLC 1, 2, 10, 13, 31,**
105; DAM POP
See also CA 17-20R; CANR 25, 51, 74;
DA3; DLB 2, 67; MTCW 1, 2

Sophocles 496(?)B.C.-406(?)B.C. .... **CMLC 2;**
DA; DAB; DAC; DAM DRAM, MST;
DC 1; WLCS
See also DA3; DLB 176

Sordello 1189-1269 .... **CMLC 15**

Sorel, Georges 1847-1922 .... **TCLC 91**
See also CA 118

Sorel, Julia
See Drexler, Rosalyn

Sorrentino, Gilbert 1929- .. **CLC 3, 7, 14, 22,**
40
See also CA 77-80; CANR 14, 33; DLB 5,
173; DLBY 80; INT CANR-14

Soto, Gary 1952- .... **CLC 32, 80; DAM**
MULT; HLC 2; PC 28
See also AAYA 10; CA 119; 125; CANR
50, 74; CLR 38; DLB 82; HW 1, 2; INT
125; JRDA; MTCW 2; SATA 80

Soupault, Philippe 1897-1990 .... **CLC 68**
  See also CA 116; 147; 131
Souster, (Holmes) Raymond 1921- .... **CLC 5,**
  14; DAC; DAM POET
  See also CA 13-16R; CAAS 14; CANR 13,
  29, 53; DA3; DLB 88; SATA 63
Southern, Terry 1924(?)-1995 .... **CLC 7**
  See also CA 1-4R; 150; CANR 1, 55; DLB
  2
Southey, Robert 1774-1843 .... **NCLC 8**
  See also DLB 93, 107, 142; SATA 54
Southworth, Emma Dorothy Eliza Nevitte
  1819-1899 .... **NCLC 26**
Souza, Ernest
  See Scott, Evelyn
Soyinka, Wole 1934- .... **CLC 3, 5, 14, 36, 44;**
  BLC 3; DA; DAB; DAC; DAM
  DRAM, MST, MULT; DC 2; WLC
  See also BW 2, 3; CA 13-16R; CANR 27,
  39, 82; DA3; DLB 125; MTCW 1, 2
Spackman, W(illiam) M(ode)
  1905-1990 .... **CLC 46**
  See also CA 81-84; 132
Spacks, Barry (Bernard) 1931- .... **CLC 14**
  See also CA 154; CANR 33; DLB 105
Spanidou, Irini 1946- .... **CLC 44**
Spark, Muriel (Sarah) 1918- ..... **CLC 2, 3, 5,**
  8, 13, 18, 40, 94; DAB; DAC; DAM
  MST, NOV; SSC 10
  See also CA 5-8R; CANR 12, 36, 76; CD-
  BLB 1945-1960; DA3; DLB 15, 139; INT
  CANR-12; MTCW 1, 2
Spaulding, Douglas
  See Bradbury, Ray (Douglas)
Spaulding, Leonard
  See Bradbury, Ray (Douglas)
Spence, J. A. D.
  See Eliot, T(homas) S(tearns)
Spencer, Elizabeth 1921- .... **CLC 22**
  See also CA 13-16R; CANR 32, 65, 87;
  DLB 6; MTCW 1; SATA 14
Spencer, Leonard G.
  See Silverberg, Robert
Spencer, Scott 1945- .... **CLC 30**
  See also CA 113; CANR 51; DLBY 86
Spender, Stephen (Harold)
  1909-1995 .... **CLC 1, 2, 5, 10, 41, 91;**
  DAM POET
  See also CA 9-12R; 149; CANR 31, 54;
  CDBLB 1945-1960; DA3; DLB 20;
  MTCW 1, 2
Spengler, Oswald (Arnold Gottfried)
  1880-1936 .... **TCLC 25**
  See also CA 118
Spenser, Edmund 1552(?)-1599 ..... **LC 5, 39;**
  DA; DAB; DAC; DAM MST, POET;
  PC 8; WLC
  See also CDBLB Before 1660; DA3; DLB
  167
Spicer, Jack 1925-1965 .... **CLC 8, 18, 72;**
  DAM POET
  See also CA 85-88; DLB 5, 16, 193
Spiegelman, Art 1948- .... **CLC 76**
  See also AAYA 10; CA 125; CANR 41, 55,
  74; MTCW 2; SATA 109
Spielberg, Peter 1929- .... **CLC 6**
  See also CA 5-8R; CANR 4, 48; DLBY 81
Spielberg, Steven 1947- .... **CLC 20**
  See also AAYA 8, 24; CA 77-80; CANR
  32; SATA 32
Spillane, Frank Morrison 1918-
  See Spillane, Mickey

See also CA 25-28R; CANR 28, 63; DA3;
  MTCW 1, 2; SATA 66
Spillane, Mickey .... **CLC 3, 13**
  See also Spillane, Frank Morrison MTCW
  2
Spinoza, Benedictus de 1632-1677 .... **LC 9**
Spinrad, Norman (Richard) 1940- ... **CLC 46**
  See also CA 37-40R; CAAS 19; CANR 20;
  DLB 8; INT CANR-20
Spitteler, Carl (Friedrich Georg) 1845-1924
  TCLC 12
  See also CA 109; DLB 129
Spivack, Kathleen (Romola Drucker) 1938-
  CLC 6
  See also CA 49-52
Spoto, Donald 1941- .... **CLC 39**
  See also CA 65-68; CANR 11, 57
Springsteen, Bruce (F.) 1949- .... **CLC 17**
  See also CA 111
Spurling, Hilary 1940- .... **CLC 34**
  See also CA 104; CANR 25, 52
Spyker, John Howland
  See Elman, Richard (Martin)
Squires, (James) Radcliffe
  1917-1993 .... **CLC 51**
  See also CA 1-4R; 140; CANR 6, 21
Srivastava, Dhanpat Rai 1880(?)-1936
  See Premchand
  See also CA 118
Stacy, Donald
  See Pohl, Frederik
Stael, Germaine de 1766-1817
  See Stael-Holstein, Anne Louise Germaine
  Necker Baronn
  See also DLB 119
Stael-Holstein, Anne Louise Germaine
  Necker Baronn 1766-1817 .... **NCLC 3**
  See also Stael, Germaine de DLB 192
Stafford, Jean 1915-1979 .. **CLC 4, 7, 19, 68;**
  SSC 26
  See also CA 1-4R; 85-88; CANR 3, 65;
  DLB 2, 173; MTCW 1, 2; SATA-Obit 22
Stafford, William (Edgar)
  1914-1993 .. **CLC 4, 7, 29; DAM POET**
  See also CA 5-8R; 142; CAAS 3; CANR 5,
  22; DLB 5, 206; INT CANR-22
Stagnelius, Eric Johan 1793-1823 . **NCLC 61**
Staines, Trevor
  See Brunner, John (Kilian Houston)
Stairs, Gordon
  See Austin, Mary (Hunter)
Stairs, Gordon
  See Austin, Mary (Hunter)
Stalin, Joseph 1879-1953 .... **TCLC 92**
Stannard, Martin 1947- .... **CLC 44**
  See also CA 142; DLB 155
Stanton, Elizabeth Cady
  1815-1902 .... **TCLC 73**
  See also CA 171; DLB 79
Stanton, Maura 1946- .... **CLC 9**
  See also CA 89-92; CANR 15; DLB 120
Stanton, Schuyler
  See Baum, L(yman) Frank
Stapledon, (William) Olaf
  1886-1950 .... **TCLC 22**
  See also CA 111; 162; DLB 15
Starbuck, George (Edwin)
  1931-1996 .... **CLC 53; DAM POET**
  See also CA 21-24R; 153; CANR 23
Stark, Richard
  See Westlake, Donald E(dwin)

Staunton, Schuyler
  See Baum, L(yman) Frank
Stead, Christina (Ellen) 1902-1983 ... **CLC 2,**
  5, 8, 32, 80
  See also CA 13-16R; 109; CANR 33, 40;
  MTCW 1, 2
Stead, William Thomas
  1849-1912 .... **TCLC 48**
  See also CA 167
Steele, Richard 1672-1729 .... **LC 18**
  See also CDBLB 1660-1789; DLB 84, 101
Steele, Timothy (Reid) 1948- .... **CLC 45**
  See also CA 93-96; CANR 16, 50; DLB
  120
Steffens, (Joseph) Lincoln
  1866-1936 .... **TCLC 20**
  See also CA 117
Stegner, Wallace (Earle) 1909-1993 .. **CLC 9,**
  49, 81; DAM NOV; SSC 27
  See also AITN 1; BEST 90:3; CA 1-4R;
  141; CAAS 9; CANR 1, 21, 46; DLB 9,
  206; DLBY 93; MTCW 1, 2
Stein, Gertrude 1874-1946 .... **TCLC 1, 6, 28,**
  48; DA; DAB; DAC; DAM MST, NOV,
  POET; PC 18; WLC
  See also CA 104; 132; CDALB 1917-1929;
  DA3; DLB 4, 54, 86; DLBD 15; MTCW
  1, 2
Steinbeck, John (Ernst) 1902-1968 ... **CLC 1,**
  5, 9, 13, 21, 34, 45, 75, 124; DA; DAB;
  DAC; DAM DRAM, MST, NOV; SSC
  11, 37; WLC
  See also AAYA 12; CA 1-4R; 25-28R;
  CANR 1, 35; CDALB 1929-1941; DA3;
  DLB 7, 9, 212; DLBD 2; MTCW 1, 2;
  SATA 9
Steinem, Gloria 1934- .... **CLC 63**
  See also CA 53-56; CANR 28, 51; MTCW
  1, 2
Steiner, George 1929- .. **CLC 24; DAM NOV**
  See also CA 73-76; CANR 31, 67; DLB 67;
  MTCW 1, 2; SATA 62
Steiner, K. Leslie
  See Delany, Samuel R(ay, Jr.)
Steiner, Rudolf 1861-1925 .... **TCLC 13**
  See also CA 107
Stendhal 1783-1842 .... **NCLC 23, 46; DA;**
  DAB; DAC; DAM MST, NOV; SSC
  27; WLC
  See also DA3; DLB 119
Stephen, Adeline Virginia
  See Woolf, (Adeline) Virginia
Stephen, Sir Leslie 1832-1904 .... **TCLC 23**
  See also CA 123; DLB 57, 144, 190
Stephen, Sir Leslie
  See Stephen, Sir Leslie
Stephen, Virginia
  See Woolf, (Adeline) Virginia
Stephens, James 1882(?)-1950 .... **TCLC 4**
  See also CA 104; DLB 19, 153, 162
Stephens, Reed
  See Donaldson, Stephen R.
Steptoe, Lydia
  See Barnes, Djuna
Sterchi, Beat 1949- .... **CLC 65**
Sterling, Brett
  See Bradbury, Ray (Douglas); Hamilton,
  Edmond
Sterling, Bruce 1954- .... **CLC 72**
  See also CA 119; CANR 44
Sterling, George 1869-1926 .... **TCLC 20**
  See also CA 117; 165; DLB 54

Tolstoy, Count Leo
See Tolstoy, Leo (Nikolaevich)
Tolstoy, Leo (Nikolaevich)
1828-1910 .. **TCLC 4, 11, 17, 28, 44, 79;
DA; DAB; DAC; DAM MST, NOV;
SSC 9, 30; WLC**
See also CA 104; 123; DA3; SATA 26
Tomasi di Lampedusa, Giuseppe 1896-1957
See Lampedusa, Giuseppe (Tomasi) di
See also CA 111
Tomlin, Lily .... **CLC 17**
See also Tomlin, Mary Jean
Tomlin, Mary Jean 1939(?)-
See Tomlin, Lily
See also CA 117
Tomlinson, (Alfred) Charles 1927- .... **CLC 2,
4, 6, 13, 45; DAM POET; PC 17**
See also CA 5-8R; CANR 33; DLB 40
Tomlinson, H(enry) M(ajor) 1873-1958
TCLC 71
See also CA 118; 161; DLB 36, 100, 195
Tonson, Jacob
See Bennett, (Enoch) Arnold
Toole, John Kennedy 1937-1969 ..... **CLC 19,
64**
See also CA 104; DLBY 81; MTCW 2
Toomer, Jean 1894-1967 .... **CLC 1, 4, 13, 22;
BLC 3; DAM MULT; PC 7; SSC 1;
WLCS**
See also BW 1; CA 85-88; CDALB 1917-
1929; DA3; DLB 45, 51; MTCW 1, 2
Torley, Luke
See Blish, James (Benjamin)
Tornimparte, Alessandra
See Ginzburg, Natalia
Torre, Raoul della
See Mencken, H(enry) L(ouis)
Torrence, Ridgely 1874-1950 .... **TCLC 97**
See also DLB 54
Torrey, E(dwin) Fuller 1937- .... **CLC 34**
See also CA 119; CANR 71
Torsvan, Ben Traven
See Traven, B.
Torsvan, Benno Traven
See Traven, B.
Torsvan, Berick Traven
See Traven, B.
Torsvan, Berwick Traven
See Traven, B.
Torsvan, Bruno Traven
See Traven, B.
Torsvan, Traven
See Traven, B.
Tournier, Michel (Edouard) 1924- .... **CLC 6,
23, 36, 95**
See also CA 49-52; CANR 3, 36, 74; DLB
83; MTCW 1, 2; SATA 23
Tournimparte, Alessandra
See Ginzburg, Natalia
Towers, Ivar
See Kornbluth, C(yril) M.
Towne, Robert (Burton) 1936(?)- ..... **CLC 87**
See also CA 108; DLB 44
Townsend, Sue .... **CLC 61**
See also Townsend, Susan Elaine AAYA 28;
SATA 55, 93; SATA-Brief 48
Townsend, Susan Elaine 1946-
See Townsend, Sue
See also CA 119; 127; CANR 65; DAB;
DAC; DAM MST
Townshend, Peter (Dennis Blandford) 1945-
CLC 17, 42

See also CA 107
Tozzi, Federigo 1883-1920 .... **TCLC 31**
See also CA 160
Traill, Catharine Parr 1802-1899 .. **NCLC 31**
See also DLB 99
Trakl, Georg 1887-1914 .... **TCLC 5; PC 20**
See also CA 104; 165; MTCW 2
Transtroemer, Tomas (Goesta)
1931- .... **CLC 52, 65; DAM POET**
See also CA 117; 129; CAAS 17
Transtromer, Tomas Gosta
See Transtroemer, Tomas (Goesta)
Traven, B. (?)-1969 .... **CLC 8, 11**
See also CA 19-20; 25-28R; CAP 2; DLB
9, 56; MTCW 1
Treitel, Jonathan 1959- .... **CLC 70**
Tremain, Rose 1943- .... **CLC 42**
See also CA 97-100; CANR 44; DLB 14
Tremblay, Michel 1942- .... **CLC 29, 102;
DAC; DAM MST**
See also CA 116; 128; DLB 60; MTCW 1,
2
Trevanian .... **CLC 29**
See also Whitaker, Rod(ney)
Trevor, Glen
See Hilton, James
Trevor, William 1928- .. **CLC 7, 9, 14, 25, 71,
116; SSC 21**
See also Cox, William Trevor DLB 14, 139;
MTCW 2
Trifonov, Yuri (Valentinovich) 1925-1981
CLC 45
See also CA 126; 103; MTCW 1
Trilling, Lionel 1905-1975 .... **CLC 9, 11, 24**
See also CA 9-12R; 61-64; CANR 10; DLB
28, 63; INT CANR-10; MTCW 1, 2
Trimball, W. H.
See Mencken, H(enry) L(ouis)
Tristan
See Gomez de la Serna, Ramon
Tristram
See Housman, A(lfred) E(dward)
Trogdon, William (Lewis) 1939-
See Heat-Moon, William Least
See also CA 115; 119; CANR 47; INT 119
Trollope, Anthony 1815-1882 ... **NCLC 6, 33;
DA; DAB; DAC; DAM MST, NOV;
SSC 28; WLC**
See also CDBLB 1832-1890; DA3; DLB
21, 57, 159; SATA 22
Trollope, Frances 1779-1863 .... **NCLC 30**
See also DLB 21, 166
Trotsky, Leon 1879-1940 .... **TCLC 22**
See also CA 118; 167
Trotter (Cockburn), Catharine
1679-1749 .... **LC 8**
See also DLB 84
Trotter, Wilfred 1872-1939 .... **TCLC 99**
Trout, Kilgore
See Farmer, Philip Jose
Trow, George W. S. 1943- .... **CLC 52**
See also CA 126
Troyat, Henri 1911- .... **CLC 23**
See also CA 45-48; CANR 2, 33, 67;
MTCW 1
Trudeau, G(arretson) B(eekman) 1948-
See Trudeau, Garry B.
See also CA 81-84; CANR 31; SATA 35
Trudeau, Garry B. .... **CLC 12**
See also Trudeau, G(arretson) B(eekman)
AAYA 10; AITN 2

Truffaut, Francois 1932-1984 ... **CLC 20, 101**
See also CA 81-84; 113; CANR 34
Trumbo, Dalton 1905-1976 .... **CLC 19**
See also CA 21-24R; 69-72; CANR 10;
DLB 26
Trumbull, John 1750-1831 .... **NCLC 30**
See also DLB 31
Trundlett, Helen B.
See Eliot, T(homas) S(tearns)
Tryon, Thomas 1926-1991 .... **CLC 3, 11;
DAM POP**
See also AITN 1; CA 29-32R; 135; CANR
32, 77; DA3; MTCW 1
Tryon, Tom
See Tryon, Thomas
Ts'ao Hsueh-ch'in 1715(?)-1763 .... **LC 1**
Tsushima, Shuji 1909-1948
See Dazai Osamu
See also CA 107
Tsvetaeva (Efron), Marina (Ivanovna)
1892-1941 .... **TCLC 7, 35; PC 14**
See also CA 104; 128; CANR 73; MTCW
1, 2
Tuck, Lily 1938- .... **CLC 70**
See also CA 139
Tu Fu 712-770 .... **PC 9**
See also DAM MULT
Tunis, John R(oberts) 1889-1975 ..... **CLC 12**
See also CA 61-64; CANR 62; DLB 22,
171; JRDA; MAICYA; SATA 37; SATA-
Brief 30
Tuohy, Frank .... **CLC 37**
See also Tuohy, John Francis DLB 14, 139
Tuohy, John Francis 1925-1999
See Tuohy, Frank
See also CA 5-8R; 178; CANR 3, 47
Turco, Lewis (Putnam) 1934- ..... **CLC 11, 63**
See also CA 13-16R; CAAS 22; CANR 24,
51; DLBY 84
Turgenev, Ivan 1818-1883 .... **NCLC 21; DA;
DAB; DAC; DAM MST, NOV; DC 7;
SSC 7; WLC**
Turgot, Anne-Robert-Jacques
1727-1781 .... **LC 26**
Turner, Frederick 1943- .... **CLC 48**
See also CA 73-76; CAAS 10; CANR 12,
30, 56; DLB 40
Tutu, Desmond M(pilo) 1931- .... **CLC 80;
BLC 3; DAM MULT**
See also BW 1, 3; CA 125; CANR 67, 81
Tutuola, Amos 1920-1997 ...... **CLC 5, 14, 29;
BLC 3; DAM MULT**
See also BW 2, 3; CA 9-12R; 159; CANR
27, 66; DA3; DLB 125; MTCW 1, 2
Twain, Mark ..... **TCLC 6, 12, 19, 36, 48, 59;
SSC 34; WLC**
See also Clemens, Samuel Langhorne
AAYA 20; CLR 58, 60; DLB 11, 12, 23,
64, 74
Tyler, Anne 1941- . **CLC 7, 11, 18, 28, 44, 59,
103; DAM NOV, POP**
See also AAYA 18; BEST 89:1; CA 9-12R;
CANR 11, 33, 53; CDALBS; DLB 6, 143;
DLBY 82; MTCW 1, 2; SATA 7, 90
Tyler, Royall 1757-1826 .... **NCLC 3**
See also DLB 37
Tynan, Katharine 1861-1931 .... **TCLC 3**
See also CA 104; 167; DLB 153
Tyutchev, Fyodor 1803-1873 .... **NCLC 34**
Tzara, Tristan 1896-1963 ...... **CLC 47; DAM
POET; PC 27**
See also CA 153; 89-92; MTCW 2

Uhry, Alfred 1936- .. **CLC 55; DAM DRAM, POP**
See also CA 127; 133; DA3; INT 133

Ulf, Haerved
See Strindberg, (Johan) August

Ulf, Harved
See Strindberg, (Johan) August

Ulibarri, Sabine R(eyes) 1919- .... **CLC 83; DAM MULT; HLCS 2**
See also CA 131; CANR 81; DLB 82; HW 1, 2

Unamuno (y Jugo), Miguel de 1864-1936 **TCLC 2, 9; DAM MULT, NOV; HLC 2; SSC 11**
See also CA 104; 131; CANR 81; DLB 108; HW 1, 2; MTCW 1, 2

Undercliffe, Errol
See Campbell, (John) Ramsey

Underwood, Miles
See Glassco, John

Undset, Sigrid 1882-1949 .... **TCLC 3; DA; DAB; DAC; DAM MST, NOV; WLC**
See also CA 104; 129; DA3; MTCW 1, 2

Ungaretti, Giuseppe 1888-1970 ... **CLC 7, 11, 15**
See also CA 19-20; 25-28R; CAP 2; DLB 114

Unger, Douglas 1952- .... **CLC 34**
See also CA 130

Unsworth, Barry (Forster) 1930- .... **CLC 76, 127**
See also CA 25-28R; CANR 30, 54; DLB 194

Updike, John (Hoyer) 1932- . **CLC 1, 2, 3, 5, 7, 9, 13, 15, 23, 34, 43, 70; DA; DAB; DAC; DAM MST, NOV, POET, POP; SSC 13, 27; WLC**
See also CA 1-4R; CABS 1; CANR 4, 33, 51; CDALB 1968-1988; DA3; DLB 2, 5, 143; DLBD 3; DLBY 80, 82, 97; MTCW 1, 2

Upshaw, Margaret Mitchell
See Mitchell, Margaret (Munnerlyn)

Upton, Mark
See Sanders, Lawrence

Upward, Allen 1863-1926 .... **TCLC 85**
See also CA 117; DLB 36

Urdang, Constance (Henriette) 1922- .... **CLC 47**
See also CA 21-24R; CANR 9, 24

Uriel, Henry
See Faust, Frederick (Schiller)

Uris, Leon (Marcus) 1924- .... **CLC 7, 32; DAM NOV, POP**
See also AITN 1, 2; BEST 89:2; CA 1-4R; CANR 1, 40, 65; DA3; MTCW 1, 2; SATA 49

Urista, Alberto H. 1947-
See Alurista
See also CA 45-48, 182; CANR 2, 32; HLCS 1; HW 1

Urmuz
See Codrescu, Andrei

Urquhart, Guy
See McAlmon, Robert (Menzies)

Urquhart, Jane 1949- .... **CLC 90; DAC**
See also CA 113; CANR 32, 68

Usigli, Rodolfo 1905-1979
See also CA 131; HLCS 1; HW 1

Ustinov, Peter (Alexander) 1921- .... **CLC 1**
See also AITN 1; CA 13-16R; CANR 25, 51; DLB 13; MTCW 2

U Tam'si, Gerald Felix Tchicaya
See Tchicaya, Gerald Felix

U Tam'si, Tchicaya
See Tchicaya, Gerald Felix

Vachss, Andrew (Henry) 1942- .... **CLC 106**
See also CA 118; CANR 44

Vachss, Andrew H.
See Vachss, Andrew (Henry)

Vaculik, Ludvik 1926- .... **CLC 7**
See also CA 53-56; CANR 72

Vaihinger, Hans 1852-1933 .... **TCLC 71**
See also CA 116; 166

Valdez, Luis (Miguel) 1940- .. **CLC 84; DAM MULT; DC 10; HLC 2**
See also CA 101; CANR 32, 81; DLB 122; HW 1

Valenzuela, Luisa 1938- .... **CLC 31, 104; DAM MULT; HLCS 2; SSC 14**
See also CA 101; CANR 32, 65; DLB 113; HW 1, 2

Valera y Alcala-Galiano, Juan 1824-1905 **TCLC 10**
See also CA 106

Valery, (Ambroise) Paul (Toussaint Jules) 1871-1945 ... **TCLC 4, 15; DAM POET; PC 9**
See also CA 104; 122; DA3; MTCW 1, 2

Valle-Inclan, Ramon (Maria) del 1866-1936 **TCLC 5; DAM MULT; HLC 2**
See also CA 106; 153; CANR 80; DLB 134; HW 2

Vallejo, Antonio Buero
See Buero Vallejo, Antonio

Vallejo, Cesar (Abraham) 1892-1938 .. **TCLC 3, 56; DAM MULT; HLC 2**
See also CA 105; 153; HW 1

Valles, Jules 1832-1885 .... **NCLC 71**
See also DLB 123

Vallette, Marguerite Eymery 1860-1953 **TCLC 67**
See also CA 182; DLB 123, 192

Valle Y Pena, Ramon del
See Valle-Inclan, Ramon (Maria) del

Van Ash, Cay 1918- .... **CLC 34**

Vanbrugh, Sir John 1664-1726 .... **LC 21; DAM DRAM**
See also DLB 80

Van Campen, Karl
See Campbell, John W(ood, Jr.)

Vance, Gerald
See Silverberg, Robert

Vance, Jack .... **CLC 35**
See also Vance, John Holbrook DLB 8

Vance, John Holbrook 1916-
See Queen, Ellery; Vance, Jack
See also CA 29-32R; CANR 17, 65; MTCW 1

Van Den Bogarde, Derek Jules Gaspard Ulric Niven 1921-1999
See Bogarde, Dirk
See also CA 77-80; 179

Vandenburgh, Jane .... **CLC 59**
See also CA 168

Vanderhaeghe, Guy 1951- .... **CLC 41**
See also CA 113; CANR 72

van der Post, Laurens (Jan) 1906-1996 .... **CLC 5**
See also CA 5-8R; 155; CANR 35; DLB 204

van de Wetering, Janwillem 1931- ... **CLC 47**
See also CA 49-52; CANR 4, 62

Van Dine, S. S. .... **TCLC 23**
See also Wright, Willard Huntington

Van Doren, Carl (Clinton) 1885-1950 .... **TCLC 18**
See also CA 111; 168

Van Doren, Mark 1894-1972 .... **CLC 6, 10**
See also CA 1-4R; 37-40R; CANR 3; DLB 45; MTCW 1, 2

Van Druten, John (William) 1901-1957 **TCLC 2**
See also CA 104; 161; DLB 10

Van Duyn, Mona (Jane) 1921- ...... **CLC 3, 7, 63, 116; DAM POET**
See also CA 9-12R; CANR 7, 38, 60; DLB 5

Van Dyne, Edith
See Baum, L(yman) Frank

van Itallie, Jean-Claude 1936- .... **CLC 3**
See also CA 45-48; CAAS 2; CANR 1, 48; DLB 7

van Ostaijen, Paul 1896-1928 .... **TCLC 33**
See also CA 163

Van Peebles, Melvin 1932- .... **CLC 2, 20; DAM MULT**
See also BW 2, 3; CA 85-88; CANR 27, 67, 82

Vansittart, Peter 1920- .... **CLC 42**
See also CA 1-4R; CANR 3, 49

Van Vechten, Carl 1880-1964 .... **CLC 33**
See also CA 183; 89-92; DLB 4, 9, 51

Van Vogt, A(lfred) E(lton) 1912- .... **CLC 1**
See also CA 21-24R; CANR 28; DLB 8; SATA 14

Varda, Agnes 1928- .... **CLC 16**
See also CA 116; 122

Vargas Llosa, (Jorge) Mario (Pedro) 1936- **CLC 3, 6, 9, 10, 15, 31, 42, 85; DA; DAB; DAC; DAM MST, MULT, NOV; HLC 2**
See also CA 73-76; CANR 18, 32, 42, 67; DA3; DLB 145; HW 1, 2; MTCW 1, 2

Vasiliu, Gheorghe 1881-1957
See Bacovia, George
See also CA 123

Vassa, Gustavus
See Equiano, Olaudah

Vassilikos, Vassilis 1933- .... **CLC 4, 8**
See also CA 81-84; CANR 75

Vaughan, Henry 1621-1695 .... **LC 27**
See also DLB 131

Vaughn, Stephanie .... **CLC 62**

Vazov, Ivan (Minchov) 1850-1921 . **TCLC 25**
See also CA 121; 167; DLB 147

Veblen, Thorstein B(unde) 1857-1929 .... **TCLC 31**
See also CA 115; 165

Vega, Lope de 1562-1635 .... **LC 23; HLCS 2**

Venison, Alfred
See Pound, Ezra (Weston Loomis)

Verdi, Marie de
See Mencken, H(enry) L(ouis)

Verdu, Matilde
See Cela, Camilo Jose

Verga, Giovanni (Carmelo) 1840-1922 .... **TCLC 3; SSC 21**
See also CA 104; 123

Vergil 70B.C.-19B.C. ... **CMLC 9; DA; DAB; DAC; DAM MST, POET; PC 12; WLCS**
See also Virgil DA3

Walker, Edward Joseph 1934-
See Walker, Ted
See also CA 21-24R; CANR 12, 28, 53

Walker, George F. 1947- . **CLC 44, 61; DAB;
DAC; DAM MST**
See also CA 103; CANR 21, 43, 59; DLB
60

Walker, Joseph A. 1935- .... **CLC 19; DAM
DRAM, MST**
See also BW 1, 3; CA 89-92; CANR 26;
DLB 38

Walker, Margaret (Abigail)
1915-1998 .... **CLC 1, 6; BLC; DAM
MULT; PC 20**
See also BW 2, 3; CA 73-76; 172; CANR
26, 54, 76; DLB 76, 152; MTCW 1, 2

Walker, Ted .... **CLC 13**
See also Walker, Edward Joseph DLB 40

Wallace, David Foster 1962- ..... **CLC 50, 114**
See also CA 132; CANR 59; DA3; MTCW
2

Wallace, Dexter
See Masters, Edgar Lee

Wallace, (Richard Horatio) Edgar 1875-1932
TCLC 57
See also CA 115; DLB 70

Wallace, Irving 1916-1990 .... **CLC 7, 13;
DAM NOV, POP**
See also AITN 1; CA 1-4R; 132; CAAS 1;
CANR 1, 27; INT CANR-27; MTCW 1,
2

Wallant, Edward Lewis 1926-1962 ... **CLC 5,
10**
See also CA 1-4R; CANR 22; DLB 2, 28,
143; MTCW 1, 2

Wallas, Graham 1858-1932 .... **TCLC 91**

Walley, Byron
See Card, Orson Scott

Walpole, Horace 1717-1797 .... **LC 49**
See also DLB 39, 104

Walpole, Hugh (Seymour)
1884-1941 .... **TCLC 5**
See also CA 104; 165; DLB 34; MTCW 2

Walser, Martin 1927- .... **CLC 27**
See also CA 57-60; CANR 8, 46; DLB 75,
124

Walser, Robert 1878-1956 .... **TCLC 18; SSC
20**
See also CA 118; 165; DLB 66

Walsh, Jill Paton .... **CLC 35**
See also Paton Walsh, Gillian CLR 2

Walter, Villiam Christian
See Andersen, Hans Christian

Wambaugh, Joseph (Aloysius, Jr.)
1937- .... **CLC 3, 18; DAM NOV, POP**
See also AITN 1; BEST 89:3; CA 33-36R;
CANR 42, 65; DA3; DLB 6; DLBY 83;
MTCW 1, 2

Wang Wei 699(?)-761(?) .... **PC 18**

Ward, Arthur Henry Sarsfield 1883-1959
See Rohmer, Sax
See also CA 108; 173

Ward, Douglas Turner 1930- .... **CLC 19**
See also BW 1; CA 81-84; CANR 27; DLB
7, 38

Ward, E. D.
See Lucas, E(dward) V(errall)

Ward, Mary Augusta
See Ward, Mrs. Humphry

Ward, Mrs. Humphry 1851-1920 .. **TCLC 55**
See also DLB 18

Ward, Peter
See Faust, Frederick (Schiller)

Warhol, Andy 1928(?)-1987 .... **CLC 20**
See also AAYA 12; BEST 89:4; CA 89-92;
121; CANR 34

Warner, Francis (Robert le Plastrier) 1937-
CLC 14
See also CA 53-56; CANR 11

Warner, Marina 1946- .... **CLC 59**
See also CA 65-68; CANR 21, 55; DLB
194

Warner, Rex (Ernest) 1905-1986 ...... **CLC 45**
See also CA 89-92; 119; DLB 15

Warner, Susan (Bogert)
1819-1885 .... **NCLC 31**
See also DLB 3, 42

Warner, Sylvia (Constance) Ashton
See Ashton-Warner, Sylvia (Constance)

Warner, Sylvia Townsend
1893-1978 .... **CLC 7, 19; SSC 23**
See also CA 61-64; 77-80; CANR 16, 60;
DLB 34, 139; MTCW 1, 2

Warren, Mercy Otis 1728-1814 ..... **NCLC 13**
See also DLB 31, 200

Warren, Robert Penn 1905-1989 .. **CLC 1, 4,
6, 8, 10, 13, 18, 39, 53, 59; DA; DAB;
DAC; DAM MST, NOV, POET; SSC 4;
WLC**
See also AITN 1; CA 13-16R; 129; CANR
10, 47; CDALB 1968-1988; DA3; DLB
2, 48, 152; DLBY 80, 89; INT CANR-10;
MTCW 1, 2; SATA 46; SATA-Obit 63

Warshofsky, Isaac
See Singer, Isaac Bashevis

Warton, Thomas 1728-1790 ..... **LC 15; DAM
POET**
See also DLB 104, 109

Waruk, Kona
See Harris, (Theodore) Wilson

Warung, Price 1855-1911 .... **TCLC 45**

Warwick, Jarvis
See Garner, Hugh

Washington, Alex
See Harris, Mark

Washington, Booker T(aliaferro) 1856-1915
TCLC 10; BLC 3; DAM MULT
See also BW 1; CA 114; 125; DA3; SATA
28

Washington, George 1732-1799 .... **LC 25**
See also DLB 31

Wassermann, (Karl) Jakob
1873-1934 .... **TCLC 6**
See also CA 104; 163; DLB 66

Wasserstein, Wendy 1950- .. **CLC 32, 59, 90;
DAM DRAM; DC 4**
See also CA 121; 129; CABS 3; CANR 53,
75; DA3; INT 129; MTCW 2; SATA 94

Waterhouse, Keith (Spencer) 1929- . **CLC 47**
See also CA 5-8R; CANR 38, 67; DLB 13,
15; MTCW 1, 2

Waters, Frank (Joseph) 1902-1995 .. **CLC 88**
See also CA 5-8R; 149; CAAS 13; CANR
3, 18, 63; DLB 212; DLBY 86

Waters, Roger 1944- .... **CLC 35**

Watkins, Frances Ellen
See Harper, Frances Ellen Watkins

Watkins, Gerrold
See Malzberg, Barry N(athaniel)

Watkins, Gloria Jean 1952(?)-
See hooks, bell
See also BW 2; CA 143; CANR 87; MTCW
2

Watkins, Paul 1964- .... **CLC 55**
See also CA 132; CANR 62

Watkins, Vernon Phillips
1906-1967 .... **CLC 43**
See also CA 9-10; 25-28R; CAP 1; DLB 20

Watson, Irving S.
See Mencken, H(enry) L(ouis)

Watson, John H.
See Farmer, Philip Jose

Watson, Richard F.
See Silverberg, Robert

Waugh, Auberon (Alexander) 1939- .. **CLC 7**
See also CA 45-48; CANR 6, 22; DLB 14,
194

Waugh, Evelyn (Arthur St. John) 1903-1966
**CLC 1, 3, 8, 13, 19, 27, 44, 107; DA;
DAB; DAC; DAM MST, NOV, POP;
WLC**
See also CA 85-88; 25-28R; CANR 22; CD-
BLB 1914-1945; DA3; DLB 15, 162, 195;
MTCW 1, 2

Waugh, Harriet 1944- .... **CLC 6**
See also CA 85-88; CANR 22

Ways, C. R.
See Blount, Roy (Alton), Jr.

Waystaff, Simon
See Swift, Jonathan

Webb, Beatrice (Martha Potter) 1858-1943
TCLC 22
See also CA 117; 162; DLB 190

Webb, Charles (Richard) 1939- .... **CLC 7**
See also CA 25-28R

Webb, James H(enry), Jr. 1946- ...... **CLC 22**
See also CA 81-84

Webb, Mary Gladys (Meredith) 1881-1927
TCLC 24
See also CA 182; 123; DLB 34

Webb, Mrs. Sidney
See Webb, Beatrice (Martha Potter)

Webb, Phyllis 1927- .... **CLC 18**
See also CA 104; CANR 23; DLB 53

Webb, Sidney (James) 1859-1947 .. **TCLC 22**
See also CA 117; 163; DLB 190

Webber, Andrew Lloyd .... **CLC 21**
See also Lloyd Webber, Andrew

Weber, Lenora Mattingly
1895-1971 .... **CLC 12**
See also CA 19-20; 29-32R; CAP 1; SATA
2; SATA-Obit 26

Weber, Max 1864-1920 .... **TCLC 69**
See also CA 109

Webster, John 1579(?)-1634(?) ... **LC 33; DA;
DAB; DAC; DAM DRAM, MST; DC
2; WLC**
See also CDBLB Before 1660; DLB 58

Webster, Noah 1758-1843 .... **NCLC 30**
See also DLB 1, 37, 42, 43, 73

Wedekind, (Benjamin) Frank(lin) 1864-1918
TCLC 7; DAM DRAM
See also CA 104; 153; DLB 118

Weidman, Jerome 1913-1998 .... **CLC 7**
See also AITN 2; CA 1-4R; 171; CANR 1;
DLB 28

Weil, Simone (Adolphine)
1909-1943 .... **TCLC 23**
See also CA 117; 159; MTCW 2

Weininger, Otto 1880-1903 .... **TCLC 84**

Weinstein, Nathan
See West, Nathanael

Weinstein, Nathan von Wallenstein
See West, Nathanael

Xenophon c. 430B.C.-c. 354B.C. ... **CMLC 17**
See also DLB 176

Yakumo Koizumi
See Hearn, (Patricio) Lafcadio (Tessima Carlos)

Yamamoto, Hisaye 1921- .... **SSC 34; DAM MULT**

Yanez, Jose Donoso
See Donoso (Yanez), Jose

Yanovsky, Basile S.
See Yanovsky, V(assily) S(emenovich)

Yanovsky, V(assily) S(emenovich) 1906-1989 **CLC 2, 18**
See also CA 97-100; 129

Yates, Richard 1926-1992 .... **CLC 7, 8, 23**
See also CA 5-8R; 139; CANR 10, 43; DLB 2; DLBY 81, 92; INT CANR-10

Yeats, W. B.
See Yeats, William Butler

Yeats, William Butler 1865-1939 .... **TCLC 1, 11, 18, 31, 93; DA; DAB; DAC; DAM DRAM, MST, POET; PC 20; WLC**
See also CA 104; 127; CANR 45; CDBLB 1890-1914; DA3; DLB 10, 19, 98, 156; MTCW 1, 2

Yehoshua, A(braham) B. 1936- .. **CLC 13, 31**
See also CA 33-36R; CANR 43

Yellow Bird
See Ridge, John Rollin

Yep, Laurence Michael 1948- .... **CLC 35**
See also AAYA 5, 31; CA 49-52; CANR 1, 46; CLR 3, 17, 54; DLB 52; JRDA; MAICYA; SATA 7, 69

Yerby, Frank G(arvin) 1916-1991 . **CLC 1, 7, 22; BLC 3; DAM MULT**
See also BW 1, 3; CA 9-12R; 136; CANR 16, 52; DLB 76; INT CANR-16; MTCW 1

Yesenin, Sergei Alexandrovich
See Esenin, Sergei (Alexandrovich)

Yevtushenko, Yevgeny (Alexandrovich) 1933- **CLC 1, 3, 13, 26, 51, 126; DAM POET**
See also CA 81-84; CANR 33, 54; MTCW 1

Yezierska, Anzia 1885(?)-1970 .... **CLC 46**
See also CA 126; 89-92; DLB 28; MTCW 1

Yglesias, Helen 1915- .... **CLC 7, 22**
See also CA 37-40R; CAAS 20; CANR 15, 65; INT CANR-15; MTCW 1

Yokomitsu Riichi 1898-1947 .... **TCLC 47**
See also CA 170

Yonge, Charlotte (Mary) 1823-1901 .... **TCLC 48**
See also CA 109; 163; DLB 18, 163; SATA 17

York, Jeremy
See Creasey, John

York, Simon
See Heinlein, Robert A(nson)

Yorke, Henry Vincent 1905-1974 ..... **CLC 13**
See also Green, Henry CA 85-88; 49-52

Yosano Akiko 1878-1942 .... **TCLC 59; PC 11**
See also CA 161

Yoshimoto, Banana .... **CLC 84**
See also Yoshimoto, Mahoko

Yoshimoto, Mahoko 1964-
See Yoshimoto, Banana
See also CA 144

Young, Al(bert James) 1939- . **CLC 19; BLC 3; DAM MULT**
See also BW 2, 3; CA 29-32R; CANR 26, 65; DLB 33

Young, Andrew (John) 1885-1971 ...... **CLC 5**
See also CA 5-8R; CANR 7, 29

Young, Collier
See Bloch, Robert (Albert)

Young, Edward 1683-1765 .... **LC 3, 40**
See also DLB 95

Young, Marguerite (Vivian) 1909-1995 .... **CLC 82**
See also CA 13-16; 150; CAP 1

Young, Neil 1945- .... **CLC 17**
See also CA 110

Young Bear, Ray A. 1950- ..... **CLC 94; DAM MULT**
See also CA 146; DLB 175; NNAL

Yourcenar, Marguerite 1903-1987 ... **CLC 19, 38, 50, 87; DAM NOV**
See also CA 69-72; CANR 23, 60; DLB 72; DLBY 88; MTCW 1, 2

Yuan, Chu 340(?)B.C.-278(?)B.C. . **CMLC 36**

Yurick, Sol 1925- .... **CLC 6**
See also CA 13-16R; CANR 25

Zabolotsky, Nikolai Alekseevich 1903-1958 **TCLC 52**
See also CA 116; 164

Zagajewski, Adam .... **PC 27**

Zamiatin, Yevgenii
See Zamyatin, Evgeny Ivanovich

Zamora, Bernice (B. Ortiz) 1938- .. **CLC 89; DAM MULT; HLC 2**
See also CA 151; CANR 80; DLB 82; HW 1, 2

Zamyatin, Evgeny Ivanovich 1884-1937 **TCLC 8, 37**
See also CA 105; 166

Zangwill, Israel 1864-1926 .... **TCLC 16**
See also CA 109; 167; DLB 10, 135, 197

Zappa, Francis Vincent, Jr. 1940-1993
See Zappa, Frank
See also CA 108; 143; CANR 57

Zappa, Frank .... **CLC 17**
See also Zappa, Francis Vincent, Jr.

Zaturenska, Marya 1902-1982 ..... **CLC 6, 11**
See also CA 13-16R; 105; CANR 22

Zeami 1363-1443 .... **DC 7**

Zelazny, Roger (Joseph) 1937-1995 . **CLC 21**
See also AAYA 7; CA 21-24R; 148; CANR 26, 60; DLB 8; MTCW 1, 2; SATA 57; SATA-Brief 39

Zhdanov, Andrei Alexandrovich 1896-1948 **TCLC 18**
See also CA 117; 167

Zhukovsky, Vasily (Andreevich) 1783-1852 **NCLC 35**
See also DLB 205

Ziegenhagen, Eric .... **CLC 55**

Zimmer, Jill Schary
See Robinson, Jill

Zimmerman, Robert
See Dylan, Bob

Zindel, Paul 1936- ..... **CLC 6, 26; DA; DAB; DAC; DAM DRAM, MST, NOV; DC 5**
See also AAYA 2; CA 73-76; CANR 31, 65; CDALBS; CLR 3, 45; DA3; DLB 7, 52; JRDA; MAICYA; MTCW 1, 2; SATA 16, 58, 102

Zinov'Ev, A. A.
See Zinoviev, Alexander (Aleksandrovich)

Zinoviev, Alexander (Aleksandrovich) 1922- **CLC 19**
See also CA 116; 133; CAAS 10

Zoilus
See Lovecraft, H(oward) P(hillips)

Zola, Emile (Edouard Charles Antoine) 1840-1902 .... **TCLC 1, 6, 21, 41; DA; DAB; DAC; DAM MST, NOV; WLC**
See also CA 104; 138; DA3; DLB 123

Zoline, Pamela 1941- .... **CLC 62**
See also CA 161

Zorrilla y Moral, Jose 1817-1893 .... **NCLC 6**

Zoshchenko, Mikhail (Mikhailovich) 1895-1958 .... **TCLC 15; SSC 15**
See also CA 115; 160

Zuckmayer, Carl 1896-1977 .... **CLC 18**
See also CA 69-72; DLB 56, 124

Zuk, Georges
See Skelton, Robin

Zukofsky, Louis 1904-1978 ... **CLC 1, 2, 4, 7, 11, 18; DAM POET; PC 11**
See also CA 9-12R; 77-80; CANR 39; DLB 5, 165; MTCW 1

Zweig, Paul 1935-1984 .... **CLC 34, 42**
See also CA 85-88; 113

Zweig, Stefan 1881-1942 .... **TCLC 17**
See also CA 112; 170; DLB 81, 118

Zwingli, Huldreich 1484-1531 .... **LC 37**
See also DLB 179

Literary Criticism Series
Cumulative Topic Index

This index lists all topic entries in Gale's *Classical and Medieval Literature Criticism, Contemporary Literary Criticism, Literature Criticism from 1400 to 1800, Nineteenth-Century Literature Criticism,* and *Twentieth-Century Literary Criticism.*

CLC Cumulative Nationality Index

Nationality Index

Nationality Index

Nationality Index

CLC-128 Title Index

Title Index

ISBN 0-7876-3203-1

90000

9 780787 632038